Arms Control

Readings from
SCIENTIFIC AMERICAN

Arms Control

With Introductions by
Herbert F. York
University of California, San Diego

W. H. Freeman and Company
San Francisco

Library of Congress Cataloging in Publication Data

York, Herbert Frank, comp.
Arms control.

Includes bibliographies.
1. Atomic weapons and disarmament. I. Scientific American. II. Title.
JX1974.7.Y57 327'.174 73-4963
ISBN 0-7167-0880-9
ISBN 0-7167-0879-5 (pbk.)

Many of the *Scientific American* articles in *Arms Control* are available as separate Offprints. For a complete list of more than 950 articles now available as Offprints, write to W. H. Freeman and Company, 660 Market Street, San Francisco, California 94104

Printed in the United States of America

9 8 7 6 5 4 3 2 1

PREFACE

"They shall beat their swords into plowshares, and their spears into pruning hooks," said the Prophets Isaiah and Micah. "Beat your plowshares into swords, and your pruning hooks into spears," said the Prophet Joel. Common sense says things ought to be as Isaiah and Micah projected, but the record clearly confirms Joel.

On an August day in 1945 a U.S. subsonic aircraft took off from the Marianas, arrived over Japan a few hours later, and destroyed the city of Hiroshima with an atomic bomb. Three days later the route was retravelled, with Nagasaki the victim. Soon after, statesmen solemnly agreed something should be done to prevent such events, or worse, from happening again. They said the peaceful atom must be controlled, and the military atom must be abandoned.

Nevertheless, over the next ten years, the power of individual bombs grew a thousandfold, the stock of bombs increased more than a thousandfold, and so the potential atomic fury was multiplied more than one million times. Finally in 1958, a majority of statesmen agreed that the time had come to stop testing nuclear weapons, and this did stop for a while, but the research and development of the means for delivering them was accelerated.

In the early 1960's, intercontinental rockets were introduced as the primary means of delivering nuclear bombs. That meant the speed of delivery had been multiplied more than fiftyfold since Hiroshima, and the possibilities of defense against them had been reduced to zero. Several new flurries of multimegaton nuclear tests were conducted in 1961 and 1962, after which it was agreed in 1963 to stop those tests that polluted the environment and were easy to detect, but not those that were hard to detect and that didn't have directly alarming side effects.

In 1964, the two superpowers of the world—the United States and the Soviet Union—began to discuss placing limits on delivery systems. Eight years later, after the total number of long-range rockets deployed had been further multiplied manyfold, the leaders of the superpowers agreed they had acquired about as many long-range rockets as they needed, and they made formal agreements placing ceilings on the number each power would deploy. If used in the worst possible way, the forces these countries then possessed could kill many hundreds of millions of people within a half hour after a launch signal was given.

Thus, in the almost three decades since the atomic bomb was first used, there has been progress in both arms developments and arms control. But, compared to the great crescendo of the arms race itself, the arms control successes can scarcely be detected. This collection of readings attempts to tell the story of how this situation came about and to present what some stuents on the subject think ought to be done about it.

The first part of the reader gives historical background for the subject. It focuses first on the dramatic developments in nuclear weaponry that flowed from the discovery of fission on the eve of World War II. It finishes with a discussion of the series of "first steps" toward arms control that were accomplished in the period 1958–1967.

The second part describes current progress and problems in arms control, and the attempts now being made to move eventually toward disarmament. The first section in Part II discusses the technology and strategic analyses underlying the SALT conferences. So far, SALT has been concerned solely with delivery systems. The second section in Part II discusses other current arms control and disarmament issues, including the comprehensive test ban and the elimination of biological and chemical weapons.

The third part is addressed to the matter of the interactions between the peaceful and military aspects of nuclear technology. These interactions are such as to stimulate the further development of that technology, and they contribute to making the military applications more generally acceptable than they would otherwise be. Although the specific examples used in this part of the reader all involve nuclear science and technology, other examples, such as the interaction between peaceful applications of space flight and intercontinental weapons could be given also, but *Scientific American* provides superior material about nuclear science and technology, and for that reason I have chosen to focus on nuclear scientific applications.

Much of the material used in this reader comes from the "Science and the Citizen" columns of *Scientific American*. For 25 years these columns have regularly provided the best summary of "news" in the world of technology available anywhere.

The use of this source may help to demonstrate one of the big differences between making scientific theories on the one hand, and making policy—including science and technology policy—on the other. In building a theory, the scientist usually waits until a substantial body of accurately checked information has accumulated. His intuition may have started to work earlier, but he does not "act" in the sense of proclaiming his theory until he is quite certain that it fits some extensive set of facts. The policy-maker, on the other hand, begins to act just as soon as the first datum arrives, especially if the matter is an important one, and he adjusts his policy continuously as the next and the next come in. The data he uses are as often false as true, or they may be half truths, or they may be irrelevant, but they all at least momentarily have their effect on the policies that are generated. I hope some of the cases presented here will make this important distinction clear. The episode of the first Soviet A-bomb and the reaction of the United States to it, and the episode of the 1954 fallout accident and the world reaction to it, are both examples of how information and political reactions to it build up together, and how the full truth is not known until long after the main policies are made and future actions are committed.

Of course, most of the background information necessary for understanding the new data is available before the events occur that require policy decisions. The more of this background information policy-makers have in their heads, and the better they understand it, the better will be the decisions they make. The only way decision makers and their immediate advisers can absorb the necessary background is through prior education, formal as well as informal. Therefore I hope this reader will help to put some relevant and useful information into the minds of some future decision-makers.

Herbert F. York

La Jolla, California
January 1973

Contents

I. Historical Background

II. The Current State of Arms Control

SECTION 5. *SALT* PHASE I

SECTION 6. OTHER ARMS CONTROL AND DISARMAMENT ISSUES

III. Peaceful Applications of Nuclear Technology

SECTION 7. PLOWSHARES AND PRUNING HOOKS

Note on cross-references: References to articles included in this book are noted by the title of the article and the page on which it begins; references to articles that are available as Offprints, but are not included here, are noted by the article's title and Offprint number; references to articles published by SCIENTIFIC AMERICAN, but which are not available as Offprints, are noted by the title of the article and the month and year of its publication.

I
Historical Background

"In some sort of crude sense which no vulgarity,
no humor, no overstatement can quite extinguish, the physicists have known sin;
and this is a knowledge which they cannot lose."

J. ROBERT OPPENHEIMER, 1948

"All but one of the major departures in American policy toward nuclear weapons
were initially conceived by scientists; the Baruch Plan, the hydrogen bomb,
the development of tactical nuclear weapons, the ballistic missile,
and a nuclear test ban. Only the doctrine of massive retaliation originated elsewhere."

ROBERT GILPIN,
American Scientists and Nuclear Weapons Policy, 1962

SECTION 1: THE ATOM BOMB

INTRODUCTION

After scientists in other countries had narrowly missed discovering it, nuclear fission was finally discovered by Otto Hahn* and Fritz Strassmann in Germany late in 1938. They promptly published their findings in January 1939, on the eve of World War II. Although the details of fission came as something of a surprise, the scientific world was quite ready for this discovery, and word about it spread rapidly throughout the then quite small and internationally minded community of nuclear physicists. Experiments designed to elucidate the process of nuclear fission were conducted simultaneously in several countries, and there was immediate and widespread speculation about the possibilities of using the discovery as a basis for producing a chain reaction that would lead to the release of large amounts of energy and, possibly, huge explosions.

These first experiments were made by individual scientists, acting on their own, and with the equipment they had at hand. However, it soon became apparent that government sponsorship of the work would be necessary if it was to proceed at the pace that was merited by its evident importance, and so a number of approaches were made to various levels of government. The most important of these approaches consisted of a letter written to President Roosevelt by Albert Einstein at the instigation of Leo Szilard. This letter was dated August 2, 1939, just one month before the German invasion of Poland. The letter pointed out the possibilities inherent in the new discovery, stressed that the discovery had been made in Germany, and urged the United States to undertake a serious program in the field.

As a result of this and other importunings, special committees were set up to study the matter and to coordinate scientific work, and the first transfer of federal funds, in the amount of $6,000, took place in February 1940.

As time went on, more was learned about the nature of fission, and it began to seem more and more probable that, indeed, nuclear weapons were possible. Finally, in the fall of 1941 a favorable report by the U.S. National Academy of Sciences and information from the British concerning their work in the field led to an acceleration and reorganization of the U.S. programs. By chance, the decision to reorganize and to conduct an "all out" effort was announced at a secret meeting that took place on December 6, 1941, the day before the attack on Pearl Harbor. The program continued to grow in size and complexity, and finally in the summer of 1942, the Corps of Engineers assumed control of the whole project, and placed it under a special new administrative unit with the code name "Manhattan District." Under the command of General Leslie R. Groves, the Manhattan District mobilized American science and industry and carried out what was by far the largest scientific "forced march" ever undertaken.

The response of American scientists to work on this and other military projects was prompt and general. As I. I. Rabi wrote later** in *Scientific American*:

> I would enter a laboratory where a scientist, generally a young scientist, was happily working away on his experiments and tell him that we had a laboratory

---

*Hahn described the discovery in an article "The Discovery of Fission," *Scientific American*, February 1958.

***Scientific American*, January 1951. In his review of the book *Security, Loyalty, and Science*, by Walter Gellhorn.

> in Cambridge [Massachusetts] where he was needed, that of necessity the purpose of the laboratory could not be revealed but that I was convinced that his services were necessary in the national interest. As part of the pep talk, I could assure him that the working conditions were poor and the problem had no relation to his present interest nor would it necessarily advance him scientifically. Furthermore, would he please show up in Cambridge in ten days or two weeks? The spirit in which this call to action was received can be judged by the fact that I had only one refusal in about two dozen solicitations in various parts of the country. The man who refused genuinely felt that he was not good enough for the job.
>
> The political opinions of the scientists ranged over the whole spectrum of confusion that was typical of the spring of 1941. There were those who wanted us to declare war on Germany, and others who saw Russia and Japan as the principal enemy. There were many who sincerely felt that we had already gone too far in our support of the British and the Allied cause. This group consisted chiefly of people who were strongly opposed to the Roosevelt administration. Nevertheless, they joined the Radiation Laboratory and made notable contributions to the war effort.

In England similar experiments and speculations led to similar conclusions about the importance of nuclear fission. The work was brought directly to Churchill's attention, and though he expressed himself as being "personally . . . quite content with the existing explosive," he authorized a program designed to explore the possibilities of making atomic bombs. Eventually, as the ferocity of the war increased, the British program was transferred to North America. Many British nuclear scientists spent the last years of the war at Berkeley, Oak Ridge, and Los Alamos, and contributed to the nuclear weapons development programs being carried out in those places. At Quebec, in 1943, Churchill and Roosevelt made an agreement providing for broad sharing of their nuclear knowledge once the war was over. Apparently, the only limitations they intended concerned certain industrial processes that had been entirely worked out in America.

The events of the first years after the discovery of fission, the establishment of the British program, and its merger with the American program are described more fully by James R. Newman in his review of the book *Atom Harvest* by Leonard Bertin, which follows this introduction.

Work on nuclear chain reactions in France continued until about the time the Germans breached the Maginot Line. Some of the French scientists then made their way to laboratories in England, first, and later in Canada, where they continued their research. Others, notably Frédéric Joliot-Curie, elected to stay in France. A number of the other western European scientists, including the great Danish physicist, Niels Bohr, also eventually escaped to England and to America, where they, too, participated in various ways in the by then very secret work on the bomb.

In the Soviet Union, as in the Western countries, the discovery of fission was widely known and stimulated experiments and speculations too. It is interesting to note that one of the last reports on fission to be published in an American journal, *The Physical Review*,* was submitted by two Russians working in the laboratory of I. V. Kurchatov, the man who later directed the Soviet nuclear weapons program. After the war, Kurchatov said that it was the total lack of any response to this report that convinced the Soviets that the Americans were mounting a secret, presumably large, program to produce a bomb. Shortly after, the Soviets began a secret, but very small, program to explore the same objective. However, the German onslaught and the immediate problem of survival made it impossible for them to mount a program even remotely resembling the American effort. Because of the highly isolationist policies of Stalin during the prewar period, there had been almost no personal contact between Western and Soviet scientists for some years, so it was only natural that not even any serious suggestions for a cooperative

*"Spontaneous Fission of Uranium," *The Physical Review*, July 1940.

effort arose on either side. Moreover, the formal security system that eventually replaced the earlier voluntary one that had been imposed by the scientists themselves was every bit as concerned about "leaks" to the Communists as it was about leaks to the Nazis, and any suggestion about cooperative effort would have died aborning even if it had been made.

Thus, by the time Enrico Fermi and his co-workers achieved the first nuclear chain reaction at Chicago in December 1942, the United States was the only nation to have a serious nuclear weapons program, but even those who were developing the program didn't know this. All of us in the project thought of ourselves as being in a race for survival. The work was hard and the hours long, and the great majority of those in the project were almost totally immersed in their particular technical or scientific problem. Most were content to follow the standard paradigm of science, according to which a scientist should stick to science and leave politics to the politicians. Simply stated, this meant "how to make the bomb is *our* problem; how to use it is *theirs*."

But as time went on, and the end of the project came closer, a few began to concern themselves with what it all meant. In 1944, Niels Bohr wrote a memorandum to Roosevelt warning him of the probable dangerous arms race that lay ahead. In late 1944 and early 1945, when it finally became evident that there was no "race" for the bomb with the Germans, James Franck, Eugene Rabinowitch, Glenn Seaborg, Leo Szilard and others at Chicago became similarly concerned and, in effect, suggested that the goals of the project be reconsidered. The resulting document, known as the Franck report, also warned about a future arms race, and recommended international control of the development of atomic energy as the means for preventing one. Similarly, scientists at Los Alamos, New Mexico, where the first atom bomb would be assembled and tested, began to meet and discuss the probable future and what to do about it. The spirit and content of all these discussions is made clear in R. R. Wilson's review of Robert Jungk's book *Brighter than a Thousand Suns*, and in Philip Morrison's review of Alice Kimball Smith's book *A Peril and a Hope*, both of which follow this introduction. (Wilson had been head of the Experimental Nuclear Physics Division at Los Alamos during the war, and Morrison had been a group leader there.)

Toward the end of the war, a very select few, chosen from among the scientific leaders of the project, were officially invited to advise on the manner in which the first bomb should be used and on the postwar disposition of atomic energy. They did so through a committee known by the long name of The Scientific Advisory Committee to the Interim Committee. The members were Robert Oppenheimer, Arthur Compton, Ernest Lawrence, and Enrico Fermi, all of them except Fermi persons who were playing administrative rôles in the Manhattan District's laboratories. According to Henry Stimson, then Secretary of War, and the man to whom the advice was addressed, they advised him that

> The opinions of our scientific colleagues on the initial use of these weapons are not unanimous; they range from the proposal of a purely technical demonstration to that of military application best designed to induce surrender. Those who advocate a purely technical demonstration would wish to outlaw the use of atomic weapons, and have feared that if we use the weapons now our position in future negotiations would be prejudiced. Others emphasize the opportunity of saving American lives by immediate military use, and believe that such use will improve the international prospects, in that they are more concerned with the prevention of war than with the elimination of this special weapon. We find ourselves closer to these latter views; we can propose no technical demonstration likely to bring an end to the war; we can see no acceptable alternative to direct military use.*

Finally, on August 6, 1945, an atomic bomb was dropped on Hiroshima and on August 9 another was dropped on Nagasaki. More than a hundred thousand

*"The Decision to Use the Atomic Bomb," *Harper's Magazine*, February 1947.

human beings were killed, most of them in an instant. Also on August 9 the Soviets declared war on Japan and began to move into Manchuria. This sudden concatenation of events, heaped on top of the huge destruction already wreaked upon Japan, and in conjunction with the obvious hopelessness of Japan's plight, quickly precipitated the surrender of that country and thus the end of World War II.

The war research laboratories began to demobilize, most of the scientists returned to their universities, and an increasing number of them began to ponder the political and moral significance of what they had done. Because of the special portent of their work, this concern arose much more often and with greater intensity among those who had worked on the atomic bomb than among those who had worked on radar, proximity fuses, rockets, antimine warfare, and the like. They began what can be best described as a massive and intensive educational campaign whose purpose was to inform the public and its leaders about the atomic bomb and what it meant. This campaign took many forms: the top leaders of the program became official advisers to the top political and legislative leaders and to the various governmental organizations eventually established to cope with the new situation. Others established their own organizations specifically designed to lobby and inform. Two of these, the Federation of American Scientists and the Bulletin of the Atomic Scientists both still survive to this day. Still others undertook to lecture on the subject to anyone who would listen, and luncheon groups and Rotary clubs from one end of the country to the other listened to more or less arcane lectures on nuclear physics and to sometimes naive lectures on world politics. The press, which had scarcely ever mentioned physics before, gave full coverage to stories about nuclear physicists, always placing the adjective "brilliant" before the phrase "nuclear scientist" whenever naming one of them. The events and the spirit of those early postwar days are well described in the review by Philip Morrison of Alice Kimball Smith's book, *A Peril and a Hope.*

Statesmen, political leaders, and governmental officials, nearly all of whom were utterly unprepared for what had happened, also struggled with the problem of what to do about the atom. Some of the arguments and struggles that went on among these people, and between them and the scientists, are described in the review by James Newman of two books about that period: *The New World, 1939/1946* by R. G. Hewlett and O. E. Anderson, and *Now It Can Be Told* by Leslie Groves, the wartime commander of the Manhattan District.

In sum, all these concerns and struggles resulted in two contradictory political trends. On the one hand, the drawstrings of the curtain of secrecy were pulled tighter. Scientists suspected of leftist political tendencies were removed from those parts of the projects that were still operative after the partial demobilization, rules about exchange of information and "need to know" became more restrictive, the Quebec agreements between Roosevelt and Churchill were unilaterally and secretly abrogated by the United States, and high officials and members of Congress frequently expressed their determination to protect the "secret" which had cost so much treasure to produce and on which many came to feel American security depended.

At the same time, the scientists' recommendations for international control of the atom as a means of preventing a hopeless and dangerous arms race also made headway. These ideas and hopes were shaped successively by Robert Oppenheimer and his scientific colleagues, then by David Lilienthal (the first Chairman of the United States Atomic Energy Commission) and Dean Acheson (then Secretary of State), and finally by Bernard Baruch into what became known as the Baruch Plan. In essence, this plan called for the United States eventually to give up its monopoly on the atomic bomb in return for international control over the development of all forms of atomic energy. This plan was extremely generous from the American point of view, and quite unlike any other previous proposal in history. However, it contained a number of details relating to the timing of events (the U.S. monopoly would be eliminated only after all else had been accomplished) and to infringements on sovereignty that ran counter to all Soviet principles and practices, so the Baruch Plan was rejected by the Soviets even though it was endorsed by most other members of the United Nations.

Generally speaking, those who urged international control of the atom (mostly the scientists) contended there was no "secret" that could last very long. Typically, such persons estimated it would take about five years for the Russians to achieve a nuclear weapon. Conversely, those who estimated they would need a much longer time, perhaps twenty years or more, favored protecting the "secret" in order to maintain the monopoly.

The official Soviet line during the period of the U.S. monopoly (to 1949) was that the United States was greatly exaggerating the political importance and military effectiveness of the atomic bomb. The Soviets maintained that the victor in any future war would be the side with the correct political and social system and not the side with the most sophisticated weapons. But despite this official whistling in the dark, they took strong measures designed to offset the U.S. monopoly. They did not demobilize their military forces to the same extent the United States did, they consolidated their political and military hold on the countries of eastern Europe, and they greatly accelerated the pace of their own program to develop the atomic bomb. The first two of these measures effectively solved the problem for the short run, and the last measure assured that eventually it would be solved in the long run. Thus, believing time was on its side, the Soviet Union had little incentive to make any of the compromises in its attitudes toward sovereignty that were called for by the Baruch Plan.

Writing in 1970, the Soviet historian V. M. Khaitsman described the situation at the war's end as follows:

> After the end of World War II, in conditions of political atomic blackmail, directed by the ruling classes of the U.S.A., the Soviet Government called up scientists and engineers to create an atomic bomb in the shortest possible time. Effective measures were adopted . . . under the leadership of B. L. Vannikov, I. V. Kurchatov and M. G. Pervukhin.
>
> Investigations of nuclear problems were conducted at the highest pitch. Scientists understood the importance of achieving completion of the Soviet atomic project; they knew its significance in ensuring the safety of the Soviet Union. The necessity to create an equal atomic weapon prior to the time when its mass production would be developed in the U.S.A. dictated the fast tempo of the work.*

The Cold War intensified. In central Europe, the Czech *coup* took place, and the Berlin blockade brought forth the U.S. airlift. In the United States, the Containment Theory was advanced and turned into a program of action as the Truman Doctrine. International control of the atom continued to be discussed, but the prospects of international control happening steadily grew dimmer.

Much of the argument that went on in those days about the significance of the atomic bomb, and about the prospects for controlling it, is contained in a pair of articles published in *Scientific American* in March, 1949, shortly before the first Soviet nuclear explosion. The first of these is by P. M. S. Blackett, and consists of a condensation of a part of his book *Fear, War, and the Bomb*. The article is based partly on his own considerable knowledge of the effects of the strategic bombing on Germany, but it is also interesting because it parallels in part the official Soviet line mentioned above. The other article is by Louis Ridenour and is called simply "A U.S. Physicist's Reply to Professor Blackett." Ridenour was one of the early activists in the U.S. scientists' postwar movement, and he wrote a widely discussed playlet** describing one of the grim possibilities that might lie ahead. A year and a half after writing this article, he became the first Chief Scientist of the U.S. Air Force.

The USSR and Problems of Disarmament, 1945–1959, Moscow, 1970.
**"Pilot Lights of the Apocalypse," *Fortune*, January 1946.

The Blackett book aroused much interest and raised not a few hackles in the United States, and to sample this reaction I have included two other commentaries on the book in the material that follows. These are both from the "Science and the Citizen" columns of *Scientific American*; the longer one includes comments by I. I. Rabi, Edward Shils, Philip Morrison, and Manuel Vallarta, the last a Mexican physicist.

On August 29, 1949, near Semipalatinsk in Central Asia, the Soviets exploded their first bomb. Soon after, the radioactive debris it produced was detected by a worldwide air-sampling system set up by the United States for that purpose not long before. On September 23, President Truman announced the success of the Soviets, and on September 25, Tass issued a statement responding to the news reports that had circulated through the Western nations. The text of these statements is contained in the following reports from the "Science and the Citizen" column of *Scientific American.*

Science and the Citizen, November 1949

Announcement

AT 11 a.m. on September 23 President Truman announced the end of the U.S. monopoly in atomic bombs. His announcement that the U.S.S.R. had produced an atomic explosion was based on a careful evaluation by scientists of certain unspecified evidence. Although his communiqué touched off much speculation, the only authoritative information available to the public was Truman's statement and the official U.S.S.R. comment broadcast two days later by Tass, the Soviet news agency.

The President's full statement:

"I believe the American people to the fullest extent consistent with the national security are entitled to be informed of all developments in the field of atomic energy. That is my reason for making public the following information.

"We have evidence that within recent weeks an atomic explosion occurred in the U.S.S.R.

"Ever since atomic energy was first released by man, the eventual development of this new force by other nations was to be expected. This probability has always been taken into account by us.

"Nearly four years ago I pointed out that 'scientific opinion appears to be practically unanimous that the essential theoretical knowledge upon which the discovery is based is already widely known. There is also substantial agreement that foreign research can come abreast of our present theoretical knowledge in time.' And, in the three-nation declaration of the President of the United States and the Prime Ministers of the United Kingdom and of Canada, dated November 15, 1945, it was emphasized that no single nation could, in fact, have a monopoly of atomic weapons.

"This recent development emphasizes once again, if indeed such emphasis were needed, the necessity for that truly effective and enforceable international control of atomic energy which this Government and the large majority of the members of the United Nations support."

The text of the Tass statement, broadcast in English from Moscow:

"On September 23 Mr. Truman, President of the U.S.A., announced that according to data of the Government of the U.S.A., during one of the recent weeks there had occurred in the U.S.S.R. an atomic explosion. Simultaneously, a similar statement was made by the British and Canadian Governments.

"Following the publication of these statements in the American, British and Canadian press and also in the press of other countries, there appeared numerous utterances which spread alarm among broad social circles.

"In this connection, Tass is empowered to declare:

"In the Soviet Union, as is known, building work on a large scale is in progress – the building of hydroelectric stations, mines, canals, roads, which evoke the necessity of large-scale blasting work with the use of the latest technical means.

"Insofar as this blasting work has taken place and is taking place pretty frequently in various parts of the country, it is possible this might draw attention beyond the confines of the Soviet Union.

"As for the production of atomic energy, Tass considers it necessary to recall that already on November 6, 1947, Minister of Foreign Affairs of the U.S.S.R. V. M. Molotov made a statement concerning the secret of the atom bomb, when he declared that this secret was already long ago nonexistent.

"This statement signified the Soviet Union already had discovered the secret of the atomic weapon and that it had at its disposal this weapon.

"Scientific circles of the United States of America took this statement by V. M. Molotov for bluff, considering that the Russians could not possess an atomic weapon earlier than the year 1952. They, however, were mistaken, since the Soviet Union possessed the secret of the atomic weapon already in 1947.

"As for the alarm that is being spread on this account by certain foreign circles, there are not the slightest grounds for alarm.

"It should be pointed out that the Soviet Government, despite the existence in its country of an atomic weapon, adopts and intends adopting in the future its former position in favor of the absolute prohibition of the use of the atomic weapon.

"Concerning control of the atomic weapon, it has to be said that control will be essential in order to check up on fulfillment of a decision on the prohibition of production of the atomic weapon."

Science and the Citizen, November 1949

Name and Place Unknown

IN the absence of a "Smyth Report" from the U.S.S.R., the Russian atomic explosion generated a remarkably confusing crop of descriptions of the Soviet atomic energy enterprise, which, for want of a more authoritative name, may perhaps be called the Moscow Engineering District. These accounts, garnered by the Western press from sources ranging from unnamed Washington informants to "a Yugoslav recently returned from the Soviet-Iranian border," made up in circumstantial detail what they lacked in authority. They produce the following picture:

"Atomgrad," the Soviet center of atomic energy work, is variously located "a few miles north of Erivan" in the Caucasus near the Soviet-Turkish border; at "Ukhta, deep inside Russia"; near Tobolsk, in central Russia; "beyond the Urals"; "in eastern Siberia."

The power of the Soviet explosion is described by one source as less than that of the Alamogordo bomb and by others as greater than that of any U.S. atomic bomb except the latest ones tested at Eniwetok.

The date of the explosion is stated on reliable authority to have been July 10, early in August, around September 1, and September 12. "Reliable sources" in Paris declare that French engineers recently detected not one but three atomic explosions in Russia.

The explosion was detected in (a) Germany, (b) France, (c) Iran, (d) Scandinavia, (e) Japan, or perhaps (f) Alaska. According to *Time*, "patrolling bombers, sniffing at the winds that blow out of Russia, picked up the radioactive cloud [and followed it] for thousands of miles."

The Russians learned how to make the bomb from the Smyth Report and/or spies in the U.S., Canada and Britain. Alternatively, or concurrently, they have had an atomic bomb project of their own since 1943, under the direction of NKVD Chief Lavrenti P. Beria, who would thus be the General Groves of the Moscow Engineering District.

The most detailed report, published in the Paris newspaper *Figaro* under the by-line of a Yugoslav traveler to Iran, describes "Atomgrad" as a collection of huge underground laboratories in the valley of the Sanga River 30 miles northeast of Erivan. Built in 1946, it has 70,000 workers, among them 15,000 scientists and technicians, employed in four separate sections: 1) preliminary refining of uranium, 2) purification of uranium, separation of U-235 and extraction of plutonium, 3) plutonium research laboratories, 4) a medical research center. Each section is surrounded by a high concrete wall and no one is ever discharged or allowed to leave. The Soviet's decision to place its atomic energy project in this vulnerable region near the borders of Turkey and Iran is explained on the ground that the U.S.S.R. had no other convenient water-power sites available.

How much truth there may be in this potpourri of rumor only the Soviet Government and perhaps some U.S. and British intelligence officers know. The secrets of the Soviet work in atomic energy since the war certainly have been as closely guarded as those in the U.S. Outside of intelligence circles and the custodians of high policy to whom they report, no data are available for any kind of informed guess as to how the Russians managed to build an atomic bomb so soon and what the scale of their present operations is.

Certain facts, however, are known. The underlying scientific principles and some of the technological requirements for a uranium chain reaction were widely discussed among European physicists as early as 1939. Since the war U.S. atomic energy officials have unearthed and translated a number of early technical papers by European workers which show a surprising knowledge of the problems later tackled by the Manhattan District. Thus a German physicist, S. Flugge, late in 1939 published in *Naturwissenschaften* a paper called: "Can Nuclear Energy Be Utilized for Practical Purposes?" In it he discussed the conditions for a chain reaction, the amount of energy that would be released, the measurement of the uranium capture cross-sections for thermal neutrons, the absorption of neutrons by fission products, the critical size of a bomb. The Russians were not behind the Germans in the investigation of atomic energy. At a meeting of the Soviet Physical Society in June, 1941, Soviet physicists presented seven papers on nuclear fission. These showed that the state of their knowledge in this field was close to that in the U.S. at the time.

It is known that at the end of the war the U.S.S.R. had a nucleus of first-rank physicists for nuclear research, including Peter Kapitza, Abram Yoffe, Y. I. Frenkel, Igor Tamm, P. I. Lukirsky, Lion Landau, Pavel Cherenkov and Dmitri V. Skobeltsyn. It is also known that after the war the Soviet Union recruited several German atomic physicists, among them Gustav Hertz, winner of the 1925 Nobel prize in physics. The U.S.S.R. launched intensive uranium mining operations, involving many thousands of workers, at the famous pitchblende mines of Joachimsthal, Czechoslovakia, and in Saxony, Germany.

It was upon these facts, and upon an appraisal of the technical problems to be solved and the general state of Russian technological development, that U.S. atomic scientists based their estimate that the Russians would achieve an atomic bomb in 1952. The fact that they achieved it in a much shorter time means, as Samuel K. Allison of the University of Chicago has said, that the U.S. must "revise radically upward" its estimation of Soviet technology.

The President's statement of the facts was entirely accurate, but his presentation of them was somewhat disingenuous. While many of his scientific advisers had been warning that there was no "secret" that could be held for long, the same cannot be said of his political and military advisers. Truman himself evidently found it hard to believe that the Soviets had achieved an atomic bomb, and after leaving the presidency he was reported to have said he still didn't believe they could really have done it.

The Tass announcement was of course, very much more disingenuous. In the face of what amounted to worldwide knowledge, the Soviets chose to deny by implication the whole thing. Even when they made a technological advance that normally would call for boasting, their penchant for secrecy made it impossible for them to be forthright about it. Later, after the death of Stalin, they relaxed in this as in other matters, and sometimes, they went so far as to announce (and boast about) important nuclear tests in advance.

The speculation in the report entitled "Name and Place Unknown" may help to convey to the current reader some of the uncertainty that surrounded the event at the time. Of course, the U.S. intelligence community had more specific information than is indicated here, but the politicians and statesmen of the world who had to decide what to do next were working in an atmosphere every bit as confusing as that so clearly depicted in the report.

For years, the extreme secrecy in which the Soviets hid their weapons programs resulted in exaggerated notions in the West about where they stood, and the exaggerated notions in turn often resulted in overreactions by the West. Thus, Soviet supersecrecy has operated as one of the important driving forces in the nuclear arms race. The U.S. reaction to the first Soviet nuclear explosion, the "bomber gap" of the early fifties, and the "missile gap" hysteria of 1960 are all examples of how this works. Finally, as we shall see later in this reader, the Soviets recognized this problem in 1972 and agreed not to interfere with certain nonintrusive forms of intelligence gathering systems, such as reconnaissance satellites.

It is still not entirely clear what Molotov was talking about in the November 6, 1947 statement mentioned in the Tass report, but it seems likely he was referring to progress in the development of nuclear reactors. According to information published in the Soviet Union years later, the first Soviet chain reaction was achieved on December 25, 1946, and their first microgram amounts of plutonium were produced in the following spring. Either of these could have been the "already long ago" event Molotov had in mind.

It is interesting to read a Soviet report on the event published more than ten years later, and given in I. N. Golovin's biography of I. V. Kurchatov:

> The creators of all the weapons components gathered on the test site. With their own hands, the directors—physicists and engineers—brought the parts up to the requisite level of reliability. Work went on around the clock.
>
> Kurchatov and Zavenyagin personally directed all the preparations on which the success of the test depended. Both could sometimes be seen on the spot of the future explosion, sometimes where the bomb components were being assembled, and sometimes in the concrete laboratory bunkers.
>
> At last the bomb was assembled under the tireless direction of Kurchatov and Zavenyagin. Finally, it was lifted up onto the metal tower where it was to be exploded.
>
> The test was successfully carried out on September 23, 1949 in the presence of the Supreme Command of the Soviet Army and Government leaders.
>
> When the physicist who had created the bomb saw the blinding flash, brighter than the brightest sunny day, and the mushroom cloud rising into the stratosphere, they gave a sigh of relief. They carried out their duties. No one became frightened like the physicists in the U.S.A. who had gathered from everywhere and had made the weapon for the army of a country that was foreign to many of them and whose government used it against the peaceful population of Hiroshima and Nagasaki.
>
> The Soviet physicists knew they had created the weapon for their own people and for their own army which was defending peace. Their labor, their sleepless nights, and the huge effort that had constantly increased in the course of those past years had not been in vain: they had knocked the trump card from the hands of the American atomic diplomats.*

It is curious that the date given for the explosion is incorrect, being that of the announcement Truman made four weeks after the event itself.

A reasoned view of what it all meant, particularly insofar as the first Soviet tests signalled a need to try again to control the atom, is presented in the article by Chester I. Barnard which concludes this first section of the reader. Barnard had been a member of the Board of Consultants in the State Department, a group which helped to develop the Oppenheimer-Lilienthal-Acheson-Baruch Plan. In the article, he calls for increased flexibility in the American approach. Others, including Baruch himself, opposed changes in American proposals.

---

*I. N. Golovin, *I. V. Kurchatov*, Moscow, 1967.

1

The Rift in the Anglo-American Nuclear Partnership

JAMES R. NEWMAN

June 1956

A review of *Atom Harvest,* by Leonard Bertin. London: Martin Secker and Warburg Ltd., 1956.

When a historian withholds important facts likely to influence the judgment of his readers, he commits a fraud, as an English statesman once remarked. When a government withholds important facts likely to influence the judgment of its people, it commits a graver fraud. Unfortunately these are offenses unknown to the law, though their effects are incalculable.

A prime example of official juggling—and of its consequences—is brought out in this book by Leonard Bertin, science correspondent of the London *Daily Telegraph.* The subject of his account is Britain's atomic energy industry. He describes its growth from small wartime beginnings to the great plants at Harwell, Capenhurst, Windscale and Calder Hall; the scientific and technological labors that made possible the expansion; the military and peaceful benefits that Britain hopes to derive from atomic energy. All this makes a readable and informative report. But the chief interest of the book for this reviewer lies in two chapters which present a timely recapitulation of a critical episode of recent history: the breakdown of the Anglo-American partnership in atomic energy.

Most of the facts, to be sure, are not new. They can be extracted from the Smyth report, the official British and Canadian atomic energy statements of August, 1945, Robert Sherwood's *Roosevelt and Hopkins,* Winston Churchill's war memoirs and various papers and documents made public in the last few years. But the material is put together here for the first time. While Bertin's is a partisan account, exaggerating the British contribution in atomic energy as others have exaggerated the U.S. contribution, it explains pretty well the nature, the causes and the results of the breach. It is a story worth pondering, more as a guide to the future than as another revelation, so fashionable in our period, of who killed Cock Robin.

To understand the culminating political fiasco it is necessary briefly to review the scientific background.

In January, 1939, Otto Hahn and Fritz Strassmann of Berlin announced their discovery that an isotope of barium was produced by the neutron bombardment of uranium. A couple of weeks earlier Hahn had imparted this information to Otto Frisch, who was spending Christmas with his aunt, Lise Meitner, in Stockholm. Frisch passed on the news to Niels Bohr at the Institute of Theoretical Physics in Copenhagen, but not before making a profound and fateful conjecture. "It looked [Frisch told Bertin] as if the absorption of the neutron had disturbed the delicate balance between the forces of attraction and the forces of repulsion inside the nucleus. It was as if the nucleus had first become elongated and then developed a waist before dividing into two more or less equal parts in just the same way that a living cell divides." From a U.S. biologist Frisch learned that the process by which bacteria and other organisms reproduce themselves is called "fission." He gave the same name to the newly discovered nuclear phenomenon.

Bohr brought the news with him to the U.S. and told his former student John A. Wheeler and others at Princeton University about it. The word spread to Enrico Fermi and his associates at Columbia University. Immediately several groups began a search for the massive pulses of ionization to be expected from the flying fragments of uranium. Within a few days the fission theory was experimentally confirmed by four laboratories in the U.S., by Frisch in Copenhagen and by Frédéric Joliot (later Joliot-Curie) in Paris. The race was on. Physicists in the U.S. and in Europe drove themselves furiously to broaden their knowledge of the subject; sensational stories began to appear in the press. When L. A. Turner of Princeton wrote an article on fission in the January, 1940, issue of *Reviews of Modern Physics,* he cited nearly 100 papers on the subject published during the preceding 12 months.

The crucial question was whether a chain reaction was possible. This turned, as Henry D. Smyth pointed out in his account, on the result of a competition among four processes: escape of neutrons before capture, non-fission capture by uranium, non-fission capture by impurities, fission capture. One of the first groups off the mark consisted of H. von Halban, Lew Kowarski and Joliot in France. They made experiments to ascertain the rate of production of neutrons, comparing the absorptive capacity of a uranium compound dissolved in water with that of a solution of a non-uranium salt. Their conclusions were basically correct though overoptimistic—for every neutron that split a uranium atom, they calculated, between three and four additional neutrons would be produced.

It was generally known by 1940 that to harness atomic energy two different processes would have to be achieved, depending on whether one wanted power or a bang. To get atomic power required a chain reaction induced by slow neutrons; to get a bomb required one induced by fast neutrons in separated uranium 235 or in plutonium. It was also known that fission neutrons had high speeds, that the neutrons had to be slowed to produce power and to convert U-238 into plutonium, and that various substances—including graphite, heavy water and beryllium—could be used as moderators to slow down fast neutrons. On the basis of this knowledge the French scientists in 1940 made designs of heavy-water reactors and graphite reactors to be used as sources of power. Lest anyone suppose that pure scientists are above sordid concerns, Bertin relates—not without relish—that the French team "hurriedly made the first application for patents of chain-reacting piles, not very different in general principle from those now operating in many parts of the world."

I need not devote time to the parallel U.S. developments during the period because they have been often and fully described; but the British side of the story, much less widely known, merits some attention.

The importance of the Hahn-Strassmann announcement was of course not overlooked in Britain. Within a short time after the news from Germany, Sir George Thomson, son of the famous J. J. and himself a Nobel prize winner in physics, went to the Air Ministry and asked for a ton of uranium oxide. He explained that he needed it to conduct experiments on the possibilities of atomic power and atomic bombs at the Imperial College of Science and Technology in London, where he was teaching. The Air Ministry supplied the material and he began to work, but the first results were disappointing. He concluded that unless large supplies of heavy water were made available, a chain reaction in uranium oxide could not be realized. To the end of the war, fortunately (as Sir George pointed out to Bertin), the "most distinguished physicists in Germany thought the same."

But the most distinguished physicists *in* Germany were by no means the most distinguished physicists *of* Germany. Albert Einstein, Hans Bethe and Leo Szilard were in the U.S.; Lise Meitner was in Sweden; Otto Frisch was in Copenhagen; F. E. Simon and R. E. Peierls were in Britain. These and other refugees—including Fermi from Italy—were to cost the "master races" dear. Like the Egyptians, the Germans soon had cause to ask: "Why have we done this, that we have let Israel go from serving us?" In March, 1940, word came to Thomson from Peierls and Frisch (who had moved to Britain from Denmark) that a bomb made of uranium 235 was probably feasible. A committee was promptly set up under Thomson to go into the matter. The cover name selected for the group was "Maud"—by which choice hangs an amusing tale.

When the Germans overran Denmark, Bohr sent Frisch a telegram, the last part of which said: "Tell Cockcroft and Maud Ray Kent." Knowing no "Maud Ray Kent," Frisch and Cockcroft concluded the words were an anagram for "radium taken," intended to warn that the Germans had confiscated the Danish stocks of that valuable and significant commodity. At any rate, it was the telegram that suggested the name for the committee. Years later Thomson mentioned the fact to Bohr, who was astounded. It turned out that he knew a lady named Maud Ray who lived in Kent; he had wanted word sent to her that he was safe and well. Nor was this the whole of the comedy. For among civil servants who regarded themselves in the know, the name Maud was interpreted as a block of initials representing "Military Application of Uranium Detonation." These ingenious conjectures remind one of some of the hypotheses of cosmology.

Among the problems tackled by the Maud committee were the separation of U-235, the physics of neutron capture and fission, the critical mass of U-235 needed to provide an explosion, and various related chemical matters. Peierls, Simon, James Chadwick, Norman Feather and Egon Bretscher led these studies, which made promising headway.

Meanwhile a daring plan was conceived by that extraordinarily gallant and intrepid agent, the late Earl of Suffolk. As scientific attaché in Paris he had compiled a list of 150 French scientists and technicians who were to be smuggled to Britain if France fell. When the Germans tore through the Maginot Line, the plan was put into execution, with Suffolk in charge. Halban, Kowarski and Joliot were on the list—but Joliot preferred to stay in France. In the confusion after the capture of Paris only 40 of the men Suffolk had selected reached Bordeaux. There they were taken aboard a small British collier, the *Broompark*, for the hazardous voyage across the Channel. Besides Halban, Kowarski and other scientists, the cargo included several million dollars' worth of industrial diamonds and 36 gallons of heavy water, comprising most of the then existing stock in the world. Suffolk, who numbered carpentry among his array of talents, built a raft, and the heavy water and diamonds were lashed on top. A "solemn agreement" was made that if the ship was mined or bombed, the suvivors were to cut loose the raft and try to make port; but in the event of a torpedoing, in which case the Germans would have seen the raft, it was to remain tied to the *Broompark* when it sank. The *Broompark* arrived safely in Falmouth, although a neighboring ship exploded on a mine. The Earl of Suffolk, afterwards killed in attempting to disarm a German bomb, had brought off another brilliant coup.

Halban and Kowarski set up shop in the Cavendish Laboratory at Cambridge and resumed their researches on reactors. According to Bertin they made notable progress, and by late 1940 had proved conclusively the feasibility of a chain-reacting, homogeneous, heavy water reactor. If this claim is to be credited, they anticipated by more than 18 months experimental demonstrations in the U.S. that a heterogeneous, graphite-moderated pile would sustain a chain reaction. The author says that when the Frenchmen's findings were "reported to the United States . . . they were immediately pooh-poohed." They are not mentioned in the Smyth report. Bertin seems to feel that nothing less than British and French honor were impugned by our attitude, and he emphasizes the fact that when the U.S. finally did catch up with Halban and Kowarski, it was the achievement of "foreign-born scientists working in America." This is petty stuff, but it bred resentments which even now, 15 years later, are apparently not forgotten.

The British work moved steadily forward, and there were frequent interchanges of information on their progress and ours. In the summer of 1941 Maud made a high-level report on the possibility of a U-235 bomb and a pile to produce power and plutonium. Simon prepared a cost estimate for a full-scale gaseous diffusion plant; the figures frightened him and he decided he had better forward his lowest estimate lest the Cabinet itself suffer a chain reaction. After hearing the opinions of his advisers, Churchill drafted one of his classic minutes for his Chiefs of Staff:

"Although personally I am quite content with the existing explosive I feel we must not stand in the way of improvement and I therefore think that action should be taken in the sense proposed by Lord Cherwell and that the Cabinet Minister responsible should be Sir John Anderson. I shall be glad to know what the Chiefs of Staff think."

The Chiefs recommended a "maximum priority." A decision was taken to build a pilot plant for uranium in Britain and, if possible, a full-scale plant in Canada. The Department of Scientific and Industrial Research set up a new unit called the "Directorate of Tube Alloys." This cover name corresponded to our "Development of Substitute Materials Project" in the "Manhattan District" of the Corps of Engineers. Anderson hit upon "Tube Alloys" because a diffusion plant would require miles of tubing made of a special alloy to resist corrosion.

It was one thing to create the administrative machinery, quite another to erect the plant. Britain was heavily committed in manpower and resources, and the threat of invasion was ever present. Churchill therefore welcomed President Roosevelt's proposal to "coordinate or even jointly conduct" the atomic energy program. Roosevelt's letter to Churchill was sent October 11, 1941, and it was followed shortly by a visit to Britain by Harold Urey and George Pegram. The day before Pearl Harbor the U.S. Office of Scientific Research and Development announced to "S-1," its uranium section, that a vigorous program would be undertaken to make a bomb. Vannevar Bush urged the British to move the bulk of their research and development to Canadian laboratories; as a result Halban led a team to Montreal. On August 13, 1942, the Manhattan District was born. The British assumed that the cooperation already achieved would be extended. By autumn, however, it was clear that the channels of Anglo-American communication were becoming constricted. British scientists soon discovered they could learn very little about our progress. Fermi's group in Chicago kept open a line to the Montreal group, but in general if the British were able to pick up anything at all it was only out of the corner of some amiable fellow's mouth and not through official channels. In this respect, it should be pointed out, the British were not worse off than most U.S. scientists on the project: no one was told any more than high authority thought he needed for his particular job. This practice led to certain costly blunders but was regarded as essential to security.

In due course the breakdown of communication came to the attention of the Prime Minister. It was a painful surprise. He had discussed the matter with President Roosevelt at Hyde Park in June, 1942, and had come away with the understanding, as he afterwards cabled Harry Hopkins, "that everything was on the basis of fully sharing the results as equal partners." At Casablanca in January, 1943, Churchill expressed his concern and Hopkins promised to look into the question on his return to Washington. This he failed to do, and Churchill cabled: "I should be grateful for some news about this, as at present the American War Department is asking us to keep them informed of our experiments while refusing altogether any information about theirs." Hopkins asked that Anderson "send me a full memo by pouch of what he considers is the basis of the present misunderstanding, since I gather the impression that our people feel no agreement has been breached." In a long responding cable Churchill said: "Urgent decisions about our programme both here and in Canada depend on the extent to which full collaboration between us is restored, and I must ask you to let me have a firm decision on U.S. policy in this matter very soon."

Hopkins conferred with the President, Secretary of War Stimson, Bush and James B. Conant. A memo by Bush (quoted in Sherwood's biography) stated that information would be furnished only to individuals "who need it can use it now in furtherance of the war effort." To step beyond this policy, he said, "would be to furnish information on secret military matters to individuals who wish it either because of general interest or because of its application to nonwar or postwar matters." This would "decrease security without advancing the war effort." On the surface this seemed a sound position, but the British objection, as reported by Sherwood, was equally sound. Our policy, they said, gave us the excuse to withhold from them all the fruits of joint research, including the possible industrial uses of atomic energy after the war. In the event, this is exactly what happened. After the war Congress, grossly misled by the Executive Department as to the nature of the British contribution and the Anglo-American agreements, passed legislation which forbade the transfer of atomic energy data to any foreign country.

In the early summer of 1943 Stimson and Churchill discussed the atomic energy impasse. Stimson took the position that the British pressure to obtain information was economically motivated, and that "the Americans could not see the fun of spending billions of dollars to find out things for someone else to use in a competitive postwar world." At least this put the cards on the table. The British were deeply concerned, but further discussion was postponed until the heads of state met at Quebec a month later. There an agreement provided for the setting up of a Combined Policy Committee "to keep all sections of the project under constant review" and for a "complete interchange of information and ideas on all sections of the project between members of the Policy Committee and their immediate technical advisers." The policy of compartmentalization was to be maintained, in that exchanges at the working level were to take place only "between those in the two countries engaged in the same sections of the field." Bertin makes the point that this gave U.S. authorities the excuse to withhold information on production techniques, since the British were not engaged in this "section of the field." The facts seem at least partly to bear out this contention, for no British scientist or engineer, according to Bertin, "was ever allowed to enter the plant at Oak Ridge, and our men were not even told whether the ideas that they had developed [on gaseous diffusion] had worked satisfactorily." It is not altogether clear why, under the terms of the Quebec agreement, the British members of the Combined Policy Committee were denied access to these data—if, indeed, that was the case.

The most important provision of the Quebec agreement related to the postwar uses of atomic energy. It stated that "in view of the heavy burden of production falling upon the U.S. as the result of a wise division of war effort, the British Government recognize that any postwar advantages of an industrial or commercial character shall be dealt with as between the U.S. and Great Britain on terms to be specified by the President of the United States to the Prime Minister of Great Britain. The Prime Minister expressly disclaims any interest in these industrial and commercial aspects beyond what may be considered by the President of the United States to be fair and just and in harmony with the economic welfare of the world."

Whether or not this was a wise provision; whether or not it demonstrated—as Bertin contends—Churchill's magnanimity, or Roosevelt's shrewdness; whether or not Congress would have approved it as a workable agreement after the war, one fact is certain: Never was a solemn treaty between heads of state more completely disregarded than this one. The agreement was made in secret and for many years was kept secret. Churchill made it public in April, 1954; Congressional leaders had been apprised of it somewhat earlier but not in time to inform their debates and decisions on the atomic energy legislation adopted in 1946.

As a participant in some of these events I am able to corroborate Bertin's statement that the McMahon Act was drafted, debated and passed by a Congress "completely unaware of the terms of the agreement with the British and Canadians." While serving as counsel to the Senate Committee on Atomic Energy, I learned by chance, as did Senator McMahon, that there had been an agreement at Quebec. Repeated attempts to discover its contents were unsuccessful. The Senator and I called upon President Truman early in 1946 to see whether he could enlighten us. We came away empty-handed. Neither the White House nor the State Department thought it advisable to share this knowledge. Senator McMahon, according to Bertin, "to his great embarrassment, was only shown the text of the Quebec agreement after he had accepted the chairmanship of the Joint Congressional Committee on Atomic Energy"—*i.e.*, in September, 1946.

It is unnecessary to read sinister motives into the decision of the Executive Branch not to make Congress privy to the facts. Disclosure would have loosed a storm on the Administration, and it is unlikely that Congress would have regarded itself as bound by President Roosevelt's more or less private and altogether vague commitment. Yet beyond question Congress had the right to know about it. Its provisions might not have been welcome to members of Congress, but at least they would have been able to act with knowledge, and the public would have been able to judge their action. Disclosure would also have countered the myth, still widely believed, that atomic energy was an exclusively American achievement and possession. Gordon Dean, in his book *Report on the Atom*, described the common misconception as follows: "Atomic energy was discovered and first developed in the U.S. in secret during World War II. Although we are still ahead in the field, the Russians, with the help of traitors, successfully stole enough of our key secrets during the war to develop a program of their own and are now hot on our heels. Our Allies, the British, because some of their scientists came over to help us with our wartime program, also know something of these matters, but are actually running a very poor third." No thoughtful person can fail to wonder to what extent the myth has made more difficult the attainment of international control of atomic energy.

One asks why the British kept quiet about the Quebec agreement in the face of legislation "which made no distinction between countries like Britain and Canada and our late enemies or those with whom at the time we were engaged in a cold war." The answer is fairly obvious. The British desperately needed our help and cooperation in the years after the war. They were in no position to risk strengthening isolationist sentiment by ventilating a secret treaty. The British therefore kept mum and built up their own establishment. And they did pretty well. Except in magnitude, their atomic energy industry is at least the equal of ours—as to weapons, atomic power and the uses of isotopes.

Atom Harvest is a valuable book. It contains errors of detail, improper emphases and doubtful inferences, but the key historical account is essentially dependable and always honest. There is no reason to criticize its occasional flashes of anger. This is how the British feel and we may as well know it. Bertin is to be congratulated as a journalist who has done his job in the best tradition of journalism.

[*Editor's note: Bertin's statement that the British were excluded from Oak Ridge, which Newman mentions, applies only to the Gaseous Diffusion Plant (K-25). A number of British scientists associated during the war with the University of California Radiation Laboratory made extended visits to the Electromagnetic Separation Plant (Y-12), also located in Oak Ridge.*]

2

A History of the Atomic Scientists

ROBERT R. WILSON
December 1958

A review of *Brighter than a Thousand Suns: A Personal History of the Atomic Scientists,* by Robert Jungk. New York: Harcourt, Brace and Company, 1958.

The title of Robert Jungk's *Brighter than a Thousand Suns* is adapted from the epic poem of India, the Bhagavad-Gita. Jungk's book is also a kind of epic, complete with tragically flawed heroes and a broad scene extending from the Old World villages of Göttingen and Cambridge to the pink and purple desert of New Mexico. Indeed, the birth of nuclear energy and the atomic bomb—its effect upon the men who developed it, upon the political environment which determined it and then was determined by it, upon a world which does not quite know what to do with it—is surely a subject fit for an epic.

A subtitle of the book is *A Personal History of the Atomic Scientists.* There is no doubt that the account is personal, but though Jungk is trained as a historian it is not history. It is marred by inaccuracies on nearly every page. Jungk has gone deep enough into his subject to catch something of the spirit of physics and of physicists (he has dug up a wealth of amusing anecdotes), but he has not gone sufficiently deep to acquire the understanding necessary to qualify him for the kind of analysis he attempts of awesome events and of complex personalities.

Although Jungk has interviewed quite a number of people and read quite a few documents, there is little new material in the volume except for the anecdotes. What is new is the synthesis of many stories, the tying up of many strands—a job so artfully done that the account reads like a novel and is as exciting as a murder mystery. What is also new is the interpretation of events and the analysis of the actors in the atomic drama. It is here that Jungk's subject is too big for him; his conclusions are frequently irresponsible, sensational and in questionable taste.

It is all to the good that Jungk comes to grips with the heart of the matter: the moral dilemma faced by those scientists attending the birth of the bomb. I cannot censure the author for concluding that his heroes are less than perfect; it may be the decision of history that they were evil personified. It is still too early to view the matter in its true perspective. Inasmuch as I, along with so many others, played my own role in this real-life epic, due allowance must be made for my defensive bias. Reading this book was an emotional experience for me; I found many old doubts, questions and uncertainties awakened. Sometimes Jungk touched old sores (he also succeeded in opening a few new ones), but usually I was moved not by remorse but by indignation.

Jungk takes us on a journey through the years to the quiet times when physics was a pleasant, intellectual subject, not unlike the study of Medieval French in its popular interest. At that time physicists were nonentities for the man on the street. In presenting rather carefully selected but sharply drawn vignettes of the period, Jungk is at his best. He has picked the right people and the right places at the right time to portray the beginnings of modern physics and modern physicists. He also shows a remarkable talent for discussing in adult but simple language some of the actual physics that was involved. Having sketched these idyllic times and then, I might add parenthetically, neglecting to give any account of the exceedingly important American work which bridged the period between early atomic physics and the later flowering of nuclear physics, Jungk comes directly to the atomic bomb. One of his main themes is the contrast between the wartime work of nuclear physicists in this country and of their counterparts in Germany. His extraordinary thesis seems to be this: Physicists in Germany managed, by their great diligence, *not* to build a bomb; physicists in the U.S., on the other hand, failed—they did *not* manage *not* to build a bomb. It is at this point that my indignation is aroused. Jungk's argument involves relationships of fact and moral value that are beyond the wisest of us to perceive at this stage of history. Furthermore, there is considerable artificiality about a discussion of the moral aspects of a scientific and technological development such as the atomic bomb. In the first place, there is no single-minded group which may be called "American physicists." Physicists do not look alike or think alike, nor are they of the same political persuasion. In the second place, important though physicists may have been in the making of the atomic bomb, there were a host of others—chemists, engineers, technicians, industrialists, military men—all of whom played important roles, and without whose cooperation and interaction the bomb would never have been built. Consequently it is presumptuous for me, a physicist, to discuss the ethics of the physicists who built the bomb. Obviously, however, each individual who participates in such a project does have a personal moral problem. One might also assign a measure of responsibility to each group of men in the project. If the physicists, for example, had decided not to build the atomic bomb, the bomb would probably not have been built. We physicists cast our lot with building it. We therefore bear the responsibility for our choice. Were we moral? Jungk thinks not, and by contrast praises the virtue of physicists working in Germany.

Let us consider the case of the German physicists. Because I take the optimistic view of human nature I should like to accept Jungk's views, but I cannot. The willing suspension of disbelief can go just so far. Jungk is the first person to make a serious case for the German physicists, and he makes it badly. A very different view of the matter has been presented by the Dutch-born U.S. physicist Samuel A. Goudsmit in his well-documented book *Alsos*, the result of his wartime study of German progress in developing nuclear energy. He has commented there, and elsewhere, on the conversations of the German physicists, temporarily in custody after the war, when they learned of the explosion of the atomic bomb. They were surprised. They had not believed that it was technically feasible. Goudsmit describes the German failure in terms of ineptitude, political interference and lack of support. Even if we choose not to believe this and accept Jungk's tale of a moral sit-down strike, the comparison is grossly unfair. Although it is now 15 years after the event, I still feel there is no comparison between physicists working for Nazi tyranny, which was hostile to intellectualism, and our activities in a desperate defense of a decent world. We are asked to believe that German nuclear physicists sabotaged the war effort while German rocket physicists worked enthusiastically, and successfully delivered to their armed forces what might have been a crucial weapon. Do blunted ethical perceptions go hand in hand with an interest in classical physics, and does morality march only with nuclear physics? It seems more logical that political and economic support was given to one field rather than another, and that this was decisive.

The other side of the argument, namely our failure not to make the weapon, is more complex. One should recall the atmosphere when work on the bomb began. The Germans were successful on all fronts; they were ruthless; there was a good chance that they would win the war. We knew that they were working on nuclear energy. I held pacifist views at the time, but in the light of the Nazi danger I felt that I had little moral choice. I suspect that the lines of the children of light and of the children of darkness were drawn as clearly as they ever will be. Neutrality would have been a selfish luxury.

Even if it was right to work on the Manhattan Project when the Germans were winning, was it right to continue the work after the Germans surrendered? In retrospect this question has bothered me greatly. Not at the time, however! Perhaps I should now respect myself more if I had left the work on V-E Day. The possibility simply did not occur to me. Events tumbled upon each other too quickly; the German surrender coincided with our preparations for the critical first test of the bomb in the New Mexico desert. We were the heroes of our epic, and there was no turning back. We were working on a problem to which we were completely committed; there was little time to re-examine our moral position from day to day.

In this connection I do remember calling in 1944 a meeting of my cyclotron group at Los Alamos. The subject of the meeting was rather pretentiously announced as "The Impact of the Gadget [the bomb] on Civilization." The meeting was advertised to other groups at Los Alamos, and between 50 and 100 scientists attended. We discussed what the world might be like as a result of our endeavors. At the time our work was not going very well; it was not at all evident that the bomb would be finished before the war was over. Secrecy was a necessary evil with which we lived uneasily. We imagined a world of conventional weapons and conventional world politics where the military kept the atomic bomb a secret. The best thing that we could think of—and we were all in agreement—was that it was absolutely essential to finish the bomb before the meeting in San Francisco at which the United Nations was formed. Then, it was our hope, the new world organization would be able to deal with the atomic bomb from the beginning. We failed that rendezvous. There was no consideration given at San Francisco to nuclear energy.

Those who criticize us for making the bomb might reflect on the kind of world which would have resulted had we not finished the bomb before the war was over. It seems almost certain that if we on the Manhattan Project had not built the bomb, the job would have been done by others within five or 10 years, either in this country or elsewhere. Nuclear energy was a time bomb set for the human race, and eventually the human race would have had to reckon with it. Was it not for the best that the public demonstration of the bomb, which ended World War II, came at a time when new relationships among nations were being established?

Jungk goes to considerable lengths to demonstrate the international origins of nuclear physics. Yet by implication he would have U.S. physicists bear the full responsibility for the bomb. During the war Los Alamos was as international a community of scientists as has ever existed. Our agreement in recognizing the hazards of nuclear energy was as complete as our agreement in purely scientific matters.

If Jungk is critical of the physicists who made the bomb, he is positively censorious of the decision to drop the bomb on Hiroshima and Nagasaki. There are many who share this view; I count myself among them. It is only with his conclusion that I am in agreement, however, for here, as usual, Jungk oversimplifies and distorts history. I recognize that my own feeling about the military use of the bomb was and remains largely sentimental rather than rational. I felt betrayed when the bomb was exploded over Japan without discussion or some peaceful demonstration of its power to the Japanese. More common, and possibly as rational, is the opinion held by many of my colleagues: that the war was ended by the atomic bomb and that more lives, both American and Japanese, would have been lost had the war been permitted to continue. Henry L. Stimson, who had more to do with the decision to drop the bomb than anyone else, perhaps expressed their sentiments when he wrote: "The face of war is the face of death; death is an inevitable part of every order that a wartime leader gives. The decision to use the atomic bomb was a decision that brought death to over 100,000 Japanese. No explanation can change that fact and I do not wish to gloss it over. But this deliberate, premeditated destruction was our least abhorrent choice. The destruction of Hiroshima and Nagasaki put an end to the Japanese war. It stopped the fire raids and the strangling blockade; it ended the ghastly specter of a clash of great land armies. The bombs dropped on Hiroshima and Nagasaki ended a war. They also made it wholly clear that we must never have another war. This is the lesson men and leaders everywhere must learn, and I believe that when they learn it they will find a way to lasting peace. There is no other choice."

Brighter than a Thousand Suns, like the Bhagavad-Gita, has its Krishna—Robert Oppenheimer. Although the author has never interviewed his subject, he has evidently discussed him at length with some physicists and has attempted what amounts to a skeletal biography. [See note at end of review. *Ed.*] Oppenheimer is of course a fascinating figure, but one so complex and with such depths that I, who worked intimately with him during the war, would quail before the task that Jungk approaches so capriciously. It is not a flattering portrait, nor is it a true one. Once more the author stoops to what must be deliberate distortion by selecting what conforms to his thesis and ignoring the rest. Unfortunately he has been aided here by the more professional efforts of those who revoked Oppenheimer's clearance in 1954 and published the proceedings. Here were indecently exposed all manner of irrelevant private details about the life of a fine scientist who had devoted his best years to serving his country. The trial of Oppenheimer was one of the last great *autos-da-fé* of the McCarthy era. Perhaps a European journalist like Jungk cannot be blamed too much for his erroneous judgment so long as this ungrateful nation's verdict, made during hysterical times, stands unrescinded.

In view of Jungk's profound errors of judgment, it is perhaps pedantic to add that he has mangled the names of many minor characters of his epic, and that he has a positively abandoned manner with dates. He has not been able to copy with any degree of accuracy a simple list from *Atomic Energy for Military Purposes*, the classic history of the Manhattan Project. He indicates that liquor was banned at Los Alamos, when in fact the only fluid in short supply there was water. (When Klaus Fuchs was arrested, many of us not only asked ourselves, "Why did he do it?," but also, "How did he dare to drink so much at Los Alamos?") Oppenheimer was not educated at the Los Alamos Ranch School for Boys. It is simply not true that "barely a dozen physicists on the bomb projects had an over-all view." Robert Serber did not collect the pool money for the most accurate prediction of the energy released by the first atomic explosion, nor was he a "visitor" to Los Alamos. I. I. Rabi won the pool, and Serber was a regular member of the Los Alamos staff. The Wilsons lived across the hall from the Serbers, and often said: "The Serbers are our nerbers." The Serbers now live across the hall from the Rabis in New York. The world of nuclear physics is rather chummy, and anyone who confuses Robert Serber and I. I. Rabi has not studied that world very carefully.

All this is not, of course, particularly important. It suggests, however, that even Jungk's anecdotal history is weak. What is more to the point, the factual errors do indicate a lighthearted and uncritical approach toward his material, which becomes serious when he attacks men and interprets events. The book lacks the documentation one expects of a historian; one never knows whether Jungk obtained some particular fact from someone's lips or from an unpublished paper or from his own vivid imagination.

Although I have criticized Jungk's book, I respect his motives in attempting to understand the forces that shape science and scientists. Assuming that civilization survives the invention of this ultimate weapon, the human spirit will be challenged often and perhaps even more seriously by future developments in science and technology. For me the question is: Are scientists to attain the heightened sense of moral values which will enable them to determine the direction of these developments with humanistic and humanitarian ends in view, or will humanists and humanitarians attain an understanding of scientific values that will allow them to determine the wise direction of science? I suspect that civilization will best be served by a true fusion—or at least a close mutual understanding—of science, the humanities and politics. There are many who are presently preoccupied with exactly this problem. Jungk has struck out boldly, if not carefully, in this direction by his provocative analysis of this case history of science, scientists and civilization.

[*Editor's note: A letter from Jungk appearing in* Scientific American *following the publication of this review made it clear that Jungk had in fact interviewed Robert Oppenheimer in the course of preparing his manuscript. His letter was followed by one from Wilson acknowledging the correction but expressing his amazement over how Jungk could have been so wrong about Oppenheimer in that case.*]

Atomic Scientists as Policy Advisers

PHILIP MORRISON

September 1965

A review of *A Peril and a Hope: The Scientists' Movement in America, 1945–1947*, by Alice Kimball Smith. Chicago: The University of Chicago Press, 1965.

Bernal Diaz, an old soldier, once sat down to bequeath us with his pen what he recalled of those cunning, cruel and resolute years when he followed his general Cortes to conquer Mexico. The old man's narrative, spare and eloquent, remains a marvel. I too was a private soldier, in a quick and cruel campaign of 20 years ago. My recollection of faded and inchoate; I saw only a small sector of the battle, in Los Alamos, postwar Hiroshima and the Senate Office Building. Today we have a few memoirs by the great captains but no chronicles of the soldiers. Alice Kimball Smith, who knew wartime Los Alamos and postwar Chicago as a friend of the scientists and a trained historian, and who was a cool and yet concerned eyewitness of the battles, has here produced a professional's narrative. Beginning in December of 1943, when Niels Bohr and his son Aage came to the Manhattan project in their flight from that final solution intended for Danes of Jewish ancestry, she carries forward a clear story of the complex events that led first to the dropping of the bomb and then to the development of the political role of the laboratory scientist in the first two years after the close of the war. I shall summarize and comment on her fine account, writing as a participant and a partisan. No review, however, can replace this book itself—fully and critically documented, compassionately written, painstakingly detailed. It is both lively and exact, although the large and shifting cast, the narrowness of the issues joined month by month and the elision of the high matters that resulted from the events she has chosen to detail make it by no means smooth reading. Nonetheless, all who want seriously to study recent history will need to build on what Dr. Smith has written.

The first sixth or so of the book ends with Hiroshima. It tells the story of the decision to drop the bomb, a tale "written from the scientists' point of view." The official Atomic Energy Commission history (*The New World*), General Leslie R. Groves's candid memoirs and the excellent journalistic history of the decision by Fletcher Knebel and Charles Bailey (*No High Ground*) are of course major sources for Dr. Smith. But the keystone of her work is the famous Franck report, dated June 11, 1945, in which James Franck, Eugene Rabinowitch, Leo Szilard and a few Chicago colleagues presciently outlined the international issues the bomb would ignite. This document is printed here uncut for the first time.

It was Niels Bohr who first among the scientists undertook to predict and shape the postbomb world. He hoped to persuade the Anglo-American leaders to tell Stalin early about the bomb, and on this basis to organize a shared control of the weapon. Early in 1944 he began to write down his ideas, by then strengthened in talks with a few leaders (particularly, it is curious to relate, Justice Frankfurter, who was not "cleared"). Whatever hope lay in his scheme, in the light of the realities of Stalin's U.S.S.R. and its uneasy alliance with the West, was broken by Churchill's "unalterable opposition to talks with Russia." Bohr acquired the faint aura of a security risk, belied by his scrupulous discretion and by the delicacy of his actual proposals. These were published as an open letter only in 1950, during the blizzard of the cold war.

Other men had a similar vision, largely independent of Bohr's but in all likelihood not entirely so. They included the leaders of all American war research, Vannevar Bush and James Bryant Conant, who wrote in September of 1944 that international control, and not an illusory Anglo-American monopoly of knowledge and uranium, ought to hold the bomb's future. The Chicago laboratory of the Manhattan project, partly because its work had essentially been completed, partly out of the initiative of men such as Franck and Szilard, had by then developed both an official and an unofficial concern with postwar policy. The Franck memorandum argues, without knowing it, in the same vein as Bohr and the leaders argued behind the scenes: Secrecy and control of resources will not preserve a monopoly. An arms race will ensue. The U.S.—even with more, bigger and better bombs—will be unsafe. Five hundred square miles might be destroyed utterly! (It is worth observing that today an estimate of the area would be hundreds of times greater.) Franck, however, was still more concrete. An early attack on Japan would merely precipitate the arms race, whereas a solemn public demonstration might set the stage for an internationally controlled renunciation of the awful weapon. So the paper runs.

Two points stand out as limits to the accuracy of the Franck report's prophecies. One is a technical matter; the authors speak of an imminent second stage of the technology, conversion to the use of the more common isotopes uranium 238 and thorium 232 instead of depending on the rare uranium 235 as the sole direct or indirect basis for the nuclear chain reaction. This stage —"breeding"—has still not come anywhere. Second, they consider as an alternative to a demonstration the withholding of any weapon explosion until later, even until after the "five or six years" of the breeding stage. I personally recall Bohr's insistence that the bomb be exploded somehow in 1945, so that the postwar world would not be built on a poisonous fear among governments that the public would have no basis to understand. Surely, said Bohr, all the governments will know that nuclear bombs are at hand. Here he seems to me clearly to have been right.

A tangle of committees and discussions slides fatefully toward the use of the bomb against Japan. Inevitability and the momentum of the enterprise seem to carry everyone. The wise and well-informed conclude there is no other path, although patently there were many. The winning of the war without paying too large a price for Soviet arms is shown as a strong motive, yet the bombing dates were fixed far in advance of Yalta. Szilard, farseeing and quixotic at once, pulls wires to gain access to Truman, the new President. A young Manhattan-project mathematician had worked for Truman's friends the Pendergasts in Kansas City. The President gets the message that Chicagoans are waiting to see him, but he diverts them to James Byrnes. And Byrnes, as late as early March, had asked President Roosevelt for an impartial review of the Manhattan project to protect the Administration from the scandal of the $2-billion waste! Not much can happen now. The story unfolds until the whole world knows.

The major portion of Dr Smith's book details the movement of the scientists from laboratories and guarded offices to hearing chambers and press conferences, from coded teletypes to rushed press statements, from disputing with colonels and reconnaissance experts to persuading congressmen and reporters. So the scientists moved, at least the majority of them. It seems to me that one finds in the story two distinct ways of meeting the sense of responsibility—indeed, of grave duty—that the Manhattan-project scientists as a whole felt then and feel still. One way I shall call the way of the insider It is a way that was shared by such disparate figures as Szilard and Robert Oppenheimer. Oppenheimer—lucid, persuasive, wonderfully analytical—works in secret with generals and diplomats, trying in a thousand ways to demonstrate what the facts imply. Szilard brings along to talk to the congressmen the courageous, influential, witty and able Edward Condon, president-to-be of the American Physical Society, "because he looks like an honest farm boy." Szilard lived beside the phone, talking to Beardsley Ruml or officials of the CIO. In buttonholing lobbyists he became himself the lobbyist par excellence. But both Oppenheimer and Szilard acted as men of inside knowledge, personally bringing their schemes, their devices and their new formulations before the individuals of power who wrote and passed laws.

On the other side, but not really an opposing side, were the rest of us: younger, less famous and less able. Ours was the way of the dissenter. The telephone calls were briefer and the secret teletypes wholly closed off. In the way we acted there was a sense less of knowledge than of commitment. William Higinbotham and Joseph Rush and Louis Ridenour and John Simpson and scores of others in Washington spoke and wrote publicly for 3,000 scientists back home, still at the project laboratories or crowding back into the universities, and also for the physicists and chemists who had not been in the project at all but felt about as we did. On that base, from shabby rented offices always overcrowded and littered with mimeographed statements and pamphlets, the "atomic scientists" floated off in the eddying stream of American public opinion. The Federation of American Scientists —lobbyists like Szilard—rose to prominence within the year or two of Dr Smith's tale. It is all here: the birth of the scientists' dissent, the petitions, the organizing of talks and the seeking of publishers, the telegram campaigns, the search for allies down the alphabetical rosters of unions and churches and fund raisers. The time was mostly stolen time; the executive secretary worked for a promise more than for a salary. When he left, the staff present was an empty wallet.

The issues are no longer clear, although they are scrupulously explained in this clear history. The early legislation to establish control over atomic energy was stillborn. Its Department of War drafters mistook the temper of the times and tried a broad and vague formula that excited fears of military control and of unreasonable emphasis on security But the McMahon Act [a law written in large part by the same James Newman who, until the time of his death in 1966, was editor of the book department of SCIENTIFIC AMERICAN] cannot be said in hindsight to have prevented an obsession with secrecy, a capitulation to obscurantist fears and a military preoccupation in the postwar development of atomic energy. In the TVA David Lilienthal was a brilliantly constructive reformer; once in the AEC he was perforce an embattled and cautious bureaucrat. It was the struggle, and not the triumph, that we can still celebrate.

It is Dr. Smith's view that there *is* something to celebrate. On the first page of her introduction one reads: "The message . . . seemed at the time . . . to fall largely on deaf ears. And yet nearly two decades later their ideas and their phraseology had so far permeated the general thinking about international problems that in preparing this book it was often necessary to remind myself whether I was reading the first mimeographed declarations of worried Manhattan Project scientists or the columns of the daily paper in 1964." When there are atomic-bomb tests at Lop Nor and hydrogen-bomb tests scheduled in the French atolls, no one can contend there is a mystical secret. The 20 years General Groves estimated it would take the Russians to get a bomb have just passed, and Soviet cosmonauts walk in space. Defense against atomic attack still seems hopeless, although dispersal and shelters remain possible unchosen options, just as was foreseen in the Franck report. Antimissile missiles, a topic not raised in the years covered by the book, still seem not worth their cost, according to Secretary McNamara's reckoning. So these cornerstones of the arguments we all made in so many speeches 18 or 20 years ago remain well set.

Less viable than the peril in Dr. Smith's title has been the hope: international control seems remote. It is quite true that the "Pugwash" meetings and the President's Science Advisory Committee, which put forward the test-ban treaty are the offspring of two parents. These institutions, both of which have now acquired the trappings of the insiders—secrecy official attention, smooth travel—owe their origins both to the inside way and to the way of dissent. If it was I. I. Rabi and his diplomacy and insight that gave rise to the Science Advisory Committee, it was the tone of the scientists' unofficial movement, and the very unofficial Cyrus Eaton, that set the stage for Pugwash. The test ban became the battlefield of the scientists long after the formative years. Edward Teller, who has practiced as both an insider and a dissenter on terms of intimacy with the generals of the Strategic Air Command and also with brilliant public advocacy, is already by the end of 1947 shown wary of international agreements, speaking for strong controls and for vigorous weaponry. How far this attitude carried him and the nation I need not detail.

Mutual deterrence, that symmetry of kill which lies behind Soviet-American relations, was not the vision of 1946. The scientists sought stability then, not mere metastability, not the top-heavy balancing rock on which we all breathlessly sit. Ridenour in a playlet he wrote for *Fortune*, had missiles in orbit, a state still less stable than our present condition. It is not for want of proposals that they are not whirling up there today; some steps logical enough in Dr. Strangelove's race for arms have not been taken, perhaps because the desire for survival keeps getting in the way The earnestness and hope of those early years—in the inside lines coming from the bold proposals of control and in the lines of dissent coming from a thousand talks and meetings with men and women of any motley grouping who would listen—gave something to the present. They gave that chiseled mental picture, reworked by the crater and the fallout of the Eniwetok hydrogen-bomb test: the view of that terrible mushroom. The peaceful uses of atomic energy even to the real electric power now flowing in a dozen city grids, have gained much less hold on us.

"The principal motive power behind the scientists' movement," writes Dr. Smith "was the feeling of responsibility, and in some sense and in some people of regret, for the part played by science . . . in the orgy of destruction." The Federation of American Scientists, whose early travail and triumph are the burden of the later chapters of the book, is, she says, a watchdog now. It can bark, but it is a bit old, like its members, and I hope it need never be asked to test its bite. The inside path has drained off from the dismaying haphazardness of dissent the best leaders, the most fluent spokesmen; the laboratory has eaten years off all of us. And still the years 1964 and 1965 see a dissenting professoriat, to be sure passing well beyond the laboratory men to the political specialists, more able and more widely heard by means of television and teach-in than we ever were when we argued as members of the Federation of American Scientists and the Federation of Atomic Scientists and breakfasted with senators. Today the technical professionals play their part in running the country—or, as it looks to me, in misrunning it—with their computers and Comsats and B-52 sorties. Professors are in the seats of power, and we laboratory men no longer can tell the Administration anything it doesn't know. Or can we?

The last word shall be Professor Rabi's. Acute, faintly acid, reflective, having had the deepest successes inside the Government of any scientist-in-policy I know of, he is the very symbol of the inside path. Yet he explained to Dr. Smith, in an interview in 1962, why the senior scientists, the project chiefs, were not leaders of the federation of the dissenting. "They didn't need us," he said. "They were doing just fine, and we older men would have spoiled the show. I was all for them, and I wish the young scientists would go to Washington and do it again." I expect I believe Rabi now, though it didn't seem that way to me back then.

Do it again? This time it is more difficult, but it is also more urgent. The new section of the press manual can be brief: in the next few years China and the U.S., like the U.S.S.R. and the U.S. in the past few years, can somehow learn to live without hot war.

4

The Early History of the Nuclear Age

JAMES R. NEWMAN

August 1962

A review of *The New World, 1939/1946*, by Richard G. Hewlett and Oscar E. Anderson, Jr., University Park (Penn.): The Pennsylvania State University, 1962; and *Now It Can Be Told*, by Leslie R. Groves, New York: Harper and Row, 1961.

These two books tell the story of an advance in technology comparable to none in its potential impact on every living person and on future generations. The story is of course not yet ended. Its full meaning will be unfolded in future chapters. If they are bright, mankind will gain much; if they are dark, mankind may perish.

Hewlett and Anderson's narrative, which gets its title from Arthur Compton's rather stagy telephone report to James Conant on the successful operation of Fermi's chain-reacting pile at Stagg Field ("Jim," he said, "you'll be interested to know that the Italian navigator has just landed in the New World") is the first volume of what is to be a multivolume history of the U.S. Atomic Energy Commission. The period covered here is from 1939 through 1946. When the story opens, scientists in the U.S. were just beginning to reckon the results of the epochal breakthrough of Hahn, Strassmann and Meitner. They were confirming, exploring and charting paths into unknown territory. Seven years later controlled atomic energy was a reality; the proof was the dead of Hiroshima and Nagasaki. The process of scientific digestion had gone forward at an astonishing rate; that of social digestion had scarcely begun.

Official histories are often more official than historical, especially when they are written so close in time to the events they purport to describe that large portions of the archives are still closed and the feelings of many living persons have to be protected. On the whole, however, the authors of this book, who are on the staff of the Atomic Energy Commission, have treated their subject frankly, openly and in considerable detail.

Two major themes constitute the survey of this period. The first concerns the scientific, technical and industrial aspects of separating uranium 235, making plutonium and designing and constructing the bomb; the second deals with the postwar period during which a legislative policy was evolved for the domestic control of atomic energy and attempts were made to achieve international control. The political theme is undoubtedly the more difficult to handle. It is one thing to tell how a plant came to be built, another to describe how a policy evolved and Congress made a law. Anyone who has spent some time in the Government and has tried to discover how things get done and who does them, to make sense of the crazy quilt of executive and legislative interaction, of lobbyists and pressure groups, of high officials who are short on time and ideas but make the decisions, of assistants who do the donkey work but remain anonymous, of nosy and cynical journalists who sometimes do harm and sometimes do good but rarely lubricate the processes of government—in short, anyone who has had the misfortune and the exhilaration of taking part in a legislative jamboree will appreciate the reportorial task that confronted Hewlett and Anderson. They write with verve and a lively appreciation of the difficulties, crosscurrents and tense conflicts that marked this first political phase of the atomic age. They re-create effectively the atmosphere of this exciting time when many different groups, with scientists in the vanguard, strove to educate the U.S. public, the press and members of Congress in the somber and challenging implications of the atomic bomb, in the importance of incorporating "an incredibly dangerous, mysterious force into the life of a nation" and in the beneficent possibilities of this force.

One of the most colorful and vehement struggles was over the civilian control of atomic energy. The control bill drafted by the War Department and approved by a group of prominent outside advisers had been perfunctorily inspected in the White House and then sent to Congress as the Administration's program. This was called the May-Johnson bill. It was seriously defective in many respects. It was essentially indifferent to the right of the American people to reap the fruits of a technological advance they had paid for. Its patent provisions were drafted so as to endow private and not public interests. Its administrative structure was almost incredibly naïve in envisaging ultimate control over atomic energy by a group of part-time consultants. It failed to establish proper safeguards against the possibility that military men might become the effective atomic energy decision makers. The bill that superseded the May-Johnson bill (introduced by Senator Brien McMahon and Congresswoman Helen Gahagan Douglas), which gained the President's support and which, after many vicissitudes, was finally enacted into law, was the product of many hands. It was threaded with compromises, some small, some serious, but it was a much better piece of legislation than that which the Administration had first offered. A large part of the credit for pushing Mcmahon's bill through Congress belongs to a group of energetic young scientists, most of whom for the first time found themselves in the political arena and for the first time deeply sensed their social responsibility. All this is ably described by Hewlett and Anderson.

It is likely, to be sure that some of those who participated in the legislative battle will fault the authors, partly for inaccuracies, more for their interpretations. I was on the scene myself, and I would criticize the book's evaluation of several of the political skirmishes. But I would prefer not to put too fine a point on the matter. Facts and details are pale, poisonous little things. If you get one wrong, your critics will hang you; even if you get all the others right, they will not cut you down. When I compare material in my own files with the authors' account, I note discrepancies; but I cannot always be certain where the error lies, and in any case only trivial items are at issue. As regards interpretations, thornier questions arise; in a few instances I am convinced that the authors have not caught quite the right note. A sequence of events did not follow the causal chain attributed to it, a decisive turning did not take place for the reasons given. But this represents only my point of view, and just as a mountain or a feature of the landscape may look radically different to observers at different vantage points, so may a series of events be interpreted differently by historians standing in different places or making their judgments at different times. Considering the mass of material that had to be sifted in preparing this work, the complexity of the issues, the fallibility of human memory, the effects of individual bias and the almost insuperable difficulty of describing accurately what happens in the smoke and swirl of battle—the reporters have done admirably. I have learned much from their account, and although I was involved in many of the happenings they describe and felt I had as complete a grasp of them as anyone, Hewlett and Anderson have broadened my perspective. By any reasonable standard theirs is an honorable and worthy accomplishment and must form the basis for future historical appraisals.

This cannot be said for General Groves's book, a singularly self-important account of his role in directing the Manhattan Project. *Now It Can Be Told*, I wish to emphasize, is not a dull book. It is clearly written. It presents a good deal of material that illuminates the growth of this horridly fascinating project and its culminating success. It has amusing cloak-and-dagger stories about the activities of the "Alsos" agents in Europe, whose task it was to discover how much progress the Nazis had made in building a bomb. But Groves's limitations and prejudices intrude at every turn.

His function in the Manhattan Project was that of administrator and expediter. Trained as an Army engineer, he makes no claim to any real understanding of the scientific side of the project. It is surprising, however, how imperfectly he seems to have grasped even the technological side. This is revealed more plainly in his postwar testimony before Congressional committees than it is in his book. Groves's myopia manifested itself not only in his opinions on how the atomic energy project should be run after the war but also in his wrong-headed notions about the possibility of the U.S. maintaining a monopoly in bomb making and the capacity of the U.S.S.R. for making its own atomic weapons.

Obsessively concerned with secrecy and proud of his policy of compartmentalization (pursuant to which no one working in any division of the enterprise was permitted to know about the work in other divisions), Groves was faintly—and not always so faintly—contemptuous of the majority of the project scientists, except for the Nobel prize winners, J. Robert Oppenheimer and a handful of others highly placed. Resentful and egotistical, he neither understood the issues of the legislative battle nor has he to this day forgiven those who had the temerity to challenge him. The following paragraph exemplifies his attitude:

"In spite of the record, since the very start of the postwar period there has been a continuous stream of propaganda calculated to lead the American people and the people of the world to believe that the War Department—and General Groves in particular—was determined to retain close control of atomic energy. The effect of this propaganda has been truly remarkable, despite the fact that it was entirely false, and was known to be false by those who first originated it and by many of those who constantly repeated it. It made no difference how many times they were corrected to their faces, often quite bluntly, or in writing; they continued to put the idea forward. Even today many of them keep up the sham and appear likely to do so as long as they live. In retrospect, this seems to have been one of the most perfect brainwashing operations in modern times, and it has been particularly effective among the better-educated Americans. Those who continue to spread it even after the facts were brought to their attention were obviously doing so deliberately with the intent of gaining political advantage from propaganda that they could not help but know was absolutely without foundation."

Groves had great energy and determination and was bent on succeeding in the task assigned him. He was given extraordinary powers and an almost unlimited budget. He brought into the program not only the industrial corporations that planned, constructed and operated the huge plants at Oak Ridge and Hanford but also the best-qualified scientists and technicians. He never lost sight of the main objective; he spared no effort to get supplies and priorities; he brooked no opposition. His significant contributions to the making of the "Little Boy" and the "Fat Man" (respectively the uranium bomb detonated over Hiroshima and the plutonium bomb detonated over Nagasaki) were his singleness of purpose, his drive and the fact that he was never fazed by the immensity of the job. Had he been more sympathetic, more modest, more reflective, more concerned with the human problems of the scientists under his control, he might not have reached the goal as quickly as he did. Some think it would be a better world if he had not succeeded. The complexion of his qualities colors his writing and makes his book at times very hard to take. But both as a self-portrait and as the story of an almost incalculably fateful undertaking it is worth reading.

5

Is the Atomic Bomb an Absolute Weapon?

P. M. S. Blackett maintains it is not, and derives therefrom some unusual conclusions. *A reply to his argument follows on page 30*

P. M. S. BLACKETT

March 1949

THERE seem to have been many people who were so deeply impressed by the results of dropping two atomic bombs on Japan that they came to believe that the use of even a few atomic bombs would decide the course of future wars. If this were true, it would indeed seem rational to single them out from all other weapons and armaments for special treatment. If, on the other hand, one concludes from an analysis of the past that even a large number of atomic bombs will not by themselves decide the course of future wars between great powers, and that there exist other weapons of comparable power, then the problem of the control of atomic energy becomes part of the problem of general disarmament.

Since only two atomic bombs were used in the Second World War, and then only at a very late stage and under very special circumstances, it is by no means sufficient only to study what happened at Hiroshima and Nagasaki; on the contrary, it is essential to study the war as a whole and to attempt to assess the part played by other arms.

The combined Anglo-American bombing offensive in Germany had as its objective "The destruction and dislocation of the German military, industrial, and economic system and the undermining of the morale of the German people to the point where their capacity for armed resistance is fatally weakened." The results of this bombing offensive were analyzed by the U. S. Strategic Bombing Survey. The remarkable and unexpected result was the discovery that German total war production continued to increase till the summer of 1944 in spite of the very heavy bombing. The report comments as follows:

"These figures demonstrate that German cities had a surprising resilience and extraordinary ability to recover from the effects of ruinous attacks. The raids on Hamburg in July-August 1943 were among the most devastating of the war. Yet, despite the deaths of over 60,000 people, the total destruction of one third of all houses in the city and the disruption of normal processes of living, Hamburg as an economic unit was not destroyed. It never fully recovered from the bombing, but in five months it had regained 80 per cent of the former productivity, despite the fact that great areas of the city lay, and still lie, in dust and rubble. As in the case of industrial plants, when it was found much easier to destroy the buildings than the machines in them, so also it is much easier to destroy the physical structure of a city than to wipe out its economic life."

A major success of the bombing offensive was the precision attack in 1944-1945 on transportation targets and specific industrial targets such as oil installations. The Survey sums this phase up as follows:

"Not until the war in the air had been won, and the landings in the Mediterranean and France successfully accomplished, were the heavy bombers free to exploit the victory in the air and attack in full force the centers of oil production, the centers of transport and other sustaining sources of military strength within the heart of Germany. . . . The greatest single achievement of the air attack on Germany was the defeat of the German Air Force."

SO MUCH has been written of the effects on Hiroshima and Nagasaki of the explosion of the two bombs that it is only necessary here to survey briefly the main facts. A plutonium bomb produces a blast wave comparable to that which would be produced by the explosion of one lump of 20,000 tons of TNT. From careful surveys of the damage to various types of buildings, it has been calculated, however, that only a little over 2,000 tons of high-explosive bombs —for example, 10-ton blockbusters— would be required to produce the same structural damage as one plutonium bomb. The reason why this figure is so much lower than the figure of 20,000 tons for the equivalent amount of TNT when exploded in one mass lies in the fact that such a very large explosion pulverizes nearby objects to a quite unnecessary degree; in fact, it "overhits" the central part of the target area, and so wastes a large part of the energy.

It is less easy to give a reliable equivalence for the civilian casualties produced by atomic and ordinary bombing. These depend to a very large extent on the distribution of the people at the time of the attack between open places, ordinary houses, reinforced concrete buildings or specially constructed shelters, and so will be much greater for a surprise attack on an unprepared city than for an expected attack on a prepared city. The

U. S. Strategic Bombing Survey, however, equates one plutonium bomb to some 2,000 tons of ordinary bombs in effect on personnel, and we will adopt this on a provisional basis, remembering that in some circumstances the figure may require considerable modification.

In order to assess the influence of atomic bombs on the course of a future war, it is necessary to estimate what changes are likely to occur by a given date in the destructiveness of the bombs, the methods of conveying the bombs to the target, and the defense. In general we will consider mainly advances that are likely to be achieved, firstly, within the next five years, that is, by 1953, and secondly within the next 10 years, that is, by 1958. For the choice of these time scales there are certain definite reasons.

It is clear that the only war in which atomic bombs are likely to be used is one in which the main contestants are the U. S. A. and the U. S. S. R. A period of five years from now is the latest possible date at which one could reasonably expect that the U. S. S. R. would not possess at least some atomic bombs. The period of 10 years is chosen as the latest date at which it is at all reasonable to attempt to predict the pattern of events.

THERE HAS been much discussion of the possibility of a "super bomb" probably using a nuclear reaction involving hydrogen or lithium initiated by the explosion of a plutonium or uranium-235 bomb. By this means scientists believe that an explosive power many times as great might be produced. However, this has so far not yet apparently been achieved, and its likely performance is still highly speculative. An increase in the explosive power of a bomb would yield increased results when the target is a large city, but it must be remembered that the present bombs are already unnecessarily powerful for use against many small but important targets such as a single factory or a single large ship.

Though rockets of the German V-2 type might possibly be built to carry an atomic war-head a distance of a few hundred miles, the technical problem of making such a rocket with a range of 1,000 miles or more is very formidable. The view of the American Navy has been expressed as follows: "For these and other reasons not here touched upon, it seems a wholly reasonable and safe assumption that rockets with atomic war-heads capable of thousands of miles of range are not to be expected for at least 25 years." Certainly for ranges over 1,000 miles and probably also for ranges over 400 miles, the only vehicle for the delivery of an atomic bomb with adequate accuracy within the next 10 years will be the conventional aircraft.

Within the shorter of our two periods, that is, within the next five years, piloted

P. M. S. BLACKETT is a distinguished nuclear physicist who served as a member of the British Advisory Committee on Atomic Energy until last year.

bombers with a range over, say, 1,500 miles, which can be expected to be in service in large numbers, will be so inferior in speed and maneuverability as to be extremely vulnerable to contemporary fighters, and probably also to improved anti-aircraft weapons. We conclude, therefore, that repeated deep penetration of a heavily defended territory is likely to be an expensive operation. This is likely to be true both by day and by night. For the development of radar has made the night fighter nearly as efficient as the day fighter. So in this period we must conclude that effective intercontinental air war is not possible.

In the latter part of our period, that is, from 1953 to 1958, the prospects are not quite so clear. It is possible that the speed advantage of fighters will be drastically reduced. But it is also possible that new and improved defense measures will be developed. So it is likely that, certainly till 1953 and probably also till 1958, any long-range bombing campaign must be carried out in very great force.

An estimate of the scale of an atomic bomb attack which would have to be launched on a major continental power to have an important effect on its power to wage war can be made by noting the loss of territory and of industrial capacity by the Soviet Union in 1941 and 1942, and recalling that this still did not prevent her from eventually defeating the German armies and driving them from her territories. A huge number of atomic bombs would have been necessary to inflict on Russia as much damage as she actually suffered by the German invasion. In Germany some 400 atomic bombs would have been required to produce as much damage as was actually done by the Allied bombing offensive, which played by no means the decisive role in the defeat of Germany.

IT MIGHT be argued that such a calculation of the number of atomic bombs, which are to be taken as equivalent to a given weight of ordinary bombs, is inadequate, on the grounds that it does not take into account the special properties of the atomic bomb. For instance, it has often been argued that the time factor is of great importance: the argument is that atomic bombs could be dropped, say, on all the major cities of an enemy country within a few hours, and that such an attack would have an altogether greater effect than if an equivalent weight of ordinary bombing were spread out over many months.

Though it is impossible to be quite sure of the effect of such an intense but short attack, the following considerations are relevant. Firstly, it is most improbable that such a widespread attack could be launched within a few hours against a well-defended country, owing to the huge air effort involved. For each atomic bomber would have to be accompanied by many other bombers, in order to have a good chance of reaching a distant target against heavy opposition.

Then again, it is not certain that it would be a sound policy to concentrate the atomic bombs in time, even if it was possible. For the disadvantage to the enemy of having a large number of attacks to compete with at once would be partially, at any rate, offset by the shortening of the time during which defense measures, civilian evacuation, etc., would have to be maintained. In fact, one can see strong arguments for a deliberate policy of spreading the attacks over a considerable period of time, in order to tire out the defense and weary the population. Only if large armies were ready for an immediate invasion would a very short-duration attack be advisable.

The other common criticism of such numerical comparisons is that they neglect the psychological factor; this presumably means that the "horror" of the atomic bomb is so great that a nation's will to resist will be rapidly sapped. To this one can reply that, from the point of view of most of the individual victims, there is not much to choose between the experience of heavy ordinary bombing and atomic bombing. Selected survivors of Hamburg, Dresden or Tokyo could have provided equally poignant material for the pen of a John Hersey as the survivors of Hiroshima. Those who remember the exaggerated expectations of the effect of the British bombing offensive on German morale current in the early days of the war will be skeptical of many of the easy predictions about the effect on morale of atomic bombs. The power of human beings to "take it" is immense; a determined people will learn to stand atomic bombardment, if that is their fate.

It is clear that if Russia thought it a sound policy to drop bombs on America, she would certainly consider that it would be essential to accumulate a minimum stockpile of a few thousand before starting. Now the magnitude of the technical and industrial problems of producing bombs makes it likely that it will be many years before the Soviet Union will possess a large enough stockpile of atomic bombs to be useful against American cities. So, on this ground alone, an atomic attack on the U. S. A. by the U. S. S. R. is in the highest degree unlikely for very many years.

The next question to be answered is how the U. S. S. R. would deliver them. In the heated imagination of the enthusiasts for atomic warfare, it would only be necessary for thousands of long-range atomic bombers to take off secretly from airfields within the Soviet Union to destroy the main cities of America within a few hours. We know now that the facts are different. Even if Russia at an early stage of such an imagined war had occupied the countries of Western Europe —a far from unlikely contingency if they were allies of America—she would still have no bases from which to launch effectively such an attack.

IT SEEMS improbable that Russia would plan an attack on America, except as part of a coordinated offensive with all arms, which must necessarily include invasion. A Soviet invasion of America is militarily impossible. Even if Russia controlled the whole of Europe including Great Britain, the invasion of America across the Atlantic would require an enormous amount of shipping to carry the millions-strong invasion force required, and further would be extremely easy to repulse since complete air superiority would rest with the defenders.

Even if the technical possibility of destroying American cities from European bases is much higher than we have here estimated, such destruction, not followed up by invasion and occupation, would leave America time to recuperate and rearm, bitterly determined to take eventual revenge. Further, such action would alienate world opinion and tend to solidify a grand alliance against Russia. The first Russian atomic bomb that fell on an American city would be a decisive political success for the enemies of Russia all over the world. The lesson of Pearl Harbor is clear. To strike a heavy but indecisive blow at a powerful enemy, without possessing the resources to follow it up by invasion and occupation of the homeland, is to court disaster.

Though many authoritative statements have been made discounting the possibility of "push-button war," clearly the possibility exercises a great fascination for many Americans. To be more concrete, the atomic bomb is seen in many British and American circles as the answer to the power of the Soviet armies, and the only answer that does not seem to involve large overseas military commitments. If not the atomic bomb, then "What else?"

It is necessary to consider the possibility that in the event of war breaking out, America might begin her offensive with an atomic bomb attack on Russian cities. Though, judging by the press, such a move would be widely accepted in many American circles as a natural one, it might well be opposed by the armed services for very strong military reasons. For the military, who after all have the responsibility of carrying through such a war to a successful conclusion, cannot fail to ask: "What happens next?"

It is clear that to any sustained atomic bomb attack on Russia within the next decade, there are possible Russian countermeasures, mainly with land forces, which would have the object of capturing the bases from which the atomic bombers were operating, or if this were not possible, of neutralizing them as far as possible by pushing forward her air-defense zone. Even the destruction of all the major cities of Russia would not impair the striking power of the Soviet armies until many months had elapsed. If one discounts the possibility—and all our calculations have shown that we must discount it—that an initial atomic bomb attack would cause Russia to capitulate, then it is certain that such a war would be fought out in Europe on land, as were the last two World Wars.

If a war of this type did occur, acute controversy would be certain to arise between the military staff of America, on the one hand, and France and England on the other, as to the advisability of the use of Anglo-French bases for attacks on Russian cities by American atomic bombers. For, if that happened, England and France would expect to get atom-bombed—not America. And the military staffs of both European countries would certainly be made aware by their political colleagues of the difficulty of convincing the public of each country that such a role was a reasonable one for their countries to undertake.

THE MOST important deduction that must inevitably be drawn from our analysis is that any future war in which America and Russia are the chief contestants—and this clearly is the only major war which needs serious consideration—would certainly not be decided by atomic bombing alone. On the contrary, a long-drawn-out and bitter struggle over much of Europe and Asia, involving million-strong land armies, vast military casualties and widespread civil war, would be inevitable.

Unless our analysis has been greatly in error, the danger of a Third World War in the next few years is much less than is generally thought.

Meanwhile America's stockpile of bombs will continue to grow ever bigger and bigger, and at some uncertain date Russia's will start to grow too. Responsible American statesmen will be bound to weigh very carefully the delicate question of when to begin again negotiations for the control of atomic energy, which they have just broken off. For the danger of waiting too long is great. When Russia has accumulated a stockpile of a few thousand bombs, her military strength, already very great by the size and efficiency of her armies, will be much enhanced. We have already noted that atomic bombs may prove valuable tactical weapons and even a hundred or so would be of great military value when used in conjunction with large-scale land operations, whereas such a number would bring no decisive results if used for area bombing of cities unrelated to other military operations. If negotiations do not start until this situation has arisen, Russia will hold most of the cards.

Let us consider what are the essential conditions for future negotiations to have a reasonable chance of success. It is undeniable that any settlement between America and Russia must be based essentially on a bargain between the two States. The bargain must be one in which both sides make comparable sacrifices and reciprocally receive comparable advantages at all stages. If America continues to insist, as she appears to have done in the past, on treating atomic energy in isolation, then clearly there will be no possibility of a bargain, and so none for an agreement, until Russia has drawn more nearly even with America in the field of atomic energy.

If, however, atomic energy is not again treated in isolation, if, that is, atomic bombs are considered along not only with other weapons of mass destruction but with conventional armaments and land armies as well, then it is easy to see the possibilities of an agreement acceptable to both America and Russia at a much earlier date.

On this broader basis, Russia with her strong land army has something to bargain against America's atomic bombs. By taking conventional weapons and armed forces into consideration at the same time, it should not be impossible, though undeniably it would not be easy, to reach an agreement to reduce armaments generally. For instance, some kind of bargain might be struck between America and Russia, in which so many American atomic bombs and their carriers are held to be the military equivalent of so many Russian divisions.

When Russia has approached more nearly to the level of industrialization of America, there will be a better chance of reaching an agreement within the single field of weapons adaptable to mass destruction. For the present it seems more hopeful to tackle the problem of general disarmament, even though this means the continued existence in the world of some limited number of atomic bombs, rather than to attempt to abolish all atomic bombs, leaving all other arms uncontrolled.

[Editor's note: This discussion of the military and political implications of the atomic bomb by the Nobelist in physics for 1948 is condensed from his much-discussed book, published in the U.S. (February 1949) with the title Fear, War, and the Bomb. *Some of the important issues raised by the British scientist are debated in this article and the one on page 30. The U.S. publisher of the book is Whittlesey House. The book, and the material taken from it here, are copyrighted by Dr. Blackett.]*

Science and the Citizen, January 1949

The Blackett Book

THE challenging and controversial work by the British physicist Patrick M. S. Blackett, *Military and Political Consequences of Atomic Energy,* which was recently published in England, will be brought out in the U.S. in February 1949 by Whittlesey House under the title *Fear, War, and the Bomb.* A February selection of the Book Find Club, the book is certain to receive considerable attention among scientists and laymen in the U.S.

Blackett's volume, already widely discussed on both sides of the Atlantic, presents a detailed analysis of the atom bomb's impact on war and politics, and sharply criticizes the U.S. proposals for the international control of atomic energy. Its author, winner of the 1948 Nobel prize in physics, is a former member of the British Government's Advisory Committee on Atomic Energy and was a leader in wartime tactical research. The importance of his book was emphasized by the fact that the day after it was published in England, the British delegation to the UN Atomic Energy Commission issued a refutation of his views. The U.S.S.R., on the other hand, warmly applauded them. Recently the book was vigorously attacked by Frederick H. Osborn, U.S. delegate to the UN Atomic Energy Commission, in a radio debate with Blackett in England.

Science and the Citizen, April 1949

The Blackett Book

A HEAVY cannonade of criticism has greeted P. M. S. Blackett's *Fear, War, and the Bomb*, which was published in the U.S. last month (and debated in the March 1949 issue of SCIENTIFIC AMERICAN [see the articles beginning on pages 24 and 30]).

In an article titled "Playing Down the Bomb," in the April issue of *The Atlantic*, I. I. Rabi, chairman of the Columbia University physics department, attacks the book as an "extraordinary piece of special pleading." Rabi declares that Blackett, in comparing atomic explosives with the bombs dropped on Germany, neglected the saturation effect made possible by atomic bombs. Rabi disputes Blackett's estimate of the importance of atomic energy and its possible role in enabling the U.S.S.R. to catch up industrially with the U.S. He says: "Professor Blackett did not work on the atomic bomb project during the war, and his professional interest in recent years has not been primarily in nuclear physics. There are many points in the book which show that his thinking in this field is that of an outsider. . . . Atomic power is not around the corner." Rabi also criticizes Blackett's suggestion that a general disarmament cannot be negotiated until Russia has its own bombs. "This," he says, "is exactly the kind of dreaded armed truce American scientists have sought to avoid."

The *Bulletin of the Atomic Scientists* devotes a third of its latest issue to reviews by Edward A. Shils of the University of Chicago sociology department; Chairman Brien McMahon of the Joint Congressional Committee on Atomic Energy; Philip Morrison of the Cornell University physics department; and M. Marinin, a Russian writer whose favorable review of Blackett's book originally appeared in *Pravda.*

Shils, who has been active in support of the Baruch plan, denounces Blackett's volume as an apology for Soviet policy "which states a defense for the Soviet Union position . . . much better than any Soviet delegate has ever stated." Shils concedes that the book contains "some very impressive pieces of analysis. . . . It is therefore necessary that this gift to Soviet propaganda be studied and understood. . . . It cannot be refuted or dismissed by self-righteous clichés."

Senator McMahon remarks that he is not reassured but frightened by Blackett's data "debunking" the bomb. "Taking 400 bombs as the least quantity needed to duplicate the ruin visited upon Germany," he observes, "how can we conclude that atomic energy is an exaggerated menace? Must we not conclude, rather, that 400 bombs is a terrifyingly small number?"

Morrison, who is in general agreement with the British physicist's thesis and conclusions, adds two footnotes. One is a calculation of the number of atomic bombs that would be required to equal the damage done by the German army in Russia. He arrives at an estimate of 800 to 1,200. Allowing for interceptions, delivery of these would require "the launching of many more than a thousand under present conditions." Concludes Morrison: "A major war will not be a three-week aerial expedition." His other footnote concerns Blackett's charge that the dropping of the bomb on Hiroshima was timed to occur before the scheduled entrance of the U.S.S.R. into the war against Japan. Morrison, a staff physicist at the Los Alamos bomb laboratory during the war, recalls that August 10 had been set as an absolute deadline for completion of the bomb, to be met regardless of cost.

The Mexican physicist Manuel Sandoval Vallarta, former member of the United Nations Atomic Energy Commission, terms the volume "an absorbing book." He disagrees, however, with Blackett's assessment of the bomb and his political analysis. Writing in *Physics Today,* Vallarta declares his conviction that the atomic bomb is qualitatively a new weapon and that acceptance of the U.S. proposals for control of atomic energy would have speeded up its development for peaceful purposes.

6

A U.S. Physicist's Reply To Professor Blackett

Challenging the Briton's strategic assumptions, he argues that a sudden air attack on military objectives would be decisive in any future war

LOUIS N. RIDENOUR
March 1949

P.M.S. BLACKETT, Nobel Laureate in physics for 1948, is a scientist of distinction and outstanding ability. He is therefore capable, as all good scientists should be, of careful and objective reasoning concerning matters that do not impinge too closely upon his faiths and implicit beliefs. Unfortunately, the subject matter of his book, *Fear, War, and the Bomb,* suggests that Blackett has allowed his pronounced political sympathies to warp his observations and his reasoning. They have apparently led him to suppress large numbers of pertinent facts, to ignore many crucial technical and political possibilities, and to depreciate the honesty and good faith of his government and of ours to an absurd degree.

Blackett attempts to establish three main theses: First, that the effectiveness of strategic bombardment has been greatly overrated, through a misinterpretation of the evidence of World War II. Second, that the atomic bomb will by no means have the impressive role in future wars which enthusiasts predict for it. Third, that the Soviet reaction to the Anglo-American proposals for atomic energy control has been entirely reasonable, for detailed reasons which we shall examine later.

Most writers who have commented on *Fear, War, and the Bomb* (which was published in England last fall) have paid attention mainly to the political matters that come under the heading of the third thesis. They have usually ignored, or even applauded, Blackett's views on strategic air power and on the atomic bomb. Since he minimizes the military usefulness of these two components of armed strength, and since both are, for the moment, substantially U. S. monopolies, his assertions are a matter of sincere and immediate concern to every American.

Let us first consider the military significance of the strategic air campaign conducted in World War II. Blackett discusses the area attacks upon centers of population which were carried out by the Royal Air Force; he concludes, in agreement with the findings of the U. S. Strategic Bombing Survey, that the great destruction and loss of life produced by such attacks had little direct effect upon German war production. The U. S. Army Air Forces, however, devoted their attention not to such area attacks but to an attack upon target systems selected as being vital to the enemy war economy.

Blackett dwells at considerable length upon the well-established fact that the American bombings had little economic effect during all the months that preceded the summer of 1944. He gives this result its correct explanation: The American air commanders, who had started the strategic air war in the belief that attacks on enemy industry could bring a quick decision, soon learned that heavy opposition from defensive fighters of the German Air Force so deranged the bombardment that its accuracy, and therefore its economic effect, was small. This difficulty being appreciated, attention was focused on destroying the GAF. It was required of the bombers only that their attacks be sufficiently annoying to draw the German fighters into battle.

BY the spring of 1944, the GAF was wrecked. Just before the Normandy invasion (the success of which hinged largely on Allied air superiority), German ventures into the air were so hazardous that a German pilot would be credited with an operational mission—a sortie in the face of the enemy—when he had merely ferried an airplane from one field in Occupied France to another. The Germans owned the land of France, but we owned the air over it. Once the GAF was finished, the accuracy, weight and effectiveness of our bombardment promptly rose, and Germany's war economy was disrupted. Nearly three quarters of the total weight of bombs dropped on Germany were dropped after July 1, 1944. The attacks on transportation and on the oil industry were especially effective. On March 15, 1945, the German Minister of Armament and War Production Albert Speer reported to Hitler that the total collapse of German industry was only four to eight weeks away.

Though Blackett describes all this, his conclusion from it is based upon the first phase of the air war over Germany, when the economic effects were small. He thus assumes that in any future war it will be necessary to fight for and win air superiority before substantial economic damage can be inflicted by strategic bombardment. While this may be true of the stable phase of any future war, it is almost entirely beside the point, since effective air superiority will always exist for a few days at the beginning of an air attack, and the atomic bomb is so effective that the destruction which took place in the 300 days that finished Germany can be compressed into those few initial days. Let us examine the background for this view, which differs so sharply from Blackett's.

Blackett justifies his faith in the effectiveness of air defense by an assessment of the future technical developments which he predicts for the next few years. He concludes (a) that piloted aircraft are the only proximate vehicles capable of delivering atomic bombs to strategic targets, (b) that they are of relatively short range, and will require forward bases within one or two thousand miles of the targets, and (c) that piloted defensive fighters can deal capably with attacks by piloted subsonic bombers.

It is possible to quarrel with all but perhaps the first of these assertions. Admittedly the accurate thousand-mile guided missile will not be available until some time in the future. How far off it is, under the present circumstances of vigorous technical development, is hard to predict; Blackett chooses to put it more than 10 years away, and let us join him.

The second conclusion is wrong on the record. It is perfectly true that the B-29s of World War II needed bases within 1,500 miles of their targets. However, the standard heavy bomber of the U. S. Air Force today is the formidable B-36, the actual combat range of which, on the basis of published statements, appears to be at least 3,000 miles. Also, Blackett's book was written too early to include any observations on the bomber range which can be attained by refueling in the air. The USAF has recently announced trials which indicate that this simple technique will give B-29s and B-50s substantially a global range.

Thus today's USAF bombers will deliver today's atomic bombs from here to anywhere, provided that they are not successfully intercepted. Blackett contends that they will be, and that the cost of operating unescorted long-range bombers in the face of enemy opposition will be prohibitive. This contention, too, can be debated. It rests upon an assumption that the fighter's advantage over the bomber depends only upon the fighter's edge in speed, and that this advantage is essentially independent of the actual speed at which the interception must be made. The assumption is grossly wrong, for reasons so lengthy and so technical that they are only hinted here. At high speeds, the maneuverability of a fighter is greatly reduced by the pilot's tolerance for acceleration in a turn, and by the danger of stalling out of a high-altitude turn that is too sharp. This reduced maneuverability requires that interception commence at ranges which are often greater than the maximum distance at which a fighter pilot can see a bomber, even under perfect visibility conditions. Several other major difficulties beset the problem of bomber interception at high subsonic speeds, even granting that the interceptors have a substantial speed advantage.

In any case, the point need not be labored. Granting that unescorted bombers would not be safe against air defenses in the stable phase of an air war fought in the near future, it is important to turn our attention to the conditions that would obtain during the early days of an attack. It is my contention that the entire strategic air effort could be carried out without effective opposition in those few days.

ALL defenses in all history, particularly such complicated coordinated defenses as those involved in air defense, have required time and actual combat experience to build up to maximum efficiency. Thus, for example, the German daylight air attack on England in 1940, quickly opposed and mastered by the RAF as it was, nevertheless deposited on its targets a weight of bombs which would have been decisive if they had been atomic bombs. So did the German night campaign of late 1940 and early 1941, though improving RAF defenses made the raids so costly that they were soon abandoned. I have documented this point with other examples in my chapter "There is No Defense," in the symposium *One World or None* (Whittlesey House, 1946). Blackett quotes extensively from that book, but nowhere refers to or refutes the present argument. The reason for the early failure of the defense is not far to seek. The defense must be eternally alert everywhere against any form of attack, while the offense chooses its time and place and weapons, and thus achieves initial surprise in most instances, and local superiority in all.

So long as the initial unmolested air attack had to be delivered in terms of old-fashioned "high explosives" and incendiaries, it could achieve a significant local success (as at Pearl Harbor), but could not be decisive. With atomic bombs, all this is changed. Blackett quotes, and agrees with, current estimates that one bombing aircraft carrying one atomic bomb is equivalent in terms of practical destructive power to between 50 and 250 heavy bombers with old-fashioned bombs. Unlike most other experts, he asks us to take comfort from the circumstance that the number is not bigger. The German economy was destroyed completely, according to the argument which Blackett himself makes, in the 300 days from July, 1944, to April, 1945; since there had been no significant economic effect earlier, we can draw no other conclusion. This means that the bomber forces of World War II could have achieved the same result in perhaps two days if they had used atomic bombs.

What targets would be attacked in those two days? Blackett assumes that we would desire to destroy the cities of the enemy. He even depreciates the value of strategic air attack on the grounds that the Russians might, in another war, occupy the whole of Europe; he argues that we would not, and dare not, bomb the cities of our friends.

In terms of capabilities, we could surely use our brief initial air superiority to lay waste all the major cities of an enemy. In terms of military realities, we would almost certainly not do so. Blackett himself has shown that attacks on cities had small result in World War II, while attacks on specific industrial target systems brought the Germans to collapse. This being so, even though there is some evidence that an atomic-bomb attack on civilian populations might be much more effective than were such attacks with old-time "high explosives," our decision would undoubtedly be to launch our strategic attack against carefully chosen points in the fabric of the enemy's industry. There would be two cogent reasons for making this choice: 1) the proved military value of such attacks; 2) the fact that the tremendous loss of irrelevant lives in city bombing is repugnant to any proper conscience.

Since industries are not usually *in* cities but on the periphery, they could be attacked even though they were in occupied friendly countries. In the absence of effective opposition during the first apocalyptic days, the bombing would be accurate, and there need be little indiscriminate killing of people living in the nearby cities. It is even possible that the raids could be announced beforehand, as Major General Curtis E. LeMay announced his targets in a late phase of the Pacific air war, without such an announcement aiding the initial air defense in any significant way. This,

LOUIS RIDENOUR was assistant director of the M. I. T. Radiation Laboratory (radar development) and a War Department consultant during the war.

however, is speculation, and the risk might be regarded as too great to take.

IN any case, another war is likely to involve, early in the conflict, the destruction by one power of certain vital economic target systems of the other. The aircraft producing this destruction would carry atomic bombs; one of them would be more terrible than an entire old-fashioned combat wing, while half a dozen would be equivalent to an old-time thousand-plane raid. The weapons could be so used that the lingering radioactivity spewed over the factories and the installations that were hit would deny their use for months or years.

Other arms, no doubt, would be involved in such a conflict. There is no quarrel on that point; indeed, our present pattern of military expenditure suggests that we put no complete reliance on strategic bombing with atomic weapons. But to say, as Blackett does, that long-range bombers cannot be decisive, and that the atomic bomb changes nothing, is to assert that the war economy of a nation is of no value to that nation in a war. Reduced to these basic terms, Blackett's contentions are preposterous.

The view here presented is not a pleasant one to take. Yet in today's nervous and hostile world, we are committed to a national policy of maintaining our armed strength. The long-range striking arm of that military strength is the strategic bomber, with its atomic weapons. Blackett does the Western world no service when he affects to deny the usefulness of strategic bombardment.

It may be that the very curious nature and the obvious bias of Blackett's political remarks will warn the reader that the military considerations he advances are also suspect. In the latter part of the book, Blackett presents the following astonishing arguments: First, that the dropping of two atomic bombs on Japan in August, 1944, was the first move in the cold war, designed to forestall a Russian offensive in the Far East. Second, that the Baruch proposals for the international control of atomic energy, based with devilish ingenuity on the altruistic program of a group of high-minded men, were another move in the same game, and were designed to put the Soviet Union at a moral disadvantage. Third, that the scheme for control contained a thinly disguised attempt to deprive the Russians of an unparalleled opportunity to raise the living standards of their masses by the peaceful exploitation of atomic power.

The usual reason given in the U. S. for the timing of the use of the first atomic bombs is that the bombs were not ready earlier. The reason advanced to explain the nature of their use is that a dramatic demonstration of the bomb's power was felt to be necessary to convince the enemy of its effectiveness, as promptly as could be done. The whole affair is said to have been calculated to result in the speediest termination of the war, and the smallest loss of American and Japanese lives. We have all this on the solemn public testimony of the men responsible for the decisions. Blackett brushes it aside; he does not even summarize these arguments as meriting serious attention. The closest that he comes to them is in what he calls the "Roman holiday" theory: that, having spent two billion public dollars on a weapon, the American people were entitled to the bloodiest possible demonstration of its effectiveness. He states that many Americans espouse this view; I know one who does not.

ON Blackett's assumption that we dropped the bombs to prevent the Russian grab in Manchuria (he does not call it that), how did we succeed? Russia took Manchuria, a proceeding that we could not have prevented even though we wished to do so. Consider also how we held back at Berlin and Prague until the Russians got there, in accordance with our agreements that their troops could enter these cities first.

The second of Blackett's political assertions that I have mentioned above is best dealt with by stating it in his own words. He says, comparing the Baruch and the Gromyko proposals for atomic energy control. "It is hardly likely that either the American or the Russian Governments had serious expectations that their proposals for control would be accepted by the other. As has already been emphasized, the American proposals constituted a very shrewd move in the diplomatic cold war, promising concrete advantages in the event either of their acceptance or their rejection. American diplomacy had maneuvered Russia into the disadvantageous position of having to reject a speciously fair offer."

Nothing I can say will make this assertion seem more absurd than it shows itself to be. Quite apart from the obvious sincerity with which the U. S. approached this problem, it is more than I can manage to believe that our democratically cumbersome and bumbling foreign policy can have reached the heights of guile suggested by Blackett.

As to his argument concerning the industrial applications of atomic energy, and Russia's need for atomic power, one can only say that this is nonsense. To be the great industrial nation that she hopes to become, Russia needs power, indisputably; but the sources of it now lie ready to her hand. Her coal reserves are the second largest in the world; her potential of water power is the largest; by her own assertion her petroleum resources are larger than those of any other country. With this great wealth in the conventional power sources, Russia should be less dependent on atomic power than any other country.

Further, the development of power from conventional sources is a straightforward business which is well understood by engineers. We are only in the faltering beginnings of the engineering of atomic power. How shall we deal with the great intensity of lethal radiation? What structural materials best resist it without change and failure? How do we transfer heat efficiently in a structure the design of which is dominated by the necessities of its service as a reactor? How shall we dispose of the intensely radioactive wastes? Can we make a reactor that will both deliver useful power and "breed" new atomic fuel? How shall we guard against explosions? In view of these and other vital questions, practical atomic power is too far off to be a factor of significance in past or current policy.

ALTOGETHER, Blackett's book appears to be an elaborate and lengthy defense of a set of fixed ideas held at the start. J. B. S. Haldane, one of Blackett's colleagues in the British left, has said of him: "He has a mind which seems to be much happier with real things, which he can count and measure, than with the more abstract forms. . . . What is more, he finds the things he is looking for." Haldane's remark, made in an altogether different context, is particularly apt as a description of the way in which the ideas and arguments of Blackett's book must have been arrived at.

His ideas coincide remarkably with the standard Russian views. He belittles the atomic bomb—which Russia has not got, but wants. He depreciates strategic air power—which is the only arm we have that can strike a blow at Russia (she does not fear our armies, surely, and she has no vital seaborne commerce to defend). He indulges in the most remarkable gymnastics of rationalization to convict us of chicanery in our external atomic policy—despite a U. S. proposal the generosity of which is unparalleled in the history of diplomacy. Blackett, and the Russians too, consistently refer to the limited world government which so many Americans desire as a "world hegemony" dominated by the U. S.

Blackett's argument carries its own antidote. The excesses and the absurdities of the political views he urges are so clearly the result of bias, and so clearly dominated by pro-Soviet prejudice, that the whole work is suspect, and will appear so even to the least discerning.

7

Arms Race v. Control

Does the atomic explosion in Russia require the U.S. to modify its position in regard to the international control of atomic energy?

CHESTER I. BARNARD

November 1949

WHEN President Truman announced that an atomic explosion was known to have occurred somewhere in the area of Soviet dominion, my immediate reaction was that the chances of attaining the international control of atomic energy under the aegis of the United Nations had increased rather than decreased. It is in many ways an advantageous thing that parties looking to an agreement should enter the discussion without either one being at too great a disadvantage. One man with a gun finds it hard not to assume a superiority which hampers negotiation. Two men with guns are not necessarily going to shoot it out. Thus, though the use of atomic weapons is now more dangerously imminent than before, the dilemma of the United Nations is less acute and the possibilities of successful negotiation are measurably improved.

In 1946 the State Department board of which David E. Lilienthal was chairman and I was a member arrived quickly at agreement on a general plan for the international control of atomic energy. Yet it seemed to me at the time that, logical and sound as the plan was, the chances of its adoption were very small. This estimate was not by any means based exclusively on the possibility of determined opposition to the plan by the Soviet Union. It appeared likely that every country, including our own, would encounter extreme technical and popular difficulties in renouncing that considerable portion of its national sovereignty which acceptance of the contemplated pact would require. The fact that substantially the plan proposed by our board finally proved acceptable to all members of the United Nations Atomic Energy Commission except the Soviet Union and its immediate satellites was heartening. It must be remembered, however, that approval of the plan by representatives of these nations in the United Nations Atomic Energy Commission is by no means the same thing as the final and formal approval required for the execution of the necessary multilateral treaties to carry the plan into effect.

It was also obvious from the outset that so long as one of the negotiators possessed a preponderance of knowledge of atomic energy science and technology, as well as an actual monopoly of production resources and of fissionable materials, the chances of agreement could not be high, for the parties lacked the equality of status that makes for success in bargaining. The position of the U. S. involved one of the most extraordinary dilemmas in history. Though our plan embodied the most generous ultimate intentions of relinquishing our preferred position, actual possession of the bomb could be given up only in consideration of comprehensive and genuine guarantees that, in the end, all nations would forego the use of weapons employing atomic energy. This inevitably meant that other nations would have to relinquish, step by step and voluntarily, important elements of sovereignty in advance of the relinquishment of the bomb by the U. S. It is hard to imagine conditions less favorable to successful negotiation by proud and equal nations. And the difficulty was not reduced by the exaggerated importance that our temporary monopoly of atomic energy knowledge assumed in the minds of the American people.

Now that the Soviet Union apparently also has the bomb, there will have to be some changes in our tactics and our attitude. It has always seemed to me a most dangerous delusion to suppose that our preferred position in the field of knowledge and technology could last very long or that our superiority with respect to the stock of fissionable materials could be maintained indefinitely. It is surely no great surprise that the essential knowledge is held by several, if not by many, nations and that in fact an atomic explosion has now occurred under other auspices than our own. The status of the participants in the attempt to negotiate an international agreement has become less unequal and with the lapse of time presumably will become progressively more nearly equal.

It would be a mistake to focus all attention on the atomic bomb to the exclusion of the other terrible modern weapons of warfare. When a British commentator observed wryly that "the Russians have devalued the bomb," his remark was true in more than one sense; it was more than the mere devaluation of a monopoly. Once the atomic bomb becomes an international weapon, so that it confers no overriding advantage upon its possessors, the result must be to increase the pressure upon all nations in any universal arms race to develop even more effective weapons of mass destruction. Already, in the short period since the end of the war, this effort has got under way. Guided missiles and rocket bombs, chemical and biological means of warfare are presumably being advanced every day, not by a few nations but by many nations. Dangerous biologicals could be made in small laboratories in small countries. Chemical poisons could be produced and assembled anywhere. And it must be remembered, after all, that the squadrons of B-29 bombers carrying conventional explosives and fire bombs produced more casualties in Tokyo in one night than the two atomic bombs on separate days in Hiroshima

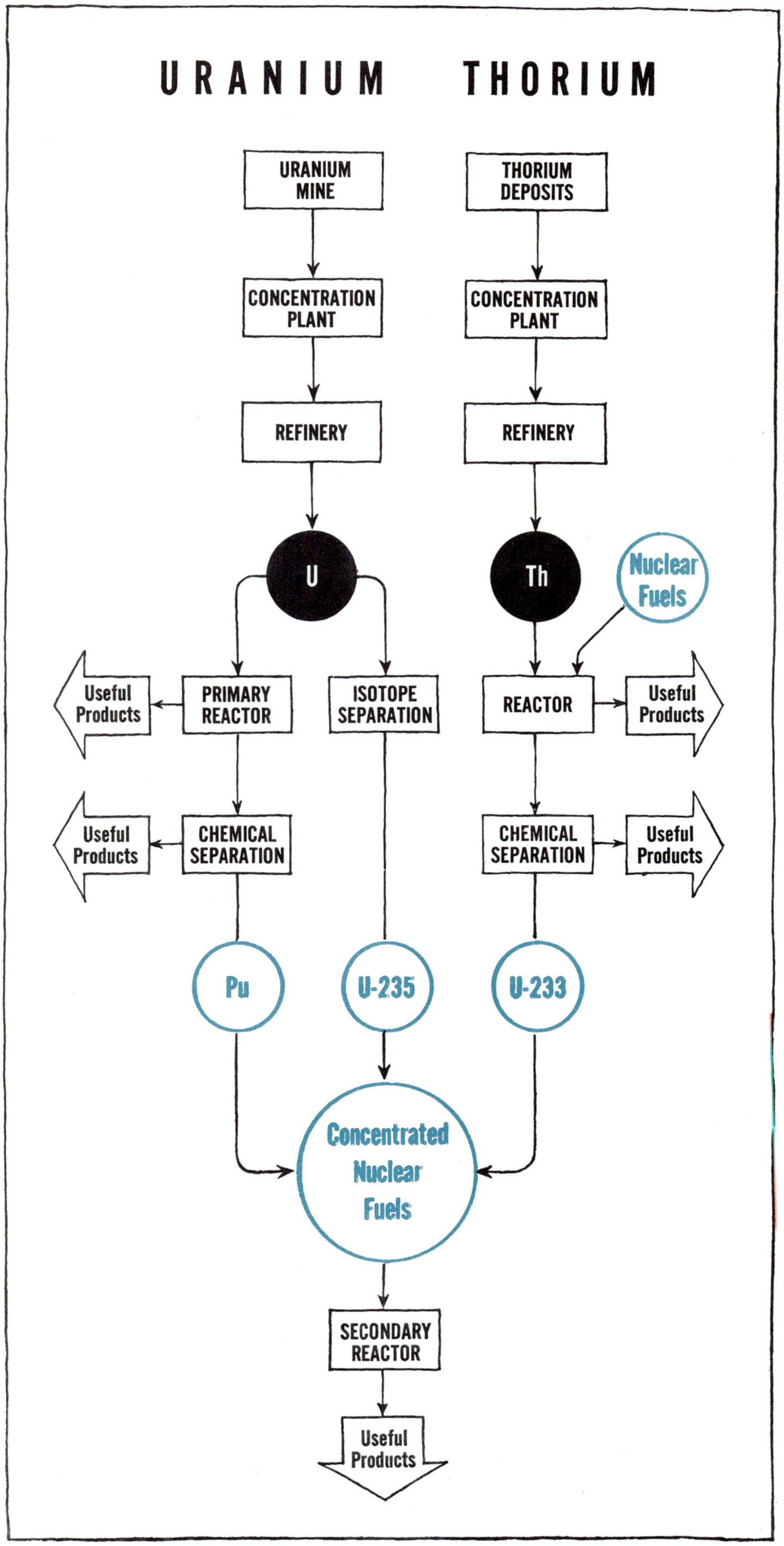

PROCESSES required to obtain power and other useful products from uranium and thorium outline the problem of control. Uranium yields two nuclear fuels: U-235 and plutonium. Thorium yields U-233. Under the Acheson-Lilienthal plan individual nations could use "denatured" fuels, but an Atomic Development Authority would control stages of their manufacture.

and Nagasaki. For the present, swift improvements in all these weapons are as likely as epoch-making changes in the atomic bomb or other destructive uses of atomic energy.

Thus the control of atomic energy is only a part of the much larger problem of the control of war itself. But in many symbolic and practical ways it occupies perhaps a decisive position in the larger problem. The atomic bomb so far is unmatched as a means of surprise attack. Aside from general dispersal of the population and industry, little or no defense against it seems in prospect. Moreover, from the military point of view it is a remarkably economical weapon; at $1 million per bomb it is a far cheaper method of destruction than its equivalent in chemical explosives and the extra planes to carry them.

At the same time, in certain respects the control of the atomic bomb might not be as difficult as that of other modes of warfare. Its spectacular character makes it not too hopeless to expect that we may arrive eventually at some sort of an agreement on the curbing of this one most vivid form of warfare.

What makes the atomic bomb unique is that, as recent statements by naval officers in Washington have reminded us, this is the first weapon primarily directed to the indiscriminate annihilation of civilian populations. As such it introduces an entirely new concept of warfare. To be sure, the concept of total destruction has long been discussed by theoreticians and was put into practice to some extent in the last war, but now that the atomic bomb has made it practically realizable, this concept must inevitably dominate all military strategy—unless the bomb is placed beyond the pale. So the curbing of atomic weapons would go a long way toward controlling the menace of annihilative war, including bacteriological warfare and all the rest.

The stakes are enormously high. In my opinion, they involve not only peace but also whether we shall be forced to have a totalitarian government. If dispersal of the population is the only immediate means of reducing vulnerability that we can hope for, then we should have to carry the control of private lives to unheard-of lengths in this country. We should recall that governments in the past have always found that the hardest thing for any central authority to undertake is the deliberate shifting of a population against its wishes. The defense measures that would be absolutely necessary in the event of a protracted failure to get international agreement would mean an intolerable central management of our lives. Such control has already progressed to the point where it threatens the freedom of science.

The principal issues in the international control of atomic energy that have been under discussion in the UN can be stated succinctly in a series of questions: Shall an international authority take ownership of the raw materials (uranium and thorium) and operate all potentially dangerous projects in atomic energy, or shall each nation develop its own atomic energy program, with international inspectors to see that it does not make atomic weapons? Shall atomic disarmament proceed in a series of stages, or shall atomic bombs be outlawed and existing stockpiles be destroyed by immediate agreement? Shall charges and penalties against a nation accused of violating the control agreement ultimately be decided by a majority or by a unanimous vote of the UN Security Council?

Obviously the present new situation reduces the significance of some of the points that have been strenuously debated in the past, notably the question of stages. It seems safe to say that too much has been made of the veto question, especially in the beginning. Time has passed and there has been less debate about the veto, for one thing because there was no great clarity on just which form of veto people were talking about. The entire veto problem has no cogent connection, so far as I can see, with the central question at issue. Of course it offends our sense of the proprieties to be told that anyone accused of committing a crime should be able to veto an inquiry into the facts. But if some nation violates an international agreement, others are not going to wait the months and months which may be required for the Security Council to complete a thorough investigation. If under these conditions a violation should occur, to all intents and purposes war would already have been declared. The veto would then be irrelevant; all rules would be off. Under the United Nations Charter all nations can, in certain circumstances, defend themselves. The violation of an international atomic energy agreement would certainly be such a circumstance.

ALTHOUGH international atomic energy control is not equivalent to the abolition of war, it is a step in that direction. It is a step that should be taken, and a step from which no quibbling, not even quibbling of the more serious sort, or any hurt feelings, should deter us. In the years since the close of the war some of our neighbors have begun to develop inferiority complexes, and America more than once has shown evidences of a high-hat complex. We have not been quite aware of how difficult it is for others not to become oversensitive, and how easy it is for us to offend.

Perhaps the major reason why the discussions of atomic energy control have heretofore been doomed to reach a stalemate is that out of sheer pride not every big power has been willing to give up its efforts to develop atomic energy. The Soviet Union now feels itself in a happier position. At the same time, although we have become more vulnerable, the Soviet Union is not less vulnerable than before. Although each nation now possesses the crucial weapon of attack, it has less direct incentive to use it—since it is an axiom of warfare that attack calls for retaliation. Even if we were to assume that we were certain to win a war because we could use the atomic bomb on a larger scale than anybody else, would such a victory be worth taking? Could any nation, however greedy, rejoice or even benefit from possession of a land in which all the works of civilization had been destroyed?

With two large and rival nations in possession of deadly atomic weapons, the peace of the world is grimly endangered, especially since tensions have been developing apace and there has thus far been no progress on an international agreement. But if we look back to various junctures in our own history and note how dark things must have looked to those who were then facing an unknown future, we should take heart. After reading about our nation's past crises in our history books, even today we do not see how it could have worked out its destiny—but it did. Concrete reality is easier to face than remote possibilities. At least we are now confronting a concrete situation. And what is even better, discussions have now been resumed.

In our panic over the destructive potentialities of atomic energy we have been inclined to lose sight of its potentialities for progress. So far we have had only glimpses of what atomic energy can do for mankind—as a source of power, as an aid to medicine, as a tool for basic research. Before these more hopeful aspects of atomic energy can receive our undivided attention, it is necessary to remove the clouds of apprehension now more than ever darkening the international sky. No one can or should be too sanguine about the ease of the task—or wait too passively for something to happen. It is always a good thing not to assume too early that a situation is entirely hopeless. Here we can say literally that while there is life there is hope. Four or five years ago the chance of achieving successful international control seemed to me about one in 100. Now it is perhaps one in 50, and it may get better as time goes on.

SECTION 2: THE HYDROGEN BOMB

"There is an immense gulf between the atomic and hydrogen bombs. The atomic bomb, with all its terrors, did not carry us outside the scope of human control or manageable events, in thought or action, in peace or war. . . . [but with the coming] of the hydrogen bomb, the entire foundation of human affairs was revolutionized, and mankind placed in a situation both measureless and laden with doom."

SIR WINSTON CHURCHILL, 1955

INTRODUCTION

Generally, politicians and government officials were about as unprepared for the Soviet A-bomb as they had been for that of the Unites States. The factor of surprise, coupled with the increasing intensity of the Cold War, made a strong U.S. response seem necessary. After a brief period of intensive but secret studies, the U.S. response was determined: the development of a "super" hydrogen-fusion bomb, or H-bomb. Long known as a possibility but never the objective of a serious program, now the development of such a bomb was to be actively pursued.

For a flavor of the times, in order better to understand the U.S. reaction to the Soviet explosion, we turn again to the news of the events just as this was presented in the "Science and the Citizen" columns of *Scientific American.*

Science and the Citizen, December 1949

The Smoldering Atom

THE Russian atomic explosion faded from the front pages rather quickly, apparently leaving a minimum of residual activity. Despite its seemingly small diplomatic effects so far, however, it set off some new chain reactions which behind-the-scenes observers in Washington, the United Nations and other world capitals have followed with considerable interest.

The opening propaganda move was made by the U.S.S.R. Soon after President Truman's announcement of the Russian explosion, the Soviet representative on the UN Atomic Energy Commission proposed that the U.S. offer "new concrete proposals" for the international control of atomic energy. The five other permanent members of the Commission (the U.S., Great Britain, France, Canada and China) countered by reasserting their support of the "Baruch" plan, insisting that it was essential to any effective system for atomic control. That neither the Commission majority nor the U.S.S.R. was ready to change its position was emphasized in reports made to the UN General Assembly by both sides a month after the Russian explosion. The majority, laying entire responsibility for the deadlock on the U.S.S.R., declared: "The Government of the U.S.S.R. puts its sovereignty first and is unwilling to accept measures which may impinge upon or interfere with its rigid exercise of unimpeded state sovereignty." There was a wide difference between the majority and U.S.S.R. plans for the restriction of atomic energy to peaceful purposes. Stripped of minor issues, the difference was this: international ownership and operation of critical atomic energy activities (the majority plan) *v.* national ownership and operation with periodic inspection by an international agency (the U.S.S.R. plan).

Could any compromise be found between such divergent points of view? The author of the Baruch plan and official spokesmen for the Truman Administration evidently thought not. Frederick Osborn, deputy U.S. representative on the Commission, declared that any agreement on atomic weapons short of "operating and managerial control" would be merely an ineffectual "expression of good intention." Bernard Baruch (speaking for himself) urged the U.S. to accept no substitute for his plan; he held that agreement on a lesser plan would only "create a false sense of security."

It was clear, however, that many U.S. students of the atomic energy control problem did not share these views. One indication of this was the stir created by Chester I. Barnard's article "Arms Race *v.* Control" [see the article beginning on page 34], in which Mr. Barnard, a coauthor of the Acheson-Lilienthal plan, urged "some changes in our tactics and our attitude." The article was widely discussed in Washington, in the UN and by unofficial commentators. Some critics of U.S. foreign policy went so far as to charge that the U.S. control plan, as presented to the UN, had been deliberately designed to make it unacceptable to the U.S.S.R. In the New York *Daily Compass* the columnist I. F. Stone declared: "I believe the Truman Administration never wanted an agreement on atomic disarmament and does not want one now."

Among U.S. atomic scientists and groups not connected with the Administration there was increasing discussion of compromise plans. Taking the realistic view that agreement on a comprehensive plan for atomic control was impossible at the present stage of cold-war tensions, they proposed that an attempt be made to obtain a limited agreement, such as a five-year convention outlawing atomic arms coupled with some method of international regulation of the mining of uranium and thorium.

Within the UN itself there appeared to be an increasing disposition to discuss compromises, particularly among the smaller nations. Carlos P. Romulo, president of the General Assembly, proposed a truce or moratorium in the production of atomic bombs while negotiations proceed on atomic energy control. A hint of a compromise in the control plans that had been actively discussed was given by Lester B. Pearson of Canada. The proposal was to reduce the scope of international ownership and operation of atomic facilities, in return for which the U.S.S.R. would be asked to agree to permit continuous inspection of atomic plants instead of periodic inspection. Said Mr. Pearson: "If it were possible to give more powers of operation to nations, and take away some powers from the international agency, that would make it all the more important to have complete international powers of inspection at any time without any reservation. . . . Our Russian friends . . . have given no indication whatever at any time that they are willing to accept that kind of international supervision or inspection, and that seems to me to be the fundamental difference between the two positions now."

As this issue of *Scientific American* went to press, a public debate of the atomic energy control problem began in the UN. It was obvious that the debate would serve merely as an occasion for polemical attacks on the rival positions. Thus Andrei Y. Vishinsky, Soviet Foreign Minister, delivered an hour and a half speech denouncing the U.S.-sponsored plan. He asserted that the plan "would make it impossible to use atomic energy for peaceful purposes" and that U.S. policy-makers had no intention of agreeing to a prohibition of atomic weapons. As for the U.S.S.R., Vishinsky declared that it was using atomic energy not for stock-piling bombs but for constructive purposes: "We are razing mountains; we are irrigating deserts; we are cutting through the jungle; we are spreading life, happiness, prosperity and welfare in places where the human footstep had not been seen for thousands of years."

Coupled with apparently Soviet-inspired stories in the Soviet-licensed Berlin newspaper *Nacht Express*, which said that the U.S.S.R. had used atomic bombs to blast channels through the Turgai Mountains to divert two Siberian rivers to desert areas, Vishinsky's statement made sensational headlines. Whether or not the U.S.S.R. had enough bombs to "raze mountains," or could use them in this way without creating prohibitive radiation hazards, the statement dramatized the fact that the U.S.S.R. intended to make an emphasis on the constructive uses of atomic energy the keystone of its atomic propaganda strategy.

U.S. Step-Up

IN the U.S. atomic energy program, the Russian explosion had two observable results. One was an acceleration of plans for expansion of plants producing atomic bombs. To enlarge the Oak Ridge and Hanford facilities for production of fissionable materials, the President authorized the Atomic Energy Commission to draw $30 million immediately from budget reserves. When Congress reconvenes in January he will ask for the appropriation of $300 million more for this purpose.

The other result was an assurance from Great Britain and Canada that the U.S. would continue to get a full supply of uranium from the Belgian Congo and Canadian mines. The three countries have been discussing for several months the renewal of an agreement permitting the U.S. to purchase most of the output of these mines [see "Science and the Citizen," SCIENTIFIC AMERICAN, September 1949]. Both the British and Canadians, who had sought a fuller exchange of atomic information with the U.S. in return for this renewal, informed the U.S. negotiators after the Russian explosion that the agreement would be renewed without conditions. The Executive Branch of the U.S. Government, including the AEC, favors a more liberal exchange of atomic data, not only with Canada and Great Britain but also with one or two other countries, but has been blocked by opposition within the Congressional Joint Committee on Atomic Energy. When Congress reconvenes the Administration may seek revision of the Atomic Energy Act of 1946 to obtain a clear authorization for the exchange of more atomic information with friendly nations.

Meanwhile the AEC received a clean bill of health in the final report of a majority of the Joint Committee on its investigation of Republican Senator Bourke B. Hickenlooper's charges of "incredible mismanagement." After 45 hearings, the Joint Committee put the charges to a vote. The 10 Democrats voted to clear the Commission; the six Republicans voted against it. The majority, in its 35,000-word report, took occasion to review the entire AEC operation. It credited the AEC with "taking a vast enterprise which was falling apart at the seams and reshaping it into a formidable deterrent against aggression." On the security question, it said: "[There is] no evidence hinting that Russia obtained secrets from the Commission which advanced by one day the date when she completed her first atomic bomb. Likewise, no evidence hints that Russia has acquired information from the Commission which would enable her to improve, by so much as mucilage and tissue paper, the current Soviet bomb designs."

Senator Hickenlooper submitted a brief minority report, supported by his Republican colleagues, which did not repeat the "incredible mismanagement" charge but insisted that "widespread opportunity has been provided for infiltration of subversives" in the AEC and accused the Commission of a "leisurely" approach and "indecision" in development of its program. The majority and minority reports agreed on one thing: research and development in the field of application of nuclear fission to useful power has not been pushed hard enough.

The formal mechanism for obtaining scientific advice on nuclear matters, including weaponry, was the Atomic Energy Commission's General Advisory Committee. This committee was chaired from the beginning by J. Robert Oppenheimer. Its members included a number of very distinguished scientists and engineers, nearly all of whom had been deeply involved in nuclear physics from the beginning. It heard much testimony from proponents of the H-bomb as well as proponents of other possible ways of responding to the Soviet bomb. Two months after the Soviet detonation, the General Advisory Committee issued its report. The first part of the report endorsed giving high priority to developing tactical atomic weapons and to the development of a new nuclear reactor for producing various special materials for use in nuclear weapons. The second part took up technical questions related to the "super bomb." It recommended against a priority program to develop such a bomb at that time because theoretical studies were not yet complete and at least some of the ideas proposed would require a large diversion of reactor capacity away from the atomic bomb programs they considered very important. They did, however, conclude that a "concerted attack had a better than even chance of producing a weapon within five years."

Appended to the technical report were two statements about political and moral issues. The first, signed by Oppenheimer and five others, said "In determining not to proceed to develop the Super bomb, we see a unique opportunity of providing by example some limitations on the totality of war and thus eliminating the fear and arousing the hopes of mankind." The second, signed by Fermi and Rabi, said "The fact that no limits exist to the destructiveness of this weapon makes its very existence and the knowledge of its construction a danger to humanity as a whole. It is necessarily an evil thing considered in any light. For these reasons, we believe it important for the President of the United States to tell the American people and the world we think it is wrong on fundamental ethical principles to initiate the development of such a weapon."

However, there were other equally effective though less formal ways of presenting scientific advice on the matter. Edward Teller had long urged development of the H-bomb, and when the first Soviet atomic bomb was exploded, he and some others intensified their advocacy. They counseled directly with Senator McMahon, chairman of the powerful Congressional Joint Committee on Atomic Energy, and with AEC Commissioner Lewis Strauss. Partly as a result of this advice, McMahon and Strauss and some other officials became convinced that the General Advisory Committee was wrong, and that the United States should initiate an energetic program to develop the hydrogen bomb. In a report refuting the General Advisory Committee's report, Senator McMahon wrote in part, "If we let Russia get the super first, catastrophe becomes all but certain—whereas, if we get it first, there exists a chance of saving ourselves."

President Truman finally received an opinion from the Atomic Energy Commissioners that was split, and he received additional advice on the matter from the Joint Chiefs of Staff, the Secretaries of Defense and State, and from McMahon's Joint Committee. Then, on January 30, 1950, the President said "I have directed the AEC to continue its work on all forms of atomic weapons, including the so-called hydrogen or super bomb." Despite the strange understatement in its wording, Truman's message was taken to be, as it was meant to be, an order to commence a serious program to develop the super bomb.

With very few exceptions, members of Congress had no hard information on the subject, nor were they allowed to read the report of the General Advisory Committee. Even so, *The New York Times* reported that "no presidential announcement since Mr. Truman entered the White House seemed, in the opinion of many observers, to strike such an instant and nonpartisan congressional support . . . the repeatedly expressed theme was that regardless of how dreadful the hydrogen weapon might be, Mr. Truman had no other course in view of the failure so far of negotiations for international control of atomic energy, and the 'atomic explosion' some months ago in the Soviet Union."

For some other contemporary reactions, we turn again to "Science and the Citizen."

Science and the Citizen, March 1950

The Superbomb

"EXCEPT for the atomic bomb itself, the existence of which was a wartime secret until it was dropped at Hiroshima, no weapon in the history of mankind became a national policy with so little understanding and discussion, though none so awful was ever projected before."

In these words Arthur Krock, the chief Washington correspondent of *The New York Times*, described the reaction of many to President Truman's announcement that he had ordered the Atomic Energy Commission to made a hydrogen bomb. Even after the decision had been made, men found it difficult to grasp its awful potentialities, or to believe that the project could be anything but a bad dream. In the short space of two months the specter of the new superweapon had developed with the swiftness and hypnotic inevitability of Greek tragedy.

As Washington correspondents pieced the story together from indirect sources, the President himself had raised the question of the hydrogen bomb soon after the explosion of the Soviet atomic bomb last fall. He called in a few of his top atomic, military and diplomatic advisers for consultations in strictest secrecy. The first public intimation of the matter came when Senator Edwin C. Johnson, a member of the Joint Congressional Committee on Atomic Energy, said in a television broadcast last November 1 that U.S. scientists had made "considerable progress" on a super-bomb 1,000 times as powerful as the Hiroshima model. On December 2 the syndicated Washington columnists Joseph and Stewart Alsop revealed that a hydrogen bomb which would devastate hundreds of square miles was under discussion, and that the President faced a decision on whether to undertake a project costing "$2 to $4 billion" to make it. This revelation was followed by further horrifying details from Drew Pearson; the story then became general, though there was still no Washington official who would permit himself to mention the words hydrogen bomb for quotation.

The debate, conducted almost exclusively in the gossip arena of newspaper columnists, developed a remarkable confusion of information: There was dispute as to whether the superbomb would employ hydrogen "fission" or hydrogen fusion; whether it would be thousands of times or only twice as powerful as the uranium-plutonium bomb; whether it would cost $4 billion or only $200 million. It was generally assumed that the possibility of creating the bomb itself had already been proved; all that remained was to manufacture it. The columnists divided the top officialdom of Washington into two camps: one for and one against making the bomb. Pearson had it that David Lilienthal and Lewis Strauss headed opposing factions in the Atomic Energy Commission, and that Lilienthal had resigned his chairmanship in protest against the hydrogen-bomb project. (After the President's decision, Strauss announced his own resignation from the Commission as of April 15, saying: "The issues involving national security which are my primary concern are now resolved as I had hoped and recommended.")

To White House visitors President Truman expressed strong displeasure that the hydrogen bomb had become a subject of public discussion. Lilienthal, denying that he had opposed making the bomb, assured reporters that the issue was not "the naked question: Do we or don't we?" It involved military, political and other considerations. What these considerations were never emerged, although the Joint Committee on Atomic Energy, the AEC's General Advisory Committee and other agencies held extended discussions of them. In the midst of the babble of private discussion in Washington, Harvard University's President James Bryant Conant, a member of the General Advisory Committee, made some public remarks that were taken to refer to the hydrogen-bomb issue. Speaking to a Harvard club in Rochester, he said: "The simple fact is that many important decisions are being made in Washington today without adequate evaluation." The Government, he added, had not developed "even the first approximation to a satisfactory procedure for evaluating technical judgments on matters connected with national defense."

In Washington the President told a press conference that when a decision was made on the hydrogen bomb it would be made by him, and by no one else. Four days later, on January 31, the President announced his decision in these words:

"It is part of my responsibility as Commander-in-Chief of the armed forces to see to it that our country is able to defend itself against any possible aggressor. Accordingly I have directed the Atomic Energy Commission to continue its work on all forms of atomic weapons, including the so-called hydrogen or superbomb. Like all other work in the field of atomic weapons, it is being carried forward on a basis consistent with the over-all objectives of our program for peace and security.

"This we shall continue to do until a satisfactory plan for international control of atomic energy is achieved. We shall also continue to examine all those factors that affect our program for peace and this country's security."

The President's decision won almost unanimous endorsement in Congress; it was accepted as inevitable by most scientists. The columnist Walter Lippmann declared: "The President's statement should put an end to a public discussion which was bound to be very foolish when it was not very dangerous, and in any event was sure to be misleading." But the public discussion was only beginning. Whether the military strategists liked it or not, the hydrogen bomb was a matter of inquisitive interest to its potential victims in all countries, including the U.S.

Many U.S. citizens quickly expressed the feeling that the President's "naked" announcement had failed to do full justice to the opportunity to promote peace and security. Senator Arthur H. Vandenberg urged the President to assure the world that the U.S. would "suspend all our activities in respect to mass destruction the first moment these weapons can be dependably outlawed." The columnist David Lawrence pleaded: "The President has an unexampled opportunity to call for a re-examination of Russian-American relations in every aspect. . . . Has our diplomacy always been fair and just? Is it really helpless to find even an unorthodox approach to a solution? Is ingenuity confined solely to the laboratories of nuclear physics? The conscience of a Christian world may soon begin to press for the answers."

At a session of the American Physical Society in New York 12 of the nation's outstanding physicists, led by Hans A. Bethe of Cornell University, urged that the U.S. Government "make a solemn declaration that we shall never use this bomb first." The physicists said: "Few of the men who publicly urged the President to make this decision can have realized its full import. . . . We shall not have a monopoly of this bomb; it is certain that the Russians will be able to make one too. In the case of the fission bomb the Russians required four years to parallel our development. In the case of the hydrogen bomb they will probably need a shorter time. . . . Even if the power [of the bomb] were limited to 1,000 times that of a present atomic bomb, the step from an A-bomb to an H-bomb would be as great as that from an ordinary TNT bomb to the atom bomb. . . . New York, or any other of the greatest cities of the world, could be destroyed by a single hydrogen bomb."

Among others who did not believe that the President's statement should put an end to public discussion of the hydrogen bomb was Senator Brien McMahon, chairman of the Joint Committee on Atomic Energy. Two days after the President's announcement McMahon delivered an address before an attentive session of the Senate. With an enthusiasm rare on cynical Capitol Hill, Senators of both parties rushed to shake his hand when he had finished. By a single bold, constructive proposal McMahon showed that the prospect was not hopeless if men did not think so. He proposed that the U.S. spend $50 billion to launch "a moral crusade for peace," end the atomic armaments race and "save mankind from destruction by fire." His suggestion was that $10 billion of the $15 billion the U.S. now spends annually for armaments be used during each of the next five years for the Point Four program, for useful development of atomic energy and for "general economic aid and help to all countries, including Russia." In return for this "global Marshall Plan" other nations would be asked to accept an effective program for international control of atomic energy and to divert two thirds of their present spending on armaments to constructive purposes.

The alternative, McMahon observed, would be the destruction of free institutions in the U.S. and the necessity of remaining "ceaselessly poised to meet an attack that might incinerate 50 million Americans—not in the space of an evening but in the space of minutes." The Senator said: "Let me warn with all the solemnity at my command that building hydrogen bombs does not promise security for the U.S.; it only promises the negative result of averting, for a few months or years, well-nigh certain catastrophe."

Although the spirit of McMahon's approach elicited a warm response, the conditions of his proposal were widely questioned. Lippmann noted that in effect the Senator had proposed to attempt to buy acceptance by the U.S.S.R. of "the obsolete Baruch plan" for international control of atomic energy—an unrealistic hope. Said Lippmann: "I venture to believe that nothing would accomplish so much to restore the confidence of mankind as a statement by the President that he had not only instructed the Atomic Energy Commission to proceed with the hydrogen bomb but that he had also instructed the Secretary of State to institute a new inquiry into the American policy and the American proposals [for atomic energy control]. . . . That . . . would revive hope and open the minds of men, now frozen in the awful realization that we have nothing to offer except an obsolete plan to deal with the new horrors to which we are committed."

The Federation of American Scientists asked the President to appoint a commission of experts in various fields, like the board that drafted the Acheson-Lilienthal plan of 1946, to restudy U.S. atomic policy and "make a fresh start, looking toward a policy which offers some real hope of breaking the present stubborn deadlock."

The answer of the White House to all these pleas was No. Secretary of State Dean Acheson replied that agreement with the U.S.S.R. was impossible; the only possible choice for the U.S. was to build up its strength. President Truman told a press conference that the position of the U.S. was unchanged; he saw no reason to reconsider the Baruch plan; no new approach or commission to restudy the question was necessary.

Immediately after Truman's decision to proceed with development of the H-bomb, *Scientific American* published a series of articles that discussed the technical, strategic, political, and moral issues involved. Three of these articles are reprinted in this section of the reader. Each was written by a physicist who had been deeply involved in research on nuclear or other modern weapons for a number of years, and the work each had done required him to think about what these weapons meant as well as how they worked. All three of the authors had close personal connections with many of the officials and advisers who carried the responsibility for advising the President about development of the H-bomb. Each also was "cleared" to receive much of the relevant information upon which the advice was based. Thus, these articles present not only the personal opinions of the authors, they also reflect much of the secret argument that had surrounded the issue.

While reading the articles today, it is important to bear in mind that they were written at a time when, though the nature of the nuclear reactions that would take place in an H-bomb were reasonably well understood, no one knew precisely about how to produce the conditions necessary to make them take place. Despite this lack of knowledge, each of the authors refers to H-bombs a thousand times as big as A-bombs, and that magnitude was commonly used in other discussions. All the arguments over the political, strategic, and even the moral issues revolve around this fantastic thousandfold increase that had gripped everyone's mind.

The first article, called simply "The Hydrogen Bomb," was written by Louis Ridenour, whose background was sketched briefly in the introduction to Section 1. Ridenour's article, like the two that follow it, first discusses and elucidates some of the technical problems involved, and then moves on to discuss implications of the bomb. Ridenour writes as one who understands the great dangers inherent in an arms race, but he clearly feels that, given an arms race, we must strive to win it. Thus, he agrees in his article that the

Soviet A-bomb does call for some kind of a reply, but he questions the logic of responding with an H-bomb program since the likeliest targets for such a bomb are to be found in the United States. He suggests that a better response, for instance, would be a program to improve the means of delivering A-bombs to their targets. If an H-bomb is really both necessary and feasible, he goes on to ask, why did the United States wait so long before starting to work on it? He concludes that a large part of the answer lies in the secrecy that surrounded the whole matter and prevented rational discussion of it. It is interesting at this point to note that Edward Teller, who has long been well known as a strong advocate of further weapons development, has also long expressed the belief that excessive secrecy on the part of the United States prevents rational discussion of the technological arms race and thus inhibits the development of important new weapons.

The second article, "The Hydrogen Bomb: II," was written by Hans Bethe, who in 1967 won the Noble Prize for work he had done earlier in elucidating the mechanisms by which hydrogen is burned in nuclear reactions in the interiors of stars. Bethe was head of the Theoretical Division at Los Alamos during the war. He continued to function in an advisory capacity afterward and was one of the persons consulted by the General Advisory Committee in its study of the question of whether an H-bomb should be developed. He has continued since then to be a leading advocate of arms control measures designed to moderate or stop the arms race. In his article in this section, after going into further details about thermonuclear reactions, Bethe also turns to the moral issue, clearly stating his view that developing an H-bomb is a wrong means for achieving our ends. Turning to strategic issues, he argues that even if the Soviets were to possess a few H-bombs before the United States had any, the prevailing strategic balance, based on U.S. possession of many A-bombs, would not be upset. His article ends with a plea for the control of all atomic weapons.

The third article in this series, "The Hydrogen Bomb: III," was written by Robert Bacher. He had been head of the Bomb Physics Division at Los Alamos during the war. Later, he was the first nuclear scientist to become a member of the U.S. Atomic Energy Commission (1946–1949). Like Ridenour and Bethe, Bacher first makes some technical speculations about what a hydrogen bomb might be like, and then turns to the other issues. He too questions the logic of responding to an A-bomb development by the Soviets with an H-bomb development by the United States. He reasons that A-bombs are already big enough and numerous enough for warfare needs and suggests that other technical problems be given higher priority, specifically, anti-submarine warfare and development of long-range guided missiles. Like Ridenour, Bacher is especially critical of the secrecy that surrounded the decision-making process, but unlike Ridenour, Bacher writes that more openness would have resulted in less support for the program.

Of all the results of Truman's decision to build an H-bomb, the reorientation of the research program at Los Alamos was by far the most important, and in later paragraphs of this introduction that reorientation will be discussed. It and some of the other events resulted from Truman's decision were reported in the "Science and the Citizen" columns of *Scientific American.*

Science and the Citizen, June 1950

AEC Reorientation

THE hydrogen bomb project and other military plans have caused substantial changes in the U.S. atomic energy program during the past two months. Sumner T. Pike, acting AEC chairman, observed in a public address that "we are doing some reshuffling of the projects and the personnel in the whole atomic energy program in order to bring the utmost weight to bear on the specific weapons development work which the President has recently directed us to pursue." In a series of guarded subsequent announcements, the AEC indicated the nature of some of these revisions. The most noteworthy announced change was the laying aside of the intermediate breeder reactor project, which many engineers consider to be a keystone in the experimental program for development of atomic power for industrial purposes.

The Commission first announced that it had "temporarily deferred" construction of this reactor, being designed by the General Electric Company Knolls Laboratory, in order to obtain "firmer costs estimates" and permit the Knolls Laboratory to turn to work on "the expanded atomic energy production program." Two weeks later the Commission disclosed that the Knolls Laboratory was shifting to the construction of an intermediate reactor for the Navy. The revised project will not test the breeding principle but will be devoted to the single purpose of developing a nuclear power plant using intermediate-speed neutrons for a ship's engine. Thus the AEC now has two naval reactor projects; the Westinghouse Electric Corporation is soon to build a prototype of a ship reactor using slow neutrons at the AEC reactor testing ground in Idaho. A House committee last month approved a request by the Navy for funds to construct a submarine to be powered by such a reactor.

The AEC further announced that a new $7-million particle accelerator for secret research will be built at a Naval Air Station in the San Francisco Bay area. The project will be carried out jointly by a subsidiary of the Standard Oil Company of California and the Radiation Laboratory of the University of California.

Science and the Citizen, December 1950

The Mathematics of Doom

UNTIL last February few persons seriously thought that atomic weapons might actually annihilate the human race. Then Leo Szilard, a wartime worker on the atomic bomb who is now a biophysicist at the University of Chicago, suggested a means: a 500- to 10,000-ton hydrogen bomb that would produce enough radioactive dust to poison the entire atmosphere.

Szilard's suggestion has now been critically examined by James R. Arnold of the University of Chicago's Institute for Nuclear Studies. Writing in the *Bulletin of the Atomic Scientists,* Arnold breaks Szilard's argument down into six points:

1. *The necessary deuterium can be produced.* True, says Arnold, although making 10,000 tons of this isotope of hydrogen would require $40 billion and a 5- to 10-year all-out effort by a major industrial nation.

2. *If produced, this amount of deuterium can be exploded, either in one package or in many.* Perhaps, says Arnold. He quotes Sumner Pike of the Atomic Energy Commission, who has called the hydrogen bomb "between possible and probable."

3. *In such an explosion, about 50 tons of neutrons will be produced.* Correct, says Arnold.

4. *These neutrons can be absorbed in an element giving rise to a dangerous radioactive isotope.* Maybe, says Arnold. Such an isotope must be sufficiently radioactive, must have a half-life neither too short nor too long and must be made from an element available in sufficient quantity. Arnold finds only two elements that meet these conditions: zinc and cobalt. Cobalt, which would yield eight times more gamma radiation than zinc, is the poison of choice. The problem is to guarantee that enough of the neutrons are actually absorbed by the cobalt and not dissipated uselessly by the explosion. For this purpose Arnold sees a need for a shell of 100,000 tons of cobalt around the exploding deuterium.

5. *The amount of radioactivity produced, if distributed uniformly as a dust layer over the earth, would irradiate every human being intensely enough to cause death.* True, says Arnold.

6. *The radiation could be effectively distributed in this manner.* Here Arnold disagrees with Szilard. Because dust will be removed from the atmosphere by rain, and from the land by runoff into rivers and oceans, "many areas will be left relatively clean." For this reason Arnold concludes: "It is almost certainly not true that a weapon of the type described can wipe out the human race com-

pletely." But he tempers this optimistic note: "It is possible, however, that the vast majority of the race can be killed off in this way. . . . Moreover, it is apparent that advances are to be expected, and a repetition of this discussion 10 years from today may give very different results."

Science and the Citizen, November 1951

Varieties of Atom Bombs

BOTH in Washington and in Moscow there was more official news on atomic-weapons developments last month than at any time since Hiroshima. In Moscow Premier Joseph Stalin, following an announcement by President Truman that the Russians had exploded a second atomic bomb, publicly confirmed for the first time that the U.S.S.R. was producing atomic weapons. And in the U.S. Gordon Dean, chairman of the Atomic Energy Commission, disclosed that the Commission was well along in the development of new types of atomic weapons which amounted to a "revolution" in atomic warfare. He said that atomic weapons which could be employed against troops in battle were already available and that "serious consideration" should be given to their use.

The second Soviet atomic explosion, like the first one in 1949, presumably was detected by U.S. observers by means of radiation monitoring devices. Stalin's confirmation, presented through the medium of an interview in *Pravda*, said that the U.S.S.R. had tested "a type of atom bomb," and he added that further "tests of atomic bombs of various calibers will be made in the future."

Dean's disclosures, made in a speech at the University of Southern California and through the publication of parts of his testimony before a House Appropriations subcommittee, were the most circumstantial account yet to come from the Commission on its weapons work. He said:

"We think of the great mushroom-shaped clouds and the devastation that lay below them. We think of them as weapons to be used against cities or large areas, and we don't think of them for use in a battle zone against troops. But all this is changing.

"What we are working toward here is a situation where we will have atomic weapons in almost as complete a variety as conventional ones, and a situation where we can use them in the same way. This would include artillery shells, guided missiles, torpedoes, rockets and bombs for ground-support aircraft among others and it would include big ones for big situations. . . . Given the right situation, and a target of opportunity, we could use an atomic bomb today in a tactical way against enemy troops in the field, against military concentrations near battle areas and against other vital military targets without risk to our own troops. We are steadily increasing, through our technological and production progress, the number of situations in which atomic weapons can be effectively employed in battle areas."

Dean added a prediction that the U.S. would develop atomic-powered airplanes within a decade.

Senator Brien McMahon, chairman of the Joint Congressional Committee on Atomic Energy, has presented to Congress a proposal for an increase in the atomic-weapons appropriation to $6 billion a year, about six times the appropriation the AEC received last year. His proposal was supported by Secretary of Defense Robert A. Lovett and the Joint Chiefs of Staff. McMahon argued that both on military and economic grounds atomic arms should replace conventional arms in U.S. defense plans.

"At the rate we are moving," he said, "I can see ahead only two ultimate destinations: military safety at the price of economic disaster or economic safety at the price of military disaster." The solution he proposed was "an atomic army, an atomic navy and an atomic air force in place of the conventional defenses we now maintain to the tune of 50 or 60 billion dollars a year."

Science and the Citizen, December 1951

Exercise Desert Rock

FIVE atomic test bombs were exploded by the Atomic Energy Commission last month at its Nevada proving ground. The experiments were designed to provide information on possible tactical uses of atomic weapons. The first explosion apparently was much smaller than any previous nuclear detonation; to newspaper reporters watching from mountainsides at a distance it looked smaller than the blast of a few tons of TNT which was set off for purposes of comparison just before. The four subsequent tests, all much more powerful, included studies of the effects of the new bombs on guns, tanks and dug-in positions at various distances from the explosion.

Army troops took part in some of the tests, called "Exercise Desert Rock." In one exercise 1,200 paratroopers set up battle positions on the test range, withdrew for the explosion and then returned for lessons in decontaminating the equipment they had left at the site.

A photographic paper factory of E. I. du Pont de Nemours and Company in Rochester, N.Y., 2,000 miles from the test site, closed down because the paper was being ruined by exposure to radioactive dust particles blown all the way from Nevada and caught in the plant's air-conditioning system.

The Atomic Energy Commission has resumed the exchange of research information, on a limited scale, with other countries. By an amendment to the Atomic Energy Act Congress has relaxed the almost total ban that was imposed in 1946; it gives the AEC permission to exchange atomic data, excluding weapon construction, with countries that do not "threaten the security" of the U.S. and that adopt approved secrecy precautions. The information the U.S. is willing to give, according to Congressional spokesmen, has to do with the refining of ores and the purification of fissionable material. In return the AEC expects to get data on reactor research from Great Britain and Canada.

Science and the Citizen, March 1952

AEC

PRESIDENT Truman announced a five-year program of expansion of atomic energy facilities which will cost $5 to $6 billion and more than quadruple the nation's investment in atomic energy. The new program will start in July, 1953, after the supply of uranium and trained technicians has been increased to the necessary strength.

In its 11th Semiannual Report, issued last month, the AEC noted that the Paducah and Savannah plants under construction, together costing over $1.7 billion, will nearly equal the value of all the plants, real estate and equipment of the General Motors Corporation. The Savannah plant alone will be worth $1,250 million—almost as much as Bethlehem Steel and considerably more than all the fixed assets of E. I. du Pont de Nemours. The report says: "The total amount of earth excavated at the two sites by December 31, 1951, would build a solid wall 5 feet wide and 7 feet high reaching from New York to San Francisco."

Science and the Citizen, April 1952

Britain's Bomb

WHEN Prime Minister Churchill visited the U.S. in January, his advisers sounded out U.S. authorities again on the delicate and painful question of a resumption of U.S.-British cooperation in atomic research. They got nowhere, as the present Atomic Energy Act in the U.S. forbids exchange of atomic energy information with other countries. During the following month hints began to appear in the press that Britain was producing an atomic bomb of her own and was ahead of the U.S. in theoretical work on atomic artillery and guided missiles. Mr. Churchill finally capped the hints with a formal announcement that his

Government would test a British-made "atomic weapon" in Australia sometime during 1952.

Mr. Churchill informed the House of Commons that the British bomb was produced some months ago, during the Labor administration. He said he was astonished to learn when he took office "that not only had the Socialist Government made the atomic bomb as a matter of research, but that they had created . . . important plant necessary for its regular production." He upbraided ex-Prime Minister Clement Attlee for having hidden Britain's light under a Socialist bushel. Mr. Attlee replied that the work was no secret within the Government and that Mr. Churchill's adviser, Lord Cherwell, should have kept the Conservative leader informed. He added that the U.S. Government had been "told about everything in order to get their cooperation."

In the U.S. officials were disappointed that Britain was making an independent test of its bomb in Australia. Senator Brien McMahon, chairman of the Joint Committee on Atomic Energy, remarked: "I might have wished that the British had seen fit to take advantage of our offer to make available a test site, subject to conditions which our law lays down."

Science and the Citizen, December 1952

British Bomb

PRIME MINISTER Winston Churchill last month announced a few details of the first British atomic bomb test, made in the Monte Bello Islands off the Australian coast in October. The bomb was exploded inside a small frigate in a harbor. The ship, said Churchill, was completely vaporized, except for some red hot fragments that scattered over one of the islands. Measurements of the radiation energy as the blast broke out of the hull showed that the temperature at the hull was almost one million degrees.

Observers from the mainland reported that the cloud thrown up by the bomb, unlike the mushroom clouds characteristic of U.S. bombs, had the shape of a ragged "Z." Churchill said that "thousands of tons of water and of mud and rock from the sea bottom were thrown many thousands of feet into the air and a tidal wave was caused." He added that damage effects were tested in specimen structures erected at various distances from the explosion.

The bomb project cost the British well over $280 million. It was directed by W. G. Penney, a physicist who had worked at Los Alamos during World War II. Churchill said he hoped the successful test would lead to "a much closer American interchange of information" with Britain about atomic energy.

As remarked earlier, the most important effect of Truman's decision of January 30, 1950 was to reorient the research and development program at the Los Alamos Scientific Laboratory. This laboratory had been established at the end of 1942 so that the work on atom-bomb design then being started at the University of California in Berkeley could be expanded in a more secluded location near Santa Fe, New Mexico. And it was at the Los Alamos Laboratory that the first atomic bombs had been produced. After the war ended, it continued to work on nuclear weapons but at a much slower pace. Most of the scientist "stars" of the period of wartime research, including Director J. Robert Oppenheimer, had returned to their universities. A substantial cadre of excellent but less well-known scientists, engineers, and technicians remained, and Norris Bradbury became the Director. Some who had spent the war years at Los Alamos returned from time to time as consultants or merely to reminisce. Work at the laboratory was largely devoted to the development of new modifications of the atomic bomb, and tests at Bikini in 1946 and Eniwetok in 1948 supported that part of the program. But ideas about the "super," or H-bomb, largely lay fallow.

Following Truman's decision, Edward Teller, who had been agitating for an H-bomb program for some time, urged some leading nuclear scientists to return to Los Alamos to work on the new program. Only a handful responded and most of those came only for extended visits during the next several summers. Among these were John von Neuman, John A. Wheeler, Gregory Breit, George Gamow, and Emil Konopinski. And Bethe and Fermi came. Both Bethe and Fermi had opposed the development of the H-bomb before the decision to go ahead with it was made. In conjunction with this new work at Los Alamos, several outside laboratories, notably the Radiation Laboratory of the University of California at Berkeley and the Naval Research Laboratory in Washington, D.C., organized teams to conduct "diagnostic" experiments to learn what actually happened at the instant of explosion. Later, the work done by John A. Wheeler expanded into Project Matterhorn which, while located in Princeton, New Jersey, functioned as an adjunct of the Theoretical Group at Los Alamos. In addition, the Berkeley team, co-directed by Hugh Bradner and myself, eventually became what is now known as the Lawrence Livermore Laboratory. With its regular staff augmented in these ways, the Los Alamos Laboratory ultimately produced a series of three crucial results.

The first of these was an experimental nuclear detonation conducted at Eniwetok, an atoll in the Marshall Islands in the Pacific, in the spring of 1951, only a little more than a year after the President's decision to proceed with H-bomb development. This detonation resulted in the first thermonuclear reactions ever produced by man. But these made only a small contribution to the amount of energy released in that particular explosion. This experiment and much of what followed is described at greater length in Teller's book, *The Legacy of Hiroshima*. A review of that book by Szent-Györgyi concludes the readings of this section. While the final preparations for this 1951 test were being made and while the theoretical ideas behind it were being restudied, Teller invented the final step in the series of ideas that made it possible to produce the conditions necessary to ignite the large masses of thermonuclear fuels needed for more powerful bombs.

The second of the three crucial results was another experimental detonation at Eniwetok Atoll, this one on Elugelab Island on November 1, 1952. The conditions necessary for igniting large masses of nuclear fuel proved effective and resulted in an explosion that released an amount of energy approximately equal to that contained in ten million tons (or 10 megatons) of TNT. The particular thermonuclear fuels used in the experiment required massive, unwieldy refrigeration equipment and other complicated gear, and the device was not a practical "bomb." However, converting this basic design into a practical bomb required no really new ideas, only the working out of certain details. Since Teller had already left Los Alamos for Chicago shortly after the 1951 experiments (he joined the Livermore group in the Fall of 1952), the final work was done by the permanent Los Alamos staff, importantly assisted by Wheeler's group at Princeton.

The third crucial event was the detonation of a very powerful, and practical, H-bomb at Bikini Atoll in the Pacific on March 1, 1954. This bomb yielded energy equivalent to 15 megatons of TNT and thus fulfilled the early common estimate that the H-bomb would be 1000 times as big as an A-bomb. The first atom bomb test explosion, at Trinity (Alamogordo, New Mexico) July 16, 1945, is listed as yielding 19 kilotons; the yield of the Hiroshima bomb the following month is unknown but has been estimated at 12.5 kilotons.

In the Soviet Union, developments followed a roughly similar course. Much less is known about the details, but what follows has been put together from official U.S. information plus the description of events given in the Kurchatov biography by Golovin cited in the introduction to Section 1.

No one in the United States really knows exactly when or why the Soviet H-bomb program began. On the one hand, Golovin says the Soviet government asked Kurchatov to explain the scare stories in the American press about a super bomb that supposedly was being developed there: Kurchatov's reported response was that the Americans were not making an empty threat: a hydrogen bomb was possible. This seems to say the Soviet program was stimulated by the United States' program. On the other hand, Golovin also says that calculations made *before* the first Soviet A-bomb test showed that a hydrogen weapon might be hundreds and thousands of times more powerful than an atomic one. He later adds that after a two-month rest following the first A-bomb test, Kurchatov launched a new project which apparently included operations necessary for making a hydrogen bomb. Taken literally, this seems to mean that the Soviet Union started its program shortly before the United States started one and that the Soviets were stimulated to do so at least partly by some early premature reports about the Americans' doing so. The fact is that just two months after the first Soviet A-bomb test, Senator Edwin Johnson mentioned the "super" on a TV program, and two weeks after that it was discussed again in a feature article in the *Washington Post*. Unfortunately, it is quite impossible to sort out cause and effect from the information available.

The rest of the record is clearer. The first Soviet test detonation involving thermonuclear reactions took place on August 12, 1953. U.S. authorities have reported that it involved fission and thermonuclear—or fusion—reactions, but they have never said anything about its power. The Soviets do not mention its power either, but Golovin does say it was detonated on a tower, and his description of the explosion and its results is definitely not that of a very big bomb. At the time, Premier Malenkov simply said "The U.S. no longer has a monopoly on the hydrogen bomb." Later the Soviets sometimes boasted about its being "the first hydrogen bomb in the world," a claim they justified by emphasizing the cumbersome and nontransportable nature of the November 1952 device detonated at Eniwetok. Some American officials have found it convenient to let that claim stand because it helps to justify both the American haste in getting on with the project and also the subsequent persecution of J. Robert Oppenheimer, who had led the opposition to doing so.

The first Soviet thermonuclear explosion that the USAEC classifies as being in the "megaton range" and as being an "air burst"—and so, both powerful and practical—did not occur until November 23, 1955, a year and a half after the U.S. spring 1954 series. Shortly after that explosion, Soviet authorities boasted about its great power, and characterized it as an important new achievement of Soviet scientists and engineers. They added that they had attempted "to achieve the maximum explosive results with the minimum amount of material." Clearly, this 1955 bomb is the first one that can be properly compared to those the United States tested in its 1954 series.

The Hydrogen Bomb

Presenting an account of the theoretical background of the weapon and a discussion of some questions it has raised in regard to our present policy of security

LOUIS N. RIDENOUR

March 1950

DURING the first weeks of 1950 the national scene was enlivened by discussions of the so-called "hydrogen bomb." Should a full-scale effort, perhaps comparable to that required to develop the fission bomb, be invested in attempting to create the potentially much more powerful hydrogen bomb? What is the morality of doing this? How would it affect our national position in an uneasy world to undertake this task? Should we not seek agreement with the U.S.S.R. on atomic energy control before embarking on a development of such significance and magnitude? Americans were asking themselves and one another these questions.

On January 31 the President of the U. S. announced that he had instructed the Atomic Energy Commission to work on the hydrogen superbomb. Thus a major issue of public policy, one quite possibly involving our national existence, was decided in a fully authoritarian way. Not without public discussion, to be sure; but without anything that could have been called informed public discussion. The public did not even know, and still does not, what the actual questions at issue were. Indeed, the matter became accessible to public discussion only because a careless reference to it was made on a television broadcast by a Senator who professes devotion to the principle of suppressing important information from the public, in the name of what he calls "national security." But the Senator did not reveal the nature of the issues and alternatives presented for decision.

The military and political questions that are either raised anew or brought to their apotheosis by the possibility of the hydrogen bomb are important, and cannot be dissociated from the physical problems surrounding the bomb's design. Let us consider the physical problems first, for they lead to certain conclusions that bear directly on the other questions.

In the President's first announcement of the Hiroshima atomic bomb, it was stated that the bomb drew its energy from the same source that fuels the sun and the stars. This statement is true only in the loosest sense. To be sure, a uranium-fission bomb, like the sun, derives energy from the transformation of one atomic species into others, but the types of reaction involved in the two cases are quite different.

As R. E. Marshak explained in "The Energy of Stars," SCIENTIFIC AMERICAN, January, 1950, there is excellent reason to believe that the enegy source of most stars, including the sun, is a rather complicated chain of nuclear transformations whose end result is to form one atom of helium out of four atoms of hydrogen. An atom of carbon, which plays an intermediate role in this chain of reactions is finally recovered unchanged, and is thus available to participate once more in the stellar energy cycle. In the sun and the stars, then, the source of energy is a chain of so-called thermonuclear reactions that ends in fusing four light hydrogen nuclei into the heavier and more complicated helium nucleus. The old-fashioned atomic bomb, on the other hand, uses as its explosive the nuclei of some of the heaviest elements known to man: uranium and plutonium. Energy is released when one of these heavy nuclei splits, or fissions, into two lighter, simpler nuclei. Thus the lightest atoms liberate energy if they are combined into heavier atoms; the heaviest atoms liberate energy when they are split into lighter ones. Only near the middle of the periodic table of the chemical elements do we find atomic species that are fully stable, in the sense that energy cannot be liberated either by combining them into heavier atoms or by splitting them into lighter ones.

To paraphrase a remark of the physicist George Gamow, we live in the midst of an atomic powder magazine, where immense amounts of energy are locked in every bit of matter. Why, then, are we safe? Why does common matter, possessed as it is of tremendous stores of energy, seem so inert, so permanent? The answer is that in order to liberate the energy of a fusion or a fission reaction we must ourselves invest some energy, just as we must expend energy to strike a match.

IN the case of nuclear fission, the energy investment is small. Fission occurs when an atom of uranium 235, plutonium 239, or uranium 233 captures a neutron, even one of very slow speed. But these neutrons must be somehow produced, since they do not occur free in nature, and are in fact unstable. The nuclear "chain reaction" that is exploited in atomic bombs and in nuclear reactors like those at Hanford is possible only because the fission reaction itself releases neutrons, the very particles that are needed to keep it going.

If the lump of uranium or plutonium in which these neutrons are liberated is

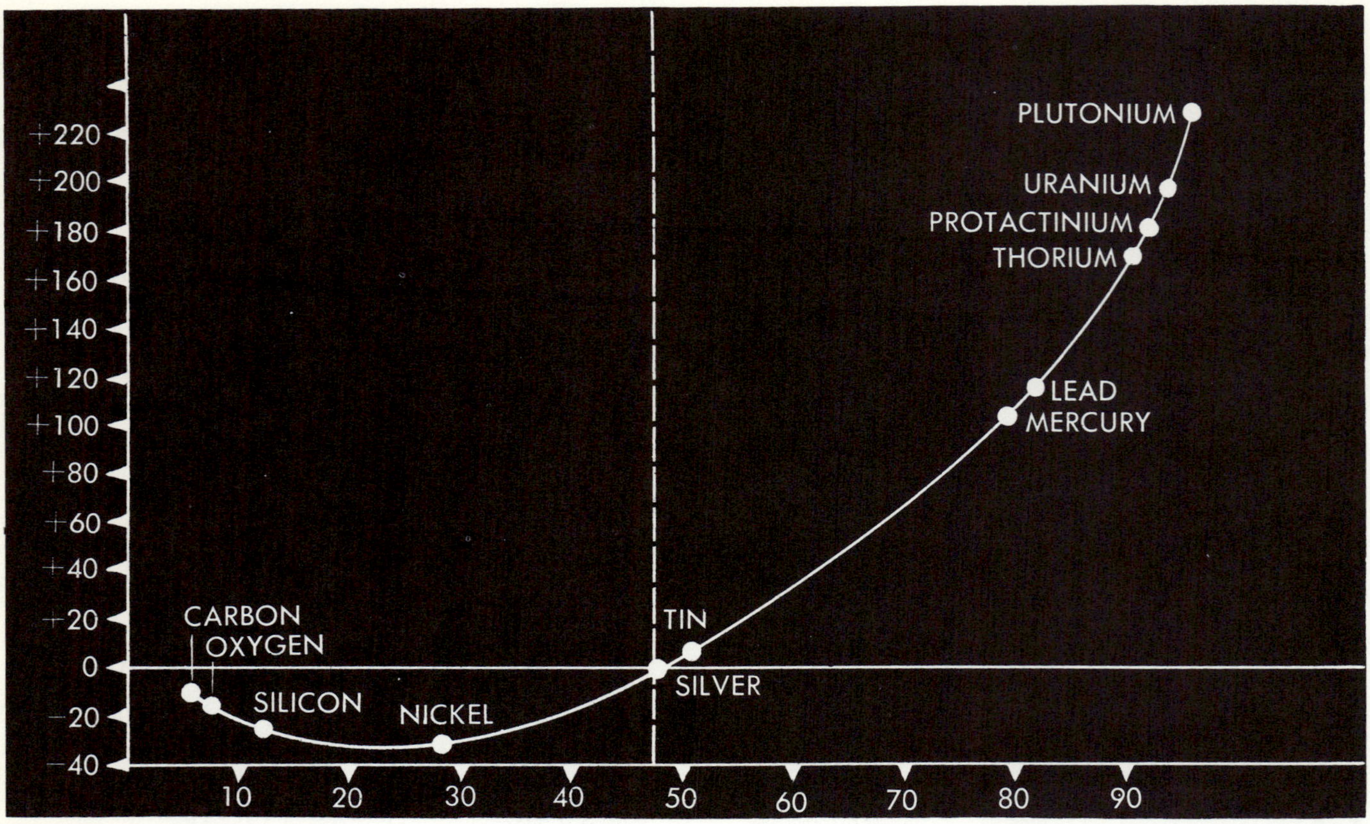

FISSION AND FUSION of nuclei are both energy-releasing processes. This diagram shows the amounts of energy released by the fission of various nuclei. The horizontal coordinate is atomic number; the vertical coordinate, the energy released in millions of electron volts. The fission of a nucleus with an atomic number larger than that of silver releases energy; the fission of a nucleus with an atomic number smaller than that of silver absorbs energy. Fusion of the lighter elements, the opposite of fission, releases large amounts of energy.

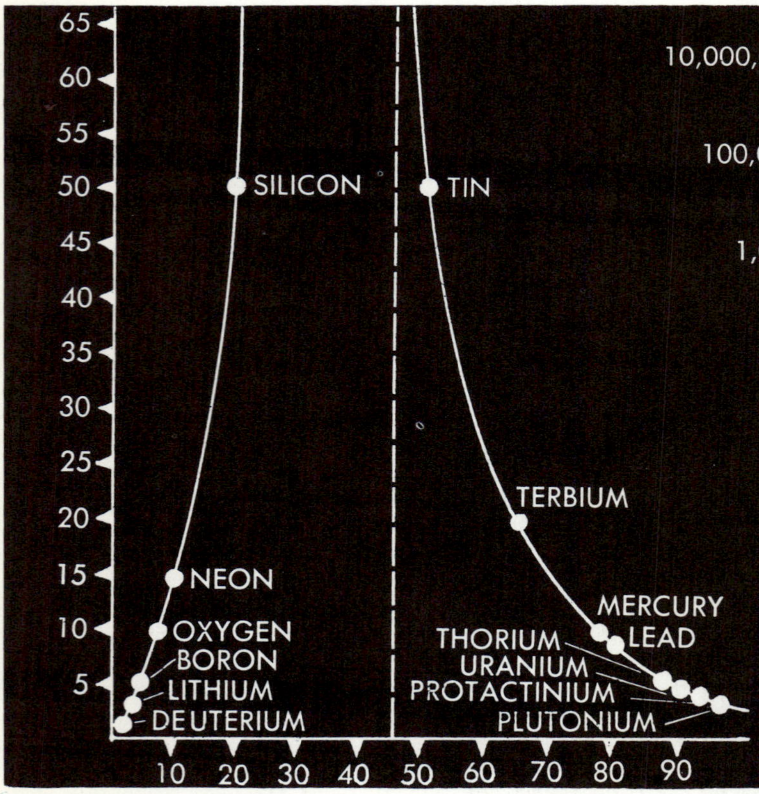

ENERGY REQUIRED to bring nuclei together so that they release energy is plotted against the same two coordinates. The lightest and heaviest elements require the least activation energy. The energy is released by two processes: fission for heavy elements and fusion for light.

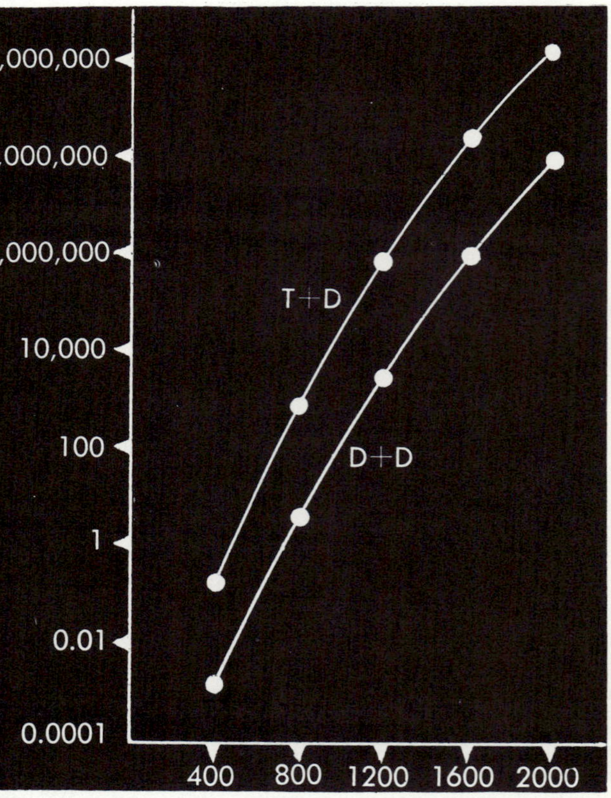

ENERGY RELEASED by the fusion of deuterium with deuterium (*bottom curve*) and tritium with deuterium (*top curve*) is plotted against temperature. The vertical coordinate is energy in calories per second. The horizontal coordinate is thousands of degrees Centigrade.

large enough, the neutrons released by one fission process will cause other fissions before they escape from the lump, and the process will go on faster and faster until an atomic explosion has been produced. The lump of uranium is then said to have exceeded the "critical size."

This limitation on critical size dictates the design of fission bombs. Detonation of such a bomb requires the rapid assembly of an overcritical mass; as soon as this is assembled, it blows up in about half a millionth of a second. The greatest ingenuity is needed to achieve an instantaneous condition exceeding the critical by as much as a few per cent; no amount of ingenuity has yet allowed the design of an efficient fission bomb so much as two or three times critical size. Thus there are inherently narrow limits to the size of a fission bomb: as it begins to exceed the critical, it explodes at once; if it is smaller, it cannot be exploded at all.

At the opposite end of the scale, among the light elements, the explosive conversion of mass into energy is not so easily achieved in terrestrial laboratories. To cause two light atoms to fuse into a heavier one, we must overcome powerful forces of electrical repulsion, since each nucleus is positively charged. Up to now this has been accomplished by scientists only laboriously, with poor efficiency and on an extremely small scale, by striking target atoms with a fast-moving beam of atoms accelerated in an electronuclear machine, or "atom-smasher." Only at energies of hundreds of thousands or millions of volts do collisions between most types of light atoms produce fusion reactions with substantial likelihood.

In the centers of the stars fusion reactions go on all the time, because the temperature there is some 20 million degrees Centigrade. The average energy of an atom at this temperature is only some 1,700 electron volts, but some atoms have several times this energy, and collisions between atomic nuclei are so frequent that fusion reactions are produced in substantial numbers. We cannot maintain stellar temperatures on the earth, but we can produce them for very small fractions of a second. In the explosion of a uranium or plutonium bomb, the central temperature of the exploding mass has been estimated as high as 50 million degrees C. At such a temperature fusion reactions in a dense mass of light atoms occur often enough to liberate significant amounts of energy.

OBVIOUSLY the fusion reactions that are likely to be most effective for producing energy are those that will go best at relatively low collision energies, since even the highest temperatures reached in the explosion of an atomic bomb correspond to rather modest bombarding energies from the laboratory standpoint. For this reason, the stellar-energy reaction cycle is out of the question; this cycle involves the fusion of hydrogen with heavy atoms such as carbon and nitrogen, and therefore proceeds relatively slowly even at temperatures of millions of degrees. It has been known for some time, however, that fusion reactions between the rarer, heavier isotopes of hydrogen can take place much more rapidly at substantially lower temperatures.

A few years ago the reaction that would have been chosen as the most promising for a hydrogen bomb was the fusion of two atoms of deuterium, or hydrogen of mass 2, containing one proton and one neutron. This results in the formation of helium 3, with the emission of a neutron and the release of about four million electron volts of energy. Gamow has calculated the thermonuclear energy release from this reaction; the results were given in his 1946 book *Atomic Energy*. He remarked that if the reaction took place at a temperature of something over one million degrees C., "a small charge of deuterium could be used as an explosive with tremendous destructive power."

Nowadays we know that a more effective reaction can be obtained with hydrogen 3, known as tritium, a radioactive but long-lived isotope of hydrogen that has one proton and two neutrons in its nucleus. Tritium not only reacts faster than deuterium at low temperatures, but also liberates more energy when it does so. A fusion reaction of tritium with deuterium produces helium 4, with the emission of a neutron; its energy yield is 17.6 million electron volts. Tritium can also fuse with tritium, yielding helium 4, two neutrons and 11.4 million electron volts of energy; the cross section for this reaction is not available in the published literature, but it is probably large.

Ponderable amounts of tritium have been and are being made by the Atomic Energy Commission in its huge facilities. The designer of a fusion bomb clearly would start with a fission bomb of uranium or plutonium, the explosion of which would produce the high temperatures required for the thermonuclear fusion reaction. To the fission bomb he would add a certain mixture of deuterium and tritium to fuel the fusion process. The final energy release of the bomb—its total deadliness—would be determined by the amount of deuterium added. To say that the fusion bomb would be 2, 7, 10, 100 or 1,000 times as devastating as the conventional fission bomb is to speak from ignorance; the effective size of a fusion bomb will depend upon the intentions and the skill of its designers.

Note, however, that there is here no concept like that of critical size. The size of the bomb depends, and depends exactly, on the amount of the reacting elements built into it. The fission detonator itself must be made overcritical in order to explode, but the happenings thereafter will depend on the amount of fuel provided for the fusion reaction.

HERE, then, are the technical conclusions that one must draw about the fusion bomb:

First, it can be made.

Second, there is no limit, in principle, to the size of a fusion bomb. It cannot be smaller than a fission bomb, since it must use a fission bomb as detonator, but it can be many times, perhaps thousands of times, bigger.

Third, while fission can be controlled in an orderly way to produce useful power in a reactor, the fusion reaction offers no prospect at the present time of any use except in terms of an explosion. We cannot find in the development of the fusion bomb any such peacetime values as are inherent in the development of nuclear fission. Except where the uses of peace demand the detonation of an explosive equivalent to, say, a million tons of TNT, there is no use for a fusion reaction. Thus when we discuss the "hydrogen bomb" we are clearly speaking of a weapon, and a weapon only.

Fourth, we are speaking of a very special type of weapon—one that is appropriate only to the destruction of large targets. A weapon of this sort is clearly of much greater significance to other nations, such as the U.S.S.R., than it is to us. We have several large targets; the U.S.S.R. has only one or two.

Fifth, the fusion bomb is not a brand-new possibility that has suddenly burst upon the minds of men. For example, J. Robert Oppenheimer, wartime director of the bomb laboratory at Los Alamos, wrote cryptically in late 1945 in the book *One World or None*: "In this connection it is clearly relevant to ask what technical developments the future might have in store for the infant atomic-weapon industry. . . . Proposals that appear sound have been investigated in a preliminary way, and it turns out that they would reduce the cost of destruction per square mile probably by a factor of 10 or more, but they would involve a great increase in the unit power of the weapons. Such weapons would clearly be limited in application to the destruction of very major targets, such as greater New York." Oppenheimer was talking of the fusion bomb. Physicists knew it then, of course; we all know it now. And it would be naive indeed to suppose that the U.S.S.R. has not given thought to it on its own account.

In view of all this, it seems a little curious that the fusion bomb should have been proposed—as it apparently was—in terms of a reply to the Soviet achievement of the fission bomb. To the detached observer, it would appear to be

TRITIUM AND DEUTERIUM reaction would release more energy than any other reaction involving these heavy isotopes of hydrogen. Tritium is H^3, or the hydrogen isotope of mass 3. Its nucleus is composed of one proton (*small white circle*) and two neutrons (*small black circles*). Deuterium is H^2, or the hydrogen isotope of

potentially a Pyrrhic reply, involving as it does the production of a weapon uniquely suited to the destruction of the great cities around which our own economy and our own civilization are built.

Be that as it may, the decision to make the superbomb has been taken, and in the world of hotly nationalistic fear and jealousy that we now inhabit, one can suppose that it is the right decision—that is, for the arms race. We can be sure that a decision by us to forego making the bomb would not have persuaded the U.S.S.R. to forego it, unless she saw that her own self-interest lay in that direction. And we can dispose of the "morality" argument at once. Once it is decided that people are to be killed, the "moral" question is fully settled; the instruments of that killing are not at all affected with humane or moral questions. It was probably more unpleasant to be disemboweled by the 18-inch sword of the Roman soldier than it will be to vanish in the flash of a nuclear reaction.

YET important questions remain, even if one considers the superbomb only in the realistic terms of national self-preservation. Although the expense and trouble of designing this instrument of national policy cannot be very great, there are good arguments to show that, if national policy is our concern, other technical developments are more important. We are far more in need of means for the sure and accurate delivery of the bombs we already know how to make than we are of an improved and more destructive bomb, provided we intend to make a good showing in the current arms race. There is indeed a question, as James Bryant Conant has pointed out, whether the technical decisions being made in Washington are being arrived at in a manner to inspire confidence that they will promote the greatest security.

We have surrounded the atomic energy field with unusual safeguards designed to protect the national security, and the practical effect has been to cut off that field from the assistance of the majority of the nation's technical community. We have given the Atomic Energy Commission unusual powers, encroaching thereby on many of the principles basic to Western democracy. One gathers from recent news reports that, even after these sacrifices, we have still failed to obtain from the Commission the "efficiency" and boldness of decision that are sometimes urged as the major benefits of totalitarianism. Our general security policy plainly bears re-examination.

One may, for example, ask: If the decision to make the superbomb was necessary and inevitable, why has it been delayed until now? Why were the "sound proposals" mentioned by Oppenheimer in 1945 allowed to gather dust? The technical possibility of a hydrogen bomb has been discussed in whispers by our scientists for years. European scientists, of course, have not been so restrained. In 1946 an Austrian physicist named Hans Thirring published a semipopular book on atomic energy that contained a chapter discussing the design of such a superbomb. Yet reviews of the book published in the U. S. deliberately refrained from mentioning that chapter or anything it contained. It is difficult to see how any sensible person could have supposed that "national security" had anything to gain from this curious ostrichism, but the secrecy-lovers in this country are not accustomed to give

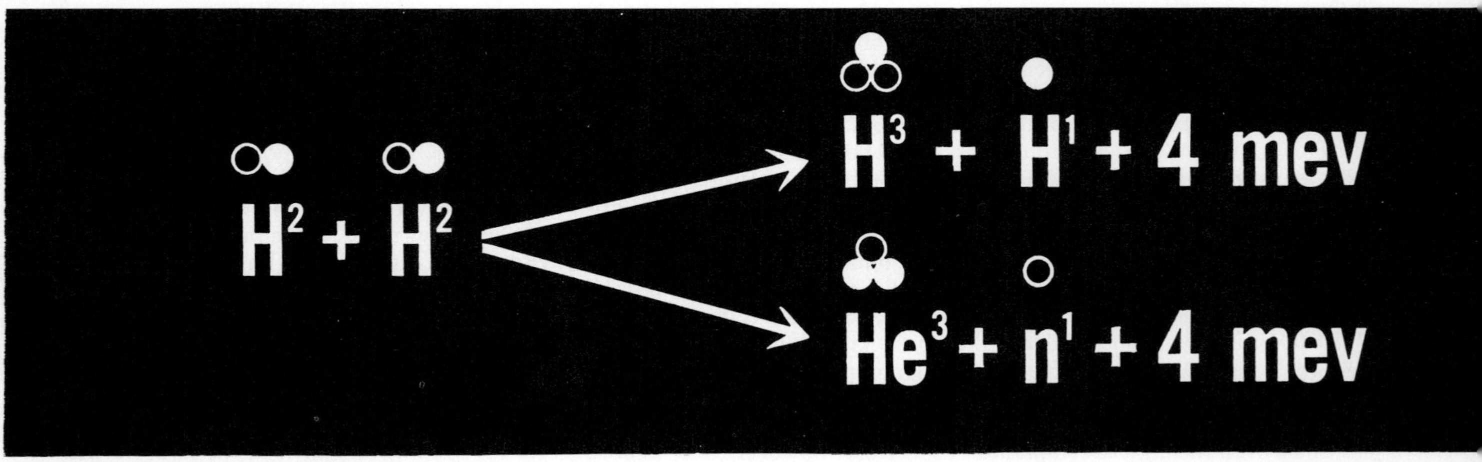

DEUTERIUM AND DEUTERIUM reaction can proceed in two directions that release approximately the same amount of energy. When two nuclei of deuterium are brought together, they yield (1) tritium, a proton and about four million electron volts; or (2) the light isotope of helium, a neutron and about the same energy.

$$\rightarrow He^4 + n^1 + 17.6 \text{ mev}$$

mass 2. Its nucleus is composed of one proton and one neutron. When these two nuclei are brought together, they form helium of mass 4 (He^4), a neutron (n^1) and 17.6 million electron volts of energy (mev). Unlike the reaction of a neutron and a plutonium nucleus, this reaction does not yield products that can perpetuate it.

thought to sensible considerations.

So the hydrogen bomb was not delayed because we lacked the idea. The effort to make it must, therefore, have been postponed by a deliberate policy decision. What were the issues or facts on which such a decision was based? About that we have no information whatever. The decision could hardly have been made on moral grounds, since the moral question nowhere enters into the present decision to make the bomb. Nor could there be any question about where the duty of the policy-making officials lay in an arms race; to make a unilateral decision not to do one's best in that race is a luxury permitted no citizen.

It is conceivable that the delay was due simply to the failure of responsible officials to make the most of their opportunities and responsibilities. This answer is strongly suggested by the AEC's patent and depressing failure with the important reactor program, which has only recently been rescued from the desuetude in which it rested for some time. On the other hand, it is also conceivable that the decision to postpone the superbomb was based on a sound judgment as to the urgency of pushing the development of old-fashioned fission bombs as against turning to work on a distant superbomb.

The main point is that you and I cannot know what considerations have influenced these most important decisions in national policy. In the present pattern of public knowledge, one may draw any of several quite different conclusions. But of one thing we can be sure: the whole experience demonstrates once more the truth for which the outcome of World War II provided such compelling evidence—an informed democracy is the strongest and most viable political form. A government does not adequately protect its citizens by taking decisions for them that they can neither know about nor take part in. Almost certainly, we would be better off to treat the atomic energy field like any other normal part of our complicated technology, such as the steel or the automotive industry.

Possibly the shock of the news about the superbomb may at last bring us face to face with reality. We may appreciate the bankruptcy of our secrecy policy when we see how it excludes us from decisions vital to us without in any way hiding the question under discussion. We may also see that an agreement for the control of atomic energy, or for the limitation of any other specific weapon, is not what we require for long-term safety. What we need is an international agreement amounting to the resolve of men not to kill other men, and we ourselves are not ready to sign that one today. Until all nations are ready to do so, the question of whether to make superbombs can have only one answer, and that answer has been given.

$$H^3 + H^3 \longrightarrow He^4 + 2n^1 + 11.4 \text{ mev}$$

TRITIUM AND TRITIUM reaction would yield a nucleus of helium and two neutrons. It would also generate approximately 11.4 million electron volts, an amount of energy less than that given up by the tritium and deuterium reaction above but more than that yielded by the deuterium and deuterium reaction at the left.

9

The Hydrogen Bomb: II

In which the technical and strategic discussion begun by Louis N. Ridenour is continued, and a proposal is made for a first step toward the international control of atomic weapons

HANS A. BETHE

April 1950

The discussion of the hydrogen bomb begun in the preceding article by Louis N. Ridenour is continued in this second article because of the tremendous importance of the issue. Ridenour described the essential parts of the theory of the nuclear reactions in the hydrogen bomb, and also discussed the likely effects of the bomb on our military security. I agree entirely with his view that the creation of the H-bomb makes our country more vulnerable rather than more secure. It remains for me to discuss two things: On the technical side, I shall try to clarify the many misconceptions that have crept into the discussions of the H-bomb in the daily press. On the political side, I wish to take up the moral issue and the meaning of the bomb in the general framework of our foreign relations.

Everybody who talks about atomic energy knows Albert Einstein's equation $E=Mc^2$: *viz.*, the energy release in a nuclear reaction can be calculated from the decrease in mass. In the fission of the uranium nucleus, one tenth of one per cent of the mass is converted into energy; in the fusion of four hydrogen nuclei to form helium, seven tenths of one per cent is so converted. When these statements are made in newspaper reports, it is usually implied that there ought to be some way in which all the mass of a nucleus could be converted into energy, and that we are merely waiting for technical developments to make this practical. Needless to say, this is wrong. Physics is sufficiently far developed to state that there will never be a way to make a proton or a neutron or any other nucleus simply disappear and convert its entire mass into energy. It is true that there are processes by which various smaller particles—positive and negative electrons and mesons—are annihilated, but all these phenomena involve at least one particle which does not normally occur in nature and therefore must first be created, and this creation process consumes as much energy as is afterwards liberated.

All the nuclear processes from which energy can be obtained involve the rearrangement of protons and neutrons in nuclei, the protons and neutrons themselves remaining intact. Hundreds of experimental investigations through the last 30 years have taught us how much energy can be liberated in each transformation, whether by the fission of heavy nuclei or the fusion of light ones. In the case of fusion, only the combination of the very lightest nuclei can release very large amounts of energy. When four hydrogen nuclei fuse to form helium, .7 per cent of the mass is transformed into energy. But if four helium nuclei were fused into oxygen, the mass would decrease by only .1 per cent; and the fusion of two silicon atoms, if it ever could occur, would release less than .02 per cent of the mass. Thus there is no prospect of using elements of medium atomic weight for the release of nuclear energy, even in theory.

THE main problem in the release of nuclear energy in those cases that we can consider seriously is not the amount of energy released—this is always large enough—but whether there is a mechanism by which the release can take place at a sufficient rate. This consideration is almost invariably ignored by science reporters, who seem to be incurably fascinated by $E=Mc^2$. In fusion the rate of reaction is governed by entirely different factors from those in fission. Fission takes place when a nucleus of uranium or plutonium captures a neutron. Because the neutron has no electric charge and is not repelled by the nucleus, temperature has no important influence on the fission reaction; no matter how slow the neutron, it can enter a uranium nucleus and cause fission. In fusion reactions, on the other hand, two nuclei, both with positive electric charges, must come into contact. To overcome their strong mutual electrical repulsion, the nuclei must move at each other with great speed. Ridenour explained how this is achieved in the laboratory by giving very high velocities to a few nuclei. This method is very inefficient because it is highly unlikely that one of the fast projectiles will hit a target nucleus before it is slowed down by the many collisions with the electrons also present in the atoms of the target. Therefore the energy released by nuclear reactions in these laboratory experiments is always much less than the energy invested in accelerating the particles.

The only known way that energy can be extracted from light nuclei by fusion is by thermonuclear reactions, *i.e.*, those which proceed at exceedingly high temperatures. The prime example of such reactions occurs in the interior of stars, where temperatures are of the order of 20 million degrees Centigrade. At this temperature the average energy of an atom is still only 1,700 electron volts—much less than the energies given to nuclear particles in "atom smashers." But all the particles present—nuclei and electrons—have high kinetic energy, so they are not slowed down by colliding with one another. They will keep their high speeds. Nevertheless, in spite of the high temperature, the nuclear reactions in stars proceed at an extremely slow rate; only one per cent of the hydrogen in the sun is transformed into helium in a billion years. Indeed, it would be catastrophic for the star if the reaction went much faster.

The temperature at the center of a star is kept high and very nearly constant by an interplay of a number of physical forces. The radiation produced by nuclear reactions in the interior can escape from the star only with great difficulty. It proceeds to the surface not in a straight line but by a complicated, zigzag route, since it is constantly absorbed by atoms and re-emitted in new directions. It is this slow escape of radiation that maintains the high interior temperature, which in turn maintains the thermonuclear reactions. Only a star large enough to hold its radiations for a long time can produce significant amounts of energy. The sun's radiation, for example, takes about 10,000 years to escape. A star weighing one tenth as much as the sun would produce so little energy that it would not be visible, and the largest planet, Jupiter, is already so small that it could not maintain nuclear reactions at all. This rules out the possibility that the earth's atmosphere, or the ocean, or the earth's crust, could be set "on fire" by a hydrogen superbomb and the earth thus be converted into a star. Because of the small mass of the bomb, it would heat only a small volume of the earth or its atmosphere, and even if nuclear reactions were started, radiation would carry away the nuclear energy much faster than it developed, and the temperature would drop rapidly so that the nuclear reaction would soon stop.

If thermonuclear reactions are to be initiated on earth, one must take into consideration that any nuclear energy released will be carried away rapidly by radiation, so that it will not be possible to keep the temperature high for a long time. Therefore, if the reaction is to proceed at all, it must proceed very quickly. Reaction times of billions of years, like those in the sun, would never lead to an appreciable energy release; we must think rather in terms of millionths of a second. On the other hand, on earth we have a choice of materials: whereas the stellar reactions can use only the elements that happen to be abundant in stars, notably ordinary hydrogen, we can choose any elements we like for our thermonuclear reactions. We shall obviously choose those with the highest reaction rates.

The reaction rate depends first of all, and extremely sensitively, on the product of the charges of the reacting nuclei; the smaller this product, the higher the reaction rate. The highest rates will therefore be obtainable from a reaction between two hydrogen nuclei, because hydrogen has the smallest possible charge —one unit. (The principal reactions in stars are between carbon, of charge six, and hydrogen.) We can choose any of the three hydrogen isotopes, of atomic weight one (proton), two (deuteron) or three (triton). These isotopes undergo different types of nuclear reactions, and the reactions occur at different rates.

The fusion of two protons is called the proton-proton reaction. It has long been known that this reaction is exceedingly slow. As Robert E. Marshak stated in his article, "The Energy of Stars," SCIENTIFIC AMERICAN, January, 1950, the proton-proton reaction takes 100 billion years to occur at the center of the sun. Ridenour pointed out that the situation is quite different for the reactions using only the heavy isotopes of hydrogen: the deuteron and triton. A number of reported measurements by nuclear

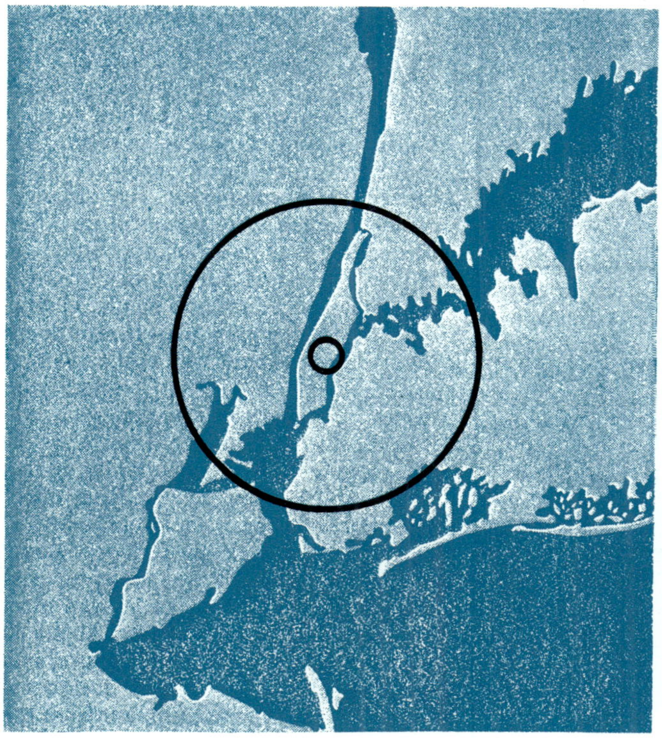

BLAST EFFECT of present and proposed atomic weapons is projected on a map of New York City and the surrounding area. A uranium bomb set off above the SCIENTIFIC AMERICAN office in midtown would cause severe destruction within a radius of a mile (*small circle*); a hydrogen bomb 1,000 times more powerful would cause severe destruction within 10 miles (*large circle*).

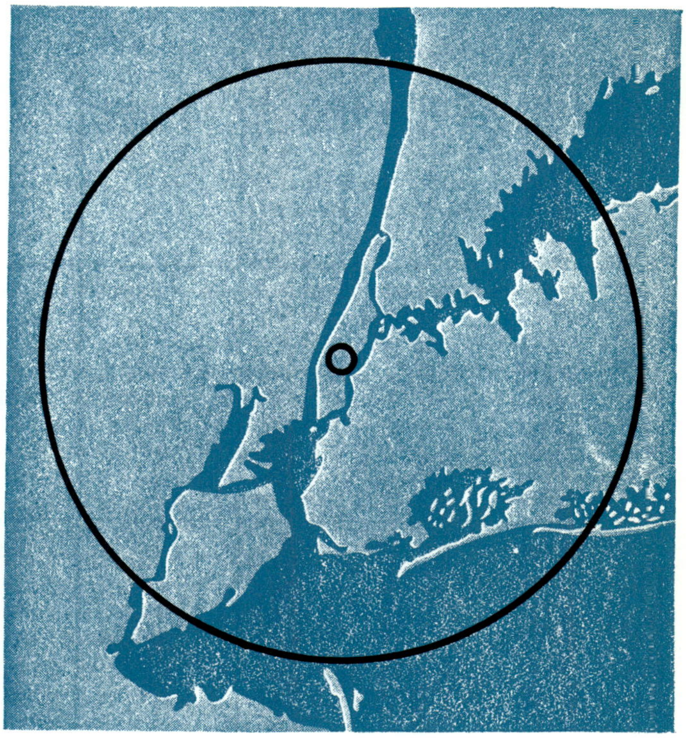

FLASH EFFECT of a hydrogen bomb 1,000 times more powerful than present bombs would be relatively greater than its blast effect. The Hiroshima bomb caused fatal burns at distances up to 4,000 to 5,000 feet (*small circle*). A hydrogen bomb would cause fatal burns at distances of 20 miles or more (*large circle*). The inhabitants of Chicago and its suburbs could thus be wiped out.

$H^1 + H^1 \rightarrow H^2 + e^+$ 	1.4 mev	100,000,000,000 years
$H^2 + H^1 \rightarrow He^3 + h\nu$ 	5 mev	.5 second
$H^3 + H^1 \rightarrow He^4 + h\nu$ 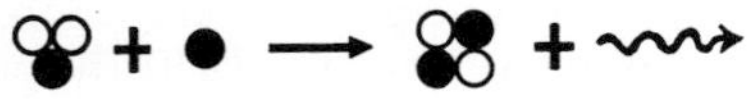	20 mev	.05 second
$H^2 + H^2 \rightarrow He^3 + n$ 	3.2 mev	.00003 second
$H^2 + H^2 \rightarrow H^3 + H^1$ 	4 mev	.00003 second
$H^3 + H^2 \rightarrow He^4 + n$ 	17 mev	.0000012 second
$H^3 + H^3 \rightarrow He^4 + n + n$ 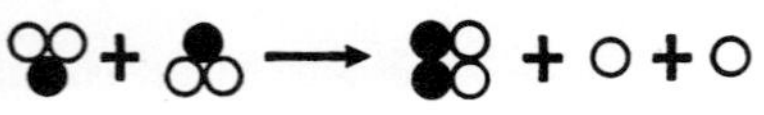	11 mev	?

THE NUCLEAR REACTIONS involving the three isotopes of hydrogen, H^1, H^2 (deuterium) and H^3 (tritium) illustrate a fundamental consideration in making a hydrogen bomb. The reactions are at left, the energy released by each is in center, the time required for each is at right. The reactions involving the heavier isotopes of hydrogen proceed at a much faster rate.

physicists have shown that the reaction rates for this type of fusion are high.

A further variable governing the rate of the reaction is the density of the material. The more atoms there are per unit volume, the higher the probability for nuclear collisions.

It is also well known, as Ridenour noted, that the reactions would require enormous temperatures. Whether the temperature necessary to heat heavy hydrogen sufficiently to start a thermonuclear reaction can be achieved on the earth is a major problem in the development of the H-bomb. To find a practical way of initiating H-bombs will require much research and considerable time.

WHAT would be the effects of a hydrogen bomb? Ridenour pointed out that its power would be limited only by the amount of heavy hydrogen that could be carried in the bomb. A bomb carried by a submarine, for instance, could be much more powerful than one carried by a plane. Let us assume an H-bomb releasing 1,000 times as much energy as the Hiroshima bomb. The radius of destruction by blast from a bomb increases as the cube root of the increase in the bomb's power. At Hiroshima the radius of severe destruction was one mile. So an H-bomb would cause almost complete destruction of buildings up to a radius of 10 miles. By the blast effect alone a single bomb could obliterate almost all of Greater New York or Moscow or London or any of the largest cities of the world. But this is not all; we must also consider the heat effects. About 30 per cent of the casualties in Hiroshima were caused by flash burns due to the intense burst of heat radiation from the bomb. Fatal burns were frequent up to distances of 4,000 to 5,000 feet. The radius of heat radiation increases with power at a higher rate than that of blast, namely by the square root of the power instead of the cube root. Thus the H-bomb would widen the range of fatal heat by a factor of 30; it would burn people to death over a radius of up to 20 miles or more. It is too easy to put down or read numbers without understanding them; one must visualize what it would mean if, for instance, Chicago with all its suburbs and most of their inhabitants were wiped out in a single flash.

In addition to blast and heat radiation there are nuclear radiations. Some of these are instantaneous; they are emitted by the exploding bomb itself and may be absorbed by the bodies of persons in the bombed area. Others are delayed; these come from the radioactive nuclei formed as a consequence of the nuclear explosion, and they may be confined to the explosion area or widely dispersed.

The bombs, both A and H, emit gamma rays and neutrons while they explode. Either of these radiations can enter the body and cause death or radiation sickness. It is likely, however, that most of the people who would get a lethal dose of radiation from the H-bomb would be killed in any case by flash burn or by collapsing or burning buildings.

There would also be persistent radioactivity. This is of two kinds: the fission products formed in the bomb itself, and the radioactive atoms formed in the environment by the neutrons emitted from the bomb. Since the H-bomb must be triggered by an A-bomb, it will produce at least as many fission products as an A-bomb alone. The neutrons produced by the fusion reactions may greatly increase the radioactive effect. They would be absorbed by the bomb case, by rocks and other material on the ground, and by the air. The bomb case could be so designed that it would become highly radioactive when disintegrated by the explosion. These radioactive atoms would then be carried by the wind over a large area of the bombed country. The radioactive nuclei formed on the ground would contaminate the center of the bombed area for some time, but probably not for very long because the constituents of soil and buildings do not form many long-lived radioactive nuclei by neutron capture.

Neutrons released in the air are finally captured by nitrogen nuclei, which are thereby transformed into radioactive carbon 14. This isotope, however, has a long half-life—5,000 years—and therefore its radioactivity is relatively weak. Consequently even if many bombs were exploded, it is not likely that the carbon 14 would become dangerous.

THE decision to proceed with the development of hydrogen bombs has been made. I believe that this decision settles only one question and raises a hundred in its place. What will the bomb do to our strategic position? Will it restore to us the superiority in armament that we possessed before the Russians obtained the A-bomb? Will it improve our chances of winning the next war if one should come? Will it diminish the likelihood that we should see our cities destroyed in that war? Will it serve to avert or postpone war itself? How will the world look after a war fought with hydrogen bombs?

I believe the most important question is the moral one: Can we who have always insisted on morality and human decency between nations as well as inside our own country, introduce this weapon of total annihilation into the world? The usual argument, heard in the frantic week before the President's decision and frequently since, is that we are fighting against a country which denies all the human values we cherish, and that any weapon, however terrible, must be used to prevent that country and its creed from dominating the world. It is argued that it would be better for us to lose our lives than our liberty, and with this view I personally agree. But I believe this is not the choice facing us here; I believe that in a war fought with hydrogen bombs we would lose not only many lives but all our liberties and human values as well.

Whoever wishes to use the hydrogen bomb in our conflict with the U.S.S.R., either as a threat or in actual warfare, is adhering to the old fallacy that the ends justify the means. The fallacy is the more obvious because our conflict with the U.S.S.R. is mainly about means. It is the means that the U.S.S.R. is using, both in dealing with her own citizens and with other nations, that we abhor; we have little quarrel with the professed aim of providing a decent standard of living for all. We would invalidate our cause if we were to use in our fight means that can only be termed mass slaughter.

We believe in personal liberty and human dignity, the value and importance of the individual, sincerity and openness in the dealings between men and between nations, prosperity for all and peace based on mutual trust. All this is in great contrast to the methods which the Soviet Government uses in pursuing its aims and which it believes necessary in the "beginning phase" of Communism —which by now has lasted 33 years. Regimentation of the private lives of all citizens, systematic education in spying upon one's friends, ruthless shifting of populations regardless of their personal ties and preferences, inhuman treatment of prisoners in labor camps, suppression of free speech, falsification of history in dealing both with their own citizens and with other nations, violation of promises and treaties and the distorted interpretations offered in excuse of these violations—these are some of the methods of the U.S.S.R. which are hateful to the people of the Western World. But if we wish to fight against these methods, *our* methods must be clean.

We believe in peace based on mutual trust. Shall we achieve it by using hydrogen bombs? Shall we convince the Russians of the value of the individual by killing millions of them? If we fight a war and win it with H-bombs, what history will remember is not the ideals we were fighting for but the methods we used to accomplish them. These methods will be compared to the warfare of Genghis Khan, who ruthlessly killed every last inhabitant of Persia.

WHAT would an all-out war fought with hydrogen bombs mean? It would mean the obliteration of all large cities and probably of many smaller ones, and the killing of most of their inhabitants. After such a war, nothing that resembled present civilization would remain. The fight for mere survival would dominate everything. The destruction of the cities might set technology back a hundred years or more. In a generation even the knowledge of technology and science might disappear, because there would be no opportunity to practice them. Indeed it is likely that technology and science, having brought such utter misery upon man, would be suspected as works of the devil, and that a new Dark Age would begin on earth.

We know what physical destruction does to the moral values of a people. We have seen how many Germans, already demoralized by the Nazis, lost all sense of morality when during and after the war the bare necessities of life, food, clothing and shelter were lacking. Democracy and human decency were empty words; there was no reserve strength left for such luxuries. If we have learned any lesson from the aftermath of World War II, it is that physical destruction brings moral destruction.

We have also learned that prosperity is the best shield against communism and dictatorship, and in this knowledge we have poured billions into Western Europe to restore her economy. This generosity has won us more friends than anything else we have done. But after the next war, if it were fought with atomic and hydrogen bombs, our own country would be as grievously destroyed as Europe and the U.S.S.R., and we could no longer afford such generosity. It would be everyone for himself, and everyone against the other.

It is ironical that the U. S. of all countries should lead in developing such methods of warfare. The military methods adopted by this nation at the outset of the Second World War had the aim of conserving lives as much as possible. Determined not to repeat the slaughter of the First World War, during which hundreds of thousands of soldiers were sacrificed in fruitless frontal attacks, the U. S. high command substituted war by machines for war by unprotected men. But the hydrogen bomb carries mechanical warfare to ultimate absurdity in defeating its own aim. Instead of saving lives, it takes many more lives; in place of one soldier who would die in battle, it kills a hundred noncombatant civilians. Surely it is time for us to reconsider what our real intentions are.

One may well ask: Why advance such arguments with reference to the H-bomb and not atomic bombs in general? Is an atomic bomb moral and a hydrogen bomb immoral, and if so, where is the dividing line? I believe there was a deep feeling in this country right after the war that the use of atomic bombs in Japan had been a mistake, and that these bombs should be eliminated from national armaments. This feeling, indeed, was one of the prime reasons for President Truman's offer of international control in 1945. We know that the negotiations for control have not led to success as yet. But our inability to eliminate atomic bombs is no reason to introduce a bomb which is a thousand times worse.

When atomic bombs were first introduced, there was a general feeling that they represented something new, that the thousandfold increase of destructive power from blockbuster to atom bomb required and made possible a new approach. The step from atomic to hydrogen bombs is just as great again, so we have again an equally strong reason to seek a new approach. We have to think how we can save humanity from this ultimate disaster. And we must break the habit, which seems to have taken hold of this nation, of considering every weapon as just another piece of machinery and a fair means to win our struggle with the U.S.S.R.

I HAVE reviewed the moral issues that should deter us from using hydrogen bombs even if we were sure that we alone would have them, and that they would contribute to our victory. As Ridenour explained, the situation is rather the opposite. We can hardly expect to have a monopoly on hydrogen bombs. If we ever had any illusions about this, the events of the past few months should have destroyed them. The U.S.S.R. has the atomic bomb. She was undoubtedly helped in her efforts by the secret information she received from Klaus Fuchs, which presumably included many of the vital "secrets" of our project. But knowing how a group of scientists put the bomb together would not by itself enable a nation to make one. If Fuchs had given his information to Spain, for instance, it would hardly have been understood; it would presumably not have been used, and even if used it would almost certainly not have led to success. The prime requirements for the job still are a group of highly capable scientists, a country determined to make the weapon and a great industrial effort. We know now, if we ever doubted it, that the U.S.S.R. has all of these. For the Soviet scientists the information must simply have resolved many doubts as to which steps to take next and saved a number of costly and futile parallel developments.

Their obvious competence will presumably again bring success to the Russians when they try to develop the H-bomb. Yet their decisions and their successes are not independent of our own. Our decision to make the H-bomb, which showed that we considered the project feasible, may well have prompted them to take the same decision. For this reason I think that our decision, if taken at all, should have been taken in secret. This became impossible, however, when the advocates of the H-bomb used public statements as a means of exerting pressure on the President. If the Russians were already working on the H-bomb before our decision, they will now have increased their effort.

It is impossible to predict whether we or the Russians will have the hydrogen bomb first. We like to assume that we shall. If so, I refuse to believe that the U. S. would start a preventive war. That would violate all the fundamental beliefs of this nation, and that these beliefs are still strong is shown by the history of the past four years: although we had a monopoly of the atomic bomb we did not start a war. Clearly, then, the time will come when both the U.S.S.R. and this country will have H-bombs. Then this country will be much more vulnerable than the U.S.S.R.: as Ridenour explained, we have many more large cities that would be inviting targets, and many of these lie near the coast so that they could be reached by submarine and perhaps a relatively short-range rocket. I think it is therefore correct to say that the existence of the hydrogen bomb will give us military weakness rather than strength.

BUT, say the advocates of the bomb, what if the Russians obtain the H-bomb first? If the Russians have the bomb, Harold Urey argued in a speech just before the President's decision, they may confront us with an ultimatum to surrender. I do not believe we would accept such an ultimatum even if we did not have the H-bomb, or that we would need to. I doubt that the hydrogen bomb, dreadful as it would be, could win a war in one stroke. Though it might devastate our cities and cripple our ability to conduct a long war with all modern weapons, it would not seriously affect our power for immediate retaliation. Our atomic bombs, whether "old style" or hydrogen, and our planes would presumably be so distributed that they could not all be wiped out at the same time; they would still be ready to take off and reduce the country of the aggressor to at least the same state as our own. Thus the large bomb would bring untold destruction but no decision. I believe that "old-fashioned" A-bombs would be sufficient to even the score in case of an initial Soviet attack with H-bombs on this country. In fact, because of the greater number available, A-bombs may well be more effective in destroying legitimate military targets, including production centers. H-bombs, after all, would be useful only against the largest targets, of which there are very few in the U.S.S.R.

So we come finally to one reason, and only one, that can justify our building the H-bomb: namely, to deter the Russians from using it against us, if only for fear of our retaliation. Our possession of the bomb might possibly put us in a better position if the U.S.S.R. should present us with an ultimatum based on their possession of it. In other words, the one purpose of our development of the bomb would be to prevent its use, not to use it.

If this is our reason, we can contribute much to the peace of the world by stating this reason openly. This could be done in a declaration, either by Congress or by the President, that the U. S. will never be the first to use the hydrogen bomb, that we would employ the weapon only if it were used against us or one of our allies. A pledge of this kind was proposed in a press statement by 12 physicists, including myself, on February 4, 1950. It still appears to me as a practical step toward relief of the international tension and toward freedom from fear for the world. The pledge would indicate our desire to avoid needless destruction; it would reduce the likelihood of the use of the hydrogen bomb in the case of war, and it would largely in the case of war, and it would largely eliminate the danger that fear of the H-bomb itself would precipitate a war.

If we do not make this pledge, the hydrogen bomb would almost surely be used. Once war broke out, our military leaders would be blamed, in the absence of a pledge, if they did not immediately initiate a full-scale hydrogen-bomb attack. But if such a pledge existed, they would be blamed if they did use the bomb first. To be sure, the pledge might not be relied on by our adversaries, but at least it would create a doubt in their minds and they might decide to wait and see. Perhaps they would not wish to provoke the certain use of the bomb by dropping the first one. Moreover, if they started a war, they would probably hope to capture our country and to exploit its wealth rather than to conquer a heap of rubble.

We have proposed unilateral action rather than an international treaty on this pledge. We have done this because negotiations with the U.S.S.R. are known to be long and frustrating. A unilateral pledge involving only this country could be made quickly, and it could not again lead to the disappointment of a breakdown of negotiations. On the other hand, we certainly would not want to exclude a pact with the U.S.S.R. on this subject. This might be the first point on which the two countries could agree, and this in itself would be important.

Obviously the pledge can only be a first step. What we really want is a workable agreement on atomic energy, as part of our efforts toward a lasting peace. Much has been said in the last few weeks about new negotiations on atomic control. Opinions vary from that of Senator Brien McMahon, who proposed to spend $50 billion for rehabilitation of war-devastated countries including the U.S.S.R. in exchange for an atomic settlement, to that of Senator Millard Tydings, who declared that an atomic settlement would not be acceptable to this country unless it was coupled with general disarmament, which he has advocated for a long time. Both of these viewpoints, and those of many other Senators, show the desire of this country for some agreement. At the same time there are persistent reports, clearly indicated in recent dispatches from the New York *Times* correspondent in Moscow, that the Russians might like to negotiate. It seems to me that too much is at stake to miss any such opportunity.

On the other hand, President Truman voiced the fears of many of us when he stated recently that there is no security in agreements with the Russians because they break them at will. He referred to the agreements of Yalta and Potsdam in 1945. Since then we have learned much about Soviet methods, and the Russians have found that we do not retreat as easily as they apparently imagined in 1945. This more realistic mutual appraisal makes it much more likely that we could now come to arrangements which neither side would regret afterward. Obviously in any negotiation each side must be willing to make concessions and to consider primarily proposals directed to mutual advantage rather than superiority over the other.

The situation in atomic energy has changed, both because of the Soviet development of the A-bomb and because of our decision on the H-bomb. To leave atomic weapons uncontrolled would be against the best interests of both countries. If we can negotiate seriously with the U.S.S.R., the scope of the negotiations should probably be as broad as possible. But the situation would be greatly eased even if we could agree only to eliminate the greatest menace to civilization, the hydrogen bomb.

[Editor's note: The author is responsible only for the statements that appear in the text of this article. The illustrations and the captions that accompany them were prepared by the editors. The information contained in the illustrations was compiled on the basis of previously published material.]

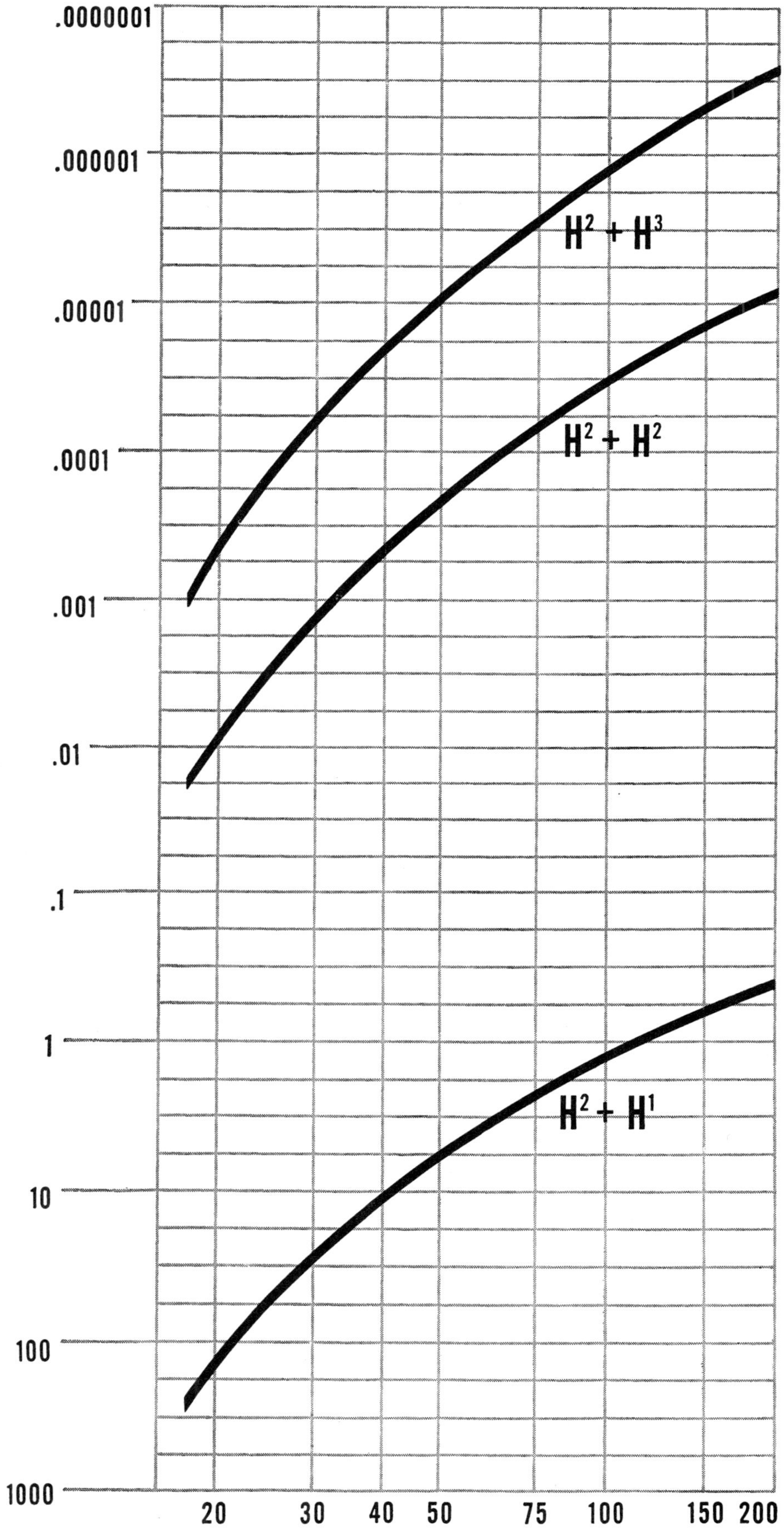

THE TIME REQUIRED for the nuclear reactions between deuterons (H^2 nuclei) and each of the three hydrogen isotopes is plotted against temperature. The vertical coordinate is in seconds; the horizontal coordinate in millions of degrees Centigrade. Deuteron-triton reaction proceeds fastest. Sun's temperature is 6,000 degrees at surface, 20 million degrees at center.

Science and the Citizen, May 1950

Concerning H-Bomb Reactions

THE first major extension of censorship over scientific information in the U.S. since the end of the war was instituted last month. The Atomic Energy Commission directed its employees and consultants to cease public discussion of thermonuclear reactions in relation to the projected hydrogen bomb. The Commission explained that its request applied to unclassified as well as classified information. It was addressed to all persons now or recently associated with the atomic energy project, which would include most of the atomic physicists of the U.S.

This policy was made known in telegrams sent on March 14 and 20 to AEC managers. The second telegram explained that the purpose was "to avoid release of technical information which, even though itself unclassified, may be interpreted by virtue of the project connection of the speaker as reflecting the Commission's program with respect to thermonuclear weapons."

The Commission applied the policy last month to censor an article written for SCIENTIFIC AMERICAN and the *Bulletin of the Atomic Scientists* by Hans A. Bethe, professor of physics at Cornell University, who is a consultant to the Commission. Dr. Bethe had sent copies of his manuscript to a number of his colleagues in physics, among them a member of the Commission. Neither the author nor the editors of the two publications considered it appropriate to submit the article to the AEC for review, since all the technical information in it was well known to physicists the world over and had been widely published. Physicists who read Dr. Bethe's original manuscript, including several associated with the atomic energy program, concurred in the view that it involved no question of security of information. On March 15, after the April issue of SCIENTIFIC AMERICAN containing Dr. Bethe's article, titled "The Hydrogen Bomb: II," had gone to press [see article beginning on page 56], a telegram was received from the Atomic Energy Commission requesting that the technical part of the article be withheld from publication. SCIENTIFIC AMERICAN stopped its presses and asked the Commission to specify its objections. After reviewing the article the Commission requested the deletion of several sentences. In order to proceed with publication of the issue, the editors complied with the Commission's request. The Commission then asked that all copies of the original article be destroyed. An AEC security officer visited the printing plant and supervised the destruction of the type and printing plates with the deleted material and the burning of 3,000 copies of the magazine which had been printed before the presses were stopped.

In response to inquiries from the press after the incident had become known, Gerard Piel, publisher of SCIENTIFIC AMERICAN, observed that the material deleted by the Commission included "statements which had already been widely quoted in the press and statements which have since been made by Robert Bacher, a former member of the Commission, in a speech in the Los Angeles Town Hall on March 27." Piel added:

"We consider that the Commission's action with regard to the Bethe article and the sweeping subsequent prohibition issued to the nation's atomic scientists raises the question of whether the Commission is thus suppressing information which the American people need in order to form intelligent judgments on this major problem. While there are certainly areas of information which must be protected for reasons of national security, there is a very large area of technical information in the public domain which is essential to adequate public participation in the development of national policy, and on which the American people are entitled to be informed by such recognized authorities as Dr. Bethe."

SCIENTIFIC AMERICAN is continuing the discussion of the hydrogen bomb with the article by Dr. Bacher in this issue [see "The Hydrogen Bomb: III," by Robert Bacher, beginning on page 63]. A fourth article in this series of discussions is "The Hydrogen Bomb: IV," by Ralph E. Lapp, SCIENTIFIC AMERICAN, June 1950.

The Hydrogen Bomb: III

The physical, strategic and moral discussion of the hydrogen bomb is continued. In this article: the question of whether the weapon enhances our military security

ROBERT F. BACHER

May 1950

THERE have been many conflicting statements about hydrogen bombs and what we should do about them. Some of these statements have become distorted in repetition. Others, while clearly stating physical possibilities, concern events which are so improbable as not to warrant serious consideration at the moment. Some of the statements made by scientists, whether intentionally or otherwise, have been very frightening to our citizens. Back of such statements seems to be the idea, expressed by some, that if the U. S. citizen will just become sufficiently frightened somehow we will not have any war in the future.

There is no question that the hydrogen bomb has terrifying possibilities and I shall try to give some estimate of what such a bomb might be like. It is our very deep obligation, however, as citizens in a democratic country to consider this whole question objectively, dispassionately, and as carefully as we can under the circumstances to decide intelligently just what our country should be doing. It will not improve the judgment of the citizen to scare him to death first. This is a very serious time for the U. S. We cannot afford any irrational or purely emotional action. Our future safety and security depend today on keeping our heads and using wise judgment.

Many people in considering the national policy on the hydrogen bomb have been able to formulate their opinions of this weapon very quickly on moral grounds alone. They say, and with justice, that the hydrogen bomb is a weapon of tremendous mass destruction and that accordingly no civilized country should consider its possible development and use. This is a comfortable position and one very easy to take, but where do we stop? Atomic bombs also are weapons of mass destruction. Are they moral or immoral? Nothing could be more gruesome and immoral than the reports that many of us have heard of some of the hand-to-hand conflicts during the past war. Nothing could be more uncivilized than some of the torture to which war, conflict and slave states have led.

War inevitably leads to many acts which are immoral. The relative immorality of various weapons and acts of war becomes difficult to assess. The hydrogen bomb, being a weapon of tremendous destruction, is more to be condemned on these grounds than lesser weapons if used for needless mass destruction. Indeed, no one can argue that the moral position of the U. S. will be improved by the possession or use of this bomb. Immoral as it is, war consumes a large part of the efforts of the people of the world. Situations arise in which war seems to be the lesser of two evils.

There are of course many other questions about the hydrogen bomb, but let us consider here primarily the practical problem of its effect on our national security. How important is it to our security, and what is the relative value of work on this development as compared with other measures of defense?

BEFORE trying to answer these questions let us look briefly at a little of the technical background of the hydrogen bomb. It has been known for a great many years that if one could somehow find a way of putting light atomic nuclei together to make heavier nuclei, it would be possible to extract energy. The first indication that this process might be important as a source of energy came from the suggestion by Hans A. Bethe that the fusion of the light elements was our fundamental source of energy in the sun and stars. Bethe worked his ideas out in some detail and scientists now believe that this is the origin of solar energy. There is no possibility that the energy release from this type of reaction can be controlled on the earth, as it can be in the case of the fission of a heavy element such as uranium. In the stars the reaction is controlled because of their great size. On the earth these self-sustaining thermonuclear reactions will give either an explosion or nothing at all.

Whether a hydrogen bomb can be made depends upon whether it is possible to create on earth an assembly of materials that will produce a nuclear reaction if heated to a sufficiently high temperature, and then to devise a way to raise these materials to that temperature.

The temperature required is comparable to that reached in the interior of the sun—more than 20 million degrees Centigrade. The only way that we know to reach such a temperature today is in a fission atomic bomb, where the sudden release of energy causes the materials of the bomb to be heated to an extremely high temperature.

The main light element to which I have been referring, of course, is hydrogen. Now ordinary hydrogen will not work. The scientific evidence for this seems to be quite clear. But hydrogen as it is found in nature has another isotope, heavy hydrogen of mass 2, which is a possibility for a fusion-bomb reaction. In recent years heavy hydrogen, as contained in water, has been separated in relatively large quantities.

There is another possibility. For more than 15 years it has been known that a still heavier isotope of hydrogen, called tritium because it has mass 3, is produced in nuclear reactions. This material is radioactive, with a half-life of only 12 years, and ordinarily does not exist in nature. But its nuclear properties are such that it is of basic interest in the release of energy by fusion.

It has been known for many years that tritium could be produced in a nuclear reaction in which neutrons are absorbed. The big nuclear reactors now in operation produce neutrons in large quantity. These neutrons are ordinarily used in the production of plutonium, but they could be used just as well to produce quantities of tritium. Any nuclear physicist can sit down and figure out the theoretical limit of the amount of tritium that can be produced with a given number of neutrons. It would be necesssary, of course, to know a great deal about the actual workings of a nuclear reactor in order to say just how much tritium could be produced in that reactor if one were willing to forego the production of a certain amount of plutonium. It appears that the production of tritium in quantity is at least a fairly expensive if not formidable process. And it is a point worth emphasizing that tritium could be produced only at the cost of using neutrons that might otherwise be employed to make plutonium.

That the heavy isotopes of hydrogen can possibly play a fundamental role in the release of nuclear energy by fusion is well known. Just exactly what relative role they play and how they might play it is not a subject for open discussion today. These questions are secret and we can have no discussion of them. But any nuclear physicist will quickly grasp the requirements as far as the basic science is concerned, even though the actual technology of making a bomb on these principles is more complicated.

THE real problem in developing and constructing a hydrogen bomb is: "How do you get it going?" The heavy hydrogens, deuterium and tritium, are suitable substances if somehow they could be heated hot enough and kept hot. This problem is a little bit like the job of making a fire at 20 degrees below zero in the mountains with green wood covered with ice and with very little kindling. Today scientists tell us that such a fire can probably be kindled with the heavy isotopes of hydrogen. Once you get the fire going, of course, you can pile on the wood and make a very sizable conflagration. Similarly the hydrogen bomb could be built up with more heavy hydrogen. It has been called an open-ended weapon, meaning that more materials can be added and a bigger explosion obtained.

Let us look for a moment at what sort of an explosion is imagined. Here I shall take the figures that have been commonly reported in the press and stick to round numbers. In 1945 President Truman stated that the atomic bomb was equivalent to 20,000 tons of TNT. A hydrogen bomb 1,000 times as powerful as the Hiroshima bomb, which is the number most commonly used in public speculation, would have an explosive effect equivalent to about 20 million tons of TNT. Its radius of comparable blast damage would be about 10 times as great as that at Hiroshima. The radius of severe blast damage at Hiroshima was about one mile, so for a bomb 1,000 times as powerful it would be about 10 miles. Appraisal of the flash-burn effect of the more powerful bomb is somewhat more complicated. If we neglect the absorption of heat radiation by smoke or smog, and do not take into account the shadow effect, we may estimate that the flash-burn effect of the bigger bomb would extend about 100 times as far as that at Hiroshima. The effects of absorption and of the shadows of buildings are important, especially at a distance, but they are most difficult to estimate. In any case, it is clear that the flash-burn effect would be important over a considerably greater area than the blast damage.

There has been a great deal of speculation about the radioactive products of a hydrogen bomb. Since an atomic bomb would be needed to get the conflagration going, some fission products from that bomb would doubtless be present. The hydrogen nuclear conflagration itself would yield neutrons which would produce large quantities of radioactivity if they were absorbed in some material that becomes artificially radioactive. On the other hand, many of these neutrons might be absorbed in material that did not become radioactive. If the neutrons escaped into the air, many of them would be absorbed by nitrogen and produce radioactive carbon. This material is most disagreeable as a radioactive contaminant, since it has a half-life of many thousands of years. If the bomb were exploded under water, very few of the neutrons would escape; most of them would activate sodium and other elements in the sea water, or convert the ordinary hydrogen in the water into heavy hydrogen.

The radioactivity effects of a hydrogen bomb are difficult to estimate, since they depend very much on where the bomb is exploded and what material surrounds it. If the bomb is surrounded with a material selected to yield a maximum of artificial radioactivity, the radiations will be a dangerous hazard over

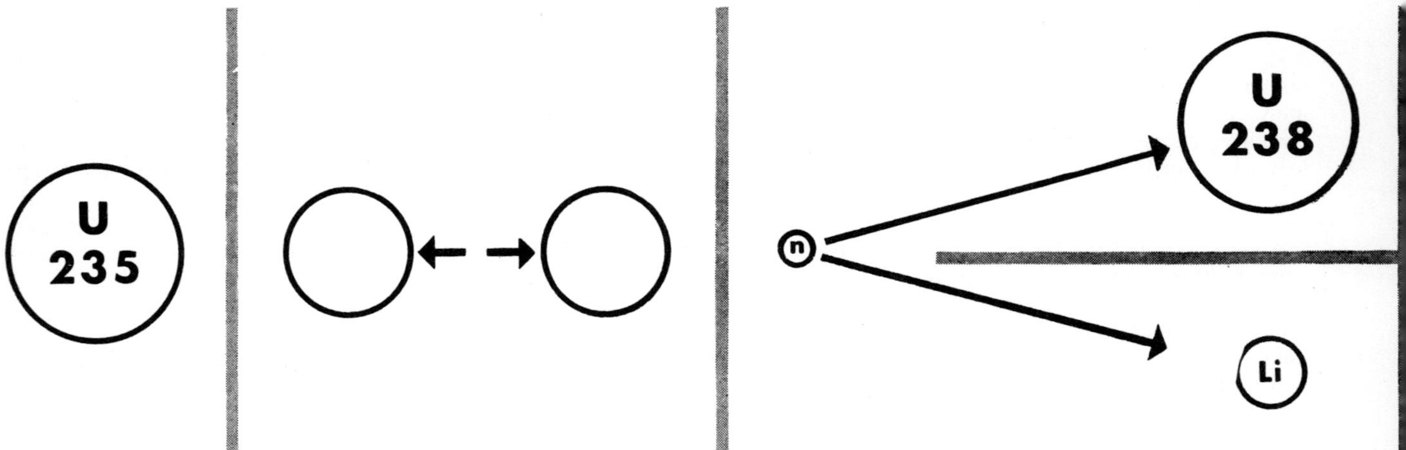

UNECONOMICAL USE OF NEUTRONS is a production shortcoming of the hydrogen bomb. In the first stage of this schematic representation of the problem is a nucleus of uranium 235, the primary fuel of all nuclear reactors. In the second stage U-235 fissions, producing the surplus neutron of the third stage. This neutron may now be used for capture by a nucleus of U-238, which shortly decays into plutonium 239. The fission of Pu-239 yields 200 million electron volts. The same neutron, however, might be used to bombard the nucleus the bombed region. One of the real scare stories about the effects of radioactivity has postulated the complete explosion of 500 tons of deuterium. While this is not impossible, as far as anyone can say, it is stretching probabilities a long way.

This brief analysis of well-known scientific information shows, then, that a hydrogen bomb would require a considerable quantity of heavy hydrogen, perhaps both deuterium and tritium, as well as an atomic bomb to set it off by raising the temperature sufficiently so that a nuclear conflagration can exist. Technically the problem is to figure out how a sizable fraction of the energy of the heavy hydrogen can be released before the material is cooled too much by emitted radiation or dispersed by the explosion. In the stars the radiation is retained because the stellar material is relatively opaque and there is an enormous temperature difference between the center and the outside of the star. In a hydrogen bomb there is no such protective layer. Thus the central problem is to get a large fraction of the energy released while the temperature is still high enough.

Whether this can be done will of course not be certain until it has been done. There are many opinions as to how difficult it may be. Since the President has directed the Atomic Energy Commission to continue with the development, we can assume that it is regarded as both possible and feasible.

SO MUCH for the technical problems that must be solved in order to develop a hydrogen bomb. Assuming that the problems can be solved, let us try to determine whether or not hydrogen bombs will add materially to our national security by considering their effectiveness as military weapons and comparing them with atomic bombs already in existence.

If we assume that the hydrogen bomb is a thousand times as powerful as the Hiroshima bomb, we can easily see that a hydrogen bomb is capable of destroying any major city, with the exception perhaps of some of the outlying districts. How does this compare with what could be done with atomic bombs? We have been comparing the hydrogen bomb with the fission bomb used at Hiroshima, but it has been stated that since the war there have been significant improvements in fission bombs. These improvements have resulted in more powerful bombs and in a more efficient use of the valuable fissionable material.

Most large metropolitan areas include many sections that are covered by water or otherwise unsettled. Thus a hydrogen bomb would blast many square miles whose destruction would contribute in no way to the effectiveness of the bomb. Atomic bombs, on the other hand, could presumably be dropped so as to avoid overbombing uninhabited areas. Furthermore, it was found in the last war that a saturation raid which greatly hampered fire-fighting forces caused damage far beyond the areas of immediate blast effects. Considering all these factors, it seems likely that there is no metropolitan area which could not be thoroughly destroyed with 25 atomic bombs at most, and perhaps as few as 10. It also appears that two atomic bombs would completely paralyze a city, even a large one.

Except for the psychological effects and for the most unpleasant and somewhat unpredictable effects of the radioactivity produced, it appears that a hydrogen bomb 1,000 times more powerful than an ordinary fission bomb would probably not be much more effective than 10 fission bombs. For smaller industrial targets it would not be much more effective than a single fission bomb.

In view of this, one begins to wonder just how useful a military weapon the hydrogen bomb would be. Would it really revolutionize warfare, as some say? Certainly it is a terrible weapon, and large numbers of these bombs could cause untold destruction; even a relatively small number could deal a major blow to any highly industrialized and centralized country. But what about the fission bomb and the damage that a sizable stockpile of these weapons could inflict? Suppose, just to take a round number, that the U. S. possessed 1,000 fission bombs of the improved variety. If they could be delivered to military objectives at all, they would go a long way at the rate of 10 for a major metropolitan area and perhaps an even smaller number for major cities. With 1,000 bombs, there would be a great many for relatively minor military objectives, and I imagine that the military commanders would have a hard time figuring out what to do with the last hundred.

It appears that if any nation has as many as 1,000 atomic bombs, the world is already in the position where any nation could be blasted thoroughly and completely, insofar as bombing alone can be effective. If this is the case, just what additional military use is a hydrogen bomb? It looks very much as if everyone is simply fascinated by the idea of "the bigger the better." There are some examples in the history of the world that should lead us to question this view. We should not forget the dinosaur nor the dodo. Indeed, we should not forget the battleship, now almost extinct.

Actually it might turn out that in a shooting war it would not be possible to deliver hydrogen bombs, atomic bombs or any other kind of big bomb to the targets. Hence if atomic bombs or any

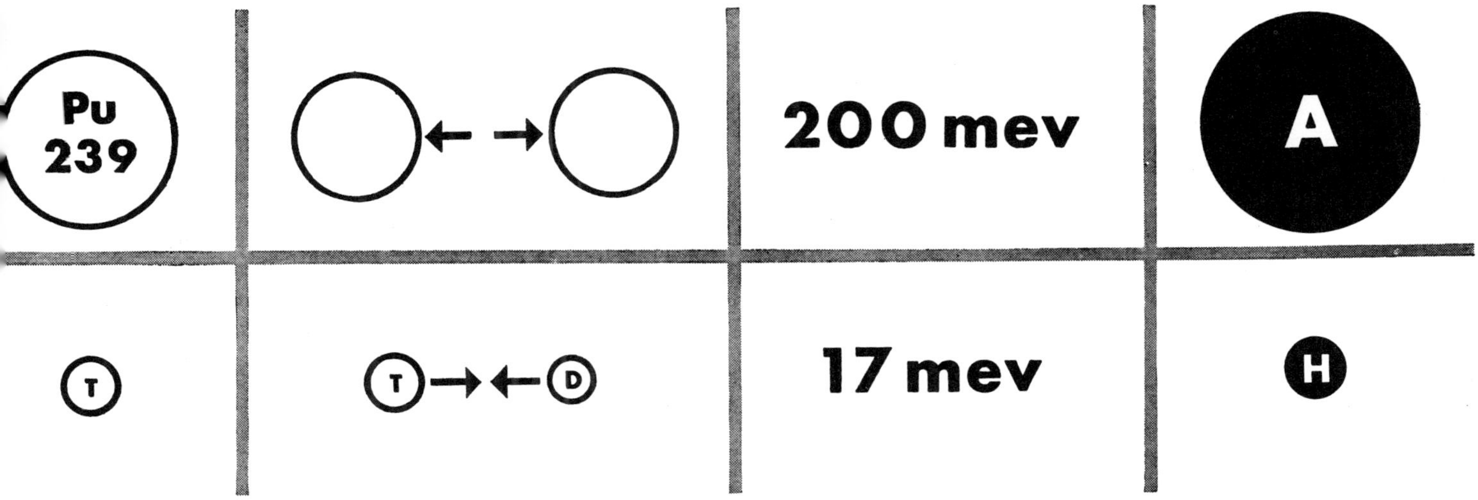

of lithium. This capture yields tritium (T), the hydrogen isotope of mass 3. The fusion of tritium and deuterium (D), assumed here to be essential in a hydrogen bomb, releases 17 million electron volts. On this basis the expenditure of a neutron in the manufacture of tritium produces much less energy than in the manufacture of plutonium. The relative energy release of A- and H-bombs per neutron is symbolized at the far right. This diagram was prepared by the editors on the basis of statements by the author and other unclassified material.

big bombs are to be a major part of our military preparation, from the military standpoint the solution of the delivery problem is vastly more important than exactly what kind of bombs would be carried if they could be delivered.

IF HYDROGEN bombs would not add very much to the military effectiveness of the U. S., would they add much to the U S.S.R.'s military potential? Here, of course, one gets involved in even more uncertain speculation. It is extremely difficult to judge whether the Russians would have an appreciable chance of delivering the hydrogen bomb by air against the radar defense which we are now constructing. Even if a reasonably effective system of air defenses is built, however, there is another method of delivery which would perhaps be quite effective for the Russians. Many of the big cities of the U. S. are on the seacoast. Into any one of these harbors, or at least reasonably close to it, a hydrogen bomb might easily be brought in the hold of a tramp steamer or in a relatively small unmanned craft. While this might not be the most effective place to detonate a hydrogen bomb, it would be a simple method of delivery for a surprise attack. On the other hand, practically no Soviet cities could be reached in this way. This means that the hydrogen bomb would be a more effective weapon for the Russians than for the U. S.

Some people have argued that if we develop the hydrogen bomb and can really keep its details secret, the Russians will never be able to develop it. There is absolutely no reason to believe this. Recent experience has shown that the Russians have an atomic energy enterprise adequately developed to make a sizable atomic explosion. In addition they probably have fairly detailed information about our work on atomic weapons and about at least some of the early thoughts on the possibility of a hydrogen bomb, obtained from the blundering indiscretions of some months ago, espionage activity and the widely known basic scientific principles. Given adequate time they can surely make a hydrogen bomb if it is possible at all.

The President's decision to go ahead with the development of the hydrogen bomb created a tremendous stir in the nation. From the standpoint of its military effectiveness, there seems to be little reason to attach such great significance to the hydrogen bomb. While it is a terrible weapon, its military importance seems to have been grossly overrated in the mind of the layman.

What is probably much more serious about the hush-hush subject of the hydrogen bomb is that here is a weapon about which the average citizen is so ill-informed that he thinks it can save the country from attack. Pumped full of hysteria by Red scares, aggravated by political mud-slinging, the average citizen is easily convinced that he can find some security and relief from all of this in the hydrogen bomb. The most tragic part is that the hydrogen bomb will not save us and is not even a very good addition to our military potential.

Here we have the outcome of what can happen in a democracy when decisions of far-reaching national significance are made without public scrutiny of pertinent information. While most of the pertinent information is not at all secret, some of the information the citizen should have in order to judge whether our national policy is sound is being kept secret. One of the most important facts the citizen should have to make a reasonable judgment is the approximate number of atomic bombs in our stockpile. It would be quite surprising if the Russians could not figure this out from the information they have obtained. Senator Brien McMahon, chairman of the Joint Committee on Atomic Energy, raised the question of making the number of atomic weapons available generally. He was vigorously criticized. As of last spring, not even the members of the Joint Committee knew how many atomic bombs the U. S. had.

ANOTHER item of information that would help the citizen appreciate the relative cost of hydrogen bombs and atomic bombs is the amount of fissionable material needed to get the hydrogen reaction started and the plutonium equivalent of the tritium to be used in a hydrogen bomb. Since neutrons are required to produce either plutonium or tritium, the neutron cost of a hydrogen bomb may be larger than first appears. The diversion of neutrons from the manufacture of plutonium to make tritium would mean a very real sacrifice of potential atomic bombs in order to obtain the ingredients for hydrogen bombs. As for the money cost of the hydrogen bomb, there have been such wide discrepancies in the estimates that the citizen can reach no sensible conclusion about it at all.

It is most important in our democracy that our government be frank and open with the citizens. In a democracy it is possible to have good government only when the citizens are well informed. It is difficult enough for them to become well informed when the information is easily available. When that information is not available, it is impossible. While it may well be that some of the information the citizen needs to make an intelligent judgment of national policy must be kept secret for military reasons, the present use of secrecy far exceeds this minimum. These are the methods of an authoritarian government and should be vigorously opposed in our democracy.

The hydrogen bomb and its potential usefulness to the U. S. as a military weapon is a subject on which citizens should be much more fully informed. It is a weapon whose effectiveness has been grossly exaggerated, and one in which we can place relatively little reliance for the future. Quantities of hydrogen bombs will not contribute very much to the security of the U. S. Unfortunately the citizen today believes that they will.

What, then, might be done to improve our military security in an important way? There are probably many answers to this question, but let me just make one suggestion that I am sure is clear to anyone who has thought seriously about the problem.

If the Russians should decide to move into Western Europe, we would immediately be faced with the prospect of fighting a war. Presumably we could use atomic bombs. It would not be long, however, before we would need a large army, and supplies not only for that army but also for our allies in Europe. We would have to send these supplies to Europe. But just how would we get them there? During the last war the Germans came dangerously close to shutting off our supplies to England on at least two occasions. This was before the development of the Schnorkel type of submarine, which we are told the Russians now have in quantity. It is well known that this Schnorkel submarine, while not absolutely impervious to detection by radar, is most difficult to run down. No method of detection has been developed that can locate it at any great distance under water. It appears that a determined enemy with adequate bases and Schnorkel submarines could go a long way toward preventing us from delivering men and supplies to Europe. We could presumably deliver a certain amount of material by air, but when it comes to delivering millions of tons, our experience with the Berlin air lift should show us that this is not a feasible solution.

Here is a problem whose solution would contribute greatly to our military strength and therefore to our security. Its solution might even deter the Russians from overrunning Western Europe if they planned to do so. Hence it seems much more important to devote our attention to this problem than to the more spectacular hydrogen-bomb development.

THERE exist a great many other problems that are probably almost as important. For example, there is the matter of the development of long-range guided missiles. This development is clearly important to military strength. During the last war both the Germans and the Russians were very successful in the tactical use of airplanes with ground troops. New technical work might greatly increase the effectiveness of airplanes in tactical use.

In the field of atomic energy itself we need to make a choice between weapons and other developments of nuclear power which may have long-range peacetime significance as well as military applications. These long-range peacetime assets may add to our industrial strength and thereby make a greater contribution to our security than the more immediate development of weapons.

At the present time it is most difficult to ascertain how our government decides what policies to follow regarding national security. High government officials find themselves beset with advice to pursue this or that development or construct this or that weapon without being very sure how one weapon compares with another. Where the development of a weapon may compete with a long-range industrial development the problem is still more difficult. Although the U. S. is a rich country, we cannot afford to follow every recommendation that anyone believes will increase our national security.

The best way to make sure that a reasonable policy is followed is to have those policies and the information on which they are based open for public scrutiny. The citizen must choose, insofar as that is possible. Today if he tries to come to some conclusion about what should be done to increase national security, he runs up against a high wall of secrecy. He can of course take the easy solution and say that these questions should be left to the upper echelons of the military establishments to decide. But these decisions are so important today that to leave them to the military men is for the citizen essentially to abrogate his basic responsibility. If in time of peace decisions on which the future of our country depends are left to any small group not representative of the people, we have gone a long way toward authoritarian government.

The U. S. has grown strong under a Constitution that wisely has laid great emphasis upon the importance of free and open discussion. Under the influence of a large number of people who have fallen for the fallacy that there is security in secrecy, and of many, including, I regret to say, eminent scientists, who prophesy doom just around the corner, we are dangerously close to abandoning those principles of free speech and open discussion that have made our country great. The democratic system depends on intelligent decisions by the electorate. Our heritage can only be carried on if the citizen has the information with which to make an intelligent decision.

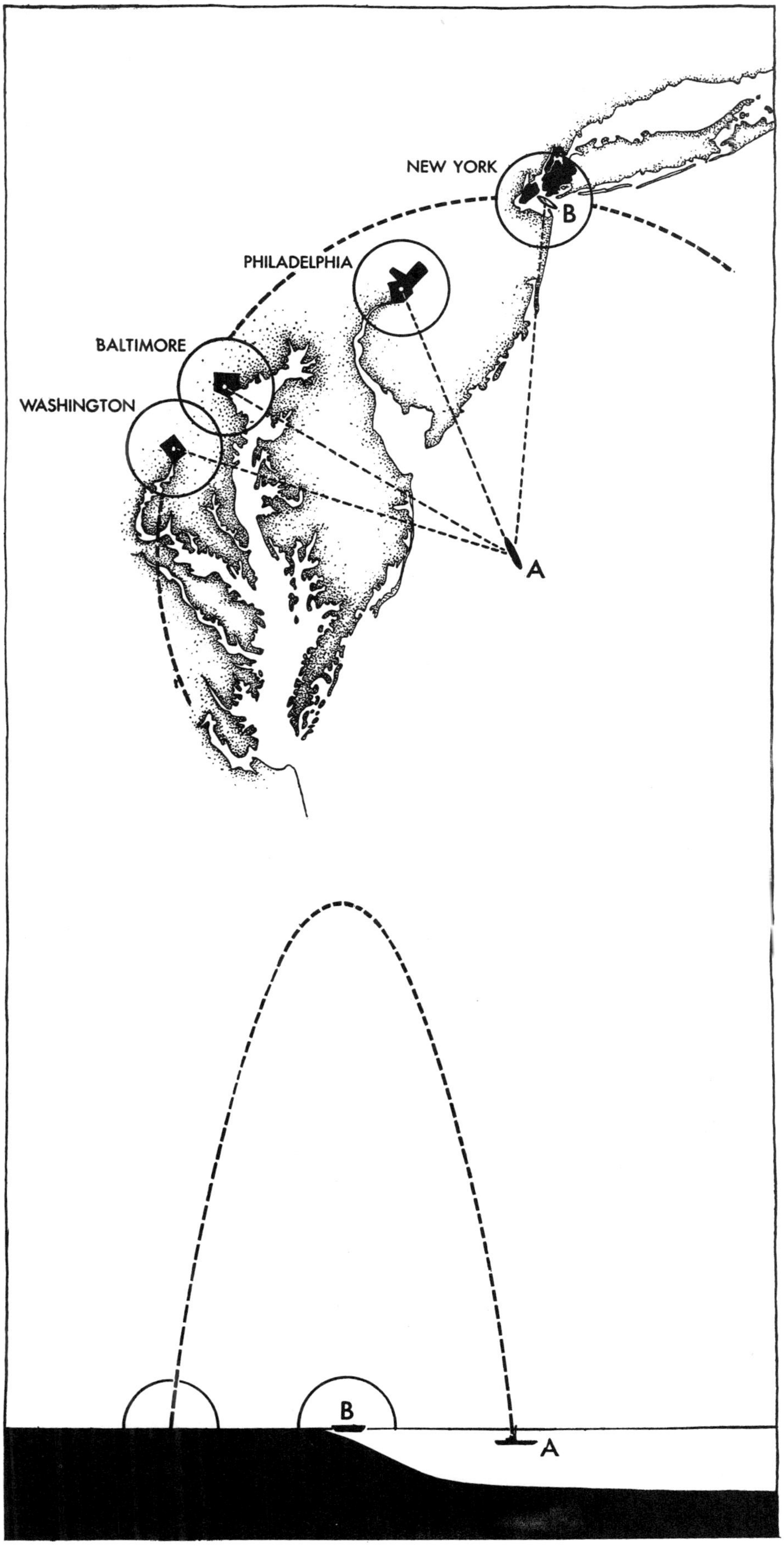

U.S. DISADVANTAGE in a war involving hydrogen bombs is illustrated in this map and section drawing. Cities on or near the coast would be vulnerable to a submarine (A) firing a hydrogen bomb in a rocket or to a hydrogen bomb-carrying robot ship (B). Range of rocket is assumed to be 150 miles.

11

Edward Teller's View of the Nuclear Age

ALBERT SZENT-GYÖRGYI
May 1962

A review of *The Legacy of Hiroshima*, Edward Teller with Allen Brown. Garden City, N.Y.: Doubleday and Company, Inc., 1962.

Edward Teller is an outstanding scientist who has made many valuable contributions to physics. I would accept his opinions about the science with the utmost confidence. During World War II he turned to weaponry and nuclear technology, and he has become, with his remarkable versatility, a leading authority in this field. I would accept his opinions about the applications of science with the same confidence. The main theme of the present book, however, is from neither of these two fields. The book is essentially a vehicle for Teller's political ideas in their relation to armaments.

Science and technology produce new tools and release new forces, but the question of what use these tools and forces are put to—construction or destruction—has little to do with science or technology proper, and so Teller's ideas and opinions in this field are as good (or as bad) as your or mine.

One of the most puzzling characteristics of the human mind is its ability to produce coherent thoughts in one field and to be irrational in another, once biased by sentiment, ambition or interest. Louis Pasteur, for instance, who was one of the clearest scientific thinkers the human species has produced, said himself that in matters of religious thought he was on a level with the peasant women of Brittany. I have often had to smile at the childish nonsense about communism uttered by some leading English physicists, who were sentimentally biased in favor of this doctrine, about the application of which I have had a firsthand knowledge.

Teller's political opinions seem to be biased by his hatred for the Russians and his love for his children, the H-bombs, whose father he is said to be. He would like to see more bombs and better bombs, bigger and deeper shelters. He would like to see our children brought up underground and in underground schools. What gives undue weight to his opinions is that he has become the "voice" of the military-industrial complex, with its enormous vested interest in political tension and distrust, its political influence and virtually inexhaustible means. President Eisenhower sounded a warning in his "farewell address" about this complex, which amplifies the voice of Teller and magnifies his figure, while the public takes the political opinions of Teller with the confidence and homage due only to Teller the scientist or military technologist and not Teller the politician and strategist. All this makes Teller's book recommended reading for those who would like to see a world of hatred and distrust, with more bombs, bigger and better bombs, deeper shelters, with mankind marching under the deepening shadow of mushroom clouds. Those who would like to see the U.S. find its idealistic self again and assume the moral leadership of our fragmented world, and who would like to see mankind marching toward a brighter future, will put this book aside with a saddened heart.

The book is well written and easy to read. The authors try to discuss all the problems of relations between the U.S. and the U.S.S.R., and to give all the answers. They foget only one possibility: an honorable peace.

The first chapters of the book deal with the story of atomic energy and armaments and make interesting reading, flavored by anecdotes and firsthand personal experience. Nonetheless, the reader is left, so to speak, empty-handed, not being told what the problems really were. Here the authors were evidently limited by secrecy. Some of the later chapters, such as the one on education, deserve full attention, although I prefer that education be discussed for its own sake, without an edge turned against the Russians.

In at least one way the authors are guilty of an unscientific attitude. They deal with all their problems from the standpoint of current technology. They seem to forget that the present is only a point on a rapidly rising curve. This curve expresses itself, for instance, in the steady growth of the destructive power of nuclear bombs, which has increased 2,500-fold since Hiroshima, a rate of growth that shows no sign of slowing down. The authors also make the improbable assumption that in a world conflict there will be a winner and a loser. To support their argument they give a distorted picture of the biological effects of ionizing radiation, and they deal with world conflict as though it were a storm that quickly blows over, leaving social structures unchanged and the atmosphere cleared, with every problem solved.

So far as I am aware, Teller's political opinions do not represent those of the great majority of scientists. Science is the fruit of the work of a group of people, who form a unified intellectual community that knows no boundaries in time or space and knows no limitation by color, creed, race or passport. The basic moral rule of this community is uncompromising intellectual honesty, good will and mutual respect. Most scientists would like to see this spirit extended to political relations and wish for a wider human understanding that would mark the way toward higher levels of human existence. Some of us even believe that the formidable forces released by science can be handled without catastrophe only by the same mentality that created them. Teller sees the final solution in the establishment of a world government after a full democratic or communist victory. He seems unable to visualize a family of man with its temporary chasms bridged, and so he takes us back to the mentality of the religious wars, the problems of which must have seemed, in their time, as insoluble as ours.

SECTION 3: FALLOUT

> *"If [the hydrogen bomb program is] successful, radioactive poisoning of the atmosphere and hence annihilation of any life on earth has been brought within the realm of technical possibilities. The ghostlike character of this development lies in its apparently compulsory trend. Every step appears as the unavoidable consequence of the preceding one. In the end, there beckons more and more clearly general annihilation. . . ."*
>
> ALBERT EINSTEIN, 1950

INTRODUCTION

In *Scientific American*, September 1901, we find one of the earliest reports on the harmful effects of radiation. The "H. Becquerel" in the following quotation from that issue is the man who discovered radioactivity in 1896, and "P. Curie" is Pierre Curie, the husband of Marie Sklowdowska Curie. The Curies are familiar, of course, as the discoverers of radium, the culprit in Becquerel's report.

> H. Becquerel has confirmed, by an unpleasant experience, the fact first noted by Walkoff and Giesel, that the rays of radium have an energetic and peculiar action on the skin. Having carried in his waistcoat pocket for several periods, equal in all to about six hours, a carboard box enclosing a small sealed tube containing a few decigrammes of intensely active radiferous barium chloride, in ten days' time a red mark corresponding to this tube was apparent on the skin; inflammation followed, the skin peeled off and left a suppurating sore which did not heal for a month. A second burn subsequently appeared in a place corresponding to the opposite corner of the pocket where the tube had been carried on another occasion. P. Curie has had the same experience after exposing his arm for a longer period to a less active specimen. The reddening of the skin at first apparent gradually assumed the character of a burn; after desquamation a persistent suppurating sore was left which was not healed fifty-six days after the exposure. In addition to these severe "burns" the experimenters find that their hands, exposed to the rays in the course of their investigations, have a tendency to desquamate, the tips of the fingers which have held tubes or capsules containing very active radiferous material often become hard and painful; in one case the inflammation lasted for fifteen days and ended by the loss of the skin; and the painful sensation has not yet disappeared after the lapse of two months. . . ."*

When a nuclear weapon explodes, enormous amounts of radioactive debris are produced. If a large nuclear bomb is exploded well above the ground, the boiling cloud that rises high into the atmosphere in the aftermath of the explosion condenses into very fine radioactive particles, most of which stay suspended in the atmosphere for a very long time. Over a period of many years, this fine radioactive dust gradually settles to the ground all over the earth, sometimes combined with water as rain and snow. However, if a nuclear bomb is exploded on or close to the ground, the results are quite different. Enormous masses of earth or water are also vaporized and carried up to great heights along with the radioactive bomb debris. Together, they condense into larger radioactive particles, many of which fall to the ground within hours after the explosion, laying down a carpet of intense radioactive fallout in an

*This quotation was reprinted in "50 and 100 Years Ago," *Scientific American*, September 1951.

elongated pattern immediately downwind from the site of the explosion. Roughly speaking, the radioactive fallout from a one-megaton explosion is strong enough to kill people over an area of five hundred to one thousand square miles. The precise shape, area, and location of the region made lethal is difficult to predict, and depends on the direction and intensity of the winds not just near the ground but at all altitudes. Furthermore, the effect of the radiation on the people in a region depends on additional factors, such as the roughness of the ground, the amount of time during which inhabitants are outdoors rather than indoors, and whether the construction and size of buildings provide some shelter for their inhabitants.

Nuclear weapons scientists and engineers had known about the potential dangers of fallout from the start of the nuclear weapons program. Accordingly, beginning with the very first, nuclear tests have always been conducted so as to avoid to the extent practical irradiating populations near test sites. Tests were conducted only in areas of low population, explosions took place on towers (and balloons) high enough to avoid entrainment of much earth in the mushroom cloud, and the weather was carefully watched so that shots would be fired only when the predicted fallout patterns would avoid populated places in the area of the tests.

The dangers of fallout had not been kept secret from the public. Fallout was often mentioned in speeches, articles, and testimony prepared by nuclear scientists for the purpose of informing the public and government officials about the realities of nuclear weapons. Indeed, reference to it is made in some of the reports and articles in previous sections in this book. However, as far as government officials and the general public were concerned, it was all a highly theoretical matter. The concept of "fallout" simply did not relate in any way to the common human experience, and so it was very largely ignored outside the very small group directly responsible for nuclear tests.

On March 1, 1954, the day the very first 15-megaton bomb was tested, a slight shift in the wind caused a radical shift in public opinion. The reports from the "Science and the Citizen" columns of *Scientific American* that follow show just how the problem of radioactive fallout forced its way into the consciousness of the world public, and how scientific and political leaders reacted to it.

Science and the Citizen, May 1954

Total Danger

IN the vast, lonely wilds of the Pacific Ocean, far—but not far enough—from civilization, man was at last playing last month with forces sufficiently powerful to destroy the human race with satisfactory speed. From behind the "security" curtain around the test area came reports of explosions which astonished scientists and satisfied even the military—of islands decapitated, of immense craters blown in the ocean floor, of fireballs large enough to engulf a city, of shock waves thunderous enough to travel around the globe. Among all the phenomena, nothing kindled more terror in the hearts of the peoples of the earth than a gentle rain of burning ash that fell from the blue upon 23 men peacefully going about their business in a Japanese fishing boat. The Thermonuclear Age fell upon mankind without mercy, if not entirely without warning.

The shock wave of fear brought its train of panic—but as yet only a small-sized panic. Mixed with the fear there were still large portions of complacency and incredulity. Yet there was a rising demand for information which could not long be denied. Just as war is too important to be left to the generals, so the Thermonuclear Bomb had become too big to be entrusted any longer to the executive sessions of rulers or technicians. If the means of doom for mankind had become a reality, the population at least wanted to know how and in what form that doom might come.

The surface events were but a faint echo of what had really happened; after the bang there came only whimpers. On March 1 the Atomic Energy Commission announced that it had just made another "routine atomic test" at its explosion grounds in the Marshall Islands. Soon came reports that it was something more than routine. A Marine corporal on Kwajalein, nearly 200 miles from the test at Bikini, wrote home to his mother that the blast had shaken his barracks like an earthquake. The AEC announced that 28 of its observers and 236 natives on islands scores of miles from the test had been showered with a radioactive "fall-out." Congressmen began to inform reporters that the explosion had been three or four times as large as expected, that it had got "out of control." It was said to be far larger than the first thermonuclear experiment in November, 1952, which had blown an island from the face of the sea. Its power was reported equivalent to 12 million tons of TNT—600 times as forceful as the Hiroshima atomic bomb. Its radius of total destruction might be 10 miles or more; its blast wave of sound was detected by far-off British monitors.

The immediate brunt fell on a Japanese fishing vessel called *The Fortunate Dragon*, carrying a harvest of tuna and shark in its open hold. Caught 80 miles from the explosion, it was showered with a white ash of particles which blistered the 23 fishermen's skin and made the fish radioactive. When the ship made port, some of the fish were sold before the government could stop it. Overnight the Japanese people stopped eating fish; housewives shopped with Geiger counters; the price of tuna fell to one third with few takers. As for the fishermen, Professor Masao Tzuzuki of Tokyo University and others who examined them found that they had inhaled and swallowed radioactive fission products. The Japanese doctors predicted that some of the victims would die. The Japanese newspapers looked upon the shower of "death dust" as the third atomic bombing of Japan. Government officials and the Japanese people demanded an international ban upon all atomic weapons and control of energy. The great Japanese physicist Hideki Yukawa said sadly: "Atomic power has grown up like a ferocious animal its master cannot completely control. The issue appears to transcend differences of social systems and to concern the very fate of the human race itself."

Premier Malenkov of the U.S.S.R. had voiced much the same conclusion, acknowledging to the Soviet people for the first time that atomic war would mean "the destruction of world civilization." In India Prime Minister Nehru urged the U.S. to end its hydrogen bomb experiments. He likened the new weapon to "the genie that came out of the bottle, ultimately swallowing man." And in Great Britain 104 members of Parliament signed a petition calling for control of all nuclear weapons by the United Nations and immediate cessation of the hydrogen bomb experiments. Lord Hore-Belisha, returning to Parliament from a 10-year retirement, said solemnly: "I want to know, and I am sure the country does, too, in what conditions the U.S. are going to use the atomic bomb." Prime Minister Churchill, called up for a full-dress questioning by the House of Commons, brokenly told the stern House that he was in "almost hourly correspondence" with the U.S. Government but had been unable to obtain the facts about the new weapons because of the secrecy strictures in the U.S. Atomic Energy Act. "I am sure," he added, "that the American people are equally anxious to be informed."

On March 26 the AEC and its military associates set off the second thermonuclear explosion in the "current series." For this one they had cleared several times as large a danger area in the Pacific—nearly half a million square miles—ignoring British and Japanese cries of violation of "the freedom of the seas." Chairman Lewis L. Strauss of the AEC witnessed the test and hastened to Washington to deliver a report for which Congressmen and the public were clamoring. Standing beside President Eisenhower at a press conference, Admiral Strauss endeavored to reassure the nation. The reports of the thermonuclear explosions, he said, had been "exaggerated." The "yield" had been about twice the estimate—"a margin of error not incompatible with a totally new weapon." No large island had been blown up—only small sand bars. *The Fortunate Dragon* had been the victim of an unfortunate wind shift; its fishermen's wounds were probably not due to radioactivity but chemical burns caused by lime particles from the blasted coral; the Japanese had not allowed U.S. doctors to examine them; the U.S. was prepared to indemnify the victims. There was no evidence of widespread contamination of fish in the Pacific. He had visited the showered island natives and found them apparently "well and happy." As for the tests themselves, they had been successful; "the results which the scientists at Los Alamos and Livermore had hoped to obtain . . . were fully realized," and the U.S. could be assured that it was keeping pace with the Russians, who "had begun work on this weapon substantially before we did." Admiral Strauss concluded that the hydrogen bomb development had enhanced "our military capability to the point where we should soon be more free to increase our emphasis on the peaceful uses of atomic power."

But the peaceful use of atomic power was not the thing that was on everyone's mind. A reporter asked how destructive the bomb would be.

Admiral Strauss; "An H-bomb can be made large enough to take out a city."

Question: "How big a city?"

Admiral Strauss: "Any city."

Question: "New York?"

Admiral Strauss: "The metropolitan area, yes."

Released next day was a film of the November, 1952, shot, which by comparison with the 1954 successes must be counted a thermonuclear fizzle. The explosion (fission plus a little fusion) disintegrated an islet half a mile long, left a hole more than a mile in diameter and 175 feet deep and created a fireball three and a half miles in diameter. The estimated radius of annihilation was three miles; of damage, 10 miles.

It seemed that H-bombs would be comparatively cheap, perhaps composed of lithium and deuterium or some such combination, and not difficult to manufacture. In their New York *Herald Tribune* column the Alsop brothers divulged, however, that physicists foresaw a limit to the effective power of the H-bomb: beyond about 50 megatons (the power of 50 million tons of dynamite) the blast could spread no farther sideways and would blow clear through the roof of our atmosphere—"the limit of blowout." The H-bomb's limitations of range are not, however, irreparable; the *New York Times* science reporter William L. Laurence quickly pointed out that the addition of a cobalt shell could sow lethal radioactivity over a continent.

In the dazed City of New York the Civil Defense Director, Herbert O'Brien, said in despair: "Air-raid shelters are obsolete." The only hope would be to flee the city—but New York would need at least three days' warning of a raid to evacuate its population in time. Val Petersen, the U.S. National Civil Defense Administrator, had no better prospect to offer. "The cities," he said, "are finished." He had made a survey of the probable toll of a thermonuclear attack on the major U.S. cities, and had concluded that at least nine million people would be killed. "Just as a practical matter," he observed, "how in hell are you going to bury nine million corpses?"

U.S. Senator Stuart Symington expressed the frozen state of mind of people throughout the world: "We are now in that era some of us have predicted with dread for a long time—the period of total danger."

No realistic statesman was lulled by the notion that the H-bomb automatically made war improbable. In the House of Commons Clement Attlee said: "We have only recently seen a great nation, Germany, putting all its resources in the hands of a paranoiac. Who can doubt, after reading of Hitler's last days, that even at the very end of that war if he had had the atomic bomb he would have used it? There is no guarantee that in some country at some time there may not arise to power a fanatic. . . . The only way open to us seems to be to make a new approach to world problems. . . . It is not too late."

Science and the Citizen, November 1954

Pandora's Box

AIKICHI Kuboyama, one of the 23 Japanese fishermen exposed to radioactive fallout from the hydrogen bomb exploded at Bikini on March 1, died in a Tokyo hospital last month.

His death gave evidence that the thermonuclear weapon's lethal effects are not limited to the vicinity of the explosion. According to the newspaper columnists Joseph and Stewart Alsop, physicists have been increasingly disquieted by their calculations of the potential coverage of a hydrogen bomb's fall-out. A superbomb of five megatons (equivalent to five million tons of TNT) would, they estimate, shower lethal radioactivity over 6,000 square miles. Thus a hydrogen bomb dropped on the city of Hartford, say, would not only pulverize that city but would make the atmosphere deadly for two days afterward in the entire state of Connecticut.

A distinguished British scientist has suggested that if enough bombs are dropped it will make no difference what country they are aimed at or whether they hit the target. In his presidential address to the British Association for the Advancement of Science, the physiologist E. D. Adrian said: "The human race cannot stand more than a few thousand large atomic explosions. . . . Repeated explosions will lead to a degree of general radioactivity which no one can tolerate or escape."

In the opinion of A. H. Sturtevant, a California Institute of Technology geneticist, the contamination of the atmosphere is already sufficient to cause concern. He told a sectional meeting of the American Association for the Advancement of Science that every test explosion of a fission or a fusion bomb will increase the "ultimate harvest of defective individuals" in future generations. Genetically, Sturtevant declared, there is no "safe" level of radioactivity, "no threshold value below which radiation is ineffective." He deplored a recent statement by Lewis Strauss, chairman of the Atomic Energy Commission, that the increase in background radioactivity due to the bomb tests was far too small to be harmful. Said Sturtevant: "Every geneticist familiar with the facts knows that any level whatsoever is certain to be at least genetically harmful to human beings when it is applied to most or all the inhabitants of the earth. . . . I regret that an official in a position of such responsibility should have stated that there is no biological hazard from low doses of high-energy radiation."

Science and the Citizen, April 1955

Fall-Out

THE only "defense" against the hydrogen bomb, authorities agree, is not to be where it explodes. Last month the Atomic Energy Commission finally released information showing how difficult it will be to run far enough away. Radioactive fall-out from the March 1, 1954, test in the Pacific contaminated an area 220 miles downwind from the explosion and 40 miles wide. Within the first 120 miles, all persons who failed to take shelter would probably have been killed. The report said: "About 7,000 square miles of territory downwind from the point of burst was so contaminated that survival might have depended upon prompt evacuation of the area or upon taking shelter and other protective measures."

Partial shelter would be afforded by any building far enough away from the blast to remain standing. The radiation level on the first floor of an ordinary frame house would be about half that outdoors, the Commission said. In the basement the level would be cut to a tenth, and in an "old-fashioned cyclone cellar with a covering of earth about three feet thick" it would be reduced to one 5,000th. "Designs of shelters of simple yet effective construction have been prepared by the Civil Defense Administration and are available to the public," the Commission declared.

Regarding the possibility that test explosions threaten the genetic heritage of all the earth's peoples, the report admitted that no conclusive data were available. However, the average dose of radiation received by U.S. residents from all nuclear weapons tests to date was said to be no more than that received in one chest X-ray. The Commission reiterated its belief that controlled tests give no "basis for serious concern." A similar opinion had been expressed a few weeks earlier by the University of California geneticist Curt Stern.

The AEC disclosures on fall-out were accurately anticipated by Ralph Lapp in an article in the *Bulletin of the Atomic Scientists*. The author said that persons caught in a fall-out area would have to spend two or three days underground, in cellars or even foxholes. Then they might venture out and begin to decontaminate their homes, for example by washing down the roof and plowing under the lawn. Lapp recommended that the Government undertake a $2 billion program for building a ring of concrete shelters around the outskirts of all large cities.

Last month Great Britain became the third nation to announce that it knew how to make hydrogen bombs. It is proceeding with "development and production." Not all Englishmen found much cheer in the news. C. F. Powell, a Nobel prize winner in physics, pointed out that 10 or 20 hydrogen bombs dropped on Great Britain would make "ordinary organized life impossible. . . . It would be a poor consolation to the pathetic remnant of our country that we had been able to reduce other lands to a similar condition of ruin." Powell estimated that the U.S. has 4,000 fission bombs and the U.S.S.R. 1,000. Each is a potential H-bomb.

Science and the Citizen, May 1955

Perils of Radioactivity

PUBLIC debate about the hazards of nuclear weapon tests increased last month.

The magazine *U.S. News and World Report* published an article, said to have been "cleared for publication as factually accurate" by the Atomic Energy Commission, which declared that the tests created no danger. H-bombs could be tested once a week indefinitely, said the article, without "raising the amount of strontium 90 to a dangerous level." It added that children of parents exposed to radiation at Hiroshima and Nagasaki have not shown an abnormal number of defects, and that a strain of fruit flies which has gone through 128 generations in highly radioactive containers has become "a much improved race of fruit flies with more vigor, hardiness, resistance to disease, better reproductive capacity." The article concluded: "The fear that people are supersensitive to mutations through radioactivity is not borne out. There is agreement among geneticists working with AEC that some changes in future generations are likely to result only from heavy or successive doses. . . . Some experts believe that mutations usually work out in the end to improve species."

From other quarters came other opinions.

The Nobel-prize-winning British physicist Frederick Soddy asserted that hydrogen explosions are "fouling the air with radioactivity. . . . It is nonsense to say it is harmless. . . . Politicians and technicians are rushing into experiments without the faintest idea of what the results may be."

Linus Pauling, professor of chemistry at the California Institute of Technology, said: "Continued dispersal of radioactive materials into the atmosphere is creating a critical situation. Irradiation may have started a new cycle of leukemia victims or new hereditary mutations."

According to Joseph Rotblat, professor of physics at the University of London, "we are sailing much closer to the wind than any of us thought" so far as genetic effects of H-bomb tests are concerned. Writing in the *Atomic Scientists Journal,* Rotblat estimated that a radioactivity level double the present natural background rate might be genetically tolerable. Any higher rate would be "rather risky." Explosion of 75 hydrogen bombs over the whole world in the course of the next 30 years, he said, would double the level of radiation.

The Federation of American Scientists proposed that to settle the question a United Nations commission be set up to assess the potential dangers from fission and thermonuclear bomb tests.

Science and the Citizen, June 1955

Radiation Study

THE National Academy of Sciences announced last month that it will undertake a broad study of the effects of atomic radiation on living organisms. Funds will be provided by the Rockefeller Foundation. The Academy's investigators will collect and evaluate the available information, decide what conclusions are now warranted, pick out problems needing further research and initiate the necessary studies. The Academy said it will also "evaluate the availability of information to scientists, physicians and the general public."

A note on radiation effects appeared recently in the English medical journal *The Lancet.* It said that all 22 of the surviving Japanese exposed to fall-out from the 1954 H-bomb test were completely sterile nine months after their exposure. Their sperm counts showed a steady fall after the accident and by December of last year "had in every case fallen to zero." The condition is not permanent, the article said, but may last as long as two years, as it did in some of the Hiroshima and Nagasaki victims.

Science and the Citizen, July 1955

Fission-Fusion-Fission

RECENT speculation in the daily press about a new type of nuclear weapon—the so-called uranium bomb—has now been carried further by the British physicist J. Rotblat. In an article in the English *Atomic Scientists Journal* (reprinted by *Bulletin of the Atomic Scientists*) he discussed the evidence for such a device and its probable effects.

From the Atomic Energy Commission's description of fallout after the thermonuclear test of March 1, 1954, Rotblat calculated that the total radioactivity released in the explosion was about 400 billion curies. Japanese measurements showed that almost all the radioactivity came from fission products rather than from materials irradiated by neutrons in a fusion reaction. The most powerful modern atomic bomb should release no more than 10 billion curies. Assuming that such a bomb was used to trigger a fusion reaction, this reaction must in turn have triggered more fission.

The commonest species of uranium (U-238) is not split by slow neutrons, but it is easily disrupted by faster ones with energies of several million electron volts. A fusion reaction liberates neutrons in this energy range. Rotblat suggests that the Bikini device consisted of a plutonium core, a shell of lithium deuteride for the fusion reaction and an outer shell of U-238.

If this is the case, the radioactive contamination from an "H-bomb" explosion must be very much greater than had been supposed. (Fission products emit more radiation, and for a longer period, than the materials in which a fusion reaction incidentally induces radioactivity.) The AEC has stated that all bomb tests to date have exposed each individual to no more radiation than he would receive from a single chest X-ray. Says Rotblat: "Most of this radiation must have come from the very few hydrogen bombs tested less than a year ago. This means that one year of H-bomb tests at the present scale about doubles the natural background. . . . If our guess is correct, the hydrogen-uranium bomb is a kind of cobalt bomb; in fact, in some respects, it is even worse."

Science and the Citizen, August 1955

Hush and Tush

SPECULATION about the "fission-fusion-fission" bomb [see the preceding "Science and the Citizen" excerpt] was indirectly confirmed last month by Atomic Energy Commissioner Willard F. Libby. This weapon is said to consist of a fission bomb which triggers a thermonuclear reaction which in turn causes ordinary uranium (238) to fission. In a speech at the University of Chicago, Libby mentioned "a nuclear explosion releasing 10 megatons of fission energy." The energy of the fission bombs in the pre-thermonuclear period was reckoned in tens of thousands of tons of TNT, not millions.

Science and the Citizen, July 1956

Radiation Study

IN the peacetime development of atomic energy, man has been lucky. Except for some tragic accidents to a relatively few people, he has suffered little biological damage from the immense radiation he has already released. As the atomic age advances at an accelerating pace, man must learn how best to cope with the inherently dangerous radioactivity he is releasing in ever-increasing quantities. This is the principal message of a report on the biological effects of atomic radiation that was released by the National Academy of Sciences last month.

The report is the first publication in what is to be a continuing study sponsored by the Academy and financed by the Rockefeller Foundation. For the past year six scientific committees have been investigating radiation problems in the fields of genetics, pathology, meteorology, oceanography, agriculture and the disposal of radioactive waste products. Each committee has issued a report summarizing present knowledge in its field and outlining the areas in which further research is most urgently needed.

The Academy has also issued a popular summary of the reports. The purpose is to provide the layman with technical background against which he can consider the "ethical, political, economic or military questions" which he will be called upon to decide in connection with atomic energy.

The genetics committee emphasizes the importance of the total amount of radiation absorbed by the human population. The cumulative effect of radiation on future generations is likely to be the same whether a great many people are exposed to tiny doses or a few people receive considerably larger amounts. In either case the total number of mutations will be the same.

A child's genetic make-up can be affected by any mutations in its parents' genes from the time they are born until it is conceived. For this reason the report recommends that, as an average for the population as a whole, the amount of radiation to which an individual's reproductive glands are exposed from conception to the age of 30 be limited to 10 roentgen units. (To give the reader an idea of the size of this unit, the average dental X-ray delivers five roentgens to the patient's jaw, but only five thousandths of a roentgen of stray radiation to such remote parts of the body as the reproductive glands.) The 10-roentgen figure is over and above the unavoidable "background" radiation that comes from naturally radioactive elements in the earth's crust and from cosmic rays. The average 30-year exposure from background in the U.S. is 4.3 roentgens.

As a maximum for the exposure of individuals, the report sets a gonad dose of 50 roentgens before the age of 30 and not more than 100 before the age of 40. It also recommends that a record be kept for every individual showing how much radiation he has accumulated in his lifetime. The geneticists advise physicians to use X-rays as sparingly as possible.

The pathologists of the National Academy study call attention to the fact that radiation shortens the span of life. Aside from the specific diseases, such as cancer and leukemia, that can be triggered by radiation, there are more diffuse effects. Radiation appears to lower immunity, damage connective tissue and generally to accelerate aging. There is no evidence that doses up to about 100 roentgens spread over years can shorten human life. Nevertheless, the pathologists warn that if very large numbers of people were exposed to a gradually accumulated dose of 100 roentgens or even less, statistics might show that their life expectancy had been reduced.

A picture of how radiation may reach the human population, and of the steps necessary to minimize the amount that does, is provided by the committees on meteorology, oceanography, agriculture and waste disposal. So far as atmospheric contamination is concerned, the chief problem comes from atomic explosions. The immediate fallout of radioactive particles covers an area that is comparatively small and, for controlled tests, closely predictable. However, the lighter material remains in the air for long periods and spreads over most of the earth. Some of it is washed out of the air by rain or snow, and so may be unevenly distributed, depending on variations in local precipitation. Following a single bomb explosion in Nevada, rain showered the cities of Albany and Troy, N.Y., with one tenth of a roentgen of fallout. It is unlikely that a single region would be so unlucky more than once, but it is possible.

The lightest particles are blown up into the stratosphere, where they remain for years. Meteorologists know little as yet about how, when or where this material gets back to the lower atmosphere and to the ground.

The report states that weapons tests have not produced dangerous world-wide levels of radioactivity, nor should they do so in the future if continued at the same rate as in the past. Nevertheless, the geneticists point out, any increase in radiation levels is genetically undesirable and should be held to an absolute minimum.

Fallout from weapons tests has measureably raised the "natural" level of radioactivity in plants. The amount is biologically negligible thus far. But no one yet knows what levels of radiation can be tolerated in plants that serve as animal or human food. Research in this field is urgently needed, the agricultural experts say.

They also sound a reminder that the biological effects of radiation are not all bad. In their science, as in many other branches of biology and medicine, controlled use of radiation is leading to remarkable advances, both in fundamental knowledge and in applied work.

As the atomic power industry develops, some of its accumulating radioactive wastes will almost certainly be dumped into the oceans. Before this happens, the oceanographers warn, we need to know much more than we do about circulation patterns and the rates of mixing between different parts of the seas. It may be that some sections of the ocean deeps mix so slowly with the surface waters that radioactive material dumped there would have a chance to "cool" before it entered the general circulation.

The problem of ocean contamination is complicated by the fact that marine life concentrates many of the elements in sea water. Radioactive substances are taken up by the smallest plants and animals, which in turn serve as food for larger creatures and so on up to the fish eaten by man. Each stage may result in an increase in concentration. Thus a comparatively low level of contamination of the oceans' surface waters could cause comparatively high contamination of food taken from the sea.

Radioactive tracers will be valuable in charting ocean currents and in studying marine life. But this research must be undertaken at once. "Because of the increasing radioactive contamination of the sea and the atmosphere," the oceanography committee points out, "many of the necessary experiments will only be possible within 10 or 20 years."

The report makes several recommendations for controlling waste disposal. Techniques for monitoring world-wide fallout should be further improved. Measurements of the storage of radiation in the stratosphere should be continued and extended. A national agency should control and record the dumping of radioactive material in the ocean. An international body should set up safe standards for the disposal of radioactive materials. As long as reactors remain potentially hazardous, those that are built near populated areas should be sealed so that in the event of an accident no radioactive materials can escape.

"The development of atomic energy is a matter for careful, integrated planning," the report concludes. "A large part of the information that is needed to make intelligent plans is not yet at hand. There is not much time left to acquire it."

The chairmen of the study committees are: Warren Weaver of the Rockefeller Foundation (genetics), Shields Warren of the New England Deaconess Hospital in Boston (pathology), A. Geoffrey Norman of the University of Michigan (agriculture and food supplies), Roger Revelle of the Scripps Institution of Oceanography (oceanography and fisheries), Harry Wexler of the U.S. Weather Bureau (meteorology), Abel Wolman of the Johns Hopkins University (disposal and waste).

Science and the Citizen, September 1957

British View of Radiation

THE British Medical Research Council released its own summary of radiation hazards simultaneously with the report of the National Academy of Sciences (see the following "Science and the Citizen" excerpt). Although the two reports agreed in most details and reached virtually the same conclusions, public reaction in the two countries has differed considerably.

Most U.S. commentators seemed reassured by the Academy's estimate that the fallout of strontium 90 from weapons tests had added only a negligible amount of radioactivity to the atmosphere. The British press, on the other hand, was alarmed by the same figures.

New Statesman and Nation declared this section of the report to be "the writing on the wall. Statesmen will ignore it at our peril." The publication said the report shows that persistent weapons testing will "raise to a danger point the amount of radiostrontium stored in the world's atmosphere."

The Times Weekly Review endorsed the rationing of weapons testing but expressed doubt that nations could reach agreement on the subject. "The danger is that rationing will always be supported by the power that believes itself to be temporarily in the lead and opposed by those which hope by the next experiments to catch up."

The Economist took issue with Prime Minister Anthony Eden's decision to carry out next year's hydrogen bomb tests as scheduled. "Britain's aim seems to be to get its own series of tests over and done with before any rationing system enters into force. This sets a bad example to other countries and may well make it more difficult to reach an agreement."

Science and the Citizen, August 1957

Fallout

THE views of U.S. scientists on fallout were aired and debated in eight full days of hearings before the Joint Congressional Committee on Atomic Energy last month. In general the witnesses agreed that the atomic weapons tests carried out so far have not released enough radioactivity to menace the world's present or future population to any substantial degree. But there was disagreement among the scientists on how dangerous further testing would be.

The argument turned chiefly on the question of "permissible" levels of exposure and the effects of very small amounts of radiation. Is there a "threshold" dose of radioactivity below which there is no biological damage? If so, tests could continue with safety until that level was approached. But if the effects merely decrease proportionately with the dose, then any permissible figure is a compromise that admits some damage. The hearings dealt with three effects of radiation: hereditary defects caused by mutation of reproductive cells; leukemia and bone cancer caused by strontium 90, and shortening of life caused by irradiation of the body as a whole. The witnesses generally agreed that radiation causes some genetic damage however small the world-wide dose. But they split on the other two effects. Some believed that there was almost certainly a threshold; others, including most of the geneticists, argued that even small doses could produce body damage.

The latest estimates on the total fallout to date were reported by workers engaged in the Atomic Energy Commission's project for determining its amount and effect, which is called "Project Sunshine." They said that significant levels of general radioactivity have accumulated only in the immediate vicinity of the test sites. In some inhabited areas in Nevada a person living constantly out of doors would have been exposed to four roentgens of radiation over the past four years—about equal to the average dose a person accumulates from natural background radiation in 30 years. In the rest of the U.S. and the world the concern is not with general radioactivity but with strontium 90. Merrill Eisenbud, manager of the AEC's New York Operations Office, told the Committee that about one million curies of the isotope have now fallen on the earth and another 2.4 million are still floating in the stratosphere and will have fallen by 1970. The distribution is not uniform; more has fallen in mid-northern latitudes than elsewhere. In the northeastern U.S. the soil now contains 20 millicuries per square mile, and will have 45 in 1970, assuming no further testing.

The concentrations in food (mainly milk) and in human bones resulting from this soil contamination are measured in "sunshine units." A sunshine unit is one micromicrocurie (a millionth of a millionth of a curie) of strontium 90 per gram of calcium. The present maximum permissible concentration of strontium 90 for atomic energy workers is 1,000 sunshine units. For the population as a whole, the National Academy of Sciences has recommended a maximum of 100, and perhaps 50 for children. The British Medical Research Council has said that an average concentration above 10 sunshine units in children would be cause for concern.

Concentrations of strontium 90 in human bone samples are being measured by J. Laurence Kulp of Columbia University. He estimates that the average child under the age of four in North America has seven tenths of a sunshine unit in his bones, and that the world average in children up to four is half a unit. Adults have only about one seventh as much. Kulp predicted that without further bomb tests the concentration in the bones of children will rise to three sunshine units by 1970, and if tests continue at the present rate it will go up to 24 sunshine units in 50 years.

William F. Neuman of the University of Rochester calculated that, assuming 50 sunshine units was the maximum permissible concentration, no more than 2.2 megatons of fission explosions should be set off annually from now on; this would balance the radioactive decay of strontium 90 against new production at a tolerable level. The average rate of fission explosions during the past five years has been about 10 megatons a year.

Shields Warren, former director of the AEC's Division of Biology and Medicine, argued that a 10-megaton rate was safe and that this might not be "an absolute upper limit." Atomic Energy Commissioner Willard F. Libby and others agreed with him.

The witnesses' assessment of damage from fallout radiation depended on their opinion as to a threshold. Those who, like Warren, believe there is a threshold for bodily injury, held that there will be essentially no damage from a testing program continuing at the present rate. On the other hand, Walter Selove of the University of Pennsylvania estimated that current levels of strontium 90 might increase the deaths from leukemia and bone cancer by 1 per cent. This would mean an additional 100 deaths per year in the U.S. He quoted a British study which predicted that the tests already held would eventually cause 50,000 deaths throughout the world. James F. Crow, a University of Wisconsin geneticist, estimated that, at the present rate of exposure, the next generation of parents over the world will bear 8,000 gross defectives because of fallout.

Many witnesses testified that if all the bomb-testing nations turned to "clean" thermonuclear bombs, employing comparatively little fissionable fuel, the fallout hazard would become negligible. But Alvin C. Graves, test director at the Nevada proving grounds, told the Committee that there could be no such thing as a completely clean bomb: some fission energy would always be required to set off the fusion process.

The hearings were conducted under the chairmanship of Representative Chet Holifield of California. In a recent speech in the House of Representatives Holifield said: "The Atomic Energy Commission has continually given out assurances that we had nothing to worry about and yet we find, using testimony from their own experts, that there is reason to worry. . . . Obviously some control and limitation of weapons testing is now mandatory!"

Science and the Citizen, September 1957

Meeting at Pugwash

FOR six days last July, 22 scientists from 10 countries met in the hamlet of Pugwash in Nova Scotia to talk about "the perils to humanity posed by the development of weapons of mass destruction." Financed by the Cleveland industrialist Cyrus Eaton, a native of Pugwash, the conference was the culmination of an appeal for such a meeting made two years ago by Albert Einstein and Bertrand Russell.

The group included scientists from the U.S., the U.S.S.R., China and Japan. They began by agreeing to "say nothing which might seem to favor one rather than the other of the two great groups of powers into which the world is divided"; then they split into three committees, which considered (1) the hazards of the peaceful and military uses of atomic energy, (2) the problems in the control of nuclear weapons, (3) the social responsibility of scientists. The conference produced a general statement emphasizing that every possible effort should be expended to prevent war and recommending suspension of nuclear bomb tests, special attention to disagreements between small nations, which could lead to global war, and education in each country on the necessity for international cooperation.

Present at the conference, by invitation of Lord Russell, were: M. L. E. Oliphant of Australia; H. Thirring of Austria; G. Brock Chisholm and John Stewart Foster of Canada; Chou Pei Yuan of China; A. M. B. Lacassagne of France; C. F. Powell and J. Rotblat of Great Britain; I. Ogawa, H. Yukawa and S. Tomonaga of Japan; M. Danysz of Poland; D. F. Cavers, H. J. Muller, P. Doty, E. I. Rabinowitch, W. Selove, L. Szilard and V. F. Weisskopf of the U.S.; A. M. Kuzin, D. F. Skobeltzyn and A. V. Topchiev of the U.S.S.R.

Science and the Citizen, December 1958

Pugwash III at Kitzbühel

EIGHTY scientists, including 20 from the U.S. and 10 from the U.S.S.R., met in Austria from September 14 to 21 in the third of the informal conferences which began last year at Pugwash, Nova Scotia. Pugwash III, held at Kitzbühel and Vienna, had more than three times as many participants as Pugwash I or II. The conferees were guests of the President of Austria, who recently urged scientists throughout the world to get together to avert the menace of nuclear warfare. Despite its size and semi-official sponsorship, the meeting went almost unreported in the U.S. press, though both Soviet and Western European newspapers gave it considerable coverage.

Like its predecessors, the conference had as its main purpose the informal exchange of views between scientists of East and West. As one U.S. participant put it: "It helped us to understand the attitude of the Soviet scientists." Despite the fears of some participants that the meeting might become a forum for nationalistic views, the conference confined itself to technical discussions on nuclear war and disarmament, plans for international cooperation, and the drafting of a concluding statement on some of the problems discussed.

Previous Pugwash meetings had laid great stress on the dangers of nuclear testing. The Kitzbühel conference found strong confirmation for these misgivings in the recent report of the United Nations Scientific Committee on the Effects of Atomic Radiation. But they noted that biological damage from a war would be incomparably larger than from tests, especially since military considerations would make likely the use of "dirty" bombs now stockpiled by major states. "Mankind," the scientists declared, "must . . . set itself the task of eliminating all wars, including local wars. . . . Any step that mitigates the arms race and leads to even small reductions in armaments and armed forces . . . is therefore desirable." The conferees agreed that disarmament "requires measures of control to protect every party from possible evasion."

Observing that "the increasing material support which science now enjoys in many countries is due mainly to its importance . . . to the military strength of the nation and to its success in the arms race," they called on scientists to promote public understanding of the dangers and potentialities of science. "Studies and programs for the effective industrialization of [underdeveloped] countries," they declared, "would not only improve the level of living of the majority of the population of the world but would also help reduce the sources of conflict between highly industrialized powers."

Among the participants were Brock Chisholm and Sir Robert Watson-Watt (Canada); Lord Boyd-Orr and Bertrand Russell (Great Britain); Max Born (Germany); H. J. Bhabha (India); Hideki Yukawa (Japan); David Cavers, H. J. Muller, Linus Pauling, Alvin Weinberg, Victor Weisskopf and Eugene Wigner (U.S.); N. N. Bogolubov and A. V. Topchiev (U.S.S.R.).

Science and the Citizen, January 1959

Carbon 14 in Fallout

LINUS Pauling of the California Institute of Technology has calculated that radioactive carbon 14 generated in the atmosphere by nuclear-weapons tests will ultimately do more biological damage than all of the fission products combined. Writing in *Science*, he states that at the present rate of testing a single year's output of C-14 will cause 55,000 children to be born with gross physical or mental defects, and will result in 170,000 stillbirths and 425,000 deaths of embryos and newborn babies. Says Pauling: "These numbers are about 17 times the numbers usually estimated as the probable effects of fallout fission products from one year of testing." In addition, Pauling reckons that C-14 will cause as much leukemia and bone cancer as fission products, including strontium 90.

The effects of C-14 had been discounted in earlier speculation on fallout. Two years ago Atomic Energy Commissioner Willard F. Libby estimated in *Science* that a small portion of the 10 grams of neutrons produced by a 20-kiloton fission weapon would react with atmospheric nitrogen to yield 1.05 kilograms of C-14. More recently Libby has estimated that the higher neutron flux from a thermonuclear weapon would yield 7.4 kilograms of C-14 per megaton of energy release.

Basing his present calculation on these estimates, Pauling predicts that most of the harm will come in the next generation. Because carbon is a universal constituent of cells, he points out, the radioactive effect of C-14 is not restricted to certain cells, as is the effect of radioactivity from the fission products.

Libby, meanwhile, has reported progress in a research effort aimed at minimizing the effects of strontium 90. In experiments performed in his off-hours at the Geophysical Laboratory of the Carnegie Institution of Washington, he has found that potassium fertilizers have a "possible effect" in reducing the amount of strontium that plants absorb. Libby estimates that as little as 30 pounds of potassium per acre could reduce the uptake of radioactive strontium by 40 per cent.

Science and the Citizen, June 1959

Strontium in the Skeleton

A WEEK of hearings before a subcommittee of the Joint Congressional Committee on Atomic Energy produced testimony that the fallout of fission products already injected into the upper atmosphere will ultimately double the population's exposure to radiation from this source. Witnesses agreed that resumption of tests at the rate prevailing during the past five years would ultimately constitute a world-wide threat to public health. But there was dispute as to the standards of permissible exposure to fission products (especially strontium 90), and so no agreement as to the hazard created by atomic-weapons tests.

According to the General Advisory Committee of the Atomic Energy Commission, nuclear explosions totaling 65 megatons of fission energy have burdened the atmosphere with fission products equivalent to 100 pounds of strontium 90.

About 50 pounds have already fallen out, and most of the balance will come down over the next few years. Nearly three quarters of the fallout, the A.E.C. reported in a separate statement, is of Western, primarily U.S., origin. The General Advisory Committee noted, however, that the average lifetime exposure to external radiation from fallout would come to "less than 5 per cent as much as the average exposure to . . . background radiation." (The equivalent A.E.C. estimate in 1956 was 2.3 per cent.) It described internal radiation from strontium 90 in food and water as being "less of a hazard than the amount of radium normally present in public drinking water supplies in certain places in the United States."

Before the hearings began the National Committee on Radiation Protection and Measurements had issued a report downgrading the strontium-90 hazard. The Committee recommended that the permissible concentration of strontium 90 in the human skeleton might safely be doubled. At the same time the principal assumption underlying prevailing standards of permissible exposure was sharply questioned by W. O. Caster, a physiological chemist of the University of Minnesota. Writing in the *Minnesota Chemist*, he pointed out that these standards invariably assume uniform distribution of strontium in the human skeleton. Swedish investigators have shown, however, that local "hot spots" in the skeleton may contain up to 60 times the average concentration. Current standards of permissible concentration, Caster concludes, may be 60 times too high for safety. Thus an average concentration of 180 strontium units, which the A.E.C. now regards as "safe," would "double and perhaps triple a person's chances of having leukemia and place him just above the threshold for bone damage." Caster believes that the standard might well be set as low as three strontium units.

In the Joint Committee hearings Wright Langham of the Los Alamos Scientific Laboratory presented estimates showing that the average world level of strontium in human skeletons will rise to a maximum of seven strontium units in the mid-1960's. The level will be higher in the countries of the Far East because of differences in diet.

Another witness, Charles L. Dunham, director of the A.E.C. Division of Biology and Medicine, testified that strontium in the bones of young children in this country might reach an average of 10 units. Over the next 70 years, he said, this dosage could produce 3,500 to 7,000 cases of bone cancer, and perhaps twice as many cases of leukemia. He later indicated that these estimates assume uniform distribution of strontium in the skeleton.

Science and the Citizen, July 1962

The Effects of Weapons Tests

TWO reports with somewhat different points of view toward radiation from fallout (and other sources) have been published in the past few weeks. The Federal Radiation Council, a group set up to advise the President on radiation health problems, has concluded that "nuclear testing through 1961 has increased by small amounts the normal risks of adverse health effects." One of the "principal purposes" of the council's report, according to *The New York Times*, was "to help end the public confusion and fears resulting from the varying and often contradictory estimates made by individual scientists." The second report, by the National Advisory Committee on Radiation, a body that advises the U.S. Surgeon General, pointed to "important gaps within current [radiation] surveillance operations," called for improvement of "radiation protection standards" and, "most important of all," for the development of "safe, effective countermeasures against all radiocontaminants of public health importance." "At present," said the committee, "the nation's countermeasure capability is inadequately developed and largely uncoordinated. It is a serious weakness which demands prompt correction."

In the Federal Radiation Council report it is estimated that the average U.S. radiation dose for a single year from fallout due to all tests through 1961 ranges from 10 to 25 millirems (a unit designed to take into account both the physical properties of radiation and its biological effects). Natural background radiation gives a dose of 100 millirems in the same period, and the "radiation protection guide" (RPG) for the general population is 170 millirems. This last is a figure set by the council and described by the Surgeon General as "the total radiation dose in one year considered to be an acceptable risk—that is, a risk of adverse radiation effects which is judged to be low enough to be justified by the need to release radioactive materials in connection with nuclear energy operations." Over a 30-year period the fallout dose (for all pre-1962 tests) is only 60 to 130 millirems as against 3,000 from natural background and 5,000 "allowed" under the RPG.

Since even small quantities of radiation are thought to have harmful effects, both somatic and genetic, the council estimates the damage that may be produced in the U.S. population by the above fallout levels. In the next 70 years, it finds, fallout radiation may be responsible for between zero and 2,000 cases of leukemia, compared with between zero and 84,000 cases expected in the same period from natural radiation. For bone cancer the comparable numbers are between zero and 700 cases for fallout; between zero and 14,000 for natural background. As to genetic effects, the number of "gross physical or mental defects" caused by fallout in the next generation is placed at 110. For all future generations the number is 3,000, of which 2,000 are attributed to the radioactive isotope carbon 14. "Any further testing," the report points out, "will of course increase the exposure."

Not mentioned in the council's summary tables, although it is discussed in the body of the report, is the radioactive isotope iodine 131. This isotope has a short life, decaying by half every eight days. If present in fallout, however, it finds its way into the human diet through milk, and it tends to concentrate in the thyroid gland, particularly in infants. There sufficiently large amounts of radiation can cause cancer. According to the report, "doses to the thyroid [in infants] from the major past tests were estimated to have ranged from 100 to 200 millirems per year during the immediately following periods of testing," but "it is likely that there was much geographic variation and in some limited areas of the U.S. the average thyroid doses were probably many times the national average." The RPG for radioiodine dose is 500 millirems.

In testimony last month before the Joint Congressional Committee on Atomic Energy it was revealed that fallout from the recent tests carried out by the U.S.S.R. in the Arctic returned to earth much sooner than fallout from the tests conducted by the U.S. near the Equator, and that therefore iodine 131 represented an unexpectedly large fraction of the total radioactivity during the period of the tests and the weeks following. The fallout was particularly intense in the Middle Western region of the U.S., and some infants there are believed to have received as much as four-fifths of the RPG of radioactive iodine.

Largely because the half life of iodine 131 is so short, effective countermeasures are available against the effects of the isotope. These are discussed at some length in the report of the National Advisory Committee on Radiation. Infants, nursing mothers and pregnant women in a contaminated area can drink powdered or canned milk until the iodine in the area decays to safe levels. Moreover, threatened individuals can take large doses of ordinary, nonradioactive iodine, thus saturating their thyroid glands and preventing the uptake of radioactive iodine. The latter measure is not recommended for large groups but rather for a limited number of people who might, for example, be exposed in a nuclear-reactor accident.

Although countermeasures exist, clear-cut legal authority and responsibility for putting them into effect do not. This was brought out before the Joint Committee by Russell H. Morgan, professor of radiology at Johns Hopkins University and chairman of the National Advisory Committee on Radiation. If the U.S.S.R. resumes testing soon, Morgan pointed out, the dose of radioactive iodine will probably exceed the RPG in several cities, but no agency or other branch of the Government has the responsibility for countermeasures, nor has any policy been formulated on the matter.

In the case of another constituent of fallout, the widely discussed strontium 90, the Advisory Committee report says that "there are no countermeasures . . .

which fulfill all of the primary requirements of effectiveness, safety and feasibility." (Strontium, chemically akin to calcium, is deposited in bone. Because of its long half life—28 years—it continues to produce radiation during the lifetime of the affected individuals.)

The Advisory Committee concludes that the Public Health Service does not have sufficient funds to discharge its major responsibilities in the field of radiation: (1) to develop adequate countermeasures against strontium 90 and other potentially important radioactive species, (2) to expand monitoring facilities for radioactivity, (3) to speed up the detection and reporting of dangerously high levels of radioactivity and (4) to conduct the research necessary for the formulation of adequate radiation protection standards. These activities will require a budget of $25 million in the fiscal year 1962–1963 (the Administration has requested $16 million), and "increasing amounts each year thereafter until an annual budget of $100 million is reached by 1970."

Some concern about fallout was expressed by Soviet scientists also, but in the United States people knew little about it at the time. One of the more interesting comments on the situation is the following, by Andrei Sakharov:

What moral and political conclusions should one draw . . . ?

One of the arguments of those who uphold the theory of the "harmlessness" of the tests is that cosmic rays produce larger doses of irradiation than the doses from the tests. But this argument does not eliminate the fact that, to the present sufferings and deaths of the people in this world, will be added the sufferings and deaths of hundreds of thousands of more people, including those in neutral countries, also those of future generations. Two world wars added less than 10 percent to the mortality figures in the twentieth century, but this does not make war a normal phenomenon.

Another argument, well known in the literature of several countries, is that the progress of civilization, the development of technology and many other instances inevitably cause human sacrifice. Often, the example is cited of the victims of automobile traffic accidents. However, the analogy here is not accurate and neither is it justifiable. Automobile transport improves the living conditions of the people, and accidents occur only in individual cases as the result of the negligence of specific persons, who are responsible for this to the criminal law. On the other hand, accidents which are caused by the tests are the inevitable consequence of each explosion. In the opinion of the author, the unique element in the moral aspect of this problem is the complete impunity for the crime, inasmuch as, in each specific case of the death of a person, it is not possible to prove that the cause was radiation; also because of the complete defenselessness of our descendants against our actions.

Cessation of the tests will directly preserve the lives of hundreds of thousands of persons and, indirectly, will help to ease international tension by decreasing the danger of a possible nuclear war, which is the principal danger of our epoch.

That quotation is from a contribution by Sakharov to a collection of articles on fallout from nuclear tests written by a number of Soviet scientists.* At the time, Sakharov enjoyed the favor of the Soviet government (he is reputed to have been a leader in Soviet H-bomb program) and the Soviet government then favored ending nuclear tests. When the Soviets resumed testing in 1961 after a pause of almost three years (as is discussed in Section 4) he protested, and by 1964 he was no longer in the government's favor.**

Two articles summarizing much of what was known in 1959 about some of the effects of radiation on human beings are reprinted in this section. They are taken from the September 1959 issue of *Scientific American* which was devoted in its entirety to the subject of "Ionizing Radiation."

The first of these articles, entitled "Ionizing Radiation and the Whole Animal," is by John F. Loutit, a radiobiologist and an M.D. whose other advanced

**Soviet Scientists on the Dangers of Testing Nuclear Weapons.* Moscow, 1959.

**According to an interview of Sakharov published in *Newsweek*, Nov. 13, 1972, page 55.

degrees reflect experience that encompasses several fields. He was director of the Radiobiological Research Unit of the Atomic Energy Research Establishment at Harwell, England from 1947 until 1958, shortly before the article was published. At that time, Harwell was one of the two principal applied nuclear research centers in the United Kingdom, the other being at Aldermaston. The article discusses the effects of radiation on whole animals, including particularly man. It takes up, *inter alia*, the important and difficult question of "threshold" effects, that is, the question of whether very low radiation doses applied to very large populations produce proportionately the same effects as larger doses to individuals. He does not reach a definite conclusion. Unfortunately, even today, more than a decade after the article was written in 1959, the matter is still uncertain and controversial.

The second article, entitled "Ionizing Radiation and the Citizen" was written by George W. Beadle. At the time he wrote the article he was head of the Biology Division at the California Institute of Technology in Pasadena. He received the Nobel Prize in Medicine in 1958 for his work in the biochemistry of genetics. Subsequently he was appointed President of the University of Chicago. His article discusses the hazards of radiation from all sources then considered important, including bomb tests, and raises questions about what public policy toward these hazards should be. At one point he writes that nuclear testing is the first way in which the actions of one nation have altered "the global environment in a manner clearly harmful to others." Since that time other actions causing harm to the environment on a global scale have been discovered, but I believe it is true that radioactive fallout is the one that can be said to have given first evidence of global environmental damage.

After these two articles, the section concludes with a review by James R. Newman of Linus Pauling's book, *No More War!* Both the review and Pauling's book demonstrate the kind of combination of intelligence and informed passion that apparently had to be focused on the matter in order to attract sufficient attention to it before some action would result. The next section will deal with the most important political consequences deriving from realization of the fallout episode: the first successful steps toward arms control and disarmament.

Ionizing Radiation and the Whole Animal

The cells of the whole animal form an interconnected society, making the effects of radiation more difficult to trace. Some effects are apparent; others can only be inferred indirectly

JOHN F. LOUTIT
September 1959

What the effects of ionizing radiation are on the living cell was the topic of a September 1959 article titled "Ionizing Radiation and the Living Cell," by A. Hollaender and G. E. Stapleton [SCIENTIFIC AMERICAN Offprint 57]. An organism such as a mouse or a man consists of course of many cells. But such an organism is much more than that. It is a society of specialized and interdependent cells. What happens when a society of cells is exposed to ionizing radiation? Even if we knew exactly how each of the cells is affected, we could not answer the question for the organism as a whole. Radiation damage to one organ can disturb the functioning of another. The cooperative action of cells and tissues in a many-celled organism profoundly complicates the primary effects of radiation. Given time, this action can also mitigate or reverse some of the effects.

There is a great deal we do not know about these processes, and our ignorance has more to do with fundamental biochemistry and physiology than with radiation. Obviously more investigation is needed. Meantime ionizing radiation produced by human activities raises problems that may affect all the organisms that now inhabit the earth. These problems must be appraised with the help of the biological and medical tools currently at hand.

The range of the problems should be clearly understood at the outset. At one extreme we are concerned with doses of radiation large enough, and delivered quickly enough, to produce detectable effects in an individual organism. Here there are symptoms for the physician to perceive, tissue changes for the pathologist to examine or for the chemist to analyze.

At the other extreme we have to do with doses so small or so slowly delivered that their direct physiological effects, if any, are too faint for us to recognize. In such cases we can try a statistical approach; for example, we irradiate a large number of mice and try to find out whether more of them develop leukemia than do an equal number of nonirradiated animals. In the absence of statistical data for small doses, as is usually the case for human beings, a dubious form of extrapolation is sometimes attempted: If a dose of 500 rads (defined in terms of absorbed energy) of mixed gamma rays and fast neutrons from an atomic bomb appears to cause 3,500 cases of leukemia per million people exposed, then one ray of X-rays should cause seven cases. Such a calculation has an appealing simplicity. It is easy for the layman to understand and may even be tempting to the nonmedical investigator. To those who have investigated the complex problems of cancer, however, the simple computation seems unwarranted. It is in this area, therefore, that much

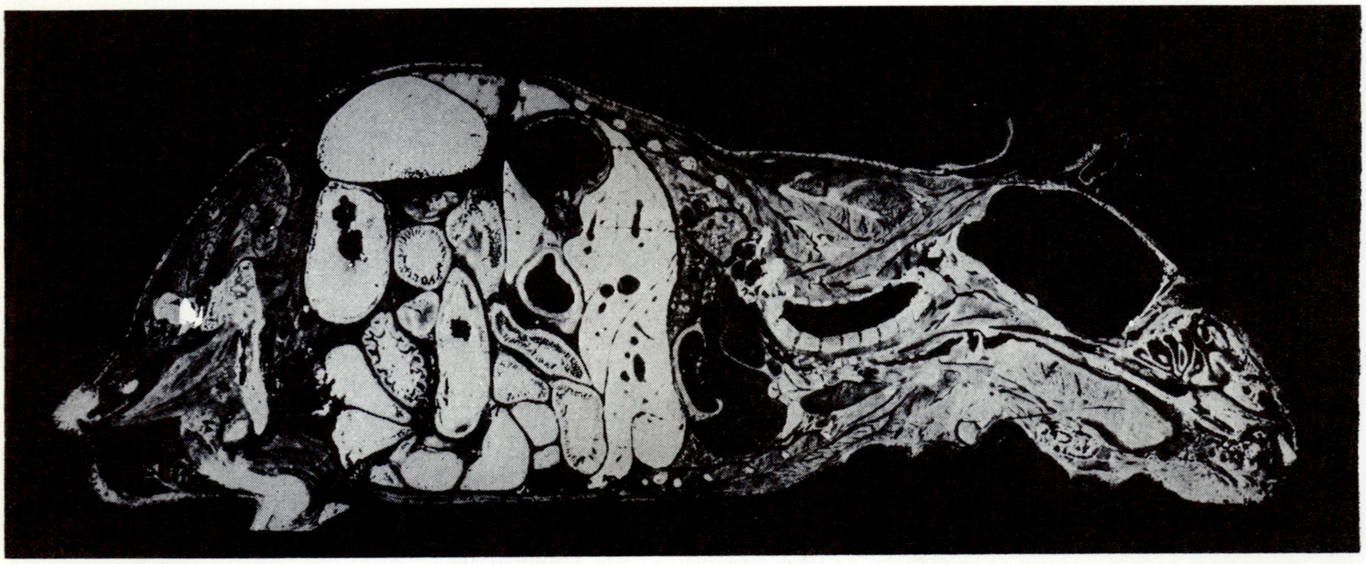

RADIOAUTOGRAPH OF MOUSE given radioactive tetracycline shows that distribution depends on biochemical behavior of the molecules to which radioactive atoms (in this case tritium) are attached. Here the concentration was greatest in liver, kidneys, lymphoid tissue and skeleton. The autograph, by Torsten André, was made by placing section of mouse on photographic plate.

WHOLE-BODY IRRADIATION OF MICE is carried out at the Oak Ridge National Laboratory in this room. The cylindrical shielding-can on the floor contains a cobalt-60 source. The animals are placed in their cages on racks above and around the source.

misunderstanding arises. We shall have more to say about the matter later. Let us begin, however, by considering the more apparent effects.

Enough radiation will kill any organism. An overwhelming dose kills instantly; a smaller, but still lethal, dose causes death within hours, days or weeks. Organisms vary widely in their sensitivity to radiation—much more widely than the cells of which they are constituted. In general, the more complex the organism, the more vulnerable it is. It takes about 20,000 rem to kill a snail, a few thousand to kill a lizard, a few hundred to kill most mammals.

Furthermore, individuals of the same species react differently. Because of this variation we frequently use as a measure the dose that is lethal to 50 per cent of the individuals exposed, abbreviating it as LD_{50}. The "acute LD_{50}" (the single dose that will be fatal to 50 per cent of the exposed individuals within 30 days) for man is 300 or 400 r for 250-kilovolt X-rays; for monkeys, about 500 r; for mice, about 600 r [*see top chart on page 90*]. Immature and senile animals are more sensitive than young adults.

These figures refer to a single burst of radiation delivered to the whole body. As might be expected, much higher doses are tolerated when only a part of the body is exposed. Here the effect will depend on the amount and kind of tissue that is irradiated, its vulnerability to radiation and its role in the economy of the organism. A man could absorb a few hundred rads in his hand, say, with virtually no effect on his body as a whole. However, an equal dose to the abdomen would have serious consequences. Moreover, the rate at which radiation is received has a great deal to do with its effect. A much larger quantity of radiation can be tolerated if it is divided into small fractions and delivered at intervals than if it is administered all at once. By dividing and spreading the dose radiotherapists can treat cancerous tissue with thousands of rads without excessive damage to the patient.

What happens to the body of an animal when it receives a dose of radiation in or near the lethal range? The most critically sensitive tissues are the lining of the intestine and the bone marrow and lymphoid tissues that manufacture blood cells. Intestinal damage causes the body to lose water and salts. If the dose is big enough, say two or three times LD_{50}, the injury is irreversible and death follows in a few days. At smaller but still lethal doses the situation corrects itself and the most serious problem becomes the loss of blood-manufacturing tissue. Death is now delayed for several weeks. It may be due directly to anemia, or to infection following the destruction of white blood cells.

Accompanying these specific effects, whether or not they are severe enough to be fatal, is a generalized reaction called the radiation syndrome. Its first manifestation is radiation sickness, characterized by nausea and vomiting, usually together with a profound lassitude. Subsequently the patient may bleed from the gums or nose, and after 10 days or so may lose some hair. The initial radiation sickness does not seem to depend on damage to specific organs. It follows whenever too much tissue receives too big a dose, whether accidentally or deliberately, as in cancer therapy. The whole clinical picture suggests a general intoxication. Presumably substantial masses of tissue break down, releasing into the general circulation substances that are normally bound within the cells. But even in 1959 this explanation remains a hypothesis subject to further research. No one has thus far identified the toxic substances.

Is there any treatment for these acute reactions to exposure? So far as the radiation syndrome is concerned, we cannot hope to find a specific treatment until we

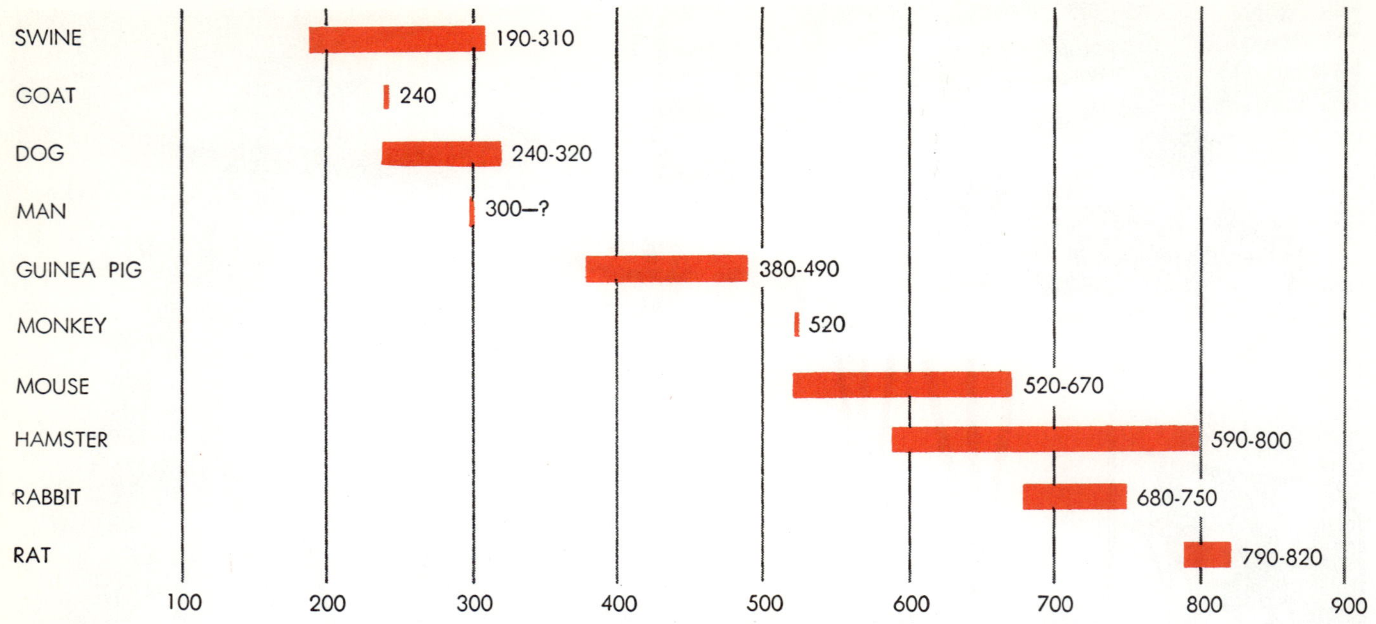

ACUTE LD50 (the single dose of radiation that will kill 50 per cent of the exposed individuals within 30 days) has been estimated for various mammals in a number of experiments. The sharp values for the goat, man and monkey reflect limitations in the amount of experimental data rather than precise knowledge. The figure for man is subject to considerable uncertainty. The dose unit in this chart is a biological measure called the rem. As used here the rem is roughly equivalent both to the rad and the r.

DISTANCE FROM CENTER (METERS)	DOSE (REM)	PERSONS EXPOSED	CASES OF LEUKEMIA
UNDER 1,000	1,300	1,241	15
1,000-1,499	500	8,810	33
1,500-1,999	50	20,113	8
2,000-2,999	2	32,692	3
OVER 3,000	0	32,963	9

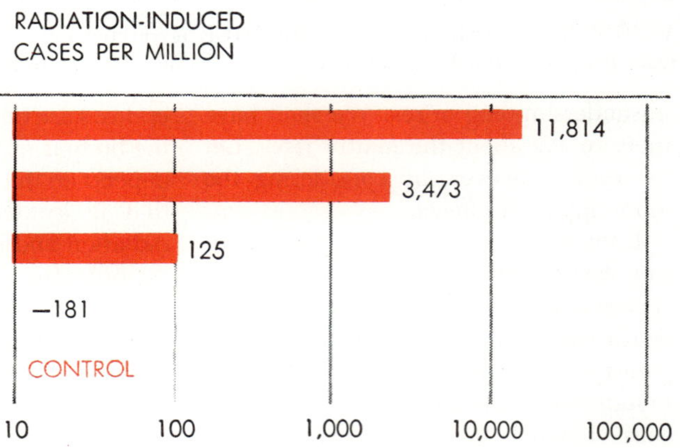

HIROSHIMA SURVIVORS within 2,000 meters of the point above which the atomic bomb was exploded developed more cases of leukemia than in the general population. Bars show incidence (per million people) attributable to radiation for the period 1950–57.

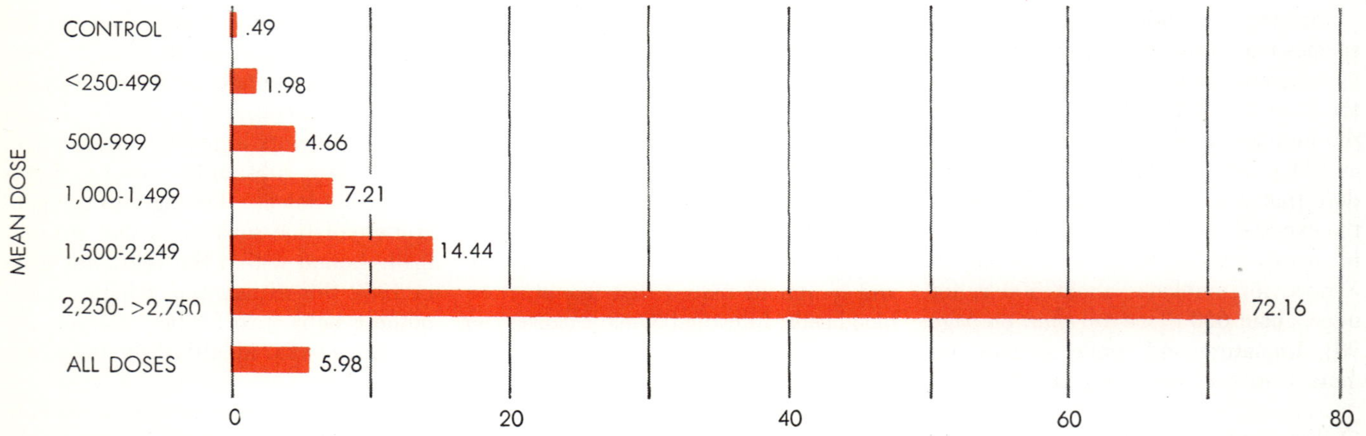

FRACTIONATED DOSES OF X-RAYS to the spines of British patients suffering from an arthritic disease called ankylosing spondylitis also produced an increased incidence of leukemia. Bars show number of cases of leukemia per year per 10,000 men.

have a clearer picture of its cause. We do know that rest and proper diet promote recovery. Antibiotics help control infection. As to intestinal damage, no method has yet been found to assist the body's own repair mechanisms. The situation is more hopeful, however, in the case of the blood-forming tissues.

Ten years ago Leon O. Jacobson, then at the University of Chicago, showed that mice whose blood-manufacturing system had been destroyed by a lethal dose of radiation could be kept alive by implanting or injecting normal blood-forming tissue from healthy animals. Subsequent investigation has proved that this tissue acts as a functioning graft in the irradiated mouse. Under ordinary circumstances this could not happen; the host would become "immune" to foreign tissue and reject it. But the same radiation that affects the blood-forming system also destroys the capacity to produce an immune response. Thus it seems that the cells of the donor actually repopulate the bone marrow and the pulp of the spleen, where blood cells are manufactured, and in addition the lymphoid tissue responsible for immunity.

Whether the procedure would be equally effective in man is not certain. It happens that the dose of radiation necessary to inactivate the mouse's immunological system permanently is very nearly the same as the lethal dose. In the dog, however, it is considerably greater than the lethal dose, and in man it may also be greater. Even so, tissue transplants can be of some help. This was demonstrated recently after an accident at a nuclear reactor in Yugoslavia. Several persons exposed to intense radiation were treated in Paris. The French physicians judged from biological reactions that five of the Yugoslav workers had received lethal doses, and gave them transfusions of normal bone marrow. Four of the patients improved dramatically and eventually recovered. Subsequent studies showed that the marrow grafts were not permanent, and possibly did not include the lymphoid system. Apparently the irradiation had blocked the immune response of these individuals for a limited time only, and had not injured their blood-forming system beyond repair. Temporary acceptance of the foreign cells gave time for the repair to operate.

In addition to seeking cures for radiation damage, we should like to find ways to prevent or reduce it in the first place. At present this is only a hope. As other authors have pointed out in other articles, ionizing radiation produces many of its effects indirectly, by form-

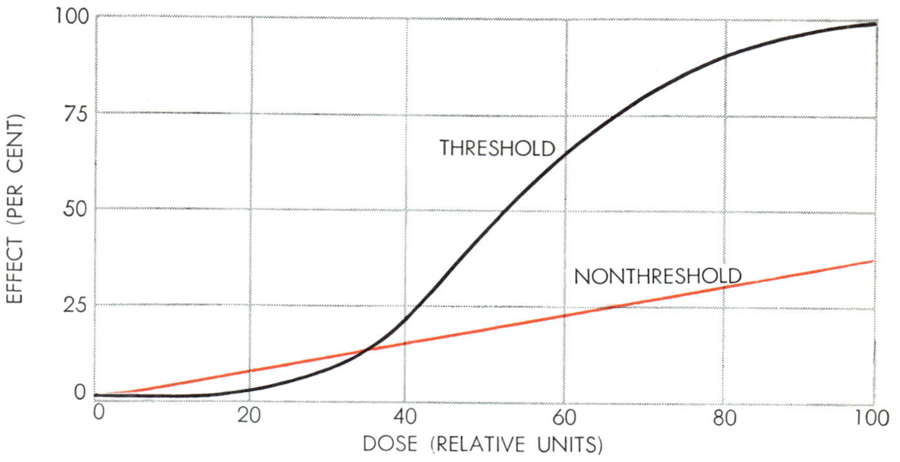

EFFECT OF RADIATION can be of two types, threshold or nonthreshold. In the former case small doses produce no detectable effect, shown by the fact that the S-shaped curve runs along the baseline for some distance before turning upward. In the latter case any dose, no matter how small, has some effect. In practice the shape of the curve is often uncertain.

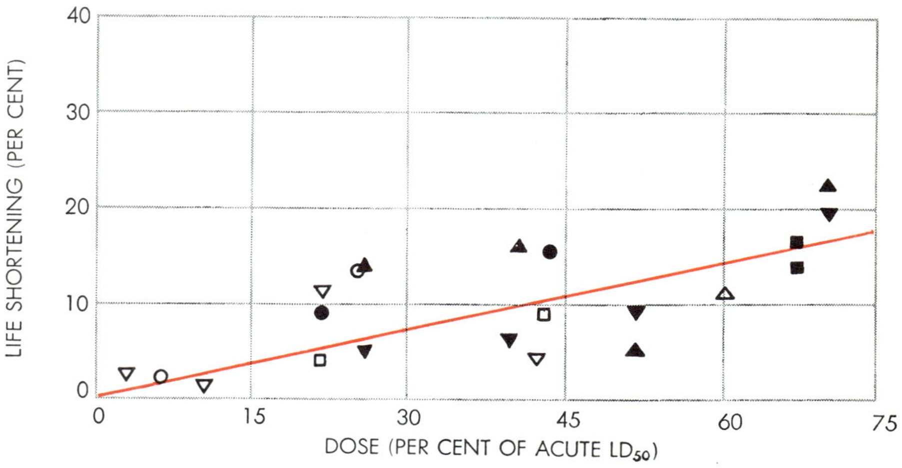

SINGLE DOSES of radiation have shortened the lives of mice and rats in a variety of controlled experiments. The effect may have no threshold. Acute LD_{50} is the dose fatal to 50 per cent of the subjects in 30 days. Various symbols represent data from different experiments. This graph and the one below, as well as the charts on page 90, are based on the 1958 Report of the United Nations Scientific Committee on the Effects of Atomic Radiation.

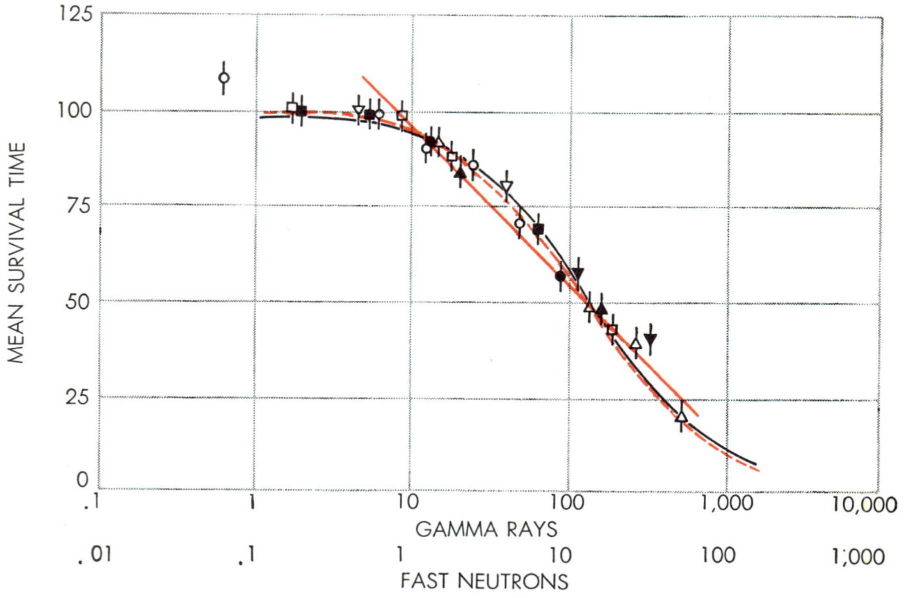

WEEKLY DOSES of fast neutrons or gamma rays have also shortened the lives of mice and rats. Three curves appear to fit the data almost equally well. All indicate that there may be a threshold for the life-shortening effect when small, repeated exposures are involved.

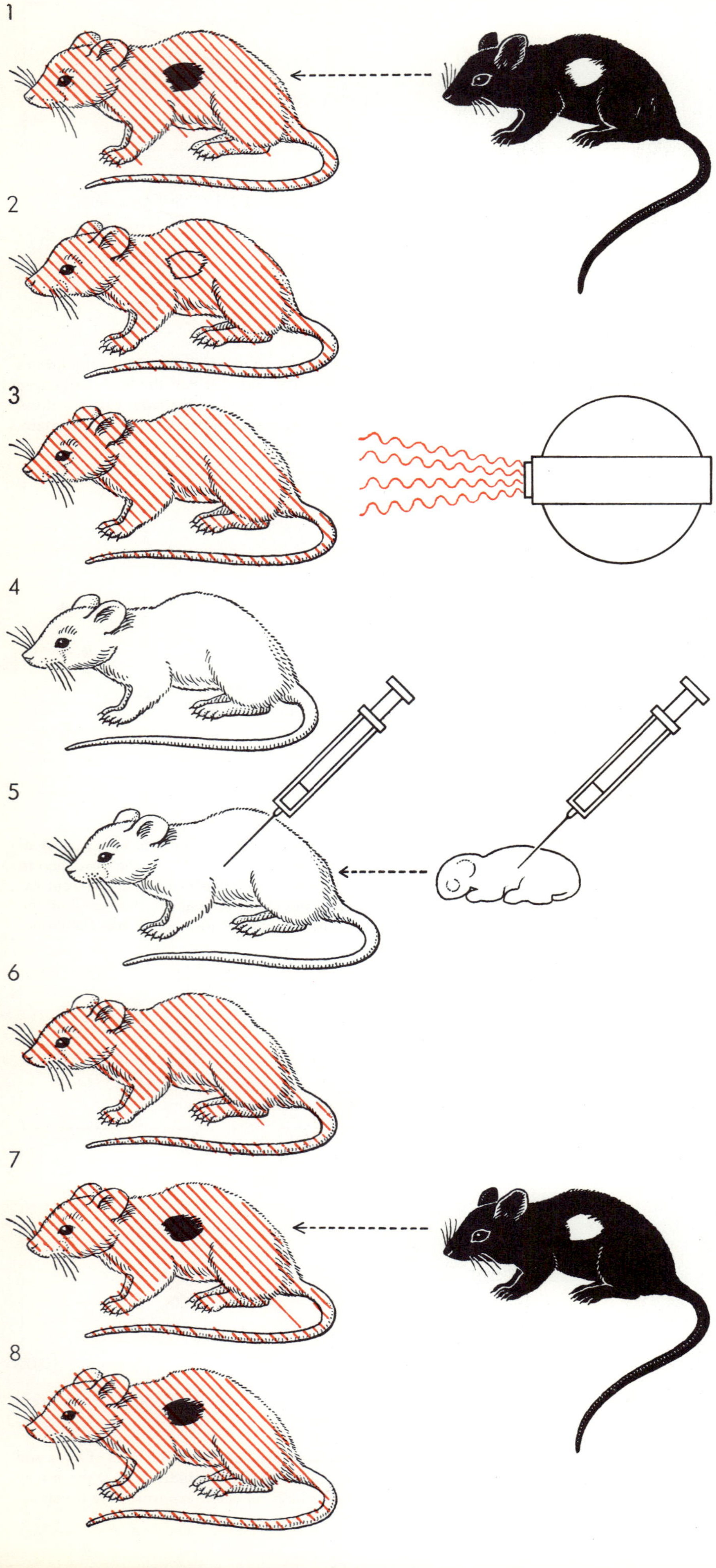

ing free radicals and peroxides. In individual cells it is possible to reduce these effects several-fold by cutting off the oxygen supply or by adding certain substances. Only some of the substances can be used on intact animals. Most of them are toxic, and even in limited doses lower the body temperature profoundly. They do seem to give some protection against radiation, but how they operate is uncertain. Possibly they reduce the supply of oxygen in radiation-sensitive tissue, but other physicochemical mechanisms have also been proposed. In any case, none of them has practical value as yet.

Thus far we have been speaking of the immediate response of the organism as a whole to a massive dose of radiation. This is only part of the story. Some effects manifest themselves more slowly, appearing months or years after exposure. Furthermore, repeated doses that are too small to produce any immediate reaction may eventually have an effect. Many of the early workers in radiation learned this by fatal experience.

Radiologists, then working with low-voltage X-ray machines, were exposed to radiation of low penetrating power. They absorbed most of their dosage in the skin. After a time they developed superficial lesions that resembled a sunburn but were much slower to appear and to heal. When the burns did heal, they left permanent scars. And the process of repair often carried with it further long-term changes. Years later many of the scars became cancerous.

Those researchers who dealt with more penetrating radiation also suffered delayed effects. As might be expected, most of the injuries were to the blood-forming tissues. Death from anemia and its complications was not uncommon. And as with the skin, so with the bone

TISSUE TRANSPLANTS that would be impossible in normal mice will "take" in irradiated animals. In the experiment represented schematically at left, skin from a mouse of one strain is grafted onto a normal animal of another strain (1). (Colored hatching indicates that animal has functioning blood-forming tissue.) The graft is rejected (2). Mouse is given a lethal dose of radiation (3), which destroys its blood-forming tissue (4) and the tissue responsible for its immune reaction to foreign grafts. Blood-forming tissue from the liver of a fetal mouse is injected (5), the blood-building system is restored (6) and the mouse recovers. The irradiated animal will also accept a foreign skin graft (7 *and* 8).

marrow. If the original injury repaired itself, malignant changes later led in a number of cases to leukemia.

This disease, in which the blood-forming tissue produces too many white cells, takes several forms in man. It can be acute, leading to death shortly after its appearance, or chronic but ultimately fatal. Two different types of white cell, known as granulocytes and lymphocytes, may be involved. Chronic lymphoid leukemia, the incidence of which increases with age, has not been shown to be induced by radiation. But there is good evidence both from the early radiologists and from more recent experience that chronic granulocytic leukemia and various types of the acute disease have followed overexposure to radiation.

The atomic bomb explosions at Hiroshima and Nagasaki undoubtedly increased the incidence of leukemia among survivors who were within a mile or so of the explosion center [*see middle chart on page 90*]. These people received doses of from 50 to 1,300 rads, presumably to the whole body. Intermittent exposures of parts of the body can also cause the disease. A British study has documented this in a group of men suffering from an arthritic spinal disease known as ankylosing spondylitis, or "poker back." The patients had been treated with X-rays concentrated on the spine, the total dose varying from 250 r to more than 2,500 r. Again the subsequent incidence of leukemia was substantially greater than that for the general population [*see bottom chart on page 90*]. On "a working hypothesis that, for low doses, the incidence of leukemia bears a simple proportional relationship to the dose of radiation," the authors of the study concluded that a dose of 30 to 50 r to the whole marrow would be likely to double the natural incidence of leukemia.

According to a recent report from the University of Oxford, the human fetus is very much more sensitive in this respect. The Oxford investigators studied the fetal history of children who had died of leukemia or other forms of cancer before the age of 10. A preponderance of these children proved to have been exposed to radiation during pelvic X-ray examinations of their mothers. Such an examination gives a dose of about two r to the fetus. Those receiving it proved about twice as likely as other children to die of malignant disease before their 10th birthday.

We should note that in all these instances, including the small doses to unborn children, the radiation was received at a substantial rate. Whether very much lower dose-rates can also cause leukemia is a question to which we shall return later.

Delayed effects of radiation are also observed in bone. Large therapeutic doses (1,000 r or more) have destroyed bone tissue and led to fractures. Much of what we know about bone damage, however, we have learned from the famous U. S. case of the luminous-watch-dial painters, who were chronically exposed to radiation from within their own bodies. They had inhaled and swallowed radium and mesothorium which were used in luminous paint. From the lungs and gut these elements passed into the general circulation. Being chemically similar to calcium, they were eventually incorporated more or less permanently in the bones of the workers.

Those whose skeletons had taken up more than 10 microcuries of radioactive material suffered acute destruction of bone and marrow, and died within a few years as a result of this direct damage. (Each microcurie of radium delivers an average dose of about 30 rads per year.) For "burdens" of one to 10 microcuries the bone lesions were less acute; the affected workers lived longer, some long enough to develop bone cancers. There were very few cases of leukemia, however. At levels below one microcurie only rarely have serious changes been noted, and below a third of a microcurie no changes of significance have been observed. Some of the workers have now been under observation for as long as 30 years after their contamination.

Nuclear fission has added to the environment another bone-seeking radioactive isotope: strontium 90. Workers actively handling this material might conceivably take enough of it into their bodies to produce long-term damage. As practically everyone knows, strontium 90 has been released into the atmosphere by the testing of nuclear weapons, and small quantities of it have found their way through the food cycle into the bodies of human beings. The amounts involved, however, are very much smaller than those we have been discussing. Measurements on young children, whose rapidly growing bones incorporate strontium at a maximum rate, have shown burdens up to a few thousandths of a microcurie. The corresponding dose-rate is in the neighborhood of .01 rad per year.

Various human tissues in addition to those already mentioned exhibit special reactions and sensitivity to radiation. For example, cataracts have been produced in the lens of the eye by doses of a few hundred rads to parts of the body which include the eyes. Heavy irradiation of the lungs in radiotherapy causes a slowly developing, progressive inflammation known as radiation pneumonitis. The gonads are particularly vulnerable. Single exposures as low as 30 r can produce temporary sterility. Smaller, repeated doses have a similar effect, and larger exposures lead to permanent loss of fertility, especially in females.

In general, cells in the process of division are especially sensitive to radiation. In the adult organism division is responsible for the continuous renewal of blood cells, skin and intestinal lining and for the production of sperm. These systems, as we have seen, are among the most easily affected by radiation. As would be expected, the developing embryo (particularly at the stage where the various tissues are being organized) is liable to damage that is irremediable. Doses of 25 r or more at this stage may lead to serious malformations.

As a final comment on the detectable effects of radiation, it should be said that neither individual organisms nor their descendants seem able to develop tolerance, as is the case with some other poisons. Small doses, given steadily or repeatedly at intervals, do not increase the body's resistance to radiation, whatever else they may do.

We turn now to effects of very small quantities of radiation on the human organism. In studying the biological effects of chemical agents such as drugs, we generally use a particular type of graph to analyze the experimental data. Along the horizontal axis of the graph we measure dose on a logarithmic scale; along the vertical, the effect as a per cent of the maximum. In almost every case the resulting curve is S-shaped, running closely parallel to the horizontal axis for some distance before it turns upward. This means that below a certain dose we can detect no effect whatever [*see top chart on page 91*]. In other words, there is a threshold for the action of the agent. Not all dose-effect curves have the standard shape, however. Another possibility is a straight line running up from the zero point or from a point on the vertical axis. Such a line indicates that any dose, however small, has a measurable effect.

Now in the case of radiation effects, especially the effects of high dose rates on mammals, the lines on the graphs usually turn out to be curved, not straight. On the other hand, it has been suggested that certain effects may be of the linear, nonthreshold type. This is perhaps more likely where dose rates are low (and where experimental data are difficult to obtain).

The capacity of X- and gamma-rays to cause point mutation in germ cells has been classically considered a universally linear effect. Any dose, no matter how small, was supposed to yield its proportionate share of mutations. Now, as has been mentioned by A. Hollaender and G. E. Stapleton, studies at the Oak Ridge National Laboratory indicate that the matter is not so simple. The mutability of the germ cell varies with its stage of development, and at some (but not all) stages the mutability may apparently change with dose rate.

Potentially valuable sources of information on the effects of low dose rates are to be found in human populations living in areas with a relatively high background of radiation. Such populations exist in parts of Kerala, in southern India, where the soil contains unusually large concentrations of thorium. It would be most desirable to compare the records of vital statistics for these people with records for similar groups living in regions of normal background-radiation. As yet, however, the necessary records are not in existence.

Lacking direct evidence as to very low dose-rates we can only fall back on the scanty records of human beings whose occupations have exposed them to intermediate but uncertain quantities of radiation, and on inferences, carefully drawn, from animal experiments. What can we say about leukemia, one of the radiation effects for which a linear relationship has been suggested? U. S. radiologists, but apparently not their British colleagues, have suffered a significantly higher death rate from the disease than have appropriate controls. Their total exposure is unknown, but it must have been intermittent, not uniform over the body, and received at substantial dose-rates.

Leukemia is a spontaneous disease of animals other than man. Mice are subject to both the lymphoid and the granular types; the former is more common. A suitable course of whole-body irradiation will greatly increase the incidence of lymphoid leukemia in mice: Given a series of intermittent exposures at high dose-rates, nearly 100 per cent of experimental animals will die of the disease. On the other hand, my colleague R. H. Mole has found a different situation at lower dose-rates. The induction of leukemia in mice receiving a total of 1,000 r in the same over-all period varies from the substantial, when the dose is given in fractions at a high rate, to the negligible when given continuously at a low rate. Such experiments lend support to the concept of a threshold; they are certainly at variance with a linear relationship unrelated to dose rate.

Another matter that has received a good deal of attention is the possibility that small doses of ionizing radiation may shorten life. Of course a person who dies of leukemia or bone cancer has been cut off before his time. But it is suggested that, in addition to such obviously lethal damage, radiation can cause a nonspecific reduction in longevity. It may accelerate the process of aging throughout life, or hasten the onset of senescence.

As always, we have very little evidence concerning human beings. A study of a few years ago indicated that U. S. radiologists die younger than other medical workers. However, upon further analysis the age distribution within the two groups proved to be different. The radiologists were generally younger, and the age of death of curates is notoriously less than that of bishops. British radiologists, an even smaller population than those in the U. S., live a normal term. Those of the earliest generation had a high rate of skin cancer, as one might expect. But there is no evidence of a nonspecific reduction in their life span.

Many investigators are working on the problem with animals. In some experiments the subjects are given single doses of various sizes and their subsequent term of life compared with that of nonirradiated controls. In others the animals are exposed at regular intervals starting at various ages and continuing for the rest of their lives. On the whole, a single irradiation appears to shorten the life span by an amount proportional to the dose; that is, the effect appears linear. However, in animals receiving daily irradiations of varying amounts, the results tend to exhibit a threshold. No significant change has been measured in mice that were subjected to five rads or less per week.

In any event all such results should be interpreted with the greatest caution. So far as nonspecific aging effects are concerned, we must be certain that the pattern of death is the same for the different experimental groups. For instance, if one scheme selectively produces a crop of radiation-induced leukemias where another does not, a comparison of the two sets of data will prove little about nonspecific aging. Until we know more about the causes of death in the various populations, the pathologist like myself profoundly distrusts those who juggle numbers. Still more does he distrust those who attempt to translate the results of animal experiments directly to man. A man is not a mouse multiplied in size, life span and other biological characteristics. Each has its own racial character. At best the mouse is a model; it can easily become a siren. Experiments with mice can elucidate principles that may apply to man, but they cannot by themselves supply numbers to put into a human equation.

Since time is a factor for which there is as yet no substitute, many of our questions are likely to remain open for generations. Meanwhile we can say that dose-rates 1,000 times greater than background produce no demonstrable shortening of life in mice. Radiologists of a former generation probably took as great a dose with no decrease in life span.

Each advance in man's power over nature has brought with it an element of danger. Atomic energy is no exception. Consciously or unconsciously we adopt a policy of acceptable risk in every facet of our lives. Society must decide what risk it will accept in the development of atomic energy; the scientist must make clear the potential gains and losses.

Thus far, as we have seen, the limits of risk are not completely outlined, and research continues on the biological effects of ionizing radiation. Some problems, such as life-shortening, may not be solved completely for a long time. Others we are liquidating more quickly. Among these we might mention the accurate measurement of dose, particularly from internal sources, and the determination of the relative effectiveness of various kinds of radiation.

In the meantime we continue to explore the beneficent possibilities of nuclear fission and other aspects of radiation. Certainly we should proceed cautiously, within limits that seem reasonable in the light of expanding knowledge. If one microcurie of radium causes only minor effects in the body, and a third causes none that we can observe, is it not reasonable to set .1 microcurie as a limit for occupational exposure? If external radiation 1,000 times background produces no apparent damage, is not 50 times background an acceptable risk for radiation workers, as has been recommended? Perhaps the figures will need revising as time goes on. But they seem to be adequate guideposts for the present.

Ionizing Radiation and the Citizen

How can mankind secure the demonstrated benefits of radiation and minimize the hazards that attend it? The question assumes that the species will not exterminate itself in a nuclear war

GEORGE W. BEADLE

September 1959

In a few short years the science and technology of nuclear physics have come to affect the lives of all men. As the authors of the preceding chapters in this book have made abundantly clear, the nuclear age is attended by unprecedented new risks and hazards.

By far the greatest hazard, as everyone knows, is the threat of nuclear war. Nuclear weapons could bring civilization to a catastrophic end. Yet no one seems able to find a workable formula for avoiding this danger that is at once foolproof and acceptable to all nations. To many men the complete abolition of nuclear weapons is the only sure solution. This must remain an unrealistic hope until ways are found for extending the ban to armed conflict itself. What is to prevent nations that have not renounced war from rebuilding their armories of nuclear weapons?

In their failure to settle their differences by peaceable agreement the major nations are engaged in a mad nuclear arms race. Each hopes to deter potential enemies by the threat of instantaneous and annihilating retaliation. All know the danger of the game. None appears to see how to stop in a manner that will guarantee security for all.

Meanwhile the hazard of nuclear armament becomes progressively more grave. Existing weapons are more widely dispersed, and the responsibility for using them is delegated to lower ranks of command. The risk of accident or poor judgment increases correspondingly. In the recent report issued by the American Academy of Arts and Sciences (*The Nth Country Problem: A World-Wide Survey of Nuclear Weapons Capabilities*) it is made clear that at least a dozen nations, in addition to the Big Three, have economic resources and manpower sufficient to arm themselves with these weapons. Will they not be tempted to enter the race in increasing numbers for national prestige if not for defense? Can they be dissuaded by any real hope of a just and effective solution? Failing this,

UNITED NATIONS SCIENTIFIC COMMITTEE on the Effects of Atomic Radiation meets periodically. A U. S. representative at this March, 1959, session was Shields Warren (*at left, chin in hand*), who guided study of casualties at Hiroshima and Nagasaki.

can they be convinced that they will be better off if they do not join the competition? It is true that capability of small-scale retaliation is a highly vulnerable intermediary position along the road to full retaliatory power. But will this argument carry conviction, coming from nations that have already arrived at the latter stage, or think they have?

The only practicable solution may lie in a pedestrian step-by-step approach. Certainly the present attempts to effect a permanent ban on the testing of nuclear weapons deserve full support, if only because this is the sole first step that appears to have a reasonable chance of acceptance.

Termination of the tests, which have increased exponentially in number for 14 years, will eliminate one nuclear hazard. The hazard of fallout is quantitatively

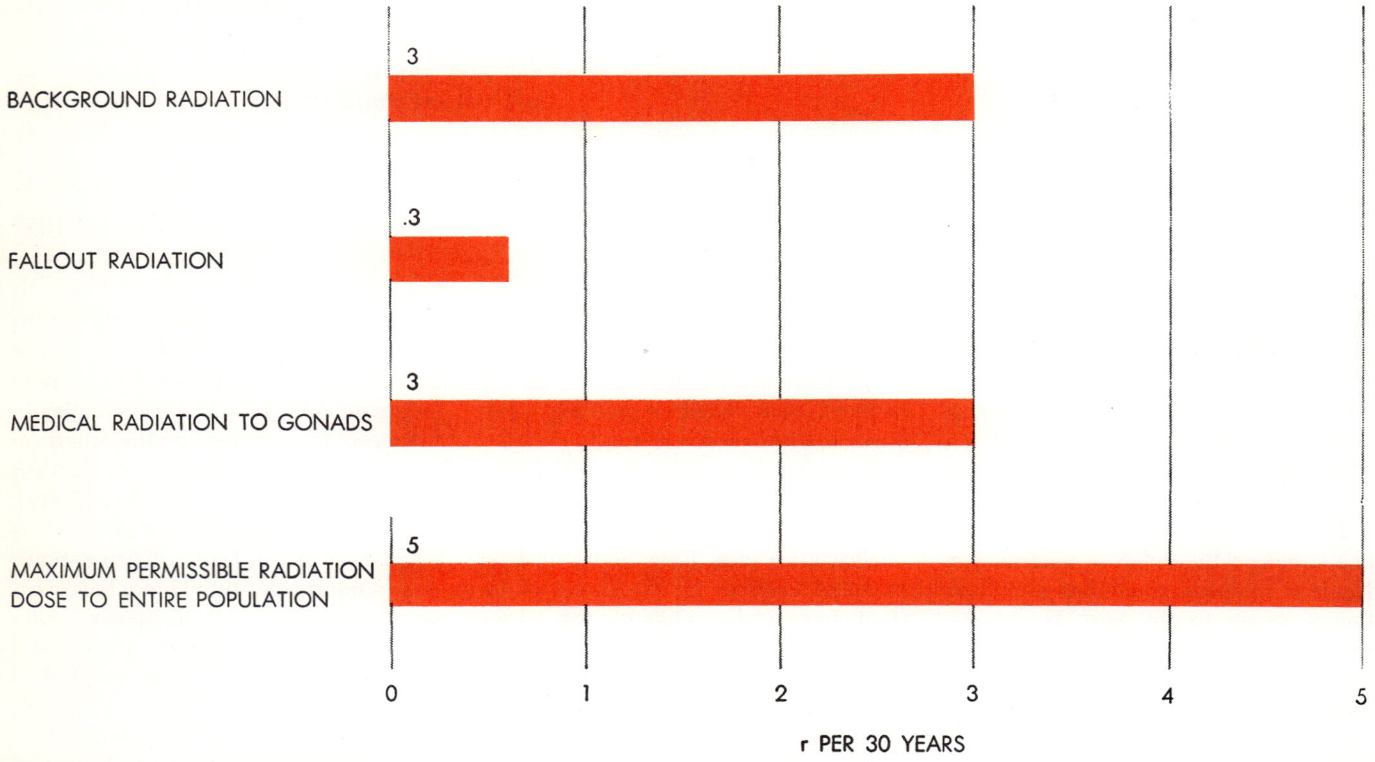

ESTIMATED RADIATION DOSE for average U. S. resident during reproductive years is represented by top three bars. Fallout estimate applies only if nuclear weapons tests cease. Permissible dose at bottom is in addition to medical and background doses.

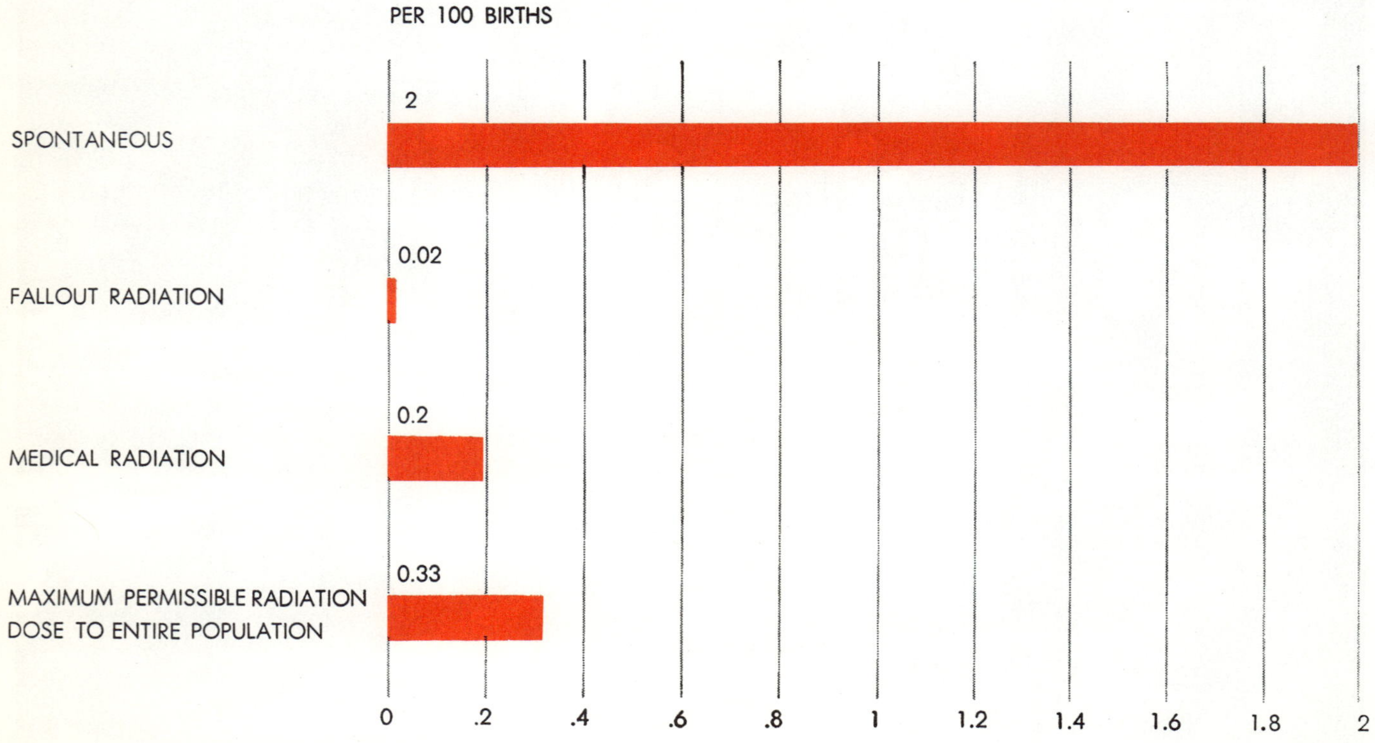

INDIVIDUALS BORN WITH NEW MUTATIONS, per 100 births, and causes of mutations are charted at left. At far right are totals of new mutations. Background radiation is responsible for some of the spontaneous mutations. All the figures on this chart are very

small but qualitatively large, because of its embarrassing moral aspects. In addition, the mere fact of agreement will encourage negotiation on other issues.

But even if we succeed in taking this step and all the ones that must follow to achieve permanent peace, we will by no means be done with the hazards of radiation. We will have greatly reduced the risk of exposing large segments of the world population to high-level radiation. But there will remain the delayed effects of fallout and the increasingly important hazards of the peacetime uses of radiation. Power-reactor accidents may occur, as they already have; the radioactive by-products and spent fuels of reactors will need to be contained and safely disposed of; radiation and radioisotopes will be finding wider use in technology as well as in scientific and industrial research. The medical profession must continue its evaluation of the risks attending diagnostic and therapeutic irradiation of patients and its efforts to reduce these risks to the essential minimum.

What are the hazards to health of ionizing radiation and how great are they in given situations? After the millions of words that have been written and spoken there remain much uncertainty and confusion in public understanding. Why is it not possible to give simple answers to straightforward questions?

We are told at various times and by investigators of repute that fallout does no biological harm; that there is some damage but that it is negligible with respect to our defense needs; that present fallout levels, by producing several hundred thousand genetic mutations per generation on a world-wide basis, do enormous biological harm. Whom shall we believe?

We read in a reputable scientific journal that present and foreseeable levels of strontium 90 in human bone are unlikely to produce a single case of leukemia. But in another issue of the same journal we find it argued that the concentration of strontium 90 may already be approaching harmful levels in the bones of some individuals and may well be responsible for hundreds of new cases of leukemia in the next generation. Is there a "right" answer?

Should school children be given annual X-ray examinations? The truck continues to make its rounds and many schools still request its services. Do the advantages outweigh the risks?

In occupational exposure to ionizing radiation, is there a zone of greater danger as exposure approaches "permissible" levels? "Permissible" implies no risk, but the maximum permissible occupational exposure is several hundred times larger than fallout exposure per given period. Is this not inconsistent with the statement that even low exposure—as from fallout—produces mutations?

To arrive at sensible assessments of radiation hazards it is necessary to understand the reason for the conflict in opinion and information. Such assessments are imperative; the health and survival of hundreds of thousands of individuals are at stake. As for succeeding generations, if we now seriously underestimate genetic hazards, the harm that is done will persist, in some degree, for centuries to come. Nor can we postpone decisions until we have final and complete answers.

It is not in the nature of science to give final and complete answers. The probability is that there will always be diverse, tentative or contradictory answers to fundamental scientific questions. The best that can be hoped is that responsible citizens will make a greater effort to understand the knowledge at our disposal at any given time and to comprehend the social implications of this knowledge. To place this knowledge in the perspective of public policy it will be useful to summarize here the biological aspects of the situation.

Whole-body exposure of man to penetrating ionizing radiation in large doses of 400 to 600 or more r units delivered over a short period of hours or days causes cell and tissue damage so extensive that successful repair may be impossible. Death results within days or weeks, the interval depending on the exposure. On the other hand, the same amount of radiation received over a much longer time, say months or years, permits such recovery processes as the replacement of cells by the division of still-viable cells and the successful resorption and elimination of breakdown products. Consequently the individual may survive and show little direct evidence of injury.

The chance of death after exposure to lethal radiation doses may be greatly reduced by certain therapeutic measures now under development. Of these the replacement of blood-cell-forming tissues by means of bone-marrow transplantation is one of the most promising. Nonlethal doses of something like 100 r units given at one time produce immediate damage, but it is to a considerable extent reparable. Such symptoms as change in the number and proportion of blood cells of various types, subcutaneous bleeding and loss of hair provide means of estimating exposure where this is not otherwise known.

In experimental animals, the mouse for example, sublethal doses of radiation appreciably reduce the life span. It is almost certain that this also occurs in man. Most investigators agree that there is no threshold below which ionizing radiation has no effect on living matter. On the other hand, some believe that there may be a minimum effective dose or dose rate for particular effects such as life-shortening, as John F. Loutit points out in the preceding chapter. Unfortunately the quantitative relation between the degree of exposure and the reduction in longevity is difficult to determine even in experimental animals. If the relation is linear—that is, directly and simply proportional to exposure—down to low levels of radiation, and if the reduction of longevity in man is proportionately the same as in the mouse, the life-span reduction per r of total-body exposure could be something like one to 10 days.

In mice and in men heavy radiation-exposure increases the incidence of various forms of cancer. Radiologists and heavily irradiated survivors at Hiroshima

IN U. S. PER YEAR PER 4,000,000 TOTAL BIRTHS	IN WORLD PER YEAR PER 80,000,000 TOTAL BIRTHS	IN WORLD PER GENERATION PER 2,400,000,000 TOTAL BIRTHS
80,000	1,600,000	48,000,000
800	16,000	480,000
8,000	160,000	4,800,000
13,000	270,000	8,000,000

rough estimates, and are subject to at least a five-fold uncertainty in either direction.

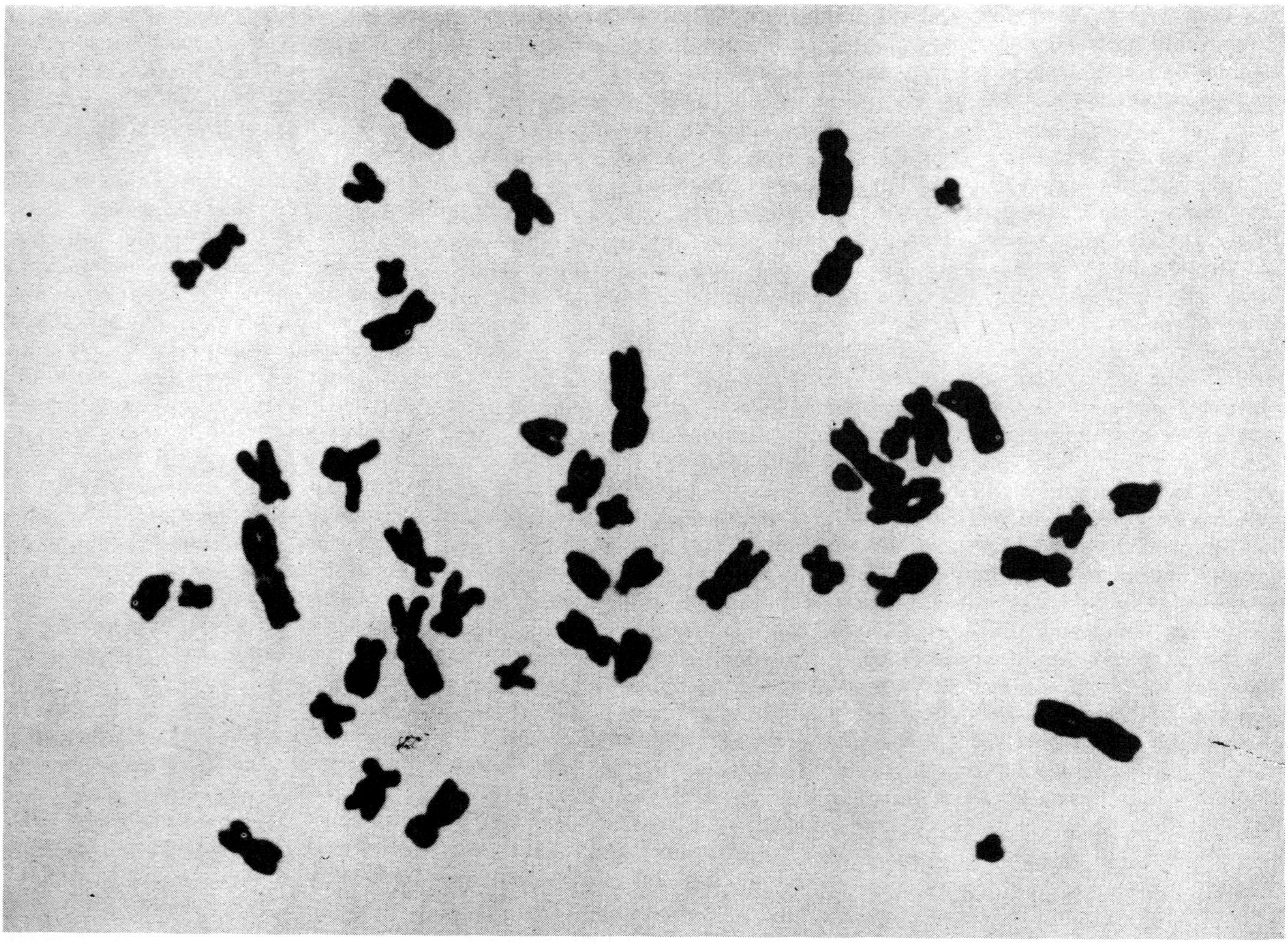

HUMAN CHROMOSOMES are enlarged some 2,000 diameters in this photomicrograph made by J. H. Tjio and T. T. Puck at University of Colorado Medical Center. The chromosomes are from a female body cell grown in tissue culture. There are 46 of them.

and Nagasaki, for example, show an incidence of leukemia 10 or more times higher than that of roughly comparable but unexposed individuals. Here again the exact relation between dose and incidence is not known; measurements are subject to large sampling errors. Even in mice the data are ambiguous. It may well be that the relation differs for different types of malignant disease. The most pessimistic assumption holds that the relation of disease to exposure is linear down to the lowest possible doses, and that the effect of intermittent and slowly delivered radiation is strictly cumulative. If this is the case, the probability that a person will develop leukemia appears to be approximately one in one million for each r of exposure per year. There is some evidence that prenatal exposure results in an even higher incidence of leukemia per r during the childhood years.

In several respects the genetic hazard is the most difficult and serious aspect of the problem of radiation. Genetic mutations are almost always harmful. Transmitted to descendants, they may express themselves over many successive generations.

It is now almost certain that in all cellular organisms (and in some viruses) molecules of deoxyribonucleic acid (DNA) bear the primary hereditary directions for the numerous processes that interact in development and function. Thus in man the DNA molecules in the chromosomes of the fertilized egg-cell are believed to carry the specifications by which the egg cell grows into an individual.

These specifications are "written" in a kind of molecular code; its basic symbols are the four kinds of units called nucleotides. Genetic directions are somehow spelled out by the sequence of these units, of which there are about 200 million in the 46 chromosomes of a human body-cell. Each grouping of 1,000 or so units of DNA is called a gene; each gene "tells" the body how to conduct some vital function; for example, how to assemble the proper amino acids (from the 20-odd kinds available) in the proper sequence to make an essential protein constituent of hemoglobin.

The individual's total DNA code is multiplied many times in the course of his life cycle and is ultimately passed on to the next generation. The details of this replication process are beginning to be understood; in fact, the process will proceed under relatively simple conditions in a test tube. Its precision is high. The probability of a genetically significant and easily detectable mistake during the 20 to 40 successive replications per generation is estimated at about one in a million for each gene. If there are 10,000 kinds of genes (an estimate subject to a large error), the chance that there will be a mistake of any kind in a given egg or sperm is only about one in 100.

Such mistakes are, like typographical errors, changes in the sequences of symbols in the code. The replication of DNA molecules is purely mechanical; therefore a sequence of incorrect symbols will be replicated as faithfully as if it were a correct sequence. Errors of this sort—

mutations—are not repaired except by the rare reversal of the process by which they occurred. There is no proofreader in the system. And such errors are likely to lead to significant errors of development or function; for example, defective hemoglobin. Since there are many ways to make hemoglobin incorrectly and only one way, or possibly a few ways, to make it correctly, mutations are much more likely to be deleterious than neutral or favorable.

If the mutant genes are replicated faithfully, with no correcting mechanism in the system, they should accumulate progressively generation after generation. Why then do species not mutate themselves out of existence? The answer is that natural selection rejects those individuals in whom deleterious mutations occur. Selection is a kind of inspector that discards the bad sets of specifications. This rejection of unfavorable mutations has been called "genetic death" by H. J. Muller. In man it may occur in many ways: death in the embryonic stage, death near or after birth, death prior to reproduction, failure to produce an average number of offspring, or failure to reproduce at all. L. S. Penrose of the University College London has estimated that in Europe and the U. S. the members of a given generation are the offspring of only 50 per cent of the members of the preceding generation. Thus "genetic death" may not mean literal premature death of individuals; it may, and frequently does, mean elimination of a particular line of descent on the instalment plan over many generations, without anyone being quite aware that it is happening.

The genes of all species, including man, are subject to varying rates of "spontaneous" mutation of which we do not know the cause. There are many ways, however, to increase the frequency of mutation, among them high temperatures, a variety of chemical treatments, and high-energy radiation. Ionizing radiation sufficiently penetrating to reach sperm and egg cells or their precursors is a particularly effective way of increasing mutation.

We may now summarize with some assurance the genetic hazard of radiation as follows: Radiation-induced mutations, like other mutations, however induced, are mostly deleterious. Under a given set of conditions, mutations appear to be induced in linear proportion to exposure; thus there is probably no threshold below which radiation will produce no mutations. Since there is no repair mechanism, once the mutation process is complete, mutations induced at different times will tend to accumulate in a line of descent until this tendency is just counterbalanced by natural selection. Ultimately, therefore, each new deleterious mutation must be compensated for by genetic death in the Muller sense.

From data on mice, fruit flies and other organisms it is estimated that the level of exposure of sperm and egg cells or their precursors to ionizing radiation sufficient to double the spontaneous-mutation rate probably lies between 10 and 100 r. Taking 30 r, the geometric mean, as a reasonable guess for the doubling dose in man, it is possible to estimate in a very rough way the number of mutations for various levels of exposure to radiation.

If there is one spontaneous mutation in each 100 egg or sperm cells per generation, as suggested above, there will be two such mutations in every 100 individuals. Exposure to 30 r would double this. The exposure from fallout to date is liberally estimated at a cumulative .3 r in the 30 years of the average human reproductive lifetime. According to this estimate, fallout would increase the spontaneous-mutation rate by 1 per cent. The mutation rate calculated in a similar way for medical radiation runs considerably higher: at 10 per cent of the spontaneous rate, as shown in the bottom chart on pages 96 and 97. The maximum permissable occupational exposure allows for an increase of more than 50 per cent over the spontaneous rate. It should be emphasized that these are exceedingly rough estimates and may be too high or too low by a factor of five or more.

Although most geneticists will agree that the foregoing statements about radiation-induced mutations are reasonably well established, and that the estimates of the number of new mutations resulting from given amounts of radiation are at least plausible guesses, there remain many unanswered questions. For example, are malignant diseases the result of mutations in ordinary body cells, as contrasted with those that occur in germ cells? Although there is sufficient circumstantial evidence to convince many geneticists that some malignant diseases are the result of mutations in body cells, the answer is in most cases not positively known. Until recently no effective techniques were available for the genetic investigation of body cells. In whatever way malignant diseases arise, however, there is no doubt that high levels of radiation induce them effectively. As for low levels of exposure, the question of exact relation of exposure to incidence must remain open until better data are available.

A difficult question is: What is the magnitude of the burden added to society by a given increase in mutation rate? Suppose, for example, that fallout were to add 5,000 to 120,000 additional mutations and perhaps five to 40 additional deaths from leukemia in each generation in the U. S. What would this mean in terms of social burden?

The answer is not known. Perhaps it cannot be, for social burden consists of diverse components that cannot be summed. The cost of caring for a mentally defective person in an institution may be calculable in dollars, but how does one assess the unhappiness and mental anguish of the victim and the victim's family? Furthermore, even though we have some notion of the manner in which genetic deaths occur, and even if we could evaluate them in terms of social burden, we still could not arrive at a proper accounting, because we do not know in what relative proportions the various kinds of genetic deaths occur. It is also important to remember that the more considerate of its unfit individuals a society becomes, the greater will be the burden of a given mutation rate. On the other hand, there is a correction of unknown magnitude for coincidental elimination of two or more unexpressed mutations in single individuals who merely fail to reproduce. What we do know with some confidence is that the social burden of mutation will be increased by radiation in approximate proportion to the increase in mutation.

In view of these uncertainties about the harmful effects of exposure to low levels of radiation, is it possible to arrive at safe "permissible" upper limits of exposure for such groups as industrial workers, X-ray technicians and the public at large? If there is no threshold, the answer is clearly that it is impossible to establish any "safe" exposure other than zero, in the sense of having eliminated all risk. The best alternative is to establish permissible levels for which risks are below specified levels. This is exactly what the various commissions and committees responsible for setting permissible exposures attempt to do. The task is not an easy one, for adequate data are difficult to obtain even with animals.

A recent study by Carol W. Buck of the University of Western Ontario will serve to illustrate some of the difficulties. Let us suppose that the relation of leukemia to radiation is linear at all levels, and that for each r of total-body exposure the annual increase in deaths from this disease is one for every million individuals. This is a value that appears reasonable for high levels of exposure. If a population were exposed prior to age 30 to an average of five r above the natural and medical background, how many individuals would have to be observed to establish a statistically significant increase in leukemia?

The answer is six million people, and they would have to be observed for a period of at least a year. In this number there would be, on the average, 30 new cases of leukemia each year attributable to the five r. This additional number, over and above the 200 cases expected without those added by radiation, would be just statistically significant. To be certain that the added radiation was responsible, there would of course have to be a control rate based on an unirradiated population similarly observed and comparable in all other respects. Even if one observed a smaller population for a correspondingly longer time, say 600,000 people for 10 years, the difficulties in meeting these requirements in human populations are formidable. They are so great that the study has not been done at this level of radiation even with an animal as favorable as the mouse.

It is obvious that we cannot for a long time arrive at better than the roughest kind of approximation in establishing permissible exposures. Right now it is difficult to see how we can improve on what the International Commission on Radiological Protection has done. This agency defines the maximum permissible dose for an individual as "that dose, accumulated over a long period of time or resulting from a single exposure, which in the light of present knowledge carries a negligible probability of severe somatic or genetic injury." It recommends that the total permissible genetic dose prior to age 30 "to the whole population from all sources additional to the natural background should not exceed five r plus the lowest practicable contribution from medical exposure."

Buck's calculations show how difficult it would be to establish whether this level of radiation to the general population would increase the incidence of leukemia by as many as five cases per million persons per year. If the entire population of the U. S. were to be exposed for generations to the maximum permissible level, it would be exceedingly difficult to exclude the possibility that the incidence of leukemia would increase by as many as 850 cases per year, or 50,000 per generation.

In addition to these difficulties, it should be remembered that ionizing radiation cannot be detected by the unaided human senses. Furthermore, overt signs of its harmful effects are often delayed for many years.

From the beginning of man's experience with ionizing radiation he has consistently underestimated its hazards. In fact, the tendency has been to underestimate not only the effects of a given exposure but often the amount of exposure as well. The exposures due to medical radiation have often been found to exceed estimates. And more recently there has been underestimation of the radiation from strontium 90 and carbon 14, two of the biologically most significant radioisotopes produced in tests of nuclear weapons. Permissible exposures have been revised downward repeatedly. Have we now reached the end? Many informed persons think not.

Incomplete knowledge thus plays a large part in public confusion and misunderstanding. It is easy to see why a qualified investigator inclined to look at the matter in the most favorable light could reasonably say that the number of persons genetically affected by fallout per year in the U. S. population might be less than 200; that the majority of these might be counterbalanced by such factors as early embryonic deaths and slight reductions in fertility; that genetic deaths of this kind would be largely undetected, even in individual cases; that the added social burden could be negligibly small. He might reason: Why worry until more compelling evidence requires it?

At the other extreme an equally qualified worker could easily feel obligated to emphasize the least favorable possibility: that fallout might well be producing as many as 800 or more new mutations per year in the U. S., or 400,000 or more per generation on a world-wide basis. On this basis he could well argue that the fallout hazard is by no means an unimportant problem for society.

It is clear that the tendency to take one or the other of these extreme positions with regard to genetic and other hazards will be strongly influenced by attitudes toward the problem of world peace. The individual who is convinced that national defense through massive build-up of nuclear weapons is at the moment the only tenable safe position will be likely to regard the development and testing of such weapons to be of such overriding importance that the uncertain, unmeasurable and possibly small damage to the population seems of relatively little importance. In contrast, another individual who is convinced that the only completely safe position will be attained through nuclear disarmament, and that we must get on with it immediately, tends to look for all possible arguments against nuclear weapons and will therefore be likely to cite the grimmer estimates.

There is no effortless way for the concerned citizen to arrive at an opinion. He must consider all aspects of the problem—risk of nuclear war included—hear all arguments, weigh all evidence and hope to arrive at a conclusion that makes sense to him. The scientist with special knowledge has a responsibility to make the facts available in as objective a manner as possible. As a citizen he has the obligation to help interpret them in terms of public policy.

The area of scientific confusion regarding radiation hazards can of course be greatly reduced by the direct procedure of adding to present knowledge. This work now engages many investigators in government agencies, industry and academic institutions. The process can and should be speeded up in all reasonable ways. Additional manpower is needed and, above all, new ideas. For example, the application of the techniques of microbiology to human-cell populations *in vivo* and *in vitro* promises a new approach to questions about human genetics. Existing manpower can be used to better advantage and at little additional expense.

Members of the medical profession are in an especially favorable position for learning about human genetics. Collectively they have occasion each year to examine millions of individuals. Unfortunately most physicians are not sufficiently well prepared to ask the right questions and make the right observations to add to the store of genetic knowledge of man. With only a little effort they could be equipped for the task. For example, medical records as kept by private practitioners, by clinics and by hospitals could be enormously improved from the standpoint of their genetic information.

In the long run more nearly adequate genetic training in medical schools will be the answer. Entirely aside from radiation hazards, this is necessary and desirable; it is increasingly apparent that the relative importance of genetic disease is great and will become greater as other diseases are conquered. Already some 160,000 infants are born each year in the U. S. with significant genetic defects, many of which constitute important medical problems.

For these reasons census procedures

and records should also be revised to encompass genetic data. A pilot study is now under way in Canada, designed to find out how this might best be done. There is every reason for other nations to consider such actions.

It is well known that unambiguous communication is difficult even among investigators in the same scientific discipline. This is true especially in the area of radiation hazards, where probability arguments are so often involved. Since the incidences of radiation damage are often very low, the evaluation of their significance usually involves statistical methods of the most sophisticated kind. Scientists, who should understand statistics, have been known to be confused about them.

Consider a specific example. Shortly after World War II geneticists were asked whether long-term studies of the survivors of the bombing of Hiroshima and Nagasaki should be made to see if evidence of genetic damage could be found. Simple preliminary calculations suggested that significant results would be hard to obtain. On the assumption that man is about as mutable per unit of radiation as the fruit fly or mouse, the detectable genetic effects would be near the borderline of statistical significance —maybe just over, maybe just under. Despite this and other difficulties the study was made, for there was both a clear obligation and an opportunity to add significantly to knowledge of the genetic hazards of radiation.

The results were pretty much as predicted: There were at first no demonstrable effects that were statistically significant. What did this mean to laymen—and, it should be added, to some scientists? The result was often taken to mean that there was no effect. The correct interpretation was that from this study alone it could not at the time be said whether the effect was zero, or as great as that expected in mice, or at a level between the two. We are not in any way justified in concluding that radiation is less effective in producing mutations in man than in mice. The data do indicate that the genes of man are not more sensitive than those of the mouse by any large amount, and that is gratifying to know.

World-wide radioactive contamination by the testing of nuclear weapons raises moral problems of a new kind. It has not previously been possible for any one nation to alter the global environment in a manner clearly harmful to other nations. A nation accused of such contamination is naturally reluctant to face the issue squarely. The temptation is rather to avoid the issue by alleging that the harm does not exist or that it is insignificantly small. Once significant harm is admitted, the issue can no longer be evaded, for morality is qualitative, not quantitative.

During war, standards shift. Mutual harm is then inflicted in the name of self-defense or rightful causes. Neutrals inadvertently caught between belligerents may then accept injury that would not otherwise be tolerated. There is a close analogy in the case of individuals. Society permits individuals to commit acts in self-defense that would not otherwise go unpunished. Again, innocent bystanders may be hurt in the process.

A large portion of the confusion that arises in disagreements about nuclear weapons results from failure of the adversaries to make clear whether they are arguing on the basis of a peacetime or wartime moral standard. Which moral standard is applicable during a cold war? Does the potential enemy follow the same standard? Although attempts to define moral standards may not help in arriving at final agreement, they may nevertheless establish that the basic issue is not one of science at all.

What should the citizen conclude about ionizing radiation? Having heard what the scientist has to say about it, and having checked a few references to be sure that what he has been told is good science, he might find the following considerations decisive in his thinking: Ionizing radiation has always been with us and will be for all foreseeable time. Our genetic system is probably well adjusted by natural selection to normal background-radiation. Added radiation will increase the frequency of mutations; most of these will be harmful. Exposure to radiation in large amounts will increase malignant disease; small amounts may possibly do the same, in proportionately lesser degree. In view of these potentially harmful effects every reasonable effort should be made to reduce the levels of ionizing radiation to which man is exposed to the lowest levels that can reasonably be attained.

As to fallout from nuclear-weapons tests, the citizen will conclude that it contributes in a small way to world-wide levels of radiation. For this reason alone the tests should be discontinued, or conducted in such a way as not to lead to atmospheric contamination. Additionally, as a hopeful first step toward a final solution of the problem of nuclear war, every possible effort should be made to discontinue the tests altogether.

Medical radiation, if properly used, is of great benefit to man. The citizen will accordingly support the investigation of ways to reduce the exposure, especially to the gonads of persons who may still reproduce, without sacrifice of clearly established diagnostic or therapeutic benefits. Radiologists estimate that progress in this direction can be expected before many years to reduce medical radiation to the gonads by a factor of five to 10—perhaps to an average value for the entire population of .5 r per reproductive generation. For the same reason exposure from industrial and experimental radiation sources should be held at minimum levels. This means that adequate shielding must be engineered into power reactors and other sources of radiation. Safe, permanent methods of waste disposal can and must be developed.

If all reasonable measures are taken, it does not seem an unreasonable hope that present levels of radiation exposure in the U. S. can be appreciably reduced —perhaps to an average level of less than one r above natural background.

With the millennium—when the citizenry has achieved sophistication in science, when wars have been abolished, when populations are stabilized at levels compatible with food supplies, when medicine has conquered the last infectious disease and corrected most genetic ailments—it may at last become essential to take a hard look at man's long-term evolutionary past and his prospects for the future.

Painful questions will have to be asked. It may become important, for example, to determine whether conquest through war, with subsequent replacement of one population by another, has been important in man's evolution. Did the conquerors differ genetically from the conquered? If so, was the effect favorable for the species (assuming that man will by then have arrived at some sensible definition of "favorable")? For the same reasons it may become essential to ask whether man's evolution has been held back because his system of controlling populations has made insufficient provision for natural selection.

Finally, assuming that medicine will have become highly successful in circumventing genetic death, will the net effect of medical practice have been unfavorable to the genetic capital of mankind? It is not inconceivable that by asking such questions man may one day find himself in the paradoxical position of searching for wiser and more humane ways than he now knows to counteract the undesirable evolutionary effects of too much success.

Preventing a Third World War

JAMES R. NEWMAN
February 1959

A review of *No More War!*, By Linus Pauling. New York: Dodd Mead and Company, 1958.

Linus Pauling's book is a powerful statement of the case for nuclear disarmament.

That war is today an insane method of solving disputes is a truth so obvious that it is hard to prove. Men are apt to acknowledge it, as they acknowledge their mortality, and then go about their business. But the proposition that we all have to die some day is not the same as that we all have to die the same day. Until now it had always been assumed that, though men were mortal, man would endure. This assumption, as Pauling shows, has become questionable.

Five chapters of his book discuss fallout. They give one of the clearest summaries of the problem I have seen. While there is considerable disagreement as to what constitutes "safe" limits of radiation with respect both to somatic and genetic injury, no responsible scientist doubts that wide "margins of uncertainty" (these words are from the United Nations report on radiation) surround all estimates. Before the subject became a hot military and political potato, it was accepted that even small amounts of radiation produce mutations, and that almost all mutant genes are bad. But because quantitative estimates of population exposure and of effects are so wide-ranging, it is easy for those who for official reasons wish to minimize the danger to becloud and confuse the issues. It cannot be foretold whose genes will be altered, or in what way, so let's all stop worrying and keep our fissionables dry.

The physicist Edward Teller, who has sought and gained wide publicity for his views, as Pauling's prime example of a public misinformer. Teller regards radiation from nuclear tests as a negligible threat to world health. World-wide fallout is, in his phrase, "as dangerous as being an ounce overweight." So far as possible genetic damage is concerned, Teller has stated that "radiation in small doses need not necessarily be harmful—indeed may conceivably be helpful." This puts fallout in roughly the same category as Lydia Pinkham's remedy. His views on radiation are of course essential to his general political position. He is convinced that the bigger the bombs the better the chance for peace. If the next war kills everyone, the world will again be peaceful; but this is not, I think, what Teller has in mind. He pins his hopes to "clean" bombs, which would leave survivors. Continued tests are needed, he says, to develop such bombs, and the tests themselves are harmless. Another reason he gives for not suspending tests is that atomic explosions can be concealed; we could never be sure therefore that an international agreement prohibiting tests would not be secretly violated by the Soviets. Because of his eminence as "father of the H-bomb," Teller's opinions have carried considerable weight. Lately their prestige has waned, Pauling's arguments having contributed to this result.

The statement that fallout is as dangerous as being an ounce overweight Pauling characterizes as "ludicrous." It is based, he says, on a gross statistical blunder and represents a 1,500-fold underestimate of the hazard. One of Teller's points is that the people of Tibet, though exposed to much more intense cosmic radiation than people who live at lower altitudes, are as healthy as we are (or, at any rate, used to be). Pauling replies that the Tibetan exposure to increased amounts of cosmic radiation should produce an increase in the incidence of seriously defective children from 2 percent—the average U.S. figure—to 2.3 per cent. But since there are no medical statistics for Tibet, Teller's statement is simply out of the blue. (He advanced it in a magazine article in order, as he said in a television debate with Pauling, merely to "quiet excessive fears.") Another of Teller's assertions is that the radiation danger to the average person is 10 times as great from luminous-dial wrist watches as from fallout. Pauling demolishes this statistic. Teller it may be felt, is better at bombs than at arithmetic.

Pauling gives examples of official misstatements. Merril Eisenbud, an Atomic Energy Commission official, wrote an article in 1955 which stated that "the total fallout to date from all tests would have to be multiplied by a million to produce visible, deleterious effects except in areas close to the explosion itself." He was later asked by a chairman of a Congressional subcommittee if he remembered how much radioactivity had fallen on the city of Troy, N. Y., following a test held in Nevada a few days before. Eisenbud estimated the amount as "something under .1 roentgen" and finally settled on .01 roentgen. Ralph Lapp, who was present at the hearing, pointed out that a million times .01 roentgen is 10,000 roentgens. Where upon one of the Senators observed that this amount would have the "visible and deleterious" effect of killing everbody in the region.

Commissioner Willard F. Libby of the AEC said in 1955 that "the fallout dosage rate as of January 1 of this year could be increased 15,000 times without hazard." This is not as cheering as Eisenbud's figure, but cheering enough. Pauling is less reassuring. He notes that 10 hours after the detonation of a small fission bomb at the Nevada test site, the level of gamma radiation at St. George, Utah, was .004 roentgen per hour, which is .1 roentgen a day. Multiplied by 15,000, this gives an exposure of 1,500 roentgens—a dose that will produce death within a few days from radiation sickness.

Pauling's own estimates of the effects of fallout are somber. He predicts an annual death rate of 8,000 if tests continue at the present rate. Moreover, 15,000 seriously defective children will be born each year whose defects must be attributed to the tests (this number does not include embryonic and neonatal deaths and stillbirths). It is possible, he admits, that his estimates are 10 times too large or 10 times too small. Perhaps then only 1,500 children will have to be sacrificed annually to the maintenance of peace; on the other hand, if the figures are too small, 150,000 children may be required. Even if no more tests are carried out, a lethal legacy of radioactive carbon 14 already released into the atmosphere will be handed on for thousands of years. According to Pauling's calculations, based to a large extent on data provided by Libby and others, the quantities of this long-lived isotope discharged in the period 1952 to 1958 will ultimately produce about one million seriously defective children and about two million embryonic and neonatal deaths, "and will cause many millions of people to suffer from minor hereditary defects." Our generation will be remembered.

When in April of last year Pauling first called attention to the menace of bomb-produced carbon 14, he was sharply criticized by three geneticists in a letter to *The New York Times* for making "erroneous" and "exaggerated" statements that "only add to the public's confusion and do not contribute to the solution of the problem." Libby dismissed Pauling's warning by saying that the effect of carbon 14 from nuclear tests "is equivalent to an increase in altitude of a few inches." But the ridicule backfired when the AEC's Division of Biology and Medicine issued a document, "The Biological Hazard to Man of Carbon 14 from Nuclear Weapons," whose conclusions agree quite closely with Pauling's. This document was unaccompanied by a press release and no enterprising reporter nosed it out. Lapp brought it to public attention in a letter to *The New York Times*.

Like Mills [C. Wright Mills, whose *The Causes of World War Three* was reviewed in paragraphs preceding the Pauling review], Pauling makes a general appeal for peace and for international agreements on the cessation of bomb tests and on disarmament. His words are a *cri de coeur*, sustained by moral authority and reason. But there is little evidence that such pleas, uttered by those who know most about the dangers involved in a nuclear war, have persuaded leaders of states of the necessity of making radical changes in their policies. The argument is often heard that those responsible for the safety of the state are in a hopeless dilemma, for even if they are sincere in wanting peace and favor disarmament it is impossible to frame enforceable disarmament agreements. If no inspection system is workable, as Teller and others have claimed, what is the practical value of test bans and treaties to outlaw weapons?

[One reply] . . . to this argument . . . is that of the noted German physicist Max von Laue. "Suppose," he said, "I live in a big apartment house and burglars attack me; I am allowed to defend myself and, if need be, I may even shoot, but under no circumstances may I blow up the house. It is true that to do so would be an effective defense against burglars, but the resulting evil would be much greater than any I could suffer. But what if the burglars have explosives to destroy the whole house? Then I would leave them with the responsibility for the evil, and would not contribute anything to it."

II
The Current State of Arms Control

SECTION 4: FIRST STEPS IN ARMS CONTROL

"Proclaiming as their principal aim the speediest possible achievement of an agreement on general and complete disarmament under strict international control in accordance with the objectives of the United Nations which would put an end to the armaments race and eliminate the incentive to the production and testing of all kinds of weapons, including nuclear weapons,

"Seeking to achieve the discontinuance of all test explosions of nuclear weapons for all time, determined to continue negotiations to this end, and desiring to put an end to the contamination of man's environment by radioactive substances, . . ."

FROM PREAMBLE, LIMITED TEST-BAN TREATY, 1963

INTRODUCTION

The most important political result of the concern about fallout was the development of the idea of a ban on nuclear tests as a separate first step toward nuclear arms control and disarmament. It was thought that subdividing the problem might make it easier to make progress toward solutions, and it seemed that a test ban would be an especially good start because of the growing public concern over fallout. Many American scientists, including the leadership of the Federation of American Scientists, supported the idea. Linus Pauling personally led a remarkably successful campaign to gain support for the idea. He obtained thousands of signatures of leading scientists on a petition calling for a test ban as a first step to general disarmament, and he even managed to carry his fight to the United Nations.

On the international scene, a humanitarian plea by Albert Schweitzer for a test cessation, and the Russell-Einstein manifesto (1955) had important impacts on world and U.S. opinions. The Russell-Einstein manifesto called for the renunciation of war in general and the abolition of nuclear war in particular, and proposed a test ban as a first step to those goals. This manifesto was signed by a group of leading scientists from England, France, Japan, Poland, and West Germany, as well as by four Americans: Albert Einstein, Percy Bridgeman, Herman Muller, and Linus Pauling. One of the direct results of the manifesto was the establishment of the Pugwash Movement, named after the site of its initial meeting in Pugwash, Nova Scotia in 1957. There, at a time when almost no other provisions for such discussions existed, leading scientists from East and West were able to discuss face-to-face the arms race and other problems of peace and war. (See the "Science and the Citizen" excerpt entitled "Pugwash," from the September 1957 *Scientific American*, in the previous introduction). The Pugwash meetings have continued nearly annually to this day.

Such a widespread attack on testing naturally called forth a reply from those who favored continued testing, who proposed two steps to mitigate the fallout problem. First came a proposal to develop "clean" weapons, that is, nuclear weapons that would produce much less radioactive debris per unit of explosive power. Proponents of continued testing said such weapons were badly needed in order to reduce the far more serious fallout problem that would otherwise accompany a nuclear war, and that since such weapons had not yet been developed and tested, the danger of fallout called for further tests in which bombs producing less fallout could be perfected. As a second means of reducing fallout, they proposed to test bombs underground whenever possible and the first such test was in fact conducted by the United States in September 1957.

By that time the worldwide public concern over fallout had led to some movement toward breaking the long deadlock over nuclear arms control. In April 1957, the Soviet Union proposed that the question of nuclear testing be isolated from other issues and settled without delay. In August the United States agreed that a test ban should be the first step to disarmament and announced it would agree to a two-year suspension of testing, provided that during the suspension the Soviets would permit the establishment of an international control system to supervise the termination of production of nuclear materials. The kind of control system that was being generally discussed at the time would have required substantial intrusions on national sovereignty. For that reason, the Soviets summarily rejected consideration of a control system just as they had rejected all previous similar proposals, and the following month they withdrew from what they called "fruitless disarmament talks."

Although the 1954 fallout episode and its political consequences had been enough to initiate a movement toward disarmament, the movement had not gained enough momentum to be effective. Then another Soviet technological surprise, *Sputnik*, created the remaining force necessary to achieve "the first step."

The Soviets had instituted a serious program to develop long-range rockets immediately following the conclusion of World War II. At first, the Soviet program, like the American program, relied in part on German personnel and equipment captured during the war or made accessible to either the Soviets or the Americans at the end of the war. Like everything else in the Soviet Union at the time, the rocket program was shrouded in deep secrecy. Even so, the U.S. intelligence community had been able to follow it in some detail at least from the time the Germans taken to Russia in 1945 started returning home around 1952. In fact, the growing knowledge in the United States of the Soviet program was one of the reasons the United States initiated a high-priority program of rocket development in 1954.

In addition to conducting their secret program, the Soviets also had publicly announced they were developing an earth satellite they intended to launch as part of the Soviet contribution to the scientific program of the International Geophysical Year to begin in July, 1957. Thus, when Sputnik was launched on October 4, 1957, it was not literally a surprise to those scientist engineers and officials in charge of the U.S. missile program, nor to those responsible for the U.S. contributions to the International Geophysical Year program.

However, for the first time the Soviets had obviously bested the Americans technologically, and at a most spectacular sort of technology to boot, and it was this irrefutable proof of Soviet supremacy that produced a strong shock in America even among those who were privy to what was going on in the field of rocket development. The majority of the U.S. population and the majority of its leaders were aware neither of the secret missile program nor of the public satellite program, and so they were stunned to an even greater degree. The initial shock produced an immediate reaction from the public, the press, the Congress, and from what President Eisenhower later, in his last public address as President, called the military-industrial complex. All demanded that the government "do something" to solve the Sputnik problem (whatever that might be) and to make sure nothing like it ever happened again.

President Eisenhower was almost as unprepared for the public reaction to Sputnik as the public had been to Sputnik itself. He met with his principal military and scientific advisers to discuss both Sputnik and the reaction to it. Among those he met with was the Science Advisory Committee of the Office of Defense Mobilization, whose chairman was I. I. Rabi. As Eisenhower later recalled it, "Dr. Rabi had another suggestion. Many policy matters coming to the President, he said, included a strong scientific component. He therefore recommended the appointment of an outstanding, full-time scientific adviser to the White House Staff." Shortly after, on November 7, Eisenhower addressed the nation over radio and TV about science and security and announced the appointment of James R. Killian, Jr. as his Special Assistant for Science and Technology. Killian, who was then President of the Massachusetts Institute of Technology, was a most fortunate choice. He had wide experience on government committees and was very well informed about both science and national security matters. In addition, he enjoyed the personal confidence of the President and his national security advisers as well as the confidence of the scientific community. Soon after, the Science Advisory Committee was expanded and elevated from the Office of Defense Mobilization to the White House Office. There it became known as the President's Science Advisory Committee (PSAC), and Killian himself became its Chairman. For the first time since World War II, a science adviser and a science advisory committee functioned in the innermost policy circles of the Executive Branch of the national government.

Prior to Sputnik, Eisenhower had relied, for advice on nuclear science affairs, on Lewis Strauss, who was simultaneously Chairman of the Atomic Energy Commission and Special Assistant to the President for Atomic Energy. Strauss had earlier been one of the strongest proponents of the H-bomb program, and later was one of the strongest opponents of a test ban. He, in turn, turned for scientific advice on nuclear science matters to Teller, E. O. Lawrence, W. F. Libby and a few others who were personally committed to nuclear testing and who strongly supported Strauss' opposition to a ban. Ironically, Harold Stassen, who was Eisenhower's Disarmament Adviser for several years before Sputnik, relied on these very same scientists to advise him about the feasibility and nature of an international control system for monitoring production of nuclear materials. In marked contrast, the new members of the new PSAC, to whom the President turned for advice on such matters after Sputnik, were not committed to a single technological approach to national security and they were able to take a more detached view of the situation. Among themselves, they had an excellent and very broad understanding of the complex issues of military security. Most important, and in contrast to most other top presidential advisers, most of the members of the PSAC, including Killian himself, shared President Eisenhower's own growing concern over the course of the arms race.

As a result, shortly after the orbiting of Sputnik, the PSAC, acting on the President's specific request, initiated a full review of the test ban question. After a study of the problem by the committee as a whole, it was referred to a special inter-agency panel chaired by PSAC member Hans Bethe. In essence, the panel was asked two questions: would a test ban be in the best interests of the national security of the United States and could a system for monitoring a test ban be created so that the risk of violation would be reduced to an acceptable level? The panel gave a positive answer to both questions. As a result, the President then proposed that an international conference of experts be convened to study the specific problem of how to monitor such a ban and to propose an acceptable plan for doing so. After a relatively brief argument over what had become a standard Soviet-American contention about the proper sequence of events (should the problem be studied thoroughly before testing stopped, or vice versa?), the conference of experts was convened in Geneva in July, 1958. The conference of experts, the ensuing political conference, the establishment of the nuclear-test moratorium in 1958, the sudden ending of the moratorium in 1961, the further conferences in 1962 and 1963, and the final achievement of the limited test-ban in 1963 are all accurately recorded in the following excerpts from the "Science and the Citizen" columns of *Scientific American*.

Science and the Citizen, October 1958

Scientific Diplomacy

LEADING scientists for the first time held an international diplomatic conference when the scientific representatives of eight nations met in Geneva to decide how to patrol the world for nuclear explosions. As diplomatic meetings go, this one went smoothly. For eight weeks in July and August the scientists discussed methods of detecting explosions from afar. In the end they agreed on recommendations to guide the statesmen convening in Geneva in September to draw up an international ban on the testing of nuclear weapons.

For the first month the scientists reviewed and evaluated possible ways of detecting nuclear explosions. They decided that a detection network should rely on four types of instruments:

1. Sensitive pressure-gauges to pick up shock waves in the air.
2. Seismographs to register ground waves generated by explosions under or near the surface of the earth.
3. Air-sampling devices to collect and analyze radioactive debris.
4. Photocells and radio receivers to pick up electromagnetic radiation.

There was then some disagreement as to how dense the detection network ought to be. The U.S. representatives, James B. Fisk of Bell Telephone Laboratories and Robert F. Bacher of the California Institute of Technology, wanted the stations to be more closely spaced than the Soviet delegates thought necessary. After about three weeks of discussion Yevgeny K. Federov, head of the Soviet delegation, yielded on this point.

The detection network finally recommended should, in the scientists' opinion, disclose a major nuclear detonation set off anywhere on earth. Very small explosions (equivalent to less than 1,000 tons of TNT) might escape notice, particularly if they took place deep underground or high in the atmosphere. The scientists envisioned a world-wide network of 180 stations: 37 in Asia, 24 in North America, 16 in South America, 16 in Africa, six in Europe, four in Antarctica, 60 on islands and 10 on ships at sea. In areas where earthquakes are rare, the stations would be spaced 1,050 miles apart; elsewhere they would be 620 miles apart. There would probably be 10 or 11 stations in the U.S., and 16 or 17 in the U.S.S.R.

The nations represented at the conference, in addition to the U.S. and the U.S.S.R., were Great Britain, Canada, Czechoslovakia, France, Poland and Rumania.

Science and the Citizen, April 1959

The Feasibility of Inspection

A PANEL on Seismic Improvement last month submitted to the White House recommendations for increasing the efficiency of detecting underground nuclear explosions. The group, under the chairmanship of Lloyd V. Berkner, president of Associated Universities, Inc., held its deliberations in secret, and its conclusions were not made public. This left as a matter of conjecture the feasibility of the inspection system recommended by an international conference of experts in Geneva last summer.

The Geneva experts had based their study on data from a single underground atomic explosion in the U.S. They concluded that a world-wide network of 180 seismographic stations would be sufficient to detect any major atomic blast. After two further test explosions last fall the U.S. announced that such detonations are much harder to distinguish from earthquakes than had been thought. According to the announcement, there would be about 10 times as many doubtful cases, requiring on-the-spot inspection, as the Geneva committee had contemplated. The reappraisal has helped to stall the current Geneva discussions of a ban on nuclear-weapons tests.

From the information made public the chief problem seemed to concern the use of "first motion" to distinguish earthquakes from explosions. The first waves that an earthquake sends through the body of the earth are compressions in certain directions and rarefactions in others. An explosion sends out compressions in all directions. Any disturbance that results in rarefactions at some of the stations can therefore be written off as an earthquake. If the source of the waves is too weak or too far from the observing station, however, extraneous vibrations will mask the nature of the first motion. Since the latest results on underground explosions indicate that they send out less energy than had been estimated, more of them will apparently fall into the uncertain category.

Some possible measures to reduce the uncertainty were discussed by Hans A. Bethe, a member of the Panel and of its parent body, the President's Science Advisory Committee, before the Senate Disarmament Subcommittee. Placing the detecting instruments in deep holes such as dry oil wells would reduce the background of random vibrations, he pointed out. Also, increasing the number of seismographs at each station to 100 would help average out this "noise." Instruments to detect surface as well as body waves would increase the amount of useful information.

Furthermore, Bethe said, the network of manned stations might be supplemented by automatic stations spaced 100 miles apart. At least one unmanned station is already operating. The U.S. Coast and Geodetic Survey office in Tucson, Ariz., has been getting regular radio reports from a seismograph sunk in bedrock 15 miles away.

Whether such an expansion of the detecting network will actually be necessary is not clear. A statement by the State Department has said that the data from the two most recent test explosions "did not invalidate the system agreed upon at Geneva last summer." According to the Federation of American Scientists, testimony before the Disarmament Subcommittee "makes it clear that the same detection capability envisioned by the Experts' Conference can be obtained with the original number of stations proposed, with some improvements in the techniques used."

Science and the Citizen, August 1959

The Test Conference

AS it began the second year of talks on stopping nuclear tests, the Geneva Conference had before it new technical data on the sorest point under discussion: the detection of underground explosions. The report of the U.S. Panel on Seismic Improvement was transmitted last month to the delegates of the three participating nations: Great Britain, the U.S. and the U.S.S.R.

Appointed by President Eisenhower and under the chairmanship of geophysicist Lloyd V. Berkner, the Panel had addressed itself to three main problems: (1) whether presently available techniques can increase the efficiency of the 180-station detection network proposed by a group of experts at Geneva last summer; (2) whether research in seismology could lead to further improvements; (3) whether it is possible to muffle underground explosions, increasing the difficulty in distinguishing them from earthquakes.

In their original proposal the experts at Geneva relied chiefly on "first motion" to separate explosions from earthquakes. The first deep traveling-wave emitted by a quake is a compression in some directions and a rarefaction in others; an explosion produces compression in all directions. Thus if both rarefactions and compressions were picked up by a net of seismic stations, the source could be identified as an earthquake. The experts estimated that there would be only 20 to 100 quakes per year with an energy equivalent to that of 5,000 or more tons of TNT that could not be positively identified. However, according to U.S. authorities last fall's tests in Nevada indicated that these figures are far too low. The probable number was said to be several thousand.

The Panel's report suggests two improvements on the original Geneva system. The first would increase the number of seismometers at each station from 10 to 100; this would make it easier to distinguish first motion from the background noise of random vibrations. The second improvement would involve using surface waves to help separate the two types of events. The peak frequency of horizontal surface-waves is said to be twice as high for explosions as for earthquakes. With these changes, the report estimates, the network of 180 stations would have about the same capability for earthquakes with an energy equivalent of 10,000 tons and over as was originally estimated for 5,000-ton events. Furthermore, a supplementary system of unmanned seismic stations spaced at intervals of 100 miles in earthquake areas would make it possible to identify 98 percent of earthquakes down to 1,000-ton events.

Seismological research, the Panel believes, would turn up several ways to increase efficiency of detection. In particular it mentions placing seismometers in holes several thousand feet deep to reduce background noise. In addition, computers might be helpful in reconstructing original wave-forms out of the disturbed patterns reaching distant seismic stations. The Panel recommends setting up a prototype detection-station where existing techniques could be tested and new ones tried out. Pointing out that all underground explosions thus far have been set off at one location, the group called for tests at other sites, using both ordinary and nuclear explosives.

According to the report, calculations show that the energy sent out by previous explosions can be cut 10-fold or more. Factors that influence the output are the location of the explosion, the type of rock in which it is set off and the design of the underground chamber. Further tests are needed to determine how effective the muffling can be.

Soviet delegates at Geneva continue to insist on the original experts' report as the basis for an initial agreement. They have steadily resisted any suggestion for increasing the number of inspections that would be necessary to establish the source of unidentified events.

In the opinion of the Federation of American Scientists, any agreement to ban nuclear tests will become more difficult if present U.S. plans for sharing nuclear weapons with NATO countries go into effect. Knowledge of the construction of nuclear devices will make it easier for other countries to undertake their own programs, the Federation says. Furthermore, if their armed forces are reorganized for nuclear warfare, these countries will have added incentive to develop their own weapons.

Science and the Citizen, September 1959

Test-Ban Developments

A GROUP of experts from the U.S.S.R., Great Britain and the U.S. last month recommended the use of satellites for detecting high-altitude nuclear explosions. Their report to the Geneva conference stated that five or six vehicles, weighing several thousand pounds each and traveling at altitudes of more than 18,000 miles, could survey the entire earth and the space around it. The necessary instruments for satellites and associated ground stations were said to require no fundamental advances in technology. However, the experts acknowledged that the system would be very expensive and technically difficult to achieve. They also proposed less ambitious schemes with orbits only 300 to 450 miles above the earth. These would leave some gaps in surveillance at lower altitudes.

As the talks at Geneva continued, the U.S. Atomic Energy Commission was reported by *The New York Times* to be "quietly preparing for immediate resumption of nuclear testing if the negotiations with the Soviet Union for a ban collapse." The preparations include the digging of tunnels in Nevada for underground explosions and maintenance work on the Eniwetok proving grounds.

The voluntary one-year moratorium on U.S. tests, which began with the Geneva talks, expires on October 31. At a recent committee hearing in the House of Representatives AEC chairman John A. McCone said he "would not continue this present type of ban" if negotiations extended beyond that date. "I would think," he continued, "that at the end of the year this policy should be very carefully reconsidered. I feel that we have been extremely patient in those negotiations and I do not think that we should find ourselves in a position of stopping testing just for the purpose of sitting at a conference table."

Science and the Citizen, October 1959

Test Suspension

AS the Geneva Conference on banning nuclear weapons tests recessed last month to await the outcome of President Eisenhower's talks with other heads of state, the conferring governments agreed to continue their existing moratorium on testing. The meetings were adjourned for six weeks from August 26 to October 12. On the day of adjournment the U.S. announced that the term of its voluntary suspension, which was to have expired on October 31, would be extended to December 31 "to allow a reasonable period of time for the negotiations to proceed following their resumption." Great Britain said that it would hold off so long as the Geneva talks showed some prospect of success. The U.S.S.R. declared that it would not resume testing unless the Western powers did. Attributing the stalemate at Geneva "exclusively" to "the positions of the Western powers," the U.S.S.R. went on to "reaffirm that it is willing immediately to sign an agreement with the U.S. and the United Kingdom on the cessation of the testing of all types of nuclear weapons for good."

The next nuclear detonation may be set off not by the existing nuclear powers but by France. That government has reiterated its intention to develop its own atomic weapons and to conduct an early test explosion in the Sahara.

Science and the Citizen, January 1960

Nuclear-Test Negotiations

HAVING agreed to join in keeping the Antarctic free of nuclear explosions, Great Britain, the U.S. and the U.S.S.R. last month resumed their efforts to abolish bomb tests over the rest of the earth. After almost a year of debate the U.S.S.R. consented to a review by a committee of experts of the technical problem of identifying underground explosions. It had previously insisted on a 180-station network, proposed in 1958, as the sole basis for negotiation, and had refused to consider U.S. data indicating that the ability of this system to distinguish explosions from earthquakes had been overestimated.

The experts began deliberations in Geneva with instructions to "consider all data and studies relevant to the detection and identification of seismic events" and to "consider possible improvements of the techniques and instrumentation." James B. Fisk, executive vice-president of the Bell Telephone Laboratories, is the leader of the U.S. delegation, which also includes Wolfgang K. H. Panofsky of Stanford University and Carl F. Romney of the Air Force Applications Center. Yevgeny K. Federov heads the Soviet team and Sir William Penney the British.

In a statement to the United Nations the U.S.S.R. reiterated that it would not resume testing unless the Western powers do so. The U.S. had formally agreed to suspend tests through the end of 1959. Henceforth, according to reports from Washington, it will be guided by the progress of the Geneva talks.

As long ago as last May the conferees had framed 17 articles of a treaty to outlaw bomb tests. While the experts were meeting they agreed on an additional measure: to set up a control organization as soon as the treaty is signed, without waiting for its ratification. Under the provisions of the treaty the three nuclear powers will be permanent members of the control commission and four places will rotate among other countries every two years. The U.S. and Great Britain have proposed that the rotating memberships be filled by one "Western" nation, one country of the Soviet bloc and two neutrals. The U.S.S.R. wants two places assigned to Communist countries.

Resolutions adopted by the U.N. General Assembly called upon the Geneva negotiators to "intensify their efforts to reach an agreement" and to continue their voluntary suspension of tests. The U.N. also appealed to other states to desist from tests. The only vote against the latter declaration was cast by France, which is going ahead with its own development of atomic weapons and plans an explosion in the Sahara. Another U.N. resolution expressed "grave concern" over the Sahara test.

Science and the Citizen, February 1960

Disagreement on Testing

THE problem of distinguishing underground explosions from earthquakes continues to obstruct progress in the Geneva talks on outlawing nuclear-weapons tests. What level of uncertainty would necessitate on-the-spot inspections to determine the source of doubtful "seismic events"? How many doubtful cases would arise through the use of the 180-station seismic-detection network proposed by a committee of experts in 1958?

A second committee of experts from Great Britain, the U.S. and the U.S.S.R., convened late last year to consider these and related questions, has left matters where it found them—with the U.S. and the U.S.S.R. at loggerheads. The group's report was classified shortly after its submission. From published excerpts and official comments it was difficult to determine how much the experts had disagreed on the political consequences of technical data and how much on the data themselves.

"The Soviets agreed on all things that make the control system look better and on nothing that makes the system look worse," said James B. Fisk of Bell Telephone Laboratories, leader of the U.S. delegation. President Eisenhower spoke of "the recent unwillingness on the part of the politically guided Soviet experts to give serious scientific consideration to the effectiveness of seismic techniques for the detection of underground nuclear explosives." "Indeed," he added, "the atmosphere of the talks has been clouded by the intemperate and technically unsupportable Soviet annex to the report of the technical experts."

This annex accused the U.S. scientists of being "on the brink of absurdity" in proposing inspection criteria that would "leave under suspicion the overwhelming majority of the earthquakes registered by the control system." It "categorically repudiated" U.S. interpretations of data from the "Hardtack" series of underground nuclear tests in 1958. According to these interpretations the ability of the 180-station network to recognize nuclear detonations would be much less than originally supposed. The Soviet experts, however, maintain that criteria can be established that would "unquestionably insure the detection of truly suspicious events, on which the control system's future activity will be concentrated." "Shortcomings" in the U.S. data, said the annex, cannot be regarded "as resulting from carelessness or coincidence," and the Soviet experts "have come to the conclusion that there has been tendentious use of one-sidedly developed material for the purpose of undermining confidence in the control system, whose basic characteristics were determined by the 1958 Geneva conference of experts."

In addition to the Hardtack results the U.S. presented theoretical studies indicating that underground explosions can be very largely muffled by "seismic decoupling," *i.e.*, setting them off in very large, hollow chambers. The theory, dismissed by the Soviet group as unproved and of no practical importance, was discussed in some detail at the winter meeting of the American Physical Society in Pasadena, Calif. A panel of physicists and seismologists reported that the disturbance set up in the solid earth by a subterranean explosion might be reduced 300 times by a sufficiently large chamber. To muffle an explosion equivalent to 100,000 tons of TNT would require a spherical hole some 3,000 feet deep and 800 feet in diameter. Assuming that such an enormous excavation could be made (it would involve scooping out a 20th as much earth and rock as was removed in digging the Panama Canal) and the factor of 300 could actually be realized, one physicist asserted, a 100,000-ton explosion "would not even be detected and located by the proposed Geneva network."

Negotiations are continuing at Geneva, but "no satisfactory agreement is yet in sight," President Eisenhower declared. As of the beginning of 1960 the U.S. feels "free to resume nuclear weapons testing," he added, but advance notice will be given of any such resumption.

Science and the Citizen, April 1960

Geneva Conference Resumes

POLITICAL representatives of Great Britain, the U.S.S.R. and the U.S. at the Geneva conference on cessation of nuclear-weapons tests have resumed negotiations after a recess of several months. They took up where the technical experts from these countries who met last December left off—debating problems of the detection and inspection of underground tests.

When the conference reconvened, the U.S. proposed a new agreement to cover only "controllable" explosions. This would have included all surface, atmospheric and ocean tests, tests in space out to great distances and all underground explosions "which cause seismic magnitude readings of 4.75 or more." Smaller explosions were to come under the agreement as means of detecting and of distinguishing them from earthquakes improved. The minimum size was expressed in terms of a seismometer reading rather than in kilotons of explosive power because "Soviet and Western scientists are in substantial agreement as to the measurement of signals but not on the equivalent kiloton yields of seismic disturbances." According to U.S. calculations the proposed reading is roughly equivalent to a 20-kiloton explosion.

The U.S. proposal was rejected by Soviet negotiators twice; once unofficially after it had been described (unofficially) in the U.S. press and again when it was formally presented to the conference. Then the U.S.S.R. made a new offer of its own. It would accept criteria suggested by the West for deciding whether a "seismic event" was suspicious enough to merit inspection. Previously the Soviet negotiators and their experts had called for technical criteria limiting much more severely the number of events eligible for inspection. Under the new offer, however, only a few of all the suspicious events could actually be inspected. The quota would be decided on the basis of political negotiations rather than technical considerations. It seemed likely that the two Western nations and the U.S.S.R. would differ widely on an acceptable quota.

A discussion of the experts' conference at Geneva appeared recently in *Bulletin of the Atomic Scientists* together with complete transcripts of the conclusions of the technical groups from the three countries. An article by Jay Orear, a physicist at Cornell University, appraised the disagreement among the experts as being due more to their purposes than to technical uncertainties. The Soviet experts originally put forth inspection criteria that, according to U.S. estimates, would leave less than one natural earthquake per year eligible for inspection. They were trying, says Orear, "to find . . . limitations that would safeguard their country from the thousands of yearly on-site inspections our country was talking about." Although they eventually dropped this demand, the Soviet experts refused to accept the criteria offered by the West, which "made eligible almost any natural disturbances that could be located."

Eugene Rabinowitch, editor of the *Bulletin*, sees some hope that a compromise can be reached on the quota problem. It will require a reduction of Soviet suspicions that inspections would in fact be espionage expeditions, and a willingness on the part of the West to be satisfied with a small chance of catching a violation; "say, one chance in 50." In any case, urges Rabinowitch, there should be more information on the degree of risk represented by clandestine testing. "American public opinion, . . . not to speak of American political leadership, . . . should be given some sober authoritative information on the possible importance of further tests, instead of vague hints that something terrible is likely to follow from clandestine Soviet testing, and something wonderful from our own resumption of tests."

While the conference continued, the U.S. announced that it is starting to build two experimental seismic stations such as might be incorporated in a control network. One will conform to the specifications recommended for the 180-

station network proposed by an earlier conference of experts in 1958. This one is located in "the central part of the U.S." and is expected to be ready this summer. The second, which will take longer to build, will include some of the refinements suggested last year by the U.S. Panel on Seismic Improvement headed by Lloyd V. Berkner.

Science and the Citizen, June 1960

The Test Ban and "the Hole"

WHEN President Eisenhower was queried at a recent press conference about the "driving force" behind his determination to reach an agreement outlawing nuclear weapons tests, he replied: "The driving force behind me is the belief that we should try to stop the spreading of this, what you might say, the size of the club. . . . As of now, I assure you, the power that exists in the arsenals, certainly of our own, and we know of Russia's, is such a tremendous thing that I don't think that testing will necessarily make destruction more likely, I mean of your enemy or of yourself. I don't mean enemy; I mean of anyone, any nation, or this one. . . . If we continue to do that [test], others are going to test in the fields we have already covered, you see, and finally there will be any number of nations that have it, and I think it ought to be stopped."

The President had just issued a joint statement with British Prime Minister Macmillan declaring their readiness to "institute a voluntary moratorium of agreed duration" on small underground tests if two conditions are met: (1) that a treaty be concluded with the U.S.S.R. to ban surface and large underground explosions and to provide for "an adequate quota of on-site inspections"; (2) that arrangements be made "for the purpose of progressively improving control methods for events below a seismic magnitude of 4.75" (equivalent to an unmuffled underground explosion of about 19 kilotons of TNT).

In the following weeks it became apparent that official U.S. opinion is not unanimous on the subjects of suspension and control. "Many responsible officials in the U.S. Government—particularly in the Atomic Energy Commission and in the Defense Department—view the decision [of the President and Prime Minister] with pessimism and alarm for several reasons," reported *The New York Times.* Joseph Alsop in the *New York Herald Tribune* quoted A.E.C. chairman John A. McCone as saying: "If their word is good, then our position of nuclear superiority is secure. If the Soviet's word is not good, the past 18 months will have given them time to catch up in nuclear weapons development. Another two or three years would place them well ahead of us." As to the advances in weapons that can be expected from further testing, they "are second only to the historic advance from the atomic to the hydrogen bomb."

The Joint Congressional Committee on Atomic Energy conducted hearings to air "the available facts" as to "various technical problems that may or may not exist in the operations of an adequate control and detection system." More than 20 scientific witnesses presented their views. Summarizing the hearings, the Committee declared: "It appears from the testimony that for the next several years at least it will not be possible to identify underground events whose seismic signals record the equivalent of a nonmuffled explosion of 20,000 tons or less, although they may be detected. Further, it appears that for this same time period it will not be possible to detect muffled tests of 100,000 tons or more set off deep underground in large cavities. Therefore, it seems that for the next several years onward there could be a race between improved means of detection and identification as against improved means of concealing and muffling nuclear tests."

Newspaper reports of the testimony emphasized that both Edward Teller, who has opposed the cessation of testing, and Hans A. Bethe, who has favored it, agreed that the original network of 180 seismic stations, proposed by an experts' conference in 1958, is now inadequate. Bethe was said to have "advocated" a 600-station network in the U.S.S.R. alone (as compared with 21 stations contemplated in the original scheme).

After the hearings an expanded U.S. program of research on seismic detection methods, known as Project Vela, was announced by the White House. During this year and next about $76 million will be spent on "increased basic research in seismology, procurement of instruments for a world-wide seismic research program, development of improved seismic instruments, construction and operation of prototype seismic detection stations, and an experimental program of underground detonations encompassing both high-explosive and, where necessary, nuclear explosions." The nuclear explosions will "produce no radioactive fallout."

In a speech before the Philosophical Society of Washington, Bethe, who is professor of physics at Cornell University and a former member of the President's Science Advisory Committee, reviewed the detection problem. He pointed out some of the practical questions raised by the large cavity: the only "reasonable" way to make it is by washing out a salt dome; this would take two and a half years and cost $10 million for a hole big enough to hide a 20-kiloton explosion; the washed-out salt could be detected in any river into which it is dumped; salt domes, especially ones accessible to rivers or oceans are not very common, and so on. Bethe concluded: "So I really think that the big hole is not quite as easy as it sometimes is represented to be."

As to his "advocacy" of a 600-station net in the U.S.S.R., he had mentioned it "only in order to show that the detection system is technically—technically, not politically—capable of dealing even with the newly decoupled shots." Such a net "would be able not only to detect but to identify explosions of 20 kilotons carried out under the extreme decoupling."

However, Bethe added, "I really think that we are all behaving like a bunch of lunatics to take any such thing as the big hole seriously. . . . The opponents of a test-cessation agreement have forced us into considering more and more, and smaller and smaller, technical details which become more and more absurd. . . . I think the problem is not a technical problem; [it is] a political problem."

At present, Bethe continued, the U.S. has "nuclear weapons of all sizes and shapes: heavy ones and particularly light ones. There is, in my opinion, very little of military value that we do not have." The U.S.S.R., being less advanced in nuclear-weapons technology, has more to gain than the U.S. from a continuation of testing. If the U.S.S.R. wished to develop small, tactical weapons, it would be better advised to accept the U.S. proposal to allow small tests rather than to undertake the necessary long series of tests clandestinely. In fact, Bethe believes, if negotiations break down, the Russians will not test small weapons but large thermonuclear weapons. "These are the ones which threaten our homeland."

The supremely important goal is to reach agreement on limitation of armaments. A test ban would constitute a first step. "We have the Russians in a frame of mind now where they are quite willing to talk about such matters. . . . But how can we expect the Russians to be willing to negotiate, or to agree to other measures of disarmament which might be more far-reaching and might be more important for the peace of the world than this one, if already in this little one, where we risk so very little, we are as sticky as we have been?"

Science and the Citizen, August 1961

N-bomb?

WITH negotiations on a nuclear-test ban stalled in Geneva, it was suggested in a number of quarters last month that the U.S. resume nuclear-weapons testing. Representative Chet Holifield of California, long a member of the Joint Congressional Committee on Atomic Energy, said the U.S. "should relieve itself" of the voluntary moratorium and start tests as soon as possible. Among the results that might be achieved he mentioned lighter warheads for missiles, better small-yield weapons and improved safety features. In addition, he declared, "concepts are now being considered by our scientists which could be as revolutionary as the H-bomb in 1949."

Holifield did not identify the concepts, but there was speculation in the press that a major one is the "neutron bomb," said to have been the "clean bomb" originally proposed by Edward Teller and his associates at the University of California Radiation Laboratory. In a recent speech Senator Thomas J. Dodd of Connecticut described the bomb as follows: "The neutron bomb could be produced by tailoring the energy of a fusion explosion so that instead of heat and blast, its primary product would be a burst of neutrons. Such a burst would operate as a kind of death ray. It would do next to no physical damage, it would result in no contamination, but it would immediately destroy all life in the target area. This, of course, would make it an ideal battlefield weapon. It would, in fact, make it a far more effective battlefield weapon than any now in existence." As for the possibility of making such a device, Dodd remarked: "Today I doubt there is a single nuclear physicist of repute who would challenge the neutron bomb from the standpoint of scientific feasibility."

According to *The New York Times*, information "pieced together" from hints "dropped over the last four years" indicates that the neutron bomb would be essentially a small hydrogen bomb in which the fusion reaction is somehow set off without a fission explosion. The fusion process releases neutrons with an energy of about 14 million electron volts. These fast neutrons have a small probability of being absorbed by atomic nuclei; hence they have high penetrating power and induce correspondingly little radioactivity in the materials, per unit of depth, through which they pass. They do, however, produce a number of high-speed secondary particles, particularly protons, by colliding with atomic nuclei. The secondary particles are responsible for the lethal effect of the neutron beam.

"There are still several unanswered technical questions about how the bomb would be built," said the *Times*. "Probably the most important is how the scientists plan to achieve the temperatures . . . necessary to ignite the thermonuclear reaction without the fission trigger." Some physicists of repute also have raised questions: whether a fissionless trigger, which so far has eluded the substantial research program in thermonuclear power, can be developed in weapons testing; whether the fusion reaction can be "tailored" to increase the output of neutrons relative to heat; whether radioactivity induced by neutrons, although much less than that from a fission bomb, would not still constitute substantial contamination; and whether resumption of testing will not help the U.S.S.R. more than the U.S.

Science and the Citizen, October 1961

More Bombs

THE first blast set off by the U.S.S.R. over Siberia last month marked the end of a hopeful epoch. For three years the major atomic powers had refrained from playing actively with nuclear fire. President Kwame Nkrumah of Ghana, addressing the Belgrade meeting of "nonaligned" powers, spoke for many aligned individuals as well when he said: "It is a shock which forcibly brings home to us the supreme danger facing mankind."

The U.S.S.R.'s avowed intention of developing rocket-carried "superpowerful nuclear bombs of 20, 30, 50 and 100 million tons of TNT" underscored the size of the potential conflagration. Big nuclear bombs are incendiary weapons: the heat radiation from the Hiroshima bomb, which was equivalent to about 20,000 tons of TNT, caused fatal burns at distances up to nearly a mile—about the same as the radius of the destructive blast. Since the effective range of radiation increases as the square root of the explosive energy, whereas blast increases only as the cube root [see "The Hydrogen Bomb: II," by Hans A. Bethe, beginning on page 56], the deadly heat of a 100-megaton bomb would reach out some 70 miles: a single bomb that flattened New York City could incinerate people from Bridgeport to Trenton, covering an area of about 15,000 square miles. Whatever the size of the weapons used—as several observers have pointed out, four 25-megaton bombs would cover the same area—the ability of men to burn up whole metropolitan regions seemed about to be realized.

Science and the Citizen, December 1961

A Hundred Million More

WITH an explosion at the end of October estimated at 57 megatons the U.S.S.R. brought to about 100 megatons the energy released in its latest series of nuclear-weapons tests (the energy equals the output of 100 million tons of TNT). The total of air explosions by all countries prior to the present Soviet series is estimated at 170 megatons, approximately two-thirds of which was set off by the U.S. and Britain and one-third by the U.S.S.R. Although it is now responsible for well over half the energy released in nuclear-weapons tests, the Soviet Union still trails in the number of individual detonations: the U.S. has carried out about 170 and the U.S.S.R. about 100.

In all pre-1961 tests, an average of 50 per cent of the yield of so-called thermonuclear devices came from fission reactions. (The devices are actually fission-fusion-fission bombs, in which a small fission charge triggers a thermonuclear reaction, which in turn sets off another fission explosion in a surrounding blanket of material.) Following the first tests in the latest series, measurements of the amount and kind of contamination in the lower atmosphere were said to indicate about the same proportion. Most of the fallout, however, will come from the two largest explosions—some 30 and 50 megatons. If these too were 50 per cent fission, the U.S.S.R. will have injected 60 per cent as much radioactivity into the atmosphere in two months as had been put there during all the rest of the atomic age. If, as some observers think likely, the Russians have succeeded in increasing the fusion-to-fission ratio in their high-yield devices, the explosions will turn out to be somewhat cleaner and the fallout correspondingly lower.

The U.S. Public Health Service has said it does not expect "dangerous" levels of fallout radiation from the tests, although the levels might occasionally reach "Range Two"—a newly established classification that calls for checks in the amount of radioactive materials entering the human food chain. One official estimated that the strontium 90 in the bones of children in the Northern Hemisphere might increase 50 per cent, but that the amount will remain comfortably below the currently accepted "maximum permissible concentration."

Elsewhere, particularly in countries nearer the high latitudes where the explosion took place, reaction was sharper. Before the big explosion the Scandinavian countries had set up emergency monitoring networks. Norway had installed radioactivity warning sirens; Britain and the Netherlands were storing food, especially dried milk; the Japanese rushed to harvest fruits and vegetables. At the United Nations, Canada's Secretary of State for External Affairs, Howard C. Green, announced that after the Soviet tests in September radiation counts in Toronto were up 1,000-fold. "The time has come," he told the General Assembly, "when it is not sufficient merely to express concern and record blame. We must find a means of compelling the countries responsible to cease the testing of nuclear weapons." The French physicist Frances Perrin said that fallout from the 50-megaton weapon could kill 10,000 persons over the next 30 years.

Science and the Citizen, January 1962

Quarantining the Atom

AS the nuclear powers resumed their deadlock at the Geneva test-ban conference, most of the nations of the world were maneuvering to keep themselves clear of the atomic incubus. Acting through the United Nations, these countries passed a quick succession of anti-atom resolutions.

First, the General Assembly voted 71 to 20 to request all powers to stop nuclear testing immediately and permanently. Voting against the measure were the nuclear powers—the U.S., Great Britain, France and the U.S.S.R.—who also declared that they would not be bound by the resolution. They were joined in the balloting by seven other Western and nine communist countries.

Next the General Assembly declared the use of nuclear weapons in war "a direct violation of the United Nations Charter." This statement was passed 55 to 20, with 26 nations abstaining and two absent. It was supported by the U.S.S.R. and opposed by the U.S., whose representative said "the Soviet Union has not the slightest intention of heeding it, despite the enthusiastic vote in its favor." At the same time the Assembly voted 55 to 0, with 44 abstaining, including the U.S., "to consider and respect the continent of Africa as a denuclearized zone," calling on member states to refrain from nuclear tests in Africa and from storing or transporting atomic weapons there.

Finally, the Political Committee of the General Assembly passed two resolutions aimed at preventing the spread of nuclear weapons. One, sponsored by Sweden, provided that no state not already in possession of nuclear weapons should acquire them, manufacture them or permit other countries to store them in its territory. The vote was 57 in favor, 12 (including the U.S.) against and 32 abstentions. The second resolution, offered by Ireland, acknowledged "the necessity of an international agreement, subject to inspection and control, whereby the powers producing nuclear weapons would refrain from relinquishing control of such weapons to any nation not possessing them and whereby powers not possessing such weapons would refrain from manufacturing them." It called for "all states, and particularly on the states at present possessing nuclear weapons, to use their best endeavors to secure the conclusion of an international agreement." Speaking on behalf of the resolution, the Irish representative told the committee "we remain firmly convinced that if nonnuclear states become one by one the possessors of nuclear weapons, war is inevitable."

Meantime at Geneva the test-ban talks got under way after time out for the Soviet test series, when the U.S.S.R. accepted a formal proposal to resume from the U.S. and Britain. Simultaneously with the proposal the Western powers declared that they would in no circumstances consent to a halt in testing, temporary or permanent, except under an agreement subject to international control and inspection. In return the U.S.S.R. proposed a new agreement in which the nuclear powers would "solemnly pledge themselves not to hold tests of any types . . . in the atmosphere, in outer space and under water." This pledge would be policed by individual states, using their own detection systems. At the same time the parties would "assume the obligation" not to test underground pending agreement on a control system. At the next meeting of the conference the negotiations appeared to be stalled as before, and the chief Western delegates announced that they were leaving Geneva temporarily. The talks were scheduled to continue, however.

Science and the Citizen, February 1962

Less Chance to Hide

IT appears increasingly doubtful that an atomic-weapons test of significant dimension can be concealed either underground or in outer space. A five-kiloton nuclear explosion in an underground salt cavern near Carlsbad, N.M., last December 10 was clearly recorded by seismographs as far away as Tokyo, New York, Uppsala in Sweden and Sodankyla in Finland. The seismograph records included tracings of the "first motion," considered critical in distinguishing between earthquakes and underground explosions. In explosions the first motion is always outward from the site of the blast. In earthquakes some seismic stations will record the first motion as an outward movement of the earth's crust and some as a movement toward the site of the earthquake, since earthquakes involve faulting and slipping rather than a uniform outwardly directed force.

During the atomic-test-ban negotiations in 1958 a number of specialists suggested that clandestine underground tests could be made virtually impossible to detect by conducting them in a large chamber. Albert L. Latter of the Rand Corporation, an author of the "big hole" theory, estimated that such "decoupling" would reduce the seismic waves from the explosion by a factor of 300 – more than enough to put large underground shots well below the threshold of the detection system under discussion at Geneva. Proponents of the big-hole possibility argued that a cavern of sufficient size could most easily be excavated by flushing a salt dome with water.

Clandestine shots in space appear to be entirely open to detection. In a report at the meeting of the American Association for the Advancement of Science, Herman Hoerlin and Donald R. Westervelt of the Los Alamos Scientific Laboratory produced figures to show that the auroral glow produced when gamma rays from a nuclear burst strike the upper reaches of the atmosphere would betray tests conducted at great distances from the earth. With the aid of a horizon-to-horizon scanner and suitable photo-multiplier equipment, Hoerlin and Westervelt said, a 20-megaton burst could be detected as much as 14 million miles from the earth, and a 100-megaton burst could be recorded at a distance of 28 million miles. Larger bursts could be monitored at still greater distances, possibly up to twice the distance from the earth to the sun.

The Atomic Energy Commission released preliminary results of its monitoring of the recent series of tests conducted in the atmosphere by the U.S.S.R. The tests proved to be "cleaner" than anticipated, with a fission yield of "about 25 megatons, out of the total yield of about 120 megatons for the approximately 50 atmospheric tests." "Of special interest," the commission said, "is the small fission yield of the 55–60 megaton test conducted on October 30." This finding indicates that the U.S.S.R. "has made advances in certain areas, especially in improving the yield-to-weight ratios of weapons in the megaton range."

Science and the Citizen, September 1962

Follow the Leader

IN the past 12 months the nuclear testing game of follow-the-leader has loosed more megatons of nuclear energy than all the explosions in the entire 17-year period since Alamogordo. The latest round began last September 1, when the U.S.S.R. broke the three-year test moratorium with a series of multimegaton atmospheric explosions. The U.S. retaliated first with a series of small underground tests and then, beginning in April, with atmospheric tests. The U.S. series was drawing to a close when in early August the U.S.S.R. started up again with a test in the atmosphere. At Geneva meanwhile the U.S. reopened negotiation of a ban on further testing of nuclear weapons, citing a "considerable amount of new data" on the problem of detecting underground tests.

U.S.-Soviet negotiations toward a test ban got under way in 1958, when scientists of the two nations drew up the specifications for the technical measures necessary to police such a ban. In particular they agreed that a network of 180 seismic stations would suffice to detect and identify any underground nuclear explosion. Soon afterward U.S. investigators reported new data indicating that the "Geneva network" would be inadequate for the identification of low-yield underground explosions or of larger shots concealed by detonation in certain kinds of geological formation or in natural or man-made caverns. The U.S. called for reconsideration of the technical agreement, and negotiations bogged down for two years.

The broad outlines of the present U.S. position were sketched by President Kennedy at his press conference on August 1. He said that "new technical assessments . . . give promise that we can work toward an internationally supervised system of detection and verification for underground testing which will be simpler and more economical" than that contemplated in previous U.S. proposals. The system would call for fewer seismic stations (perhaps as few as 80), would permit them to be manned by the nationals of the countries in which they are located and would require fewer on-site inspections by an international control agency. At Geneva these proposals brought the U.S. closer to the compromise position advanced by the eight neutral participants in the disarmament conference. The first Soviet response was negative, but the negotiation of a test ban was under way again.

Science and the Citizen, October 1962

The Test Ban

AS disarmament negotiations moved from Geneva to the U.N. General Assembly last month there was a selection of test-ban proposals on the table, but none, apparently, on which the U.S. and the U.S.S.R. could agree. The obstacle was underground testing.

The U.S. and Britain stood on two proposals. One called for prohibition of all tests, with mandatory on-site inspection of underground events certified as "unidentified" by an international commission. The other would ban tests in the atmosphere and space and under water—all of which are readily identifiable—but allow underground tests to continue.

The U.S.S.R., having turned down inspection on the ground that it is a pretext for espionage and the partial ban on the ground that it would provide a stimulus to the arms race, insisted that any test ban would have to meet one of three conditions. An across-the-board agreement would be acceptable, according to Soviet representative Vasily V. Kuznetsov, only if inspection of underground events were at the invitation of the country concerned. Alternatively, the U.S.S.R. would agree to a formal ban on the readily identifiable tests only if they were accompanied by a moratorium on underground tests until general disarmament is negotiated. In the absence of any formal agreement, said Kuznetsov, the U.S.S.R. would settle for a moratorium on all testing.

Science and the Citizen, January 1963

The Black Box

THE "black box" robot seismographic station for detecting underground nuclear explosions was placed on the table at the Geneva disarmament conference last month. This idea had been put forward by three U.S. and three Soviet scientists during the nongovernmental "Pugwash" conference in London last September. It contemplated the installation at various points in the U.S.S.R. and the U.S. of unmanned, sealed, automatic seismographic stations—enough "so that seismic events will be seen on many instruments." The records from the instruments would be turned over periodically to an international commission for inspection. The Pugwash scientists suggested that the black boxes might "provide a new basis for negotiation in the Geneva discussions and ease the problem of resolving the on-site inspection issue."

That problem has been the major point of contention in devising a policing system for underground tests, which remains the principal barrier to a treaty to end all testing. The U.S. has held out for detection stations manned by international teams and mandatory on-site inspection of any unidentifiable seismic events they detect. The U.S.S.R. has insisted that detection stations should be manned by nationals of the country involved and that there must be no obligatory on-site inspection. The neutral nations at the Geneva conference have suggested compromises involving national detecting stations controlled by an international commission, with inspections on a quota basis or by invitation of the country accused of an infraction. The Pugwash suggestion was advanced to provide "minimal interference with the host country" and "a maximum amount of completely objective seismic information," which would "substantially reduce the number of necessary on-site inspections."

Semiofficial comment from Moscow favorable to the idea drew semiofficial expressions of reserve from Washington. Then, on December 10, Soviet delegate Semyon K. Tsarapkin said his government would permit installation of "two or three" robot stations in earthquake-prone regions of the country and would permit "international personnel" to visit the stations to bring in and take out the sealed recording apparatus. This offer he said, contained "some elements" of the international control demanded by the U.S. But the U.S.S.R. still rejected any "compulsory on-site inspection." The Soviet proposal—implying that black boxes could serve in the place of manned international stations and inspection—was completely unacceptable, according to Charles C. Stelle of the U.S. delegation, although he welcomed the possibility that the U.S.S.R. was ready to discuss "precise details" of a system involving the robot stations. Other U.S. spokesmen pointed out that any Western proposal for such a system would call for hundreds of black boxes rather than two or three.

Although the two great nuclear powers had yet to find a solution to the problem of policing an underground-test ban, they found themselves under increasing pressure from the neutrals and from the United Nations to write a treaty. The mood on both sides seemed favorable: Stelle spoke of "the tenuous barriers between us" and *Izvestia* suggested that a "relatively small push" could achieve an agreement. Meanwhile the U.S. and the U.S.S.R. had each completed a major series of atmospheric tests and presumably felt no pressing need to resume in the near future.

Science and the Citizen, March 1963

Nuclear Politics

A new note of hope was injected into the nuclear testing negotiations in January by Soviet acceptance of the principle of on-site inspection. But the concession failed to bring quick agreement, and no early break in the long impasse seemed likely. At the same time both the U.S. and the U.S.S.R. were troubled by nuclear-weapons controversies within their respective alliances; the nuclear ambitions of France and Communist China were likely to complicate any progress at Geneva toward a ban on nuclear testing.

Ever since the beginning of the negotiations in 1958 the U.S. and Great Britain have insisted on inspection of suspicious seismic events to guard against the possibility of secret underground testing. At first the U.S.S.R. agreed, but since November, 1961, Soviet representatives have refused to discuss the issue, arguing that inspection was merely an excuse for espionage. Last December, during a recess in the Geneva disarmament talks, Premier Khrushchev conceded the point. In a letter to President Kennedy he said the U.S.S.R. would allow two or three inspections a year. He also confirmed the Soviet offer, made at Geneva last fall, to permit the installation of three automatic seismic stations ("black boxes") in regions of the U.S.S.R. where earthquakes occur frequently. These would be inspected periodically by an international commission for evidence of testing.

President Kennedy welcomed Premier Khrushchev's proposals but said that three inspections would not be enough. He added, however, that although the U.S. had originally demanded between 12 and 20 a year, it might now settle for eight to 10. There was a feeling of optimism as representatives of the U.S., Great Britain and the U.S.S.R. met in New York and Washington in January to pursue the matter. President Kennedy ordered a temporary suspension of underground testing and there were hints that a compromise should be possible between three and eight inspections.

Early in February, however, the Soviet representatives broke off the meetings, because, *Pravda* reported, the U.S. and Great Britain had "no intention" of ending tests. The Russians apparently objected to U.S. insistence on discussing details of the inspection system before agreeing to a specific number of inspections. The U.S. resumed underground testing and the issue was returned to the 18-nation disarmament conference at Geneva, where the U.S.S.R. expected that its concession on inspection would attract neutral support and bring pressure on the Anglo-U.S. delegates.

Nuclear power-politics was being played within each of the two great blocs as well as between them. The U.S., having got Great Britain to accept the submarine-based Polaris missile system instead of the Skybolt air-to-ground missile, hopes to make the Polaris the basis of an eventual NATO nuclear force that will forestall the development of more national nuclear forces. Turkey and Italy appeared to be willing to accept Polaris submarines in the Mediterranean Sea as a substitute for U.S. intermediate-range missiles now based on their territory. But France turned down Polaris and announced it would have its own nuclear striking force by the end of the year. On the Communist side, Moscow was reported to have withdrawn from China the Soviet technicians who had been helping to develop nuclear weapons. China was nonetheless expected to have its first atomic devices ready for testing within the year.

Science and the Citizen, April 1963

Power Politics and Nuclear Power

NUCLEAR power has become inextricably tangled with power politics, and last month the combination of the two dominated the international scene and even played a large role in the domestic politics of several countries. In Geneva the U.S. and the U.S.S.R. were still wrestling with the old and difficult issue of safeguards against clandestine underground testing. The U.S.S.R., having agreed to the principle of inspection, stood on its offer of two or three inspections a year. The U.S., having come down from its 12 to 20 a year to seven, tried in vain to get the Soviet representatives to bargain away the difference. The U.S. indicated that a spelling out of inspection procedures and the details of a "black box" automatic detection system would facilitate such bargaining; the Russians demanded initial agreement on a specific number of inspections.

While the two sides in the cold war debated how to stop testing the bomb, the Western allies were arguing among themselves about how to deploy it. France is shaping its own nuclear force, and President de Gaulle's close relation with West Germany has raised fears of a Bonn-Paris axis armed with the bomb. Under the Nassau plan agreed to by President Kennedy and Prime Minister Macmillan, Great Britain is expected to buy Polaris submarines and use them as the basis of its own nuclear deterrent. In an effort to prevent the Balkanization of Europe into rival nuclear powers, the U.S. last month proposed the formation of a NATO deterrent force armed with Polaris-bearing surface ships and submarines. Even if the plan is accepted by the NATO governments, it seems likely to run into political difficulties within many of the countries: in Canada and Great Britain it is a hot political issue.

While it negotiates in Geneva and the NATO capitals, the Kennedy Administration is having trouble protecting its rear in Washington. Republican opposition to test-ban concessions was formalized by a House "Republican Conference Committee on Nuclear Testing" report accusing the Administration of endangering U.S. security by moving toward an inadequately policed test suspension. As for the NATO force, it too seemed likely to run up against Congressional objections on the ground that it would place too many fingers on the nuclear trigger and would violate the Atomic Energy Act.

Science and the Citizen, August 1963

Test Ban and Overkill

AS U.S., British and Soviet negotiators assembled in Moscow in mid-July for a renewed effort to negotiate a ban on further testing of nuclear weapons, comments by officials in the U.S. and U.S.S.R. suggested that advances in military technology may have facilitated the task of arriving at an agreement. Unnamed U.S. officials, according to *The New York Times*, have said that the Administration has begun to explore the possibility of curtailing the production of nuclear weapons. In the U.S.S.R. Premier Khrushchev stated that his country had stopped producing surface warships and long-range bombers.

Behind the U.S. discussions lies the belief that the nuclear arsenal may have reached the point of "overkill." As one official put it to the *Times*: "We have tens of hundreds of times more weapons than we would ever drop even in an all-out war." Another official estimated that it might be possible to cut $1 billion from the Atomic Energy Commission's $1.8 billion annual budget for the production of nuclear weapons.

Premier Khrushchev made his disclosure to Harold Wilson, British Labor Party leader, during the latter's recent visit to Moscow. Wilson quoted Khrushchev as saying that the U.S.S.R. had decided to stop making surface warships and long-range bombers "because of their total vulnerability" in the missile age. The plain implication was that Moscow regards itself as adequately armed with submarine-borne and intercontinental ballistic missiles. Earlier this year U.S. Defense Secretary Robert S. McNamara had declared in the same vein that "our forces today could still destroy the Soviet Union without any help from the deployed tactical air units, or carrier task forces, or Thor or Jupiter intermediate-range ballistic missiles."

Science and the Citizen, September 1963

The Test Ban

THE limited nuclear-test-ban treaty signed last month by Great Britain, the U.S. and the U.S.S.R. at the very least promises a sharp reduction in the pollution of the atmosphere with radioactive debris. Beyond that it is, as President Kennedy observed, "an important first step—a step toward peace—a step toward reason—a step away from war." Premier Khrushchev said the treaty should produce "a situation favorable to the long-overdue solutions of international problems." At the level of nuclear power politics the agreement institutionalizes the great-power nuclear stalemate and tends to align the U.S. and the U.S.S.R. against all "*n*th countries" seeking to acquire a nuclear capability—most specifically against Communist China.

Although the treaty curbs tests in the atmosphere, in space and under water (those that produce widespread fallout), it does not stop testing; the long-standing Soviet-U.S. argument on inspection was settled by simply exempting underground tests, the only context in which inspection is an issue. There are still graver reasons why, as President Kennedy said, "the treaty is not the millennium." It does not halt the production of nuclear weapons or of missiles to carry them and, as President de Gaulle pointed out, "nothing is changed in the terrible threat that the nuclear armaments of the two rivals suspends over the world." The treaty is, however, the first fruit of 17 years of on-and-off efforts to control the nuclear arms race, and it capped with almost anticlimactic speed five years of tortuous Big Three negotiations on a suspension of nuclear testing. There is the possibility, President Kennedy said, that "both sides can by this treaty gain confidence and experience in peaceful collaboration."

Aside from pressure to respond to world-wide fears of fallout, the three powers were motivated primarily by a desire to prevent the proliferation of nuclear weapons in the hands of other countries. To abjure atmospheric testing is in effect to agree not to develop fission or fusion weapons. On the first day on which the treaty was opened for accession, representatives of 31 nations signed the copy on deposit in Washington, including Israel and the United Arab Republic, Yugoslavia, Japan, Canada, Australia and several European members of NATO and the Warsaw Pact; about 100 countries are expected eventually to subscribe to it.

Two countries refused to sign. France, which considers a nuclear capability an essential element of an independent foreign policy, has already tested atomic weapons and is reported to be preparing for its first thermonuclear test in the South Pacific. China, which is developing atomic weapons without Soviet assistance, denounced the treaty as a bargain between the U.S.S.R. and the "imperialists" to monopolize nuclear weapons and warned that the monopoly would be broken "in the not too distant future."

Science and the Citizen, November 1963

Beyond the Test Ban

AS the partial ban on nuclear testing went into effect last month two modest "second steps" were taken toward international control of the atom. One limited the means of delivery of nuclear weapons and the other marked the first vote by the U.S.S.R. in favor of international supervision of nuclear installations.

After a series of talks in New York, the U.S. and the U.S.S.R. joined in sponsoring a UN resolution calling on all nations not to place in orbit or otherwise station in space "any objects carrying nuclear weapons or other weapons of mass destruction." This agreement by the great powers was not considered a major advance in arms control because apparently neither nation had been attracted to satellites as a means of delivering nuclear warheads; missiles can presumably do the job more efficiently. But a nation might achieve a devastating psychological advantage by placing in a hovering orbit a huge nuclear device subject to detonation at any moment. This eerie specter, at least, was banished by the agreement, which was generally welcomed as an indication that the big powers were anxious to maintain the atmosphere established by the test-ban treaty.

The Soviet vote on nuclear installations came at a meeting in Vienna of the International Atomic Energy Agency. The delegates voted, 57 to four, to extend the agency's safeguards system to large nuclear reactors that produce significant amounts of plutonium. All the Soviet-bloc nations except Albania voted with the majority. The safeguards procedures, which require strict accountability for plutonium production, are designed to prevent the diversion to weapons purposes of nuclear equipment or materials supplied through the agency or placed under its jurisdiction. These procedures had previously applied only to small research and training reactors of less than 100,000 kilowatts of thermal output.

As for the test-ban treaty itself, in which the signatories undertook not to conduct nuclear tests except underground, the U.S. Senate approved it on September 24 by a vote of 80 to 19. It went into effect on October 10, having been signed by more than 100 countries.

Following this introduction two articles describe in more detail various aspects of the nuclear test ban relating to arms control and disarmament.

The first article, entitled "National Security and the Nuclear-Test Ban" was written by Jerome Wiesner and myself shortly after the limited test-ban went into effect. In the article we give our views about the relationship of the test ban to national security, and we also analyze the problems of active defense, as exemplified by ABM (anti-ballistic missile) systems, and passive defense (shelters), from a technico-strategic point of view. We point out that both superpowers are confronted with a dilemma: for years the military power of these countries has been steadily increasing but the national security of each has been steadily decreasing. We conclude that this dilemma has no technical solution, and that if the great powers continue to look for solutions in the area of science and technology only, the result will be to worsen the situation. Wiesner and I had both been intimately involved in arms development since early in World War II, and we had served together on the President's Scientific Advisory Committee after its reorganization following Sputnik. Wiesner had been for some time one of the primary advocates of nuclear arms control. He also was one of the principal advocates of the formation of a special agency devoted specifically to the development and promotion of arms control and disarmament policies to be operative at the highest levels of national government. The United States Arms Control and Disarmament Agency was finally created at the end of 1961 when Wisner was serving as President Kennedy's Special Assistant for Science and Technology.

The second article is by Sir Edward Bullard. It is entitled "The Detection of Underground Explosions" and was originally published in the July 1966 issue of *Scientific American.* As is plainly evident from the foregoing reports on the moratorium and test ban negotiations, arguments over the detection and identification of underground explosions were the major cause for the failure of the test moratorium to evolve directly into a test ban treaty. Furthermore, it only became possible to achieve a test ban treaty in 1963 when it was agreed to forego for the time being a ban on underground tests. The Bullard article reviews technical and political elements of the problem of test detection and identification both as they were seen at the time negotiations began and as they had progressed to the time the article was written. Bullard frequently served as a member of the British delegations to the various test ban conferences from the very beginning of serious discussions in 1958. Thus, his article is based not only on his qualifications as a geophysicist but also on his personal knowledge of what the most serious problems were from a geopolitical point of view.

One of the principal arguments in favor of a nuclear test ban was that it would serve as a "first step" and would create a climate that would make the achievement of additional steps easier and more probable. It did indeed work out that way; the first step, the test moratorium of 1958–1961, has been followed by a number of others.

The second step was the Antarctic Treaty. It was signed in Washington December 1, 1959, roughly one year after the first test moratorium went into effect. The signatories agreed that "Antarctica shall be used for peaceful purposes only." To this end all measures of a military nature, such as building bases, conducting maneuvers, and testing all types of weapons are prohibited. The treaty provided for direct inspection of any kind of base in the region, and there have been inspections of scientific bases by American teams.

The third step was the Hot-Line Agreement, which resulted in the establishment of a direct communications link between the national command centers of the two nuclear superpowers. The purpose of this link was to help avoid misunderstandings during crisis situations. The original Hot-Line Agreement was signed in 1963; it was modified and supplemented by two additional agreements in 1971.

The fourth step was the Limited Test-Ban Treaty of 1963, which replaced the moratorium on testing that had been instituted in 1958 and terminated in 1961. The 1963 treaty banned all nuclear tests except those that were conducted underground. It thus avoided the knotty problem of international on-site inspection by banning only those tests that took place in media where remote detection and verification means were judged to be adequate by themselves. More important, by eliminating tests that produce fallout, the limited test-ban also eliminated that part of the protest ban constituency that had placed primary emphasis on that secondary issue. As a result, progress toward a comprehensive test-ban has been glacially slow since then. The Limited Test-Ban Treaty has been ratified by three of the five nuclear powers—the United States, Britain, and the Soviet Union—and by more than one hundred other nations. The most important of the nonsigners are the remaining two nuclear powers, France and China. These two countries had only recently begun programs to develop nuclear weapons in 1963, and they were entirely unwilling to stop their programs when they were still so far behind the other three. Both France and China have continued to test nuclear weapons in the atmosphere up to the present time.

The fifth step was the Outer Space Treaty signed at Washington, London, and Moscow in 1967. It states that "outer space, including the moon and other celestial bodies, is not subject to national appropriation by claim of sovereignty, by means of use or occupation, or by any other means." It further states that none of the signatories shall place any nuclear weapon, or any other weapon of mass destruction, in orbit around the earth, and that they shall not install such weapons on the moon and other celestial bodies.

The sixth step was the Treaty for the Prohibition of Nuclear Weapons in Latin America. The purpose of this rather complicated treaty is to make Latin America a nuclear free zone. It was signed in 1967 and 1968 by all the independent Latin American and Caribbean nations except Cuba. The treaty contains a complex set of provisions designed to allow at some future time the use of so-called peaceful nuclear explosives. The implications of these provisions will be discussed in Section 7. The treaty also has additional protocols designed to insure support for the maintenance of the "free zone" by other powers having special interests in the region. The appropriate protocols have been signed by the United States, Britain, and the Netherlands.

The seventh step was the Non-Proliferation Treaty of 1968. This treaty has as its purpose prevention of the spread of nuclear weapons beyond the five powers then having them. A signatory not currently possessing nuclear weapons agrees not to take any action designed to produce or acquire weapons, and a signatory that currently has nuclear weapons agrees not to help any nonnuclear power acquire them. This treaty also includes a complex set of provisions designed to allow for the possible future use of so-called peaceful nuclear explosives (see Section 7). To date, the treaty has been signed by less than ninety nations. Among the nonsigners are France and China, and also Cuba, Israel, India, Argentina, Brazil, and South Africa. The nonsigners have given a number of reasons for their refusals to sign. Some accuse the United States and the Soviet Union of hypocrisy, pointing out that on the one hand these nations tell the rest of the world that nuclear weapons are unnecessary while on the other hand they continue to test weapons underground and in other ways make it clear they regard nuclear weapons as exceedingly important to themselves. Some of the countries that have refused to sign the non-proliferation treaty charge that the provisions in the treaty for peaceful uses of nuclear explosives are unfair and inadequate.

The eighth step was the Seabed Arms Control Treaty of 1971. It is similar to the Outer Space Treaty; it prohibits placing of weapons of mass destruction on "the seabeds, the ocean floor and in the subsoil thereof." As in the other cases, France and China have not yet signed.

The ninth step was the Biological Weapons Convention of 1972 signed in London, Moscow, and Washington. All the prior agreements and treaties listed above are *arms control* agreements. They do not call for the destruction or removal of any existing weapon. The Biological Weapons Convention differs from these in that for the first time nations have signed a true *disarmament* measure. It calls for the total prohibition of such weapons in the future and the *destruction* of any which may have existed at the time it went into force. Specifically, it bans:

> 1. Microbial or other biological agents, or toxins whatever their origin or method of production, of types and in quantities that have no justification for prophylactic, protective or other peaceful purposes;
> 2. Weapons, equipment or means of delivery, designated to use such agents or toxins for hostile purposes or in armed conflict.

The tenth and last step to date consists in the SALT Treaty, governing deployment of antiballistic missiles, and the SALT Interim Agreement, pertaining to offensive weapons, of 1972. Both of these are discussed separately in Section 5. Of the other steps mentioned in this introduction, the texts of the Limited Test-Ban Treaty and the Non-Proliferation Treaty are reprinted at the end of this section, just as they were published by the U.S. Arms Control and Disarmament Agency.

National Security and the Nuclear Test Ban

Two scientific advisers to the Eisenhower and Kennedy administrations present the reasons why further nuclear tests are unnecessary and why there can be no technical solution to the problem of national security

JEROME B. WIESNER and HERBERT F. YORK

October 1964

The partial nuclear-test ban—the international treaty that prohibits nuclear explosions in the atmosphere, in the oceans and in outer space—has been in effect for a little more than a year. From July, 1945, when the first atomic bomb was set off in New Mexico, until August, 1963, when the U.S. completed its last series of atmospheric bomb tests in the Pacific, the accumulated tonnage of nuclear explosions had been doubling every three years [*see top illustration on page 131*]. Contamination of the atmosphere by fission products and by the secondary products of irradiation (notably the long-lived carbon 14) was approaching a level (nearly 10 percent of the natural background radiation) that alarmed many biologists. A chart plotting the accumulation of radioactive products can also be read as a chart of the acceleration in the arms race.

Now, for a year, the curve has flattened out. From the objective record it can be said that the improvement of both the physical and the political atmosphere of the world has fulfilled at least the short-range expectations of those who advocated and worked for the test ban. In and of itself the treaty does no more than moderate the continuing arms race. It is nonetheless, as President Kennedy said, "an important first step—a step toward peace, a step toward reason, a step away from war."

The passage of a year also makes it possible to place in perspective and evaluate certain misgivings that have been expressed about the effect on U.S. national security of the suspension of the testing of nuclear weapons in the atmosphere. These misgivings principally involve the technology of nuclear armament. National security, of course, involves moral questions and human values—political, social, economic and psychological questions as well as technological ones. Since no one is an expert in all the disciplines of knowledge concerned, it is necessary to consider one class of such questions at a time, always with the caution that such consideration is incomplete. As scientists who have been engaged for most of our professional lifetimes in consultation on this country's military policy and in the active development of the weapons themselves, we shall devote the present discussion primarily to the technological questions.

The discussion will necessarily rest on unclassified information. It is unfortunate that so many of the facts concerning this most important problem are classified, but that is the situation at this time. Since we have access to classified information, however, we can assure the reader that we would not have to modify any of the arguments we present here if we were able to cite such information. Nor do we know of any military considerations excluded from open discussion by military secrecy that would weaken any of our conclusions. We shall discuss the matter from the point of view of our country's national interest. We believe, however, that a Soviet military technologist, writing from the point of view of the U.S.S.R., could write an almost identical paper.

Today as never before national security involves technical questions. The past two decades have seen a historic revolution in the technology of war. From the blockbuster of World War II to the thermonuclear bomb the violence of military explosives has been scaled upward a million times. The time required for the interhemispheric transport of weapons of mass destruction has shrunk from 20 hours for the 300-mile-per-hour B-29 to the 30-minute flight time of the ballistic missile. Moreover, the installation of the computer in command and control systems has increased their information-processing capacity by as much as six orders of magnitude compared with organizations manned at corresponding points by human nervous systems.

It has been suggested by some that technological surprise presents the primary danger to national security. Yet recognition of the facts of the present state of military technology must lead to the opposite conclusion. Intercontinental delivery time cannot be reduced to secure any significant improvement in the effectiveness of the attack. Improvement by another order of magnitude in the information-processing capacity of the defending system will not make nearly as large a difference in its operational effectiveness.

The point is well illustrated by the 100-megaton nuclear bomb. Whether or not it is necessary, in the interests of national security, to test and deploy a bomb with a yield in the range of 100 megatons was much discussed during the test-ban debates. The bomb was frequently referred to as the "big" bomb, as if the bombs now in the U.S. arsenal were somehow not big. The absurdity of this notion is almost enough by itself to settle the argument. A one-megaton bomb is already about 50 times bigger than the bomb that produced 100,000 casualties at Hiroshima, and 10 megatons is of the same order of magnitude as the grand total of all high explosives used in all wars to date. Other technical considerations that surround this question are nonetheless illuminating and worth exploring.

There is, first of all, the "tactics" of the missile race. The purpose of a missile system is to be able to destroy or, perhaps more accurately, able to threaten to destroy enemy targets. No matter what the statesmen, military men and moralists on each side may think of the national characteristics, capabilities and morality of the other side, no matter what arguments may be made about who is aggressive and who is not or who is rational and who is not, the military planners on each side must reckon with the possibility that the other side will attack first. This means that above all else the planner must assure the survival of a sufficient proportion of his own force, following the heaviest surprise attack the other side might mount, to launch a retaliatory attack. Moreover, if the force is to be effective as a deterrent to a first strike, its capacity to survive and wreak revenge and even win, whatever that may mean, must be apparent to the other side.

Several approaches, in fact, can be taken to assure the survival of a sufficient missile force after a first attack on it. The most practical of these are: (1) "hardening," that is, direct protection against physical damage; (2) concealment, including subterfuge and, as in the case of the Polaris submarine missiles, mobility, and (3) numbers, that is, presenting more targets than the attacker can possibly cope with. The most straightforward and certain of these is the last: numbers. For the wealthier adversary it is also the easiest, because he can attain absolute superiority in numbers. A large number of weapons is also a good tactic for the poorer adversary, because numbers even in the absence of absolute superiority can hopelessly frustrate efforts to locate all targets.

There is an unavoidable trade-off, however, between the number and the size of weapons. The cost of a missile depends on many factors, one of the most important being gross size or weight. Unless one stretches "the state of the art" too far in the direction of sophistication and miniaturization, the cost of a missile turns out to be roughly proportional to its weight, if otherwise identical design criteria are used. The protective structures needed for hardening or the capacity of submarines needed to carry the missile also have a cost roughly proportional to the volume of the missile. Some of the ancillary equipment has a cost proportional to the size of the missile and some does not; some operational expenditures vary directly with size or weight and some do not. The cost of the warhead generally does not, although the more powerful warhead requires the larger missile. It is not possible to put all these factors together in precise bookkeeping form, but it is correct to say that the cost of a missile, complete and ready for firing, increases somewhat more slowly than linearly with its size.

On the other hand—considering "hard" targets only—the effectiveness of a missile increases more slowly than cost as the size of the missile goes up. The reason is that the radius of blast damage, which is the primary effect employed against a hard target, increases only as the cube root of the yield and because yield has a more or less direct relation to weight. Against "soft" targets, meaning population centers and conventional military bases, even "small" bombs are completely effective, and nothing is gained by increasing yield. Given finite resources, even in the wealthiest economy, it would seem prudent to accept smaller size in order to get larger numbers. On any scale of investment, in fact, the combination of larger numbers and smaller size results in greater effectiveness for the missile system as a whole, as contrasted to the effectiveness of a single missile.

This line of reasoning has, for some years, formed the basis of U.S. missile policy. The administration of President Eisenhower, when faced with the choice of bigger missiles (the liquid-fueled Atlas and Titan rockets) as against smaller missiles (the solid-fueled Minuteman and Polaris rockets), decided to produce many more of the smaller missiles. The administration of President Kennedy independently confirmed this decision and increased the ratio of smaller to larger missiles in the nation's armament. During the test-ban hearings it was revealed that the U.S. nuclear armament included bombs of 23-megaton yield and higher, carried by bombers. Recently Cyrus R. Vance, Under Secretary of Defense, indicated that the Air Force has been retiring these large bombs in favor of smaller ones. There are presumably no targets that call for the use of such enormous explosions.

The argument that says it is now critical for U.S. national security to build very big bombs and missiles fails completely when it is examined in terms of the strictly technical factors that determine the effectiveness of a missile attack. In addition to explosive yield the principal factors are the number of missiles, the overall reliability of each missile and the accuracy with which it can be delivered to its target. The effectiveness of the attack—the likelihood that a given target will be destroyed—can be described by a number called the "kill probability" (P_k). This number depends on the number of missiles (N) launched at the target, the reliability (r) of each missile and the ratio of the radius of damage (R_k) effected by each missile to the accuracy with which the missiles are delivered to the target (CEP). The term "CEP," which stands for "circular error probable," implies that the distribution of a large number of hits around a given target will follow a standard error curve; actually, for a variety of reasons (which include the presence of systematic errors, coupling between certain causes of error and the sporadic nature of the larger error factors) the distribution does not really follow a standard error curve. The term "CEP" is still useful, however, and can be defined simply as the circle within which half of a large number of identical missiles would fall.

Now, in the case of a soft target, R_k is very large for the present range of warhead yields in the U.S. arsenal. The reason is that soft targets are so highly vulnerable to all the "prompt" effects (particularly the incendiary effects) of thermonuclear weapons. The range of these effects, modified by various attenuation factors, increases approximately as the square root or the cube root of the yield at large distances. Under these circumstances, given the accuracy of existing fire-control systems, the ratio R_k/CEP is large and the likelihood that the target will be destroyed becomes practically independent of this ratio. Instead P_k depends primarily on r, the reliability of the missile. If r is near unity, then a single missile ($N = 1$) will do the job; if r is not near unity, then success in the attack calls for an offsetting increase in the number of missiles $[P_k = 1 - (1 - r)^N]$. In either case changes in R_k make little difference. That is to say, a "big" bomb cannot destroy a soft target any more surely than a "small" one can.

When it comes to hard targets, the ratio R_k/CEP becomes much smaller even for bombs of high yield. The blast effects—including the ground rupture, deformation and shock surrounding the crater of a surface burst—have comparatively small radii at intensities sufficient to overcome hardening. Moreover, as mentioned above, the radii of these effects increase only as the cube root of the yield. This rule of thumb is modified somewhat in both directions by the duration of the blast pulse, local variations in geology and other factors, but it is sustained by a voluminous record from weapons tests. Since the radius of blast damage is of the same order of size as the circular error probable, or smaller, the ratio R_k/CEP must be reckoned with in an attack on a hard target. Yet even in this situation the cube root of a given increase in yield would contribute much less to success than a comparable investment in numbers, reliability or accuracy.

Yield is of course a product of the yield-to-weight ratio of the nuclear explosive employed in the warhead multiplied by the weight of the warhead. In order to gain significant increases in the first of these two quantities further nuclear tests would be necessary. Increase in the weight of the warhead, on the other hand, calls for bigger and more efficient missiles. In the present state of the art, efforts to improve CEP and reliability as well as weight-carrying capacity hold out more promise than efforts to improve the yield-to-weight ratio. The reason is that missile design and control involve less mature and less fully exploited technologies than the technology of nuclear warheads. Finally, an increase in the number of missiles, although not necessarily cheap, promises more straightforward and assured

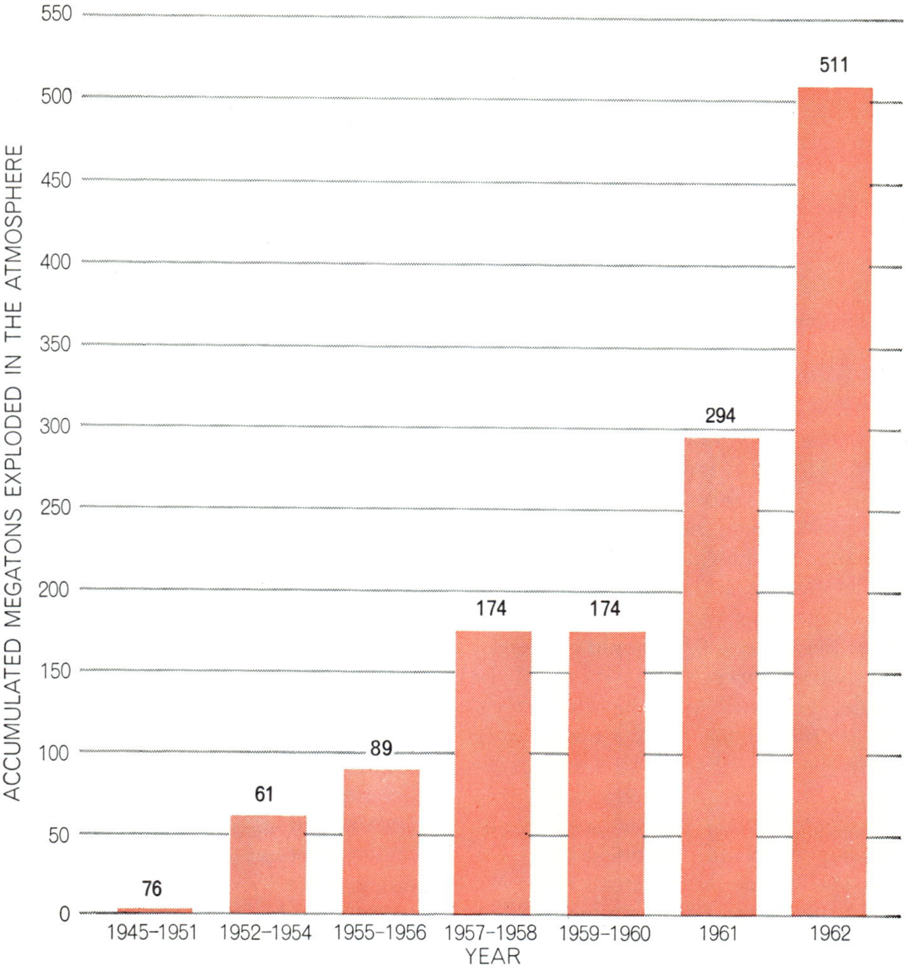

NUCLEAR EXPLOSIONS IN THE ATMOSPHERE from 1945 to 1962, the last full year in which the U.S. and the U.S.S.R. set off such explosions, are presented on the basis of accumulated megatons. The bars of equal height for the periods 1957–1958 and 1959–1960 reflect the informal moratorium on testing. The overall increase in megatons has doubled every three years. The data for this chart are from *Federal Radiation Council Report No. 4.*

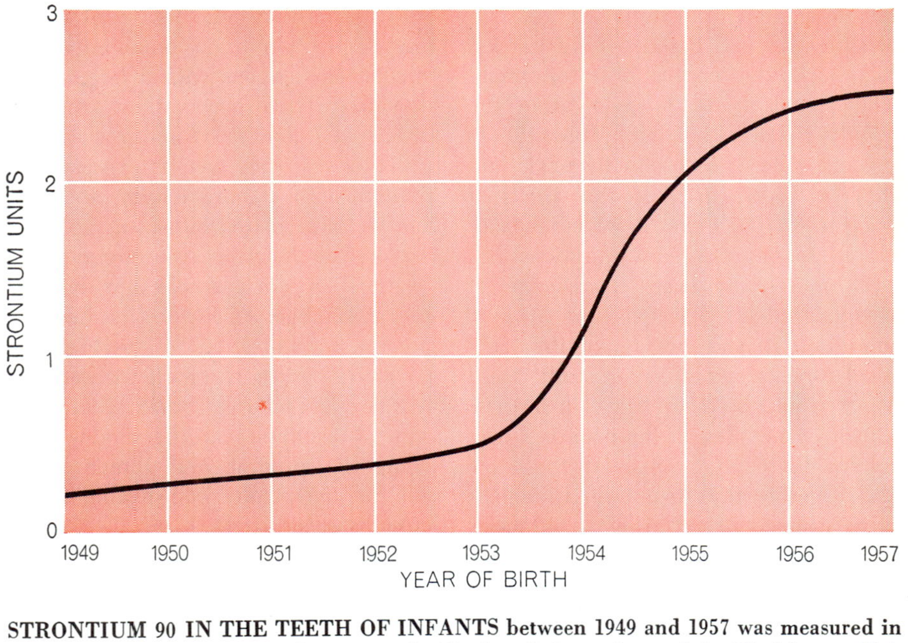

STRONTIUM 90 IN THE TEETH OF INFANTS between 1949 and 1957 was measured in a cooperative project of the Committee for Nuclear Information and the Washington University and St. Louis University schools of dentistry. This curve shows the strontium-90 activity in the deciduous teeth of bottle-fed infants. Because such teeth can be collected only some six years after the birth of the child, the curve does not come up to the present. The sharp rise in strontium-90 activity coincides with the period of extensive nuclear testing beginning in 1953. In the course of the project 110,000 teeth were collected.

results than a fractional increase in yield-to-weight ratio. Of all the various possible technical approaches to improving the military effectiveness of an offensive missile force, therefore, the only one that calls for testing (whether underground or in the atmosphere) is the one that offers the smallest prospect of return.

Suppose, however, a new analysis, based on information not previously considered, should show that it is in fact necessary to incorporate the 100-megaton bomb in the U.S. arsenal. Can this be done without further weapons tests? The answer is yes. Because the U.S.S.R. has pushed development in this yield range and the U.S. has not, the U.S. 100-megaton bomb might not be as elegant as the Soviet model. It would perhaps weigh somewhat more or at the same weight would produce a somewhat lower yield. It could be made, however, and the basic techniques for making it have been known since the late 1950's. The warhead for such a bomb would require a big missile, but not so big as some being developed by the National Aeronautics and Space Administration for the U.S. space-exploration program. Such a weapon would be expensive, particularly on a per-unit basis; under any imaginable circumstances it would be of limited use and not many of its kind would be built.

The extensive series of weapons tests carried out by the U.S.—involving the detonation of several hundred nuclear bombs and devices—have yielded two important bodies of information. They have shown how to bring the country's nuclear striking force to its present state of high effectiveness. And they have demonstrated the effects of nuclear weapons over a wide range of yields. Among the many questions that call for soundly based knowledge of weapons effects perhaps none is more important in a discussion of the technical aspects of national security than: What would be the result of a surprise attack by missiles on the country's own missile forces? Obviously if the huge U.S. investment in its nuclear armament is to succeed in deterring an attacker, that armament must be capable of surviving a first strike.

A reliable knowledge of weapons effects is crucial to the making of rational decisions about the number of missiles needed, the hardening of missile emplacements, the degree of dispersal, the proportion that should be made mobile and so on. The military planner must bear in mind, however, that such decisions take time—years—to carry out and require large investments of finite physical and human resources. The inertia of the systems is such that the design engineer at work today must be concerned not with the surprise attack that might be launched today but rather with the kind and size of forces that might be launched against them years in the future. In addition to blast, shock and other physical effects, therefore, the planner must contend with a vast range of other considerations. These include the yields of the various bombs the attacker would use against each target; the reliability and accuracy of his missiles; the number and kind of weapons systems he would have available for attack; the tactics of the attacker, meaning the number of missiles he would commit to a first strike, the fractions he would allocate to military as against civilian targets and the relative importance he would assign to various kinds of military targets, the effects of chaos on the defender's capacity to respond, and so on. In all cases the planner must project his thinking forward to some hypothetical future time, making what he can of the available intelligence about the prospective attacker's present capabilities and intentions. Plainly all these "other considerations" involve inherently greater uncertainties than the knowledge of weapons effects.

The extensive classified and unclassified literature accumulated in two decades of weapons tests and available to U.S. military planners contains at least some observations on all important effects for weapons with a large range of yields. These observations are more or less well understood in terms of physical theories; they can be expressed in numerical or algebraic form, and they can be extrapolated into areas not fully explored in the weapons tests conducted by the U.S., for example into the 100-megaton range. As one departs from the precise circumstances of past experiments, of course, extrapolation becomes less and less reliable. Nonetheless, some sort of estimate can be made about what the prompt and direct effects will be under any conceivable set of circumstances.

Consider, in contrast, the degree of uncertainty implicit in predicting the number and kind of weapons systems that might be available to the prospective attacker. Such an uncertainty manifested itself in the famous "missile gap" controversy. The remarkable difference between the dire predictions made in the late 1950's—based as they were on the best available intelligence—and the actual situation that developed in the early 1960's can be taken as indicating the magnitude of the uncertainties that surround the variables other than weapons effects with which the military planner must contend. Moreover, these factors, as they concern a future attack, are uncertain not only to the defender; they are almost as uncertain to the attacker.

Uncertainties of this order and kind defy reduction to mathematical expression. A human activity as complex as modern war cannot be computed with the precision possible in manipulation of the data that concern weapons effects. What is more, the uncertainties about this single aspect of the total problem are not, as is sometimes assumed, multiplicative in estimation of the overall uncertainty. Most, but not all, of the uncertainties are independent of one another. The total uncertainty is therefore, crudely speaking, the square root of the sum of the squares of the individual uncertainties.

In our view further refinement of the remaining uncertainties in the data concerning prompt direct physical effects can contribute virtually nothing more to management of the real military and political problems, even though it would produce neater graphs. Furthermore, if new effects should be discovered either experimentally or theoretically in the future, or if, in certain peculiar environments, some of the now known effects should be excessively uncertain, it will be almost certainly possible to "overdesign" the protection against them. Thus, although renewed atmospheric testing would contribute some refinement to the data on weapons effects, the information would be, at best, of marginal value.

Such refinements continue to be sought in the underground tests that are countenanced under the partial test ban. From this work may also come some reductions in the cost of weapons, modest improvements in yield-to-weight ratios, devices to fill in the spectrum of tactical nuclear weapons and so on. There is little else to justify the effort and expenditure. The program is said by some to be necessary, for example, to the development of a pure fusion bomb, sometimes referred to as the "neutron bomb." It is fortunate that this theoretically possible (stars are pure fusion systems) device has turned out to be so highly difficult to create; if it were relatively simple, its development might open the way to thermonuclear armament for the smallest and poorest powers in the world. The U.S., with its heavy investment in fission-to-fusion technology, would be the last nation to welcome this development and ought to be the last to encourage it. Underground testing is also justified for its contribution to the potential peaceful uses of nuclear explosives. Promising as these may be, the world could forgo them for a time in exchange for cessation of the arms race. Perhaps the best rationale for the underground-test program is that it helps to keep the scientific laboratories of the military establishment intact and in readiness—in readiness, however, for a full-scale resumption of the arms race.

Paradoxically one of the potential destabilizing elements in the present nuclear standoff is the possibility that one of the rival powers might develop a successful antimissile defense. Such a system, truly airtight and in the exclusive possession of one of the powers, would effectively nullify the deterrent force of the other, exposing the latter to a first attack against which it could not retaliate. The possibilities in this quarter have often been cited in rationalization of the need for resuming nuclear tests in the atmosphere. Here two

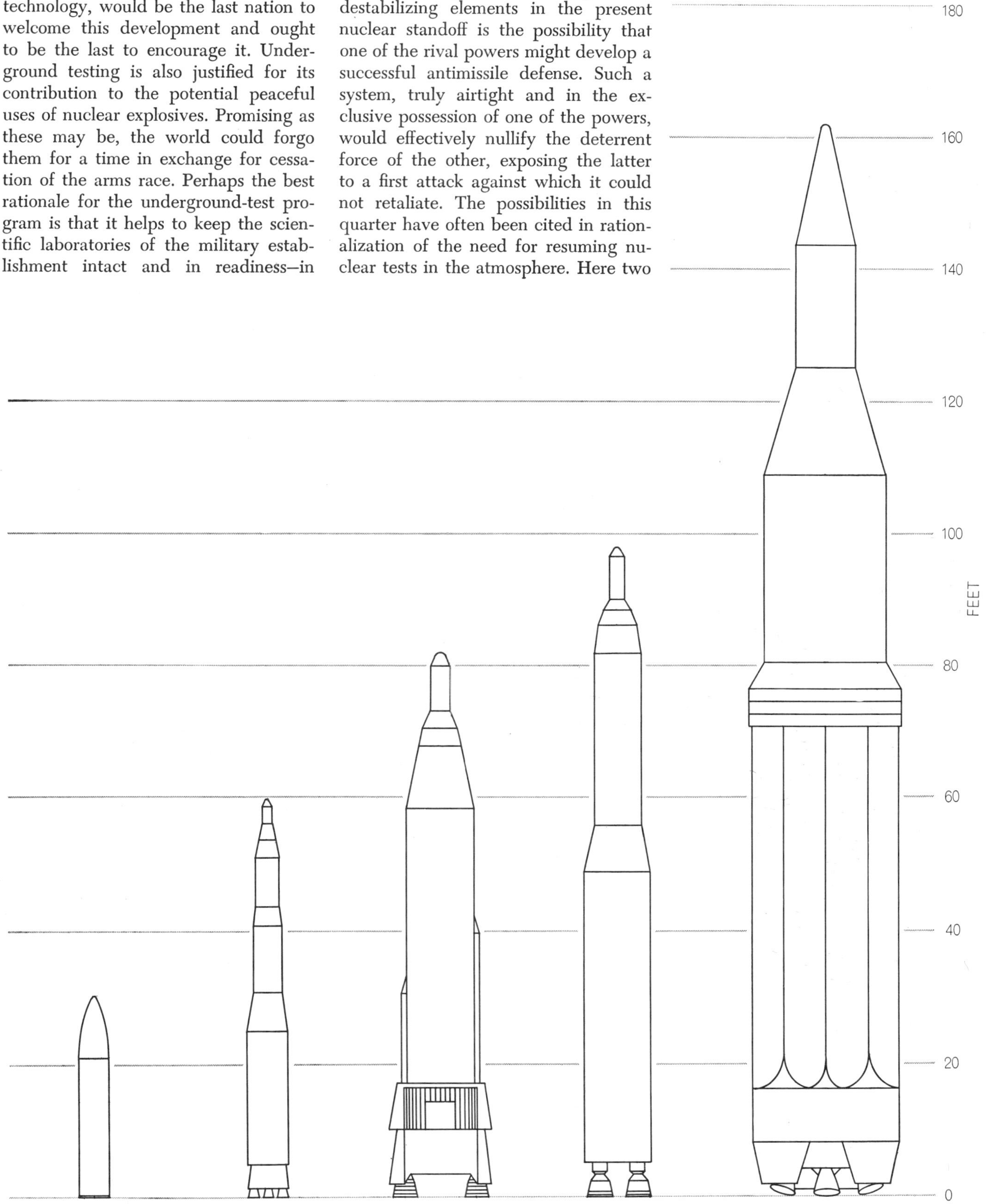

PAYLOAD OF EXISTING ROCKETS sets a limit on the size of nuclear weapons that can be used in a rocket attack. The five U.S. rockets shown here are drawn to scale. At left is the Polaris Type A-3, designed for launching from submarines; it weighs 30,000 pounds, has a range of 2,500 nautical miles and can carry a nuclear warhead of about one megaton. Second from left is Minuteman II; it weighs 65,000 pounds, has a range of 6,300 nautical miles and can carry a warhead of about one megaton. Third is Atlas; it weighs 269,000 pounds, has a range of 9,000 nautical miles and can carry a warhead of about five megatons. Fourth is Titan II; it weighs 303,000 pounds, has a range of 6,300 nautical miles and can carry a warhead of about 20 megatons. To lift a larger warhead would require a rocket such as Saturn I (*right*), which weighs 1,138,000 pounds. Data are from the journal *Missiles and Rockets.*

questions must be examined. One must first ask if it is possible to develop a successful antimissile defense system. It then becomes appropriate to consider whether or not nuclear weapons tests can make a significant contribution to such a development.

Any nation that commits itself to large-scale defense of its civilian population in the thermonuclear age must necessarily reckon with passive modes of defense (shelters) as well as active ones (antimissile missiles). It is in the active mode, however, that the hazard of technological surprise most often lurks. The hazard invites consideration if only for the deeper insight it provides into the contemporary revolution in the technology of war.

The primary strategic result of that revolution has been to overbalance the scales in favor of the attacker rather than the defender. During World War II interception of no more than 10 percent of the attacking force gave victory to the defending force in the Battle of Britain. Attrition of this magnitude was enough to halt the German attack because it meant that a given weapons-delivery system (bomber and crew) could deliver on the average only 10 payloads of high explosive; such a delivery rate was not sufficient to produce backbreaking damage. In warfare by thermonuclear missiles the situation is quantitatively and qualitatively different. It is easily possible for the offense to have in its possession and ready to launch a number of missiles that exceeds the number of important industrial targets to be attacked by, let us say, a factor of 10. Yet the successful delivery of only one warhead against each such target would result in what most people would consider an effective attack. Thus where an attrition rate of only 10 percent formerly crowned the defense with success, a penetration rate of only 10 percent (corresponding to an attrition rate of 90 percent) would give complete success to the offense. The ratio of these two ratios is 100 to one; in this sense the task of defense can be said to have become two orders of magnitude more difficult.

Beyond this summary statement of the situation there are many general reasons for believing that defense against thermonuclear attack is impossible. On the eve of attack the offense can take time to get ready and to "point up" its forces; the defense, meanwhile, must stay on the alert over periods of years, perpetually ready and able to fire within the very few minutes available after the first early warning. The attacker can pick its targets and can choose to concentrate its forces on some and ignore others; the defense must be prepared to defend all possible important targets. The offense may attack the defense itself; then, as soon as one weapon gets through, the rest have a free ride.

The hopelessness of the task of defense is apparent even now in the stalemate of the arms race. A considerable inertia drags against the movement of modern, large-scale, unitary weapons systems from the stage of research and development to operational deployment. The duration and magnitude of these enterprises, whether defensive or offensive, practically assure that no system can reach full deployment under the mantle of secrecy. The designer of the defensive system, however, cannot begin until he has learned something about the properties and capabilities of the offensive system. Inevitably the defense must start the race a lap behind. In recent years, it seems, the offense has even gained somewhat in the speed with which it can put into operation stratagems and devices that nullify the most extraordinary achievements in the technology of defense. These general observations are expensively illustrated in the development and obsolescence of two major U.S. defense systems.

Early in the 1950's the U.S. set out to erect an impenetrable defense against a thermonuclear attack by bombers. The North American continent was to be ringed with a system of detectors that would flash information back through the communications network to a number of computers. The computers were to figure out from this data what was going on and what ought to be done about it and then flash a series of commands to the various interceptor systems. In addition to piloted aircraft, these included the Bomarc (a guided airborne missile) and the Nike-Hercules (a ballistic rocket). By the early 1960's this "Sage" system was to be ready to detect, intercept and destroy the heaviest attack that could be launched against it.

The early 1960's have come and yet nothing like the capability planned in the 1950's has been attained. Why not? Time scales stretched out, subsystems failed to attain their planned capabilities and costs increased. Most important, the offense against which the system was designed is not the offense that actually exists in the early 1960's. Today the offensive system on both sides is a mixture of missiles and bombers. The Sage system has a relatively small number of soft but vital organs completely vulnerable to missiles—a successful missile attack on them would give a free ride to the bombers. As early as 1958 the Department of Defense came to realize that this would be the situation, and the original grand plan was steadily cut back. In other words, the Sage system that could have been available, say, in 1963 and that should have remained useful at least through the 1960's would in principle have worked quite well against the offense that existed in the 1950's.

To answer the intercontinental ballistic missile, the Department of Defense launched the development of the Nike-Zeus system. Nike-Zeus was intended to provide not a defense of the continent at its perimeter but a point defense of specific targets. To be sure, the "points" were fairly large—the regions of population concentration around 50 to 70 of the country's biggest cities. The system was to detect incoming warheads, feeding the radar returns directly into its computers, and launch and guide an interceptor missile carrying a nuclear warhead into intersection with the trajectory of each of the incoming warheads.

Nike-Zeus was not designed to defend the 1,000 or so smaller centers outside the metropolitan areas simply because there are too many of these to be covered by the resources available for a system so huge and complicated. Nor was the system designed to defend the retaliatory missiles, the security of these forces being entrusted to the more reliable protection of dispersal, concealment, mobility and number. In principle, the defense of a hardened missile silo would have presented by far the simplest case for proof of the effectiveness of Nike-Zeus as advanced by those who contend that such a system can be made to "work." There would be no ambiguity about the location of the target of the incoming warhead. By the same token Nike-Zeus might have been considered for the defense of a few special defense posts, such as the headquarters of the Air Defense Command of the Strategic Air Command. These special cases are so few in number, however, that it had to be concluded that the attacker would either blast his way through to them by a concentration of firepower or ignore them altogether.

At the time of the conception of the Nike-Zeus system its designers were confronted with a comparatively simple problem, namely that of shooting down

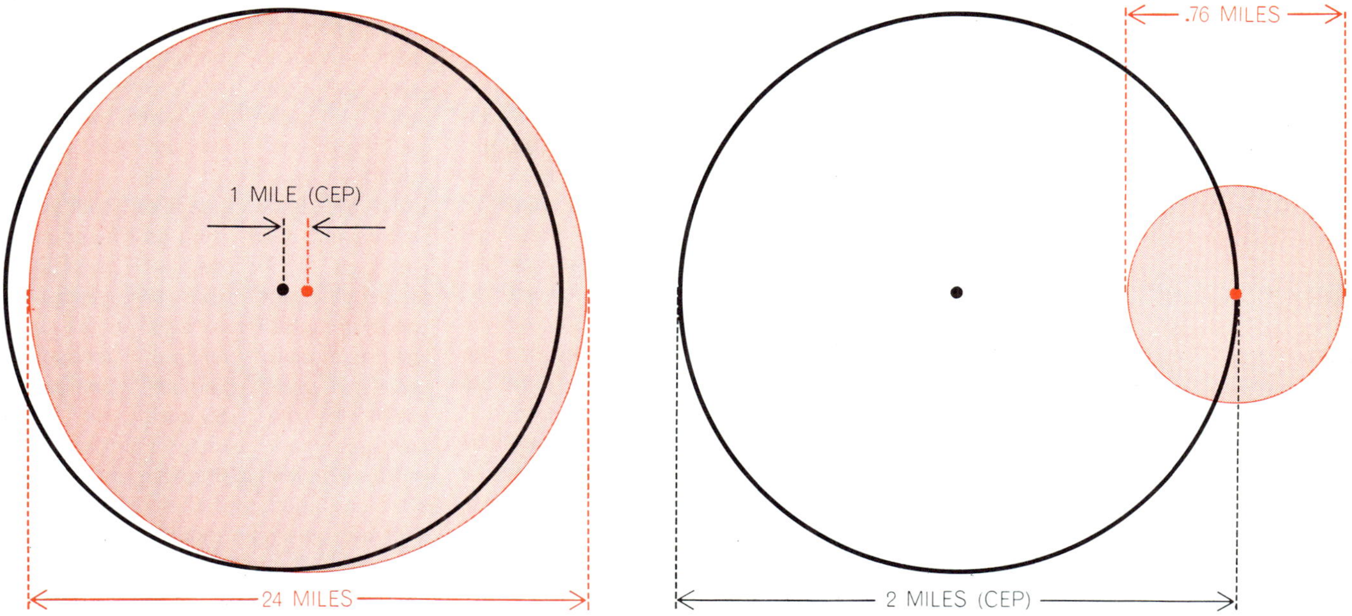

ACCURACY OF MISSILES has far more relevance for hard targets than for soft. It has been estimated that at maximum range both U.S. and Soviet rockets have a "circular error probable" of about a mile, that is, there is a probability of 50 percent that a rocket will hit within a mile of the target. The radius of fire damage for a one-megaton bomb will not be greatly affected by a near miss (*circles at left*). The radius of kill for a one-megaton bomb aimed at a target hardened to 300 pounds per square inch, however, is so much smaller than the circular error probable (*circles at right*) that a number of weapons would have to be used to assure a hit. The illustrations in this article and the figures on which they are based are not the responsibility of the authors but of the editors.

the warheads one by one as they presented themselves to the detectors. Even this simple problem had to be regarded as essentially unsolvable, in view of the fact that a 90 per-cent success in interception constitutes failure in the inverted terms of thermonuclear warfare. At first, therefore, the designers of the offensive system did not take the prospect of an antimissile system seriously. Then the possibility that the problem of missile interception might be solved in principle gave them pause. Thereupon the designers of the offense began to invent a family of "penetration aids," that is, decoys and confusion techniques. The details of these and the plans for their use are classified, but the underlying principles are obvious. They include light decoys that can be provided in large numbers but that soon betray their character as "atmospheric sorting" separates them from the heavier decoys (and actual warheads) that can be provided in smaller numbers to confuse the defending detectors down to the last minute. Single rockets can also eject multiple warheads. Both the decoys and the warheads can be made to present ambiguous cross sections to the radar systems. These devices and stratagems overwhelmed the designed capability of the Nike-Zeus system and compelled its recent abandonment.

If the installation of the system had proceeded according to plan, the first Nike-Zeus units would have been operational within the next year or two. This could have been celebrated as a technical milestone. As a means of defense of a substantial percentage of the population, however, the system would not have reached full operational deployment until the end of the decade. In view of its huge cost the system should then have looked forward to a decade of useful life until, say, the late 1970's. Thus, in inexorable accordance with the phase-lag of the defense, the U.S. population was to be defended a decade too late by a system that might have been effective in principle (although most probably not in practice) against the missiles of the early 1960's.

The race of the tortoise and the hare has now entered the next lap with the development of the Nike-X system as successor to Nike-Zeus. The Advanced Research Projects Agency of the Department of Defense has been spending something on the order of $200 million a year on its so-called Defender Program, exploring on the broadest front the principles and techniques that might prove useful in the attempt to solve the antimissile problem. Although nothing on the horizon suggests that there is a solution, this kind of work must go forward. It not only serves the forlorn hope of developing an active antimissile defense but also promotes the continued development of offensive weapons. The practical fact is that work on defensive systems turns out to be the best way to promote invention of the penetration aids that nullify them.

As the foregoing discussion makes clear, the problems of antimissile development are problems in radar, computer technology, missile propulsion, guidance and control. The nuclear warheads for the antimissile missile have been ready for a long time for delivery to the right place at the right time. Although it is argued that certain refinements in the existing data about weapons effects are needed, the other uncertainties all loom much larger than the marginal uncertainties in these physical effects. The antimissile defense problem, then, is one in which nuclear testing can play no really significant part.

The pursuit of an active defense system demands parallel effort on the passive defense, or shelter, front because the nature of the defense system strongly conditions the tactics of the offense that is likely to be mounted against it. To take a perhaps farfetched example, a Nike-Zeus system that provided protection for the major population centers might invite the attacker to concentrate the weight of his assault in ground bursts on remote military installations and unprotected areas adjacent to cities, relying on massive fallout to imperil the population centers. This example serves also to suggest how heavily the effectiveness of any program for sheltering the civilian population depends on the tactics of the attacker. Fallout shelters by themselves are of no avail if the attacker chooses to assault the population centers directly.

In any speculation about the kind of attack to which this country might be exposed it is useful to note where the military targets are located. Most of the missile bases are, in fact, far from the largest cities. Other key military installations, however, are not so located. Boston, New York, Philadelphia, Seattle, San Francisco, Los Angeles (Long Beach) and San Diego all have important naval bases. Essential command and control centers are located in and near Denver, Omaha and Washington, D.C. The roll call could be extended to include other major cities containing military installations that would almost certainly have to be attacked in any major assault on this country. The list does not stop with these; it is only prudent to suppose still other cities would come under attack, because there is no way to know in advance what the strategy may be.

The only kind of shelter that is being seriously considered these days, for other than certain key military installations, is the fallout shelter. By definition fallout shelters offer protection against nothing but fallout and provide virtually no protection against blast, fire storms and other direct effects. Some people have tried to calculate the percentage of the population that would be saved by fallout shelters in the event of massive attack. Such calculations always involve predictions about the form of the attack, but since the form is unknowable the calculations are nonsensical. Even for the people protected by fallout shelters the big problem is not a problem in the physical theory of gamma-ray attenuation, which can be neatly computed, but rather the sociological problem of the sudden initiation of general chaos, which is not subject to numerical analysis.

Suppose, in spite of all this, the country were to take fallout shelters seriously and build them in every city and town. The people living in metropolitan areas that qualify as targets because they contain essential military installations and the people living in metropolitan areas that might be targeted as a matter of deliberate policy would soon recognize that fallout shelters are inadequate. That conclusion would be reinforced by the inevitable reaction from the other side, whose military planners would be compelled to consider a massive civilian-shelter program as portending a first strike against them. Certainly the military planners of the U.S. would be remiss if they did not take similar note of a civilian-shelter program in the U.S.S.R. As a step in the escalation of the arms race toward the ultimate outbreak of war, the fallout shelter would lead inevitably to the blast shelter. Even with large numbers of blast shelters built and evenly distributed throughout the metropolitan community, people would soon realize that shelters alone are not enough. Accidental alarms, even in tautly disciplined military installations, have shown that people do not always take early warnings seriously. Even if they did, a 15-minute "early" warning provides less than enough time to seal the population into shelters. Accordingly, the logical next step is the live-in and work-in blast shelter leading to still further disruption and distortion of civilization. There is no logical termination of the line of reasoning that starts with belief in the usefulness of fallout shelters; the logic of this attempt to solve the problem of national security leads to a diverging series of ever more grotesque measures. This is to say, in so many words, that if the arms race continues and resumes its former accelerating tempo, 1984 is more than just a date on the calendar 20 years hence.

Ever since shortly after World War II the military power of the U.S. has been steadily increasing. Throughout this same period the national security of the U.S. has been rapidly and inexorably diminishing. In the early 1950's the U.S.S.R., on the basis of its own unilateral decision and determination to accept the inevitable retaliation, could have launched an attack against the U.S. with bombers carrying fission bombs. Some of these bombers would have penetrated our defenses and the American casualties would have numbered in the millions. In the later 1950's, again on its own sole decision and determination to accept the inevitable massive retaliation, the U.S.S.R. could have launched an attack against the U.S. using more and better bombers, this time carrying thermonuclear bombs. Some of these bombers would have penetrated our defenses and the American casualties could have numbered in the tens of millions.

Today the U.S.S.R., again on the basis of its own decision and determination to accept the inevitable retaliation, could launch an attack on the U.S. using intercontinental missiles and bombers carrying thermonuclear weapons. This time the number of American casualties could very well be on the order of 100 million.

The steady decrease in national security did not result from any inaction on the part of responsible U.S. military and civilian authorities. It resulted from the systematic exploitation of the products of modern science and technology by the U.S.S.R. The air defenses deployed by the U.S. during the 1950's would have reduced the number of casualties the country might have otherwise sustained, but their existence did not substantively modify this picture. Nor could it have been altered by any other defense measures that might have been taken but that for one reason or another were not taken.

From the Soviet point of view the picture is similar but much worse. The military power of the U.S.S.R. has been steadily increasing since it became an atomic power in 1949. Soviet national security, however, has been steadily decreasing. Hypothetically the U.S. could unilaterally decide to destroy the U.S.S.R. and the U.S.S.R. would be absolutely powerless to prevent it. That country could only, at best, seek to wreak revenge through whatever retaliatory capability it might then have left.

Both sides in the arms race are thus confronted by the dilemma of steadily increasing military power and steadily decreasing national security. *It is our considered professional judgment that this dilemma has no technical solution.* If the great powers continue to look for solutions in the area of science and technology only, the result will be to worsen the situation. The clearly predictable course of the arms race is a steady open spiral downward into oblivion.

We are optimistic, on the other hand, that there is a solution to this dilemma. The partial nuclear-test ban, we hope and believe, is truly an important first step toward finding a solution in an area where a solution may exist. A next logical step would be the conclusion of a comprehensive test ban such as that on which the great powers came close to agreement more than once during 10 long years of negotiation at Geneva. The policing and inspection procedures so nearly agreed on in those parleys would set significant precedents and lay the foundations of mutual confidence for proceeding thereafter to actual disarmament.

Commentary

Although we scientists often pride ourselves that our familiarity with the "scientific method" enables us to form more rational political views and to raise the level of political discussions, most of our writings on the problems that confront our nation today resemble the monologues that men in politics use. We state our views and desires but do not point out the areas of disargreement with our opponents, or the extent, or the reasons therefor. No fruitful scientific discussion could proceed on such a basis, and in the following paragraphs, in which I comment on the article "National Security and the Nuclear-Test Ban," by Jerome B. Wiesner and Herbert F. York, I hope to come closer to a dialogue. Thus I shall attempt to specify both the areas in which I agree with the authors and those in which I disagree, and to give my reasons for disagreeing.

In the early stages of writing this letter it appeared that only the views expressed by Wiesner and York on policies, attitudes and technical questions would have to be discussed. It soon became apparent, however, that there is a third subject that could not be disregarded: the inferences the daily press drew from the article and the extrapolations it attached thereto.

Turning first to *questions of broad policy expressed in the article itself,* there is much with which it would seem a vast majority of our colleagues can agree. The principal area of agreement concerns the success of the test-ban treaty. One would have to be blind not to see that the tensions between the U.S.S.R. and our country have much relaxed since this treaty has been in effect. It would be stretching a point to say that the cessation of testing is only the consequence, and not at the very least partially a *cause*, of the relaxation of tensions. As to the delay that peaceful uses of atomic explosives suffer as a result of the test cessation, the article says, "Promising as peaceful uses of nuclear explosives may be, the world could forgo them for a time" in exchange for a quieter international atmosphere, and I can only concur.

On the other hand, it would be a mistake to overlook the fact that the test-ban treaty is the result of extensive negotiations in which *both* parties made significant concessions. There is no evidence that generous acts of the U.S. through which it unilaterally weakens itself on *mutual* concessions have to create an unfriendly atmosphere. On the contrary, the constant pressure on our government, by means of public statements, to give in, raises false hopes in the negotiators of the U.S.S.R. The thwarting of these hopes, and the irritation of our own negotiators because of these pressures, do create an unhappy atmosphere. It is to be hoped that the article by Wiesner and York, with its insistence on a comprehensive test-ban treaty but without equal insistence on policing and inspection, will not have such an effect. It certainly counsels moderation not only to our government but also to that of the U.S.S.R. (An apt description of the adverse circumstances under which our negotiators often labor was given by R. Gilpin in his *American Scientists and Nuclear Weapons Policy.*)

Another statement of the article with which few will quarrel is that "if the great powers continue to look for solutions in the area of science and technology only, the result will be to worsen the situation." It is unfortunate that the subtitle of the article abbreviates this to "there can be no technical solution to the problem of national security." This subtitle, whether written by the authors or by a somewhat careless editor, printed as it is in large italics, could give the impression, and has given the impression to some of the daily press, that technical problems will play no further role in the future. This is, of course, not the meaning of the statement quoted. In fact, the sentence "Today as never before national security involves technical questions" stands just three inches below the subtitle.

Actually the great powers have never confined themselves to looking for solutions in the area of science and technology only but have initiated extensive negotiations toward easing tensions. As we have seen, some of these were successful.

If one is asked whether one agrees or disagrees with the policies recommended by the article, one soon discovers that the article does not recommend any policies. It leaves its reader with a sense of frustrated disorientation coupled with the impression that the past policies of this country were fundamentally wrong and something fundamentally new has to be tried. Some passages even carry the implication that our defense preparations have aggravated the danger to our freedom, independence and survival. "Ever since shortly after World War II the military power of the U.S. has been steadily increasing. Throughout the same period the national security of the U.S. has been rapidly and inexorably diminshing." Does this suggest that the decrease of our security is a *result* of the increase of our military power? To some who wish to think so it apparently does; to the people of countries whose military power did not grow adequately—to the people of Czechoslovakia, Hungary and Tibet—it would not. When I maintained in a discussion with one of the top scientific negotiators of the U.S.S.R. that the U.S. used its early atomic monopoly with great restraint, he answered, "I don't know. We wanted to do many things that [as a result of your atomic strength] we [the U.S.S.R.] could not." I am afraid that the borders of Stalinist Russia would have moved *much* farther to the West in Europe had the military power of the U.S. not been "steadily increasing."

Furthermore, is it really true that the national security of the U.S. has been "rapidly and inexorably diminishing"? If one thinks only in terms of physical possibilites, in terms of a fanatical enemy who takes seriously Lenin's dictum "Better only one-third of the world's population surviving if those are then good communists," the security has decreased. But is that a valid picture? Have we not spoken of the relaxation of tensions before? True, we still hear the threats of burying us, alone or in collaboration with the Chinese brothers, the praise of the "irreconcilable class hatred that exposes and strikes the enemies of our social system," and the glorification of the sparks flying from the sabers of cavalrymen (both in Khrushchev's speech on culture of March 8, 1963). But one also hears, with an increasing volume, the realization of the need for coexistence and of peaceful competition. One does not have to shut one's ears to the threats in order to hear also the voice of reason and adjustment. Furthermore, is it not clear that the realization of the need for coexistence is in large measure the result of the understanding that the sparks flying from the sabers of cavalrymen can ignite other fires? A U.S. that is not only strong but *evidently* strong is in the interests of all: it is reassuring to the West and should turn the interest of the rulers of the East away from domination and toward the true welfare of their people. Are there no signs that it is at least beginning to do so?

To put the preceding point more pragmatically: Although the worst conceivable alternative may have become worse with the progress of time, the probablity of such an alternative has decreased sharply. As a result, from the point of view of the most likely turn of events, the security of the U.S. has probably greatly increased, particularly in the course of the past few years.

Let us now turn to the *technical points of the article.* I am sorry to say that I find it more difficult to agree with them than with the general statements discussed before. The first remark that comes to mind is that the alleged need for developing the 100-megaton bomb was not the only, in fact not the principal, argument against the test-ban treaty. Personally I feel that this treaty was worth what we paid for it, and that it benefits both the U.S. and the U.S.S.R. It would be only fair toward those who opposed the treaty, however, to state that they were chiefly concerned with the testing of certain defense measures against antiballistic missiles, not with the development of the 100-megaton bomb.

Nevertheless, we must recall in connection with this bomb that the U.S.S.R. found it worthwhile to break the test moratorium in order to test it. In addition, the statement of the article that "on any scale of investment, the combination of larger numbers and smaller size results in greater effectiveness of the missile system" cannot be maintained. The cost of a missile is approximately proportional to the square root of its explosive yield. The illustration in the article that shows a linear relation is incorrect (and is contradicted in the text). Hence the yield is proportional to the square of the cost. The range of destruction is proportional to the cube root of the yield and hence to the 2/3 power of the cost. Finally, the area of destruction is proportional to the *square* of the range of destruction and hence to the 4/3 power of the cost. It follows that if one disregards soft targets that can be destroyed by a single smaller bomb, the cost effectiveness of weapons actually *increases* somewhat with their yield. Even this is not the complete picture. A hardened defense installation can be destroyed with a smaller explosion only if this takes place closer by and at lower altitudes. It is easier to prevent such an explosion by antimissile measures, or otherwise, than an explosion at the larger distances and high altitudes at which a very large bomb can still destroy the installation.

Drs. Wiesner and York state that we do not need tests in order to design a 100-megaton bomb. This is true but disregards the time element. The time schedules for the production of a bomb with the characteristics that exploit the inherent advantages of size are extremely long in the absence of tests. If the bomb should be needed, it would be meager comfort to know that, given only a few more years, we could have had it.

The cases for and against the big bomb remain unproved and I personally cannot become enthusiastic about it. I do feel strongly, however, that the rejection of defense measures, in particular the rejection of civil defense, is unjustified. Drs. Wiesner and York recognize that the instability that has to be overcome is due to the "overbalance [of] the scales in favor of the attacker rather than defender." If this is so, a wholehearted effort should be made to redress the overbalance. It does not seem, however, that they have explored the possibilities of civil defense even halfheartedly. Most readers will be struck by the contradiction between the postulates that, on the one hand, the retaliatory installations are invulnerable and, on the other hand, that shelters are useless. In fact, when discussing civil defense, the authors say: "The only kind of shelter that is being seriously considered these days, for other than certain key military installations, is the fallout shelter." They then proceed to show that fallout shelters by themselves do not suffice to render the position of the defender strong enough. Although they do not state this explieitly, they give the impression that they would not be opposed to abandoning altogether the fallout shelter program as insufficient. The opposite alternative, to strengthen the civil defense program by the installation of blast shelters at important locations, is dismissed all too easily with arguments that are in no way convincing. Thus the writers mention the danger of a short warning time in a surprise attack but do not mention that a complete surprise is difficult to achieve, and in fact the two world wars did not break out without warning. In addition, the shelters could well be located in such a way that they could be reached by most people in the 15-minute warning time the writers concede. Similarly, the writers mention the possibility of chaos and disorientation in shelters but fail to mention either that the history of past disasters does not bear out their fears of antisocial behavior as long as proper leadership is provided. During the siege of Budapest people stayed in shelters for many weeks but continued to cooperate and help each other. The authors emphasize throughout the article that, in contrast to an attack of World War II, a nuclear atack that is 10 percent effective would be considered successful. This would hardly be the case if the population were well sheltered. Hence a combination of antiballistic missiles and shelters seems to hold more promise of reducing the "overbalance" of offense over defense than any other measure known to me.

Finally, and perhaps most importantly, the authors do not mention that no nation will dare to disarm if its population remains exposed to the awesome dangers the authors so well depict. Hence civil defense is also a prerequisite to disarmament.

Let us come finally to the "extrapolations" contained in the *reports of the daily press.* Many of these were crude exaggerations that may have served a useful purpose, however, by attracting attention to the article. They were encouraged by the mode of communication of the article, which made most of its points by implication. However, the result often approached the bizarre. Even *The New York Times* headline reads "Disarmament Is Called the Answer to 'Stalemate,'" as if it were desirable to have a checkmate ending to the game. The words "stalemate" and "disarmament" occur once each in the article, the former toward the middle and the latter as the last word.

A more nearly justified "extrapolation" made from the article is that no further methods of offense or defense need be explored, that is, that military science is a complete and closed book. Even this is only implied by the article. To evaluate it, it may be useful to recall similar statements about other areas, in particular about physics. These were made around the turn of the century, before the advent of atomic theory, before virtually any knowledge of the nucleus, before quantum and relativity theories, before any inkling of the results of almost all areas that are at present at the center of interest of research in physics. Statements of this sort mean partly that those who make them have, at the time of making the statements, no promising ideas in the field about which they speak. Others may have such ideas, and those making the statements may themselves conceive such ideas at a later time. The statements in question also appear to herald the impending initiation of new lines of endeavor. In the case of physics this was the turn toward microscopic phenomena; in the area of "weaponry" it may well be the exploration of a more effective defense.

Having stated the areas of disagreement, it would be well to reemphasize the agreement with what appears to be the main thesis of Wiesner and York: the importance of not relying on physical power alone. It is a truism that the purpose of power is only the achievement of certain goals, called national objectives. However, military power, like police power, works best when it works through its presence rather than by active involvement, and when it is supporting persuasion to follow rules of conduct that are just and reasonable. Certainly included is the rule to leave our country free to follow its own path of independence and individual freedom.

EUGENE P. WIGNER

Princeton University
Princeton, N.J.
December, 1964

The Detection of Underground Explosions

New methods make it possible to identify as such the great majority of earthquakes and explosions. Thus the technical basis for extending the ban on nuclear tests is established

SIR EDWARD BULLARD

July 1966

Serious interest in the detection of underground explosions dates from 1958. In that year a conference of "experts" was held in Geneva to study methods of detecting violations of a possible agreement on the suspension of nuclear tests. At that time the interest in an agreement to stop testing came mostly from a wish to slow the arms race and to moderate the "cold war"; it was thought that it might be relatively easy to reach an agreement in this field and that it might then be possible to make progress in related fields of disarmament and arms control. The wish to halt the contamination of the atmosphere was also a powerful motive, but this is not relevant to underground testing. Since the conclusion of the treaty prohibiting atmospheric tests both France and China have exploded nuclear devices, thus increasing the membership of the "nuclear club" from three to five. The main reason today for wishing to stop underground testing is the desire to hinder additional nations from developing nuclear weapons by persuading them to join in a test-ban treaty.

The 1958 conference showed how

SUBSIDENCE CRATER was left by a nuclear explosion set off 1,620 feet belowground at the Nevada test site of the U.S. Atomic Energy Commission. The explosion, of "intermediate yield," took place in a formation of volcanic tuff. The "chimney" produced by the explosion, however, extended upward into alluvium, a loosely consolidated material, with the result that the chimney collapsed.

little anyone knew about underground explosions. To remedy this situation large programs of investigation were started in both the U.S. and Britain. My purpose is not to describe the renewal of the whole field of seismology that has followed from this work but to summarize the present state of affairs as it relates to the detection of clandestine tests of nuclear weapons below the surface of the earth. The detection of such tests has three aspects: detection, location and identification. Has anything happened? If it has, where did it happen? Was it a nuclear explosion?

When a nuclear explosion occurs in a cavity within the earth, the explosive device is converted to a very hot gas that reaches the wall of the cavity as a shock wave. The pressure exerted on the wall produces stress differences much exceeding the strength of the rock, and the temperature near the wall rises above the melting point. A "plastic" wave travels through the rock, leaving it permanently distorted. The wave spreads for a few hundred meters until it is so attenuated by spreading and absorption that it can no longer permanently distort the rock. Beyond this point the plastic wave becomes an elastic wave and is propagated much as if it had been produced by an earthquake. Some seconds or minutes after the explosion the roof of the cavity collapses, leaving a chimney-like hole filled with debris and with a puddle of molten rock at the bottom. Much work has been done on the processes occurring in the immediate neighborhood of the explosion, and the main features of these processes are understood.

From the point of view of detection the important result of an underground explosion is the motion of the ground produced by the seismic wave at distant points. It is customary to use the measured ground motions at such points to calculate a quantity known as the magnitude of the earthquake or explosion causing the seismic waves. The magnitude is intended to be a measure of the energy in these waves. Owing to the large range of energies to be covered the scale is a logarithmic one; each increase of one unit in the magnitude corresponds to an increase of 250-fold in the total seismic energy. The relation of magnitude to seismic energy is very uncertain, perhaps by as much as a factor of four. Our interest, however, is not in the seismic energy but in the ground motions. In spite of the uncertainty in the relation of the magnitude to energy, the magnitude does constitute

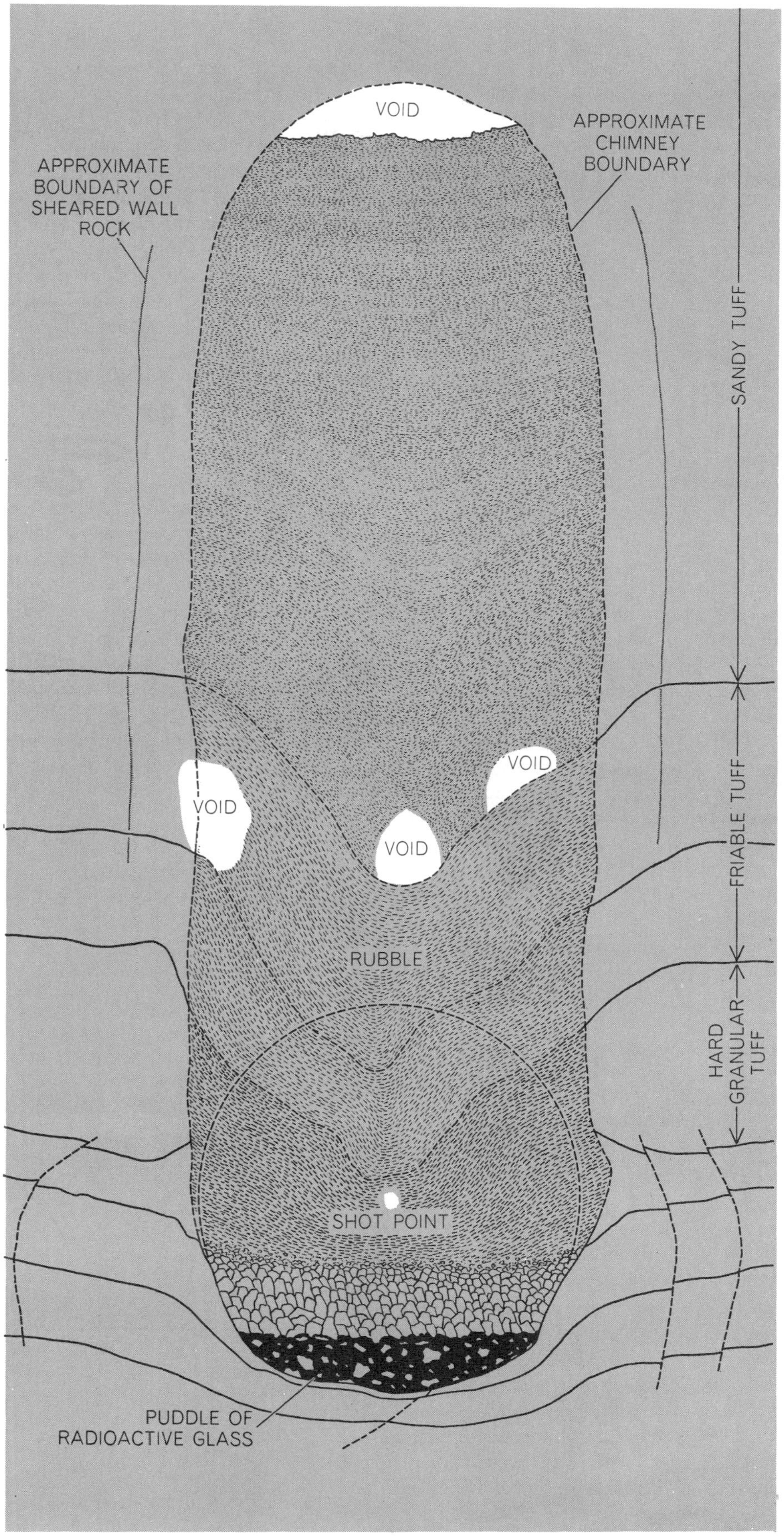

UNDERGROUND NUCLEAR EXPLOSION leaves a rubble-filled chimney above a puddle of radioactive glass. The explosion that produced this result at the Nevada test site was named "Rainier." The shot was fired at a depth of about 800 feet. Because the yield of the Rainier explosion was so low (1.7 kilotons) its effects did not extend upward into the alluvium above the chimney and thus the chimney did not collapse to produce a crater at the surface. The explosion created a temporary cavity (*white dot*) 19.8 meters in radius.

a useful summary of the observed ground motions.

The energy in the seismic waves is of course only a part of all the energy released by an explosion; in smaller explosions it is commonly a few parts per thousand of the entire energy. The principal matter of practical significance is the energy of the explosion—the "yield"—needed to produce seismic signals of a given magnitude. This energy depends on the nature of the material in which the explosion occurs. The explosive energy needed to produce a given seismic effect in alluvium—unconsolidated material of the kind deposited by a river—is about 10 times the energy needed in granite. The volcanic tuff of the test site in Nevada requires twice the explosive energy that is needed in granite. It is unlikely that a clandestine explosion would be made in alluvium; the unconsolidated material above the cavity made by such an explosion usually collapses, leaving a crater at the surface that could be photographed by a reconnaissance satellite [*see illustration on page 140*].

There has been considerable difference of opinion as to the true relation between explosive energy and seismic magnitude. From the study of a large number of explosions it appears that the amplitude of the first few cycles of ground motion at distant stations is proportional to the energy released by the explosion. From this it may be deduced that the magnitude increases by one for a tenfold increase in the explosive energy [*see illustration at right*]. Most relations previously proposed gave a slower increase in magnitude with explosive energy. The revision is due to the results from the 80-kiloton explosion ("Longshot") recently set off in hard rock in the Aleutian Islands, which gave records of amplitude comparable to a magnitude-six earthquake.

There is little room for difference of opinion concerning smaller magnitudes, for which data are available from numerous test explosions: an explosion of one kiloton in hard rock produces a magnitude-four seismic signal. The size of the smallest underground explosion that would be important in verifying a test-ban agreement is not well defined; in most discussions the lower limit has been considered to be a yield of a few kilotons, corresponding to a seismic signal of about magnitude four.

Because the surface of the earth is in continuous motion all seismic signals have to be detected against a background of seismic noise. The main advances in recent years have resulted from improvements in the ratio of signal to noise. These improvements are of three kinds: the choice of quiet sites, the use of arrays of instruments and the processing of the recorded signals.

The background noise has many causes, among which are storms at sea, waves breaking on the shore, the rocking of trees and buildings by the wind, vibrations from traffic and machinery and the effects of innumerable earthquakes too small to be detected individually. The amount of disturbance varies greatly from place to place, and one of the most useful seismological discoveries of recent years is that there exist sites where the noise level is exceptionally low. As might be expected, such sites are on hard rock, in the interiors of continents and remote from industrial activity. Excellent sites have been found at Yellowknife in northwestern Canada, in the mountain states of the U.S., in the Sahara, in India and in Australia; doubtless others could be found in the U.S.S.R., Africa and South America.

The background noise has a spectrum with a broad maximum at periods of oscillation between five and 10 seconds, whereas the bulk of the energy in the initial part of a seismic record (the *P* wave, or compressional wave) has periods between .5 and 1.5 seconds. A considerable improvement in the ratio of signal to noise can therefore be obtained by passing the signal through a filter that removes signals with periods greater than about one second. It is also desirable to remove signals whose frequencies are above 10 cycles per second; there is appreciable noise and almost no signal in this frequency range. When this filtering has been done, the ground motion at the best sites is less than 10^{-7} centimeter—only a few times the diameter of an atom—for a large part of the time. A poor site may give values 10 or 100 times greater.

Background noise is not the only impediment to obtaining a clear record of an explosion or earthquake. As a seismic wave travels through the earth it is reflected and scattered by discontinuities. Such reflected and scattered waves complicate the signal and increase the difficulty of extracting information about the source. A rather similar effect is produced by scattering

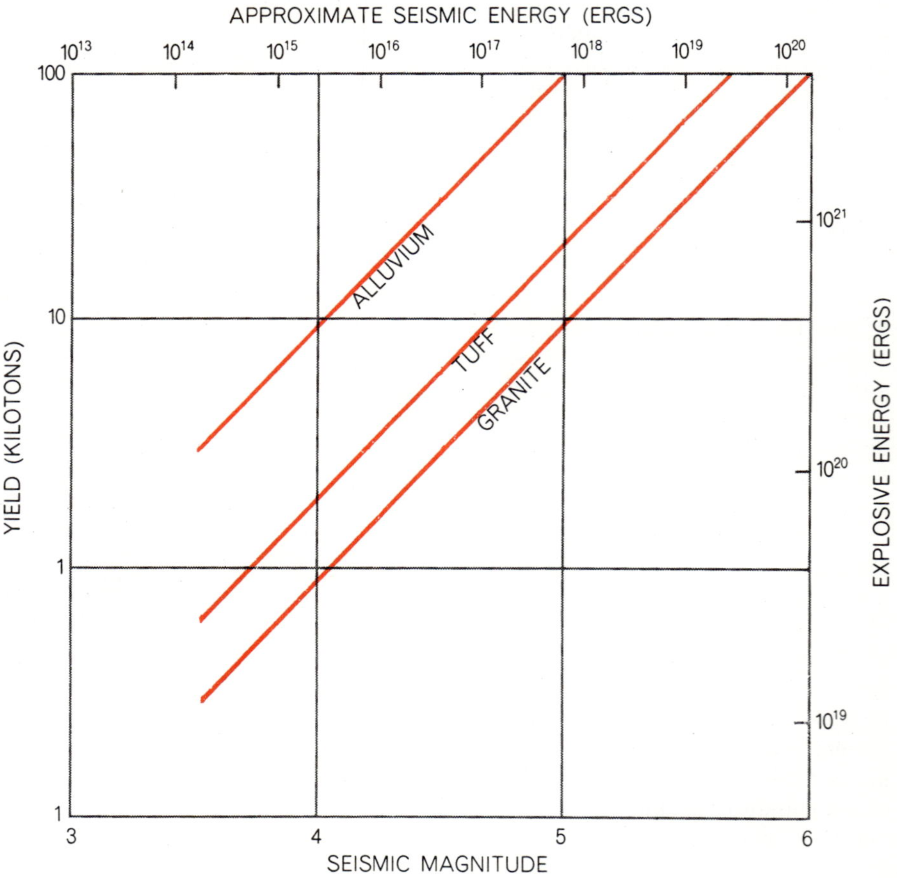

EXPLOSIVE ENERGY required to produce a seismic disturbance of a given magnitude is shown for three kinds of material. There is some evidence that the curves for alluvium and tuff should bend upward to give lower magnitudes for large explosions. A kiloton is the energy released by the explosion of 1,000 tons of TNT, equivalent to about 4.2×10^{19} ergs.

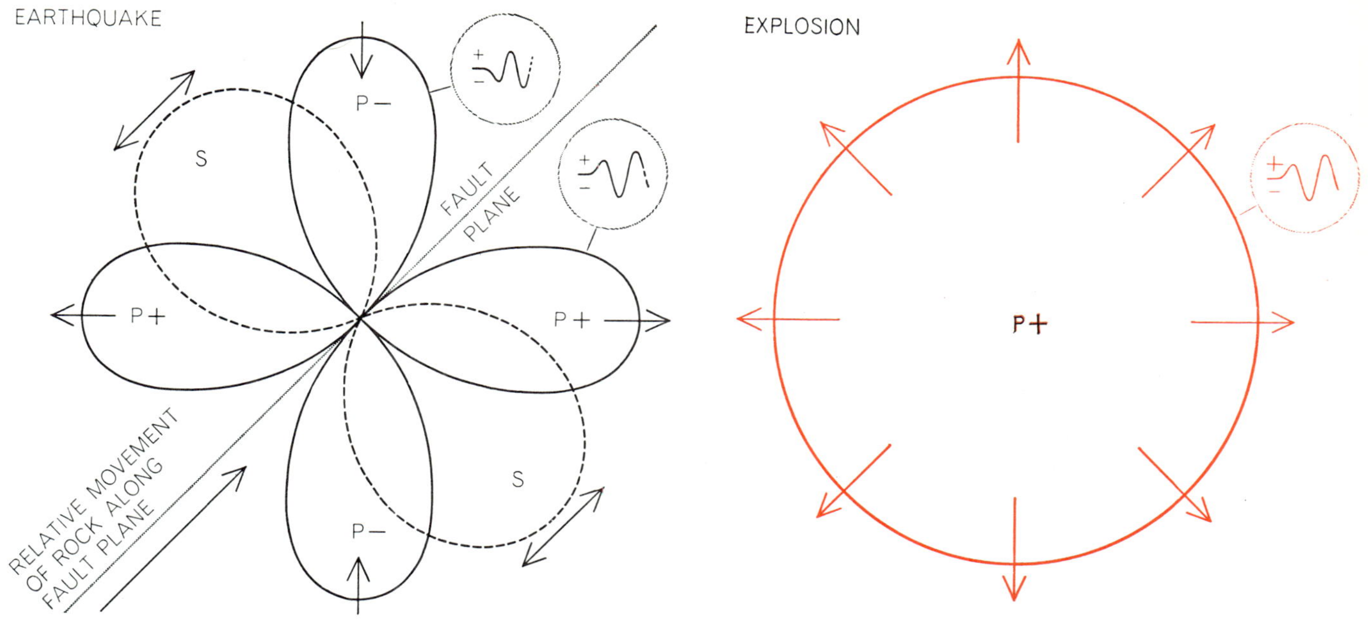

COMPARISON OF EXPLOSION WITH EARTHQUAKE shows that an earthquake (*left*) characteristically produces compressional *P* waves and distortional *S* waves, both of which vary with direction. In contrast, an explosion (*right*) produces an initial outward compressional motion in all directions. An earthquake normally originates in a fault where two bodies of rock slip past each other.

from topographic irregularities at the surface of the earth near the seismograph. This "signal-generated noise" is particularly troublesome when a large part of the path of the signal from source to seismograph runs through the outermost part of the earth. At greater distances the seismic ray goes steeply down from the source and steeply up to the seismograph [*see illustration below*]. There is then only a small part of its path over which it is affected by the complications of geology; the greater part is deep in the earth's mantle, where the material is more uniform than it is near the surface. Accordingly if one wishes to study the structure of the earth's crust, one should make measurements within, say, 1,000 kilometers of the seismic source, but if one wishes to study the nature of seismic sources or to detect clandestine explosions, one should observe at distances beyond 3,000 kilometers.

Between 3,000 and 10,000 kilometers the amplitudes of the first few cycles of the seismic signals are as great as or greater than they are between 1,000 and 2,000 kilometers. Beyond 10,000 kilometers the earth's core casts a shad-

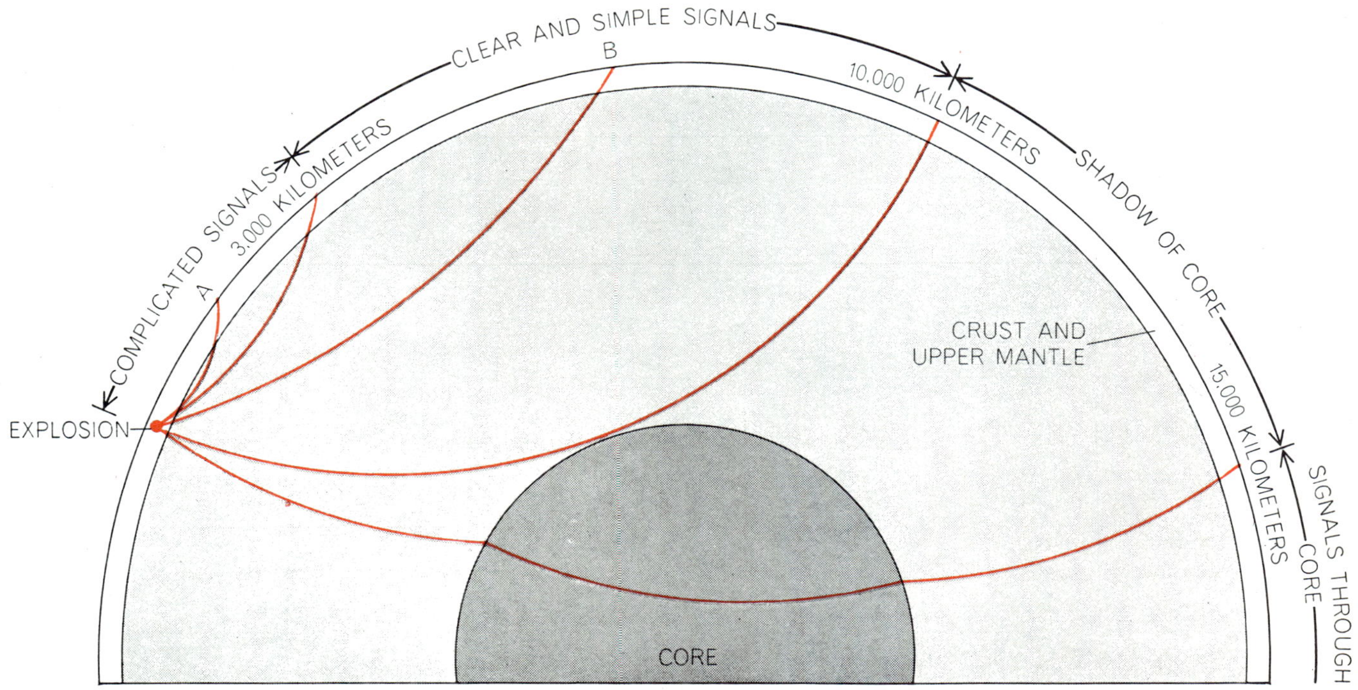

SEISMIC WAVES, whether produced by an earthquake or an explosion, can be recorded at great distances. In fact, the signals received at distances between 3,000 and 10,000 kilometers from an event are usually clearer than signals received within 3,000 kilometers. A ray received at *A* has its entire path in the crust and upper mantle of the earth, where irregularities in the rocks scatter the energy and complicate the record. The ray to *B* has most of its path deep in the earth, where the irregularities are few.

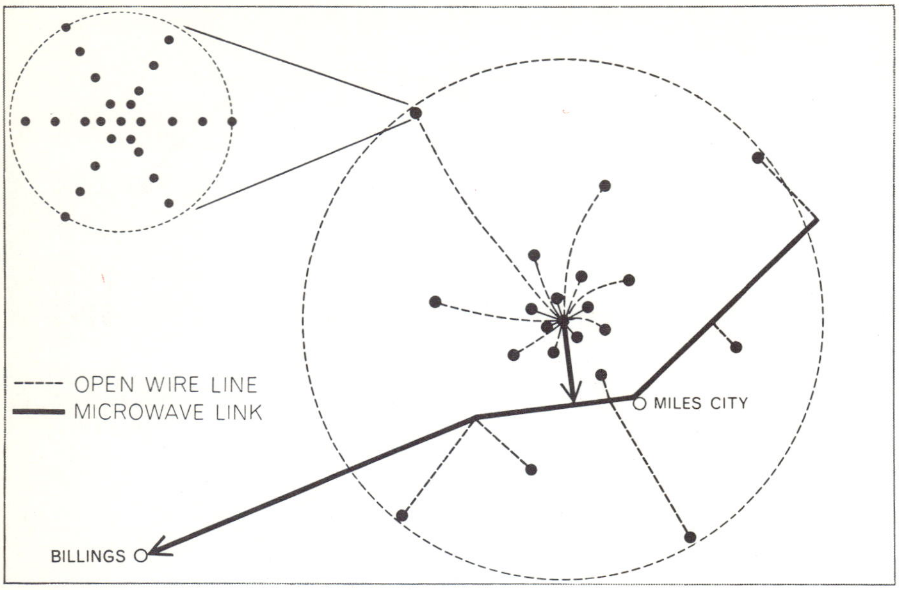

LARGE SEISMIC ARRAY recently installed by the AEC near Billings, Mont., consists of 21 clusters, each containing 25 seismometers. The clusters are seven kilometers in diameter. The entire seismic array is spread over a circular area 200 kilometers in diameter.

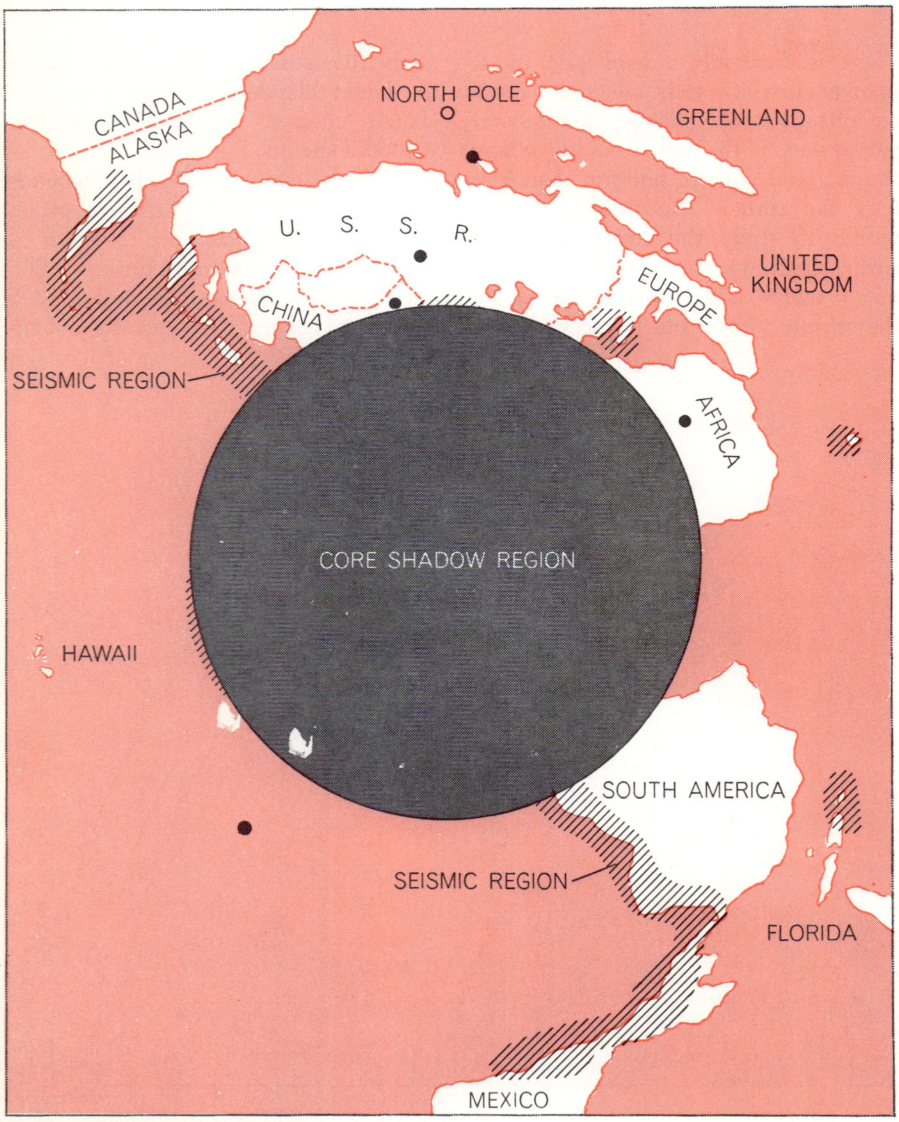

SEISMIC VIEW OF THE EARTH from the center of the Montana array shows the region in which seismic events can be detected and that in which they cannot be. Earthquake regions are hatched. Black dots indicate nuclear test sites in the U.S.S.R. and elsewhere.

ow, making satisfactory observations of the earlier part of the seismogram impossible. Between 14,000 kilometers and the antipodes (20,000 kilometers) waves can be received through the core and could probably be used in the study of seismic sources, but this range of distances has been little studied for purposes of bomb-test detection. The range from 3,000 to 10,000 kilometers is convenient because the whole of the U.S.S.R. lies within this range from stations in the U.S.

A large improvement in the ratio of signal to noise can be obtained by the use of an array of seismographs instead of a single instrument. The idea of an array is not a new one; arrays have been employed for many years in the reception of short radio waves and in radio astronomy. If a row of n detectors receives a signal, and if the outputs from all the detectors are combined (after delaying the outputs to allow for different times of arrival at the different instruments), all the signals will add up to give a signal with an amplitude n times the amplitude of that from a single detector [*see illustration on next page*]. The array can be regarded as a telescope that selects signals coming from a given direction or, what is the same thing, as a device that selects signals arriving with a given apparent velocity of propagation over the ground. By adjusting the correction for the time lag it is possible to accentuate different parts of the seismogram, for example the compressional *P* waves or the distortional *S* waves. If the instruments of the array are not all on a single line but are spread out in two dimensions on the surface of the earth, the time lags can be adjusted so as to pick out signals coming from a given compass direction as well as those coming at a given angle to the vertical.

Obviously there would be no advantage in using an array if it enhanced the noise as much as it enhanced the signal. Provided that the noise at the different detectors is uncorrelated, an array of n detectors will yield a total value for noise that is roughly the square root of n times the noise received by a single detector. As a consequence the ratio of signal amplitude to noise amplitude will be increased in the ratio of n divided by the square root of n, that is, by a factor equal to the square root of n. For a real array the noise, particularly the signal-generated noise, will be partially correlated at the different detectors, and the improvement attainable may be greater or less than the

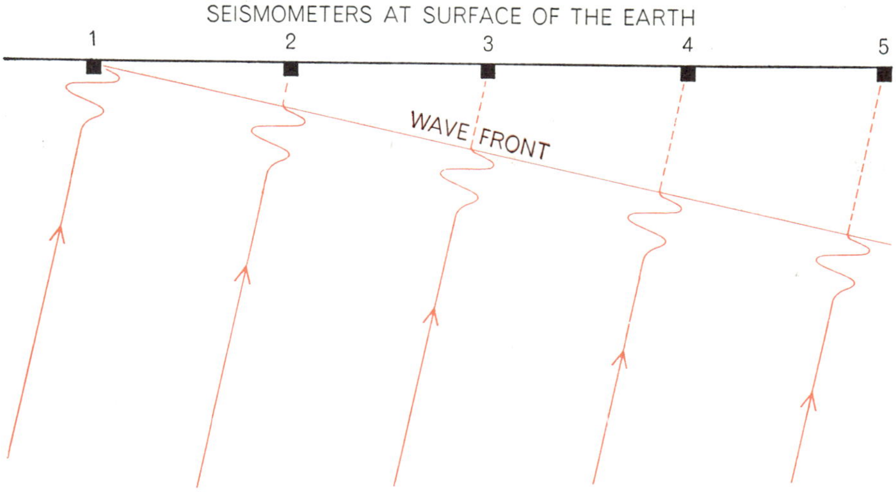

FUNCTION OF SEISMIC ARRAY is to enhance the signal from a seismic event while suppressing noise. The diagram shows a seismic wave traveling upward to a line of five seismometers near the surface of the earth. The signal arrives first at the detector at the far left. To reach the next detector the wave must travel an extra distance. If the signals from the detectors are suitably delayed before they are added together, the combined output from the five detectors will have an amplitude five times that from a single detector.

square root of *n*. In practice it is usually possible to reach an improvement equal to the square root of *n* by using an array whose diameter is 20 kilometers or more. Since the number of detectors, *n*, in an array can exceed 100, the factor represented by the square root of *n* may represent a very large improvement.

An array can be organized in many ways to meet particular requirements, and much work has been done on the properties of different layouts. A common arrangement is to put two lines of instruments on the arms of a cross each about 20 kilometers in length. In the large-aperture seismic array recently installed in Montana the array consists of 21 clusters of seismometers spread over a circle 200 kilometers in diameter; each cluster contains 25 detectors spread over a circle seven kilometers in diameter. All 525 detectors are at the bottom of holes 200 feet deep to reduce noise generated at the surface by wind and other causes [*see top illustration on preceding page*].

Filtering and adding the outputs from a number of instruments is a linear process, and is especially suitable for improving the ratio of signal to noise when the signal is smaller than the noise, or not much larger. When the signal has been raised well above the noise level by these methods, it is advantageous to use nonlinear methods to "clean up" the record.

A particularly useful technique is to take the two records produced by summing all the instruments on each arm of a cross array, to accentuate the parts of these records that are similar and to reduce the parts that are dissimilar. This can be done by feeding the two records into a multiplier, multiplying them point by point and smoothing the product over time intervals of 1.5 or two seconds [*see illustration on following page*]. Such a record is called a correlogram.

With the aid of correlograms it has been possible to separate the signal of a small (400-pound) underground chemical explosion from the seismic disturbance produced by a small earthquake, both recorded by an array 2,400 kilometers distant [*see top illustration on page 149*]. If the array had been located several hundred kilometers farther away from the disturbances, the record of the explosion would probably have been even simpler. The detection of so small an explosion even though it was obscured by a preceding earthquake is remarkable. It shows that an explosion of the size of significance for bomb-test detection will usually be detected; the main difficulty is to identify it as an explosion.

Information on the accuracy with which a seismic event can be located is not as complete as could be wished. The onset of the signals from an explosion can be determined to within a few tenths of a second. If a network of 10 or 20 stations could achieve this accuracy, the source would be located within a few kilometers. In practice the accuracy is degraded by local variations in the velocity of seismic waves, about which information is largely lacking. If data from stations distant from the event are used, it seems realistic to estimate that the site can be located within a circular area whose radius is about eight kilometers. Stations that are 500 to 2,000 kilometers from the event may give much larger errors, owing to irregularities in seismic velocities in the crust and upper mantle.

Since the great majority of events recorded at seismic stations are earthquakes, the critical problem in attempting to detect clandestine explosions is to distinguish a very few explosions among a great many earthquakes. Not surprisingly, small earthquakes are much more numerous than large ones. Roughly speaking, the number decreases by a factor of 10 for each increase of one unit in seismic magnitude. Throughout the world each year there are about 10,000 earthquakes of magnitude between four and five and only 10 or 20 of magnitude seven or greater [*see bottom illustration on page 149*].

About 1.5 percent of the world's earthquakes occur in the U.S.S.R. In an average year some 170 of these will be above magnitude four and only two or three will be above magnitude six. These numbers are only estimates of mean rates; the actual numbers fluctuate considerably from year to year. The fluctuations exceed the statistical expectancy for random events because in some years there may be 100 or more aftershocks following a single large earthquake. In a given year the total number of earthquakes above magnitude four in the U.S.S.R. might be as high as 300 or as low as 100.

The distribution of earthquakes over the world is extremely nonuniform; the great bulk of them occur along the Alpine-Himalayan chain, on the margins of the Pacific Ocean and along the mid-ocean ridges. In the U.S.S.R. earthquakes are practically confined to a belt along the southern border of the country and to the Kamchatka Peninsula, with a few on a north-south line to the east of the Lena River [*see illustration on pages 146 and 147*]. The areas of older rocks that constitute the greater part of the country appear to be completely free from earthquakes. The Russian testing ground near Semipalatinsk is just north of the earthquake belt and the testing ground in Novaya Zemlya is in an almost earthquake-free region.

Some earthquakes cause fractures at the surface of the earth; others cause fracturing entirely below the surface, commonly at depths of from 10 to 60 kilometers. The deepest earthquakes are about 750 kilometers below the surface.

The deep earthquakes occur only in certain places, particularly on the inner side of the earthquake belt surrounding the Pacific. This can be seen in the map below: in the Kamchatka region the earthquakes just offshore are shallow and most of those inland are deep.

At first it seems that it should not be too difficult to distinguish an earthquake from an explosion. The mechanism at the source is quite different. An earthquake normally has its origin in a fault where two bodies of rock slip past each other, whereas an explosion produces a sudden and spherically symmetrical pressure pulse. The first motion from an explosion is always an outward-moving compressional pulse, which is similar in all directions. A fault, on the other hand, generates both compressional *P* waves and distortional S waves whose motion differs in different directions. The first motion is inward in some places and outward in others [*see top illustration on page 143*]. Moreover, the motion produced by an explosion is much simpler than that from an earthquake. This is not unexpected; an explosion is localized in both space and time, whereas a fault extends for some distance and may take some seconds to complete its movement.

These criteria have been considerably sharpened by the development of seismic arrays. The initial wave form can now be seen with great clarity, largely freed from the effects of the transmission path. For example, an underground explosion near Semipalatinsk on May 16, 1964, produced closely similar records at stations at Eskdalemuir in Scotland and Yellowknife in Canada [*see top illustration on page 150*]. The first few seconds of the records are almost

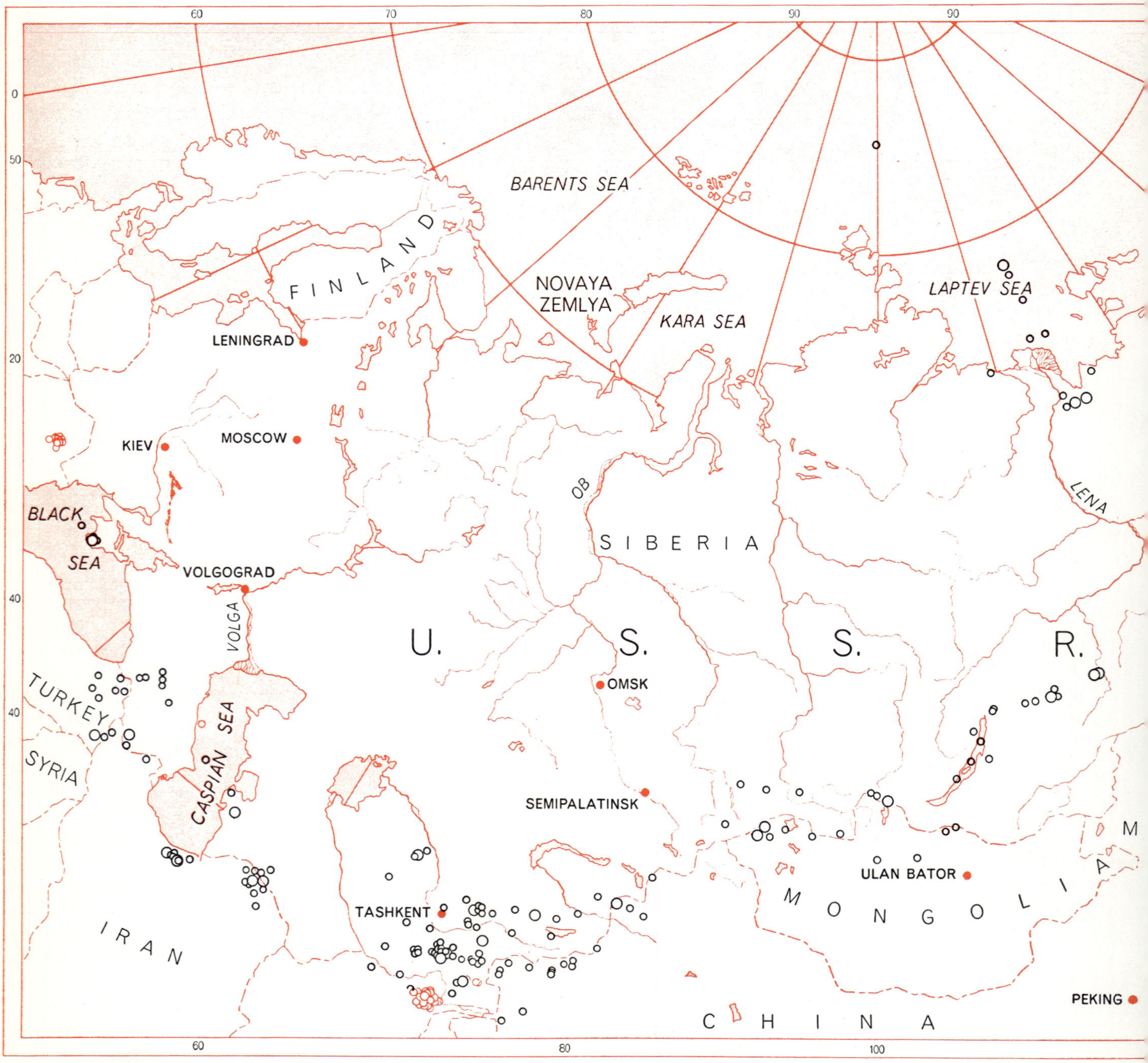

SEISMIC MAP OF U.S.S.R. shows earthquakes above magnitude 5¼ that occurred from 1911 to 1959. The shocks above magnitude 6½ are represented by larger circles, those of 5¼ to 6½ by smaller circles. Black circles indicate shallow earthquakes: depth less than 35 kilometers. Open colored circles indicate depths of between 35 and 300 kilometers; colored circles with dots indicate depths exceeding 300 kilometers. The map is based on one published by the Soviet Academy of Sciences. Novaya Zemlya and Semipalatinsk,

identical at the two stations in spite of the widely separated paths followed by the seismic waves and the completely different geological setting of the two arrays. The wave form must therefore be determined largely by the events at the source of the energy.

Another striking example is given by comparing the records of the seismic waves from an explosion at the French testing ground in Algeria with those from an earthquake in Libya. The arrays at Eskdalemuir, Yellowknife and a station at Pole Mountain, Wyo., gave very similar records of the explosion and much more complicated and dissimilar records of the earthquake [*see bottom illustration on page 150*].

It has been suggested that the complexity in the wave form of earthquakes is due not to the source mechanism but to the tendency of earthquakes to occur in more complex geological settings than those in which explosions are fired. The recent Longshot explosion in the Aleutians has demonstrated that this is not so. This shot gave characteristic explosion records in spite of being fired in the circum-Pacific earthquake belt. The suggestion that it is only earthquakes of magnitude above 4.5 that have complicated records also appears to have no foundation.

The determination of depth is another criterion that enables a large number of earthquakes to be eliminated. An event occurring at a depth exceeding eight kilometers is certainly an earthquake. About 30 percent of all earthquakes occur at depths exceeding 50 kilometers. The number with depths between eight kilometers and 50 kilometers is not easy to determine because the complexity of the wave form makes it difficult to detect the wave reflected from the surface above the site of the fault. If an earthquake with a simple wave form occurred in this depth range, it should be possible to determine its depth and thus demonstrate that it is not an explosion. By a careful examination of records from arrays it is sometimes possible to estimate the depth of an explosion fired at a depth of as little as one kilometer below the surface of the earth. The determination of depth is of particular importance for detecting explosions in Kamchatka, where most of the shallow earthquakes occur in the sea just offshore and most of those on land are deep.

Attempts to use criteria depending on S waves and surface waves have not been very successful. The horizontally polarized S waves from an explosion are smaller than those from an earthquake, but there are many small earthquakes without detectable S waves or surface waves. The probable explanation is that the period of these waves falls near the peak in the frequency distribution of background noise. It is also true that less effort has been put into such methods than has been devoted to the study of *P* waves; moreover, the instruments used in the arrays are designed to respond to vertical motions and thus are unsuitable for detecting horizontally polarized waves. It may be that the matter deserves closer attention. It would be particularly interesting to see what results could be obtained from a cross array equipped with instruments capable of responding along three coordinate axes.

The critical question is whether, when all these criteria have been used, there is a residuum of earthquakes that are indistinguishable from explosions. The results of an examination of a worldwide sample of 161 earthquakes with depths of less than 50 kilometers have been published by the United Kingdom Atomic Energy Authority. There were seven earthquakes, or 4.5 percent, that could not be distinguished from explosions. This would give an average of eight "suspicious events" per year in the U.S.S.R. Estimates by some other authorities are about twice as high. The discrepancy is not surprising. "Suspicious" is not a precisely defined concept; how many events one regards as suspicious will depend to some extent on how suspicious one is.

The number of arrays used in the Atomic Energy Authority's investigation was three, but for a large part of the time only one was in operation. Five of the seven explosion-like earthquakes were recorded while only one array was in operation. Some improvement is to be expected from the use of more arrays, particularly from those recently established in Australia and India, which receive signals from the U.S.S.R. in directions differing widely from the directions of signals received in Britain, Canada and the U.S. The arrays themselves are also susceptible to improvement; those employed in gathering the sample had only 20 detectors, compared with the total of 525 in the array in Montana. The use of more refined determinations of focal depth would also probably remove some ambiguous events.

It is clearly possible to chip away at the number of earthquakes within the U.S.S.R. that might be mistaken for explosions, but there is no reason to suppose that this number can be reduced to zero. Even if there are no earthquakes that virtually duplicate explosions, there may be earthquakes whose fault planes lie at such an angle that they give an initial outward motion at all distances beyond 3,000 kilometers. If one of these happened to give a simple wave form and to be shallow, it might not be distinguished from an explosion. With a system as complicated as the earth almost anything can happen occasionally. It seems prudent to assume that we shall not get a system that never mistakes an earthquake for an explosion.

In a sample of 35 underground explo-

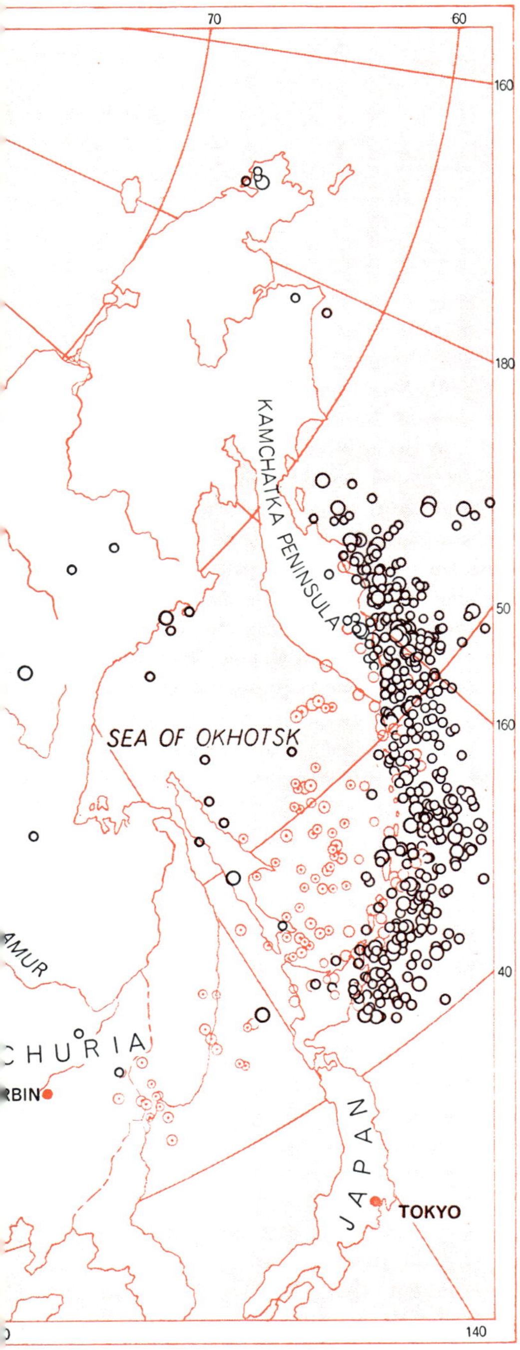

used as nuclear-test sites, are in regions that are free from earthquakes. In the Kamchatka area the earthquakes just offshore are shallow and most of those inland are deep.

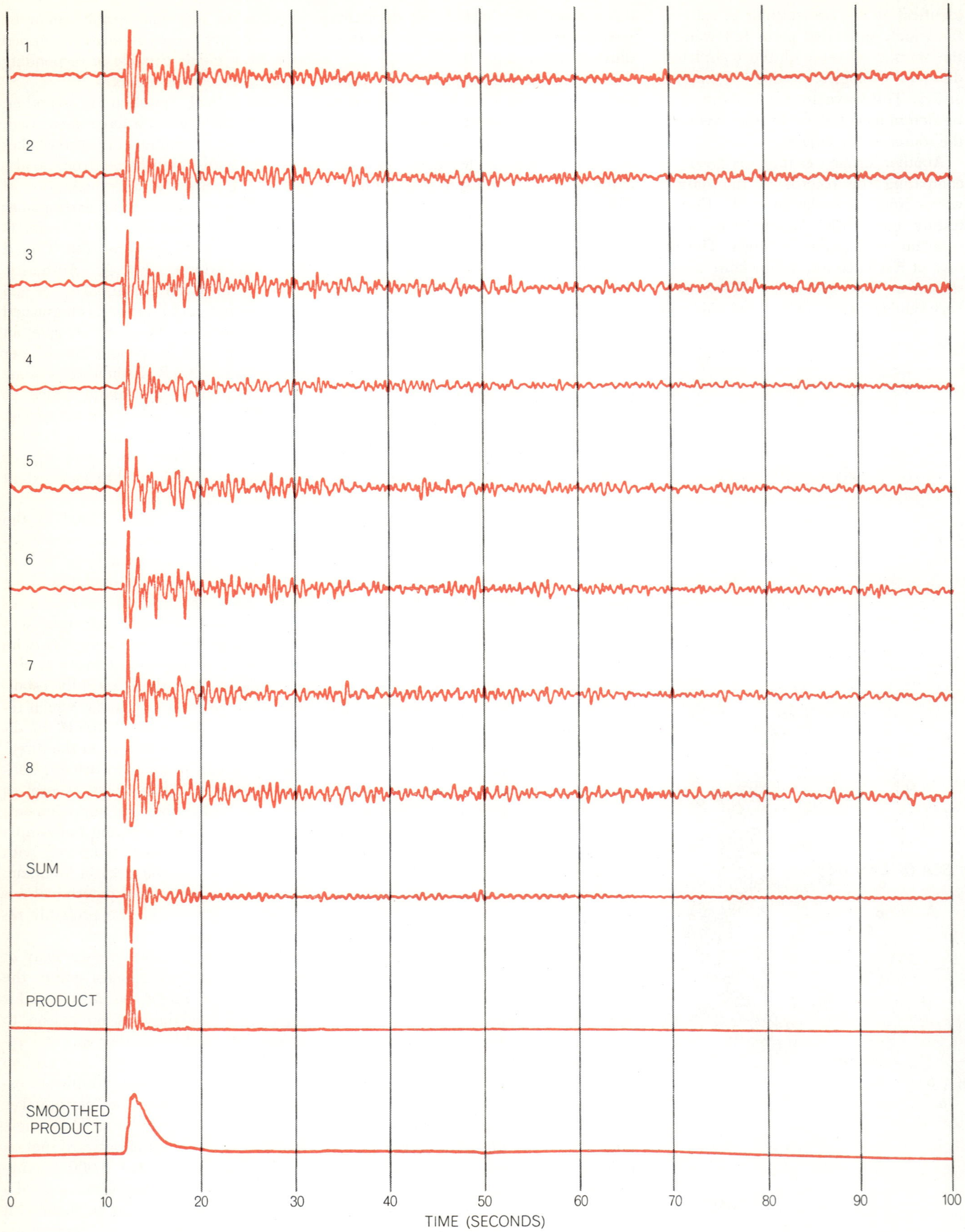

EXPLOSION NEAR SEMIPALATINSK, a test site in the U.S.S.R., produced these records at a seismic array at Eskdalemuir in Scotland, 5,300 kilometers from the event. The first eight traces are from single instruments on one arm of the cross array. The next trace shows the sum of all instruments on both arms of the array. The next trace gives the product of the records from the two arms; the bottom trace shows the product after smoothing. The first wave to arrive is the compressional *P* wave of the explosion. The oscillations that are removed in the last two traces are noise generated by the signal itself. The explosion took place on May 16, 1964.

sions studied by seismological means, one on Novaya Zemlya would have been regarded as an earthquake if it had occurred in a seismic region. Such misinterpretation is not, however, of much significance. In order to take advantage of it one would have to know beforehand that the conditions were such that an explosion would be misinterpreted as an earthquake.

Much attention has been given to the possibility that the seismic effects of an explosion could be reduced or modified so that it was undetectable or appeared to be an earthquake. The most promising method is to set off the explosion in a very large cavity. If this were done, theory suggests that the amplitude of the seismic signal would be reduced by a factor of 100.

The theory has been verified for chemical explosions of up to about one ton and there is no reason to suppose that it would not apply to nuclear explosions. In spite of the importance of the matter no experiments have been made with kiloton explosions. This is probably because of the great engineering difficulties involved in making cavities several hundred feet in diameter and also because of the possibility that such a cavity would collapse after an explosion and form a detectable crater at the surface. If the method were to be used for concealing a clandestine explosion, there would also be great difficulty in removing millions of cubic feet of material from the cavity without leaving conspicuous signs on the surface.

Other methods of concealment that have been proposed are to set off several explosions in a short interval or to set off an explosion just after an earthquake has occurred. Neither method is likely to be effective. The second entails a wait of years before a suitable earthquake occurs near the place where the test has been prepared.

It may be that it is possible to devise a method of concealing a nuclear explosion. As far as is known, however, this has not been done. To do it would itself involve an extensive series of tests. One of the reasons for wishing that a comprehensive test ban be not too long delayed is that the ban would prevent the development of methods of concealment that, if they were discovered before tests stop, would make agreement more difficult.

This article is not the place to discuss at length the influence that the facts presented here should have on international negotiations. The main political

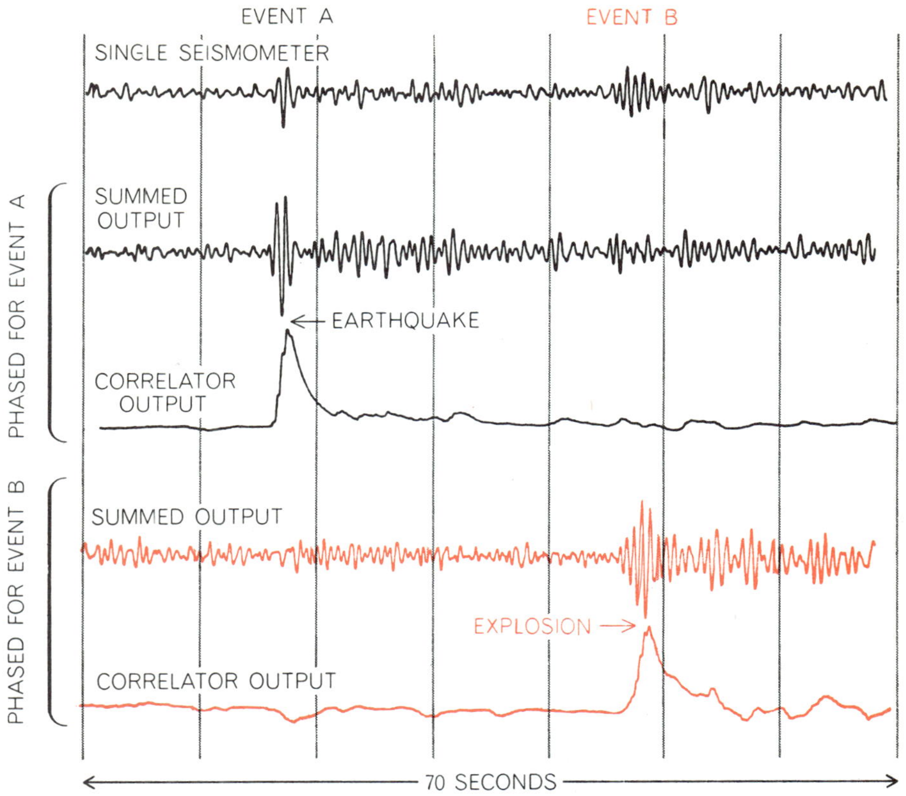

EARTHQUAKE FOLLOWED BY SMALL EXPLOSION at a distance of some 2,400 kilometers were clearly distinguished by the seismic array at Yellowknife in Canada. The explosion was produced by .2 kiloton of chemical explosive set off belowground at Climax, Colo. The top trace shows the output of a single seismometer. The second trace shows the effect of adding the traces from 20 detectors with time lags chosen to emphasize the earthquake. In the fourth trace the lags emphasize the explosion. The remaining traces are "correlograms" obtained by multiplying and smoothing the summed output from the two arms of the array. Had the explosion been farther away the record probably would have been simpler.

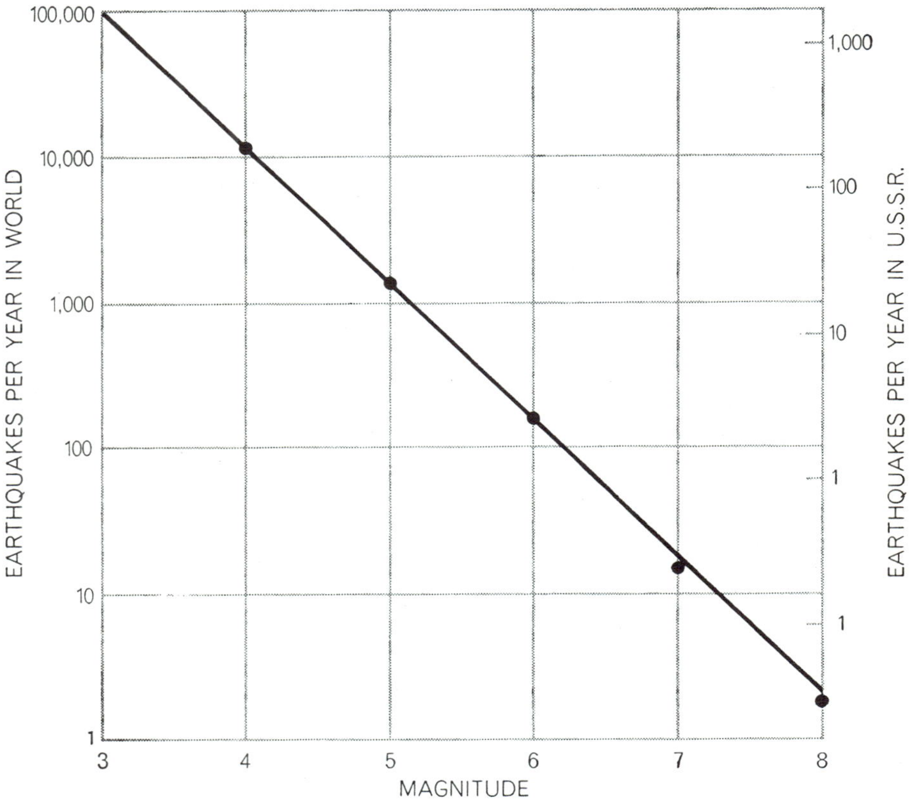

ANNUAL NUMBER OF EARTHQUAKES above a given magnitude are shown for the entire world and for the U.S.S.R. It is assumed that 1.4 percent of all earthquakes occur inside Russian territory. There are sizable annual fluctuations around these mean rates.

problem is to decide what means of verification, if any, are needed to ensure that a "suspicious event" is not a clandestine explosion. The only effective means of verification is to inspect the neighborhood of the event. The exact nature of the inspection is not of the first importance; a violator of a test ban would be unlikely to allow an inspection of a real explosion. Rather than be caught red-handed he would incur the odium of refusing access to the site or of abrogating the treaty. The object of having the right of inspection is to demonstrate to ourselves and to the world in general that suspicious events are not explosions, and to get a strong indication of a violation from the obstruction that would occur if a proposal were made to inspect the site of an actual explosion.

A formal theory can be set up: If there are *N* suspicious events in country *A* per year, and country *B* is allowed *n* inspections, what is the probability of *A*'s conducting *M* tests in a year without *B*'s asking to inspect one or more of them? *A* will require this probability to be quite high, say .95, since the consequences of being caught cheating on a matter concerned with nuclear weapons are serious. *B*, on the other hand, requires a high probability of detecting *A*'s violation before too many tests have been carried out. In other words, *B* wants the probability formula to produce a low number. The following figures show for various numbers of inspections the probabilities that *B* will *not* ask to inspect one or more of the tests when there are five tests among 15 suspicious events:

Number of inspections	1	2	3	4
Probabilities	.67	.43	.26	.15

In summary, one can say that the technical facts are as clear as can be expected for a complicated subject and that there are now no very serious differences of opinion about them. Some further improvements in equipment are possible, particularly in the provision of more seismographic arrays. These, however, can hardly affect the political decisions, which must depend on a balance between the desirability of a test ban and the disadvantages of knowing that a few ambiguous events will occur in the U.S.S.R. each year, any of which could be an explosion but all or most of which are earthquakes. In practice the choice is among the following three courses:

First, to say that the real risks exceed the hypothetical gains and that we therefore do not want to seek a test ban.

Second, to accept something like the Russian offer (since withdrawn) of "two or three" inspections a year.

Third, to say that no nation is likely to conduct clandestine tests in circumstances where there is an appreciable probability of their opponent's knowing that they are doing so, even if the violation cannot be proved in a court of law, and that a treaty without inspection is therefore acceptable.

Most informed opinion would accept the second course. The difficulty is that the Russians have stated categorically and recently that it is not acceptable to them. It is therefore not a possible choice for the U.S. The acceptance of the third course would be made easier if there were little chance of making important improvements in weapons by underground testing. In the absence of detailed knowledge one can only say that it is difficult to imagine what the improvements could be. It might be objected that acceptance of a test ban without inspection would leave us on a slippery slope where, if we were sufficiently lacking in judgment or firmness, we might find it hard to refuse unverified agreements about matters vital to our security.

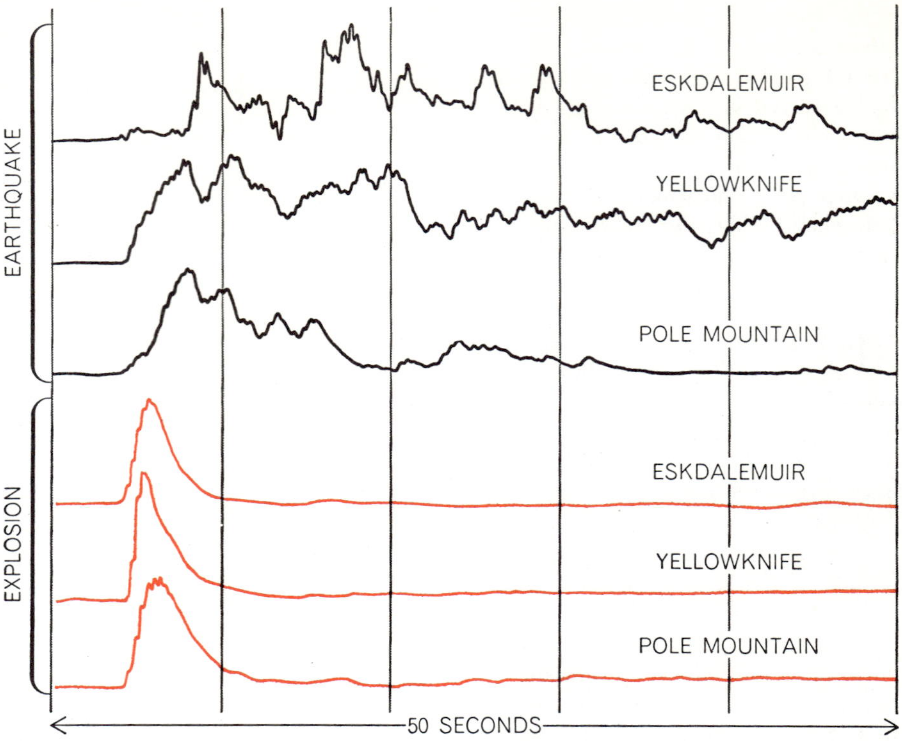

EARTHQUAKE AND EXPLOSION are compared in the correlograms obtained from seismic arrays at Eskdalemuir, Yellowknife and Pole Mountain, Wyo. The earthquake (*top*), which occurred in Libya, gives a long-drawn-out, complicated record that is visibly different at different stations. The nuclear explosion (*bottom*), which was conducted by the French government at its test site in Algeria, gives simple and similar records at all stations.

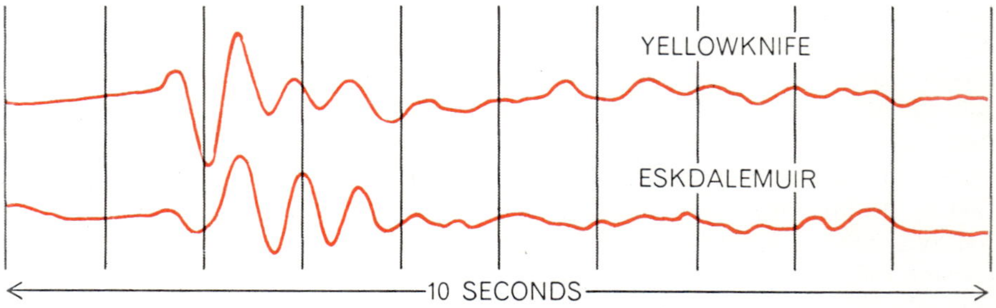

FRENCH UNDERGROUND EXPLOSION produced these records at Yellowknife and Eskdalemuir, respectively 9,000 and 3,500 kilometers from the event. The two traces are the summed output of all the instruments at each site. It can be seen that the initial wave form depends on the character of the original signal and is largely independent of the distance and the path from the source to the seismic arrays and of the geology near the arrays.

17

Treaty Banning Nuclear Weapons in the Atmosphere, in Outer Space, and under Water

Text of treaty done at Moscow
on August 5, 1963.
U.S. ratification deposited October 10, 1963.
Entered into force October 10, 1963.
Not published in Scientific American.

The Governments of the United States of America, the United Kingdom of Great Britain and Northern Ireland, and the Union of Soviet Socialist Republics, hereinafter referred to as the "Original Parties,"

Proclaiming as their principal aim the speediest possible achievement of an agreement on general and complete disarmament under strict international control in accordance with the objectives of the United Nations which would put an end to the armaments race and eliminate the incentive to the production and testing, of all kinds of weapons, including nuclear weapons,

Seeking to achieve the discontinuance of all test explosions of nuclear weapons for all time, determined to continue negotiations to this end, and desiring to put an end to the contamination of man's environment by radioactive substances,

Have agreed as follows:

Article I

1. Each of the Parties to this Treaty undertakes to prohibit, to prevent, and not to carry out any nuclear weapon test explosion, or any other nuclear explosion, at any place under its jurisdiction or control:

(a) in the atmosphere; beyond its limits, including outer space; or underwater, including territorial waters or high seas; or

(b) in any other environment if such explosion causes radioactive debris to be present outside the territorial limits of the State under whose jurisdiction or control such explosion is conducted. It is understood in this connection that the provisions of this subparagraph are without prejudice to the conclusion of a treaty resulting in the permanent banning of all nuclear test explosions, including all such explosions underground, the conclusion of which, as the Parties have stated in the Preamble to this Treaty, they seek to achieve.

2. Each of the Parties to this Treaty undertakes furthermore to refrain from causing, encouraging, or in any way participating in, the carrying out of any nuclear weapon test explosion, or any other nuclear explosion, anywhere which would take place in any of the environments described, or have the effect referred to, in paragraph 1 of this Article.

Article II

1. Any Party may propose amendments to this Treaty. The text of any proposed amendment shall be submitted to the Depositary Governments which shall circulate it to all Parties to this Treaty. Thereafter, if requested to do so by one-third or more of the Parties, the Depositary Governments shall convene a conference, to which they shall invite all of the Parties, to consider such amendment.

2. Any amendment to this Treaty must be approved by a majority of the votes of all the Parties to this Treaty, including the votes of all of the Original Parties. The amendment shall enter into force for all Parties upon the deposit of instruments of ratification by a majority of all the Parties, including the instruments of ratification of all of the Original Parties.

Article III

1. This Treaty shall be open to all States for signature. Any State which does not sign this Treaty before its entry into force accordance with paragraph 3 of this Article may accede to it at any time.

2. This Treaty shall be subject to ratification by signatory States. Instruments of ratification and instruments of accession shall be deposited with the Governments of the Original Parties—the United States of America, the United Kingdom of Great Britain and Northern Ireland, and the Union of Soviet Socialist Republics—which are hereby designated the Depositary Governments.

3. This Treaty shall enter into force after its ratification by all the Original Parties and the deposit of their instruments of ratification.

4. For States whose instruments of ratification or accession are deposited subsequent to the entry into force of this Treaty, it shall enter into force on the date of the deposit of their instruments of ratification or accession.

5. The Depositary Governments shall promptly inform all signatory and acceding States of the date of each signature, the date of deposit of each instrument of ratification of an accession to this Treaty, the date of its entry into force, and the date of receipt of any requests for conferences or other notices.

6. This Treaty shall be registered by the Depositary Governments pursuant to Article 102 of the Charter of the United Nations.

Article IV

This Treaty shall be of unlimited duration.

Each Party shall in exercising its national sovereignty have the right to withdraw from the Treaty if it decides that extraordinary events, related to the subject matter of this Treaty, have jeopardized the supreme interests of its country. It shall give notice of such withdrawal to all other Parties to the Treaty three months in advance.

Article V

This Treaty, of which the English and Russian texts are equally authentic, shall be deposited in the archives of the Depositary Governments. Duly certified copies of this Treaty shall be transmitted by the Depositary Governments to the Governments of the signatory and acceding States.

IN WITNESS WHEREOF the undersigned, duly authorized, have signed this Treaty.

DONE in triplicate at the city of Moscow the fifth day of August, one thousand nine hundred and sixty-three.

For the Government of the United States of America

Dean Rusk

For the Government of the United Kingdom of Great Britain and Northern Ireland

Alex Douglas-Home

For the Government of the Union of Soviet Socialist Republics

A. Gromyko

18

Treaty on the Non-Proliferation of Nuclear Weapons

Text of treaty signed at Washington, London, and Moscow on July 1, 1968. U.S. ratification deposited March 5, 1970. Entered into force March 5, 1970. Not published in Scientific American.

The States concluding this Treaty, hereinafter referred to as the "Parties to the Treaty,"

Considering the devastation that would be visited upon all mankind by a nuclear war and the consequent need to make every effort to avert the danger of such a war and to take measures to safeguard the security of peoples,

Believing that the proliferation of nuclear weapons would seriously enhance the danger of nuclear war,

In conformity with resolutions of the United Nations General Assembly calling for the conclusion of an agreement on the prevention of wider dissemination of nuclear weapons,

Undertaking to cooperate in facilitating the application of International Atomic Energy Agency safeguards on peaceful nuclear activities,

Expressing their support for research, development and other efforts to further the application, within the framework of the International Atomic Energy Agency safeguards system, of the principle of safeguarding effectively the flow of source and special fissionable materials by use of instruments and other techniques at certain strategic points,

Affirming the principle that the benefits of peaceful applications of nuclear technology, including any technological by-products which may be derived by nuclear-weapon States from the development of nuclear explosive devices, should be available for peaceful purposes to all Parties to the Treaty, whether nuclear-weapon or non-nuclear-weapon States,

Convinced that, in furtherance of this principle, all Parties to the Treaty are entitled to participate in the fullest possible exchange of scientific information for, and to contribute alone or in cooperation with other States to the further development of the applications of atomic energy for peaceful purposes,

Declaring their intention to achieve at the earliest possible date the cessation of the nuclear arms race and to undertake effective measures in the direction of nuclear disarmament,

Urging the cooperation of all States in the attainment of this objective,

Recalling the determination expressed by the Parties to the 1963 Treaty banning nuclear weapons tests in the atmosphere in outer space and under water in its Preamble to seek to achieve the discontinuance of all test explosions of nuclear weapons for all time and to continue negotiations to this end,

Desiring to further the easing of international tension and the strengthening of trust between States in order to facilitate the cessation of the manufacture of nuclear weapons, the liquidation of all their existing stockpiles, and the elimination from national arsenals of nuclear weapons and the means of their delivery pursuant to a treaty on general and complete disarmament under strict and effective international control,

Recalling that, in accordance with the Charter of the United Nations, States must refrain in their international relations from the threat or use of force against the territorial integrity or political independence of any State, or in any other manner inconsistent with the Purposes of the United Nations, and that the establishment and maintenance of international peace and security are to be promoted with the least diversion for armaments of the world's human and economic resources,

Have agreed as follows:

Article I

Each nuclear-weapon State Party to the Treaty undertakes not to transfer to any recipient whatsoever nuclear weapons or other nuclear explosive devices or control over such weapons or explosive devices directly, or indirectly; and not in any way to assist, encourage, or induce any non-nuclear-weapon State to manufacture or otherwise acquire nuclear weapons or other nuclear explosive devices, or control over such weapons or explosive devices.

Article II

Each non-nuclear-weapon State Party to the Treaty undertakes not to receive the transfer from any transferor whatsoever of nuclear weapons or other nuclear explosive devices or of control over such weapons or explosive devices directly, or indirectly; not to manufacture or otherwise acquire nuclear weapons or other nuclear explosive devices; and not to seek or receive any assistance in the manufacture of nuclear weapons or other nuclear explosive devices.

Article III

1. Each non-nuclear-weapon State Party to the Treaty undertakes to accept safeguards, as set forth in an agreement to be negotiated and concluded with the International Atomic Energy Agency in accordance with the Statute of the International Atomic Energy Agency and the Agency's safeguards system, for the exclusive purpose of verification of the fulfillment of its obligations assumed under this Treaty with a view to preventing diversion of nuclear energy from peaceful uses to nuclear weapons or other nuclear explosive devices. Procedures for the safeguards required by this article shall be followed with respect to source or special fissionable material whether it is being produced, processed or used in any principal nuclear facility or is outside any such facility. The safeguards required by this article shall be applied on all source or special fissionable material in all peaceful nuclear activities within the territory of such State, under its jurisdiction, or carried out under its control anywhere.

2. Each State Party to the Treaty undertakes not to provide: (a) source or special fissionable material, or (b) equipment or material especially designed or prepared for the processing, use or production of special fissionable material, to any non-nuclear-weapon State for peaceful purposes, unless the source or special fissionable material shall be subject to the safeguards required by this article.

3. The safeguards required by this article shall be implemented in a manner designed to comply with article IV of this Treaty, and to avoid hampering the economic or technological development of the Parties or international cooperation in the field of peaceful nuclear activities, including the inter-

national exchange of nuclear material and equipment for the processing, use or production of nuclear material for peaceful purposes in accordance with the provisions of this article and the principle of safeguarding set forth in the Preamble of the Treaty.

4. Non-nuclear-weapon States Party to the Treaty shall conclude agreements with the International Atomic Energy Agency to meet the requirements of this article either individually or together with other States in accordance with the Statute of the International Atomic Energy Agency. Negotiation of such agreements shall commence within 180 days from the original entry into force of this Treaty. For States depositing their instruments of ratification or accession after the 180-day period, negotiation of such agreements shall enter into force not later than eighteen months after the date of initiation of negotiations.

Article IV

1. Nothing in this Treaty shall be interpreted as affecting the inalienable right of all the Parties to the Treaty to develop research, production and use of nuclear energy for peaceful purposes without discrimination and in conformity with articles I and II of this Treaty.

2. All the Parties to the Treaty undertake to facilitate, and have the right to participate in, the fullest possible exchange of equipment, materials and scientific and technological information for the peaceful uses of nuclear energy. Parties to the Treaty in a position to do so shall also cooperate in contributing alone or together with other States or international organizations to the further development of the applications of nuclear energy for peaceful purposes, especially in the territories of non-nuclear-weapon States Party to the Treaty, with due consideration for the needs of the developing areas of the world.

Article V

Each Party to the Treaty undertakes to take appropriate measures to ensure that, in accordance with this Treaty, under appropriate international observation and through appropriate international procedures, potential benefits from any peaceful applications of nuclear explosions will be made available to non-nuclear-weapon States Party to the Treaty on a non-discriminatory basis and that the charge to such Parties for the explosive devices used will be as low as possible and exclude any charge for research and development. Non-nuclear weapon States Party to the Treaty shall be able to obtain such benefits, pursuant to a special international agreement or agreements, through an appropriate international body with adequate representation of non-nuclear-weapon States. Negotiations on this subject shall commence as soon as possible after the Treaty enters into force. Non-nuclear-weapon States Party to the Treaty so desiring may also obtain such benefits pursuant to bilateral agreements.

Article VI

Each of the Parties to the Treaty undertakes to pursue negotiations in good faith on effective measures relating to cessation of the nuclear arms race at an early date and to nuclear disarmament, and on a treaty on general and complete disarmament under strict and effective international control.

Article VII

Nothing in this Treaty affects the right of any group of States to conclude regional treaties in order to assure the total absence of nuclear weapons in their respective territories.

Article VIII

1. Any Party to the Treaty may propose amendments to this Treaty. The text of any proposed amendment shall be submitted to the Depositary Governments which shall circulate it to all Parties to the Treaty. Thereupon, if requested to do so by one-third or more of the Parties to the Treaty, the Depositary Governments shall convene a conference, to which they shall invite all the Parties to the Treaty, to consider such an amendment.

2. Any amendment to this Treaty must be approved by a majority of the votes of all the Parties to the Treaty, including the votes of all nuclear-weapon States Party to the Treaty and all other Parties which, on the date the amendment is circulated, are members of the Board of Governors of the International Atomic Energy Agency. The amendment shall enter into force for each Party that deposits its instrument of ratification of the amendment upon the deposit of such instruments of ratification by a majority of all the Parties, including the instruments of ratification of all nuclear-weapon States Party to the Treaty and all other Parties which, on the date the amendment is circulated, are members of the Board of Governors of the International Atomic Energy Agency. Thereafter, it shall enter into force for any other Party upon the deposit of its instrument of ratification of the amendment.

3. Five years after the entry into force of this Treaty, a conference of Parties to the Treaty shall be held in Geneva, Switzerland, in order to review the operation of this Treaty with a view to assuring that the purposes of the Preamble and the provisions of the Treaty are being realized. At intervals of five years thereafter, a majority of the Parties to the Treaty may obtain, by submitting a proposal to this effect to the Depositary Governments, the convening of further conferences with the same objective of reviewing the operation of the Treaty.

Article IX

1. This Treaty shall be open to all States for signature. Any State which does not sign the Treaty before its entry into force in accordance with paragraph 3 of this article may accede to it at any time.

2. This Treaty shall be subject to ratification by signatory States. Instruments of ratification and instruments of accession shall be deposited with the Governments of the United States of America, the United Kingdom of Great Britain and Northern Ireland and the Union of Soviet Socialist Republics, which are hereby designated the Depositary Governments.

3. This Treaty shall enter into force after its ratification by the States, the Governments of which are designated Depositaries of the Treaty, and forty other States signatory to this Treaty and the deposit of their instruments of ratification. For the purposes of this Treaty, a nuclear-weapon State is one which has manufactured and exploded a nuclear weapon or other nuclear device prior to January 1, 1967.

4. For States whose instruments of ratification or accession are deposited subsequent to the entry into force of this Treaty, it shall enter into force on the date of the deposit of their instruments of ratification or accession.

5. The Depositary Governments shall promptly inform all signatory and acceding States of the date of each signature, the date of deposit of each instrument of ratification or of accession, the date of the entry into force of this Treaty, and the date of receipt of any requests for convening a conference or other notices.

6. This Treaty shall be registered by the Depositary Governments pursuant to article 102 of the Charter of the United Nations.

Article X

1. Each Party shall in exercising its national sovereignty have the right to withdraw from the Treaty if it decides that extraordinary events, related to the subject matter of this Treaty, have jeopardized the supreme interests of its country. It shall give notice of such withdrawal to all other Parties to the Treaty and to the United Nations Security Council three months in advance. Such notice shall include a statement of the extraordinary events it regards as having jeopardized its supreme interests.

2. Twenty-five years after the entry into force of the Treaty, a conference shall be convened to decide whether the Treaty shall continue in force indefinitely, or shall be extended for an additional fixed period or periods. This decision shall be taken by a majority of the Parties to the Treaty.

Article XI

This Treaty, the English, Russian, French, Spanish and Chinese texts of which are equally authentic, shall be deposited in the archives of the Depositary Governments. Duly certified copies of this Treaty shall be transmitted by the Depositary Governments to the Governments of the signatory and acceding States.

SECTION 5: *SALT* PHASE I

"The United States of America and the Union of Soviet Socialist Republics, . . .

"Proceeding from the premise that nuclear war would have devasting consequences for all mankind,

"Declare their intention to achieve at the earliest possible date the cessation of the nuclear arms race and to take effective measures toward reductions in strategic arms, nuclear disarmament, and general and complete disarmament. . . ."

RICHARD NIXON
LEONID BREZHNEV
Moscow, May 26, 1972

INTRODUCTION

The Strategic Arms Limitations Talks (SALT) began in November 1969. Their first phase ended in May 1972 and resulted in a treaty and an agreement signed personally in Moscow by President Nixon and Chairman Brezhnev. The bold words above are from the preamble to the treaty. They clearly call for *disarmament.* Yet, *no disarmament whatsoever was achieved by SALT Phase I*: not a single weapon is to be destroyed or even moved. Nor can we expect any disarmament in Phase II, the discussions of which began late in 1972.

Even so, we must count the results of SALT so far as progress in the right direction. Phase I did help to stablize the arms race, and Phase II could result in a real arms freeze. Further, Phase I is not only a step in the right direction, it is the first step in a new direction. For the first time, arms control measures pertain not only to nuclear explosives but also to some of the vehicles for delivering them; in this case, the modern large rocket. Highest priority during the Phase I deliberations was given to achieving a treaty specifying the maximum number of *defensive* missiles the United States and the Soviet Union would deploy. Limitations on the number of *offensive* missiles were not only set much higher, but so far these limits are controlled only by a temporary executive agreement rather than by a treaty. To understand how this state of affairs came to be, we must briefly turn back to an earlier period.

During the 1940's and 1950's attempts to control the nuclear arms race focused almost exclusively on nuclear explosives themselves, but the means for delivering them were largely ignored. The reasons for this derived from the unique nature of the nuclear explosives, from the plans for their use, and from their rarity. Atomic bombs were perceived as terror weapons. The first and only use of these weapons in warfare was as weapons of unprecedented terror designed to push a nation already thoroughly familiar with the horrors of war over the brink to surrender. The first formal statement of a strategy for their use, the "massive retaliation" doctrine of Eisenhower's Secretary of State, John Foster Dulles, reinforced the notion. Some of those who helped to develop nuclear bombs justified doing so by claiming that these new weapons would so increase the horror of war that politicians would be forced to abandon war as a means of achieving goals and extending power. Analysts spoke of a "balance of terror" and argued, variously, about how stable, or precarious, it might be.

The attitudes of the public and politicians toward other modern weapons was quite different. Many of the other high-technology weapons, such as radar and antisubmarine devices, seemed to have primarily defensive purposes. Other weapons had multiple purposes, of which sowing terror was only one. Aircraft, for example, were used for defense as well as offense, for transportation as well as for killing and destroying. None of these other weapons, and rightly so, attracted the alarmed concern that nuclear explosives did. In the forties and fifties, then, the nuclear might of a nation was reckoned by the number and size of its nuclear bombs, and not by measures of its delivery systems.

By the early 1960's the situation had shifted greatly. On the one hand, officials began to speak of a stockpile of many tens of thousands of nuclear weapons designed and programmed for a wide variety of uses: defensive as well as offensive, tactical as well as strategic. On the other hand, new weapons systems, designed exclusively for delivering nuclear explosives, were just beginning to enter the military inventories. These were the long-range ballistic missiles: the land-based Atlas, Titan, Thor, Jupiter, and Minuteman, and the sea-based Polaris. The inaccuracy of the early versions of these weapons was such that they were suitable only for attacking so-called "soft" targets. There are a few military targets of this type (bomber bases are an example) but the commonest and most widely discussed such targets were cities—areas of civilian habitation. Thus, the introduction of these new missiles reemphasized the terror of nuclear weapons.

In addition to the general trends, two special events focused further attention on long-range rockets. One was the missile gap controversy of 1958–1960. As mentioned in the introduction to Section 4, the almost universal belief, shared by insider and outsider alike, was that the Soviets were technologically more advanced than the Americans in the development of long-range rockets. This belief focused Americans' fears directly on the rockets themselves rather than solely their cargoes. The other special event was the Cuban Missile Crisis of 1962. The Soviets' introduction of medium-range missiles into Cuba, and the American reaction to it, once again riveted popular and official attention on this particular type of weapon. As a result, the nuclear might of a nation came to be reckoned by the number, size, and type of its missiles, and not only by the size of its inventory of nuclear explosives. In this, there was little difference between insiders and outsiders, between those who urged ever greater weapons deployment and those who advocated arms control.

Since about 1960, many of those most concerned and best informed about the arms race and the implications of new weapons systems focused special attention on the anti-ballistic missile, or ABM. Since the ABM is a defensive weapon, designed to intercept incoming ballistic missile warheads, it may at first seem strange that this should be the case. There were, however, two good reasons for it. First of all, in the early sixties there were no ABM's deployed, and in the United States, at least, there were no approved plans for deploying them. For advocates of disarmament, it seemed, therefore, easier to attempt to hold this number at zero than to attempt to convince the Military to reduce the numbers of other, already deployed missiles to zero. Anyone with any experience in arms control knew that "nonarmament" was much easier to achieve than disarmament. The other, and more important, reason for being especially concerned about ABM systems dealt with the dynamics of the arms race and the rôle of the ABM in accelerating it. The substance of the second reason is not, however, immediately obvious, and so nuclear strategists and arms race analysts have long argued about it both at home and in international meetings, and both in secret and in public. Several of the articles included in this section have been included because they analyze the problem in detail, so I will not go into the details of the argument here.

One of the earliest international discussions about the significance of

ABM deployment took place at the Eleventh Pugwash Conference at Dubrovnik in 1963. There Matthew Meselson presented a paper in which he asked whether the introduction of missile defense systems might not have the effect of inflaming the competition for the accumulation of nuclear weapons delivery systems. The problem was analyzed again in greater detail at the next conference by Murray Gell-Mann and Jack Ruina. At first the reaction of participants from other countries was the "obvious" one: ABM's are defensive weapons and therefore of no concern to persons worried about the arms race. After further discussion, however, the idea that deployment of ABM's can accelerate the arms race came to be generally accepted there.

Four years later, when Soviet Premier Kosygin and President Johnson met at Glassboro, New Jersey, in 1967, Secretary of Defense Robert McNamara tried to persuade Kosygin that both countries should forego ABM deployment. McNamara again argued that ABM deployment could accelerate the arms race. By that time the Soviets had already installed a few ABM's (of doubtful value) around Moscow, and Kosygin could not be persuaded.

In late 1967, President Johnson, despite much contrary technical advice, decided the United States should also deploy an ABM system and he ordered this. President Nixon, after reconsidering the problem when he took over in 1969, reconfirmed the decision to deploy ABM's but made a number of major changes in the detailed plans.

Given this background of controversy, it is not surprising that consideration of controlling deployment of ABM systems was given the highest priority during the first phase of the SALT talks when they began in late 1969.

The SALT talks are bilateral talks, strictly between the two so-called superpowers, the United States and the Soviet Union. Prior to their start in 1969, the only important forum for discussing problems of arms control and disarmament had been the United Nations. There, detailed work is delegated to a special subcommittee, known from 1962 to 1969 as the Eighteenth National Disarmament Committee (ENDC), and known as the Conference of the Committee on Disarmament (CCD) since then. The ENDC–CCD is responsible for all kinds of disarmament matters. It considers proposals for controlling and eliminating not only nuclear armaments, but also biological and chemical warfare, nuclear testing, and other issues that come under the rubric of "general and complete disarmament."

In 1964, the United States proposed that the ENDC explore a verifiable freeze on both offensive and defensive strategic missiles. At the time, the United States had a very much larger stock of such weapons than did the Soviet Union. That gross imbalance, plus the usual argument over "verification," which the United States continued to insist meant some kind of on-site inspection, resulted in the rejection of such a freeze by the Soviets. Various modifications of the idea were presented, but to no avail. Finally, it became evident that, if any progress in controlling strategic delivery systems was to be made, the problem would have to be taken up in a purely bilateral Soviet-American forum. A specific proposal for doing so was made by President Johnson in January 1967, but the growing fury of the war in Southeast Asia and the invasion of Czechoslovakia in 1968 made it impossible to arrange a formal conference. Eventually, the spirit of détente that developed during the Nixon administration made such a conference possible, and the Strategic Arms Limitation Talks (SALT) began in late 1969 in Helsinki.

The articles in this section elucidate many of the political, strategic, and technical issues I have mentioned, in greater detail.

The first article, entitled "Anti-Ballistic-Missle Systems", was written by Richard Garwin and Hans Bethe shortly after President Johnson's decision to deploy what was known as the Sentinel ABM system. The authors discuss this particular system in terms of the specific purposes claimed for it at the time the article was first published, in 1968. Even so, most of what is said applies broadly to other ABM systems as well. Bethe will be familiar to readers of this book as the author of an article in Section 2 about the hydrogen bomb. Garwin has an exceptional record of service as an adviser on national security problems. He has twice been a member of the president's Advisory Committee, where he chaired or served on panels dealing with practically all aspects of national security, including strategic weapons, aircraft, and naval warfare. He has also worked directly with various offices of the Defense Department, the Atomic Energy Commission, and with other agencies and organizations directly involved with national security matters. He has frequently been invited to testify before Congressional committees faced with problems having important technical aspects. Probably no one else at the present time brings to the discussion of these issues as great breadth and depth of knowledge about their technical elements.

The second article, entitled "The Dynamics of the Arms Race," was written by George Rathjens, who earned his Ph.D. in chemistry and is now a professor of political science at the Massachusetts Institute of Technology. He wrote this article just as the Senate ABM debates of 1969–1970 were beginning. It discusses the way the deployment of ABM's and MIRV's (multiple-independently-targetable-reentry-vehicles) affect the arms race. Rathjens has had a remarkably broad career of public service. He has served on the staff of the President's Special Assistant for Science and Technology, as Chief Scientist of the Advanced Research Projects Agency of the Department of Defense, as an adviser to the Joint Chiefs of Staff, and as a member of the staff of the U.S. Arms Control and Disarmament Agency.

"Military Technology and National Security," the third article, is one I wrote after the 1969 Senate debates about ABM deployment. It summarizes and expands on the issues as they were understood at that time. In addition, I devote special attention to what I consider to be the very dangerous trend toward "automatization" of the strategic forces, a trend exemplified by suggestions made by many defense planners that the United States should develop a "launch-on-warning" doctrine for our strategic forces: automatically an enemy attack would be sensed and automatically missiles would respond.

George Rathjens and George Kistiakowsky are the authors of the fourth article, "The Limitation of Strategic Arms." It directly addresses the substance of the SALT talks with special attention to ABM's (which were discussed) and MIRV's (which were not). Kistiakowsky worked on development of the atomic bomb at Los Alamos during World War II. He subsequently served in many advisory capacities, including membership in the so-called "Teapot Committee" which initiated the high priority long-range missile program in 1953–1954, and on the President's Science Advisory Committee. In 1960 he was simultaneously chairman of the latter committee and Special Assistant to the President for Science and Technology. From 1962 to 1969 he served as a member of the General Advisory Committee on Arms Control and Disarmament. Rathjen's collaboration with Kistiakowsky dates from the time both worked in Washington after the launching of Sputnik.

The fifth article, entitled "The Limitation of Offensive Weapons," was written by Herbert Scoville, Jr. In it he first discusses the several possible forms a limitation on offensive weapons might take, and then discusses some of the ways in which these results could, if not reinforced by further controls, lead to undesirable and detrimental results. He puts special emphasis on the unsolved MIRV problem. Scoville's article is also based on the knowledge gained through a long career in national security matters. He was one of the first officials in the Armed Forces Special Weapons Project, an agency created in the Defense Department at the end of World War II after the termination of the Manhattan Project to sponsor and conduct research on nuclear weapons effects. Later he worked in the Central Intelligence Agency, where he became Deputy Director for Science and Technology. In 1963 he joined the staff of the U.S. Arms Control and Disarmament Agency and served as its Assistant Director for Science and Technology.

"Reconnaissance and Arms Control," the sixth article, is by Theodore Greenwood, currently a student of Rathjens at the Massachusetts Institute of Technology. Very little has been written on the subject of use of satellites for reconnaissance and on what reconnaissance satellites can and already do contribute to military intelligence in general and to the verification of arms control agreements in particular. The reason for this lack is the especially high level of classification that surrounds such matters and the consequent inhibitions that prevent persons who have direct knowledge of the subject from saying much about it. Greenwood has not had access to classified information and therefore is able to discuss general and theoretical problems freely. He has been able to take what little has been revealed over the years and turn it into a worthwhile article.

The seventh and eighth articles form a pair that set forth a difficult problem facing the second phase or later phases of SALT. The first of these two is entitled "Missile Submarines and National Security" and is by Herbert Scoville, Jr.; the second is entitled "Antisubmarine Warfare and National Security" and is by Richard Garwin. The trend in recent years has been to assign more and more importance to the submarine-launched-missile component of the deterrent. The reason is straightforward: technologists *can* now foresee how the land-based missile force *might* be overwhelmed in a preemptive attack, they *cannot* now foresee how the sea-based force *could* be similarly overwhelmed. In the long run, then, the stability of the balance of terror may increasingly depend on the invulnerability of the missile submarines. Research on antisubmarine warfare (ASW) threatens this invulnerability and hence the stability of the deterrent. In brief, ASW can effect the arms race in the same way as ABM, and the articles by Scoville and Garwin elucidate that problem.

After the articles, I have included the text of the two SALT Phase I agreements—the treaty limiting ABM's and the interim agreement limiting offensive arms—and the protocol, interpretations, and statements that were published with them. In conjunction with the publication here of those texts, it is interesting to look behind the specific agreements in an attempt to ascertain the broader understandings that underlie them, and so I conclude this section with a Postscript that does this.

19

Anti-Ballistic-Missile Systems

The U.S. is now building a "light" ABM system. The authors argue that offensive tactics and cheap penetration aids could nullify the effectiveness of this system and any other visualized so far

RICHARD L. GARWIN
and HANS A. BETHE

March 1968

Last September, Secretary of Defense McNamara announced that the U.S. would build "a relatively light and reliable Chinese-oriented ABM system." With this statement he apparently ended a long and complex debate on the merits of any kind of anti-ballistic-missile system in an age of intercontinental ballistic missiles carrying multimegaton thermonuclear warheads. Secretary McNamara added that the U.S. would "begin actual production of such a system at the end of this year," meaning the end of 1967.

As two physicists who have been concerned for many years with the development and deployment of modern nuclear weapons we wish to offer some comments on this important matter. On examining the capabilities of ABM systems of various types, and on considering the stratagems available to a determined enemy who sought to nullify the effectiveness of such a system, we have come to the conclusion that the "light" system described by Secretary McNamara will add little, if anything, to the influences that should restrain China indefinitely from an attack on the U.S. First among these factors is China's certain knowledge that, in McNamara's words, "we have the power not only to destroy completely her entire nuclear offensive forces but to devastate her society as well."

An even more pertinent argument against the proposed ABM system, in our view, is that it will nourish the illusion that an effective defense against ballistic missiles is possible and will lead almost inevitably to demands that the light system, the estimated cost of which exceeds $5 billion, be expanded into a heavy system that could cost upward of $40 billion. The folly of undertaking to build such a system was vigorously stated by Secretary McNamara. "It is important to understand," he said, "that none of the [ABM] systems at the present or foreseeable state of the art would provide an impenetrable shield over the United States.... Let me make it very clear that the [cost] in itself is not the problem: the penetrability of the proposed shield is the problem."

In our view the penetrability of the light, Chinese-oriented shield is also a problem. It does not seem credible to us that, even if the Chinese succumbed to the "insane and suicidal" impulse to launch a nuclear attack on the U.S. within the next decade, they would also be foolish enough to have built complex and expensive missiles and nuclear warheads peculiarly vulnerable to the light ABM system now presumably under construction (a system whose characteristics and capabilities have been well publicized). In the area of strategic weapons a common understanding of the major elements and technical possibilities is essential to an informed and reasoned choice by the people, through their government, of a proper course of action. In this article we shall outline in general terms, using nonsecret information, the techniques an enemy could employ at no great cost to reduce the effectiveness of an ABM system even more elaborate than the one the Chinese will face. First, however, let us describe that system.

Known as the Sentinel system, it will provide for long-range interception by Spartan antimissile missiles and short-range interception by Sprint antimissile missiles. Both types of missile will be armed with thermonuclear warheads for the purpose of destroying or inactivating the attacker's thermonuclear weapons, which will be borne through the atmosphere and to their targets by reentry vehicles (RV's). The Spartan missiles, whose range is a few hundred kilometers, will be fired when an attacker's reentry vehicles are first detected rising above the horizon by perimeter acquisition radar (PAR).

If the attacker is using his available propulsion to deliver maximum payload, his reentry vehicles will follow a normal minimum-energy trajectory, and they will first be sighted by one of the PAR's when they are about 4,000 kilometers, or about 10 minutes, away [*see illustration on page 169*]. If the attacker chooses to launch his rockets with less than maximum payload, he can put them either in a lofted trajectory or in a depressed one. The lofted trajectory has certain advantages against a terminal defense system. The most extreme example of a depressed trajectory is the path followed by a low-orbit satellite. On such a trajectory a reentry vehicle could remain below an altitude of 160 kilometers and would not be visible to the horizon-search radar until it was some 1,400 kilometers, or about three minutes, away. This is FOBS: the fractional-orbit bombardment system, which allows intercontinental ballistic missiles to deliver perhaps 50 to 75 percent of their normal payload.

In the Sentinel system Spartans will be launched when PAR has sighted an incoming missile; they will be capable of intercepting the missile at a distance of several hundred kilometers. To provide a light shield for the entire U.S. **about half a dozen PAR units will be deployed along the northern border of the country to detect missiles approaching from the general direction of the North Pole [*see illustration on page 166*].** Each PAR will be linked to several "farms" of long-range Spartan missiles, which can be hundreds of kilometers away. Next to each Spartan farm will be a farm of Sprint missiles together with missile-site radar (MSR), whose function is to help guide both the Spartans and the shorter-range Sprints to their targets. The task of the Sprints is to provide terminal protection for the important Spartans and MSR's. The PAR's will also be protected by Sprints and thus will require MSR's nearby.

Whereas the Spartans are expected to intercept an enemy missile well above the upper atmosphere, the Sprints are designed to be effective within the atmosphere, at altitudes below 35 kilometers. The explosion of an ABM missile's thermonuclear warhead will produce a huge flux of X rays, neutrons and other particles, and within the atmosphere a powerful blast wave as well. We shall describe later how X rays, particles and blast can incapacitate a reentry vehicle.

Before we consider in detail the capabilities and limitations of ABM systems, one of us (Garwin) will briefly summarize the present strategic position of the U.S. The primary fact is that the U.S. and the U.S.S.R. can annihilate each other as viable civilizations within a day and perhaps within an hour. Each can at will inflict on the other more than 120 million immediate deaths, to which must be added deaths that will be caused by fire, fallout, disease and starvation. In addition more than 75 percent of the productive capacity of each country would be destroyed, regardless of who strikes first. At present, therefore, each of the two countries has an assured destruction capability with respect to the other. It is usually assumed that a nation faced with the assured destruction of 30 percent of its population and productive capacity will be deterred from destroying another nation, no matter how serious the grievance. Assured destruction is therefore not a very flexible political or military tool. It serves only to preserve a nation from complete destruction. More conventional military forces are needed to fill the more conventional military role.

Assured destruction was not possible until the advent of thermonuclear weapons in the middle 1950's. At first, when one had to depend on aircraft to deliver such weapons, destruction was not really assured because a strategic air force is subject to surprise attack, to problems of command and control and to attrition by the air defenses of the other side. All of this was changed by the development of the intercontinental ballistic missile and also, although to a lesser extent, by modifications of our B-52 force that would enable it to penetrate enemy defenses at low altitude. There is no doubt today that the U.S.S.R. and the U.S. have achieved mutual assured destruction.

The U.S. has 1,000 Minuteman missiles in hardened "silos" and 54 much larger Titan II missiles. In addition we have 656 Polaris missiles in 41 submarines and nearly 700 long-range bombers. The Minutemen alone could survive a surprise attack and achieve assured destruction of the attacker. In his recent annual report the Secretary of Defense estimated that as of October, 1967, the U.S.S.R. had some 720 intercontinental ballistic missiles, about 30 submarine-launched ballistic missiles (excluding many that are airborne rather than ballistic) and about 155 long-range bombers. This force provides assured destruction of the U.S.

Secretary McNamara has also stated that U.S. forces can deliver more than 2,000 thermonuclear weapons with an average yield of one megaton, and that fewer than 400 such weapons would be needed for assured destruction of a third of the U.S.S.R.'s population and three-fourths of its industry. The U.S.S.R. would need somewhat fewer weapons to achieve the same results against the U.S.

It is worth remembering that intercontinental missiles and nuclear weapons are not the only means of mass destruction. They are, however, among the most reliable, as they were even when they were first made in the 1940's and 1950's. One might build a strategic force somewhat differently today, but the U.S. and the U.S.S.R. have no incentive for doing so. In fact, the chief virtue of assured destruction may be that it removes the need to race—there is no reward for getting ahead. One really should not worry too much about new means for delivering nuclear weapons (such as bombs in orbit or fractional-orbit systems) or about advances in chemical or biological warfare. A single thermonuclear assured-destruction force can deter such novel kinds of attack as well.

Now, as Secretary McNamara stated in his September speech, our defense experts reckoned conservatively six to 10 years ago, when our present strategic-force levels were planned. The result is that we have right now many more missiles than we need for assured destruction of the U.S.S.R. If war comes, therefore, the U.S. will use the excess force in a "damage-limiting" role, which means firing the excess at those elements of the Russian strategic force that would do the most damage to the U.S. Inasmuch as the U.S.S.R. has achieved the level of assured destruction, this action will not preserve the U.S., but it should reduce the damage, perhaps sparing a small city here or there or reducing somewhat the forces the U.S.S.R. can use against our allies. To the extent that this damage-limiting use of our forces reduces the damage done to the U.S.S.R. it may slightly reduce the deterrent effect resulting from assured destruction. It must be clear that only surplus forces will be used in this way. It should be said, however, that the exact level of casualties and industrial damage required to destroy a nation as a viable society has been the subject of surprisingly little research or even argument.

One can conceive of three threats to the present rather comforting situation of mutual assured destruction. The first would be an effective counterforce system: a system that would enable the U.S. (or the U.S.S.R.) to incapacitate the other side's strategic forces before they could be used. The second would be an effective ballistic-missile defense combined with an effective antiaircraft system. The third would be a transition from a bipolar world, in which the U.S. and the U.S.S.R. alone possess overwhelming power, to a multipolar world including, for instance, China. Such threats are of course more worrisome in combination than individually.

American and Russian defense planners are constantly evaluating less-than-perfect intelligence to see if any or all of these threats are developing. For purposes of discussion let us ask what responses a White side might make to various moves made by a Black side.

SENTINEL ANTI-BALLISTIC-MISSILE SYSTEM, described as a "relatively light and reliable Chinese-oriented ABM system," is now under construction at an estimated cost exceeding $5 billion. Designed to defend the entire U.S., Sentinel will depend on perhaps six perimeter acquisition radars (PAR's) along the country's borders to detect enemy missiles as they come over the northern horizon. The arcs at the end of the radar "fans" show where an enemy reentry vehicle (RV) would be detected if it were in a low, satellite-like orbit. The PAR's will alert Spartan interceptors located at some 10 or a dozen sites around the U.S. The sites shown on the map are not actual ones but indicate how the U.S. could be covered by a pattern of 10 Spartan sites, assuming that the Spar-

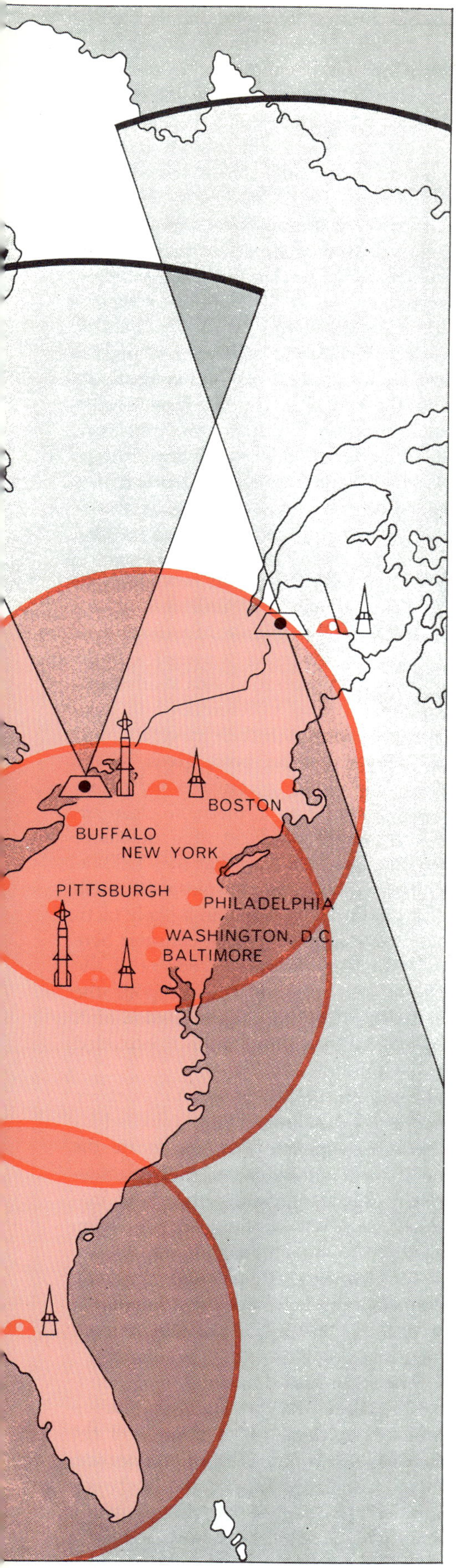

tans have an effective range of 600 kilometers. Each Spartan site will be protected by short-range Sprint missiles and will include missile-site radar (MSR) to help guide both types of missiles. Sprints and MSR's will also guard the PAR installations.

Assume that Black has threatened to negate White's capability of assured destruction by doing one of the following things: (1) it has procured more intercontinental missiles, (2) it has installed some missile defense or (3) it has built up a large operational force of missiles each of which can attack several targets, using "multiple independently targetable reentry vehicles" (MIRV's).

White's goal is to maintain assured destruction. He is now worried that Black may be able to reduce to a dangerous level the number of White warheads that will reach their target. White's simplest response to all three threats—but not necessarily the most effective or the cheapest—is to provide himself with more launch vehicles. In addition, in order to meet the first and third threats White will try to make his launchers more difficult to destroy by one or more of the following means: by making them mobile (for example by placing them in submarines or on railroad cars), by further hardening their permanent sites or by defending them with an ABM system.

Another possibility that is less often discussed would be for White to arrange to fire the bulk of his warheads on "evaluation of threat." In other words, White could fire his land-based ballistic missiles when some fraction of them had already been destroyed by enemy warheads, or when an overwhelming attack is about to destroy them. To implement such a capability responsibly requires excellent communications, and the decision to fire would have to be made within minutes, leading to the execution of a prearranged firing plan. As a complete alternative to hardening and mobility, this fire-now-or-never capability would lead to tension and even, in the event of an accident, to catastrophe. Still, as a supplemental capability to ease fears of effective counterforce action, it may have some merit.

White's response to the second threat —an increase in Black's ABM defenses— might be limited to deploying more launchers, with the simple goal of saturating and exhausting Black's defenses. But White would also want to consider the cost and effectiveness of the following: penetration aids, concentrating on undefended or lightly defended targets, maneuvering reentry vehicles or multiple reentry vehicles. The last refers to several reentry vehicles carried by the same missile; the defense would have to destroy all of them to avoid damage. Finally, White could reopen the question of whether he should seek assured destruction solely by means of missiles. For example, he might reexamine the effectiveness of low-altitude bombers or he might turn his attention to chemical or biological weapons. It does not much matter how assured destruction is achieved. The important thing, as Secretary McNamara has emphasized, is that the other side find it credible. ("The point is that a potential aggressor must himself believe that our assured destruction capability is in fact actual, and that our will to use it in retaliation to an attack is in fact unwavering.")

It is clear that White has many options, and that he will choose those that are most reliable or those that are cheapest for a given level of assured destruction. Although relative costs do depend on the level of destruction required, the important technical conclusion is that for conventional levels of assured destruction it is considerably cheaper for White to provide more offensive capability than it is for Black to defend his people and industry against a concerted strike.

As an aside, it might be mentioned that scientists newly engaged in the evaluation of military systems often have trouble grasping that large systems of the type created by or for the military are divided quite rigidly into several chronological stages, namely, in reverse order: operation, deployment, development and research. An operational system is not threatened by a system that is still in development; the threat is not real until the new system is in fact deployed, shaken down and fully operative. This is particularly true for an ABM system, which is obliged to operate against large numbers of relatively independent intercontinental ballistic missiles. It is equally true, however, for counterforce reentry vehicles, which can be ignored unless they are built by the hundreds or thousands. The same goes for MIRV's, a development of the multiple reentry vehicle in which each reentry vehicle is independently directed to a separate target. One must distinguish clearly between the *possibility* of development and the development itself, and similarly between development and actual operation. One must refrain from attributing to a specific defense system, such as Sentinel, those capabilities that *might* be obtained by further development of a different system.

It follows that the Sentinel light ABM system, to be built now and to be operational in the early 1970's against a possible Chinese intercontinental ballistic

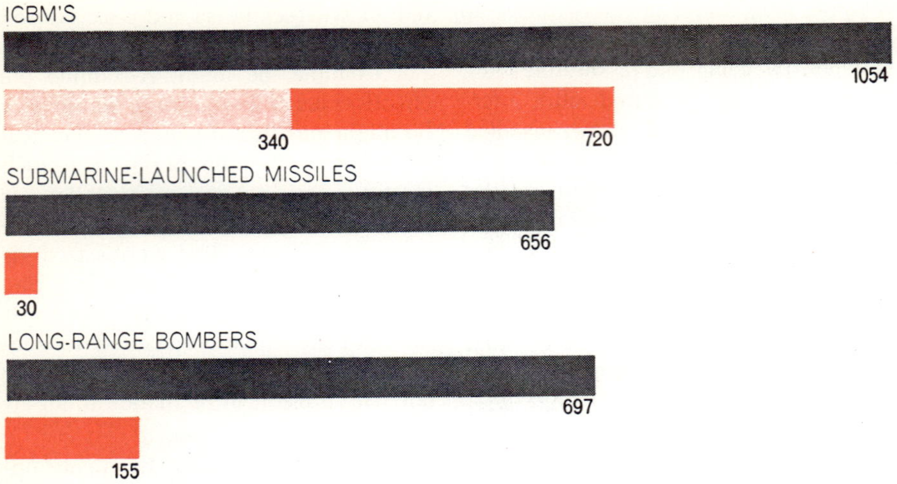

COMPARISON OF NUCLEAR WEAPON CARRIERS shows that the U.S. (*gray bars*) outweighs the U.S.S.R. in every category. These figures, representing U.S. intelligence estimates as of October 1, 1967, appear in the Secretary of Defense's latest annual report. The report notes that the number of Soviet ICBM's had increased from 340 a year earlier. Of the 1,054 U.S. ICBM's, 1,000 are Minutemen and 54 are Titan II's. The 30 submarine-launched ballistic missiles credited to the U.S.S.R. are believed to have a range considerably less than the range of some 2,500 kilometers for the 656 Polaris missiles aboard 41 nuclear-powered U.S. submarines. The report states that the combined U.S. force could deliver up to 4,500 nuclear warheads compared with about 1,000 larger warheads for the U.S.S.R. force.

missile threat, will have to reckon with a missile force unlike either the Russian or the American force, both of which were, after all, built when there was no ballistic-missile defense. The Chinese will probably build even their first operational intercontinental ballistic missiles so that they will have a chance to penetrate. Moreover, we believe it is well within China's capabilities to do a good job at this without intensive testing or tremendous sacrifice in payload.

Temporarily leaving aside penetration aids, there are two pure strategies for attack against a ballistic-missile defense. The first is an all-warhead attack in which one uses large booster rockets to transport many small (that is, fractional-megaton) warheads. These warheads are separated at some instant between the time the missile leaves the atmosphere and the time of reentry. The warheads from one missile can all be directed against the same large target (such as a city); these multiple reentry vehicles (MRV's) are purely a penetration aid. Alternatively each of the reentry vehicles can be given an independent boost to a different target, thus making them into MIRV's. MIRV is not a penetration aid but is rather a counterforce weapon: if each of the reentry vehicles has very high accuracy, then it is conceivable that each of them may destroy an enemy missile silo. The Titan II liquid-fuel rocket, designed more than 10 years ago, could carry 20 or more thermonuclear weapons. If these were employed simply as MRV's, the 54 Titans could provide more than 1,000 reentry vehicles for the defense to deal with.

Since the Spartan interceptors will each cost $1 million to $2 million, including their thermonuclear warheads, it is reasonable to believe thermonuclear warheads can be delivered for less than it will cost the defender to intercept them. The attacker can make a further relative saving by concentrating his strike so that most of the interceptors, all bought and paid for, have nothing to shoot at. This is a high-reliability penetration strategy open to any country that can afford to spend a reasonable fraction of the amount its opponent can spend for defense.

The second pure strategy for attack against an ABM defense is to precede the actual attack with an all-decoy attack or to mix real warheads with decoys. This can be achieved rather cheaply by firing large rockets from unhardened sites to send light, unguided decoys more or less in the direction of plausible city targets. If the ABM defense is an area defense like the Sentinel system, it must fire against these threatening objects at very long range before they reenter the atmosphere, where because of their lightness they would behave differently from real warheads. Several hundred to several thousand such decoys launched by a few large vehicles could readily exhaust a Sentinel-like system. The attack with real warheads would then follow.

The key point is that since the putative Chinese intercontinental-ballistic-missile force is still in the early research and development stage, it can and will be designed to deal with the Sentinel system, whose interceptors and sensors are nearing production and are rather well publicized. It is much easier to design a missile force to counter a defense that is already being deployed than to design one for any of the possible defense systems that might or might not be deployed sometime in the future.

One of us (Bethe) will now describe (1) the physical mechanisms by which an ABM missile can destroy or damage an incoming warhead and (2) some of the penetration aids available to an attacker who is determined to have his warheads reach their targets.

Much study has been given to the possibility of using conventional explosives rather than a thermonuclear explosive in the warhead of a defensive missile. The answer is that the "kill" radius of a conventional explosive is much too small to be practical in a likely tactical engagement. We shall consider here only the more important effects of the defensive thermonuclear weapon: the emission of neutrons, the emission of X rays and, when the weapon is exploded in the atmosphere, blast.

Neutrons have the ability to penetrate matter of any kind. Those released by defensive weapons could penetrate the heat shield and outer jacket of an offensive warhead and enter the fissile material itself, causing the atoms to fission and generating large amounts of heat. If sufficient heat is generated, the fissile material will melt and lose its carefully designed shape. Thereafter it can no longer be detonated.

The kill radius for neutrons depends on the design of the offensive weapon and the yield, or energy release, of the defensive weapon. The miss distance, or distance of closest approach between the defensive and the offensive missiles, can be made small enough to achieve a kill by the neutron mechanism. This is particularly true if the defensive missile and radar have high performance and the interception is made no more than a few tens of kilometers from the ABM launch site. The neutron-kill mechanism

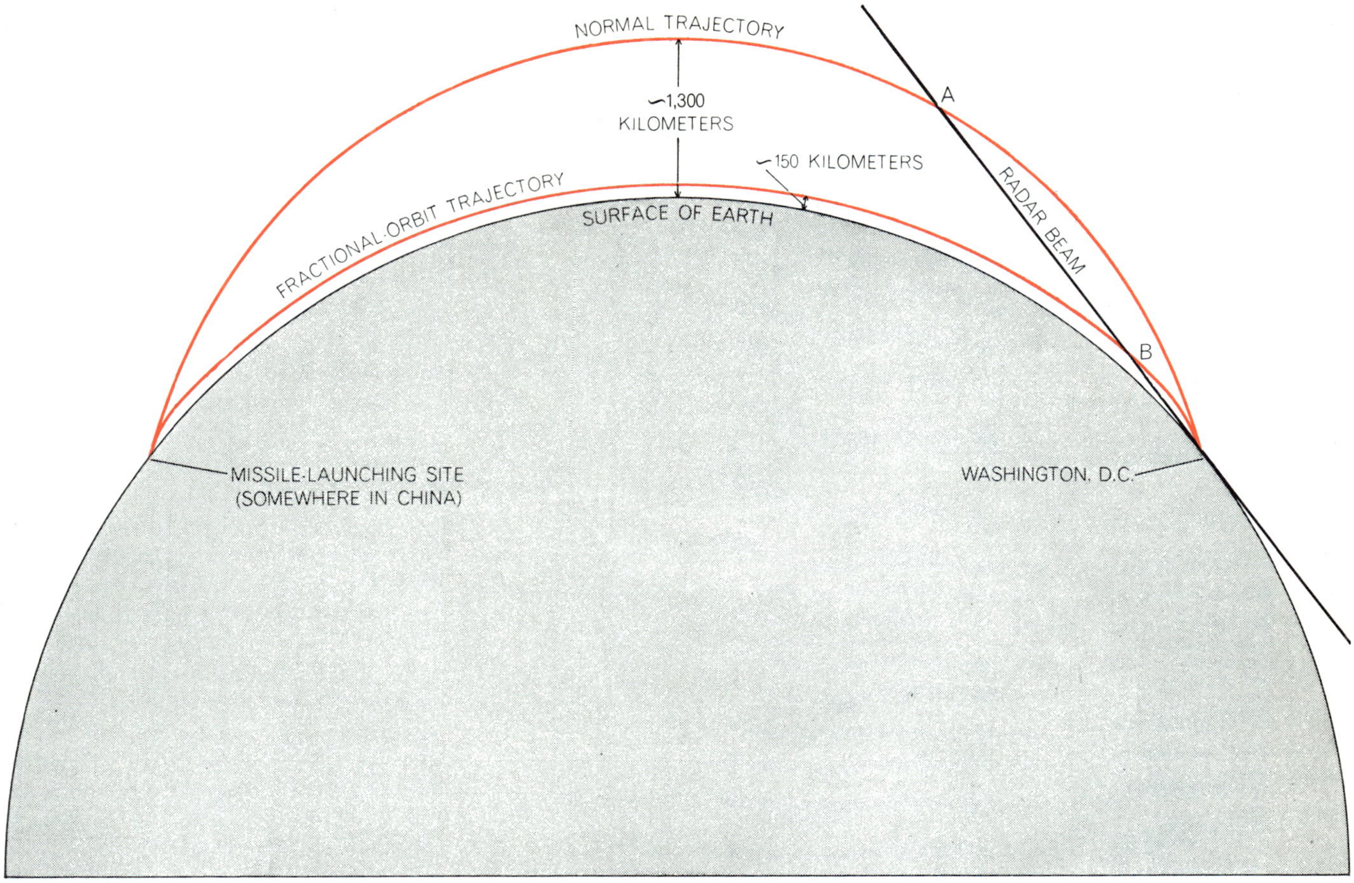

MISSILE TRAJECTORIES can be chosen by the attacker to reduce the effectiveness of the defender's radar. The normal trajectory, which requires the least fuel, carries an ICBM to an altitude of about 1,300 kilometers. On its return to the earth the missile would intersect the path of a horizon-search radar at a distance of about 4,000 kilometers (*A*), when the missile was about 10 minutes away. Longer-range but less precise radars may be able to detect the missile earlier. On a fractional-orbit trajectory the missile would stay so close to the earth that it would not cross the radar horizon (*B*) until it was about 1,400 kilometers, or about three minutes, away.

is therefore practical for the short-range defense of a city or other important target. It is highly desirable that the yield of the defensive warhead be kept low to minimize the effects of blast and heat on the city being defended.

The attacker can, of course, attempt to shield the fissile material in the offensive warhead from neutron damage, but the mass of shielding needed is substantial. Witness the massive shield required to keep neutrons from escaping from nuclear reactors. The size of the reentry vehicle will enable the defense to make a rough estimate of the amount of shielding that can be carried and thus to estimate the intensity of neutrons required to melt the warhead's fissile material.

Let us consider next the effect of X rays. These rays carry off most of the energy emitted by nuclear weapons, especially those in the megaton range. If sufficient X-ray energy falls on a reentry vehicle, it will cause the surface layer of the vehicle's heat shield to evaporate. This in itself may not be too damaging, but the vapor leaves the surface at high velocity in a very brief time and the recoil sets up a powerful shock wave in the heat shield. The shock may destroy the heat shield material or the underlying structure.

X rays are particularly effective above the upper atmosphere, where they can travel to their target without being absorbed by air molecules. The defense can therefore use megaton weapons without endangering the population below; it is protected by the intervening atmosphere. The kill radius can then be many kilometers. This reduces the accuracy required of the defensive missile and allows successful interception at ranges of hundreds of kilometers from the ABM launch site. Thus X rays make possible an area defense and provide the key to the Sentinel system.

On the other hand, the reentry vehicle can be hardened against X-ray damage to a considerable extent. And in general the defender will not know if the vehicle has been damaged until it reenters the atmosphere. If it has been severely damaged, it may break up or burn up. If this does not happen, however, the defender is helpless unless he has also constructed an effective terminal, or short-range, defense system.

The third kill mechanism—blast—can operate only in the atmosphere and requires little comment. Ordinarily when an offensive warhead reenters the atmosphere it is decelerated by a force that, at maximum, is on the order of 100 *g*. (One *g* is the acceleration due to the earth's gravity.) The increased atmospheric density reached within a shock wave from a nuclear explosion in air can produce a deceleration several times greater. But just as one can shield against neutrons and X rays one can shield against blast by designing the reentry vehicle to have great structural strength. Moreover, the defense, not knowing the detailed design of the reentry vehicle, has little way of knowing if it has destroyed a given vehicle by blast until the warhead either goes off or fails to do so.

The main difficulty for the defense is the fact that in all probability the offensive reentry vehicle will not arrive as a single object that can be tracked and fired on but will be accompanied by many other objects deliberately placed there by the offense. These objects come under the heading of penetration aids. We shall discuss only a few of the many types of such aids. They include fragments of the booster rocket, decoys, fine metal wires called chaff, electronic countermeasures and blackout mechanisms of several kinds.

The last stage of the booster that has propelled the offensive missile may disintegrate into fragments or it can be fragmented deliberately. Some of the pieces will have a radar cross section comparable to or larger than the cross section of the reentry vehicle itself. The defensive radar therefore has the task of discriminating between a mass of debris and the warhead. Although various means of discrimination are effective to some extent, radar and data processing must be specifically set up for this purpose. In any case the radar must deal with tens of objects for each genuine target, and this imposes considerable complexity on the system.

There is, of course, an easy way to discriminate among such objects: let the whole swarm reenter the atmosphere. The lighter booster fragments will soon be slowed down, whereas the heavier reentry vehicle will continue to fall with essentially undiminished speed. If a swarm of objects is allowed to reenter, however, one must abandon the concept of area defense and construct a terminal defense system. If a nation insists on retaining a pure area defense, it must be prepared to shoot at every threatening object. Not only is this extremely costly but also it can quickly exhaust the supply of antimissile missiles.

Instead of relying on the accidental targets provided by booster fragments, the offense will almost certainly want to employ decoys that closely imitate the radar reflectivity of the reentry vehicle. One cheap and simple decoy is a balloon with the same shape as the reentry vehicle. It can be made of thin plastic covered with metal in the form of foil, strips or wire mesh. A considerable number of such balloons can be carried uninflated by a single offensive missile and released when the missile has risen above the atmosphere.

The chief difficulty with balloons is putting them on a "credible" trajectory, that is, a trajectory aimed at a city or some other plausible target. Nonetheless, if the defending force employs an area defense and really seeks to protect the entire country, it must try to intercept every suspicious object, including balloon decoys. The defense may, however, decide not to shoot at incoming objects that seem to be directed against nonvital targets; thus it may choose to limit possible damage to the country rather than to avoid all damage. The offense could then take the option of directing live warheads against points on the outskirts of cities, where a nuclear explosion would still produce radioactivity and possibly severe fallout over densely populated regions. Worse, the possibility that reentry vehicles can be built to maneuver makes it dangerous to ignore objects even 100 kilometers off target.

Balloon decoys, even more than booster fragments, will be rapidly slowed by the atmosphere and will tend to burn up when they reenter it. Here again a terminal ABM system has a far better chance than an area defense system to

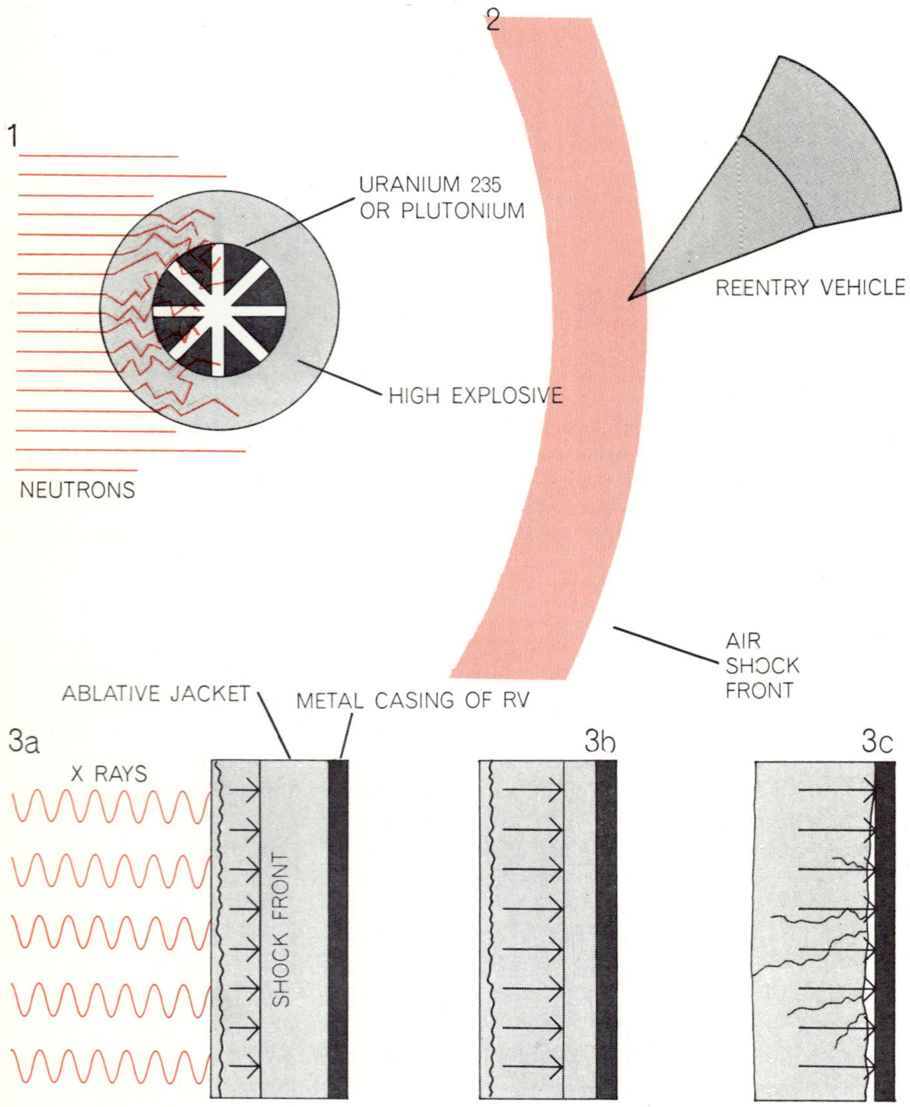

MECHANISMS FOR KILLING REENTRY VEHICLES include the neutrons, blast and X radiation from a thermonuclear explosion. Neutrons (*1*) can penetrate the fission trigger of an enemy warhead, causing the uranium 235 or plutonium to melt and lose its shape. It can then no longer be assembled for firing. If the defensive warhead is fired inside the atmosphere, the resulting shock front of air (*2*) can cause the incoming reentry vehicle (RV) to decelerate with a force equivalent to several hundred times the force of gravity, thereby leading to its destruction or malfunction. If the explosion is outside the atmosphere, the X rays travel unimpeded to their target. On striking an RV (*3a*) they are absorbed by and intensely heat a thin layer of the RV's heat jacket. This creates a shock front that travels through the jacket (*3b, 3c*) and may cause the jacket to break up or detach from the RV.

discriminate between decoys and warheads. One possibility for an area system is "active" discrimination. If a defensive nuclear missile is exploded somewhere in the cloud of balloon decoys traveling with a reentry vehicle, the balloons will either be destroyed by radiation from the explosion or will be blown far off course. The reentry vehicle presumably will survive. If the remaining set of objects is examined by radar, the reentry vehicle may stand out clearly. It can then be killed by a second interceptor shot. Such a shoot-look-shoot tactic may be effective, but it obviously places severe demands on the ABM missiles and the radar tracking system. Moreover, it can be countered by the use of small, dense decoys within the balloon swarms.

Moreover, it may be possible to develop decoys that are as resistant to X rays as the reentry vehicle and also are simple and compact. Their radar reflectivity could be made to simulate that of a reentry vehicle over a wide range of frequencies. The decoys could also be made to reenter the atmosphere—at least down to a fairly low altitude—in a way that closely mimicked an actual reentry vehicle. The design of such decoys, however, would require considerable experimentation and development.

Another way to confuse the defensive radar is to scatter the fine metal wires of chaff. If such wires are cut to about half the wavelength of the defensive radar, each wire will act as a reflecting dipole with a radar cross section approximately equal to the wavelength squared divided by 2π. The actual length of the wires is not critical; a wire of a given length is also effective against radar of shorter wavelength. Assuming that the radar wavelength is one meter and that one-mil copper wire is cut to half-meter lengths, one can easily calculate that 100 million chaff wires will weigh only 200 kilograms (440 pounds).

The chaff wires could be dispersed over a large volume of space; the chaff could be so dense and provide such large radar reflection that the reentry vehicle could not be seen against the background noise. The defense would then not know where in the large reflecting cloud the reentry vehicle is concealed. The defense would be induced to spend several interceptors to cover the entire cloud, with no certainty, even so, that the hidden reentry vehicle will be killed. How much of the chaff would survive the defensive nuclear explosion is another difficult question. The main problem for the attacker is to develop a way to disperse chaff more or less uniformly.

An active alternative to the use of chaff is to equip some decoys with electronic devices that generate radio noise at frequencies selected to jam the defensive radar. There are many variations on such electronic countermeasures, among them the use of jammers on the reentry vehicles themselves.

The last of the penetration aids that will be mentioned here is the radar blackout caused by the large number of free electrons released by a nuclear explosion. These electrons, except for a few, are removed from atoms or molecules of air, which thereby become ions. There are two main causes for the formation of ions: the fireball of the explosion, which produces ions because of its high temperature, and the radioactive debris of the explosion, which releases beta rays (high-energy electrons) that ionize the air they traverse. The second mechanism is important only at high altitude.

The electrons in an ionized cloud of gas have the property of bending and absorbing electromagnetic waves, particularly those of low frequency. Attenuation can reach such high values that the defensive radar is prevented from seeing any object behind the ionized cloud (unlike chaff, which confuses the radar only at the chaff range and not beyond).

Blackout is a severe problem for an area defense designed to intercept missiles above the upper atmosphere. The problem is aggravated because area-defense radar is likely to employ low-frequency (long) waves, which are the

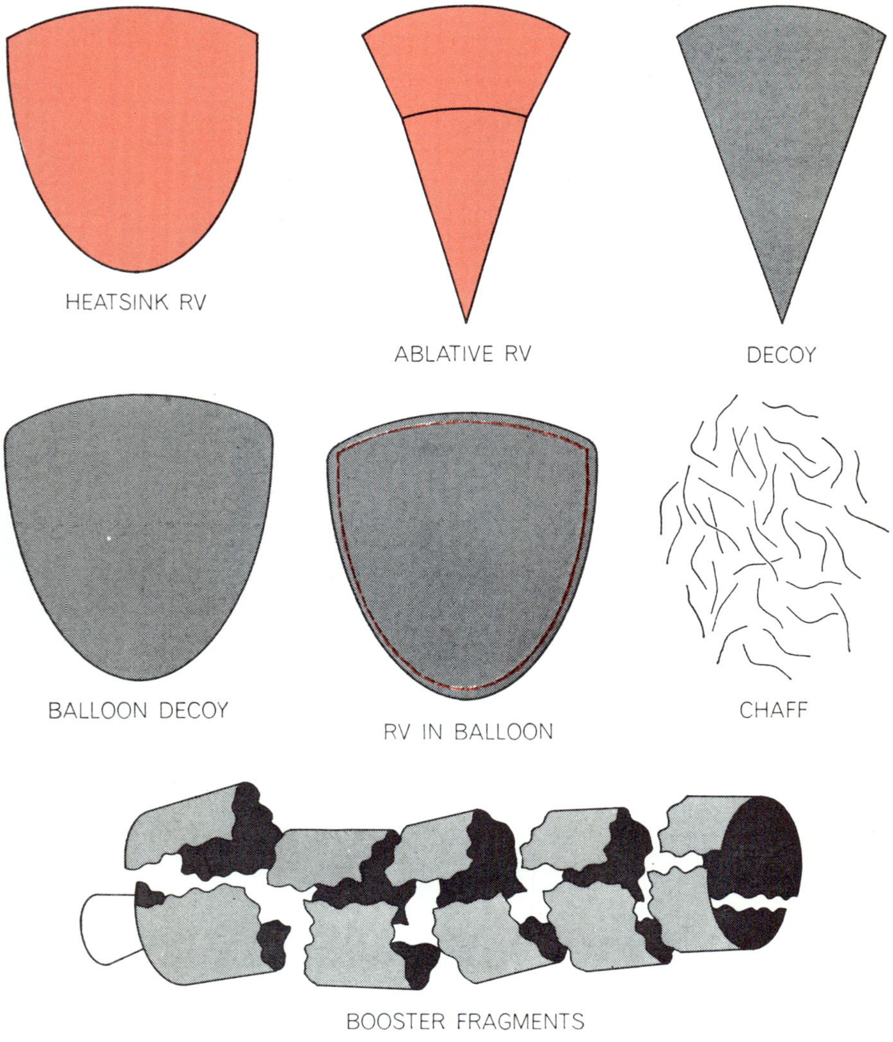

PENETRATION AIDS include objects that will reflect radar signals and thus simulate or conceal actual reentry vehicles (*color*). A decoy might be a simple conical structure or even a metallized balloon. RV's could be placed inside the same kind of balloon. Fragments of the launching vehicle and its fuel tank provide radar reflectors at no cost. Short bits of metal wire, called chaff, also make a cheap and lightweight reflector of radar signals.

most suitable for detecting enemy missiles at long range. In some recent popular articles long-wave radar has been hailed as the cure for the problems of the ABM missile. It is not. Even though it increases the capability of the radar in some ways, it makes the system more vulnerable to blackout.

Blackout can be caused in two ways: by the defensive nuclear explosions themselves and by deliberate explosions set off at high altitude by the attacker. Although the former are unavoidable, the defense has the choice of setting them off at altitudes and in locations that will cause the minimum blackout of its radar. The offense can sacrifice a few early missiles to cause blackout at strategic locations. In what follows we shall assume for purposes of discussion that the radar wavelength is one meter. Translation to other wavelengths is not difficult.

In order to totally reflect the one-meter waves from our hypothetical radar it is necessary for the attacker to create an ionized cloud containing 10^9 electrons per cubic centimeter. Much smaller electron densities, however, will suffice for considerable attenuation. For the benefit of technically minded readers, the equation for attenuation in decibels per kilometer is

$$\alpha = \frac{4.34}{3 \times 10^5} \frac{\omega_p{}^2}{\omega^2 + \gamma_c{}^2} \gamma_c \, .$$

Here ω_p is the plasma frequency for the given electron density, ω is the radar frequency in radians per second and γ_c is the frequency of collisions of an electron with atoms of air. At normal tempera-

RADAR BLACKOUTS can be created if enough free electrons are released in a sizable volume of space. An attacker can use thermonuclear explosions to generate the electrons required. A fireball blackout results when the heat from a nuclear explosion strips electrons from atoms and molecules of air. In this diagram a high-altitude fireball has been created by an enemy missile launched in a low orbit. The beta rays (electrons) released in the decay of fission products can create another type of blackout. If the beta rays are released at high altitude, they travel along the lines of force in the earth's magnetic field (*parallel colored lines*) and remove electrons from molecules in the atmosphere below. An effective beta blackout could be produced by spreading the fission products of a one-

tures this frequency γ_c is the number 2×10^{11} multiplied by the density of the air (ρ) compared with sea-level density (ρ_0), or $\gamma_c = 2 \times 10^{11}\ \rho/\rho_0$. At altitudes above 30 kilometers, where an area-defense system will have to make most of its interceptions, the density of air is less than .01 of the density at sea level. Under these conditions the electron collision frequency γ_c is less than the value of $\omega = (2\pi \times 3 \times 10^8)$ and therefore can be neglected in the denominator of the equation. Using that equation, we can then specify the number of electrons, N_c, needed to attenuate one-meter radar waves by a factor of more than one decibel per kilometer: $N_c > 350\rho_0/\rho$. At an altitude of 30 kilometers, where ρ_0/ρ is about 100, N_c is about 3×10^4, and at 60 kilometers N_c is still only about 3×10^6. Thus the electron densities needed for the substantial attenuation of a radar signal are well under the 10^9 electrons per cubic centimeter required for total reflection. The ionized cloud created by the fireball of a nuclear explosion is typically 10 kilometers thick; if the attenuation is one decibel per kilometer, such a cloud would produce a total attenuation of 10 decibels. This implies a tenfold reduction of the outgoing radar signal and another tenfold reduction of the reflected signal, which amounts to effective blackout.

The temperature of the fireball created by a nuclear explosion in the atmosphere is initially hundreds of thousands of degrees centigrade. It quickly cools by radiation to about 5,000 degrees C. Thereafter cooling is produced primarily by the cold air entrained by the fireball as it rises slowly through the atmosphere, a process that takes several minutes.

When air is heated to 5,000 degrees C., it is strongly ionized. To produce a radar attenuation of one decibel per kilometer at an altitude of 90 kilometers the fireball temperature need be only 3,000 degrees, and at 50 kilometers a temperature of 2,000 degrees will suffice. Ionization may be enhanced by the presence in the fireball of iron, uranium and other metals, which are normally present in the debris of nuclear explosion.

The size of the fireball can easily be estimated. Its diameter is about one kilometer for a one-megaton explosion at sea level. For other altitudes and yields there is a simple scaling law: the fireball diameter is equal to $(Y\rho_0/\rho)^{1/3}$, where Y is the yield in megatons. Thus a fireball one kilometer in diameter can be produced at an altitude of 30 kilometers (where $\rho_0/\rho = 100$) by an explosion of only 10 kilotons. At an altitude of 50 kilometers (where $\rho_0/\rho = 1{,}000$), a one-megaton explosion will produce a fireball 10 kilometers in diameter. At still higher altitudes matters become complicated because the density of the atmosphere falls off so sharply and the mechanism of heating the atmosphere changes. Nevertheless, fireballs of very large diameter can be expected when megaton weapons are exploded above 100 kilometers. These could well black out areas of the sky measured in thousands of square kilometers.

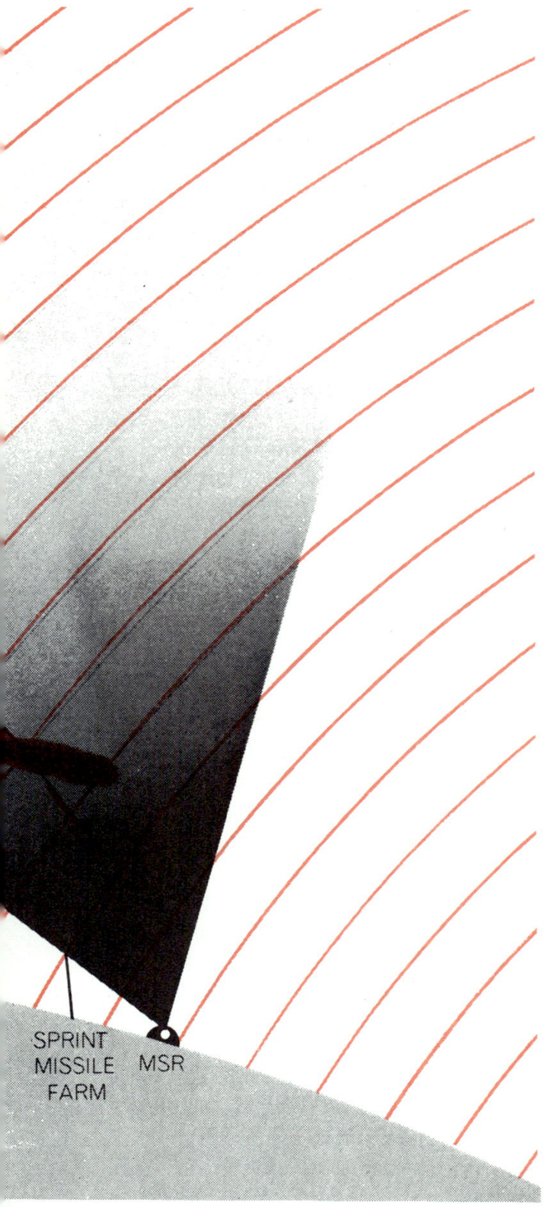

megaton explosion over an area 200 kilometers in radius. For several minutes the electron cloud would heavily absorb the long waves emitted by a PAR unit, here aimed to the north. The shorter MSR waves, however, would be attenuated only briefly.

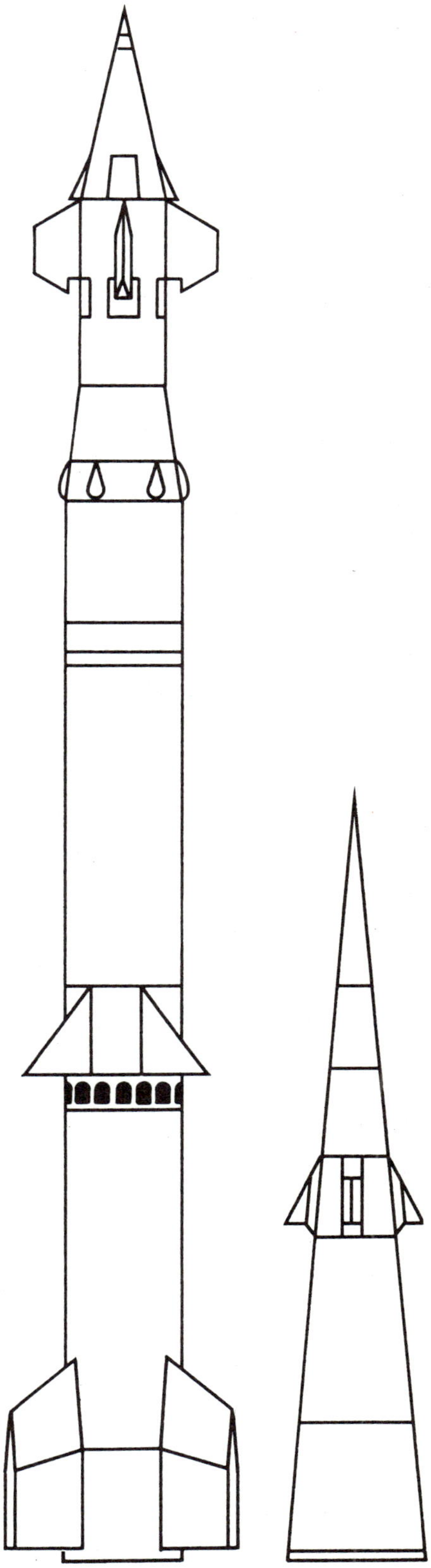

SENTINEL MISSILES are the long-range Spartan (*left*), with a reported range of several hundred kilometers, and the Sprint (*right*), which will be used for terminal defense, usually below 35 kilometers. Both will be equipped with thermonuclear warheads designed to destroy or disable the attacker's bomb-carrying reentry vehicles. The Spartan, about 55 feet long, is a three-stage solid-fuel rocket. The smaller and faster Sprint missile uses two stages of solid fuel.

For explosions at very high altitudes (between 100 and 200 kilometers) other phenomena become significant. Collisions between electrons and air molecules are now unimportant. The condition for blackout is simply that there be more than 10^9 electrons per cubic centimeter.

At the same time very little mass of air is available to cool the fireball. If the air is at first fully ionized by the explosion, the air molecules will be dissociated into atoms. The atomic ions combine very slowly with electrons. When the density is low enough, as it is at high altitude, the recombination can take place only by radiation. The radiative recombination constant (call it C_R) is about 10^{-12} cubic centimeter per second. When the initial electron density is well above 10^9 per cubic centimeter, the number of electrons remaining after time t is roughly equal to $1/C_R t$. Thus if the initial electron density is 10^{12} per cubic centimeter, the density will remain above 10^9 for 1,000 seconds, or some 17 minutes. The conclusion is that nuclear explosions at very high altitude can produce long-lasting blackouts over large areas.

The second of the two mechanisms for producing an ionized cloud, the beta rays issuing from the radioactive debris of a nuclear explosion, can be even more effective than the fireball mechanism. If the debris is at high altitude, the beta rays will follow the lines of force in the earth's magnetic field, with about half of the beta rays going immediately down into the atmosphere and the other half traveling out into space before returning earthward. These beta rays have an average energy of about 500,000 electron volts, and when they strike the atmosphere, they ionize air molecules. Beta rays of average energy penetrate to an altitude of about 60 kilometers; some of the more energetic rays go down to about 50 kilometers. At these levels, then, a high-altitude explosion will give rise to sustained ionization as long as the debris of the explosion stays in the vicinity.

One can show that blackout will occur if $y \times t^{-1.2} > 10^{-2}$, where t is the time after the explosion in seconds and y is the fission yield deposited per unit horizontal area of the debris cloud, measured in tons of TNT equivalent per square kilometer. The factor $t^{-1.2}$ expresses the rate of decay of the radioactive debris. If the attacker wishes to cause a blackout lasting five minutes ($t = 300$), he can achieve it with a debris level y equal to 10 tons of fission yield per square kilometer. This could be attained by spreading one megaton of fission products over a circular area about 400 kilometers in diameter at an altitude of, say, 60 kilometers. Very little could be seen by an area-defense radar attempting to look out from under such a blackout disk. Whether or not such a disk could actually be produced is another question. Terminal defense would not, of course, be greatly disturbed by a beta ray blackout.

The foregoing discussion has concentrated mainly on the penetration aids that can be devised against an area-defense system. By this we do not mean to suggest that a terminal-defense system can be effective, and we certainly do not wish to imply that we favor the development and deployment of such a system.

Terminal defense has a vulnerability all its own. Since it defends only a small area, it can easily be bypassed. Suppose that the 20 largest American cities were provided with terminal defense. It would be easy for an enemy to attack the 21st largest city and as many other undefended cities as he chose. Although the population per target would be less than if the largest cities were attacked, casualties would still be heavy. Alternatively the offense could concentrate on just a few of the 20 largest cities and exhaust their supply of antimissile missiles, which could readily be done by the use of multiple warheads even without decoys.

It was pointed out by Charles M. Herzfeld in *The Bulletin of the Atomic Scientists* a few years ago that a judicious employment of ABM defenses could equalize the risks of living in cities of various sizes. Suppose New York, with a population of about 10 million, were defended well enough to require 50 enemy warheads to penetrate the defenses, plus a few more to destroy the city. If cities of 200,000 inhabitants were left undefended, it would be equally "attractive" for an enemy to attack New York and penetrate its defenses as to attack an undefended city.

Even if such a "logical" pattern of ABM defense were to be seriously proposed, it is hard to believe that people in the undefended cities would accept their statistical security. To satisfy everyone would require a terminal system of enormous extent. The highest cost estimate made in public discussions, $50 billion, cannot be far wrong.

Although such a massive system would afford some protection against the U.S.S.R.'s present armament, it is virtually certain that the Russians would react to the deployment of the system. It would be easy for them to increase the number of their offensive warheads and thereby raise the level of expected damage back to the one now estimated. In his recent forecast of defense needs for the next five years, Secretary McNamara estimated the relative cost of ABM defenses and the cost of countermeasures that the offense can take. He finds invariably that the offense, by spending considerably less money than the defense, can restore casualties and destruction to the original level before defenses were installed. Since the offense is likely to be "conservative," it is our belief that the actual casualty figures in a nuclear exchange, after both sides had deployed ABM systems and simultaneously increased offensive forces, would be worse than these estimates suggest.

Any such massive escalation of offensive and defensive armaments could hardly be accomplished in a democracy without strong social and psychological effects. The nation would think more of war, prepare more for war, hate the potential enemy and thereby make war more likely. The policy of both the U.S. and the U.S.S.R. in the past decade has been to reduce tensions to provide more understanding, and to devise weapon systems that make war less likely. It seems to us that this should remain our policy.

Commentary

As one who has been intimately associated with the U.S. Anti-Ballistic-Missile (ABM) Defense System Program for the past five years and who has participated in many constructive dialogues on the program with Drs. Garwin and Bethe, I should like to offer some comments regarding their article "Anti-Ballistic-Missile Systems."

As a general comment, let me note that neither the authors nor myself are arguing about technical facts, since in this complex area we are dealing at most with technical judgments, and more often with political opinion. Further, there are limits placed on our discussion by the necessary security classification that exists regarding the details of the program. Drs. Garwin and Bethe make three primary points, and I should like to comment on each of these in turn.

1. An ABM system designed to counter a potential Chinese ICBM threat is unnecessary because our overwhelming nuclear offensive power "should restrain China indefinitely from an attack on the U.S."

An opposing political judgment to that presented by the authors would state that deterrent power only has meaning if the potential enemy believes it will be used. I believe it is well within the realm of possibility that some future Chinese leaders might not believe we would use our nuclear power in a crisis, when we would know that we could be destroyed with certainty by a much less potent force. I readily admit that this is only opinion, but I believe it to be no more or no less credible than that expressed by the authors. The fact is that neither they nor I nor our present government leadership will be making the decisions on either side at the time of some future crisis. I believe the main purpose of our light anti-China defense system should be to give our future leadership more options in order to lend credibility to our deterrent.

2. The Sentinel system will "nourish the illusion that an effective defense against ballistic missiles is possible and will lead almost inevitably to demands that the light system . . . be expanded into a heavy system."

This argument has been repeated time and again, and I believe it is a toothless old saw. This country has resisted the expansion of weapon systems, both offensive and defensive, time and again by sound arguments against the necessity of such expansion. There is no reason why this pressure, if it exists at all, cannot be countered by effective leadership. The point is further clouded by the lack of precise definition of the word "ineffective." Somehow we only pay attention to the extremes; either the system is so "ineffective" that it does not work at all or it is so "effective" that there must be an insatiable demand for more of this good thing. Let me first state unequivocally that I agree with the authors that I cannot foresee a system so effective that by expanding the system we would have any real chance of negating the deterrent power of a sophisticated enemy such as the U.S.S.R. To attempt such an objective would truly be a waste of resources; but I should like to define an effective system as one that is able to successfully counter light attacks, and I would contend that this is a very necessary one in the situation when the U.S.S.R. has some ballistic-missile defense. I do not believe it is adequate for us to only have the power to use any force en masse to overwhelm the defense and produce "assured destruction." Suppose, for example, for any reason a potential enemy sent over a couple of missiles, perhaps to take out a military target with very few civilian casualties. Would we respond by an overwhelming attack against their cities, knowing full well that the counterresponse would lead to our destruction? The light defense goes a long way toward removing the military credibility of any light attacks and thus introduces a firebreak that makes the ballistic missile useful solely as a deterrent, which is a situation we have grown to accept.

3. Our Sentinel Chinese-oriented system is, or will be, penetrable by the Chinese.

No discussion of this subject is possible in any depth without getting into classified material. Certainly there are possible penetration aids, as the authors have pointed out, that could be attempted to defeat the Sentinel system, but the uncertainties are not all on the side of the defense. The decision to deploy the Sentinel system was a very conscious one, with a great deal of analysis done to provide reasonable assurance that the system could evolve to handle future penetration aids that could be adopted by the Chinese. This does not mean an expansion of the system to the $40-billion variety but a continued technical upgrading as necessary to include and counter advances in technology. Certainly there is no guarantee that this is possible, but there were adequate possibilities to warrant the deployment decision.

While the subject of ballistic-missile defense may be an unusual one for your journal, it is appropriate since it is primarily the technical community that has expressed opinions on the subject. I would only hope that future treatment of ABM would present both sides of this very complicated and important issue.

DANIEL J. FINK

General Manager
Space Systems
Valley Forge Space Technology Center
Missile and Space Division
General Electric Company
Philadelphia, Pa.
May, 1968

It is always helpful to know what is being said by eminent scientists about our major weapons system developments. I deeply regret that military classification prevents the scientists and engineers who know most about ballistic-missile defense capabilities from publication of a better-informed treatment of this whole subject.

What concerns me about the Garwin-Bethe approach to ballistic-missile defense is to read again about all those clever tricks that a theoretical physicist can invent on paper for an enemy to use to defeat a defensive system—ideas that have been around for 10 years to my knowledge and possibly longer. The inference is that these clever tricks are easy to do with high confidence of real-world effectiveness, and that defense is helpless to react. Nothing could be further from the truth. The U.S. Air Force and the U.S. Navy are able to draw on 20 years of ballistic-missile technology and 10 years of space technology, and they still find that achievement of effective penetration aids takes years and hundreds of millions of dollars of development and testing to have *high confidence* in penetration aids. Surely no nation, not even the Chinese, would be so foolish as to plan to produce and deploy a weapons system as expensive as the ICBM without the years of painstaking and costly testing effort needed to give them high confidence that their systems would work if called on.

The fact of the matter is that the Army-proposed level of defense and our estimates of its probable effectiveness in the 1975-to-1980 time frame were carefully reviewed by technically competent and well-informed groups outside of the Army before the Secretary of Defense recommended approval of production and deployment of the Nike Sentinel system. There is nothing in the Garwin-Bethe analysis that was not known and adequately considered at that time.

A. W. Betts

Lieutenant General, GS
Chief of Research and Development
Department of the Army
Washington, D.C.
May, 1968

We agree with Dr. Fink that competent proponents and opponents of ABM systems differ primarily not on technical facts but in technical judgments and political opinions.

Dr. Fink's Point 2 is the crux of the matter. Within a few weeks after the decision to deploy Sentinel, demands were made by influential persons to expand the system as soon as possible to the $40-billion variety. Certainly effective leadership has in the past sometimes sucessfully resisted the expansion of weapons systems or of other programs, but the effectiveness of governments varies, and a moment of weakness or of political horse trading could saddle us with a costly, useless and dangerous system. We think the existence of a light ABM will make it more difficult to resist pressure for its expansion.

General Betts and Dr. Fink note that successful penetration aids require more than invention, and take a lot of effort on development and testing. They also point out that a defense can be modified technically to deal with any of them. Security classification precludes meaningful technical problems, that in general the required reaction by the defense is slower, much more costly and less certain than the action of the offense. We do not agree that a system on the scale of Sentinel can long stay ahead of Chinese penetration aids.

The elements of the Sentinel system and the production capacity we build to produce it, together with the avowed possibility of technical upgrading of the system, may lead the U.S.S.R. to consider it as directed against themselves. Whether warranted or not, such a conclusion on their part would lead to a revived and intensified arms race. In the words of former Secretary McNamara, "the Soviets and ourselves would be forced to continue on a foolish and feckless course."

The other half of the arms race deserves mention as well. Should the U.S. become convinced, rightly or wrongly, of an expansion and increased capability of the Soviet ABM system around Moscow, our present deterrent policy would require high assurance as to the adequacy of our penetration aids and perhaps even an increase in numbers of missiles as well. As a consequence of our maintaining a high-confidence assured-destruction capability, if war actually comes, the U.S.S.R. would very likely suffer even more complete destruction than if they had not built an ABM system. Like the U.S., the U.S.S.R. would be well advised not to build an ABM system that could present even the appearance of effectiveness against a deterrent force.

Richard L. Garwin

IBM-Watson Laboratory
at Columbia University
New York, N.Y.

Hans A. Bethe

Laboratory of Nuclear Studies
Cornell University
Ithaca, N.Y.
May, 1968

The Dynamics of the Arms Race

Recent decisions by the U.S. and the U.S.S.R. threaten to upset the stability of the present strategic military balance. The net result may be simply to decrease the security of both countries

GEORGE W. RATHJENS

April 1969

The world stands at a critical juncture in the history of the strategic arms race. Within the past two years both the U.S. and the U.S.S.R. have decided to deploy new generations of offensive and defensive nuclear weapons systems. These developments, stimulated in part by the emergence of China as a nuclear power, threaten to upset the qualitatively stable "balance of terror" that has prevailed between the two superpowers during most of the 1960's. The new weapons programs portend for the 1970's a decade of greatly increased military budgets, with all the concomitant social and political costs these entail for both countries. Moreover, it appears virtually certain that at the end of all this effort and all this spending neither nation will have significantly advanced its own security. On the contrary, it seems likely that another upward spiral in the arms race would simply make a nuclear exchange more probable, more damaging or both.

As an alternative to this prospect, the expectation of serious arms-limitation talks between the U.S. and the U.S.S.R. holds forth the possibility of at least preventing an acceleration of the arms race. In the circumstances it seems worthwhile to inquire into the nature of the forces that impel an arms race. In doing so we may determine how best to damp this newest cycle of military competition, either by mutual agreement or by unilateral restraint, before it is beyond control.

There are a number of new weapons systems under development in both the U.S. and the U.S.S.R., but the possibilities that are likely to be at the center of discussion not only in the forthcoming negotiations but also in the current Congressional debate are the anti-ballistic-missile (ABM) concept and the multiple-independently-targeted-reentry-vehicle (MIRV) concept. These systems, one defensive and the other offensive, can usefully be discussed together because of the way they interact. In fact, the intrinsic dynamics of the arms race can be effectively illustrated by concentrating on these two developments.

It is now 18 months since former Secretary of Defense McNamara announced the decision of the Johnson Administration to proceed with the deployment of the Sentinel system: a "thin" ABM system originally described as being intended to cope with a hypothetical Chinese missile attack during the 1970's. The technology of the Sentinel system and some of the means a determined adversary might employ to defeat it were discussed in some detail a year ago in this magazine [see "Anti-Ballistic-Missile Systems," by Richard L. Garwin and Hans A. Bethe, the article beginning on page 164]. At this point I should like to review some of the background of the ABM problem.

Before the Sentinel decision most of the interest in a ballistic-missile defense for the U.S. was focused on the Nike-X program. This concept involved the use of two kinds of interceptor to protect the population and industry of the country against a hypothetical Russian missile attack. Interception would first be attempted outside the earth's atmosphere with Spartans, long-range missiles with nuclear warheads in the megaton range. The effectiveness of the defense, however, would depend primarily on the use of Sprints, short-range missiles with kiloton-yield warheads designed to intercept incoming missiles after they have reentered the atmosphere. The system also envisaged suitable radars and computers to control the engagement.

The Spartans could in principle defend large areas; indeed, about a dozen sites could defend the entire country. A defense based solely on them could be rendered ineffective, however, by fairly simple countermeasures, in particular by large numbers of lightweight decoys (which would be indistinguishable to a radar from an actual reentry vehicle containing a warhead) or by measures that would make the radar ineffective, for example the use of nuclear explosions, electronic jammers or light, widely dispersed metal "chaff."

The effectiveness of a Sprint defense would be less degraded by such countermeasures. Light decoys could be distinguished from actual reentry vehicles because they would be disproportionately slowed by the atmosphere and possibly because their wake in the atmosphere would be different. Radar blackout would also be much less of a problem. Because of their short range, however, Sprints could defend only those targets in their immediate vicinity. Thus an adversary could choose to attack some cities with enough weapons to overwhelm the defense while leaving others untargeted. Heavy radioactive fallout could also be produced over large parts of the country by an adversary's delivering large-yield weapons outside the areas covered by Sprint defenses. A nationwide defense of the Sprint type would therefore require a nationwide fallout-shelter program.

Although combining Sprints and Spartans in a single system, as was proposed for the Nike-X system, would complicate an adversary's penetration problem, in a competition with a determined and resourceful adversary the advantage in an offense-defense duel would still lie with the offense. As a result, in spite of strong advocacy by the Army and support from the other branches of the military and from members of Congress, the decision to deploy the Nike-X system was never made.

At the heart of the debate about whether or not to deploy the Nike-X system was the question of what the Russian reaction to such a decision would be. It was generally conceded that the system might well save large numbers of lives in the event of war, if the U.S.S.R. were simply to employ the forces projected in the available intelligence estimates. On that basis proponents argued in favor of deployment in spite of the high costs, variously estimated as being from $13 billion to $50 billion. Such deployment was opposed, particularly by Secretary McNamara, because of the belief that the U.S.S.R. could and would improve its offensive capabilities in order to negate whatever effectiveness the system might have had. Indeed, because the deployment of a U.S. ABM system would introduce large uncertainties into the calculus of the strategic balance, there were occasional expressions of concern that the U.S.S.R. might overreact. Hence the damage inflicted on us in the event of war might even be greater than it would be if the Nike-X system were not deployed.

The Sentinel system announced in 1967 would have far less capability than

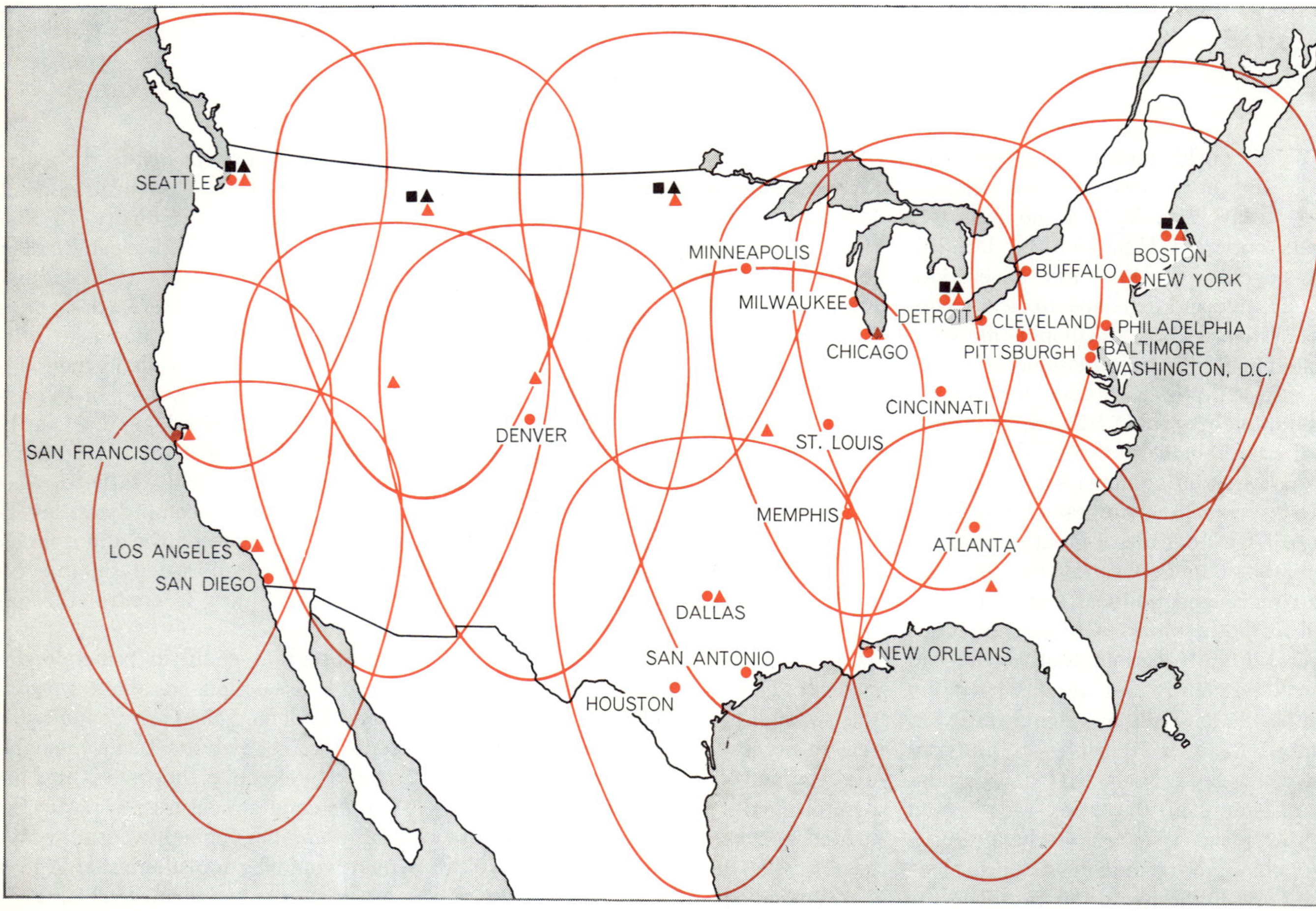

▲ SPARTAN SITE

▲ SPRINT SITE

■ PAR SITE

● 25 LARGEST CITIES

SENTINEL SYSTEM, a "thin" anti-ballistic-missile (ABM) system described by the Johnson Administration as being intended to defend the U.S. against a hypothetical Chinese missile attack in the 1970's, is depicted on this map in its original form. The main defense would be provided by Spartan missiles, long-range ABM missiles with nuclear warheads in the megaton range, designed to intercept incoming missiles outside the earth's atmosphere. The Spartans would be deployed at about 14 locations in order to provide a "thin" or "light" area defense of the whole country. The range of each "farm" of Spartans is indicated by the egg-shaped area around it; for missiles attacking over the northern horizon, the intercept range of the Spartan is elongated somewhat to the south. The Sentinel system would also include some Sprint missiles, short-range ABM missiles with much smaller warheads, designed to intercept incoming missiles after they have reentered the atmosphere. The Sprints were originally to be deployed to defend only the five or six perimeter acquisition radars, or PAR's, which were to be deployed across the northern part of the country. In President Nixon's proposed modification of the Sentinel scheme Spartans, Sprints and PAR sites would be deployed in a somewhat different array to provide additional protection for our land-based retaliatory forces against a hypothetical surprise attack by the Russians.

the Nike-X system. It would include some Sprint missiles to defend key radars (five or six perimeter acquisition radars, or PAR's, to be deployed across the northern part of the country), but the main defense would be provided by Spartan missiles located to provide a "thin" or "light" defense for the entire country [*see illustration on opposite page*]. Spokesmen for the Johnson Administration argued that such a deployment would be almost completely effective in dealing with a possible Chinese missile attack during the 1970's, but that it would be so ineffective against a possible Russian attack that the U.S.S.R. would not feel obliged to improve its strategic offensive forces as a response to the decision. Both arguments were seriously questioned.

Garwin and Bethe, for example, contended that even the first-generation Chinese missiles might well be equipped with penetration aids that would defeat the Sentinel system. Other experts pointed out that the system, like the Nike-X system, could never be tested adequately short of actual war, and that in view of its complexity there would be a high probability of a catastrophic failure.

The contention that the U.S.S.R. would not react to the Sentinel decision seemed at least as questionable as the assertions of great effectiveness against the Chinese. Whatever the initial capability of the Sentinel system, it seemed clear that the Sentinel decision would at least shorten the lead time for the deployment of a system of the Nike-X type. Moreover, the fact that Sentinel was strongly and publicly supported as a first step toward an "anti-Soviet" system could hardly escape the attention of Russian decision-makers.

Since the announcement of the Sentinel decision, and particularly since the change in the Administration, the arguments in favor of the decision have become confused. It has been variously suggested by Administration spokesmen that the primary purpose would be (1) to defend the American population and industry against a possible Chinese attack, (2) to provide at least some protection for population and industry against a possible Russian attack, (3) to defend Minuteman missile sites against a possible Russian attack and (4) to serve as a bargaining counter in strategic-arms-limitation talks with the U.S.S.R. It might be noted that no one in recent months has seriously suggested that a Russian reaction to the decision is unlikely. In fact, all but the first

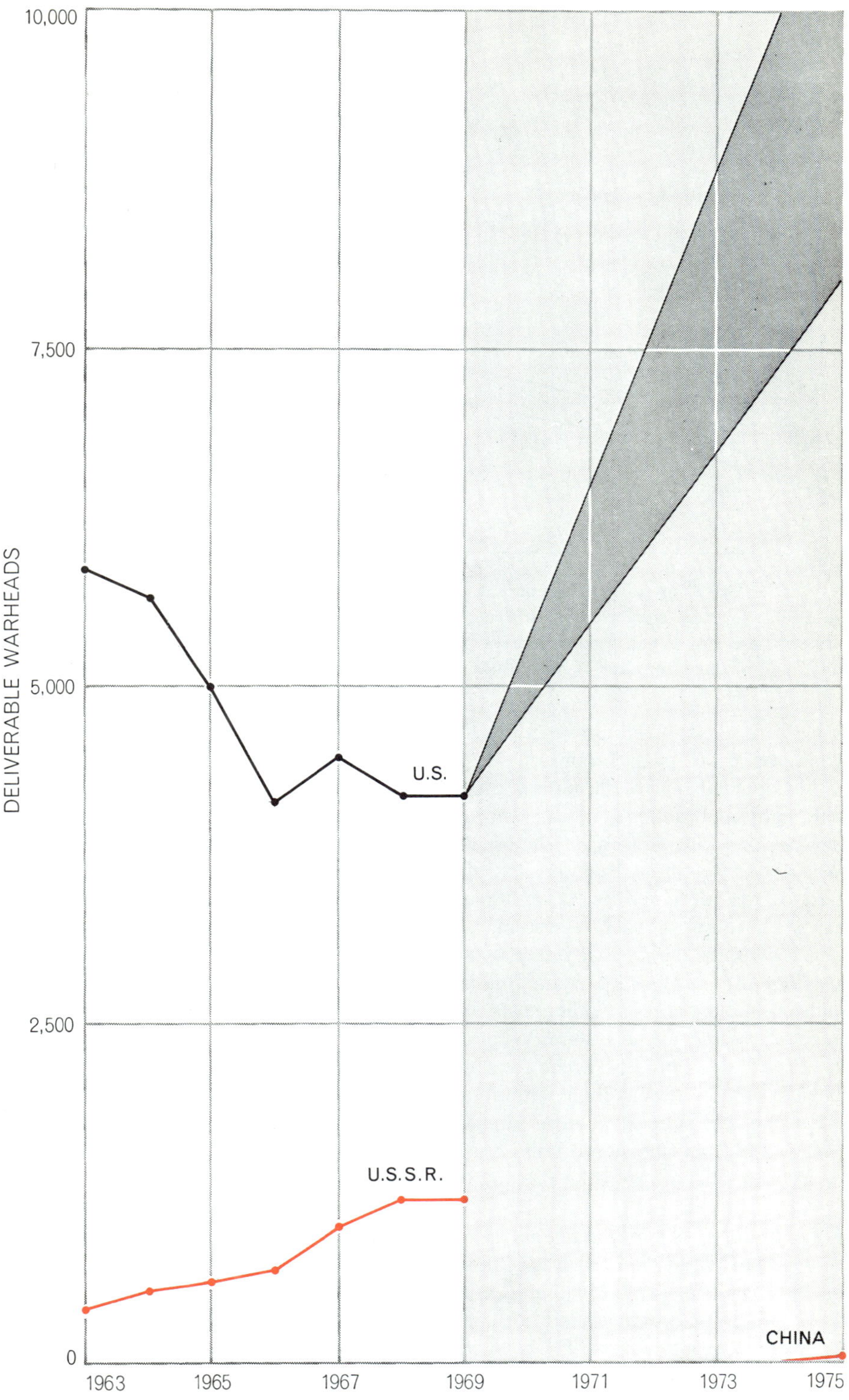

STRATEGIC OFFENSIVE FORCES of the U.S., the U.S.S.R. and China are compared here in terms of the number of megaton-range nuclear warheads the U.S. could deliver against either of the two other powers as of a given date, and vice versa. The U.S. missile force grew rapidly during the 1960's, offsetting a partial phasing-out of intercontinental bombers. The Russian bomber force, meanwhile, has remained at a constant level, while their missile force has grown steadily and shows no sign of leveling off. Thus at present the U.S. maintains a superiority over the U.S.S.R. of about four to one in numbers of deliverable warheads. The hypothetical Chinese strategic force was recently estimated by Secretary of Defense Laird to be 20 to 30 deliverable warheads by the mid-1970's. The effect of the present U.S. program to equip its Minuteman III and its Poseidon missiles with multiple independently targeted reentry vehicles (MIRV's) would be to increase greatly the number of U.S. deliverable warheads by 1975 (*dark gray area*). It is not known what compensating actions, if any, will be taken by the other powers in response to this development. It has been estimated by former Secretary of Defense McNamara that 400 one-megaton warheads would suffice to destroy 75 percent of the industry and 33 percent of the population of the U.S.S.R.

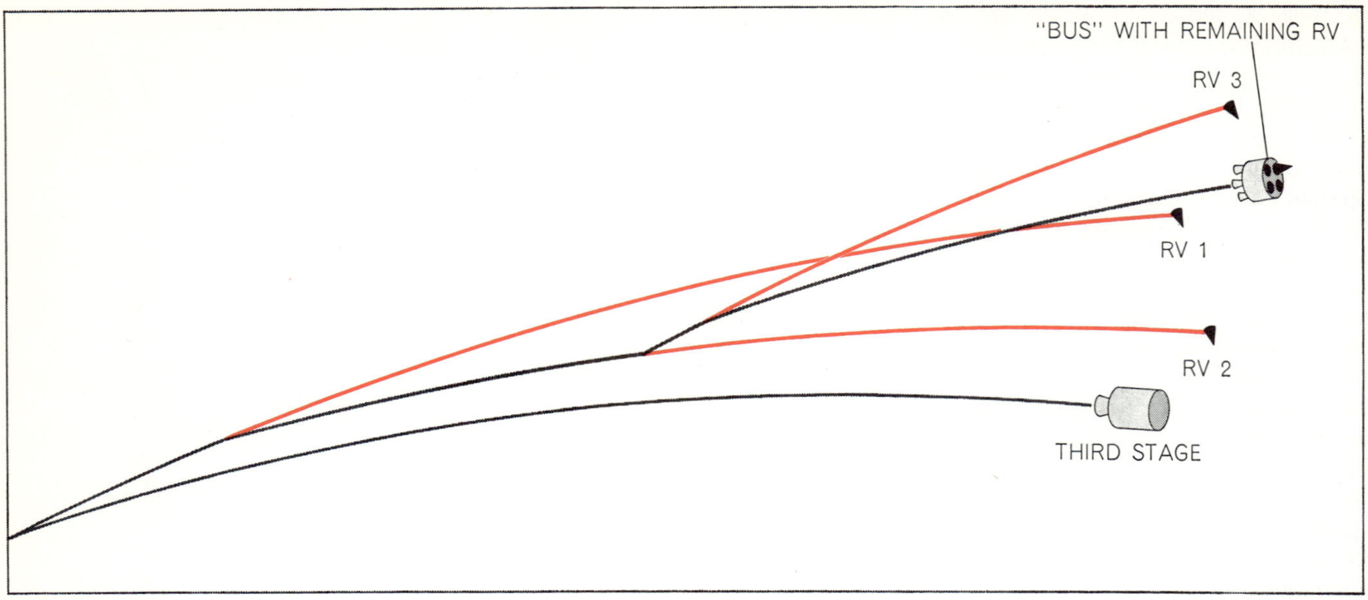

MIRV CONCEPT on which the current U.S. Minuteman III and Poseidon programs are based is illustrated by the idealized drawings on these two pages. Each offensive missile will carry aloft a "bus," containing a number of individual reentry vehicles, or RV's (in this example four are shown). A single guidance and propulsion system will control the orientation and velocity of the bus, from which the reentry vehicles will be released sequentially (*left*). After each release there will be a further adjustment in the velocity

of the arguments cited above imply the likelihood of a Russian response.

President Nixon's reaffirmation, albeit with some modification, of the Sentinel decision was presumably made on the basis of his judgment that the first and third of the aforementioned arguments justify the costs of such a system, not only the direct dollar cost but also the cost in terms of the impact on Russian decision-making and any other costs that may be imputed to the system. Whether or not his decision is correct depends strongly on how serious the possibility of a Russian reaction is. Before dealing further with that question it will be useful to bring MIRV's into the picture.

The problem of simulating an actual warhead reentry vehicle is a comparatively easy one, provided that the attacker need not be concerned with differences in the interaction of decoys and warheads with the atmosphere during reentry. If one wishes to build decoys and warheads that will be indistinguishable down to low altitudes, however, the problem is a formidable one, particularly if one demands high confidence in the indistinguishability of the two types of object. Improved radar resolution and increased traffic-handling and data-processing capability make the problem of effective decoy design increasingly difficult. The development of interceptors capable of high acceleration will also complicate the offense's problem. With such interceptors the decision to engage reentering objects can be deferred until they are well down into the atmosphere; the longer the defense can wait, the more stringent are the demands of decoy simulation on the offense.

As the problem becomes more difficult, the ratio of decoy weight to warhead weight increases. There comes a point at which, if one wants really high confidence of penetration, one might just as well use several warheads on each missile rather than a single warhead and several decoys, each of which may be as heavy, or nearly as heavy, as a warhead. Hence multiple warheads are in a sense the ultimate in high-confidence penetration aids (assuming that one relies on exhaustion or saturation of defense capabilities as the preferred tactic for defeating the defense). To be effective, however, multiple warheads must be sufficiently separated so that a single interceptor burst will not destroy more than one incoming warhead. Moreover, the utility of multiple warheads for destroying targets, particularly small ones that would not justify attack by more than one or two small warheads, will be greatly enhanced if they can be individually guided.

In principle each reentry vehicle could have its own "post-boost" guidance and propulsion system. That, however, is not the concept of the MIRV's in our Poseidon and Minuteman III missile systems, which are now under development. Rather, a single guidance and propulsion system will control the orientation and velocity of a "bus" from which reentry vehicles will be released sequentially [*see illustration on these two pages*]. After each release there will be a further adjustment in the velocity and direction of the bus. Thus each reentry vehicle can be directed to a separate target. The targets can be rather widely separated, the actual separation depending on how much energy (and therefore weight) one is willing to expend in the post-boost maneuvers of the bus. It is an ingenious—and demanding—concept.

Two rationales have been advanced for the decision to proceed with the U.S. MIRV programs. One is that with MIRV's the U.S. can have a high confidence of being able to penetrate an adversary's ABM defenses. The apparent deployment of a limited Russian ABM system in the vicinity of Moscow and U.S. concern about a possibly more widespread Russian ABM-system deployment have been important considerations in the decision to go ahead with the U.S. MIRV programs.

The second rationale is that a MIRV system enables one to strike more targets with a given number of boosters than would be the case if one were using one warhead per missile. This rationale has been important for two reasons.

First, it enabled spokesmen for the Johnson Administration to argue against expanding the size of our strategic missile force during a period when Russian forces were growing rapidly. They were able to contend in the face of political opposition on both flanks that, whereas

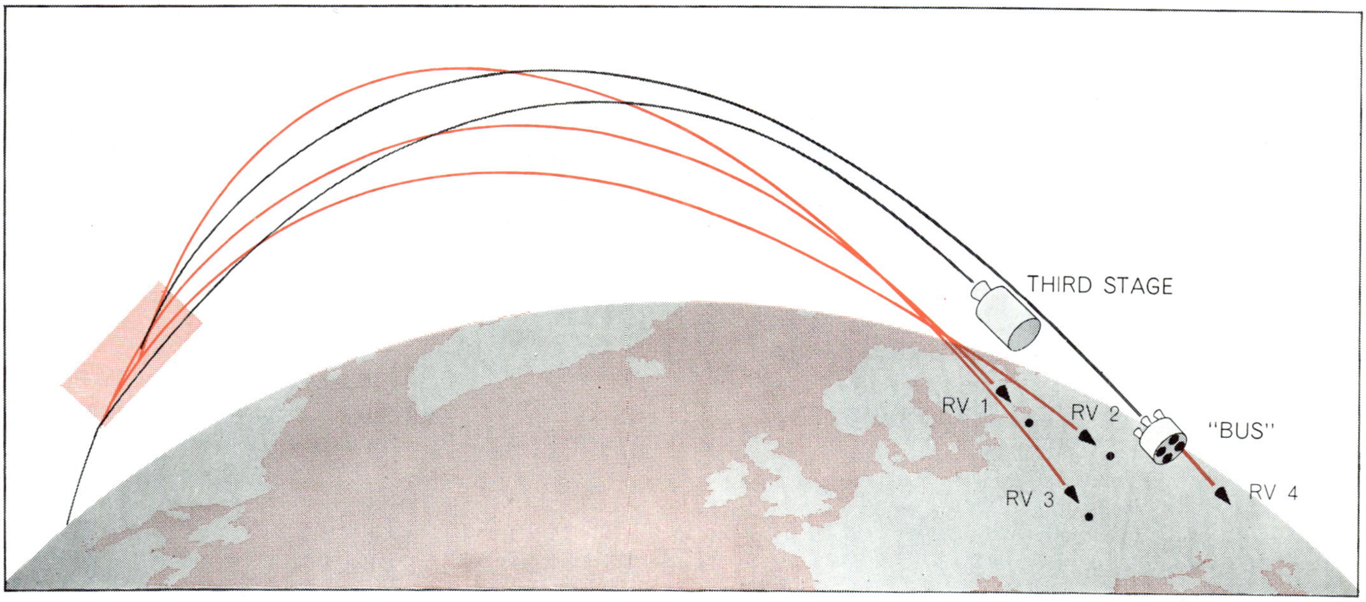

and the direction of the bus. Thus each reentry vehicle can be directed to a separate target (*right*). The actual separation of the targets depends on how much energy (and therefore weight) one is willing to expend in the post-boost maneuvers of the bus. Besides being a potentially attractive means of penetrating an adversary's ABM defenses, MIRV's could conceivably be effective some day as a "counterforce" weapon, that is, a system capable of destroying the adversary's strategic offensive forces in a preemptive attack.

we did not contemplate expanding the number of our offensive missiles, the number of warheads we could deliver would increase rapidly.

Second, it raised the prospect of a missile force that could be used as a very effective "counterforce" weapon. This means that with MIRV's a limited number of missiles might be capable of destroying a larger intercontinental-ballistic-missile (ICBM) force in a preemptive attack. To achieve this performance, however, particularly against hardened offensive missile sites, would require a substantial improvement in accuracy and a high post-boost reliability—no mean feats with a device as complicated as the MIRV bus.

What bearing will the deployment of the ABM and the MIRV systems have on the future of the arms race? In attempting to answer this difficult question it is instructive to consider the extent to which the choices of each of the superpowers regarding strategic weapons have been influenced by the other's decisions.

The actual role of this action-reaction phenomenon is a matter of considerable debate in American defense circles. Indeed, the differences in views on this question account for most of the dispute of the past few years regarding the objectives to be served by strategic forces and their desired size and qualities. Thus whether the U.S. should be content with an adequate retaliatory, or "assured destruction," capability or go further and try to build a capability that would permit us to reduce damage to ourselves in the event of war must clearly depend on a judgment on whether Russian defense decisions could be influenced significantly by our decisions. Those who have felt that Russian defense planning would be responsive to our actions have held that for the most part any attempt by us to develop such "damage-limiting" capabilities with respect to the U.S.S.R. would be an effort doomed to failure. The U.S.S.R. would simply improve its offensive capabilities to offset the effects of any measures we might take. This was the basis for the rejection by the American leadership of the requests by the Army for large-scale ABM-system deployment and for the rejection of requests by the Air Force for much larger ICBM forces.

Although there is considerable evidence to support the claim that the action-reaction phenomenon does apply to defense decision-making, to explain all the major decisions of the superpowers in terms of an action-reaction hypothesis is an obvious oversimplification. The American MIRV deployment has been rationalized as a logical response to a possible Russian ABM-system deployment, but there were also other motivations that were important: the desire to keep our total missile force constant while increasing the number of warheads we could deploy, the long-term possibility of MIRV's giving us an effective counterforce capability, and finally the simple desire to bring to fruition an interesting and elegant technological concept.

Nevertheless, the action-reaction phenomenon, with the reaction often premature and/or exaggerated, has clearly been a major stimulant of the strategic arms race. Examples from the past can be cited to support this point: (1) the American reaction, indeed overreaction, to uncertainty at the time of the "missile gap," which played a central role in the 1960 Presidential election but was soon afterward shown by improved intelligence to be, if anything, in favor of the U.S.; (2) the Russian decision to deploy the "Tallinn" air-defense system, possibly made in the mistaken expectation that the U.S. would go ahead with the deployment of B-70 bombers or SR-71 strike-reconnaissance aircraft; (3) the U.S. response to the Tallinn system (which until recently was thought to be an ABM system) and to the possible extension of the Moscow ABM system into a countrywide system. It was in order to have high assurance of its ability to get through these possible Russian ABM defenses that the U.S. embarked on the development of various penetration aids and even of new missiles: Minuteman III and Poseidon.

These examples have in common the fact that if doubt exists about the capabilities or intentions of an adversary, prudence normally requires that one respond not on the basis of what one expects but on a considerably more pessimistic projection. The U.S. generally

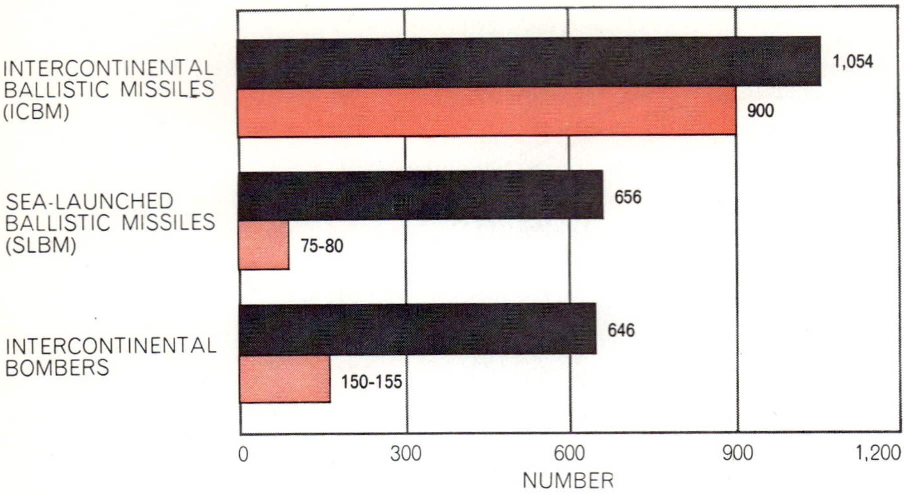

INVENTORY of the intercontinental delivery vehicles possessed by the U.S. (*gray*) and the U.S.S.R. (*color*) as of October, 1968, shows that in this category also the U.S. continues to hold a clear superiority over the U.S.S.R. This measure is not entirely satisfactory, however, in that it does not take into account qualitative differences in the various systems, the expected interactions during a nuclear exchange or the match of the weapons with the targets. When such factors are taken into account, the differences between the U.S. and the U.S.S.R. are not significant. In his final "posture" statement for fiscal 1969, for example, former Secretary McNamara estimated that, barring drastic changes in the strategic balance, in an all-out nuclear exchange in the mid-1970's each country could inflict a minimum of 120 million fatalities on the other—regardless of which country struck first.

bases its plans—and makes much of the fact—on what has become known as the "greater-than-expected threat." In so doing, the Americans (and presumably the Russians) have often overreacted. The extent of the overreaction is directly dependent on the degree of uncertainty about any adversary's intentions and capabilities.

The problem is compounded by lead-time requirements for response. According to the Johnson Administration, the decisions to go ahead with Minuteman III, Poseidon and Sentinel had to be made when they were because of the possibility that in the mid-1970's the Russians might have a reasonably effective ABM system and the Chinese an ICBM capability. The Russians had to make a decision to develop the Tallinn system (if the decision was made because of the B-70 program) long before we ourselves knew whether or not we would deploy an operational B-70 force.

Once the decisions to respond to ambiguous indications of adversary activity were made it often proved impossible to modify the response, even when new intelligence became available. For example, between the time the Sentinel decision was announced and the first Congressional debate on the appropriation took place during the summer of 1968, evidence became available that the Chinese threat was not developing as rapidly as had been feared. Yet in spite of this information those in Congress who attempted at that time to defer the appropriation for Sentinel failed. Similarly, at this writing, as the Poseidon and Minuteman III programs begin to gain momentum, it seems much less likely than it did at the time of their conception that the U.S.S.R. will deploy the kind of ABM system that was the Johnson Administration's main rationale for these programs. On the Russian side, the Tallinn deployment continued long after it became clear that no operational B-70 force would ever be built.

Of the kinds of weapons development that can stimulate overresponse on the part of one's adversary, it is hard to imagine one more troublesome than ABM defenses. In addition to uncertainty about adversary intentions and the need (because of lead-time requirements) for early response to what the adversary might do, there is the added fact that the uncertainties about how well an ABM system might perform are far larger than they are for strategic offensive systems. The conservative defense planner will design his ABM system on the assumption that it may not work as well as he hopes, that is, he will overdesign it to take into account as fully as he can all imaginable modes of failure and enemy offensive threats. The offensive planner, on the other hand, will assume that the defense might perform much better than he expects and will overdesign his response. Thus there is overreaction on both sides. These uncertainties result in a divergent process: an arms race with no apparent limits other than economic ones, each round being more expensive than the last. Moreover, because of overreaction on the part of the offense there may be an increase in the ability of each side to inflict damage on the other.

All one needs to make this possibility a reality is a triggering mechanism. The Russian ABM program, by stimulating the Minuteman III and Poseidon programs, may have served that purpose. The Chinese nuclear program may also have triggered an action-reaction chain, of which the Sentinel response is the second link [*see illustration on page 186*].

It can be assumed that there will be considerable pressure and effort to make Sentinel highly effective against a "greater than expected" Chinese threat. Such a system will undoubtedly have some capability against Russian ICBM's. Russian decision-makers, who must assume that Sentinel might perform better than they expect, will at least have to consider this possibility as they plan their offensive capabilities. More important, they will have to respond on the assumption that the Sentinel decision may foreshadow a decision to build an anti-Russian ABM system. Hence it is probably not a question of whether the U.S.S.R. will respond to Sentinel but rather of whether the U.S.S.R. will limit its response to one that does not require a U.S. counterresponse, and of whether it is too late to stop the Sentinel deployment.

It is apparent that reduction in uncertainty about adversary intentions and capabilities is a *sine qua non* to curtailing the strategic arms race. There are a number of ways to accomplish this (in addition to the gathering of intelligence, which obviously makes a great contribution).

First, there is unilateral disclosure. In the case of the U.S. there has been a conscious effort to inform both the American public and the Russian leadership of the rationale for many American decisions regarding strategic systems and, to the extent consistent with security, of U.S. capabilities. This has been done particularly through the release by the Secretary of Defense of an annual "posture" statement, a practice that, it is hoped, will be continued by the U.S. and will be emulated someday by the U.S.S.R. This would be in the interest of both countries. Because there has been no corresponding effort by the Russians the U.S. probably overreacts to Russian decisions more than the U.S.S.R. does to American decisions. (At least it is easier to trace a causal relationship between Russian decisions and U.S. reactions than it is between U.S. decisions and Russian reactions.)

Second, negotiations to curtail the arms race (even if abortive) or any other dialogue may be very useful if such efforts result in a reduction of uncertainty about the policies, capabilities or intentions of the parties.

Third, some weapons systems may be less productive of uncertainty than others that might be chosen instead. For example, it is likely to be less difficult to measure the size of a force of submarine-launched or fixed missiles than it is to measure the size of a mobile land force. Similarly, it would be easier to persuade an adversary that a small missile carried only a single warhead than would be the case with a large vehicle. Such considerations must be borne in mind in evaluating alternative weapons systems.

In short, although uncertainty about adversary capabilities and intentions may not always be bad (in some instances the existence of uncertainty has contributed to deterrence), the U.S. and the U.S.S.R. would seem well advised to make great efforts to avoid giving each other cause for overreacting to decisions because of inadequate understanding of their meaning.

The importance of somehow breaking the action-reaction chains that seem to drive the arms race is obvious when one considers the enormous resources involved that could otherwise be used to meet pressing social needs. In addition, there is particular importance in doing so at present because the concurrent deployment of MIRV's and ABM systems is likely to have drastic destabilizing consequences. It is conceivable that one of the superpowers with an ABM system might develop MIRV's to the point where it could use them to destroy the bulk of its adversary's ICBM force in a preemptive attack. Its air and ABM defenses would then have to deal with a much degraded retaliatory blow, consisting of the sea-launched forces and any ICBM's and aircraft that might have survived the preemptive attack. The problems of defense in such a contingency would remain formidable. They would be significantly less difficult, however, than if the adversary's ICBM force had not been seriously depleted. In fact, the defense problem would be relatively simple if a large fraction of the adversary's retaliatory capability were, as is true for the U.S. and to a far greater degree for the U.S.S.R., in its land-based ICBM's, most of which would presumably have been destroyed.

It may seem unlikely that either superpower would initiate such a preemptive attack, in view of the great uncertainties in effectiveness (particularly with respect to defenses) and the disastrous consequences if even a comparatively small fraction of the adversary's retaliatory force should get through. With both MIRV's and an ABM system, however, such a preemptive attack would not seem as unlikely as it does now. It might not appear irrational to some, for example, if an uncontrollable nuclear exchange seemed almost certain, and if by striking first one could limit damage to a significantly lower level than if the adversary were to strike the first blow. In short, if one or both of the two superpowers had such capabilities, the world would be a much more unstable place than it is now.

Obviously neither superpower would permit its adversary to develop such capabilities without responding, if it could, by strengthening its retaliatory forces. The response problem becomes more

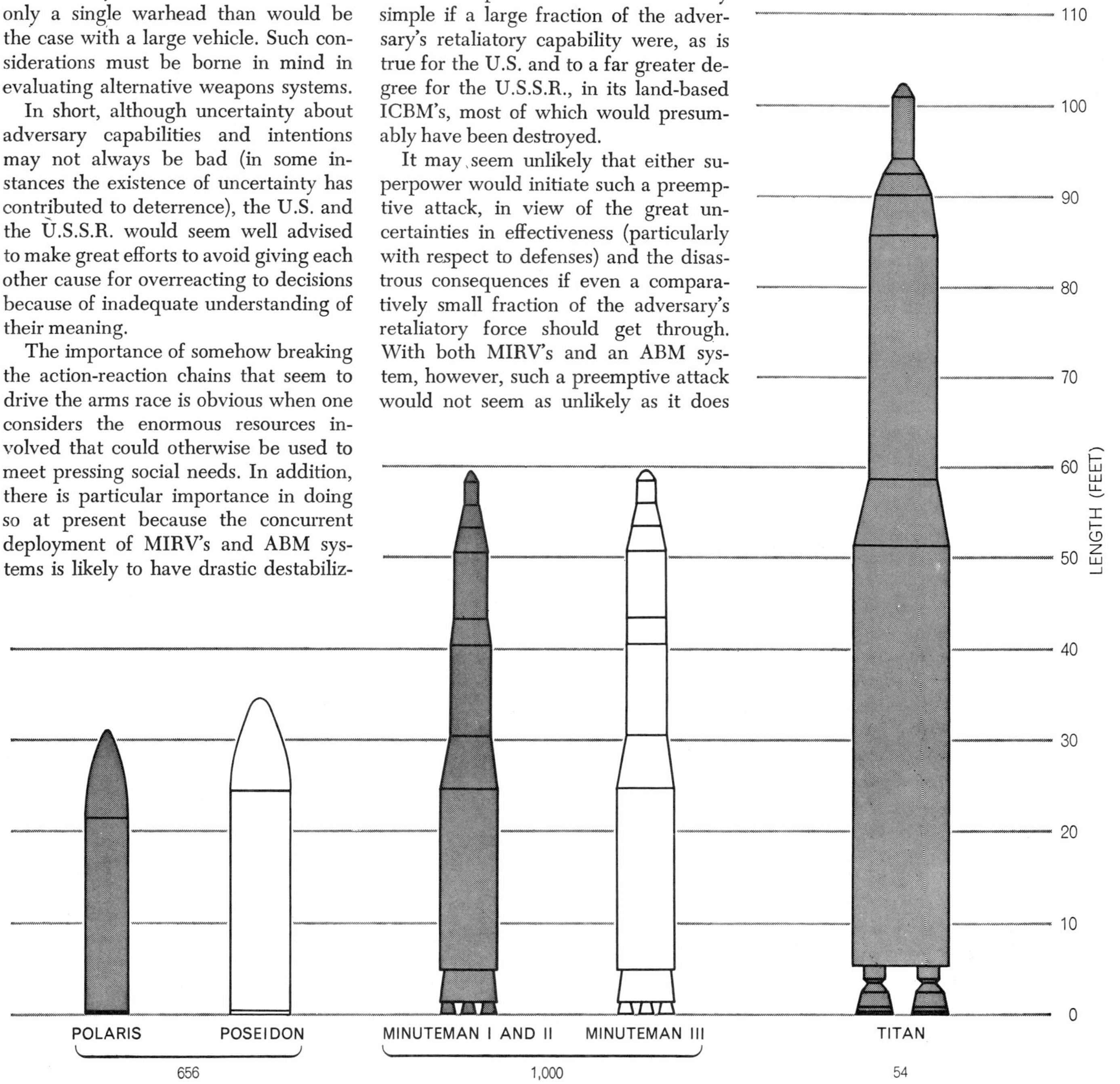

U.S. OFFENSIVE MISSILES currently deployed or under development are drawn here to scale. The sea-based Polaris and Poseidon and the land-based Minutemen are capable of carrying warheads with a total explosive yield of about one megaton each. The land-based Titan II can carry a warhead of more than five megatons. Poseidon and Minuteman III, which are under development, are designed to carry MIRV warheads. The total number of missiles scheduled for deployment in each category is indicated at the bottom.

difficult, however, if the adversary develops both MIRV's and an ABM system than if only one is developed.

Against a MIRV threat alone there are such obvious responses as defense of ICBM sites or greater reliance on sea-launched or other mobile systems. Such responses are likely to be acceptable because, whereas the costs of highly invulnerable systems are large (perhaps several times larger than the costs of simple undefended ICBM's), only relatively small numbers of such secure retaliatory weapons would be required to provide an adequate "assured destruction" capability. Indeed, a force the size of the present Polaris submarine fleet would seem to be more than adequate. The response to an ABM system alone might also be kept within acceptable limits because the expenditures required to offset the effects of defense are likely to be small compared with the costs of the defense.

If it is necessary to acquire retaliatory capabilities that are comparatively invulnerable to MIRV attack in numbers sufficient to saturate or exhaust ABM defenses, however, the total cost could be very great. In fact, if one continued to rely heavily on exhaustion of defenses as the preferred technique for penetration, the offense might no longer have a significant cost-effectiveness advantage over the defense. Thus the concurrent development of MIRV's and ABM systems raises the specter of a more precarious balance of terror a few years hence, a rapidly escalating arms race in the attempt to prevent the instabilities from getting out of hand, or quite possibly both.

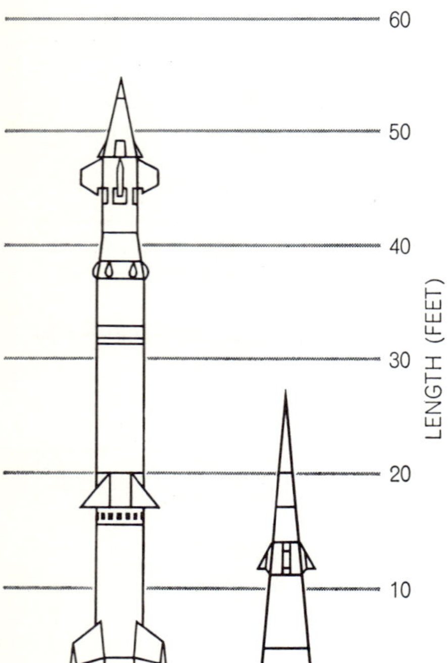

U.S. DEFENSIVE MISSILES currently being deployed as part of the modified Sentinel system are drawn here to scale. The Spartan and Sprint carry warheads in the megaton range and kiloton range respectively.

With this background about the roles of uncertainty and the action-reaction phenomenon in stimulating the arms race, one can draw some general conclusions about the functions and qualities of future strategic forces. We must first recognize that two kinds of instability must be considered: crisis instability (the possibility that when war seems imminent, one side or the other will be motivated to attack preemptively in the hope of limiting damage to itself) and arms-race instability (the possibility that the development or deployment decisions of one country, or even the possibility of such decisions, may trigger new development or deployment decisions by another country).

The first kind of instability is illustrated in the chart on the opposite page, which is based on former Secretary McNamara's posture statement for fiscal 1967. This shows that—assuming two possible expanded Russian threats, various damage-limiting efforts by the U.S. and failure of the U.S.S.R. to react to extensive U.S. damage-limiting efforts by improving its retaliatory capability—American fatalities in 1975 would be only about a third as great in the event of a U.S. first strike as they would be in the case of a Russian first strike. (In the present situation the advantage of the attacker is negligible.) Obviously if war seemed imminent, with the strategic balances assumed in this example, there would be tremendous pressure on the U.S. to strike first. There would be corresponding pressure on the U.S.S.R. to do likewise if a Russian first strike could result not only in a much higher level of damage to the U.S. but also in a diminution in damage to the U.S.S.R. The incentives would be mutually reinforcing.

To minimize the chance of a failure of deterrence in a time of crisis, it seems important for both the U.S. and the U.S.S.R. to develop strategic postures such that preemptive attack would have as small an effect as possible on the anticipated outcome of a thermonuclear exchange. Actually, of course, it is extremely unlikely that the Russians would passively watch the U.S. develop the extensive damage-limiting postures assumed in the foregoing example. Instead they would probably react by modifying their posture so that the advantage to the U.S. of attacking preemptively would be less than is indicated in the chart. Thus the example can also be used to illustrate the second kind of instability.

To the extent that one accepts the action-reaction view of the arms race, one is forced to conclude that virtually anything we might attempt in order to reduce damage to ourselves in the event of war is likely to provoke an escalation in the race. Moreover, many of the choices we might make with damage-limitation in mind are likely to make preemptive attack more attractive and war therefore more probable. The concurrent development of MIRV's and ABM systems is a particularly good example of this.

One is struck by the fact that there is an inherent inconsonance in the objectives spelled out in our basic military policy, namely "to deter aggression at any level and, should deterrence fail, to terminate hostilities in concert with our allies under conditions of relative advantage while limiting damage to the U.S. and allied interests." Hard choices must be made between attempting to minimize the chance of war's occurring in a time of crisis and attempting to minimize the consequences if it does occur.

The decisions made by U.S. planners in recent years with respect to new weapons development and deployment reflect a somewhat inconsistent philosophy on this point. The U.S. has generally avoided actions whose primary rationale was to limit damage that the U.S.S.R. might inflict on it, actions to which the Russians would probably respond. Accordingly the U.S. has not deployed an anti-Russian ABM system and has given air defense a low priority.

On the other hand, where there were reasons other than a desire to improve American damage-limiting capability with respect to the U.S.S.R., the U.S. has proceeded with programs in spite of their probably escalating effect on the arms race or their effect on first-strike incentives. This was true in the case of the MIRV's and Sentinel.

The U.S. will face more such decisions. For example, it may appear necessary to change the U.S. strategic offensive posture in order to make American forces less vulnerable to possible Russian MIRV attack. The nature of these decisions will depend on the importance attached to the action-reaction phenomenon and to the effect of improved counterforce capabilities on the probability of war. Emphasis on these two factors

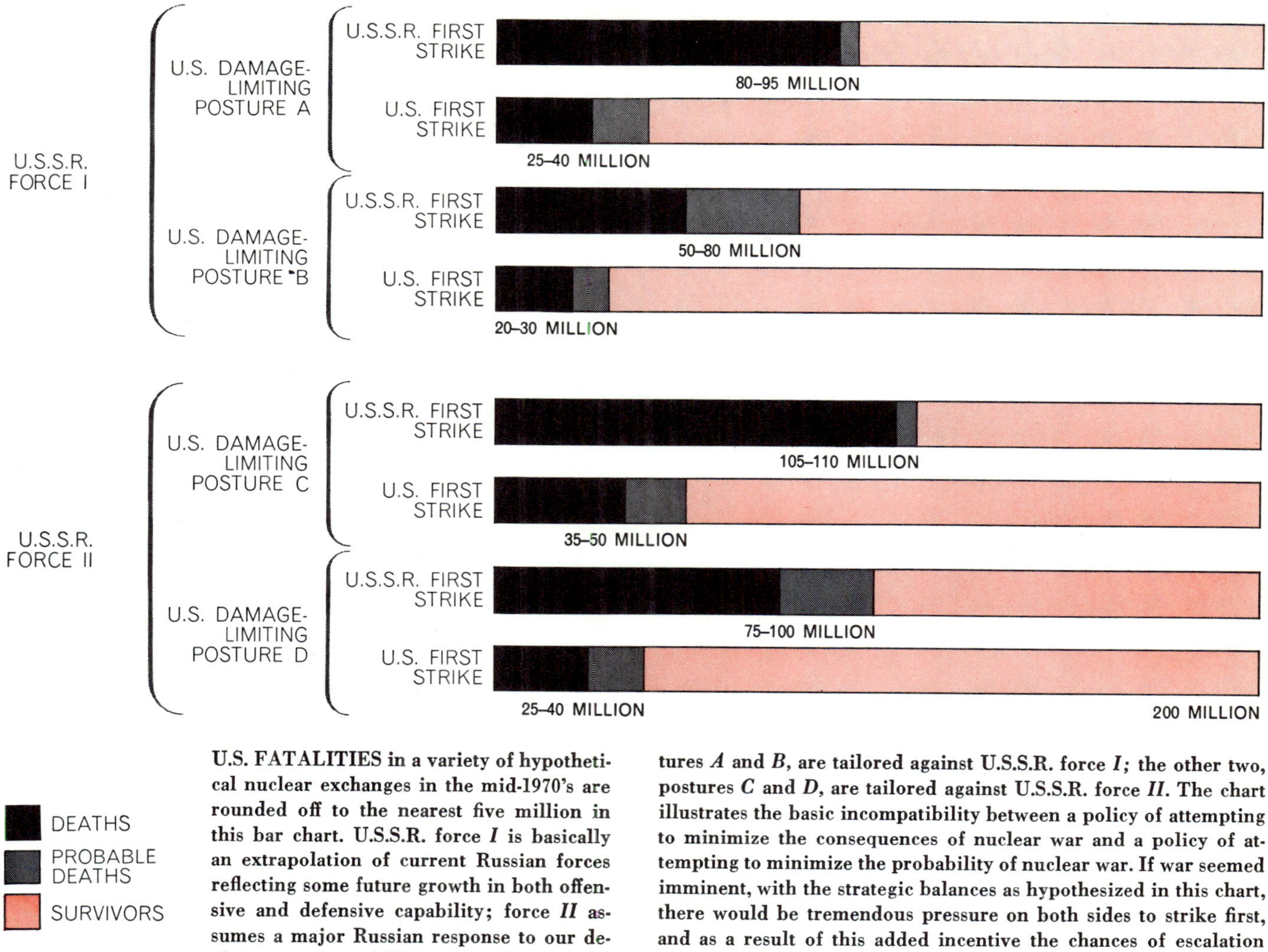

U.S. FATALITIES in a variety of hypothetical nuclear exchanges in the mid-1970's are rounded off to the nearest five million in this bar chart. U.S.S.R. force *I* is basically an extrapolation of current Russian forces reflecting some future growth in both offensive and defensive capability; force *II* assumes a major Russian response to our deployment of an ABM system. Two of the four U.S. damage-limiting programs, postures *A* and *B*, are tailored against U.S.S.R. force *I*; the other two, postures *C* and *D*, are tailored against U.S.S.R. force *II*. The chart illustrates the basic incompatibility between a policy of attempting to minimize the consequences of nuclear war and a policy of attempting to minimize the probability of nuclear war. If war seemed imminent, with the strategic balances as hypothesized in this chart, there would be tremendous pressure on both sides to strike first, and as a result of this added incentive the chances of escalation would be enhanced. The chart is based on information contained in former Secretary McNamara's posture statement for fiscal 1967.

implies discounting options that would increase U.S. counterforce capability against Russian strategic forces, which in turn might provoke an expansion of Russian offensive forces. Options requiring long lead times would also be discounted, since decisions regarding them might have to be made while there was still uncertainty about whether the U.S.S.R. was developing MIRV's.

Should more weight be given in the future to developing damage-limiting capabilities? Or should more weight be given to minimizing the probability of a thermonuclear exchange and curtailing the strategic arms race? It is hard to see how one can have it both ways.

In spite of some changes in technology, there is little to indicate that the U.S. could get very far with damage-limiting efforts, considering the determination of the Russians and the options available to them for denying the attainment of such U.S. capabilities. The emergence of new nuclear powers, the rapid pace of technological advance and the other important demands on American resources suggest that a clear first priority should be assigned to moderating the action-reaction cycle. Moving toward greater emphasis on damage-limitation would seem justified only if the U.S. can persuade itself that the Russians will not react to American moves as the U.S. would to theirs, and if means can be chosen that will not increase the probability of war.

No treatment of the dynamics of the strategic arms race would be complete without some discussion of the possibility of ending it, or at least curtailing it, through negotiations. Both the urgency and the opportunity are great, but the latter may be waning. This opportunity is in part a consequence of the present military balance, as well as of somewhat changed views in both the U.S. and the U.S.S.R. about strategic capabilities and objectives.

With the rapid growth in its strategic offensive forces during the past few years, the U.S.S.R. can at long last enter negotiations without conceding inferiority or (which is worse from the Russian point of view) exposing itself to the possibility of being frozen in such a position. Moreover, the U.S.S.R. may at long last be prepared to accept the prevailing American view about the action-reaction phenomenon, and about the intrinsic advantage of the offense and the futility of defense. The apparent decision of the Russians not to proceed with a nationwide ABM system at present, and their professed willingness to enter into negotiations to control both offensive and defensive systems, may be evidence of this convergence of viewpoints.

On the American side there is at long last a quite general, if not yet universal, acceptance of the concept of nuclear "sufficiency": the idea that beyond a certain point increased nuclear force cannot be translated into useful political power. Acceptance of this concept is an almost necessary condition to termination of the arms race.

In considering negotiations with the U.S.S.R. on the strategic arms problem, the first factor to be kept in mind is the objectives to be sought. It would be a mistake to expect too much or to aspire to too little. One obvious aim is to re-

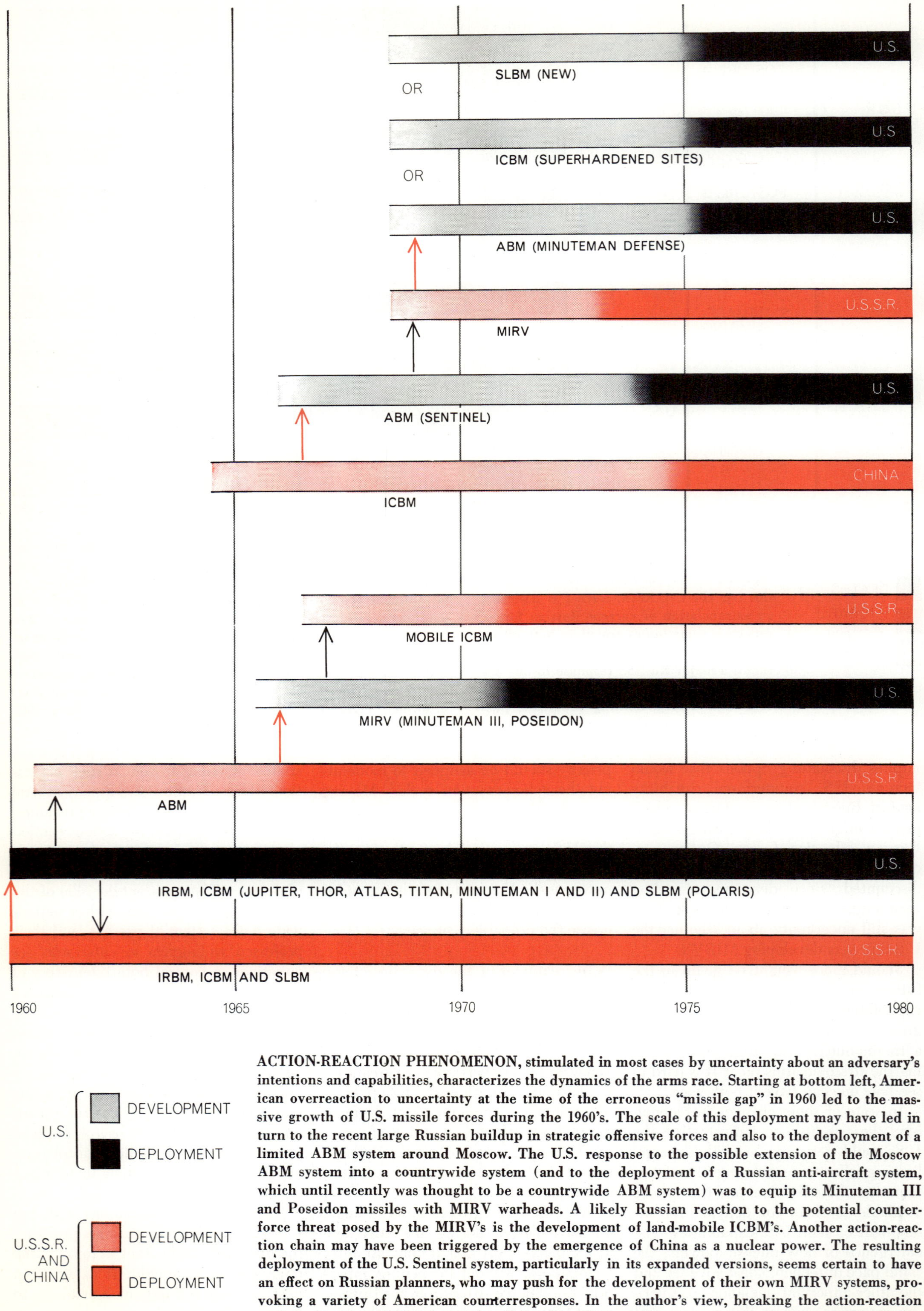

ACTION-REACTION PHENOMENON, stimulated in most cases by uncertainty about an adversary's intentions and capabilities, characterizes the dynamics of the arms race. Starting at bottom left, American overreaction to uncertainty at the time of the erroneous "missile gap" in 1960 led to the massive growth of U.S. missile forces during the 1960's. The scale of this deployment may have led in turn to the recent large Russian buildup in strategic offensive forces and also to the deployment of a limited ABM system around Moscow. The U.S. response to the possible extension of the Moscow ABM system into a countrywide system (and to the deployment of a Russian anti-aircraft system, which until recently was thought to be a countrywide ABM system) was to equip its Minuteman III and Poseidon missiles with MIRV warheads. A likely Russian reaction to the potential counterforce threat posed by the MIRV's is the development of land-mobile ICBM's. Another action-reaction chain may have been triggered by the emergence of China as a nuclear power. The resulting deployment of the U.S. Sentinel system, particularly in its expanded versions, seems certain to have an effect on Russian planners, who may push for the development of their own MIRV systems, provoking a variety of American counterresponses. In the author's view, breaking the action-reaction cycle by limiting ABM defenses should be given first priority in any forthcoming arms-control talks.

duce strategic armaments in order to lessen significantly the damage that would be sustained by the U.S. (and the U.S.S.R.) in the event of a nuclear exchange. Regrettably this goal is not likely to be realized in the near future. In the first place, any initial understandings will probably not involve reductions in strategic forces. Even if they did, the reductions would be limited. One cannot expect potential damage levels to be lowered by more than a few percent, even with fairly substantial cuts in strategic forces, because the capabilities of the superpowers are already so great.

Other objectives have been considered: reducing the incentives to strike preemptively in time of crisis, reducing the probability of accident or miscalculation, and increasing the time available for decision-making in the hope that the increased opportunity for communication might prevent a nuclear exchange from running its full course. Last but not least, one might also hope to change the international political climate so as to lessen tension, to reduce the incentive for powers that currently do not have nuclear weapons to acquire them and to increase the possibility for agreement by the superpowers on other meaningful arms-control measures.

It is reasonable to expect that successful negotiations might to some degree achieve all these objectives except the first: the reduction of potential damage. To focus on any one objective, or combination of objectives, however, is to obscure the immediate problem. In spite of the restraint of the U.S. in its choices regarding strategic weapons development and deployment during the first two-thirds of this decade, it now appears that in the absence of some understanding between the U.S. and the U.S.S.R. the action-reaction sequence that impels the arms race will not be broken. Therefore the immediate objective of any negotiations must be simply to bring that sequence to a halt, or to moderate its pace so that there will be a better chance of ending the arms race than is offered by continuing the policies of the past two decades.

In retrospect, controlling or reversing the growth of strategic capabilities could have been accomplished more easily a few years ago, when the possibility of ABM-system deployment seemed to be the main factor that would trigger another round in the arms race. Now the prospect of ABM systems is more troublesome because of technological advances. In addition, there are the two other stimuli already discussed: the possibility of effective counterforce capabilities as a result of the development of MIRV's, and the possibility that the Chinese nuclear capability may serve as a catalyst to the Russian-American action-reaction phenomenon.

Obviously, short of destroying China by nuclear attack, there is little the U.S. can do about Chinese capabilities except to make sure that it does not give them more weight in its thinking than they deserve. This leaves the option of trying to break the ABM-MIRV chain by focusing on the control of MIRV's or ABM defenses.

Whereas one might hope to limit both, if a choice must be made the focus should clearly be on the control of ABM defenses. Verification of compliance would be relatively simple and could probably be accomplished without intrusive inspection. In addition, the incentive to acquire MIRV's for penetrating defenses would be eliminated, although the incentive to acquire them for counterforce purposes would remain.

The problems of verifying compliance with an agreement to control MIRV's would be much more difficult. Moreover, if an ABM system were deployed, there would be great pressure to abrogate or violate any agreement prohibiting MIRV deployment because MIRV's offer high assurance for penetrating defenses. Although reversing the MIRV decision would be difficult, reversing the Sentinel one would present less of a problem.

To be attractive to the U.S.S.R. any proposal to limit defenses would almost certainly have to be coupled with an agreement to limit, if not reduce, inventories of deployed strategic offensive forces. In principle this should not be difficult, since it need not involve serious verification problems.

Complicating any attempt to reach an understanding with the U.S.S.R. on the strategic balance, however, is the fact that the American and Russian positions are not symmetrical. The U.S. has allies and bases around the periphery of the U.S.S.R., whereas the latter has neither near the U.S., unless one counts Cuba. It is clear that a Pandora's box of complications could be opened by any attempt in the context of negotiations on the strategic balance to deal with the threat to America's allies posed by short-range Russian delivery systems, and with the potential threat to the U.S.S.R. of systems in Europe that could reach the U.S.S.R. even though they are primarily tactical in nature. One may hope that initial understandings will not have to include specific agreements on such thorny issues as foreign bases and dual-purpose systems.

Virtually all the above is based on the premise that for the foreseeable future each side will probably insist on maintaining substantial deterrent capabilities. For some time to come there will unfortunately be little basis for expecting negotiations with the U.S.S.R. to result in a strategic balance with each side relying on a few dozen weapons as a deterrent. The difficulties and importance of verification of compliance at such low levels, the problem of China, the existence of large numbers of tactical nuclear weapons on both sides and the general political climate all militate against this. At the other extreme, negotiations would almost necessarily fail if either party based its negotiating position on the expectation that it might achieve a significant damage-limiting capability with respect to the other.

Thus the range of possible agreement is quite narrow. There is a basis for hope, if both sides can accept the fact that for some time the most they can expect to achieve is a strategic balance at quite high, but less rapidly escalating, force levels, and if both recognize that breaking the action-reaction cycle should be given first priority in any negotiations, and also in unilateral decisions.

There will be risks in negotiating arms limitation. These must be weighed not against the risks that might characterize the peaceful world in which everyone would like to live, or even against the risks of the present. Rather, the risks implicit in any agreement must be weighed against the risks and costs that in the absence of agreement one will probably have to confront in the 1970's.

Whether the superpowers strive to curtail the strategic arms race through mutual agreement or through a combination of unilateral restraint and improved dialogue, they should not do so in the mistaken belief that the bases for the Russian-American confrontation of the past two decades will soon be eliminated. Many of the sources of tension have their origins deep in the social structures and political institutions of the two countries. Resolution of these differences will not be accomplished overnight. Restraining the arms race, however, may shorten the time required for resolution of the more basic conflicts between the two superpowers, it may increase the chances of survival during that period, and it may enable the U.S.S.R. and the U.S. to work more effectively on the other large problems that confront the two societies.

Military Technology and the National Security

The ABM debate is analyzed in the context of a larger dilemma: the futility of searching for technological solutions to what is essentially a political problem

HERBERT F. YORK

August 1969

The recent public hearings in the Senate and the House of Representatives on anti-ballistic-missile (ABM) systems have provided an unprecedented opportunity to expose to the people of this country and the world the inner workings of one of the dominant features of our time: the strategic arms race. Testimony has been given by a wide range of witnesses concerning the development and deployment of all kinds of offensive and defensive nuclear weapons; particular attention has been paid to the interaction between decisions in these matters and the dynamics of the arms race as a whole.

In my view the ABM issue is only a detail in a much larger problem: the feasibility of a purely technological approach to national security. What makes the ABM debate so important is that for the first time it has been possible to discuss a major aspect of this larger problem entirely in public. The reason for this is that nearly all the relevant facts about the proposed ABM systems either are already declassified or can easily be deduced from logical concepts that have never been classified. Thus it has been possible to consider in a particular case such questions as the following:

1. To what extent is the increasing complexity of modern weapons systems and the need for instant response causing strategic decision-making authority to pass from high political levels to low military-command levels, and from human beings to machines?

2. To what extent is the factor of secrecy combined with complexity leading to a steadily increasing dominance of military-oriented technicians in some vital areas of decision-making?

3. To what extent do increasing numbers of weapons and increasing complexity—in and of themselves—complicate and accelerate the arms race?

My own conclusion is that the ABM issue constitutes a particularly clear example of the futility of searching for technical solutions to what is essentially a political problem, namely the problem of national security. In support of this conclusion I propose in this article to review the recent history of the strategic arms race to evaluate what the recent hearings and other public discussions have revealed about its present status and future prospects, and then to suggest what might be done now to deal with the problem of national security in a more rational manner.

The strategic arms race in its present form is a comparatively recent phenomenon. It began in the early 1950's, when it became evident that the state of the art in nuclear weaponry, rocket propulsion and missile guidance and control had reached the point in the U.S. where a strategically useful intercontinental ballistic missile (ICBM) could be built. At about the same time the fact that a major long-range-missile development program was in progress in the U.S.S.R. was confirmed. As a result of the confluence of these two events the tremendous U.S. long-range-missile program, which dominated the technological scene for more than a decade, was undertaken. The Air Force's Thor, Atlas and Titan programs and the Army's Jupiter program were started almost simultaneously; the Navy's Polaris program and the Air Force's Minuteman program were phased in just a few years later.

More or less at the same time the Army, which had had the responsibility for ground-based air defense (including the Nike Ajax and Nike Hercules surface-to-air missiles, or SAM's), began to study the problem of how to intercept ICBM's, and soon afterward initiated the Nike Zeus program. This program was a straightforward attempt to use existing technology in the design of a nuclear-armed rocket for the purpose of intercepting an uncomplicated incoming warhead. The Air Force proposed more exotic solutions to the missile-defense problem, but these were subsequently absorbed into the Defender Program of the Department of Defense's Advanced Research Projects Agency (ARPA). The Defender Program included the study of designs more advanced than Nike Zeus, and it also incorporated a program of down-range measurements designed to find out what did in fact go on during the terminal phases of missile flight.

By 1960 indications that the Russians were taking the ABM prospect seriously, in addition to progress in our own Nike Zeus program, stimulated our offensive-missile designers into seriously studying the problem of how to penetrate missile defenses. Very quickly a host of "penetration aid" concepts came to light: light and heavy decoys, including balloons, tank fragments and objects resembling children's jacks; electronic countermeasures, including radar-reflecting clouds of the small wires called chaff; radar blackout by means of high-altitude nuclear explosions; tactics such as barrage, local exhaustion and "rollback" of the defense, and, most important insofar as the then unforeseen consequences were concerned, the notion of putting more than one warhead on one launch vehicle. At first this notion simply involved a "shotgun" technique, good only against

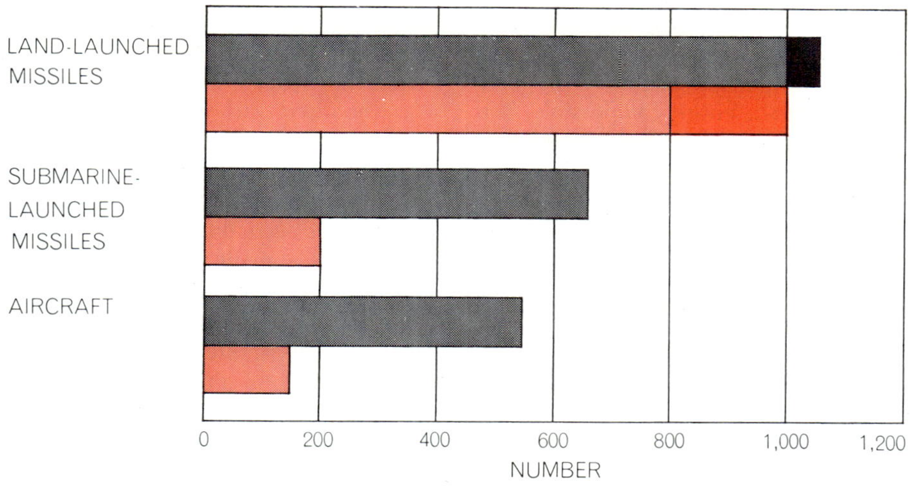

PRESENT STATUS of the deployment of strategic offensive forces by the U.S. (*gray*) and the U.S.S.R. (*color*) shows that the two superpowers are about even in numbers of intercontinental ballistic missiles (ICBM's), and that the U.S. is ahead in both long-range aircraft and submarine-launched ballistic missiles (SLBM's) of the Polaris type. The U.S. ICBM's consist almost entirely of Minutemen (*light gray*), which carry a nuclear warhead with an explosive yield in the megaton range; there currently remain only 54 of the larger Titans (*dark gray*) in our strategic forces. The smaller Russian missiles (*light color*) are mostly SS-11's, which are roughly equivalent in size to our Minutemen. The larger Russian missiles (*dark color*) are SS-9's, which are comparable in size to our Titans. The figures used are from a speech given by Secretary of Defense Melvin R. Laird on March 25.

large-area targets (cities), but it soon developed into what we now call MIRV's (multiple independently targeted reentry vehicles), which can in principle (and soon in practice) be used against smaller, harder targets such as missile silos, radars and command centers.

This avalanche of concepts forced the ABM designers to go back to the drawing board, and as a result the Nike-X concept was born in 1962. The Nike-X designers attempted to make use of more sophisticated and up-to-date technology in the design of a system that they hoped might be able to cope with a large, sophisticated attack. All through the mid-1960's a vigorous battle of defensive concepts and designs versus offensive concepts and designs took place. This battle was waged partly on the Pacific Missile Range but mostly on paper and in committee meetings. It took place generally in secret, although parts of it have been discussed in earlier chapters in this book [see "National Security and the Nuclear-Test Ban," by Jerome B. Wiesner and Herbert F. York, on page 129, "Anti-Ballistic-Missile Systems," by Richard L. Garwin and Hans A. Bethe, on page 164, and "The Dynamics of the Arms Race," by George W. Rathjens, on page 177].

This intellectual battle culminated in a meeting that took place in the White House in January, 1967. In addition to President Johnson, Secretary of Defense Robert S. McNamara and the Joint Chiefs of Staff there were present all past and current Special Assistants to the President for Science and Technology (James R. Killian, Jr., George B. Kistiakowsky, Jerome B. Wiesner and Donald F. Hornig) and all past and current Directors of Defense Research and Engineering (Harold Brown, John S. Foster, Jr., and myself). We were asked that simple kind of question which must be answered after all the complicated ifs, ands and buts have been discussed: "Will it work?" The answer was no, and there was no dissent from that answer. The context, of course, was the Russian threat as it was then interpreted and forecast, and the current and projected state of our own ABM technology.

Later that year Secretary McNamara gave his famous San Francisco speech in which he reiterated his belief that we could not build an ABM system capable of protecting us from destruction in the event of a Russian attack. For the first time, however, he stated that he did believe we could build an ABM system able to cope with a hypothetical Chinese missile attack, which by definition would be "light" and uncomplicated. In recommending that we go ahead with a program to build what came to be known as the Sentinel system, he said that "there are *marginal* grounds for concluding that a light deployment of U.S. ABM's against this possibility is prudent." A few sentences later, however, he warned: "The danger in deploying this relatively light and reliable Chinese-oriented ABM system is going to be that pressures will develop to expand it into a heavy Soviet-oriented ABM system." The record makes it clear that he was quite right in this prediction.

Meanwhile the U.S.S.R. was going ahead with its own ABM program. The Russian program proceeded by fits and starts, and our understanding of it was, as might be supposed in such a situation, even more erratic. It is now generally agreed that the only ABM system the Russians have deployed is an area defense around Moscow much like our old Nike Zeus system. It appears to have virtually no capability against our offense, and it has been, as we shall see below, extremely counterproductive insofar as its goal of defending Moscow is concerned.

Development and deployment of offensive-weapons systems on both sides progressed rapidly during the 1960's, but rather than discuss these historically I shall go directly to the picture that the Administration has given of the present status and future projection of such forces.

Data recently presented by the Department of Defense show that the U.S. and the U.S.S.R. are about even in numbers of intercontinental missiles, and that the U.S. is ahead in both long-range aircraft and submarines of the Polaris type [*see illustration on this page*]. The small Russian missiles are mostly what we call SS-11's, which were described in the hearings as being roughly the equivalent of our Minutemen. The large Russian missile is what we call the SS-9. Deputy Secretary of Defense David Packard characterized its capability as one 20-megaton warhead or three five-megaton warheads. Our own missiles are almost entirely the smaller Minutemen. There currently remain only 54 of the larger Titans in our strategic forces. Not covered in the table are "extras" such as the U.S.S.R.'s FOBS (fractional orbital bombardment system) and IRBM's (intermediate-range ballistic missiles), nor the U.S.'s bombardment aircraft deployed on carriers and overseas bases in Europe and elsewhere. There are, of course, many important details that do not come out clearly in such a simple tabular presentation; these include payload capacity, warhead yield, number of warheads per missile and, often the most important, warhead accuracy.

In the area of defensive systems designed to cope with the offensive systems outlined above, both the U.S. and the

U.S.S.R. have defenses against bombers that would probably be adequate against a prolonged attack using chemical explosives (where 10 percent attrition is enough) and almost certainly inadequate against a nuclear attack (where 10 percent penetration is enough). In addition the U.S.S.R. has its ineffective ABM deployment around Moscow, usually estimated as consisting of fewer than 100 antimissile missiles.

What all these complicated details add up to can be expressed in a single word: parity. This is clearly not numerical equality in the number of warheads or in the number of megatons or in the total "throw weight"; in fact, given different design approaches on the two sides, simultaneous equality in these three figures is entirely impossible. It is, rather, parity with respect to strategic objectives; that is, in each case these forces are easily sufficient for deterrence and entirely insufficient for a successful preemptive strike. In the jargon of strategic studies either side would retain, after a massive "first strike" by the other, a sufficiently large "assured destruction capability" against the other in order to deter such a first strike from being made.

There is much argument about exactly what it takes in the way of "assured destruction capability" in order to deter, but even the most conservative strategic planners conclude that the threat of only a few hundred warheads exploding over population and industrial centers would be sufficient for the purpose. The large growing disparity between the number of warheads needed for the purpose and the number actually possessed by each side is what leads to the concept of "overkill." If present trends continue, in the future all or most missiles will be MIRVed, and so this overkill will be increased by perhaps another order of magnitude.

Here let me note that it is sometimes

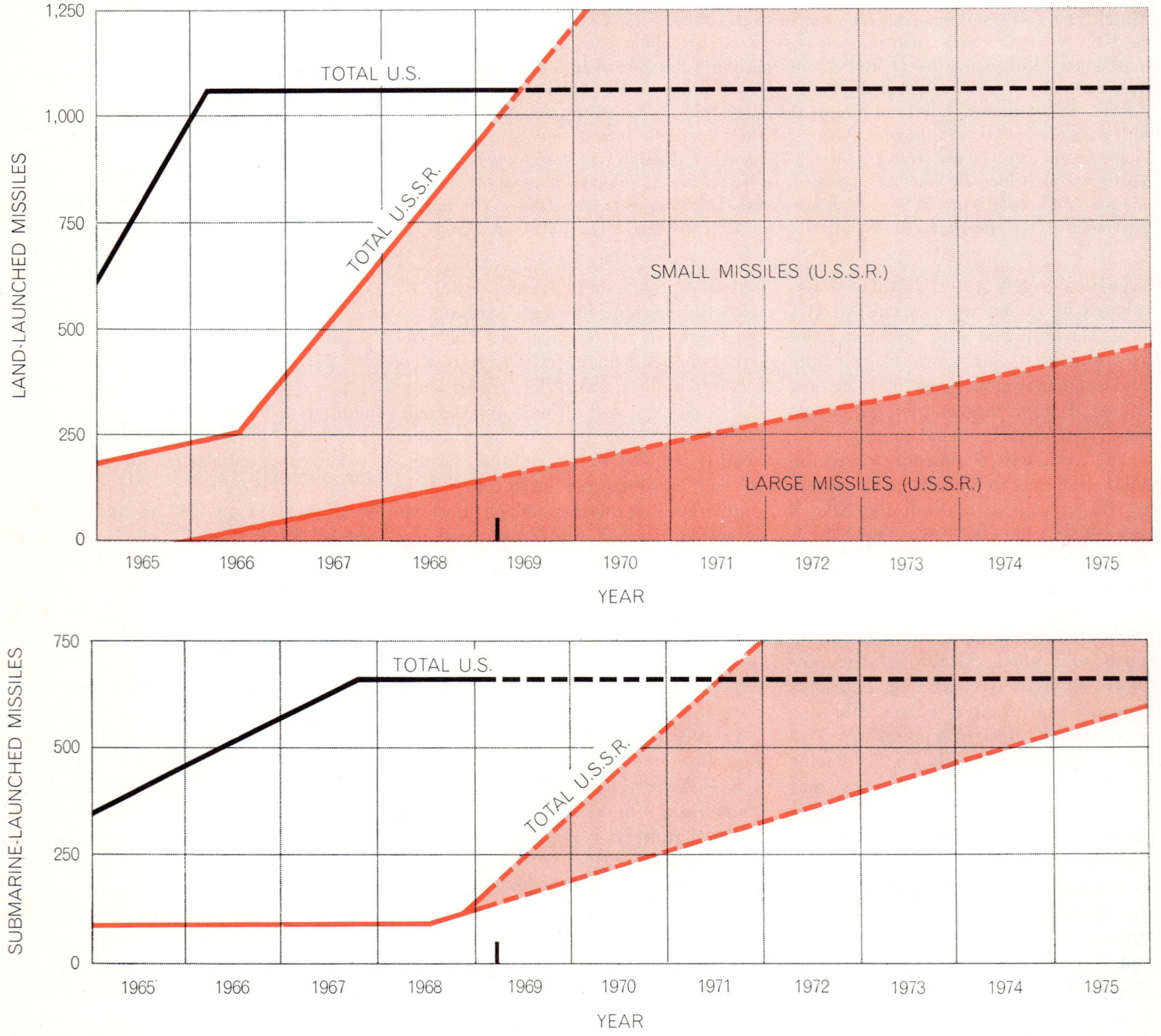

EXTRAPOLATED TRENDS in the deployment of strategic offensive missiles by the U.S. and the U.S.S.R. are indicated by the broken lines in this pair of charts, which are based on a presentation by Deputy Secretary of Defense David Packard to the Senate Foreign Relations Committee on March 26. The chart at top shows the numbers of deployed ICBM's for both sides during the period 1965–1975. The Russian total is broken down into "small" missiles (the one-megaton SS-11's) and "large" missiles (the multimegaton SS-9's). The chart at bottom shows the deployed SLBM's during the same period. The extrapolations suggest that the Russians will be even with us in ICBM's quite soon and will catch up in SLBM's sometime between 1971 and 1977. One important factor omitted from the charts is the imminent deployment by both sides of MIRV's (multiple independently targetable reentry vehicles).

argued that there is a disparity in the present situation because Russian missile warheads are said to be bigger than U.S. warheads, both in weight and megatonnage; similarly, it is argued that MIRVing does not increase overkill because total yield is reduced in going from single to multiple warheads. This argument is based on the false notion that the individual MIRV warheads of the future will be "small" when measured against the purpose assigned to them. Against large, "soft" targets such as cities bombs *very much* smaller than those that could be used as components of MIRV's are (and in the case of Hiroshima were proved to be) entirely adequate for destroying the heart of a city and killing hundreds of thousands of people. Furthermore, in the case of small, "hard" targets such as missile silos, command posts and other military installations, having explosions bigger than those for which the "kill," or crater, radius slightly exceeds "circular error probable" (CEP) adds little to the probability of destroying such targets. Crater radius depends roughly on the cube root of the explosive power; consequently, if during the period when technology allows us to go from one to 10 warheads per missile it also allows us to improve accuracy by a little more than twofold, the "kill" per warhead will remain nearly the same in most cases, whereas the number of warheads increases tenfold.

In any case, it is fair to say that in spite of a number of such arguments about details, nearly everyone who testified at the ABM hearings agreed that the present situation is one in which each side possesses forces adequate to deter the other. In short, we now have parity in the only sense that ultimately counts.

Several forecasts have been made of what the strategic-weapons situation will be in the mid-1970's. In most respects here again there is quite general agreement. Part of the presentation by Deputy Secretary Packard to the Senate Foreign Relations Committee on March 26 were two graphs showing the trends in numbers of deployed offensive missiles beginning in 1965 and extending to 1975 [*see illustrations on page 190*]. There is no serious debate about the basic features of these graphs. It is agreed by all that in the recent past the U.S. has been far ahead of the U.S.S.R. in all areas, and that the Russians began a rapid deployment program a few years ago that will bring them even with us in ICBM's quite soon and that, if extended

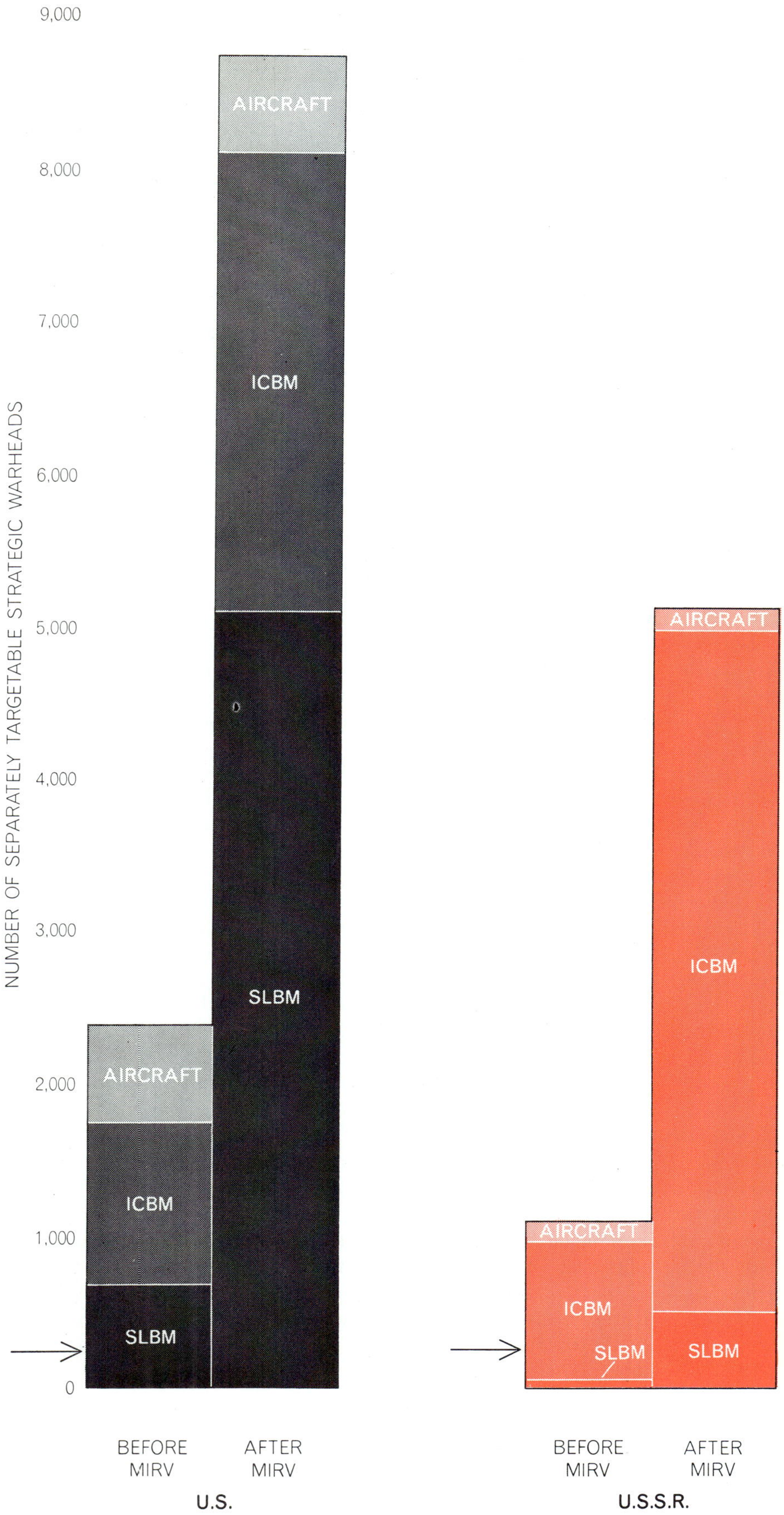

IMPACT OF MIRV on the strategic balance is emphasized in this chart, which is based on one prepared by the staff of the Senate Foreign Relations Committee and presented by Senator Albert Gore of Tennessee on March 26. The chart depicts the strategic balance in terms of separately targetable strategic warheads before and after MIRVing, which is expected to take place in the next five years. The two black arrows near the bottom indicate the number of warheads that could devastate the 50 largest cities on each side.

ahead without any slowdown, would bring them even in submarine-launched ballistic missiles (SLBM's) sometime between 1971 and 1977.

One important factor that the Department of Defense omitted from its graphs is MIRV. Deployment plans for MIRV's have not been released by either the U.S. or the U.S.S.R., although various rough projections were made at the hearings about numbers of warheads per vehicle (three to 10), about accuracies (figures around half a mile were often mentioned, and it was implied that U.S. accuracies were better than Russian ones) and about development status (the U.S. was said to be ahead in developments in this field). A pair of charts emphasizing the impact of MIRV was prepared by the staff of the Senate Foreign Relations Committee [*see illustration on page 191*].

One could argue with both of these sets of charts. For example, one might wonder why the Senate charts show so few warheads on the Russian Polaris-type submarine and why they show only three MIRV's on U.S. Minutemen; on the other hand, one might wonder whether the Department of Defense's projected buildup of the Russian Polaris fleet could be that fast, or whether one should count the older Russian missile submarines. Nonetheless, the general picture presented cannot be far wrong. Moreover, the central arguments pursued throughout the ABM hearings (in both the Senate Foreign Relations Committee hearings in March and the Senate Armed Services Committee hearings in April) were not primarily concerned with these numerical matters. Rather, they were concerned with (1) Secretary of Defense Melvin R. Laird's interpretation of these numbers insofar as Russian *intentions* were concerned, (2) the validity of the Safeguard ABM system as a response to the purported strategic problems of the 1970's and (3) the arms-race implications of Safeguard.

As for the matter of intentions, those favoring the ABM concept generally held that the only "rational" explanation of the Russians' recent SS-9 buildup, coupled with their multiple-warhead development program and the Moscow ABM system, was that they were aiming for a first-strike capability. One must admit that almost anything is conceivable as far as intentions are concerned, but there certainly are simpler, and it seems to me much more likely, explanations. The simplest of all is contained in Deputy Secretary Packard's chart. The most surprising feature of this chart is the fact that the Russians were evidently satisfied with being such a poor second for such a long time. This is made more puzzling by the fact that all during this period U.S. defense officials found it necessary to boast about how far ahead we were in order to be able to resist internal pressures for still greater expansion of our offensive forces.

Another possible reason, and one that I believe added to the other in the minds of the Russian planners, was that their strategists concluded in the mid-1960's that, whatever the top officials here might say, certain elements would eventually succeed in getting a large-scale ABM system built, and that penetration-aid devices, including multiple warheads, would be needed to meet the challenge. Whether or not they were correct in this latter hypothetical analysis is still uncertain at this writing. Let us, however, pass on from this question of someone else's intentions and consider whether or not the proposed Safeguard ABM system is a valid, rational and necessary response to the Russian deployments and developments outlined above.

To many of those who have recently written favorably about ABM defenses or who have testified in their favor before the Congressional committees, Safeguard is supported mainly as a prototype of something else: a "thick" defense of the U.S. against a massive Russian missile attack. This is clearly not at all the rationale for the Safeguard decision as presented by President Nixon in his press conference of March 14, nor is it implied as more than a dividend in the defense secretaries' testimony. The President said that he wanted a system that would protect a *part* of our Minuteman force in order to increase the credibility of our deterrent, and that he had overruled moving in the direction of a massive city defense because "even starting with a thin system and then going to a heavy system tends to be more provocative in terms of making credible a first-strike capability against the Soviet Union. I want no provocation which might deter arms talks." The top civilian defense officials give this same rationale, although they put a little more emphasis on the "prototype" and "growth potential" aspects of the system. For simplicity and clarity I shall focus on the Administration's proposal, as stated in open session by responsible officials.

From a technical point of view and as far as components are concerned, President Nixon's Safeguard system of today is very little different from President Johnson's Sentinel system [*see illustrations on page 195*]. There are only minor changes in the location of certain components (away from cities), and elements have been added to some of the radars so that they can now observe submarine-launched missiles coming from directions other than directly from the U.S.S.R. and China. As before, the system consists of a long-range interceptor carrying a large nuclear weapon (Spartan), a fast short-range interceptor carrying a small nuclear weapon (Sprint), two types of radar (perimeter acquisition radar, or PAR, and missile-site radar, or MSR), a computer for directing the battle, and a command and control system for integrating Safeguard with the national command. I shall not describe the equipment in detail at this point but pass on directly to what I believe can be concluded from the hearings and other public sources about each of the following four major questions: (1) Assuming that Safeguard could protect Minuteman, is it needed to protect our deterrent? (2) Assuming that Safeguard "works," can it in fact safeguard Minuteman? (3) Will it work? (4) Anyway, what harm can it do?

First: Assuming that Safeguard could protect Minuteman, is it needed to protect our deterrent?

Perhaps the clearest explanation of why the answer to this first question is "no" was given by Wolfgang K. H. Panofsky before the Senate Armed Services Committee on April 22. He described how the deterrent consists of three main components: Polaris submarines, bombers and land-based ICBM's. Each of these components alone is capable of delivering far more warheads than is actually needed for deterrence, and each is currently defended against surprise destruction in a quite different way. ICBM's are in hard silos and are numerous. Polarises are hidden in the seas. Bombers can be placed on various levels of alert and can be dispersed.

Since the warning time in the case of an ICBM attack is generally taken as being about 30 minutes, the people who believe the deterrent may be in serious danger usually imagine that the bombers are attacked by missile submarines, and therefore have only a 15-minute warning. This is important because a 30-minute warning gives the bombers ample time to get off the ground. In that case, however, an attack on all three components cannot be made simultaneously; that is, if the attacking weapons are launched simultaneously, they

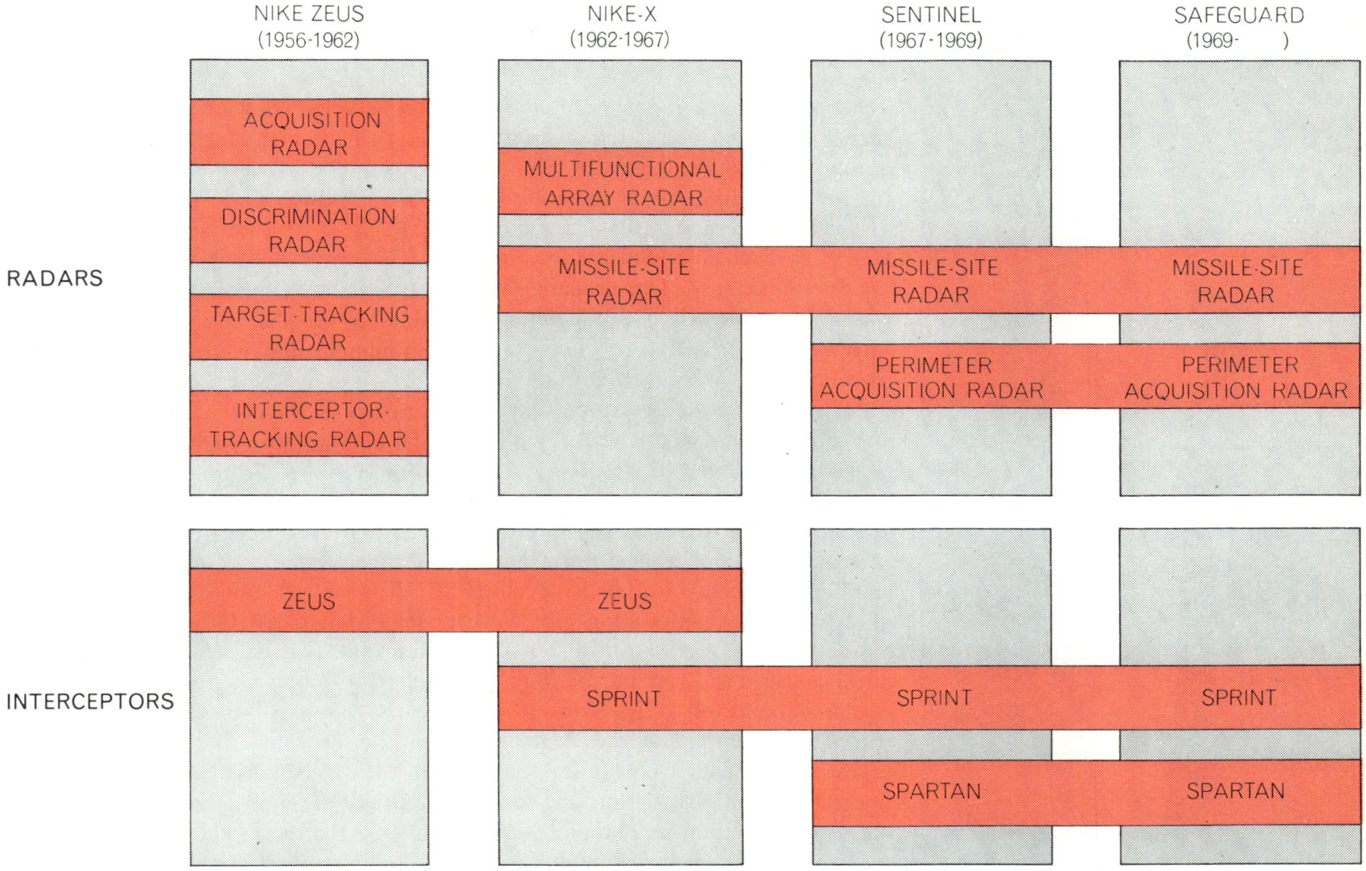

EVOLUTION OF U.S. ABM SYSTEMS is represented in this illustration, which is adapted from a chart introduced by Daniel J. Fink in his testimony before the Senate Foreign Relations Committee on March 6. In general the radar components of the successive designs have progressed from slow, mechanically steered, single-function radars to fast, electronically steered, multifunction radars. The slow Zeus ABM missile has been superseded by the short-range Sprint (for terminal defense) and the long-range Spartan (for area defense). The components of the Safeguard system are the same as those that were originally intended for the earlier Sentinel system.

cannot arrive simultaneously, and vice versa.

Thus it is incredible that all three of our deterrent systems could become vulnerable in the same time period, and it is doubly incredible that we could not know that this would happen without sufficient notice so that we could do something about it. There is, therefore, no basis for a frantic reaction to the hypothetical Russian threat to Minuteman. Still, it is sensible and prudent to begin thinking about the problem, and so we turn to the other questions. We must consider these questions in the technological framework of the mid-1970's, and we shall do this now in the way defense officials currently seem to favor: by assuming that this is the best of all possible technological worlds, that everything works as intended and that direct extrapolations of current capabilities are valid.

Second: Assuming that Safeguard "works," can it in fact safeguard Minuteman?

One good approach to this problem is the one used by George W. Rathjens in his testimony before the Senate Armed Services Committee on April 23. His analysis took as a basis of calculation the implication in Secretary Laird's testimony that the Minuteman force may become seriously imperiled in the mid-1970's. Rathjens then estimated how many SS-9's would have to be deployed at that time in order to achieve this result. From this number, and the estimate of the current number of SS-9's deployed, he got a rate of deployment. He also had to make an assumption about how many Sprints and Spartans would be deployed at that time, and his estimates were based on the first phase of Safeguard deployment. These last numbers have not been released, but a range of reasonable values can be guessed from the cost estimates given. Assuming that the SS-9's would have four or five MIRV warheads each by that time, Rathjens found that by prolonging the SS-9 production program by a few months the Russians would be able to cope with Safeguard by simply exhausting it and would still have enough warheads left to imperil Minuteman, if that is indeed their intention [*see illustration on page 200*].

The length of this short safe period does depend on the numbers used in the calculations, and they of course can be disputed to a degree. Thus if one assumes that it takes fewer Russian warheads to imperil Minuteman (it can't be less than one for one!), then the assumed deployment rate is lower and the safe period is lengthened; on the other hand, if one notes that the missile-site radars in our system are much softer than even today's silos, then the first attacking warheads, fired directly at the radars, can be smaller and less accurate, so that a higher degree of MIRVing can be used for attacking these radars and a shorter safe period results. To go further, it was suggested that the accuracy/yield combination of the more numerous SS-11's might be sufficient for attacking the missile-site radars, and therefore, if the Russians were to elect such an option, there would be no safe period at all. In short, the most that Safeguard can do is either delay somewhat the date when Minuteman would be imperiled or cause the attacker to build up his forces at a somewhat higher rate if indeed imperiling Minuteman by a fixed date is his purpose.

In the more general case this problem

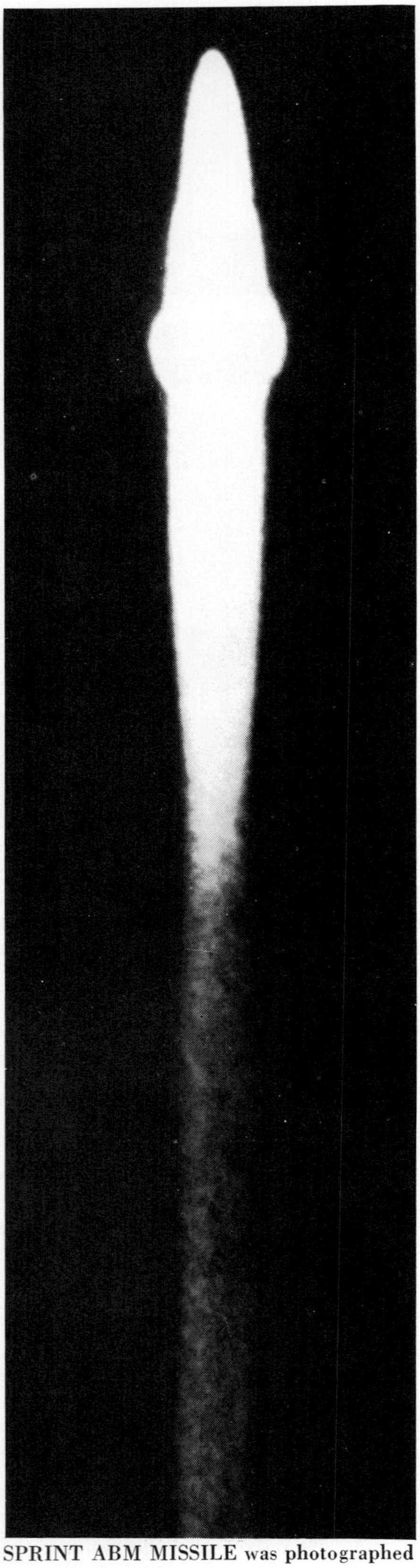

SPRINT ABM MISSILE was photographed during a test flight at the White Sands Missile Range in New Mexico. The photograph, which was released by the U.S. Army's Nike-X Project Office in March, 1966, shows the second stage of the missile heated to incandescence by friction with the atmosphere. Because of the extremely high speed of the Sprint, the missile's skin in places reaches temperatures hotter than inside its rocket motor. The bulges are created by the guidance fins at the rear of the second stage.

is often discussed in budgetary terms, and the "cost-exchange ratio" between offense and defense is computed for a wide variety of specific types of weapon. Such calculations give a wide variety of results, and there is much argument about them. However, even using current offense designs (that is, without MIRV), such calculations usually strongly favor the offense. This exchange ratio varies almost linearly with the degree of MIRVing of the offensive missiles, and therefore it seems to me that in the ideal technological future we have taken as our context this exchange ratio will still more strongly favor the offense.

Third: Will it work? By this question I mean: Will operational units be able to intercept enemy warheads accompanied by enemy penetration aids in an atmosphere of total astonishment and uncertainty? I do not mean: Will test equipment and test crews intercept U.S. warheads accompanied by U.S. penetration aids in a contrived atmosphere? A positive answer to the latter question is a necessary condition for obtaining a positive answer to the former, but it is by no stretch of the imagination a sufficient condition.

This basic question has been attacked from two quite different angles: by examining historical analogies and by examining the technical elements of the problem in detail. I shall touch on both here. Design-oriented people who consider this a purely technical question emphasize the second approach. I believe the question is by no means a purely technical question, and I suggest that the historical-analogy approach is more promising, albeit much more difficult to use correctly.

False analogies are common in this argument. We find that some say: "You can't tell me that if we can put a man on the moon we can't build an ABM." Others say: "That's what Oppenheimer told us about the hydrogen bomb." These two statements contain the same basic error. They are examples of successes in a contest between technology and nature, whereas the ABM issue involves a contest between two technologies: offensive weapons and penetration aids versus defensive weapons and discrimination techniques. These analogies would be more pertinent if, in the first case, someone were to jerk the moon away just before the astronauts landed, or if, in the second case, nature were to keep changing the nuclear-reaction probabilities all during the development of the hydrogen bomb and once again after it was deployed.

Proper historical analogies should involve modern high-technology defense systems that have actually been installed and used in combat. If one examines the record of such systems, one finds that they do often produce some attrition of the offense, but not nearly enough to be of use against a nuclear attack. The most up-to-date example is provided by the Russian SAM's and other air-defense equipment deployed in North Vietnam. This system "works" after a fashion because both the equipment designers and the operating crews have had plenty of opportunities to practice against real U.S. targets equipped with real U.S. countermeasures and employing real U.S. tactics.

The best example of a U.S. system is somewhat older, but I believe it is still relevant. It is the SAGE system, a complex air-defense system designed in the early 1950's. All the components worked on the test range, but by 1960 we came to realize, even without combat testing, that SAGE could not really cope with the offense that was then coming into being. We thereupon greatly curtailed and modified our plans, although we did continue with some parts of the system. To quote from the recent report on the ABM decision prepared by Wiesner, Abram Chayes and others: "Still, after fifteen years, and the expenditure of more than $20 billion, it is generally conceded that we do not have a significant capability to defend ourselves against a well-planned air attack. The Soviet Union, after even greater effort, has probably not done much better."

So much for analogies; let us turn to the Safeguard system itself. Doubts about its being able to work were raised during the public hearings on a variety of grounds, some of which are as follows:

First, and perhaps foremost, there is the remarkable fact that the new Safeguard system and the old Sentinel system use virtually the same hardware deployed in a very similar manner, and yet they have entirely different primary purposes. Sentinel had as its purpose defending large soft targets against the so-called Chinese threat. The Chinese threat by definition involved virtually no sophisticated penetration aids and no possibilities of exhausting the defense; thus were "solved" two of the most difficult problems that had eliminated Nike Zeus and Nike-X.

Safeguard has as its primary purpose defending a part of the Minuteman force against a Russian attack. It is not credible that a Russian attack against the part of the Minuteman force so defended would be other than massive and sophisticated, so that we are virtually right back to trying to do what in 1967 we said we could not do, and we are trying to do it with no real change in the missiles or the radars. It is true that defending hard points is to a degree easier than defending cities because interception can be accomplished later and at lower altitudes, thus giving discrimination techniques more time to work. Moreover, only those objects headed for specific small areas must be intercepted. These factors do make the problem somewhat easier, but they do not ensure its solution, and plenty of room for doubt remains.

Second, there is the contest between penetration aids and discrimination techniques. This was discussed at length by Richard L. Garwin and Hans A. Bethe in the article beginning on page 164 and mentioned also in varying degrees of detail by many of those who testified recently concerning the ABM issue. The Russian physicist Andrei D. Sakharov, in his essay "Thoughts on Progress, Coexistence and Intellectual Freedom," put the issue this way: "Improvements in the resistance of warheads to shock waves and the radiation effects of neutron and X-ray exposure, the possibility of mass use of relatively light and inexpensive decoys that are virtually indistinguishable from warheads and exhaust the capabilities of an antimissile defense system, a perfection of tactics of massed and concentrated attacks, in time and space, that overstrain the defense detection centers, the use of orbital and fractional-orbital attacks, the use of active and passive jamming and other methods not disclosed in the press—all of this has created technical and economic obstacles to an effective missile defense that, at the present time, are virtually insurmountable."

I would add only MIRV to Sakharov's list. Pitted against this plethora of penetration aids are various observational methods designed to discriminate the real warheads. Some of the penetration devices obviously work only at high altitudes, but even these make it necessary for the final "sorting" to be delayed, and thus they still contribute to making the defense problem harder. Other devices can continue to confuse the defense even down to low altitudes. Some of the problems the offense presents to the defense can no doubt be solved (and have been solved) when considered separately and in isolation. That is, they can be

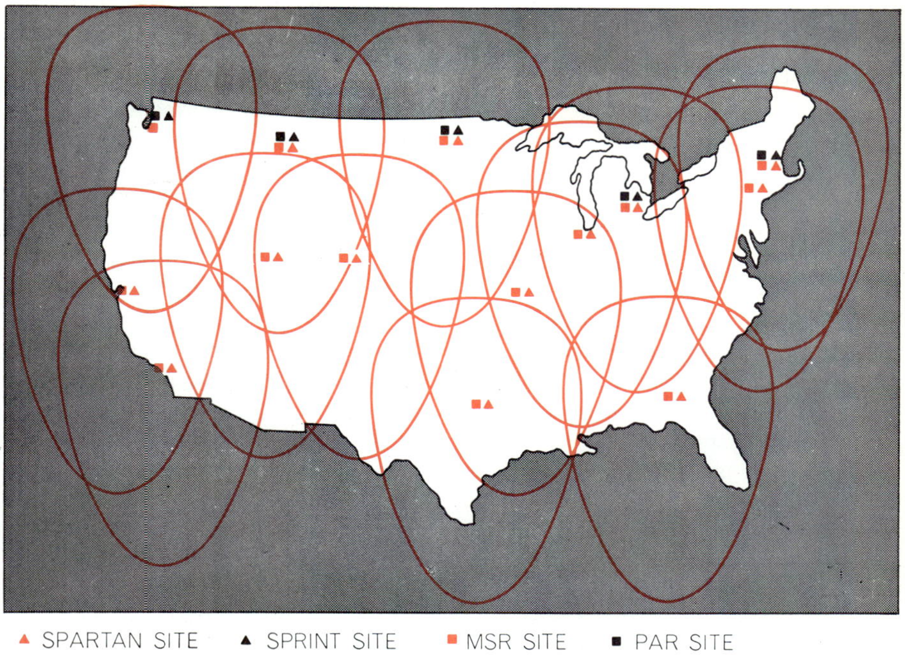

SENTINEL SYSTEM was described by the Johnson Administration as a "thin" ABM system designed to defend the U.S. against a hypothetical Chinese missile attack in the 1970's. The main defense was to be provided by long-range Spartan missiles. The Spartans would be deployed at about 14 locations in order to provide an area defense of the whole country. The range of each "farm" of Spartans is indicated by the egg-shaped area around it; for missiles attacking over the northern horizon the intercept range of the Spartan is elongated somewhat to the south. The Sentinel system would also include some short-range Sprint missiles, which were originally to be deployed to defend the five or six perimeter acquisition radars, or PAR's, which were to be deployed at five sites located across the northern part of the country. Missile-site radars, or MSR's, were to be deployed at every ABM site.

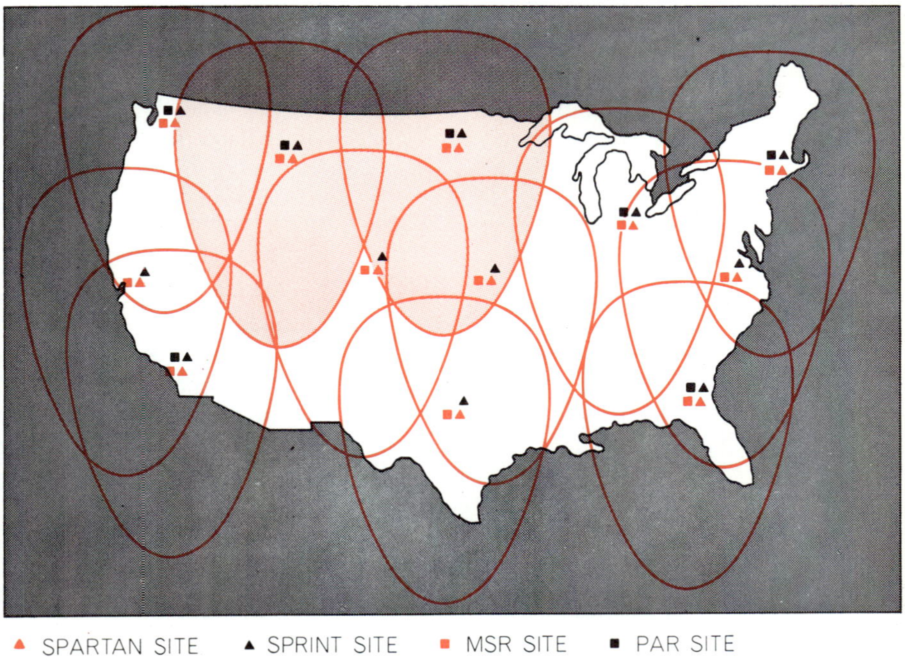

SAFEGUARD SYSTEM, President Nixon's proposed modification of the Sentinel scheme, uses essentially the same components in a slightly different array to accomplish an entirely different primary purpose: the defense of a part of our Minuteman force against a hypothetical surprise attack by the Russians. Phase I of Safeguard covers the construction of ABM sites at two Minuteman "fields": one near Malmstrom Air Force Base in Montana and the other near Grand Forks Air Force Base in North Dakota (*colored areas*). The completed system would have a total of 12 sites, each with Sprint and Spartan coverage, located somewhat farther away from the cities. In addition two new PAR sites would be included in order to observe submarine-launched missiles coming from directions other than due north.

solved for a time, until the offense designers react. One must have serious reservations, however, whether these problems can ever be solved for any long period in the complex combinations that even a modestly sophisticated attacker can present. Further, such a contest *could* result in a catastrophic failure of the system in which all or nearly all interceptions fail.

Third, there is the unquantifiable difference between the test range and the real world. The extraordinary efforts of the Air Force to test operationally deployed Minutemen show that it too regards this as an important problem. Moreover, the tests to date do seem to have revealed important weaknesses in the deployed forces. The problem has many aspects: the possible differences between test equipment and deployed equipment; the certain differences between the offensive warheads and penetration aids supplied by us as test targets and the corresponding equipment and tactics the defense must ultimately be prepared to face; the differences between the installation crews at a test site and at a deployment site; the differences in attitudes and motivation between a test crew and an operational crew (even if it is composed of the same men); the differences between men and equipment that have recently been made ready and whom everyone is watching and men and equipment that have been standing ready for years during which nothing happened; the differences between the emotional atmosphere where everyone knows it is not "for real" and the emotional atmosphere where no one can believe what he has just been told. It may be that all that enormously complex equipment will be ready to work the very first time it must "for real," and it may be that all those thousands of human beings have performed all their interlocking assignments correctly, but I have very substantial doubts about it.

Fourth, there is the closely related "hair-trigger/stiff-trigger" contradiction. Any active defense system such as Safeguard must sit in readiness for two or four or eight years and then fire at precisely the correct second following a warning time of only minutes. Furthermore, the precision needed for the firing time is so fine that machines must be used to choose the exact instant of firing no matter how the decision to fire is made. In the case of offensive missiles the situation is different in an essential way: Although maintaining readiness throughout a long, indefinite period is necessary, the moment of firing is not so precisely controlled in general and hence human decision-makers, including even those at high levels, may readily be permitted to play a part in the decision-making process. Thus if we wish to be certain that the defense will respond under conditions of surprise, the trigger of the ABM system, unlike the triggers of the ICBM's and Polarises, must be continuously sensitive and ready—in short, a hair trigger—for indefinitely long periods of time.

On the other hand, it is obvious that we cannot afford to have an ABM missile fire by mistake or in response to a false alarm. Indeed, the Army went to some pains to assure residents of areas near proposed Sentinel sites that it was imposing requirements to ensure against the accidental launching of the missile and the subsequent detonation of the nuclear warhead it carries. Moreover, Army officials have assured the public that no ABM missiles would ever be launched without the specific approval of "very high authorities."

These two requirements—a hair trigger so that the system can cope with a surprise attack and a stiff trigger so that it will never go off accidentally or without proper authorization—are, I believe, contradictory requirements. In saying this I am not expressing doubt about the stated intentions of the present Army leaders, and I strongly endorse the restrictions implied in their statements. I am saying, however, that if the system cannot be fired without approval of "the highest authorities," then the probability of its being fired under conditions of surprise is less than it would be otherwise. This probability depends to a degree on the highly classified technical details of the Command and Control System, but in the last analysis it depends more on the fact that "the highest authority" is a human being and therefore subject to all the failures and foibles pertaining thereto.

This brings us to our fourth principal question: Anyway, what harm can it

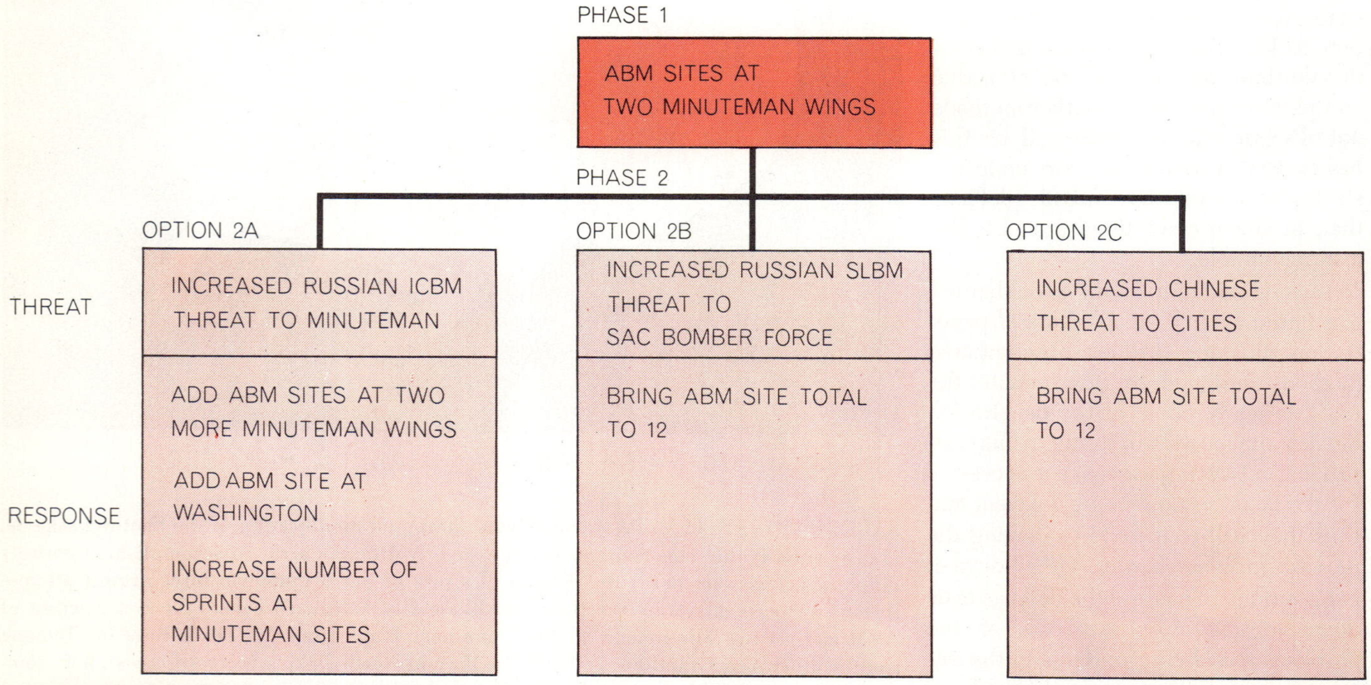

SAFEGUARD PHASE II provides for three different optional responses to various potential threats in the 1970's. A possible further addition would be sites in Alaska and Hawaii. This chart is also adapted from Deputy Secretary Packard's testimony on March 26.

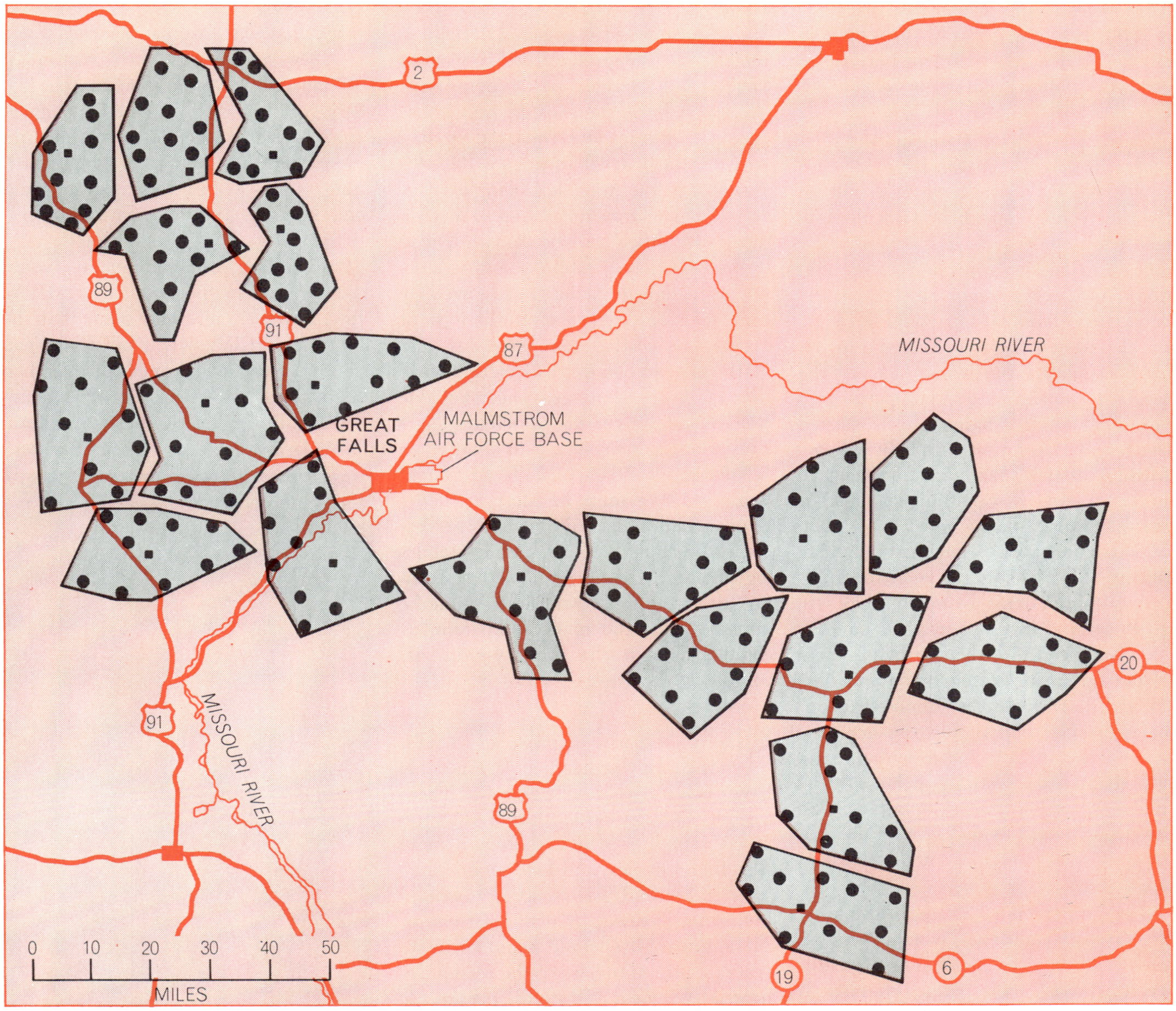

■ CONTROL CENTER ● MINUTEMAN SILO

MINUTEMAN MISSILE BASE in the vicinity of Malmstrom Air Force Base is shown on this map, which is based on information released by the Department of the Air Force. The Minuteman missiles are grouped in 20 flights of 10 missiles each for a total of 200 missiles. Every flight has its own control center, each of which is capable of launching an entire squadron of 50 missiles.

do?

We have just found that the total deterrent is very probably not in peril, that the Safeguard system probably cannot safeguard Minuteman even if it "works," that there is, to say the least, considerable uncertainty whether or not it will "work." Nonetheless, if there were no harm in it, we might be prudent and follow the basic motto of the arms race: "Let us err on the side of military safety." There seem to be many answers to the question of what harm building an ABM system would do. First of all, such a system would cost large sums of money needed for nondefense purposes. Second, it would divert money and attention from what may be better military solutions to the strategic problems posed by the Administration. Third, it would intensify the arms race. All these considerations were discussed at the hearings; I shall comment here only on the third, the arms-race implications of the ABM decision.

It is often said that an ABM system is not an accelerating element in the arms race because it is intrinsically defensive. For example, during the hearings, Senator Henry M. Jackson of Washington, surely one of the best-informed senators in this field, said essentially that, and he quoted Premier Kosygin as having said the same thing. I believe such a notion is in error and is based on what we may call "the fallacy of the last move." I believe that in the real world of constant change in both the technology and the deployed numbers of all kinds of strategic-weapons systems, ABM systems are accelerating elements in the arms race. In support of this view let us recall one of the features of the history recited at the start of this article.

At the beginning of this decade we began to hear about a possible Russian ABM system, and we became concerned about its potential effects on our ICBM and Polaris systems. In response the MIRV concept was invented. Today there are additional justifications for MIRV besides penetration, but that is how it started. Now, the possibility of a Russian MIRV is used as one of the main arguments in support of the Safeguard system. Thus we have come one full turn around the arms-race spiral. No one in 1960 and 1961 thought through the potential destabilizing effects of multiple warheads, and certainly no one predicted, or even could have predicted, that the inexorable logic of the arms race would carry us directly from Russian talk in 1960 about defending Moscow against missiles to a requirement for hard-point defense of offensive-missile sites in the U.S. in 1969.

By the same token I am sure the Russians did not foresee the large increase in deployed U.S. warheads that will ultimately result from their ABM deployment and that made it so counterproductive. Similarly, no one today can describe in detail the chain reaction the Safeguard deployment would lead to, but it is easy to see the seeds of a future acceleration of the arms race in the Nixon Administration's Safeguard proposal. Soon after Safeguard is started (let us assume for now that it will be) Russian offense planners are going to look at it and say something such as: "It may not work, but we must be prudent and assume it will." They may then plan further deployments, or more complex penetration systems, or maybe they will go to more dangerous systems such as bombs in orbit. A little later, when some of our optimistic statements about how "it will do the job it is supposed to do" have become part of history, our strategic planners are going to look at Safeguard and say something such as: "Maybe it will work as they said, but we must be prudent and assume it will not and besides, *now* look at what the Russians are doing."

This approach to strategic thinking, known in the trade as "worst-case analysis," leads to a completely hopeless situation in which there is no possibility of achieving a state of affairs that both sides would consider as constituting parity. Unless the arms race is stopped by political action outside the two defense establishments, I feel reasonably sure there will be another "crash program" response analogous to what we had in the days of the "missile gap"—a situation some would like to see repeated.

I also mentioned in my own testimony at the ABM hearings that "we may further expect deployment of these ABM systems to lead to the persistent query 'But how do you know it *really* works?' and thus to increase the pressures against the current limited nuclear-test ban as well as to work against amplifying it." I mentioned this then, and I mention it again now, in the hope that it will become a self-defeating prediction. It is also important to note that the response of our own defense establishment to the Russian ABM deployment, which I have outlined above, was not the result of our being "provoked," and I emphasize this because we hear so much discussion about what is a "provocative" move and what is not. Rather, our response was motivated by a deep-seated belief that the only appropriate response to any new technical development on the other side is further technical complexity of our own. The arms race is not so much a series of political provocations followed by hot emotional reactions as it is a series of technical challenges followed by cool, calculated responses in the form of ever more costly, more complex and more fully automatic devices. I believe this endless, seemingly uncontrollable process was one of the principal factors President Eisenhower had in mind when he made his other (usually forgotten) warning: "We must be alert to the... danger that public policy could itself become the captive of a scientific-technological elite." He placed this other warning, also from his farewell address, on the same level as the much more familiar comment about the military-industrial complex.

Several alternative approaches to Safeguard for protecting Minuteman have been discussed recently. These include superhardening, proliferation, a "shell game" in which there are more silos than missiles, and land-mobile missiles. Although I was personally hopeful before the hearings that at least one of these approaches would maintain its invulnerability, a review of the recent debates leaves me now with the pessimistic view that none of them holds much promise beyond the next 10 years.

Silo-hardening most probably does work now, in the sense that the combination of SS-11 accuracy and yield and Minuteman silo-hardening works out in such a way that one incoming warhead (and hence one SS-11 missile) has less than a 50-50 chance of destroying a Minuteman. If one considers the technological trends in hardening, yield per unit weight, MIRVing and accuracy, however, it does seem convincing that this is a game in which the offense eventually will win. Albert Wohlstetter, testifying in favor of the Safeguard system before the Senate Armed Services Committee, quoted a paper he wrote with Fred Hoffman in 1954 (long before any ICBM's were actually in place anywhere) predicting that the ability of silo-hardening to protect offensive missiles would run out by the end of the 1960's. That was a remarkably prescient study and is wrong only in numerical detail.

If we take the same rosy view of technology that was taken in almost all the pro-ABM arguments, then hardening will not work for more than another five years. My own view of the technological future is clearly much less rosy, but I do believe that the situation in which hardening is no longer the answer could come by, say, 1980 or, more appropriately, 1984.

Proliferation of Minuteman would have worked in the absence of MIRV. Now, however, it would seem that the ability to MIRV, which no doubt can eventually be carried much further than the fewfold MIRV we see for the immediate future, clearly makes proliferation a losing game as well as the dan-

FIRST SALVO LAUNCH of Minuteman ICBM's was made at Vandenberg Air Force Base in California on February 24, 1966. Photograph was released by U.S. Air Force.

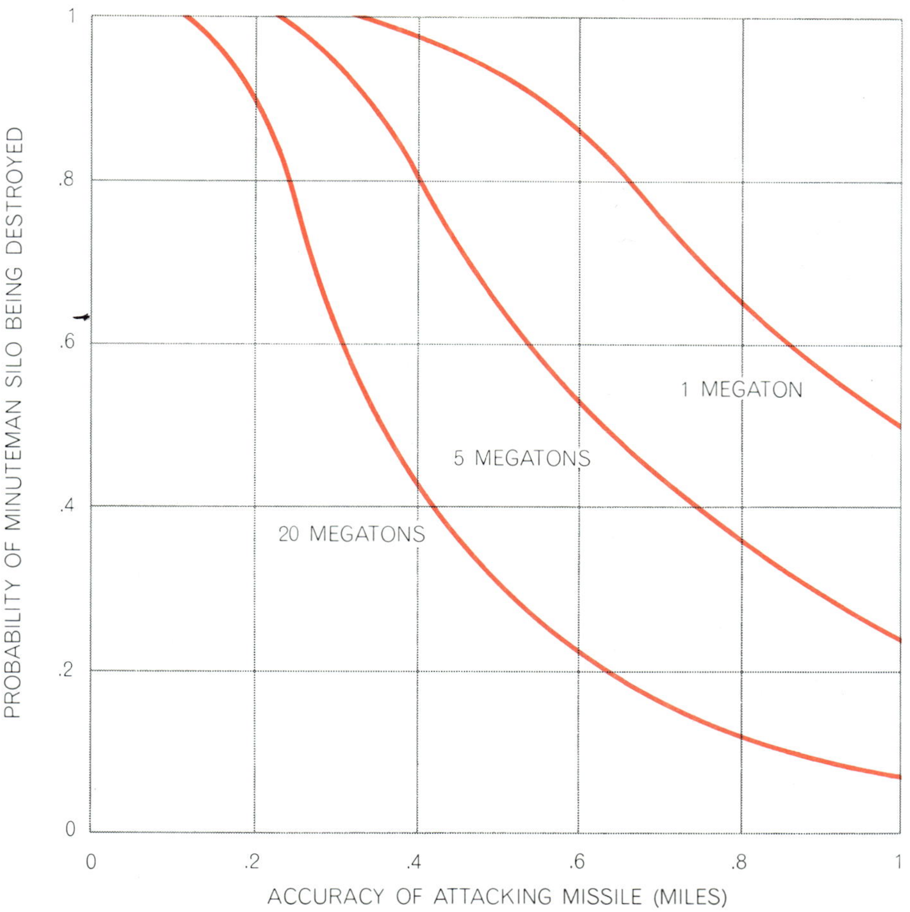

VULNERABILITY OF MINUTEMAN is revealed in this graph, which relates probability of destruction of a hardened Minuteman silo to accuracy for three different sizes of attacking warhead. This graph was interpreted by Deputy Secretary Packard as demonstrating the seriousness of the threat to Minuteman posed by the large Russian SS-9 missile, which he said is capable of carrying either one 20-megaton warhead or three five-megaton warheads.

gerous one it always was.

The "shell game" has not in my view been analyzed in satisfactory detail, but it would appear to have a serious destabilizing effect on the arms race. Schemes have been suggested for verifying that a certain fraction of the missile holes are in fact empty, but one can foresee a growing and persistent belief on each side that the "other missiles" must be hidden somewhere.

Road-mobile and rail-mobile versions of Minuteman have been seriously studied for well over a decade. These ideas have always foundered on two basic difficulties: (1) Such systems are inherently soft and hence can be attacked by large warheads without precise knowledge of where they are, and (2) railroads and highways all pass through population centers, and large political and social problems seem unavoidable.

Where does all this leave us insofar as finding a technical solution for protecting Minuteman is concerned? One and only one technically viable solution seems to have emerged for the long run: Launch on warning. Such an idea has been considered seriously by some politicians, some technical men and some military officers. Launch on warning could either be managed entirely by automatic devices, or the command and control system could be such as to require authorization to launch by some very high human authority.

In the case of the first alternative, people who think about such things envision a system consisting of probably two types of detection device that could, in principle, determine that a massive launch had been made and then somewhat later determine that such a launch consisted of multiple warheads aimed at our missile-silo fields. This information would be processed by a computer, which would then launch the Minutemen so that the incoming missiles would find only empty holes; consequently the Minutemen would be able to carry out their mission of revenge. Thus the steady advance of arms technology may not be leading us to the ultimate weapon but rather to the ultimate absurdity: a completely automatic system for deciding whether or not doomsday has arrived.

To me such an approach to the problem is politically and morally unacceptable, and if it really is the only approach, then clearly we have been considering the wrong problem. Instead of asking how Minuteman can be protected, we should be asking what the alternatives to Minuteman are. Evidently most other people also find such an idea unacceptable. As I mentioned above, the Army has found it necessary to reassure people repeatedly that ABM missiles would not be launched without approval by "the highest authorities," even though this is clearly a far less serious matter in the case of the ABM missiles than in the case of Minuteman.

The alternative is to require that a human decision-maker, at the level of "the highest authorities," be introduced into the decision-making loop. But is this really satisfactory? We would be asking that a human being make, in just a few minutes, a decision to utterly destroy another country. (After all, there would be no point in firing at *their* empty silos.) If, for any reason whatever, he was responding to a false alarm, or to some kind of smaller, perhaps "accidental," attack, he would be ensuring that a massive deliberate attack on us would take place moments later. Considering the shortness of the time, the complexity of the information and the awesomeness of the moment, the President would himself have to be properly preprogrammed in order to make such a decision.

Those who argue that the Command and Control System is perfect or perfectable forget that human beings are not. If forced to choose, I would prefer a preprogrammed President to a computer when it came to deciding whether or not doomsday had arrived, but again I feel that this solution too is really unacceptable, and that once again, in attempting to defend Minuteman, we are simply dealing with the wrong problem. For the present it would seem the Polarises and the bombers are not, as systems, subject to the same objections, since there are now enough other approaches to the problem of ensuring their invulnerability to sudden massive destruction.

In my view, all the above once again confirms the utter futility of attempting to achieve national security through military technology alone. We must look elsewhere. Fortunately an opportunity does seem to be in the offing. There appears to be real promise that serious strategic-arms-limitation talks will begin soon. The time is propitious. There is in the land a fairly widespread doubt about the strictly military approach to security problems, and even military-minded politicians are genuinely interested in exploring other possibilities. The essay by Academician Sakharov, as well as the statements of Russian officials, indicate genuine interest on the other side. The time is propitious in another sense: both sides will be discussing the matter from a position of parity. Moreover, this parity seems reasonably stable and likely to endure for several years.

Later, however, major deployments of sophisticated ABM systems and, even more important, widespread conversion of present single-warhead systems to MIRV will be strongly destabilizing and will at least give the impression that parity is about to be upset. If so, the motto of the arms race, "Let us err on the side of military safety," will come to dominate the scene on both sides and the present opportunity will be lost. Therefore in the short run we must do everything possible to ensure that the talks not only start but also succeed. Although the ABM decision may not forestall the talks, it would seem that success will be more likely if we avoid starting things that history has shown are difficult to stop once they are started.

Such things surely include deployment of ABM missiles and MIRV's. There have been successes in stopping programs while they were in the development phase, but seldom has anything been stopped after deployment had started. The idea of a freeze on deployment of new weapons systems at this time and for these reasons is fairly widespread already, but achieving it will require concerted action by those believing strongly in the validity and necessity of arms limitations as a means of increasing national security. Thus the principal result of the recent national debate over the ABM issue has been to make it clear that Safeguard will safeguard nothing, and that the right step for the immediate future is doing whatever is necessary (such as freezing present deployments and developments) to ensure the success of the coming strategic-arms-limitation talks.

In addition, the ABM debate has served to highlight more serious issues (for example the implications of MIRV for the arms race) and to raise serious questions about other weapons systems. For instance, I suggest that we have also found that silo-based missiles will become obsolete. The only sure method for defense of Minuteman beyond, say, the mid-1970's seems to be the unacceptable launch on warning. As long as we must have a strategic deterrent, we must find one that does not force us to turn the final decision over to either a computer or a preprogrammed President. Minuteman was conceived in the 1950's and served its purpose as a deterrent through the 1960's, but it appears that in the 1970's its threat to us will exceed its value, and that it and other silo-based missiles will have to go. The deterrent must have alternatives other than "go/no-go," and for the 1970's at least it would now appear that other strategic weapons (Polaris/Poseidon and bombers) could provide them. I expect, however, that as the continuing national debate subjects the whole matter of strategic arms to further public scrutiny we shall learn that these other alternatives also have dangerous flaws, and we shall see confirmed the idea that there is no technical solution to the dilemma of the steady decrease in our national security that has for more than 20 years accompanied the steady increase in our military power.

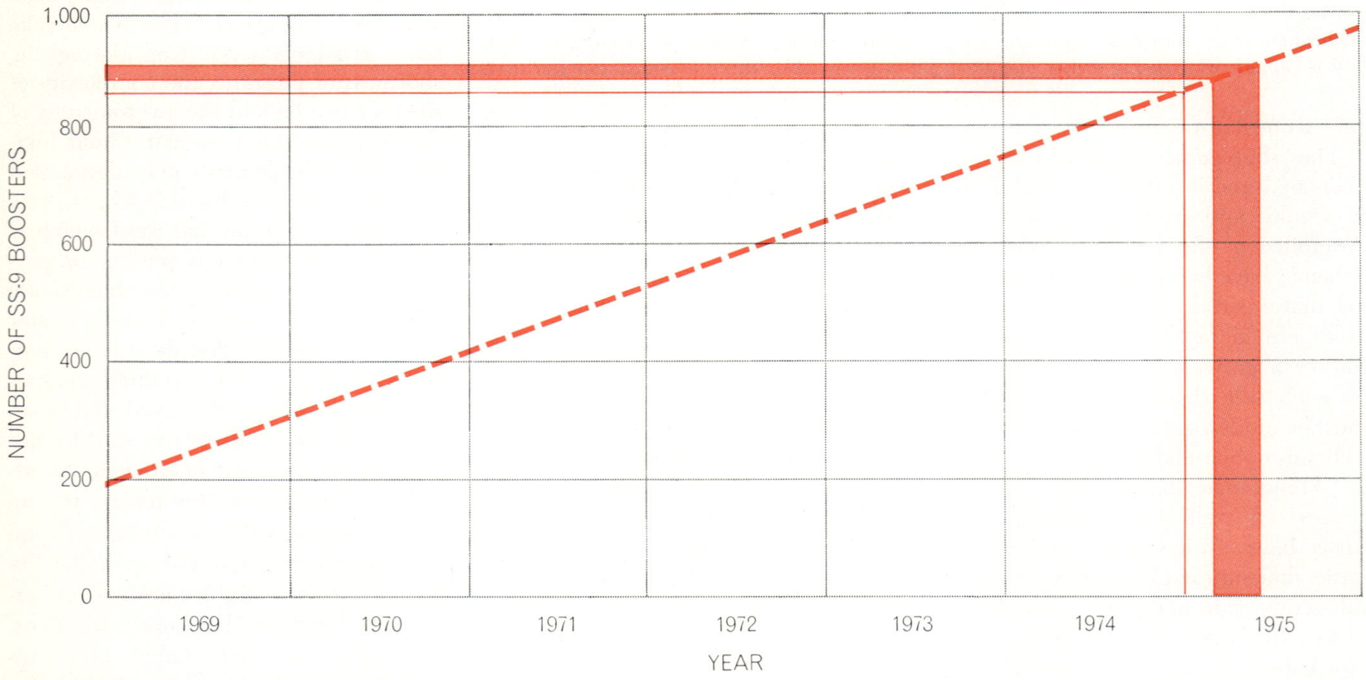

SAFEGUARD COULD BE NULLIFIED within a few months after its Phase I deployment, according to this graph, which is based on calculations presented by George W. Rathjens in his testimony before the Senate Armed Services Committee on April 23. His analysis took as a basis of calculation the implication in Secretary Laird's testimony that the Minuteman force may become seriously imperiled in the mid-1970's. Assuming that the Russian SS-9's would have four or five MIRV warheads each by that time, Rathjens then estimated that approximately 850 SS-9's would have to be deployed in order to achieve this result. From this number, and the estimate of the current number of SS-9's deployed (about 200), he got a rate of deployment (about 100 per year). Making certain assumptions about the numbers and effectiveness of the Spartan and Sprint ABM missiles that would be deployed at that time, Rathjens found that by prolonging the SS-9 production program by two to five months the Russians would be able to cope with Safeguard by simply exhausting it and would still have enough warheads to imperil Minuteman. Recently different numerical assumptions have been made, but they do not change the general conclusion that the proposed Safeguard system is much too thin to safeguard Minuteman.

The Limitation of Strategic Arms

The long-term prospects for the strategic-arms-limitation talks would be greatly enhanced by an early agreement to ban further tests of multiple independently targeted reentry vehicles (MIRV's)

G. W. RATHJENS
and G. B. KISTIAKOWSKY

January 1970

The preliminary phase of the strategic-arms-limitation talks ("SALT") between the U.S. and the U.S.S.R. was conducted in a convivial atmosphere and with a refreshing lack of familiar rhetoric. The road ahead for the negotiations nonetheless remains a steep and slippery one. The fact that the talks were delayed for as long as they were by both sides is not an encouraging sign. The initial unwillingness of the Russian leadership to negotiate because of the American involvement in Vietnam and the subsequent unwillingness of the American leadership to negotiate because of the Russian intervention in Czechoslovakia both reflect a failure to perceive the extraordinary and possibly fleeting nature of the opportunity presented at this particular juncture in the arms race and a failure to recognize that the strategic-arms confrontation can and should be largely decoupled from other sources of conflict between the two superpowers. More recent delays, first by the U.S. and then by the U.S.S.R., reinforce the view that on both sides there has been a fundamental failure in the ordering of priorities—a failure to recognize that the dangers to national security associated with arms-control agreements can be far less than those inherent in the ongoing arms race.

As the substantive phase of the arms talks is about to begin, it is still not obvious that policy-making circles of the two superpowers have consonant views about such basic questions as what objectives strategic forces serve, what relative roles offensive and defensive strategic forces play and what the desired effects of limitations on such forces are. If it should develop that there is no agreement on these points, it may not be possible to negotiate any meaningful limitation on strategic forces.

This article is written in the hope that by stimulating discussion of these questions the differences between the two powers may become more clearly understood and in time narrowed. Even if the talks fail to produce significant agreement, a better grasp of the issues involved will be in the ultimate interest of everyone.

A number of recent developments make the prospects for successful negotiations seem to be more favorable now than they might have been some years ago. Advances in the strategic reconnaissance capabilities of the superpowers (chiefly in the area of surveillance by artificial satellites) are steadily reducing the need for intrusive inspection to establish the degree of compliance with possible future agreements. Thus the thorny issue of verification may be less of a barrier to agreed arms limitation than it has been in the past. In addition the rapid growth of Russian offensive-missile forces has effectively erased a disparity with the U.S. that existed in the past, thereby making an arms-limitation agreement a more realistic possibility. Finally, there is the growing popular realization—at least in the U.S. and presumably also in the U.S.S.R.—that each side already has an enormous "overkill" capacity with respect to the other, and that further escalation in strategic-force levels would entail tremendous costs and new dangers at a time when both countries are confronted with a host of other pressing demands on their resources.

Although these developments would seem to favor successful negotiations, they are possibly outweighed by developments on the other side of the ledger. The most troublesome items are two emerging technical capabilities: multiple independently targeted reentry vehicles (MIRV's) and anti-ballistic-missile (ABM) defenses. It is frequently argued that the development and deployment of either (or particularly both) of these systems by one superpower could lead to a situation in which a decision to attempt a preemptive attack against the other's strategic forces might be considered rational. Indeed, some strategic planners contend that the threat is so great that offsetting actions must be started even before it is clear whether or not the adversary intends to acquire either a MIRV or an ABM capability. It is our belief that such arguments are largely fallacious and are made without real appreciation of the fact that a thermonuclear war between the superpowers, considering the vulnerability of the two societies, is a totally irrational policy choice. No combination of tactics and

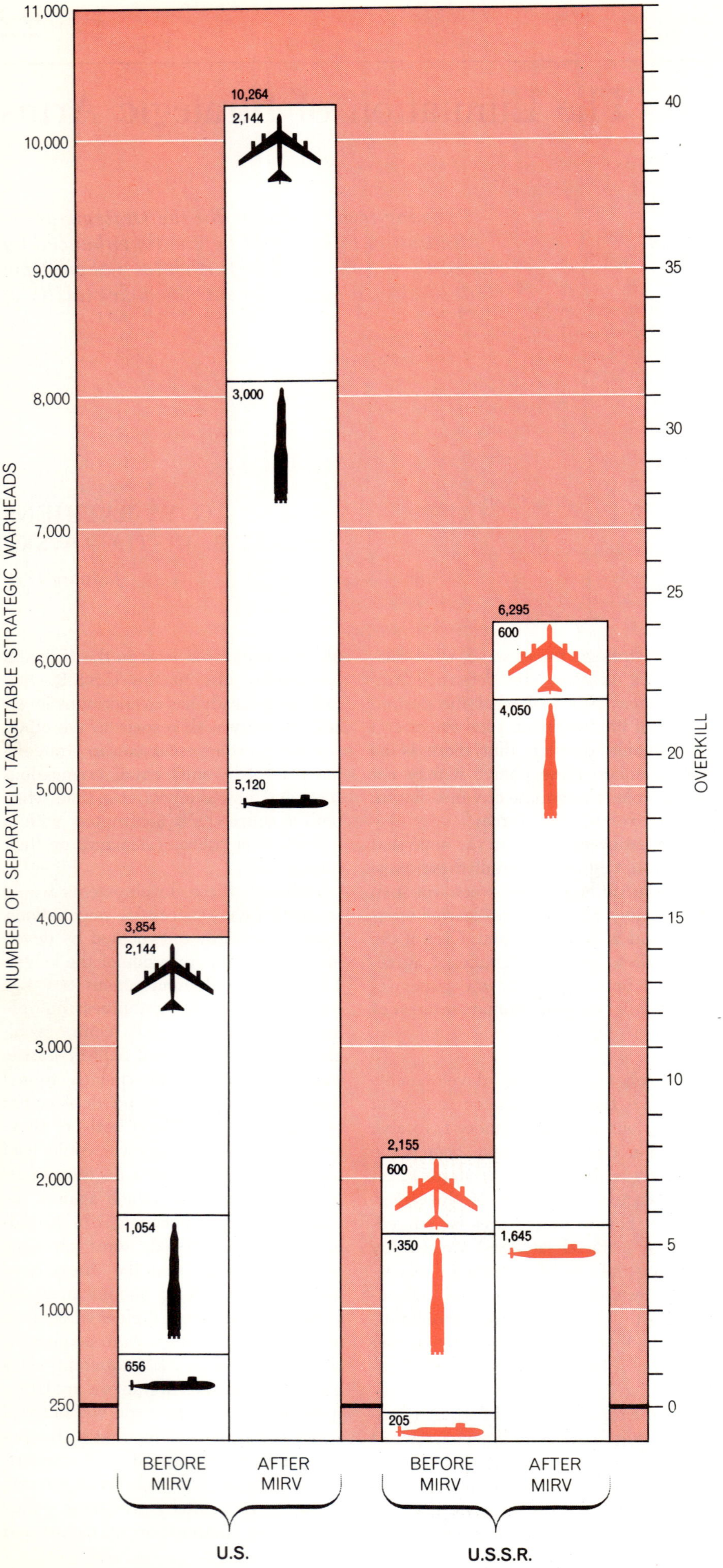

weapons, offensive and defensive, could provide either power with sufficient assurance that at least a small fraction of its adversary's weapons would not be successfully delivered, thus inflicting in retaliation damage that would be clearly unacceptable.

We are confronted here, however, with a paradox that will haunt the rest of this discussion. Unilateral decisions regarding the development and procurement of strategic-weapons systems, and hence planning for arms-control negotiations, have been and will continue to be greatly influenced by a fundamentally simpleminded, although often exceedingly refined, form of military analysis. This approach, sometimes characterized as "worst-case analysis," invariably ascribes to one's adversary not only capabilities that one would not count on for one's own forces but also imputes to him a willingness to take risks that would seem insane if imputed to one's own political leadership. Thus the U.S. will react to Russian MIRV and ABM programs, and vice versa, whether or not national security demands it. Even if the reaction is totally irrational, it nonetheless becomes as much a part of reality as if the decision were genuinely required to preserve a stable strategic balance. We reluctantly accept the fact that in both the U.S. and the U.S.S.R. policy will be influenced excessively by those military planners and their civilian allies who persist in behaving as if a thermonuclear war could be "won," and in asserting that responsible political leaders on the other side may initiate it on that assumption.

The development of a strategic nuclear capability by lesser powers, particularly China, seems also destined to complicate efforts to curtail the strategic-

STRATEGIC BALANCE between the U.S. and the U.S.S.R. is shown at left in terms of the numbers of separately targetable strategic nuclear warheads already deployed and the numbers projected for 1975 if present plans to deploy multiple independently targeted reentry vehicles (MIRV's) go into effect. The symbols indicate the means of delivery; the numbers give the actual total of deliverable warheads in each category. The scale at right suggests the enormous "overkill" capacity possessed by each side in either circumstance; it is calibrated in units of 250—a highly conservative estimate of the number of nuclear warheads required to devastate the 50 largest cities on each side. The chart includes only strategic (that is, intercontinental) nuclear warheads, not tactical or intermediate-range nuclear weapons.

arms race between the superpowers. Here there are essentially two problems. First, what was said earlier about the unacceptability of nuclear war between the superpowers may be less applicable to conflicts between emerging nuclear powers, because their political leadership will be less knowledgeable about the effects of nuclear warfare and because the nuclear stockpiles involved will, at least initially, not be large enough to ensure the destruction of entire societies. Thus, with proliferation, the probability of thermonuclear war is likely to increase, and the superpowers will have a real basis for concern about their becoming involved. Second, a phenomenon not unlike the much discussed action-reaction effects of ABM defenses and MIRV's is likely to come into play. Nuclear proliferation may complicate Russian-American efforts to curtail the strategic-arms race even more than the objective facts warrant, as each superpower overreacts not only to the development of new centers of nuclear power but also to the other's reaction to them.

In fact, the rising threat of nuclear proliferation is already increasing the pressure in the U.S. (and probably in the U.S.S.R.) to develop defenses that might be effective at least for a few years against emergent nuclear powers. The enthusiasts talk about neutralizing completely the effects of such developments; the realists propose measures aimed at reducing the damage that might be inflicted in the unlikely event of a nuclear attack by a smaller power. Unfortunately the capabilities that might prove effective, for instance an ABM system adequate to cope with first-generation Chinese missiles, would probably lead the other superpower to expand or qualitatively improve its strategic forces.

The other major considerations that will have a bearing on the prospects for SALT are domestic. As the failure of American policy in Southeast Asia and its implications become apparent, it seems likely that there will be a sharp reaction in an important segment of American society, with the polarization of attitudes proceeding even further than it has in the past year or two. It will be a difficult time for arms-control negotiations. Indeed, the strategic-arms-limitation talks are likely to be a divisive factor in the same way that the recent debate on the Safeguard ABM system was.

The situation in the U.S.S.R., although less clear, seems no more promising. The controversy between China and the U.S.S.R. might lead one to expect that accommodation and cooperation with the West would be increasingly attractive to the Russian leadership. But that controversy, like the recent Russian difficulties in eastern Europe, is also likely to be a factor in reinforcing the trend toward orthodoxy and conservatism within the U.S.S.R., which is hardly a favorable augury for an arms-control agreement.

Thus for SALT to be successful will require not only that the two governments be sincere in approaching the talks but also that they be prepared to display leadership and steadfastness of purpose in dealing with domestic opposition. On both sides there will have to be a rejection of many of the premises on which military policy has been at least partially based for two decades, for example the importance of "superiority" in strategic strength, the concept of "winning" a thermonuclear war, and the view that one can build meaningful defenses against a thermonuclear attack. The leadership in each nation will be confronted with arguments about the great risks inherent in various kinds of agreement—barely feasible (or at least not provably unfeasible) developments that might be taken advantage of by an adversary. Such arguments will undoubtedly resemble those to which the Kennedy Administration had to respond, when in connection with the nuclear-test-ban treaty it was asserted that the U.S.S.R. might conduct nuclear tests behind the moon or behind the sun to our great disadvantage. If agreement is to be reached, such arguments will have to be judged for what they are: nightmares of people who have focused so narrowly on such problems that they simply lack the perspective for weighing the risks of agreement against the risks implicit in continuing the arms race without any agreed constraints.

In the case of the U.S. the President will have a special problem and a formidable challenge, perhaps the greatest faced by any American leader since President Wilson's effort at the end of World War I to gain acceptance for his views regarding the Treaty of Versailles and the League of Nations. Although most Americans, including probably a majority of those who supported President Nixon in his campaign for the Presidency, would support him in his efforts to reach an arms-control agreement, almost certainly the conservative wing of the President's political supporters will counsel him to exercise extreme caution in approaching SALT. In so doing this latter group will give unwarranted weight to the technical and military risks that might be involved in any agreement under consideration. It is equally certain that the military will attempt to influence him with similar arguments, both through its direct channels and through its Congressional allies.

It is inconceivable that any meaningful agreement can be reached if the views of these groups should prevail. They need not, of course. Exercising broader judgment, the President can reject such advice and, as suggested above, draw on very substantial nationwide support for an agreement. Should he choose to do so, he will be in a better position to make his decision politically acceptable than would have been the case for any of his recent predecessors, or for that matter for his opponent in the last election. There is almost certainly a sizable segment of the American body politic that could accept a decision by President Nixon to conclude a very far-reaching agreement as a result of SALT that would not accept a similar position were it offered by, say, a liberal Democratic president.

President Nixon's prospects for such an achievement will be enhanced if the SALT negotiators make substantial progress in the next few months. With momentum established as a result of some limited agreement, and with the prospects of broader agreements before them, both the American and the Russian leadership might well make the judgment that it would be worthwhile to expend the political capital that might be required to effect broader agreements. If, on the other hand, the talks bog down in procedural discussions or in defense of obviously non-negotiable positions, the political leadership in both the U.S. and the U.S.S.R. will be in a weakened position in dealing with those who are most skeptical and fearful of an agreement. Thus the importance of early limited agreement in connection with SALT cannot be overestimated.

In what areas might such limited agreement be immediately feasible? In order to answer this question we must first examine some of the technical realities of the present strategic balance. We believe that for the foreseeable future technological considerations will continue to make nuclear offensive forces dominant over nuclear defensive forces. In other words, we assert that, as has been the case since the initial deployment of thermonuclear weapons, it will be easier to destroy a technologically advanced society than to defend one. What can and should be done both in structuring strategic forces in the absence of agreement and in agreeing to limitations is critically dependent on whether or not this judgment is correct. There is some dispute about its correctness in the U.S. For example, some assert that with recent developments in ABM technology it may be possible to offset the effects of an incremental expenditure on offensive capabilities by a similar or even lesser expenditure on defenses. Nonetheless, we share the prevailing view that defense of population, at least against a determined adversary with comparable resources, is essentially hopeless.

To facilitate discussion we shall now define two terms that have come to be applied to strategic forces and to their uses. By "damage limitation" we mean the prevention of damage to industry and population in a nuclear war or the reduction of such damage to below the levels that might be expected without the use of certain damage-limiting measures or systems. Antiaircraft or ABM defenses of cities would be categorized as being damage-limiting systems. The use of civil defense measures such as population shelters or evacuation of threatened cities would be regarded as damage-limiting measures. So would be attempts to limit the adversary's ability to inflict damage by preemptively attacking any component of his offensive strategic forces. By "assured destruction" we mean the destruction with high confidence of the adversary's society. Measures to achieve such destruction, or systems that might be used for the purpose, would be characterized as assured-destruction measures or systems. They include the use of offensive missiles and bombers against civilian targets, as distinguished from strictly military targets.

With these definitions we recast our earlier statement about the relative roles of offensive and defensive strategic weapons to assert: *In the superpower confrontation any attempt to build significant damage-limiting capabilities can be offset by changes in the adversary's assured-destruction capabilities.* To take a specific example, attempts to limit and reduce the damage to American society by deploying ABM defenses (including appropriate civil defense measures) can be offset by qualitative and quantitative improvements in the adversary's offensive capabilities at a cost to him certainly no greater than the cost of the damage-limiting measures taken. What is more, we believe that by and large such responses will occur, in spite of the fact that realistic security considerations do not necessarily require a response. Even a very large-scale and technically sophisticated American ABM system could not be counted on to prevent totally unacceptable destruction in the U.S. by a Russian attack—even by an attack launched in retaliation after the Russian forces had already been preemptively struck. Such an American ABM system would in no way make our strategic forces more useful as political instruments, and hence no Russian response would really be required to preserve the effectiveness of the U.S.S.R.'s assured-destruction forces. Because of fear, conservatism and uncertainty, however, it seems a foregone conclusion that a fully compensating buildup in Russian strength would follow.

There may, of course, be circumstances in which damage-limiting efforts will be effective. Each of the superpowers would temporarily be able to maintain a strategic posture that might greatly limit the damage to it in a conflict with a lesser nuclear power such as China. This will be particularly true if a preemptive, or "counterforce," attack against the lesser power's strategic nuclear forces is not excluded.

Moreover, if a nuclear exchange between the two superpowers should ever occur, parts of the strategic forces in being at that time probably would be used for active defense or in attacks on the strategic forces of the opponent. Thus they would be used in a damage-limiting role. Their effect would not be great, however, simply because the overkill capacity of each superpower's assured-destruction capabilities is so enormous. Both superpowers almost certainly now have the ability to destroy at least half of the adversary's population and three-quarters of his industrial capacity in spite of any damage-limiting measures that might be undertaken by the other. This situation has come about as a result of two factors. A strategic doctrine has developed, at least in the U.S., that has called for the maintenance of a very great assured-destruction capability under all conceivable circumstances. The doctrine has been one that could be easily implemented simply because thermonuclear weapons and strategic delivery systems are cheap in terms of the damage they can inflict on civilian targets.

This tremendous buildup of offensive forces means that the effectiveness of the last weapons used in destroying another society (in fact, the effectiveness of something like the last 90 percent of all weapons used) would be relatively small, since those already expended would have left so little to destroy. The amount of life and property saved by damage-limiting efforts would be dwarfed by the amount destroyed by weapons whose delivery could not be prevented.

We believe this situation will not change significantly in the near future. Any realistic approach to limitations on strategic armaments in the near future must almost certainly be in the context of the maintenance of very great assured-destruction capabilities. Agreements that would embody quite different strategic balances might result if any of several changes were to occur: technological breakthroughs that would lead to the dominance of the defense over the offense, the development of a high degree of trust between the U.S. and the U.S.S.R., the willingness of both nations to accept intrusive inspection, or an increased appreciation that strategic forces designed to inflict much lower damage levels would also serve effectively as a deterrent. We do not see any of these changes as short-term possibilities.

Because the assured-destruction, or damage-inflicting, capabilities of the two superpowers are so large and so varied, the present strategic balance is remarkably insensitive to either qualitative or quantitative changes in strategic forces. Even major changes in force levels, including the neutralization of entire systems (for example all bomber aircraft), would not be likely to have major effects on the damage levels one would expect each of the superpowers to suffer in a nuclear war. Worldwide radioactive fallout might be reduced significantly, but as far as the superpowers are concerned, cross-targeting with other systems would ensure that all major population and industrial centers would continue to be in jeopardy. When considered in the framework of the virtually certain collapse of an entire society, changes of a few percent in fatalities, which is all one might expect with foreseeable changes in strategic-force levels, are not likely to affect political decisions. Although it may have been correct some years ago to characterize the balance of terror as a "delicate" one, it is not so today, nor is it likely to be so in the foreseeable future. It will not be easily upset. Opponents of the Safeguard ABM decision have argued with some effect (although obviously not with complete success) that the U.S. deterrent was most unlikely to be in jeopardy at any time in the near future simply because of its diversity and because of the improbability of the U.S.S.R.'s being able to develop damage-limiting capabilities and tactics that would effectively neutralize all the deterrent's components.

We have argued so far that one general premise on whose acceptance a successful SALT outcome depends is

RELATIVE DESTRUCTIVENESS of several currently deployed thermonuclear weapons is illustrated here in relation to the damage caused by the nuclear bomb that was exploded over Hiroshima on August 5, 1945. The colored circles superposed on the map denote each weapon's "lethal area": the area within which the number of survivors equals the number of fatalities outside the circle. For a perfectly uniform population distribution the lethal area times the population density gives the total number of people killed in the explosion. At present most of the strategic warheads deployed by the U.S. and the U.S.S.R. are in the megaton range or larger. Even after MIRVing all the strategic warheads on both sides will exceed the estimated 15-kiloton explosive yield of the Hiroshima bomb.

that the offense will continue to dominate the defense for the foreseeable future. A second technical generalization that may be equally important is: *The uncertainty about the effectiveness of damage-limiting capabilities will be considerably greater than about assured-destruction capabilities.* This statement can be supported by a number of arguments. First, the characteristics of the target against which assured-destruction capabilities would be used (population and industry) will be known with some precision and will change only slowly with time. On the other hand, the characteristics of the systems (and the environment) against which damage-limiting capabilities must operate (adversary's warheads, delivery vehicles and launch facilities) will be generally less well known and more susceptible to rapid variation, both in quality and in number, at the option of the adversary. Second, some of the damage-limiting systems (such as ABM defenses, antiaircraft defenses and under some circumstances antisubmarine warfare, or ASW, systems) must function at the time chosen by the adversary for his offensive, whereas for assured destruction there is a much bigger "time window" during which performance will be acceptable. The effectiveness of submarine-launched missiles in destroying cities will not depend much on the instant of launch. Third, damage limitation generally will involve the use of more intimately coupled systems (for example the radars, computers and missiles of an ABM system), inviting the possibility of "catastrophic" technical failures. All these factors tend to make the advance estimates of the effectiveness of assured-destruction systems far more reliable than estimates of damage-limiting systems.

The inherent uncertainty in effectiveness that characterizes the performance of damage-limiting systems has been of profound importance in the Russian-American strategic-arms race. Each side has reacted to the development, or even the possible development, by the other of damage-limiting capabilities by greatly strengthening its offensive forces—to the point of overreaction because of the conservative assumption that the adversary's damage-limiting forces will be far more effective than they are in fact likely to be. For example, the uncertainty about the possible deployment and effectiveness of a large-scale Russian ABM defense has provided the primary rationale for the U.S. decision to introduce MIRV's into both land-based and sea-based missile forces, the net effect being a severalfold increase in the number of warheads these forces will be able to deliver. Barring unforeseeable technical developments, we must expect that the great uncertainty that characterizes the performance of damage-limiting systems will continue, and we must base our approach to SALT on that assumption.

If one accepts the judgments we have made about the relative effectiveness of defense and offense, about the insensitivity of assured-destruction capability to changes in force levels and about the uncertainty that characterizes damage-limiting efforts, one is led to some possibly useful generalizations about the forthcoming substantive phase of SALT.

First, the level of damage that each of the superpowers can inflict on the other is not likely to be altered significantly in the near future. Measures that might possibly be agreed on could change the level of damage that each side could inflict on the other by at most

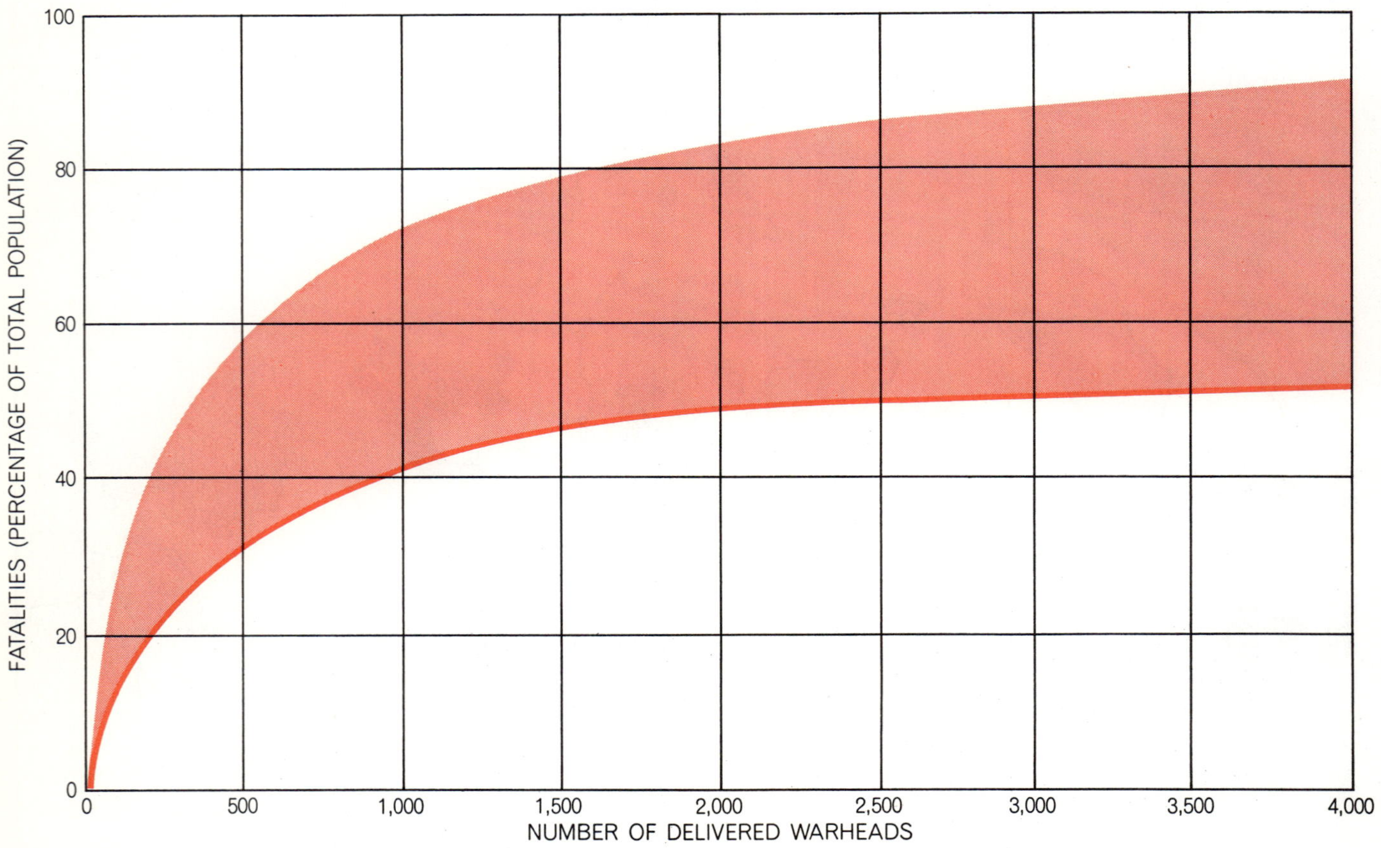

FUTILITY of seeking to mitigate the consequences of a full-scale nuclear exchange between the two superpowers by negotiating modest reductions in strategic-force levels or by resorting to moderately effective "damage-limiting" measures is illustrated in this graph, in which the expected fatalities in the U.S.S.R. are plotted as a function of the number of U.S. megaton-range warheads delivered. The solid curve indicates the immediate, easily calculable fatalities; the shading represents the fact that the total fatalities would probably be much larger. In either case, because of the very large number of deployed weapons, the effects of small changes in the total of delivered weapons would be negligible. The expected effects of a Russian attack against the U.S. would be similar.

a few percent. Therefore the problem of the reduction in damage in the event of war should probably be given low priority as a short-term negotiation objective. More realistic objectives of the negotiations could be to lower the level of tension between the superpowers and so reduce the probability of nuclear war.

Second, apart from possible worldwide fallout effects and domestic political considerations, neither side need be much concerned about the possibility of modest, or even substantial, expansions in the strategic offensive forces of the other side, nor about precise limitations on those forces, as long as the other side does not have a damage-limiting capability. Because of the large overkill capacities discussed above, even large increases in strategic forces will have little military effect.

Third, measures to constrain the introduction or improvement of damage-limiting systems, particularly those whose performance is expected to be highly uncertain, merit high priority. The introduction or improvement of damage-limiting capabilities by either side is likely to result, as we have noted, in an excessive reaction by the other. Because of the insensitivity of the strategic balance to modest changes in force levels, a move toward the development of a narrowly circumscribed damage-limiting capability by one side could in principle be tolerated without undue concern by the other. Such a move might be perceived, however, as an indicator of the adversary's intent to develop an across-the-board damage-limiting capability. (Witness Secretary of Defense Laird's public reaction to a possible Soviet SS-9 MIRV capability.) This, coupled with the fact that a development of damage-limiting capabilities can be offset rather quickly and cheaply, virtually ensures a reaction. The overall effect of such an action-reaction cycle on the ability of each side to inflict damage on the other is likely to be small, but the expenditures of both sides on strategic armaments are likely to be much increased, as will be the tensions between them.

Fourth, owing to the large uncertainty that characterizes the effectiveness of damage-limiting systems and tactics, the two superpowers will face a very troublesome dilemma if, on the one hand, they try to develop effective damage-limiting capabilities with respect to emerging nuclear powers and, on the other, they attempt to limit the strategic-arms race between themselves. With a few exceptions, such as a deployment of Russian intermediate-range ballistic missiles (IRBM's) in Siberia, the measures that could have long-term effectiveness against a third country's nuclear strength would appear to the other superpower to foreshadow an erosion in its own assured-destruction, or deterrent, capability. This creates an authentic problem of conflicting desires. We would hope that in efforts to deal with this problem the usefulness of damage-limiting capabilities with respect to the lesser nuclear powers would not be overrated. Although such damage-limiting capabilities probably would be effective in reducing damage in the event that a lesser power attempted a nuclear attack against one of the superpowers, we question whether either superpower would ever be willing to take action against a lesser power on the assumption that damage-limiting efforts would be 100 percent effective, that is, on the assumption that "damage denial" with respect to a lesser power could be achieved. Considering one's inability to have high confidence in the effectiveness of damage-limiting measures, and considering the effects of even a single thermonuclear weapon on a large American or Russian city, we doubt that efforts to develop damage-limiting capabilities with respect to the smaller powers would materially increase the options the superpowers would have available for dealing with these powers.

With this background in mind one would be in a good position to evaluate the relative desirability of limiting various strategic systems if each were unambiguously useful only for damage limitation or assured destruction. Unfortunately many existing or prospective strategic systems may play several roles, a factor that greatly complicates the problem.

Of all the ambiguous developments now under way none is more troublesome than MIRV. The development of a MIRV capability may facilitate the maintenance of an assured-destruction capability by providing high assurance that ABM defenses of industry and population can be penetrated. Given sufficient accuracy, reliability and yield, however, MIRV's may also make it possible for a small number of missiles to destroy a larger number of fixed offensive facilities, even if they are "hardened" against the effects of nuclear weapons.

Although the effectiveness of a given missile force in a damage-limiting preemptive attack against an adversary's intercontinental ballistic missile (ICBM) force might be much increased through the use of such MIRV's, it does not necessarily follow that the deployment of the MIRV's would make such a strike more likely. As we have noted, in the context of a confrontation between superpowers such an attack would surely be irrational, no matter how severe the crisis, simply because no responsible political leader could ever have high confidence in the effectiveness of the attack and in the effectiveness of the other damage-limiting measures that would be required to keep the damage from a retaliatory response down to acceptable levels. Although MIRV's are not likely to have much actual effect on the willingness or ability of nations to use strategic nuclear forces to attain political objectives, we must accept the fact that arms policies will, to a substantial degree, be based on the assumption that they might be so used.

Beyond that, there is the problem of the impact of MIRV's on events if a crisis should ever escalate to the point where limited numbers of nuclear weapons will have been employed by the superpowers against each other. At some point in the process of escalation it is likely that one or both powers would initiate counterforce attacks against the other's remaining offensive forces. Such an attack would probably come earlier if one or both sides had counterforce-effective MIRV's than if neither did.

Because of what we regard as unwarranted, but nevertheless real, concern about MIRV's being used in a preemptive counterforce attack, and because of more legitimate concern that once a thermonuclear exchange has begun MIRV's may make further escalation more likely, MIRV development may well have a critical impact on the outcome of SALT, and for that matter on the force levels of the two sides independent of the talks. It is generally, although not universally, accepted that the tests of MIRV's have not yet gone far enough for one to have confidence that their reliability and accuracy would be sufficient to assure their effectiveness in a counterforce role against hardened ICBM's. On the other hand, the MIRV principle is now demonstrated, and the expectation is common that with perhaps the second generation of such systems, if not with the first, MIRV's will be effective as counterforce weapons.

If no constraints are put on the development of MIRV's, it is likely that each superpower will go ahead with such development and (in the case of the U.S. at least) an early deployment program. This will be regarded as particularly urgent if ABM deployment continues, or even if there continues to be evidence of significant research and development that might later lead to ABM deployment. Assuming that MIRV programs do continue, each superpower will perceive in the other's deployment a possible threat to its fixed-base ICBM's and will react to counter that threat. The U.S. has already begun to do so in deciding to go ahead with an active ABM defense of Minuteman sites: the Safeguard program. Acceleration in the U.S.S.R.'s missile-launching submarine program and a possible mobile-ICBM program are plausible reactions to the U.S. MIRV programs.

We anticipate that in the absence of agreements the technological race will go much further. It seems likely that the arguments to "do something" about the vulnerability of fixed ICBM's will increase in tempo and will carry the day in both the U.S. and the U.S.S.R. Superhardening alone will be perceived to be a losing game, considering how easily any moves in that direction could be offset by further improvements in missile accuracy. A defense of the Safeguard type will probably also be judged to be a losing proposition. A very heavy defense with components specifically optimized for the defense of hardened ICBM's might be one response. There is likely to be even further reliance on mobile systems: missile-launching submarines, new strategic bombers and, in the case of the U.S.S.R., probably mobile ICBM's. It is conceivable that fixed ICBM's may be given up altogether, although the arguments we have advanced against the acceptability of attacking them preemptively would still be valid.

It is also likely in the absence of agreements that one or the other of the superpowers will deploy ABM systems that will provide more extensive and effective defense of population and industry than either the present Russian defenses around Moscow or the projected Phase II of Safeguard. Defense against a Chinese missile capability may be the rationale, but it is to be expected that the other superpower will respond to any such deployment both by emulation and by increasing its strategic offensive capabilities.

Whereas the strategic-forces budget of the U.S. now amounts to about $9 billion per year (excluding some rather large items for nuclear warheads, research and development, command and control, communications and intelligence activities), outlays for strategic systems could well double by the mid-1970's. Continuing large expenditures on strategic systems are probably also to be expected in the U.S.S.R.

As we have stated, there appears to be no basis for expecting SALT to lead to significant reductions in the assured-destruction capabilities of the superpowers. Therefore other objectives must command our attention. The most important objective is of course to reduce the probability that a thermonuclear exchange will ever take place.

The major factors affecting that probability are likely not to be simply technical but to be largely political. They involve the degree of tension that will exist between the superpowers based on international political considerations, on domestic politics in each country and in an important sense on the strategic-arms race itself. We believe that in contrast to some previous eras, when the motivations for continuing arms races were largely political and economic conflicts, the strategic-arms race now has a life of

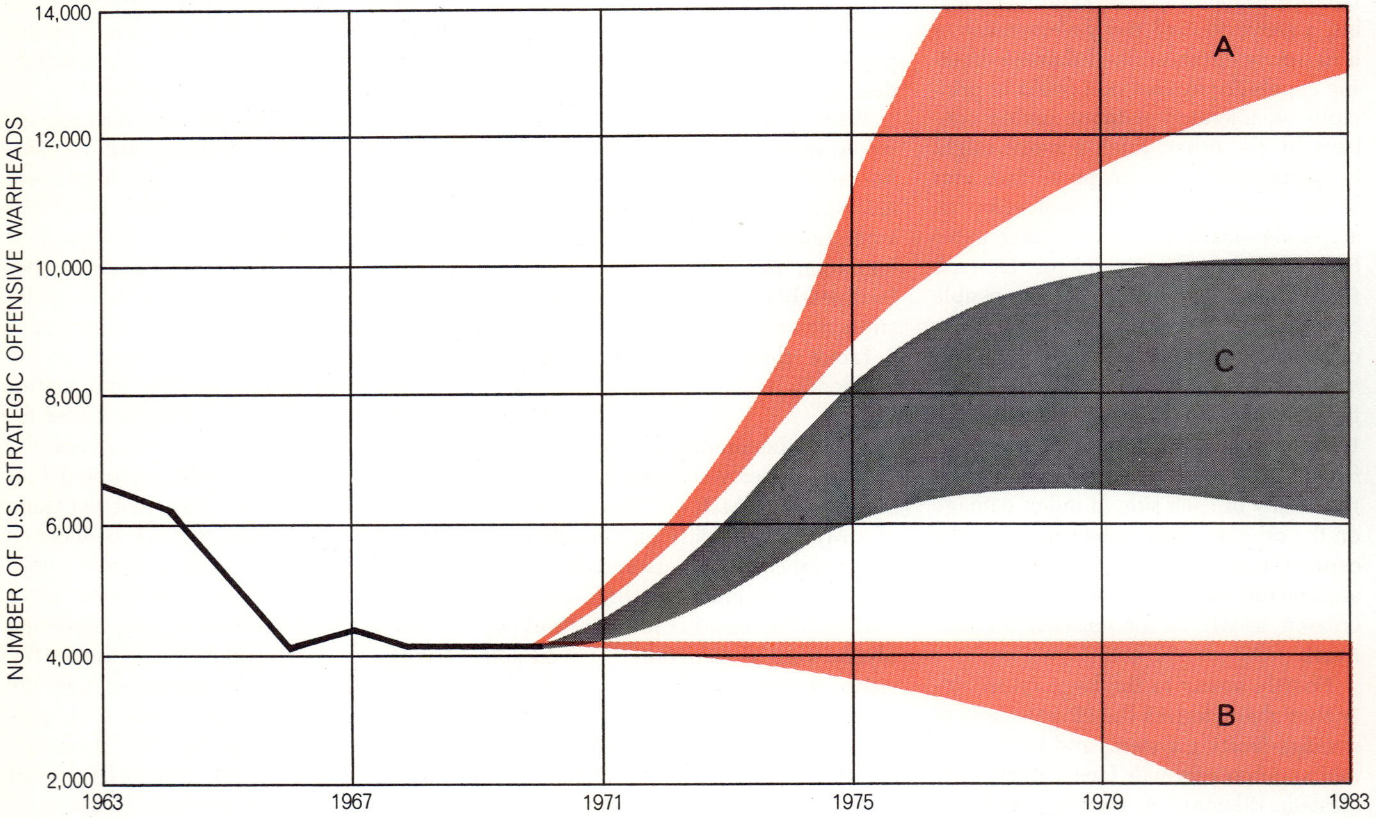

PROJECTED EFFECTS associated with three possible outcomes of the strategic-arms-limitation talks are expressed in the graphs on these two pages in terms of the number of U.S. strategic offensive warheads (*left*) and the U.S. budget for strategic forces (*right*). With no agreement (*A*) the number of weapons and the strategic-forces budget are likely to grow with no obvious limit. A SALT agreement that included a prohibition on the development and deployment of MIRV's (*B*) could lead to stability in strategic forces and a reduction in the budget to a level required to maintain them. With an agreement that did not constrain MIRV's (*C*) there would certainly be an increase in the strategic-forces budget for a few years as the composition of these forces changed, probably accompanied by the replacement of some fixed-base offensive missiles by mobile systems (either land-based or sea-based) or possibly by its own. For instance, the strategic-weapons programs of each superpower are more dependent on the programs of the other than on the levels of tension between the two countries. If this race can be attenuated, it would have a number of effects that would result in a diminution of tensions and hence in a reduction in the risk of war. That is perhaps the major reason for the urgency of a serious SALT effort. Keeping budgets for strategic forces at low levels is desirable in its own right in that significant resources, both financial and intellectual, will be freed for more constructive purposes. More important, in the U.S. lower military budgets will diminish the role of what President Eisenhower termed the military-industrial complex: those who have a propensity for, and in some cases obviously a vested interest in, the acquisition of more armaments and in exciting and maintaining an often unwarranted attitude of alarm and suspicion regarding an adversary's intentions. Lower military budgets in the U.S.S.R. would almost certainly have a similar desirable effect.

A poorly designed agreement could of course prove to be a vehicle for increasing suspicion and tension. Venturing into the realm of unprovable value judgments, however, we assert that it is not beyond the wit of man to design agreements that would result in there being less objective cause for concern than if the strategic-arms race continues unabated. In general, it would seem that any understanding that slowed the rate of development and change of strategic systems would have an effect in the right direction.

Beyond affecting the probability of a nuclear exchange's beginning, one would like to see strategic forces structured so that there would be at least some possibility that, if an exchange started, it would not have to run its course. A necessary but of course not sufficient condition for this is that there be no particular advantage to be gained from precipitate launch of more nuclear weapons after a few have been dispatched. By this criterion vulnerable ICBM's would seem to be the quintessence of undesirability. If both sides have them, each will recognize that if they are withheld, they may be destroyed.

Whether or not MIRV development and deployment will be controlled may not be a question for the SALT negotiators to consider, because of the inability of one side or the other to decide in a timely fashion the position it wishes to take on the issue. The rate of MIRV development is so rapid that the question may thus be settled before the substantive phase of the talks is well advanced. If such development is still in doubt, however, either because the talks get to such substantive issues very quickly or because of a moratorium on MIRV testing, MIRV limitation should be an issue of the highest priority.

The arguments for preventing deployment of MIRV's advanced enough to be effective counterforce weapons are persuasive. They have been made at great length elsewhere (for example in public hearings before committees of the Senate and the House of Representatives). We simply summarize here by pointing out that if MIRV deployment is prevented, it may be possible to freeze the strategic balance at something approximating its present level. Most of the incentive to defend hardened ICBM's or to replace them with mobile systems will

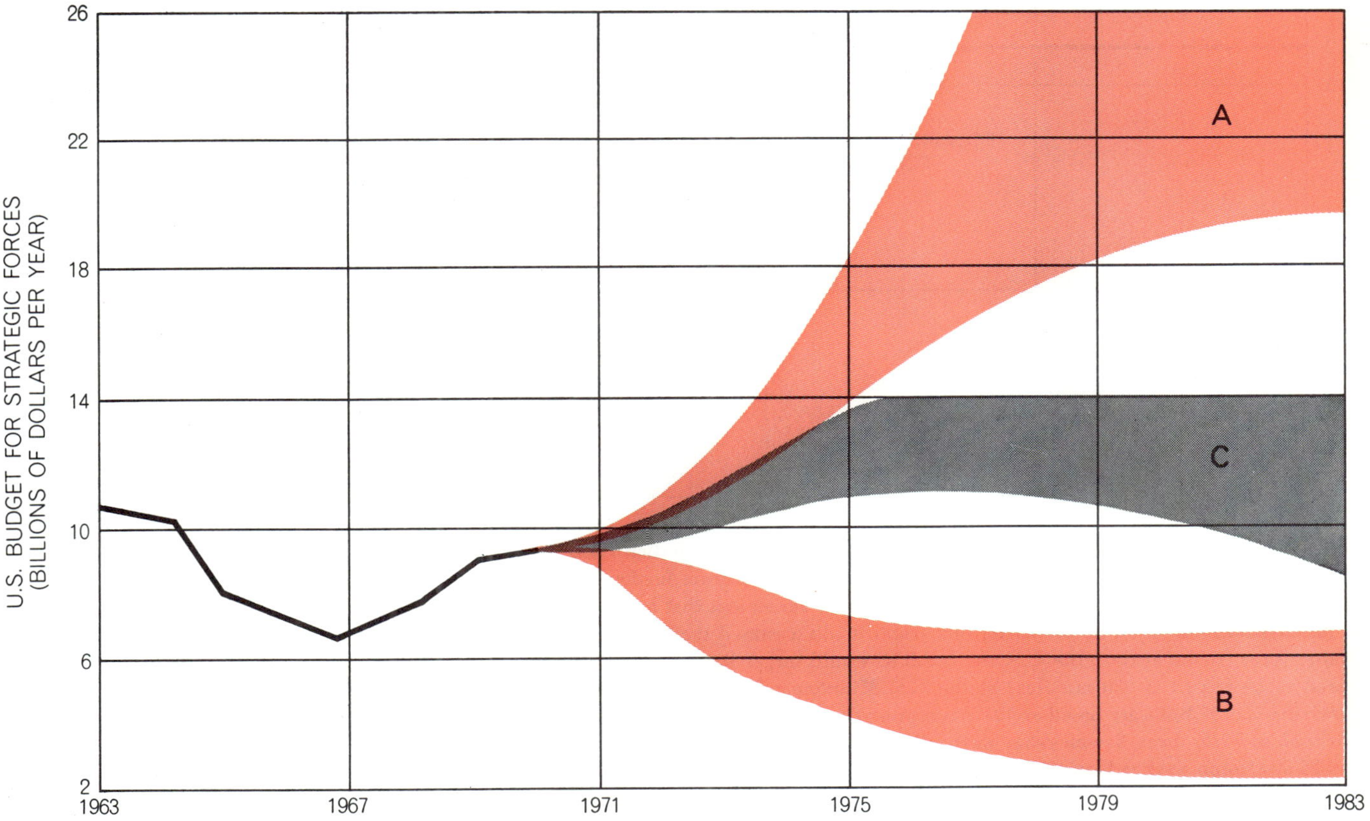

"superhardening" and heavy specialized ABM defense of missile sites. Assuming under case *C* that a large-scale ABM defense of population is prohibited, there would be little military rationale for either side to acquire large additional numbers of offensive warheads. Nonetheless, the numbers might increase significantly with the implementation of present plans to deploy MIRV's. Future Russian strategic-forces levels would probably display similar trends, but budget projections would differ somewhat. The Russian budget for strategic weapons is possibly at an unprecedentedly high level now, considering the present rapid rate of growth in their strategic systems. Thus in case *B* the drop in the strategic-forces budget for the U.S.S.R. might be sharper than for the U.S., and in the two other cases there would be a less pronounced increase. Estimates are in constant-value 1969 dollars.

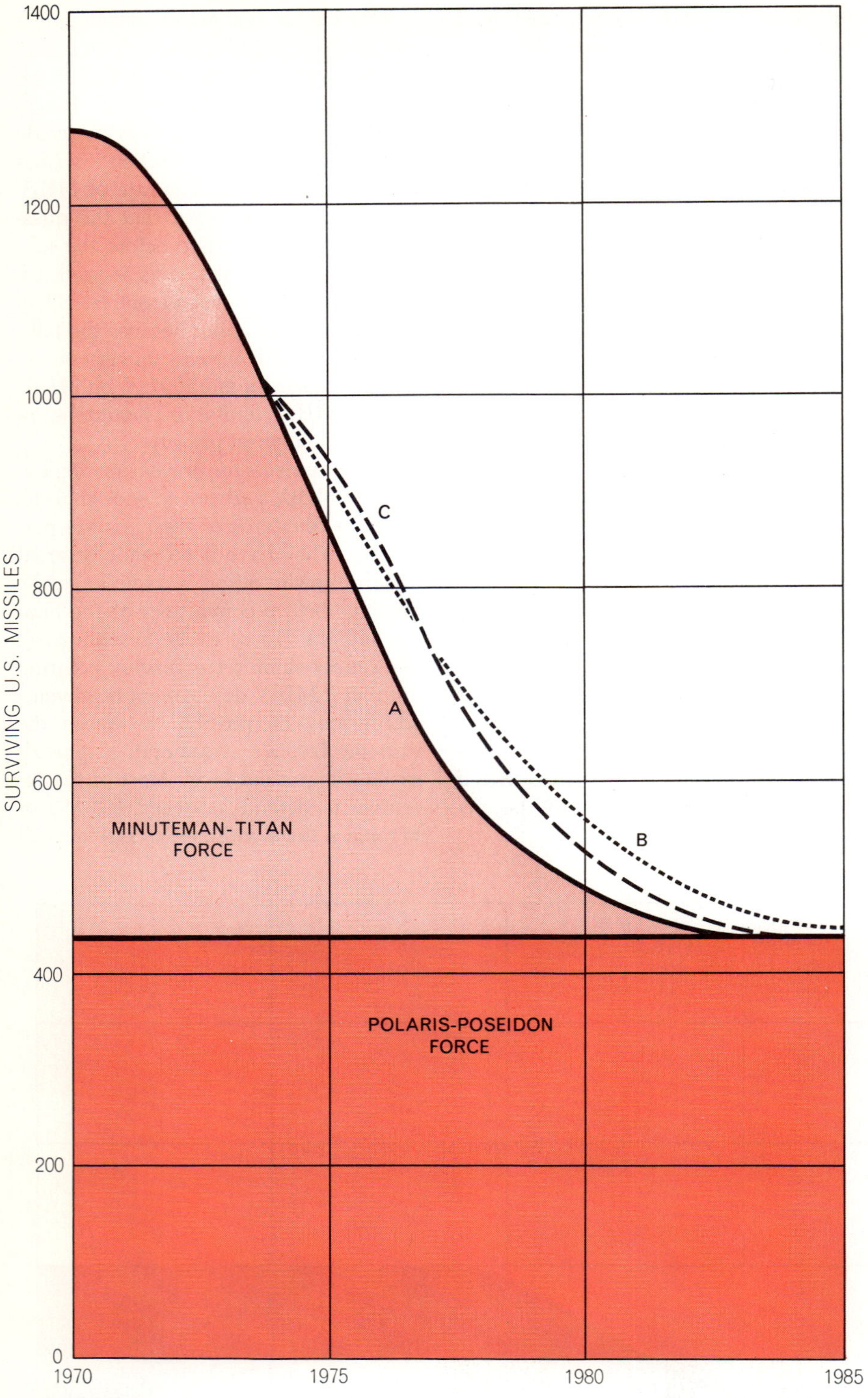

DIMINISHING UTILITY of fixed-base intercontinental ballistic missiles (ICBM's) as a component of the U.S. "assured-destruction" forces would result from further development and deployment of MIRV's, even in the event of a SALT agreement that freezes the number of missiles on both sides. In preparing this graph it was assumed that in a preemptive, or counterforce, strike against the U.S. the U.S.S.R. would target its SS-9 missile force (estimated to be frozen at 280 missiles) at the U.S. Minuteman-Titan force. The numbers of surviving U.S. ICBM's are based on the assumption that each SS-9 will carry one 25-megaton warhead in 1970, three five-megaton warheads in 1975, nine 500-kiloton warheads in 1980 and 25 50-kiloton warheads in 1985; delivery accuracies are assumed to improve by a factor of two every five years. Curve *A* assumes that no additional measures are taken to protect the already "hardened" U.S. ICBM force. Curve *B* assumes that the blast resistance of the ICBM sites is improved by "superhardening" so that by 1972 they can withstand three times the overpressure sustainable in 1970. Curve *C* assumes full operational capability (and a generous estimate of performance) of the Safeguard ABM system by 1978. It is apparent that neither superhardening nor active defense (unless many times more effective than Safeguard) is likely to extend the period of invulnerability for U.S. ICBM's by very much. (The number of surviving submarine-launched missiles is based on the assumption that a third of the Polaris-Poseidon force is destroyed in port by the Russian preemptive attack.)

have been reduced, if not eliminated.

The arguments for continuing MIRV testing and then deployment because MIRV's may someday be required to penetrate an adversary's ABM defenses are not convincing. There is little doubt that currently designed U.S. MIRV's could be deployed on a time scale short compared with that required for deployment of any significant Russian ABM defenses. Accordingly there is no need for any MIRV deployment pending firm evidence that the U.S.S.R. is beginning the construction of such defenses. And there is no need for further research and development tests unless a counterforce capability is intended. For similar reasons the U.S.S.R. should also abstain from further multiple-warhead tests and deployment, which it can do at no great risk to its security.

Essential to the survival of an agreement not to test MIRV's would be a prohibition of large-scale ABM deployment. If ABM systems were deployed, the pressures to deploy MIRV's and to test them frequently in order to maintain confidence in their reliability would be overwhelming. Furthermore, there would undoubtedly be great domestic pressures to develop and test more sophisticated penetration aids. Under such circumstances neither side could have any confidence that the other was not developing counterforce-effective MIRV's. An ABM freeze would be a logically required companion measure to any agreement prohibiting MIRV's.

Assuming that ABM deployment and MIRV testing are both frozen, the other important component of a strategic-arms-limitation agreement would be an understanding to maintain something like parity in ICBM-force levels by freezing these levels or preferably reducing them, and if necessary permitting replacement of fixed-base ICBM's by mobile systems whose levels could be verified by unilateral means. In the absence of such a measure there would be the possibility of one side's gaining such a superiority in missile strength that, with improved accuracies and even without MIRV's, would enable it to knock out a large fraction of its adversary's forces by delivering a counterforce attack against them. The reasons for concern about such a possibility have been identified above: the probability of arms-race escalation and the reduction in whatever small chance there may be of a nuclear exchange's being terminated short of running its suicidal course.

If the development of MIRV's that are perceived by the adversary to have counterforce capability cannot be prevented (and we are pessimistic about preventing it), the relative importance of some of the measures discussed above will be changed materially. A prohibition on large-scale ABM deployment would still be desirable, but it would be less important; it would not in this case prevent the MIRV genie from escaping the bottle. Moreover, continuing development and deployment of MIRV's would make a large-scale ABM defense unattractive simply on cost-effectiveness grounds.

A provision permitting the replacement of fixed ICBM's by mobile systems would seem virtually unavoidable because of concern about the vulnerability of the ICBM's to counterforce attack. Indeed, in the interest of stabilizing arms at low levels, and to minimize concern about damage-limiting strikes, agreements could probably include measures that would enhance the viability of mobile systems. An area of agreement that would seem to merit most serious consideration would be prohibition on certain improvements in antisubmarine-warfare capabilities. Actually the possibility of breakthroughs in antisubmarine warfare is extremely remote. It is probable that through noise reduction, extension of missile range and other techniques the gap between ASW capability and the capability of the missile-launching submarine to escape detection and destruction will widen rather than narrow. Yet it seems likely from recent debate in the U.S. that the present American leadership, and presumably the leadership of the U.S.S.R. as well, would be reluctant to rely solely on a missile-launching submarine force for deterrence, given the possibility of further ASW development by its adversary. Constraints on ASW such as a limitation on the number of hunter-killer submarines would increase the acceptability to both sides of relying more heavily on missile-launching submarines for deterrence.

Similar arguments might be made for limitations on or curtailment of air defense. Such moves would seem less realistic on three counts. First, compliance with limitations on air-defense capabilities could probably not be verified with unilateral procedures as well as could limitations on ASW systems, or for that matter on ABM systems. Intelligence on short-range antiaircraft systems is likely to be poorer than on hunter-killer submarines, specialized ASW aircraft or large-sized components of ABM systems. Second, the overlap between tactical and strategic antiaircraft capabilities is considerable, and neither superpower is likely to be willing to greatly reduce tactical antiaircraft capabilities in the context of SALT. ASW capabilities (except for destroyers) would, on the other hand, have little role other than attack against an adversary's missile-launching submarines. This is far truer now than it was a few years ago because the realization is more widespread that a major war involving large antishipping campaigns is extremely unlikely. Third, neither the U.S. nor the U.S.S.R. is likely to have enough confidence in bombers to rely much on them in a missile age even if air defenses are constrained, whereas both superpowers obviously are prepared to rely heavily on submarine-launched missiles.

Finally, if counterforce-effective MIRV's were a reality, and if as a consequence both sides were to place reliance very largely on mobile systems, additional offensive weapons on one side could not be used effectively to limit the other side's ability to retaliate. Considering this fact and the fact that since strategic-force levels are already at least an order of magnitude larger than is rationally required for deterrence, there would be little incentive for either side to acquire additional offensive capabilities. Also in this situation it would hardly matter if either side were to introduce new assured-destruction systems such as, for example, small mobile ICBM's that could not be easily counted.

Even this incomplete discussion shows that the strategic balance between the superpowers is likely to be very different depending on whether or not MIRV development and ABM deployment are allowed to continue. Both possibilities will have a serious impact on future strategic postures, but with respect to ABM deployment nothing much is going to happen overnight. Dealing with the issue of MIRV development, although perhaps no more important, is far more urgent. That is why it is the watershed issue for SALT. If counterforce-effective MIRV's (and large-scale ABM deployment) can be stopped, the present strategic balance of force levels may endure for some time. If such MIRV's are deployed, the balance will unavoidably change in qualitative ways. How large an escalation in the arms race will result will depend on whether agreement to constrain or cut back other strategic systems could still be negotiated.

We have attempted here to present an objective analysis of the prospects for various agreements to limit strategic armaments. In so doing we are aware that many of our readers will be dismayed that our discussion has been in the context of each superpower's preserving the capability of destroying the other. This has been so not because we ourselves favor the continuing retention of huge stocks of thermonuclear weapons but because we have tried to be realistic. The distrust that exists between the U.S. and the U.S.S.R. will induce both to preserve the capability of destroying the other; such a capability, as we have noted, is unfortunately easier to attain than an effective defense of one's own society, whether or not there are agreements on strategic armaments. Both superpowers will preserve this capability because they see it as the only effective deterrent to the war that neither wants or could win.

The most that can reasonably be expected of the forthcoming talks is a move toward a strategic balance where (1) uncertainties about the adversary are reduced and with them some of the tensions; (2) each side can inflict a level of damage on the other sufficient to destroy its society but neither feels a need to maintain a great overkill capability as a hedge against possible damage-limiting efforts by the other; (3) there will be an improved chance that a thermonuclear exchange, should one begin, would be terminated short of running its course, and (4) the levels of expenditure on strategic armaments are lower, so that larger fractions of the resources available to each society can be used for more constructive endeavors.

We believe that the realization of these objectives would be a tremendous accomplishment and one that is possible without the solution of the deep-seated political problems of the Russian-American confrontation. To go further will require dealing with those problems. We do not believe, however, that the superpowers can afford to delay attacking the strategic-arms race while trying to solve political differences. Regrettably the situation with respect to technical developments (MIRV's, ABM defenses and nuclear proliferation), and quite possibly with respect to domestic politics as well, will probably make strategic-arms-limitation negotiations less likely to be successful several years hence than now. Time is of the essence, and we write with a feeling of urgency. Although our tone is pessimistic, we do not despair. We are convinced that latent public support for an agreement could be exploited by effective political leadership on both sides to reverse the trends we have lived with for two decades.

23

The Limitation of Offensive Weapons

It is argued that the best possible outcome that can be expected to emerge from the current strategic-arms-limitation talks (SALT) would be a freeze on the existing offensive forces of both sides

HERBERT SCOVILLE, JR.

January 1971

Recent public debate in the U.S. on the control of strategic weapons has been mainly focused on anti-ballistic-missile (ABM) systems. Apart from the limited and so far unsuccessful effort to halt further testing by this country of multiple independently targeted reentry vehicles (MIRV's), there has been little open discussion of how offensive strategic weapons might also be controlled. It appears to have been generally assumed that reaching an international agreement to limit the deployment of offensive weapons systems would be a comparatively straightforward matter not requiring such extensive analysis.

In reality, however, a number of different approaches to the limitation of offensive weapons are possible, and these could have very different effects on the future course of the strategic-arms race. Certain approaches could raise serious issues of national security for one side or the other, whereas others could actually accelerate the arms race instead of curtailing it. The economic gains from the banning of certain activities could be completely nullified by rechanneling arms expenditures into new developments. Some types of agreement would be extremely difficult to verify and could even lead to increased tensions by arousing fears that the agreements were not being honored. Other possible agreements, although superficially attractive to one side or the other, would be extremely difficult to negotiate.

In any attempt to evaluate the various approaches to the problem of limiting offensive weapons it is important to bear in mind the stated objective of the U.S. strategic forces: to deter the initiation of nuclear war by maintaining a credible capacity to cause unacceptable destruction to the other side even after any conceivable surprise attack. In theory this "assured-destruction capacity" can be achieved by having enough offensive forces so that those that survive a "counterforce" strike are enough to penetrate the enemy's defenses. At present both the U.S. and the U.S.S.R. possess such forces in the form of a combination of submarine-launched ballistic missiles (SLBM's), fixed, land-based intercontinental ballistic missiles (ICBM's) and long-range strategic bombers. Neither side has an ABM system that can threaten the other's deterrent. The primary goal of any arms-control agreement is to provide greater confidence that this state of mutual deterrence is maintained and at the same time conserve scarce resources that both nations need for many other programs.

In general the methods of offensive-arms limitation that have been proposed so far can be grouped under three broad headings. First, an agreement could be reached setting a ceiling on the total number of delivery vehicles that would be allowed for each side. Such an agreement would not place any limitation on the mix of weapons that could be included in the total number. Thus replacement of an existing weapon with another type of weapon would be allowed. A variation of this approach would further restrict the number of weapons in specific categories, such as bombers or land-based ICBM's; alternatively, such an agreement might limit the replacement of an existing weapon by one of a radically different size.

The second general approach would be to limit the total useful payload deliverable by each side; payload in this case would include both warheads and penetration aids.

The third approach would be to freeze the strategic forces of both sides at their present levels, without formally stating any specific allowed numbers. Substitution of existing delivery vehicles or launchers by new types would not be permitted. A possible variation would be to allow only those replacements that did not alter the external configuration of the delivery vehicle or launcher.

It is important to analyze each of these approaches in detail in order to develop an understanding of the significance of any agreement that might be reached as a result of the current strategic-arms-limitation talks (SALT) between the U.S. and the U.S.S.R.

Before proceeding with such an evaluation, it is necessary to review the present levels of the deployed strategic forces on both sides and consider how these levels might change in the event that no arms-limitation agreement is reached [*see illustration on next page*].

For the purpose of this review a land-based delivery vehicle is considered strategic if it has the range to deliver a warhead to a substantial part of the territory of one nation from its deployed launching point on the territory of the other nation; in addition delivery vehicles launched from nuclear-powered submarines are regarded as strategic. Systems that are only capable of being fired between Siberia and Alaska are normally not considered to be part of this total. Similarly, manned aircraft that are only capable of one-way missions, short-range, medium-range and intermediate-range missiles that are capable of being used only against allied nations, and tactical aircraft that are based either overseas or on carriers are not included in the total. (The U.S. FB-111's, which have been classed as strategic bombers by Secretary of Defense Laird, are now being deployed in Britain, so that these are a somewhat marginal case.) Although any such definitions are of necessity somewhat arbitrary and would of course be the subject of negotiation, they help to simplify the analysis and do not alter the basic conclusions.

Since the U.S. and Russian missiles do not have identical characteristics, numbers alone are not sufficient to analyze the security implications of any potential agreement. The U.S. Minuteman I and Minuteman II missiles, which comprise most of our deployed ICBM force, can each carry a warhead with an explosive yield in the megaton range. Roughly half of these missiles, however, are in the process of being replaced with the Minuteman III, which will have approximately the same payload but will carry three MIRV's, each with a yield in the range of hundreds of kilotons. The 54 Titan missiles have a larger payload capacity: each can deliver more than five megatons on the U.S.S.R. No plans exist for modernizing these Titans. The Russian SS-11's and SS-13's have nearly the same payload capability as the Minuteman. Just recently Secretary Laird announced that the Russians were testing an SS-11 system with three multiple reentry vehicles (MRV's), which lack the capability for being independently targeted. The Russian SS-9, a much larger missile capable of delivering a 25-megaton warhead on the U.S., has been tested for a period of about two years with three MRV's, each of which might have a warhead yield of about five megatons.

The U.S. has no plans to deploy additional land-based missile launchers, although many design studies have been carried out for advanced systems that might be either mobile or in "superhardened" rock silos (or both). The U.S.S.R., on the other hand, is continuing to deploy SS-11's and SS-13's at the rate of about 100 per year and SS-9's at the rate of about 50 or fewer per year. Although there is some evidence that the rate of this deployment has decreased somewhat in the past year, it is not known at what point the Russians would unilaterally halt these programs in the absence of an arms-control agreement. There is some possibility that they are continuing the deployment of the SS-9 in order to emulate the U.S.'s example of being able to negotiate at SALT "from a position of strength."

The U.S. SLBM force consists of 41 submarines equipped with Polaris missiles, a large fraction of which are the A-3 model with three MRV's. Of the existing Polaris submarines 31 will be modified to carry the new Poseidon missile, which will be capable of delivering 10 MIRV's with yields of somewhat less than 100 kilotons each. At present eight submarines are undergoing such modification; the first will go to sea in January, 1971. The early Russian ballistic-missile submarines could handle only three missiles each, but the later versions, some 14 of which are now reported to be operational and 16 more to be under construction, are equipped to carry 16 missiles of the early Polaris type. No Russian testing of MRV's or MIRV's for this system has been reported. The Russians have the capability of increasing this fleet by approximately six or eight submarines per year and so could have a force with a numerical, but not qualitative, equivalence of the U.S. fleet before 1975. The U.S. has no firm plans for building new ballistic-missile submarines but has in the design stage a replacement for Polaris-Poseidon called the underwater long-range missile system (ULMS). Secretary Laird has stated that without an agreement at SALT a decision will have

U.S.

DELIVERY VEHICLES		NUMBER	APPROXIMATE EXPLOSIVE YIELD (MEGATONS)
ICBM'S	TITAN	54	5+
	MINUTEMAN	1,000	1
SLBM'S	POLARIS	656	1
BOMBERS	B-52, FB-111	550	
TOTAL		2,260	

U.S.S.R.

DELIVERY VEHICLES		APPROXIMATE NUMBER	APPROXIMATE EXPLOSIVE YIELD (MEGATONS)
ICBM'S	SS-9	270	25
	SS-11, SS-13	825	1
	OLD MODELS	220	1+
SLBM'S		254	1
BOMBERS	BISON, BEAR	150	
TOTAL		1,719	

STRATEGIC OFFENSIVE FORCES of the U.S. and the U.S.S.R. as of January 1, 1971, are listed in this table. The three major categories on both sides are fixed, land-based intercontinental ballistic missiles (ICBM's), submarine-launched ballistic missiles (SLBM's) and long-range bombers. The approximate explosive yield of each type of missile is given in equivalent megatons of TNT; megatonnage is not indicated for the bombers, since this value varies from mission to mission, but the U.S. is known to have a substantial advantage in this category. In addition to the figures shown the U.S.S.R. is believed to have under construction about 40 SS-9's, 100 SS-11's and SS-13's, and 16 submarines carrying 256 SLBM's. The SS-9 has been tested with three multiple reentry vehicles (MRV's), each with a yield of about five megatons. The SS-11 has also been tested with three MRV's, with a total yield of less than one megaton. About 50 percent of the Minutemen are currently being converted to carry three multiple independently targeted reentry vehicles (MIRV's), again with a total yield somewhat less than one megaton. Some Polaris SLBM's currently carry three MRV's with a total yield less than one megaton, and the U.S. is in the process of replacing the Polaris missiles on 31 of its submarines with Poseidon missiles capable of carrying 10 roughly 100-kiloton MIRV's. No additional bomber deployment is taking place on either side. The U.S. now has a total of more than 4,300 strategic nuclear weapons in the form of missile warheads and bombs, whereas the U.S.S.R. has about 2,000. With the completion of the MIRV program in the mid-1970's the U.S. total will rise to about 9,000.

to be made in 1971 on whether to proceed with the deployment of ULMS.

The U.S. currently has a force of 550 B-52 and FB-111 intercontinental bombers. Since there has been no new production of B-52 aircraft for many years, the size of this force is gradually decreasing, but it is estimated that it will still total several hundred aircraft into the 1980's. The B-52's are being modernized to carry air-to-surface missiles and improved penetration aids. Originally the nuclear weapons for these bombers had yields greater than 20 megatons, but it has been found more efficient to load them with several bombs having considerably smaller yields. The smaller Russian long-range bomber force is composed of a mix of turboprop Bears and jet Bisons. The U.S.S.R. has tested a nuclear device with a potential yield of 100 megatons deliverable by a Bear aircraft, but no information is available concerning whether or not such a weapon has been deployed. In all likelihood the majority of the bombs for the Russian aircraft are of much lower yield. The U.S. is in the early development stage of a new long-range intercontinental bomber, the B-1, but there is no known Russian program for the development of a replacement for the U.S.S.R.'s existing aircraft.

Perhaps the simplest type of arms agreement to limit offensive strategic weapons would be one in which both nations agreed to a common ceiling on the total number of deployed launchers or delivery vehicles without regard to what types would be included within the total. Replacement of existing weapons by new models of the same type or by substitution with a different type would be allowed provided that the total number of operational weapons at any given time did not exceed the agreed number. No restrictions would be placed on qualitative improvements or on the number of warheads or bombs that could be carried by any giver delivery vehicle. In the case of missiles it would be assumed that each completed launcher contained one delivery vehicle, and no restrictions would be placed on missiles that were not associated with a launching platform. In the case of bombers each aircraft would be regarded as a single delivery vehicle.

There are several alternative ways such a ceiling on numbers might be selected. If the ceiling were very high, say 2,500, it would provide no limitation at all. If it were initially chosen to be very low, say 1,000, it would involve widespread scrapping of existing weapons and might raise questions in some minds as to the viability of the deterrent. Intermediate levels would satisfy the security requirements of both nations but, depending on the exact terms, might present negotiating problems.

If such an agreement were reached with forces as of January 1, 1971, the U.S. would have a total operational force of 2,260 delivery vehicles and the U.S.S.R. about 1,720. This inequality results from the much larger U.S. bomber and SLBM forces, which outweigh the numerical advantage that the U.S.S.R. has in land-based ICBM's. The U.S.S.R. would also have approximately 400 additional missile launchers under construction. It is conceivable that the Russians might be willing to agree that the allowed numbers should be at the existing operational levels since a rough parity in force strength does exist. The larger payload capacity of the Russian land-based missiles (specifically the SS-9's) might be said to compensate for the U.S. advantage in number of SLBM's. The Russians might worry, however, that the number of their currently deployed sea-based missiles, the least vulnerable of all strategic systems, would be dangerously low in view of the fact that, with no restrictions on MIRV's, fixed land-based systems might at some time in the future be vulnerable to complete elimination by a U.S. counterforce strike. Furthermore, under such an agreement there would be nothing to prevent the U.S., if it chose, from replacing its present small missiles with those of larger payload.

On the other hand, the agreement could require that both nations have an equal number of delivery vehicles. Since the relative Russian inferiority in numbers would be largely alleviated if the U.S.S.R. were allowed to complete those launchers now under construction, a freeze on new starts might be the simplest way to achieve equality. The alternative to the U.S.'s reducing its force levels to those of the U.S.S.R. might be politically more difficult for the U.S. to accept and might leave the Russians feeling insecure because of their comparatively small number of SLBM's.

None of these approaches presents any real risk to U.S. security, particularly if ABM systems are simultaneously limited to low levels, since the U.S. would still have an adequate deterrent force. Even if the Russians developed MIRV's with sufficient accuracy to provide a high probability of eliminating U.S. land-based missiles, the U.S. would still be left with 656 submarine launchers, almost 500 of which would be capable of firing Poseidon missiles, each of which in turn could carry 10 warheads. Such a weapons system could be confident of wreaking completely unacceptable devastation on the U.S.S.R. in retaliation even if the Russians had deployed a very large ABM force. In addition the U.S. would have as a backup a large bomber force, which could not be destroyed simultaneously with the ICBM force. The deterrent should therefore remain secure, but if in time concern for security developed, the U.S. would always be in a position to replace its fixed land-based systems with less vulnerable mobile or sea-based ones.

An agreement along these lines, however, would have only minor effects in curbing the offensive-arms race and would only turn it in the direction of qualitative rather than quantitative developments. Since at present the U.S. has no plans for increasing the total number of its delivery vehicles, it would unilaterally affect the U.S.S.R. Although the U.S. is doing design studies on new systems in all categories, no decisions have been made for the deployment of any of these systems, and any deployments that might occur would probably serve to replace existing systems. On the other hand, such an agreement would have considerable effect on present Russian programs since the U.S.S.R. is continuing to deploy both land-based ICBM's and new submarines with SLBM's. In spite of this asymmetry the Russians might be willing to negotiate such a ceiling, since they may now be almost at the point of halting additional deployments. If the total number of Russian delivery vehicles were to be kept at the January 1971 level, it is likely that the Russians would decide to replace some of their 220 older ICBM's with SLBM's in order to remedy their present deficiency in this area. They could also substitute SS-9's for some of these old missiles, thus eliminating one of the chief U.S. aims at SALT.

The failure to place restrictions on qualitative improvements in the delivery systems or on the replacement of old missiles with new ones is likely to accelerate rather than restrict the arms race. We have had the experience of an arms-control agreement being used to justify technical programs that otherwise might not have been carried out. In 1963 one of the key elements in gaining acceptance of the Limited Test Ban Treaty by the Joint Chiefs of Staff and Congress was President Kennedy's undertaking that the U.S. would maintain a standby capability to resume atmospheric testing on short notice and would vigorously prosecute those weapons-development and test programs that were still permitted under the treaty in order to be in the strongest position possible should the Russians abrogate or violate the treaty. Such programs have cost the U.S. hundreds of millions of dollars, have involved an increase in the total annual number of nuclear tests over the average for the preceding 10 years, and have in many cases been continued at a somewhat reduced level up to the present time even though many have little or no effect on national security. It is almost certain that similar requirements would be placed on the Administration in the event that an agreement were reached in SALT. The U.S.S.R. would probably be pressured to emulate such actions. Thus such a SALT agreement could become a stimulus to the arms program in the same way that SALT itself has already been used to justify continuing present programs in order to be able to negotiate from strength.

In the first place the U.S. would undoubtedly proceed with its present program to put MIRV's on a large fraction of the Minuteman and the Polaris systems. In fact, under the constrictions of a SALT agreement it is not at all unlikely that these forces would be completely MIRVed instead of only partially as now planned. The Russians, who do not yet have any MIRV systems tested, would undoubtedly feel impelled to proceed with similar programs. They probably would not be content with placing only three MIRV's on their SS-9's, the number that has been given in most threat calculations publicized by the Department of Defense, and they would undoubtedly attempt to take advantage of the larger payload of the SS-9 by plac-

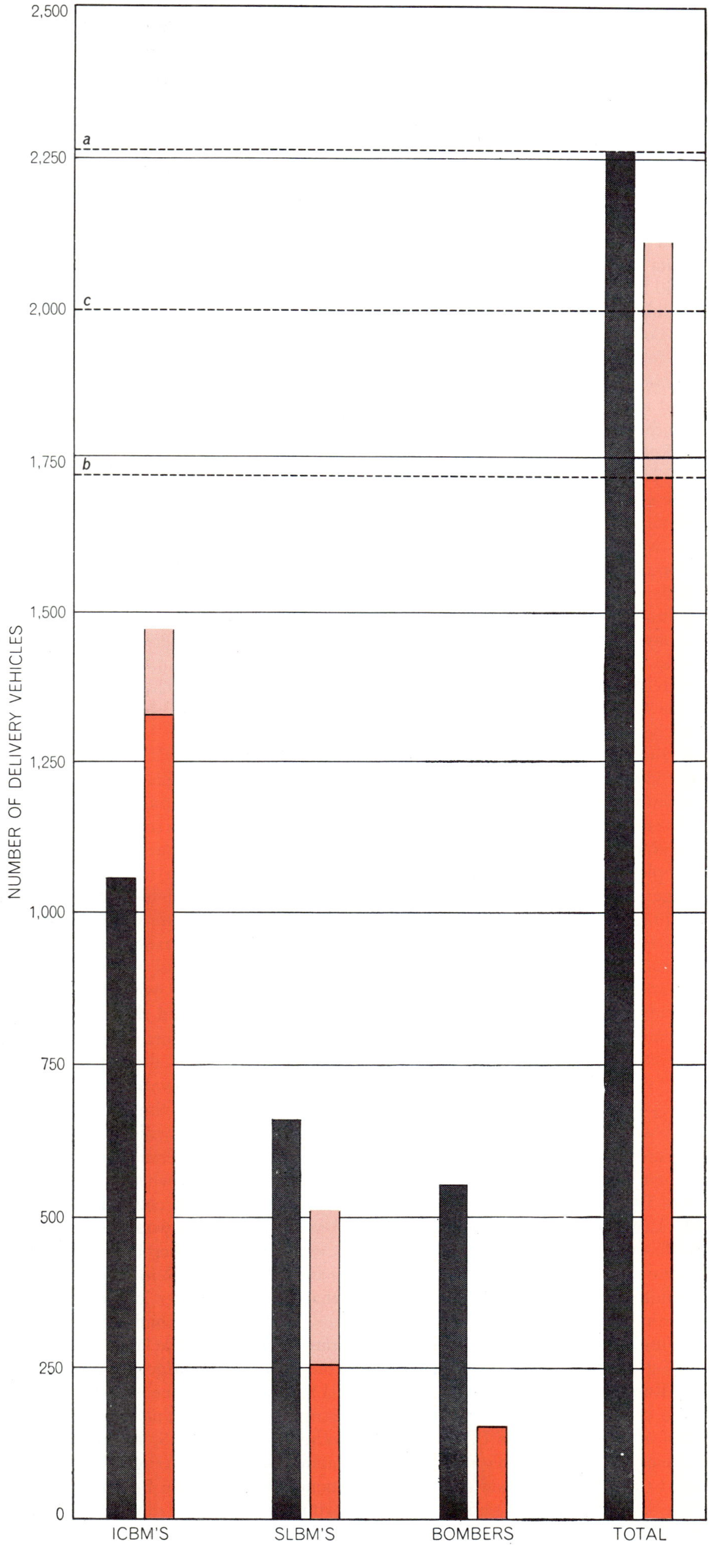

POSSIBLE NEGOTIATED CEILINGS on the strategic offensive forces of the U.S. (*black bars*) and the U.S.S.R. (*colored bars*) are indicated by the broken lines at the top of this chart. An agreement that placed a ceiling on the total number of delivery vehicles at the present U.S. level (*a*) would have to allow the U.S.S.R. to add about 150 vehicles (presumably missiles) to its forces in addition to those now under construction. An agreed ceiling at the present Russian level (*b*) would require a corresponding cutback in U.S. forces. A compromise ceiling of, say, 2,000 delivery vehicles (*c*) would allow the Russians to finish some of the missiles they now have under construction (*light-colored bars*) and would require a small U.S. reduction in total delivery vehicles. A freeze at existing force levels would leave the strategic balance substantially as it appears here.

ing 10 or more warheads on each missile. In time these could have the accuracies required to virtually ensure destruction of all U.S. fixed land-based ICBM's. The race for increasingly effective MIRV systems would be given the sanction of an arms-control agreement.

The race, however, would not be restricted to the development of MIRV's. As the threat to the U.S. land-based forces increased, an ABM defense of the missile sites, if not already banned, would begin to appear inadequate. Since it would be allowed to do so under the terms of the agreement, the U.S. would feel forced to attempt to reduce this vulnerability by replacing fixed land-based systems up to the agreed ceiling even though the existing weapons would continue to provide an adequate deterrent. The most likely replacement would be less vulnerable but more expensive submarine systems. If land-based systems were eliminated entirely, however, it would create the difficult political problem of removing the Air Force from the strategic-missile picture. Substituting sea-based missiles for land-based ones would be argued as having the security disadvantage of placing reliance on a single type of missile deterrent system. This point has already been used to justify the Safeguard ABM system. It is most likely that at least some of the conversion would include replacement with new land-based systems involving super-hardening and/or mobility. The expense of deploying such new systems would be staggering compared with that of present programs. The U.S. also might be tempted toward missiles with a larger payload in order to compensate for the Russian advantage in this area and to circumvent the restrictions imposed by the limit on the total number.

Within such an agreement the U.S.S.R. would also probably be led to deploy new systems. Certainly the Russians would be forced to take certain measures to decrease the vulnerability of their present land-based missile systems. This could be carried out by using up a larger fraction of their total number of allowed missiles in the form of submarine systems. Such a program could be quite expensive for the U.S.S.R. because submarines are costly vehicles and because the distance from ports to operating areas is considerably greater for the Russian submarines than it is for those of the U.S. From a geographical point of view alone, the U.S.S.R.'s submarines also are probably more vulnerable to anti-submarine-warfare measures than those of the U.S. since they must operate in deep-ocean areas that are surrounded by Western-controlled land masses and are more amenable to acoustic-detection techniques.

Finally, the Russians too would have the political problem of moving their deterrent from land to sea. The rocket forces are a powerful group within the Russian military hierarchy, and they are unlikely to forgo this mission. The U.S.S.R. is traditionally much more land-minded than the U.S. Therefore it is likely that the Russians would turn to a firing doctrine of "launch on warning" or to mobile land-based missile systems or to both. They have already tested some mobile missiles at short ranges and have boasted of the existence of mobile ICBM's. It would seem very likely that they would move into this area with extensive programs as they became concerned that their present forces might be threatened. Such deployment would increase the uncertainties in U.S. planning, since mobile missiles are hard to count accurately. It is also possible that the Russians would choose to increase the proportion of the large SS-9's in their missile force in order to ensure the maximum potential payload and penetration capability. This would still further increase U.S. fears of the Russian threat.

Although under this agreement both the U.S. and the U.S.S.R. would have the option of replacing their old bombers, it is not clear that either nation would choose to do so. As the present forces become obsolete or gradually become smaller because of accidents and deterioration, both nations might choose to deploy additional missiles in their place. Such a choice would be less costly than developing and deploying an entirely new bomber force, but it would in time eliminate one alternative form of deterrent. When bomber forces are no longer operational, the need for costly air-defense systems will be largely eliminated. The U.S. is already decreasing its air-defense efforts, whereas the Russian efforts in this area continue at a high level. The Russians would be faced with the decision on bomber replacement sooner than the U.S. in view of the fact that they have fewer long-range bombers. Their medium-bomber force has the range capable of attacking both Chinese and European targets, so that the U.S.S.R. does not need the very-long-range bombers for this purpose. On the other hand, the U.S. has only a small number of medium-range aircraft operational and, when the B-52's are gone, it would be forced to rely entirely on the FB-111's and carrier-based planes in the event that such aircraft were needed for lesser conflicts. The U.S., however, is known to be developing the B-1 as a replacement for its B-52's. As a result the U.S. might be less inclined to forgo bomber replacements than the U.S.S.R. would be.

Verification of an agreement limiting strategic delivery systems to a given fixed total would present a number of difficulties. Any new construction of missile launchers or of submarines carrying ballistic missiles could be observed by unilateral means (that is, without on-site inspection) well in advance of completion so that one could be confident of detecting any significant additions to the force. Nonetheless, an accurate count of the total number of operational missiles at a specific time would be harder to obtain if substitutions were allowed. This would be particularly difficult if mobile land-based missiles were deployed. Moreover, there would be some difficulty in ascertaining when a new missile system that was being constructed to replace an old one had reached operational status. If the replacement rate were very high, then concern might arise that the new facilities were being constructed without the intention of phasing out existing ones and that by so doing one side hoped to gain a temporary advantage. It is unlikely, however, that the new construction would be so extensive that such a violation could provide a real threat to anyone's security in view of the already large number of missiles available to both sides. Procedures for replacements could perhaps be negotiated to reduce the risks from a violation, but such a situation is likely to create a climate for accusations of bad faith and to increase tensions, which of course is the exact opposite of what a well-designed agreement should provide.

A final difficulty might arise in proving a violation. It would not be enough to point to a new site; it would also be necessary to present evidence that the total number of sites at a given time exceeded the agreed number. This might be very difficult to do and would open the way to charges and countercharges. The problem would be even more difficult if missiles were allowed to be substituted for bombers, since the operational status of the entire bomber force at any one time is difficult to determine. During the complete nuclear-test moratorium from 1958 to 1961, continued claims were made by certain groups that the Russians were violating the moratorium, and major efforts were necessary in order to provide the President with sufficient confidence that this was indeed not the case. An agreement such as the one proposed above would provide countless opportunities for misunderstandings.

In summary, an agreement that placed a ceiling on the total number of strategic delivery systems, although simple in concept and probably presenting little risk to the security of either nation, would have little if any value in controlling the strategic-arms race. In fact, the race might even be accelerated as it turned to qualitative as opposed to quantitative increases. There would clearly be little saving in funds, and in actuality new and expensive programs might be more easily justified under such an agreement than they would be without any agreement at all. At a minimum some additional restrictions on the replacement of existing systems should be added to this approach. It would be far better for both sides to agree to phase out their fixed, land-based missiles as they became vulnerable than to allow their replacement with new weapons. Although it is difficult to imagine any violation that could escape detection seriously affecting the security of either nation, it is likely that many misunderstandings and disputes would arise through misinterpretation of the programs allowed under the agreement.

In view of the numerous difficulties and risks that an agreement allowing complete freedom to shift strategic forces from one type to another presents, consideration could be given to agreeing not only on the total number of systems but also on the numbers within the various categories. The simplest such scheme would involve an agreement on specific numbers of aircraft and specific numbers of missiles; it would allow the option to vary the types of missiles or aircraft within the agreed numbers. This approach would represent a considerable improvement, since it would separate out the disparity in the numbers of aircraft, which is less significant, from the more critical missile problems. At present both nations have approximately the same number of missiles, the Russian advantage in land-based systems almost compensating for the U.S. advantage in sea-based systems. If closer equality were essential, the Russians could be allowed to complete the missile submarines now under construction until they had the same total number of missiles as the U.S. This separating of missiles and aircraft would avoid many of the difficulties in negotiating an agreed total number of delivery vehicles.

Such a variation would, however, still have many of the disadvantages of a simple agreement on total number. Strong pressures would still hold for replacing existing systems with more modern ones. With complete freedom to continue development and deployment of MIRV's, both sides would have strong incentives for revising their force structures to reduce the vulnerability of their land-based systems. The pressure would be particularly strong for the U.S.S.R. with its relatively weak SLBM forces. In addition there would be nothing to prevent the U.S.S.R. from continuing to build up its SS-9 force to the point where Secretary Laird's predictions about the vulnerability of the U.S. deterrent would become more credible. For this purpose the U.S.S.R. has more than 200 older missiles that could be phased out and replaced. There would then be strong pressures within the U.S. for the replacement of existing systems to neutralize this Russian threat. As in the previous approach, the arms race might only proceed faster on a new track.

Since such an agreement would freeze the U.S. with an overwhelming advantage in strategic bombers, it would certainly present the Russians with serious political difficulties even though they have no known plans to expand their present force. They would probably seek in some way to try to negotiate a reduction in the number of U.S. bombers to reduce this inequality. The U.S. in turn might be quite reluctant to do so and could use the argument that this U.S. advantage was compensated by the large Russian medium-range bomber force. Once this class of aircraft becomes a subject of negotiation, however, the Rus-

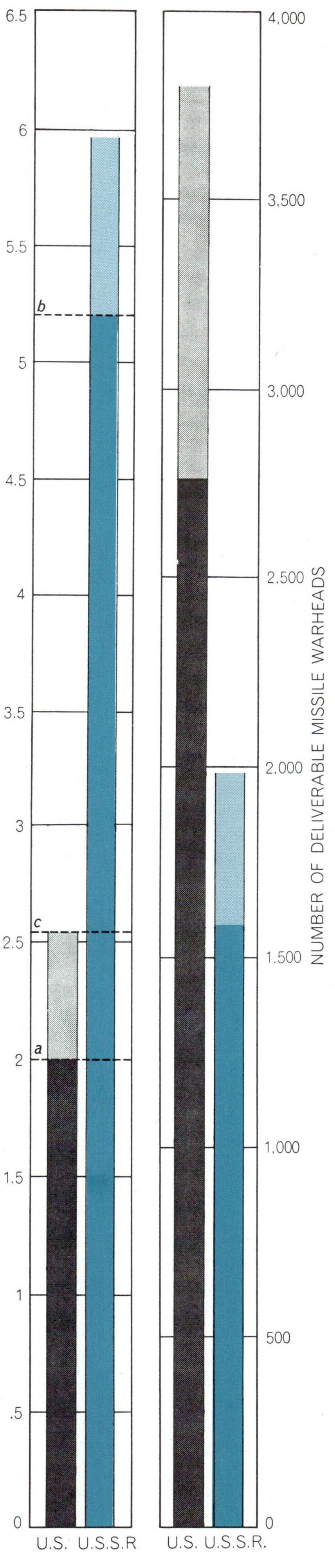

ALTERNATIVE CEILINGS on strategic offensive forces are shown in this pair of bar charts; systems currently under construction are indicated by the lighter gray and lighter colored bars. In terms of deliverable missile payload the Russians have a significant lead (*left*), but this is outweighed by the large U.S. advantage in bomber capacity (*not shown*). In terms of deliverable warheads the U.S. currently has about a 50 percent lead (*right*). An agreed ceiling on payload could require that the U.S.S.R. greatly reduce the size of its missile force (*a*), or that the U.S. greatly expand its force (*b*), or that some combination of these two approaches be put into effect (*c*). A freeze on warheads that put no restrictions on MIRV's would allow the U.S.S.R. to make more effective use of its payload advantage and would eventually enable it to surpass the U.S. in deliverable warheads as well.

sians are likely to press many complicating questions pertaining to U.S. carrier-based and European-based systems. Although the bomber discrepancy is likely to complicate the negotiation, it would probably not be an insuperable obstacle, since for both countries the bomber forces are less critical to the deterrent balance. It should not be forgotten, however, that the largest part of the total nuclear yield that can be delivered by the U.S. on the U.S.S.R. comes from the U.S. bomber force, and the Russians are extremely conscious of that fact. This undoubtedly accounts for their large concentration of effort on antiaircraft defenses even now when the major threat is from missiles.

An additional variation of this approach would be to limit the further deployment of very large missiles such as the SS-9. If the SS-9's could be kept at their present number, the threat to the U.S. Minuteman would be greatly reduced, since extensive MIRVing would be required before the present force could approach a first-strike capability. Certainly as long as the Russians could not deploy more than three MIRV's per missile an important fraction of the Minuteman force could not be threatened. On the other hand, a limitation on Russian SS-9 deployment is not easily balanced by any similar U.S. limitation. This country has no plans for deploying larger ICBM's, and the Russians are not likely to agree to any restrictions on their SS-9's without some parallel restriction on the part of the U.S. The most obvious limitation would be on the further replacement of the Polaris missile with the larger Poseidon missile or the possible eventual deployment of an underwater long-range missile system. Such a proposal, however, is likely to be strongly opposed by the U.S. since the Poseidon system is considered the most critical element in the U.S. deterrent. The ability of this missile to carry more than 10 MIRV's ensures penetration of any ABM system the U.S.S.R. would be able to construct for many years to come. If ABM's were also limited to low levels by the agreement, however, then the U.S. requirement for the Poseidon MIRV's to penetrate a Russian ABM system would be removed. Furthermore, if the SS-9's were limited, the Minuteman missiles could be relied on to supplement the sea-based deterrent. Thus from a strict security point of view the U.S. could afford an agreement that limited SS-9's and Poseidons simultaneously, even taking into account the risks from a possible clandestine ABM program. Nevertheless, there would be strong opposition in the U.S. from those groups that have insisted on the necessity for continued U.S. MIRV testing and deployment. This opposition would have to be overcome, because unless some limitations were imposed to prevent present missiles from being replaced by larger ones the arms race would continue almost unabated and U.S. security would not be improved.

One proposal that has been suggested in order to place some limitations on qualitative improvements on existing strategic systems would be to agree that each nation would be restricted to a total payload that could be delivered on the other nation. Payload, sometimes referred to as throw weight, is here defined as the total useful weight that can be delivered to a target area from a launcher. This can be in the form of nuclear warheads or penetration aids to overcome defenses. For a given missile there will be a tradeoff between range and payload (since the longer the range is, the lower will be the deliverable payload) so that the payload would have to be tied to some nominal range.

Such an agreement would have the advantage of preventing the replacement of existing small missiles with much larger ones. It would not, however, prevent the replacement of single-warhead missiles by MIRV's since this could be done without increasing the payload of existing missiles. In actuality the threat to the U.S. from the SS-9, which has created such concern on the part of Secretary Laird, results from the assumption that MIRV's will replace the existing reentry vehicles without requiring any increase in the total payload.

If the agreement were such that the U.S. and the Russian missile forces were frozen with the existing payloads, the U.S.S.R. would be left with an advantage of about two to one in the missile payload that could be delivered on the U.S. This disparity would be somewhat alleviated if the U.S. were allowed to complete the conversion program for 31 of its Polaris submarines from the present missiles to the larger Poseidon. It is highly unlikely that the U.S.S.R. would agree to the continued buildup on the part of the U.S. without being allowed some concession in return. This could take the form of allowing the U.S.S.R. to complete its present submarine construction program to the point where it approached the Polaris fleet in size, if not in payload capacity. This would involve a very significant addition to the total number of missiles available to the Russian forces, however, and would then provide a disparity in favor of the U.S.S.R. in total number of strategic delivery vehicles. Although none of these inequalities would present serious security problems—in fact, greater emphasis on submarine-based systems improves the reliability of the deterrent—they would certainly present serious political problems in the U.S. or the U.S.S.R. and might therefore be difficult if not impossible to negotiate.

Another alternative might be to allow both nations to have the same total payloads without any restrictions on how this was divided among various missile systems. That, however, would either enable the U.S. to build up unilaterally to the present Russian level by doubling its present payload capacity or require the U.S.S.R. to reduce the size of its forces. Neither of these alternatives appears to be negotiable. If bomber load were included in the total payload for strategic systems, the tables would be turned and the U.S. would have an advantage. Perhaps the simplest solution would be to leave the Russians with their present advantage in missile payload and consider that this was compensated for by the present U.S. advantage in long-range bombers. Such an agreement would not threaten U.S. security even if the U.S.S.R. exploited its missile advantage by MIRVing its larger payload capacity. Provided that ABM defenses were simultaneously controlled at zero or very low levels, the Polaris fleet would by itself be able to provide an adequate deterrent even if the Poseidon conversion was not completed. The large U.S. bomber force would offer an additional safety factor, although this would not be vital.

If the limitation were restricted to payload only without any simultaneous restrictions on the number of delivery vehicles, then each nation would have the option of increasing the total number of its delivery vehicles, provided that it reduced the average payload of each individual vehicle. Such a conversion would not increase the threat and in fact might in some cases add a greater reliability to the deterrent. The more potential launch points and the greater the number of potential retaliatory warheads there are, the greater will be the certainty that the deterrent will not be eroded by a combination first strike and ABM defense. It does, however, mean that there would be few restrictions on the development of new missile systems to replace existing ones. Uncertainty would always be created during these transition periods concerning whether or not the limitation was being abided by.

Therefore a more satisfactory arrangement might be to combine the payload limitation with one on total number. This would tend to freeze present forces at their existing strength and would provide fewer opportunities for misunderstanding. There would certainly be less excuse for a broad expansion of the arms race. In qualitative areas the most serious development that this type of agreement would not control is MIRV's. In fact, the result would probably be a race to develop the most efficient MIRV system within the agreed limitations on payload and number. Whether or not in the face of such a situation it will be possible to maintain a prolonged halt to other parts of the arms race is open to serious question. As mentioned above, it is likely that there would still be strong incentives for replacing existing systems with less vulnerable ones, for example the replacement of fixed land-based Minuteman or SS-11 missiles with sea-based systems or with mobile or superhardened land-based ones.

Finally, one should consider whether or not a limitation on payload can be adequately verified without requiring unacceptably intrusive inspection. Within a given missile silo, either on land or in a submarine, it would be possible to replace an existing missile with one having a somewhat greater payload capacity. This might be accomplished by increasing the energy available from the fuel, by better utilization of the launch-tube volume or by using different techniques for ejecting the missile from the launcher. None of these changes is particularly susceptible to observation by unilateral means, although evidence of wide-scale conversions that might significantly affect security might be difficult to conceal. If replacement of existing systems were allowed for other purposes,

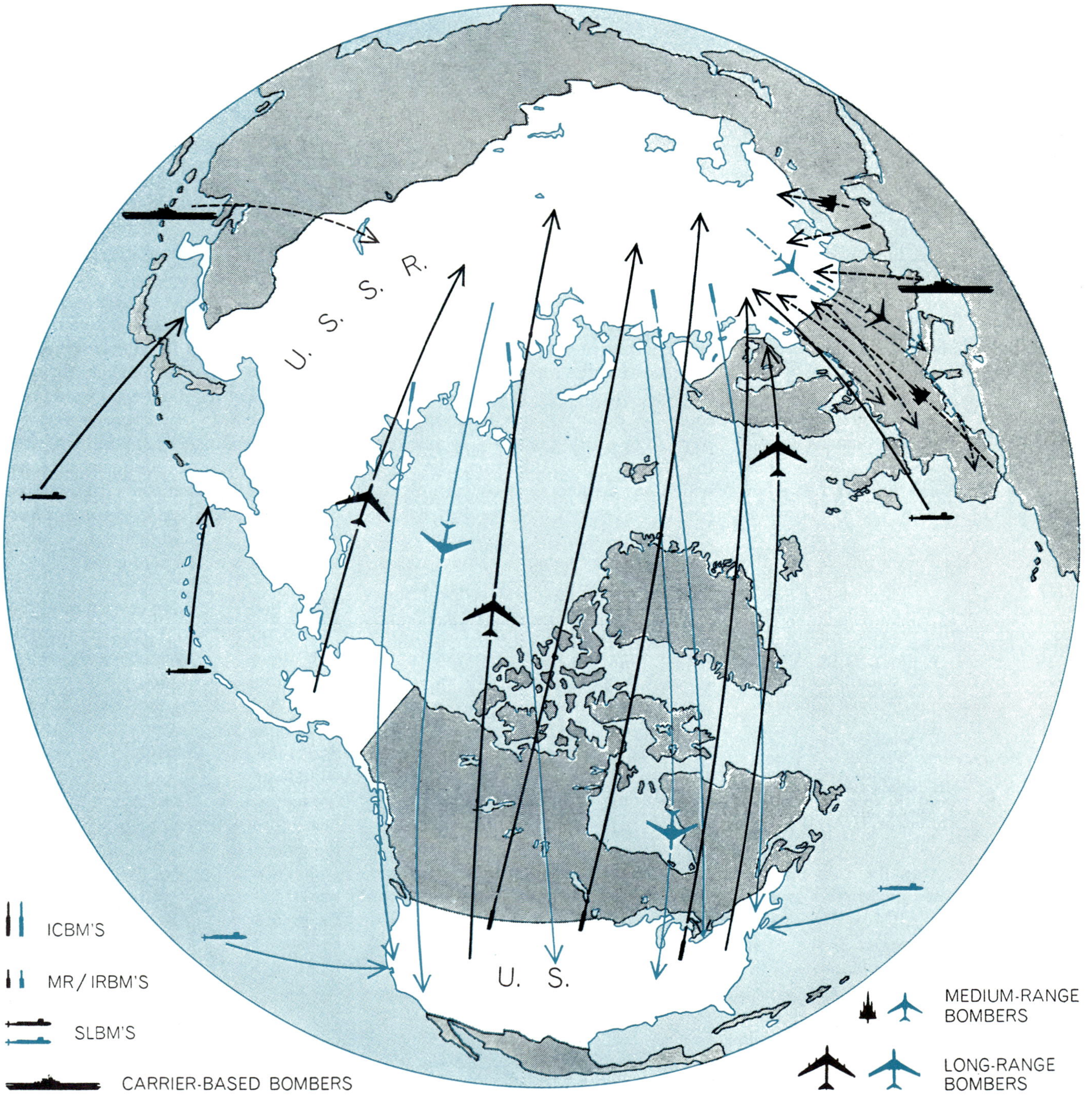

STRATEGIC OFFENSIVE WEAPONS ARE DEFINED for the purpose of this article to include only those long-range nuclear weapons indicated by the solid black and colored arrows on this map. Various other medium-range, intermediate-range and tactical weapons systems, indicated by the broken arrows, are nevertheless available to both sides and could be discussed at SALT.

however, it might be almost impossible to detect those that involved an increase in payload capacity. Thus it would appear that for a deployment ban alone it would at a minimum be necessary to carry out rather extensive on-site inspections if one was to be certain that the agreement was being abided by. This verification problem has also been the major stumbling block in developing controls on MIRV deployment.

As in the case of MIRV's, however, there are opportunities for dealing with the problem by limiting the testing of missiles with larger payloads. At present the U.S. has a reasonably reliable estimate of the payload capacity of the Russian missiles. This has been obtained by observation of test programs over the years and is partially the basis for Secretary Laird's being able to announce that the Russian SS-9 is capable of delivering a payload of 13,500 pounds and a single warhead of 25 megatons on the U.S. Therefore, providing that the Russians did not change their test procedures, it is likely that the U.S. would be able to determine if they tested a new missile with a significantly increased payload.

On the other hand, it is possible that by changing its test procedures the U.S.S.R. could test a missile with a larger payload capacity without U.S. knowledge. Development testing could proceed under conditions where observations from outside the U.S.S.R. might not be able to determine that the payload of the operational system had been increased. Any new missile system on which the Russians intended to rely for a major part of their strategic power, however, would require testing under closely simulated operational conditions, and such tests might be more easily monitored and provide opportunities for detection of an increased payload capability. Such detection would be significantly more difficult than the detection of MRV and MIRV testing; yet the verification problem has been used by some as a justification for on-site inspection in order to control MIRV's. Therefore, if verification considerations are sufficient to prevent the achievement of a MIRV ban, such considerations should also militate against the negotiation of a ban that limited payload capacity.

Another approach to limiting the deployment of strategic arms would be an agreement that froze existing delivery systems at their current status. The levels of the agreed freeze need not be specified since the ban would be directed at changes in the existing balance rather than at limitations to agreed numbers. Ideally the prohibition should be all-inclusive, not only banning the substitution of one launcher by another of a different type but also preventing the replacement of the present missiles and aircraft. This would be most satisfactory from the point of view of security, of halting the arms race and of economic savings. It would, however, present serious problems of verification, since extraordinarily intrusive and almost certainly impractical inspection would be required to ensure that new weapons having some enhanced capabilities were not being substituted for those currently deployed. For example, to detect the deployment of an improved guidance system in a missile would require dismantling the missile and inspecting its interior. Even then one could not be sure that violations were not occurring. An agreement, however, could partially cope with the problem of qualitative improvements by restricting the launchers to those now in existence, by not allowing their replacement by new systems and by restricting any modifications to these launchers and their missiles to those that did not change their external configuration or that of the missiles they contained.

Under such a freeze it would be possible to replace single warheads by MIRV's in existing missiles, since this could be accomplished without any alteration in the external configuration of the launcher or missile; enlarging the missiles to still further improve MIRV capability would be constrained. Some other improvements in the missile systems might be possible, but these would also be restricted by the necessity of keeping the configuration of the launcher and the envelope of the missile unchanged. Since the replacement of old launchers by new ones would not be allowed, wholesale changes in the force structure would be prohibited. Fixed land-based missiles could not be replaced by submarine systems or by mobile ones. This might be considered a disadvantage, since in time such land-based systems would become vulnerable to highly accurate MIRV's, although this would be less likely with a freeze than without one. In any case, as long as ABM systems were simultaneously limited to low levels the deterrent would not be threatened. The U.S. would still have 656 SLBM's, supplemented by a large bomber force, which would be more than enough to produce unacceptable damage to the U.S.S.R. in a retaliatory strike. Since it is not possible to destroy either the bomber or the Minuteman forces without providing advance warning to the other, the combination of these two forces would still provide deterrence even if they were individually vulnerable. Pressures for new strategic systems could probably be contained. The conversion of the Polaris to the Poseidon would, however, be halted at the point it had reached at the time the agreement went into effect. The halt in submarine construction might be a more serious problem for the Russians, since their SLBM program lags considerably behind that of the U.S.

Such a freeze would leave both nations with a secure deterrent force (provided that ABM systems were simultaneously controlled). Furthermore, at the present time both nations have an approximate parity in overall force strengths in spite of inequalities within individual systems. Thus such an agreement should be politically acceptable to both sides. Any changes that would be allowed under the agreement or carried out clandestinely could not upset the present strategic balance.

From the point of view of controlling the arms race this proposal would be the most far-reaching. There would be greatly reduced opportunities or incentives for replacing existing missile systems with new ones. Although MIRV's would be allowed, the replacement of the fixed land-based system by a mobile or a sea-based one would be precluded, and there would be few incentives for increasing the payload capacity of the existing missiles within the agreed limitations. Such an agreement would therefore also be by far the most effective in terms of economic savings.

Verification of a freeze of this nature would also be relatively easy. New deployments of missile launchers or long-range aircraft are comparatively easy to observe by unilateral means, and since any change in visible characteristics would be banned, it would be relatively easy to determine if a violation had occurred. To determine a violation it would not be necessary to present evidence on the total number of deployed systems but only that a change had occurred from the situation that existed at the time the agreement went into effect. This would avoid the extensive disclosure of unilateral information available on the programs of the other side and would greatly simplify making a case for a violation before the world. Furthermore, sources of misunderstanding and confusion would be much reduced. Since no new missile-site construction would be allowed, there would be no question of whether a given activity was an allowed replacement or not. The only possible source of confusion would be in connection with the external configuration of the missiles themselves. Once the missile was emplaced within the hole, it would be very difficult to determine whether or not it had the same external configuration as an older missile. There would, however, always be some risk of detection of such replacement during the emplacement phase; evidence that a new missile was available for this purpose could be obtained during testing. Furthermore, since the dimensions of the launcher would be kept constant, the opportunities and incentives for significant cheating would be kept to a minimum. Thus old Russian missiles could not be replaced by SS-9's. In sum, it would appear that such a freeze could be adequately verified without fears that security was being eroded.

None of the foregoing proposals for limiting the deployment of offensive strategic weapons provides any limitations on the deployment of MIRV's. The proposals for limiting payload or banning changes in the external configuration of missiles or launchers would still allow replacement of single warheads with MIRV's, although they would provide some limitations on the number of MIRV's that could be associated with any one missile, since the number is dependent on the payload available and the external configuration of the missile. The proposed Poseidon missile, however, is planned to carry 10 or more MIRV's, each one admittedly of low yield (although still several times greater than the Hiroshima bomb). The SS-9, which is much larger than the Poseidon, could be adapted to hold at least 10 MIRV's.

Analyses of the foregoing proposals also show that the most destabilizing element would in all cases be the ability to obtain a MIRV capability. MIRV's threaten the viability of the fixed land-based missile component of the strategic force and provide pressures for the development and deployment of new systems. A Russian MIRV capability presents a much greater potential threat to the U.S. than vice versa because of the greater payload of the Russian missiles. Therefore it should be an extremely important U.S. objective to see that MIRV's are controlled. The problems of MIRV's have been discussed in detail elsewhere [see "The Limitation of Strategic Arms," by G. W. Rathjens and G. B. Kistiakowsky, the article beginning on page 201]. Heretofore the major problem facing the U.S. in this connection has been fears that a MIRV ban could not be adequately verified. Clearly this is true for deployment of previously tested systems, since this would require at a minimum extremely extensive and probably impractical inspection. Nonetheless, it would take the Russians at least a year and probably several years before they could have a tested, deployable MIRV system that could threaten the Minutemen. Hence this provides an opportunity to extend the ban to include testing. Although there are differences of opinion on the adequacy of unilateral verification techniques, such techniques would certainly be much more satisfactory for verifying a ban on the testing of MRV's and MIRV's than they would be for verifying a limitation on total missile payload. A strong case can be made that it is technologically possible to verify a MIRV test ban adequately by unilateral means in order to protect U.S. security without on-site inspections. These means should clearly provide greater confidence against significant violations than would the on-site inspections that have been proposed for the detection of clandestine deployment of MIRV's, since it is not clear how any procedure could provide confidence that

POSSIBLE SALT AGREEMENT	EFFECT ON U.S. SECURITY	ECONOMIC SAVINGS FOR U.S.	EFFECT ON ARMS RACE	NEGOTIABILITY
1 CEILING ON NUMBERS OF DELIVERY VEHICLES				
a NO LIMITATION ON REPLACEMENT	LITTLE, IF ANY, IMPROVEMENT	NONE (MIGHT INCREASE MILITARY EXPENDITURES)	LITTLE, IF ANY (MIGHT ACCELERATE)	VERY EASY (VERIFICATION COMPLICATED)
b SEPARATE CEILINGS ON MISSILES AND BOMBERS	SLIGHTLY BETTER THAN 1a	LITTLE, IF ANY	SLIGHTLY BETTER THAN 1a	EASY (VERIFICATION COMPLICATED)
c LIMITATION ON LARGE ICBM'S	SOME IMPROVEMENT	LITTLE, IF ANY	BETTER THAN 1b BUT LIMITS ONLY ONE SYSTEM	HARD (UNLESS U.S. IS ALSO WILLING TO HALT POSEIDON)
2 FREEZE ON DEPLOYED PAYLOAD	NO IMPROVEMENT (FREEZES U.S. INFERIORITY)	SOME	GOOD BUT DOES NOT HALT MIRV'S	HARD (VERIFICATION HARD)
3 FREEZE ON DELIVERY VEHICLES				
a NO REPLACEMENT	SIGNIFICANT IMPROVEMENT	VERY LARGE	EXCELLENT	POSSIBLE (VERIFICATION MARGINAL)
b NO CHANGE IN EXTERNAL CHARACTERISTICS	SIGNIFICANT IMPROVEMENT (LESS THAN 3a)	LARGE (LESS THAN 3a)	VERY GOOD	EASIER THAN 3a (VERIFICATION EASY)
4 LIMITATION ON MIRV'S				
a BAN ON DEPLOYMENT	IMPROVEMENT	SIGNIFICANT	VERY GOOD	HARD (VERIFICATION ALMOST IMPOSSIBLE)
b BAN ON PRODUCTION TESTING AND DEPLOYMENT	GREAT IMPROVEMENT	SIGNIFICANT	VERY GOOD	EASIER THAN 4a (VERIFICATION POSSIBLE)

VARIOUS APPROACHES to a strategic-arms-limitation agreement are evaluated in this table in very general terms. The best agreement possible under the present circumstances would appear to be one in which the strategic forces of both sides would be frozen at their existing levels, ABM systems would be banned and further production, testing and deployment of MIRV's would be halted.

a single warhead was not substituted for a deployed MIRV warhead before the inspectors visited the launching site.

As time has passed, another obstacle has arisen to the success of achieving a MIRV limitation. The U.S. has now completed more than two years of testing on its first-generation MIRV system for the Minuteman III and Poseidon missiles. Beginning in June, 1970, the deployment of Minuteman III with MIRV's was begun at an operational site in North Dakota. Eight Polaris submarines are now in the yards being modified to fire the Poseidon missile, and the first of these will be going to sea in January, 1971. Even if the U.S. were willing to stop this program and actually withdraw these MIRV missiles from the inventory, it would seem highly unlikely that the Russians would be willing to accept an agreement that would leave them so far behind the U.S. in this particularly critical strategic area. Past experience has clearly shown that the Russians are unwilling to negotiate from a position of significant inferiority. They steadfastly refused to seriously discuss strategic-arms limitations until they had approached general parity with the U.S. Therefore there should be no optimism that it will be possible to reach an agreement on MIRV's until the Russian program is considerably more advanced. The clock on the U.S. development cannot be turned back. Unfortunately when the Russians have a capability equivalent to the present U.S. one, an agreement will still be extremely hard to achieve, since then they would be able to deploy an already tested system and the verification problems would be greatly compounded. Hence the U.S. should make an urgent, all-out effort to attempt to persuade the U.S.S.R. to accept a MIRV limitation at this time. Otherwise U.S. security could in the long run be reduced and the arms race would continue, while scarce funds would be expended on more advanced weapons systems. An agreement to ban the production, testing and deployment of MIRV's would be in the mutual interest of both sides; the U.S. could still verify such a ban in the testing phase and the Russians in the production and deployment phases.

Although it is not the purpose of this article to discuss limitations on ABM systems, it is clear in analyzing the various alternative methods of limiting offensive systems that their adequacy is strongly dependent on whether or not ABM systems are limited at the same time. In fact, ABM limitations would be desirable even if no controls could be placed on offensive weapons. Without controls on such defenses, fears could develop that an ABM system might be deployed that could successfully handle those residual offensive weapons that might survive a first strike. If this came to pass, the deterrent would be threatened. Thus without controls on ABM systems, and particularly without also having controls on MIRV's, strong pressures will exist for the deployment of new offensive systems that will be less vulnerable to a first strike: mobile land-based missiles and more SLBM's. There will also be increased pressures to deploy more MIRV's on the existing systems, particularly on the SLBM's. These would not be needed if ABM defenses were also limited to low levels.

From the point of view of arms control, a complete ban on ABM systems would be most satisfactory, but if these were limited to defense of capitals, then they should not require an escalation of the offensive-arms race. Whereas the present Moscow ABM system might be politically justifiable by the U.S.S.R., in view of its existence and in view of that city's role as the center of the Russian nation, it is harder to justify the large U.S. expenditure of funds for a future defense of Washington, which does not occupy the same position in American minds. Security considerations allow the U.S. to leave the Moscow ABM system as it is and to forgo the Washington ABM system and perhaps extract some parallel concession from the Russians in another area. If ABM defenses were limited to defense of Minuteman sites, they should, like capital defenses, not be destabilizing, since these would not provide significant protection of U.S. urban centers. Unfortunately the same would not be the case for a parallel Russian ICBM defense, because their ICBM deployment is relatively close to urban centers; hence such a system could provide nationwide coverage and could be viewed as a potential threat to the U.S. deterrent. If either nation built a thin area defense to handle even a small Chinese threat, this too would be destabilizing and militate against U.S.-U.S.S.R. controls on offensive weapons, since it could be viewed as being expandable into a system that could cope with a limited second-strike capability.

In summary, it appears that the ideal method of limiting offensive strategic weapons would be to freeze currently deployed forces at present levels and types of weapons. This would maintain the present security that exists in a stable strategic balance; it would have the greatest damping effect on the arms race, and it would provide the largest economic savings. On the other hand, such an agreement would present numerous problems of verification, since many qualitative improvements cannot be detected without very intrusive inspection.

The most immediately practical method of controlling offensive weapons would involve a freeze on existing systems, a ban on the construction of new launchers and a restriction on any changes in deployed systems to those that do not change their external characteristics. Such an agreement would provide some valuable limitations on qualitative improvements and would be adequately verifiable by unilateral means.

A limitation that restricted both the number of weapons and the payload they could deliver would also provide some useful restriction on qualitative improvements but would present certain verification problems. It might also prove difficult to find a mutually satisfactory negotiating formula for such a concept in view of the present large Russian lead in missile payload and the U.S. lead in bomber payload.

An agreement that limited strategic weapons to specific numbers without any restrictions on replacement or substitution would do little if anything to halt the arms race and in fact might provide strong incentives for accelerating it along new directions. Placing additional limitations on specific types of weapons might overcome some of these defects, but it would be difficult to achieve an arrangement that would satisfy both the security and the political requirements of both nations. Furthermore, this type of agreement would provide opportunities for misunderstandings concerning whether or not it was being abided by.

Although limitations on MIRV's may now be increasingly difficult to achieve both because of problems of verification and because of the present U.S. technological lead, the risks they present to the strategic balance and to almost any long-term arms-limitation agreement make it important that no opportunities be overlooked to attempt to reach some limitation on these weapons. The risks from no limitation would seem to far outweigh the risks from possible undetected violations of a ban on MIRV production, testing and deployment.

Finally, a prerequisite to any useful long-term limitation on offensive forces requires a simultaneous ban on ABM systems or at least a limitation that precludes rapid expansion to provide nationwide coverage.

Reconnaisance and Arms Control

Reconnaissance satellites are the chief means relied on by the U.S. and the U.S.S.R. to verify each other's compliance with the SALT I accords. What bearing will they and related systems have on SALT II?

TED GREENWOOD

February 1973

The two major arms-control agreements signed last May in Moscow as a result of the first round of the strategic-arms-limitation talks (SALT I) between the U.S. and the U.S.S.R. both incorporate sections designed to deal with the problem of verification. For example, Article XII of the treaty on the limitation of anti-ballistic-missile (ABM) systems states: "1. For the purpose of providing assurance of compliance with the provisions of this Treaty, each Party shall use national technical means of verification at its disposal.... 2. Each Party undertakes not to interfere with the national technical means of verification of the other Party.... 3. Each Party undertakes not to use deliberate concealment measures which impede verification by national technical means of compliance with the provisions of this Treaty...." Article V of the SALT I interim agreement "on certain measures with respect to the limitation of strategic offensive arms" uses virtually identical language to make the same three points.

What are the "national technical means of verification" mentioned in these documents? How are these systems now being used by each side to unilaterally monitor the other side's compliance or noncompliance with the SALT I accords? What bearing does this mutual capability have on further arms-control agreements, in particular on those that might emerge from the current SALT II negotiations?

In attempting to answer such questions this article will of necessity focus primarily on the subject of observation satellites, since the main restrictions imposed by both of the SALT I agreements can be, and undoubtedly are being, monitored largely by means of sensors carried on board such orbiting photoreconnaissance systems. The primary SALT I restrictions limit each side's ABM missile launchers to 200 at two widely separated sites, impose numerical ceilings on both land-based intercontinental ballistic missiles (ICBM's) and submarine-launched ballistic missiles (SLBM's), regulate the replacement of old ICBM's and SLBM's with new SLBM's and prohibit the exchange of old ICBM's or light ICBM's for heavy ICBM's.

In addition the ABM treaty bans the testing of new types of ABM systems or of other systems or components "in an ABM mode." The monitoring of activities of this type involves not only observation satellites but also other methods specifically suited for the surveillance of missile launchings. Hence systems such as advanced land-based radars, early-warning satellites and shipboard tracking sensors are the second major concern of this article. Such systems are of particular importance to any discussion of the prospect that SALT II will result in meaningful qualitative restrictions of strategic offensive missiles.

In spite of the official secrecy that almost completely hides from public view the observation-satellite programs of both the U.S. and the U.S.S.R., it is possible to make some general observations about the theoretical capabilities of such systems and about their actual performance. For example, it is known that because of the fundamental electromagnetic properties of the earth's atmosphere, satellite-borne sensors are restricted to three spectral "windows": the visible-light wavelengths, a broad infrared band centered on a wavelength of eight microns and certain radar wavelengths. Over the years, as larger booster rockets have made it possible to put heavier instrument packages into orbit, there has been an increase in the number of different sensors and in their resolution and film capacity. At the same time the associated communications systems have also become more sophisticated and their data-transmission rate has increased.

The most useful measure of the quality of an airplane or satellite photoreconnaissance system is ground resolution, a value that is equivalent to the smallest object that can be distinguished on the ground with good contrast. For a camera pointing vertically downward the expression for ground resolution, G, is given by the equation $G = A/300\,FR$, where A is the altitude of the airplane or the satellite in feet, F is the focal length of the camera in feet, R is the joint resolution of the film and optics in lines per millimeter and 300 is a numerical constant characteristic of the units used for the other quantities.

To cite a recent example of space photography, the panoramic camera built by the Itek Corporation for the last three Apollo missions to the moon had a focal length of two feet and photographed the lunar surface from an altitude of approximately 60 miles. The resulting photographs had a ground resolution of about three feet [*see illustration, pages 232 and 233*]. These numbers, inserted in the equation given above, suggest an optical resolution for the system of better than 180 lines per millimeter.

By way of comparison, it has been reported unofficially that the high-resolution cameras used in the newest generation of observation satellites have a focal length of more than eight feet. Taking eight feet as the focal length and 180 lines per millimeter as the optical resolution, one can calculate that the ground resolution of such a system from a nominal altitude of, say, 100 miles would be 1.2 feet. Actually there is reason to believe that the resolution of the most advanced systems now in service may be even better; as early as 1960 experts in the field were talking about prospective U.S. Air Force cameras with focal lengths on the order of 20 feet. Furthermore, films with a resolution considerably better than 180 lines per millimeter are currently available. A compromise must be made, however, between film resolution and film speed, and rather fast film is needed for satellite photography.

Another factor that must be taken into consideration is the aperture of the camera's optics. Diffraction effects place an upper limit on the optical resolution of any lens system (a limit never attainable in practice). The limit is given by the ratio $.82d/\lambda F$, where d is the aperture in feet and λ is the wavelength in millimeters of the radiation to which the system is sensitive. For a camera with a focal length of eight feet an aperture of one foot would result in a diffraction-limited resolution of 180 lines per millimeter, assuming that one is working with visible light at a wavelength of .55 micrometer.

In practice a much larger aperture would be employed in order to ensure that the optical system is not limited by diffraction. Therefore a camera with a focal length of eight feet and an aperture of three feet would (assuming that it uses film with a resolution of 180 lines per millimeter) provide a ground resolution of 1.6 feet from an altitude of 100 miles. With the same film a camera having a focal length of 20 feet and an aperture of five feet would yield a ground resolution of .7 foot. To achieve a ground resolution of .5 foot the same camera would require film with a resolution of about 330 lines per millimeter.

These simple calculations are based on the assumption that the overall resolution of the system is poorer than the poorest contributing factor, which may be either the diffraction-limited resolution of the optics or the line resolution of the film. Moreover, the results do not take into account various operational degradations, nor do they involve the intrinsic limitation on ground resolution presented by the scattering of light in the atmosphere. The latter limitation amounts to a few inches for an altitude of 100 miles. Nonetheless, it seems clear that the latest U.S. photoreconnaissance satellites are close to achieving resolutions that are limited only by atmospheric effects.

Ground resolution is not the only relevant measure of picture quality. It characterizes an image only at the threshold of what can be barely distinguished. The color and light contrast of the objects being photographed strongly affect their distinguishability. The angle of the sun and the intrinsic reflectivity of an object are also important, since these factors influence the object's apparent brightness. In general the task of identifying an object in a photograph is always more difficult than simply locating it. On the other hand, extended objects such as roads or rail lines can often be distinguished even though their dimensions

RUSSIAN MULTIPLE-WARHEAD TEST was photographed from a U.S. Air Force plane in the vicinity of the projected impact point somewhere in the Pacific Ocean. The three separate reentry vehicles, which were launched by a single SS-9 missile from the Russian missile-testing center at Tyuratam, east of the Aral Sea, are equipped with protective head shields that glow as the vehicles reenter the atmosphere. As a result the vehicles (which for tests of this type bear dummy nuclear warheads) are visible as bright dots in the photograph. The three fainter streaks at lower left were made by fragments of the booster rocket burning up on reentry into the atmosphere. U.S. radars routinely monitor Russian missile tests near both ends of their trajectory, after which specially equipped aircraft and vessels are dispatched to make such photographs. This picture was released by the Department of Defense in 1971.

may be far below the calculated ground resolution.

Two different techniques are currently employed by the U.S. to retrieve photoreconnaissance information from space. The first is to return the film itself for processing on the ground. This method preserves all the information that is recorded on the film and is therefore employed for very-high-resolution photographs. The exposed film is ejected from the satellite and is returned to the earth in a special reentry package, which is caught in midair by specially equipped aircraft as it floats by parachute through the latter part of its descent [*see illustration on page 228*].

For lower-resolution pictures the film can be developed on the satellite and scanned by a television camera or a laser system. This information is temporarily stored and then transmitted to the earth when the satellite passes over one of several ground and shipboard stations around the world. Clearly in order to transmit all the necessary information during the short time in which the satellite is in view of these stations a communications system with a high data-transmission rate is needed.

Once a film pack is returned to the earth it must be developed to maximum advantage and then interpreted. The transmitted pictures must also be recreated and then interpreted. With a ground resolution measured in inches or feet and with a film resolution measured in the hundreds of lines per millimeter, it is clear that by the time enlargements of the photographs are made many man-hours must be expended to interpret them. Indeed, photographic interpretation must be a very large enterprise today both in the U.S. and in the U.S.S.R. It is also no wonder that systems are used to make photographs at less than maximum resolution in order to identify interesting targets for further photography at higher resolution.

In addition to visible-light cameras infrared sensors are used in reconnaissance satellites. Since all bodies at terrestrial temperatures radiate energy that is predominantly in the infrared part of the spectrum, infrared photography is not dependent on the sun for illumination. It is therefore useful for night applications or in polar regions. (Low-light systems have been developed and may also be in service for these purposes.) Perhaps the greatest significance of infrared sensors is their ability to detect things (such as missile silos) that are underground or may be camouflaged. As long as the ground immediately around the object is at a different temperature or has emission characteristics different from those of the surrounding terrain, an underground silo will stand out in an infrared picture. For this reason multispectral photography, a technique for making pictures simultaneously at several wavelengths, is increasingly employed in observation satellites. Although longer-wavelength infrared photography would require much larger optics to achieve resolutions comparable to those attainable with visible-light systems, such high resolution is probably not needed to accomplish the tasks assigned to the infrared sensors.

One of the major obstacles for satellite reconnaissance is, of course, cloud cover. Certain locations, for example the location of Moscow, are rarely free of clouds. The coordination of observation-satellite launchings with information received from weather satellites can overcome this problem to some extent. Moreover, observation satellites currently in service probably have the capability of changing their orbit to take advantage of breaks in the cloud cover.

Observation satellites contribute to the verification of the SALT agreements in a variety of ways. By photographing missile test sites they help to identify new missile systems, to detect changes in operational procedure that may suggest a change in hardware and to monitor testing programs. They can watch industrial facilities, including shipyards for the construction of submarines and plants for the assembly of missiles. Intermittent information on critical aspects of transportation networks can be obtained. The progress of construction of missile silos, ABM radars or ABM launcher sites can be monitored. Wide-area surveys can be made to determine if any activity is underway that violates the agreements.

Although the possibility of artificial earth satellites and their potential for military reconnaissance were recognized immediately after World War II, not until the mid-1950's was the future availability of rocket boosters assured and a satellite program actually initiated. On March 16, 1955, under the sponsorship of the Central Intelligence Agency, the U.S. Air Force issued a formal operational requirement for a strategic satellite system. After a year-long competition the Air Force selected the Lockheed Aircraft Corporation to develop a self-powered satellite vehicle, later named the Agena. This vehicle (along with several later models) was for many years the workhorse of the U.S. observation-satellite program.

The U.S. did not wait for the availability of satellites, however, before beginning a strategic-reconnaissance program. By 1956 U-2 reconnaissance aircraft were making their first flights over the U.S.S.R. Their photographic information supplemented the radar data on Russian missile tests, provided the basis for the gradual downgrading of estimates of the size of the Russian bomber force and eventually convinced most informed observers that the Russian ICBM buildup was proceeding at a much slower pace than had been anticipated. In spite of the considerable usefulness of the U-2 flights, the aircraft had two weaknesses as a sensor platform. First, the limited range of the plane, the endurance of the pilot and the provocative nature of the mission imposed a severe limitation on the area of the U.S.S.R. that could be photographed. As a result of this limitation the lack of U-2 evidence for large numbers of deployed Russian ICBM's was not conclusive proof that only a few existed. Not until reconnaissance satellites had provided much greater coverage of the landmass of the U.S.S.R. could the U.S. intelligence community be certain that missiles had not been deployed and remained undetected. The second weakness of the airplane was its vulnerability. Eventually the Russians developed an antiaircraft missile that could hit the U-2 at 70,000 feet. When Francis Gary Powers was shot down in May, 1960, the U-2 overflights ended, except for certain minor incursions. Satellites, on the other hand, were known to be invulnerable, and would remain so for the then foreseeable future.

Among the many technical problems that had to be solved in order to develop an operational reconnaissance satellite were the stabilization and orientation of the spacecraft, the design and production of light cameras with a long focal length and a large aperture, and the recovery of the data. The possibility of using a television camera was considered very early but was rejected because the desired resolution was not attainable with available technology. In 1957 the decision was made to pursue two parallel approaches: first, direct recovery of a film package, and second, on-board developing and scanning of film followed by radio transmission to ground stations. Techniques for direct recovery were developed using Discoverer satellites as test vehicles. The first successful reentry package was recovered from *Discoverer*

13 on August 11, 1960. Either this package or the one recovered from *Discoverer 14* the following week probably yielded the first satellite photographs of the U.S.S.R. That was just three months after the last U-2 overflight of the U.S.S.R. The first successful radio-transmission observation satellite was *Samos II,* which was put in a polar orbit varying in altitude between 300 and 350 miles on January 31, 1961; this spacecraft carried between 300 and 400 pounds of instruments.

These early successes almost certainly were responsible for the final laying to rest of the myth of the "missile gap." On February 6, 1961, Secretary of Defense Robert S. McNamara told reporters at an informal, off-the-record briefing that a study had yielded no evidence of such a gap. A White House spokesman denied the report, saying that the studies were not yet complete. Intelligence sources, however, soon began to reduce their estimates of the number of Russian missiles. By September, 1961, after the successful recovery of additional Discoverer capsules and with time to analyze the *Samos II* data, the number of deployed Russian ICBM's was reportedly put at 14.

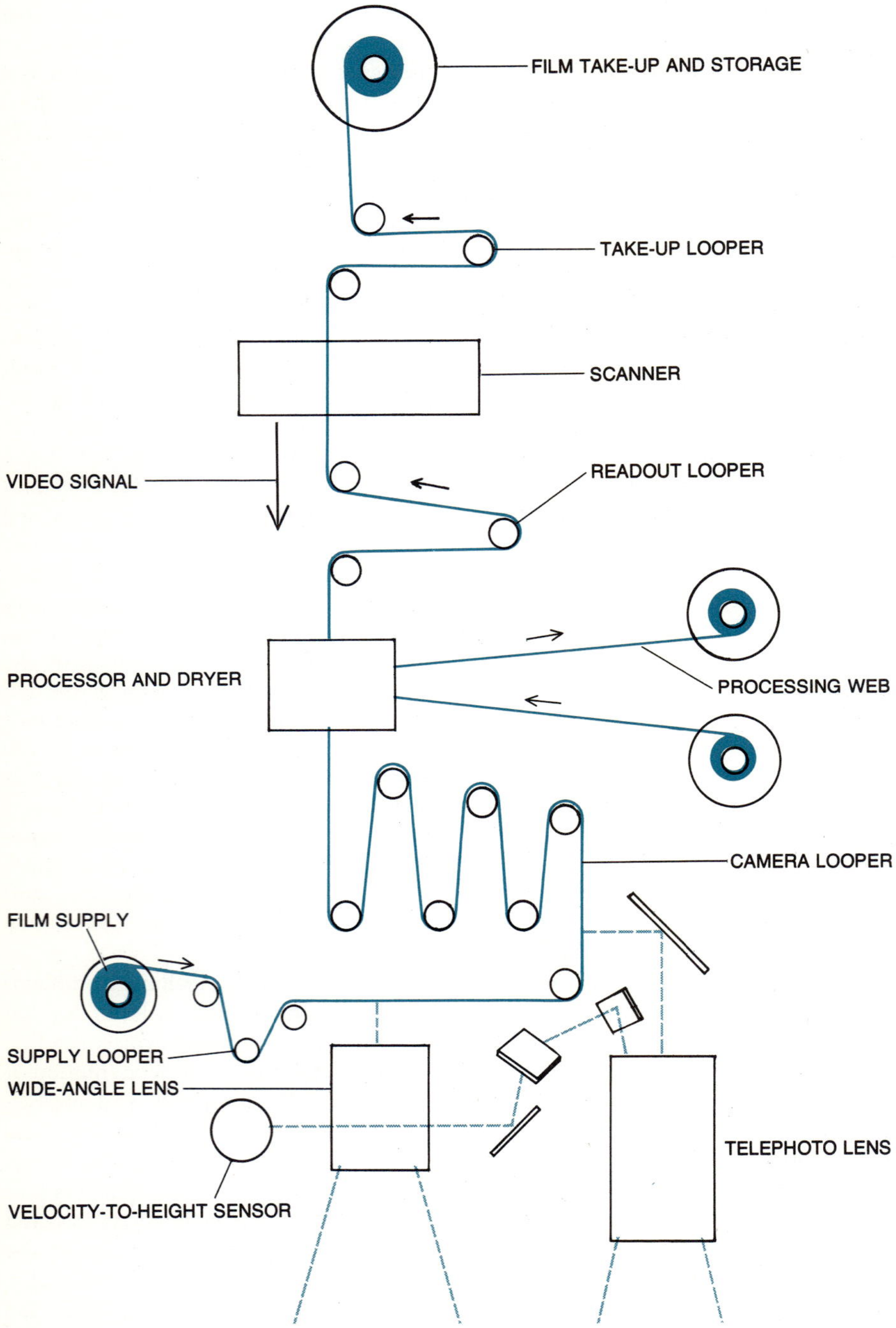

AREA-SURVEILLANCE SYSTEM similar to the system used in the early U.S. Samos reconnaissance satellites is represented here by a schematic diagram of the interior mechanism of a Lunar Orbiter, the spacecraft used to make a photographic survey of the surface of the moon preparatory to selecting the Apollo landing sites. In both systems the film is exposed and developed by the optical and film-processing elements of the camera subsystem; the developed photographs are then scanned by a television camera, converting the picture into electrical signals for radio transmission back to earth. Cameras for both Lunar Orbiter and Samos were built by the Eastman Kodak Company; film scanners for both spacecraft were built by CBS Laboratories, a division of the Columbia Broadcasting System.

The descendants of the early Samos satellites have been comparatively small radio-transmission observation satellites whose sensors and orbital characteristics are chosen to maximize their degree of coverage. They stay in orbit for three to four weeks. Although their perigee (lowest orbital point) is about 100 miles above the earth's surface, the ellipticity of their orbit greatly reduces their atmospheric drag, thereby increasing their lifetime. With an inclination of 80 to 92 degrees with respect to the Equator, they provide virtually full coverage of the U.S.S.R. and complete coverage of China. These "area surveillance" satellites provide low-resolution coverage of wide regions, and the radio transmission of data makes possible the rapid recovery of intelligence information. Particular areas of interest are identified on the basis of this information and higher-resolution pictures are later made by another satellite with a recoverable film capsule. By early 1962 the size and weight of the camera system had been reduced sufficiently to allow the area-surveillance satellites to be launched by the Thor/Agena booster rather than by the more powerful Atlas/Agena booster used earlier.

The use of the Thrust-Augmented-Thor/Agena D, beginning in May, 1963, indicates that a new generation of satellites was then introduced. The greater throw weight of this booster rocket enabled the satellite to carry a larger camera and more of a consumable payload (including film), resulting in an increase in useful lifetime. These satellites were launched at roughly one-month intervals beginning in the middle of 1963. Until the end of 1965, however, two or more area-surveillance satellites were frequently in orbit at the same time, and occasional delays in the regular launch schedule can be identified. This suggests that problems of reliability necessitated the replacement of satellites that had failed before the completion of their mission and also that problems had sometimes occurred at ground level. Since 1966 one of these satellites has been in orbit for almost half the days of

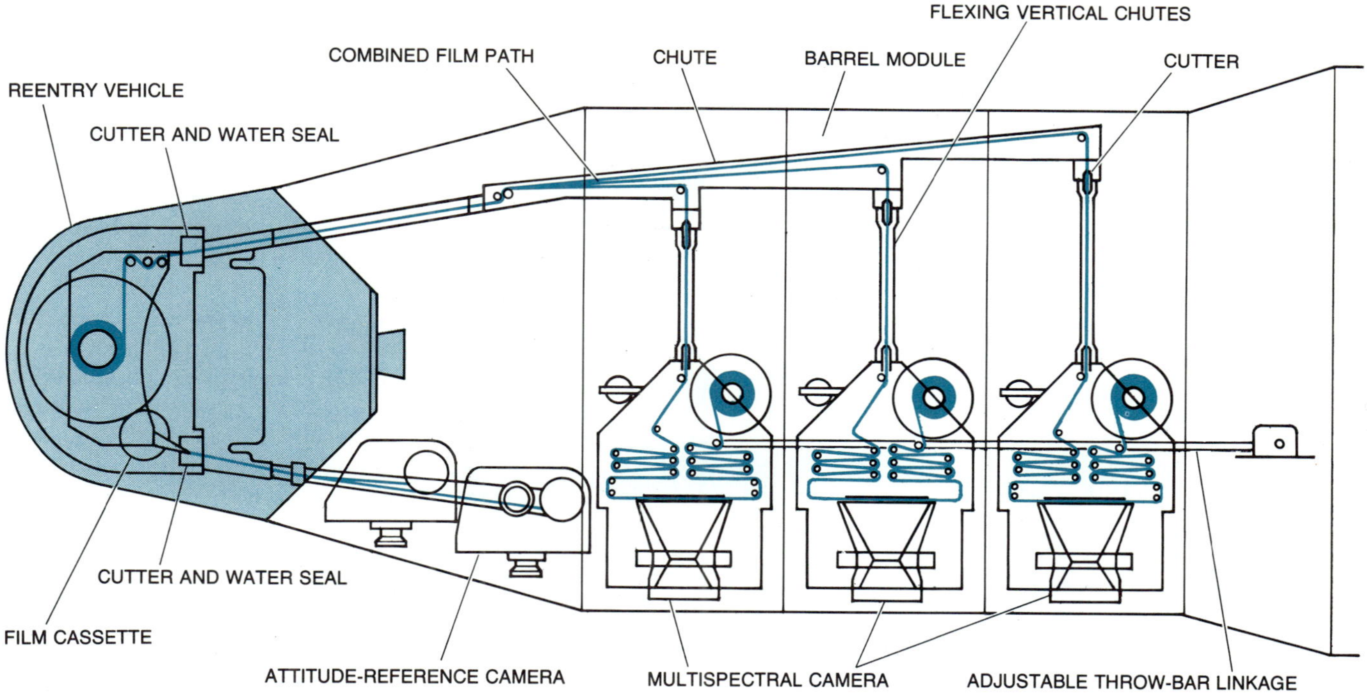

CLOSE-LOOK SYSTEM similar to the system used in the U.S. second-generation Discoverer reconnaissance satellites is represented here by a schematic diagram of the interior mechanism of a proposed nonmilitary satellite. The scheme shown was submitted by the General Electric Company to the National Aeronautics and Space Administration in 1969 for possible use in NASA's earth-resources survey program. In both systems exposed film is fed from several cameras into a recoverable capsule, which is ejected from the satellite and returned to earth for processing. Since this method preserves all the information on the film, it is preferable for high-resolution photography. The recoverable-film system for the Discoverer reconnaissance satellites was produced by General Electric.

the year, and there has been hardly any overlap. One can therefore probably fix the beginning of 1966 as the date of a fully operational status for the area-surveillance satellites.

The first test launch employing the even more powerful Long-Tank-Thrust-Augmented-Thor/Agena was in August, 1966, and that booster was introduced into regular service in May, 1967. The use of this booster also marks the arrival of a heavier, third-generation satellite. It was probably equipped with a camera of longer focal length, a larger film supply, an infrared optical system and a new transmission system with an increased data rate.

The task of these satellites has been to survey wide areas with sensors of moderate resolution and to reveal targets that merit a closer look at higher resolution. In order to provide that closer look, a different type of satellite is used.

The descendants of the Discoverer recoverable-capsule satellites are the close-look satellites. They are heavier than the area-surveillance satellites, reflecting the fact that they carry a camera with a longer focal length and a wider aperture. They are also in a lower orbit, with a perigee of typically about 80 miles, in order to maximize resolution. With this more powerful telescopic system interesting targets identified by an earlier area-surveillance satellite can be rephotographed and examined more closely. To minimize information losses introduced by electronic data storage and transmission, the close-look satellites send their film packs back to the earth in a reentry capsule for midair recovery by aircraft.

The first launching of a close-look satellite appears to have been on April 26, 1962, when a Thor/Agena booster put into orbit a satellite carrying a recovery capsule designated *E*-6. Three days later the capsule and its film were recovered. Judging from the frequency of launchings, this program seems to have achieved operational status by the middle of 1963. With their shorter lifetime in orbit, the close-look satellites had less stringent reliability requirements than the area-surveillance models and were therefore able to reach full operational status more quickly. By 1964 the Atlas/Agena had been introduced as the program's booster, ensuring that heavier satellites with improved capabilities could be placed in orbit. These second-generation high-resolution satellites were launched about once a month and remained in orbit for three to five days before sending their film package back to the earth.

The Titan 3B began to be used for test launches in July, 1966, and came into regular service in August, 1967. With the introduction of this still larger booster the lifetime of the close-look satellites began to increase until by 1968 they remained in orbit for a period averaging some two weeks. This clearly shows that a third-generation satellite had been introduced with a much greater film capacity and the ability to raise its orbit in order to avoid early burnup. It has been suggested that the new satellite could alter its orbit to take advantage of breaks in cloud cover; moreover, it seems likely that several new types of sensor were included in the satellites. Infrared sensors and multispectral photography appear to be the most likely candidates because of their ability to discover and penetrate camouflage and, in the case of the infrared sensors, to operate in the dark. An accurate mapping camera for the purpose of pinpointing the location of strategic targets in the U.S.S.R. may also have been included.

In the past 18 months or so an entirely new fourth generation of observation satellites has been introduced and is now reaching operational status. This satellite, unofficially called Big Bird, weighs more than 20,000 pounds, which makes it much heavier than any previous observation satellite. The spacecraft itself is a modified Agena rocket 10 feet in diameter and 50 feet long. It is launched by the powerful Titan 3D booster.

The extra weight and size of this sys-

MIDAIR RECOVERY of a film capsule from a Discoverer-type reconnaissance satellite is accomplished by means of specially equipped aircraft as the capsule floats by parachute through the latter part of its descent. This photograph, released by the Air Force in 1961, shows a C-119 transport aircraft "as it approaches a Discoverer capsule... somewhere over the Pacific Ocean." At present larger C-130 aircraft are used routinely to recover the much heavier film capsules dropped by the latest-model close-look reconnaissance satellites.

tem result from joining the separate functions of area-surveillance and close-look photography into the one satellite. Big Bird is reported to carry an area-surveillance camera made by the Eastman Kodak Company and an on-board film processor and scanner. The resulting data are reportedly transmitted by means of a new 20-foot unfurlable antenna, which would represent an increase in capacity by a factor of 16 over the older five-foot antennas. In the past, several months would go by before a close-look satellite could be launched to rephotograph an area of interest identified by a low-resolution photograph and its film pack could be recovered. Now, however, Big Bird can be directed to turn on its high-resolution camera (made by the Perkin-Elmer Corporation) during a subsequent pass. Film from this camera, said to have a resolution of less than one foot from an altitude of 100 miles, is returned in one of several recovery capsules. The delay time should now be cut to several weeks.

This dual capability requires that Big Bird remain aloft for a much longer period than earlier close-look satellites. In order to accomplish this result the satellite is placed in a higher and more elliptical orbit. The orbital characteristics of the first Big Bird, launched on June 15, 1971, were a perigee of 111 miles and an apogee of 180 miles. To compensate for this higher altitude and to improve resolution both the focal length and the aperture of the high-power camera had to be increased over those of earlier models. To further increase the satellite's lifetime it has been equipped with an on-board rocket to raise its orbit and prevent early burnup. The times in orbit for the first three satellites were respectively 52 days, 40 days and 68 days. The fourth launching was on October 10, 1972.

Certainly since 1962, and probably earlier, the U.S. has had detailed information on the number and location of Russian strategic missiles. In 1967 President Johnson told a meeting of educators in Tennessee that satellite reconnaissance was worth 10 times the money the U.S. had spent in space. "I know how many missiles the enemy has," Johnson said. He suggested that this knowledge had prevented the country from harboring fears that otherwise might have arisen. From the late 1960's to the present the Department of Defense has regularly published information on the level of Russian ICBM, SLBM and ABM deployment. Both Congress and the public have come to expect such information as part of the Department's budget justification, and in recent years both the Administration and its critics have used the published figures to support their own arguments.

The major task assigned by SALT I to these now protected "national technical means of verification" is to monitor the quantitative limits imposed on the number of ABM launchers, large radars, ICBM's and SLBM's. This is the arms-control task for which observation satellites are best suited. From satellite photographs intelligence analysts are able to monitor silo construction and the transport of missiles to their deployment sites. With multispectral and infrared photography they can detect or penetrate camouflage and monitor nighttime activity. Submarine shipyards are observed on a routine basis to monitor new construction. Similarly, ABM launchers and radar deployments can be observed. There seems to be no doubt that these aspects of the SALT I agreements can be verified by satellite reconnaissance with a high degree of confidence, as long as the Russians live up to their pledge "not to use deliberate concealment measures which impede verification by national technical means."

The more important question, however, is whether or not the Russians could find ways clandestinely to circumvent the restrictions and thereby achieve a military or political advantage over the U.S. Although the actual deployment of prohibited weaponry secretly seems quite impossible, could the Russians simply manufacture additional missiles or radars and then abrogate the treaty at a time of their own choosing and deploy them on a time scale too short for a U.S. response? A full discussion of this problem would have to include an assessment of the internal pressures that might lead the U.S.S.R. to such actions, the possible international political repercussions and an analysis of what the Russians would have to do that would make any difference either militarily or politically.

Although such considerations lie outside this discussion, one can still go part of the way toward dealing with the problem. The continuous monitoring of Russian transportation networks, power-generation plants and manufacturing facilities by observation satellites would make it unlikely that the U.S. could not detect such clandestine activity in time to react in some way. The decrease in delay time provided by Big Bird between the first indication of suspicious activity in an area-surveillance photograph and further photography with a high-resolution camera will certainly reduce the uncertainties involved. Although photography cannot penetrate buildings, infrared and multispectral techniques can often reveal a great deal about activities inside, particularly since activities of special interest may be indicated by changes in standard operating procedures.

Cloud cover remains an impediment to observational activities, but with longer orbital lifetimes and the capability of changing orbit the newer satellites are less constrained than their predecessors. For the clarification of ambiguities both the unilateral techniques of electronic and communications intelligence and the bilateral apparatus of the Standing Consultative Commission (also set up by the SALT I agreements) may be useful. To summarize, the very size and complexity of construction and industrial activity required to build and deploy modern strategic weapons, combined with the breadth of coverage, resolution and multispectral aspects of observation satellites, guarantee that the agreements of SALT I can be verified unilaterally with high confidence. The cost of hardware and manpower for photointerpretation, however, will remain high.

If a future agreement were to impose qualitative restrictions on strategic systems, the U.S. would have to rely on other verification techniques to augment the observation satellites. The usefulness in this regard of systems that monitor missile tests will be considered below. Observation satellites would also, however, have a role to play in monitoring such agreements. Any qualitative improvement in missile weaponry, whether it is new guidance systems, multiple warheads, improved ABM radar, new SLBM's or advanced ICBM's, must be reflected in changes from former manufacturing and testing procedures and equipment. Any new hardware must be delivered to an operational site and

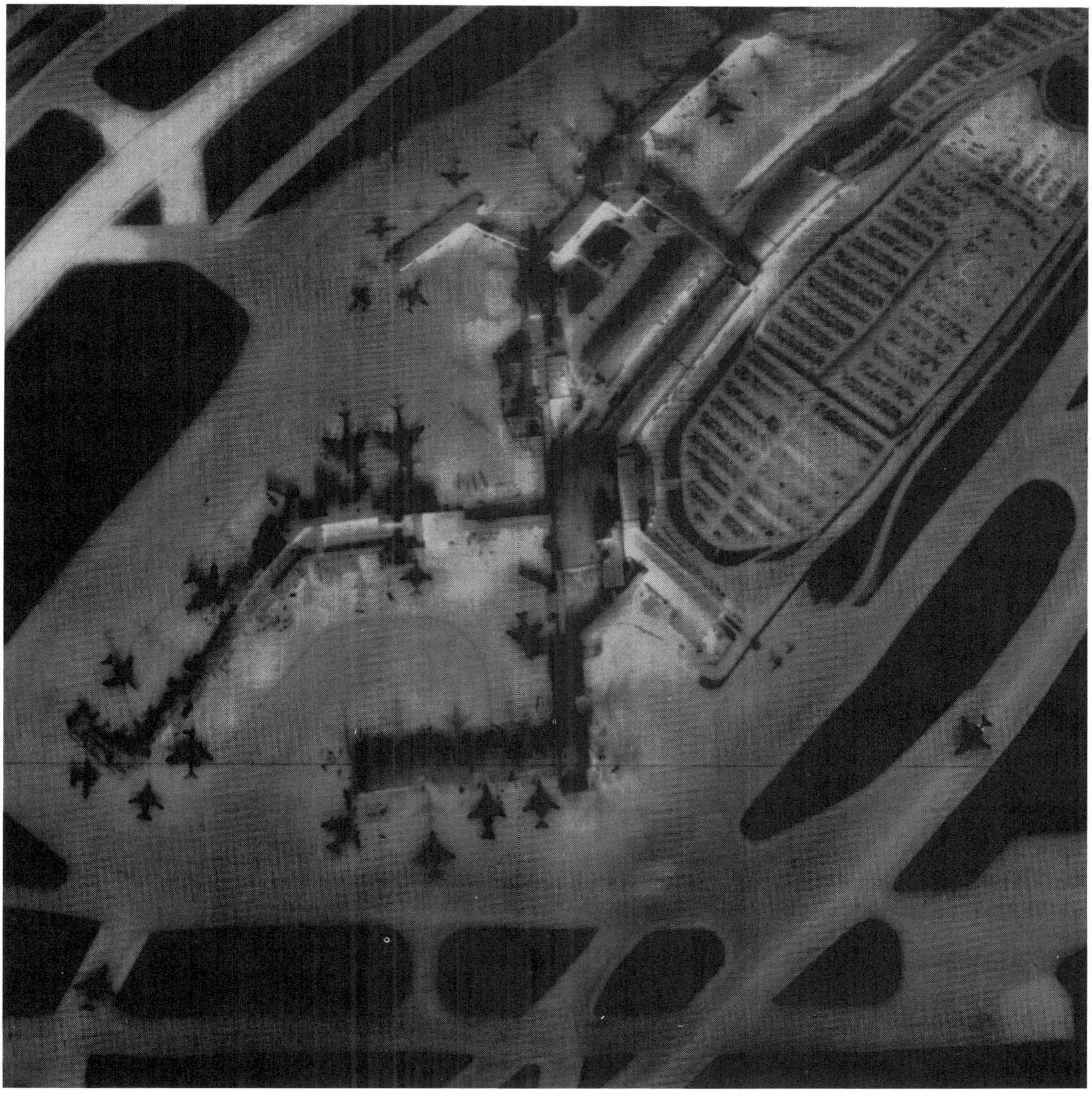

INFRARED PHOTOGRAPH of an airport in Texas was made from an aircraft flying at an altitude of 2,000 feet. Since infrared photography is not dependent on the sun for illumination, it is used in reconnaissance satellites for night applications or in polar regions. The ability of infrared sensors to detect the heat from missile exhausts is suggested by the bright images of the jet exhausts from the aircraft on the runway at lower right. This unusual unclassified photograph was supplied by Texas Instruments Incorporated.

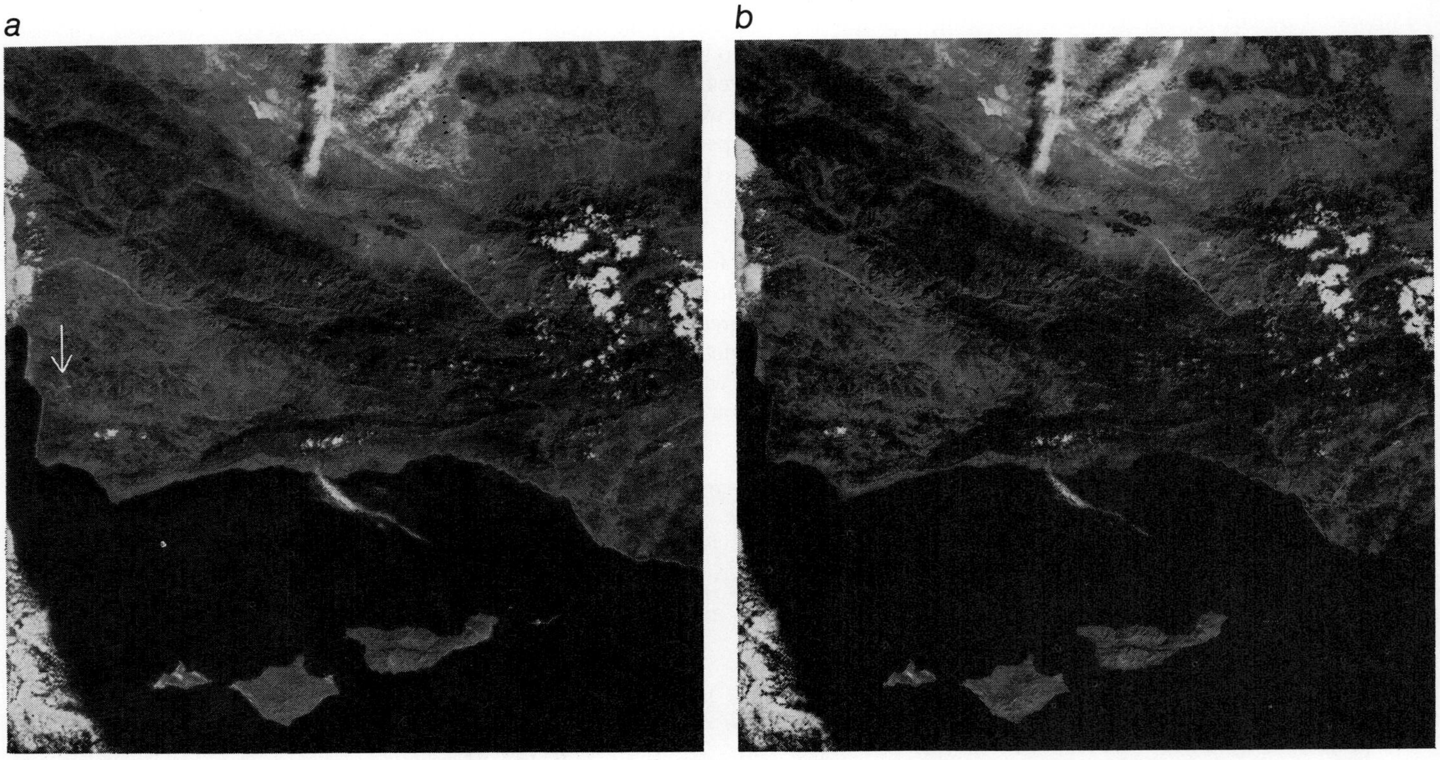

MULTISPECTRAL PHOTOGRAPHY, a technique for making pictures simultaneously at several wavelengths, is increasingly employed in reconnaissance satellites. The four sample photographs shown on these two pages were made by a multispectral scanner on board NASA's Earth Resources Technology Satellite; the line-scanning device employed in this case uses an oscillating mirror to simultaneously record the terrain passing under the spacecraft in four spectral bands: .5 to .6 micrometer (*a*), .6 to .7 micrometer (*b*), .7 to .8 micrometer (*c*) and .8 micrometer to 1.1 micrometers (*d*). The electronic signals produced by this television system are

installed. These activities can be monitored by satellites.

The surveillance systems that would be useful in the verification of an agreement imposing qualitative restrictions on ballistic missiles include certain land-based line-of-sight radars, over-the-horizon radars, satellite systems and particularly shipboard sensors for terminal observations. As early as the summer of 1955 a U.S. radar at Samsun in Turkey was tracking missile tests from the Russian launch site at Kapustin Yar, northwest of the Caspian Sea. As a result of this monitoring the launching of *Sputnik I* in October, 1957, and the Russian ICBM tests of the same year came as no surprise to the U.S. intelligence community and Government officials with access to such data. They were well aware of the Russian capabilities in this area. By late 1963 or early 1964 a longer-range radar had been installed in Diyarbakir in Turkey, bringing into view missiles launched from the newer Russian test center at Tyuratam, east of the Aral Sea.

Several fixed land-based radars are also available to observe Russian tests near the end of their flights. One of these has been operational on Shemya Island, far out in the Aleutian chain, since at least 1959. This radar can track and provide data on the Russian reentry vehicles that impact either in the test area on Kamchatka Peninsula or in the North Pacific area northwest of the Midway Islands. For the longer-range tests that end in the Pacific southwest of Johnston Island several radars that have been installed for other purposes at the Midway Islands, Bikini Atoll, Kwajalein Atoll and Johnston Island can be employed.

Unlike conventional radar, over-the-horizon, or OTH, radar is not restricted in its range by the curvature of the earth. By reflection from the ionosphere OTH radar can penetrate to great distances, making possible the detection of missiles soon after they are launched. The currently deployed "forward scatter" OTH radar detects the disturbances in the ionosphere caused by the ionized jet of gas emanating from a rocket's motor. Since each type of missile disturbs the ionosphere somewhat differently, a detected missile can be identified by its characteristic OTH signature. In the currently operational system three transmitters are deployed in Taiwan, Japan and the Philippines. These transmitters are matched with corresponding receivers in Italy, Germany and another European country. Although the system was originally intended as an early-warning system for a massive missile attack, it has detected a high percentage of the known single events since 1968. All long-range missiles fired from test sites in the U.S.S.R. are detectable.

Parallel to the observation-satellite developments of the late 1950's and early 1960's there was an expensive and unsuccessful program to develop a satellite early-warning system. For years this program was plagued by unreliabilities in its hardware and by the inability of its infrared sensors to distinguish between rocket-exhaust plumes and sunlight reflected from high clouds. By 1963 an interim capability had been achieved, but not until recently did a high-confidence system exist. The first two operational vehicles of the satellite early-warning network were launched on May 5, 1971, and were placed in near-synchronous orbits over the Indian Ocean at about 65 degrees east longitude. Their orbits have a 10-degree inclination to provide more northern coverage than a truly synchronous orbit would allow. A slight ellipticity of orbit increases the time they spend over the Northern Hemisphere. Two satellites are required to provide continuous coverage. Although the primary mission of these satellites and others deployed at different longitudes is to provide early warning of an ICBM attack, they are of interest here because they also provide a capability to monitor Russian missile tests.

Both the OTH radars and the early-warning satellites can be used to help verify the testing restrictions included in

c

d

then transmitted back to the earth, where they are converted to black-and-white images. The latter in turn can be used to make color composites by registering the images sequentially on color film through the appropriate filters. These particular photographs are shown here only to help illustrate the multispectral technique; their ground resolution (roughly 200 feet from an altitude of 569 miles) in no way compares with the ground resolution obtainable with the current generation of close-look reconnaissance satellites (roughly one foot from an altitude of 100 miles). The region viewed in the photographs includes Vandenberg Air Force Base (*arrow*).

the SALT I ABM treaty. Beyond that they can be used in conjunction with land-based line-of-sight radars to indicate when and where missile tests are taking place and to provide some information about the type of test. These systems would therefore be used to monitor any agreement that imposed numerical or geographical restrictions on missile-testing. As long as a missile test is within view of a line-of-sight radar its point of ballistic impact can be determined. Some characteristics of the reentry vehicle, such as its size and shape, can also be determined from radar observation. The precision of such determinations would depend on the detailed characteristics of both the radar and the reentry vehicle.

The most useful observations for monitoring long-range missile tests are those made from ships and aircraft in the region of impact of the reentry vehicle. From terminal radar and photographic observations detailed information about the reentry system can be derived. If one compares the calculated impact point with the observed impact point and knows the local weather conditions at the point of impact, one can make estimates of the mode of reentry through the atmosphere. For example, one can estimate whether the reentry vehicle has been designed to glide past its ballistic-impact point or to fall short of it. From the close-range radar pictures of the reentry vehicle and its observed speed of passage through the atmosphere, estimates can be made of its weight and ballistic coefficient (a constant that represents the efficiency of the reentry vehicle in overcoming air resistance). If a powered terminal maneuver is attempted, observing radar and infrared sensors should be able to detect it. Multiple-warhead tests can be easily detected near the impact site, if they are not detected earlier by other techniques.

With all this information readily available to observers near the impact area, it is not surprising that such observations have been made for many years. Since 1961 U.S. ships have monitored Russian missile shots into the Pacific. These observations not only have allowed the intelligence community to keep abreast of qualitative improvements in Russian missile technology but also have provided data on the radar "signatures" of Russian missiles, supplying an important input for the design of ABM radars. The sophistication of current capabilities was demonstrated on April 23, 1970, when a set of photographs of a Russian multiple-warhead test was released to the press by the Department of Defense. It was reported that after shipboard radar had detected the incoming reentry vehicles, aircraft and vessels were dispatched to make the photographs.

The verification of any qualitative restrictions on ICBM's that might emerge from SALT II would rely chiefly on these land-based line-of-sight radars, OTH systems, early-warning satellites and shipboard sensors. An examination of their possibilities and limitations is important to any realistic assessment of what may be possible and desirable in SALT II.

One approach that has been suggested in order to inhibit qualitative improvements in offensive missiles is to restrict the number of missile tests that each side is allowed each year. It is argued that if the restricted number were small enough, the competition between the testing of existing hardware and the development of new hardware would eliminate most or all new developments. Putting aside the questions of uncertainties and asymmetries to which such a limitation might give rise, one can say with high confidence that the limitation itself could be verified. Counting missile firings is just what the early-warning satellites, OTH radar and fixed land-based radars do best. If the purpose of such an agreement is to restrain qualitative improvements, however, a useful extension would be to insist that all sanctioned tests be conducted along designated flight corridors and at preannounced times. Such an extension would

RECENT EXAMPLE of high-resolution space photography is provided by this photograph of a strip of the lunar surface made from the *Apollo 15* command ship after the lunar landing module containing the two Apollo astronauts had already landed on the moon. A panoramic camera with a focal length of two feet, built by the Itek Corporation, was used to photograph the lunar surface from a

facilitate the task of ensuring that qualitative improvements have not been made in spite of the numerical limitations.

Where qualitative restrictions themselves are concerned the verification problem becomes much more difficult. The far-reaching development restrictions built into the ABM treaty, however, may be cause for encouragement. In general a prohibition against new types of boosters, front-end configurations or reentry vehicles could probably be verified with high confidence, particularly if it were imposed on top of the previously suggested restrictions. Since the various identifying signatures of current systems are either well known or will become so with time, any new hardware would be distinguishable by an unrecognized signature. Such an across-the-board standstill might be very useful and perhaps even feasible if both the U.S. and the U.S.S.R. could reconcile themselves to accepting certain technical asymmetries.

Other less restrictive prohibitions can also be considered. For example, since terminal maneuvering can probably be detected, either directly with infrared and radar sensors or indirectly by comparing the calculated and the observed trajectories, such maneuvering might be prohibitable. A prohibition of this type would automatically rule out terminal guidance, which would serve no purpose without corrective terminal maneuvering.

Another possibility, although it would be more difficult to verify, would be to restrict improvements in accuracy. Although an observer can tell where a reentry vehicle lands and probably can tell whether the vehicle went through deliberate terminal maneuvers or exploited an aerodynamic shape in order to arrive at its target, he cannot tell from his own observations alone where it was supposed to land. Therefore information on missile accuracy must come from second-order inference. One way to estimate the accuracy of the guidance systems, but not the reentry techniques, is to monitor the apparent accuracy of the inertial guidance on space missions. Presumably the technology available for space shots is also available for ICBM's. The U.S. has a very capable worldwide network of radars in the Space Detection and Tracking System, and these systems can be used for making such inferences. Nonetheless, trying to limit accuracy by constraining inertial-guidance systems does not seem to be a fruitful approach. Instead, prohibitions against giving reentry vehicles terminal-maneuvering capabilities and high ballistic coefficients might be used to indirectly inhibit improvements in accuracy.

Another concern for the SALT II agenda is multiple-warhead tests. The presence of several warheads can be detected by terminal radar, shipboard radar and possibly by other systems. Could a multiple-warhead system be tested with only one warhead at a time, however, thereby avoiding detection? The full answer must depend on both the detailed structure of the hardware and the confidence required in such a system. A partial answer can be formulated by recognizing that in a world characterized by mutual deterrence the major concern of each side is that the opponent not achieve a capability that can be used for a preemptive, counterforce attack. It seems unlikely that such a capability could be developed and brought to a status of high reliability without a large number of full-system tests. There is a problem, however, in translating the likelihood that the U.S.S.R. could not create such a high-confidence system while it was constrained by an arms-control treaty into a certainty on the part of the U.S. that such a system has not been developed.

In this connection the distinction between MRV's (multiple reentry vehicles) and MIRV's (multiple independently targetable reentry vehicles) may be quite inconsequential, depending on the nature of the systems. For a small separation of the reentry vehicles, systems with either mechanical separation or independent guidance could be conceived. To distinguish one such system from another would be difficult and of little value. For a wide separation, however, independent guidance would be required in order to prevent a degradation of accuracy. Presumably a system that can produce wide separation could also be programmed for small separation and could perhaps be tested without being recognized for what it was. In general it seems very difficult to impose verifiable restrictions on multiple-warhead systems except by a total prohibition or a freezing of present systems.

This article has been concerned with national technical means of verification because these are the techniques mentioned in and protected under the SALT I accords. The conclusion should not be drawn, however, that such technical means of verification are the only means available. Other national (or unilateral, as opposed to on-site, or cooperative) verification techniques include economic analysis, diplomacy, content analysis of documents and speeches, interviewing travelers and participants in scientific meetings, and espionage. Although the utility of these information sources cannot be denied, they do have the disadvantage of relying on inference. Reconnaissance and surveillance, on the other hand, are dependent primarily on the physical properties of electromagnetic sensors and therefore provide less ambiguous information and broader coverage than other techniques.

This discussion cannot even claim to have exhausted the national technical means of verification. Specifically omitted because of the lack of sufficient unrestricted information have been the ships, the aircraft, the satellites and the

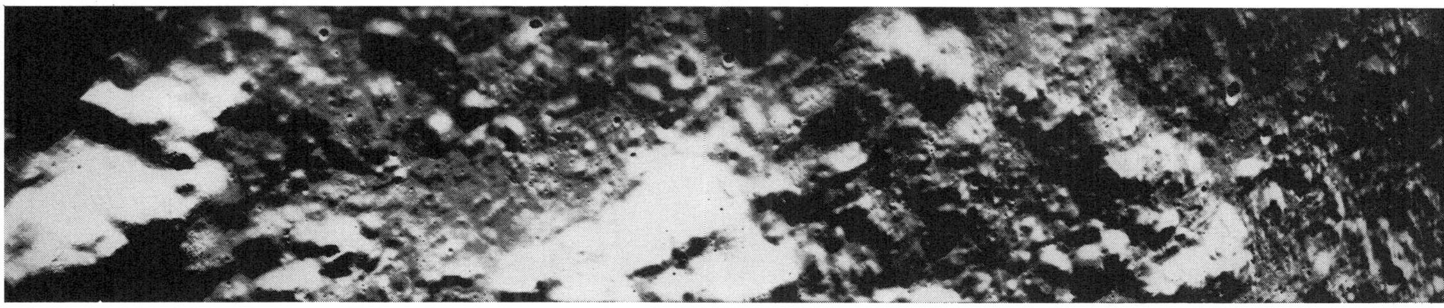

height of about 60 miles. The reproduction of the complete strip photograph shown here is approximately a third of the size of the original film. The original has a ground resolution of about three feet, suggesting an optical resolution for the system of better than 180 lines per millimeter of film. The *Apollo 15* landing site is within the small white square at lower center (*see illustration at bottom*).

land-based receivers used for electronic and communications intelligence. The information gathered by these devices, such as radar transmission frequencies and the nature of Russian and Chinese communications networks, may be of greater relevance to military planning than to the verification of the SALT agreements. To the extent that communications can be intercepted and decoded, however, the intelligence community may be able to go beyond its assessment of technical capabilities to clues about political intention.

The major conclusion that can be drawn from the analysis presented here is that the U.S. can, with its observation satellites and missile-test-surveillance systems, verify Russian observance of the SALT I ABM treaty and interim agreement with high confidence. Although the focus of this article has been exclusively on the U.S. capability, the Russians have comparable observation-satellite systems that they also can rely on to verify U.S. compliance. The mutual benefits of verifying each other's activities by national technical means have now been formally recognized in the noninterference and nonconcealment stipulations of the current agreements.

The conclusion of verifiability is not dependent, however, on Russian cooperation in nonconcealment. Although it is much easier to monitor a cooperative target nation, the possibility of cheating on an arms-control agreement must not be ruled out. In fact, the purpose of reconnaissance systems is precisely to detect or deter such cheating.

The next major arms-control negotiations, SALT II, are now under way. There is a widespread hope that in this round of talks the interim SALT I agreement can be transformed into permanent numerical limitations on offensive systems. The verification of such an agreement presents the same issues as SALT I has and could also be accomplished with high confidence by observation satellites and missile-surveillance systems. Even a prohibition of land-mobile systems could probably be verified, although a nonzero numerical limitation might be very difficult to monitor because of the intermittent nature of satellite reconnaissance.

The hope has also been expressed that SALT II may be able to restrain the qualitative arms race in offensive missiles. In this connection there may be a rather attractive package of verifiable restrictions, including a blanket prohibition against the testing of new ICBM boosters and new reentry systems. Since each type of booster or reentry system has a set of unique signatures, the introduction of new hardware could be detected. Such a prohibition would best be accompanied by a numerical limit on the number of tests allowed each year and by a requirement that all allowed tests be both preannounced and along prearranged flight corridors. The first limitation would reduce the opportunities for cheating and increase the incentives for compliance, since the testing of new hardware could only be done if the opportunity to test existing hardware were given up. The second restriction would make the task of verifying the prohibition against new hardware easier. Both restrictions could themselves be verified, since with current surveillance systems no unauthorized test could be conducted clandestinely.

BLOWUP of the *Apollo 15* landing site made from the panoramic strip shown at the top of these two pages clearly reveals the lunar landing module (*dead center*). The resolution of this reproduction, made from third-generation negatives, is considerably poorer, of course, than that of the original, in which the individual experiments set out by the astronauts can be distinguished. In other photographs made with this system the tracks of the "lunar rover" used by the astronauts are also visible. Even so, the intrinsic optical resolution of the system is still much poorer than that of the most advanced satellite-reconnaissance cameras, which are probably close to achieving resolutions that are limited only by atmospheric effects.

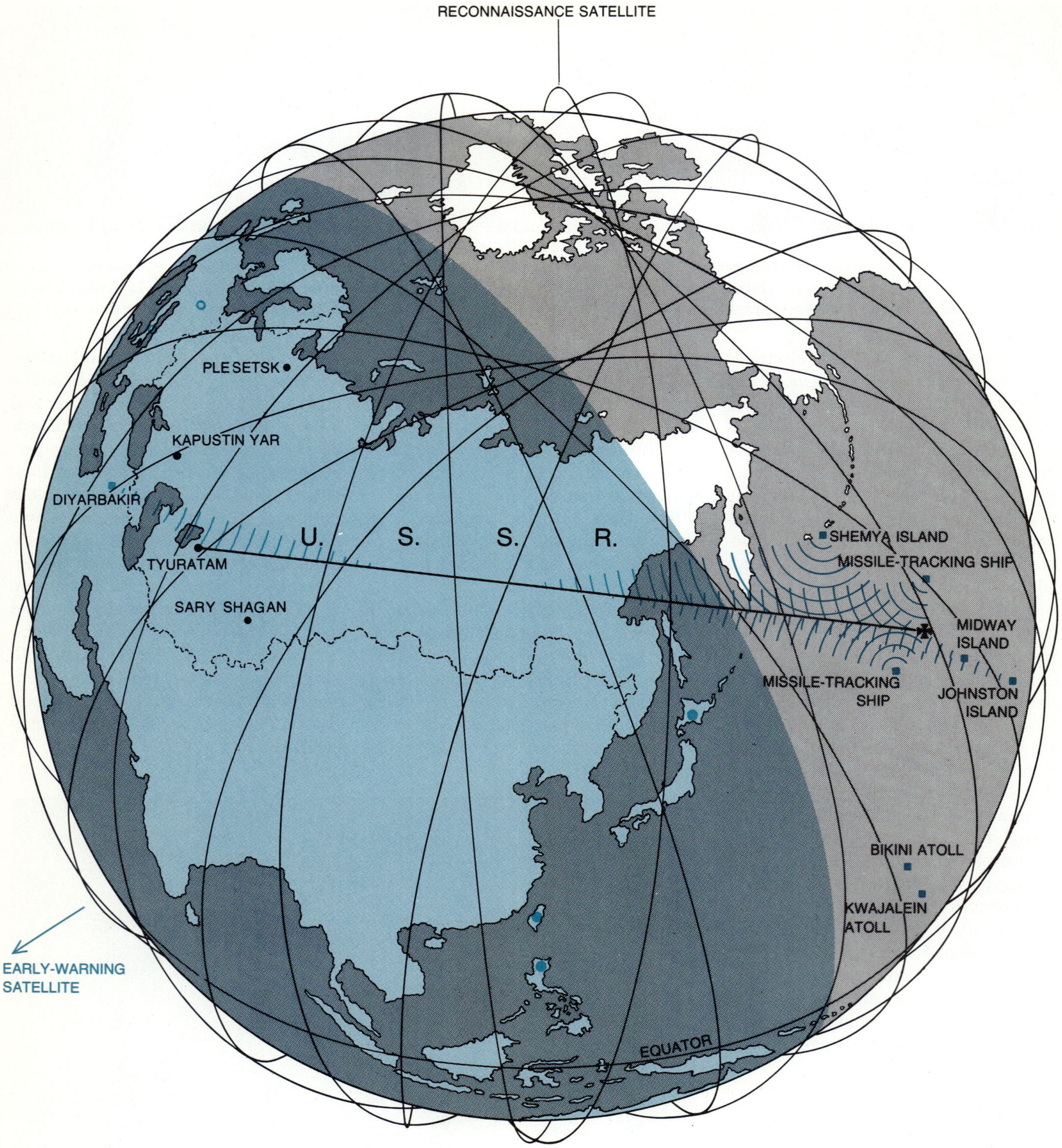

RECONNAISSANCE AND SURVEILLANCE SYSTEMS currently used by the U.S. to verify Russian compliance with the terms of the SALT I agreements are represented schematically in this illustration. U.S. photoreconnaissance satellites are typically launched (from Vandenberg Air Force Base in California) into a near-polar elliptical orbit with an orbital period of approximately 90 minutes and a perigee (lowest point) on the order of 100 miles. The latest, fourth-generation U.S. observation satellite, unofficially called Big Bird, combines the separate functions of area-surveillance photography and close-look photography and hence is required to stay aloft for a much longer period than earlier close-look satellites; orbital times to date have averaged about seven weeks. The orbit of such a satellite remains essentially fixed in space while the earth rotates, with the result that to an earth-based observer the satellite appears to move westward on each successive orbit. Hence most of the earth's surface passes under the orbital path of the satellite. U.S. early-warning satellites, in contrast, are typically launched into near-equatorial, near-synchronous "parking" orbits at altitudes of about 22,300 miles. Two such satellites, launched into identical "figure eight" orbits at the same fixed longitude over the Indian Ocean but lagging each other by 12 hours, can provide continuous infrared coverage of most of the U.S.S.R. and all of China (*light colored area*). The value of early-warning satellites from the point of view of arms control is that they are also capable of monitoring missile tests. The black dots indicate the locations of the major Russian missile-testing launch centers; the black line shows a typical trajectory for a Russian long-range missile test. Also shown are two types of U.S. radar used to monitor Russian missile tests: over-the-horizon transmitters (*colored dots*) and receivers (*open colored circles*), and conventional, or line-of-sight, radars (*colored squares*).

Missile Submarines and National Security

Land-based missiles are giving way to submarine missiles as a secure deterrent to a nuclear first strike. The question now is whether or not the U.S. should spend perhaps $40 billion on a new missile fleet

HERBERT SCOVILLE, JR.

June 1972

In recent years, as the nuclear-weapons arsenals of both the U.S. and the U.S.S.R. have continued to grow, the concept of deterrence has become almost universally accepted as the key to maintaining national security and preventing the outbreak of a nuclear war. "Winning" a nuclear exchange is no longer regarded as a rational strategic objective; in such an exchange everyone, participant and nonparticipant alike, would be a loser. In keeping with the deterrence principle President Nixon affirmed in his State of the World Message of February 9 that "our forces must be maintained at a level sufficient to make it clear that even an all-out surprise attack on the U.S. by the U.S.S.R. would not cripple our capability to retaliate." For the Russians to feel secure they must have a similar capability; only then would a stable strategic balance exist.

The primary attribute required of any deterrent force is the ability to survive a "counterforce," or preemptive, attack. Ballistic-missile submarines are almost ideally suited to satisfying this requirement. Although they are expensive compared with other strategic weapons (more than $100 million per submarine exclusive of the missiles), their mobility and invisibility make them virtually immune to destruction in a surprise attack. In contrast, land-based intercontinental ballistic missiles (ICBM's) can readily be located with the aid of surveillance satellites, so that they must be regarded as "targetable" in the event of an enemy first strike. Attempts to "harden" such fixed missile-launchers (that is, to increase their resistance to the effects of nuclear explosions) are in the long run doomed to futility, since in the absence of qualitative arms-control agreements improvements in offensive missiles, particularly improvements in accuracy, will inevitably make fixed missile-launchers vulnerable and hence reduce confidence in their deterrence value.

The advent of multiple independently targetable reentry vehicles (MIRV's),

	SUBMARINES	MISSILES	WARHEADS		MAXIMUM TARGETS	
			BEFORE MIRV	AFTER MIRV	BEFORE MIRV	AFTER MIRV
U.S.	41	656	1,712	5,440	656	5,120
U.S.S.R.	26 (42)	416 (672)	416 (672)		416 (672)	

MISSILE-SUBMARINE FORCES of the U.S. and the U.S.S.R. are compared in this table. The submarines of both fleets are designed to carry 16 ballistic missiles each. The U.S. is currently in the process of converting 31 of its total of 41 deployed Polaris submarines to carry Poseidon missiles, each of which is capable of carrying up to 14 multiple independently targetable reentry vehicles (MIRV's); on the average each Poseidon will be able to deliver 10 nuclear warheads on 10 separate targets or at intervals on the same target. (The remaining payload can be devoted to various "penetration aids" intended to foil a potential enemy anti-ballistic-missile, or ABM, system.) Before the MIRV program began the bulk of the U.S. missile-submarine fleet was armed with Polaris *A-3* missiles, which feature a multiple reentry vehicle (MRV) capable of carrying three warheads; these warheads are not, however, widely separable and are aimable only in shotgun fashion at a single target. After MIRVing is complete the remaining 10 ships in the Polaris fleet will continue to be armed with *A-3* missiles. The Russian missile-submarine fleet consists at present of 26 ships deployed and about 16 more under construction, but this program could continue. (Known future submarine and missile totals are given in parentheses.) Since its missiles carry only one warhead each, however, the number of warheads it can launch is no greater than the total number of its missiles. Moreover, in a crisis military strategists in the U.S.S.R. must add to the U.S. totals the missile-submarine forces of France and Great Britain, each of which may eventually consist of four submarines and 64 missiles.

which are currently being deployed on a large scale by the U.S., creates a situation in which the "exchange ratio" strongly favors the attacker. Thus a single missile with, say, six warheads can potentially destroy six enemy ICBM's if they are caught in their silos. Moreover, strategic bombers are extremely vulnerable while they are on the ground and would therefore be very susceptible to annihilation in a surprise missile attack. Attempts to avoid this weakness by maintaining aircraft on continuous airborne alert have proved to be expensive and potentially dangerous. Even the current 15-minute ground alert is not completely satisfactory, since adequate warning would be more difficult to obtain if fractional-orbital-bombardment systems (FOBS) or depressed-trajectory missiles launched from submarines were used to attack the bombers.

Hence given the present state of military technology and reasonable anticipated advances, the primary element in the strategic-deterrent forces of both the U.S. and the U.S.S.R. will continue to be the ballistic-missile submarine. All other strategic systems will remain secondary. Moreover, it seems likely that any agreement that may emerge in the near future from the strategic-arms-limitation talks (SALT) will further enhance the relative importance of the missile-submarine forces. Since the chances that MIRV's will be limited by a SALT agreement are extremely low, ICBM's will become increasingly vulnerable. The more likely limitations on anti-ballistic-missile (ABM) systems, on the other hand, would guarantee the retaliatory capability of even a comparatively small number of submarine-launched ballistic missiles (SLBM's). The expected failure to limit antiaircraft defenses and to restrain qualitative improvements in offensive-missile systems would further decrease the value of strategic bombers. Although there will probably not soon be restrictions on antisubmarine-warfare (ASW) measures, the technology in this area is so far behind that it could not possibly threaten the submarine deterrent, if it can threaten it at all, until far in the future. In sum, the Navy will increasingly be the principal military guardian of our national security.

What characteristics must an SLBM force have in order to fulfill its function as a deterrent against the initiation of nuclear warfare by the U.S.S.R.? (Since China is so far behind both the U.S. and the U.S.S.R. in this respect, the same forces would be more than adequate to deter China as well.) First of all, the submarines should be designed to operate in, and fire their missiles from, large enough ocean areas in a variety of directions around the U.S.S.R. so as to decrease their vulnerability to ASW detection and tracking and to facilitate the penetration of any ABM system. The closer these areas are to ports in the U.S., the less will be the time lost in moving to and from operational stations and the less will be the need for overseas bases. Higher submarine speeds will also reduce this travel time and increase the ability to break contact with a trailing ASW submarine or surface vessel. The gains here may be marginal, particularly since tracking vessels will probably be faster than any missile submarine. The faster a submarine moves through the water, however, the more noise it will produce, and in countering ASW measures quietness may be much more important than speed. The reduction of submarine noise is the most critical element in preventing detection and continuous covert tracking, both of which must rely on passive acoustic sensors.

If an ABM defense is a realistic possibility, then the submarine missiles must have enough payload capacity to allow the use of multiple warheads and other penetration aids. The entire submarine force should be large enough so that the destruction of a few submarines by a concerted enemy attack, by slow attrition or perhaps by a series of accidents does not seriously degrade its overall capability. If continuous tracking by antisubmarine submarines or other ASW

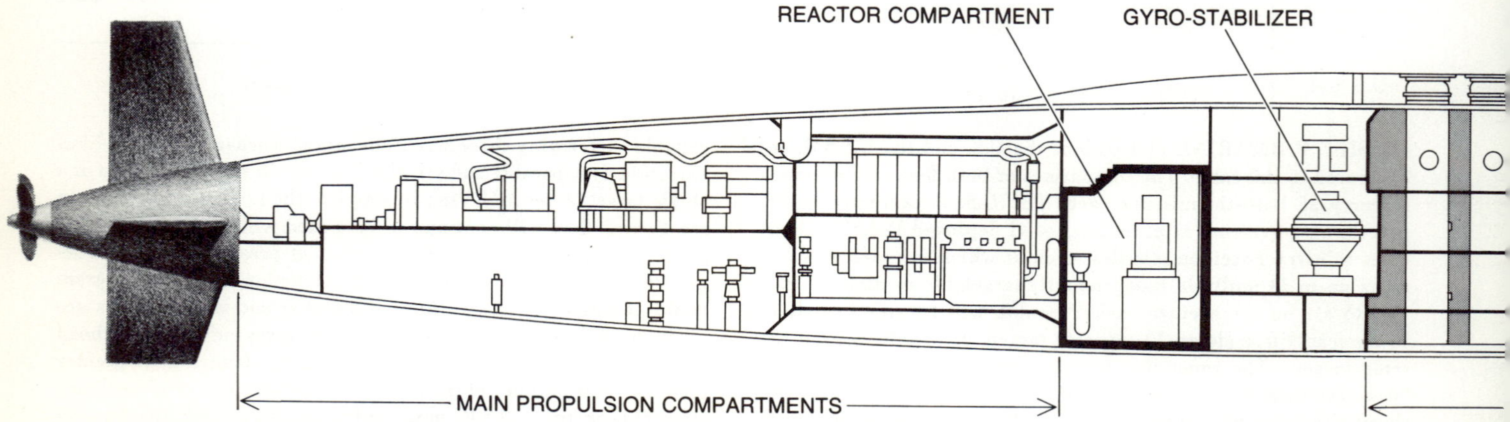

TYPICAL POLARIS SUBMARINE, in this case an advanced model belonging to the Lafayette, or 616, class is shown schematically in the cutaway drawings on these two pages. The nuclear-powered submarine has a length of 425 feet, a beam of 33 feet and a submerged displacement of 8,250 tons. In addition to its 16 ballistic-missile silos it is equipped with four bow torpedo tubes. Each of its

vessels ever becomes a realistic operation on a large scale, then the more vessels there are in the missile-submarine fleet, the harder it will be for this tactic to be successful in destroying the entire force. Ballistic-missile submarines cannot be used to attack other submarines and are no threat to the SLBM deterrent of the other side.

In addition to an adequate number of submarines, missiles and warheads, it is essential to have secure and reliable communications between these vessels and their command authorities. It is not enough to send the submarines to sea with sealed orders. Controls to prevent inadvertent or unauthorized firing are an absolute necessity, and reliable methods for ordering retaliation in the event of a surprise attack are required. These communications must be jam-proof; the potential attacker cannot be allowed to hope that a communications failure might prevent a retaliatory strike.

The submarines must also be able to navigate accurately, so that after they have moved through the oceans into their operational areas they will always be in a position to fire their missiles at predetermined targets. High navigational accuracy is not as great a requirement for a retaliatory strike against cities as it would be if the submarines were to be used in a counterforce role for destroying such "hard" targets as enemy missile sites. In fact, if one side wishes to use missile submarines only as deterrent weapons, then it is important that the accuracy-yield combination of the system not be so great as to give the other side concern that the submarines have a first-strike capability against land-based ICBM's; otherwise the position of mutual stable deterrence will be eroded.

With these general principles in mind, let us examine how the U.S. missile-submarine forces have developed over the years. The U.S. launched the first nuclear-powered submarine, the *Nautilus*, in 1955, but it was not until the late 1950's that development of long-range missiles had proceeded to the point that these could be installed in such submarines. The first ballistic-missile submarine, the *George Washington*, became operational in November, 1960. It was armed with 16 solid-fuel Polaris *A-1* missiles, which could be fired at a rate of about one per minute. The range of this missile was about 1,200 nautical miles and the warhead yield about one megaton. The submarines were designed to fire their missiles while submerged, using compressed gases to expel the missile; the rocket engine is then ignited after the missile has cleared the surface. By 1963, 12 more Polaris submarines were operational.

Meanwhile the development of more advanced missiles continued. The next-generation missile, the *A-2*, had a range of about 1,500 nautical miles. The first test of the *A-3* missile, with a range of 2,500 nautical miles and a "triplet" reentry vehicle, was conducted from a submerged submarine in the fall of 1963. The triplet reentry vehicles, which could carry three individual nuclear warheads each, did not have independent guidance; the three warheads were intended to reenter the atmosphere in a shotgun pattern with the target at the center. Since such warheads cannot be aimed at separate targets, they do not alter the exchange ratio and do not provide any first-strike advantage. Their advent was therefore not in itself regarded as destabilizing.

In the early 1960's there was considerable debate over the appropriate size of the Polaris fleet. The Navy originally sought 48 ships, and the final decision was to build 41. One factor limiting the number of submarines is the problem of manpower recruitment. Nuclear-submarine duty, which involves 60-day underwater cruises, calls for a certain type of person who is not easy to find and who must be highly trained. Normally each vessel has two crews of about 140 men who go on alternate patrols.

By the end of 1966 all 41 Polaris submarines were operational; eight carried *A-2* missiles and 33 were eventually

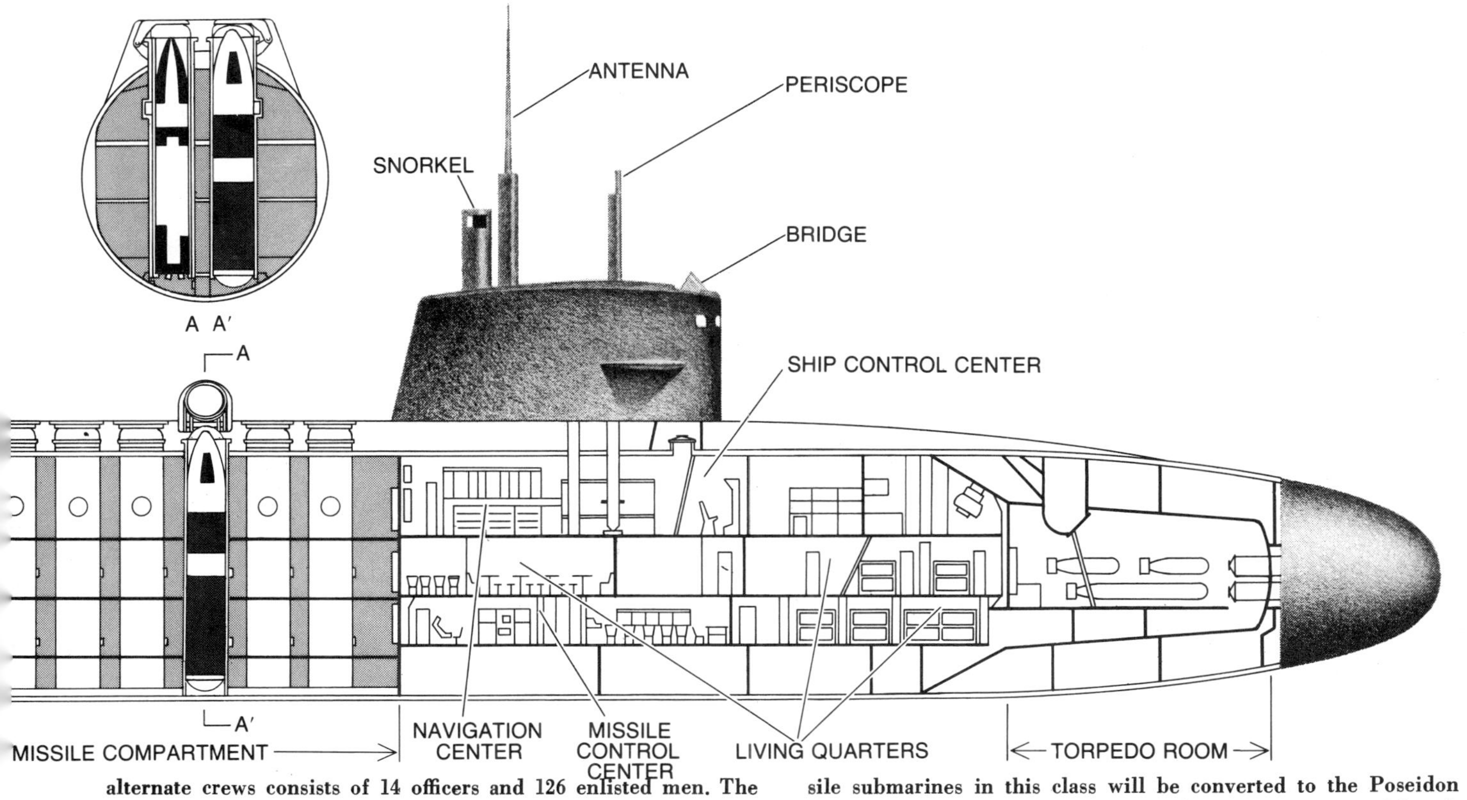

alternate crews consists of 14 officers and 126 enlisted men. The transverse section (*AA′*) shows the relative sizes of the Polaris *A-3* missile (*left*) and the Poseidon *C-3* missile (*right*). All the 31 missile submarines in this class will be converted to the Poseidon MIRV system by 1976. The Russian *Y*-class submarines, although not as advanced, are believed to be roughly similar in design.

fitted out with *A-3*'s. Thus the force carried a total of 1,712 warheads, but since the triplet warheads cannot be aimed separately, 656 was the maximum number of separate targets that could be hit. Of course, not all of these submarines can be kept at operational stations at all times. In general a submarine spends 60 days at sea and 30 days in port for maintenance. In addition the submarine might take five or more days to move from the U.S. to its launch point and the same period to return. If a submarine wished to avoid detection by moving quietly and therefore slowly, the travel time would be even greater. Thus the number of submarines at launch stations at any one time could be reduced to some 20 to 25 ships. The situation is improved by using forward bases (on Guam, at Holy Loch in Scotland and at Rota in Spain), which reduces the time needed to reach launch stations from five or six days to one or two days.

With a range of 2,500 nautical miles, a submarine-launched missile can hit Moscow from most of the North Atlantic (inside an arc extending from the tip of Greenland to North Africa), from the Mediterranean and even from some parts of the Indian Ocean, a total sea area of about six million square miles [*see illustration below*]. The sea area from which a submarine-launched missile could hit important targets other than Moscow, say targets only 200 miles inside the U.S.S.R., is even larger [*see illustration on opposite page*]. One high-ranking Navy officer reported in 1964 that a Polaris submarine equipped with the *A-3* missile could operate in 15 million square miles of ocean area while

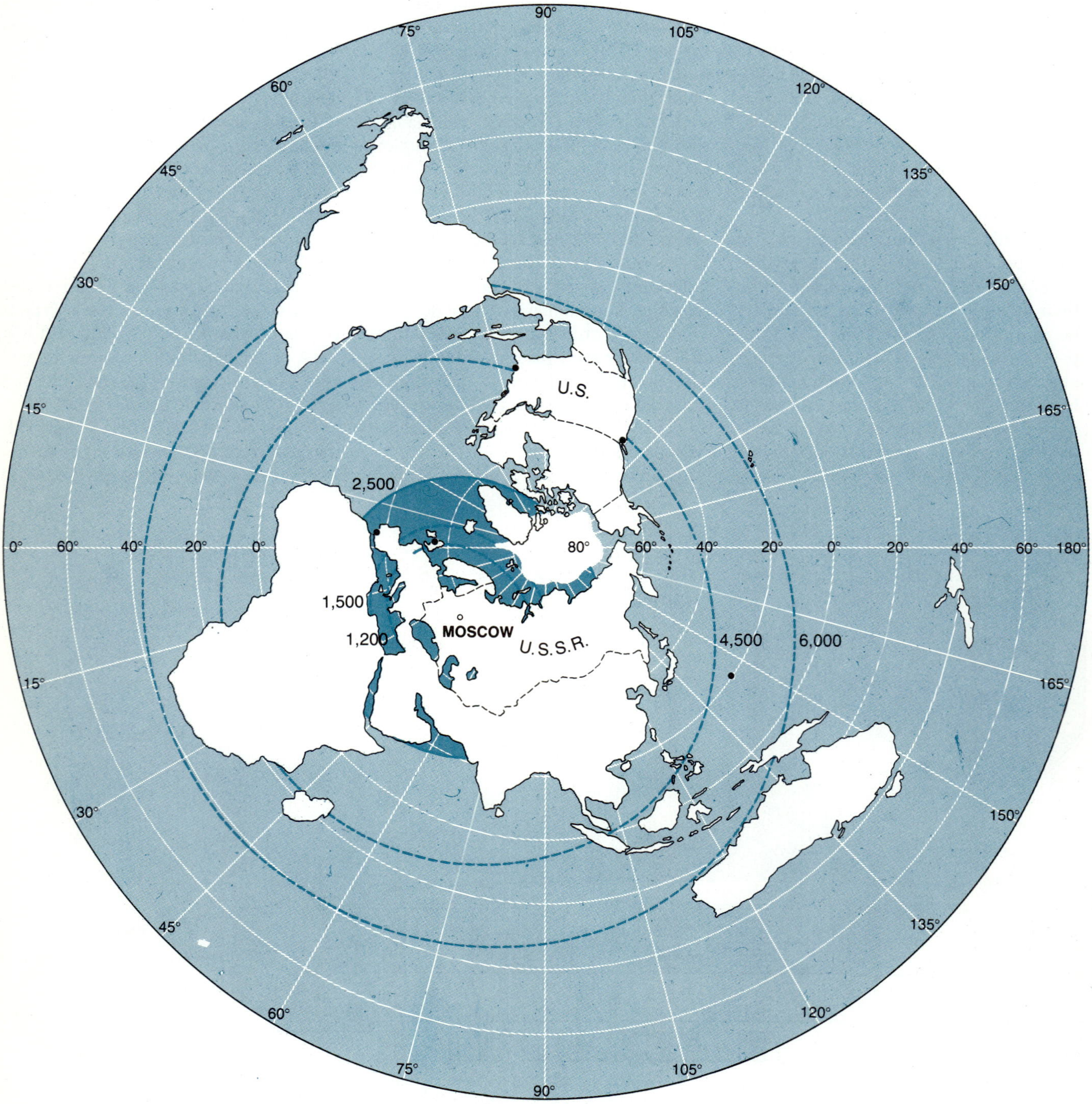

RANGE OF U.S. SUBMARINE MISSILES defines the operational sea areas from which submarine-launched ballistic missiles (SLBM's) could hit strategically important targets in the U.S.S.R. In the map at left the target is assumed to be Moscow; in the map at right the targets are assumed to include population centers and industrial complexes within 200 miles of the border of the U.S.S.R. (*gray areas*). The contours in the map at left are actually circles; their somewhat misshapen appearance is caused by the polar projection used in plotting the map. The contours in the map at right are concentric with the border of the U.S.S.R. The solid colored

covering its targets in the U.S.S.R. No land target anywhere in the world is inaccessible from attack by the *A-3* missile.

Although mobility provides a submarine with the tremendous advantage of improving its survivability, it creates a new problem: the determination of its location at the moment when the missile is to be launched toward its target several thousand miles away. Unless the missile is provided with some means of determining its position during flight or with a terminal-homing capability, the accuracy at the impact point can never be better than the uncertainty in the launch point. To determine the launch position calls for accurate submarine navigation, which is made more difficult by the requirement that in order to avoid disclosing its presence the submarine should not surface to determine its location. The attitude of the ship with respect to the vertical and true north at the time of the launch is also needed. When the missile force is being used for deterrent purposes, an accuracy greater than a few thousand feet is not needed; it is only necessary to be able to hit a large urban complex. Today this order of accuracy in locating the position and attitude of a submarine can be readily achieved. The U.S. has made tremendous advances in the development of inertial-navigation systems in recent years, and reasonably accurate position fixes can be obtained even after the submarine has been submerged at sea for many days.

The inertial-navigation system in a Polaris submarine is a complex system of gyroscopes, accelerometers and com-

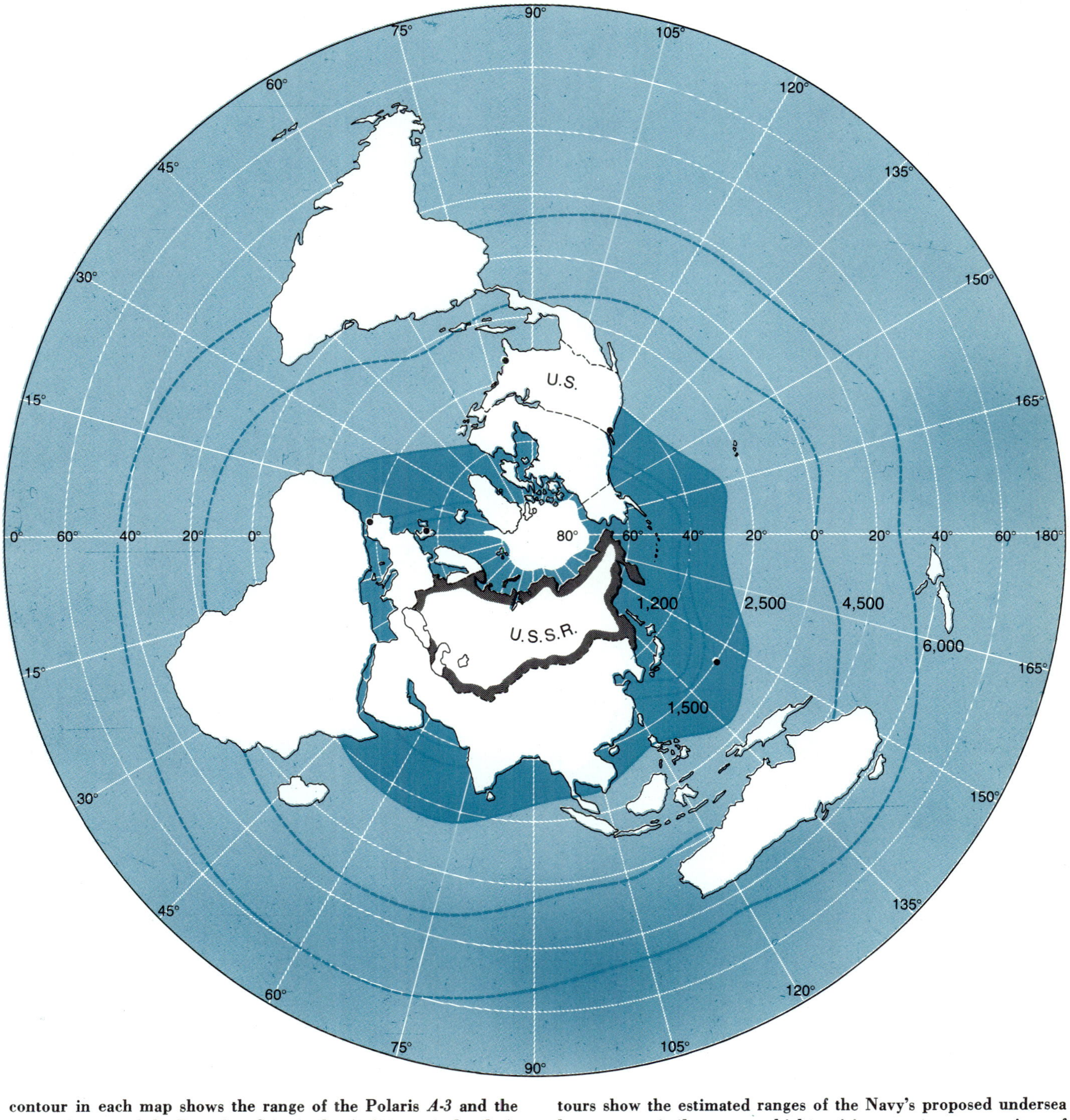

contour in each map shows the range of the Polaris *A-3* and the nominal range of the Poseidon *C-3* missiles (2,500 nautical miles). The two inner broken colored contours in each case show the ranges of the older Polaris *A-1* and *A-2* missiles (1,200 and 1,500 nautical miles respectively). The two outer broken colored contours show the estimated ranges of the Navy's proposed undersea long-range missile system, which envisions two new generations of missiles, the ULMS 1, with a range of 4,500 nautical miles, and the ULMS 2, with a range of 6,000 nautical miles. Black dots denote home ports and forward bases of the U.S. missile-submarine fleet.

puters that relate the movement and the speed of the ship in all directions with respect to true north. If an initial position is known, then this system will provide continuous data on the ship's position. For an absolutely stationary submarine, or one whose motion can be corrected for, inertial sensors can determine without external data the vertical, the true north, the latitude and all velocity components by inertially sensing the earth's gravitational and rotational vectors, but there is no way of determining the longitude by inertial means. Submarines that have been voyaging at sea for protracted periods and whose inertial-navigation errors may have become unacceptably large can, by trailing an antenna while they are still submerged, get a radio "position fix" from navigation satellites or land-based transmitters. It may also be possible to locate a submarine by reference to accurately known geographical landmarks on the ocean bottom such as seamounts. In sum, the present technology has advanced to the point where the location and attitude of the submarine could in principle no longer be the critical factor in obtaining missile accuracies down to less than an eighth of a mile.

A deterrent force must also be able to receive communications from national command centers. Direct command and control originating with the President and with many verification checks is vital to prevent unauthorized launching; it is also essential that command authorities be able to communicate in times of crisis with the submarine captains without fear of interference by the other side. Otherwise communication would

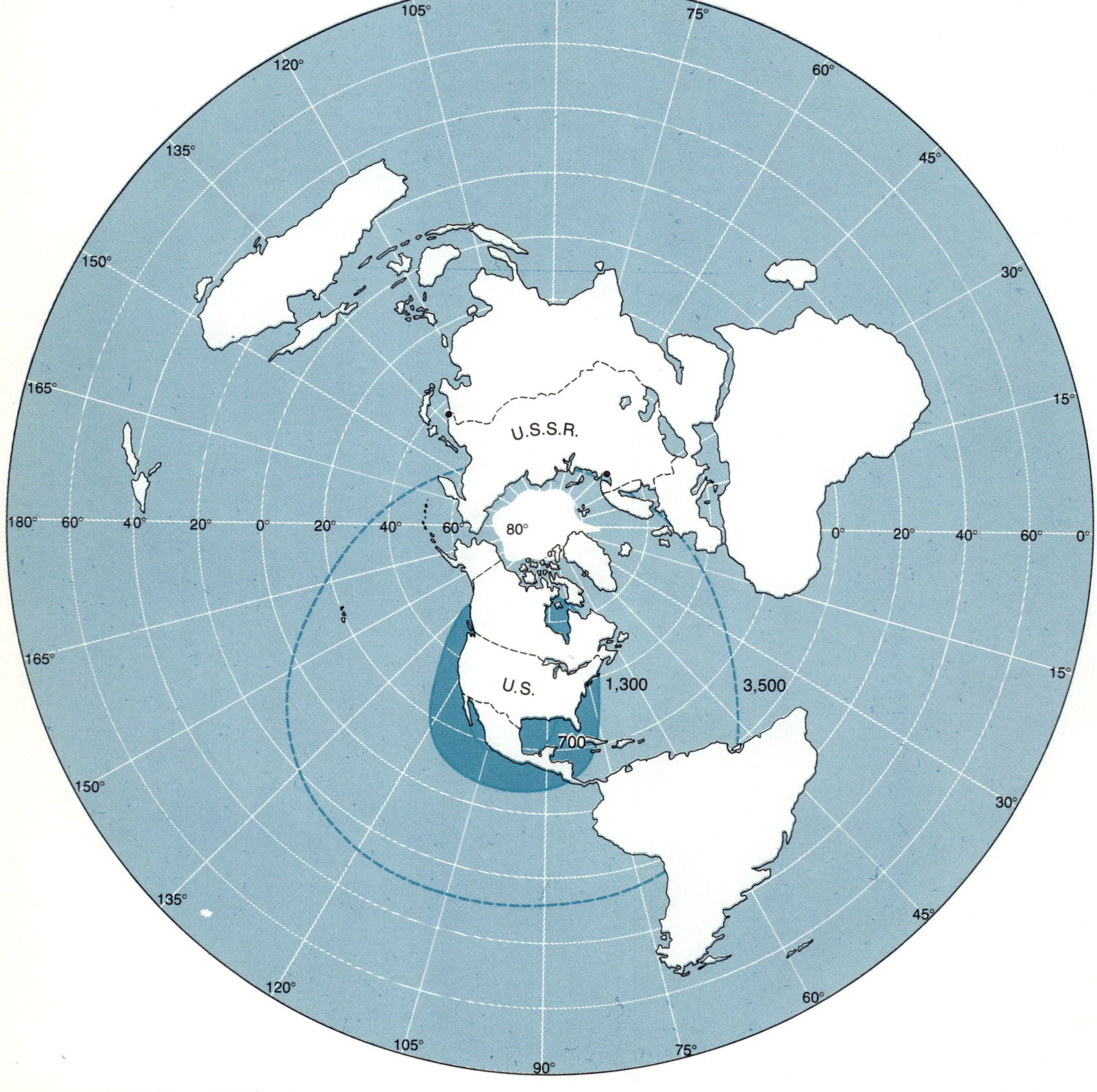

RANGE OF RUSSIAN SUBMARINE MISSILES is estimated in these two maps in order to show the operational sea areas from which their SLBM's could hit targets anywhere in the U.S. (*left*) and targets within 200 miles of the U.S. border (*right*). Alaska and Hawaii are excluded from consideration. Again the solid colored contour in each map shows the present range of the Russian Y-class missiles (1,300 nautical miles). The inner broken colored contour in each case shows the range of the previous generation of Russian SLBM's (700 nautical miles). The outer broken colored contour in each case shows the range of a new Russian missile that be the Achilles' heel of the submarine deterrent. There are a number of means of communicating with a submarine, at least one way from shore to ship, that do not require the submarine to surface. Very-low-frequency (VLF) radio waves can penetrate a short distance into the water, so that a receiving antenna does not need to be exposed at the surface. Moreover, the submarine can operate at a considerable depth, since it can trail an antenna as much as several hundred feet above its deck. The U.S. has a number of land-based VLF transmitters at various locations around the world for communication with Polaris submarines, and more recently an airborne VLF system has been devised in order to eliminate the possibility that the fixed land-based stations would be destroyed in a surprise attack.

The use of satellites for relaying messages to submarines provides an alternative means of communication. Recently much research has been devoted to extremely-low-frequency (ELF) waves, which can penetrate even deeper into the water. The Navy project named Sanguine proposed to set up a vast antenna for this purpose in Wisconsin. The data rate of such a system would be quite low, but it would be adequate for command-communication purposes. The project has run into difficulties with local residents because of the large antenna currents and the potential hazard to living things. For communication from a submarine to the command center the problem is more difficult; it calls at the very least for trailing an antenna close to the surface and must in any case be avoided in order to prevent disclosure of

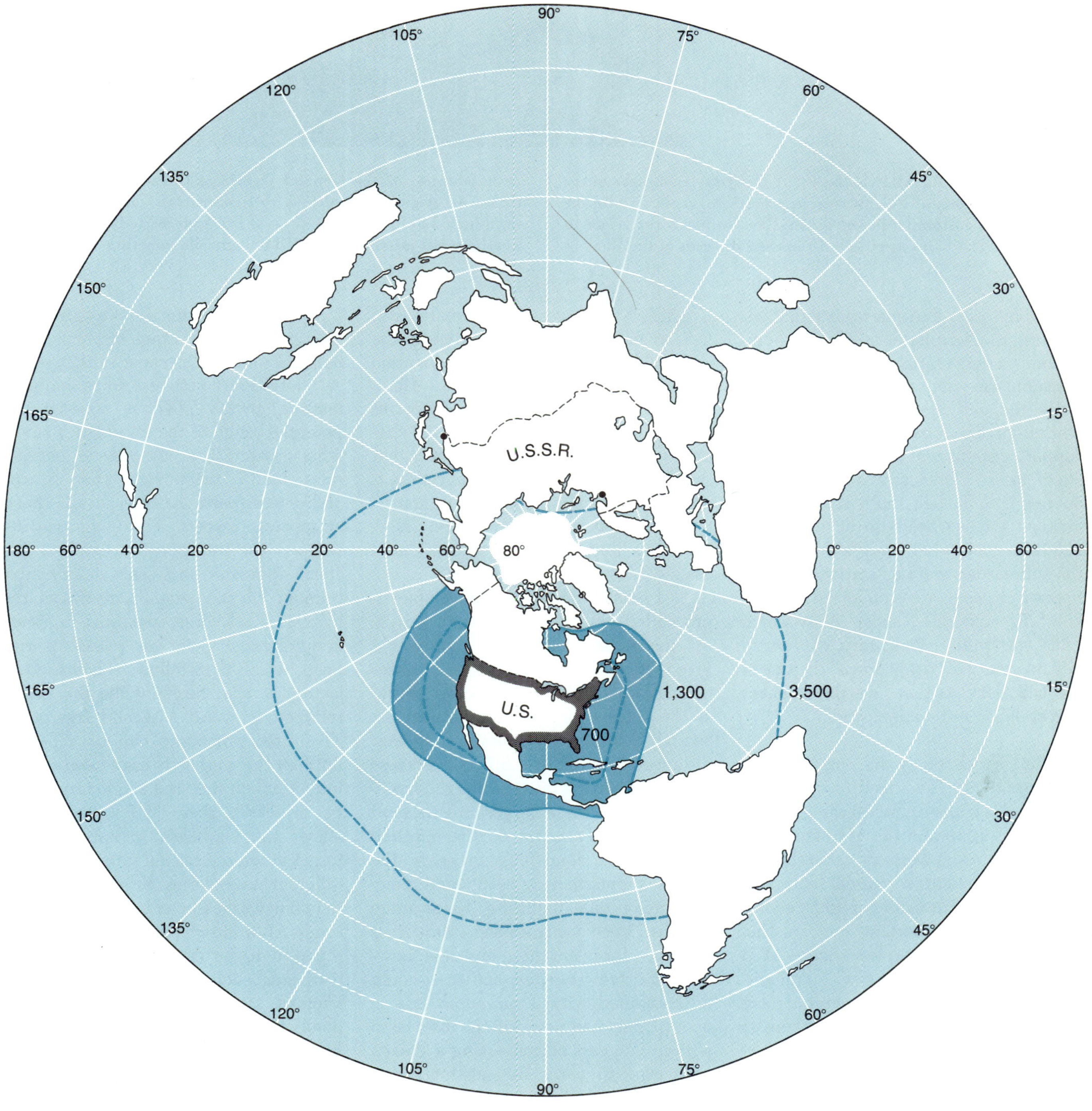

has recently been tested; this missile, however, is believed by U.S. strategic planners to be too long to fit readily in the present *Y*-class missile submarines. The black dots indicate the shipyards of the Russian missile-submarine fleet; the U.S.S.R. has no forward bases for its missile submarines. In general the greater distance from the Russian missile-submarine fleet's home ports to their operational launching areas, combined with their lack of forward bases, means that their submarines waste more time in getting "on station." Hence the U.S.S.R. requires more missile submarines than the U.S. to maintain the same deterrent force operational at any one time.

U.S. MISSILE SUBMARINE, the U.S.S. *Lafayette*, namesake of the advanced 616 class of Polaris vessels, was photographed while she cruised in the Atlantic Ocean during her builder's sea trials in April, 1963. The *Lafayette* was built in the shipyards of the Electric Boat Division of the General Dynamics Corporation in Groton, Conn. As originally deployed, this submarine was armed with 16 solid-fueled Polaris *A-2* missiles; it is scheduled to be converted to Poseidon *C-3* missiles with MIRV warheads sometime before 1976.

the submarine's location to listening enemy radios. Fortunately such communication is not essential to the viability of the submarine deterrent force.

By the end of 1966 the U.S. submarine-missile force together with its support systems was by itself more than adequate to deter any nuclear attack on the U.S. It had more than enough missiles and warheads to devastate the U.S.S.R. even when only a fraction of the submarines were on station. It could operate in ocean areas on all sides of the U.S.S.R., and the Russian ASW capability was quite rudimentary, with virtually no ability to "draw down" the size of the U.S. fleet. At that time the Russians had no ABM system deployed.

Military technology did not, however, stand still. The need to operate in restricted sea areas close to the northern coast of Europe and the Mediterranean in order to reach Moscow and other interior Russian cities created fears that someday ASW measures might become a threat. More important, concern that the U.S.S.R. might deploy a large ABM system capable of coping with our missile-submarine force was becoming more acute every day. The Russians were in the process of deploying an ABM defense around Moscow, using a large interceptor missile estimated to have a single-warhead yield large enough to destroy all three warheads of the Polaris *A-3*. In addition they were deploying radars and defensive missiles in the "Tallinn system" widely throughout the U.S.S.R. Some "worst case" analyses of U.S. planners, particularly during the early phases when factual information was limited, postulated that these facilities were for ABM defense. Later, as more data became available, the predictions were scaled down to the effect that the Tallinn system was an antiaircraft defense that could perhaps be upgraded to provide an ABM capability. (Now even this upgrading is not considered practicable by most experts.)

As a result research and development proceeded on a next-generation missile for the Polaris submarine that would give increased future assurance of penetrating any ABM defense and would at the same time give the submarines enough flexibility to operate at greater distances from the U.S.S.R. To increase either the payload or the range significantly called for a larger missile, and the resulting Poseidon missile required enlarging the launching tubes in the Polaris submarines, a costly and time-consuming task requiring 13 or more months. Since many of the submarines were due for overhaul in any case, however, the two shipyard activities could be combined with a minimum loss in operational readiness for the fleet as a whole. The cost of converting a Polaris submarine to carry the advanced Poseidon missiles is on the average $29 million, with another $38 million for normal submarine overhaul and replacement of the nuclear fuel.

The new Poseidon missile is about twice as heavy as the Polaris *A-3* and has a payload about four times as great. Although its nominal range of about 2,500 nautical miles is the same as that of the *A-3*, a trade-off between range and payload is always possible, so that the potential range of the Poseidon is somewhat greater. The new missile incorporates MIRV technology, that is, the ability to disperse many warheads aimed at separate targets. The technique developed for this purpose employs the "bus" approach, in which shortly after burnout of the propulsion stages the missile's final stage (the bus) is aimed at a first target point and releases a warhead, which then follows a ballistic trajectory to that target while the bus is redirected toward a second aim point. The same procedure can be repeated until all the warheads have been sent to individual targets. If a single target is to be attacked, then MIRV technology allows the warheads to approach the target at widely spaced intervals and on different trajectories so that no more than one warhead can be destroyed by a single ABM interceptor. The Poseidon is reported to be capable of carrying 14 warheads, each with a yield of about 50 kilotons, several times the yield of the bomb that destroyed Hiroshima. Warheads can be traded off for either ABM penetration aids or increased range. The nominal complement is usually taken as being 10 MIRV warheads. Department of Defense officials have repeatedly stated that these warheads do not have the accuracy-yield combination to provide a first-strike capability against hardened silos (a "circular-error probability" of about an eighth of a mile or better would be needed with that yield), but the Russians might still be concerned on this score.

As with the Polaris *A-3*, a Poseidon missile with a range of 2,500 nautical miles can launch warheads at Moscow not only from large areas of the North Atlantic and the Mediterranean but also from some parts of the Indian Ocean, a total area of about six million square miles. Targets within 200 miles of the border of the U.S.S.R. can be reached from some 15 million square miles. These large ocean areas present great problems for any possible future ASW system. To deploy detection and tracking systems throughout these waters is a prodigious, if not impossible, task. Furthermore, on short notice these areas might be somewhat enlarged if it ever became critical by reducing the Poseidon payload, either by eliminating penetration aids or by cutting down the number of warheads in each missile.

The first Poseidon missile was tested in August, 1968, and the development of the entire Poseidon system was completed two years later. The first Polaris submarine went to sea with Poseidon missiles in March of last year. At present about 10 submarines have been converted. The program calls for modifying 31 submarines to carry these new missiles, leaving 10 to be equipped with the older *A-3*'s. When the program is completed in 1976, the U.S. submarine force will be able to launch 5,440 warheads at 5,120 separate targets. It should be possible to keep considerably more than half of these submarines on station at all times, and in times of crisis the operational readiness can be stepped up if necessary. This is an awesome force, capable of overwhelming even a massive ABM defense system. There is, of course, no evidence that the Russians have any intention of building a large ABM system with nationwide coverage, and it is highly likely that such a system will be precluded in the first stage of a strategic-arms-limitation treaty.

Even one missile submarine can launch 160 warheads at separate industrial centers in the U.S.S.R., an attack that the Russians could not afford even if the U.S. had been annihilated. This means that any ASW system would have to be able to eliminate almost instantaneously every single submarine, a herculean task. Today it is difficult, if not impossible, to destroy even a single submarine that follows skilled evasion tactics. Yet if ABM defenses were forbidden by treaty, an ASW system that has still to be devised would be the only threat to the submarine deterrent. That is one reason why an ABM agreement at SALT would by itself be such an important gain to the security of both the U.S. and the U.S.S.R.

The U.S.S.R. has always lagged considerably behind the U.S. in the development of nuclear submarines and SLBM's. The first Russian nuclear submarine was built about four years after the *Nautilus,* and Admiral Hyman G. Rickover, the director of the U.S. nuclear-submarine program from the beginning, has made it clear he believes the Russian submarines are technically inferior to the U.S. ships. The first Russian ballistic-missile submarines were diesel-powered and therefore had limited endurance and cruising range. Their first nuclear-powered missile submarine carried only three missiles with a 300-nautical-mile range, which in later models was extended to about 700 nautical miles.

By the late 1960's it must have been obvious to military planners in the U.S.S.R. that their land-based ICBM's would become increasingly vulnerable to the U.S. MIRV's, which were then under development and which had been publicly justified as providing an improved counterforce capability. The Russian deterrent needed shoring up with a more effective SLBM force, whose value had been demonstrated by the U.S. In 1966 the U.S.S.R. launched its first *Y*-class submarine, which carries 16 missiles with a reported range of 1,300 miles. This class of vessels was similar to the Polaris submarines, which the U.S. had put into operation seven years earlier. All the Russian SLBM's deployed so far have had storable liquid fuels,

RUSSIAN MISSILE SUBMARINE, a representative *Y*-class vessel, is remarkably similar in appearance and general dimensions to the earlier U.S. Polaris designs. The ship carries 16 liquid-fuel missiles with a reported range of about 1,300 nautical miles. Each missile is armed with a single nuclear warhead with a yield of about one megaton. This photograph was released by the U.S. Navy in 1970.

whereas all the U.S. missiles have had solid fuels. The Russians apparently decided to continue with the *Y*-class design and began building submarines at a rapid pace, initially at the rate of six to eight per year and currently at nine per year. Two shipyards are engaged in this work, one at Severodvinsk on the Arctic Sea and one in Siberia on the Pacific. At present the Russians have about 26 *Y*-class submarines operational and another 16 under construction.

Although the Russians have tested a new missile with a range of about 3,500 miles, John Stuart Foster, Jr., chief research scientist for the Department of Defense, recently reported that this missile was so long that he did not believe the *Y*-class submarine could be modified to launch it. The Russians have never even tested multiple warheads on their submarine missiles, let alone MIRV's. Their missiles are each armed with a single warhead with a yield of about one megaton. These missiles have no capability for attacking our ICBM silos, but it has been postulated that they might be employed to attack our bombers on the ground and our command and control centers, using a depressed trajectory to achieve the necessary surprise. The missiles have not, however, been tested in this mode, and this approach would, in any case, entail a reduction in their already limited range.

The U.S.S.R. will have a slightly larger ballistic-missile submarine fleet than the U.S. when it completes those vessels now under construction (42 to 41). Even then, however, the capabilities of the Russian fleet will be far inferior to those of the U.S. Polaris fleet. President Nixon in his 1972 State of the World Message said that "our missiles have longer range and are being equipped with multiple independently targetable warheads. Moreover, our new submarines are now superior in quality." The shorter range of the Russian missiles requires that their submarines operate fairly close to the U.S. coast in order to be able to strike inland U.S. targets; this makes the Russian submarines potentially more vulnerable to a U.S. ASW system [*see illustration on page 240*]. On the other hand, the population centers and industrial complexes on the east and west coasts of the U.S. can be reached from much larger ocean areas, and these targets would be quite satisfactory if the SLBM's were to be used for deterrent purposes [*see illustration on page 241*]. The restricted range would be a serious factor only if the SLBM's were to be used against our bomber bases or missiles in the interior of the U.S.

There are other reasons why the parity between the U.S. and the U.S.S.R. in operational submarines cannot be evaluated on numerical grounds alone. Since bases in the U.S.S.R. are farther from the operational launching areas and since the Russians have no locations available for forward bases, more time is wasted getting submarines on station and it takes more submarines to maintain the same deterrent force operational at any one time. It would take Russian submarines a minimum of six days in the Atlantic and eight days in the Pacific to reach the nearest launch stations, so that the transit time to and from home ports, in many cases a quarter to a third of the duration of the patrol, seriously degrades the operational readiness of the Russian fleet. This disadvantage can be only partly alleviated by using submarine tenders for maintenance and crew exchange at sea. Moreover, in any East-West comparison the small British and French missile-submarine fleets, each of which may eventually consist of four submarines and 64 missiles, must be added to the U.S. total. Thus, whereas the Russians now have an adequate missile-submarine deterrent, their fleet is markedly inferior to that of the U.S. and its allies and provides no threat to the U.S. deterrent.

As the first phase of SALT is drawing to an end, then, it is becoming universally recognized that ballistic-missile

ARRANGEMENT OF MISSILE SILOS in a Lafayette-class Polaris submarine is revealed by the open silo doors in this view. The submarine, the U.S.S. *Sam Rayburn*, was photographed at Newport News, Va., at about the time of her commissioning in December, 1964.

CONVERSION of the Polaris submarine U.S.S. *James Madison* to accommodate the new, larger Poseidon missile was undertaken in February, 1969, and was completed in June, 1970. This photograph shows the *Madison*, the first of 31 such missile submarines to be converted, being test-fitted for the new Poseidon missile system at the Groton shipyards of the General Dynamics Electric Boat Division.

submarines are the essential foundation of a secure and stable strategic balance. Under these circumstances it is only natural to investigate ways to still further improve submarine missile systems. The U.S. has had a research and development program in this area for several years, so that the developments at the frontiers of technology could be incorporated in the successor to the Polaris-Poseidon system. The particular system proposed by the Navy for this role has been called ULMS, for undersea long-range missile system.

One obvious way to improve the present submarine missile would be to extend its range, making possible the launching of missiles from larger ocean areas in all directions around the U.S.S.R. Increasing the missile's payload would allow the incorporation of more warheads per missile or additional ABM-penetration aids. Payload can, of course, always be traded off for range. A longer-range missile would reduce the time required to move from U.S. ports to launching areas and thereby reduce the need for overseas basing in order to maintain the submarines on station for a larger fraction of their cruising time. With a range of 4,500 nautical miles a missile could reach Moscow shortly after the submarine leaves the U.S., whereas with a range of 2,500 nautical miles at least three days' travel would be required. Thus for a 60-day cruise lengthening the missile range by 2,000 miles could increase the period of operational effectiveness by about 10 percent if forward bases were abandoned.

More advanced guidance systems employing terminal control (the ability to change the path of the warhead during reentry) are being developed to avoid interception by ABM systems or to improve accuracy. Higher accuracy obtained by this means or others is not required if missiles are to be used as deterrent weapons. Indeed, it might be construed by the other side as an attempt to attain a counterforce capability for a first strike. Although it is more difficult to acquire such a capability with a submarine missile system than with an ICBM because of the inherent limitations on the payload and the nuclear explosive yield and because of navigational complications, there are no scientific barriers to its achievement. The greatest technical restriction on the use of SLBM's for a counterforce first strike may lie in command and control. It may be feasible to preprogram and command the initial launchings, but there will inevitably be failures. The difficulties of directing subsequent firings to destroy the silos missed the first time appear to be virtually insurmountable.

The submarine itself can be improved

by making it quieter as it moves through the water, thereby rendering detection and tracking by passive acoustic techniques more difficult. Although increasing the speed of the submarine will make it somewhat harder for enemy ASW ships to follow it, the higher speed will also raise the level of noise produced by the submarine. In any case it is probably a losing proposition for a missile submarine to try to outrun an ASW vessel, which can always be designed to move faster. High speed will enable the submarine to reach its launch area more rapidly and thus reduce the time it spends in a nonoperational condition, but again the potential gains are not large, and they may be outweighed by the disadvantages. If all other factors are equal, it will require a bigger power plant and larger submarine, both of which will increase cost and detectability. Increasing the depth at which a submarine can operate is not particularly significant, at least for the depths that are likely to be achieved in the next generation of submarines; submarines can be detected acoustically and destroyed by nuclear depth charges or homing torpedoes at any reasonable depth.

FIRST SUCCESSFUL TEST LAUNCH of a Poseidon missile from a submerged submarine was carried out in October, 1970. The missile was launched from the *James Madison*. The Poseidon missile, like the earlier Polaris models, is expelled from its silo by compressed gas; its rocket engine is then ignited after the missile has cleared the surface of the water.

If space for more and larger missiles is needed to increase the destructive capacity and the ABM-penetrability of any single submarine, then larger submarines with bigger power plants will be required. The larger the submarines, however, the fewer the ships that will be available for the same investment. Therefore if funds are limited (and they always are), this means a smaller fleet, which is more vulnerable to being wiped out in a simultaneous surprise attack. Thus there are many trade-offs in system design, and the final decision on a successor to the Polaris-Poseidon system should be based only on the nature of the specific threat.

In 1971 $104.8 million was appropriated for the advanced development of ULMS. Although this expenditure still left options open, it was a major step on the path toward procuring a specific new submarine system. This year the Department of Defense is seeking $977 million for ULMS. If that amount is authorized, the U.S. will be irrevocably committed to a large and very expensive new shipbuilding program. Unclassified details of the proposed ULMS program are still scarce, but it appears that the submarine in the system would be quite large (more than twice the size of the Polaris ships) and that it would be capable of launching 20 to 24 large missiles equipped with MIRV's. It is proposed to have a higher maximum speed and to incorporate the latest available silencing techniques, although these two objectives are competitive.

The ULMS program has been divided into two parts. The first stage (ULMS 1) would involve a new missile with a range of about 4,500 nautical miles capable of being deployed in the present Polaris submarines as well as in any new vessel. The second stage (ULMS 2) would include the development of the new submarine and a still more advanced missile with a range of about 6,000 miles that would be too big to be substituted for the Poseidon in the existing Polaris ships. A maneuvering reentry vehicle (MARV) is also being developed for the new ULMS missiles. According to one estimate, the total cost of a program for 30 such ULMS vessels would be $39.6 billion [*see illustration at right*].

RESEARCH, DEVELOPMENT, TEST AND EVALUATION	MILLIONS OF DOLLARS
SUBMARINE	$800
MANEUVERING REENTRY VEHICLE (MARV)	$600
ULMS 1 MISSILE	$2,100
ULMS 2 MISSILE	$1,500
PROCUREMENT	
SUBMARINES (30 AT AVERAGE COST OF $400 MILLION EACH)	$12,000
ULMS 1 MISSILES (ENOUGH FOR 500 LAUNCHERS AT AVERAGE COST OF $8 MILLION EACH)	$4,000
ULMS 2 MISSILES (ENOUGH FOR 600 LAUNCHERS AT AVERAGE COST OF $11 MILLION EACH)	$6,600
SUPPORT	
ULMS REFIT FACILITIES (ONE PER 15 SHIPS AT COST OF $1,800 MILLION FOR FIRST, $1,200 MILLION FOR SECOND)	$3,000
OPERATION AND MAINTENANCE (FOR 30 SHIPS AT AVERAGE COST OF $30 MILLION PER YEAR FOR 10 YEARS)	$9,000
TOTAL	$39,600

ESTIMATE OF TOTAL COST of the Navy's proposed ULMS program was prepared by Members of Congress for Peace through Law. The first stage of the ULMS program (ULMS 1) would involve a new missile with a range of about 4,500 nautical miles capable of being deployed in the present Polaris submarines as well as in any new vessels. The second stage (ULMS 2) would include the development of a new, larger submarine and a still more advanced missile with a range of about 6,000 miles. A special maneuvering reentry vehicle (MARV) is being developed for these new, larger missiles. The entry under research, development, test and evaluation for the submarine includes the cost of all nonmissile subsystems and integration work. The procurement estimates assume that the new program would eventually involve 30 new submarines. The support estimates assume a need for two special refit facilities for the ULMS ships and include crew-related costs for 10 years. The cost of the ULMS 1 missile program by itself is estimated to come to about $6.7 billion.

So far no convincing case has been made for the need to proceed with a replacement for the Polaris-Poseidon system and for making a commitment to a new large, high-speed submarine. Russian construction of SLBM's is no justification for ULMS; the Russian missile submarines do not in any way threaten the Polaris deterrent. Numerical superiority in launchers is meaningless; all authorities agree that the U.S. is far ahead qualitatively and can deliver from submarines about 5,000 warheads to fewer than 700 for the U.S.S.R. Even if we foolishly choose to race the Russians in the number of SLBM's, ULMS is certainly not the way to do it; each ULMS system will probably cost five or more times per missile launched than the Russian *Y*-class system.

The Poseidon with 10 or more MIRV's on each missile has a far greater capability than is needed to overwhelm any Russian ABM system that can be foreseen at present. Admiral Thomas H. Moorer, chairman of the Joint Chiefs of Staff, testified in February that "the Moscow ABM system even with improved radars and more and better interceptors could still be saturated by a very small part of our total missile force. In any event, the programmed Minuteman III and Poseidon forces, with their large number of reentry vehicles, provide a hedge against a future large-scale Soviet ABM deployment." Since such a large-scale ABM deployment will almost certainly be precluded by a first-stage SALT agreement, there is nothing in the ABM area that would require replacement of the Poseidon; in fact, even the Poseidon MIRV's will not be needed if a SALT ABM treaty is realized.

Therefore it is necessary to examine antisubmarine warfare to determine if there is anything that would currently justify the major ULMS step. Without going into a detailed analysis of possible ASW measures and countermeasures, suffice it to say that no evidence has yet been presented that the Russian ASW program could present a threat to the Polaris deterrent in the next decade. [See "Antisubmarine Warfare and National Security," by Richard L. Garwin, the article beginning on page 248]. Admiral Levering Smith, director of the Navy's Strategic Systems Project, testified in 1969 that even the new generation of Russian ASW submarines will not be able to follow our Polaris submarines, and that the U.S.S.R. has no specific new ASW methods that would make the Polaris fleet vulnerable to attack. That is still true today. The U.S. has spent tens of billions of dollars on ASW efforts over the past 20 years and still does not have any system that could even begin to approach the kind of capability that would be needed to eliminate 20 to 30 missile submarines almost simultaneously. The Russians are far behind the U.S. in this area, and they have the serious geographical disadvantages of remoteness from and unavailability of land areas contiguous to the oceans in which their ASW systems would have to operate. Since the nature of the potential ASW threat to the Polaris-Poseidon system cannot even be foreseen at this point, ULMS, if built now, may be designed to cope with the wrong threat. The most obvious improvement to Polaris-Poseidon would be to increase the range of the missile in order to enlarge the ocean areas from which missiles could be launched. The deployment of such a new long-range missile might cost nearly seven billion dollars, however, and in any case, as the maps on pages 6 and 7 show, the Poseidon system already has a tremendous operational flexibility and is not threatened in its present launch areas.

Thus there are strong arguments for keeping both the ULMS missile and the ULMS submarine options in the research and early development stage. This would allow the exploration of all approaches, including smaller, slower but quieter submarines, and would avoid the making of a premature commitment to a large, expensive submarine and missile program. We must not fall into the trap of buying new military hardware just because we have made technological advances; there is no quicker way to price ourselves out of the security market. The submarine missile force is the backbone of our deterrent; its present strength and invulnerability obviate the need for its replacement for at least a decade.

Antisubmarine Warfare and National Security

The missile-submarine deterrents of the U.S. and the U.S.S.R. are not threatened by current antisubmarine technology. It is argued that this state of affairs should be maintained by the two powers

RICHARD L. GARWIN

July 1972

The treaty and executive agreement recently signed by the U.S. and the U.S.S.R., the culmination of three years of the strategic-arms-limitation talks (SALT), formally recognize that the two countries accept the military and political value of mutual deterrence as a means of forestalling an all-out nuclear war. The accords remove one potential threat to the effectiveness of strategic offensive missiles, on which deterrence rests, by prohibiting the U.S. and the U.S.S.R. from constructing nationwide anti-ballistic-missile (ABM) defenses. By ensuring the effectiveness of our offensive missiles, the ABM treaty greatly enhances our future security. The SALT accords, however, do not prohibit either country from qualitatively improving its offensive missile forces, for example by equipping missiles with multiple independently targeted reentry vehicles (MIRV's) or by improving the accuracy or explosive yield of missile warheads, perhaps to the point where the offensive missiles have a high probability of being able to destroy land-based missiles in their silos (if they were to remain there until they were hit). The U.S. could in fact replace Minuteman with a larger missile in the same silo, thereby multiplying the "throw weight" of the Minuteman force by a factor of three or four. As a result of this possibility each country will be concerned to maintain the invulnerability of its submarine-based strategic missiles, which are essentially immune to attack from land-based weapons [see "Missile Submarines and National Security," by Herbert Scoville, Jr., the article beginning on page 235].

A potential threat to the submarine-based deterrent already exists in the antisubmarine-warfare (ASW) forces that both the U.S. and the U.S.S.R. possess. Fortunately, in the present state of the art, the technology of antisubmarine warfare is even less effective in a disabling strike against ballistic-missile-launching submarines than it is against nuclear-powered submarines designed to attack surface ships. Nevertheless, given the importance of the submarine-based deterrent, it is not too early to examine the feasibility of arms-control limitations on possible methods of antisubmarine warfare that might eventually threaten the survivability of missile-launching submarines.

In this article I shall distinguish between antisubmarine-warfare techniques whose utility is tactical (the protection of surface shipping) and techniques that would be specifically useful against submarines carrying strategic offensive missiles. I hope to show that one could limit antisubmarine-warfare methods that would threaten the submarine-based deterrent without impairing one's ability to protect surface shipping from submarine attack. The precedent set by the prohibition of nationwide ABM systems shows that both the U.S. and the U.S.S.R. have a strong interest in preserving a controllable, survivable force of submarine-launched ballistic missiles (SLBM's). Even if a conventional war were to break out between the two powers, one could hope to continue to deter mutual nuclear annihilation by arranging for the SLBM forces of the two countries to survive. To that end one might now consider a possible SALT II agreement to provide safe passage for missile-launching submarines along designated routes to the open ocean. This is only one example of what might be in the interest of both the U.S. and the U.S.S.R.

Mutual acceptance of invulnerability for ballistic-missile submarines of the U.S. and the U.S.S.R. does not extend, however, to all possible roles for those submarines. For instance, a deterrent role for the ballistic-missile submarine does not require that all boats be in firing position near the surface and able to coordinate their fire within seconds. Nor does it require that they all be able to survive for several months after the outbreak of a major war without suffering any losses, deliberate or inadvertent, through antisubmarine warfare. The principle of deterrence would seem to be adequately served if ballistic-missile submarines on station could survive a full first-strike onslaught for a few hours in order to fire their weapons and if submarines not on station but in sanctuary or in the broad ocean reaches had a good probability of surviving a prudent trip of five or 10 days to firing position.

If war should break out between the U.S. and the U.S.S.R. and if nuclear weapons were used only at sea, the major consequence would be the destruction of each country's relatively few capital surface ships. Submarines, by and large, would survive. Although one cannot exclude the use of nuclear weapons against missile-carrying submarines, they do not change the conclusions. I shall argue the compatibility of an invulnerable submarine-based deterrent force with the active conduct of a tactical, nonnuclear and antisubmarine war.

Antisubmarine warfare involves at least four activities that proceed in logical sequence: intelligence, detection, localization and destruction. An optional tracking stage of hours or days can be imagined between localization and destruction. If the antisubmarine weapon is an antisubmarine mine, of course, no tracking is involved and the other activities are collapsed in time (although potentially intelligence can be fed into the mine from outside in advance or at arbitrary intervals).

Intelligence includes such information as the number of enemy submarines of each class, for example attack submarine (SS), nuclear-powered attack submarine (SSN), ballistic-missile-launching submarine (SSB), nuclear-powered ballistic-missile-launching submarine (SSBN) or cruise-missile-launching submarine (SSG or SSGN). Other kinds of information include number and range of missiles, number and type of torpedoes, speed and endurance, noise level, and sonar and radar capability. In addition to this intelligence on force levels and technical characteristics there is tactical intelligence, dealing broadly with the number of enemy submarines out of port, the number in each ocean basin, operating tactics, special vulnerabilities and so on. Tactical intelligence shades into detection and localization when a submarine can be limited to a certain area.

Over the years various methods have been employed for detecting submarines, including the detection of periscopes by radar, radio-frequency direc-

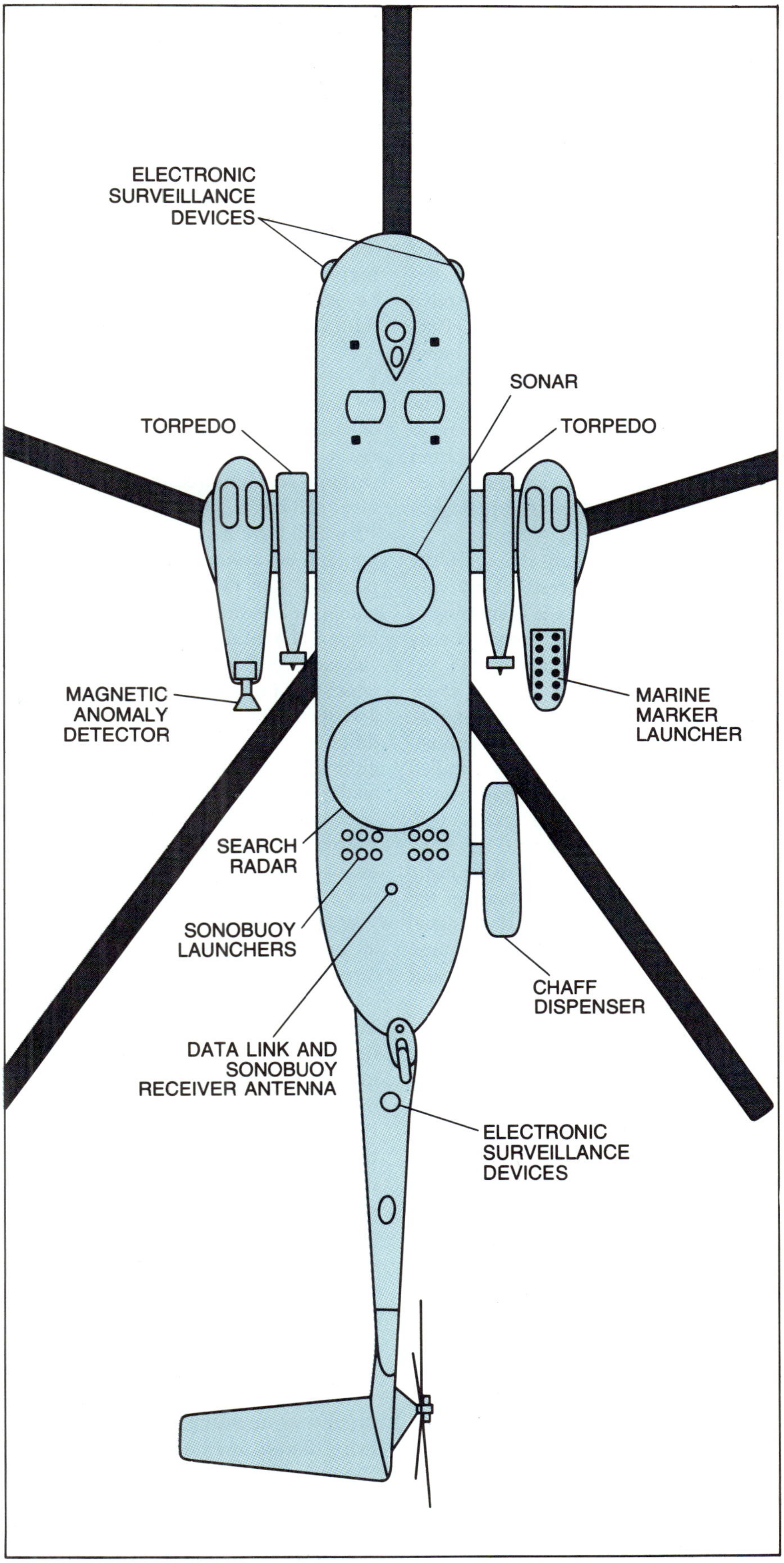

ADVANCED ANTISUBMARINE HELICOPTER, designated the SH-3H, is viewed from below in this schematic diagram. The helicopter is equipped with five different submarine-detection systems and is armed with a pair of lightweight 12-inch Mark 46 active acoustic homing torpedoes. The first eight SH-3H helicopters, built by the Sikorsky Aircraft Division of United Aircraft Corporation, are scheduled to be delivered to the U.S. Navy in mid-1972.

tion finding and visual sighting from aircraft. Although all play a role in tactical antisubmarine operations, the only currently effective way to locate a submerged submarine from any distance is by the use of acoustic methods, which can be either passive or active. Passive techniques include dispersed or concentrated arrays of fixed hydrophones, sonobuoy fields and hydrophones mounted either on surface vessels (usually destroyers) or on other submarines. Active techniques all require some kind of sonar gear: a sound generator combined with a hydrophone to receive reflected sound waves. Sonar systems can be mounted on submarines, surface ships or on devices towed at various depths from ships or helicopters. In addition sonar gear can be deployed in fixed underwater systems.

Passive techniques rely simply on the detection of noise generated by a submarine. When a submarine is running at high speed, the principal sound energy detectable at long range is radiated primarily by the propeller and by water flowing around the hull of the ship. At low speeds the major source of submarine noise is sound generated by installed machinery of various kinds, particularly rotating machinery that is unbalanced. Even a very noisy submarine, however, radiates less than one watt of acoustic power. One can therefore imagine the problem of detecting this tiny signal at long range in the presence of noise from waves and wind, undersea life and hundreds—even thousands—of surface vessels.

The propagation of sound in the ocean is extremely complex. Since the velocity of sound under water varies with temperature, pressure and salinity, it also varies with depth, position and season. These variations in sound velocity under some conditions bend underwater sound waves as much as 15 degrees, so that there is no guarantee that noise radiated from a submarine will consistently reach even the most sensitive passive listening post. On the other hand, sound waves are guided for thousands of miles with surprisingly little loss if they happen to be generated in the deep sound channel, a plane of minimum sound velocity lying at a depth of some 4,000 to 6,000 feet. A sound signal can travel 3,000 miles in the deep sound channel and still retain 1 percent of the intensity it had after traveling only 30 miles (suffering only cylindrical spreading loss). The existence of the deep sound channel is of no direct help in submarine detection, however, because existing submarines cannot safely descend to that depth and would be unwise to do so even if they could. When a near-surface hydrophone is moved away from a near-surface submarine sound source, the received signal often drops rapidly beyond a few kilometers and then rises to a high level again in successive "convergence zones" at multiples of about 50 kilometers (the distance required for a sound wave initially horizontal to be refracted through and beyond the deep sound channel and to return again to the surface).

Detecting a submarine in the immense background of ocean noise requires discrimination or processing gain. The desired source is known to be a point within a few hundred meters of the surface. Moreover, the source can be assumed to have a stationary spectrum in which there are usually strong line components. For decades large cadres of competent technicians have been working on the problems of extracting the submarine's "signal" from the noise in which it is immersed; the result has been a large variety of systems emphasizing different choices of available parameters, guided by operational considerations, analysis or tradition.

Basically the signal received from a source at a given assumed point can be enhanced with respect to noise or other point sources by adding in a coherent way the signals received at hydrophones located in different places. In a fixed dispersed array hundreds or thousands of hydrophones could be distributed throughout an entire ocean basin. The signals detected by the various instruments could be fed into a large computer provided with a program that assumes that a submarine, located somewhere in the detection area, successively occupies many possible points; for each point the program could introduce an appropriate time delay in the electrical output from each hydrophone. The computer could then add delayed electrical signals and ask whether the resulting integrated signal resembles the sound from a submarine or is simply just noise.

In a fixed concentrated array the hydrophones might be spread in a line no more than a few hundred meters long. Here the computer tests the result of integrating the various signals after inserting time delays allowing for the sound source to lie in some n number of distinguishable directions in a 360-degree arc. With processing equipment of sufficient size and power one can arrange for the beams from n directions to be formed simultaneously rather than sequentially, thereby ensuring that no signal is lost. Both dispersed and concentrated fixed arrays can incorporate hydrophones at various depths; by introducing vertical directivity the signal from distant sources is enhanced and locally generated surface noise is reduced.

Sonobuoy fields are most expeditiously sown from and monitored by aircraft. The U.S. has both shore-based aircraft (the P-3C) and sea-based aircraft (the S-2 and soon the S-3) equipped to drop sonobuoys weighing a few kilograms from either low or high altitude. A hydrophone, dangling from each sonobuoy at a substantial depth, picks up pressure signals that are then relayed by radio to the aircraft. In principle the signals could be added coherently, as are the signals from fixed arrays, but this would be difficult with sonobuoy fields since the buoys have considerable freedom of movement. The alternative is to monitor the field by listening to one sonobuoy after another to determine whether or not a submarine is in the vicinity. Processing gain can still be obtained from a single hydrophone by making a time or frequency analysis of the sound signal. An aircraft will have a search rate of so many thousand square kilometers per hour, limited not so much by its flight speed as by its ability to monitor each sonobuoy effectively.

The most highly regarded vessel for passive acoustic detection of submarines is another submarine, since it is far quieter than a surface ship. Moreover, a hunter-killer submarine is large enough to carry an array of hydrophones to produce a narrow listening beam for long-range detection. Depending on the sound-velocity profile and the noise level of the hunted and the hunter, the effective range for passive detection can vary from less than a kilometer to 100 kilometers or more. Factors affecting range include the reflection of sound waves from the ocean surface and ocean bottom and the signal-processing capability of the hunter submarine. As might be expected, passive acoustic measures become less effective as submarine designers learn to build quieter vessels and submarine commanders learn how to minimize the radiation of noise. In any event a submarine lying "dead" in the water cannot be detected by passive techniques. As a result the U.S. and the U.S.S.R. both rely heavily on active acoustic-detection, or sonar, systems.

Although sonar gear is installed routinely on both surface vessels and submarines, one of the potentially most effective antisubmarine measures makes

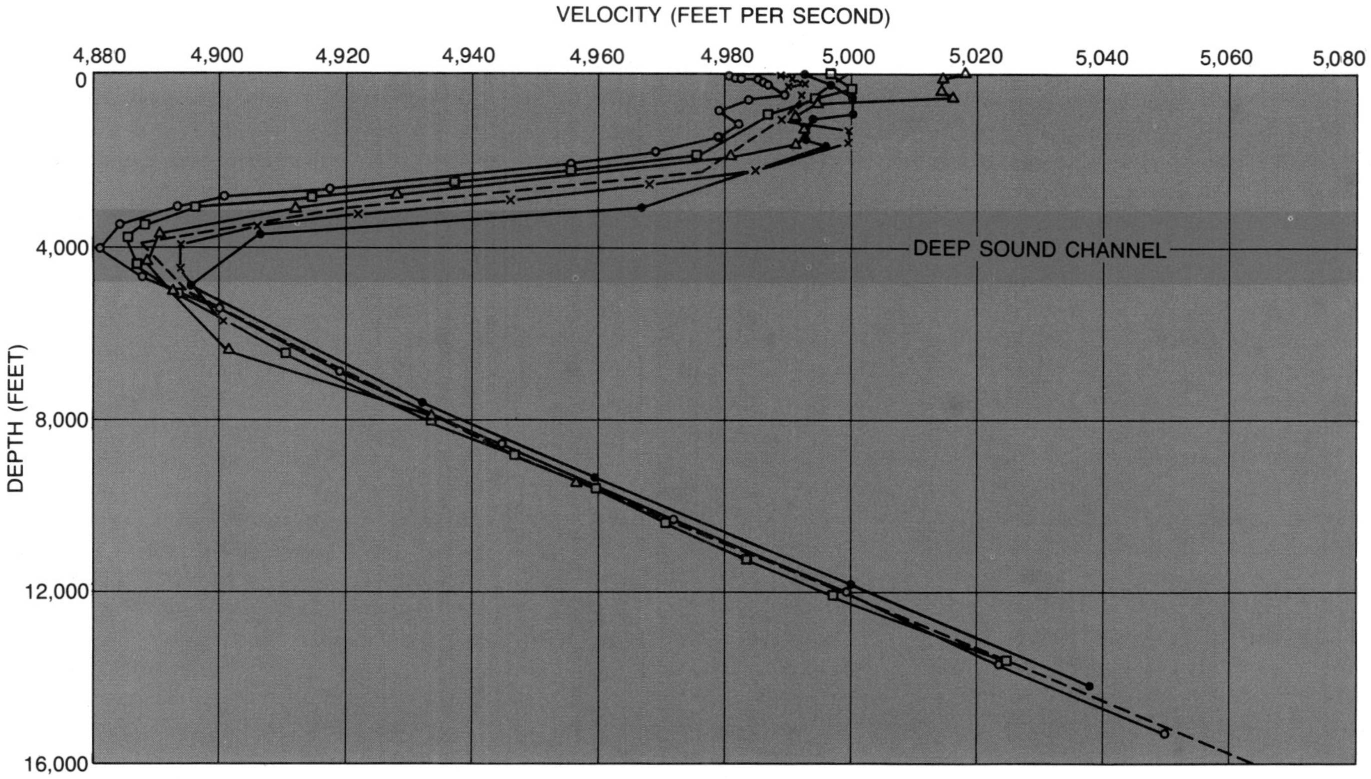

VELOCITY OF SOUND IN THE OCEAN varies with temperature, pressure and salinity, and hence also with depth, as can be seen from this record of a series of measurements made at several locations in the North Atlantic Ocean. As a consequence of the complex nature of underwater acoustic conditions there is no guarantee that noise radiated from a submarine will consistently reach even the most sensitive acoustic-detection device. Sound waves generated in the deep sound channel, a plane of minimum sound velocity lying at a depth of approximately 4,000 feet in this part of the Atlantic (*dark colored band*), can be guided for thousands of miles with little loss, but this is of no direct help in submarine detection, since existing submarines cannot operate at that depth.

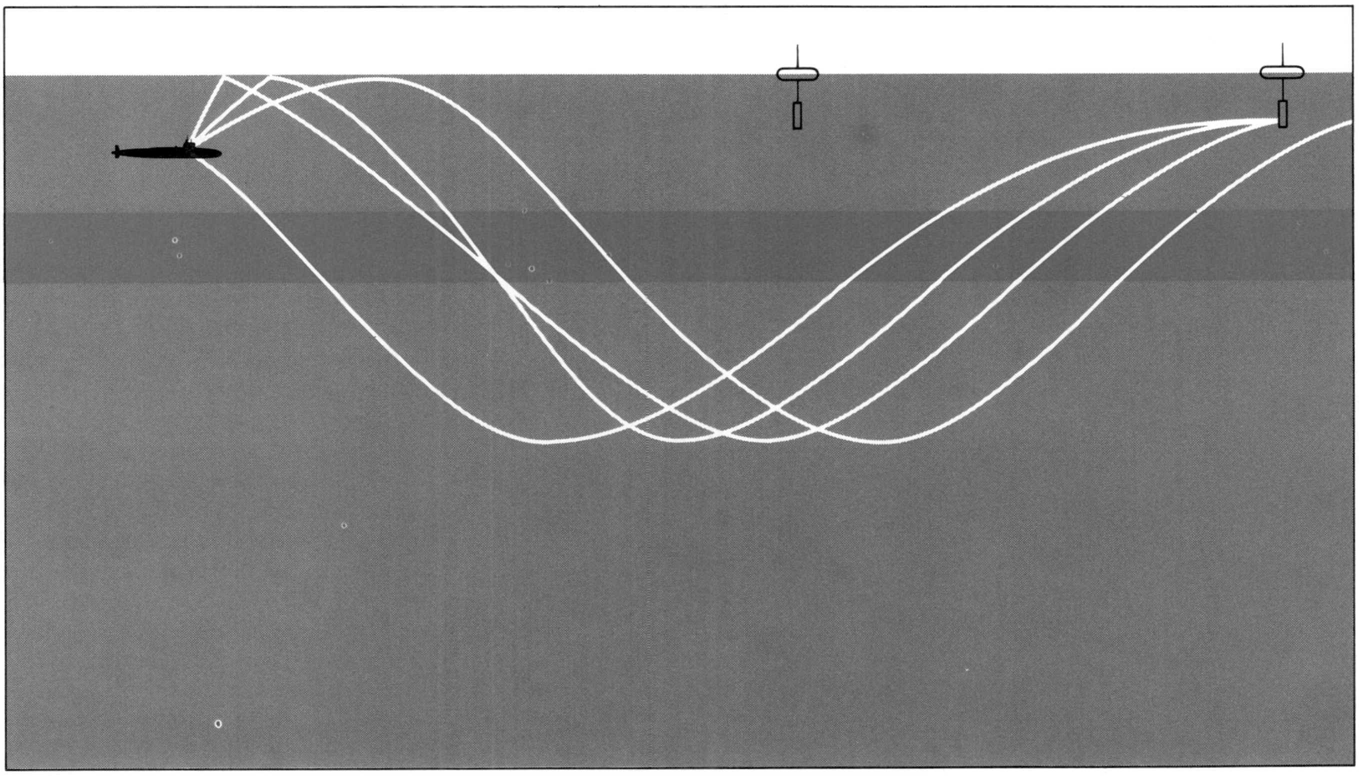

"CONVERGENCE ZONES" are observed when a near-surface acoustic detector is moved away from a near-surface submarine sound source. The received signal often drops rapidly beyond a few kilometers and then rises to a high level again at multiples of about 50 kilometers. The successive intervals that mark the convergence zones correspond to the distance required for a sound wave initially horizontal to be refracted through and beyond the deep sound channel and to return again to the surface of the ocean.

use of helicopters operating from carriers, destroyers or other sea platforms. The sonar devices are lowered from the helicopter by winch and can descend to depths of several hundred meters. An explosive charge can be detonated to produce an omnidirectional sound wave, or magnetostrictive or piezoelectric systems can be used to generate narrow beams of sound. The sound-wave probe is reflected from the sea surface, the sea bottom and marine animals, large and small, as well as from any submarine in the vicinity. The reflected signals are picked up and transmitted by way of the hoist cable to the helicopter for processing and display. To achieve efficient radiation and useful angular discrimination from helicopter-suspended platforms one uses sound frequencies in the range between one and 10 kilohertz (1,000 and 10,000 cycles per second) as compared with the subkilohertz waves employed for long-range detection. Signals in the range of 100 kilohertz to one megahertz attenuate so rapidly and become so scattered that they are not useful for submarine detection at long range.

In principle active sonars can detect moving objects more readily than stationary objects, because the Doppler shift in the sonar echo can be used to enhance the signal. On the other hand, even when the acoustic energy is confined to an ocean layer including the submarine, active sonars suffer a two-way loss: the power illuminating the target falls off directly with the distance, which means that the return signal decreases as the square of the distance. In other words, for equivalent received signals an active sonar must illuminate the target with at least as much energy as the target is radiating by itself (assuming that it is radiating and not just lying dead in the water), although detection can be accomplished with weaker signals because the precise form of the signal is known and often chosen to be best adapted to signal processing.

The purpose of active sonar is not necessarily to sweep the oceans clear of submarines; such systems are often employed to provide a submarine-free region a few kilometers in diameter in which merchant or military ships can be free from attack. When submarines had only unguided torpedoes to attack shipping, active sonars mounted on destroyers or suspended from helicopters provided reasonable protection. Now, however, submarines carry acoustic homing torpedoes with a range of 10 kilometers or more. And the cruise missiles carried by many Russian submarines have an effective range of hundreds of kilometers, which means that active sonar cannot provide a point defense against such submarines.

In the past decade much work has been done on active sonar systems anchored to the ocean bottom in an effort to provide detection of submarines at ranges of hundreds of kilometers. These fixed-active systems, as they are called, emit a narrowly focused beam of sound at frequencies of a few hundred hertz and a power level of several megawatts. Such installations not only are expensive but also have the drawback of broadcasting their location, which makes them vulnerable to countermeasures. The opposition need not even destroy the installation; by sampling the pulses emitted by the system it can contrive to "spoof" or jam it.

An alternative to the fixed-active sonar system is the semiactive, or bistatic, system, in which the transmitters and receivers are widely separated. Such systems are probably harder to spoof or jam than ordinary active sonars and they provide more leeway in the depth at which the transmitter can be located. At very high power levels a deep transmitter is less limited by cavitation: the rapid expansion and collapse of bubbles that arise from gases dissolved in the water.

After a submarine has been detected in a certain target area, say an area 50 kilometers square, the next step is to pinpoint its position. Localization can be done from the air, from the surface or from below the surface. If an aircraft such as a P-3 or an S-2 is employed, it can drop directional sonobuoys that are capable of indicating the bearing from the sonobuoy to the submarine. The aircraft then follows along this line by dropping more sonobuoys. When the submarine has been located to an accuracy of one kilometer or so, its position can be determined still more precisely by low-level passes with a magnetic-anomaly detector (MAD) to sense the presence of a large mass of submerged steel.

If localization is conducted by helicopter, the preferred detector is active sonar suspended from the aircraft, which can determine range accurately and bearing somewhat less accurately. If one assumes that the sonar has a range of three kilometers and that five minutes of listening are needed each time the sonar unit is lowered into the water, one can estimate that one helicopter can search 300 square kilometers per hour. Thus within an hour six helicopters should have a 50 percent chance of finding a single submarine known initially to be in a square area 50 kilometers on a side.

If the search is conducted by surface ships, active sonar is used in essentially the same way as by helicopters except that a surface ship does not have nearly

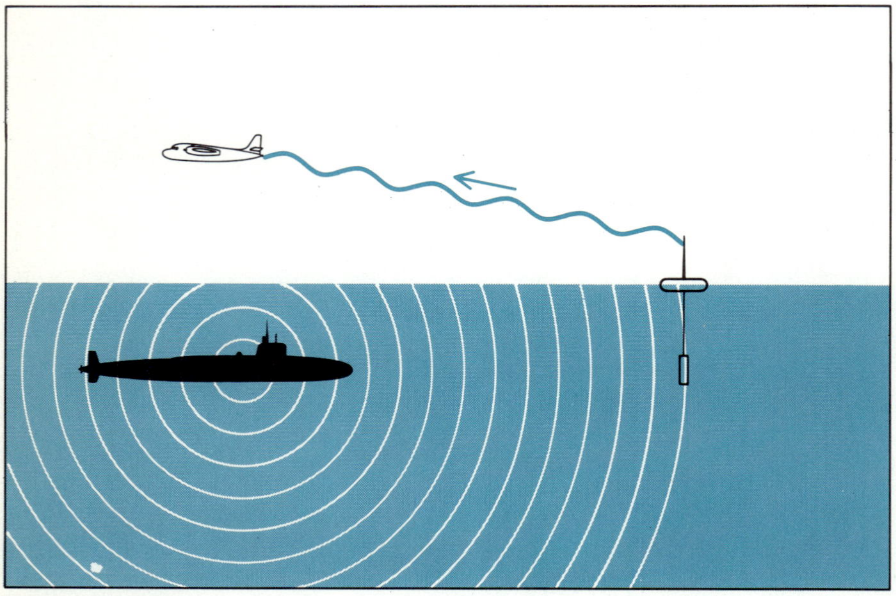

PASSIVE ACOUSTIC DETECTION of a submerged submarine relies on picking up the noise radiated by the submarine itself. In this case the passive acoustic detector is a hydrophone dangling from a buoy at a substantial depth; signals detected by the hydrophone are relayed by radio to the aircraft for analysis. Hydrophones of this type and size can be sown by aircraft in either dispersed or concentrated arrays. Larger hydrophones can also be mounted on the hulls of surface vessels (usually destroyers) or on other submarines.

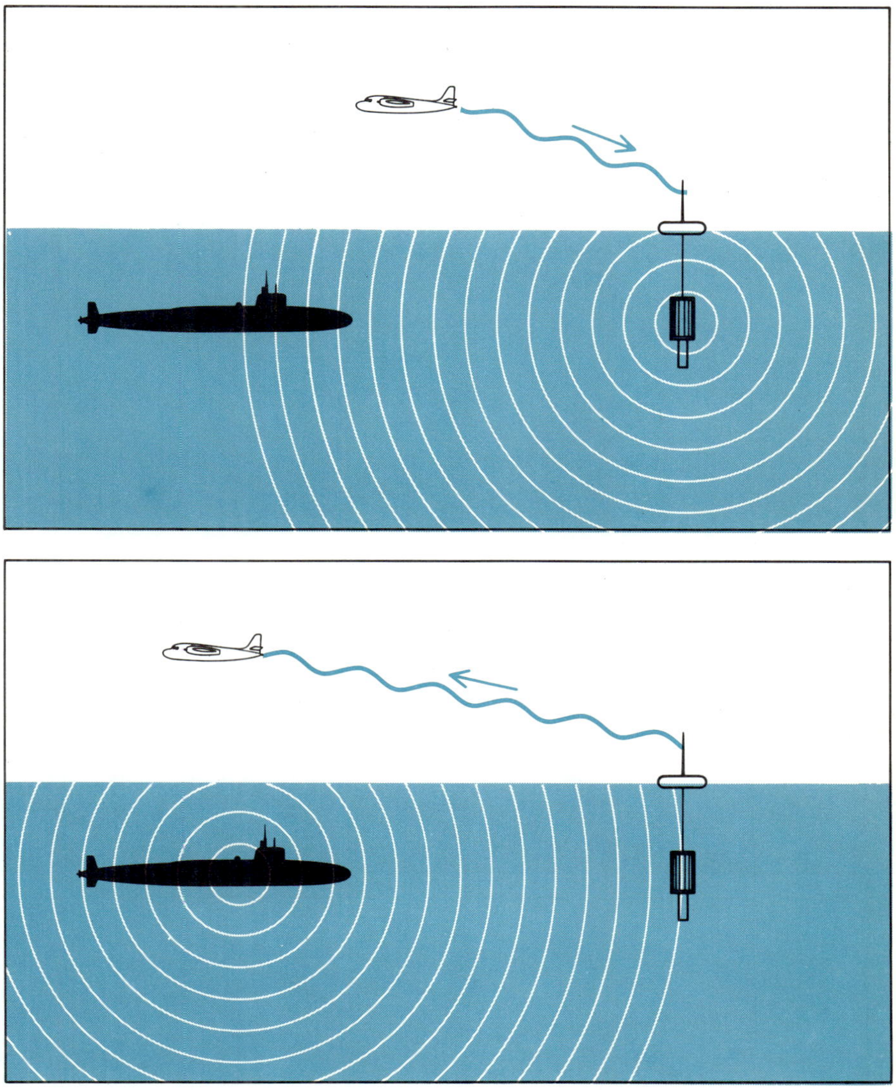

ACTIVE ACOUSTIC DETECTION of a submerged submarine requires a sound generator combined with a hydrophone to receive reflected sound waves. "Sonar" systems of this type suffer a two-way loss: in a near-surface sound channel the power illuminating the target (*top*) falls off directly with the distance, which means that the return signal (*bottom*) decreases as the square of the distance. Deep or bottom-mounted sonars suffer spherical spreading of the sound energy; hence the illuminating power falls off as the square of the distance, and the total energy received at the sonar falls off as the fourth power. Besides being deployed in aircraft-sown sonobuoy fields, sonar systems can be mounted on other submarines, surface ships or on devices towed at various depths from ships or helicopters.

the speed advantage over a submarine that a helicopter has. This disadvantage is partly compensated for by the surface ship's ability to carry a sonar of much higher power and effectiveness than the equipment a helicopter can carry.

Underwater search by one or more hunter-killer submarines is perhaps the slowest but not necessarily the least effective way of localizing a submarine. A hunter-killer submarine has an optimum search speed of between five and 15 knots. For a given sonar range the area searched increases linearly with speed, but the self-noise generated as speed increases reduces the effective sonar range. Hence the optimum search speed is a compromise.

In antisubmarine-warfare exercises an "enemy" submarine that with much effort has been detected and localized is often tracked for hours or even days. The tracking skill thus developed in peacetime, however, has little applicability in wartime. Under wartime conditions an enemy submarine would ordinarily be sunk as soon as it was localized. As for tracking the other side's ballistic-missile submarines 24 hours a day in peacetime, the simultaneous tracking of 30 to 50 modern submarines is so difficult that its feasibility seems doubtful. Even if the job could be done, it is the thesis of this article that continuous tracking is distinctly undesirable if one concedes that the nuclear deterrent is valuable and should be preserved.

Let us see nonetheless what continuous tracking involves. Antisubmarine warfare is the primary mission of the U.S. fleet of nuclear-powered hunter-killer submarines, numbering some 57 vessels. Their chief sensor is low-frequency passive sonar. Depending on the state of the sea, they are probably able to detect a moving Russian submarine at distances ranging from a few kilometers to perhaps 20 or 30 kilometers under more favorable conditions. An effort to carry out passive acoustic tracking reliably at a range of 10 kilometers or more in the face of changing sea conditions, normal variations in sound velocity, sea noise and the evasive measures readily available to the quarry seems doomed, however, to failure. If such tracking could be accomplished at all, several hunter-killer submarines would probably have to be assigned to each hunted submarine. Moreover, if the necessity should arise, the destruction of an enemy submarine at a range of 10 kilometers or more before it could fire its missiles might call for a weapon faster than the standard torpedo. For these and other reasons, including the possibility of acoustic countermeasures, my own view is that effective covert tracking is not a plausible disarming threat to the submarine-based deterrent forces of either the U.S. or the U.S.S.R.

Active sonar tracking from submarines, surface vessels or aircraft is another story. Given the mission to maintain at all times the ability to destroy the enemy fleet of ballistic-missile submarines before it could launch its weapons, one would immediately think of active trailing from extremely short range, say a few hundred meters. At that distance a sonar operating at a frequency of 100 to 1,000 kilohertz would be compact and low-powered and could provide a clear pictorial representation of the target. For example, a 1,000 kilohertz (one megahertz) sonar would provide a resolution of 30 centimeters on a target 200 meters away. Mounted on a specialized trailing vehicle (submerged, on the surface or airborne), such a sonar could provide a detailed picture of its quarry every few seconds. The tracker could therefore sail in formation with the quarry without fear of collision.

This is not the place to describe the command-and-control arrangements that would enable the small specialized tracking ship to destroy its quarry on

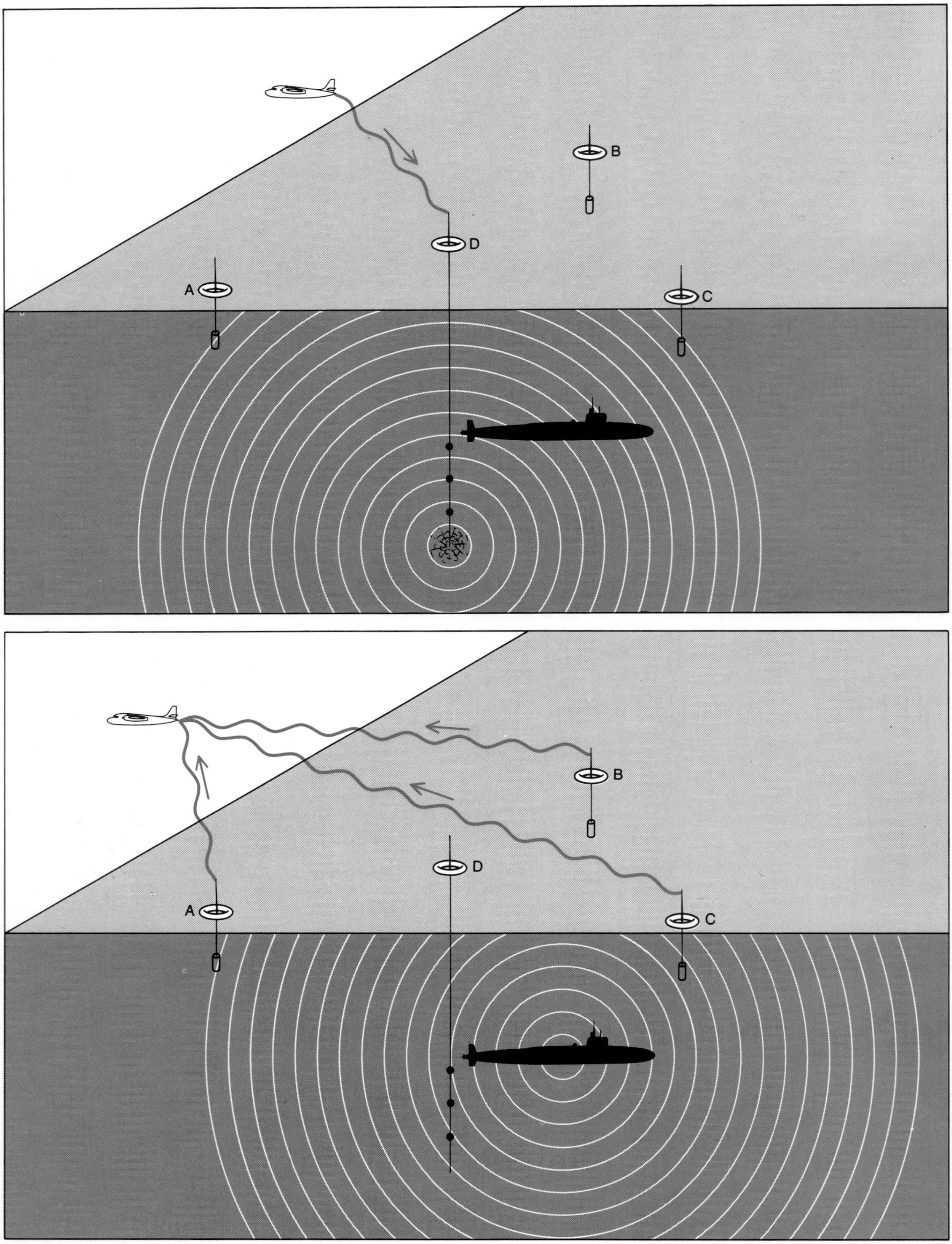

SEMIACTIVE ACOUSTIC DETECTION involves systems in which the transmitters and the receivers are widely separated. In the idealized system portrayed in the pair of diagrams on this page an ASW aircraft has sown a field of passive hydrophones in the vicinity of a submerged submarine. A string of explosive charges is suspended from a similar aircraft-delivered buoy to a depth of several hundred meters. The charges are detonated singly on command to produce a series of omnidirectional sound waves (*top*). The reflected signals, or echoes, are picked up by the hydrophones and transmitted to the aircraft for processing and display (*bottom*).

command or that would lead to the destruction of both ships if the quarry should attempt to use force against the tracker. The important fact is that the characteristics of such a close-in tracking ship (be it a submarine, a surface vessel or an aircraft) are quite different from those of any craft deployed in large numbers today. The craft would need to have endurance and good seakeeping qualities; it would have no need for more than a few torpedoes or other destructive weapons, and none for a large crew or great flexibility of operation.

The chief difficulty in this type of active tracking seems to lie not in maintaining tracking but in ensuring that a tracker is assigned to every ballistic-missile-launching submarine that leaves the home port and crosses a detection barrier of some kind. Obviously the other side will seek to avoid detection by employing various stratagems, perhaps by sending its missile submarines across the barrier in clumps or by mixing them with non-missile-submarine decoys. The many possibilities need not concern us here. As I have argued above, tracking (particularly active tracking) has little application to tactical antisubmarine warfare, but if done successfully and without opposition, it could jeopardize the survivability of the ballistic-missile-submarine forces of the U.S. and the U.S.S.R.

The U.S. Navy has two principal weapons for destroying enemy submarines: the lightweight 12-inch Mark 46 active acoustic homing torpedo and the full-size 21-inch Mark 48 active-passive acoustic homing torpedo (which is just coming into service). The 12-inch torpedo is essentially the only effective antisubmarine weapon available to aircraft and helicopters. It can also be launched from the deck of a ship or delivered by a drone helicopter. A rocket-boosted version has more range and can get to its target faster than the standard Mark 46. The Mark 48 is a long-range torpedo with a large warhead; when it is launched by a hunter-killer submarine, it can be guided electrically by means of a control wire. Like any other weapon, a homing torpedo will not be perfectly reliable in actual combat, and it may be vulnerable to countermeasures.

Specialists in antisubmarine warfare have long been attracted to more effective antisubmarine mines. Such mines could be planted defensively to protect harbors or to cordon off a landing area for an expeditionary force. They could also be used to keep enemy submarines

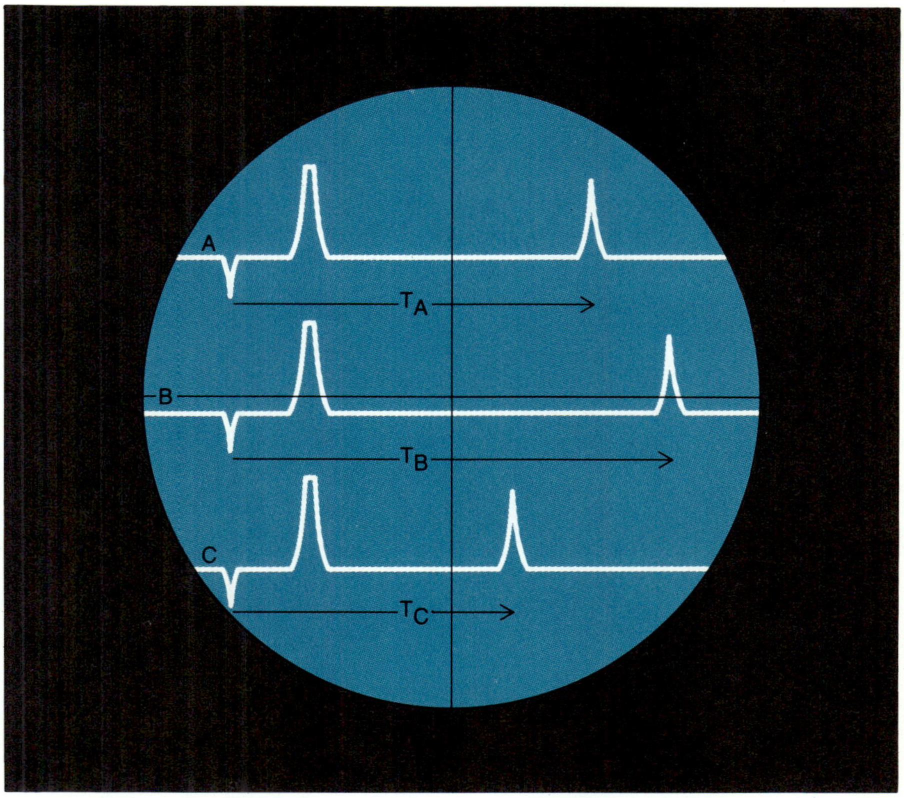

RECEIVED SIGNALS from the semiactive detection system shown in the illustration on the opposite page are processed on board the monitoring aircraft and displayed on a cathode ray tube. The times at which the signals are received from the various hydrophones are then used by an operator to plot the location of the submarine (*see illustration at bottom*).

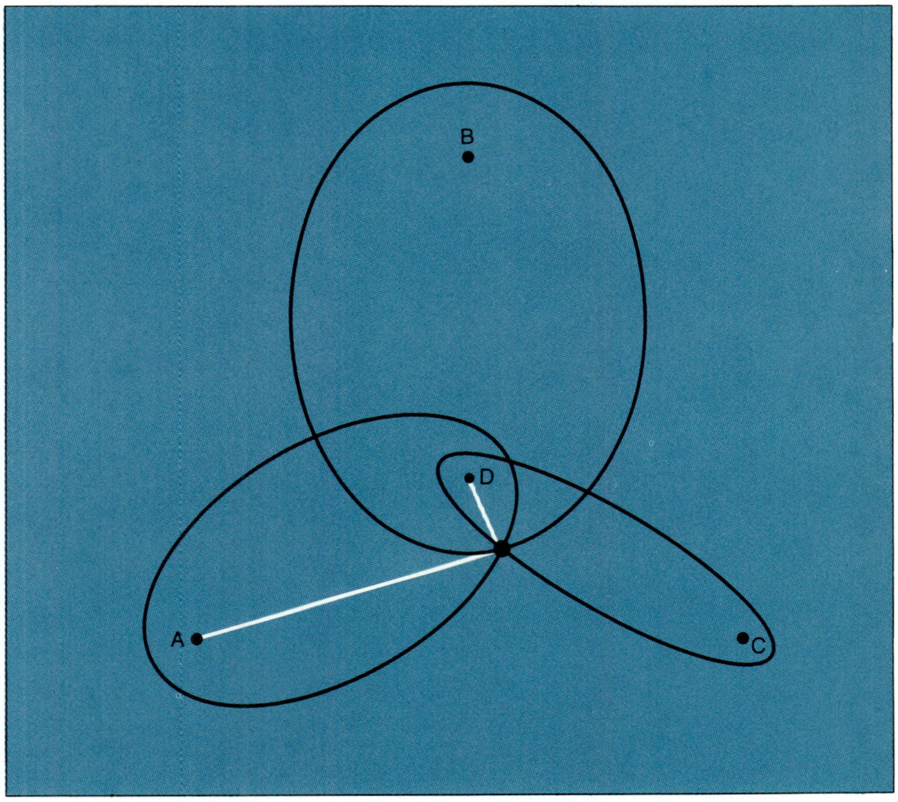

SUBMARINE IS LOCATED on the basis of the times at which the hydrophones picked up the signals reflected from the submarine. The observed time interval T_A between the explosion at D and the reception of the echo at sonobuoy A defines an ellipse with foci at A and D. (The sum of the distances from any point on an ellipse to the two foci is constant.) The information from each hydrophone is used to draw an ellipse on which the submarine is situated. The intersection of the three ellipses indicates the exact location of the quarry.

ANTISUBMARINE MINE of a type that is probably under development in both the U.S. and the U.S.S.R. would have a much greater radius of effectiveness than ordinary mines. The hypothetical device shown incorporates an acoustic homing torpedo, which is designed to drive itself upward when a submarine is detected above it. Such a mine would cost well under $100,000 and have a 50 percent chance of destroying any submarine passing within one kilometer of it.

from leaving their home ports, to create a barrier across straits or even to limit travel in the open ocean.

Since ordinary mines have a limited radius of effectiveness (submarines could pass above or below them), such mines can be used against submarines only in shallow water. There have been recurrent proposals, however, for a mine that would either drive itself downward when a trip wire indicated a submarine was passing below it or drive itself upward when a submarine was detected above it. Mines with this capability are probably under development in both the U.S. and the U.S.S.R.

If such a mine were based on the Mark 46 torpedo, it should cost well under $100,000 and have a 50 percent chance of destroying any submarine passing within one kilometer of it. Thus 500 mines would be enough to cover the gap of 1,000 kilometers between Greenland and the British Isles. Actually the mines would not be sown cheek by jowl in a thin line; they could better be deployed in a minefield 100 kilometers deep with a density of one mine per two kilometers of front so that 500 mines would still suffice.

The mines would allow surface ships to pass without harm, and the commanders of friendly submarines could traverse the minefield safely with the aid of charts. The mines could be remotely activated and deactivated. They could be laid by aircraft, surface ships or submarines. For about $50 million (less than the cost of one destroyer) it should be possible to provide a robust, effective barrier 1,000 kilometers long with low physical and political vulnerability.

Let us now try to distinguish between the kind of antisubmarine force needed to protect surface shipping and the kind of specialized capability needed to find, track and destroy on signal ballistic-missile submarines. Because these two needs impose conflicting requirements on the design of antisubmarine-warfare forces it is not surprising that the U.S. Navy sometimes takes a self-contradictory position when it tries to argue on the one hand the invulnerability of its Polaris-Poseidon submarine fleet and on the other the effectiveness of its antisubmarine forces. I shall argue that one can develop antisubmarine measures sufficient to protect surface shipping during an actual conflict without developing an antisubmarine capability of such a nature that it jeopardizes the other side's submarine-based nuclear deterrent.

Unlike major cities or even aircraft carriers, merchant ships are plentiful and of modest value; they are substantially less costly and easier to replace than nuclear-powered attack submarines. A merchant ship delivered in 1972 with a speed of 22 knots and a deadweight of 29,000 tons costs about $23 million. A U.S. nuclear submarine costs more than $150 million. The average crew size of nuclear submarines also substantially exceeds that of modern merchant ships. The U.S. has some 100 attack submarines; the U.S.S.R. has about 300 oceangoing submarines of all types. During World War II Germany lost about 700 submarines and sank 2,600 merchant ships, accounting for 13 million tons of shipping in the North Atlantic. Therefore in round numbers Germany lost one submarine for every 17,000 tons of Allied shipping sent to the bottom. If in another war U.S. antisubmarine forces were able to destroy one enemy nuclear-powered attack submarine for every 10 merchant ships sunk, we should probably regard the exchange ratio as being in our favor. In such a war of attrition the nonnuclear-powered submarine could be the greater threat.

A well-protected convoy remains a principal means for protecting surface vessels. With the various antisubmarine measures described above it should be possible to achieve a kill ratio of one enemy submarine for every 10 merchantmen sunk. Although this ratio might be acceptable for ordinary military and civilian cargoes, it would not be satisfactory if the surface vessels carried troops or critical materiel required at a specific time by troops being ferried by air.

Protection for such vessels is ordinarily imagined to be provided by destroyer-escort vehicles with extra-powerful sonars that provide a moving screen extending well beyond torpedo range and within which enemy submarines would have a high probability of being located and destroyed. In my own opinion the best way to create such a screen would be to improve the capability of antisub-

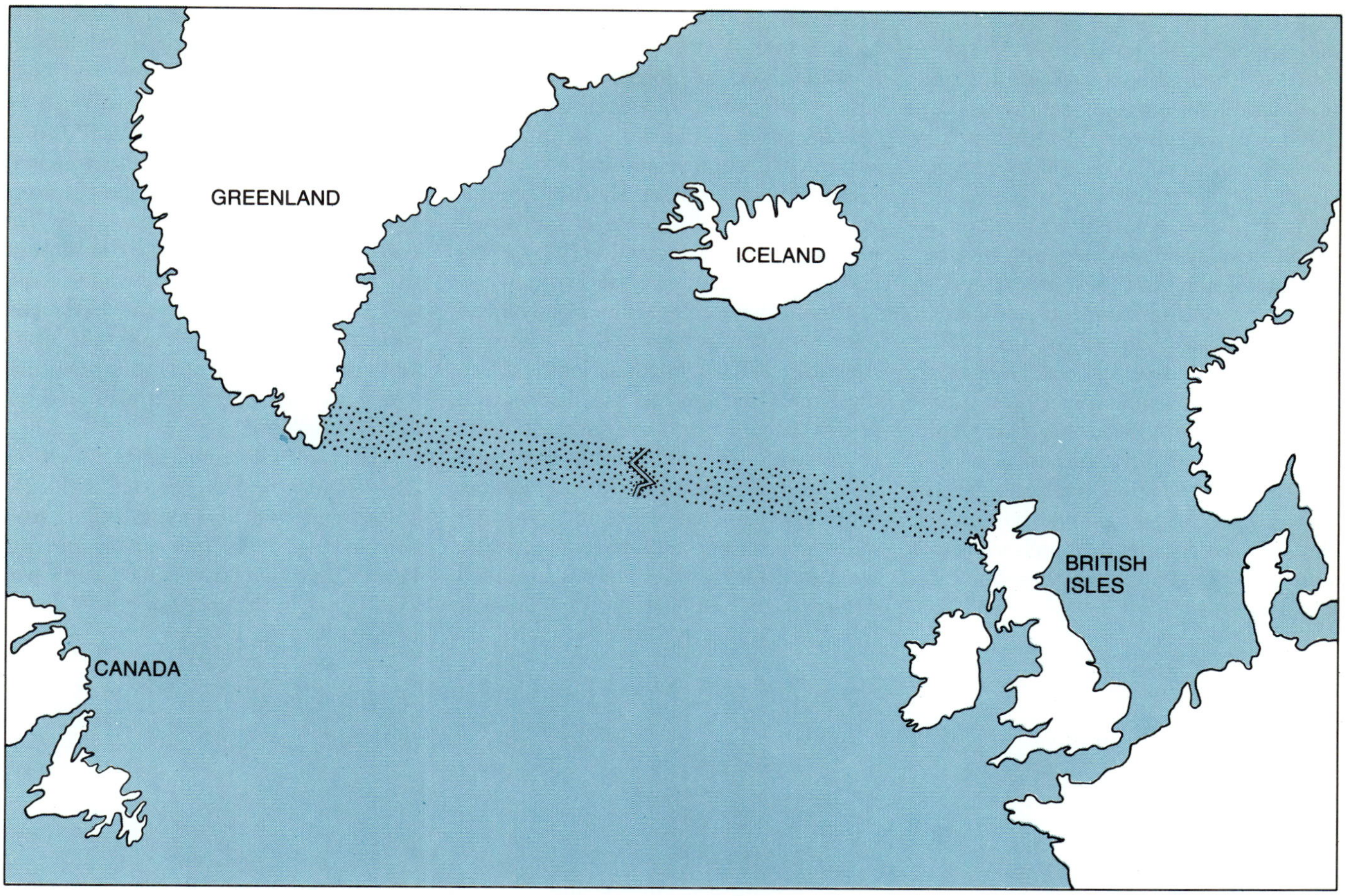

ANTISUBMARINE MINEFIELD based on the use of mines such as the one shown on the opposite page could be laid to create a barrier across the 1,000-kilometer strait between Greenland and the British Isles. For a minefield 100 kilometers deep with a density of one mine per two kilometers of front 500 mines would be needed. The mines would allow surface ships to pass without harm, and friendly submarines could traverse the minefield safely along mine-free lanes with the aid of charts. The mines could be remotely activated and deactivated. The production cost of such an ASW measure (about $50 million) would be less than the cost of one destroyer.

marine helicopters by placing the analysis and data-processing equipment for each helicopter in a van on the deck of a ship rather than in the helicopter itself. With the room saved each helicopter could be provided with several active sonars, which could be deployed by a single helicopter in leapfrog fashion, with the control and signal analysis transmitted by radio between ship and sonars. In this way it should be possible to increase the effectiveness of antisubmarine helicopters by a factor of five, while reducing the crew from four to no more than two persons. Although such improved helicopters can provide a potent local defense, a ballistic-missile-launching submarine could easily move out of range when it detected the approach of such a convoy.

Because a convoy has certain inherent vulnerabilities, such as inviting attack by straight-running torpedoes or by cruise missiles launched from a considerable distance, it is sometimes preferable to allow fast merchant ships to sail independently at maximum speed. The threat to such ships from torpedo attack might be reduced to negligible proportions if each ship carried some retaliatory homing torpedoes that would be launched automatically from the deck of the ship if the ship were struck by a torpedo. This tactic could deter torpedo attack (without defending against it) in just the same way that the strategic offensive force reliably deters a first strike.

The defense of aircraft carriers presents a special problem. An aircraft carrier can scarcely be hidden. Its screws can be heard all the way across an ocean; it is highly visible on radar and can be detected by other means. For these reasons carriers are built to resist damage; as many as a dozen torpedoes are said to be needed to sink one. A close-in defense against torpedo-launching submarines can be provided by the same helicopter-sonar screen already described for the protection of convoys. As some additional protection against cruise missiles launched from a distance of hundreds of kilometers carriers are already equipped with rapid-firing automatic weapons that provide a last-ditch defense. These defenses against cruise missiles could be further improved. One should probably consider installing active antitorpedo defenses directly on the carrier's hull. None of these measures for the defense of aircraft carriers poses any threat to the ballistic-missile submarine.

In any readily foreseeable war between the U.S. and the U.S.S.R. a major part of the conflict at sea will be asymmetrical: an essential mission of the U.S. Navy will be to keep the sea lanes open and an essential mission of the Russian navy will be to close them. Only in preserving the security of their submarine-based ballistic-missile forces are the missions of the two navies symmetrical. By emphasizing the antisubmarine measures discussed here, the U.S. can carry out its two missions; it should be able to protect surface shipping and nullify the Russian attack-submarine force without creating a credible threat to Russia's submarine-based nuclear deterrent. It is this freedom to pursue their individual and opposing interests, while not jeopardizing their common interest in an invulnerable sea-based deterrent, that could lead to arms-control agreements to provide enhanced and equal security for the SLBM deterrent forces.

As we have seen, neither country as yet has the means for negating that deterrent. Even if the U.S. were to improve its tactical antisubmarine techniques to the level I have described, they could not be regarded as a threat to Russia's ballistic-missile submarines. For example, antisubmarine measures that would require, say, 10 days to destroy half of the enemy's ballistic-missile submarines in the open ocean cannot be said to threaten the deterrent. If such measures required only 10 minutes, they would be a real threat.

Moving cordons of antisubmarine vehicles around convoys or aircraft carriers, designed to protect at most 1,000 square kilometers of ocean at a time, can be easily avoided by ballistic-missile-carrying submarines and hence present no threat to them. By the same token the statistical defense of individual merchant ships, triggered only by a torpedo explosion, is no threat.

Would the emplacement of advanced mine barriers be regarded as a threat? A barrier 1,000 kilometers long extending from Greenland to the British Isles could undoubtedly take a substantial toll of deterrent-force submarines that tried to cross it after hostilities began. We are assuming here that the conflict is originally nonnuclear and that both sides want to preserve their submarine-based deterrent to keep it that way. Even if the U.S. did not deliberately cooperate in helping deterrent-force submarines through the minefield, at least half should survive the one-way trip needed to reach firing position. The SLBM force could be stationed behind the minefield without suffering attrition; its deterrent power would not be impaired by the losses suffered on a one-way trip through a barrier if the order were given to move to firing position and launch. On the other hand, the minefield would take a prohibitive toll of antishipping submarines, which must make many trips in and out of their home port.

The question sometimes raised is: How should the U.S. respond if the Polaris-Poseidon fleet should suffer attrition during peacetime under circumstances that seemed suspicious? My personal view is that neither the U.S. nor

ASW AIRCRAFT CARRIER, the U.S.S. *Intrepid*, is capable of launching both ASW aircraft and ASW helicopters. The U.S. has four such carriers, the U.S.S.R. none. The photograph was made during an inspection cruise in the Atlantic Ocean in February, 1971.

the U.S.S.R. has any incentive to covertly reduce the size of the other's deterrent fleet. Furthermore, it is difficult to guarantee that such a covert action is not exposed. Finally, each side has equal vulnerability in its submarine-deterrent fleet.

A more difficult problem is to know how to conduct active, conventional ocean war, including tactical antisubmarine warfare, without an accompanying and unintended attrition of the opponent's submarine-based nuclear deterrent. Let us turn to that problem.

The first step in reducing unintentional attrition would be formal recognition that it is in the mutual interest of the two countries to preserve the submarine-based deterrent not only in peacetime but also indefinitely during a conflict to forestall the escalation to all-out nuclear war. One can imagine many possible arms-control agreements that would then contribute to the continued invulnerability of the submarine-based deterrent.

Such an agreement might have two goals. First, it might prohibit either side from building or deploying a force that is technically capable of destroying the other side's submarine deterrent in a matter of minutes, hours or even a few days. The second goal, which might be more difficult to achieve, would be a set of measures that would reduce or perhaps eliminate the attrition of missile-launching submarines during a conventional war without restricting vigorous warfare to protect (or attack) surface shipping.

The first goal—the peacetime one—might be aided by prohibitions against the active tracking of missile submarines and by the creation of sanctuary areas. There are so many possible technical ways to discourage active tracking unilaterally that it is by no means assured that one side, invest what it will, could follow nearly all its opponent's submarines. It would nonetheless be valuable to reach an early agreement to eliminate fear of this threat, which seems to have no utility other than to threaten the survival of the strategic deterrent. Moreover, such an agreement seems readily verifiable. It should not be difficult for a submarine that is being tracked to recognize that it has (or has not) at all times a companion at a distance of a few hundred to a few thousand meters.

Additional protection for the submarine deterrent force in peacetime could be achieved by creating wide-ocean sanctuaries in which ballistic-missile submarines of one side or the other would be free to patrol, immune from surveillance of any kind. Clearly the sanctuaries must be large compared with the range of antisubmarine detection and attack devices, yet they must not be so large that they interfere with merchant shipping or with the transit routes of naval vessels, including deterrent-force submarines. Problems may arise in connection with third parties but these do not appear insoluble.

To limit the attrition of deterrent-force submarines during a conventional war, the U.S. and the U.S.S.R. might agree to provide safe-conduct routes through minefields or other barriers for each other's ballistic-missile submarines. The problem here is to distinguish between strategic missile submarines entitled to safe passage and attack submarines, which would still be fair game. The simplest solution would be to provide safe passage to any submarine that was effectively running on the surface and could thus be inspected.

Because surfaced submarines are not very good at traversing heavy seas, a submarine could be allowed to travel submerged provided that it towed a buoy emitting a distinctive radio signal. The signal could be monitored by surface ships, aircraft or even by satellites, and the position of such submarines could thus be known precisely and instantaneously. Buoy-towing submarines would be allowed to pass without harassment (although subject to surfacing on call) through clearly marked lanes in barriers; all other submarines would be subject to attack. The number of safe-conduct trips per month could be only enough to permit normal rotation of submarines in the deterrent force.

These three schemes only suggest the scope of possibilities for a SALT II agreement that would enhance the survivability of submarines designed specially for carrying long-range ballistic missiles. I should emphasize that in my opinion such submarines are probably adequately survivable in the absence of a new agreement. An important function of the agreement, however, would be to allay exaggerated fears that our Polaris-Poseidon fleet might suddenly be neutralized by a dramatic advance in the effectiveness of antisubmarine warfare. As a nonnegligible by-product of such an agreement both the U.S. and the U.S.S.R. would be enabled to reallocate either within or outside the military sphere much of the money that is likely to be spent in attempting to endanger the deterrent, if no agreement is forthcoming.

NEWEST ASW AIRCRAFT, the S-3A, was photographed during a test flight earlier this year. The jet-powered aircraft is scheduled to join the U.S. ASW forces in 1974, replacing the propeller-driven S-2. The carrier-based S-3A will carry a digital computer to enable its four-man crew to better analyze underwater sounds and other data. It will be armed with a variety of weapons: acoustic homing torpedoes, mines, depth charges, rockets and missiles.

Treaty between the United States of America and the Union of Soviet Socialist Republics on the Limitation of Anti-Ballistic-Missile Systems

Text of treaty done at Moscow on May 26, 1972.
Not published in Scientific American.

The United States of America and the Union of Soviet Socialist Republics, hereinafter referred to as the Parties,

Proceeding from the premise that nuclear war would have devastating consequences for all mankind,

Considering that effective measures to limit anti-ballistic missile systems would be a substantial factor in curbing the race in strategic offensive arms and would lead to a decrease in the risk of outbreak of war involving nuclear weapons,

Proceeding from the premise that the limitation of anti-ballistic missile systems, as well as certain agreed measures with respect to the limitation of strategic offensive arms, would contribute to the creation of more favorable conditions for further negotiations on limiting strategic arms,

Mindful of their obligations under Article VI of the Treaty on the Non-Proliferation of Nuclear Weapons,

Declaring their intention to achieve at the earliest possible date the cessation of the nuclear arms race and to take effective measures toward reductions in strategic arms, nuclear disarmament, and general and complete disarmament,

Desiring to contribute to the relaxation of international tension and the strengthening of trust between States,

Have agreed as follows:

Article I

1. Each Party undertakes to limit anti-ballistic missile (ABM) systems and to adopt other measures in accordance with the provisions of this Treaty.
2. Each Party undertakes not to deploy ABM systems for a defense of the territory of its country and not to provide a base for such a defense, and not to deploy ABM systems for defense of an individual region except as provided for in Article III of this Treaty.

Article II

1. For the purposes of this Treaty an ABM system is a system to counter strategic ballistic missiles or their elements in flight trajectory, currently consisting of:

   (a) ABM interceptor missiles, which are interceptor missiles constructed and deployed for an ABM role, or of a type tested in an ABM mode;

   (b) ABM launchers, which are launchers constructed and deployed for launching ABM interceptor missiles: and

(c) ABM radars, which are radars constructed and deployed for an ABM role, or of a type tested in an ABM mode.

2. The ABM system components listed in paragraph 1 of this Article include those which are:
(a) operational;
(b) under construction;
(c) undergoing testing;
(d) undergoing overhaul, repair or conversion; or
(e) mothballed.

Article III

Each Party undertakes not to deploy ABM systems or their components except that:

(a) within one ABM system deployment area having a radius of one hundred and fifty kilometers and centered on the Party's national capital, a Party may deploy: (1) no more than one hundred ABM launchers and no more than one hundred ABM interceptor missiles at launch sites, and (2) ABM radars within no more than six ABM radar complexes, the area of each complex being circular and have a diameter of no more than three kilometers; and

(b) within one ABM system deployment area having a radius of one hundred and fifty kilometers and containing ICBM silo launchers, a Party may deploy: (1) no more than one hundred ABM launchers and no more than one hundred ABM interceptor missiles at launch sites, (2) two large phased-array ABM radars comparable in potential to corresponding ABM radars operational or under construction on the date of signature of the Treaty in an ABM system deployment area containing ICBM silo launchers, and (3) no more than eighteen ABM radars each having a potential less than the potential of the smaller of the above-mentioned two large phased-array ABM radars.

Article IV

The limitations provided for in Article III shall not apply to ABM systems or their components used for development or testing, and located within current or additionally agreed test ranges. Each Party may have no more than a total of fifteen ABM launchers at test ranges.

Article V

1. Each Party undertakes not to develop, test, or deploy ABM systems or components which are sea-based, air-based, space-based, or mobile land-based.

2. Each Party undertakes not to develop, test, or deploy ABM launchers for launching more than one ABM interceptor missile at a time from each launcher, nor to modify deployed launchers to provide them with such a capability, nor to develop, test, or deploy automatic or semi-automatic or other similar systems for rapid reload or ABM launchers.

Article VI

To enhance assurance of the effectiveness of the limitations on ABM systems and their components provided by this Treaty, each Party undertakes:

(a) not to give missiles, launchers, or radars, other than ABM interceptor missiles, ABM launchers, or ABM radars, capabilities to counter strategic ballistic missiles or their elements in flight trajectory, and not to test them in an ABM mode; and

(b) not to deploy in the future radars for early warning of strategic ballistic missile attack except at locations along the periphery of its national territory and oriented outward.

Article VII

Subject to the provisions of this Treaty, modernization and replacement of ABM systems or their components may be carried out.

Article VIII

ABM systems or their components in excess of the numbers or outside the areas specified in this Treaty, as well as ABM systems or their components prohibited by this Treaty, shall be destroyed or dismantled under agreed procedures within the shortest possible agreed period of time.

Article IX

To assure the viability and effectiveness of this Treaty, each Party undertakes not to transfer to other States, and not to deploy outside its national territory, ABM systems or their components limited by this Treaty.

Article X

Each Party undertakes not to assume any international obligations which would conflict with this Treaty.

Article XI

The Parties undertake to continue active negotiations for limitations on strategic offensive arms.

Article XII

1. For the purpose of providing assurance of compliance with the provisions of this Treaty, each Party shall use national technical means of verification at its disposal in a manner consistent with generally recognized principles of international law.

2. Each Party undertakes not to interfere with the national technical means of verification of the other Party operating in accordance with paragraph 1 of this Article.

3. Each Party undertakes not to use deliberate concealment measures which impede verification by national technical means of compliance with the provisions of this Treaty. This obligation shall not require changes in current construction, assembly, conversion, or overhaul practices.

Article XIII

1. To promote the objectives and implementation of the provisions of this Treaty, the Parties shall establish promptly a Standing Consultative Commission, within the framework of which they will:

(a) consider questions concerning compliance with the obligations assumed and related situations which may be considered ambiguous;

(*b*) provide on a voluntary basis such information as either Party considers necessary to assure confidence in compliance with the obligations assumed;
(*c*) consider questions involving unintended interference with national technical means of verification;
(*d*) consider possible changes in the strategic situation which have a bearing on the provisions of this Treaty;
(*e*) agree upon procedures and dates for destruction or dismantling of ABM systems or their components in cases provided for by the provisions of this Treaty;
(*f*) consider, as appropriate, possible proposals for further increasing the viability of this Treaty, including proposals for amendments in accordance with the provisions of this Treaty;
(*g*) consider, as appropriate, proposals for further measures aimed at limiting strategic arms.
2. The Parties through consultation shall establish, and may amend as appropriate, Regulations for the Standing Consultative Commission Governing procedures, composition and other relevant matters.

ARTICLE XIV

1. Each Party may propose amendments to this Treaty. Agreed amendments shall enter into force in accordance with the procedures governing the entry into force of this Treaty:

2. Five years after entry into force of this Treaty, and at five year intervals thereafter, the Parties shall together conduct a review of this Treaty.

ARTICLE XV

1. This Treaty shall be of unlimited duration.

2. Each Party shall, in exercising its national sovereignty, have the right to withdraw from this Treaty if it decides that extraordinary events related to the subject matter of this Treaty have jeopardized its supreme interests. It shall give notice of its decision to the other Party six months prior to withdrawal from the Treaty. Such notice shall include a statement of the extraordinary events the notifying Party regards as having jeopardized its supreme interests.

ARTICLE XVI

1. This Treaty shall be subject to ratification in accordance with the constitutional procedures of each Party. The Treaty shall enter into force on the day of the exchange of instruments of ratification.

2. This Treaty shall be registered pursuant to Article 102 of the Charter of the United Nations.
DONE at Moscow on May 26, 1972, in two copies, each in the English and Russian languages, both texts being equally authentic.
For the United States of America:

RICHARD NIXON,
President of the United States of America.

For the Union of Soviet Socialist Republics:

L. I. BREZHNEV,
General Secretary of the Central Committee of the CPSU.

Interim Agreement between the United States of America and the Union of Soviet Socialist Republics on Certain Measures with Respect to the Limitation of Strategic Offensive Arms

Text of interim agreement done at Moscow on May 26, 1972. Not published in Scientific American.

The United States of America and the Union of Soviet Socialist Republics, hereinafter referred to as the Parties,

Convinced that the Treaty on the Limitation of Anti-Ballistic Missile Systems and this Interim Agreement on Certain Measures with Respect to the Limitation of Strategic Offensive Arms will contribute to the creation of more favorable conditions for active negotiations on limiting strategic arms as well as to the relaxation of international tension and the strengthening of trust between States,

Taking into account the relationship between strategic offensive and defensive arms,

Mindful of their obligations under Article VI of the Treaty on the Non-Proliferation of Nuclear Weapons,

Have agreed as follows:

Article I

The Parties undertake not to start construction of additional fixed land-based intercontinental ballistic missile (ICBM) launchers after July 1, 1972.

Article II

The Parties undertake not to convert land-based launchers for light ICBMs, or for ICBMs of older types deployed prior to 1964, into land-based launchers for heavy ICBMs of types deployed after that time.

Article III

The Parties undertake to limit submarine-launched ballistic missile (SLBM) launchers and modern ballistic missile submarines to the numbers operational and under construction on the date of signature of this Interim Agreement, and in addition to launchers and submarines constructed under procedures established by the Parties, replacements for an equal number of ICBM launchers of older types deployed prior to 1964 or for launchers on older submarines.

Article IV

Subject to the provisions of this Interim Agreement, modernization and replacement of strategic offensive ballistic missiles and launchers covered by this Interim Agreement may be undertaken.

Article V

1. For the purpose of providing assurance of compliance with the provisions of this Interim Agreement, each Party shall use national technical means of verification at its disposal in a manner consistent with generally recognized principles of international law.

2. Each Party undertakes not to interfere with the national technical means of verification of the other Party operating in accordance with paragraph 1 of this Article.

3. Each Party undertakes not to use deliberate concealment measures which impede verification by national technical means of compliance with the provisions of this Interim Agreement. This obligation shall not require changes in current construction, assembly, conversion, or overhaul practices.

Article VI

To promote the objectives and implementation of the provisions of this Interim Agreement, the Parties shall use the Standing Consultative Commission established under Article XIII of the Treaty on the Limitation of Anti-Ballistic Missile Systems in accordance with the provisions of that Article.

Article VII

The Parties undertake to continue active negotiations for limitations on strategic offensive arms. The obligations provided for in this Interim Agreement shall not prejudice the scope or terms of the limitations on strategic offensive arms which may be worked out in the course of further negotiations.

Article VIII

1. This Interim Agreement shall enter into force upon exchange of written notices of acceptance by each Party, which exchange shall take place simultaneously with the exchange of instruments of ratification of the Treaty on the Limitation of Anti-Ballistic Missile Systems.

2. This Interim Agreement shall remain in force for a period of five years unless replaced earlier by an agreement on more complete measures limiting strategic offensive arms. It is the objective of the Parties to conduct active follow-on negotiations with the aim of concluding such an agreement as soon as possible.

3. Each Party shall, in exercising its national sovereignty, have the right to withdraw from this Interim Agreement if it decides that extraordinary events related to the subject matter of this Interim Agreement have jeopardized its supreme interests. It shall give notice of its decision to the other Party six months prior to withdrawal from this Interim Agreement. Such notice shall include a statement of the extraordinary events the notifying Party regards as having jeopardized its supreme interests.

DONE at Moscow on May 26, 1972, in two copies, each in the English and Russian languages, both texts being equally authentic.

For the United States of America:

RICHARD NIXON,
President of the United States of America.

For the Union of Soviet Socialist Republics:

L. I. BREZHNEV,
General Secretary of the Central Committee of the CPSU.

Protocol to the Interim Agreement between the United States of American and the Union of Soviet Socialist Republics on Certain Measures with Respect to the Limitation of Strategic Offensive Arms.

Text of protocol done at Moscow on May 26, 1972.
Not published in Scientific American.

The United States of America and the Union of Soviet Socialist Republics, hereinafter referred to as the Parties,

Having agreed on certain limitations relating to submarine-launched ballistic missile launchers and modern ballistic missile submarines and to replacement procedures, in the Interim Agreement,

Have agreed as follows:

The Parties understand that, under Article III of the Interim Agreement, for the period during which that Agreement remains in force:

The U.S. may have no more than 710 ballistic missile launchers on submarines (SLBMs) and no more than 44 modern ballistic missile submarines. The Soviet Union may have no more than 950 ballistic missile launchers on submarines and no more than 62 modern ballistic missile submarines.

Additional ballistic missile launchers on submarines up to the above mentioned levels, in the U.S.—over 656 ballistic missile launchers on nuclear-powered submarines, and in the U.S.S.R.—over 740 ballistic missile launchers on nuclear-powered submarines, operational and under construction, may become operational as replacements for equal numbers of ballistic missile launchers of older types deployed prior to 1964 or of ballistic missile launchers on older submarines.

The deployment of modern SLBMs on any submarine, regardless of type, will be counted against the total level of SLBMs permitted for the U.S. and the U.S.S.R.

This Protocol shall be considered an integral part of the Interim Agreement.

DONE at Moscow this 26th day of May, 1972.

For the United States of America:

RICHARD NIXON,
President of the United States of America.

For the Union of Soviet Socialist Republics:

L. I. BREZHNEV,
General Secretary of the Central Committee of the CPSU.

Agreed Interpretations and Unilateral Statements

Text of interpretations and statements done at Moscow on May 26, 1972.
Not published in Scientific American.

1. AGREED INTERPRETATIONS

(*a*) *Initialed Statements.*—The texts of the statements set out below were agreed upon and initialed by the Heads of the Delegations on May 26, 1972.

ABM TREATY

[A]

The Parties understand that, in addition to the ABM radars which may be deployed in accordance with subparagraph (a) of Article III of the Treaty, those non-phased-array ABM radars operational on the date of signature of the Treaty within the ABM system deployment area for defense of the national capital may be retained.

[B]

The Parties understand that the potential (the product of mean emitted power in watts and antenna area in square meters) of the smaller of the two large phased-array ABM radars referred to in subparagraph (b) of Article III of the Treaty is considered for purposes of the Treaty to be three million.

[C]

The Parties understand that the center of the ABM system deployment area centered on the national capital and the center of the ABM system deployment area containing ICBM silo launchers for each Party shall be separated by no less than thirteen hundred kilometers.

[D]

The Parties agree not to deploy phased-array radars having a potential (the product of mean emitted power in watts and antenna area in square meters) exceeding three million, except as provided for in Articles III, IV and VI of the Treaty, or except for the purposes of tracking objects in outer space or for use as national technical means of verification.

[E]

In order to insure fulfillment of the obligation not to deploy ABM systems and their components except as provided in Article III of the Treaty, the Parties agree that in the event ABM systems based on other physical principles and including components capable of substituting for ABM interceptor missiles, ABM launchers, or ABM radars are created in the future, specific limitations on such systems and their components would be subject to discussion in accordance with Article XIII and agreement in accordance with Article XIV of the Treaty.

[F]

The Parties understand that Article V of the Treaty includes obligations not to develop, test or deploy ABM interceptor missiles for the delivery by each ABM interceptor missile of more than one independently guided warhead.

[G]

The Parties understand that Article IX of the Treaty includes the obligation of the US and the USSR not to provide to other States technical descriptions or blueprints specially worked out for the construction of ABM systems and their components limited by the Treaty.

INTERIM AGREEMENT

[H]

The Parties understand that land-based ICBM launchers referred to in the Interim Agreement are understood to be launchers for strategic ballistic missiles capable of ranges in excess of the shortest distance between the northeastern border of the continental U.S. and the northwestern border of the continental USSR.

[I]

The Parties understand that fixed land-based ICBM launchers under active construction as of the date of signature of the Interim Agreement may be completed.

[J]

The Parties understand that in the process of modernization and replacement the dimensions of land-based ICBM silo launchers will not be significantly increased.

[K]

The Parties understand that dismantling or destruction of ICBM launchers of older types deployed prior to 1964 and ballistic missile launchers on older submarines being replaced by new SLBM launchers on modern submarines will be initiated at the time of the beginning of sea trials of a replacement submarine, and will be completed in the shortest possible agreed period of time. Such dismantling or destruction and timely notification thereof, will be accomplished under procedures to be agreed in the Standing Consultative Commission.

[L]

The Parties understand that during the period of the Interim Agreement there shall be no significant increase in the number of ICBM or SLBM test and training launchers, or in the number of such launchers for modern land-based heavy ICBMs. The Parties further understand that construction or conversion of ICBM launchers at test ranges shall be undertaken only for purposes of testing and training.

(*b*) *Common Understandings.*—Common understanding of the Parties on the following matters was reached during the negotiations:

A. INCREASE IN ICBM SILO DIMENSIONS

Ambassador Smith made the following statement on May 26, 1972:

> The Parties agree that the term "significantly increased" means that an increase will not be greater than 10–15 percent of the present dimensions of land-based ICBM silo launchers.

Minister Semenov replied that this statement corresponded to the Soviet understanding.

B. LOCATION OF ICBM DEFENSES

The U.S. Delegation made the following statement on May 26, 1972:

> Article III of the ABM Treaty provides for each side one ABM system deployment area centered on its national capital and one ABM system deployment area containing ICBM silo launchers. The two sides have registered agreement on the following statement: "The Parties understand that the center of the ABM system deployment area centered on the national capital and the center of the ABM system deployment area containing ICBM silo launchers for each Party shall be separated by no less than thirteen hundred kilometers." In this connection, the U.S. side notes that its ABM

system deployment area for defense of ICBM silo launchers, located west of the Mississippi River, will be centered in the Grand Forks ICBM silo launcher deployment area. (See Initialed Statement [C].)

C. ABM TEST RANGES

The U.S. Delegation made the following statement on April 26, 1972:

Article IV of the ABM Treaty provides that "the limitations provided for in Article III shall not apply to ABM systems or their components used for development or testing, and located within current or additionally agreed test ranges." We believe it would be useful to assure that there is no misunderstanding as to current ABM test ranges. It is our understanding that ABM test ranges encompass the area within which ABM components are located for test purposes. The current U.S. ABM test ranges are at White Sands, New Mexico, and at Kwajalein Atoll, and the current Soviet ABM test range is near Sary Shagan in Kazakhstan. We consider that non-phased array radars of types used for range safety or instrumentation purposes may be located outside of ABM test ranges. We interpret the reference in Article IV to "additionally agreed test ranges" to mean that ABM components will not be located at any other test ranges without prior agreement between our Governments that there will be such additional ABM test ranges.

On May 5, 1972, the Soviet Delegation stated that there was a common understanding on what ABM test ranges were, that the use of the types of non-ABM radars for range safety or instrumentation was not limited under the Treaty, that the reference in Article IV to "additionally agreed" test ranges was sufficiently clear, and that national means permitted identifying current test ranges.

D. MOBILE ABM SYSTEMS

On January 28, 1972, the U.S. Delegation made the following statement:

Article V (1) of the Joint Draft Text of the ABM Treaty includes an undertaking not to develop, test, or deploy mobile land-based ABM systems and their components. On May 5, 1971, the U.S. side indicated that, in its view, a prohibition on deployment of mobile ABM systems and components would rule out the deployment of ABM launchers and radars which were not permanent fixed types. At that time, we asked for the Soviet view of this interpretation. Does the Soviet side agree with the U.S. side's interpretation put forward on May 5, 1971?

On April 13, 1972, the Soviet Delegation said there is a general common understanding on this matter.

E. STANDING CONSULTATIVE COMMISSION

Ambassador Smith made the following statement on May 22, 1972:

The United States proposes that the sides agree that, with regard to initial implementation of the ABM Treaty's Article XIII on the Standing Consultative Commission (SCC) and of the consultation Articles to the Interim Agreement on offensive arms and the Accidents Agreement,* agreement establishing the SCC will be worked out early in the follow-on SALT negotiations; until that is completed, the following arrangements will prevail: when SALT is in session, any consultation desired by either side under these Articles can be carried out by the two SALT Delegations; when

*See Article 7 of Agreement to Reduce the Risk of Outbreak of Nuclear War Between the United States of America and the Union of Soviet Socialist Republics, signed Sept. 30, 1971.

SALT is not in session, *ad hoc* arrangements for any desired consultations under these Articles may be made through diplomatic channels.

Minister Semenov replied that, on an *ad referendum* basis, he could agree that the U.S. statement corresponded to the Soviet understanding.

F. STANDSTILL

On May 6, 1972, Minister Semenov made the following statement:

In an effort to accommodate the wishes of the U.S. side, the Soviet Delegation is prepared to proceed on the basis that the two sides will in fact observe the obligations of both the Interim Agreement and the ABM Treaty beginning from the date of signature of these two documents.

In reply, the U.S. Delegation made the following statement on May 20, 1972:

The U.S. agrees in principle with the Soviet statement made on May 6 concerning observance of obligations beginning from date of signature but we would like to make clear our understanding that this means that, pending ratification and acceptance, neither side would take any action prohibited by the agreements after they had entered into force. This understanding would continue to apply in the absence of notification by either signatory of its intention not to proceed with ratification or approval.

The Soviet Delegation indicated agreement with the U.S. statement.

2. Unilateral Statements

(a) The following noteworthy unilateral statements were made during the negotiations by the United States Delegation:

A. WITHDRAWAL FROM THE ABM TREATY

On May 9, 1972, Ambassador Smith made the following statement:

The U.S. Delegation has stressed the importance the U.S. Government attaches to achieving agreement on more complete limitations on strategic offensive arms, following agreement on an ABM Treaty and on an Interim Agreement on certain measures with respect to the limitation of strategic offensive arms. The U.S. Delegation believes that an objective of the follow-on negotiations should be to constrain and reduce on a long-term basis threats to the survivability of our respective strategic retaliatory forces. The USSR Delegation has also indicated that the objectives of SALT would remain unfulfilled without the achievement of an agreement providing for more complete limitations on strategic offensive arms. Both sides recognize that initial agreements would be steps toward the achievement of more complete limitations on strategic arms. If an agreement providing for more complete strategic offensive arms limitations were not achieved within five years, U.S. supreme interests could be jeopardized. Should that occur, it would constitute a basis for withdrawal from the ABM Treaty. The U.S. does not wish to see such a situation occur, nor do we believe that the USSR does. It is because we wish to prevent such a situation that we emphasize the importance the U.S. Government attaches to achievement of more complete limitations on strategic offensive arms. The U.S. Executive will inform the Congress, in connection with Congressional consideration of the ABM Treaty and the Interim Agreement, of this statement of the U.S. position.

B. LAND-MOBILE ICBM LAUNCHERS

The U.S. Delegation made the following statement on May 20, 1972:

In connection with the important subject of land-mobile ICBM launchers, in the interest of concluding the Interim Agreement the U.S. Delegation now withdraws its proposal that Article I or an agreed statement explicitly prohibit the deployment of mobile land-based ICBM launchers. I have been instructed to inform you that, while agreeing to defer the question of limitation of operational land-mobile ICBM launchers to the subsequent negotiations on more complete limitations on strategic offensive arms, the U.S. would consider the deployment of operational land-mobile ICBM launchers during the period of the Interim Agreement as inconsistent with the objectives of that Agreement.

C. COVERED FACILITIES

The U.S. Delegation made the following statement on May 20, 1972:

I wish to emphasize the importance that the United States attaches to the provisions of Article V, including in particular their application to fitting out or berthing submarines.

D. "HEAVY" ICBM'S

The U.S. Delegation made the following statement on May 26, 1972:

The U.S. Delegation regrets that the Soviet Delegation has not been willing to agree on a common definition of a heavy missile. Under these circumstances, the U.S. Delegation believes it necessary to state the following: The United States would consider any ICBM having a volume significantly greater than that of the largest light ICBM now operational on either side to be a heavy ICBM. The U.S. proceeds on the premise that the Soviet side will give due account to this consideration.

E. TESTED IN ABM MODE

On April 7, 1972, the U.S. Delegation made the following statement:

Article II of the Joint Text Draft uses the term "tested in an ABM mode," in defining ABM components, and Article VI includes certain obligations concerning such testing. We believe that the sides should have a common understanding of this phrase. First, we would note that the testing provisions of the ABM Treaty are intended to apply to testing which occurs after the date of signature of the Treaty, and not to any testing which may have occurred in the past. Next, we would amplify the remarks we have made on this subject during the previous Helsinki phase by setting forth the objectives which govern the U.S. view on the subject, namely, while prohibiting testing of non-ABM components for ABM purposes: not to prevent testing of ABM components, and not to prevent testing of non-ABM components for non-ABM purposes. To clarify our interpretation of "tested in an ABM mode," we note that we would consider a launcher, missile or radar to be "tested in an ABM mode" if, for example, any of the following events occur: (1) a launcher is used to launch an ABM interceptor missile, (2) an interceptor missile is flight tested against a target vehicle which has a flight trajectory with characteristics of a strategic ballistic missile flight trajectory, or is flight tested in conjunction with the test of an ABM interceptor missile or an ABM radar at the same test range, or is flight tested to an altitude inconsistent with interception of targets against which air defenses are deployed, (3) a radar makes measurements on a cooperative target vehicle of the kind referred to in item (2) above during the reentry portion of its trajectory or makes measurements in conjunction with the test of an ABM interceptor missile or an ABM radar at the same test range. Radars used for purposes such as range safety or instrumentation would be exempt from application of these criteria.

F. NO-TRANSFER ARTICLE OF ABM TREATY

On April 18, 1972, the U.S. Delegation made the following statement:

In regard to this Article [IX], I have a brief and I believe self-explanatory statement to make. The U.S. side wishes to make clear that the provisions of this Article do not set a precedent for whatever provision may be considered for a Treaty on Limiting Strategic Offensive Arms. The question of transfer of strategic offensive arms is a far more complex issue, which may require a different solution.

G. NO INCREASE IN DEFENSE OF EARLY WARNING RADARS

On July 28, 1970, the U.S. Delegation made the following statement:

Since Hen House radars [Soviet ballistic missile early warning radars] can detect and track ballistic missile warheads at great distances, they have a significant ABM potential. Accordingly, the U.S. would regard any increase in the defenses of such radars by surface-to-air missiles as inconsistent with an agreement.

* * * * * * *

(b) The following noteworthy unilateral statement was made by the Delegation of the U.S.S.R. and is shown here with the U.S. reply:

On May 17, 1972, Minister Semenov made the following unilateral "Statement of the Soviet Side":

Taking into account that modern ballistic missile submarines are presently in the possession of not only the U.S., but also of its NATO allies, the Soviet Union agrees that for the period of effectiveness of the Interim 'Freeze' Agreement the U.S. and its NATO allies have up to 50 such submarines with a total of up to 800 ballistic missile launchers thereon (including 41 U.S. submarines with 656 ballistic missile launchers). However, if during the period of effectiveness of the Agreement U.S. allies in NATO should increase the number of their modern submarines to exceed the numbers of submarines they would have operational or under construction on the date of signature of the Agreement, the Soviet Union will have the right to a corresponding increase in the number of its submarines. In the opinion of the Soviet side, the solution of the question of modern ballistic missile submarines provided for in the Interim Agreement only partially compensates for the strategic imbalance in the deployment of the nuclear-powered missile submarines of the USSR and the U.S. Therefore, the Soviet side believes that this whole question, and above all the question of liquidating the American missile submarine bases outside the U.S., will be appropriately resolved in the course of follow-on negotiations.

On May 24, Ambassador Smith made the following reply to Minister Semenov:

The United States side has studied the "statement made by the Soviet side" of May 17 concerning compensation for submarine basing and SLBM submarines belonging to third countries. The United States does not accept the validity of the considerations in that statement.

On May 26 Minister Semenov repeated the unilateral statement made on May 24. Ambassador Smith also repeated the U.S. rejection on May 26.

The Jackson Amendment

Text adopted by the U.S. Senate
on September 14, 1972 as an amendment to the
resolution approving the interim agreement.
Proposed by Senator Henry M. Jackson and known as
the Jackson Amendment.
Not published in Scientific American.

The Government and the people of the United States ardently desire a stable international strategic balance that maintains peace and deters aggression. The Congress supports the stated policy of the United States that, were a more complete strategic offensive arms agreement not achieved within the five years of the interim agreement, and were the survivability of the strategic deterrent forces of the United States to be threatened as a result of such failure, this could jeopardize the supreme national interests of the United States; the Congress recognizes the difficulty of maintaining a stable strategic balance in a period of rapidly developing technology; the Congress recognizes the principle of United States–Soviet Union equality reflected in the anti-ballistic missile treaty, and urges and requests the President to seek a future treaty that, inter alia, would not limit the United States to levels of intercontinental strategic forces inferior to the limits provided for the Soviet Union; and the Congress considers that the success of these agreements and the attainment of more permanent and comprehensive agreements are dependent upon the maintenance under present world conditions of a vigorous research and development and modernization program as required by a prudent strategic posture.*

*As adopted—see *Congressional Record—Senate,* September 14, 1972; pp. 14870, 14885–14886, and 14893.

POSTSCRIPT

The Common Understandings Implicit in SALT Phase I

On May 26, 1972, President Nixon and Chairman Brezhnev signed a treaty pertaining to ABM's and an executive agreement about deployment of offensive missiles. These agreements constitute the net result of the first phase of SALT, the Strategic Arms Limitation Talks, which lasted from November 1969 to the very day of their signing two and one-half years later. These agreements accomplish no disarmament: not a single weapon must be destroyed or even moved because of them.

But these agreements do help to stabilize the present arms balance by setting ceilings on the deployment of certain critical strategic weapons. Most important, they contain in clear though implicit form some common understandings about some of the most basic issues in the arms race.

The ABM treaty limits each party to one hundred ABM's at each of two sites, one protecting the national capital and the other protecting a part of the nation's offensive forces. This fixes a precise and relatively low ceiling on deployment, but it is not clear whether this ceiling is lower than the deployment that would have resulted in the absence of a treaty. At the time they signed the treaty the Soviets had fewer than 100 ABM missiles deployed around Moscow, and progress on that system had been very slow for a long time. Also, they had no missiles deployed in protection of their main offensive forces, and nothing they have said or done implied they previously intended to put any there. As for the United States, it is true that it had planned to deploy more than 200 ABM's to protect its offensive forces, but the Senate had approved doing so only by a single vote—51 to 50—and the roll-call resulting in that tally came after a long debate in which a major argument had been the purported need for approval of an ABM system as a "bargaining chip" at the SALT talks. Thus, there is no way of being certain about whether SALT has resulted in a higher or lower ABM deployment in either country. One thing is clear, however: the ABM limitations does *prohibit* the deployment of the massive nationwide ABM systems that *might* otherwise have occurred. And that by itself is a very good thing, since it removes a major potential instability in the pre-SALT situation.

In addition, the ABM treaty contains clauses designed (1) to prevent the upgrading of a local ABM system into something more nearly national in scope, (2) to prevent the upgrading of the ubiquitous Soviet air defenses into ABM systems, and (3) to prevent or at least to inhibit the deployment of entirely new kinds of ABM's.

The executive agreement similarly places ceilings on the deployment of certain kinds of offensive weapons, namely, intercontinental land-based missiles and missiles launched from submarines. These limitations apply both to numbers and to the size of individual missile-launching facilities. The numerical ceilings are supposed to be equal to the present deployments plus the number of missiles currently being built for deployment. Precisely, there are some small allowable variations within these totals that account for substitutions of certain new weapons for older ones. In the United States, for practical purposes the ceiling is equal to the deployment at the time of the signing. In the Soviet Union, the ceiling is substantially higher than the deployment at that time because during the time the agreement was being negotiated the Soviet Union was still in the build-up phase of its deployment

"The Common Understandings Implicit in SALT Phase I" is based on a paper Professor York originally prepared for the Southern California Arms Control and Foreign Policy Seminar.

of submarine-based missiles. The net result is a larger ceiling for the Soviet Union (2358) than for the United States (1710). The ceiling on size refers to the maximum allowable dimensions of the launch facilities rather than of the missiles themselves. Again, it sets a ceiling in accordance with the current situation. However, since the missiles now installed within underground silos are not the largest that could be installed in them, quite substantial increases in payload capability are allowed.

It is important to note, while discussing the limitations both nations agreed to, the many important systems and programs that SALT Phase I did *not* limit. I present this list of omissions, not to criticize SALT conferees, but to point out how much more there is to be done even in simply limiting the arms race, to say nothing of reversing it and finally achieving some actual disarmament.

SALT Phase I placed no limits of any kind on intercontinental bombers, nor on sea-based bombers, nor on short-range bombers deployed and deployable on forward bases, nor did it place any limits on the number or types of bombs or missiles that would be carried by such vehicles. The United States is far better equipped than the Soviet Union with strategic bombers and sea-based bombers. Each side has many bombers of shorter range, but though the Americans can readily deploy bombers to bases in allied countries, from which they can reach the Soviet Union itself, Soviet bombers generally can only reach as far as U.S. allies and not the United States itself.

SALT Phase I placed no limitations on short- and intermediate-range land-based missiles. Both the United States and the Soviet Union have such missiles, but the most important are the 700 or so intermediate-range ballistic missiles (IRBM's) said to be in western Russia and targeted on western Europe.

Nor did SALT Phase I place limitations on MIRV, nor on any other possible modifications or improvements in warheads. Currently, only the United States has MIRV's fully developed and deployed, a fact which gives the Americans, for the present, a great superiority over the Soviets in numbers of warheads. However, the Soviets certainly can develop and use the same technology, so there is no reason to suppose this lead will be maintained indefinitely. Currently, the Soviets have a superiority as to the total weight that can be thrown by missiles and, consequently, in the total megatonnage of the warheads. This derives simply from the large size of their delivery vehicles. However, as remarked above, the size limitations are on "land-based ICBM silo launchers" and not on the missiles themselves. Therefore, the United States could, if it wanted to, substantially increase the weight of its missiles and thus the weight and megatonnage of its warheads. However, so far there seems to have been no substantial interest in doing so.

No limitations of any kind were placed by SALT Phase I on research and development except for the development of certain specific kinds of ABM's. Most military research and development will therefore continue unfettered, and may even increase, as a result of the SALT first stage agreements. This research includes general research and development of nuclear weapons, antisubmarine warfare weapons and methods, penetration aids for missiles and bombers, stand-off weapons, chemical weapons, and air-defense systems. It also includes developments specifically aimed at new and improved strategic offensive systems such as the B-1 Bomber and ULMS (undersea long-range missile system), the Navy's proposed follow-on to the already deployed Poseidon missiles.

SALT Phase I also failed to carry out the previous commitments made by both the Soviet Union and the United States to proceed promptly to convert the limited nuclear test ban to a complete test ban. Such a commitment was formally undertaken by the two powers when they signed the Limited Test Ban Treaty in 1963 and again when they signed the Non-Proliferation Treaty in 1968.

This list of things SALT I did not limit is, of course, not exhaustive, and anyone interested in the subject can add his own favorite omissions to it.

But the omissions should not obscure the very important common understandings about basic issues that are clearly implicit in the SALT Phase I agreements. I believe the most important of these are: (1) the deployment of defensive weapons can accelerate the arms race just as much as the deployment of offensive weapons; (2) defense of the nation against a massive nuclear attack is impossible; (3) a strategic situation of approximate parity and mutual deterrence is the best that is now within reach; and (4) too much secrecy can unnecessarily stimulate the arms race, and therefore certain forms of intelligence gathering are necessary and legitimate.

Strategic Defense and the Arms Race

A large number of the people connected with making U.S. defense and arms control policy have long held that the development and deployment of defensive weapons leads directly to the development and deployment of new offensive weapons, and vice versa. Many years ago Jerome Wiesner remarked that the extensive deployment of defensive weapons by the Soviets around Moscow simply induced the United States to aim a great many more weapons against that particular very special target; American offense planners were just as determined to maintain the capability of destroying it as Soviet defense planners were determined to save it. The net result of such situations is that if the defense works perfectly, a special target such as a nation's capital will be hurt at least as badly as it would be if it were undefended, but if the defense fails partially, the failure would lead to very much worse devastation than would result had no defense been planned at all.

Overall the dynamics of the arms race are the same as those for an individual special target like Moscow. The perceptions of American technologists in the late 1950's about the potentialities of Soviet ABM's in the mid-1960's was the stimulus for the introduction of multiple warheads (multiple reentry vehicles or MRV) on some of our missiles. Similarly, the perceptions of American technologists in the mid-1960's about the potentialities of Soviet ABM's in the 1970's was one of the main stimuli for converting MRV's to multiple independently targeted reentry vehicles (MIRV's). Conversely, the first observations of Soviet MRV tests, and the anticipation in the United States that the Soviets planned further development and eventual deployment of MIRV's, was interpreted by Secretary of Defense Melvin Laird in 1969 and 1970 to mean the Soviets were attempting to develop a first-strike capability, and this in turn was used as one of the main arguments in open hearings in support of the U.S. Safeguard System of ABM's.

The Soviets were slow to reach similar views about the effect of weapons development on the arms race. Premier Kosygin's rebuff at Glassboro of Secretary McNamara's suggestions that both countries hold off on ABM deployment appears to have based on Kosygin's belief that deployment of defensive systems was only natural and could not be considered as an accelerating move in the arms race. Discussions in Pugwash meetings in the early sixties confirm that this same view was then also generally held by those Soviet scientists who were aware of such issues. Gradually Soviet views of the arms race changed. The priority given by both sides, but especially by the Soviets, to an agreement on ABM systems (a priority higher than that given to an agreement on offensive systems) strongly suggests that both sides now clearly recognize that ABM deployment is an accelerating step in the arms race, and that limiting its deployment is a good way to begin to limit the entire process.

The Unfeasibility of Defense

The argument over the feasibility and predicted performance of ABM systems has a long history. At first, the objective set for an ABM system was analogous to the objective of other defense systems: protect the nation's people and their works by preventing enemy weapons from entering the country. However, virtually from the beginning there have been many technologists who believed that through the use of various penetration aids it would always be possible to overcome such defenses. From relatively early times (i. e., beginning in 1957) the favored way of doing so was by overwhelming and exhausting the defenses through the use of various types of barrages and multiple warheads, the latest of which are the Poseidon and Minuteman MIRV's. Again from relatively early times, the consensus has been that the technological balance strongly favored the offense and that no useful defense of the nation as a whole was feasible if this was based solely on ABM systems. As a result, proposals for defense against missiles took two different tacks.

One tack involved the proposed construction of a very large nationwide ABM system coupled with a major civil defense plan. Typically, the cost of each component of such a combined system was estimated at some modest multiple of ten billions of dollars. Because of cost, because of doubts about both the technical feasibility of ABM's as well as about the social, political, and technical feasibilities of civil defense, there was always a clear national consensus against proceeding along that tack, to the degree that almost total lack of action is a measure of a negative consensus.

The other tack involved proposals designed to defend only the most vital parts of the country. In a world where the major emphasis is on survival through the deterrence of nuclear war, perhaps the most vital part of the country is the strategic deterrent itself. The Safeguard system, proposed by the Nixon administration immediately upon Nixon's taking office, had precisely as its primary objective the defense of the country's deterrent devices. A system that could succeed in that limited objective could, in principle, probably be constructed, and some of the later versions of Safeguard (e.g., the site defense system) were widely regarded as having technical promise. However, very high costs, the availability of alternatives that many thought were both cheaper and better, continued doubts about feasibility in practice as distinct from feasibility in principle, and concerns about stimulating the arms race, have continued to engender a substantial opposition to the project. While there now is a national decision there surely is no national consensus.

In my view, giving an ABM agreement priority over an agreement on offensive systems, and setting the ceilings on ABM's at a token level that was very much lower than the ceilings on offensive weapons, means that each side clearly recognized (1) the unfeasibility of providing the nation as a whole with an active defense against nuclear attack, and (2) the greater importance of cooling the arms race as compared to one particular and controversial way of improving the security of one component of the deterrent.

Surely, if the leaders of the two countries had believed the reverse was true, the agreements would have been entirely different. Indeed, if they had even believed that defense was as cheap, as easy, as certain as offense, they would not have put primary emphasis on limiting defense and would have placed a lower limit on defense systems than on offense systems.

The Acceptance of Parity and Mutual Deterrence

The SALT I agreements guarantee that the current situation of approximate strategic parity will be maintained for at least another five years. The current agreements are essentially preliminary in nature, and they leave out a large fraction of all the weapons and megatons that can be brought to bear on strategic targets. Under such circumstances nothing more than approximate parity could possibly have been achieved. It is intended to go from here, to modify and extend the agreements until they do indeed cover all elements of the nuclear threat and yield a stable international strategic balance. Even then, such a strategic balance can result only through an overall parity, a kind of parity whose basic meaning is that mutual deterrence has been achieved and will be indefinitely maintained. Such a state of parity will, no doubt, involve approximate numerical parity, but precise equality weapon-by-weapon cannot possibly be achieved. The geography of the United States and the Soviet Union, their relations with other countries, and their technological histories make purely arithmetical forms of parity entirely impossible.

Overall parity, combined with the agreement to give up permanently further development of ABM systems, means that the two major nuclear powers have agreed that mutual deterrence is the only rational policy to pursue with respect to strategic nuclear weapons at this time. Conversely, the powers have given up any hope of winning a war in which strategic nuclear exchange is triggered. Even theoretical ideas about winning such wars always include the necessity for widely deployed defenses, and these defenses have been permanently abandoned.

The Necessity and Legitimacy of Certain Kinds of Intelligence

Uncertainties about Russian plans and capabilities have played a major role in aggravating relations and stimulating conflicts between Russia and other countries for centuries. In our time, uncertainties about Soviet capabilities and plans led to the bomber gap and missile gap hysterias in the United States, and Soviet paranoia about spying has been one of the wellsprings of their rejections of many of the arms control proposals put forward by the United States since World War II. In an effort to do something about these problems, Eisenhower made his "open skies" proposals. When these were rejected out of hand by Khrushchev, Eisenhower proceeded to approve the flights of U-2 reconnaissance planes over the Soviet Union. Eisenhower's unilateral open skies program was most unusual in peacetime, and it succeeded as long as it did only because the technological balance made it impossible for the Soviets to prevent it. When a U-2 plane was shot down in the summer of 1960, the resulting furor and personal anger on the part of Khrushchev led to the cancellation of a Summit Meeting that had then been just about to start.

At about the time of the downing of that U-2, the U.S. satellite reconnaissance program came to fruition. The technological difficulties involved in preventing satellite reconnaissance, perhaps combined with a growing recognition of the way the arms race was accelerated by excessive secrecy, led to a tacit acceptance of satellite reconnaissance. Also, the fact that Soviet Sputniks and Soviet Cosmonauts flew above the United States before American satellites similarly flew above the Soviet Union may have been helpful in setting favorable precedents. And in the United States, President Eisenhower specifically disapproved proposals to deploy an antisatellite capability by the United States. Since those early times, neither the Americans nor the Soviets have shown much interest in an antisatellite capability until very recently. Of course, satellites are by no means the only so-called "national technical means" of gaining intelligence in general or of verifying compliance with an arms limitation agreement in particular. A variety of long-distance detectors exist for detecting and identifying nuclear explosions in all environments (underground, under water, in the atmosphere, and in outer space). In addition, both the United States and the Soviet Union maintain electronic listening posts all over the world, such as have been evidenced by the "Pueblo Incident" off North Korea, the patrols made just offshore of American missile test sites by Soviet ships equipped with all sorts of electronic devices, and the revelations made by occasional dissidents and defectors on both sides. The SALT Phase I agreements for the first time formally and explicitly recognize the legitimacy of such "national technical means of verification," and limit these only by saying they must be used "in a manner consistent with generally recognized principles of international law." Moreover, the agreements go on to state, "Each Party undertakes not to interfere with the national technical means of verification of the other Party" and "Each Party undertakes not to use deliberate concealment measures which impede verification. . . ."

The specific agreements about intelligence-gathering in the SALT Phase I accords will go a long way toward making more complex and more far-reaching arms control agreements possible. In addition, they open the way for further agreements on intelligence which can supplement and complement those already achieved.

For instance, the ABM agreement limits ABM test centers to those now in existence; in the case of the Soviet Union that is said to be the one at Sary Shagan. A limitation on the location of testing contributes importantly to the ability to keep track of what is going on by "national technical means." An extension of this idea would be to limit the downrange end of offensive missile test ranges to the peripheries of the large countries or to the open oceans. This would significantly improve the capability for keeping track of any future agreements limiting missile developments.

No discussion of SALT Phase I and the future of disarmament would be complete without mention of the Jackson Amendment to the resolution adopted by the U.S. Senate in approving the Interim Agreement. This amendment calls for the United States to have not less than numerical parity with the Soviets in "intercontinental strategic systems" alone. Senator Fulbright had proposed an alternative amendment which called for "overall equality, parity, and sufficiency, taking into account all relevant qualitative and quantitative factors . . ." Senator Muskie later made a quite similar proposal. In rejecting these versions of parity in writing his amendment, Senator Jackson made it clear he intended to exclude from any future Soviet-American SALT agreements those "U.S. forces dedicated to the defense of our European allies and our friends in the Middle East." Given the great disparities in history, geography, and current deployments of weapons not yet covered by agreements, Jackson's narrower notion of parity could create an almost impossible situation. Demanding nuclear parity within just one of Jackson's categories, "intercontinental strategic systems," naturally calls forth a proposal for parity within the other, "forces dedicated to the defense of our allies and our friends. . . ." One need only recall what happened the last time the Soviets attempted to move toward that narrow definition of parity by deploying in Cuba intermediate-range missiles capable of delivering nuclear warheads to targets in the United States.

In summary, SALT Phase I has not had any large direct impact on weapons deployment and programs, but it has fixed some important ceilings, and, it has thus been a step toward limiting the arms race. More important, the clearly implied understandings about the dynamics of the arms race, about the rôle and uses of ABM, about parity and mutual deterrence, and about the need for and legitimacy of certain forms of intelligence, all are necessary conditions for future progress.

Achieving these understandings will not necessarily compel further progress, but has cleared away a number of notions that have been blocking progress for years. As a result, there is reason to hope that after 27 years of trying, some real nuclear disarmament may be in the offing at last. However, at best the odds are not high and they could easily be reduced by domestic political activities in either country that undermine the basic understandings achieved so far.

SECTION 6: OTHER ARMS CONTROL AND DISARMAMENT ISSUES

INTRODUCTION

In the public mind, the SALT conferences for several years now have overshadowed all other arms control efforts. They have also very largely preoccupied the attention of the officials responsible for the development and promotion of arms control policy in the governments of the two superpowers. Even so, work has been going ahead on other fronts, albeit rather slowly.

The Conference of the Committee on Disarmament of the United Nations (the CCD) provides today, as it has for many years, the principal forum for discussing the many arms issues that fall outside the scope of SALT. One of the more important of these other issues is the conversion of the current limited test-ban into a comprehensive test-ban, or, to put it more directly, the prohibition of underground nuclear tests.

The superpowers have repeatedly pledged themselves to try to achieve a total ban on tests. Two such pledges are presented in this book: the Limited Test-Ban Treaty itself and the Non-Proliferation Treaty, both of which are reprinted in Section 4. The failure to achieve a total test-ban in 1963 resulted from a failure to resolve the so-called verification issue. The United States insisted on a provision for on-site inspections, that is, a provision allowing the prompt dispatch of an international inspection team to the site of a suspected violation for the purpose of performing whatever kinds of tests were necessary to determine the truth of the matter. The arguments never got beyond consideration of the number of such inspections; the details of the inspections, including even the approximate size of an inspection team, were never seriously discussed. The United States insisted on a fairly large number of inspections per year; the Soviets at first refused to accept any. Eventually Khrushchev, Soviet premier at the time, proposed to allow as many as three per year and the United States offered to come down to as few as seven. There the discussions stuck; neither side was willing to close the gap, and later the Soviets even withdrew their offer of three. Finally, that issue of inspection was bypassed by agreeing to ban tests in all environments *except* underground.

In the decade since the Limited Test-Ban Treaty was signed, technology has changed greatly. Many advances in long-range verification techniques have been made. Many students of the problem believe these advances now make it possible to verify compliance to a treaty without any on-site inspections. In addition, the superpowers have conducted hundreds of additional nuclear tests since 1963. So many additional tests, one might presume, may have brought nuclear technology to a point where tests are resulting in more marginal, and hence less valuable, advances.

The other members of CCD have continually pressed the United States and the Soviet Union to meet their obligations in this matter. However, despite these major technical changes, and despite progress on other arms control issues, there has so far been no progress whatsoever toward agreement about a comprehensive ban. The official positions of the United States and the Soviet Union remain as they were before all these changes took place.

Two articles that discuss the technical and political elements of this issue are included in this section. The first article, entitled "Extending the Nuclear-Test Ban," was written by Henry R. Myers, formerly a member of the technical staff of the United States Arms Control and Disarmament Agency. He discusses recent advances in seismology and shows how they relate to the problem of detecting and verifying nuclear tests by remote means. The second article, entitled "The Great Test-Ban Debate," is one I wrote in 1972. It attempts to evaluate the need for further tests. I do this by taking a retrospective look at the arguments that were made in the period from 1957 to 1963 concerning the necessity for tests. Those arguments frequently entailed predictions about future developments, and enough time has now gone by to allow us to see the outcome of these predictions. The article similarly discusses the arguments given in the early 1960's in support of a test ban. These also included predictions that can be examined and weighed in retrospect.

Another arms issue the nations of the world have been discussing for many decades is the matter of biological and chemical warfare, commonly known by the acronyms BW and CW. The article entitled "Chemical and Biological Weapons" by Matthew Meselson discusses this problem as of early 1970. Meselson is now on the faculty at Harvard University. He has long concerned himself with these arms control questions; reference has already been made to his participation in an early discussion of the ABM issue at a Pugwash Conference. In his article on chemical and biological weapons he describes the attempts to eliminate this particularly nasty form of warfare that followed the first uses of gas in World War I, and he traces the curious but distressing failure of the United States, alone among the great nations of the world, to cooperate fully in this endeavor. In 1969, shortly before Meselson worte this article, the President of the United States did announce that the United States would renounce all biological weapons, and that it would not use *lethal* chemical weapons unless these were used first by an enemy against Americans. It has subsequently been made clear that the President intended no such restrictions for *non*lethal chemical weapons, for herbicides and other chemicals not used directly against human beings.

Since Meselson wrote his article, there has been further progress on the international front. For years, the Soviet Union and its allies, with the support of most other nations, had insisted that BW and CW be treated together, contending that it was impractical to separate them. The United States, on the other hand, had been urging that they be treated separately. Finally, in the spring of 1971, the Soviet suddenly accepted the American view. As a result, a convention on the prohibition of biological weapons was drawn up and placed before the United Nations in April 1972 for ratification by the member states. This convention was discussed in the introduction to Section 4 and the text of the convention itself is included in this section immediately following Meselson's article.

Two other articles, which form a pair, show that there are other arms control and disarmament issues besides those dealing with exotic modern weapons such as BW, nuclear explosives, or long-range rockets.

The first article in this matched set is entitled, "The Mekong River Plan." It was written in 1963 by Gilbert F. White, Professor of Geography at The University of Chicago. He has worked for the U.S. National Resources Planning Board and the U.S. Bureau of the Budget. He has been an adviser to a number of national and international water and power development study and planning groups, and in 1961–1962 he was a consultant to the committee planning the project he writes about.

The article describes a plan worked out in the United Nations for a comprehensive river-development plan drawing on social and natural science for the benefit of peoples in a very sizeable area in Southeast Asia covering much of Cambodia, Laos and Vietnam. At the time White wrote his article, the war in Vietnam was relatively small. The Mekong River plan required international cooperation in a region where political relations were recognized as unstable, and where the continuation of the plan was precarious. Despite this the plan, begun in 1957, went ahead with a confidence White describes as "incredible."

The second article in this pair, written nearly a decade after White's, is entitled "The Cratering of Indochina." It is by Arthur H. Westing and E. W. Pfeiffer. Westing is Professor of Biology at Windham College and Pfeiffer is Professor of Zoology at the University of Montana. The authors have made several trips to Indochina to study the environmental effects of modern war. The article describes what actually happened in the same area White wrote about, in the following few years. It is important to note that what Westing and Pfeiffer describe there did not result solely from the use of what we all recognize as weapons—although, in the period from 1965 to 1971 the area was bombarded with munitions amounting to approximately twice what the United States used in all theaters of World War II. An essential rôle was also played by gadgets and substances developed originally purely for peaceful purposes, specifically bulldozers and weed-killers.

Extending the Nuclear-Test Ban

Recent advances in seismological techniques for distinguishing underground nuclear explosions from earthquakes have spurred a renewal of interest in negotiating a comprehensive test ban

HENRY R. MYERS

January 1972

Treaties to ban the testing of nuclear weapons have been a subject of widespread interest since the middle 1950's. The history of the matter is marked by turgid international negotiations, conferences of scientific experts, acrimonious domestic debates, changes in position by one side or the other, a three-year informal moratorium on testing suddenly terminated by a series of Russian tests in the atmosphere, "breakthroughs" in the technology of detecting clandestine tests, supposed "breakthroughs" in the technology of conducting clandestine tests, proposals that were sincere and proposals that were not so sincere, a limited treaty banning all but underground tests, accusations of minor violations of that treaty and—most recently—renewed talk of extending the limited treaty to cover underground tests, stimulated primarily by reports of significant new advances in seismic techniques for distinguishing underground explosions from earthquakes.

Advocates of a test ban have over the years pointed out that such a treaty would be a major step toward terminating the strategic-arms race, that it would bring an end to radioactive pollution by nuclear explosions, that it would make the proliferation of nuclear weapons less likely and that it would increase barriers against the use of nuclear weapons in warfare. Those opposed to a test ban have tended to argue that a treaty would address the symptoms rather than the disease, and that whatever advantages there might be were outweighed by certain military and political disadvantages.

Throughout this meandering history there has been little consensus on answers to a series of related questions: How important are the advantages of treaties that limit the testing of nuclear weapons? Is it really a good idea to accept such limitations even if there could be confidence that other countries had done the same? How much assurance could there be that others would live up to the agreements? What developments might stem from clandestine bomb-testing by others?

Questions related to the problem of detecting violations have dominated the test-ban dialogue out of all proportion to their significance. The reasons for this anomaly are interesting in themselves. One is that the verification question is the one aspect of an otherwise complex issue that appears amenable to quantitative analysis. (Actually it is much less so than appearances suggest.) A second reason is that there seems to be a widely held obsession with the *possibility* of violations rather than with their probability or their significance. A third is that opponents of limitations on nuclear testing have exploited this obsession by encouraging fears that have little basis in fact.

Following the established tradition, much of the present discussion will be concerned with the problem of detecting violations. This is done, however, not to emphasize that aspect of the matter but to place it in proper perspective, so that the political and military implications of continued nuclear testing or a complete cessation of it may receive the greater attention they deserve.

Some people have feared that the U.S. Government, in its eagerness to make arms-control agreements, has not been concerned enough about its ability to detect violations. Such fears have never been well founded. An often-stated precondition for the U.S. to enter into a treaty limiting underground nuclear testing has been that there be adequate assurance that the national security would not be placed in jeopardy by developments growing out of clandestine testing by other countries. Indeed, the failure to arrive at a ban on underground tests has in part reflected the inability to negotiate a treaty that provided the U.S. with the assurance of compliance with the terms of the treaty that many officials and citizens believe is necessary.

Such assurance can be derived from several sources: (1) seismological records, intelligence observations or on-site inspections indicating that particular events were earthquakes and not explosions; (2) awareness that any significant clandestine program would involve a large enough number of tests so that eventually a mistake would be made that would reveal the prohibited activity; (3) knowledge of the relative insensitivity of the balance of strategic power to further developments in nuclear-weapons technology; (4) the belief that a potential violator would probably find an excuse for withdrawing from a treaty rather than run the risks inherent in violating it.

On the last point Herbert Scoville, Jr., a former deputy director of the Central Intelligence Agency and assistant director of the Arms Control and Disarmament Agency, has suggested that consideration be given to the experience of the 1958–1961 moratorium on all nuclear testing. At that time the ability to acquire information concerning violations was much inferior to what it is today. In addition, nuclear-weapons technology was less advanced, and there was more incentive to cheat. Yet even then the U.S. was willing to rely for assurance on its own verification systems. The moratorium ended not because of mutual suspicions about cheating (although these did exist) but because of the initiation by the U.S.S.R. of a massive atmospheric-testing program.

In discussing the various interacting factors that influence assurance I shall begin with the area in which the significant new developments have emerged, namely seismology.

Both earthquakes and explosions cause elastic vibrations in the ground that propagate as seismic waves through the earth (body waves) and along its surface (surface waves). Seismometers are used to detect such waves, and the data obtained from a number of instruments, separated by hundreds or thousands of miles, can be used to determine where the event took place, to define its seismic magnitude and to learn something about the nature of the source mechanism.

Seismic magnitude is an approximate indication of the energy released by an earthquake or an explosion. It is a logarithmic quantity based on the average of measurements of the amplitude of certain portions of seismic waves. For some purposes magnitude is based on measurements of the body wave; in other circumstances it is based on the surface wave.

The largest earthquakes have a body-wave magnitude slightly in excess of 7 and a surface-wave magnitude slightly in excess of 8.5. On the average there are one or two such earthquakes a year. Underground explosions in the megaton range can have a body-wave magnitude of 6.5 to 7. Explosions in the low-kiloton range typically have a body-wave magnitude of 4. The seismic magnitude associated with underground explosions depends not only on the explosive yield but also on the material in which the detonation is set off [*see top illustration on page 290*].

Determining the location of seismic events eliminates the large majority of earthquakes from the "probably suspicious" category. For example, unless there are other grounds for suspicion, it is possible to immediately eliminate events under the ocean floor or in countries where there is no reason to believe a nuclear test might have been conducted.

If an event cannot be discarded on the basis of its location, analysts can exploit the fact that in terms of the spectral distribution and the partition of energy among wave modes the seismic signals generated by explosions are quite different from those generated by earthquakes. At distances within 1,000 kilometers of an event, explosions in excess of a few kilotons can easily be differentiated from earthquakes. The effects of the paths along which the waves travel, however, are such that as the waves

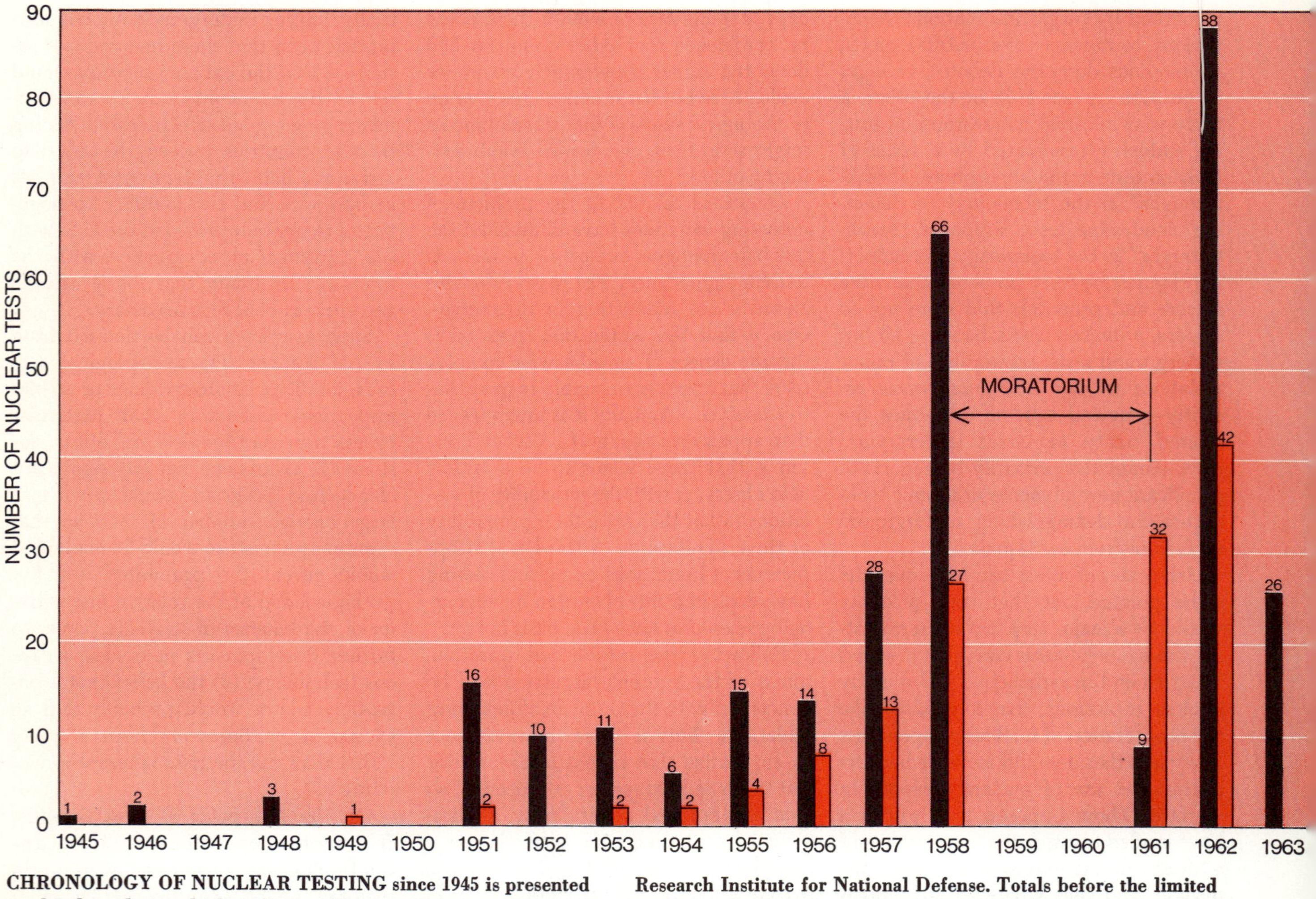

CHRONOLOGY OF NUCLEAR TESTING since 1945 is presented in this bar chart, which indicates the approximate numbers of nuclear-weapons tests conducted by the U.S. (*gray bars*) and the U.S.S.R. (*colored bars*). The estimates were compiled by the Stockholm International Peace Research Institute (SIPRI) from data provided by the U.S. Atomic Energy Commission and the Swedish Research Institute for National Defense. Totals before the limited test-ban treaty went into effect in 1963 include tests conducted in the atmosphere, in space, underwater and underground; these numbers are probably more complete than those available after the 1963 test ban. Although the totals indicated for the latter period may understate the actual rate of underground testing since 1963,

propagate they increasingly assume a form that is determined more by the characteristics of the path than by the characteristics of the source. Moreover, the seismic wave is attenuated with distance, and diagnostic features contained in it (and for small events the entire signal) can be obscured at the point of detection by seismic noise generated by winds, nearby road traffic or distant ocean waves.

An enduring tenet of the test-ban dialogue has been that the negotiability and viability of a prohibition on underground testing were related to the amount of verification information that could be extracted from the seismological data. More specifically, such a ban was dependent on the ability to understand and reduce the effects of travel paths and seismic noise. As a result the U.S. undertook in 1959 to sponsor a research program intended to lead to improved capabilities for detecting seismic events, for determining their location and for establishing whether the events were earthquakes or explosions. The ultimate objective was to develop monitoring procedures that could provide sufficient assurance in a treaty situation while calling for a minimum of provisions that would be difficult to negotiate, namely on-site inspections or internationally supervised seismological observations inside the U.S.S.R.

it is likely that they give a correct indication of the relative numbers of such tests conducted by the U.S. and the U.S.S.R. According to SIPRI there have been in addition, through 1970, a total of 21 tests conducted by Britain, 46 by France and 11 by China.

Since 1959 more than $300 million has been spent on the U.S. seismological research effort. A lesser effort was mounted by the United Kingdom. As a result there has been a considerable advance in the understanding of earthquake mechanisms and of the structure of the earth. Other significant developments have come in instrumentation, in data-handling and analysis procedures, in the ability to separate signals from noise and in the ability to determine the location of events and to isolate information that might help in determining whether the event was an earthquake or an explosion. On the other hand, the rate at which this progress has been translated into a more negotiable position at the nuclear-test-ban discussions at Geneva has not been as great as might have been hoped. Nevertheless, there have been two notable advances that have led to a substantial improvement in the ability to collect and abstract useful information from the seismological data.

The first major "breakthrough," announced in 1962, amounted to a reduction in the annual number of earthquakes in the U.S.S.R. that might be confused with explosions. Part of the basis for this reduction was a thorough study of earthquake and explosion data that resolved the existing uncertainties about the rate at which earthquakes occur and the relation between earthquake magnitude and explosive yield. In addition, it was determined that the depth of seismic events could be better inferred from the data than had been believed. It became possible to conclude that many more events were too deep to be explosions and therefore were earthquakes. These results were the basis for dropping from the U.S. negotiating position the requirement that there be manned, internationally supervised seismological observatories in the territory of the U.S.S.R.

The second such major advance has emerged in the past few years from a series of studies initiated by Jack F. Evernden, a seismologist formerly employed by the Department of Defense and now working at the Arms Control and Disarmament Agency. The most significant result of this work, which has been carried on by groups at several universities, was to verify the hypothesis that for a given total release of seismic energy, explosions were much less efficient at generating long-period surface waves than small, shallow earthquakes were [*see illustration on pages 288 and 289*]. Although there were indications before 1962 that this was a worthwhile line of investigation, the early analyses were based on limited data and were not pursued to the point where results would have had a strong impact on the U.S. position in the test-ban negotiations. Moreover, it had been suggested that as the total seismic energy released became smaller, the differences between explosions and earthquakes would tend to diminish to the point where they would not be observable.

It has now been demonstrated that the difference persists for the smallest events of any interest, and that the average ratio of surface-wave magnitude to body-wave magnitude for explosions is less than the average ratio for earthquakes at least as far down as a body-wave magnitude of 4, and probably lower [*see bottom illustration on page 290*]. For the comparatively small number of events that cannot be eliminated on the basis of location, depth or surface-wave criteria there are other diagnostic methods that can be applied to the data. These criteria include the relative complexity of the seismic wave (earthquakes generally produce more complex signals than explosions do) and the ratio of compressional-wave energy to shear-wave energy (earthquakes usually produce larger shear waves than explosions do).

Other research has demonstrated that through the use of seismometer arrays, which have the effect of enhancing seismic signals with respect to the background noise, it is possible to detect both surface waves and body waves at distances of thousands of miles from events with a body-wave magnitude of 4.

As a result of these studies it is now known that it is possible to build a network of seismological observatories, located many thousands of miles from seismic sources of interest, that will acquire data that can be used to identify "virtually all" earthquakes in the U.S.S.R. having a body-wave magnitude in excess of 4. It also means that in the absence of active evasion procedures there would be a substantial probability of detecting and identifying explosions in the U.S.S.R. with yields greater than one or two kilotons. At such yields a nuclear-

UNDERGROUND NUCLEAR EXPLOSION is chronicled in this sequence of photographs made from a helicopter circling above ground zero at the Nevada Test Site of the Los Alamos Scientific Laboratory. The first photograph, made about a minute after the nuclear explosive was detonated, shows dust rising around ground zero caused by the explosion's shock wave. At this point a 100-foot-high experimental tower began to move by rail away from ground zero to a safe position outside the anticipated crater area (*second photograph*). Some 23 minutes later the material above the temporary underground cavity formed by the explosion collapsed (*third photograph*), leaving a subsidence crater (*fourth photograph*).

test program would have little significance. The significance of these conclusions of course depends on the meaning of "virtually all." Some seismologists suggest it means that each year there will be as many as 25 earthquakes in the U.S.S.R. with a body-wave magnitude above 4 that could not be differentiated from explosions on the basis of the seismic data. Others believe that the number will be 10 or less. These estimates are to be compared with the average expected number of unidentified events, ranging from 75 to 150 events above a body-wave magnitude of 4, that would have been anticipated before the surface-wave techniques were developed.

The spread in present and past estimates is partly a reflection of natural fluctuations in the rate of occurrence of earthquakes. Mostly, however, it results from different interpretations of the data and different estimates of the likely outcome of ongoing studies. The data themselves are sometimes subject to diverse interpretations because the great variability in the source mechanisms and the transmission properties of the earth creates a corresponding variability in the observations; therefore questions are sometimes raised concerning the validity of conclusions based on a particular set of measurements. Also contributing to the diversity in estimates is the fact that there are very different views concerning the elaborateness of the seismological network that might exist at some future time. This uncertainty is important because the degree of differentiation that is possible depends directly on the number, distribution and quality of the seismometer stations providing the raw data.

The residual number of events that cannot be identified on the basis of the seismic data would be further reduced by the analysis of data supplied by intelligence systems. In particular it has been hypothesized that satellite photography should be capable of providing information that might alleviate doubts about specific occurrences. For example, a seismic event might be detected and its location determined on the basis of seismological data but without there being enough information to provide confidence that the event was an earthquake. Photography from space might indicate that in the area where the event took place there was no sign of activity of the kind associated with a nuclear test. On the other hand, if the photography were to reveal activity such as mining, it would not serve to decrease suspicion. It is therefore probable that satellite photography would serve much more to reduce suspicions about earthquakes than to provide evidence that a prohibited explosion had occurred.

Nevertheless, a country deciding to undertake clandestine tests would be constrained to do so in a way that would not be susceptible to observation. The possibility that violations might be observed from space would thus have the effect of imposing substantial restrictions on a potential violator. This would tend to deter attempts to carry out secret tests.

On-site inspections have been another omnipresent element in the test-ban dialogue. In the beginning there was a generally held belief that seismological data would be much less useful and inspections more useful than either are now known to be. By supplementing information provided by seismic instruments and intelligence systems, inspections were considered a mechanism that would make a substantial contribution to the verification process. As a result of the recent developments in seismology, inspections would apply only to the very small number of events that are large enough to be detected but that produce signals of insufficient signal-to-noise ratio to allow the application of seismic identification techniques. As usually envisioned, inspections would be conducted after the presentation of ambiguous seismic data and under the auspices of an international body. They would involve visits to the area of origin of seismic events that could not be identified after analysis of the seismic and intelligence data. The inspection area would extend over some several hundred square kilometers, an area reflecting the expected error in determining the point at which the seismic event had occurred.

The procedure for deciding that a seismic event could not be identified, and therefore should be subject to an inspection, is not easily articulated. As a practical matter it would be exceedingly difficult to specify in a treaty, in a manner that would be acceptable to all parties, the data that would need to be provided in substantiation of a claim that an inspection was necessary.

The ability of on-site inspections to uncover evidence of clandestine testing, should there be such testing, would depend on a chain of probabilities: the probability that an explosion would be selected as a candidate for inspection, the probability that the inspection area would encompass the point of detonation and the probability that the inspectors would actually uncover positive evidence should the inspection area include the shot point. The foregoing factors would in turn depend on the quality of the evidence on which the inspection decision was based, the number of inspections that might be conducted in a given time period, the accuracy of locating the source point of seismic events, the size of the area covered by an inspection, the duration of the inspection, the number and training of the inspectors and the elaborateness of the inspection

SUBSIDENCE CRATERS caused by underground nuclear explosions pock the desert at the Nevada Test Site. Viewed from space by satellites such craters would be telltale evidence that a test had occurred. Hence a country planning to violate a test-ban agreement would be compelled to detonate its nuclear explosives at sufficient depths to have confidence that there would be no such crater.

procedures.

Since a country that had violated the treaty would be unlikely to allow access to inspectors who might uncover the clandestine activity, inspections would probably be undertaken only in areas where earthquakes had actually occurred. Because the seismic data would be adequate for identifying large earthquakes, inspections would be directed toward smaller events that typically would produce no ground effects that might be found by inspectors. Moreover, Defense Department experts now say their research has indicated that careful planning and execution of a clandestine test would preclude the existence of surface manifestations that might be found by inspectors. Therefore on-site inspections could not be expected to turn up any evidence of either explosions or earthquakes. Finally, if an evader should be successful in employing active evasion techiques, there would be no seismic evidence on which a request for an inspection might be based.

If this is the case, do inspections serve any purpose even in theory? Yes, according to some. The lack of evidence of an explosion would supposedly provide a limited amount of assurance (skeptics say false assurance) that there had been no explosion. In addition, the prospect of an on-site inspection and the possibility that one might miscalculate or make a mistake would be at least a slight deterrent to a potential violator.

Whatever the theoretical utility of inspections, it is questionable that a treaty that provided for meaningful inspections was ever a realistic possibility. The Russians have always had a negative attitude toward inspections on the grounds that they are not needed and would be used as a pretext for espionage. During periods when the Russians did seem willing to consider the possibility of some small number of inspections (allegedly for the purpose of diminishing some American domestic opposition to a treaty), it was not clear that the nature of these inspections was even close to the elaborate procedures envisioned by the U.S.

With the recent advances in seismological research, doubts concerning the usefulness of inspections have been intensified. To continue to maintain that a ban on underground tests is important but that inspections are still necessary implies the acceptance of the following dubious propositions: (1) that significant tests might escape the various monitoring systems operated by the U.S., (2) that inspections would play a substantial role in deterring violations or in alleviating suspicions that might arise and (3) that the Russians would agree to inspection procedures of the kind that would be required if they were to serve their purpose.

To put the matter in perspective it should be noted that new ground would not be broken if the demand for inspections were dropped because they were deemed unnecessary. The U.S. is already a party to a series of arms-control agreements that contain either no provision for inspections or provision only for inspections of a kind that would yield virtually no assurance in addition to the assurance acquired by other means. These agreements include the ban on nuclear explosions in the atmosphere or outer space, the ban on placing nuclear weapons in orbit around the earth, on the moon or on other celestial bodies, the ban on placing weapons of mass destruction on the ocean bottom and the ban on nuclear weapons in the Antarctic. In each case unilateral means are considered adequate to provide the necessary confidence that the impact of possible undetected violations would be so minuscule as to make them not worth worrying about.

In effect the data provided by seismological and intelligence systems and, to a much lesser extent, by on-site inspections would serve to reduce the background "noise" against which the "signal," or positive evidence, of clandestine test activity would be detected. This "noise" is a factor that a potential violator would take into account in making a decision about conducting a clandestine test. Would he assume that his activity would be lost in the "noise," that it would be discounted as a spurious earthquake in the residuum of unidentified seismic events? Or would he believe that he should play a more active role in attempting to conceal his tests?

Since a complete test ban became a serious possibility several such active schemes for clandestine evasions have been proposed. These include the muffling of the explosion so that the resulting seismic signals would be unlikely to be detected, modification of the character of the seismic waves so that even though they might be detected they would not be characteristic of waves associated with explosions, and testing in the aftermath of a large earthquake so that the explosion signals would be concealed by the ground motion caused by the earthquake.

The muffling of seismic signals might be achieved by conducting the test in an underground material where a comparatively small fraction of the energy of the explosion would appear in a propagating seismic wave. For example, a 20-kiloton explosion in a dry desert alluvial deposit might produce a seismic signal as small as the one produced by a one-kiloton explosion in hard rock. If a country were to seek to test in such an alluvial deposit, it would first be confronted by the fact that a deposit deep enough and dry enough is very uncommon. There is, in fact, reason to believe these deposits do not exist in the U.S.S.R. in depths that would allow tests of more than one or two kilotons. Since dry alluvial deposits, or other dry materials that might be useful for the same purpose, are usually found in areas that are relatively free of clouds and lacking in human activity, any attempt to conduct clandestine tests in these circumstances would be particularly vulnerable to observation from space. Further restrictions arise from the fact that the alluvium must be deep enough not only to contain the immediate effects of the explosion but also to make it possible to set off the explosion at a depth that would not leave a collapse crater. This is an indirect effect in which the cavity produced by the nuclear explosion fills with material from above. The result is a propagating void that ultimately appears at the surface as a characteristic subsidence crater. Such craters are com-

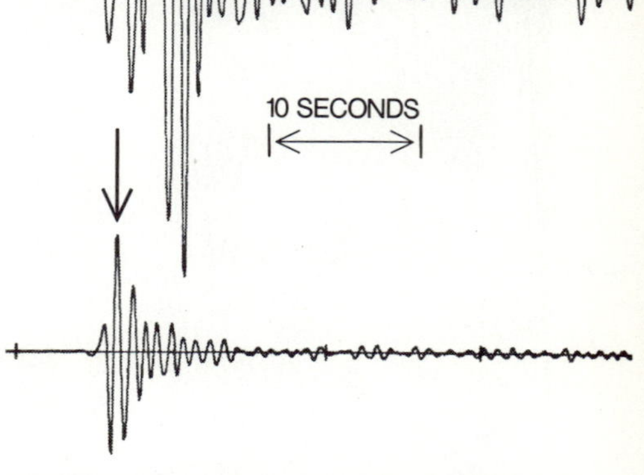

SEISMIC RECORDS produced by an earthquake (*top traces*) and an underground nuclear explosion (*bottom traces*) each located at approximately the same distance (80 degrees) and the same azimuth (350 degrees)

mon at the U.S. testing ground in Nevada [*see illustration on page 287*]. If such a crater were to be observed from space, it would be telltale evidence of a nuclear explosion.

A more elaborate muffling technique calls for detonating the nuclear device in a spherical cavity. It is predicted that with a cavity of the right size the seismic signal would be about 100 times weaker than it would be without the cavity. The diameter of the required cavity increases with the cube root of the explosive yield. A 10-kiloton explosion would call for a cavity 300 feet in diameter 3,000 feet below the surface. It is questionable whether the cost of excavating such a cavity would be commensurate with the gains that might be made from a clandestine nuclear test conducted in it.

For a time it seemed that such muffling, or decoupling, schemes had fallen out of the domain of plausible evasion possibilities. In recent Congressional testimony, however, decoupling was resurrected by Defense Department experts, who implied that decoupled detonations with yields of 50 to 100 kilotons were feasible and could be carried out at costs that were within reasonable bounds. The assertion raised the question of why, if the possibility of decoupling was considered to be significant enough to bring up, there had been only one small experiment to check out the predictions. This test had involved a 300-ton shot in a cavity created by a 5,000-ton nuclear explosion in a salt deposit in Mississippi. Because the observed decoupling was less by a factor of two than had been forecast, and because there are serious questions concerning the validity of extrapolating the results of this experiment from a yield of 300 tons to one of 50,000 or 100,000 tons, it would seem important to have conducted experiments with much larger explosions. The willingness to extrapolate results here (where the extrapolated conclusion is consistent with the desires of many Defense Department experts to avoid a complete ban on nuclear-weapons tests) conflicts with the Defense Department's usual position on nuclear-weapons development. For example, the five-megaton Cannikin test conducted on Amchitka in November was supposed to be necessary because it was not possible to base conclusions on data obtained from a one-megaton explosion.

At various times it has been suggested that a series of nuclear detonations, appropriately located and timed, would produce a composite seismic signal that was more typical of earthquakes than explosions. Although this procedure might generate waves that in some respects were similar to waves made by earthquakes, it would be difficult for a treaty violator to be confident that the similarity was sufficient to avoid creating suspicion.

A violator might also try to conceal illicit test activity by setting off an explosion almost immediately after an earthquake. If this were done properly, the seismic signals associated with the explosion would be masked by those generated by the earthquake. One disadvantage of testing in this fashion would be the need to maintain the nuclear device and the apparatus associated with the experiment in a constant state of readiness for a period that would range from months to years, depending on the size of the test detonation. It would also be necessary to determine rather quickly that the earthquake was suitable for purposes of masking. That would require an interconnected network of seismometers from which data would be fed to a computer. The computer would immediately calculate the location and size of the earthquake, and it would give a "go" signal when the earthquake met the preset conditions. As with other imagined evasion techniques, the practicality of this method would depend on how badly a country wanted to test, on the size of the test and on how the country evaluated its chances of being caught.

The usefulness of on-site inspections in deterring such efforts would be contingent on procedures that had been established for submitting requests to conduct an inspection. If it were necessary to base the request on specific kinds of seismic data indicating that an unidentified event had occurred, there would be much less deterrent value than if it were

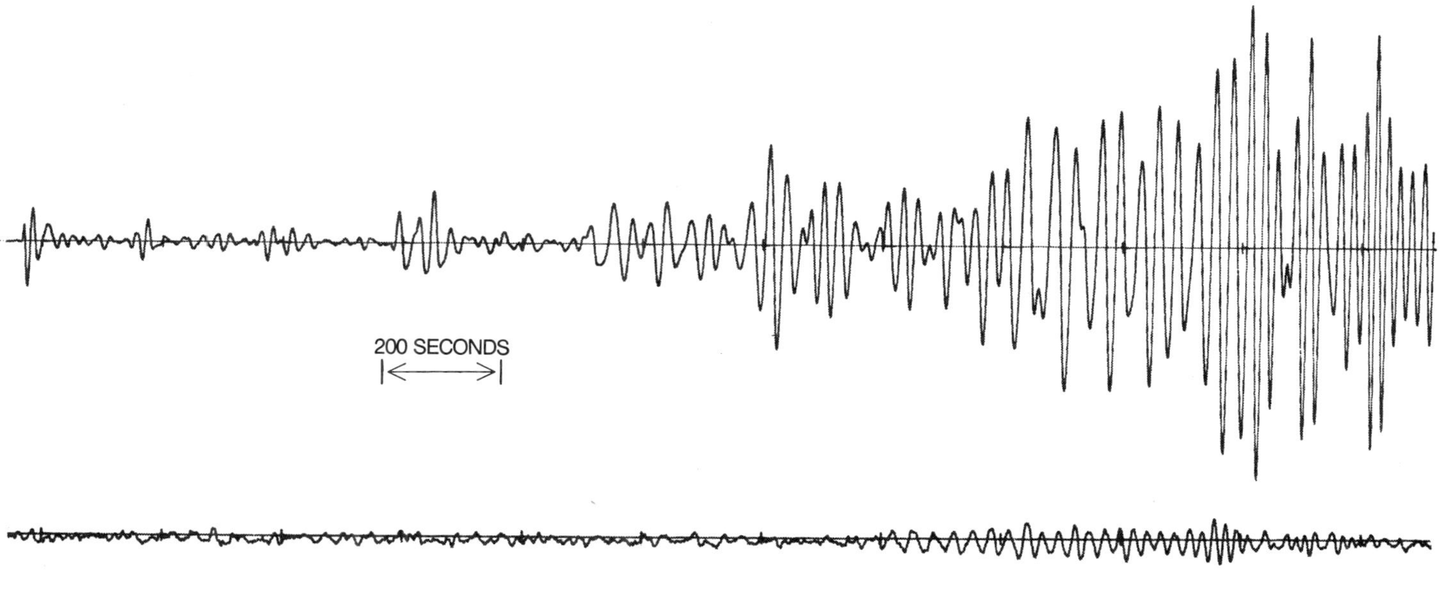

from the detection point are compared here. The two seismograms at left were produced by body waves: shock waves that traveled through the earth from each event to the seismic station. The two traces at right were produced by surface waves: shock waves that traveled along the surface of the earth. The body-wave magnitude of each event is determined from a measurement of the maximum amplitude in the first five cycles of the wave (*arrows*). In this case the body-wave magnitudes are approximately equal for the two events. As expected, however, the magnitude of the surface wave is much smaller for the explosion than it is for the earthquake.

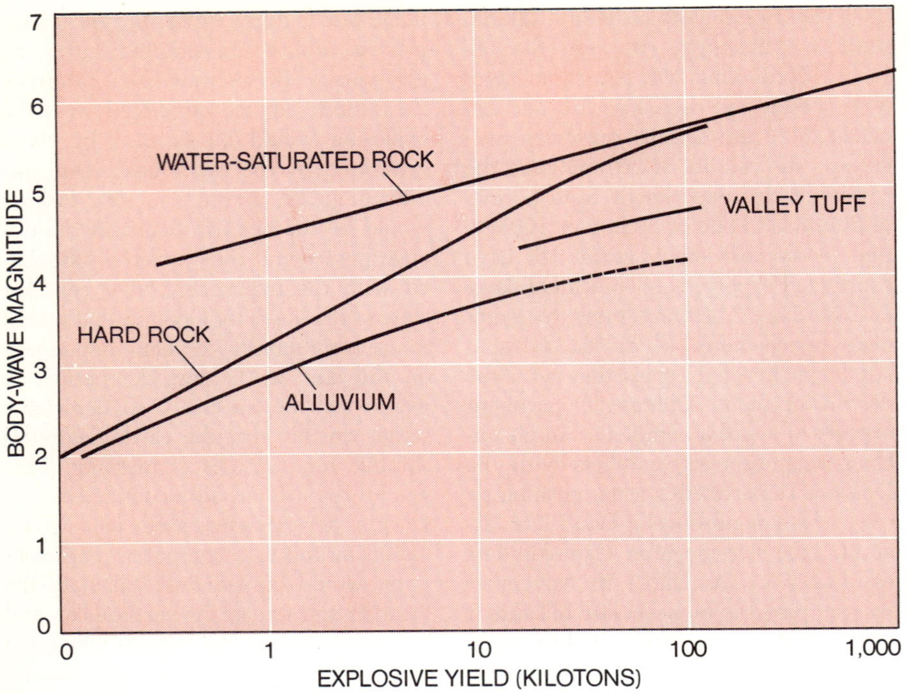

SEISMIC MAGNITUDE recorded for a particular underground explosion depends not only on the explosive yield but also on the material in which the explosion takes place. These curves illustrating that relationship are based primarily on measurements made in the eastern U.S. of explosions in Nevada. For explosions in excess of 20 kilotons the alluvial deposits at the Nevada Test Site are not deep enough to contain the immediate effects of the explosion. Hence for larger explosions it is necessary to drill beyond the alluvium into the valley tuff underlying it. This accounts for the upward shift of the right end of the alluvium curve. The fluctuations about these curves are such that any body-wave magnitude inferred from them is uncertain by .3 unit and any explosive yield is uncertain by a factor of 2.

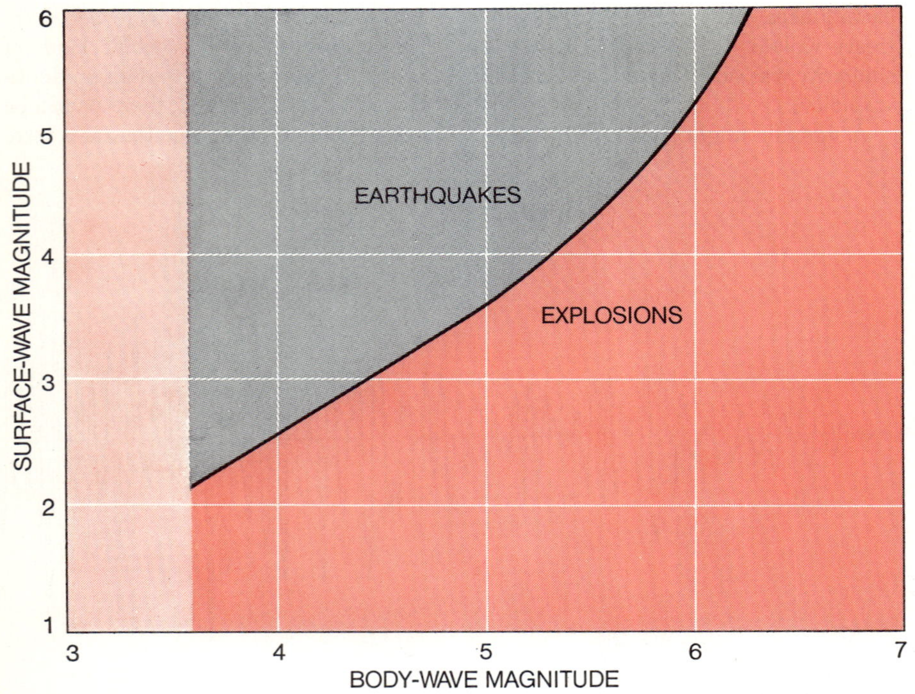

DIFFERENTIATION of underground explosions and shallow earthquakes by means of the ratio of their body-wave magnitude to their surface-wave magnitude appears to be feasible down to a body-wave magnitude of approximately 4. In this graph of that ratio, inferred from a large quantity of seismic data, virtually all explosions lie below the curve, whereas most shallow earthquakes lie above the curve. (Deep earthquakes can be identified on the basis of other properties of the seismic data.) It is generally agreed that a small number of shallow earthquakes will be within the explosion zone. Some seismologists believe there will be each year as many as 25 such events with a body-wave magnitude greater than 4 in the U.S.S.R.; others believe the number of such ambiguous seismic events will be 10 or less.

possible to base the request on unrevealed intelligence information with only scant reference to publicly available seismic data.

Scoville notes that an easy, although seldom discussed, way for a country to cheat a weapons-test ban would be for it to mount a program of setting off nuclear devices for peaceful purposes, such as the U.S. Plowshare program. One part of Plowshare is the development of nuclear explosive devices for use in nonmilitary projects. Since these devices are in many ways identical with weapons, it would be virtually impossible to determine the kind of development activity being undertaken without being given access to the experimental apparatus. Such access is not likely to be granted by either the Russians or ourselves. Therefore if there is going to be a complete ban on nuclear-weapons tests, it will be necessary either to live with the possibility of some weapons development under the shelter of Plowshare-like programs or to forgo the yet to be established economic benefits of this type of activity.

A further consideration affecting a country's assurance that it could detect clandestine tests (or evade detection) is the possibility that there might be a mistake or an accident in such a test. An unexpected collapse crater or the venting of radioactive debris could lead to the discovery of prohibited activities. There is a significant chance of unintentional venting and a significant probability that such venting, if it occurs, will be detected. In the past radioactive debris has been unintentionally emitted from underground explosions conducted by both the U.S. and the U.S.S.R. The possibility of such accidents would tend to deter violations.

A useful device for summarizing the concepts that enter into evaluations of the likelihood of detecting clandestine test activity or of escaping detection is represented by the graph on the opposite page. The abscissa represents the product of the annual number of tests and their average yield; for instance, a value of 10 could mean 10 tests with an average yield of one kiloton or two tests with an average yield of five kilotons. The ordinate is a measure of the confidence that a test or series of tests with the specified yield-number product would be detected.

The "deterrence" curve represents the situation as it might be viewed by a country undertaking a clandestine test program. The "assurance" curve represents the situation as it might be perceived by countries concerned about their ability to detect violations by others. The deterrence curve invariably lies to the left of the assurance curve because the country concerned about violations by others will, in comparison with the evaluations of the potential violator who presumably places a high premium on not being caught, tend to underestimate the chances of a violation's being detected.

For example, the great variability in seismic data may cause a violator to "play it safe." He would assume, as actually happens, that his explosions would produce at some observation points seismic signals substantially greater than the signals suggested by the averages implied by the curves in the top illustration on the opposite page. The violator would have to conservatively evaluate his chances of being observed from space or having an accident that resulted in the venting of radioactive debris. On the other hand, countries seeking assurance might well assume that explosions would produce seismic signals of an average size implied by the average curve, that the violator would make sure that there was no substantial deviation from the average, that there would be no basis for counting on anomalously large signals to reveal a clandestine test, and that the test would be conducted in a manner so as not to produce a collapse crater or other evidence that might be collected by intelligence systems.

Such curves or their conceptual equivalent are an aid in evaluating the risks associated with a nuclear-test ban even though they are necessarily imprecise because of the large number of intangibles and uncertainties they encompass. The inability of anyone to develop more quantitative estimates has caused consternation among presidents, members of Congress and interested citizens. Adding to the uncertainty is the fact that the detection of clandestine tests must be considered an integral part of the broader question of how significant undetected violations would actually be.

It is fortunate that the recent advances in verification technology have simplified the issue. Many informed observers now conclude that the U.S. need no longer be concerned about developments that might result from *clandestine* nuclear-test activities, since such developments would not affect the strategic position of the U.S. with respect to its adversaries. It is thus possible to focus on the role of *any* nuclear tests at the present juncture of the arms-development cycle.

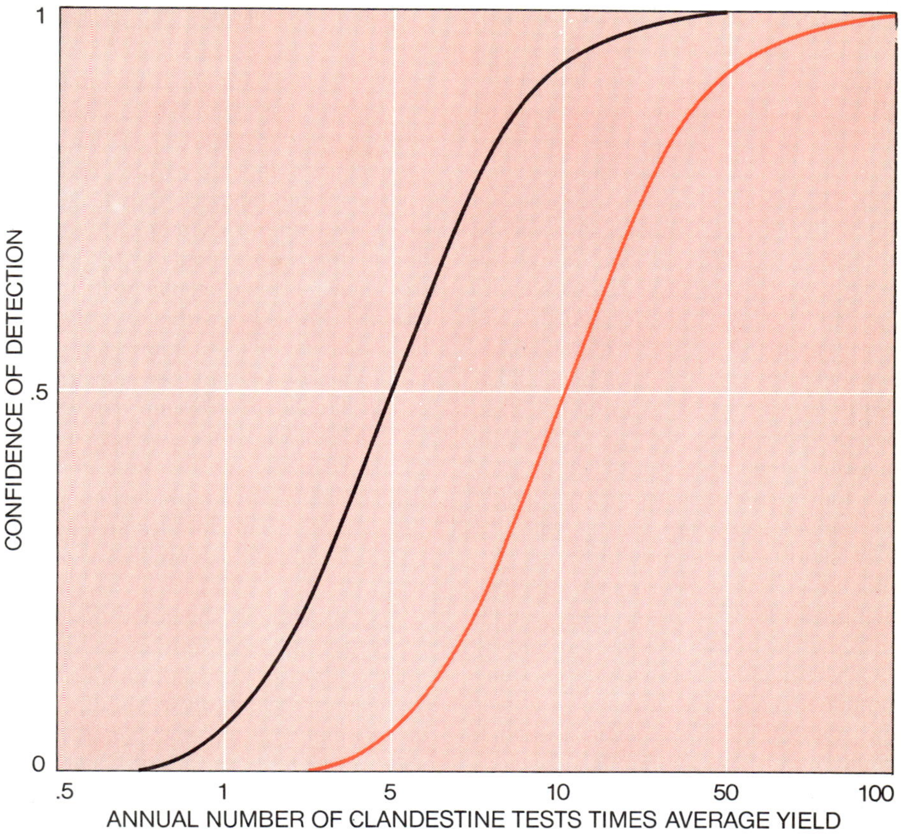

DETERRENCE AND ASSURANCE CURVES indicate the degree of confidence either party to an underground-test-ban agreement might have that at least one of a certain annual number of clandestine tests with a certain average explosive yield would be detected. The deterrence curve (*black*) represents the situation as viewed by a potential violator of the agreement; the assurance curve (*color*) represents the situation as viewed by a country concerned about detecting the violations of others. The deterrence curve lies to the left of the assurance curve because the country concerned about the violations of others will, as compared with the evaluations of a potential violator, tend to underestimate its chances of detecting violations. Although the locations of such curves are necessarily imprecise, they do serve as a useful device for evaluating the risks associated with a nuclear-test ban.

In discussing nuclear testing it is necessary to consider global questions, including what the intentions of adversaries are, how nuclear testing would influence the probability of a nuclear war's starting and what effect nuclear testing would have on the outcome of the war if it should start. It is clear that such complex questions cannot be answered conclusively, but certain facts, opinions and speculations can be stated, and inferences can be drawn from them.

The public record contains very few details of the U.S. nuclear-weapons program. Information about what goes on in the U.S.S.R. is even scantier. Nevertheless, it is possible to get an idea of both the objectives and the costs of U.S. activities from official testimony before committees of Congress and from committee reports based on that testimony. From these sources it appears that during each of the past six years the U.S. has spent approximately $450 million on the development and testing of nuclear weapons. The objectives are to develop weapons that have greater explosive yield for a fixed weight, to develop weapons in which certain nuclear effects are either increased or decreased with respect to other effects, to verify that the performance of existing weapons does not decline with the passage of time and to gain confidence in safety against accidental nuclear detonations. Some nuclear explosions are used as sources of radiation and blast in experiments to determine their effects on weapons systems and their components.

Nuclear detonations for these purposes can be justified to some extent on the grounds that in the long run they will make it possible to save money. For example, it may be that a missile warhead with a certain explosive power and a specified weight could be developed only through nuclear testing. If tests were not allowed, the same destructive power would have to be put into, say, three missiles instead of two, thus preventing a saving in the cost of producing a given amount of damage.

Similarly, there could be uncertainties about the performance of stockpiled weapons or the effect of nuclear explosions on military hardware that could be resolved only by subjecting the hardware to the effects of a nuclear explosion. If such uncertainties could not be eliminated by nuclear tests, it would be necessary to eliminate them through the more costly route of conservative design. In "National Security and the Nuclear Test Ban," Scientific American, October 1964 [see article on page 129 of this book], Jerome B. Wiesner and Herbert F. York addressed the uncertainty question at some length. They pointed out that whatever uncertainties might be resolved by nuclear testing would be very small compared with those that abound in military planning. The fact that some of these uncertainties might be removed by nuclear tests would, in their view, "contribute virtually nothing more to management of the real military and political problems, even though it would produce neater graphs."

Some have argued that nuclear testing must continue because of the possibility of surprise findings: either findings that lead to important new developments or, what is more likely, findings that expose a problem where none had been expected. Others argue that tests are necessary to help ensure that the Russians do not acquire knowledge not in the possession of American experts. It is of course not possible to demonstrate that surprise results will not be obtained. Nor is it possible to prove that the Russians do not know things of which American experts are unaware. As for the likelihood of there being a surprise of the kind that suggests a new line of weapons, one may take note of York's belief that the rapid technological advances of recent decades are neither typical of the past nor predictive of the future.

It is sometimes suggested that the U.S. could not forgo testing as long as China or France was continuing its tests. This contention has little validity. For the indefinite future whatever dangers might arise from the fact of Chinese or French nuclear-weapons developments are most unlikely to be ameliorated by the products of U.S. tests. Such dangers must be countered by other means.

More generally, the need for continued testing should be considered in the light of the fact that in this 27th year of the nuclear age some thousands of nuclear weapons of proved design are fully deployed. No foreseeable weapons developments based on further nuclear tests, conducted either openly in the absence of a complete test ban or clandestinely in the presence of one, would affect the ability of either the U.S. or the U.S.S.R. to deliver a substantial portion of its strategic stockpile to an opponent's cities. McGeorge Bundy has remarked on the implications of even a small fraction of these weapons being detonated over urban targets: "In the real world of real political leaders—whether here or in the Soviet Union—a decision that would bring even one hydrogen bomb on one city of one's own country would be recognized in advance as a catastrophic blunder; 10 bombs on 10 cities would be a disaster beyond history, and 100 bombs on 100 cities unthinkable."

In brief, the advanced status of nu-

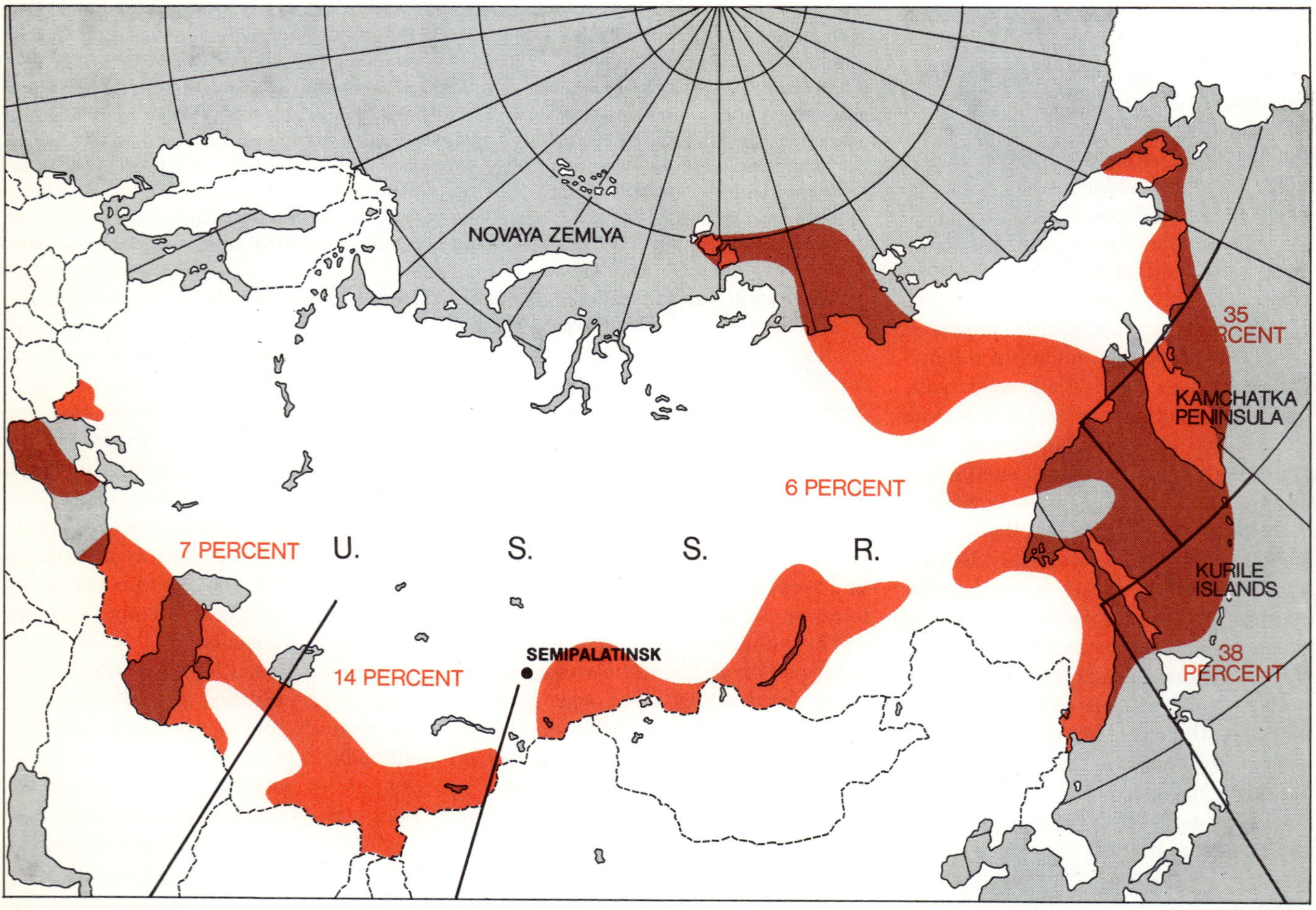

SEISMIC MAP OF U.S.S.R. indicates the principal regions of seismic activity (*colored areas*) and the approximate percentage of the total number of earthquakes that occur in each area (*colored type*). As far as is known, underground nuclear-weapons tests have been conducted by the U.S.S.R. on the arctic island of Novaya Zemlya and near the city of Semipalatinsk in south-central Siberia.

clear-weapons development, the existence of very large weapons stockpiles and the deterrent value of the ability to destroy even one city suggest that neither the continuation of nuclear-weapons tests nor the cessation of such tests will affect the strategic position of one superpower with respect to the other. If this is the case, it should mean that continued testing need not necessarily be a source of international tension and a motive force in the arms race.

Yet in spite of the decline of the substantive importance of nuclear tests, testing has developed a life of its own and, as was evident in the Cannikin episode, does exacerbate international discord. If only because there are such strong feelings concerning the need for either an indefinite continuation of testing or its elimination, the matter retains a large symbolic importance. Accordingly there is much to be said for a treaty that removes nuclear testing as an issue that obscures the real problem: how to avoid nuclear war.

The ban on atmospheric testing grew out of the fears generated by the Cuban missile crisis of 1962 and the increasing radiation levels caused by fallout. The superficial reason the treaty did not encompass underground tests was the inability of the signatories to reach agreement on verification procedures. Underlying the omission of such tests was the opposition of persons in and out of the U.S. Government who believed it was essential that this country continue its test activities. At the same time the importance of a prohibition on underground tests was recognized in the preamble of the Limited Test-Ban Treaty of 1963 and later in the Nonproliferation Treaty of 1970, both of which incorporated a commitment to continue negotiations toward a ban on all nuclear-weapons tests.

Not only has little been done to fulfill this commitment but also it is debatable that the atmospheric ban has had much effect on the development of nuclear weapons. In order to secure the endorsement of the U.S. Joint Chiefs of Staff for the Limited Test-Ban Treaty the Kennedy Administration agreed to implement a program of safeguards that included "the conduct of comprehensive, aggressive and continued nuclear-test programs designed to add to our knowledge and improve our weapons in all areas of significance to our military posture for the future." This was to counter the Joint Chiefs' concern that the treaty might presage a "euphoria in the West which will eventually reduce our vigilance and willingness of our country and of our allies to expend continued effort on our collective security." The result of these safeguards has been what many believe is a nuclear-weapons development effort that is indistinguishable in scope—if it is not even larger—from the one that had been under way before the treaty.

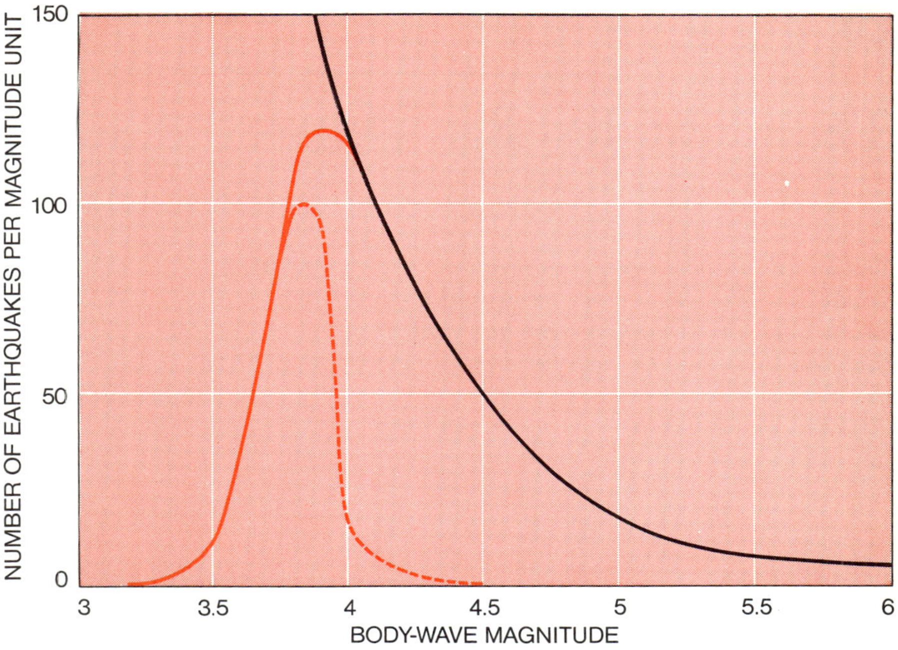

AVERAGE NUMBER OF SHALLOW EARTHQUAKES in the U.S.S.R. per magnitude unit per year is indicated approximately by the black curve in this graph. The estimated average annual number of shallow earthquakes per magnitude unit that would be detected by an appropriate network of seismological observatories located outside the U.S.S.R. is indicated by the solid colored curve; the estimated average number of shallow earthquakes per magnitude unit that would be detected but not identified by such a seismic network is indicated by the broken colored curve. The solid colored curve diverges from the black curve at a point where seismic signals become comparable in amplitude to irreducible seismic noise. If noise-suppression techniques should be further improved, the divergence of these two curves would occur at a lower magnitude. Improvements in identification techniques would have the effect of moving the broken colored curve to the left and reducing it in amplitude. The quantities represented by these curves fluctuate about the average by substantial amounts. Moreover, the curves are dependent on certain "ground rules" for considering earthquakes to be of "shallow" depth and for including certain seismic events in the waters off the Kurile Islands and the Kamchatka coast (*see map on opposite page*).

Since 1963 there has been little serious discussion of extending the Limited Test-Ban Treaty to include underground tests. The ostensible obstacle remains: the U.S.S.R. continues to maintain that on-site inspections are not needed; the U.S. asserts the contrary. The verification issue is still a pretext for not achieving agreement. As the foregoing discussion suggests, however, the plausibility of the pretext has dwindled to the vanishing point.

The failure to prohibit underground tests plays into the hands of those in the non-nuclear nations who press for the acquisition of nuclear forces; it tends to reinforce the contention that the statements of the superpowers are not matched by actions, and it undermines the credibility of the U.S. Government, which has maintained for more than a decade that unresolved verification problems are the obstacle to a ban on underground tests.

The attainment of a treaty banning underground tests would demonstrate to the non-nuclear countries that the major nuclear powers would accept substantial restrictions on their own nuclear activities, a demonstration that would strengthen arguments against the acquisition of nuclear weapons by other countries. As a result of its symbolic value, a cessation of underground testing, particularly in the absence of a major agreement at the Strategic Arms Limitation Talks, would more than any other likely step signify an almost irrevocable commitment to seek security through arms-control agreements rather than through the never ending cycle of weapons and counterweapons that has characterized the period since World War II.

The Great Test-Ban Debate

The trend of events in weaponry and in arms control tends to refute arguments presented a decade ago against a limited nuclear-test ban and to indicate that the time may be ripe for a comprehensive test ban

HERBERT F. YORK

November 1972

The modest but significant progress toward the control of nuclear weapons that has been made during the past nine years has brought to the fore the question that was raised in the first place: Is the time ripe for a treaty prohibiting all tests of nuclear weapons? Indeed, both the limited-test-ban treaty of 1963 and the nonproliferation treaty of 1968 contain clauses obligating the signatories to seek to achieve a treaty establishing a comprehensive ban. The issue is therefore being debated again [see "National Security and the Nuclear-Test Ban," by J. B. Wiesner and H. F. York, on page 129]. This time, however, it is possible to employ hindsight to sharpen foresight, because most of the arguments being made against a comprehensive test ban now are essentially the same as the ones that were put

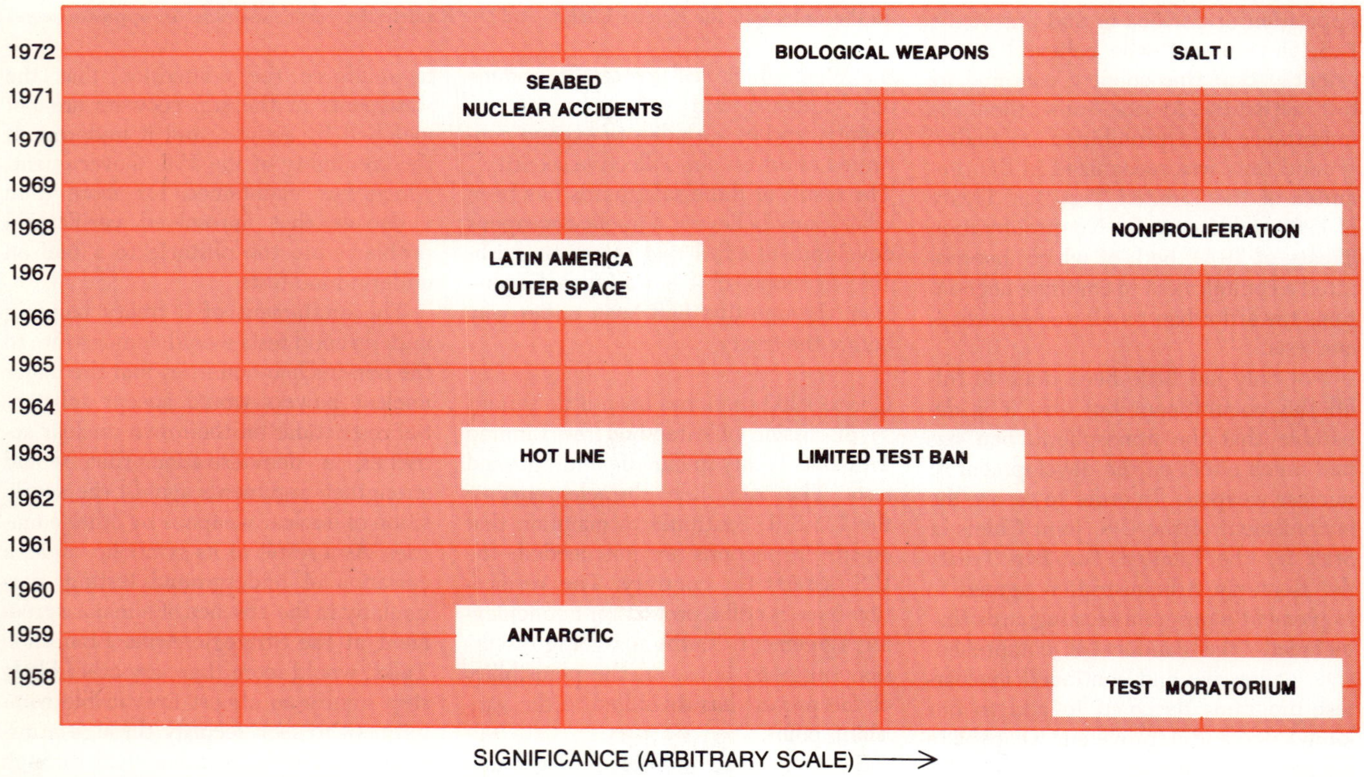

CHRONOLOGY OF ARMS-CONTROL AGREEMENTS adopted since 1958 is traced. The test moratorium lasted only from 1958 to 1961, but the work that went into it and the climate that it created provided the basis for all the other agreements. SALT stands for strategic-arms-limitation talks, which were conducted between the U.S. and the U.S.S.R. for more than two years and culminated in the agreements of last May limiting the deployment of anti-ballistic-missile systems and freezing strategic offensive missiles.

forward in the long debate preceding the adoption of the limited test ban. An examination of how those arguments look in the light of experience will help to supply a basis for estimating how much weight they should be given in the present debate.

The questions involved are of two general types. One type has to do with the means for monitoring a test ban to ensure that the signatories are complying with the treaty. That subject was recently reviewed in these pages [see "Extending the Nuclear-Test Ban," by Henry R. Myers, the article beginning on page 283]. The other type has to do with the potential effects of a test ban on the national security of the parties to a treaty or any other agreement. I shall limit my discussion to questions of this type.

In the debates of a decade and more ago (from 1957 to 1963, to be more precise) the national-security matters most frequently raised by people who opposed or seriously questioned the test ban came under the following general headings: anti-ballistic-missile (ABM) systems, weapons effects, pure fusion bombs, improvement of the yield-to-weight ratio of nuclear weapons and new knowledge, possibly involving military surprises. Let us review the arguments and the subsequent developments under each heading.

In the early 1960's claims were made by Russian officials that the U.S.S.R. had solved the problem of intercepting and destroying incoming ballistic missiles. Not long afterward U.S. intelligence activity discovered that the Russians were indeed beginning to deploy an ABM system. Moreover, the extensive series of nuclear tests conducted by the Russians during 1961 and 1962 had included explosions at altitudes that would be of interest to designers of an ABM system. The U.S. had also conducted a number of high-altitude tests, leading certain scientists and military officials to assert that this country had enough knowledge to design an ABM system. Secretary of Defense Robert S. McNamara and other high officials did not agree, however, and so no ABM-system deployment was then authorized in this country.

Opponents of a test ban contended that the reason for the difference between the Russian decision to deploy and the U.S. decision not to deploy must be that the Russians knew something we did not know. They suggested that this something had been discovered during the Russian test series. Some opponents went on to speculate that the reason the Russians were now willing to consider a test ban was that they had learned some essential secret and saw the test ban as a way of preventing the U.S. from learning it.

For example, the physicist Edward Teller said: "I think there is a disparity in knowledge, and the disparity of knowledge today means a disparity of power tomorrow.... I believe that, because they have acquired this knowledge, they don't need any more atmospheric tests, and I believe that is why Khrushchev is willing to sign the treaty at present." Senator Strom Thurmond said: "All it will take to put the Soviets in a dominant nuclear position is two

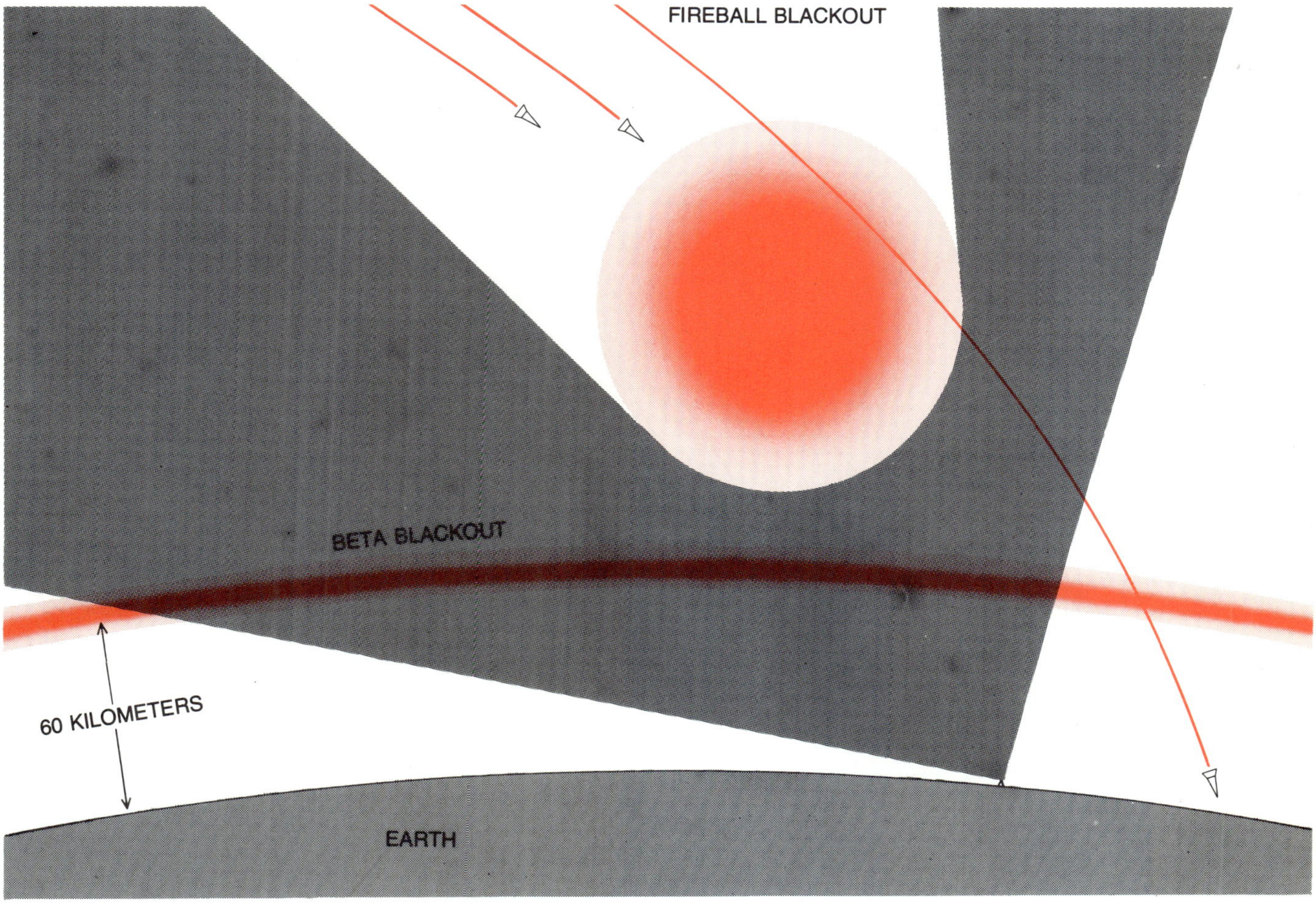

BLACKOUT PHENOMENON was a possibility raised as an argument against the limited test ban. The concern was that a nuclear explosion at high altitude would produce ionized air that would for a time be opaque to the defender's radar. "Fireball blackout" would result when heat from the explosion stripped electrons from air molecules, and "beta blackout" would result from electrons released in the decay of fission products. Continued testing was said to be needed to produce a defensive missile system that could withstand such effects. The difficulty of creating any adequate antimissile system has made the blackout argument peripheral.

things: one, enough time to build up a stockpile of the already perfected Red antimissile missile, which will render our huge arsenal of ICBM's [intercontinental ballistic missiles] useless, and second, ratification of the test-ban treaty that will prevent the United States from high-altitude tests necessary for completion of our own Nike X antimissile-missile program, thereby leaving America defenseless against Red missiles."

When pressed for details, the opponents of the test ban commonly referred to several matters on which, they said, insufficient information existed, at least in the U.S. One matter was the blackout phenomenon, in which a nuclear explosion at high altitude produces a large volume of ionized air that is for a time opaque to radar. There were also allusions to certain long-range "kill" mechanisms that would work against incoming warheads. Here it was argued that tests were needed in order to design defensive warheads that would produce such effects and offensive warheads that would survive the effects.

On the other side of the argument it was contended that the U.S.S.R. had not gained any special advantage due to some private knowledge about high-altitude effects. Harold Brown, who was then Director of Defense Research and Engineering, said: "I feel rather strongly that they [the Russians] are not substantially ahead of us." He added that it was not a defect in nuclear knowledge that had prevented the U.S. from deploying ABM systems but rather that "the U.S. decided not to deploy the Nike Zeus because its effectiveness was inadequate against U.S. penetration aids . . . and we assume the same would be true of the Soviet penetration-aid capability." The U.S. Joint Chiefs of Staff said that "development of the U.S. [ABM] system does not depend on atmospheric testing and hence this treaty will not significantly influence any imbalance that may exist."

What have subsequent events revealed about these claims and predictions? The Russian ABM program proceeded erratically from the base described in 1963. After several periods of delay that indicated indecision and uncertainty, the Moscow ABM system (now called the Galosh system) was reported early this year to have fewer than 100 ABM vehicles ready for launching. The system was generally judged to be quite inadequate for coping with an attack against it by U.S. missiles. Russian ABM installations that had at one time been reported around Leningrad and Tallinn either were dismantled or turned out to have a different purpose. Nothing that has happened since the test-ban debate has confirmed the notion that the U.S.S.R. knew something the U.S. did not know. Indeed, the Russian decision to deploy the Galosh system seems to have been due to a poor understanding of just how easy it is to penetrate systems of that type and size.

On the U.S. side the development of an ABM system continued through the 1960's at a level of about $500 million per year. The system slowly evolved, as did the political situation both domestically and internationally. Finally, near the end of the Johnson Administration, a decision was made to deploy an ABM

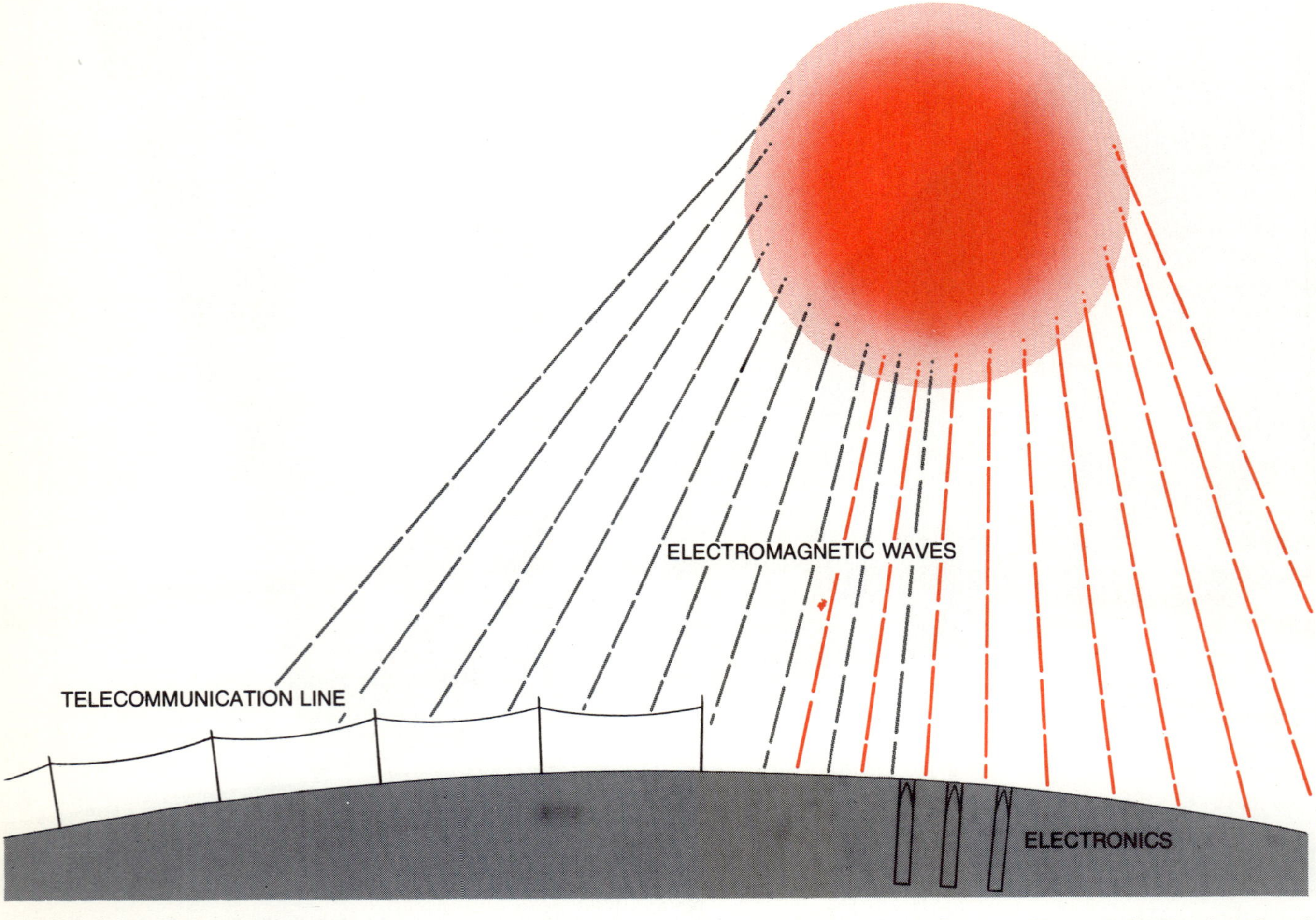

"TREE" AND "EMP" PHENOMENA have been raised as arguments for continued testing. TREE stands for transient radiation effects on electronics, and EMP stands for electromagnetic pulse. They both arise from nuclear explosions. The phenomena can disrupt electrical communications on the ground and can cause electronic equipment on missiles to malfunction. In this "pin-down" tactic the defending nation supposedly could not launch its missiles. The weakness of the argument is that the tactic would be ineffective in view of the large variety of retaliatory weapons that would be available to the defender and the extent of their dispersal.

system called Sentinel around certain cities. The main reason given was that it would provide protection against a prospective Chinese missile force.

After considerable public reaction this decision was rescinded, and a deployment of the same equipment under a new name (Safeguard) was proposed by the Nixon Administration. The Senate accepted the proposal after a long debate about the effectiveness of the system and the problems being met in developing it. In the entire debate developments in nuclear weaponry were never cited as having a crucial role in the various decisions concerning deployment. The serious questions that were raised about the feasibility of the system all had to do with such matters as the computers, the radar and the problems posed by decoys and MIRV's (multiple independently targetable reentry vehicles). When nuclear problems such as blackout were mentioned, it was only peripherally and never as constituting a major problem.

None of this proves that nuclear-weapons development and weapons-effect research are entirely irrelevant to ABM development, but it does indicate that recent research and development in this field have been far from essential. Apparently any lack of perfection in weapons can be overcome in the design of other parts of the system. Moreover, as the ABM program has shifted from Sentinel to Safeguard and now to the site-defense system (sometimes called Hardsite), the emphasis has shifted from interception at great distances and high altitudes to interception near the target at relatively low altitudes, where the phenomena to be dealt with are much better known.

I turn now to weapons effects. During the years when nuclear weapons were tested aboveground, the basic effects—blast, radiation, fallout—that kill, injure and destroy were studied in great detail. These are the weapons effects that matter; the entire concept of deterrence, which all sides cite as the main reason for maintaining nuclear forces, is based wholly on the threat of unacceptable levels of death and destruction through these effects. For decades the phenomenology of these effects has been known with a precision that far exceeds the practical use of the information.

In addition to these basic phenomena one hears of a few other more exotic effects that are of technical interest in connection with certain duels between nuclear weapons. Uncertainties about such effects are sometimes raised as an issue in test-ban debates. Among the effects are "TREE" and "EMP."

TREE stands for transient radiation effects on electronics. It is an old problem that has become relatively more important as more complex devices have been introduced into nuclear-weapons systems. It is also mainly of interest in connection with duels in outer space, where there is nothing to attenuate radiation, which therefore would far outreach other effects such as blast.

EMP stands for electromagnetic pulse. It refers to the fact that a nuclear explosion produces a large electromagnetic field, which in turn can induce large electric currents in conductors at substantial distances. Such currents, if nothing is done about them, can sometimes produce destructive effects in insufficiently protected equipment.

Some of the people who work on nuclear weapons have envisioned an attack in which an enemy explodes a series of warheads high over U.S. missile fields, producing a series of TREE and EMP phenomena (or other long-range effects) timed in such a way that the U.S. could not launch its missiles while the barrage continued. (The tactic is known as "pin-down.")

It is impossible to believe that real political or military leaders would consider such an effort in the face of the variety and dispersion of retaliatory weapons that could be employed. Even so, the claim that further research was needed on this matter was advanced in the early 1960's as an argument against the test ban. (At the time the argument was largely conducted behind the curtain of secrecy that surrounds much military activity; public discussion of the issue became possible only later.)

All the more exotic effects were observed before the partial test ban went into effect. They were not as thoroughly studied as the basic effects, however, and in addition certain new forms of interaction between these phenomena and specific weapons systems have been found since 1963. At first it was thought that it would be difficult to learn more about the exotic effects in underground explosions, and that possibility was raised as an argument against the partial test ban. Later it turned out that a good deal can be learned about the effects from underground testing and by other means. In 1968 Vice-Admiral Lloyd M. Mustin, director of the Defense Atomic Support Agency, reported to Congress: "We think we have the interaction of threats with these two systems [Minuteman and Polaris] well understood and identified and very carefully developed and sophisticated countermeasures far advanced."

In sum, no really new phenomena produced by the explosion of nuclear weapons has been discovered in about 15 years, and there is no good reason to expect that any will be forthcoming. In those years the U.S. has refined its knowledge of the effects of specific systems and in specific environmental situations. Even at that level of detail we have long since passed the point of diminishing returns. The remaining uncertainties are small compared with the

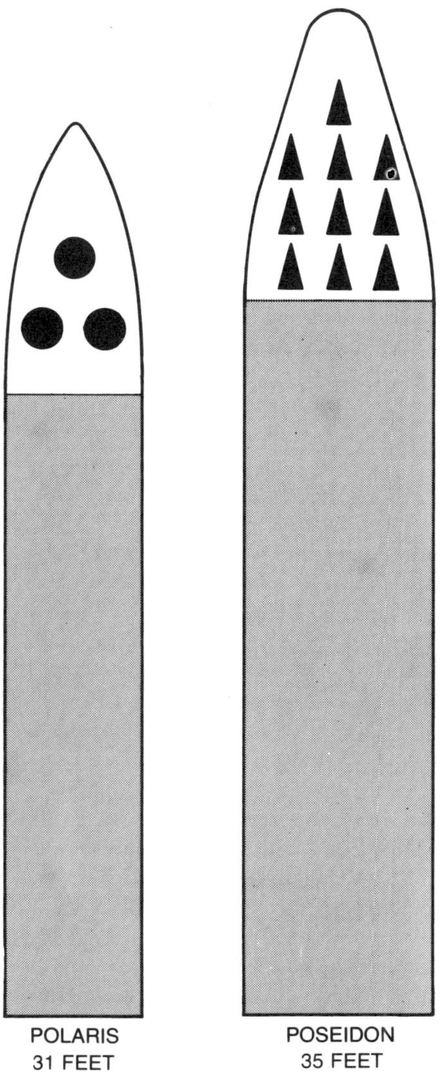

POLARIS AND POSEIDON missiles are compared. The older Polaris has three reentry vehicles that are not independently targetable, whereas the Poseidon has 10 MIRV's (multiple independently targetable reentry vehicles). It has been said that the Poseidon warhead could not have been developed under a comprehensive test ban. The author argues that the Polaris warhead could have well been adapted for the Poseidon missile.

other uncertainties about any nuclear attack: the kind, number, yield and accuracy of the weapons; the targets selected; the timing, the relation to other attacks or to political moves, and so on. These are the uncertainties that will dominate the thinking of any statesman who may one day be considering the use of nuclear weapons. No doubt there is more to be learned about weapons effects, but the matter is largely of interest to specialists, and concern about it should have no bearing on important political questions such as whether or not to ban further nuclear tests.

Pure-fusion bombs and bombs with a high ratio of fusion to fission (also called neutron bombs) were seen in the late 1950's as offering a number of advantages, and the need to develop them was therefore raised as an argument against a test ban. Teller, for example, was reported to have said to a Republican committee on nuclear testing in 1963: "We have started the development of clean and cheap nuclear explosives. We need more tests to complete this development. Clean and cheap nuclear explosives are needed for battlefield use, for peaceful applications and for missile defense." John A. Wheeler of Princeton University was reported as telling the same group: "As a physicist and specialist on nuclear fission I see a decisive loss to national security from a test ban. It will prevent us from developing a technology of pure hydrogen devices free of fission fallout.... The new technology will have important peacetime applications in mining and earth-moving and will revolutionize ground warfare. ... It is unconscionable to renounce for the free world a revolutionary device which others will then make without our knowledge."

On the other side, William C. Foster, director of the U.S. Arms Control and Disarmament Agency, said that the expert advice he had received was that pure-fusion weapons would not be of great advantage. The reason, he said, was that "they would constitute primarily a cheaper substitute for the explosive components in our already large stockpile of nuclear weapons."

How did matters turn out? The pure-fusion bomb remains undeveloped, and responsible people no longer talk much about it as being the basis of a new revolution in weaponry. When officials of the Department of Defense and the Atomic Energy Commission present arguments for continued testing now, they do not rate the need for fission-free bombs any higher than the need for other and more orthodox modifications and improvements.

A pure-fusion explosion may yet be achieved as a result of all the effort that has been expended. It would be a technological accomplishment, but the likelihood that it would have any large military or political value seems small. The basic fact is that the nuclear capability of the major nuclear powers is already supersaturated in the sense that it can produce more varieties of death, destruction and horror than anyone can seriously contemplate seeking to inflict.

It was also stated during the debate preceding the test ban of 1963 that further improvement in the yield-to-weight ratio of nuclear weapons was in prospect and that certain other improvements and modifications were both possible and necessary. Among them were decreased vulnerability to nearby nuclear explosions and increased safety of weapons. Substantial progress has indeed been made along these lines since 1963. The important question, however, is: How important and how relevant has the progress been?

The Poseidon missile provides a basis for discussion. It is more advanced than its predecessor, the Polaris A-3, in many ways. It is bigger, it can carry a larger payload a longer distance and it has improved accuracy. Moreover, its payload is of the MIRV type: each missile launches a "bus," which has on board a large number of reentry missiles, each of which can be accurately and independently targeted. None of these advances depended on nuclear tests.

M. Carl Walske, Jr., assistant to the Secretary of Defense for Atomic Energy, recently stated that the warhead for the Poseidon MIRV was developed after the limited test ban went into effect, and he argued that if the ban had been comprehensive, nothing like the present Poseidon MIRV could have been developed. I believe his statement is highly misleading. If a pre-1963 warhead such as the one for the Polaris A-3 had been adapted for the Poseidon, the Poseidon MIRV would have had either lower multiplicity (fewer independent missiles) or a shorter range, but it could have had a higher total yield.

Presumably the new Poseidon warhead has been further modified so as to reduce its vulnerability to attempts to intercept it. These modifications apparently resulted in a reduction of the yield-to-weight ratio. In any case such modifications were superfluous, since the basic multiple-warhead feature is in itself the most effective means for penetrating anti-ballistic-missile defenses of the kind that now exist. It does so simply by overwhelming the defense with larger numbers. The only requirement is that the individual warheads be hardened enough and separated enough so that one interceptor must be launched for each reentry vehicle. An A-3 warhead on a MIRV bus of the Poseidon type would easily satisfy this requirement.

Defense penetrability beyond what could be achieved in 1963 is needed only against an ABM defense consisting of very large numbers of relatively sophisticated interceptors. No such defense now exists—nor, I believe, is there any serious prospect of one in the foreseeable future. To say the least, deployment of the

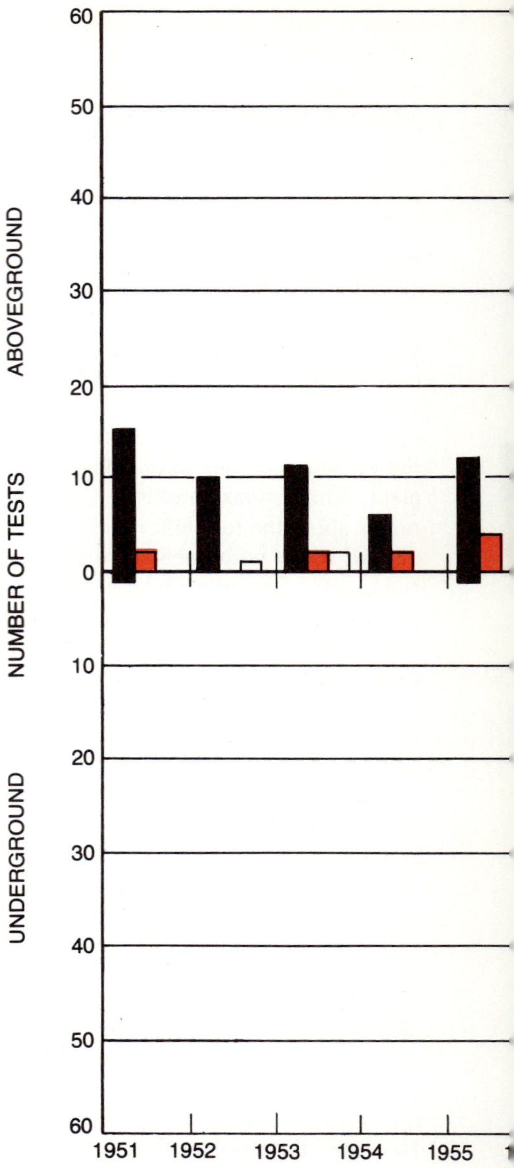

NUCLEAR TESTING by the U.S. (*black*), the U.S.S.R. (*color*) and all other nations

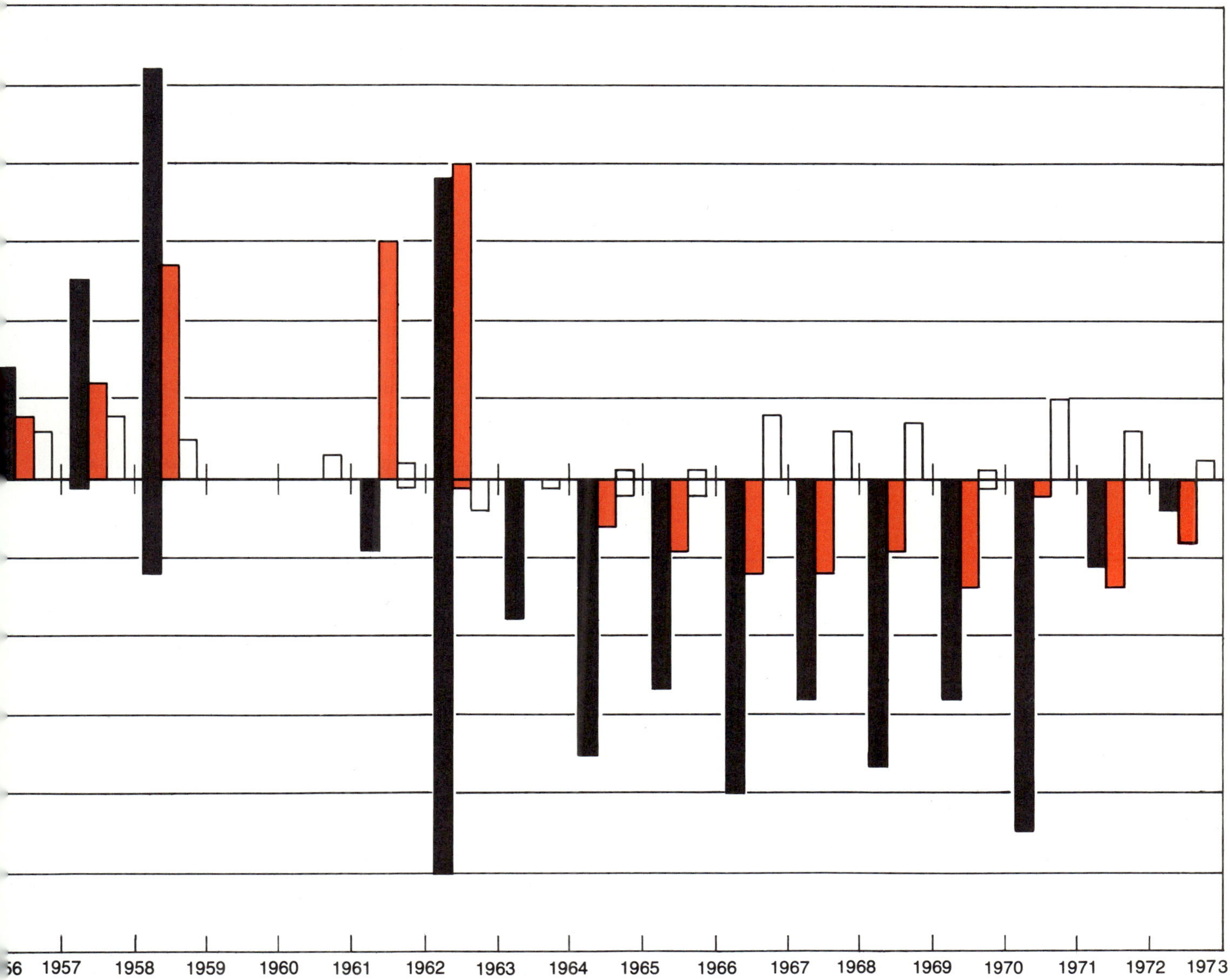

(*open bars*) is charted from 1951 to the fall of 1972. The gap near the center reflects the moratorium on testing nuclear weapons from 1958 to 1961. The figures were obtained from various sources by the Stockholm International Peace Research Institute (SIPRI).

post-1963 Poseidon warhead is premature.

It is small wonder that the concern over surprises and new knowledge persists. One need only recall the early years of nuclear development to realize that surprises and new knowledge abounded at that time. The phenomenon of nuclear fission was discovered in 1938. The first nuclear-test device was exploded only seven years later, which was also the first (and so far the only) time that nuclear bombs were employed in warfare. In terms of energy output those bombs were 1,000 times larger than the biggest chemical bombs.

Seven years later the first thermonuclear device was exploded. It was 1,000 times as large in output of energy as the first atomic bombs. Both of these huge technological steps can be characterized as breakthroughs, and they had major political and military consequences. No such huge gains in yield were made thereafter, but during the next seven years fundamentally important factors such as yield-to-weight ratio continued to improve radically. By 1960 the yield-to-weight ratio of fission bombs was two orders of magnitude (100 times) larger than it had been at the beginning. Means also had been found for both reducing the size and increasing the yield-to-weight ratio of thermonuclear weapons, again by order-of-magnitude amounts.

As a result of such developments many people came to believe politically significant technological breakthroughs had become the norm for nuclear technology. One thus finds many leaders in the field emphasizing the likelihood and importance of further technological surprises and arguing that no bars should be raised against obtaining new knowledge. In 1963, questioning the limited-test-ban treaty, John S. Foster, Jr., then director of the Lawrence Radiation Laboratory (he is now director of defense research and engineering in the Department of Defense), said: "We are involved in a field of technology that is not fully understood, nor its applications, and hence new experiments frequently bring surprises." Teller said a ban would "prohibit future science" and was "directed against knowledge." In 1961 Representative Chet Holifield, then chairman of the Joint Committee on Atomic Energy, expressed concern about "the ultimate general effect on weapons tech-

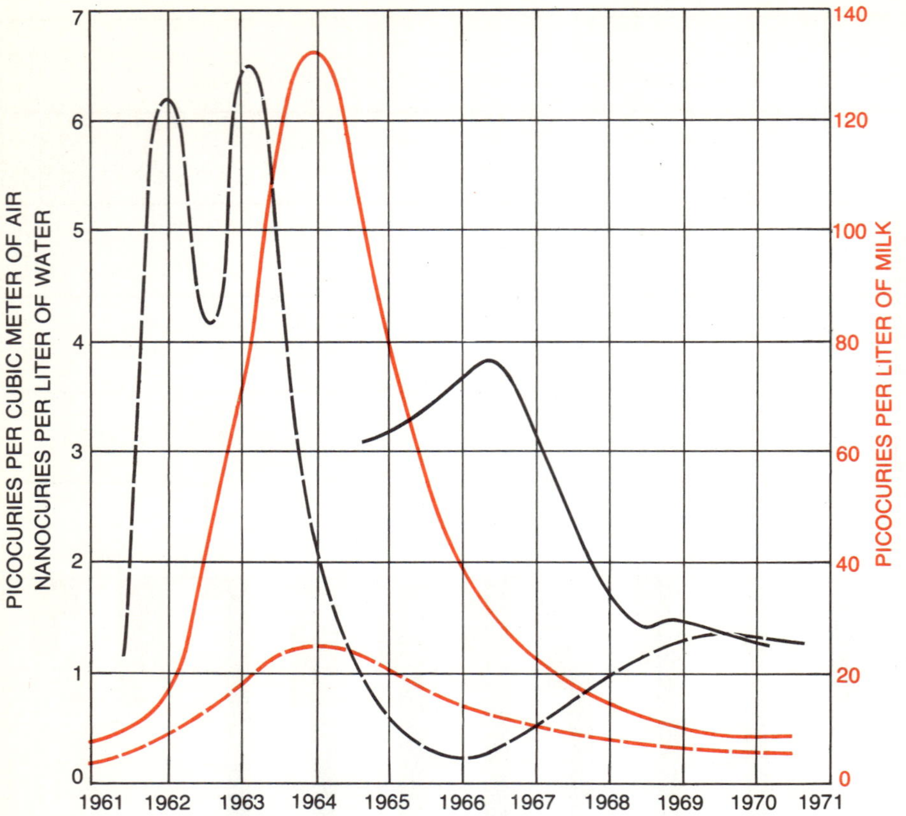

RADIOACTIVE FALLOUT has declined since nuclear testing by the U.S. and the U.S.S.R. has been done underground as a result of the limited test ban. The chart, based on data from the U.S. Environmental Protection Agency, shows gross beta radiation in the air (*broken black curve*), tritium in water (*solid black curve*), strontium 90 in milk (*broken colored curve*) and cesium 137 in milk (*solid colored curve*). Some of the radioactivity is natural.

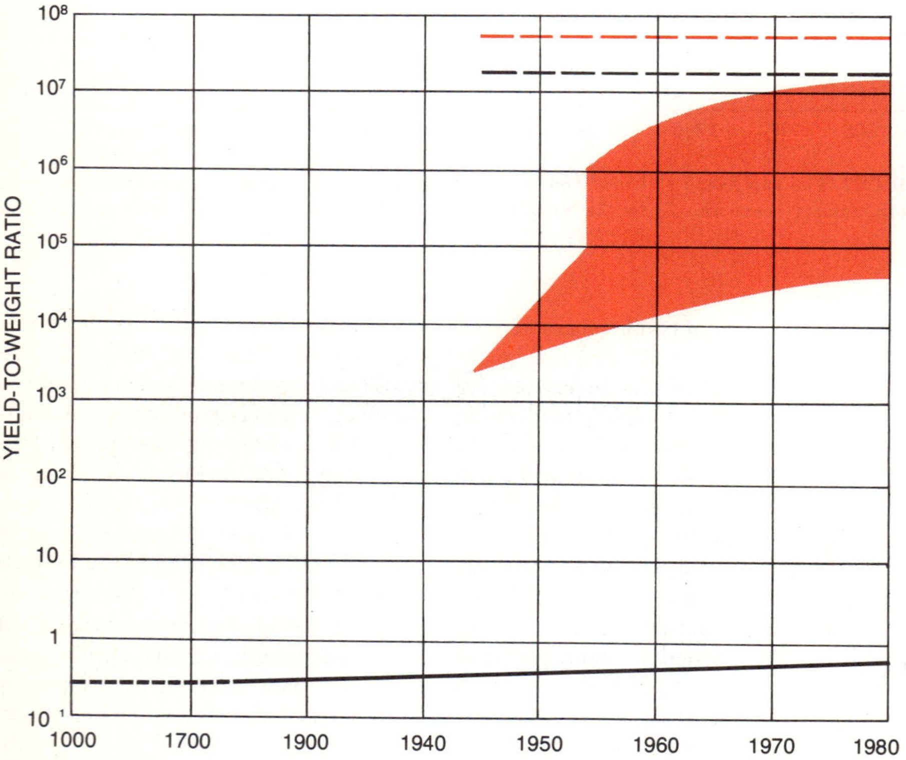

RATIO of yield to weight of nuclear weapons (*colored band*) and conventional weapons (*black line*) is charted. Lower part of nuclear-weapon band represents fission bombs; upper part, thermonuclear bombs. Broken lines represent theoretical maximum for fusion (*color*) and fission (*black*). The slowness of the rise in recent years is due in part to emphasis on other matters such as dimensions and decreasing vulnerability to nearby explosions.

nology of a continuing test ban," which would "inevitably stifle developments undreamed of at the present time." He added: "Concepts are now being considered by our scientists which could be as revolutionary as the H-bomb [was] in 1949." General Curtis E. LeMay, as Chief of Staff of the U.S. Air Force in 1963, said: "We are just at the beginning of our investigations into the nuclear-weapons field."

On the other side, proponents of a test ban expressed doubt about the importance of specific potential breakthroughs and saw as unlikely the possibility that any such development would upset the balance of power. William Foster of the disarmament agency, supporting the limited test ban, suggested that nuclear science was maturing. "The point of diminishing returns in improving weight-yield ratios is fast approaching," he said.

At the time of the debate on the partial test ban the issue of surprises and new knowledge was still difficult to resolve. On the one hand there was the record of a remarkable series of discoveries, technological advances and politically significant applications. On the other hand no further breakthroughs were then in sight, with the possible exception of the pure-fusion bomb, and of that many experts said it would be technologically novel but without great political or military significance.

Now, however, it seems to me that this issue has been resolved. Nuclear weapons have been further refined, and there is greater understanding of the details of certain effects, but no new knowledge or surprises remotely similar in kind or importance to those of the first two nuclear decades have been reported or claimed. Moreover, the nuclear arsenal is so large and varied that the significance of new inventions is small in any case. Compared with the danger of further proliferation of nuclear weapons, the danger that the U.S. will be overwhelmed by an unsuspected breakthrough seems vanishingly small.

Let us turn now to the arguments that were made in 1963 and earlier in support of the limited test ban. Five principal points were made and can be set forth here in quotations of participants: (1) "A nuclear test ban treaty would constitute a significant step in the direction of slackening the arms race" (Dean Rusk). (2) It would preserve for a "longer period our present nuclear advantage" (William Foster). (3) "The treaty will curb the pollution of the atmosphere" (President Kennedy). (4) It would create a political climate in which "new opportunities for further steps toward turning the arms race downward might well be more within the realm of possibility than at present" (Rusk). (5) "A nuclear test ban would constitute a significant first step in achieving control over the further spread of nuclear weapons" (Foster).

Each of the statements also amounted to a prediction. Let us see how the predictions stand up in 1972. The limited test ban probably did slow down the arms race between the U.S. and the U.S.S.R., but it cannot be considered to have been outstandingly successful in this respect. It probably has severely limited the further development of very large thermonuclear weapons, but the rate of nuclear testing has continued at about the same level—although the tests are now underground.

Similarly, the treaty does not appear to have done much to preserve the "nuclear advantage" of the U.S. Since the treaty was signed, the U.S.S.R. has achieved rough parity with the U.S. in strategic weapons. In any event, the degree of "overkill" in the nuclear capability of both countries is such that further technological advances would make little political or military difference.

The treaty has been quite effective in curbing radioactive pollution of the atmosphere. Although France and China have continued to conduct nuclear tests in the atmosphere, the tests are far less frequent than was the case when the U.S. and the U.S.S.R. were conducting them. Moreover, without the treaty there would be no hope of persuading those nations and other potential nuclear powers to accept similar restraints. Meanwhile, in the absence of a comprehensive test ban such hazards as underground contamination, earthquakes and leakage of radioactive substances into the atmosphere remain possible.

The record of the treaty in creating an environment that made further moves toward arms control possible is excellent. The treaty has been followed by agreements to prohibit nuclear weapons in space (1967), make Latin America a non-nuclear zone (1967), bar further proliferation of nuclear weapons (1968), rule out the seabed for the emplacement of nuclear weapons (1971) and prohibit the use of biological weapons (1972). One might also cite the "hot line" agreements of 1963 and 1971 and the recent strategic-arms-limitation talks (SALT) that resulted in agreement by the U.S. and the U.S.S.R. to put ceilings on their offensive and defensive missiles.

One should also recognize, however, that many of the treaties are peripheral to the main problem and in effect prohibit actions that no nation particularly wanted to undertake anyway. The British disarmament expert Philip J. Noel-Baker, reviewing the results of the 1959 treaty that demilitarized Antarctica, commented that "while disarming Antarctica, we put 7,000 nuclear weapons in Europe; we should have disarmed Europe and put those weapons in Antarctica." Nonetheless, all the agreements are steps in the right direction, and collectively they add up to something sig-

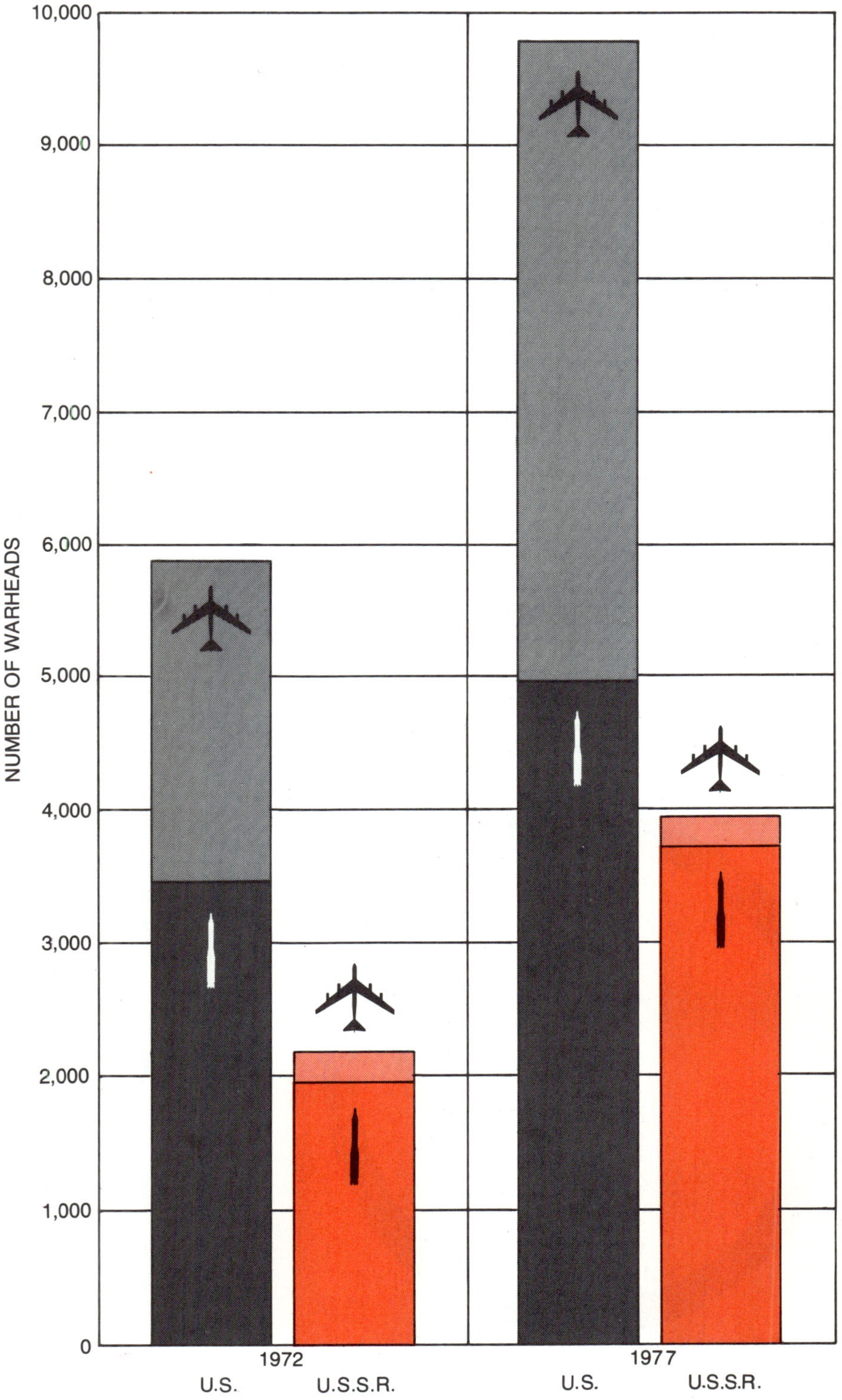

BALANCE OF POWER between the U.S. and the U.S.S.R. is charted in terms of nuclear warheads in 1972 and 1977, the end of the period for which the SALT I agreements are to remain in effect. The missile symbol represents missile-launched warheads and the airplane symbol represents bomber-launched missiles. The chart is based on data from the U.S. Arms Control and Disarmament Agency, which points out that the U.S. has more but smaller missiles than the U.S.S.R. and that the megatonnage represented is approximately equal.

nificant. Moreover, they help to make arms-control and disarmament measures seem more feasible.

Probably the most important result of the limited test ban has been its contribution to inhibiting the further proliferation of nuclear weapons. Since the treaty was signed, only China has begun testing nuclear weapons, and the Chinese program to develop nuclear weapons had been set in motion long before 1963. The cause was greatly aided by the nonproliferation treaty, which now has some 70 signatories in addition to the original adherents (the U.S., the United Kingdom and the U.S.S.R.). It also seems evident that the treaty has deterred nonsigners from testing.

Indeed, the most important reason for moving now toward a comprehensive ban on testing nuclear weapons is that it would strengthen and reinforce the nonproliferation treaty. The present situation contains elements of hypocrisy and unfairness, since the two major nuclear powers are trying to persuade other nations that nuclear weapons are unnecessary while at the same time both are conducting test programs.

To sum up, a decade of hindsight on the debates preceding the limited-test-ban treaty of 1963 suggests the following main conclusions:

1. The predictions of major surprises and ominous developments were wrong. There has been no "third revolution" in nuclear weapons. The atmospheric tests before 1963 and the underground tests since then have not produced a solution to the problem of developing an ABM system that would be likely to have more than limited success.

2. On the other hand, the passage of time has confirmed the more moderate claims that there was substantial progress to be made in improving the yield-to-weight ratio, hardening weapons against interception, making better fits to new delivery systems and so on. The questions to be asked, however, are how progress in these areas has affected the nuclear balance and whether such technical progress is politically significant. The answers seem to be that, if anything, continued testing has further degraded whatever nuclear advantage the U.S. still had in 1963 and that the political significance of nuclear weapons is derived from the huge numbers of such weapons rather than from their technical sophistication.

3. The limited test ban has not done much to slow the main arms race between the two superpowers. The reason is the limited nature of the agreement. A comprehensive ban in 1963 probably would have done much more.

4. On the other hand, the limited ban has accomplished several of the most important objectives that were were set for it. In ascending order of importance they are cleaner air, the establishment of a political climate conducive to much additional progress in arms control and disarmament and the distinct slowing of the spread of nuclear weapons.

On balance, therefore, the limited test ban can be described as a success. Clearly, however, it needs to be extended to prohibit underground testing. A comprehensive treaty may now be within grasp; we must reach for it while we can.

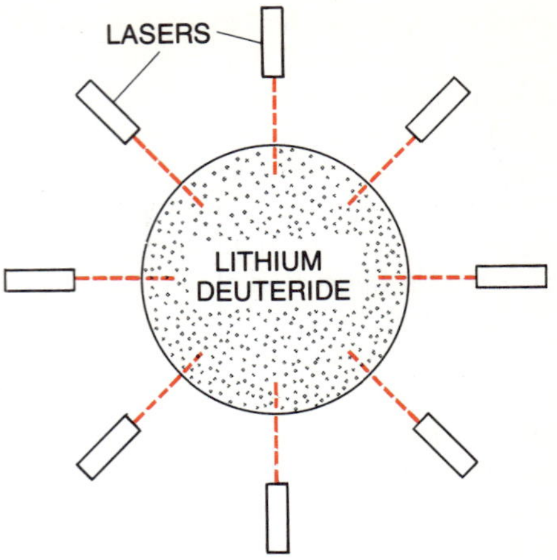

PURE-FUSION BOMB, which has yet to be developed, would entail heating the fusion material without the use of a fission explosion. Lasers could perhaps produce the necessary initial conditions, but the technology seems to be formidable. Achieving such a bomb would be a technological feat, but it seems probable that the achievement would not have any great political or military value beyond the present nuclear bombs.

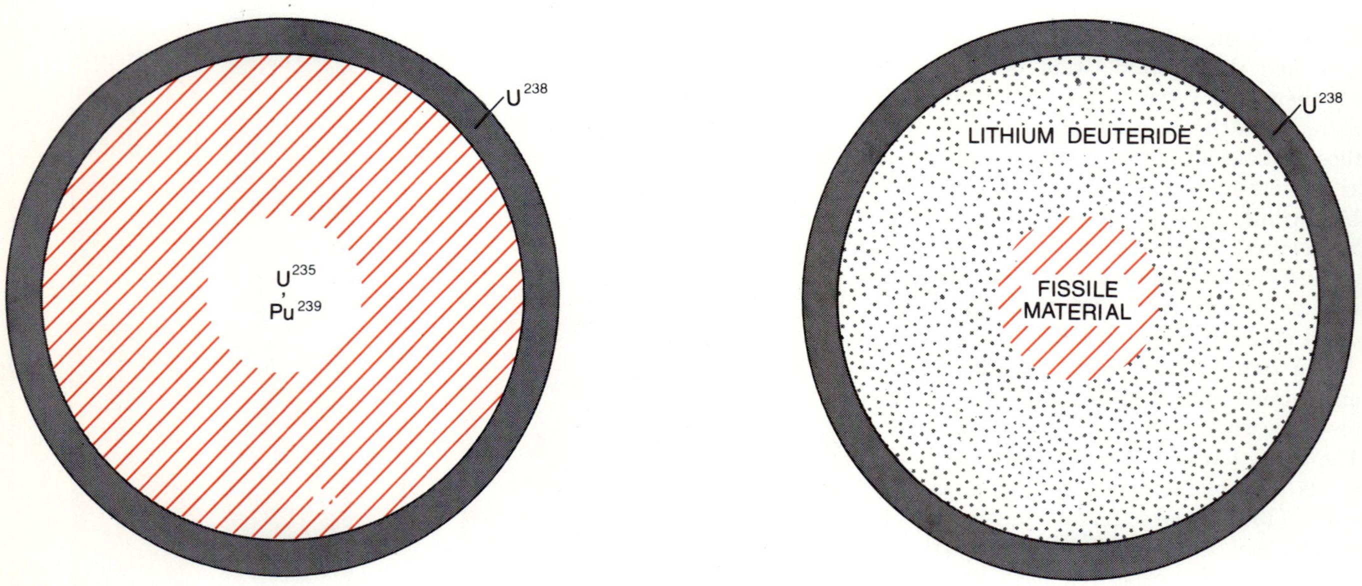

NUCLEAR WEAPONS are depicted schematically. At left a fission bomb is shown just as the nuclear explosion starts. A supercritical mass of fissile material has been rapidly assembled by means of high explosive, which is not shown, and a chain reaction is initiated by a neutron from a source near the mass. The uranium 238 reflects some neutrons and provides some additional inertia but does not otherwise participate importantly in the reaction. The drawing of a thermonuclear bomb (*right*) explains its known properties, although no detailed design has ever been made public. Fissile material in the central core explodes, producing much heat and many neutrons. The neutrons convert some of the lithium 6 surrounding the core to tritium, and the heat causes thermonuclear deuterium-deuterium and deuterium-tritium reactions to take place in the lithium deuteride. These reactions in turn produce neutrons having enough energy to cause the surrounding uranium 238 to fission, thus releasing still more energy and additional quantities of neutrons.

Chemical and Biological Weapons

The U.S. has renounced all forms of biological weapons and the first use of most chemical weapons. The issue of whether or not to include irritant gases and antiplant agents in the prohibition remains open

MATTHEW S. MESELSON

May 1970

On November 25 of last year President Nixon announced a number of major decisions regarding chemical and biological weapons. He proclaimed that the U.S. will never be the first to use lethal or incapacitating chemical weapons and will not use biological weapons under any circumstances, even in retaliation. He also announced that he would submit to the Senate the 1925 Geneva Protocol prohibiting the use of chemical and biological weapons in warfare.

The President's statement left a question whether toxins, the poisonous but nonliving substances produced by some bacteria and other organisms, were included in the unconditional renunciation of biological weapons or only in the no-first-use pledge for chemicals. The question was resolved on February 14 when the President extended the policy for biological weapons to cover toxins as well. In order to remove a possible ambiguity, it was decided to renounce toxin weapons even if advances in chemistry should make it practicable to prepare them synthetically instead of by extraction from bacteria or other organisms.

Under the new policy the U.S. will destroy existing stocks of germ and toxin weapons and will no longer engage in their development, production or stockpiling. The U.S. biological program will be restricted to research for strictly defined defensive purposes, such as techniques of immunization.

In accord with these decisions on biological and toxin weapons, White House officials have stated that there will no longer be a need for secret work and that consideration is being given to the transfer for conversion to other purposes of our sizable biological weapons facilities at Fort Detrick, Md., and Pine Bluff, Ark., from the Department of Defense to nonsecret agencies such as the Department of Health, Education, and Welfare and the Department of Agriculture.

As to chemical weapons, the restraints are less sweeping. The U.S. reserves the right to continue the development, production and stockpiling of lethal and incapacitating chemical weapons. It pledges, however, never to use them first. The same pledge is embodied in the treaty commitment by the 84 states now party to the Geneva Protocol.

There are two types of chemical weapon whose use in war has not been renounced. They are the antiplant chemicals and the "riot control" agents, such as CS, employed by U.S. forces in Southeast Asia. The U.S. has maintained that these agents are not prohibited by the Geneva Protocol. Many nations disagree, which raises problems for U.S. ratification of that treaty. The President himself has made no statement regarding CS or herbicides. White House officials have said only that the use of these chemical weapons will continue "for the time being."

The President's decisions were based on a six-month review of U.S. policies and programs for chemical and biological weapons. The review was conducted under the auspices of the National Security Council, which coordinated the efforts of the Department of State, the Department of Defense, the Arms Control and Disarmament Agency, the Central Intelligence Agency, the Office of Science and Technology and other branches of the Government. The subject was put under searching examination. The National Security Council considered the following topics: chemical and biological weapons that were already available and those that might conceivably be developed, the possible military value of each type of weapon in relation to other weapons at our disposal, the possible consequences of proliferation, strategic questions concerning the use of such weapons for threat or deterrence, the political and moral impact of their development and possible use, the potential hazards for civilian populations, possible defenses against the various weapons, and the policies and activities of other nations.

It was obvious and became more so as the review proceeded that such a study was long overdue. The U.S. had a large factory for producing germ weapons, even though no one had ever produced a convincing "scenario" for a case in which they should be used. Shortly before and during the National Security Council study, chemical weapons were involved in one disquieting incident after another, creating a political atmosphere favorable to the questioning of previous policies. A series of earthquakes that shook the city of Denver was traced to the massive subterranean disposal of chemical wastes at the Army's Rocky Mountain Arsenal. The accidental release of nerve gas in a test of an aircraft spray tank over the Dugway Proving Ground in Utah led to the death of thousands of sheep, some of them grazing as far as 40 miles away. Then there was protest against the Army's plan to ship 12,000 tons of outmoded nerve-gas bombs across the country from Colorado to be dumped in the Atlantic. Soon afterward there was an incident in which nerve gas escaped from U.S. munitions stored on Okinawa, and it was also revealed that nerve-gas munitions were stored in West Germany. Finally there had been newspaper articles to the effect that the Defense Department was testing biological weapons in the South Pacific and had conducted open-air tests of nerve gas in Hawaii without informing state officials.

The public reaction to these incidents can be gauged from the fact that the U.S. Senate voted 91 to 0 for a resolution requiring the review by the Public Health Service of any plan for the domestic transportation or open-air testing of lethal chemical agents or of any biological warfare agents. The resolution, which is now law, also requires the Defense Department to render semiannual reports to Congress on the investigation, development, testing and procurement of all agents of chemical and biological warfare.

Here I shall discuss first the nature of chemical and biological weapons (CBW) and their military implications, then the international effort that has been made to prevent their use, and finally the present situation. Although much work on CBW has been secret, the essential facts about the weapons are now in the open literature. Particularly noteworthy is the report of a United Nations group published last year and the subsequent World Health Organization report that specifically examines the potential effects on civilian populations. The UN report was prepared by a group of 14 consultant experts nominated by their respective governments. The U.S. participant was Ivan L. Bennett, Jr., director of the New York University Medical Center and former Deputy Director of the U.S. Office of Science and Technology. The American members of the WHO consultant group were Joshua Lederberg of the Stanford University School of Medicine and myself. Even more detailed than the UN and WHO reports is the forthcoming study by the Stockholm International Peace Research Institute.

Although chemical and biological weapons are linked together in the psychology, the customs and the international law that restrain their use, it is helpful to distinguish several categories for analyzing military characteristics and implications. I shall discuss five kinds of weapon: lethal biological weapons, incapacitating biological weapons, lethal chemical weapons, incapacitating chemical weapons and antiplant agents. The distinction between lethal and incapacitating is not altogether clear-cut, particularly under the extremely uncontrolled conditions of warfare. There is a continuous spectrum of agents from the highly lethal to the generally nonlethal, and even tear gas can be used together with bullets and bombs to increase ca-

HERBICIDES ARE SPRAYED by U.S. Air Force planes in South Vietnam. More than 19,000 sorties have been flown since 1962. One aircraft covers a swath nearly 300 feet wide and 10 miles long. Military officials say destruction of crops in certain areas held by Vietcong reduces food supplies for opposing forces and jungle defoliation reduces concealment.

sualties. Nonetheless, the arguments for and against lethal and nonlethal weapons deserve separate attention.

Let us first consider lethal biological weapons. They would operate by disseminating clouds of disease germs over the target area or upwind from it. The germs would then be inhaled by the target population. The disease anthrax is an example. Caused by the bacterium *Bacillus anthracis,* it is mainly encountered as a disease of domesticated animals that is occasionally transmitted to man. Because it is not very contagious among humans, natural cases of anthrax are generally localized rather than epidemic. If the bacteria were sprayed in the air in an aerosol, however, the effects could be devastating. The inhalation of approximately 50,000 spores of *B. anthracis* (total weight less than a millionth of a gram) is believed to be enough to cause a 50 percent chance of contracting pulmonary anthrax. Symptoms would first appear about a day after the attack. The onset might be mistaken for a common cold, but this would be followed by severe coughing, cyanosis, respiratory failure and death. Untreated pulmonary anthrax is almost always fatal.

The WHO report gives estimates of the area-coverage capability of various biological agents. For illustrative purposes the report assumes that one light bomber delivers in a single pass ground-functioning "bomblets" containing a total of 50 kilograms of dry powdered agent along a two-kilometer line at right angles to the wind. It is assumed that the intensity of atmospheric turbulence is less than a certain level, but not so low as to be at all unusual, particularly at night. The bomblets release the agent as an aerosol, which then drifts over the target area. Such calculations take into account the dissemination efficiency of the bomblets, the decay rate of agent infectivity, the rate of vertical dilution in the atmosphere, the rate of deposition on the ground and the dose-response curve for man. For an attack with anthrax spores the WHO report predicts a high mortality rate over at least 20 square kilometers. Although there are uncertainties in the quantities that enter into the calculation, the estimate is deliberately conservative. The UN report, in a similar estimate, considers an attack by a large low-flying bomber dispensing 10,000 kilograms of agent along a 100-kilometer line by means of a spray tank. The estimated area in which a high casualty rate would occur is as large as 100,000 square kilometers, depending on the particular agent used.

Among the lethal biological agents that might be considered for military use are the viruses of Eastern equine encephalitis and yellow fever, the rickettsia causing Rocky Mountain spotted fever, and the bacteria causing anthrax, plague, cholera, glanders and melioidosis. There are moderately effective vaccines and antibiotics against some of these diseases but none against others. Moreover, such protections might be overwhelmed by a massive attack, and for some agents antibiotics can be circumvented by the use of drug-resistant strains. Protection can be given by gas masks or air-filtered shelters if there is early warning of an attack, but no satisfactory early-warning device has yet been developed. In any case a program for supplying the civilian population with masks and shelters and maintaining discipline for their use would require a major and sustained economic and political effort—without achieving reliable protection against biological attack.

It is not to be expected that biological warfare agents would be deliberately chosen to be contagious; that would maximize the risk of spreading disease far beyond the intended target, possibly to the territory of the attacker or his allies. Nevertheless, the unnatural conditions inherent in military operations create the possibility that widespread epidemics would be unintentionally started. There is also the hazard, difficult to evaluate, that the bacteria or viruses used in an attack, or even used in a field test, could subsequently emerge from exposed populations of humans, rodents, birds or other animals with increased persistence, virulence and contagiousness for man.

From this brief account it should be clear that lethal biological weapons would present a devastating threat of killing human populations over large areas. The threat is made particularly formidable by the relative ease with which such weapons could pass into many hands if the technology becomes established and if the customs and attitudes that have generally kept nations from pursuing the development of biological weapons should change. After several years of pursuing a biological weapons program that has not had adequate review or guidance from the Executive Branch, and that has been almost entirely shielded by secrecy from public and congressional knowledge, the U.S. has decided that the best way to minimize the threat of biological weapons is to renounce them altogether. The logical case for doing so rests on the realization that the possession of such weapons would add little, if anything, to our strategic-deterrent capability, whereas their proliferation would present a major threat to the U.S. and indeed to all mankind.

The second category of weapons to be considered is incapacitating biological weapons. An example is Venezuelan equine encephalitis. It is a virus that causes severe headache, nausea and prostration but that has a case fatality rate in natural epidemics of .5 percent or lower. Methods for disseminating incapacitating biological agents and the possibilities for defending against them are essentially the same as those for lethal biological agents. The use of incapacitating biological weapons might be considered in certain unlikely and extreme situations. Perhaps the most "attractive" scenario that has been proposed imagines the entrapment of a large friendly force by enemy troops deployed over an extensive area and intermingled with civilians. In this situation the employment of incapacitating biological weapons in forward and rear areas might impede the enemy advance long enough to allow reinforcement or evacuation of the friendly troops when the alternatives might be to use nuclear weapons or to surrender.

Of course any decision to launch an incapacitating biological attack must face the fact that substantial numbers of civilians, particularly infants and the infirm, will almost inevitably be killed, even if the case fatality rate is only a few tenths of a percent. Beyond that there is the possibility that the fatality rate under military conditions might be much higher than the rate estimated from natural occurrences of the disease and from various kinds of experimental data. It is also important to note that this scenario assumes the *first* use of biological weapons rather than their employment in retaliation. This adds the additional risk of escalation and enlargement of the conflict that could result from the outbreak of germ warfare of any kind. A principal long-term cost to security of using incapacitating biological weapons, or even of maintaining them, would be stimulation of the proliferation of germ weapons, including lethal ones. The facilities for developing, producing and delivering incapacitating biological weapons are essentially the same as those required for lethal germs. International law and international custom do not distinguish between them.

To summarize, incapacitating biologi-

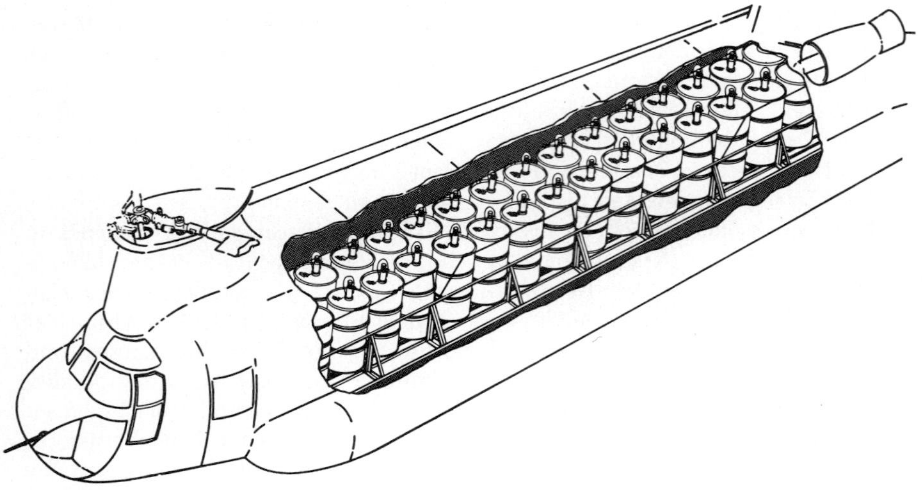

LOADING PLAN for a CH-47 Chinook helicopter employed for air-dropping the irritating agent CS is depicted as it is shown in a U.S. Army training manual. Each bomb contains 80 pounds of CS-2. Burster tube down the middle of each bomb contains an explosive charge.

cal weapons might seem logical in certain tactical situations, but such situations are most unlikely, and even then the risks would outweigh the possible gain.

Here a more general statement about germ weapons should be made. Such weapons have serious shortcomings from a military viewpoint. Their effects are not as predictable as those of other weapons. They might get out of control. Alternative and already available weapons are preferable, and the acquisition of a biological weapons capability would be an addition to, not a substitute for, preexisting military expenditures and programs.

Military officers and political leaders are strongly disinclined to use biological weapons, partly for practical reasons, partly because of unfamiliarity and partly because of the moral revulsion and apprehension that are undeniably associated with these weapons. There does not currently seem to be any serious interest in biological weapons in high military circles anywhere. Although such weapons could become a terrible menace, the likelihood of this is greatly reduced by the spectacular gesture of renunciation made by the U.S. This is the moment in history when the biological sciences, with their intimate linkage to the lifesaving ethos of medicine, may be spared from being recruited to serve military ends all over the world. Whether or not international biological disarmament can be ensured over the long run may ultimately be related to progress in chemical disarmament, for in the minds of many the two are linked.

Chemical weapons present a much more immediate problem. They were used in World War I and are stockpiled by the U.S. and the U.S.S.R. and are also possessed by several other nations. The distinction between lethal weapons and incapacitating ones has more practical importance here than it has with biological weapons. There are strong restraints against the use of lethal chemical weapons, and until recently nonlethal chemicals have been excluded from warfare as well. From an arms-control point of view there are important arguments for treating lethal and nonlethal chemicals together. Still, for the purpose of analysis it is useful to make the distinction.

Modern lethal chemical weapons employ the nerve gases first developed (but not used) by Germany during World War II. These agents are hundreds of times more poisonous than the poison gases of World War I; they kill when they are inhaled or when they are deposited as liquid droplets on the skin. The term "nerve gas" derives from the fact that these agents operate by interfering with the transmission of nerve impulses across synapses. They do so by inactivating the enzyme cholinesterase, which normally functions to terminate the transmission of a nerve impulse. In the presence of a nerve agent, nerve impulses continue without control, causing a breakdown of respiration and other functions. Death caused by nerve-gas poisoning results from asphyxiation. It is preceded by blurring of vision, intense salivation and convulsions.

The U.S. has stockpiled a variety of tactical nerve-gas weapons, and the U.S.S.R. is believed to have done so too. The weapons include mines, artillery projectiles, rockets, bombs and aircraft spray devices.

The U.S. stockpile includes two kinds of nerve agent. One is GB, a code name for isopropylmethylphosphonofluoridate. It is also known as Sarin and was produced in limited amounts by Germany during World War II. Sarin is a volatile liquid that evaporates at room temperature to a colorless and odorless gas.

Weapons containing Sarin release it as a spray, which then evaporates to create a respiratory hazard for unprotected personnel. The lethal exposure for man is estimated to be approximately 100 milligram-minutes per cubic meter. This means, for example, that a man would accumulate a lethal dose in 10 minutes if the concentration of Sarin in the air were 10 milligrams per cubic meter.

Since the hazard posed by Sarin is mainly respiratory, a gas mask provides good protection. Modern gas masks are capable of reducing the concentration of all known war gases, by a factor of about 100,000. In addition there are chemical antidotes for nerve agents that can provide protection if the dose of agent is not very great and the antidote is administered promptly.

The other kind of nerve agent in the U.S. stockpile is VX. The chemical formula of VX is still secret, although the WHO report suggests that the agent is ethyl S-dimethylaminoethyl methylphosphonothiolate. It is a member of a class of compounds first prepared in the mid-1950's in the course of a search for improved insecticides. (Sarin was also the outcome of insecticide research.) Also a liquid but several times more toxic than Sarin and much less volatile, VX is lethal either when inhaled or deposited on the skin. VX kills in a matter of minutes, and by contaminating the ground and objects on which it is deposited it can make an entire area hazardous for many days. It was VX that killed the sheep in Utah.

The lethal dose of VX applied to the skin has been estimated to be from two to 10 milligrams, depending on the site of application. Since contact with even a small droplet of VX can be fatal, adequate protection requires the wearing of a special suit as well as a gas mask. The wearing of protective suits and masks is extremely cumbersome. They are mechanically awkward, and the buildup of heat is a serious problem. Fighting efficiency would be severely reduced by the wearing of full protective equipment and also by the strict observation of various special precautions necessary for survival in a lethal chemical environment. This kind of complexity in gas warfare was clearly recognized in World War I.

In the words of one officer: "The range of problems was infinite. How would the soldier eat, drink, sleep, perform bodily functions, use his weapon, give and receive commands? How would he know when his immediate area was contaminated?"

For tactical use against an enemy without protective equipment, lethal chemicals would be devastating. Against an enemy possessing suits and masks and able to impose the wearing of such gear on one's own troops by the threat of retaliation in kind, lethal chemical weapons would enormously complicate the battlefield without giving either side a major advantage. This argues for not initiating lethal chemical warfare. It also suggests, however, a reason for possessing lethal chemical weapons as a tactical deterrent if the other side is thought to have them. For example, if conventional land warfare should ever break out in Europe, with only one side in possession of lethal chemical munitions, that side might be tempted to use them in order to force opposing troops into protective gear while its own forces, taking advantage of their knowledge of the timing and location of the chemical attack, pressed the offensive. Having this knowledge, the argument goes, their operations would be considerably less complicated. It is this kind of analysis that presumably underlies the U.S. policy of maintaining lethal chemical weapons even though it is our policy never to initiate their use.

Both the plausibility and the accuracy of the foregoing scenario can be challenged. Many would maintain that a major war in Europe is extremely unlikely. It is even more unlikely that such a war could go on for many days without resort to nuclear weapons, in which case chemicals would become unimportant. Finally, it is argued, even in the event of a large nonnuclear war the use of chemicals would be strongly deterred by the risk that using such unconventional weapons to obtain any major advantage would trigger a nuclear response.

Clearly there are some risks in either approach. The second approach, however, would allow the renunciation of the possession of lethal chemical weapons.

Lethal chemical weapons could be produced by nonnuclear nations to provide a capability for strategic attack on urban populations. Under meteorological conditions favorable to the attack, a medium bomber or a converted commercial air transport can deliver enough nerve agent to kill a high proportion of unprotected people throughout the central region of a large city. For example, the WHO report estimates that an airborne attack across the wind along a two-kilometer line, releasing four tons of chemical agent over a city, would cause high casualties over an area of between two and 40 square kilometers, depending on the type of agent and munitions used. Given adequate warning a highly disciplined population could be defended against such an attack by a combination of gas masks, protective shelters and antidote therapy. Although strategic chemical weapons would add nothing significant to the arsenals of the nuclear powers, the proliferation of such weapons among the nonnuclear nations would obviously constitute a serious hazard. Even though it is unlikely that a small nation could deliver a chemical attack over a wide area of a country that has modern air defenses, it would be much easier to penetrate the air space over one or a few coastal cities.

It is also important to consider the possible role of lethal chemical weapons

AGENTS	DISEASES	INCUBATION PERIOD (DAYS)	EFFECT OF TREATMENT	CONTAGIOUSNESS
VIRUSES	EASTERN EQUINE ENCEPHALITIS	5 TO 15	NONE	BY VECTOR
	TICK-BORNE ENCEPHALITIS	7 TO 14	NONE	BY VECTOR
	YELLOW FEVER	3 TO 6	NONE	BY VECTOR
RICKETTSIAE	ROCKY MOUNTAIN SPOTTED FEVER	3 TO 10	GOOD	BY VECTOR
	EPIDEMIC TYPHUS	6 TO 15	GOOD	BY VECTOR
BACTERIA	ANTHRAX	1 TO 5	MODERATE	LOW
	CHOLERA	1 TO 5	GOOD	HIGH
	PNEUMONIC PLAGUE	2 TO 5	MODERATE	HIGH
	TULAREMIA	1 TO 10	GOOD	LOW
	TYPHOID	7 TO 21	GOOD	HIGH

AGENTS	DISEASES	INCUBATION PERIOD (DAYS)	EFFECT OF TREATMENT	CONTAGIOUSNESS
VIRUSES	CHIKUNGUNYA FEVER	2 TO 6	NONE	BY VECTOR
	DENGUE FEVER	5 TO 8	NONE	BY VECTOR
	VENEZUELAN EQUINE ENCEPHALITIS	2 TO 5	NONE	BY VECTOR
RICKETTSIAE	Q FEVER	10 TO 21	GOOD	LOW
BACTERIA	BRUCELLOSIS	7 TO 21	MODERATE	NONE
FUNGI	COCCIDIOIDOMYCOSIS	7 TO 21	POOR	NONE

BIOLOGICAL AGENTS are shown by category and effect; those that could be expected to cause death are at top and agents that might be used to cause incapacitation are at bottom. Contagion "by vector" means transmission by certain species of mosquitoes or other insects.

COMMON NAME	SARIN	VX	MUSTARD	BZ	CS AND CS-2
MILITARY CLASSIFICATION	LETHAL AGENT (NERVE GAS)	LETHAL AGENT (NERVE GAS)	LETHAL AND INCAPACITATING AGENT	INCAPACITATING AGENT (PSYCHO-CHEMICAL)	HARASSING AGENT
PHYSICAL STATE	LIQUID	LIQUID	LIQUID	SOLID	SOLID
FORM AS DISSEMINATED	VAPOR, AEROSOL OR SPRAY	AEROSOL OR SPRAY	SPRAY	AEROSOL OR DUST	AEROSOL OR DUST
DURATION OF CONTAMINATION	HOURS OR DAYS	DAYS OR WEEKS	DAYS OR WEEKS		CS–MINUTES CS-2–WEEKS

CHEMICAL WARFARE AGENTS included in the U.S. stockpile are listed by category and some of their major characteristics. Data were assembled by the World Health Organization for its recent report on the health effects of chemical and biological weapons.

in "low level" conflicts. Today such conflicts are fought with high-explosive and flame weapons, which individually have limited area effect. Although such wars can be exceedingly destructive, they become so only when enormous quantities of weapons are used. (In Vietnam, for example, more than 6,000 tons of ammunition were expended by the U.S. daily in 1968.)

Many of the types of munitions used in limited war, however, could be filled with lethal chemicals. In such a case the "kill area" of lightweight munitions such as mortar shells and rockets could be increased by a factor of as much as 100. Even though combatants could be provided with protective equipment, such weapons would be devastating to military units caught unprepared and to civilians in urban areas. Small military units would begin to acquire strategic capabilities against cities.

It is apparent, therefore, that chemical weapons constitute a menace far beyond their possible tactical employment by the major powers. It is this menace that provides one of the chief arguments for chemical and biological disarmament. A concluding but often overriding restraint on the tactical use of lethal chemicals, particularly when the battlefield is on friendly soil, is that their large-scale employment could cause heavy casualties among undefended civilians in the combat zone and out to considerable distances downwind.

Although U.S. policy now treats toxins in the same way as biological weapons, by renouncing even their possession, the UN report classifies toxins as chemicals because they do not reproduce. Toxins are poisonous substances produced by living organisms including plants, animals and bacteria. Examples are ricin from the castor bean, tetrodotoxin from the globefish and botulin from the bacterium *Clostridium botulinum*. Some toxins, such as botulin, are highly lethal to man; others, such as the staphylococcus enterotoxin (the substance responsible for staphylococcal food poisoning), are usually only temporarily incapacitating.

Even though toxins are not capable of reproduction and therefore cannot cause epidemics, they do induce many of the same symptoms associated with infection by disease organisms. Indeed, the principal pathological symptoms of several bacteriological diseases are thought to be caused by toxins produced within the human body by the living microorganisms. Thus toxin weapons, both in terms of the means of their production and the symptoms they cause, are closely related to the biological ones.

For use as weapons toxins could be dispersed as aerosols in much the same way as biological and chemical weapons. Because toxins are not absorbed effectively through the skin, gas masks would provide protection, as would shelters fitted with special air filters. Protection can also be afforded by prior immunization with specific toxoid. Each toxoid, however, is effective only against a particular kind of toxin, and for some toxins the margin of protection is not enough to be of practical significance.

The chief military argument for having toxins is that, because of their great potency, the weight of toxin munitions needed to cover a given area would be lower than the corresponding requirement for standard chemical munitions. There are several technical reasons to question whether this is so, but even if it were, the saving would not be of very great importance for major military powers with their large logistic capability. An active U.S. toxin weapons program would have run counter to the President's decision to demilitarize and declassify U.S. biological weapons research and production facilities and would have made it impossible for the U.S. to take an unequivocal and convincing stand against the use of disease as a weapon of war.

The first chemical weapons to be employed in World War I were nonlethal. It is reported that some soldiers brought police tear-gas cartridges to the front. Soon both Germany and France began using artillery shells containing tear gas, and thousands of these shells were fired months before the famous German attack at Ypres with chlorine gas released from cylinders. Tear gas and other irritant chemicals continued to be used throughout the war—more than 12,000 tons in all. Even larger quantities of such chemicals were prepared but not employed by the belligerents on both sides in World War II.

Modern incapacitating chemical weapons are of two types, one with effects lasting considerably beyond the period of exposure and one with brief effects. President Nixon's renunciation of the first use of incapacitating chemicals has been applied only to the longer-lasting type. An example of this type is the U.S. agent BZ. This is a psychochemical, the chemical identity of which is still secret, although the WHO report speculates that it belongs to the family known as benzilates. BZ is a solid that can be dispersed as an aerosol to be inhaled by enemy personnel. It affects both physical and mental processes, causing blurred vision, disorientation and confusion. Its incapacitating effects can last for several days.

Although BZ has been standardized as a weapon by the U.S. Army and munitions have been loaded with it, it is not regarded as a very satisfactory incapacitating agent. It can elicit unpredictable and often violent behavior. Men sufficiently motivated to fight may do so more tenaciously under its influence. Furthermore, BZ has serious effects on the body's water-balance and temperature-regulation mechanisms that could lead to death, particularly under hot, dry conditions. Much effort has been devoted, without success, to finding a long-lasting incapacitant without these drawbacks or similar ones.

The principal short-term incapacitant now in military use is CS (orthochlorobenzalmalonitrile). This compound was first synthesized in the U.S. in the 1920's. After World War II it was developed by the British government as a riot-control agent and named after its American discoverers, Ben Corson and Roger Staughton of Middlebury College. When employed for military purposes, it is more accurately described as a harassing agent.

The first CS munitions operated by vaporizing the agent from a pyrotechnic mixture. The CS then condenses to form an aerosol of micron-sized particles. Pyrotechnic CS is used in grenades, rockets, artillery shells and cluster bombs. A newer form is designated CS-2. Used in both bulk-disseminating devices and bursting bombs, it is a powder consisting of micron-sized particles treated with silica gel and silicone compound to improve its flow properties and persistence in the field. CS-2 can be effective in the field for several weeks. It is reintroduced into the air by the wind and the movement of people and vehicles.

The effects of CS depend on the particle size of the aerosol. Particles larger than some 50 microns exert their predominant effect on the eyes, whereas smaller particles are more effective as lung irritants. For military use CS-2 is milled fine enough to achieve the latter effect. Exposure to either form of CS causes intense pain in the eyes and upper respiratory tract, progressing to the deep recesses of the lungs and giving rise to feelings of suffocation and acute anxiety. In humid weather moderately heavy skin exposure can cause severe blistering that requires many days for healing.

If exposure is not excessive, the symptoms usually pass within a few minutes after the exposure ends. The lethal dose for man, as estimated from animal experimentation, is very much higher than that required to cause intense irritation. Nevertheless, heavy or prolonged exposure, such as might be expected in confined spaces or in close proximity to a munition emitting the agent, could cause serious lung damage and death, particularly among infants and the infirm. No long-term aftereffects of moderate exposure to CS have been demonstrated. Although investigations of this possibility are now under way, they have not been completed.

For military purposes CS has supplanted older harassing agents such as ordinary tear gas (CN, or chloracetophenone) and the emetic and respiratory agent known as adamsite or DM.

When used in war against unmasked personnel, harassing agents are effective in forcing an enemy from cover to face capture or hostile fire, to deny him terrain or to upset his fire. Against masked personnel harassing agents are very much less effective, although they reduce fighting efficiency somewhat by forcing men to put on masks. The first major application of harassing gas in combat since World War I has come in Vietnam, where more than 14 million pounds have been used by U.S. forces. At first U.S. policy was to use CS only when its employment would be more humane than the use of more lethal weapons. For example, on March 24, 1965, following the first newspaper reports of U.S. use of nonlethal gas in Vietnam, Secretary of State Dean Rusk made the following statement: "We do not expect that gas will be used in ordinary military operations.... The anticipation is, of course, that these weapons will be used only in those situations involving riot control or situations analogous to riot control."

For five months following Rusk's statement the use of harassing agents in Vietnam ceased completely. Then an event took place that put the use of CS in the most attractive possible light and probably played an important role in bringing about authorization for its renewed employment. On September 5 a Marine officer came on a cave where civilians were thought to be intermingled with Vietcong soldiers. Faced with a choice between sending in an assault force, throwing in CS grenades or abandoning the mission, he decided on CS. It was reported that several enemy soldiers and 400 civilians emerged without

	TYPE OF WEAPON		
AGENTS	NUCLEAR	CHEMICAL	BIOLOGICAL
AREA AFFECTED	UP TO 300 SQUARE KILOMETERS	UP TO 60 SQUARE KILOMETERS	UP TO 100,000 SQUARE KILOMETERS
TIME TO EFFECTIVENESS	SECONDS	MINUTES	DAYS
DAMAGE TO STRUCTURES	WIDESPREAD DESTRUCTION	NONE	NONE
OTHER EFFECTS	PROLONGED RADIOACTIVITY IN AREA OF 2,500 SQUARE KILOMETERS	CONTAMINATION FOR DAYS OR WEEKS	POSSIBLE EPIDEMIC OR NEW FOCI OF DISEASE
NORMAL USE OF AREA	3 TO 6 MONTHS	LIMITED FOR DAYS OR WEEKS	VARIABLE
EFFECT ON MAN	90 PERCENT DEATHS	50 PERCENT DEATHS	50 PERCENT MORBIDITY

THREE WEAPONS are compared for damaging effects. The weapons are a one-megaton nuclear bomb, 15 tons of a chemical nerve agent and 10 tons of a biological agent. In each case the table assumes delivery of weapon by one bomber on an unprotected population.

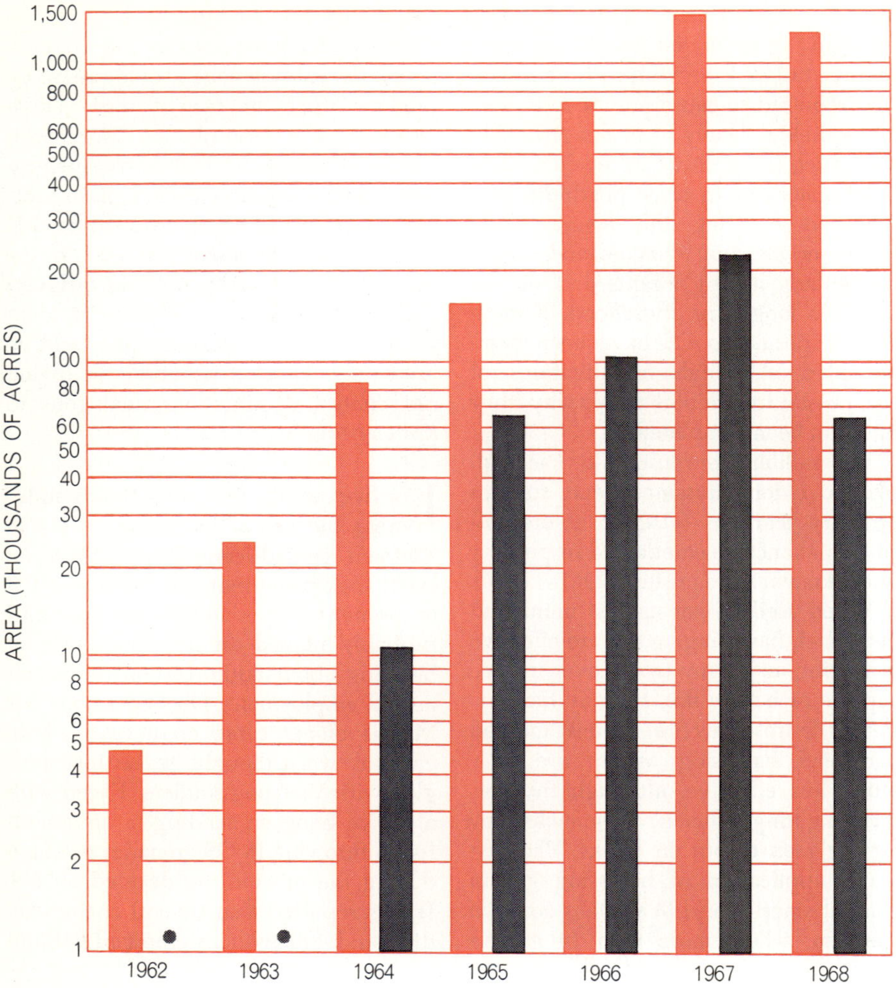

USE OF HERBICIDES in South Vietnam is stated in terms of Air Force estimates for defoliation (*color*) and crop destruction (*gray*). Dots represent less than 1,000 acres. In South Vietnam some eight million acres are under cultivation and about 14 million are forested.

injury to noncombatants. Following this incident soldiers and field commanders found a wide variety of uses for CS in regular combat. Soldiers encountered many situations in which it could be used to inflict casualties on the enemy and otherwise perform their mission while reducing their own losses. One of the major uses of CS in Vietnam is to flush enemy soldiers out of bunkers preceding high-explosive fire or infantry assault.

The overall utility of CS in Vietnam is not known, no systematic studies having been made. It has nonetheless been a popular weapon, and under this pressure from the battlefield its use has expanded greatly. One indicator is the yearly record of Army procurement of CS for Southeast Asia, which rose from 253,000 pounds in fiscal year 1965 to 6,063,000 pounds in 1969. Another indicator is the rapid proliferation of experimental and newly standardized CS munitions developed by the Army. As recently as July, 1966, military manuals listed only five types of CS weapons: two grenades and three bulk disseminating devices. Since then 18 new CS munitions have appeared, ranging from grenades with delayed-action fuzes for air drop up to 105-millimeter and 155-millimeter howitzer projectiles, various mortar and rocket munitions and a number of aircraft bombs with area coverage ranging up to a square kilometer.

It is sometimes argued that nonlethal chemical weapons would make war more humane. There is good reason, however, to expect the opposite. As long as lethal weapons are employed in war, if nonlethal chemicals are introduced, it must be expected that they will come to be employed not by themselves but rather in coordination with the weapons already in service, in order to increase the overall effectiveness of military operations. Certainly this has been so in the case of the agent CS.

The expansion of CS use in Vietnam has given rise to two widespread concerns. The first is that the U.S. has departed from its original humanitarian justification for the use of chemicals in war. Second, it is becoming increasingly clear that the long-term arms control cost to the U.S. may be severe. I shall return to this point.

The last category of chemical weapons to be considered here is antiplant agents. These agents were first developed for military purposes during World War II and subsequently came into wide use for weed control. Near the end of the war some consideration was given to using them to destroy rice being cultivated by Japanese soldiers in isolated island strongposts, but the plan was never authorized. Herbicides were used on a small scale to clear roadsides by the British in Malaya during their military operations there in the 1950's.

The use of herbicides in Vietnam was first authorized on an experimental basis in 1961. They next came to be employed there for increasing visibility along roads and waterways and on the perimeters of military installations; then for the destruction of crops thought to be destined for enemy consumption, and finally for the treatment of large areas suspected of harboring enemy base camps or supply routes. By mid-1969 approximately five million acres had been sprayed, 10 percent of it cropland. Following a peak in 1967, anticrop operations were substantially reduced, reflecting adverse criticism of both their propriety and their effectiveness.

Three principal antiplant agents or mixtures have been in service. They are designated Orange, White and Blue. Agent Orange is an equal mixture of the n-butyl esters of 2,4-dichlorophenoxyacetic acid (2,4-D) and 2,4,5-trichlorophenoxyacetic acid (2,4,5-T). The agent is mainly directed against forest vegetation. It is applied undiluted at three gallons per acre, approximately 25 times the average amount for domestic application. Within a week or more after its application the leaves fall from most jungle trees. Orange has been the antiplant agent most widely used in Vietnam, but recently its employment has been suspended because of concern that 2,4,5-T may cause human birth defects.

Agent White is a 4:1 mixture of the triisopropanolamine salts of 2,4-D and 4-amino-3,4,6-trichloropicolinic acid. The latter component is known as picloram. The agent is sprayed from a water solution at a rate of approximately 7.6 pounds of total herbicide per acre. It is generally used for the same purposes as agent Orange, although its somewhat lower volatility makes it preferable for operations where drifting would be a hazard, as in the vicinity of rubber plantations. The extreme resistance of picloram to biodegradation has been a factor in limiting its employment.

Agent Blue is a water solution of sodium dimethylarsinate, applied at the rate of nine pounds per acre. It is used mainly against rice.

Any evaluation of the military effectiveness of herbicides is made particularly difficult by the fact that they exert their effects on the enemy only indirectly and after a substantial time lag. Certainly the most dubious form of antiplant warfare from a military point of view is crop destruction. It is not generally possible to distinguish crops destined for noncombatants from those to be consumed by soldiers. Indeed, both common sense and the experience of many wars show that when the food supply is restricted, it is the civilians and not the soldiers who go on short rations, and it is the children who are most harmed by malnutrition.

There is very little quantitative information about the overall military utility of herbicides used to improve visibility. There is no doubt that the leaves drop and visibility is thereby improved. As a result an enemy will generally choose to avoid such areas. Nonetheless, an enemy commander will not withdraw his men from action; he will deploy them elsewhere. Thus for every soldier who gains protection from improved visibility there may be another soldier or civilian receiving fire from a redeployed enemy soldier. Obviously the trade-off will not be precisely equal, but this effect will act to exaggerate the apparent military effectiveness of herbicides.

Certainly in some situations there are alternatives to chemical defoliants. In Vietnam giant plows, often working under the protection of military escorts, have been used to clear more than 500,000 acres. Where possible, this method is more effective than the aerial spraying of chemical defoliants because it removes branches and trunks as well as leaves.

I have attempted to keep the foregoing discussion factual in order to define the issues. Emotions run high on the subject of chemical and biological weapons, however, and few persons can discuss the subject without expressing or evoking strong feelings about whether or not it is wise to use or even to possess such weapons. The strong feelings generated by these weapons have been responsible for the fact that historically they have been singled out for special efforts at arms control. The most important international effort to prohibit the use of such chemical and biological weapons is the Geneva Protocol of 1925. It prohibits (1) "the use in war of asphyxiating, poisonous, or other gases, and of all analogous liquids, materials or devices" and (2) "the use of bacteriological methods of warfare." The protocol does not prohibit research, development, testing or production of gas or germ weapons. It does not prohibit the use of such weapons in reprisal against their first use by the enemy. It does not prohibit the use of riot-control gases or other agents for domestic police purposes. It does not prohibit the use in war of nontoxic smokes used for concealment or of flamethrowers, napalm or other incendiary weapons. The language of the Geneva Protocol is derived from the peace treaties of World War I, which treated gas warfare as already prohibited and specifically forbade the manufacture and importation of war gases by Germany and her wartime allies. On the initiative of the U.S., an article based on the language of the peace treaties was incorporated in the 1922 Washington Treaty on Submarines and Noxious Gases. At the urging of President Harding, Secretary of State Charles Evans Hughes, Senator Elihu Root and a presidentially appointed advisory committee of prominent citizens, the Washington Treaty passed through the Senate with no dissenting votes. Although ratified by the U.S., Great Britain, Italy and Japan, this treaty never came into force because France, whose ratification was required, objected to its provisions on submarines.

The U.S. again pressed for a prohibition against gas warfare at the 1925 Geneva Conference on the Limitation of Arms, proposing language on gas essentially identical with that of the Washington Treaty. The prohibition was extended to cover "bacteriological methods of warfare" at the suggestion of Poland. The resulting treaty—the Geneva Protocol for the Prohibition of the Use in War of Asphyxiating, Poisonous or Other Gases, and of Bacteriological Methods of Warfare—was signed by representatives of 38 nations on June 17, 1925.

The Coolidge Administration and the various supporters of the protocol seem to have assumed that the Senate would give its consent as readily as it had to the Washington Treaty. Almost nothing was done to prepare the case for ratification or to mobilize public support. Meanwhile the Army Chemical Warfare Service, the American Legion, the American Chemical Society and segments of the chemical industry organized the opposition. The arguments made against ratification were that the protocol would be ignored in time of war and that poison gas was more humane than bombs and bullets. The protocol was debated but not acted on by

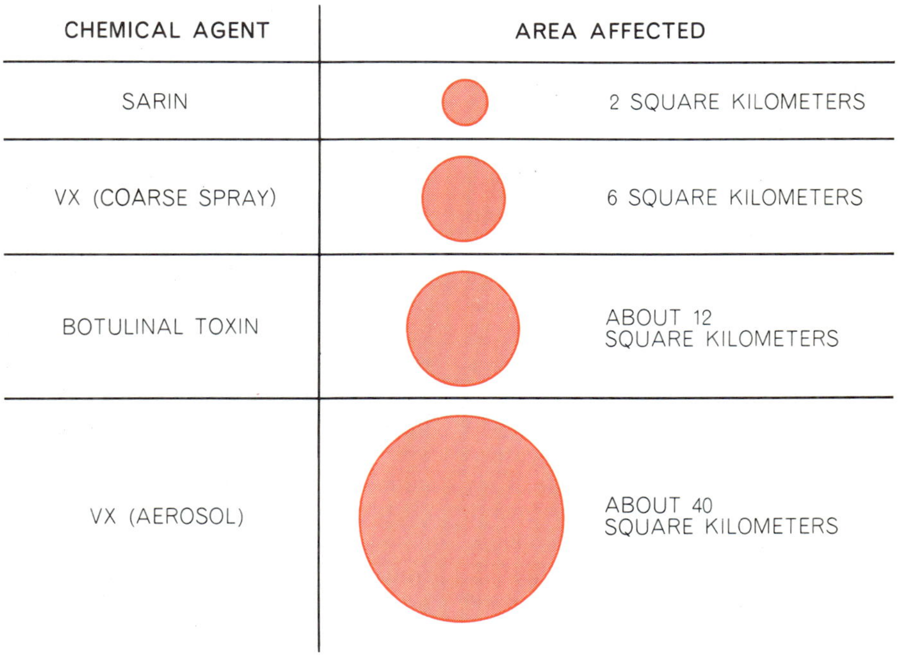

EFFECTS OF ATTACK with chemical agents are charted. The stated effects assume an attack by a single plane, along a two-kilometer crosswind line, laying down four tons of the agent. The use of VX in aerosol form would be to maximize the agent's downwind travel.

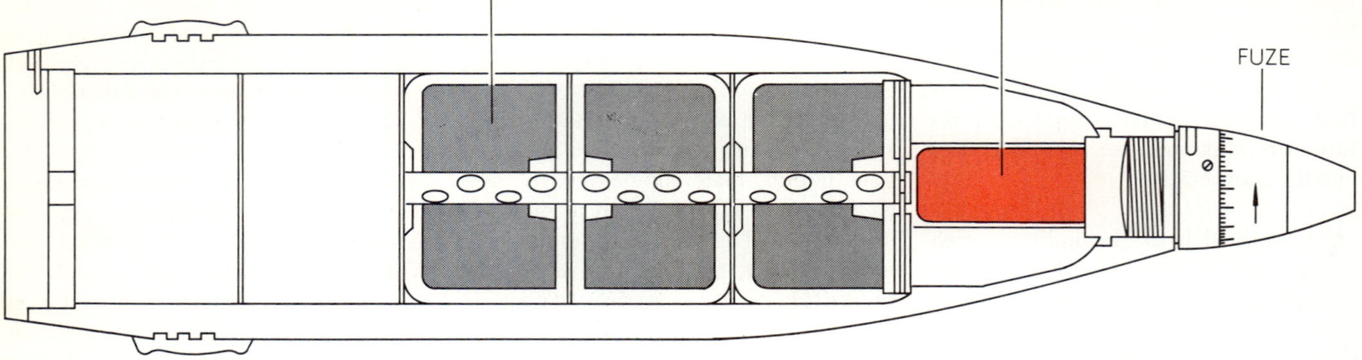

ARTILLERY SHELL designed to deliver CS irritant has the agent in canisters that are expelled when the fuze detonates the shell. The shell portrayed, which is for a 155-millimeter weapon with a range of 15 kilometers, is 60 centimeters long, weighs 44 kilograms and carries 4.4 kilograms of CS. In a normal artillery barrage several weapons are fired, delivering a number of shells to target.

the Senate—apparently because the majority leader did not have the votes. It remained on the Foreign Relations Committee docket until 1947, when President Truman withdrew it together with several other long-pending treaties.

By 1939 the Geneva Protocol had been ratified by 44 nations, including all major European powers. At the outbreak of World War II England, France and Germany exchanged assurances that they would abide by the protocol. In 1943 President Roosevelt declared that gas warfare was "outlawed by the general opinion of civilized mankind" and that "we shall under no circumstances resort to the use of such weapons unless they are first used by our enemies." Japan is believed to have used gas against China before our entry into the war but otherwise gas was not used in World War II. The threat of retaliation provided a sanction. The restraint was reinforced by widespread abhorrence of gas and germs and by military skepticism regarding their utility, but it was the protocol that placed gas and germs in a distinct category and provided a clear standard on which the belligerents could base their conduct.

Since World War II the U.S. has on numerous occasions declared its support for the no-first-use principle of the Geneva Protocol. When President Eisenhower was asked at a press conference if he planned a change in our no-first-use policy, he said: "No official suggestion has been made to me, and so far as my own instinct is concerned, it is not to start such a thing first." During President Johnson's Administration the U.S. supported resolutions passed in 1966 and 1968 by the UN General Assembly, calling for "strict observance by all states of the principles and objectives of the Protocol" and "inviting all nations that have not done so to accede to the Protocol." Some statements, however, have made the U.S. position seem ambiguous. For example, the U.S. Army manual *The Law of Land Warfare,* last issued in the 1950's, states that the Geneva Protocol is "not binding on this country."

A total of 84 nations are now parties to the Geneva Protocol; 16 of them have ratified it since the 1966 UN resolution. The parties include all North Atlantic Treaty Organization members except the U.S., all members of the Warsaw Pact including the U.S.S.R. and all nuclear powers (other than the U.S.), including the People's Republic of China. All major industrial nations except Japan and the U.S. are parties. The protocol has been signed but not ratified by the U.S., Brazil, El Salvador, Japan, Nicaragua and Uruguay.

Whether or not the protocol prohibits the use of harassing agents and antiplant chemicals is a subject of some dispute. On the first occasion when nations were canvassed for their views on the status of tear gas (at a League of Nations Commission in 1930), Canada, China, France, the U.S.S.R. and several other nations agreed with the declared British position that "the use in war of 'other' gases, including lachrymatory gases, was prohibited." None of the nations then party to the protocol made objections to this view. The U.S. delegate, however, expressed hesitation over any commitment to refrain from the use in war of agencies used in peacetime by domestic police and whose use in combat would be "more clearly humane than the use of weapons to which [nations] were formerly obliged to resort." Two years later the League Disarmament Conference unanimously recommended that the use of all gases, including tear gas, be prohibited in war. This view was accepted by the U.S. with the understanding that it did not apply to the use of tear gas for police purposes. The discussions were not directed at the Geneva Protocol but at devising a comprehensive disarmament treaty, an attempt that was disrupted by the approach of World War II. The question did not come up again until 1965, when questions were first raised about our employment of CS and herbicides in Vietnam.

Responding to these questions in 1966, the U.S. representative to the General Assembly stated that the protocol does not prohibit "the use in combat against an enemy, for humanitarian purposes, of agents that Governments around the world commonly use to control riots by their own people" or of chemicals used to control "unwanted vegetation" for agricultural and other peaceful purposes. At the time these views were contested mainly by the U.S.S.R. and its allies. As the scale of chemical operations in Vietnam has increased, however, the U.S. position has come under mounting attack. Last summer Secretary General U Thant urged the members of the UN to "make clear affirmation" that the protocol prohibits the use of all chemical agents, including tear gas, in warfare. Last winter India, Mexico, Pakistan, Sweden and 17 other nations proposed in the General Assembly a resolution holding that the Geneva Protocol prohibits the use in war of all chemical agents directed at men, animals or plants. The resolution was passed by a vote of 80 to three, with 36 abstentions. Portugal, Australia and the U.S. voted against the resolution.

Since then the British government has declared that CS is exempt from the Geneva Protocol, although Britain still considers the tear gases known in 1930 to be prohibited. The British argument was that CS is less toxic than older tear gases, but it is generally thought that the real motivation of the cabinet was to avoid risking charges that the use of CS for riot control in Ulster was illegal. If so, this reflects a confusion regarding the meaning of the Geneva Protocol, which by its terms prohibits the use of gas only in warfare. The distinction between the use of tear gas for domestic police purposes and the prohibition of its use in war has been observed without difficulty by many nations ever since World War II. Even Sweden, a nation that has led the opposition to the use of tear gas in war, uses it in riot control at home. Ironically, it may be that the massive use of CS in war and the excesses this breeds will generate serious opposition to its domestic use.

As the U.S. moves to ratify the Geneva Protocol, the Administration must decide on a policy regarding the use of harassing agents and herbicides. There is no great difficulty in identifying the pros and cons of maintaining an option to use these agents in war. The difficulty arises when one attempts to quantify the various arguments and then to place values on them in order to reach conclusions.

The principal gain to the user of these agents in war is that to some extent they enable him to increase enemy casualties and to reduce his own. These agents, however, are of significant effect almost only in counterguerilla warfare and, in the case of CS, only if opposing troops are unprotected by gas masks. Hence the arguments for keeping these weapons become important to the extent that a nation anticipates involvement in such wars. CS can be expected to lose its advantage in any case, for once the impression is created that one's forces will use gas, supplies of masks will become much more available throughout the world. North Vietnamese troops in South Vietnam are now largely equipped with fairly good Chinese Communist gas masks, and increasing numbers of the excellent Russian Shlem masks are appearing. Even for guerillas the expense of masks is not great.

The main threat to security of continuing the use of these agents is the increased likelihood of proliferation of chemical weapons and of the breakdown of the restraints against chemical warfare. Our employment of harassing gas in war, particularly when it is done on a large scale in conjunction with ordinary military operations, stimulates military planners in other nations to secure gas masks, initiate chemical training and upgrade chemical cadres and to consider acquiring for their own nations chemical weapons of various types, including lethal ones.

The large-scale military employment of antiplant chemicals poses ecological and public health problems of which we still know little but that could be most serious in the long run. The precedent of countenancing large-scale alteration of the environment in the conduct of war has obvious perils. Moreover, in many parts of the world use might be made of chemicals as agents of starvation and economic warfare against the civil population. Because of the relative ease with which this tactic can be practiced, it would be difficult to stop once the precedent is set.

The general problem of preventing chemical and biological warfare is to a large extent a psychological one. Perhaps the central problem is to prevent the application of biochemistry and biology to the opening up of a new and highly unpredictable dimension of warfare. If we can maintain and reinforce the traditional expectation that no gas or germs will be used in war, there will not be much pressure for these weapons to proliferate.

This psychological aspect of the problem has been understood by essentially all nations, including the U.S., ever since World War I. Recently, however, a dangerous break with tradition has been allowed to occur and to escalate in Vietnam. Many who have studied the problem consider the use of chemical weapons there, even though they are not lethal chemicals, to be the major and most immediate threat to the barriers that prevent chemical warfare.

If we can accept the loss of our option to use harassing agents and antiplant chemicals as weapons of war, then, judging from the recent vote in the General Assembly, it appears likely that all important nations of the world could be brought to agree. If, on the other hand, the long-observed rule of "No chemical and biological weapons" is abandoned, there will be no unique and equally simple standard on which national practice and international agreement can be based.

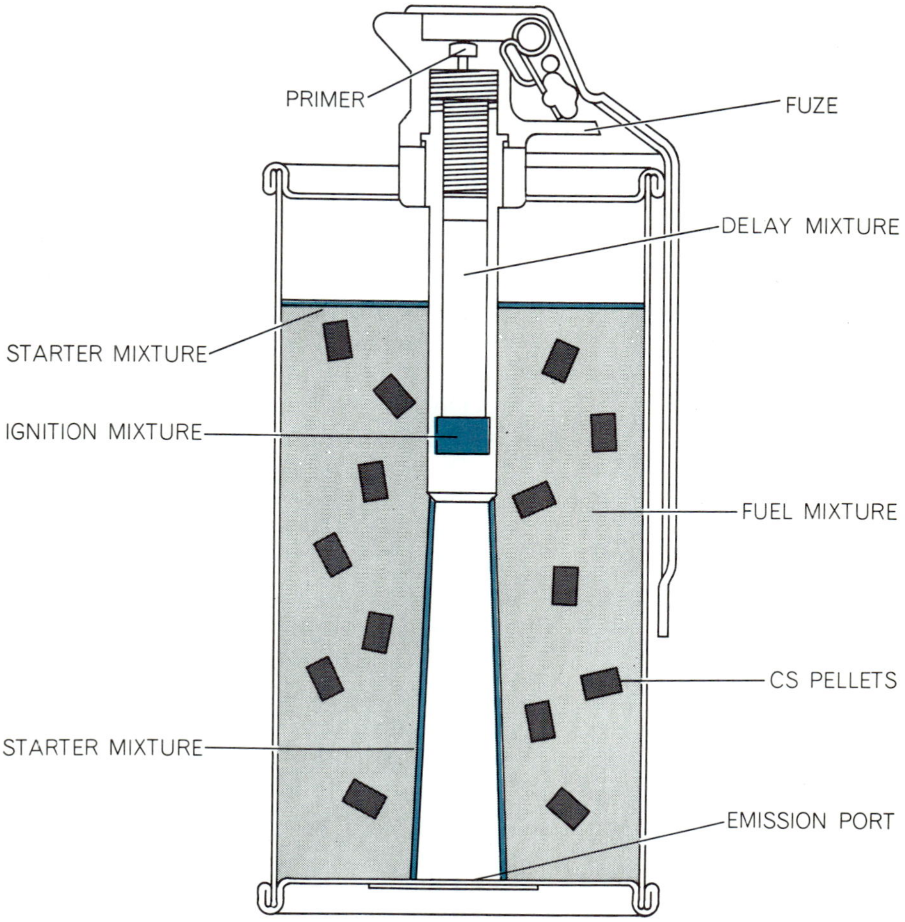

CS GRENADE with a 12-second delay fuze is designed to be delivered either by a grenade launcher or by airdrop. One of these grenades weighs one pound and holds 115 grams of CS.

Convention on the Prohibition of the Development, Production, and the Stockpiling of Bacteriological (Biological) and Toxin Weapons, and on their Destruction

Text of convention signed at Washington, London, and Moscow on April 10, 1972. Not published in Scientific American.

The States Parties to this Convention,

Determined to act with a view to achieving effective progress towards general and complete disarmament, including the prohibition and elimination of all types of weapons of mass destruction, and convinced that the prohibition of the development, production and stockpiling of chemical and bacteriological (biological) weapons and their elimination, through effective measures, will facilitate the achievement of general and complete disarmament under strict and effective international control,

Recognizing the important significance of the Protocol for the Prohibition of the Use in War of Asphyxiating, Poisonous or Other Gases, and of Bacteriological Methods of Warfare, signed at Geneva on June 17, 1925, and conscious also of the contribution which the said Protocol has already made, and continued to make, to mitigating the horrors of war,

Reaffirming their adherence to the principles and objectives of that Protocol and calling upon all States to comply strictly with them,

Recalling that the General Assembly of the United Nations has repeatedly condemned all actions contrary to the principles and objectives of the Geneva Protocol of June 17, 1925,

Desiring to contribute to the strengthening of confidence between peoples and the general improvement of the international atmosphere,

Desiring also to contribute to the realization of the purposes and principles of the Charter of the United Nations,

Convinced of the importance and urgency of eliminating from the arsenals of States, through effective measures, such dangerous weapons of mass destruction as those using chemical or bacteriological (biological) agents,

Recognizing that an agreement on the prohibition of bacteriological (biological) and toxin weapons represents a first possible step towards the achievement of agreement on effective measures also for the prohibition of the development, production and stockpiling of chemical weapons, and determined to continue negotiations to that end,

Determined, for the sake of all mankind, to exclude completely the possibility of bacteriological (biological) agents and toxins being used as weapons,

Convinced that such use would be repugnant to the conscience of mankind and that no effort should be spared to minimize this risk,

Have agreed as follows:

Article I

Each State Party to this Convention undertakes never in any circumstances to develop, produce, stockpile or otherwise acquire or retain:

(1) Microbial or other biological agents, or toxins whatever their origin or method of production, of types and in quantities that have no justification for prophylactic, protective or other peaceful purposes;

(2) Weapons, equipment or means of delivery designed to use such agents or toxins for hostile purposes or in armed conflict.

Article II

Each State Party to this Convention undertakes to destroy, or to divert to peaceful purposes, as soon as possible but not later than nine months after the entry into force of the Convention, all agents, toxins, weapons, equipment and means of delivery specified in article I of the Convention, which are in its possession or under its jurisdiction or control. In implementing the provisions of this article all necessary safety precautions shall be observed to protect populations and the environment.

Article III

Each State Party to this Convention undertakes not to transfer to any recipient whatsoever, directly or indirectly, and not in any way to assist, encourage, or induce any State, group of States or international organizations to manufacture or otherwise acquire any of the agents, toxins, weapons, equipment or means of delivery specified in article I of the Convention.

Article IV

Each State Party to this Convention shall, in accordance with its constitutional processes, take any necessary measures to prohibit and prevent the development, production, stockpiling, acquisition or retention of the agents, toxins, weapons, equipment and means of delivery specified in article I of the Convention, within the territory of such State, under its jurisdiction or under its control anywhere.

Article V

The States Parties to this Convention undertake to consult one another and to cooperate in solving any problems which may arise in relation to the objective of, or in the application of the provisions of, the Convention. Consultation and cooperation pursuant to this article may also be undertaken through appropriate international procedures within the framework of the United Nations and in accordance with its Charter.

Article VI

(1) Any State Party to this Convention which finds that any other State Party is acting in breach of obligations deriving from the provisions of the Convention may lodge a complaint with the Security Council of the United Nations. Such a complaint should include all possible evidence confirming its validity, as well as a request for its consideration by the Security Council.

(2) Each State Party to this Convention undertakes to cooperate in carrying out any investigation which the Security Council may initiate, in accordance with the provisions of the Charter of the United Nations, on the basis of the complaint received by the Council. The Security Council shall inform the States Parties to the Convention of the results of the investigation.

Article VII

Each State Party to this Convention undertakes to provide or support assistance, in accordance with the United Nations Charter, to any Party to the Convention which so requests, if the Security Council decides that such Party has been exposed to danger as a result of violation of the Convention.

Article VIII

Nothing in this Convention shall be interpreted as in any way limiting or detracting from the obligations assumed by any State under the Protocol for the Prohibition of the Use in War of Asphyxiating, Poisonous or Other Gases, and of Bacteriological Methods of Warfare, signed at Geneva on June 17, 1925.

Article IX

Each State Party to this Convention affirms the recognized objective of effective prohibition of chemical weapons and, to this end, undertakes to continue negotiations in good faith with a view to reaching early agreement on effective measures for the prohibition of their development, production and stockpiling and for their destruction, and on appropriate measures concerning equipment and means of delivery specifically designed for the production or use of chemical agents for weapons purposes.

Article X

(1) The States Parties to this Convention undertake to facilitate, and have the right to participate in, the fullest possible exchange of equipment, materials and scientific and technological information for the use of bacteriological (biological) agents and toxins for peaceful purposes. Parties to the Convention in a position to do so shall also cooperate in contributing individually or together with other States or international organizations to the further development and application of scientific discoveries in the field of bacteriology (biology) for prevention of disease, or for other peaceful purposes.

(2) This Convention shall be implemented in a manner designed to avoid hampering the economic or technological development of States Parties to the Convention or international cooperation in the field of peaceful bacteriological (biological) activities, including the international exchange of bacteriological (biological) agents and toxins and equipment for the processing, use or production of bacteriological (biological) agents and toxins for peaceful purposes in accordance with the provisions of the Convention.

Article XI

Any State Party may propose amendments to this Convention. Amendments shall enter into force for each State Party accepting the amendments upon their acceptance by a majority of the States Parties to the Convention and thereafter for each remaining State Party on the date of acceptance by it.

Article XII

Five years after the entry into force of this Convention, or earlier if it is requested by a majority of Parties to the Convention by submitting a proposal to this effect to the Depositary Governments, a conference of States Parties to the Convention shall be held at Geneva, Switzerland, to review the operation of the Convention, with a view to assuring that the purposes of the preamble and the provisions of the Convention, including the provisions concerning negotiations on chemical weapons, are being realized. Such review shall take into account any new scientific and technological developments relevant to the Convention.

Article XIII

(1) This Convention shall be of unlimited duration.

(2) Each State Party to this Convention shall in exercising its national sovereignty have the right to withdraw from the Convention if it decides that extraordinary events, related to the subject matter of the Convention, have jeopardized the supreme interests of its country. It shall give notice of such withdrawal to all other States Parties to the Convention and to the United Nations Security Council three months in advance. Such notice shall include a statement of the extraordinary events it regards as having jeopardized its supreme interests.

Article XIV

(1) This Convention shall be open to all States for signature. Any State which does not sign the Convention before its entry into force in accordance with paragraph (3) of this Article may accede to it at any time.

(2) This Convention shall be subject to ratification by signatory States. Instruments of ratification and instruments of accession shall be deposited with the Governments of the United States of America, the United Kingdom of Great Britain and Northern Ireland and the Union of Soviet Socialist Republics, which are hereby designated the Depositary Governments.

(3) This Convention shall enter into force after the deposit of instruments of ratification by twenty-two Governments, including the Governments designated as Depositaries of the Convention.

(4) For States whose instruments of ratification or accession are deposited subsequent to the entry into force of this Convention, it shall enter into force on the date of the deposit of their instruments of ratification or accession.

(5) The Depositary Governments shall promptly inform all signatory and acceding States of the date of each signature, the date of deposit of each instrument of ratification or of accession and the date of the entry into force of this Convention, and of the receipt of other notices.

(6) This Convention shall be registered by the Depositary Governments pursuant to Article 102 of the Charter of the United Nations.

Article XV

This Convention, the English, Russian, French, Spanish and Chinese texts of which are equally authentic, shall be deposited in the archives of the Depositary Governments. Duly certified copies of the Convention shall be transmitted by the Depositary Governments to the Governments of the signatory and acceding States.

32

The Mekong River Plan

In spite of many political obstacles, four southeast Asian nations helped by 14 others under UN auspices are engaged in thorough advance planning for a historic experiment in river development

GILBERT F. WHITE

April 1963

The winding yellow streams of the lower Mekong River system in southeast Asia are currently the scene of a historic international experiment in river development. Some 20 million citizens of four nations—Cambodia, Laos, Thailand and Vietnam—live within this watershed. Their numbers are bound to double in the next 25 years. The dominant rhythm of their economic life is the annual cycle of monsoon rains and dry season, of flood and drought on their land. To advance the welfare of these peoples and help them to build stable societies, 14 nations and the United Nations are assisting the four countries in a co-operative undertaking to realize the abundance of the waters of the lower Mekong. This venture is unique in three respects. It is the first such effort in the UN family. It is the first to marshal knowledge from the social as well as the natural sciences on such a large scale in setting the aims, priorities and methods of river-basin management before the moving of earth or the pouring of concrete. It exacts international co-operation in a region where political relations are unstable and where an untoward turn of events—or the mistakes of administrators—could destroy the enterprise overnight.

The Mekong is one of the world's great rivers. Exclusive of its reaches beyond the Chinese frontier, it drains an area of 307,000 square miles, a watershed greater than that of the Tigris-Euphrates of the Middle East or the Columbia of the northwestern U.S. In its volume of flow at low water it ranks with the Irrawaddy of Burma, and it is several times larger than the Indus of India and Pakistan and the Yellow River of China. Man has tampered only a little with it. A few small dams have been built on tributaries in Thailand; there are bits of levees along the main stem; the flatlands of the alluvial valleys below Sambor have been cut here and there with channels for irrigation and drainage or for navigation. Nowhere is the main channel yet crossed by a bridge; nowhere is it curbed by a dam. The great bulk of its water flows from source to sea without human use.

The present studies and the vision that inspire them had their origin in a pioneering appraisal made by P. T. Tan and his associates in the flood control bureau of the UN Economic Commission for Asia and the Far East (ECAFE). In its major outline the work reflects the findings of a reconnaissance conducted for ECAFE by the Bureau of Reclamation of the U.S. Department of the Interior and the recommendations of a UN engineering mission headed by Lieutenant General Raymond A. Wheeler, who had been deputy commander of the Allied bases in this region during World War II and was later chief of the U.S. Army Corps of Engineers. The Wheeler Mission recommended in particular that a series of detailed studies precede any construction. The four nations had signed an agreement on September 17, 1957, authorizing the work under an international co-ordinating committee operating with staff aid and sponsorship supplied by ECAFE.

During 1961 and 1962 I joined with three colleagues (Egbert de Vries, Harold B. Dunkerley and John V. Krutilla) in a study supported by the Ford Foundation of the economic and social aspects of the undertaking that we have now filed with the co-ordinating committee. This experience provides much of the factual material for the present article. It should be understood, however, that my comments on emerging problems and their political implications go beyond the committee's authority and our assignment as its consultants and are made on my personal responsibility.

Confidence in the central premise of the enterprise—that the long-run social development of the region requires the management and distribution of the lower Mekong waters on a basis that comprehends the lower basin as a whole—has grown stronger as the work has gone forward over the past half decade. Given the political history of the region during this period, the continuation of the work seems incredible. Twice since the formal planning for the Mekong began, Cambodia and Thailand have broken off diplomatic relations; Laos and Vietnam have each been divided by civil war. Even now parts of the Annamite plateau country and the delta lands of Vietnam are controlled by guerrillas. This is hardly the setting for international collaboration in resource management. Yet for the present the work is going forward, setting administrative precedents, engaging the energies of devoted people in the four nations and drawing on the human and material resources of 14 other nations.

Politics has excluded the upper basin, which lies within the People's Republic of China, from the planning to date; China, not being a member of the UN, does not participate in the activities of ECAFE. This removes from consideration 74,000 square miles of the total drainage area, all of it lying in the high, rugged Tibetan plateau and in the long, precipitous gorge cutting down through the Yunnan Plateau from altitudes of 10,000 to 5,000 feet, paralleling the upper gorges of the Salween and Yangtze rivers. Ideally the entire stretch of the river should be embraced in the planning, but for two reasons the division at the present line does not seem crippling. The excluded territory is so high and dissected that it offers little opportunity for agriculture or dense settlement and is therefore unlikely to make heavy demand on the flow of water. There are sites for large-scale hydroelectric power installations, but if these did not involve diversion of water, they would affect the river regimen chiefly by storage during periods of high flow and thus would be helpful to water management downstream.

The major portion of the Mekong waters is gathered in the lower basin, where the mean annual rainfall ranges from 40 to 150 inches a year. In 1960, a near-average year, more than 100 million acre-feet (an acre-foot of water covers one acre to a depth of one foot) flowed past Pa Mong on the Thailand-Laos border, 1,000 miles from the mouth; here is a site for a storage reservoir with a capacity three times that of Lake Mead, the reservoir behind Hoover Dam on the Colorado River. Without holdover from flood seasons and even in the driest years, the flow at this point is expected to be sufficient to irrigate more than a million acres without encroaching on flow requirements in the lower reaches.

Most parts of the basin have a pronounced wet season in the summer and early fall and a dry season in the winter and spring months of the year. Rice is the dominant crop everywhere. Its cultivation in paddy fields, with water supplied by seasonal inundation, crowds a major portion of the population into the alluvial lands of the delta and the lowlands of the main stream and its

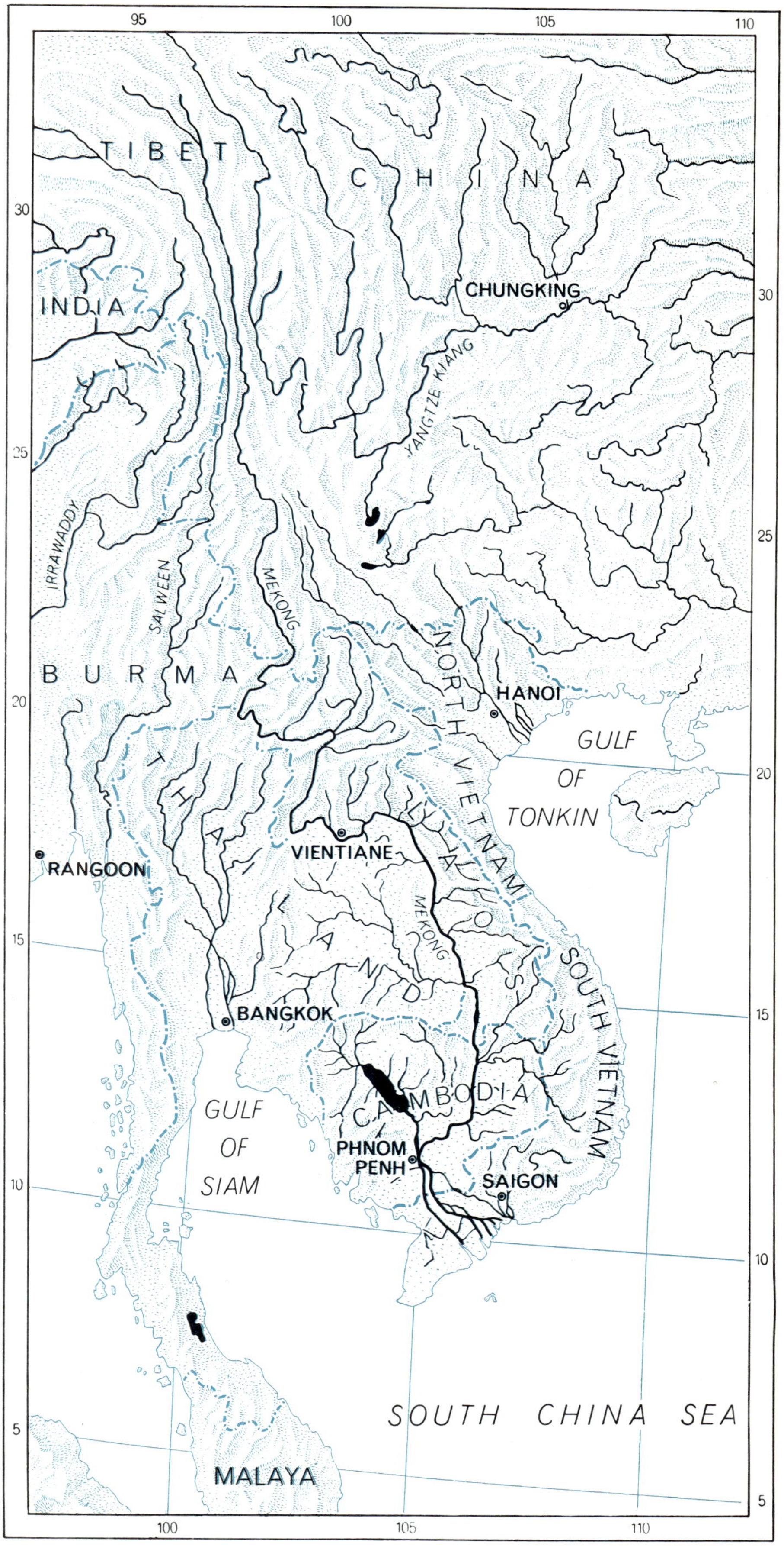

PARTS OF SIX COUNTRIES are drained by the Mekong River, which flows out of heights of the Tibetan plateau in China. The area of the proposed lower Mekong development includes most of Cambodia and Laos, about half of Vietnam and a third of Thailand. The small portions of the river basin lying in China and Burma have not been included in the plan.

numerous tributaries. In terms of area, on the other hand, more of the land in the basin is covered by the shifting cultivation of upland rice and associated crops; the forest is burned, the land is cleared and cropped for two to five years and is then abandoned for a longer period, during which regrowth of the forest restores the depleted soil. Under this primitive mode of agriculture, which prevails over much of the tropical regions of the world, it can be said that there is land to spare in the basin, in contrast to many other parts of Asia. There is little land, however, that could be claimed for intensive use without destruction of the soil or elaborate measures of conservation and improvement. Farming practice throughout the basin is adapted to the arrival, duration and volume of the monsoon rains and to the rise and fall of the rivers. In general it can be said that from season to season and year to year there is either too much water or too little. The task of water management calls at once for drainage and for irrigation—for measures that will carry over

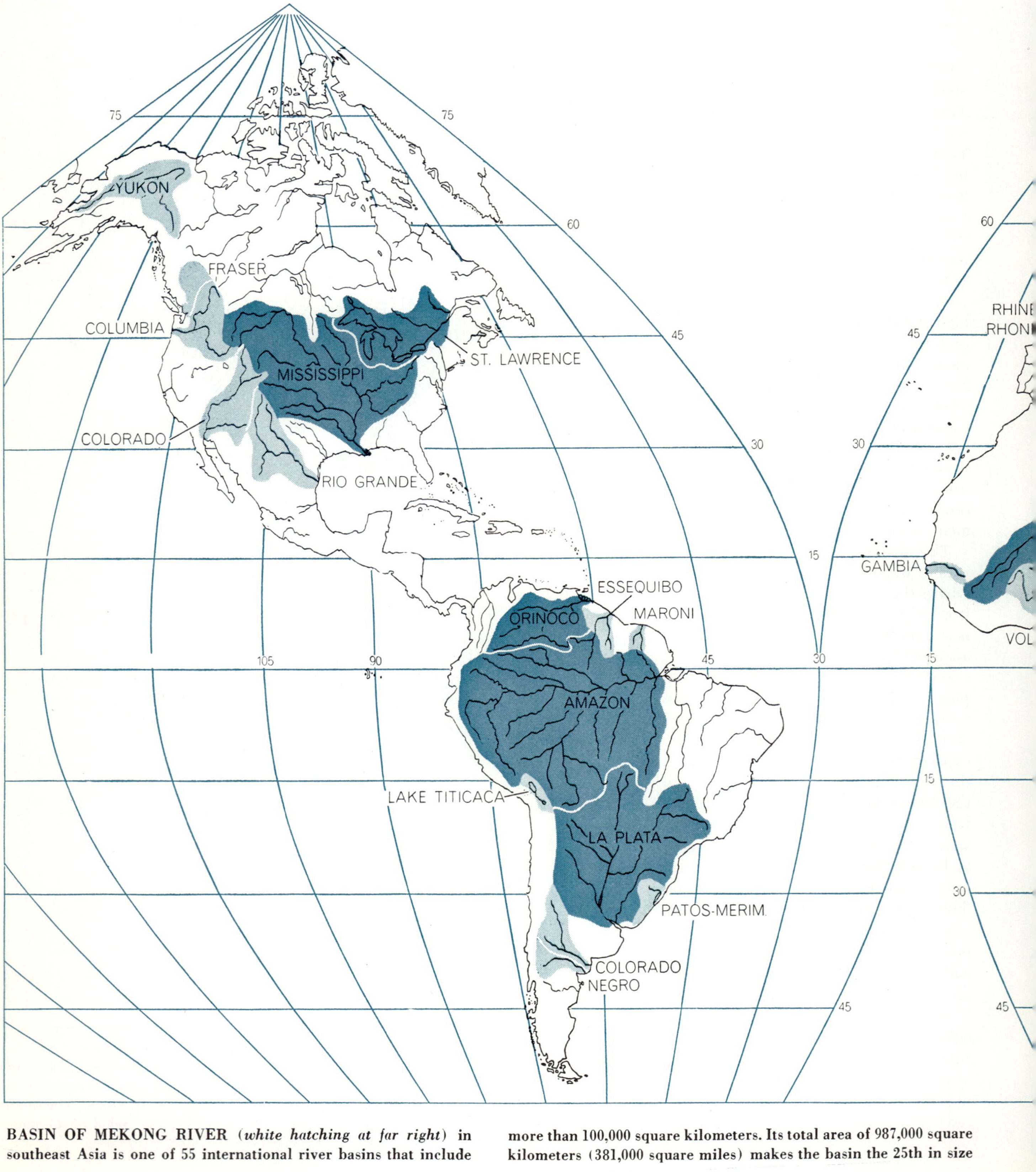

BASIN OF MEKONG RIVER (*white hatching at far right*) **in southeast Asia is one of 55 international river basins that include more than 100,000 square kilometers. Its total area of 987,000 square kilometers (381,000 square miles) makes the basin the 25th in size**

the water from the wet season to the dry and distribute it more evenly in time and on the land.

Over so vast a territory, of course, such generalizations do not hold without amendment and qualification with respect to specific local conditions. The gross patterns of present and potential water use that have emerged from the project studies divide the basin into nine regions, each with a somewhat homogeneous combination of annual water balance and water-management opportunities [*see illustration on the following page*]. In the densely populated lower delta region the flat land is beyond the reach of floods but is subject to the hazard of intruding salty water; drainage is required for intensive rice and vegetable cultivation, and irrigation is possible where the flow in the distributary streams is sufficient to prevent salt intrusion during dry periods. In the middle-delta and upper-delta–Grand Lac regions the annual flood hazard is serious, and relief will ultimately involve the entire complex of dams and storage res-

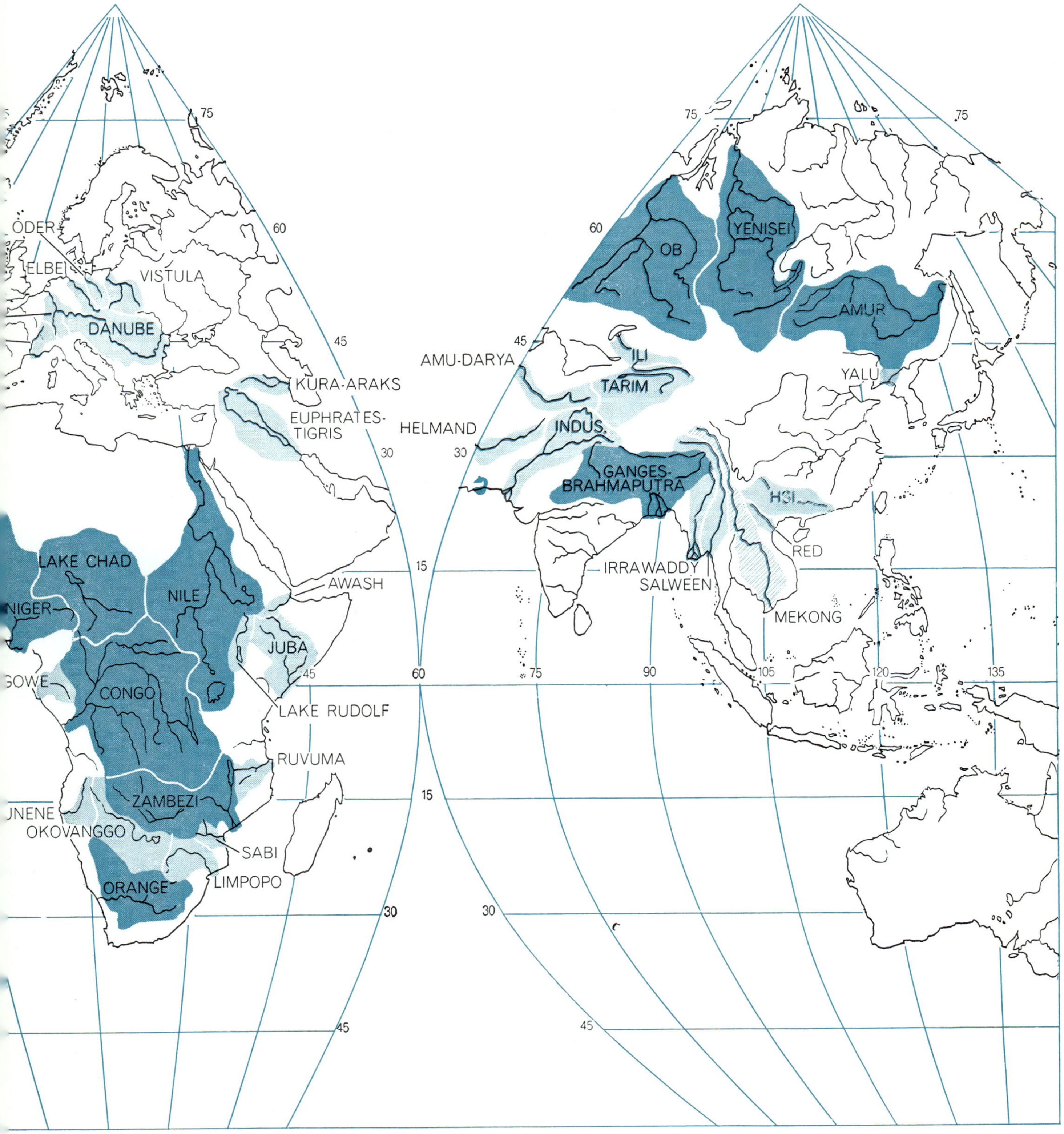

in the world, but even in the dry season the Mekong carries more water than many rivers that have larger basins. Basins of 100,000 to a million square kilometers are in lighter color; those of more than a million square kilometers are designated by darker color.

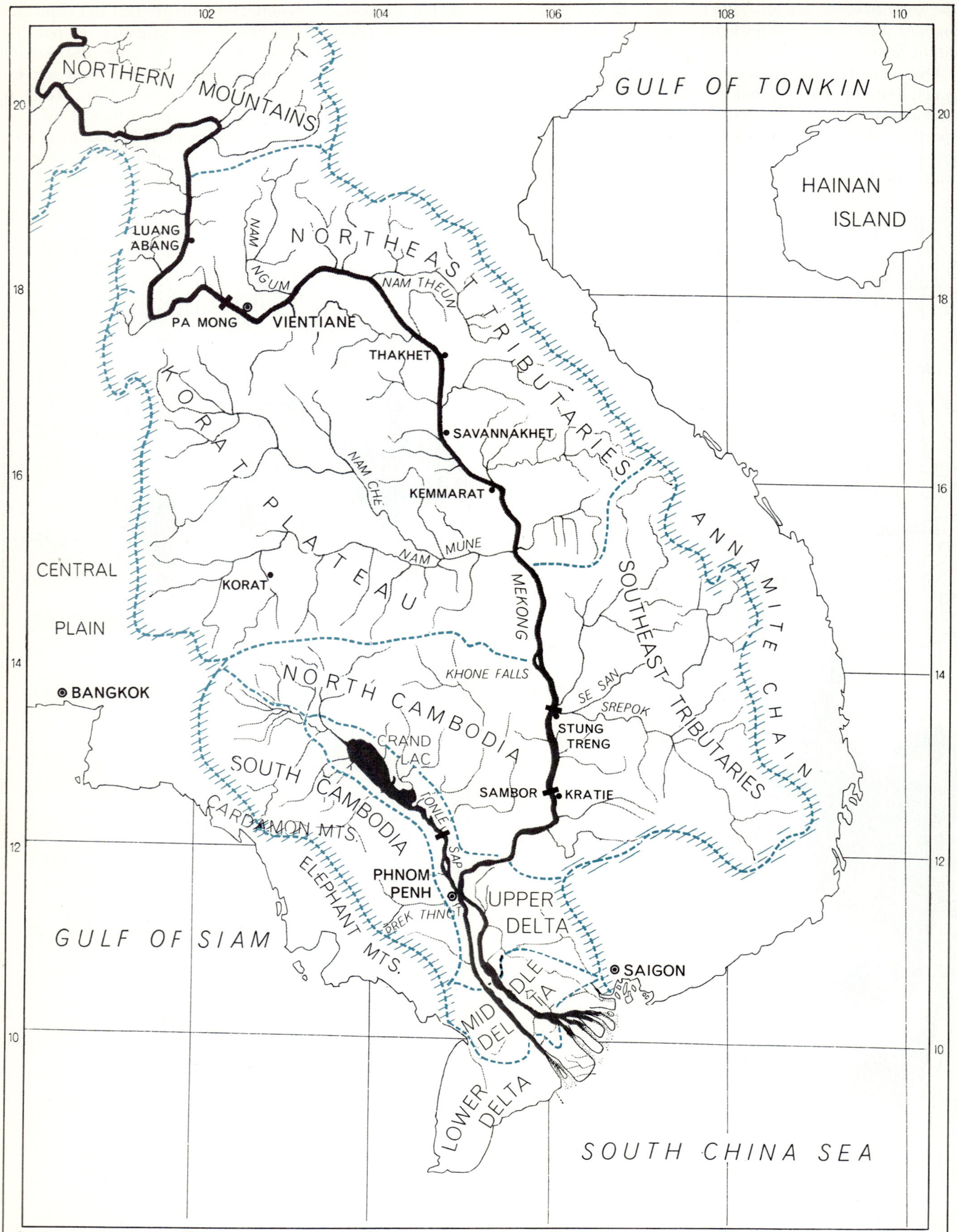

LOWER MEKONG AREA is divided into nine water-management regions, each with its own geographic, hydrographic and climatic characteristics. The map also shows cities and the proposed sites of four major dams. Flood control, irrigation and drainage would make cultivation possible in new lands and would allow second-cropping in several regions. Ultimately river could be made navigable from mouth to Vientiane, opening Laos to shipments from overseas. Most tributaries could furnish hydroelectric power.

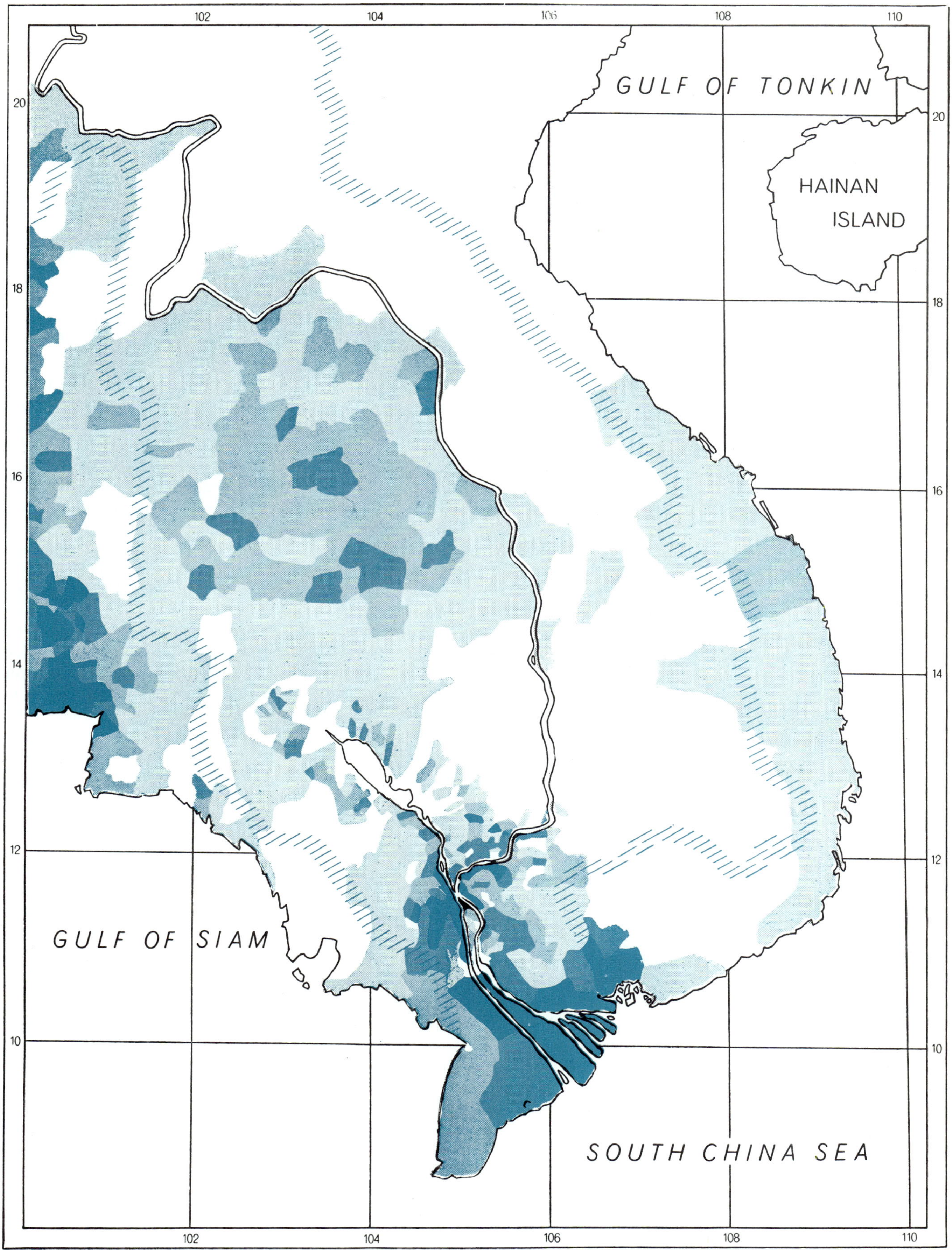

POPULATION OF MEKONG REGION is largely rural. White areas have fewer than 13 people per square kilometer. The four color gradations denote, from the lightest to the darkest, concentrations of 13 to 49 people per square kilometer, 50 to 99, 100 to 199 and more than 200. Hatching marks boundary of Mekong valley. More than 20 million people live in the region of the lower Mekong, grouped largely on the Korat Plateau and in the upper and middle delta. The map is based largely on population estimates.

ervoirs in the distant reaches of the main stream and tributaries. At the height of flood in the main stream the water actually flows upstream in the Tonle Sap into Grand Lac; project investigators are looking into the possibility of controlling the lake as a reservoir. In the streams that drain the forested Cardamon and Elephant mountains small heads of water for electric-power generation can be captured by dams and the water impounded for dry-season irrigation of the lands in the South Cambodia region. Harnessing of the flow in the main stream at the several promising sites between Sambor and Khone Falls would supply water to irrigate certain of the thin soils of the North Cambodia region, and the improvement in navigation would make the rough and sparsely settled terrain of the southeast-tributaries region more accessible to development.

In the heavily populated Korat Plateau region much of the alluvial bottom land is flooded so deep each year as to go uncultivated; yet in the dry season this area suffers the greatest water deficiency in the entire basin. Here flood control and irrigation must go hand in hand. There are only a few substantial power sites in the low-gradient tributary streams, but the Pa Mong site to the north offers a huge block of power and of water for diversion southward on the plateau. In the rugged northeast tributary and northern mountain regions the steeply falling streams provide many sites for cheap power and for the storage of water to irrigate the lands on the gentler slopes and lower plains where these streams join the main stream.

The major cities of southeast Asia—the Vietnamese capital Saigon-Cholon on the eastern edge of the Mekong delta (with a population of a million) and the Thai capital Bangkok at the mouth of the Chao Phraya (with a population of similar size)—are outside the basin. Except for the 500,000 in the Cambodian capital Phnom Penh and the 100,000 in the Laotian capital Vientiane, the population in the basin is largely rural. Although for the great majority labor in the rice paddies and upland fields yields little more than subsistence, the region depends on agricultural surplus for export. Rice, rubber, teak and a few other products of field and forest constitute the principal commodities that enter the monetary economies of the four countries and move in the channels of trade among them and with the world outside. During the past 10 years great numbers of refugees have moved from the north to the delta in Vietnam, the hill tribes of Laos have suffered displacement and there has been a steady emigration from the Korat Plateau into the central plain of Thailand and the city of Bangkok.

Estimates of present and future needs for purposes of planning development are heavily conditioned by uncertainty of data, including such basic data as population statistics. It does appear, however, that the population of the four countries now totals about 48 million. A conservative projection, assuming a continuing decline in maternal and infant death rates in a population now strongly grouped in the younger age brackets, and assuming that birth rates will be high even if birth control spreads and living levels rise, indicates that the population may grow at the rate of 3 per cent per year for the next 25 years. At that rate the population of the four countries will exceed 90 million by the last decade of this century.

To secure the food requirements for that number of people and a surplus for the foreign exchange necessary to generate a modest—50 per cent—increase in income from other economic activities will require an increase in production of milled rice from a present total of eight million tons to 17 million tons. Current exports of rice from Cambodia, Thailand and Vietnam run at about two million tons; in the interest of foreign exchange it will be desirable to increase this figure. There is reason to think that in recent years rice production in the three countries has been increasing at about 2 per cent per year; at this rate population growth will soon overtake production and eat up the surplus. It is apparent that the rate of increase in rice production must be accelerated to 3.5 or 4 per cent per year. Forecasts and plans must also reckon with concomitant increases in secondary crops and livestock products in response to changes in food habits and nutritional needs. Toward the support of economic growth, external demand for the forest products of the basin and for rubber may be expected to grow.

If the 50-per-cent improvement in income per capita is to be achieved, industrial output will have to grow at the rate of 6 or 7 per cent per year. A substantial portion of this activity is likely to be in the processing of agricultural and forest products. Without assuming the building of large industry serving regional or world markets, it appears that electric-power demand might increase five- to sevenfold.

Still another major item on the agenda of the future is transportation. At present the lack of adequate transportation routes and facilities presents a major obstacle to economic growth. Improvement is essential to the shift to monetized economy and efficient use of resources.

It is apparent that water management has a central role to play in the attainment of all of these objectives. Major increases in agricultural production, in the first place, require the balancing of the water surplus and the water deficiency that present such hazards to agriculture today. Irrigation will make possible the cultivation of a second crop of rice over large areas of the basin; drainage will improve yields from the regular wet-season crop; and flood control will reduce the risks that now discourage the investment of seed, fertilizer and labor in the single crop that is raised. In many of the tributaries and along the main stream the regulation of high and low flows will involve dams and reservoirs, because the concentration of high runoff in the valleys is little affected by small local works. Individual dams on the upper tributaries will have to be operated in conjunction with others in the same system before substantial reduction of floods can be assured in the principal valleys, and only very large installations on the main stream of the Mekong can affect flood heights appreciably in the alluvial areas below Sambor. Over large regions where slash-and-burn agriculture is now practiced, irrigation combined with careful soil management can stabilize yields and make possible the diversification of crops. As my colleague De Vries likes to put it, water may here replace fire as an agricultural tool.

Since prospecting in the sedimentary basins and plateaus has not so far revealed any major deposits of fossil fuels, the stream system offers the chief means of generating electric energy. The great opportunities are on the main stream, where there are likely dam sites that command flows the size of that on the lower Columbia River and heads of 60 to 180 feet. Virtually all the tributaries have some hydroelectric potential. The conspicuously attractive sites are in the Nam Theun and other east-bank tributaries in middle Laos that drain the heavy plateau runoff through steep, short valleys.

Dams built for water storage and power will help to open the main stream as a transportation route. In the reaches of the distributaries in the delta country below Phnom Penh the maintenance of stable, well-marked deep channels would encourage coastal and overseas shipping. Upstream there can be improvement of channels between the stretches of rapids for seasonal navigation. Conversion of the Mekong into a year-round deep-water channel to Vientiane—1,000 miles from the sea—would open up the land-locked areas of the basin to bulk shipments by water. The necessary engineering works would be too costly, however, if they were not combined in power and flood-control structures with savings from joint purpose and large scale.

Although the inhabitants of the country below Sambor have learned to live with floods—cultivating, for example, special varieties of floating rice that survive rising waters and give a harvest—the river in some years can bring catastrophe to farm and village. A number of towns, such as Phnom Penh, are built on natural levees or are protected by natural levees that may be overtopped by the rare great floods. Certainly flood control will become increasingly imperative as farming is extended and urban life spreads into new areas.

If the full array of possible measures to put the river to human use were to be applied over a period of perhaps 100 years, the total investment might run to $7 billion at current prices. Even with generous external aid, heavy local contributions would be required. To maintain such a rate of investment would call for expansion of total economic activity to levels not yet attained by any of the countries but not beyond the realm of possibility.

As of today it can be said that the first $14 million of investment in this vision has been committed. The figure is a small one, but it is larger than any previously assembled for a multilateral international enterprise under the auspices of the UN. The money has gone to finance the surveying and engineering work that must precede construction. Since this work involves skills that are still rare in the populations of the four nations of the Mekong basin, the personnel supplied by the other participating nations and by international agencies have helped to gain precious lead time.

By 1964, with Canadian and U.S. assistance, the project's planners will have at their disposal topographic maps of the basin on a scale of 1:50,000. Meanwhile the Canadians, with aid from the Filipinos, are completing large-scale maps of selected river reaches for use in dam-site and irrigation-project studies; to estab-

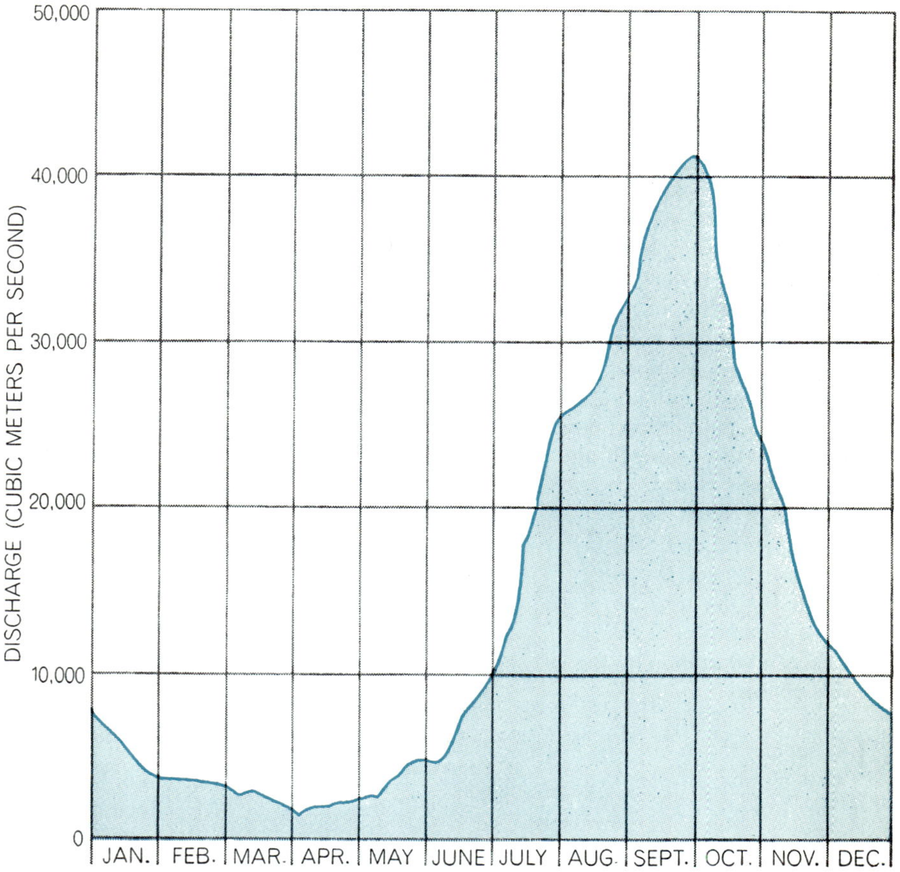

ESTIMATED DISCHARGE of the Mekong River at Phnom Penh in a wet year shows the typical long dry season and the flood period. Change is so great that Tonle Sap reverses flow.

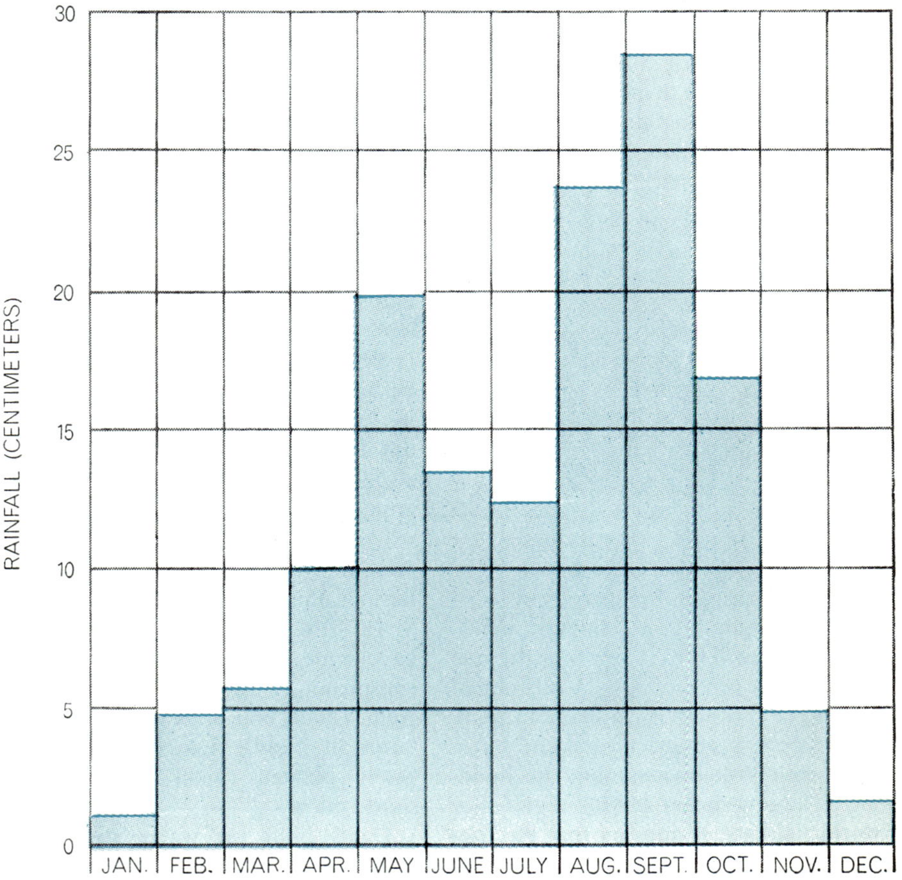

MEAN MONTHLY RAINFALL at station on the Korat Plateau in Thailand also shows wet and dry seasons. The plateau suffers from both heavy floods and severe shortages of water.

lish ground control for aerial photography precise levels have been run along the main line of the river. Geological investigation of the dam sites for several of the likely major projects has been handled by the Australians, not without personal hazard from unfriendly guerrillas. The fundamental observations of precipitation and stream flow are going forward on a network established by a U.S. engineering firm and now maintained by local personnel with assistance from the World Meteorological Organization. Improvement in navigation has been supported by the United Kingdom and New Zealand, with a hydrographic survey under a grant from the UN Special Fund for International Development.

A heavy part of the work has centered on engineering and associated studies looking to preliminary plans for dams on the main stream and on the tributaries. Three main stream sites are receiving attention at present. At Sambor in Cambodia a Japanese team is at work; engineers from the U.S. have made a preliminary examination of the Pa Mong site, and Indian engineers are preparing a comprehensive report for the Tonle Sap project in Cambodia. The last, with its possible effects on water, sediment and fish life in the Grand Lac area, requires examination of silt and fisheries data collected by French workers, and it would have major effects downstream in the delta. In that area there is a small experiment in reclamation of the land through drainage and irrigation, and a mathematical model of water volume and density is being prepared under a UNESCO contract supported by the UN Special Fund.

A Japanese group has completed a reconnaissance survey of all the tributaries, and more detailed surveys are being conducted by Japanese, French and U.S. engineers at seven sites. All of these involve irrigation and power development. At or near four of these sites the Special Fund, in collaboration with the UN Food and Agriculture Organization, is setting up experimental farms. Other countries are also taking part in the tributary studies: Pakistan is planning the irrigation-distribution system at the Nam Pong site in Thailand and Israel is helping with irrigation design and project review for the Prek Thnot in Cambodia.

Israel and the Republic of China have contributed cement. Iran has donated the petroleum for use in the land and water transport of the survey teams. The World Health Organization, the International Atomic Energy Agency, the International Labor Organization and UNESCO have sent experts to deal with special problems.

Large-scale construction of dams, canals and channels does not in itself guarantee solution to the long-term needs of the rapidly growing population in this region. Experience with several score small-scale projects built on the Korat Plateau during the past decade shows that, even though the dams, spillways and outlet works were soundly designed, the water is little used and does not reach all the paddies that ought to have benefited. There has been difficulty or delay in getting proper canals built, in laying out the distributary ditches and drains, in advising farmers on methods and seeds and in managing suitable transport, credit and market facilities for the hopefully enlarged harvest. By the same token any extensive growth in manufacturing would depend in large measure on revision of conditions and institutions, habits and outlook among people of all classes. Near the heart of the problem is education. With adult literacy at about 50 per cent in Thailand and 20 per cent in Cambodia, Laos and Vietnam and with something like the same percentages of school-age children in school in each country, the expansion of elementary and secondary schools ought to have high priority in the national development plans. Technical and physical works have highly significant roles to play, but they must be evaluated in the broader context of the less visible and tangible social transformations that must accompany them if they are to serve their purpose.

The most urgent question confronting the Mekong planners, my colleagues and I found, is to decide when the basic studies have reached a stage that warrants embarking on construction. Administrators and citizens alike yearn to see earth move, concrete structures rise and power lines make their giant strides across the green terrain. The engineer and the economist directly responsible for the study are subject to pressure not only from above and below but from all sides—from agencies competing for investigation and investment funds. As the reports from engineering teams pile up on the table of the co-ordinating committee, its members will face extremely difficult problems of choice in terms of internal feasibility and the relation of projects to one another within the basin and to other forms of national development activity. Our mission urged that the collection and analysis of social and economic data be advanced promptly to catch up with the lengthening shelves of technical and physical reports. Power markets should be assessed, agricultural measures should be appraised, land capability should be inventoried and a systems analysis should be carried out. Certain of the needed studies are already

INTENSIVE CULTIVATION of rice in Cambodia is shown in this aerial photo-

under way.

Some data of this kind cannot be assembled from archives, questionnaires or head counts. We recommended that the experimental and demonstration effort be pushed on a larger scale than that of the experimental farms. The complete village setting is necessary to test and predict the effects of some measures. It would be desirable to get a project of at least 6,000 acres in operation in connection with one of the tributary dams.

Perhaps the most urgent need is for the training of agricultural advisers to work in the villages and provincial centers. Without competent and devoted workers who are ready to get their feet wet in the paddy fields, the benefits of much engineering investment might never be developed. To train as many as 6,000 village workers and 1,000 more for service out of the provincial centers over the next 10 or 15 years would in itself be a tremendous task. Their training might be initiated at the pilot farms now being organized.

An equally critical need is for a rela-

graph made by Hunting Survey Corporation Limited for the Canadian government under the Colombo Plan program. North is at bottom. Small town *(lower right)* is Sambor, where a large dam may be built on the Mekong. Shape of fields is typical of rice paddies.

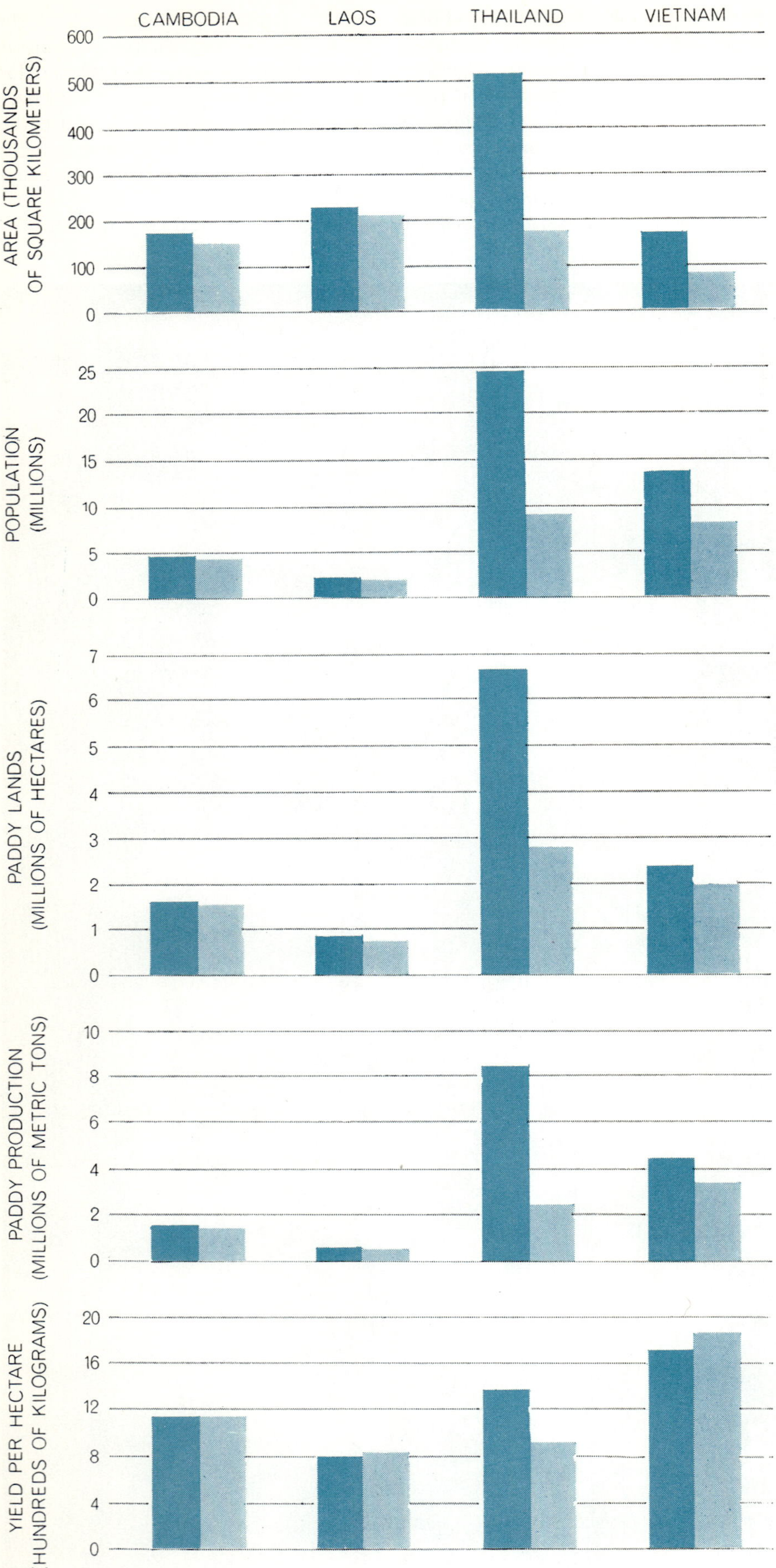

COMPARISONS are made for area, population and rice-paddy cultivation in the four Mekong countries. The light bars are for the Mekong region alone; the dark bars give totals for each country as a whole. There are 2.47 hectares to an acre and 2.2 kilograms to a pound.

tively few highly educated individuals in the agencies of the governments who are qualified to prepare, review and revise the schemes for water management in relation to the scheme for the basin as a whole and the economic policies of their countries. An expert from the outside cannot acquit responsibilities of this kind. Nor can a central lower Mekong staff, however competent and enlightened, be charged with essentially national decisions.

Some of the other personnel requirements seem easier to meet. The training of workers to handle and maintain earth-moving equipment can be accomplished in a matter of 18 to 24 months. The engineering skills are demanding, but the Royal Irrigation Department in Thailand has shown that a competent engineering office can be set up in the region. Until these skills are more widely established in the population, however, personnel equipped with them can be imported. At present the start-up of four projects on the tributary rivers would call for more professional workers than the four countries now have in their employ.

In setting human and cultural demands of this kind the program for water management in the Mekong basin becomes the organizing force behind more subtle aspects of social change. Since one cannot wait for the other and both water management and social change must go forward together, our mission recommended that the four countries should proceed forthwith on the specifications for and construction of a few tributary projects. We did so in the belief that the values of early experience and action—in the management of agricultural development as well as dam-building—would outweigh the possible social costs of undertaking a less fruitful project or one that would later hamper optimum development downstream.

Within recent weeks commitments have been made for financing the first multipurpose dam on the tributaries. The West German government has agreed to lend Thailand the equivalent of $11 million for the Nam Pong project. If political conditions are favorable and if reason and vision can find their way into the construction and administration of the lower Mekong program to the same degree that they have emerged in the study stage, this program may become the first genuinely international and peaceful venture in river-basin development. It may thereby help to remove the obstacles that stand in the way of the development of international rivers elsewhere in the world.

The Cratering of Indochina

The countries of the area are pitted with an estimated 26 million bomb and shell craters. What are the long-term ecological effects of this massive physical alteration of the terrain likely to be?

ARTHUR H. WESTING and E. W. PFEIFFER

May 1972

The unprecedented use of herbicides on a massive scale as an instrument of war in Vietnam has prompted several studies of the probable long-term effects of these chemical agents on the land of Indochina. Much less attention has been paid to the effects of the tearing up of the land by bombing and shelling. Yet the released tonnage statistics alone suggest that these effects must be sizable. In the seven-year period from 1965 to 1971 the area of Indochina, a region slightly larger than Texas, was bombarded by a tonnage of munitions amounting to approximately twice the total used by the U.S. in all the theaters of World War II.

During three tours of war zones of Indochina to assess damage done to the environment by herbicides, we became increasingly conscious of the ubiquitous scarring of the landscape by bomb and shell craters. From the air some areas in Vietnam looked like photographs of the moon. How would this cratering of the land affect life and the ecology in Indochina when its people attempted to pick up normal living after the war? It seemed that the physical alteration of the terrain by bombing might have created long-range problems fully as serious as those produced by the defoliation campaign (which had attacked more than five million acres of forest and cropland in Vietnam). In order to initiate investigation of the crater problems, the two of us went to Vietnam for a preliminary study in behalf of the Scientists' Institute for Public Information in August, 1971. From the U.S. Department of Defense we collected the limited information that was available to the public about the expenditures of munitions in Indochina. Then in the field we surveyed bombed areas on the ground and from the air (in helicopters) and interviewed many people, including farmers, lumbermen and other persons who had observed various effects of the bombing on the land, the economy and various occupations.

In the seven years between 1965 and 1971 the U.S. military forces exploded 26 billion pounds (13 million tons) of munitions in Indochina, half from the air and half from weapons on the ground. This staggering weight of ordnance amounts to the energy of 450 Hiroshima nuclear bombs. For the area and people of Indochina as a whole it represents an average of 142 pounds of explosive per acre of land and 584 pounds per person. It means that over the seven-year period the average rate of detonation was 118 pounds per second. These average figures, however, give no indication of the actual concentration; most of the bombardment was concentrated in time (within the years from 1967 on) and in area. Of the 26 billion pounds, 21 billion were exploded within South Vietnam, one billion in North Vietnam and 2.6 billion in southern Laos. The bombardment in South Vietnam represented an overall average of 497 pounds per acre and 1,215 pounds per person; the major part, however, was focused on two regions: the five northern provinces and the region around Saigon.

Craters pock every area of South Vietnam: forests, swamps, fields, paddies, roadsides. Certain areas, notably the "free fire," or "specified strike," zones, show severe cratering. We personally observed large areas that had been subjected to intensive transformation of the landscape in Tay Ninh, Long Khanh, Gia Dinh, Hau Nghia and Binh Duong provinces around Saigon and Quang Ngai, Quang Tin and Quang Nam provinces of the northern part of the country. And of course the concentration of craters is particularly marked in areas such as the demilitarized zone (DMZ) between North Vietnam and South Vietnam and the supply trails in southern Laos.

We were able to visit on foot an area in the Mekong Delta that had been until fairly recently a free-fire zone. The area was near the hamlet of Hoi Son about 30 miles south of My Tho. Farmers were being resettled there on their previously fought-over land because senior officials considered the region fairly secure. (The degree of security became evident during our stay when U.S. aircraft were observed rocketing and strafing only a few miles away.) Several families that had left the area a decade earlier because of fighting were interviewed, and they took us to three craters that they said had been made in 1967. The craters had probably been produced by 500-pound bombs dropped by fighter-bombers. Each crater was about 30 feet in diameter, filled with water, and at the time of our visit was about five feet deep in the center. The entire immediate area had been a rice paddy, but during the years when no cultivation had occurred, the rice had been replaced by

CRATERED MANGROVE FOREST in Gia Dinh province in South Vietnam was photographed from a helicopter by Westing during a trip made by the authors in August, 1971, on behalf of the Scientists' Institute for Public Information. Heavy bombing damages trees in three ways: outright destruction, riddling of the timber by missile fragments and weakening of the trees through subsequent infection. In addition this particular tract of forest had been subjected to an earlier attack with herbicides. Water-filled craters in both timberlands and croplands have greatly multiplied the available breeding areas for disease-carrying mosquitoes.

CRATERED CROPLANDS in Long An province in South Vietnam were photographed from a helicopter by Gordon H. Orians of the University of Washington, who accompanied Pfeiffer on his first inspection tour of the war zone in March, 1969. The craters were made by 500-pound bombs dropped from B-52's. Such craters, which in this region remain filled with water during much or all of the year, are unsuitable for rice cultivation. For this reason, and because of the dangers of unexploded munitions and sharp bomb fragments buried in the ground, Vietnamese farmers have generally abandoned croplands that have been pocked by craters.

a very tall reed, genus *Phragmites*, which surrounded the crater at a distance of 10 to 20 feet. Growing from the rim of the craters and into the reeds was a species of relatively short grass, *Brachiaria*, and a taller grass, *Scirpus*. The farmers were growing seed rice near the craters and were plowing under the reeds and grasses in preparation for planting rice. It was obvious that they could not use the cratered areas for rice cultivation because the water was much too deep. The only apparent solution was to bring in soil from elsewhere, but this was obviously not practical.

We also observed at close hand many craters on the flat terrace lands northwest of Saigon that had previously supported an evergreen hardwood forest. In this area the craters generally contain no water during the dry season, so that their natural history is considerably different from the history of the craters of the Delta region that are permanently filled with water. The craters were very numerous in this area; there was at least one every 100 feet. Each crater was 20 to 40 feet across and five to 20 feet deep. There were many generations of craters from different air strikes. The most recent ones were bare of vegetation but contained some rainwater. (We observed these craters in the wet season.) In the older craters a few sprigs of grass, probably *Imperata*, were sprouting in the center. As the craters age grass grows radially, eventually covering the bottom to meet vines trailing down from the peripheral vegetation. There is some filling of old craters with soil washed down from the sides, but this is limited because old craters almost completely covered with grass were still five to 10 feet deep. They thus became permanent features of the landscape.

From the data available to us on the quantity of munitions expended we calculated tentative estimates of the total area affected by cratering and other damage to the land. For these estimates we had to make some very free and general assumptions. For example, we assume that about half (by weight) of the total amount of munitions employed in Indochina consisted of bombs, shells and other missiles that would produce craters. We assume further that on the average each of the crater-producing missiles was equivalent to a 500-pound bomb and formed a crater 30 feet in diameter and 15 feet deep, displacing 131 cubic yards of earth. (A large proportion of the cratering has been produced by B-52 bomber raids; each of these big planes

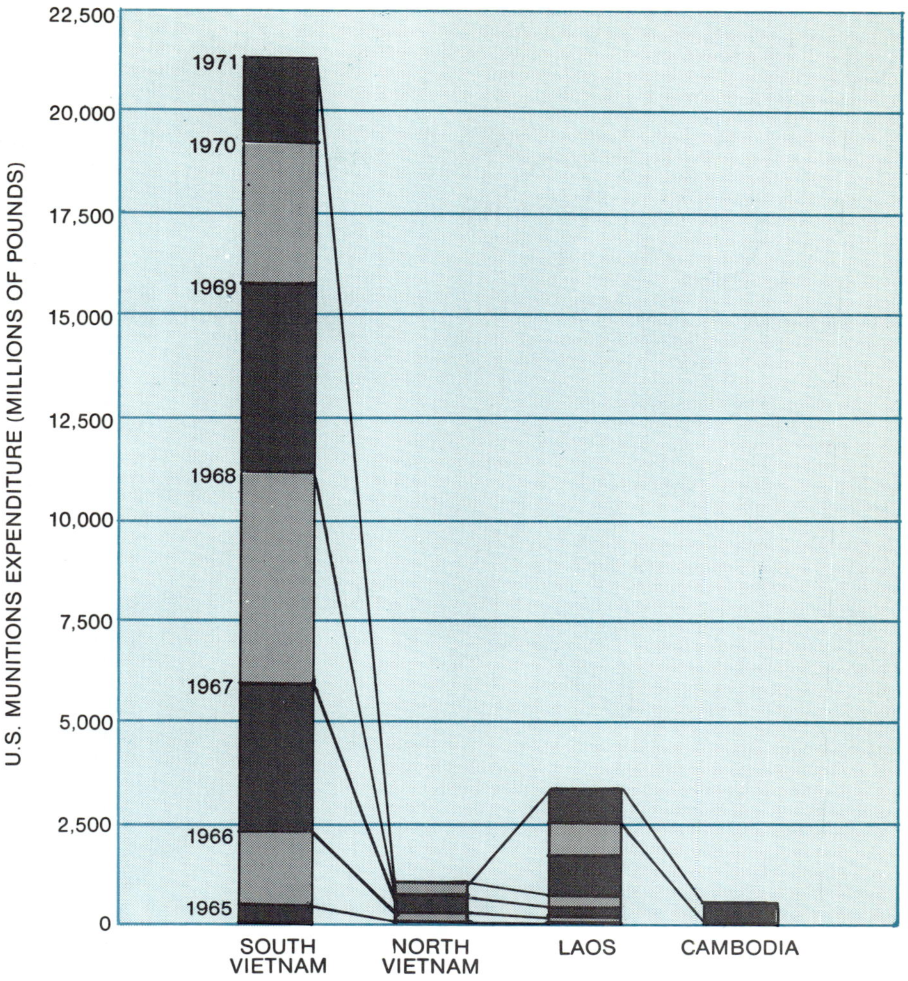

TOTAL U.S. MUNITIONS EXPENDITURES in Indochina for the seven-year period from 1965 through 1971 are broken down by country and by year in this bar chart. The bar for North Vietnam omits 1969 and 1970, years in which large-scale U.S. bombing of that country was suspended. The bar for Cambodia begins with 1970, the year in which U.S. and Republic of Vietnam forces launched a large-scale invasion of that country. The data were gathered from scattered Department of Defense sources in large part by Raphael Littauer and associates at Cornell University. (For lack of sufficient information all ground-based munitions, which comprise about half of the total, have been assigned to South Vietnam.)

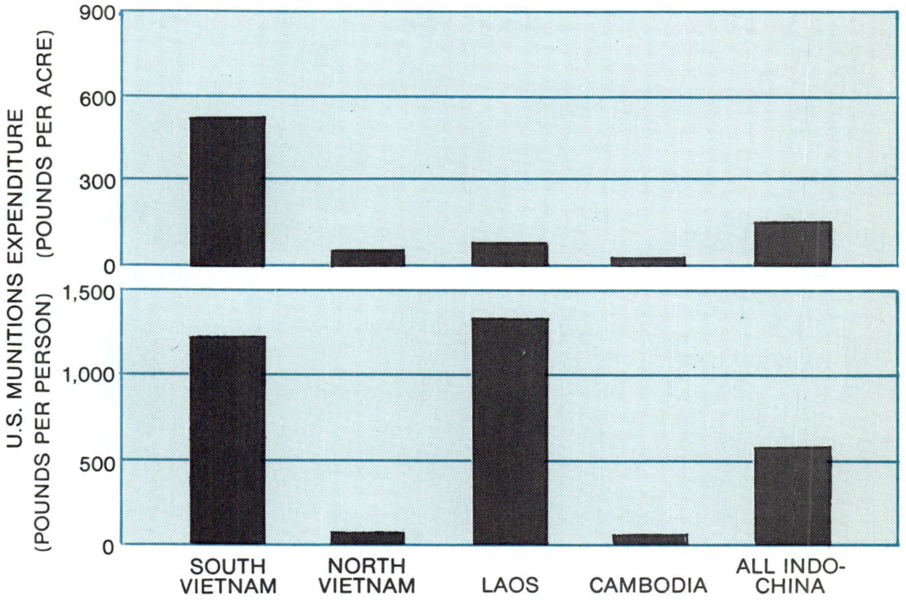

IMPACT of total U.S. munitions expenditures on the land and people of Indochina is suggested by these two bar charts. The figures shown were calculated by the authors from the available data on the total quantity of munitions expended by U.S. forces from 1965 through 1971, together with estimates of the areas and populations of recipient countries.

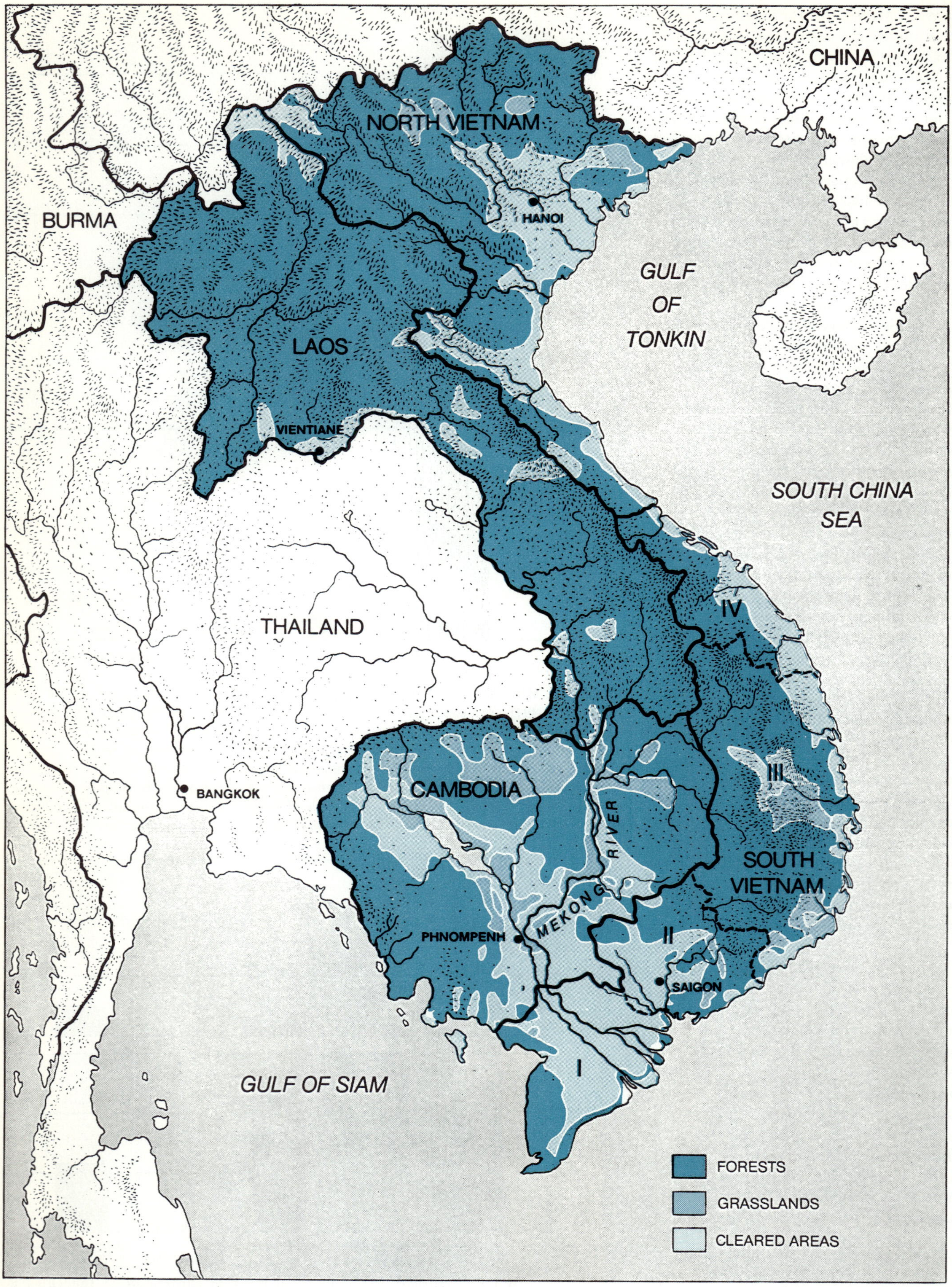

MAP OF INDOCHINA shows the general topography of the region and principal vegetation zones (*see key at lower right*). The U.S. armed forces regard South Vietnam as being divided into four major military regions, which are designated by Roman numerals.

typically carries 108 500-pound bombs.) We also estimate that the fragments from each crater-producing missile were spread over an area of 1.25 acres.

On the basis of these assumptions (some of which are supported by actual measurements) we estimate that the number of craters produced in Indochina by the bombardments from 1965 to 1971 totaled some 26 million, covering a total area of 423,000 acres and representing a total displacement of about 3.4 billion cubic yards of earth. The area of missile-fragment spread totals 32.6 million acres, if we disregard overlap. Again we note that South Vietnam has borne the brunt of this damage. In the period mentioned (through 1971) South Vietnam is estimated to have received about 21 million craters, covering all together about 345,000 acres, and to have had millions of acres contaminated by missile fragments, even allowing for overlap. The total area of the country is 42.8 million acres.

Let us now examine some specific effects, for the present and for the future, of this massive application of "landscape management" by high explosives. There is evidence from previous wars that the effects will be long-lasting. A decade after the end of World War II the craters of heavily shelled areas on Okinawa were still barren of vegetation and reddened by rusting shell fragments. On Eniwetok craters were clearly in evidence two decades after the war. Four decades after World War I vegetation in the Negev desert of Israel outlined the craters from that war, and even in France's Verdun area many of the World War I craters are still clearly visible and in some cases to this day are devoid of vegetation.

To begin with, we can see that the displacement and scattering of soil and subsoil from the craters in Indochina have given rise to harmful physical consequences. (Over the seven years the displacement of soil by bombardment in Indochina proceeded at a rate of nearly 1,000 cubic yards of soil per minute.) In hilly terrain the tearing up of the soil promotes erosion. In Indochina, where some of the soil is vulnerable to laterization (hardening to a bricklike state), the removal of vegetation and humus may make the area in and around craters permanently barren. At the least it has resulted in colonization of cratered regions by weedy, worthless grasses and shrubs. Furthermore, the deep craters have made many areas almost impassable for travel.

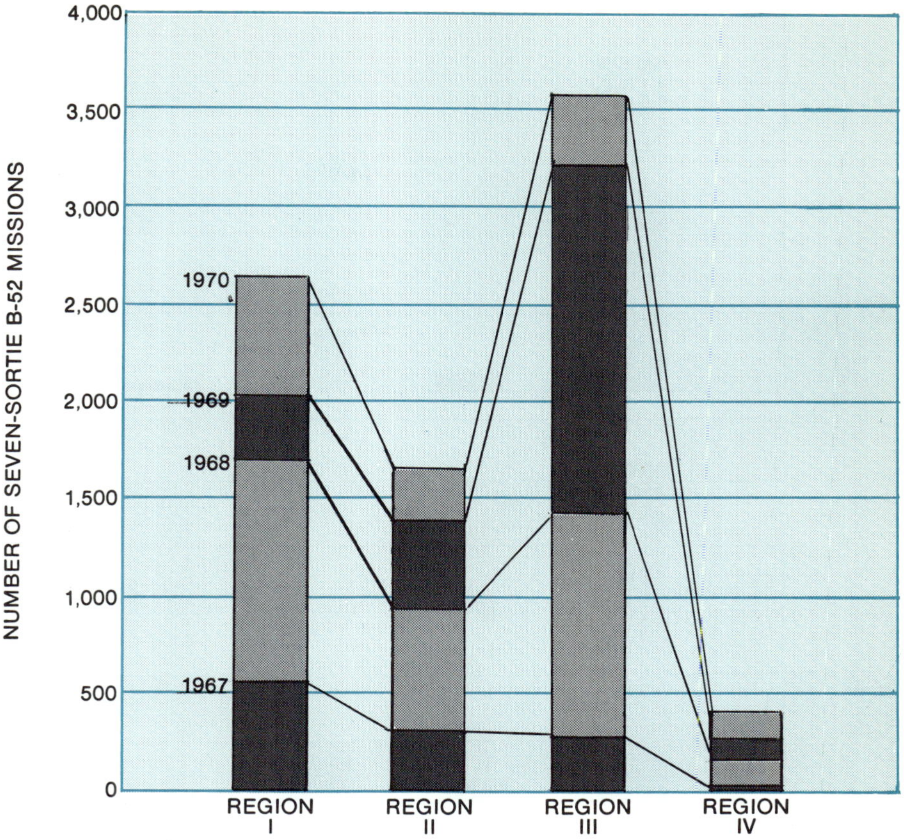

B-52 MISSIONS over South Vietnam from 1967 through 1970 are broken down by military region and by year in this bar chart, based on data gathered by Littauer and the authors. A typical B-52 mission is assumed to comprise seven planes on the average and thus to deliver a total of 756 500-pound bombs. Breakdowns for other years were not available.

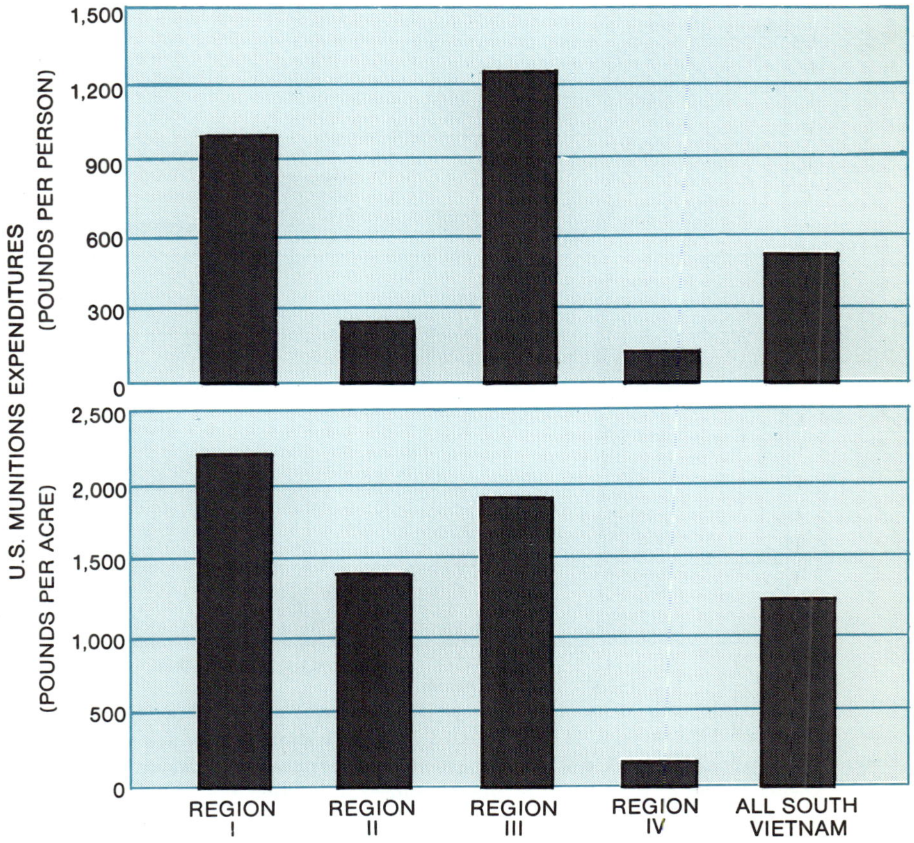

ALTERNATIVE METHOD of estimating the impact of total U.S. munitions expenditures from 1965 to 1971 on the land and inhabitants of South Vietnam by region was devised by the authors on the assumption that the relative B-52 activity from 1967 through 1971 among the four military regions of the country was proportional to overall munitions expenditures.

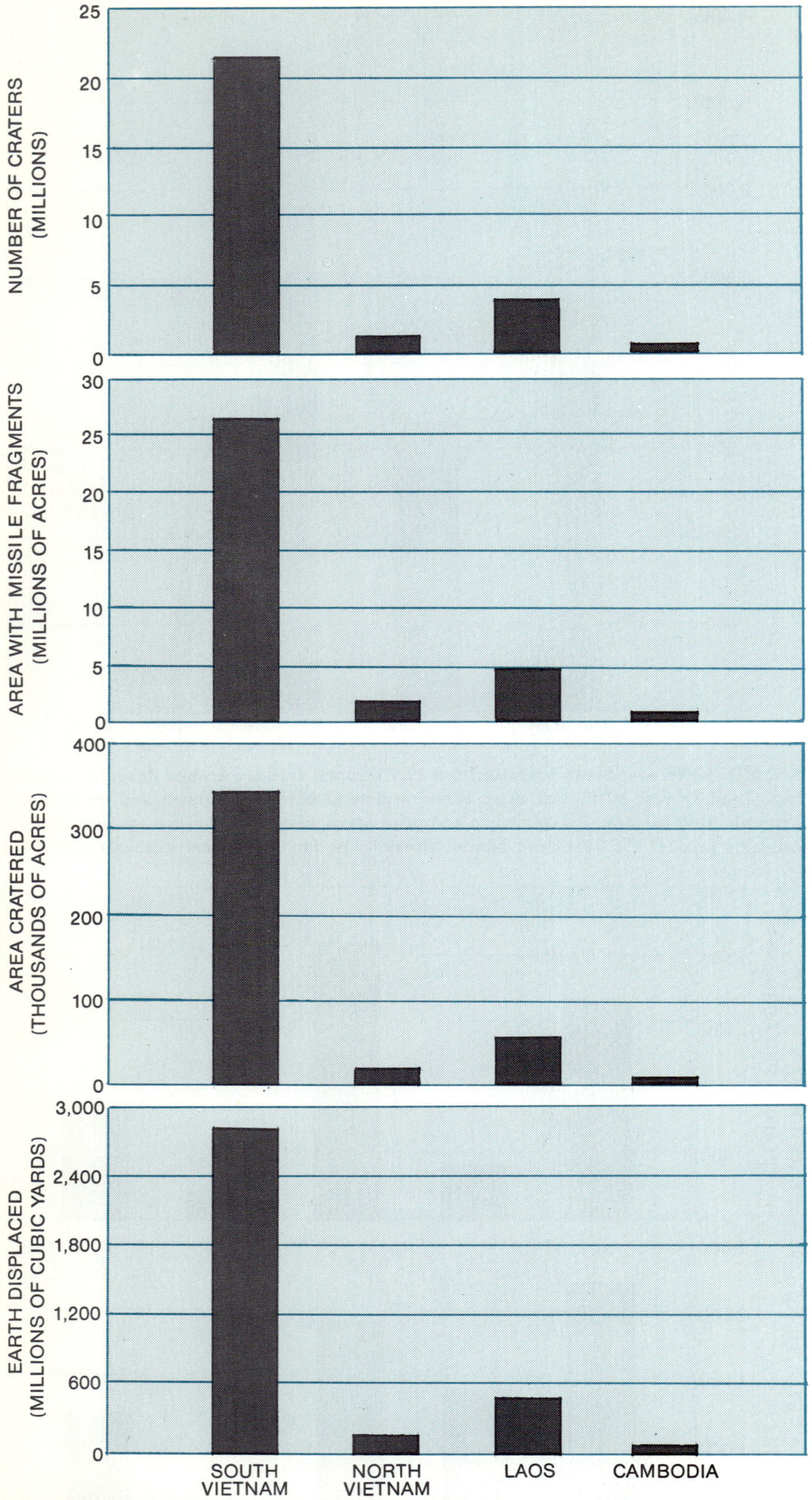

ECOLOGICAL IMPACT of bombardment on the countries of Indochina for the seven-year period from 1965 through 1971 is assessed in this illustration in terms of number of craters, area covered by bomb and shell fragments, area cratered and amount of earth displaced. Owing to the unavailability of precise information from the Department of Defense, the authors were forced to make the following assumptions: that half of all the air and ground munitions expended in Indochina have been of the kind that produce craters, and that these are all the equivalent of 500-pound bombs. (Although the number of craters is thereby underestimated, their combined dimensions and impact probably are not.) They also assumed that the zone of flying metal fragments associated with each crater is 1.25 acres. Finally, they assumed that each crater is a cone 30 feet in diameter and 15 feet deep.

Many of the craters, particularly in the Delta and coastal regions, have penetrated the water table and remain filled with water during much or all of the year. They have thereby probably become breeding grounds for mosquitoes, greatly increasing the hazards of malaria and dengue fever for the population. Reports by military authorities indeed confirm that "malaria has been causing increasing concern in Vietnam" and has spread to previously unafflicted areas.

The impact of cratering on agriculture has been substantial. Farmers in South Vietnam, notably in the Mekong Delta, have been reluctant or unable to attempt to reclaim rice paddies or other farmlands that have been pocked by craters. One of the important deterrents is the presence of unexploded munitions buried in the ground. A number of farmers have been killed by the detonation of such shells or bombs by their plows. Moreover, the ubiquitous missile fragments in the ground cut the hooves of the water buffaloes used as draft animals, causing infection and death of the animals. The unexploded bombs and shells lying about in the soil of Indochina are known to number several hundred thousand. Bombing has also disrupted rice-growing in Indochina by breaking up many of the intricate irrigation systems, and in some areas near the seacoast it has opened the land to encroachment by salt water.

The timber industry of South Vietnam, potentially one of the most important elements in the region's predominantly agricultural economy, has been particularly hard hit by the bombing. It has catastrophically slashed the values of the once prime timberlands northwest and northeast of Saigon, for example. The heavy shelling and bombing have damaged the trees in three ways: outright destruction, riddling of the timber by missile fragments and subsequent weakening of the trees through infection by wood-rotting fungi.

The forests have been bombarded by ordnance so intensively that the trees are filled with metal shards; one mill-owner told us that four out of five logs he receives have metal in them. Although the sawmill operators make laborious efforts to chop out the pieces of metal, they are only partly successful, with the result that they have a high rate of destruction of their saw blades by still embedded metal. In trees left standing the missile-fragment wounds provide ready entry for fungal rot. In some tree species the rot progresses so rapidly that if they are not harvested

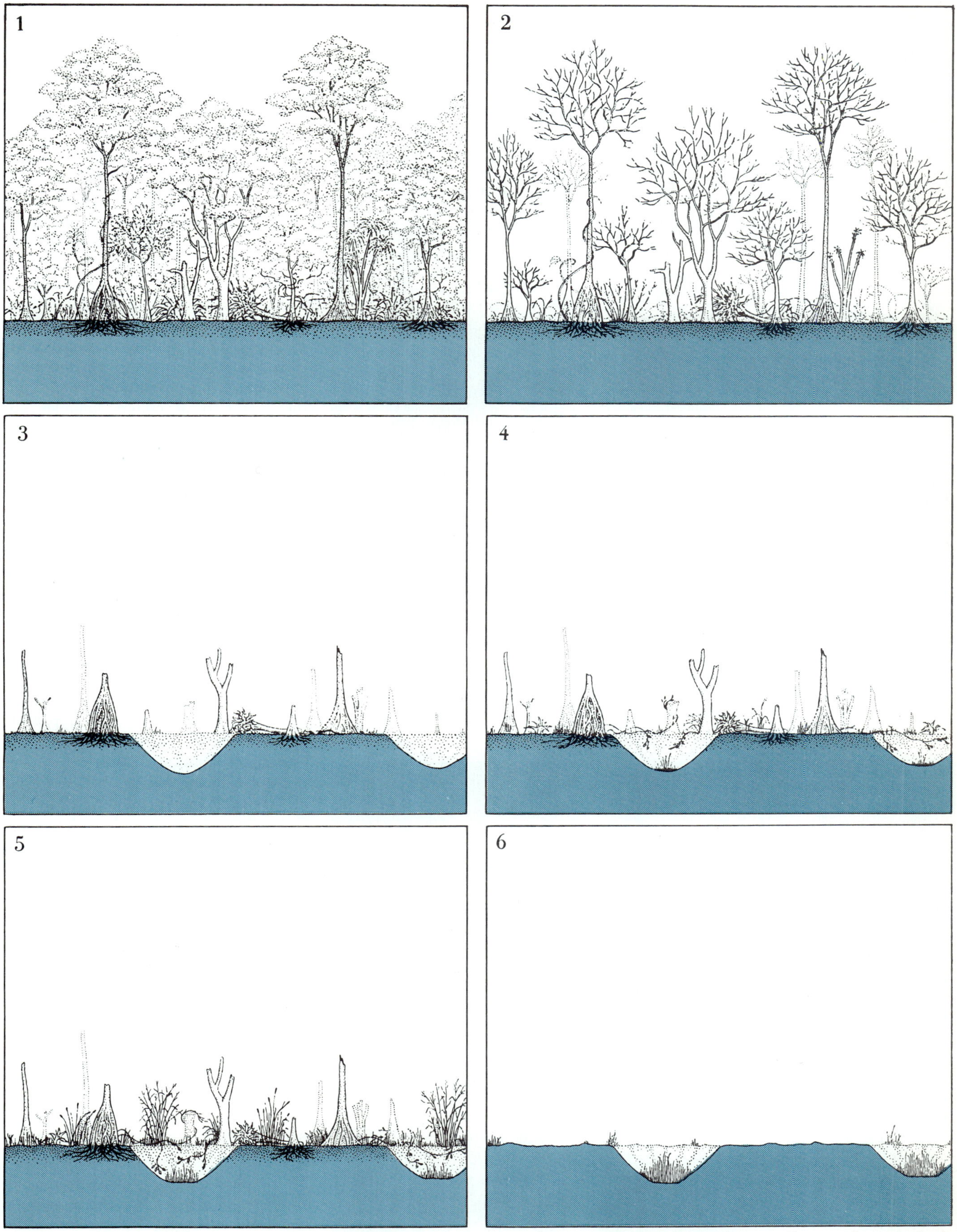

EFFECTS of defoliation, bombing and plowing on a typical evergreen hardwood forest in South Vietnam (*1*) are summarized in this sequence of highly idealized drawings. Most mature trees in such a forest are killed by defoliation (*2*), leaving a thick understory of useless broad-leafed brush, vines, bamboo and tall grass. Comparatively recent craters are bare of vegetation but often contain a little rainwater during the wet season (*3*). Somewhat later a few sprigs of grass, probably cogon grass (*Imperata*), sprout in the middle (*4*). As the crater ages further the grass grows radially, covering the bottom to meet vines trailing down from the peripheral vegetation (*5*). There is some filling of the crater with soil washed down from the sides, but this is limited. Broad-leafed plants generally do not invade these holes. Plowing is occasionally added to clear vegetation remaining between the craters (*6*).

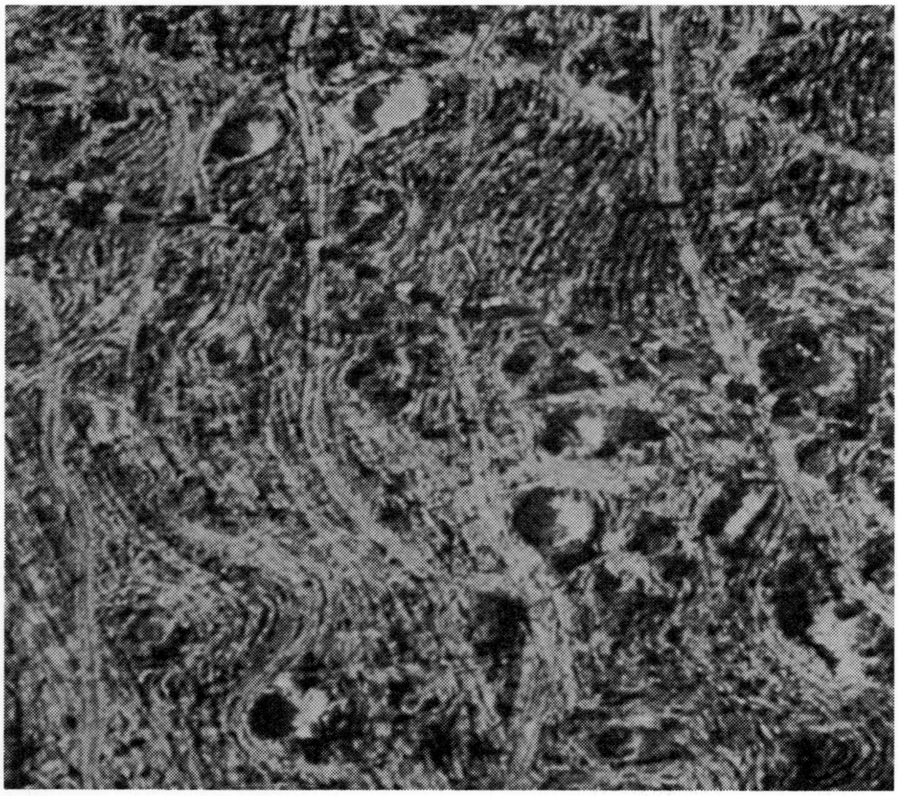

LARGE PLOWS have been used by the U.S. Army in South Vietnam to destroy vast stretches of vegetation in order to deny cover to the enemy. According to information released by the Army, at least three-quarters of a million acres were cleared in this manner through mid-1971, and this total is being added to at the rate of about 1,000 acres per day. The swaths cut by such plows, often scraped down to the infertile subsoil, are invaded by cogon grass or remain barren and subject to erosion. In this photograph, made by Westing in August, 1971, a line of heavy vehicles, including both plows and tanks, can be seen wending its way across a thoroughly cratered and plowed landscape in Tay Ninh province.

CLOSEUP AERIAL VIEW shows a U.S. Army plow clearing the area around a large B-52 bomb crater. The machine is basically a 20-ton Caterpillar tractor fitted with a massive 11-foot-wide, 2.5-ton plow blade and with 14 tons of armor plate. Crater is several years old.

immediately after the metal attack they soon become almost worthless. Apparently the main South Vietnamese timber trees lose about 50 percent of their value in two or three years from this cause. Rubber trees are particularly susceptible to the fungal rot initiated by missile-fragment wounds; they become so weakened that they are felled by any high wind. A French official of a rubber plantation told us he had lost 80 percent of his trees within two years after a bombardment of his plantation.

Loggers in the battle zones of South Vietnam find that the damaging of timber by munitions is causing them a loss of more than 30 percent in the price received for the logs (although the severance tax remains the same). In addition the profusion of craters impedes the hauling of their logs to the mill. Often they must cut the logs to a short length (instead of the desirable 90 feet that is possible under normal circumstances) to allow sufficient maneuverability to skid them around the craters. During a survey in a high-flying helicopter of a mountain forest near Da Nang we saw many craters on the mountainside and along the ridges with severe accompanying erosion; they had been produced by a single B-52 raid about a year and a half earlier. We also observed another significant type of damage: large areas of the forest had been burned out, apparently by incendiary attacks with napalm, white phosphorus and flares.

Bombardment and defoliation are by no means the only methods used by the U.S. military in its struggle with vegetation in Indochina. Beginning in the mid-1960's a vast program of systematic forest bulldozing has been developed. The employment of massed tractors organized into companies for extensive forest clearing had apparently replaced the use of herbicides to deny forest cover and sanctuary to the other side. The effectiveness of the tractors, called Rome plows, is in some ways clearly superior to that of chemicals and is probably more destructive to the environment. When we visited a land-clearing operation in August, 1971, we watched about 30 such plows (20-ton Caterpillar tractors fitted with massive 11-foot-wide, 2.5-ton plow blades and with 14 tons of armor plate) scrape clean the remaining few areas of the Boi Loi Woods northwest of Saigon. We learned that in the 26 days prior to our visit the company had cleared 6,037 acres. Four other companies were also in operation and these five units had cleared a total of 750,000 acres as of August, 1971. We visited an area that had been plowed several years previously and it had regrown to cogon grass (*Imperata*), making further successional stages to the original hardwood forest very unlikely.

A study by U.S. agents has determined that about 10 percent of the agricultural land of South Vietnam has had to be abandoned because of the destruction wrought by bombardment and other weapons used in this war. It has been a war against the land as much as against armies. Indeed, it appears that one of the main strategies of our military effort has been to disrupt and destroy the social and economic fabric of rural, agricultural Vietnam in order to drive the peasant population into areas under central control and to deprive the guerrilla enemy of a power base.

Only about 5 to 8 percent of the U.S. bombing missions in Indochina have been directed at tactical military targets, that is, in direct support of troops. The rest of the bombing missions are described as "harassing" or "interdiction" attacks. They are also referred to as strategic bombing missions. Whereas the targets of strategic bombing in World War II were the factories, port cities, railroads and so forth of the enemy, in the Indochina war the strategic targets are the land and forests of Indochina because they give cover and sanctuary to the other side. It is important to note here that whereas factories, ports and other man-made sources of production can be rapidly rebuilt, as demonstrated in Europe and Japan, it is doubtful that many of the forests and lands of Indochina can be rehabilitated in the foreseeable future.

From 1966 on the B-52's carried out incessant attacks on a schedule of almost daily missions. From an altitude of 30,000 feet, where they are usually unheard and unseen from the ground, they have been sowing systematic destruction. A typical B-52 mission, comprising seven planes on the average, delivers 756 500-pound bombs in a pattern that saturates an area about half a mile wide and three miles long, that is, nearly 1,000 acres. Thus on a schedule of four or five missions per day of seven sorties each, such as was followed during 1971, the B-52's alone were creating about 100,000 new craters each month. Unfortunately the release of air-war data is now severely restricted.

The cumulative impact of the munitions attack on the land has to be seen to be grasped fully. Reports by military

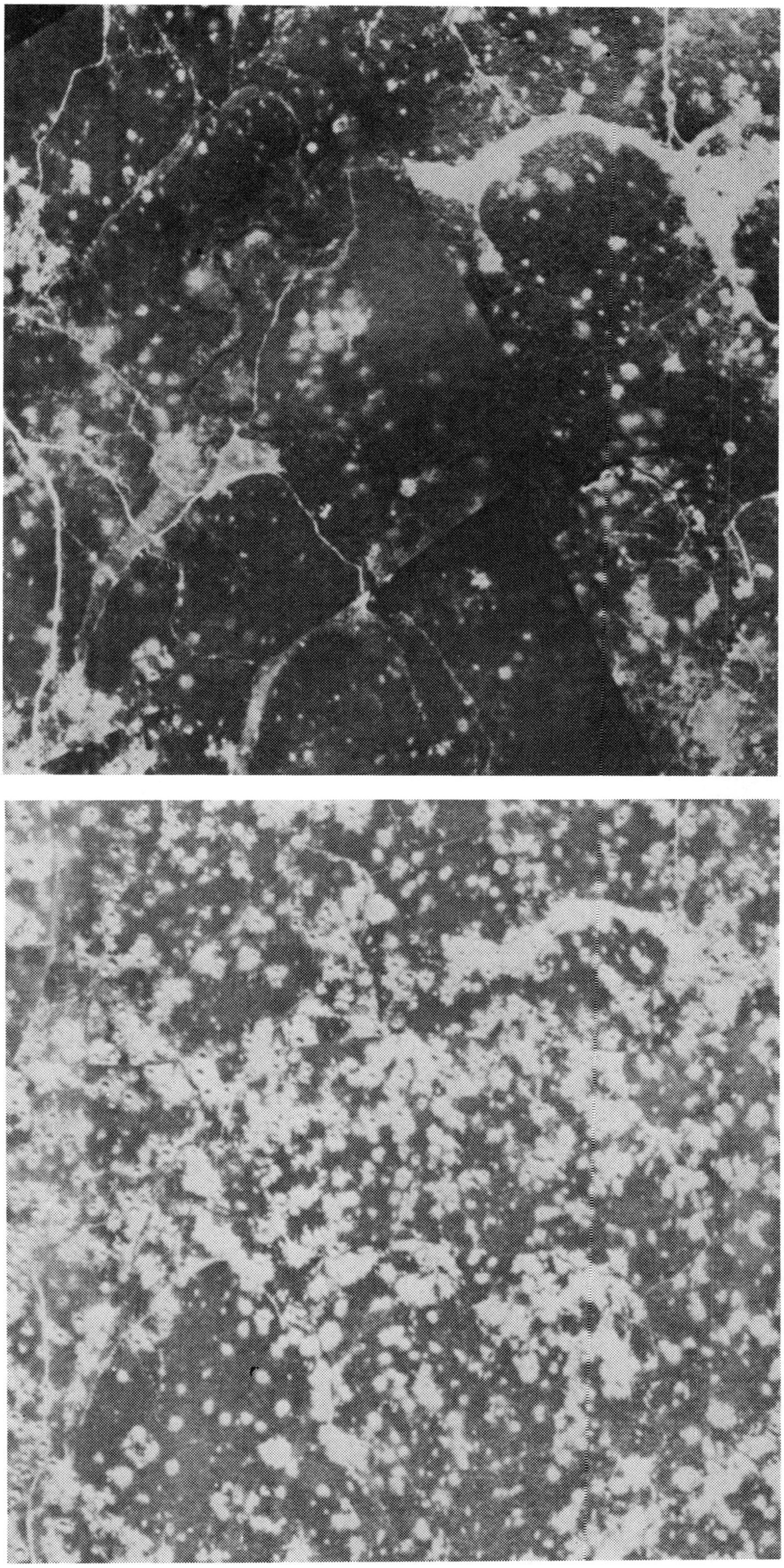

HIGH-ALTITUDE PHOTOGRAPHIC MOSAICS of an area in the demilitarized zone between North Vietnam and South Vietnam show the scene before (*top*) and after (*bottom*) a period of intense B-52 and tactical air strikes in 1967. The photographs were made by the U.S. Air Force. The larger bomb craters measure between 20 and 40 feet in diameter.

observers speak of the landscape's being "torn as if by an angry giant," and of areas of the green delta land's being pulverized into a "gray porridge." Our brief survey has only suggested some of the grim consequences for the present and future life of the inhabitants of Indochina. Still to be assessed are the effects of the persisting bombardment on the people's habitations, on the animal life and general ecology of the region. The damage caused by the large-scale disorganization of the environment may be felt for centuries.

Meanwhile the steady bombardment and shattering of the land, shielded from the Western world's view and concern by the wide Pacific Ocean and the supposed "winding down" of the war, goes on with no end in sight.

Senator Gaylord Nelson of Wisconsin has introduced in the Senate a bill to provide for a study by the National Academy of Sciences "to assess the extent of the damage done to the environment of South Vietnam, Laos and Cambodia as the result of the operations of the Armed Forces of the United States ... and to consider plans for effectively rectifying such damage."

Senator Nelson declared:

"There is nothing in the history of warfare to compare with [what we have done in Indochina]. A 'scorched earth' policy has been a tactic of warfare throughout history, but never before has a land been so massively altered and mutilated that vast areas can never be used again or even inhabited by man or animal.... These programs should be halted immediately before further permanent damage is done to the landscape.

"Our program of defoliation, carpet bombing with B-52's and bulldozing... did not protect our soldiers or defeat the enemy, and it has done far greater damage to our ally than to the enemy.

"The cold, hard and cruel irony of it all is that South Vietnam would have been better off losing to Hanoi than winning with us. Now she faces the worst of all possible worlds with much of her land destroyed and her chances of independent survival after we leave in grave doubt at best."

PERMANENCE OF SHELL CRATERS as a feature of the landscape is demonstrated by this photograph of a large number of old shell craters in a field near Verdun in northeastern France. The photograph was made in 1964 by Alfred Eisenstaedt almost five decades after the end of the World War I Battle of Verdun. It is reproduced here with the kind permission of *Life* magazine.

III
Peaceful Applications of Arms Technology

SECTION 7: PLOWSHARES AND PRUNING HOOKS

They shall beat their swords into plowshares, and their spears into pruning hooks: nation shall not lift up sword against nation, neither shall they learn war any more.

ISAIAH *2:4*

Beat your plowshares into swords, and your pruning hooks into spears: let the weak say, I am strong.

JOEL *3:10*

INTRODUCTION

Today, as in ancient times, most technologies have two aspects: one warlike and the other peaceful. The relationship between the two is not simply a matter of each deriving from a single scientific or technologic parent. In ancient times, the same piece of metal could be pounded into either a plowshare or a sword, and even once in one form, it could, if desired, be converted to the other. With modern nuclear technology, the case is more complex and more serious. The development and use of the peaceful atom has continuously reinforced the development and use of the military atom, and vice versa. And this has happened not only by feeding new ideas and new information back and forth between the two. The mere existence of the military aspect has helped to generate public backing, particularly of a fiscal kind, for research and development in support of the peaceful aspect. And conversely, the very existence of the peaceful atom has served to justify nuclear technology in the minds of many who would be repelled by it if it could only be used for destroying and killing. Thus, the peaceful atom has helped to garner a broader political acceptance for the nuclear bomb than the latter would have received solely on its own merits.

Three important ways in which engineers and scientists seek to apply nuclear technology to peaceful purposes have been aired in *Scientific American*. These are the production of electrical energy by fission, the production of electrical energy by fusion, and the use of nuclear explosives in civil engineering projects. Examining each of these more closely throws more light on the mutual relationships set forth above.

Fission Reactors

The energy production in A-bombs and in nuclear reactors depends on a multistep process commonly referred to as a "chain reaction." The chain reaction starts when a single so-called "fissile" atom (usually an atom of uranium-235 or plutonium-239) absorbs a neutron and undergoes "fission." When that happens the atomic nucleus splits into two roughly equal pieces, releasing large amounts of energy and producing approximately two new neutrons at the same time. If that first fissioning atom was somewhere near the center of a large mass of nearly pure U-235, the two new neutrons will each be very quickly absorbed by two other U-235 nuclei. Each of these will then repeat the fission process, splitting and producing two neutrons each, and producing in this round a net of four new neutrons, which will initiate four new fissions, and so on. In a massive, solid ball of U-235 (or Pu-239), it takes roughly ten one-billionths of a second for one link in the chain. Eighty such links, each doubling the number of neutrons, would result in the fissioning of approximately one kilogram of U-235, and so once the chain starts it takes only about one microsecond for the atoms in a 100-kg-ball to be consumed with an efficiency of the order of a few percent. When so much energy is released in so short a time the result is obviously an exceedingly violent explosion. The whole process can be enormously slowed down—and for controlled use of fission energy it must be—by diluting the fissile atoms with certain other lighter atoms that do not themselves readily absorb neutrons. Carbon, beryllium, and the atoms of deuterium and oxygen that make up so-called "heavy water" are quite suitable for the purpose. Thus, when small bits of metallic uranium rich in the isotope U-235 are dispersed in a matrix of pure graphite, a form of carbon, the time it takes for a small percent of the uranium to burn up can be stretched out from microseconds to years, and the energy produced in the process can be converted to some directly useful form, such as electricity.

The enormous potential of deriving energy from U-235 is offset somewhat by its scarcity in nature. Less than one percent of natural uranium is the naturally fissile isotope U-235. The rest is in the form of U-238, naturally a nonfissile material. When a neutron is absorbed by a nucleus of the more common isotope U-238, fission does not normally occur. Instead, the U-238 is converted first to U-239, which then undergoes a radioactive decay process that eventually converts it into Pu-239. This process provides the means for converting the common but nonfissile U-238 into a material that is fissile. Since all uranium metal contains both U-235 and U-238, both of these processes always occur together and compete with each other for the neutrons that keep the chain reaction going.

By choosing a suitable mixture of U-235 and U-238, and diluting the mixture with just the right amount of nonabsorbing light atoms, it is possible to set up a condition so that one of the (approximately) two neutrons produced in each fission will produce another fission and thus keep the chain going, while the remainder of the neutrons produce Pu-239. By a remarkable coincidence, the absorption characteristics of the two isotopes of uranium, which are very different from each other, turn out to be such that the naturally occurring mixture of uranium (139 atoms of U-238 for each atom of U-235) happens to work as just described when it is highly diluted by very pure graphite or heavy water.

In summary, all nuclear reactors built to date automatically and simultaneously produce both energy and new fissile material. However, in the early years of the nuclear era, reactors were built to exploit only one or the other process, either the production of energy or of new fissile material, but not both at once. Thus, the reactors built at Hanford, Washington during World War II were built for the purpose of converting the nonfissile atom U-238 into the fissile atom Pu-239, and the energy that was simultaneously produced in the form of heat was considered a nuisance and dispersed into the Columbia River. On the other hand, the Pu-239 produced by the Hanford reactors was used to make the first and third atom bombs: the one tested in Alamogordo, New Mexico on July 16, 1945, and the one exploded over Nagasaki on August 9.

Other reactors were built solely for the production of electric power. For example, part of the light I wrote these words by was produced by energy coming from the San Diego Gas and Electric Company's reactor at San Onofre, California. In that reactor, some new fissile material is being unavoidably produced along with the energy. However, the amount of that new fissile material is much less than the amount being consumed, and its production is in no way essential to the operation of the system as a whole.

More recently, special attention has been focused on building reactors in which both the production of energy and the production of new fissile material are to be accomplished together. Such reactors are called breeder reactors and are described in two of the articles included in this section.

The first, entitled "Breeder Reactors," is by Alvin Weinberg, Director of the Oak Ridge National Laboratory. Oak Ridge, Tennessee, was one of the major sites of the wartime atomic bomb program, and after the war some of its people and facilities were brought into a single unit now known as the Oak Ridge National Laboratory (ORNL). Weinberg has been associated with ORNL since its beginning, and is widely known both as one of the most knowledgeable persons in the field of reactor technology and as one of the most articulate spokesmen in support of such work. The article was published in 1960 when breeder reactors were still a fairly new development. It describes breeder reactors, tells how they work, and explains why they are so important for the long run. The other article on breeders, entitled "Fast Breeder Reactors," was written in 1970 by Glenn T. Seaborg and Justin L. Bloom. Seaborg received the Nobel Prize in Chemistry in 1951 for his work on the transuranium elements. That work included the preparation of the first visible amounts of plutonium during World War II. He was the first scientist to be Chairman of the United States Atomic Energy Commission (1961–1971), a post he held at the time the article was written. Justin Bloom was a staff assistant to Seaborg at the time the article was written. A graduate of the California Institute of Technology, he has served in the AEC since 1956. This second article updates the one by Weinberg, and places special attention on the particular variety of breeder that uses "fast," or highly energetic, neutrons.

These articles show how breeder technology goes back to wartime roots. However, neither of them mentions the very serious matter of how breeder reactors can promote military uses and complicate attempts to control the military atom. In order to get a grasp on the special significance of breeder reactors in a world where several of the major nations base their military security on nuclear weapons, it is necessary to do some "order-of-magnitude, back-of-the-envelope" calculations.

We start with the basic fact that a reactor that produces one megawatt of *heat* consumes approximately one gram of fissile material *per day*. That means that a reactor producing one megawatt of *electricity* (at, say 40 percent efficiency) *in one year* would consume about one kilogram of fissile material.

In a breeder reactor, the amount of plutonium produced in the blanket (a term explained in the reprinted articles) is a little more than the amount consumed in the core, so we will take 1 kg as the amount of fissile material produced per year in a breeder reactor generating one megawatt of electricity. Also in order-of-magnitude terms, it takes on the average about one kilowatt of centrally produced electric power to satisfy the needs of one inhabitant of a country with a modern standard of living. Therefore, when and if all the world's several billion people reach the current level of "modernity," and if, as seems quite possible, most of their electrical power will then be produced by breeders, then the annual production rate of plutonium will be several million kilograms. No one says exactly what it takes to make a relatively simple nuclear bomb, but if we assume it is about 10 kilograms, which is the critical mass of pure metallic plutonium surrounded by an appropriate neutron reflector, we can figure that at that future time the plutonium produced each year *could* be converted into several hundred thousand bombs; or, to round off the figures, the plutonium produced by the world's breeders in three years would be enough to make one million atomic bombs. Of course, no one contends that many actually *would* be produced; the number is only useful as the starting point for further estimates of what might possibly happen. To convert all the plutonium into bombs would require shutting down virtually all central power, just as pounding every plowshare into a spear would have virtually stopped agriculture. However, converting one-tenth of one percent of the plutonium would not necessarily produce an observable effect in the power industry, but it could produce, on the basis of our estimates, one thousand clandestine bombs in three years time. And one-tenth of one percent is not really very much to lose sight of; even now the USAEC seems to be unable to keep track of plutonium to an accuracy of better than about one percent, and that is in a work environment where everyone, presumably, is trying to be cooperative.*

Most of the population of the world is in countries which do not now have nuclear weapons. That means that in the long run most of the *potential* for making clandestine bombs is in countries that do not now have them. To be sure, some of these nations are not going to be producing large amounts of nuclear energy for a long time. However, others will soon be moving into important levels of nuclear power production; these include both East and West Germany, Japan, India, Israel, and many other countries readily capable of handling the pertinent technological problems.

But the production of nuclear fuels is not the only contribution breeder reactors have to make to a clandestine bomb production program. Many of the facilities and much of the technology necessary for operating breeder reactors are similar to what are needed for producing nuclear weapons. An especially important example is the means for handling, processing, and fabricating plutonium, a very difficult material under ordinary circumstances. Therefore, a country which installs an energy production system based on breeders not only acquires a means for producing nuclear fuels, but also most of the means for fabricating them into bombs. The connection between this particular peaceful use of the atom and the military atom is really a very close one.

Fusion Reactors

The sun and most of the stars produce huge outpourings of energy by fusion—or thermonuclear—reactions. In such reactions, hydrogen is converted into helium. In order for these reactions to take place spontaneously, the hydrogen must be at a temperature of many millions of degrees. Such temperatures are found in the central regions of stars, together with pressures typically equal to many billions of atmospheres. These temperatures and pressures are produced in the first place by the gratitational contraction of the mass that forms the star, and they are then maintained by the thermonuclear reactions themselves. If the hot central region of a star was exposed directly to the vacuum of outer space, the extreme temperature would cause most of the star's heat to radiate away in a matter of seconds, the extreme pressures would cause it to blow itself apart in minutes, and as the conditions that made them possible ceased, the thermonuclear reactions would abruptly cease. The thermal insulating properties and the huge weight of the relatively cooler outer layers of the star prevent such a cataclysmic disaster from happening. The outer parts of the sun, for instance, may be thought of as an enormous blanket hundreds of thousands of miles thick. The thermal insulation provided by this blanket prevents the central core from radiating its heat away too rapidly, and the enormous weight of the blanket prevents the huge internal pressure from simply blowing the whole core apart. It is clear from the foregoing that the conditions required to initiate and maintain thermonuclear reactions in a star are utterly unlike any found naturally on the earth. However, in the case of thermonuclear bombs, a means has been worked out for producing such conditions, but only for an instant. The great temperatures and pressures do indeed cause the energy to be radiated away and the reacting mass to blow itself apart. However, the fraction of a microsecond that it takes for this to happen is a sufficiently long time to enable a substantial fraction of the hydrogen to react. The reactions in bombs proceed much more rapidly than the reactions in normal stars for two reasons. First, much more reactive forms of hydrogen—deuterium and tritium—are used in bombs. And second, the reaction rates are extremely temperature-sensitive, and higher temperatures can be used in bombs than normally exist in stable stars.

*"Plutonium Reactor Proliferation Threatens a Blackmail," *Science*, April 9, 1971.

The extreme violence of the reactions in hydrogen bombs makes it impossible to convert their huge energy output directly to useful electric power. (We will later take up ways in which, in principle, the energy from a large explosion might be indirectly converted to electricity.) However, two general methods have been suggested for producing thermonuclear energy in a less violent manner.

One is to maintain small amounts of deuterium (and, usually, tritium) at very high temperature but low densities and pressures in the form of a plasma contained in what has been termed a "magnetic bottle." Under these conditions, the energy would be produced steadily rather than explosively, and it would be converted to electrical energy by any one of several means that have been suggested. The other method is to produce a semicontinuous series of discrete micro-explosions of very tiny hydrogen bombs initiated by intense bursts of laser light.

Ideas making use of magnetic bottles were bruited about in the waning years of World War II, and some small research programs were initiated at Los Alamos by James Tuck and at Harwell, England, by Peter Thoneman soon after. However, intensive work did not begin until inspired by some most surprising reports of success coming out of Argentina. In 1951, Ronald Richter, a physicist supported by Juan Perón and working in Barriloche, Argentina, issued statements in which he claimed success in producing controlled thermonuclear reactions. He gave no details, but his claims alone inspired Lyman Spitzer, of Princeton University, to ponder how Richter might have done this. Those ponderings, according to Spitzer, are what lead to the invention of the "Stellarator," an early experimental magnetic bottle, a model of which may now be seen in the Smithsonian Institution. My subsequent conversations with Soviet scientists lead me to believe that Richter's claims provoked similar interests and led to similar experiments in the Soviet Union. Richter's claims proved to be unverifiable, and he lost the confidence of Perón shortly before Perón was deposed in 1955. The moral of this story is that half of what there is to know about a new idea is simply that it can be accomplished. That information alone is enough to inspire others to try and to succeed. Moreover, the "information" need not even be true! We shall come across another instance of this phenomenon in the discussion of peaceful uses of nuclear explosions, later in this introduction.

The ideas of magnetic-bottle fusion have been explored several times by articles in the *Scientific American,* two of which are reproduced in this chapter. The first, entitled simply "Fusion Power" was written in 1957 by Richard F. Post, one of the pioneers in the field. Post, a physicist, has been at the Lawrence Livermore Laboratory since its beginning in 1952, and has led most of the work in his field at that laboratory. The article discusses the benefits that would result from the achievement of controlled thermonuclear power, and the early ideas about how it might be done, and presents the fundamental physical ideas that underlie the various schemes.

The second article, entitled "The Prospects of Fusion Power," was published in 1971 and was written by William C. Gough and Bernard J. Eastlund. It brings the discussion of the fundamentals of "plasma physics" or the magnetic bottle up to date. It also discusses in some detail what a hypothetical fusion-power plant might look like, and it attempts to consider some of the environmental aspects of the overall problem of fusion-energy production. Gough, an electrical engineer, and Eastlund, a physicist, both joined the AEC headquarters staff soon after they received their degrees in 1952 and 1963, respectively.

Many students of arms control problems believe that a world that gets its energy from controlled magnetic-bottle thermonuclear reactors would be a world safer than one that gets its energy from breeder reactors. The argument is that breeder reactors of necessity produce large amounts of plutonium and that controlled thermonuclear reactors need not. Unfortunately, that is not the whole story. The use of either fusion reactors or fission reactors on a mass scale would result in what Gough and Eastlund (and others) refer to as a "neutron-rich" economy. In each case, most of the neutrons produced in reaction must be used to keep the cycle going—by producing new plutonium for fission or new tritium for fusion. However, the gross number of neutrons produced per megawatt-day is ten times as great in a thermonuclear reactor as it is in a breeder reactor. Therefore, potentially the amount of plutonium that could be produced and diverted to use in weapons is much greater in the world powered by the thermonuclear reactors than in the world powered by breeder reactors.

The other type of controlled release of thermonuclear energy, based on laser-induced explosions of micro-deuterium-tritium bombs, is of more recent origin. The first instance of reactions in a plasma induced by lasers was reported by N. G. Basov of the Lebedev Institute in Moscow in 1963. (It is interesting to note the first public release of information about the magnetic-bottle reactor also came from a Russian source: a speech made at Harwell by Kurchatov while accompanying Khrushchev on a visit to England in 1956.) Later reports on laser-induced fusion have also issued from laboratories in other countries but most research in the field has been surrounded by a curtain of secrecy which has effectively hidden many of the critical ideas and much of the work until very recently. In June 1971, *Scientific American* published an article entitled "Fusion by Laser" by Moshe J. Lubin and Arthur P. Fraas. The article discussed what was known and publishable at the time, and is included in this section. Shortly after its first publication, the authorities declassified many more details of the U.S. work in this field but so far no new article describing them has appeared in *Scientific American.* Lubin, a plasma physicist and aeronautical engineer who joined the faculty of the University of Rochester in 1965, has worked in plasma research since then. Fraas is an aeronautical and mechanical engineer. He has been at Oak Ridge National Laboratory since 1950, and has been Associate Director of its Reactor Division since 1957.

The basic reason for keeping fusion by laser highly classified for so long is its obvious nuclear weapons potential. Clearly, if tiny thermonuclear explosions can be produced by lasers—and without the use of fission—then perhaps bigger ones can be produced that way also. If so, then small but technologically advanced countries could produce thermonuclear weapons without making the huge initial investment generally thought necessary to produce fission-based nuclear weapons. It must be emphasized that in this particular technology, the practical means are not yet in hand for making either plowshares or swords, but should either be fashioned, the other might follow soon after.

Peaceful Uses of Nuclear Explosives (Project Plowshare)

When President Truman announced the detection of the first Soviet nuclear explosion in 1949, Tass, and Soviet U.N. delegate Vishinsky, chose to beg the question of whether it was true, and instead spoke vaguely about peaceful applications of nuclear energy, about moving mountains, and other implementations (their quotations were included in Section 1). Inspired by those implied claims—which later turned out to be without substance—some of the nuclear scientists of the staff of the Los Alamos Laboratory looked into the possibilities of "moving mountains" with nuclear explosions. A 1950 paper by Fred Reines* summarized their views and concluded that it did not look like a very practical idea. In the middle of the 1950's, shortly after the Lawrence Livermore Laboratory was founded, a group of us there—Arthur T. Biehl, Harold Brown, Gerald W. Johnson, Edward Teller, and myself—looked into the matter afresh. We decided that it was promising enough to merit further study, and we initiated what Harold Brown named Project Plowshare.* In the course of the next year or so, we uncovered a number of

**Bulletin of the Atomic Scientists,* June 1950.

*After the passage from Isaiah in the Bible; he was not then aware of the passage in Book of Joel that parodies it.

other possibilities besides moving mountains.

An article describing these possibilities is reprinted in this section. Entitled "Non-Military Uses of Nuclear Explosives," it was written in 1958 by Gerald W. Johnson and Harold Brown. At the time the ideas were being worked out, they were both Division Directors at the Lawrence Laboratory; Brown's division was responsible for the development of thermonuclear weapons, and Johnson's division was responsible for testing them. Before joining the Livermore staff, Johnson had been a senior staff member of the Armed Forces Special Weapons Project (now DASA). He later became Assistant to the Secretary of Defense for Atomic Energy, and later still joined the staff of the AEC. Brown's first postdoctoral employment was at the Radiation Laboratory of the University of California at Berkeley, and he joined at its very inception the staff from Berkeley that formed the laboratory at Livermore. Later he became, successively, Director of the Lawrence Livermore Laboratory, Director of Defense Research and Engineering, Secretary of the Air Force, and President of the California Institute of Technology.

The article describes the view of non-military uses of nuclear explosives that prevailed at the time the authors wrote. They summarize the experience gained from "Rainier"—the first underground nuclear explosion—and by extrapolation, suggest a number of applications: these include energy production, mining, oil-well stimulation, construction of water storage reservoirs, recharging of underground aquifers, creation of harbors and canals, and production of special radioactive isotopes.

Since those beginnings, much more experimental and theoretical work has been conducted in the United States and the Soviet Union. With one minor exception, no really new ideas have been developed since then, but a number of variations of those listed have been explored. In the United States, two of the most important have been a thorough theoretical examination of the problem of building a new Trans-Isthmain canal to complement the Panama Canal and experiments—"Gasbuggy" and "Rulison"—in the stimulation of gas wells. These latter experiments have shown that the production rate of a gas well can be substantially increased through use of a nuclear explosion. However, the new gas wells drilled every year number in many thousands in the United States alone, and substantial stimulation of national (or world) gas production, contrasted with the stimulation of a single well, would require the use, perhaps, of thousands of nuclear bombs per year, a condition altogether different politically from the use of an occasional explosion. The net results of almost two decades of work and study are that though many of these applications are technically feasible, political, social, and economic considerations make them, in the net, not worthwhile, even from a strictly national point of view.

The Soviets have been busy exploring non-military uses of nuclear explosions too, and have recently published the results of a number of experiments. The most notable were the creation of a reservoir in a water course in Asia, and the extinction of two major gas well fires—this latter use being the only new idea for a Plowshare application that cannot be found in the earliest Livermore studies of the 1950's. Both Soviet experiments worked in the technical sense. And the extinction of the gas well fires, unique among applications so far explored, *may* have been impossible with any other means, or so the Soviets claim. The Soviets also have a favorite canal project, just as the Americans do. The Soviet canal would take the waters in a northward-flowing river and divert them south to the Volga and hence, into the Caspian Sea. Like the Trans-Isthmian canal, the Soviet project can no doubt be accomplished without the use of nuclear explosives, but it is argued by advocates of the nuclear program that the use of nuclear explosive makes construction of such a canal cheaper.*

Internationally, the problems created by Project Plowshare have proved to by very serious. Several of the nuclear-arms-control treaties have had to be

*For more on the Soviet program, see Glenn Werth's report in *Nuclear Technology*, July 1971.

distorted because influential advocates insisted that the treaties allow for the possibility of future uses of peaceful nuclear explosives. In addition, several countries, notably India and Brazil, have used these possibilities as an argument against the Non-Proliferation Treaty. They claim the treaty does not adequately provide for these possibilities, and they have used that claim as a justification, or as an alibi, for their refusal to sign it. Similar arguments have been advanced in the United States. One of the most persistent of the arguments raised in the United States against both the actual limited test-ban and a possible comprehensive test-ban has been that such bans limit our own opportunities for the use of peaceful nuclear explosives. Arms control advocates generally agree, but most of them believe that it is worth giving up those alleged opportunities if doing so improves the chances for getting the military atom under better control.

The most thorough discussion of the technology of Project Plowshare can be found in a 1969 book entitled *The Constructive Uses of Nuclear Explosives* by Edward Teller, Wilson K. Talley, Gary H. Higgins, and Gerald W. Johnson. Philip Morrison's review of that book is included as the last reading in this book.

34

Breeder Reactors

Reactors that produce more fuel than they consume make it feasible to "burn the rocks," that is, to utilize the vast supply of uranium and thorium contained not in rich ores but in rocks such as granite

ALVIN M. WEINBERG

January 1960

Even the gloomiest of contemporary Malthusians, projecting an increasingly desolate future for a rising world population, have had to concede that there is one ray of hope. If the controlled fusion of the heavy isotopes of hydrogen can be engineered on a large scale, future generations will have available in the oceans a supply of energy that will last for the lifetime of the solar system. Workers in several nations have been engaged in an effort to learn how to "burn the sea." They have learned a great deal about the behavior of matter at the very high temperatures associated with thermonuclear reactions. But it is not yet possible to assume that a successful thermonuclear reactor can be developed.

Even if such reactors cannot be built, however, mankind will not be condemned to an impasse in the problem of population *v.* resources. Closer at hand is another energy resource about as abundant as that contained in the sea. This resource consists of the enormous quantities of uranium and thorium dispersed in trace amounts throughout the rocky crust of the earth. To extract the energy the rocks contain we can draw upon an existing technology. Nuclear reactors that operate on the controlled fission of the heavy elements are already generating electrical power. We need only to perfect the breeder reactor—the reactor that "breeds" more nuclear fuel than it consumes—and we shall literally be able to "burn the rocks."

The realization that an essentially inexhaustible source of energy lies almost within our grasp has come surprisingly late in the evolution of nuclear power. It was not until 1955, at the first Geneva Conference on the Peaceful Uses of Atomic Energy, that Harrison Brown and L. T. Silver of the California Institute of Technology demonstrated that the trace amounts of radioactive elements present in the granite of the continents could vastly multiply the supply of fissionable material accessible in ores. This conclusion has been supported by Farrington Daniels and his colleagues at the University of Wisconsin.

As a result of these studies and the progress that has been made in development of breeder reactors, there is no longer any doubt that nuclear breeding offers a long-term solution to the energy problem. With the full significance of nuclear breeding now becoming apparent, the Atomic Energy Commission's research program aimed at furthering the development of breeder reactors takes on new significance: If the program is successful, we shall be able to satisfy mankind's hunger for energy, even though we never learn how to burn the sea.

Breeding Cycles

Breeder reactors have been built or are under construction in the U. S., Great Britain and the U.S.S.R. The first, the Experimental Breeder Reactor No. 1 (EBR-1) at the National Reactor Testing Station in Arco, Idaho, was also the first reactor in the world to generate electricity (on December 20, 1951). Its successor, EBR-2, is now being built at the same site, and a third reactor, the Enrico Fermi Fast Breeder, is under construction near Detroit. The U.S.S.R. has built two breeders at Obninsk, some 100 miles from Moscow. And last November the Dounreay reactor, the first breeder

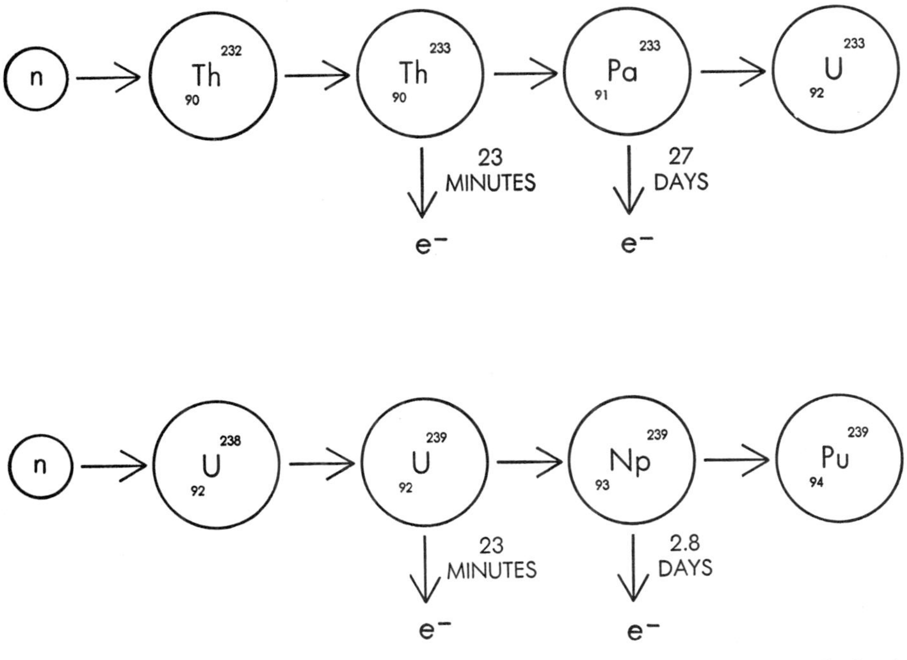

BREEDING CYCLES are based on two sets of nuclear reactions. In the thorium cycle (*top*) an atom of fertile thorium 232 absorbs a neutron and emits a beta particle (e^-) to become protoactinium, which spontaneously emits a beta particle to become fissionable uranium 233. In uranium cycle (*bottom*) fertile uranium 238 absorbs a neutron and emits a beta particle to become neptunium, which then undergoes beta decay to become fissionable plutonium 239.

LARGEST BREEDER REACTOR designed to produce electrical power is the Enrico Fermi Atomic Power Plant, now under construction near Detroit. It is expected to produce 300,000 kilowatts of heat and 100,000 kilowatts of electricity. The photograph shows the top edge of the shield tank (*large circle*) and inside it the circular shield plug that caps the reactor vessel. The flanged opening in the right side of the plug is for the reactor control-rods; the fuel-handling mechanism protrudes from the left side of the plug.

in Great Britain, began to operate at low power.

Most breeder reactors are now fueled with uranium 235, but ultimately they will burn the uranium 233 and plutonium 239 they produce. The fission of each atom of these fuels liberates, on the average, two fast (high-energy) neutrons. One of the neutrons must trigger another fission to maintain the nuclear chain-reaction; the other neutron is available to breed a new fissionable atom, that is, to transform a "fertile" isotope of one of the heavy elements into a fissionable isotope. The fertile raw materials for breeder reactions are thorium 232 (which is transmuted into uranium 233) and uranium 238 (which is transmuted into plutonium 239). As the most abundant isotopes of their elements, thorium 232 and uranium 238 are respectively present in an average of about 12 and three parts per million in the various kinds of granite.

In the thorium-uranium cycle an atom of thorium 232 captures a neutron and decays spontaneously in two steps into fissionable uranium 233 [*see top reaction on page 349*]. Similarly, in the uranium-plutonium cycle an atom of uranium 238 captures a neutron and decays in two steps into fissionable plutonium 239 [*see bottom reaction on page 349*].

With a newly bred fissionable atom to replace the one destroyed in the original fission reaction, a breeder can operate with no net loss of fissionable material. One measure of the performance of a breeder reactor is its "breeding ratio": the ratio of fissionable atoms produced to fissionable atoms destroyed. If the ratio is greater than one, the reactor will breed more nuclear fuel than it consumes; if the ratio is less than one, the fissionable fuel must be replenished to keep the reactor going.

Theoretically a breeder reactor can achieve a breeding ratio of one if it produces two neutrons for each fissionable atom destroyed. In practice, however, the neutron economy is always upset by the absorption of neutrons in the control rods and structural materials of the reactor and in the neutron-absorbing isotopes (such as xenon 135 and samarium 149) formed by the fission of uranium or plutonium. Moreover, some newly bred fissionable material is lost in the chemical processing necessary to get rid of fission products and to recover the fissionable and fertile material not yet burned or bred. Because of these losses, it is generally believed that a reactor must produce at least 2.2 neutrons per fissionable atom destroyed in order to

EXTERIOR VIEW shows the Fermi plant with Lake Michigan in the background. The steel dome that houses the reactor is 120 feet high and 72 feet in diameter. The adjoining buildings contain power-plant equipment such as heat exchangers and turbogenerators.

FIRST BREEDER REACTOR, the Experimental Breeder Reactor No. 1 (EBR-1), was built in 1951 by the Argonne National Laboratory. It was the first reactor to produce electrical power, and is still in operation at the National Reactor Testing Station at Arco, Idaho.

achieve a breeding ratio of one or better.

Many workers have seriously doubted the possibility of achieving a breeding ratio well above one, especially in the thorium-uranium cycle, because fissionable atoms do not always fission when they absorb a neutron. As Boyce D. McDaniel discovered during the wartime development of the atomic bomb at the Los Alamos Scientific Laboratory, both uranium 233 and plutonium 239 participate in so-called radiative-capture reactions, in which they absorb a neutron and emit a gamma ray to become the nonfissionable isotopes uranium 234 and plutonium 240. In addition to destroying fuel, radiative-capture reactions use up neutrons and so reduce the reactor's ability to breed.

In general the competition between fission and capture reactions tends to favor fission as the energy of the neutron that triggers the reaction increases. This consideration carries more weight in the uranium-plutonium cycle than it does in the thorium-uranium cycle. When a nucleus of plutonium 239 absorbs a thermal (low-energy) neutron, it fissions and liberates an average of only 2.09 neutrons; when it absorbs a fairly fast neutron (one with an energy of about 500,000 electron volts), it liberates an average of 2.7 neutrons—well above the 2.2-neutron minimum necessary to achieve a breeding ratio of one. In the thorium-uranium cycle, on the other hand, a thermal neutron produces an average of about 2.3 neutrons when it is absorbed by a uranium-233 nucleus, but a fast neutron increases the yield only to 2.4. The values in the thorium-uranium cycle are so close to the 2.2-

LIQUID-FUEL REACTOR, the Homogeneous Reactor Experiment No. 2 (HRE-2) was originally designed as a prototype of a liquid-fuel breeder. The core of the reactor is inside the 74-inch spherical blast shield which is visible at top center. The pipes on the shield are cooling coils. The fuel burned in the reactor consists of uranyl sulfate dissolved in heavy water. In the later stages of construction the reactor sphere was lowered into the pit directly in front of it; the reactor and the pit were then covered by slabs of shielding.

neutron minimum that a great deal of work has been done at the Oak Ridge National Laboratory and elsewhere to determine precisely how many neutrons are emitted (the so-called eta value) when a uranium-233 nucleus is fissioned by a thermal neutron. The thermal-neutron eta value of uranium 233 is now firmly established as 2.28. It is one of the most accurately measured of all nuclear constants.

The eta values for the uranium-plutonium and thorium-uranium cycles have determined the whole strategy of breeder-reactor design. Because there is obviously little to be gained by using fast neutrons to trigger the chain reaction in thorium breeders, these reactors are designed to breed with thermal neutrons, and are often called thermal breeders. Uranium-plutonium breeders, on the other hand, are designed to take advantage of the abundance of neutrons produced in fast-neutron fission; these reactors are accordingly known as fast breeders.

On the basis of breeding ratio alone, the fast breeder would appear to have a decisive superiority over the thermal breeder. As the respective eta values of the two breeding cycles suggest, the fast breeder has a theoretical breeding ratio of 1.6, and the thermal breeder has a ratio of only 1.1. There is, however, another important consideration. This is the "doubling time": the time it takes a reactor to double its original inventory of fissionable material. The doubling time is determined by two factors. One of them is of course the breeding ratio. The other is the specific power of the reactor, that is, its output in kilowatts per kilogram of fissionable material tied up in the reactor and in the chemical plant that processes its fuel. Specific power is thus a measure of the rate at which fuel is burned in the reactor. Since the burning of each fissionable atom results in a certain fractional gain (determined by the breeding ratio) in the over-all inventory of fuel, the higher the rate of burning—that is, the higher the specific power—the shorter the doubling time. The ideal reactor must therefore have a high specific power as well as a high breeding-ratio.

Unfortunately this ideal can only be approximated. The fast reactor has a high breeding-ratio, as nuclear physics shows. But engineering considerations give it an inherently low specific power. If a fast reactor is to breed at all, the fuel in its core must not be greatly diluted by coolants or structural materials; these decrease the energy of fast neutrons to the point where many are lost in useless radiative-capture reactions. The only way to prevent such losses is to design a more compact core containing more concentrated fuel. But this raises serious obstacles to the extraction of heat from the reactor, an operation necessary both to obtain power and to keep the core from melting. For efficient heat-transfer the fuel should be as dilute as possible, a requirement that can be met only by the sacrifice of fast neutrons. Thus the fast breeder is faced with the dilemma of "unusable compactness" *v.* "unworkable diluteness."

In contrast, thermal breeders are inherently dilute systems and so have excellent heat-transfer properties. The fuel in the core is always mixed with large quantities of coolant as well as with a moderator (such as graphite, beryllium or heavy water) and slows fast neutrons down to thermal energies. The thermal breeder thus has a relatively high specific power, perhaps five times as high as the fast breeder. This is enough to offset the lower breeding-ratio of the thermal system. On the basis of present data both types of reactor should have a dou-

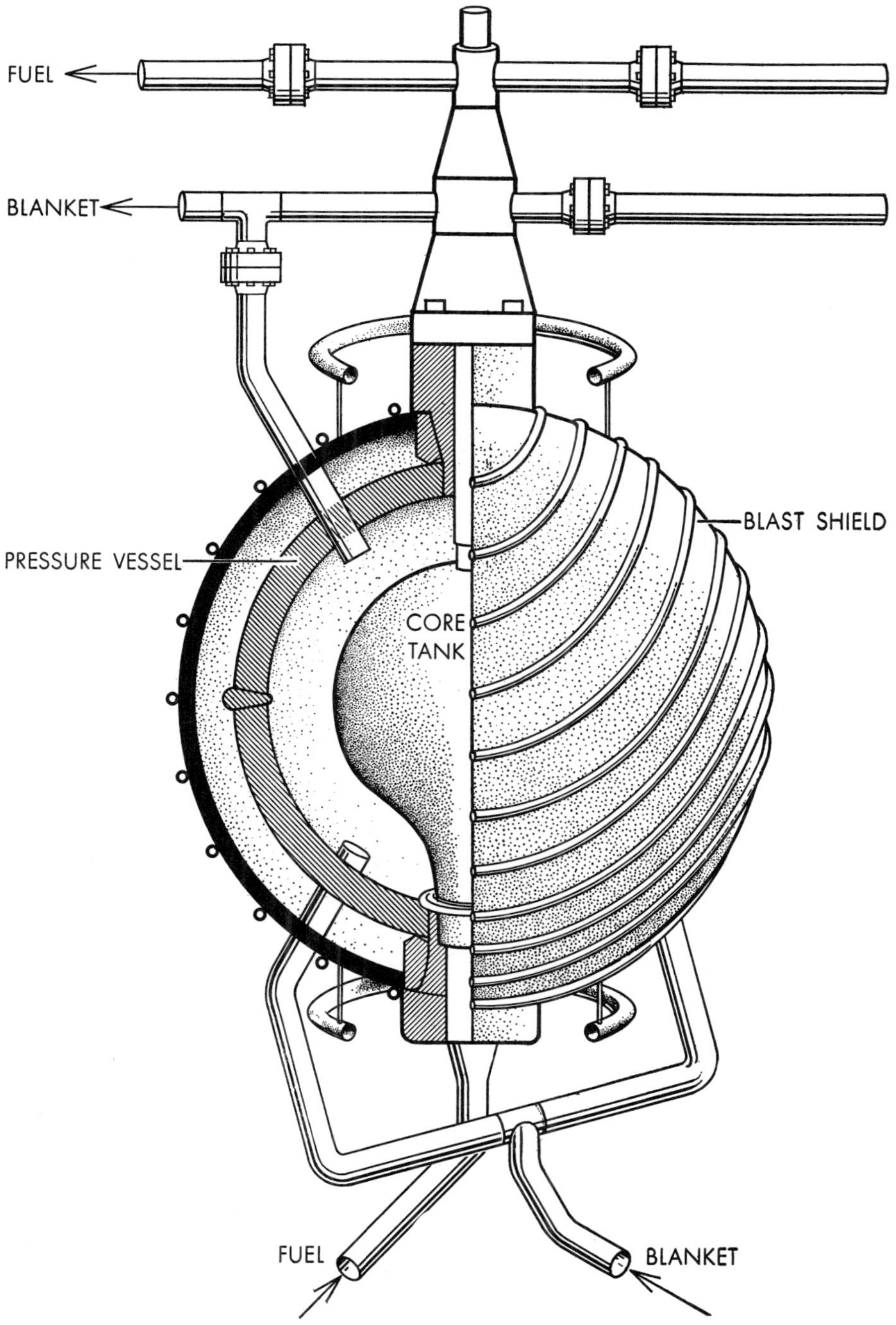

CORE OF HRE-2 is a pear-shaped tank 32 inches in diameter. It is surrounded by a steel pressure-vessel and a blast shield. Liquid fuel is pumped into the core from below and leaves at the top. The blanket, a slurry of thorium oxide suspended in heavy water, was to fill the space between core tank and pressure vessel, but a hole in the core prevented this.

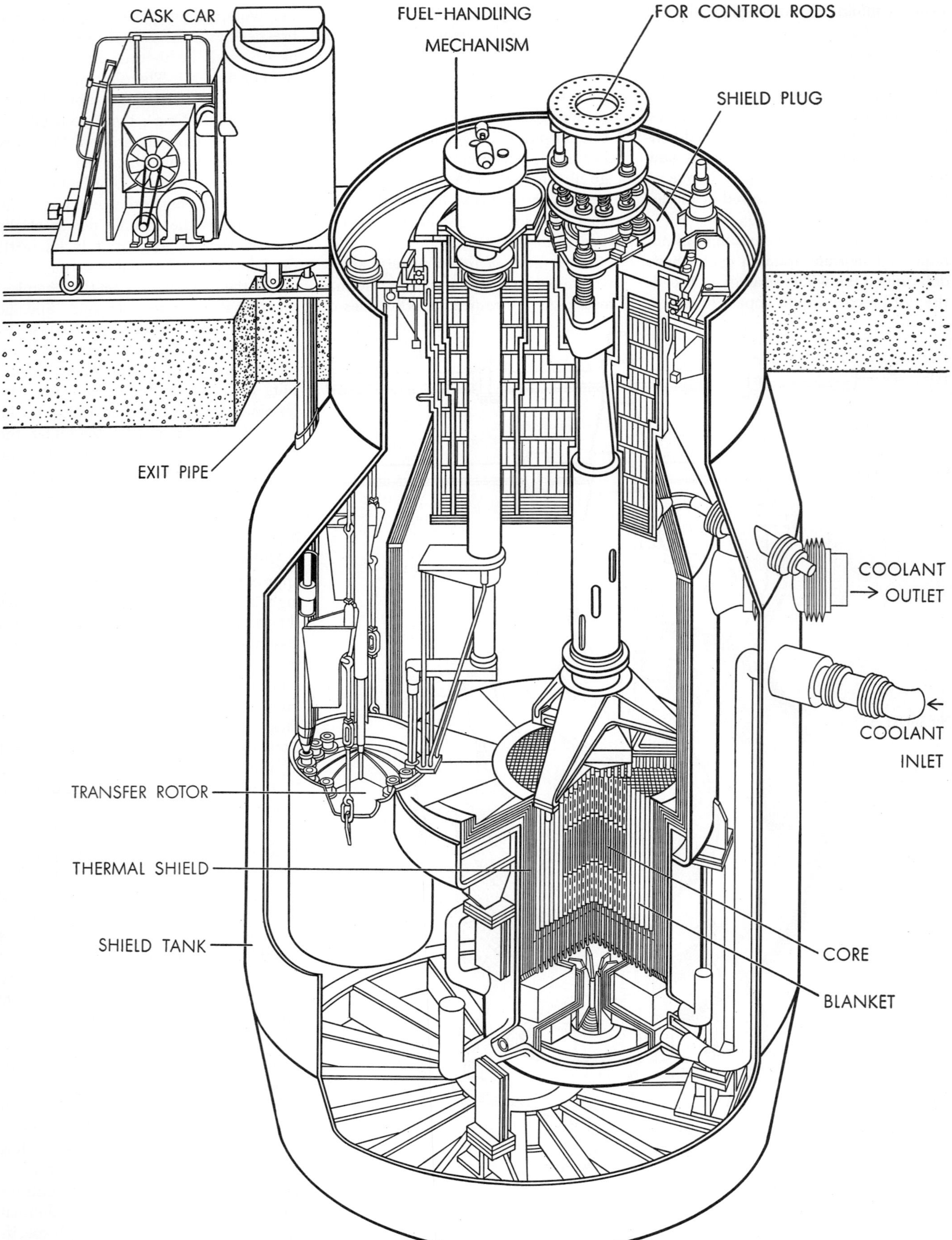

CUTAWAY VIEW of Fermi reactor shows the interior of the 40-foot shield tank with the 36-foot reactor vessel inside it. Fuel elements can be removed from the sodium-filled reactor vessel by the fuel-handling mechanism at center, which transfers the elements from the core to the transfer rotor. The elements leave the reactor via the exit pipe and cask car. By reversing the procedure, new fuel and blanket elements can be added to the reactor. Shield plug at top contains cans of neutron-absorbing borated graphite.

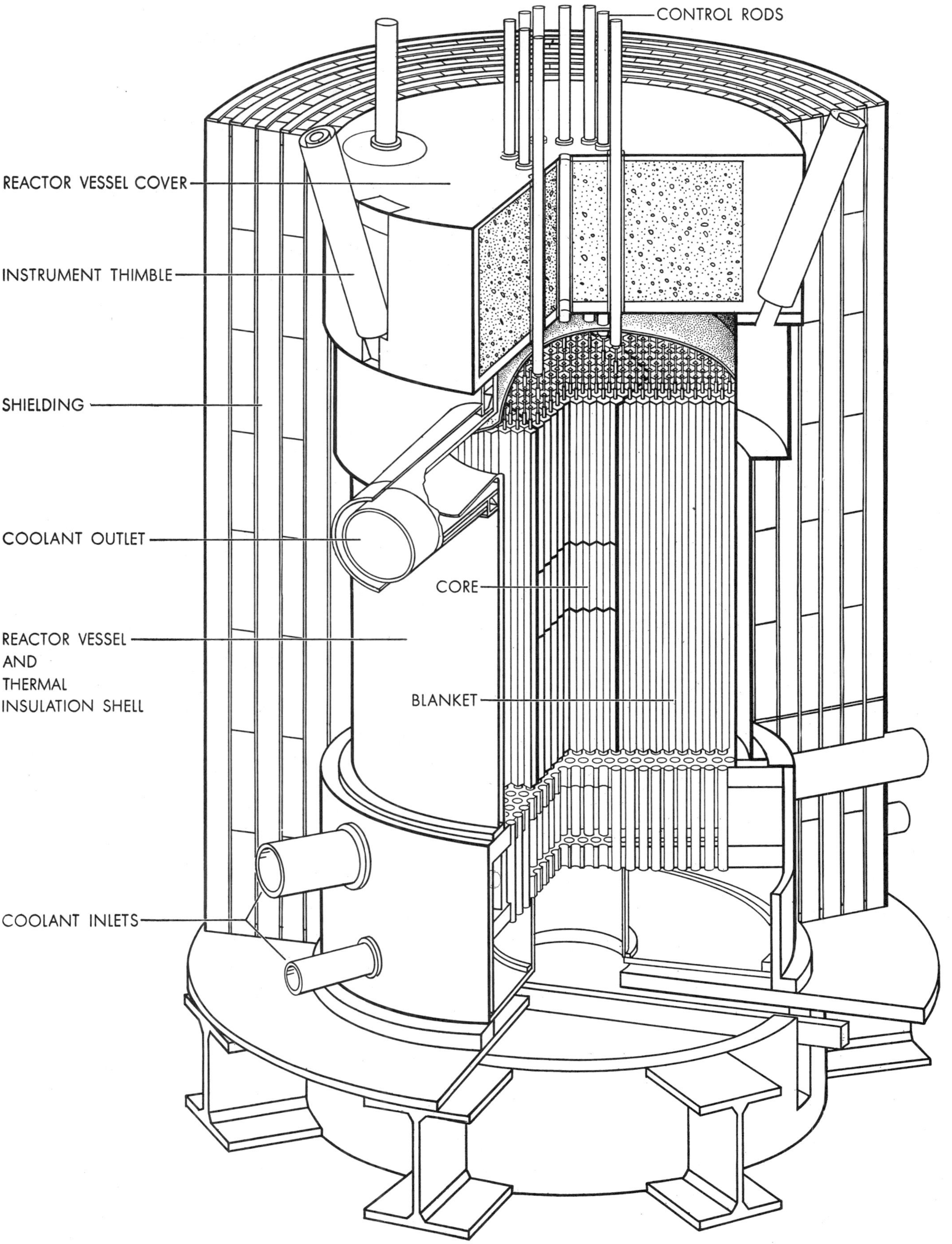

CUTAWAY OF EBR-2 shows the interior of the 13-foot reactor vessel. Sodium coolant enters at the bottom of the reactor and is pumped upward through the core (*inner hexagonal area*) and the surrounding blanket. The drive shafts of the control rods can be seen protruding through the concrete-filled reactor vessel cover. The shielding on the sides of the reactor is canned borated graphite.

NEW BRITISH BREEDER was recently completed at Dounreay, on the coast of Scotland. The reactor is housed in a steel sphere 135 feet in diameter (*center*); the surrounding buildings contain electrical generating equipment. The reactor is expected to produce

bling time of 10 to 20 years. It should be emphasized that the fast breeder gets its name from the fast neutrons that do its breeding and not from the speed at which it breeds.

Fast Breeders

The compromises that must go into the design of a fast breeder are well demonstrated in the Fermi reactor, an engineering tour de force. Like all breeders, the Fermi reactor has a blanket of fertile material that surrounds a core of fissionable fuel [*see illustrations on pages 352 and 358*]. Both core and blanket are submerged in a pool of liquid sodium, the favorite coolant for fast breeders because it does not sharply decrease the energy of fast neutrons as most other coolants do. The fuel in the core is a mixture of metallic uranium 238 and uranium 235, alloyed with a small amount of molybdenum to improve resistance to radiation. The alloy is fabricated into thin zirconium-clad fuel pins, which are arrayed side by side and far enough apart to permit coolant to flow upward between them. When the molten sodium leaves the core (at a temperature of about 400 degrees centigrade), it is pumped to specially designed heat exchangers, where it converts water into high-pressure steam. The steam drives a series of turbogenerators that produce 100,000 kilowatts of electricity, and the cooled sodium is cycled back through the core.

The conflict of compactness *v.* diluteness is evident in the design of the reactor core. Most of the reactor's 300,000 kilowatts of heat are produced in a cylinder not much bigger than a large garbage can; the cylinder is about a meter high, a meter in diameter and has a total volume of about 600 liters. The thermal-power density in the core thus reaches a level of about 500 watts per cubic cen-

60,000 kilowatts of heat and 15,000 kilowatts of electricity. It began to operate at low power last November and will be gradually worked up to full power over a period of months. The Dounreay reactor is a solid-fuel breeder that will produce plutonium 239.

timeter—one of the highest values for any reactor in the world. But considering the amount of fuel in the core (485 kilograms of uranium 235), the specific power is actually quite low. It is expected that the reactor will yield only about 650 kilowatts per kilogram of fissionable material. A full-scale thermal breeder, by contrast, would deliver about 2,000 to 3,000 kilowatts per kilogram.

The specific power of fast breeders would be even lower if the designers did not take advantage of the fact that fast neutrons can trigger the fission of uranium 238, a reaction that produces additional neutrons. By mixing uranium 238 with the fissionable material in the core, the breeding ratio can be increased by as much as .3. The resulting dilution of the fuel also serves to improve the heat-transfer characteristics of the core, increasing the reactor's thermal efficiency and easing the strain that the high power-density places on the fuel elements.

Despite these inherent engineering difficulties, fast breeders have attracted the major portion of the world's research effort. This is only natural, because the breeding ratio in the uranium-plutonium cycle is so large that there can be no question that fast-neutron breeding is possible. Almost every nation that has a reactor-development program has given serious consideration to building a fast breeder.

The first fast breeder, EBR-1 (designed and built by a group headed by Walter H. Zinn, then director of the Argonne National Laboratory), is rated at 1,400 kilowatts of heat and about 200 kilowatts of electricity [*see illustration at bottom of page 351*]. Several years ago, during experiments designed to test its response to temporary overheating, the core of the EBR-1 melted. But the reactor has since been rebuilt and has operated routinely since 1957.

As its thermal rating suggests, the

EBR-1 is much smaller than the Fermi reactor. Its core is about as large as a football and is fueled with stainless-steel-clad rods of almost pure uranium 235, about .3 inch in diameter. The blanket contains rods of uranium 238 about an inch in diameter, also clad with stainless steel. Because EBR-1 is fueled with uranium 235 instead of plutonium 239, it achieved a breeding ratio of only about one (instead of the theoretically possible 1.6). Nevertheless, the fact that the reactor operated reliably at reasonable temperature and power while achieving a significant breeding ratio was a major milestone in nuclear-energy development.

Encouraged by the success of EBR-1, several groups are now constructing much larger fast breeders. The Fermi reactor is being built by Atomic Power Development Associates, Inc., a consortium of public utilities and manufacturers, and the Argonne National Laboratory is currently completing the construction of EBR-2 [*see illustration on opposite page*]. Designed to yield 62,500 kilowatts of heat and 15,000 kilowatts of electricity, EBR-2 resembles the newly completed Dounreay reactor in Scotland, which is rated at 60,000 kilowatts of heat and 15,000 kilowatts of electricity [*see illustration on pages 356 and 357*]. Of the two breeders in the U.S.S.R., the smaller, rated at 100 kilowatts of heat, has been dismantled; the other, the BR-5, has a thermal rating of 5,000 kilowatts. All of these reactors are basically similar. They are sodium-cooled and are loaded initially with uranium 235 in the expectation that they will be fueled with plutonium when they have been thoroughly tested. The single exception is the 5,000-kilowatt Soviet reactor, which has begun operation using ceramic plutonium-oxide fuel.

So far there have been no completely satisfactory estimates of the cost of producing electrical power in these early experimental breeders. It is generally conceded, however, that the cost will be hopelessly high in comparison with that of conventional power. Much of the cost of nuclear power can be dismissed as being due to the inevitable expense of developing a new technology; we can expect these costs to fall as we gain more experience. Fast breeders are nonetheless beset by two technical problems which are inherent in their design and which must be solved before they can produce economical power. One is "high holdup": the fact that their low specific power ties up large quantities of fissionable and fertile material. The other is "low burnup," that is, their consumption of only a small percentage of the fissionable material contained in each loading.

Fast reactors must contend with low burnup so long as their fast-neutron economy requires the use of solid metallic fuel. Only about 15 per cent of the fissionable material in a solid-fuel reactor can be burned before the fuel rods become so swollen, warped and weakened by radiation and poisoned by fission products that they must be replaced and reprocessed [see "Reactor Fuel Elements," by James F. Schumar; SCIENTIFIC AMERICAN, February, 1959]. This means that each gram of fuel must go through seven cycles of reprocessing before it is at last consumed. At an initial cost of $15 per gram and a cost of $3 per gram for each reprocessing, the cost of burning one gram of uranium 235 comes to $35. The fast reactor thus runs up a fuel cost of about seven mills per kilowatt hour, perhaps two to three times the energy cost of conventional fuel.

Of course the cost of reprocessing can be charged against the value of the new plutonium fuel bred in the reactor, but this is not enough. Fast breeding will not be economical until fuel elements can be made to withstand much longer burnup, or the cost of reprocessing is reduced, or both. Work in both of these directions is proceeding at the Argonne National Laboratory. Fuel elements made of "fissium," an alloy of uranium and rare earths, seem to be less susceptible to radiation damage than uranium-molybdenum alloy. Greatly simplified fuel-recovering processes and new techniques for refabricating fuel elements, particularly the substitution of casting for machining, promise to reduce costs. Radiation-resistant plutonium-oxide ceramic fuel elements, similar to those in the Soviet BR-5 reactor, are also being tested.

The high holdup of fissionable and fertile material is a problem that stems even more directly from the essential nature of the fast-breeder cycle. In addition to the 485 kilograms of fissionable material in its core, the Fermi reactor will tie up some 40,000 kilograms of fertile material in its blanket. Such large inventories of material will represent an even heavier capital requirement when present high-grade uranium ores have been exhausted. In the Age of Granite envisioned by Harrison Brown, the cost of extracting fertile uranium 238 from rocks will force its price far above the present $5 per pound. With an inventory of half a ton of uranium 238 in the blanket for each 1,000 kilowatts of electrical output, the total capital cost of the blanket of the Fermi reactor is now $2.50 per kilowatt. The cost of extracting uranium in trace amounts from granite is likely to multiply this figure to a prohibitive value, perhaps to $500 per kilowatt of capacity. To the high fixed charge imposed by this capital burden must be added the high operating cost attributable to low burnup.

Undoubtedly future improvements in technology will reduce the inventory. But present circumstances offer a neat way around the difficulty that can reduce at least the start-up costs of nuclear breeding. The reactor can be stocked initially with cheap uranium from high-grade ores, and then be kept burning indefinitely with more costly uranium from low-grade sources to replace the minute amounts of material consumed in each burnup cycle. I can even foresee a situation in which the cheap uranium tied up as inventory in nonbreeding reactors will be transferred to breeders; this may occur when the cost of uranium goes so high that it is no longer economical to burn it in nonbreeders.

Thermal Breeders

The high specific power of the thermal breeders sets up a considerably more modest capital requirement for inventory of fuel and fertile material. Thermal breeders also circumvent the burnup problem by "homogenizing" the fuel and coolant, that is, by mixing them together in a fuel solution or by suspending finely divided fuel in a slurry. With the fuel in fluid rather than solid form, radiation damage no longer limits the burnup that can be achieved before the fuel must be reprocessed. The burnup limit is imposed by the much less stringent requirement of keeping the concentration of neutron-absorbing fission products down to an acceptable level.

Two high-power thermal reactors—the Homogeneous Reactor Experiments No. 1 and No. 2 (HRE-1 and HRE-2) have been built at Oak Ridge. The HRE-2 was originally intended to be a small-scale prototype of a thermal thorium breeder [*see illustration on page 352*]. The core is a pear-shaped zirconium-alloy tank 32 inches in diameter, through which a uranium-235 solution (uranyl sulfate in heavy water) is pumped at a pressure of 2,000 pounds per square inch. The shape of the tank allows a critical mass of fuel to accumulate, starting a nuclear chain-reaction. The heat generated by the reaction is carried away by the fluid fuel, which leaves the core at a maximum temperature of 300 degrees C. and delivers the heat to a 5,000-kilowatt heat exchanger. A small steam turbogenerator converts 300 kilowatts of the heat to electricity, and the rest is dumped into the atmosphere.

The core tank is surrounded by a heavy steel pressure-vessel. The vessel is four feet in diameter, leaving a space between it and the core. Through this space was eventually to be pumped a slurry of thorium oxide in heavy water, constituting a blanket in which uranium 233 was to be bred. Unfortunately local overheating during early power-runs melted a small hole in the core tank, allowing the uranyl sulfate fuel to mix with the blanket. For this reason HRE-2 has operated since April, 1958, as a one-region reactor with fuel in both core and blanket.

Because the radioactive fuel contaminates the entire circulating system, the HRE-2 reactor and all its cooling equipment, including the pumps and heat exchanger, are enclosed in a completely shielded steel box. During the past year and a half the reactor has been run at power levels up to 5,000 kilowatts for months at a time; during these runs it has never been necessary to enter the box for maintenance. Although this suggests that the circulating-fuel technology has been developed to the point where larger reactors are feasible, a number of engineering problems must be solved before it will be prudent to build a full-scale homogeneous thorium breeder. For example, the slurry must be well stirred throughout the system to keep it from settling out and forming cakes of fuel and fission products. Damage to the zirconium core tank by the corrosive fuel-solution is also something of a problem, although corrosion in the greater part of the system that is made of stainless steel is gratifyingly low. Still another problem is represented by the fact that the homogeneous fuel-and-coolant mixture tends to separate into two solutions under intense radiation: one rich in uranyl sulfate and the other rich in heavy water. The higher concentration of fuel in the uranium-rich solution accelerates the fission reaction, leading to local overheating and possible melting of reactor components.

None of these difficulties is unsolvable, however, and all are being vigorously attacked. The experience now being gained with HRE-2 should prove directly useful to the designers of liquid-fuel thermal breeders. Moreover, because HRE-2 is the first reactor in which the entire circulating system is contaminated with radioactivity, experience gained with it should be indirectly useful in the development of other reactors with contaminated cooling systems. Among these are the advanced gas-cooled, solid-fuel thermal breeders now being studied in Great Britain and the U. S.

The gas-cooled, solid-fuel thermal breeder is the product of an entirely different approach to the achievement of nuclear breeding. Up to this point we have been discussing what might be called the "egghead" approach. This involves starting from scratch and designing a completely new reactor patterned after the physicists' concept of how a breeder should look. The opposite, or "hardheaded," school argues that breeders should be developed by starting with existing, well-engineered nonbreeder designs (such as that of the gas-cooled British Calder Hall reactors) and improving the performance in increments, saving a tenth of a neutron here and there until the reactor has been converted into a breeder. As might be expected, the two strategies tend to overlap. All the breeders built so far, however, can be considered to be primarily egghead reactors. In the next 10 years we can expect to see a number of hardheaded reactors transformed into breeders or at least near-breeders.

Energy Economics

It seems obvious that in the long run the world will be able to use breeder energy only if it is cheaper, more abundant or more accessible than any other energy source. One of the most serious potential competitors is solar energy. But the diluteness and unpredictability of sunlight argue against it as a primary energy-source in large power stations, especially because such a station would involve a formidable capital investment. It is estimated that solar energy will require an initial investment of from $1,000 to $2,000 per kilowatt. To compete successfully, an alternative energy system should cost less than, say, $1,500 per kilowatt. Here breeder reactors have a marked advantage, for their capital cost should be no more than $750 per kilowatt even if their fertile material comes from low-grade sources such as

EBR-2, the successor to EBR-1, is now under construction at the National Reactor Testing Station in Idaho. The reactor is housed in the steel dome at left; adjoining it is a power plant that will use the reactor's heat to produce 15,000 kilowatts of electricity.

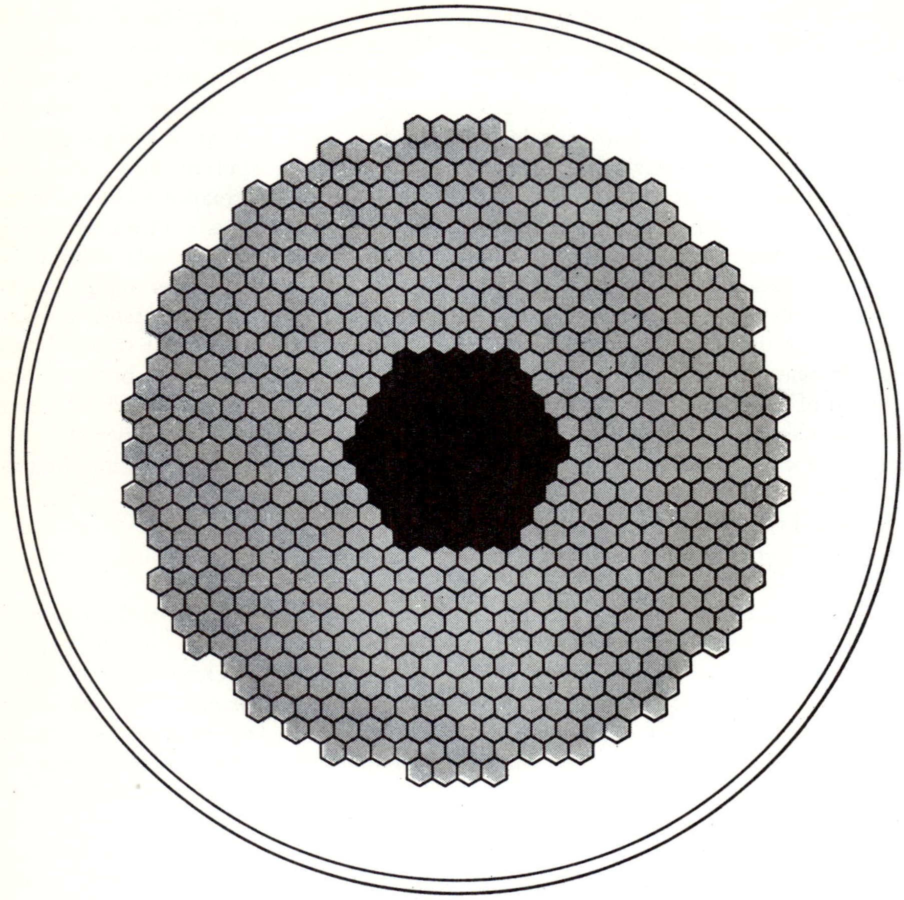

CORE AND BLANKET OF EBR-2 are typical of those in fast breeders. The core (*darker color*) consists of hexagonal fuel elements containing uranium 235; the surrounding blanket elements (*lighter color*) contain uranium 238. The small hatched hexagons represent the control rods that govern the rate of the nuclear reaction; black hexagons are safety rods.

granite. This estimate drops to about $200 to $300 per kilowatt if the reactor is started with cheap uranium from high-grade ores and kept burning with the relatively expensive materials from low-grade sources.

Controlled fusion, if it is ever achieved, will also be a strong competitor. The raw material for fusion is relatively easy to recover from the sea, the present cost of deuterium being 30 cents per gram. Burned in a fusion reactor at 25 per cent thermal efficiency, this amount of deuterium would yield about 24,000 kilowatt-hours of electricity. The burnup charge works out to about .015 mill per kilowatt-hour. This is a negligible figure, and one that should always remain negligible, because the extraction of deuterium from the sea will not significantly reduce its concentration for eons to come. Assuming, as Harrison Brown does in his book *The Next Hundred Years*, that the world will finally settle down to an energy consumption of 40 billion kilowatts per year (20 times the present rate), the energy reservoir in either the rocks or the sea will last for more than 10 billion years.

The long-term raw-material costs for breeder power are almost as clearly defined as the costs for fusion power. Because the breeder operates with no net loss of fissionable fuel, the raw materials that are actually consumed are the abundant fertile isotopes, thorium 232 or uranium 238, rather than the much rarer and far more expensive uranium 235 by which the reactions are first ignited. According to Brown, a ton of granite could be processed for $1 to $2.25, and this would lead to a cost of 30 to 80 cents per gram for fertile material. Other estimates suggest that $1 per gram is more realistic. Even at this price, however, the burnup cost would be only .18 mill per kilowatt-hour. Although such a cost is not quite negligible, it is a small fraction of the total cost of generating a kilowatt-hour of electricity.

It is conceivable that the burnup cost could go still higher, because relatively little of the earth's crust is accessible to mining: we should not count the sea bottom, nor rocks more than three kilometers below the surface, nor those heavily overlaid with thorium- and uranium-poor sediments. Yet even a 10-fold increase in fuel cost (to $10 per gram) would still leave the burnup cost at 1.8 mills per kilowatt-hour, a figure comparable to the present energy-cost of coal.

The scale of the necessary mining (or quarrying) operation would also be comparable to our present coal-mining efforts. To support an energy economy 20 times larger than our present one, we would have to obtain 40 tons or so of fertile material a day. This would require mining about 10 million tons of rock, not much more than the world's daily coal and lignite production (in 1953) of approximately six million tons.

Perhaps the strongest argument for burning the sea instead of the rocks is that fusion is a "cleaner" process than fission. Admittedly the most troublesome aspect of rock-burning is the question of what to do with the huge quantities of radioactive wastes produced by fission reactors. The methods of waste disposal now being studied involve using the earth, whence the unburned fissionable materials came, as a grave for radioactive wastes. Salt domes, deep natural wells and artificially created cracks in the earth's crust have all been suggested as possible disposal sites, but it is premature to say that any of them will prove entirely satisfactory. Nevertheless it is encouraging to note that a committee recently established by the American Petroleum Institute to examine geologic methods of waste disposal has endorsed the feasibility of the proposed deep-well and salt-dome disposal schemes.

With fusion reactors the waste problem would be considerably less severe. But to compare fission and fusion reactors is a highly speculative pastime, for we have yet to show that we can develop a fusion reactor to burn any fraction of the deuterium in the sea. Burning uranium, on the other hand, is a rather routine process. It has become so routine, in fact, that the solution of mankind's long-term energy problem by breeding, instead of by thermonuclear fission, seems almost inelegant. We need only the solutions to certain tedious engineering difficulties rather than brilliant flashes of scientific insight. As academician N. N. Bolgolyubov, head of the Institute of Theoretical Physics at the Soviet Joint Nuclear Center, said to me recently, "breeding constitutes a trivial solution to man's ultimate energy problem." Perhaps it is because of the essential simplicity implied by the word "trivial" that those of us who are interested in breeding find it such an exciting technological development.

Fast Breeder Reactors

Nuclear reactors that use fast neutrons to produce more fuel than they consume are a promising approach to producing electric power with a minimum of strain on energy resources and the environment

GLENN T. SEABORG and JUSTIN L. BLOOM

November 1970

The need to generate enormous additional amounts of electric power while at the same time protecting the environment is taking form as one of the major social and technological problems that our society must resolve over the next few decades. The Federal Power Commission has estimated that during the next 30 years the American power industry will have to add some 1,600 million kilowatts of electric generating capacity to the present capacity of 300 million kilowatts. As for the environment, the extent of public concern over improving the quality of air, water and the landscape hardly needs elaboration, except for one point that is often overlooked: it will take large amounts of electrical energy to run the many kinds of purification plants that will be needed to clean up the air and water and to recycle wastes.

A related problem of equal magnitude is the rational utilization of the nation's finite reserves of coal, oil and gas. In the long term they will be far more precious as sources of organic molecules than as sources of heat. Moreover, any reduction in the consumption of organic fuels brings about a proportional reduction in air pollution from their combustion products.

Nuclear reactors of the breeder type hold great promise as the solution to these problems. Producing more nuclear fuel than they consume, they would make it feasible to utilize enormous quantities of low-grade uranium and thorium ores dispersed in the rocks of the earth as a source of low-cost energy for thousands of years. In addition, these reactors would operate without adding noxious combustion products to the air. It is in the light of these considerations that the U.S. Atomic Energy Commission, the nuclear industry and the electric utilities have mounted a large-scale effort to develop the technology whereby it will be possible to have a breeder reactor generating electric power on a commercial scale by 1984.

Nuclear breeding is achieved with the neutrons released by nuclear fission. The fissioning of each atom of a nuclear fuel, such as uranium 235, liberates an average of more than two fast (high-energy) neutrons. One of the neutrons must trigger another fission to maintain the nuclear chain reaction; some neutrons are nonproductively lost, and the remainder are available to breed new fissionable atoms, that is, to transform "fertile" isotopes of the heavy elements into fissionable isotopes. The fertile raw materials for breeder reactions are thorium 232, which is transmuted into uranium 233, and uranium 238, which is transmuted into plutonium 239 [*see illustrations on next page*].

We have mentioned that breeding occurs when more fissionable material is produced than is consumed. A quantitative measure of this condition is the doubling time: the time required to produce as much net additional fissionable material as was originally present in the reactor. At the end of the doubling time the reactor has produced enough fissionable material to refuel itself and to fuel another identical reactor. An efficient breeder reactor will have a doubling time in the range of from seven to 10 years.

Two different breeder systems are involved, depending on which raw material is being transmuted. The thermal breeder, employing slow neutrons, operates best on the thorium 232–uranium 233 cycle (usually called the thorium cycle). The fast breeder, employing more energetic neutrons, operates best on the uranium 238–plutonium 239 cycle (the uranium cycle). Nonproductive absorption of neutrons is less in fast reactors than it is in thermal reactors, resulting in a decrease in the doubling time.

The concept of the breeder reactor is almost as old as the idea of the nuclear chain reaction. In the early stages, soon after World War II, many types of breeder reactor were visualized. Some were thermal and some were fast. Another important differentiation involved the type of coolant employed to carry off the heat of fission and deliver it to a power-generating system. Among the coolants proposed were water and molten salts for thermal breeding and inert gas (such as helium), liquid metal (such as sodium) and steam for fast breeding.

In the U.S. and several other countries decisions were made rather early that a fast breeder reactor cooled with liquid metal was the most attractive concept to pursue. This concept is known to atomic energy workers as the LMFBR (liquid-metal-cooled fast breeder reactor). Since the greater part of breeder-reactor development is now proceeding on the basis of this concept, this article is mainly devoted to the liquid-metal fast breeder. A serious alternative effort is being pursued, chiefly by utility companies, to develop the technology of a gas-cooled fast breeder reactor using pressurized helium as the coolant. In the U.S. two thermal-breeder-reactor concepts operating on the thorium cycle are being developed: the light-water breeder reactor at the Bettis Atomic Power Laboratory and the molten-salt reactor at the Oak Ridge National Laboratory.

In the design of a liquid-metal-cooled fast breeder reactor several features are noteworthy. The core of a fast reactor can be quite small. For economic reasons the reactor must be operated at a much higher power density than ordinary fission reactors are. The active core volume is therefore only a few cubic meters and is roughly proportional to the power output. The power density is about .4 megawatt per liter.

To carry off the heat while maintaining the fuel at a reasonable temperature sodium must flow through the core at a rate of tens of thousands of cubic meters per hour. In order to provide channels

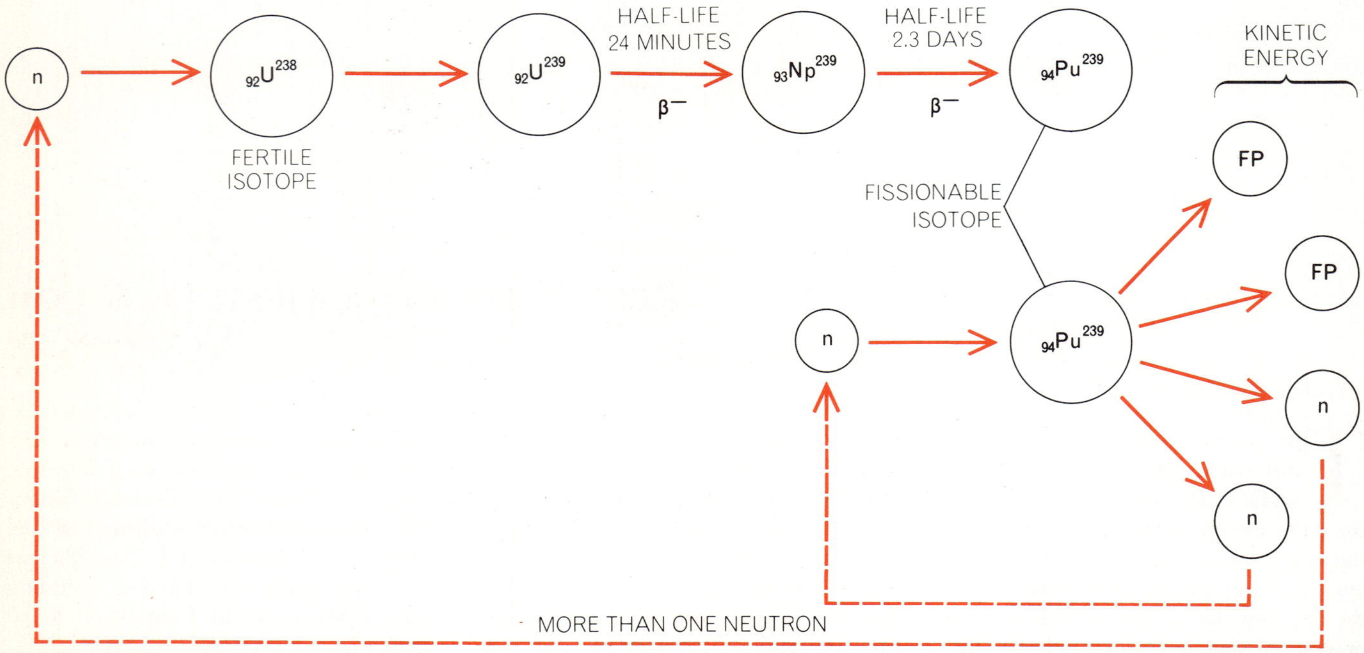

URANIUM CYCLE for breeding in a fast breeder reactor relies on fast, or highly energetic, neutrons. In the cycle an atom of fertile uranium 238 absorbs a neutron and emits a beta particle to become neptunium, which then undergoes beta decay to become fissionable plutonium 239. When an atom of plutonium 239 absorbs a neutron, it can fission, releasing energy, fission products (*FP*) and at least two neutrons. One of the neutrons is needed to continue the chain reaction, but the others are available to transform a fertile isotope into a fissionable one, thereby "breeding" fuel. Within a few years a breeder doubles its original fuel inventory.

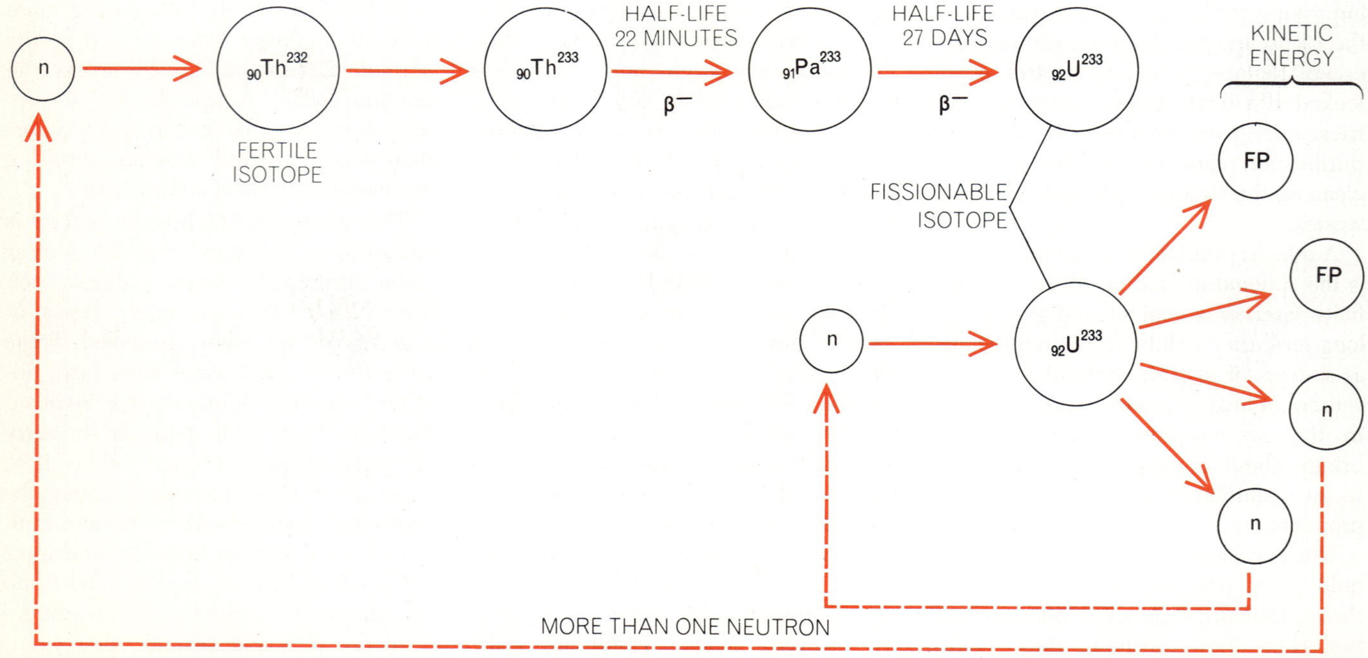

THORIUM CYCLE of breeding is similar to the uranium cycle except that it works best in a thermal breeder reactor, where it relies on thermal, or relatively slow, neutrons. Thorium 232 is the fertile isotope that becomes protactinium and then uranium 233.

for the flow of sodium the fuel is divided into thousands of slender vertical rods, which are usually referred to as pins. Each pin is sealed in stainless steel or another high-temperature alloy.

The fuel is preferably in a ceramic form such as oxide or carbide, since these ceramics are stable during long exposures to heat and radiation, have very high melting points and are relatively inert in liquid metal. The fissionable component of the fuel can be enriched uranium 235, plutonium 239 or a mixture of the two. Typically the fuel is diluted with uranium 238, so that part of the breeding takes place within the core. The uranium 238 also serves a safety function in the core, which we shall explain in more detail below. For maximum economy and performance the fuel must be able to accept neutron irradiation at many times the rate common in present nuclear reactors of commercial scale. Furthermore, the consumption of fuel between reprocessing steps is to be at least twice that of thermal reactors. The development of a fuel meeting these stringent criteria requires the testing of numerous fuel combinations in reactors and accounts for a major element of the breeder development program.

A second major feature of a fast breeder reactor is the "blanket" that surrounds the core. Much of the breeding takes place here, and so the blanket consists of uranium 238 in stainless-steel tubes. (It can be uranium that is depleted in the isotope uranium 235 as a result of enrichment procedures designed to make uranium 235 as a fuel for nuclear reactors; large stocks of such depleted uranium are now available.) Since there is a certain amount of fission in the blanket, it too must be cooled by the flow of sodium. The blanket also has an important nuclear function. Not all the neutrons entering the blanket are captured; a fairly large proportion are reflected back into the reactor core, enhancing the neutron economy there.

The sodium coolant has excellent heat-transfer characteristics. Moreover, it can be used at a fairly low pressure even though it emerges from the reactor at a temperature (above 500 degrees Celsius) that with water would give rise to high pressures. Indeed, the sodium pressure arises solely from the force required to maintain the high rate of flow through the maze of tubes in the core and the blanket. Compared with coolants such as water and gas, sodium requires low pumping power. It is not particularly corrosive to the reactor.

Sodium does, however, have certain

CORE AND BLANKET of a fast breeder reactor, Experimental Breeder Reactor II, are the heart of the breeding operation. The dark hexagonal area is the core, where fuel elements can be installed and removed by the gripper mechanism at right center. Rods clustered at left center are connected to control rods in the core. Around the core is the blanket, consisting of rods containing uranium 238, which is converted to plutonium during the breeding.

EXPERIMENTAL BREEDER REACTOR II is operated by the U.S. Atomic Energy Commission at the National Reactor Testing Station in Idaho. The primary components of the nuclear reactor are under the floor in a tank that is 26 feet high and 26 feet in diameter and contains liquid sodium, which is the coolant. Vertical assembly at right center contains mechanisms for operating the control rods and for handling fuel elements within the reactor. The reactor is used to test fuels and materials for breeder reactors of commercial scale.

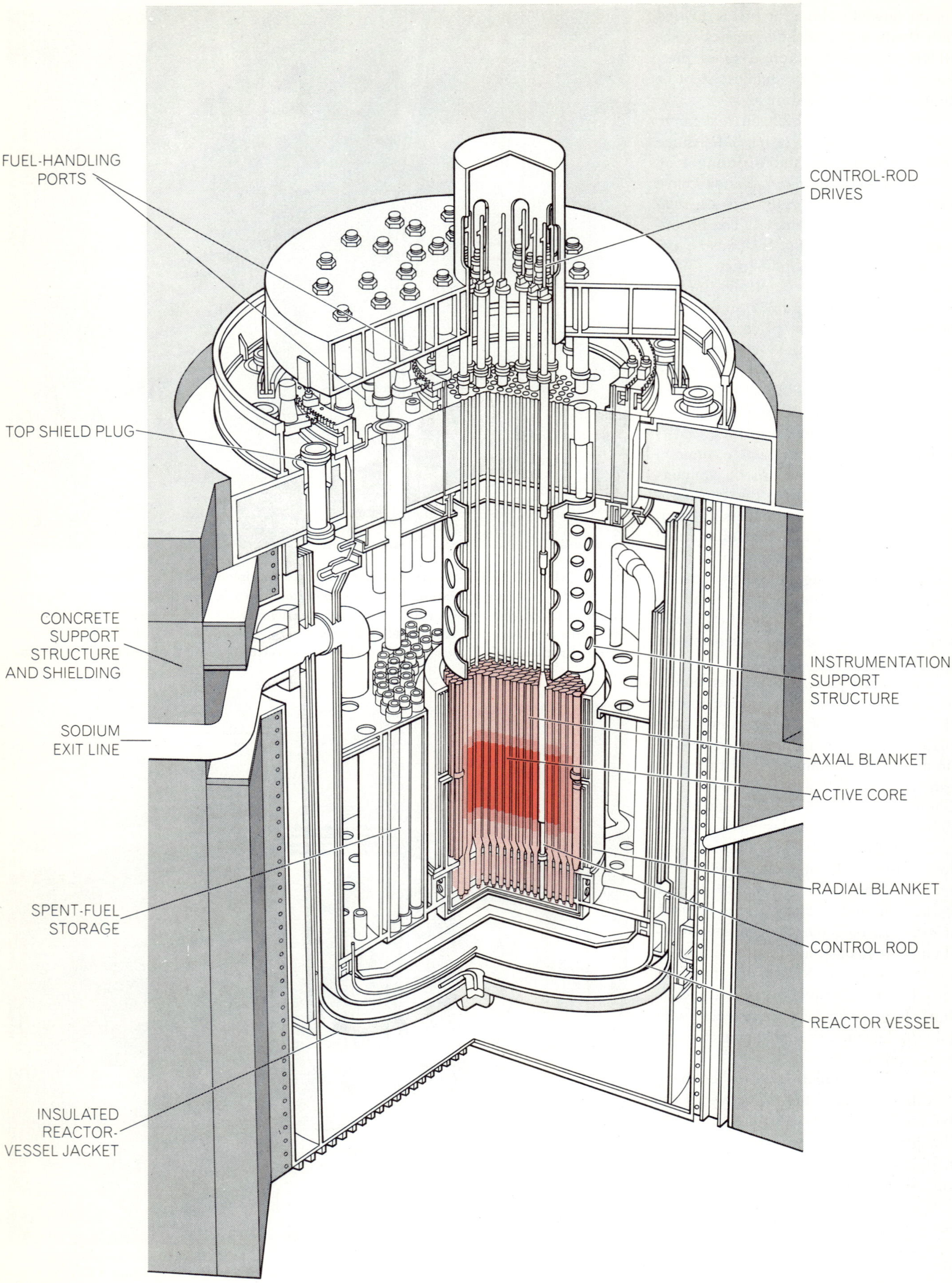

LIQUID-METAL REACTOR of the fast-breeder type is depicted on the basis of a design for a demonstration plant that would produce some 500 megawatts of electricity. A full-scale commercial plant, scheduled for operation by 1984, would be of 1,000-megawatt capacity. This design is of the loop type, meaning that the reactor proper, which is contained in a large tank of liquid sodium, is separated from the primary heat exchangers and the associated pumps by loops of piping through which sodium coolant flows.

disadvantages that markedly influence the design of a reactor. Since sodium is opaque, provision must be made for the maintenance and refueling of the reactor without benefit of visual observation. Sodium is of course highly reactive chemically, and it becomes intensely radioactive when it is exposed to neutrons, even though its "cross section," or neutron-absorption capacity, is relatively low. Hence the sodium must be kept out of contact with air or water, and radiation shielding must be used to protect workers who are near sodium that has been through the core and blanket of an operating reactor.

Interspersed through the core region are numerous rods with safety and control functions. They maintain the power output at the desired level and provide the means for starting and stopping the reactor. The rods are filled with neutron-absorbing material such as boron carbide or tantalum metal.

All materials have markedly lower neutron-absorption probabilities for fast neutrons than for thermal ones. The lower cross sections reduce the effectiveness of fast-reactor control rods of sizes comparable to those in thermal reactors. On the other hand, a large amount of excess fuel is present in the core of a thermal reactor to compensate for the fuel that will be consumed by fission and to counteract the poisoning effect of the fission products. (The fission products capture neutrons without yielding significant amounts of energy.) With extra fuel there must be extra controls. Fast breeder reactors require fewer control rods because their greater effectiveness in converting uranium 238 to fissionable plutonium 239 compensates for depletion of the initial fuel charge and because fast neutrons are not absorbed by fission products as much as thermal neutrons are.

During a fission reaction not all the neutrons are released at the precise instant that each nucleus disintegrates. A small proportion of the neutron population is created by the decay of fission products. One thus distinguishes delayed neutrons from the "prompt" neutrons emitted directly by the fissioning nuclei. It is the delayed neutrons that keep the chain reaction from escalating into an essentially instantaneous propagation of one generation of neutrons to the next.

The fraction of delayed neutrons depends appreciably on which nucleus is fissioning. Most thermal reactors are fueled with uranium 235, whereas the fast breeder will be fueled with plutonium 239. The fraction of delayed neutrons produced by the fission of uranium 235 is about .0065 and by plutonium 239 fission about .003. The smaller fraction of delayed neutrons present in a fast reactor is not of major concern under normal operation. It does increase the sensitivity of the reactor to adjustments of the control rods and to other inputs that affect reactivity, such as temperature variations in the core.

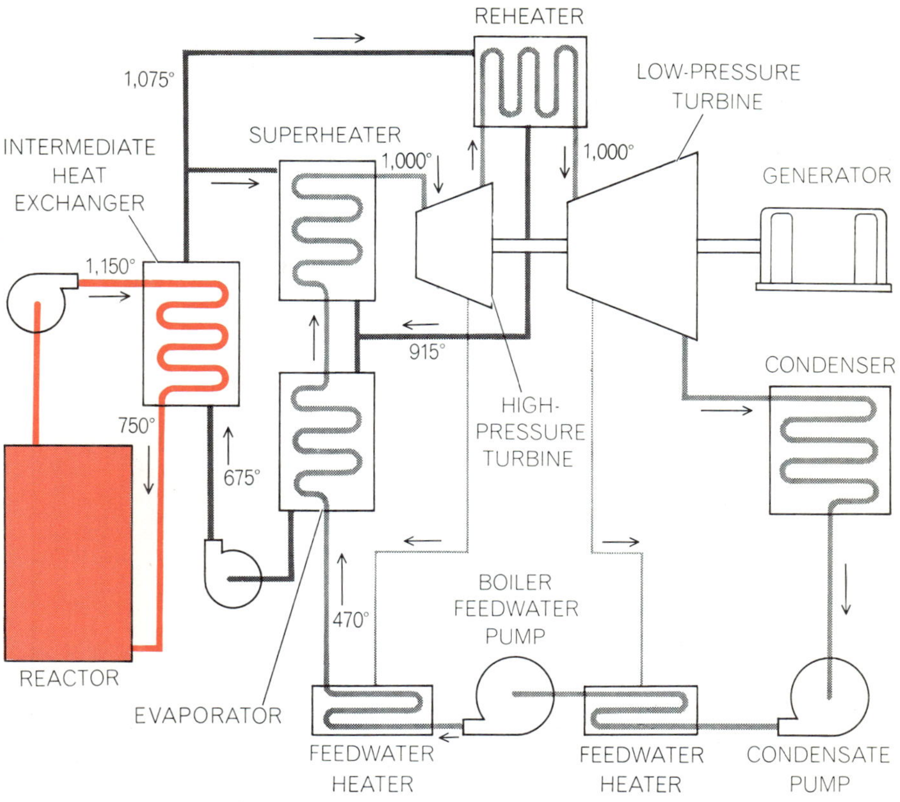

FLOW PLAN for a liquid-metal fast breeder reactor entails pumping the sodium coolant (*color*) through the reactor, where it becomes radioactive, and then to an intermediate heat exchanger, where heat is transferred to a separate stream of sodium (*dark gray*) that is not radioactive. The heat of that stream is put into a water and steam cycle (*light gray*) that is employed to generate electricity. The numerals give temperatures in degrees Fahrenheit.

Two different designs of containers for the core-and-blanket assembly and the primary heat-transfer system are under consideration: the pot type and the loop type [*see illustrations on next page*]. In the pot type a large tank filled with sodium encloses (1) the reactor vessel, (2) sodium pumps that take sodium from the pool and move it through the core and blanket and (3) intermediate heat exchangers that transfer heat from the radioactive sodium to another sodium stream. In the loop type only the reactor vessel is filled with sodium; the liquid metal is circulated by pumps through heat-exchange loops mounted outside the reactor container. The pot type has the advantage of a much greater heat capacity in the event of pump failure, but it also requires a much larger inventory of sodium.

In both the pot and the loop design the liquid-metal fast breeder reactor employs a complex heat-transfer arrangement to isolate the sodium that flows through the core from the steam-generating equipment. This is the role of the intermediate heat exchangers. They transfer heat from the radioactive sodium to nonradioactive sodium, which then flows through the steam generator. Subsidiary streams of sodium are required to superheat the steam and to reheat it from time to time as it works against the blades of the turbine.

Both the pot and the loop design require sealing of the part of the structure that is in direct contact with the radioactive core and blanket. In routine operation there would be no release of radioactive fission products to the environment. Because of the inherently low pressure of the sodium coolant, the reactor vessel and its associated piping need be designed to withstand only moderate operating stresses, in marked distinction to the pressure vessels and other primary-system components of a pressurized-water reactor, a boiling-water reactor or a gas-cooled reactor.

At present the pot design seems to be attracting the most interest. It is inherently a less complicated arrangement than the loop design. Nonetheless, it

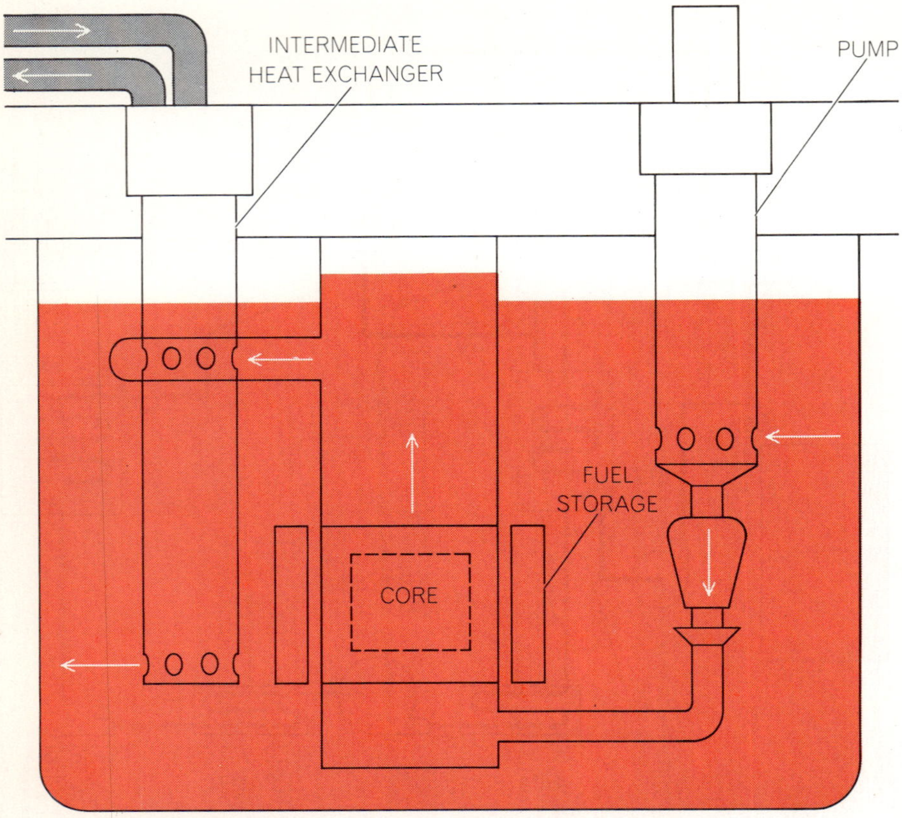

POT SYSTEM is one of two designs for containing the core-and-blanket assembly of the reactor and the primary heat-transfer system. The pot is a tank that is filled with sodium and also contains the reactor, pumps that take sodium from the pool and move it through the reactor, and intermediate heat exchanger where heat is transferred to nonradioactive sodium.

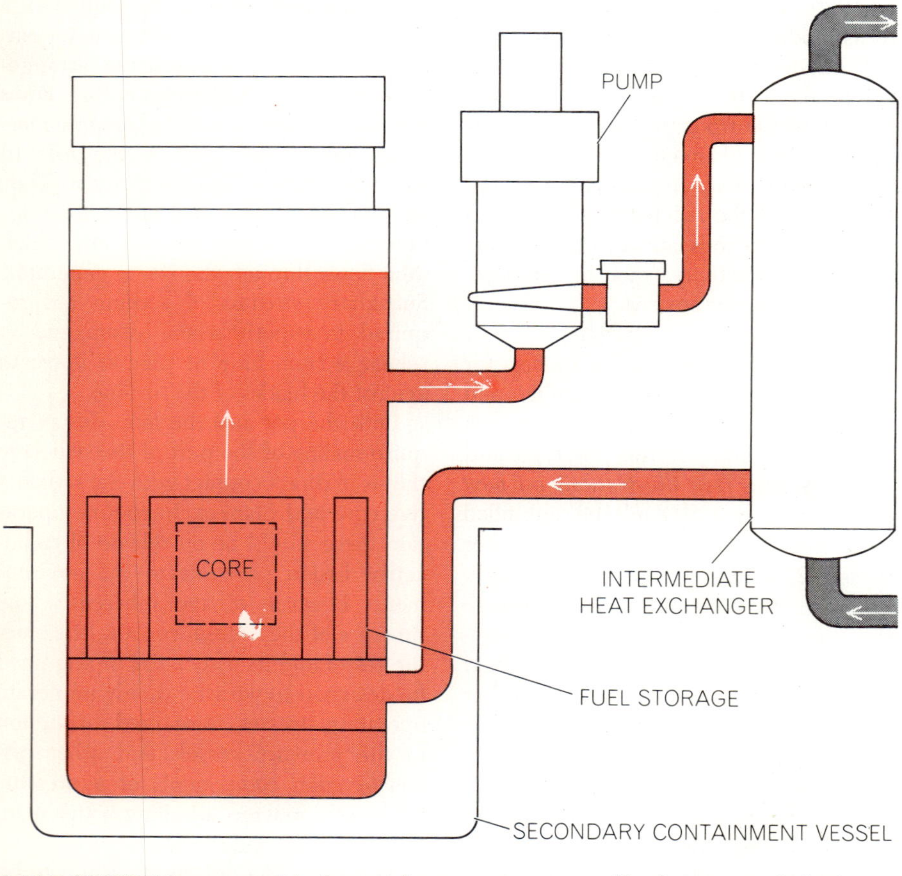

LOOP SYSTEM has most of its heat-exchange apparatus outside the reactor. Only the reactor vessel is filled with sodium, which is circulated by pumps through heat-exchange loops mounted outside the reactor vessel. In the present state of breeder-reactor technology both of the designs in the schematic illustrations on this page are being pursued.

does present certain problems, notably in gaining access to the reactor for maintenance.

The gas-cooled fast breeder reactor is receiving attention (comparatively modest so far) as a parallel and complementary concept to the liquid-metal fast breeder. Gas-cooled thermal reactors are already in operation, and a gas-cooled fast breeder would not represent a large step in terms of coolant technology. The design and testing of the fuel for a gas-cooled fast breeder have much in common with the work on fuel for the liquid-metal fast breeder.

The essential difference between the two fast breeders is that the gas-cooled one uses helium gas at a pressure of from 70 to 100 atmospheres rather than molten sodium to transport the heat from the reactor core to the steam generators. Since the gas does not become radioactive and cannot react chemically with the water in the steam generator, there is no need for an intermediate heat exchanger. The resulting simplification of the system is a helpful offset against the need to design for a higher coolant pressure with gas.

The use of helium as a coolant has other special advantages for a fast breeder reactor. Helium does not interact with the fast neutrons in the reactor core, resulting in both simplified control of the reactor and enhanced breeding of new fissionable fuel from fertile material. In addition helium is transparent and chemically inert, providing visibility during refueling and maintenance operations, a simpler engineering design and freedom from corrosion problems.

In a gas-cooled fast breeder the reactor core, helium circulators and steam generators are all contained in a prestressed-concrete reactor pressure vessel. These major components and their arrangement are almost the same as in a thermal gas-cooled reactor.

The development of a gas-cooled fast breeder reactor could result in substantial additional savings beyond those that would be achieved by liquid-metal fast breeders. Neutrons are moderated, or slowed, less in helium than they are in sodium. Hence the doubling time is short. It is also possible to foresee the development of a gas-cooled fast breeder with a direct power cycle wherein the gas coolant flows from the reactor directly to a gas turbine that drives the electrical generator. Such a cycle should help to reduce the capital cost of fast breeder reactors.

Three major reactors will carry the burden of the Atomic Energy Commission's program to develop a liquid-metal fast breeder reactor. Two of them are already in operation: the Experimental Breeder Reactor II (EBR-II) and the Zero Power Plutonium Reactor (ZPPR).

EBR-II is a fast-neutron test reactor operated by the Argonne National Laboratory at the commission's National Reactor Testing Station in Idaho. This reactor, which as of July 1 had a cumulative record of more than 35,000 megawatt-days of operation, is the focal point of the program of testing fuels and irradiating materials for the liquid-metal fast breeder reactor. At present almost 800 experimental fuel pins and more than 100 capsules containing hundreds of structural, control-rod and shield-material specimens are being irradiated in the reactor. EBR-II achieved its design power of 62.5 megawatts (thermal) last year.

The Argonne National Laboratory is also operating the ZPPR, which went into operation last year. (Zero power in this context means that the reactor does not generate a significant amount of heat.) It is the nation's largest zero-power fast reactor and the only one in the world that is big enough and has a large enough inventory of plutonium (at least 3,000 kilograms) to allow full-scale mock-ups of the plutonium fuel arrangements that will be used in the large commercial breeders envisioned for the 1980's and beyond. The reactor will provide important information on the behavior of neutrons in breeder-reactor cores.

The third reactor is now being designed on the basis of data obtained from EBR-II, the ZPPR and smaller facilities. Called the Fast Flux Test Facility, it will operate at a very high neutron flux (defined as the number of neutrons passing through a square centimeter of area per second) to produce the radiation effects on fuel and structural materials that will take place in a commercial breeder reactor. The reactor, which will cost about $100 million, will operate at a power level of 400 megawatts (thermal) with no conversion to electric power. It will be built at the Atomic Energy Commission's site in Richland, Wash.; construction should start next year and full power should be achieved by the middle of the decade.

Following the lessons learned in the development of thermal reactors, the commission has taken the first steps toward construction of one or more liquid-metal fast-breeder demonstration plants. The cost will be shared by the Government and industry. The first such plant, with a capacity of from 300 to 500 megawatts (electric), will accumulate valuable operating experience with both the reactor and the power-conversion equipment. Such a plant will not compete economically with existing nuclear or conventional plants because of its relatively small size and early stage of development. The full-scale liquid-metal fast breeder reactor of the 1980's will be rated at 1,000 megawatts (electric) or more.

Much consideration is being given to safety in the fast breeder development program. The waste products of fission are the elements in the middle of the periodic table that represent the split nuclei of the fuel atoms. Many isotopes

	NAME	COUNTRY	POWER		INITIAL OPERATION	TYPE (POT OR LOOP)
			MEGAWATTS (THERMAL)	MEGAWATTS (ELECTRICAL)		
OPERATING	BR-5	U.S.S.R.	5	—	1959	LOOP
	DFR	U.K.	60	15	1959	LOOP
	EBR-II	U.S.	62.5	20	1964	POT
	FERMI	U.S.	200	66	1963	LOOP
	RAPSODIE	FRANCE	40	—	1967	LOOP
	SEFOR	U.S.	20	—	1969	LOOP
	BOR-60	U.S.S.R.	60	12	1970	LOOP
UNDER CONSTRUCTION	BN-350	U.S.S.R.	1,000	150	1971	LOOP
	PFR	U.K.	600	250	1972	POT
	PHENIX	FRANCE	600	250	1973	POT
	BN-600	U.S.S.R.	1,500	600	1973/75	POT
	FFTF	U.S.	400	—	1974	LOOP
PLANNED	KNK-II	WEST GERMANY	58	20	1972	LOOP
	JEFR	JAPAN	100	—	1973	LOOP
	PEC	ITALY	140	—	1975	MODIFIED POT
	SNR	WEST GERMANY	730	300	1975	LOOP
	DEMO #1	U.S.	750-1,250	300-500	1976	NOT DECIDED
	JPFR	JAPAN	750	300	1976	LOOP
DECOMMISSIONED	CLEMENTINE	U.S.	.025	—	1946	LOOP
	EBR-I	U.S.	1	.2	1951	LOOP
	BR-2	U.S.S.R.	.1	—	1956	LOOP
	LAMPRE-I	U.S.	1	—	1961	LOOP

LIQUID-METAL FAST REACTORS built or planned are summarized. Those that produce electricity have far less capacity than the 1,000-megawatt commercial fast-breeder plant that the development program of the U.S. seeks to have in operation by 1984.

of these elements are radioactive. The permanent control of the fission products has been recognized as essential from the early stages of reactor development and is routinely achieved in the fuel cycle. In addition to making fission products, fast breeders will also contain large amounts of plutonium, which in certain forms is radiologically toxic. The standard procedure in both thermal and fast reactors is to ensure the confinement of all potentially hazardous substances under all foreseeable conditions, including earthquakes.

Perhaps the most significant safety feature of commercial nuclear reactors is that they are self-regulating, that is, they are designed to compensate inherently for any incident that could lead to an unintentional increase of power output. In water reactors the compensation is usually achieved through the decrease in reactivity caused by the decrease in the density of water as its temperature increases. In a fast reactor the change in density of the coolant with temperature may lead in the opposite direction.

Compensation is provided in a fast breeder by the Doppler effect, which results from the increase in the rate at which neutrons are absorbed by uranium 238 as the temperature of the fuel in the core rises. Since a sudden power increase will necessarily be accompanied by increased fuel temperature, there will be increased neutron absorption and a consequent tendency toward reduction of power. A small sodium-cooled fast reactor has been built in Arkansas with private funds to measure this effect under conditions analogous to those in a large power reactor. It is called the Southwest Experimental Fast Oxide Reactor.

The fact that a decrease in coolant density or coolant content can result in an increase in reactivity leads to other safety considerations for sodium-cooled fast reactors. For example, if one postulates a bubble of gas or another void whereby an area of the core might overheat without detection, some of the fuel pins in the area would be expected to fail. Further disturbances of flow might ensue. A continued sequence of such events would not necessarily result in an automatic shutdown of the reactor. Thus

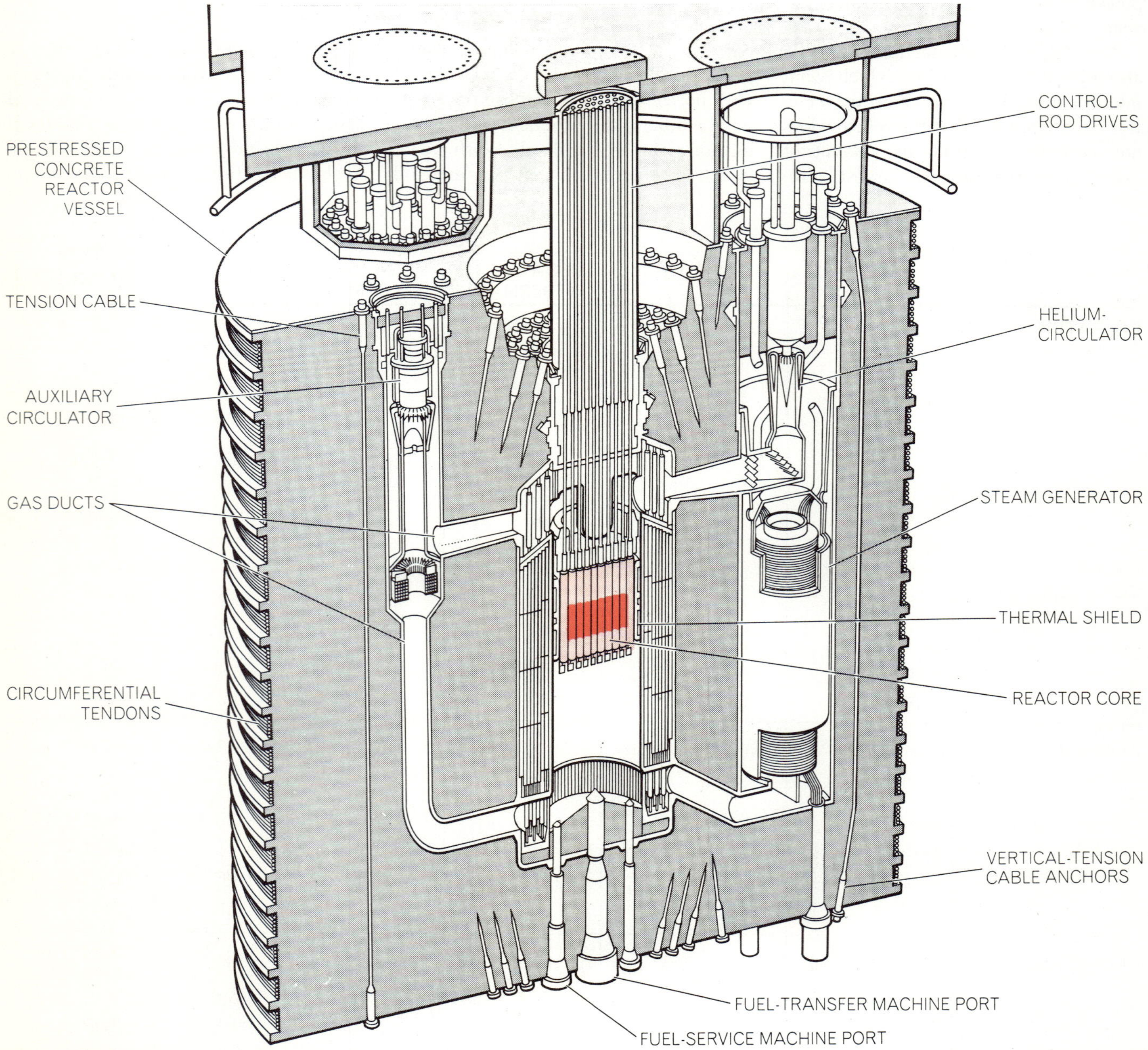

GAS-COOLED REACTOR is depicted in the form it might take for a demonstration breeder plant with a capacity of 300 megawatts of electric power. The chief difference between such a reactor and a liquid-metal one is that the coolant here is helium at high pressure instead of liquid sodium at low pressure. Because of the pressure the reactor is contained within a prestressed-concrete vessel.

it is necessary to preclude by design the propagation of fuel-pin failures.

This control can be achieved by a number of techniques. The addition of a moderator such as beryllium oxide increases the magnitude of the neutron Doppler effect. A change in the ratio of coolant to fuel can reduce the void effect. Other methods include distributing the fuel in such a way that the potential reactivity of coolant voids is decreased by increasing the number of neutrons leaking from the core.

In a gas-cooled fast reactor there is no problem with voids because a bubble cannot form in gas. There is, however, another condition to be guarded against: a sudden loss of coolant pressure resulting from an event such as rupture of the pressure vessel. This possibility is minimized by the use of the prestressed-concrete type of reactor vessel.

Having made sure that perturbations in normal operating conditions do not escalate, one looks to the possibility of other problems. One is a loss of cooling by mechanical blockage. Such accidents have occurred, but they will become less likely as engineering experience is gained. In this type of accident any significant release of fission products is precluded by providing several layers of structural containment for the entire reactor system.

Another possibility is an increase in power to the point where heat is being generated faster than it can be carried away by the coolant. Such an accident took place in EBR-I some years ago. Here again the answer has been found in improved design. Even beyond this, structural containment sufficient for any foreseeable accident will be provided.

Much consideration is also being given to environmental factors in the design of fast breeder reactors. Because fast breeder reactors will operate at far higher temperatures than are encountered in contemporary water reactors, they will have greater thermodynamic efficiency. Today's water reactors operate at an overall efficiency of about 32 percent, meaning that 32 percent of the thermal energy produced is converted to electrical energy. Modern fossil-fueled plants operate at about 39 percent efficiency. Hence water reactors add more waste heat to the environment per unit of electrical energy produced than fossil-fueled plants do. Fast breeder reactors will probably attain efficiencies equal to that of the most modern fossil-fueled plant, thereby reducing the nuclear waste-heat problem.

The release of radioactivity to the air from fast breeders will be near zero.

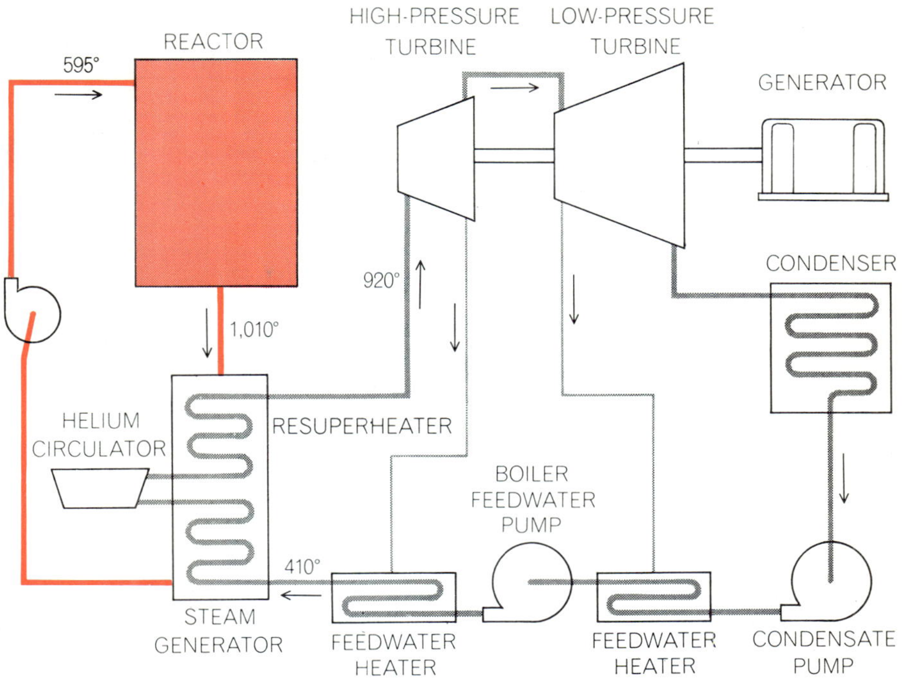

PATTERN OF FLOW in a gas-cooled fast breeder reactor entails the transfer of the heat from the helium coolant (*color*) to a water-steam cycle (*gray*). The system operates without an intermediate heat-exchange cycle. Numerals give temperatures in degrees Fahrenheit.

Even the small amounts of radioactive fission-product gases (primarily krypton 85 and tritium) now released under controlled conditions from water-moderated reactors will be eliminated because the necessity of hermetically sealing the core area will give an inherently effective method for collecting and disposing of the gases, which can then be rendered harmless. Moreover, since the coolant in a fast breeder is kept in a closed system, and since the water used to generate steam is never exposed to neutrons, there should be no formation of radioactivity in aqueous effluents from the plant.

The economic potential of fast breeder reactors lies mainly, but not entirely, in the fact that they would conserve resources of nuclear fuel. Over the next 50 years the use of breeders as planned can be expected to reduce by 1.2 million tons the amount of uranium that would be consumed without breeders. That is the energy equivalent of about three billion tons of coal.

The development of a breeder economy also appears to offer a direct dollar gain of large proportions. Studies have indicated that the cost of research and development of the liquid-metal fast breeder will be more than $2 billion through the year 2020 for the Atomic Energy Commission alone, with large industrial expenditures added. If the first commercial breeder is introduced by 1984 as planned, however, reductions in the cost of electrical energy thereafter (to 2020) are estimated at $200 billion in 1970 dollars.

The present cost of producing electricity in the U.S. ranges from five to 10 mills per kilowatt-hour delivered to the transmission system, depending on the type, age and location of the plant. This range covers most plants, although there are a few outside of either extreme. The liquid-metal fast breeder reactor is predicted to produce power at a saving of from .5 to one mill per kilowatt-hour. Large breeder-reactor systems that eventually bring the cost of electricity down by as much as two mills per kilowatt-hour will make it possible to extract, use and reuse resources in ways that cannot be afforded today. It will be possible to tap substantial resources in the oceans and on land and to use land not now habitable or productive.

Indeed, we believe breeders will result in a transition to the massive use of nuclear energy in a new economic and technological framework. The transition may be slow, and it will require the introduction of a series of innovations in the technologies of industry, agriculture and transportation. The innovations will include large-scale, dual-purpose desalting plants; electromechanization of farms and of means of transportation; electrification of the metal and chemical industries, and more effective means for utilizing wastes. The key to these possibilities is abundant low-cost electrical energy, and the route to that is by way of the breeder reactor.

Fusion Power

If man can tame the reactions in which the nuclei of atoms are fused rather than split, he will have an almost limitless source of energy. The problem is now being attacked in laboratories all over the world

RICHARD F. POST

December 1957

The effort to "tame" the hydrogen bomb reaction—to harness the energy of nuclear fusion for controlled power—is gaining momentum in many countries of the world. It is proceeding quietly, behind a screen of official secrecy, but nonetheless vigorously and on a substantial scale. Every nation has come to recognize that this research effort may well be the most important in the history of mankind. The ultimate stakes are so high, for nations individually and mankind collectively, that a growing sense of urgency and determination is infusing the work of the several nations on this problem.

The upsurge of our industrial civilization in the first half of the 20th century was founded upon fossil fuels—coal and oil. But there are many "have-not" nations, and even countries rich in these fuels are now seeing rapid inroads into their reserves. At this juncture uranium has come to the rescue as a hope for the future. Already electrical power is beginning to flow from the first nuclear fission plants. The United Kingdom expects to go over to fissionable fuels for most of its energy needs within a few decades, and many other countries are laying plans to follow suit; even the U. S., with its great reserves of coal, is spending hundreds of millions of dollars to prepare for turning to fission power at a not too distant date.

The world's uranium and thorium, it is estimated, represent an energy reserve somewhere between 10 and 100 times larger than its remaining coal. Even so, fissionable fuels, too, are an exhaustible supply. At the rate at which the world's energy needs are expanding (the U. S. has doubled its electrical power requirements every eight years) practically all of the economically recoverable uranium, as well as coal, might be exhausted within another century or so. Fission power also presents a more immediate problem: namely, disposal of its radioactive wastes. If the present power needs of the U. S. were all supplied by fission reactors, we would have to dispose each year of an amount of radioactive fission products equal to that from the explosion of 200,000 atomic bombs; by the year 2000, with increased use of power, the radioactive wastes

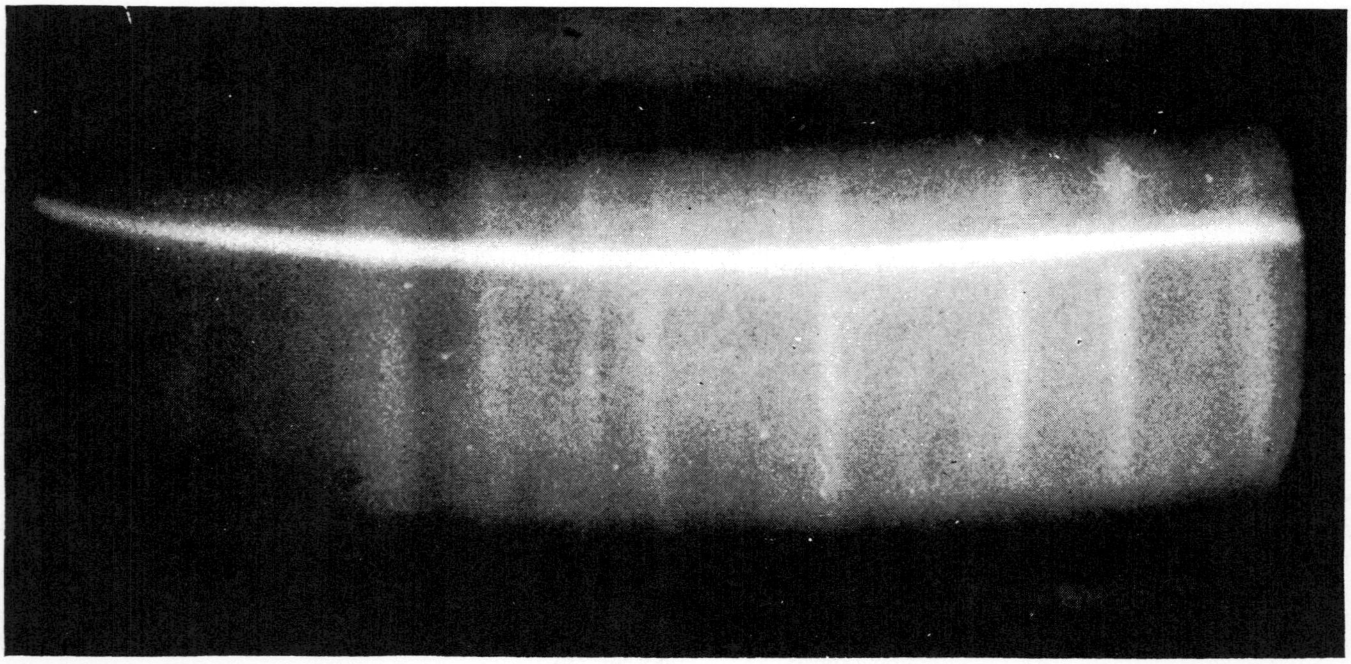

HOT PLASMA (an electrically neutral mixture of positive ions and electrons) is seen as a bright horizontal line in this image-amplifier photograph. The gas is heated and constricted by the "pinch effect," produced by a current of 8,000 amperes. This experiment, using krypton gas at a pressure of two ten-thousandths of an atmosphere, was done at the Los Alamos Scientific Laboratory.

would come to the equivalent of eight million atomic bomb explosions per year! It is clear that the problem of safe disposal of radioactive ashes and gases in the coming age of fission power will soon become staggering.

All this helps to explain the drive, if not race, to find out whether thermonuclear power can be tapped and put to work. If the fusion reaction can be made to yield power, it will solve forever both the fuel supply problem and the problem of radioactive wastes. The basic fusion fuel, deuterium, is as inexhaustible as the oceans, and fusion produces no appreciable amount of radioactive by-products.

The Fusion Reaction

Nuclear fusion is not exactly a new phenomenon. It has been generating the power of the sun and other stars for billions of years, and physicists discovered the fusion reaction in the laboratory before they did fission. But to create and control fusion power on the earth is a problem of a totally different order from harnessing fission. It is undoubtedly the most difficult project ever presented to scientists and engineers. This article is a report of the publishable progress made so far.

In the 1920s and 1930s physicists working with particle accelerators found that by accelerating protons (hydrogen nuclei) and other light nuclei to high enough energies (many thousands of electron volts) they could break through the nuclear electrical repulsion and force the projectiles to fuse with light nuclei in a target. The fusion releases energy, because part of the mass of the fusing nuclei is transformed into energy according to Einstein's famous equation $E=mc^2$. But in this sort of bombardment a great deal of energy has to be put in to make a few nuclei fuse. There can be no net yield of energy from fusion unless it proceeds by a self-sustaining reaction, as, for example, in the interior of the sun.

What is needed to produce a self-sustaining reaction? Here it is apropos to compare fusion with fission. The fission chain reaction is analogous to the explosion of TNT. A mechanical shock is sufficient to cause TNT to start exploding; the shock wave produced by fracture of its unstable molecules then touches off one molecule after another. Similarly in a fission chain-reaction the trigger for the successive fissions is supplied by neutrons, each fission releasing neutrons to attack more fissionable

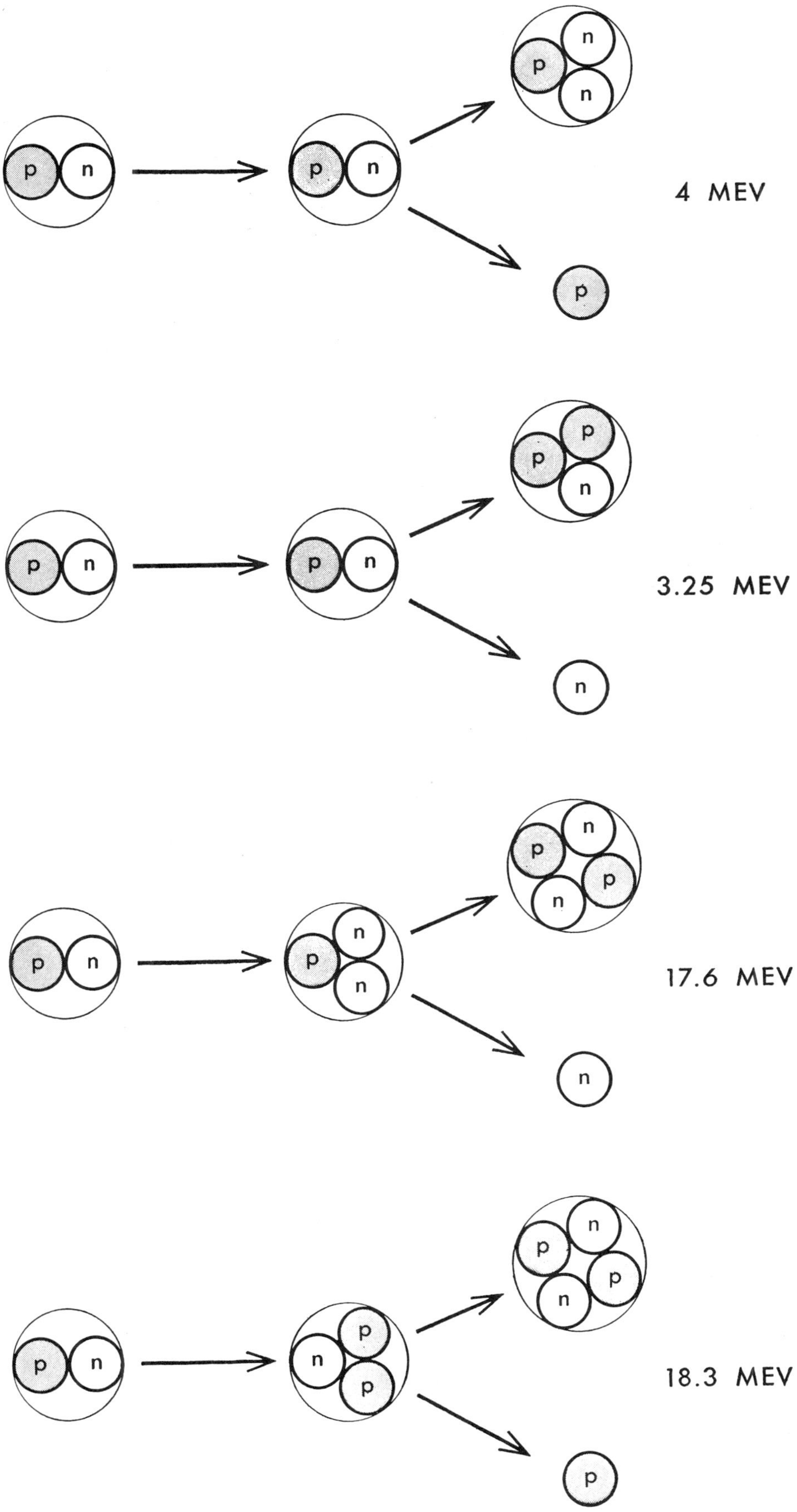

FUSION REACTIONS which promise to be useful for production of power are shown schematically. At top two deuterons merge to form a tritium nucleus (triton). Second is the equally probable reaction in which the deuterons form helium 3 and a neutron. Third, a deuteron combines with a triton to form helium 4 and a neutron. At bottom a deuteron fuses with helium 3, producing helium 4 and a proton. The amount of energy released in each reaction is listed at its right. Protons and neutrons are designated as "p" and "n".

uranium nuclei. In short, heat or kinetic energy plays no part in promoting the chain reaction.

A continuing fusion reaction, in contrast, is analogous to the familiar process of combustion. In ordinary burning, molecules combine (*e.g.*, hydrogen with oxygen, forming water), and their chemical reaction releases energy. To stick together or fuse, the molecules must collide violently, which means the material must be heated. Three conditions are needed to burn a chemical fuel and harness its heat to do work: (1) the fuel must be raised to its ignition point; (2) there must be enough of it to sustain a continuing reaction; (3) the energy released must be tapped in a controlled manner—*e.g.*, to heat water or to drive a piston. Now precisely the same conditions are needed to make a nuclear fusion reaction go and do useful work. The great difference is that for a fusion reaction the ignition point is rather high—hundreds of millions of degrees centigrade!

This one condition—the attainment of which was quite unthinkable on the earth until recently—underlies all our problems. From it stems a whole train of formidable questions. Unfortunately it seems that no one crucial experiment will tell us whether a solution is possible, as the first fission chain reaction did. We shall have to go through a long series of experiments to solve one problem after another. Most of them have to do with quantitative questions, that is, numbers. There never was a field in which the numbers were more imposing—or more important.

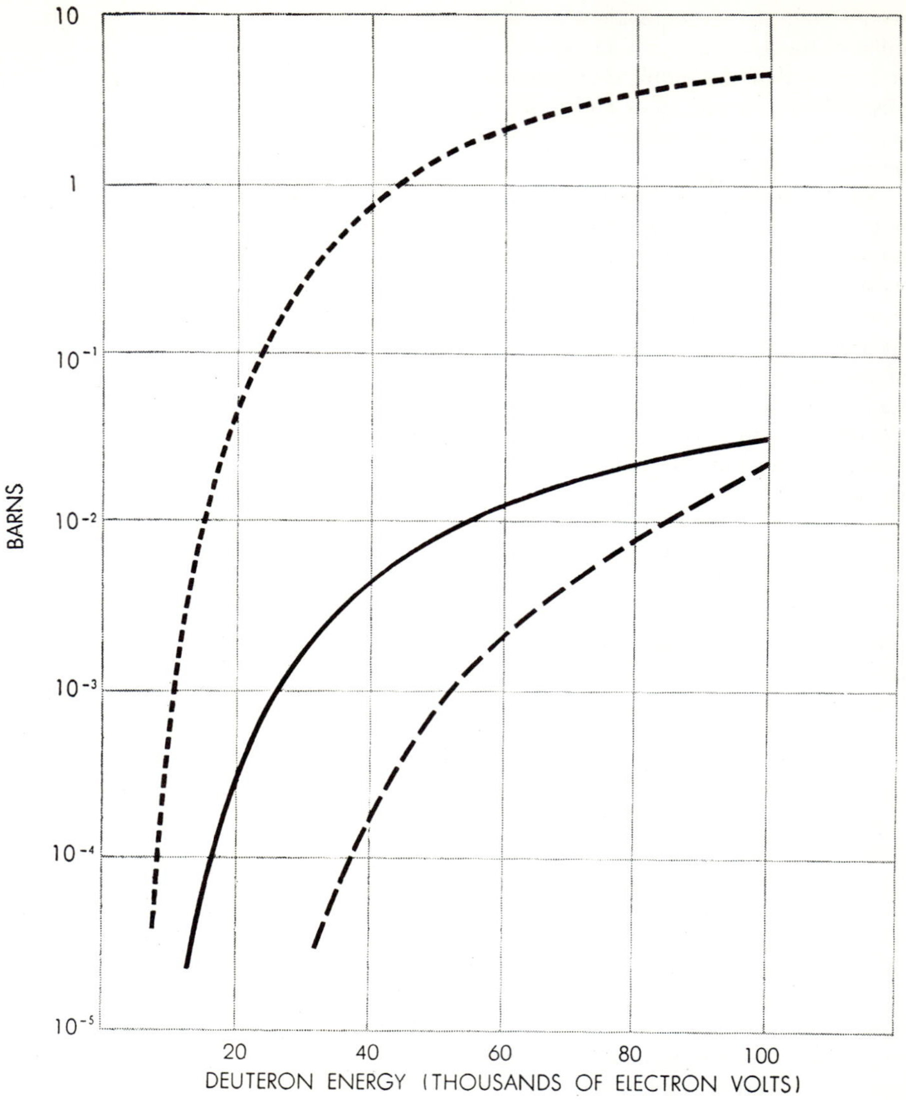

CROSS SECTIONS or probabilities of fusion reactions, as they vary with particle energy, are plotted for fusion of deuterium and tritium (*top*), deuterium and deuterium (*middle*) and deuterium and helium 3 (*bottom*). A barn is an area of 10^{-24} square centimeter.

The Fusion Fuel

Our first concern is the fuel. The most interesting candidate is deuterium, a heavy isotope of hydrogen, found in ordinary water. The nucleus of the deuterium atom consists of one proton and one neutron. When two deuterium nuclei (deuterons) collide with enough energy to fuse, one deuteron grabs either the proton or the neutron of the other—the chances are 50-50. If it fuses with the proton (freeing the neutron), it forms helium 3, releasing about 3.25 million electron volts of energy. If it combines with the neutron (this time liberating its partner's proton), it yields about four million electron-volts and becomes hydrogen 3, or tritium, the radioactive isotope of hydrogen. A deuteron and a tritium nucleus (triton) will fuse more readily than two deuterons, and this reaction releases more energy. Tritium is therefore another potential fuel for thermonuclear reactors. It would have to be manufactured, however, as plutonium is, because there are only trace amounts of tritium in nature. One possible method of breeding tritium is to expose lithium to slow neutrons: on capturing a neutron, lithium splits into tritium and helium 4.

Complete "burning" of the deuterons and their products (tritium and helium 3) in a thermonuclear cycle would produce about seven mev (million electron volts) per deuteron burned. This corresponds to 43 million kilowatt-hours per pound of fuel. By comparison gasoline, one of the best chemical fuels, yields about six kilowatt-hours per pound. Although only a small fraction of the hydrogen in natural water is deuterium, still the deuterium in one gallon of ordinary water has an energy content equivalent to 350 gallons of gasoline! The oceans contain enough deuterium to supply the world with fuel for billions of years, even at a power demand 1,000 times the present figure. For use in our atomic energy program in the U. S., according to published figures, we are already producing an amount of deuterium which would be sufficient to supply the nation's total energy needs many times over if it could be burned as fuel. The cost of extracting deuterium from water is low enough so that deuterium would be less than 1 per cent as expensive as coal as a fuel. And finally, the nuclear burning of deuterium and tritium produces only inert gases, avoiding any problem of waste disposal.

Deuterium, then, represents the "ultimate fuel." But its great promise is matched by the equally great difficulty of finding a way to burn it!

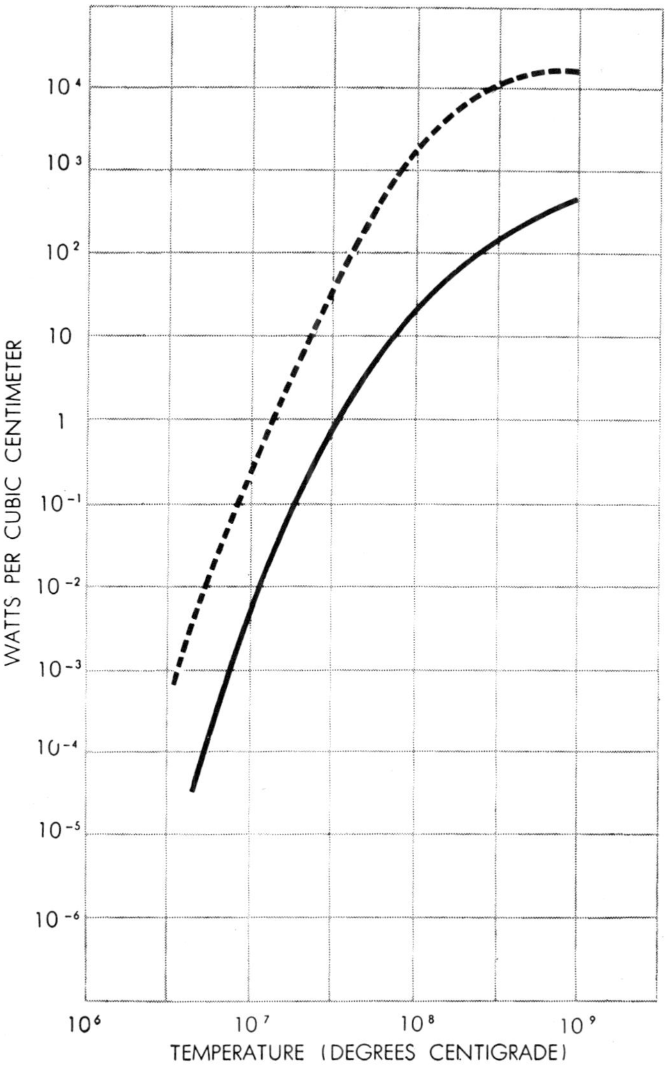

FUSION-POWER OUTPUT of plasma at one ten-thousandth of atmospheric density is plotted against temperature. Upper curve is for deuterium-tritium fusion; lower curve, for deuterium-deuterium.

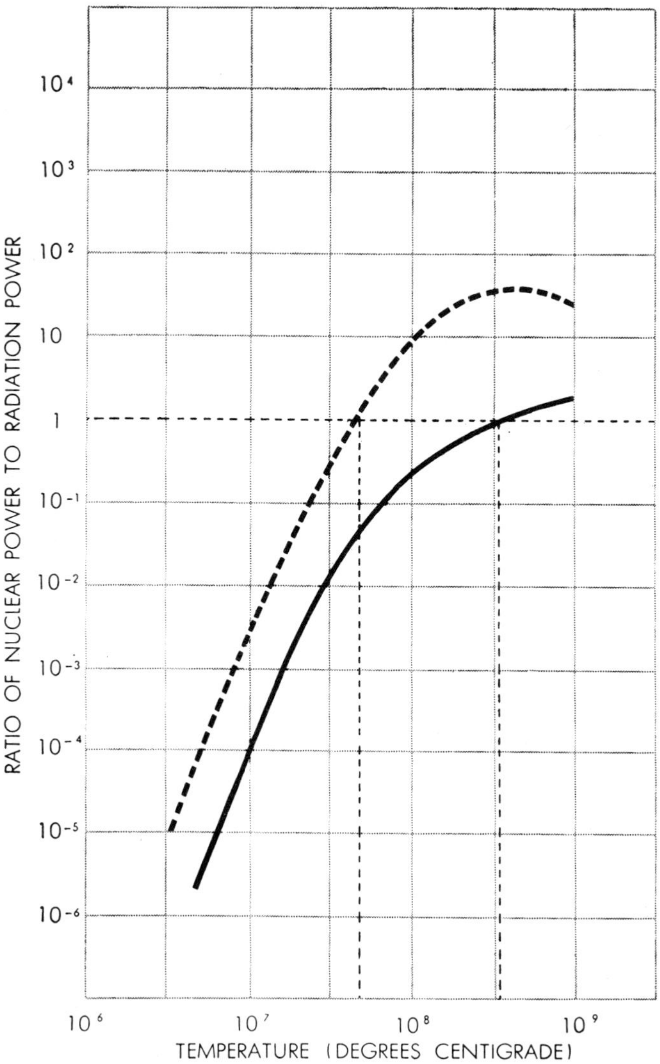

IGNITION TEMPERATURES, where nuclear power equals radiated power, are indicated by broken vertical lines for deuterium-tritium (*upper curve*) and deuterium-deuterium (*lower curve*).

The burning of thermonuclear fuel in an uncontrolled manner has been achieved with all too well known success in the hydrogen bomb. But the problem of producing a controlled fusion reaction is quite different. Let us see what the necessary conditions are. The best way to do this is to follow an imaginary experiment.

The Plasma

We take a liter of deuterium gas confined in a vessel made of a mythical material which is capable of withstanding the enormous temperatures and pressures that will arise in the course of the experiment. At room temperature and normal atmospheric pressure the deuterium gas-molecules are wandering about in the vessel with an average kinetic energy of about one 25th of an electron volt, or a velocity of about 3,000 miles per hour. Of course no fusion reactions are taking place. Now we heat the gas to 5,000 degrees C. At this temperature we no longer have molecules: the violence of their collisions has broken them apart into deuterium atoms. The pressure has risen to about 40 atmospheres (600 pounds per square inch), and the average velocity of the atoms is about 40,000 miles per hour. But we are still very far from the velocity needed to make two nuclei fuse.

Next, let us jump to 100,000 degrees. The remarkable properties of the mythical wall material are very much needed now, for any real material would long since have vaporized. Now the deuterium atoms of the gas have been broken down to the electrically charged nuclei (deuterons) and electrons: in a word, the gas has become what is known as a plasma. The gas pressure has risen to 1,500 atmospheres. The average velocity of the electrons is 10 million miles per hour, and even the much heavier deuterons are moving at the great speed of 170,000 miles per hour. Yet the deuterons still do not have sufficient energy effectively to overcome their mutual electrostatic repulsion. At this temperature there would be only about one fusion in the liter of plasma every 500 years! We still have a long way to go before we shall reach the ignition temperature of a mass of deuterons.

At one million degrees, the rate of fusion reactions will increase more than a billion billion times, but the total energy output will still be too small to be detected—only a few millionths of a watt per cubic centimeter. At 100 million degrees, however, the reaction rate will become really respectable. The pressure

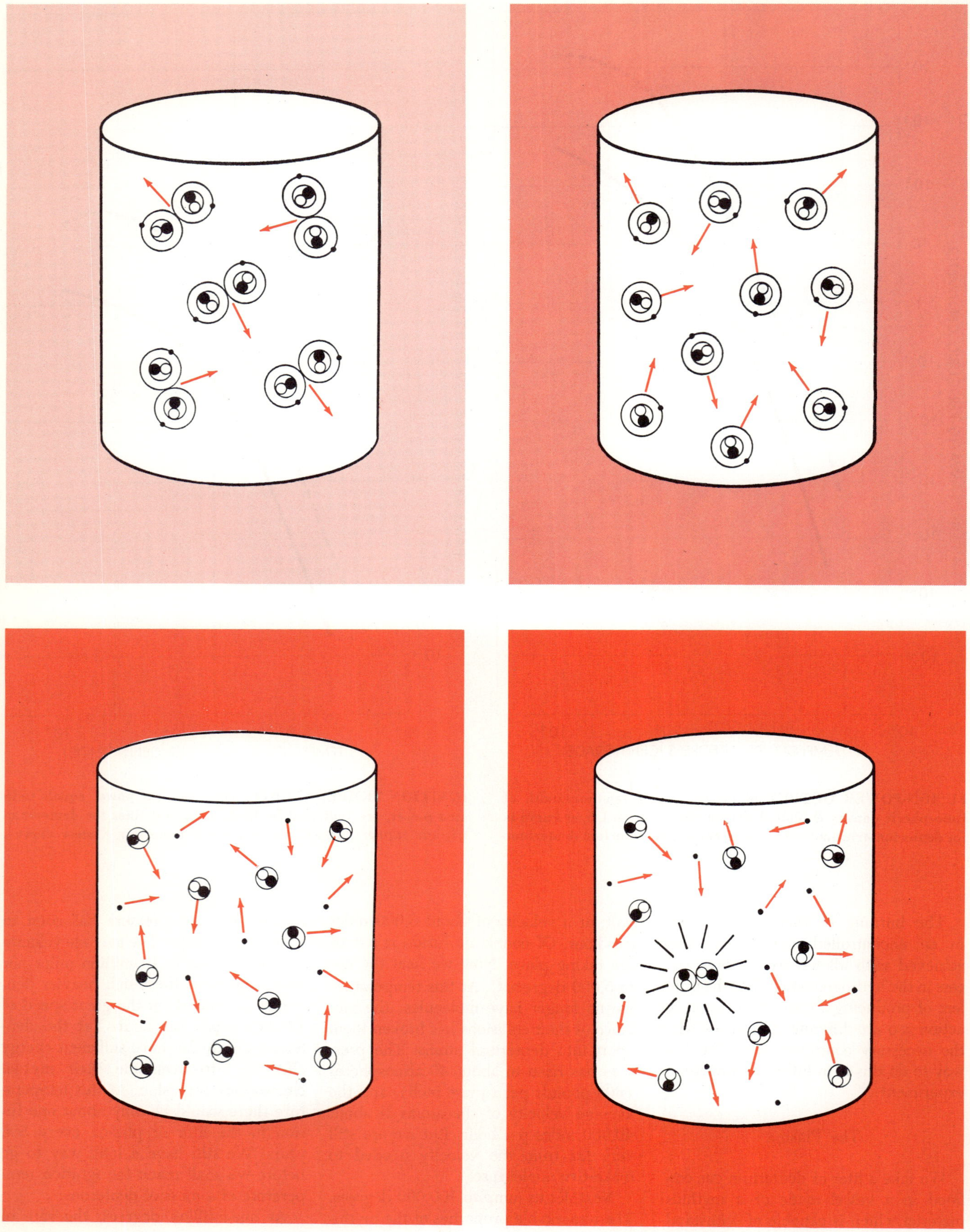

IMAGINARY EXPERIMENT shows the results of heating deuterium gas. At top left the gas is at room temperature and atmospheric pressure of 15 pounds per square inch. Heated to 5,000 degrees centigrade (*top right*), the diatomic molecules have split to form deuterium atoms and the pressure is 600 pounds per square inch. When the temperature is raised to 100,000 degrees (*bottom left*), atoms are ionized, forming a plasma of electrons and deuterons. The pressure is 20,000 pounds. At a temperature of 100 million degrees (and a pressure of 22 million pounds) some deuterons can fuse, releasing energy, but the reaction is still not self-sustaining.

then will have reached the staggering value of 1.5 million atmospheres. The electrons will be traveling at 90,000 miles per *second*, and the deuterons at 1,500 miles (around the world in 16 seconds). Essentially all of the deuterons will react with one another rapidly (within a fraction of a second), and their reactions will release energy at a fantastic rate—about 100 million kilowatts. But we shall not yet have arrived at the kindling point: to sustain the reaction we shall still have to put in more energy than the fusions release. Only at about 350 million degrees will the "fire" (*i.e.*, thermonuclear reaction) become self-sustaining.

This imaginary experiment brings out several important points. First, we need extremely high temperatures, though when we speak of high temperature here we are not thinking of heat in the usual sense but of the kinetic energy of the gas particles. Second, we could not even think of using the fuel at ordinary gas concentrations. If we are to keep the energy output and pressure of the gas within controllable bounds, we must start with a thin gas at a density much lower than at atmospheric pressure—somewhere in the neighborhood of one 10,000th of an atmosphere. But what a thin fuel this is! In a laboratory a gas at this density would be considered practically a vacuum.

One of the interesting consequences of using a very low density is that even though the plasma is very hot in terms of the speed of its particles, its heat *content* will actually be very small. A liter of deuterium plasma one 10,000th of an atmosphere in density would, at a kinetic temperature of 350 million degrees, have a heat content amounting to 18,000 calories—about enough to heat a small cup of coffee.

To calculate the rate of fusion power production from a hot plasma it is only necessary to know the reaction cross sections and to insert these as data in the theory of thermonuclear reactions in a hot gas [*see charts on page 373*]. However, calculation of this kind, important as they are in specifying the required physical conditions, shed no light on *how* to heat a gas to thermonuclear temperatures or on whether the reactions, once initiated, could be made self-sustaining. This latter question depends on how much of the energy will be lost by radiation and other mechanisms. In the sun, the energy generated within its huge volume is sufficient to maintain the reactions in spite of the radiation loss from the surface. If we could build a

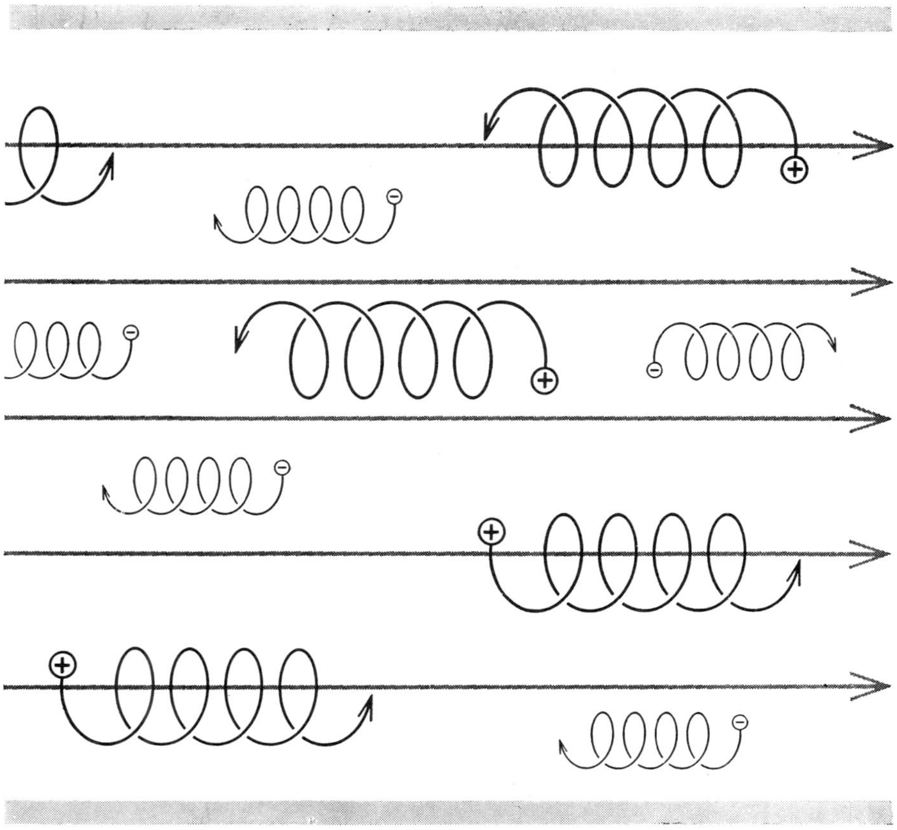

PATHS OF PLASMA PARTICLES in a magnetic field are helixes. Positive particles go counterclockwise; negative particles, clockwise looking in the direction of the field.

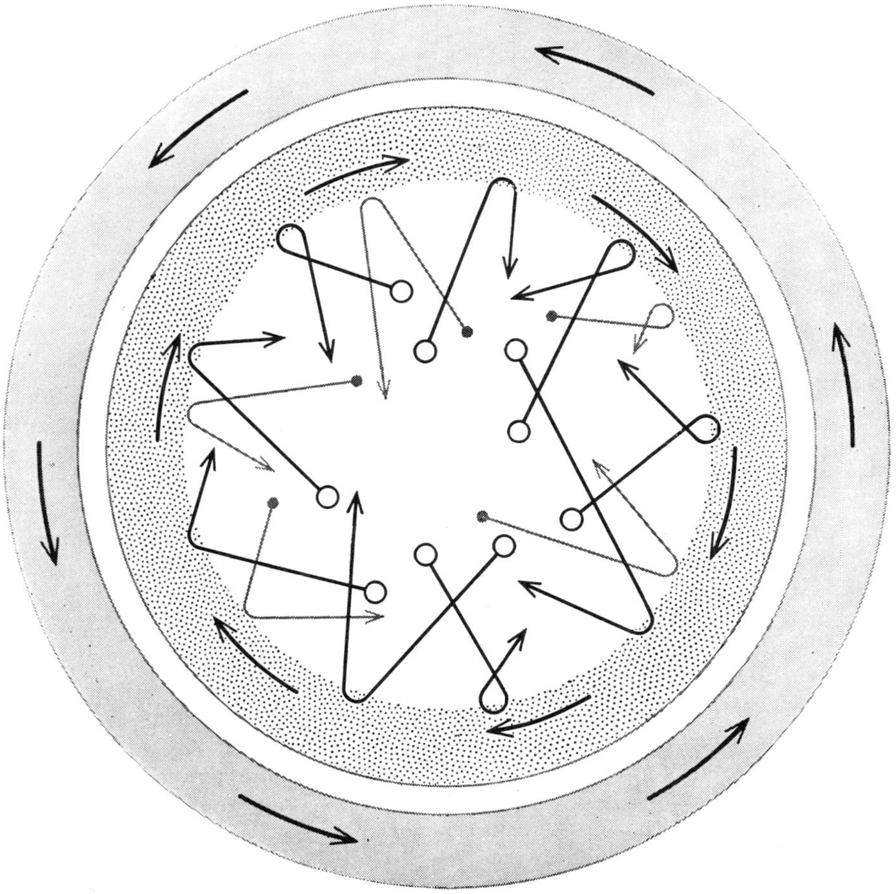

PLASMA IS CONTAINED by a magnetic field (*dotted ring*) which prevents escape of particles. Outer arrows show current in coil; inner arrows, current from deflected particles.

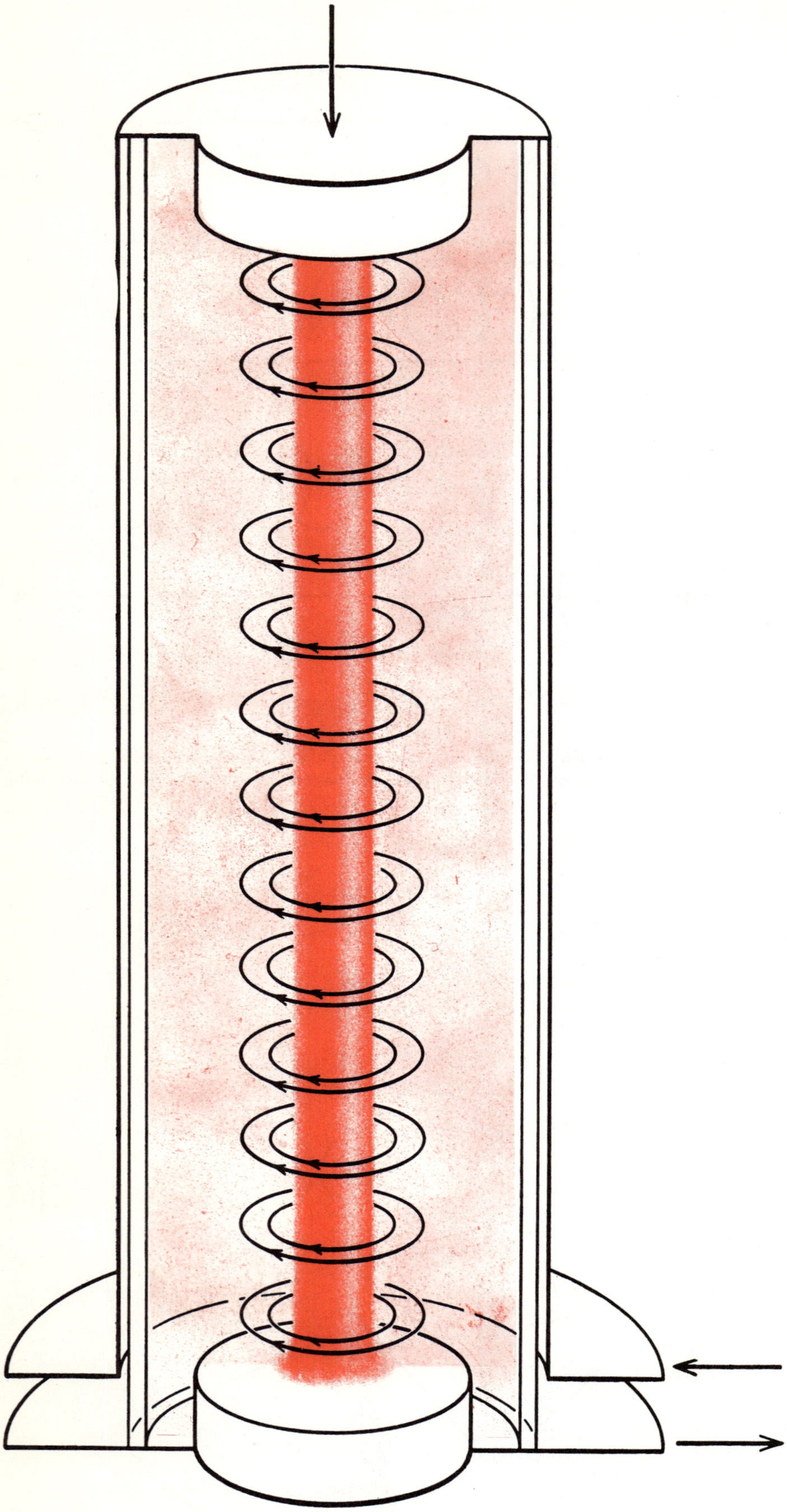

PINCH EFFECT occurs when a large electric current is sent through a plasma in a cylinder. Circular magnetic lines of force set up by the current contract and pinch the plasma into a narrow channel (*colored column*). The straight arrows show the direction of the current.

fusion reactor as big as the moon, we would not need to worry particularly about energy losses. But for a reactor of practicable size this is our key problem.

Let me first mention the unavoidable losses that must be lived with. These are the losses by radiation from the plasma—primarily in the form of X-rays emitted when electrons collide with nuclei. Now at a temperature of 100 million degrees, one cubic centimeter of dense matter would radiate energy at the unbelievable rate of three million million million kilowatts! But fortunately the rate of radiation drops very rapidly as the density of the matter falls. At the low density we have been considering, the radiation loss becomes comparatively small. The energy yield of fusion reactions increases rapidly with rise in temperature, and it will outstrip radiation losses at a temperature above 50 million degrees in the case of the deuteron-triton reaction and above 370 million degrees in the deuteron-deuteron reaction. These, then, are the ignition temperatures of the respective fuels. But the plasma must be very pure, because nuclei of higher elements (above hydrogen and helium) greatly accelerate the rate of radiation. A surprisingly small amount of impurities could poison a very large volume of plasma. For example, the metal in the head of a pin, if vaporized, would be quite sufficient to poison several railroad tank cars full of plasma. It is clear that purity will be a prime requirement in any controlled-fusion reactor.

Of the other class of energy losses—the ones we can and must reduce—the most serious is dissipation of particle energy to the walls of the reactor. We have to have a closed chamber, to hold out the atmosphere and keep our gas at low density. But consider the particles in this gas. They are so widely dispersed in our near-vacuum that each deuteron, in its random wanderings, travels thousands of miles on the average before it encounters another deuteron (or a triton). It has a far greater chance of hitting the walls of the container first. Yet if it does, this collision will immediately damp its energy. Obviously we cannot allow the particles of the plasma to touch the walls. Contrary to a common impression, the reason is not that the plasma will vaporize the walls (it does not contain much heat) but simply that contact with the walls would instantly cool the plasma and quench the reaction.

This, then, is the nub of the problem: How to confine a very hot gas within a material chamber (for at least a fraction of a second) without allowing any appreciable amount of it to reach the chamber walls. Posed in this way, it sounds like a science-fiction problem, quite unsolvable in any real world. But as is now well known, about a decade ago an ingenious solution emerged—namely, the plasma might be confined within a magnetic field, serving as a kind of furnace liner in the chamber to keep the particles away from the walls.

The Magnetic Bottle

The idea rests basically on the simple fact that a strong magnetic field will deflect charged particles from a straight path [*see diagram at top of page 375*]. Now a hot, high-pressure plasma could, under the proper circumstances, generate an internal magnetic field of its own strong enough to exclude the externally applied field. Inside such a plasma the particles would therefore move in straight lines. But at the boundary of the plasma they would be deflected back into it by the outside magnetic field [*see diagram at bottom of page 375*]. The magnetic lines of force, acting like elastic rubber bands, could resist considerable pressure. If the magnetic field were made strong enough, it should form a magnetic "wall" able to contain a high-pressure plasma, just as a steel cylinder holds a high-pressure gas. According to the theoretical calculations, a field with a strength of 50,000 gauss, for example, could withstand a plasma pressure of 100 atmospheres, and a field 10 times stronger (which has been achieved in laboratories) could support a pressure of 10,000 atmospheres.

A fusion reaction sustained in such a magnetic bottle could never "run away," as the fission chain reaction may. If the plasma pressure became stronger than the magnetic field, it would rupture the magnetic wall and the plasma would touch the material chamber wall, which would immediately quench the fusion reaction. By the very nature of the beast, then, a fusion reactor could never explode; it could only collapse.

The simplified picture we have been considering should not be taken to mean that the magnetic bottle would be leakproof. Actually the plasma and the magnetic field would gradually penetrate and intermingle with each other, and the plasma would eventually escape completely unless replenished. Fortunately this leakage should be slow enough, according to the theory, to permit the achievement of a self-sustaining fusion reaction. But, as we shall see, a magnetic bottle does not always behave as the simple theory predicts. The interactions between a high-temperature plasma and magnetic fields are a difficult problem in fundamental physics, and they have given rise to a new field of study which might be called "experimental astrophysics."

The Pinch Effect

So much for the theory. How could we actually make a magnetic bottle? It occurred independently to many investigators that an obscure electrical phenomenon known as the "pinch effect" might provide the answer. This effect, first produced experimentally only about a decade ago, requires a very large electrical current. When such a current is passed through a conducting gas in a tube, it sets up a magnetic field which tends to pinch the gas and pull it away from the tube walls [*see diagram on page 376*]. The magnetic lines of force circling the gas compress it by their tension. Since a plasma is an excellent conductor of electricity, the pinch effect looked like an attractive and ready-made means of forming a magnetic bottle.

Theoretical calculations showed that it would take a very large current indeed—millions of amperes—to confine a plasma of high temperature and low density. Not discouraged by this fact, investigators in many countries carried out experiments with simple pinch tubes [*see illustration on page 370*]. They applied a high voltage to a low-pressure gas in an insulated tube and produced an electrical discharge. This ionized the gas, and heavy current then began to flow. As they hoped, the pinch made its dramatic appearance. But with it also came a blow to their hopes. The pinch lasted only a millionth of a second or so; no sooner had the column of plasma been compressed than it writhed violently and drove itself to the tube wall. Furthermore, the tighter the pinch, the faster it destroyed itself.

This was not hard to understand, and in fact was predictable theoretically. Two different types of instability can develop. In the first place, any small kink in the pinched column will grow rapidly, because the magnetic pressure is stronger on the concave side of the kink (where the lines of force are crowded together) than on the convex side [*see diagram at left, page 378*]. The second cause of instability is a kind of

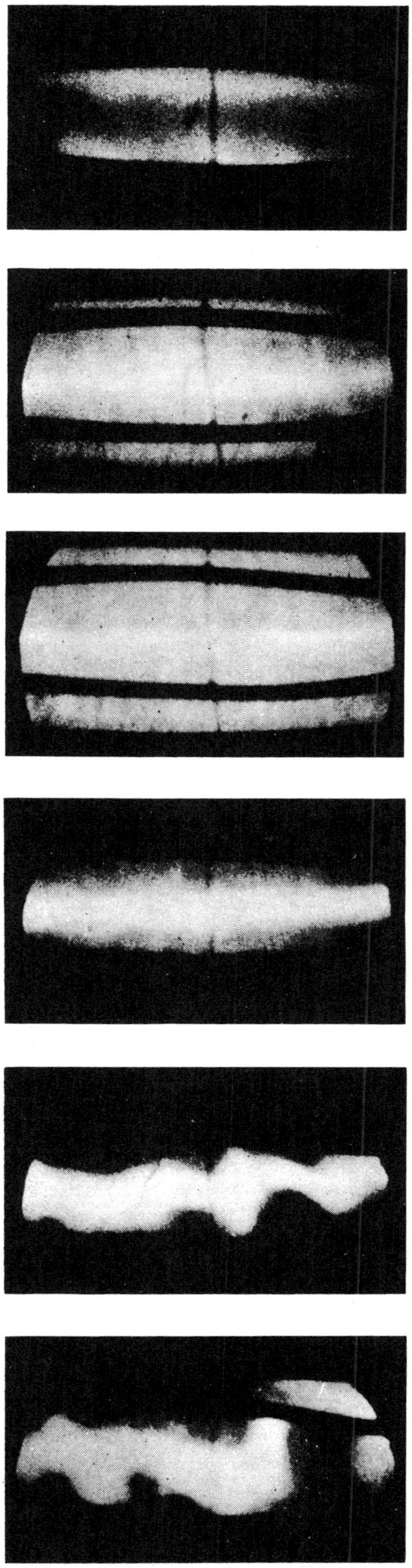

LIFE OF A PINCH is depicted in this series of image-amplifier photographs. The top three pictures show the formation of the pinched column of plasma (*bright band*) as current is sent through the gas. The remaining views show its death, brought on by the development of kink instabilities.

"sausage" effect [*middle diagram, page 378*]. The plasma tends to pinch or neck itself off at one or more points along the column, and thus cuts itself into pieces.

Incidentally, in connection with the latter phenomenon there is an interesting story which illustrates how hopes can suddenly rise and just as suddenly fall in an important but uncharted field of research such as the fusion power enterprise. When investigators first produced strong pinches in deuterium gas, they were delighted to discover bursts of neutrons—evidence of fusion reactions in the plasma. They thought they had reached thermonuclear temperatures momentarily. But on analysis they had to conclude that it was merely some obscure electrical effect, associated with the violent disruption of the pinch by the sausage instability, that had accelerated a few deuterons to fuse.

How could the pinch be stabilized? Theoretical investigations published in the U. S., in the United Kingdom and in the U.S.S.R. have suggested a possible answer, although they have not yet shown how the physical conditions necessary to make it work could be achieved. The idea is to create not only a pinching magnetic field around the plasma but also a strong longitudinal magnetic field *within* the plasma column [*see diagrams on pages 378 and 379*]. The internal field would act as a kind of stiffener. If a kink started to develop, it would tend to stretch the interior lines of force, and their elastic resistance would pull out the kink. Similarly if the sausage type of constriction tried to pinch into the column, the internal lines of force would resist being squeezed together and thus would prevent collapse of the column.

There is a third type of instability which could destroy a plasma column: namely, a long, gentle bend of the column that would grow in strength and push the column to the chamber wall [*see diagram at right, page 379*]. How-

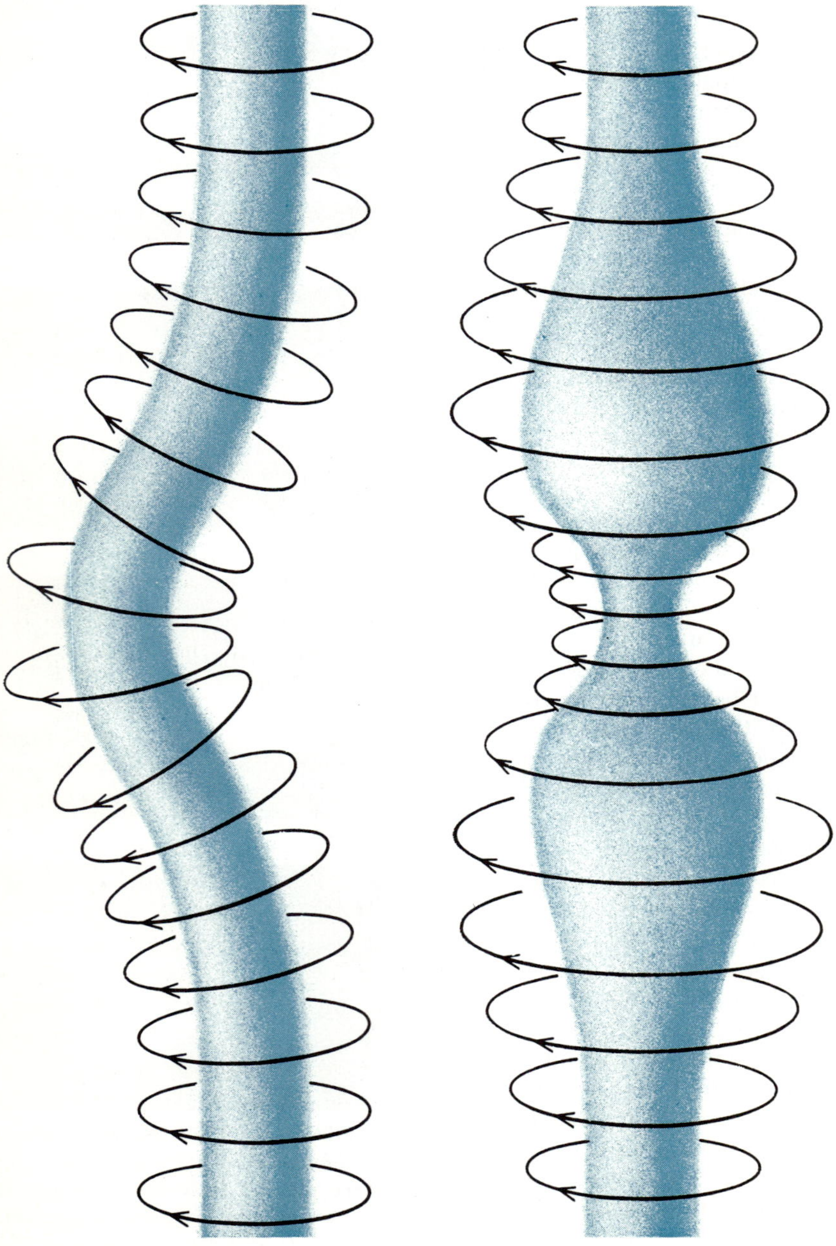

INSTABILITIES in a pinched plasma arise from kinks (*left*), where the magnetic lines are crowded on the concave side, and constrictions (*right*), where the field is also crowded.

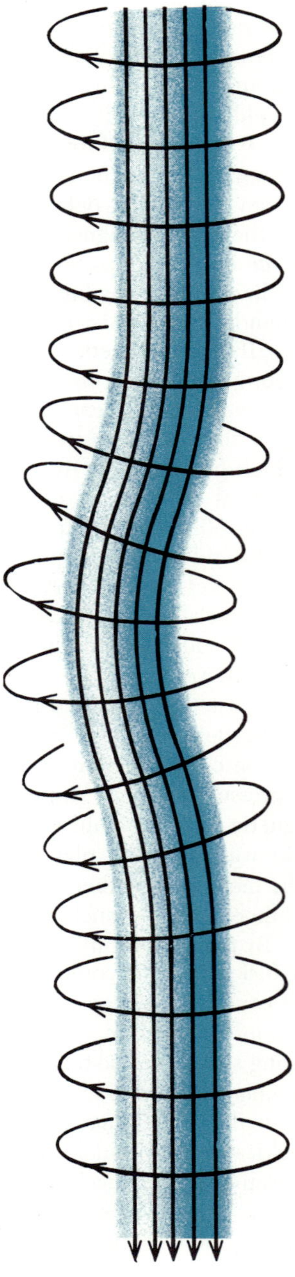

STABILIZED PINCH might be achieved by putting a magnetic field (*long arrows*)

ever, this could be counteracted by using a conducting material for the walls of the tube. Since a conductor acts as a barrier to a magnetic field, the magnetic field lines around the plasma column would be crowded against the wall where the bent column approached it, and the resulting back pressure would push the column back toward the center of the tube.

I should make clear that the straight pinch columns illustrated here are simplified systems which merely exemplify the principles. In practice it would probably not be desirable to try to produce a stable pinch in a straight tube, for several reasons: among other things, the electrodes at the ends of the tube would have a cooling (*i.e.*, quenching) effect on the plasma. Pinch experiments have already been performed with other shapes. One of these is a doughnut-shaped tube in which currents are induced and can circulate without bumping into a solid surface. A high voltage applied to the winding around a large iron transformer core in the tube produces an electrical discharge in the gas, which then functions as a one-turn secondary winding. Very heavy currents can be induced into the plasma in this way.

Besides the pinch effect, other possible methods of forming a magnetic bottle are being investigated, in the U. S. and no doubt in other countries. Most of the current research on the fusion power problem involves experiments in very complicated electromagnetic phenomena—the behavior of a high-temperature plasma in various magnetic field configurations. It is extremely hard work, taxing all the resources of our present technology. As I have mentioned, there is little likelihood of anything like a sudden "break-through" to a radically simpler approach. Since we shall make headway only by many mutually reinforcing studies and by the development of new and unusual techniques, it is evident that progress would be more rapid if the various nations involved joined in a cooperative exchange of information on all phases of the research.

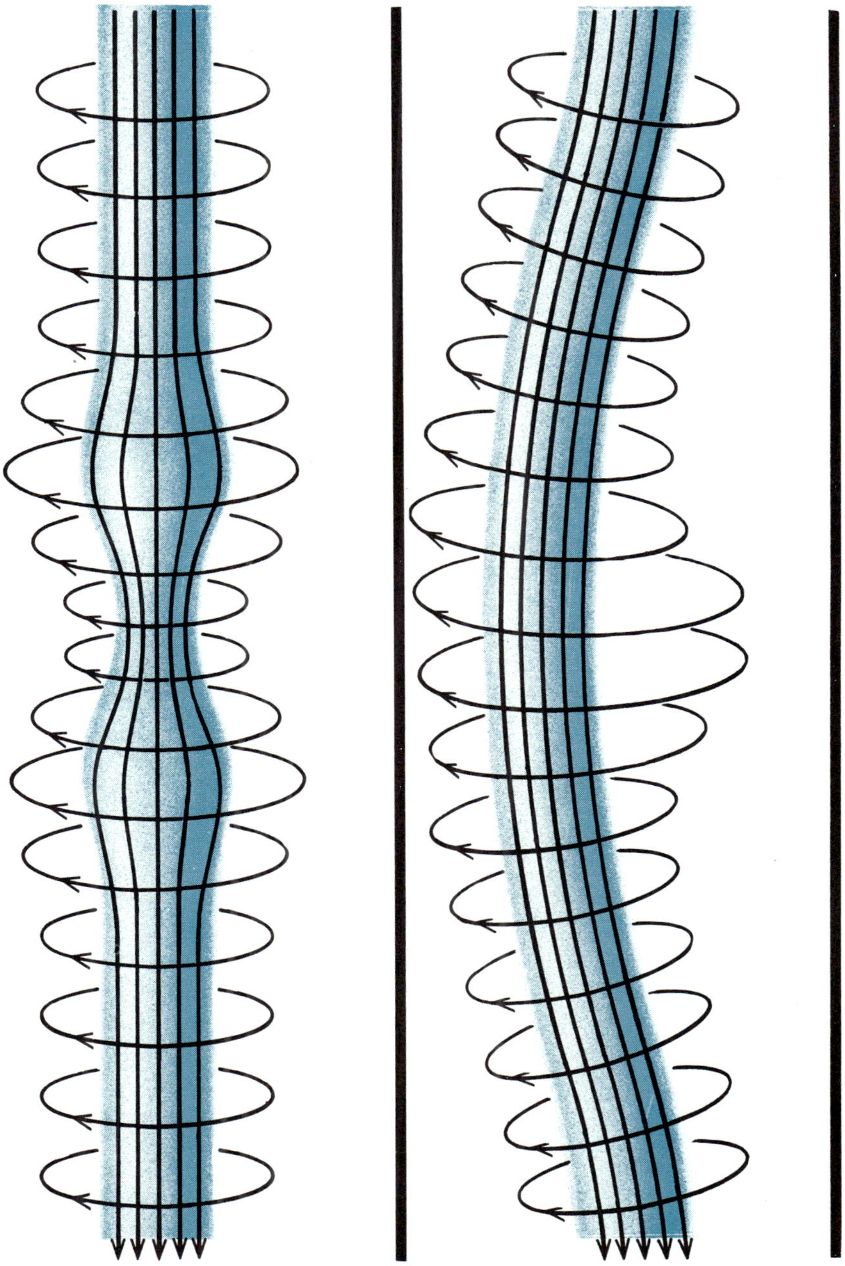

through a plasma. Tension would straighten kinks (*left*) and mutual repulsion would resist constrictions (*center*). Circular lines hold plasma away from conducting wall (*right*).

Tracing the Wisp

We are having to learn for the first time how to handle and manipulate rapidly huge quantities of electrical energy, and to build big, extremely clean vacuum systems. One of the thorniest problems is measurement. It is hard enough to create a hot plasma in the first place, but to find out what it is doing, once created, is sometimes still harder. Some new measurement techniques have already been developed. To measure the density of a plasma there is a new "microwave interferometer" using beams of millimeter radio waves as probes. The temperature of the plasma is assessed by studying its X-ray emissions, its radio "noise" and its escaping particles or reaction products. Somewhat surprisingly, a very hot plasma emits little visible light. But it has been possible to make spectroscopic studies of cooler plasmas, in which the atoms are not completely stripped of their electrons. These measurements not only indicate the temperature but also tell the velocity of the plasma's motions, by the Doppler shift. And simply by measuring changes of the magnetic field during an experiment we can get information about the temperature, density, shape and velocity of plasmas as they are formed.

To appreciate the observation problem you have to picture the scene of the events we are studying. Most of the experiments on high-temperature plasmas are carried out within antiseptic vacuum systems surrounded by conductors carrying large and rapidly varying electrical currents. And what we have to detect are the whims of an invisible, short-lived

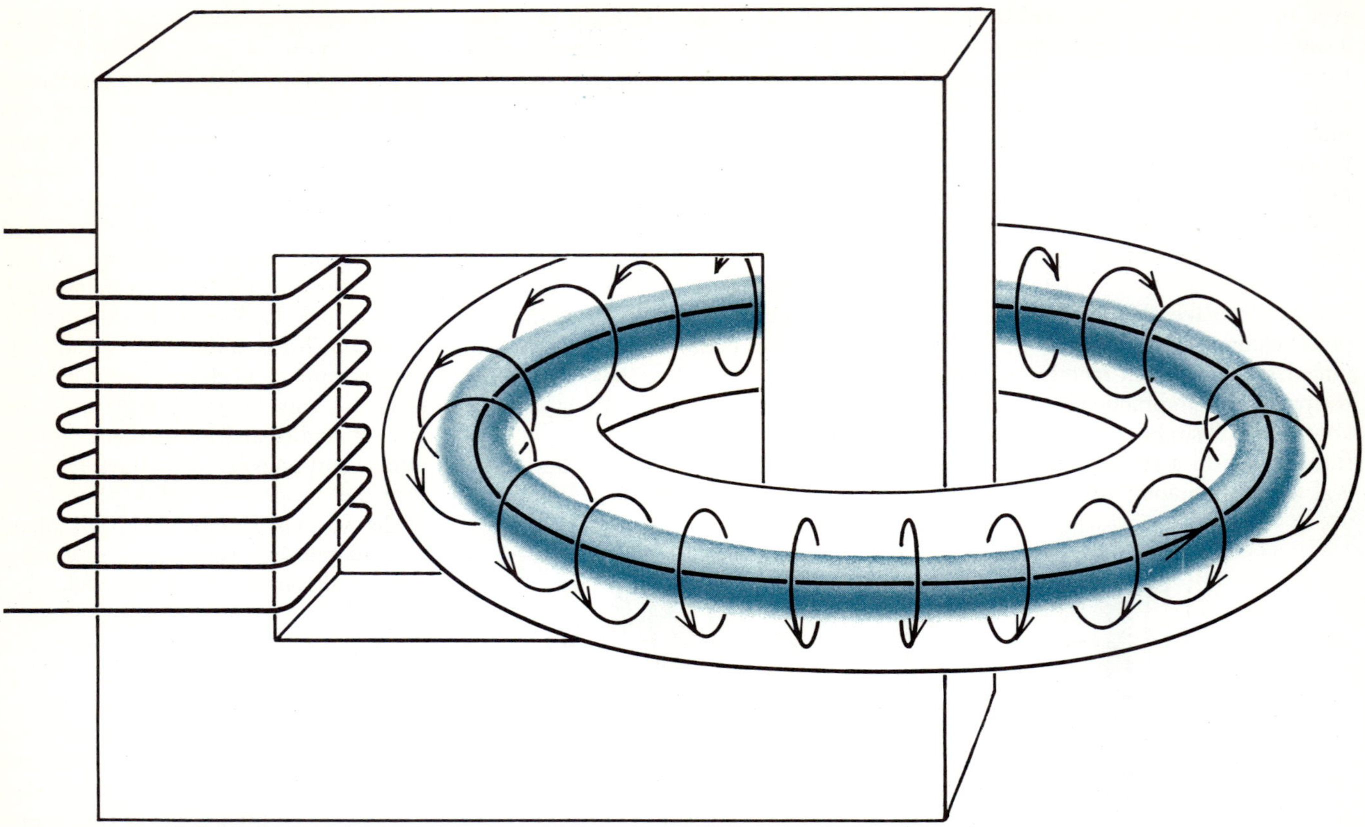

DOUGHNUT-SHAPED PINCH TUBE is made by threading a transformer core through a hollow ring containing plasma. Current through the winding at left causes a strong induced current in the plasma, which is then pinched by its own circular magnetic field.

wisp of near-nothingness somewhere in the bowels of this apparatus!

Tapping the Power

Plainly it will be several years before any fusion reactor is developed to the point where we have to face the final problem of extracting its power. But of course some thought has already been given to this matter.

If the fuel is a mixture of deuterium and tritium, the lion's share (80 per cent) of the energy released by the fusion is carried off by the neutron emerging from the reaction. This energy would be tapped by trapping the fast neutrons and feeding the resulting heat to a steam system generating electricity in the conventional way. Since such a reactor would have to breed more tritium, the neutrons would probably be trapped in a breeding blanket of lithium surrounding the reactor. Some of the electrical power generated would have to be fed back to the reactor to maintain the magnetic bottle.

If the fuel is deuterium alone, we have the intriguing possibility of turning the energy output directly into electricity. In the deuteron-deuteron fusion, 66 per cent of the energy released is imparted to the charged reaction products —helium nuclei and protons. It is quite possible that conditions could be arranged so that most of these particles stayed trapped within the plasma. In that case the heated and expanding plasma would tend to push outward against the magnetic field, and by the use of properly arranged circuits this motion could in principle be made to generate a current. In other words, in pushing against the magnetic field the expanding plasma would do work, just as steam expanding against the piston of a steam engine does work. In the case of the plasma the piston would be the "wall" of the magnetic field, and the linkages converting its energy into useful work would be electrical circuits instead of rods and wheels. It is possible that the efficiency of this engine might be much higher than that of the conventional steam cycle, for the thermodynamic principles that limit the efficiency of ordinary heat engines would not apply.

In the last analysis the feasibility of fusion power probably will hinge primarily on the size of the reactor. Very likely many potentially workable reactor schemes will have to be rejected on the basis that they would be impracticably large. On the other hand, "pocket-edition" fusion reactors are simply out of the question, on theoretical grounds. The fusion power plants of the future, if they are ever realized, will in all likelihood be large central stations for generating electrical power.

Growing Hopes

The scientists working on the fusion power project in the U. S. confidently believe that all the problems will eventually be solved, for, difficult though the problems are, they now see no really fundamental barrier standing in the way of ultimate success.

I want to mention a few of the milestones that have been passed, insofar as secrecy restrictions permit. The first group to consider the possibility of obtaining fusion power through the magnetic confinement of a hot plasma, so far as we know, were Enrico Fermi, Edward Teller, James Tuck and others at the Los Alamos Scientific Laboratory. Although they advanced their ideas around the end of World War II, no extensive experimental work was started in the U. S. until about 1951, when programs began under Tuck at Los Alamos and Lyman Spitzer at Princeton. Scientists in the United Kingdom apparently had launched some work two or three years earlier, and the U.S.S.R.

may have started about the same time. In 1952 the U. S. Atomic Energy Commission sponsored a large conference on controlled-fusion reactions. In the same year a program was initiated by Herbert York at the University of California Radiation Laboratory in Livermore. Smaller programs have since been set up at the Oak Ridge National Laboratory and New York University. Within the past year two substantial programs have been initiated with private capital: at the General Atomics Laboratory in San Diego, Calif., and at the General Electric Research Laboratory in Schenectady, N. Y.

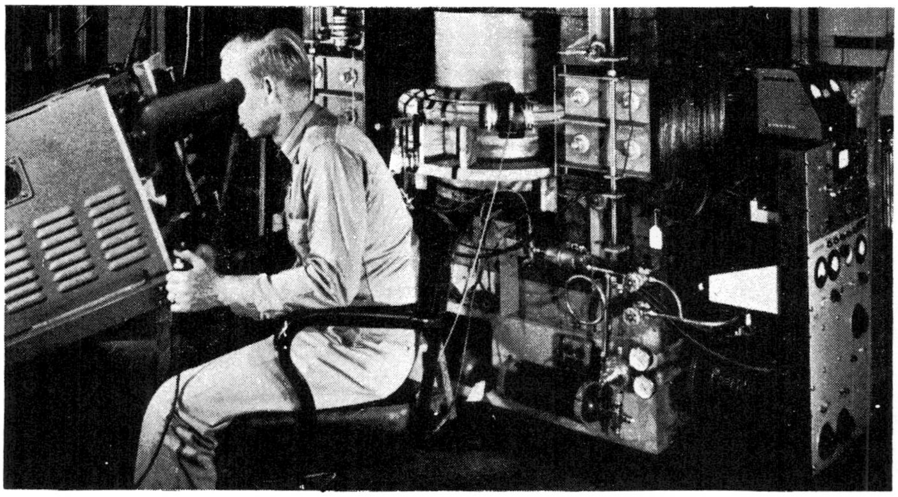

THE "PERHAPSATRON," an instrument for producing the pinch effect in a plasma, was photographed at the Los Alamos Scientific Laboratory. Doughnut tube is in the center.

Among other countries known to be engaged in studies of controlled fusion are France, Germany, the Netherlands and Sweden. It is abundantly evident that the search for fusion power is taken seriously in all parts of the world. The nature of the problems being faced, the time it will no doubt take to solve them, and the importance of the goal to be won are compelling reasons to hope for the growth of international cooperation in the research.

If the reader of this article is left with the impression that the search for fusion power is at once the most fascinating, the most difficult and potentially the most important peacetime scientific effort ever undertaken, he will be sharing the opinion of the many scientists now working on this problem.

The Prospects of Fusion Power

Recent advances in the performance of several experimental plasma containers have brought the fusion-power option very close to the "break even" level of scientific feasibility

WILLIAM C. GOUGH
and BERNARD J. EASTLUND

February 1971

The achievement of a practical fusion-power reactor would have a profound impact on almost every aspect of human society. In the past few years considerable progress has been made toward that goal. Perhaps the most revealing indication of the significance of this progress is the extent to which the emphasis in recent discussions and meetings involving workers in the field has tended to shift from the question of purely scientific feasibility to a consideration of the technological, economic and social aspects of the power-generation problem. The purpose of this article is to examine the probable effects of the recent advances on the immediate and long-term prospects of the fusion-power program, with particular reference to mankind's future energy needs.

The Role of Energy

The role of energy in determining the economic well-being of a society is often inadequately understood. In terms of *total* energy the main energy source for any society is the sun, which through the cycle of photosynthesis produces the food that is the basic fuel for sustaining the population of that society. The efficiency with which the sun's energy can be put to use, however, is determined by a feedback loop in which auxiliary energy sources form a critical link [*see illustration on page 384*]. The auxiliary energy (derived mainly from fossil fuels, water power and nuclear-fission fuels) "opens the gate" to the efficient use of the sun's energy by helping to produce fertilizers, pesticides, improved seeds, farm machinery and so on. The result is that the food yield (in terms of energy content) produced per unit area of land in a year goes up by orders of magnitude. This auxiliary energy input, when it is transformed into food energy, enables large populations to live in cities and develop new ways to multiply the efficiency of the feedback loop. If a society is to raise its standard of living by increasing the efficiency of its agricultural feedback loop, clearly it must expand its auxiliary energy sources.

The dilemma here is that the economically less developed countries of the world cannot *all* industrialize on the model of the more developed countries, for the simple reason that the latter countries, which contain only a small fraction of the world's population, currently maintain their high standard of living by consuming a disproportionately large share of the world's available supply of auxiliary energy. Just as there is a direct, almost linear, relation between a nation's use of auxiliary energy and its standard of living, so also there is a similar relation between energy consumption and the amount of raw material the nation uses and the amount of waste material it produces. Thus the more developed countries consume a correspondingly oversized share of the world's reserves of material resources and also account for most of the world's environmental pollution.

In order to achieve a more equitable and stable balance between the standards of living in the more developed countries and those in the less developed countries, only two alternatives exist. The more developed countries could reduce their consumption of auxiliary energy (thereby lowering their standard of living as well) or they could contribute to the development of new, vastly greater sources of auxiliary energy in order to help meet the rising demands for a better standard of living on the part of the rapidly growing populations of the less developed countries.

When one projects the world's long-term energy requirements against this background, another important factor must be taken into account. There are finite limits to the world's reserves of material resources and to the ability of the earth's ecological system to absorb pollutants safely. As a consequence future societies will be forced to develop "looped," or "circular," materials economies to replace their present, inherently wasteful "linear" materials economies [*see bottom illustration on page 393*]. In such a "stationary state" system, limits on the materials inventory, and hence on the total wealth of the society, would be set by nature. Within these limits, however, the standard of living of the population would be higher if the rate of flow of materials were lower. This maximizing of the life expectancy of the materials inventory could be accomplished in two ways: increasing the durability of individual commodities and developing the technological means to recycle the limited supply of material resources.

The conclusion appears radical. Future societies must *minimize* their physical flow of production and consumption. Since a society's gross national product for the most part measures the flow of physical things, it too would be reduced.

But all nations now try to *maximize* their gross national product, and hence their rate of flow of materials! The explanation of this paradox is that in the existing linear economies the inputs for increasing production must come from the environment, which leads to depletion, while an almost equal amount of materials in the form of waste must be returned to the environment, which leads to pollution. This primary cause of pollution is augmented by the pollution that is produced by the energy sources used to drive the system.

In order to make the transition to a stationary-state world economy, the wealthier nations will have to develop the technology—and the concomitant auxiliary energy sources—necessary to operate a closed materials economy. This capability could then be transferred to the poorer nations so that they could develop to the level of the wealthier nations without exhausting the world's supply of resources or destroying the environment. Thus some of the causes of international conflict would be removed, thereby reducing the danger of nuclear war.

Of course any effort to bring about a rapid change from linear economies to looped economies will encounter the massive economic, social and political forces that sustain the present system. The question of how to distribute the stock of wealth, including leisure, within a stationary-state economy will remain. In summary, the world's requirements for energy are intimately related to the issues of population expansion, economic development, materials depletion, pollution, war and the organization of human societies.

The Energy Options

What are the available energy options for the future? To begin with there are the known finite and irreplaceable energy sources: the fossil fuels and the better-grade, or easily fissionable, nuclear fuels such as uranium 235. Estimates of the life expectancy of these sources vary, but it is generally agreed that they are being used up at a rapid rate—a rate that will moreover be accelerated by increases in both population and living standards. In addition, environmental considerations could further restrict the use of these energy sources.

Certain other known energy sources, such as water power, tidal power, geothermal power and wind power are "infinite" in the sense of being continuously replenished. The total useful *amount* of energy available from these sources, however, is insufficient to meet the needs of the future.

Direct solar radiation, resulting from the fusion reactions that take place in the core of the sun, is an abundant as well as effectively "infinite" energy source. The immediate practical obstacle to the direct use of the sun's energy as an effective auxiliary energy source is the necessity of finding some way to economically concentrate the available low energy density of solar radiation. Controlled fusion is another potentially "infinite" energy source; its energy output arises from the reduction of the total mass of a nuclear system that accompanies the merger of two light

U.S. TOKAMAK, a toroidal plasma-confinement machine used in fusion research, was recently put into operation at the Plasma Physics Laboratory of Princeton University. Until about a year ago this machine, formerly known as the Model-C stellarator and now called the Model ST tokamak, had been the largest of the stellarator class of experimental plasma containers developed primarily at the Princeton laboratory. The decision to convert it to the closely related tokamak design followed the 1969 announcement by the Russian fusion-research group of some important new results obtained from their Model T-3 machine, the most advanced of the tokamak class of plasma containers developed mainly at the I. V. Kurchatov Institute of Atomic Energy near Moscow. In large part because of the cooperative nature of the world fusion-research program, this conversion was accomplished quickly and the Model ST has already produced results comparable to those obtained by the Russians. Several other tokamak-type machines are being built in this country.

RUSSIAN STELLARATOR is now the largest representative of this class of experimental plasma containers in the world. It is named the Uragan (or "hurricane") stellarator and is located at the Physico-Technical Institute of the Academy of Sciences of the Ukrainian S.S.R. at Kharkov. In both photographs on this page the large circular structures surrounding and almost completely obscuring the toroidal plasma chambers are the primary magnet coils. The main difference between the tokamak design and the stellarator design is that in a tokamak a secondary plasma-stabilizing magnetic field is generated by an electric current flowing axially through the plasma itself, whereas in a stellarator this secondary magnetic field is set up by external helical coils situated just inside the primary coils and hence not visible.

nuclei. The most likely fuel for a fusion-power energy source is deuterium, an abundant heavy isotope of hydrogen easily separated from seawater.

In addition to these two primary "infinite" energy sources, secondary "infinite" energy sources could be made by using neutrons to transmute less useful elements into other elements capable of being used effectively as fuels. Thus for fission systems the vast reserves of uranium 238 could be converted by neutron bombardment into easily fissionable plutonium 239; similarly, thorium 232 could be converted into uranium 233. For fusion systems lithium could be converted into tritium, another heavy isotope of hydrogen with a comparatively low resistance to entering a fusion reaction and a comparatively high energy output once it does.

The prime hope for extending the world's reserves of nuclear-fission fuels is the development of the neutron-rich fast breeder fission reactors [see "Fast Breeder Reactors," by Glenn T. Seaborg and Justin L. Bloom, the article beginning on page 361]. Another potential source of abundant, inexpensive neutrons is a fusion-fission hybrid system, an alternative that will be discussed further below.

Fusion Energy

Nuclear fusion, the basic energy process of the stars, was first reproduced on the earth in 1932 in an experiment involving the collision of artificially accelerated deuterium nuclei. Although it was thereby shown that fusion energy could be released in this way, the use of particle accelerators to provide the nuclei with enough energy to overcome their Coulomb, or mutually repulsive, forces was never considered seriously as a practical method for power generation. The reason is that the large majority of the nuclei that collide in an accelerator scatter without reacting; thus it is impossible to produce more energy than was used to accelerate the nuclei in the first place.

The uncontrolled release of a massive amount of fusion energy was achieved in 1952 with the first thermonuclear test explosion. This test proved that fusion energy could be released on a large scale by raising the temperature of a high-density gas of charged particles (a plasma) to about 50 million degrees Celsius, thereby increasing the probability that fusion reactions will take place within the gas.

Coincident with the development of the hydrogen bomb, the search for a more controlled means of releasing fusion energy was begun independently in the U.S., Britain and the U.S.S.R. Essentially this search involves looking for a practical way to maintain a comparatively low-density plasma at a temperature high enough so that the output of fusion energy derived from the plasma is greater than the input of some other kind of energy supplied to the plasma. Since no solid material can exist at the temperature range required for a useful energy output (on the order of 100 million degrees C.) the principal emphasis from the beginning has been on the use of magnetic fields to confine the plasma.

The variety of magnetic "bottles" designed for this purpose over the years can be arranged in several broad categories in order of increasing plasma density [*see illustration on pages 388 and 389*]. First there are the basic plasma devices. These are low-density, low-temperature systems used primarily to study the fundamental properties of plasmas. Their configuration can be either linear (open) or toroidal (closed). Linear basic-plasma devices include simple glow-discharge systems (similar in operation to ordinary fluorescent lamps) and the more sophisticated "Q-machines" ("Q" for "quiescent") found in many university plasma-physics laboratories. Toroidal representatives of this class include the "multipole" devices, developed primarily at Gulf Energy & Environmental Systems, Inc. (formerly Gulf General Atomic Inc.) and the University of Wisconsin, and the spherator, developed at the Plasma Physics Laboratory of Princeton University.

Next there are the medium-density plasma containers; these are defined as systems in which the outward pressure of the plasma is much less than the inward pressure of the magnetic field. A typical configuration in this density range is the linear magnetic bottle, which is usually "stoppered" at the ends by magnetic "mirrors": regions of somewhat greater magnetic-field strength that reflect escaping particles back into the bottle. In addition extra current-carrying structures are often used to improve the stability of the plasma. These structures were originally proposed on theoretical grounds in 1955 by Harold Grad of New York University. They were first used successfully in an experimental test in 1962 by the Russian physicist M. S. Ioffe.

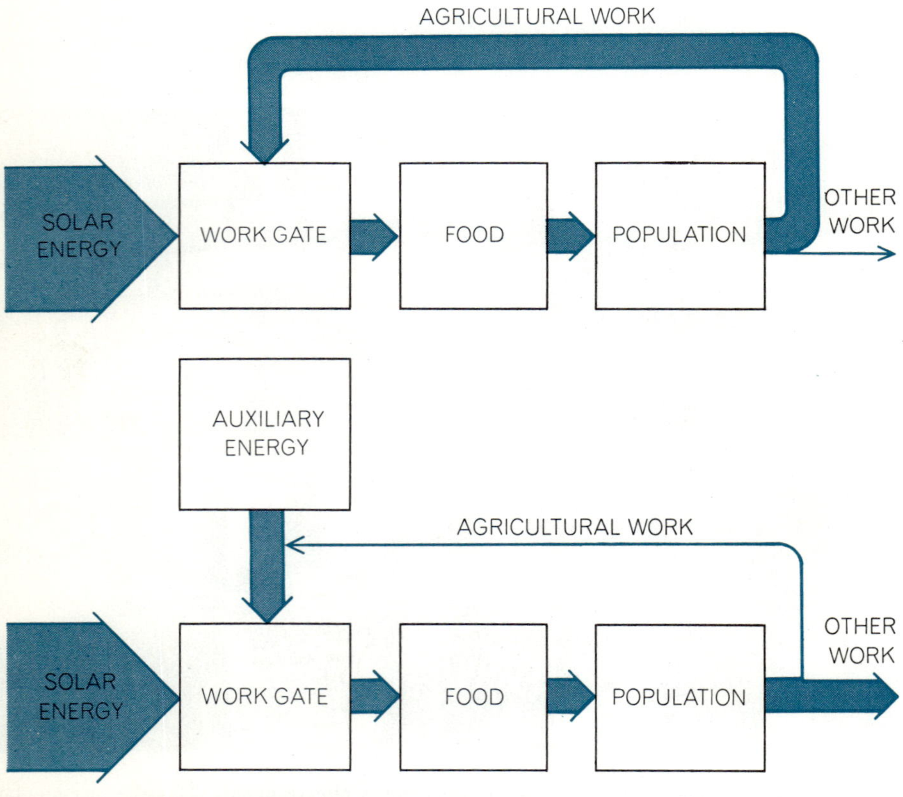

ROLE OF AUXILIARY ENERGY in determining the economic well-being of a society is illustrated by these two diagrams of agricultural feedback loops. In an economically less developed country (*top*) the bulk of the population must be devoted to the agricultural transformation of the sun's energy into food in order to support itself at a subsistence level. In an economically more developed industrial country (*bottom*) auxiliary energy sources "open the gate" to the more efficient utilization of the sun's energy, making it possible for the entire population to maintain a higher standard of living and freeing many people to live in cities and develop new ways to multiply the efficiency of the feedback loop.

		LIFE EXPECTANCY OF KNOWN RESERVES (YEARS)		LIFE EXPECTANCY OF POTENTIAL RESERVES (YEARS)		LIFE EXPECTANCY OF TOTAL RESERVES (YEARS)	
		AT .17Q	AT 2.8Q	AT .17Q	AT 2.8Q	AT .17Q	AT 2.8Q
FINITE ENERGY SOURCES	FOSSIL FUELS (COAL, OIL, GAS)	132	8	2,700	165	2,832	173
	MORE ACCESSIBLE FISSION FUELS (URANIUM AT $5 TO $30 PER POUND OF U_3O_8 BURNED AT 1.5 PERCENT EFFICIENCY)	66	4	66	4	132	8
	LESS ACCESSIBLE FISSION FUELS (URANIUM AT $30 TO $500 PER POUND OF U_3O_8 BURNED AT 1.5 PERCENT EFFICIENCY	43,000	2,600	129,000	7,800	172,000	10,400
"INFINITE" NATURAL ENERGY SOURCES	WATER POWER, TIDAL POWER, GEOTHERMAL POWER, WIND POWER	INSUFFICIENT		INSUFFICIENT		INSUFFICIENT	
	SOLAR RADIATION	10 BILLION	10 BILLION			10 BILLION	10 BILLION
	FUSION FUELS (DEUTERIUM FROM OCEAN)	45 BILLION	2.7 BILLION			45 BILLION	2.7 BILLION
"INFINITE" ARTIFICIAL ENERGY SOURCES (ELEMENTS TRANSMUTED FROM OTHER ELEMENTS BY NEUTRON BOMBARDMENT)	FISSION FUELS (PLUTONIUM 239 FROM URANIUM 238; URANIUM 233 FROM THORIUM 232)	8.8 MILLION	536,000	21 MILLION	1.3 MILLION	30 MILLION	1.8 MILLION
	FUSION FUELS (TRITIUM FROM LITHIUM) a) ON LAND b) IN OCEAN	48,000 120 MILLION	2,900 7.3 MILLION	UNKNOWN	UNKNOWN	48,000+ 120 MILLION	2,900+ 7.3 MILLION

WORLD ENERGY RESERVES are listed in this table in terms of their life expectancy estimated on the basis of two extreme assumptions, which were chosen so as to bracket a reasonable range of values. First, the assumption was made that the world population would remain constant at its 1968 level of 3.5 billion persons and that the energy-consumption rate of this population would remain constant at the estimated 1968 rate of .17 Q (Q is a unit of heat measurement equal to 10^{18} BTU, or British Thermal Units). Second, the assumption was made that the world population would eventually reach seven billion and that this population would consume energy at a per capita rate of 400 million BTU per year (about 20 percent higher than the present U.S. rate), giving a total world energy-consumption rate of 2.8 Q per year. (A commonly projected world energy-consumption rate for the year 2000 is one Q.) Current fission-converter reactors use only between 1 and 2 percent of the uranium's potential energy content, since the component of the ore that is burned as fuel is primarily high-grade, or easily fissionable, uranium 235. The world fission-fuel reserves were derived by multiplying the U.S. reserves times the ratio of world land area to the U.S. land area (approximately 16.2 to one). For fusion-converter reactors lithium-utilization studies show that natural lithium, a mixture of lithium 6 and lithium 7, would be superior to pure lithium 6 in a tritium-breeding reactor "blanket" and would yield an energy output of about 86.4 million BTU per gram. The figure for known world lithium reserves is based on a study carried out last year by James J. Norton of the U.S. Geological Survey. The potential reserves of lithium are unknown, since there has been no exploration program comparable to that undertaken for, say, uranium. Lithium, however, is between five and 15 times more abundant in the earth's crust than uranium. Finally, the life expectancy of the earth—and hence that of potentially useful solar radiation—is predicted to be at most 10 billion years.

The straight rods used by Ioffe in his experiment have come to be called Ioffe bars, but such stabilizing structures can assume various other shapes. For example, in one series of medium-density linear devices they resemble the seam of a baseball; accordingly these devices, developed at the Lawrence Radiation Laboratory of the University of California at Livermore, are named Baseball I and Baseball II.

Medium-density plasma containers with a toroidal geometry include the stellarators, originally developed at the Princeton Plasma Physics Laboratory, and the tokamaks, originally developed at the I. V. Kurchatov Institute of Atomic Energy near Moscow. The only essential difference between these two machines is that in a stellarator a secondary, plasma-stabilizing magnetic field is set up by external helical coils, whereas in a tokamak this field is generated by an electric current flowing through the plasma itself. The close similarity between these two designs was emphasized recently by the fact that the Princeton Model-C stellarator was rather quickly converted to a tokamak system following the recent announcement by the Russians of some important new results from their Tokamak-3 machine.

The astron concept, also developed at the Lawrence Radiation Laboratory at Livermore, is another example of a medium-density plasma container. In overall geometry it shares some characteristics of both the linear and the toroidal designs.

Higher-density plasma containers, defined as those in which the plasma pressure is comparable to the magnetic-field pressure, have also been built in both the linear and the toroidal forms. In one such class of devices, called the "theta pinch" machines, the electric current is in the theta, or azimuthal, direction (around the axis) and the resulting magnetic field is in the zeta, or axial, direction (along the axis). The Scylla and Scyllac machines at the Los Alamos Scientific Laboratory are respectively examples of a linear theta-pinch design and a toroidal theta-pinch design.

As the density of the plasma is increased further, one reaches a technological limit imposed by the inability of the materials used in the magnet coils to withstand the pressure of the magnetic field. Consequently very-high-density plasma systems are often fast-pulsed and obtain their principal confining forces from "self-generated" magnetic fields (fields set up by electric currents in the plasma itself), from electrostatic fields or from inertial pressures. In this very-high-density category are the "zeta pinch" machines, devices in which the electric current is in the zeta direction and the resulting magnetic field is in the theta direction. An example of this type of configuration is the Columba device at Los Alamos.

Other very-high-density, fast-pulsed systems include the "strong focus" designs, in which a stream of plasma in a cylindrical, coaxial pipe is heated rapidly by shock waves as it is brought to a sharp focus by self-generated magnetic forces, and laser designs, in which a pellet of fuel is ionized instantaneously by a pulse from a high-power laser, producing an "inertially confined" plasma. Still another confinement scheme that has been investigated in this general density range includes an electrostatic device in which the plasma is confined by inertial forces generated by concentric spherical electrodes.

The Fusion-Power Balance

What are the fundamental requirements for a meaningful release of fusion energy in a reactor? First, the plasma must be hot enough for the production of fusion energy to exceed the energy loss due to bremsstrahlung radiation (radiation resulting from near-collisions between electrons and nuclei in the plasma). The temperature at which this transition occurs is called the ignition temperature. For a fuel cycle based on fusion reactions between deuterium and tritium nuclei the ignition temperature is about 40 million degrees C. Second, the plasma must be confined long enough to release a significant net output of energy. Third, the energy must be recovered in a useful form.

In the first years of the controlled-fusion research program one of the major goals was to achieve the ignition temperature in a fairly dense laboratory plasma. Steady progress was made toward this goal, culminating in 1963, when the ignition temperature (for a deuterium-tritium fuel mixture) was reached in one of the Scylla devices at Los Alamos. This test, which was performed in a pure deuterium plasma to avoid the generation of excessive neutron flux, resulted in the release of fusion energy: about a thousandth of a joule per pulse, or 370 watts of fusion power during the three-microsecond duration of the pulse. If the test had been performed using a deuterium-tritium mixture, it would have released approximately a half-joule of fusion energy per pulse, or 180,000 watts of fusion power.

Today a large number of different devices have either achieved the deuterium-tritium ignition temperature or are very close to it [*see bottom illustration on opposite page*]. The main difficulties encountered in reaching this goal were comparatively straightforward energy-loss processes involving impurity atoms that entered the plasma from the walls of the container. A large research effort in the areas of vacuum and surface technology was a major factor in surmounting the ignition-temperature barrier.

The problem of confining a plasma long enough to release a significant net amount of energy has proved to be even more difficult than the problem of achieving the ignition temperature. Extremely rapid energy-loss processes—known collectively as "anomalous diffusion" processes—appeared to prevent the attainment of adequate confinement times. Plasma instabilities were the primary cause of this rapid plasma leakage [see "The Leakage Problem in Fusion Reactors," by Francis F. Chen; SCIENTIFIC AMERICAN, July, 1967]. Within the past few years, however, several large containment devices have reduced these instabilities to such a low amplitude that other more subtle effects, such as convective plasma losses and magnetic-field imperfections, can be studied. As a result it has been shown that there is no basic law of physics (such as an instability-initiated anomalous plasma loss) that prevents plasma confinement for times long enough to release significant net fusion energy. In fact, "classical," or ideal, plasma confinement has been achieved in several machines; this is the best confinement possible and yields a plasma-loss rate much lower than that required for a fusion reactor.

The twin achievements of ignition temperature and adequate confinement time, it should be noted, have taken place in quite different machines, each

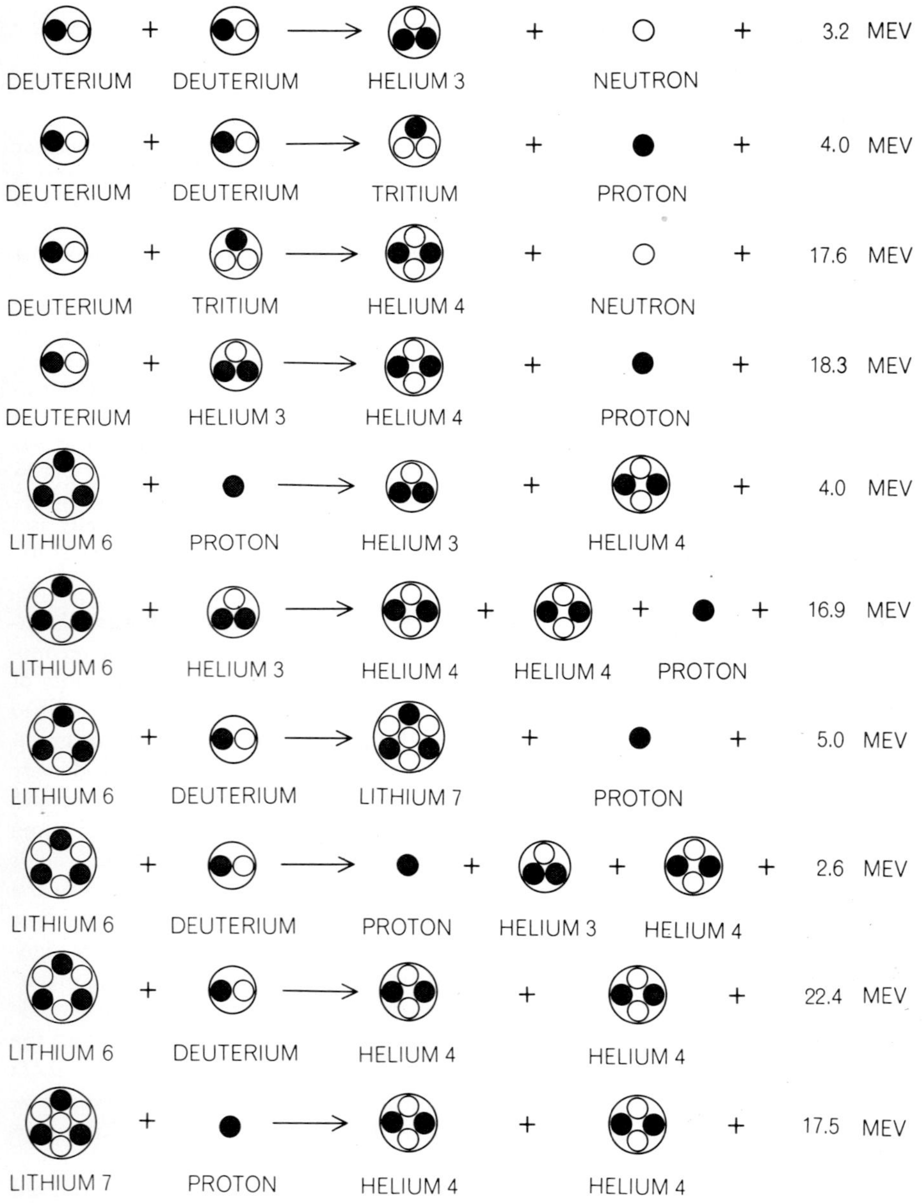

FUSION REACTIONS regarded as potentially useful in full-scale fusion reactors are represented in this partial list. The two possible deuterium-deuterium reactions occur with equal probability. The deuterium-tritium fuel cycle has been considered particularly attractive because this mixture has the lowest ignition temperature known (about 40 million degrees Celsius). Other fuel cycles, including many not shown in this list, have been attracting increased attention lately, since certain plasma-confinement schemes actually operate better at higher temperatures and offer the advantage of direct conversion to electricity. The energy released by each reaction is given at right in millions of electron volts (*MeV*).

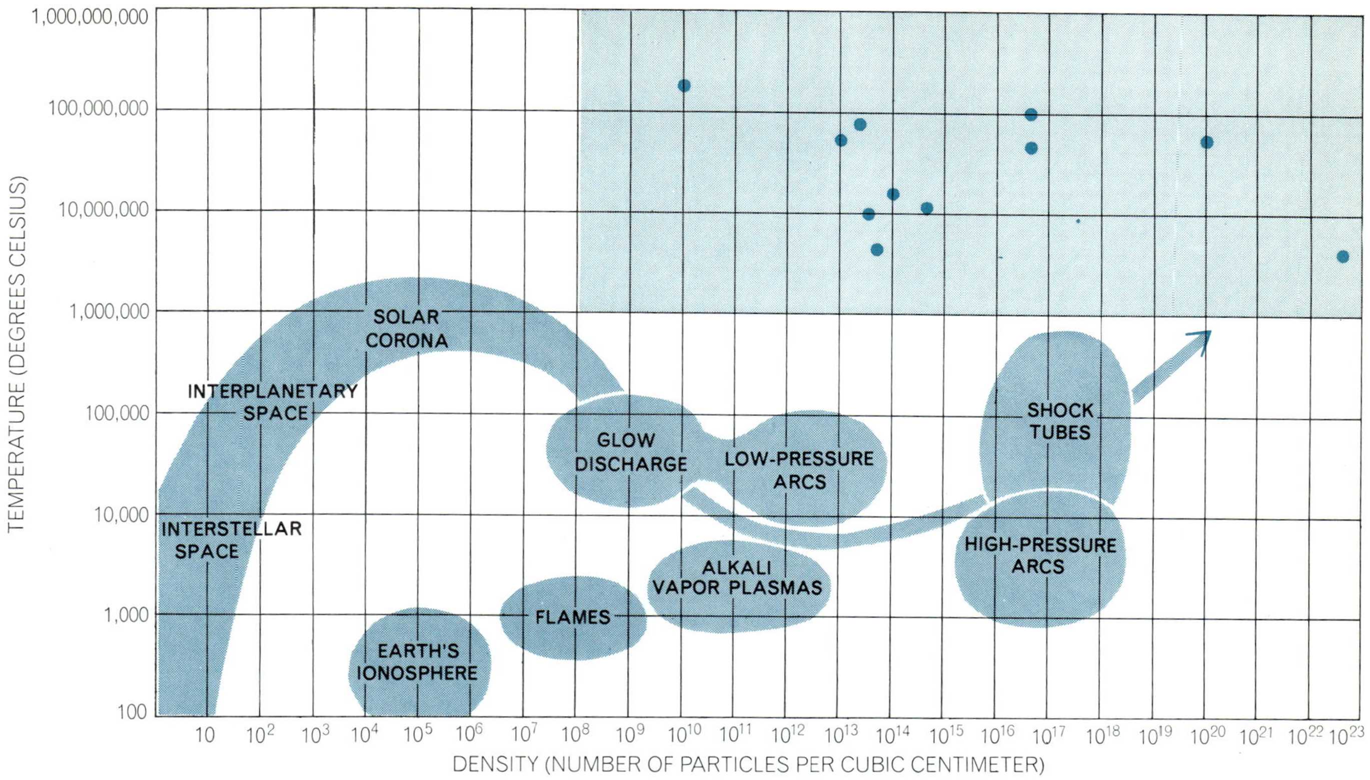

INDUSTRIALLY UNEXPLORED RANGE of plasma temperatures and densities has already been made available by the fusion-power research program. These experimental plasmas (*colored dots*), which range in temperature from 500,000 to a billion degrees C. and in density from 10^9 to 10^{22} ions per cubic centimeter, are compared here with various other industrial and natural plasmas.

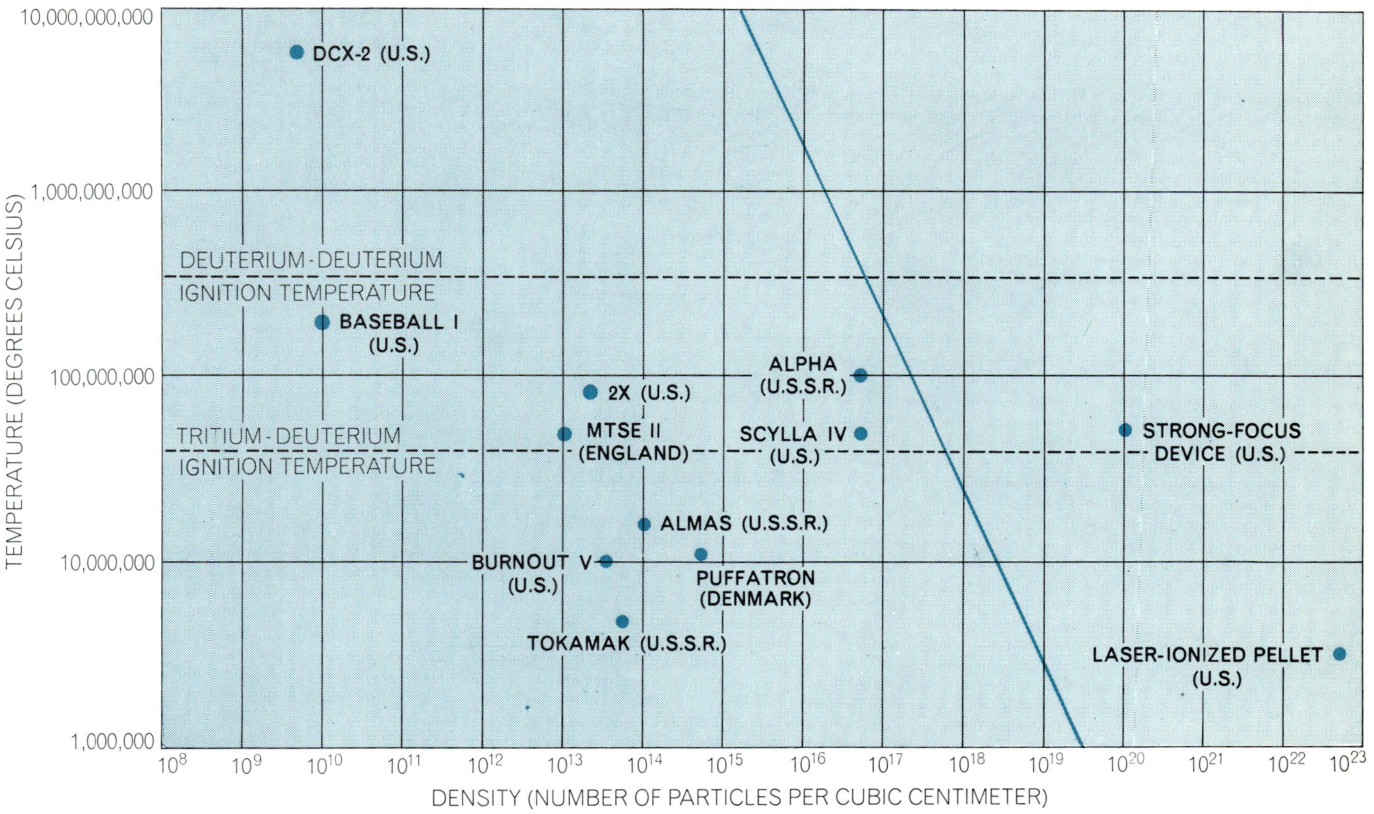

PLASMA EXPERIMENTS that have achieved temperatures near or above the fusion ignition temperatures of a deuterium-tritium fuel (*bottom horizontal line*) and a deuterium-deuterium fuel (*top horizontal line*) are identified by the name of the experimental device and the country in which the experiment took place in this enlargement of the upper right-hand section of the illustration at top. The diagonal colored line represents the limit beyond which the materials used to construct the magnet coils can no longer withstand the magnetic-field pressure required to confine the plasma (assumed to be 300,000 gauss in this case). Beyond this limit only fast-pulsed systems (in which the magnetic fields are generated by intense currents inside the plasma itself) or systems operating on entirely different principles (such as laser-produced, inertially confined plasmas) are possible. The record of six billion degrees C. was achieved with the aid of a high-energy ion-injection system associated with DCX-2 device at the Oak Ridge National Laboratory.

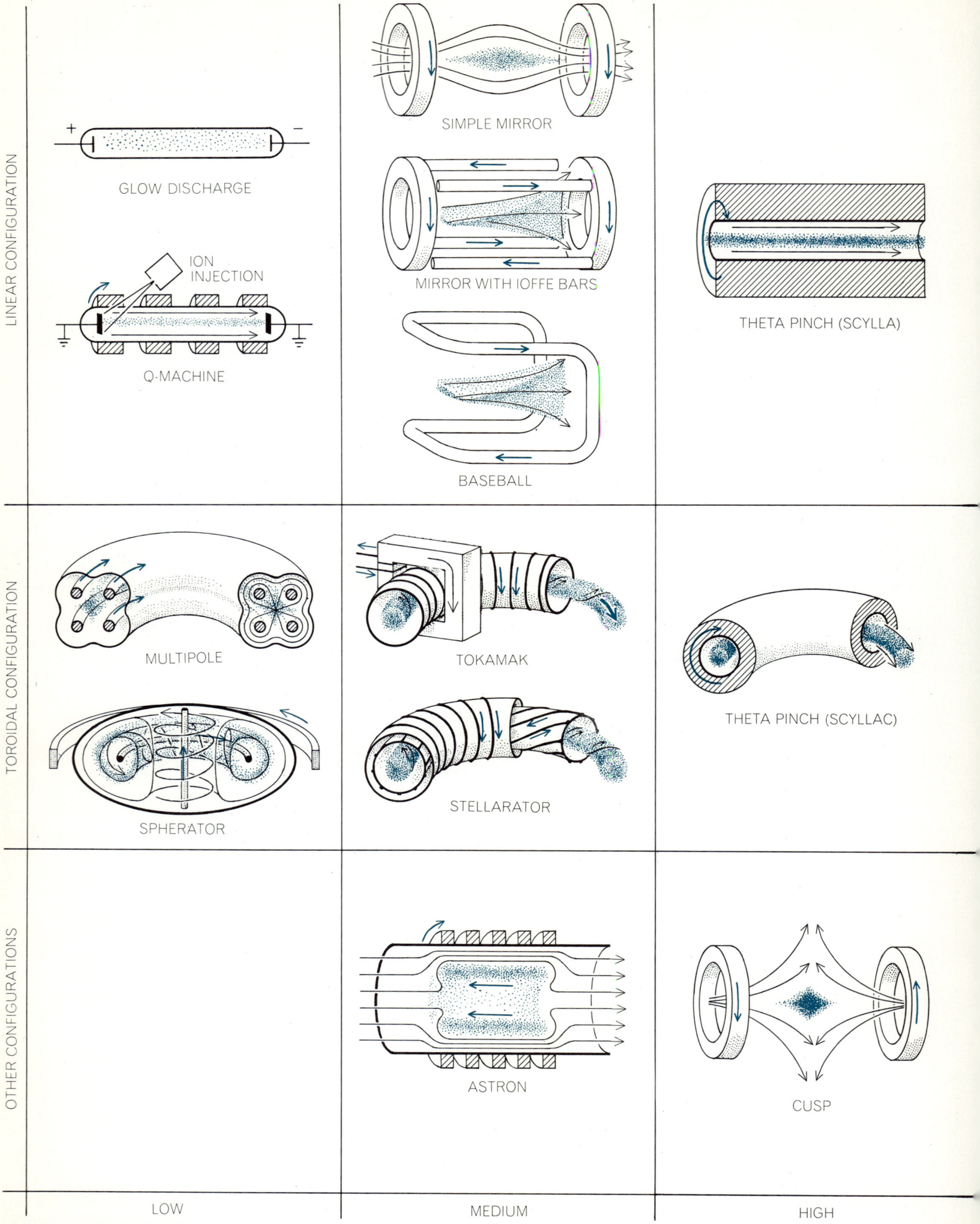

PRINCIPAL SCHEMES devised in the past 18 years to confine plasmas for fusion research are arranged in the illustration on these two pages in order of increasing plasma density (*left to right*) and overall geometry (*top to bottom*). Only a few examples are depicted in each category. In every case the plasma is in color, the colored arrows signify the direction of the electric current and the black arrows denote the direction of the resultant magnetic field. Various structural details have been omitted for clarity. For each example shown there are a large number of variations either already in existence or in the conceptual stage. Furthermore, the

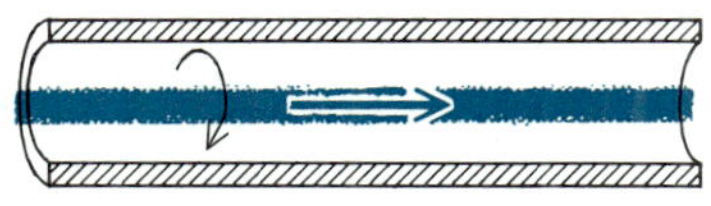

ZETA PINCH

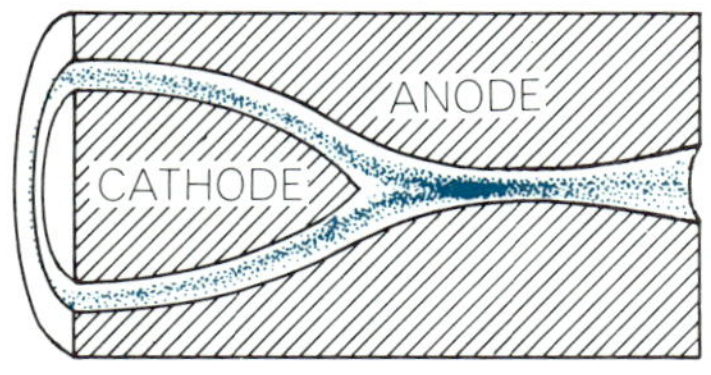

PLASMA FOCUS

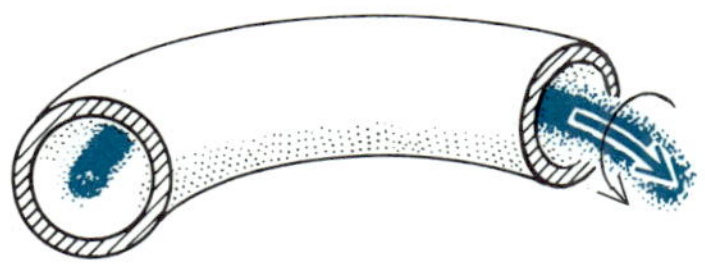

ZETA PINCH

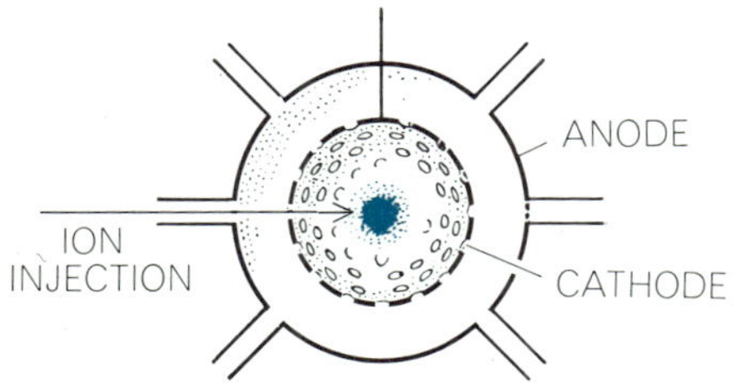

ELECTROSTATIC

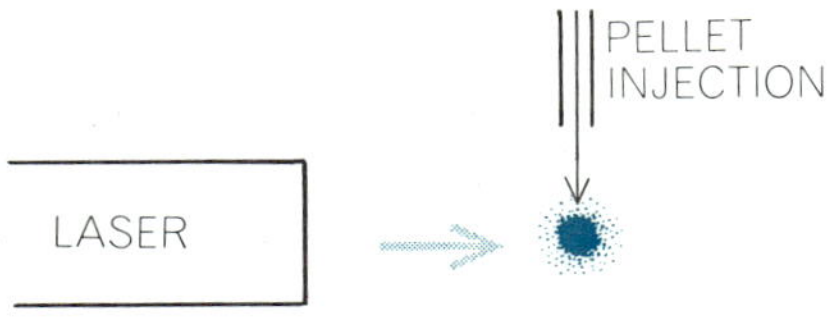

LASER-IONIZED PELLET

VERY HIGH

fact that an example is given in one category does not necessarily mean that that configuration is not applicable to some other category; there are, for instance, toroidal Q-machines and medium-density cusp designs.

specially designed to maximize the conditions for reaching one goal or the other. How does one compare the performances of these machines in order to gauge how near one is to the combined conditions needed to operate a practical fusion-power reactor? The basic criterion for determining the length of time a plasma must be confined at a given density and temperature to produce a "break even" point in the power balance was laid down in 1957 by the British physicist J. D. Lawson. Combining data on the physics of fusion reactions with some estimates of the efficiency of energy recovery from a hypothetical fusion reactor, Lawson derived a factor, which he called R, that denoted the ratio of energy output to energy input needed to compensate for all possible plasma losses. Lawson's criterion is still in general use as a convenient yardstick for measuring the extent to which losses must be controlled in order to make possible the construction of a fusion reactor. Although more recent calculations consider many other physical constraints in order to arrive at the break-even power balance, these criteria still give values very close to those derived by Lawson.

For a deuterium-tritium fuel mixture Lawson found that at temperatures higher than the ignition temperature the product of density and confinement time must be equal to 10^{14} seconds per cubic centimeter in order to achieve the break-even condition. This criterion defines a surface in three-dimensional space, the coordinates being the logarithmic values of density, temperature and confinement time [*see illustration on page 391*]. The goal of a break-even release of energy will have been achieved when the set of conditions for a given machine reaches this surface. It should be emphasized that the exact location and shape of the surface is a function of both the fuel cycle used and the recovery efficiency of the hypothetical reactor system. Fuels other than the deuterium-tritium mixture would increase the temperature needed to achieve a break-even power balance.

The extraordinary progress made recently by various groups in learning how to raise the combination of density, temperature and confinement time to a set of values approaching this break-even surface can be appreciated by referring to the illustration of the Lawson-criterion surface. The several plasma systems shown range in density from about 10^9 ions per cubic centimeter to 5×10^{22} ions per cubic centimeter. (Below a density of about 10^{11} ions per cubic centimeter the power density would be so low that it would require an impractically large reactor.) The particular density range chosen for investigation in each case is a function of the scientific preferences of the investigators concerning the best route to fusion power and the available technology (magnets, power supplies, lasers and so forth). Thus there are various trajectories to the break-even surface being followed through the three-dimensional "parameter space" of the illustration. Closing the gap between where each trajectory is now and the break-even surface depends in some cases (for example the tokamak devices) on obtaining a better understanding of the physical principles required to develop reliable scaling rules, whereas in other cases (such as the linear theta-pinch devices) all that may be required is an economic solution to the engineering problem of building a large enough system.

Fusion-Reactor Designs

How would a full-scale fusion reactor operate? In the first place fusion reactors, like fission reactors, could be run on a variety of fuels. The nature of the fuel used in the core of a fusion reactor would, however, have a decisive effect on the method used to recover the fusion energy and the uses to which the recovered energy might be put. Most research on reactor technology has centered on the use of a deuterium-tritium mixture as a fuel. The reason is that the mixture has the lowest ignition temperature, and hence the lowest rate of energy loss by radiation, of any possible fusion fuel. Nonetheless, other combinations of light nuclei have been considered for many years as potential fusion fuels. Prominent among these are reactions involving a deuterium nucleus and a helium-3 nucleus and reactions involving a single proton (a hydrogen nucleus) and a lithium-6 nucleus. Because containment based on the magnetic-mirror concept actually operates better at higher temperatures, a number of other fuels have been attracting increased attention [*see illustration on page 386*].

Depending on the fuel used, a fusion reactor could release its energy in several ways. For example, neutrons, which are produced at various rates by different fusion reactions, can cross magnetic fields and penetrate matter quite easily. A reactor based on, say, a deuterium-tritium fuel cycle would release approximately 80 percent of its energy in the form of highly energetic neutrons. Such a reactor could be made to produce electricity by absorbing the neutron energy in a liquid-lithium shield, circulating the

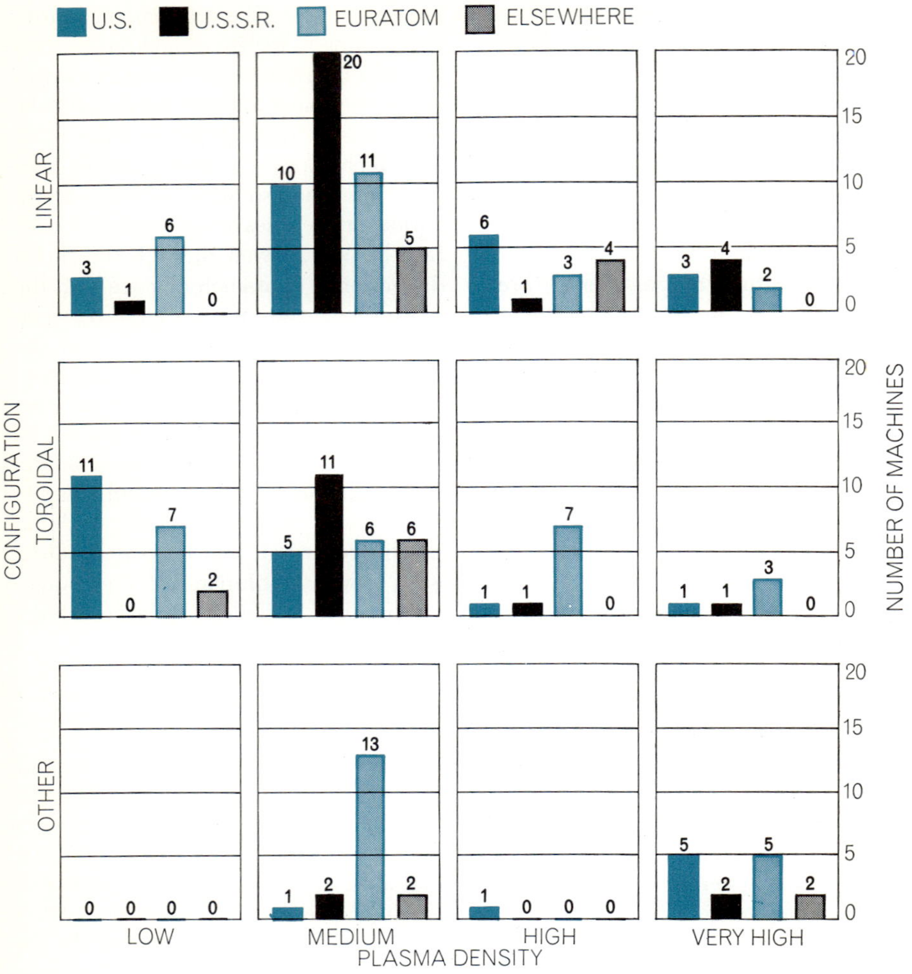

INVENTORY of the number of machines now operating throughout the world in each of the broad categories represented in the illustration on the preceding two pages is given in this table. The total number in each category is broken down into subtotals for the U.S., the U.S.S.R., the European Atomic Energy Community, or Euratom, countries (Belgium, France, Germany, Italy, Luxembourg and the Netherlands) and the rest of the world (principally Japan, Sweden and Australia). Britain, although not officially a member of Euratom, is included in the Euratom subtotal. The figures are drawn mainly from a recent survey compiled by Amasa S. Bishop and published by the International Atomic Energy Commission. The U.S. fusion-power program currently represents about a fifth of the world total.

liquid lithium to a heat exchanger and there heating water to produce steam and so drive a conventional steam-generator electric power plant [*see top illustration on page 392*].

This general approach could also lead to an attractive new technique for converting the world's reserves of uranium 238 and thorium 232 to suitable fuels for fission reactors—the fusion-fission hybrid system mentioned above. By employing the abundance of inexpensive, energetic neutrons produced by the deuterium-tritium fuel cycle to synthesize fissionable heavy nuclei, a fusion reactor could act as a new type of breeder reactor. This could have the effect of lowering the break-even surface defined by Lawson's criterion, bringing the fusion-breeding scheme actually closer to feasibility than the generation of electricity solely by fusion reactions. Cheap fuel might thus be made for existing fission reactors in systems that could be inherently safe. A "neutron-rich" economy created by fusion reactors would have other potential benefits. For example, it has been suggested that large quantities of neutrons could be useful for "burning" various fission products, thereby alleviating the problem of disposing of radioactive wastes.

Fuel cycles that release most of their energy in the form of charged particles offer still other avenues for the recovery of fusion energy. For example, Richard F. Post of the Lawrence Radiation Laboratory at Livermore has proposed a direct energy-conversion scheme in which the energetic charged particles produced in a fusion-reactor core are slowed directly by an electrostatic field set up by an array of large electrically charge plates [*see bottom illustration on page 392*]. By a judicious arrangement of the voltages applied to the plates such a system could theoretically be made to operate at a conversion efficiency of 90 percent.

J. Rand McNally, Jr., of the Oak Ridge National Laboratory has suggested that a long sequence of fusion reactions similar to those that power the stars could be reproduced in a fusion reactor. The data necessary to evaluate fuel cycles operating in this manner, however, do not exist at present.

The characteristics of a full-scale fusion reactor would depend not only on the fuel cycle but also on the particular plasma-confinement configuration and density range chosen. Thus it is probable that there eventually will exist a number of different forms of fusion reactor. For example, medium-density magnetic-mirror reactors and very-high-density laser-ignited reactors could be expected to operate at power levels as low as between five and 50 megawatts, which could make them potentially useful for fusion-propulsion schemes.

For central-station power generation the medium-density reactors would most likely operate on a deuterium-tritium fuel cycle in order to take advantage of the mixture's low ignition temperature. Because of the high neutron output associated with this fuel, a heat-cycle conversion system would be appropriate.

A reactor of this type would operate most efficiently with a power output in the billion-watt range. Before such a reactor can be built, it will be necessary to prove that the plasma will remain stable as present devices are scaled to reactor sizes and temperatures. Problems likely to be encountered in this effort involve the long-term equilibrium of the plasma, the interaction of the plasma with the walls of the container and the necessity of pumping large quantities of liquid lithium across the magnetic field.

Medium-density linear reactors would be better suited for fuel cycles that yield a major part of their energy output in the form of charged particles, since this approach would allow the direct recovery of the kinetic energy of these reaction products through schemes such as Post's. Such fuel cycles could be based on a deuterium-deuterium reaction, a deuterium-helium reaction or a proton-lithium reaction. A system operating on this principle could be made to produce direct-current electricity at a potential of about 400 kilovolts, which would be ideal for long-distance cryogenic (supercooled) power transmission.

Although the break-even conditions would be lowered in this case (because of the high energy-conversion efficiency), it still remains to be shown that existing experiments can be scaled to large sizes and higher temperatures. Some major technological obstacles that need to be overcome include the construction of large atomic-beam injectors and extremely strong magnetic mirrors.

For reactors operating on the basis of any of the higher-density schemes, such as the theta-pinch machines or the fast-pulsed systems, major technological hurdles include the development of efficient energy-storage and energy-transfer techniques and problems related to heating techniques such as lasers.

In addition to generating electric power and possibly serving in a propulsion system, fusion reactors are potentially useful for other applications. For example, fusion research has already made available plasmas that range in temperature from 500,000 to a billion degrees C. and in density from 10^9 to 10^{22} ions per cubic centimeter. Almost all industrial processes that use plasmas fall outside this range [*see top illustration on page 387*]. In order to suggest how this industrially unexplored range might be exploited, we recently put forward the concept of the "fusion torch." The gen-

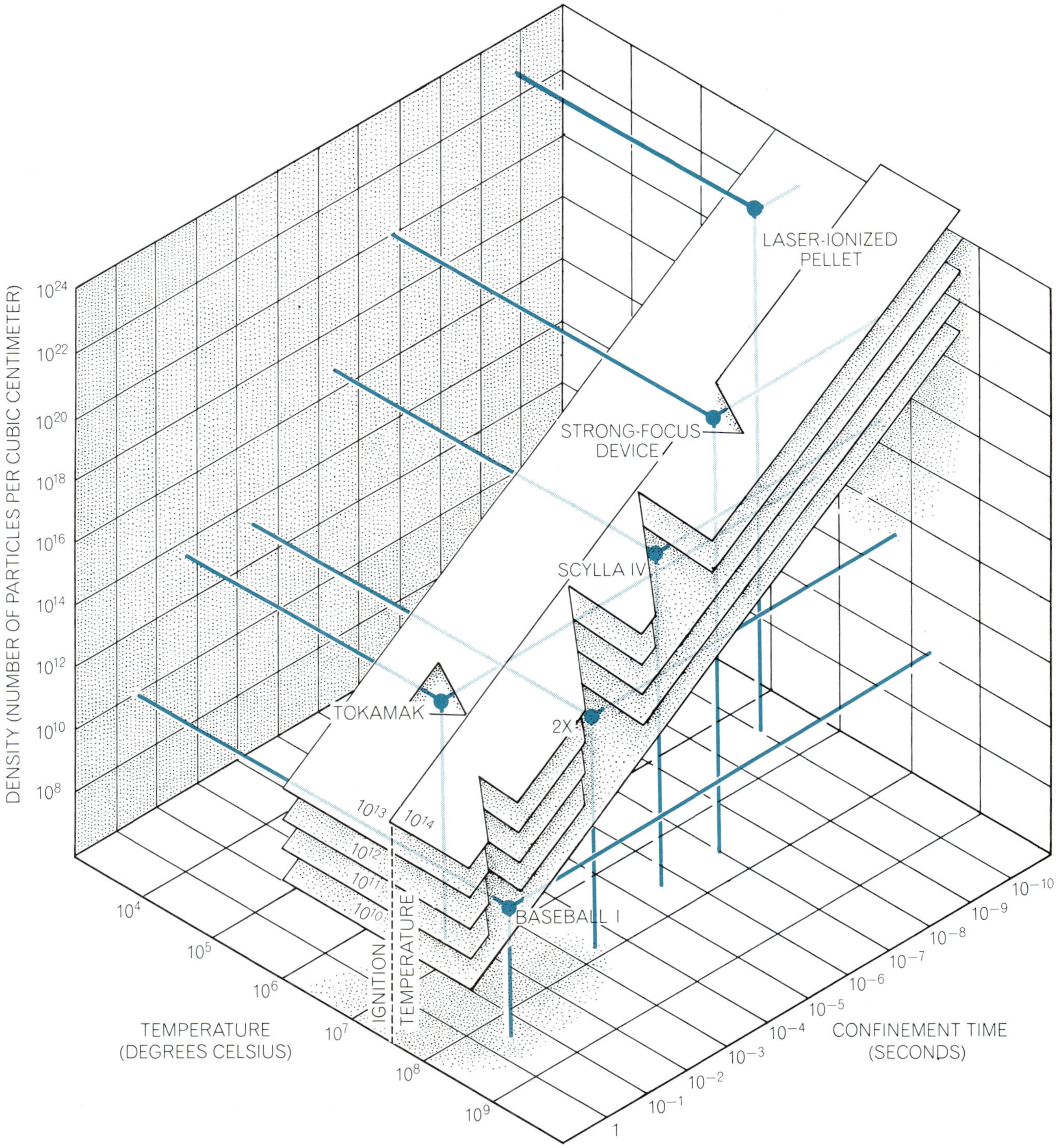

BASIC CRITERION for determining the length of time a plasma must be confined at a given density and temperature to achieve a "break even" point in the fusion-power balance is represented in this three-dimensional graph. The graph is based on a method of analysis devised in 1957 by the British physicist J. D. Lawson. For a deuterium-tritium fuel mixture in the temperature range from 40 million degrees C. to 500 million degrees C., Lawson found that the product of density and confinement time must be close to 10^{14} seconds per cubic centimeter to achieve the break-even condition (based on an assumed energy-conversion efficiency of 33 percent). This criterion corresponds to the top layer in the stack of planes in the illustration. The lower planes, which correspond to successively smaller values of density times confinement time, are included in order to give some idea of the positions of the best confirmed results from several experimental devices with respect to the combination of parameters needed to operate a full-scale fusion reactor.

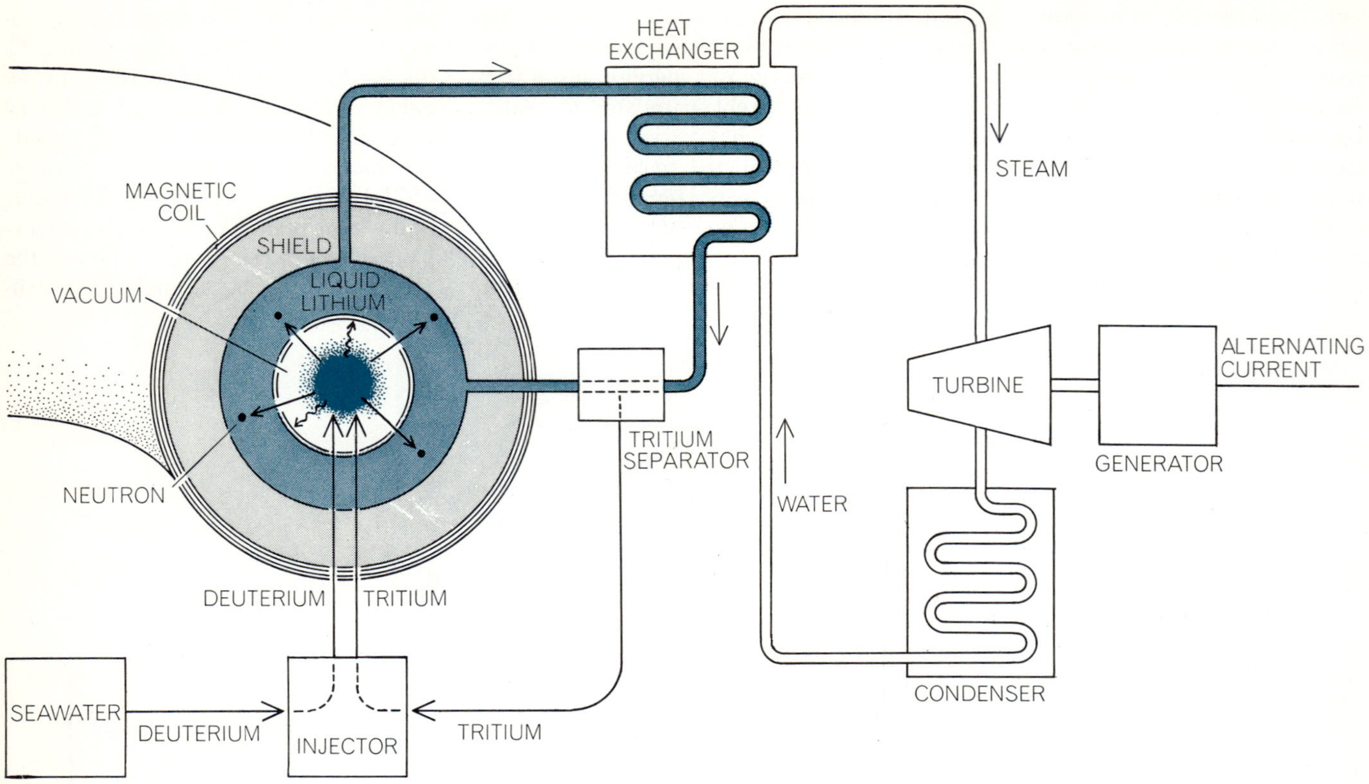

THERMAL ENERGY CONVERSION would be most effective in a fusion reactor based on a deuterium-tritium fuel cycle, since such a fuel would release approximately 80 percent of its energy in the form of highly energetic neutrons. The reactor could produce electricity by absorbing the neutron energy in a liquid-lithium shield, circulating the liquid lithium to a heat exchanger and there heating water to produce steam and thus drive a conventional steam-generator plant. The reactor core could be either linear or toroidal.

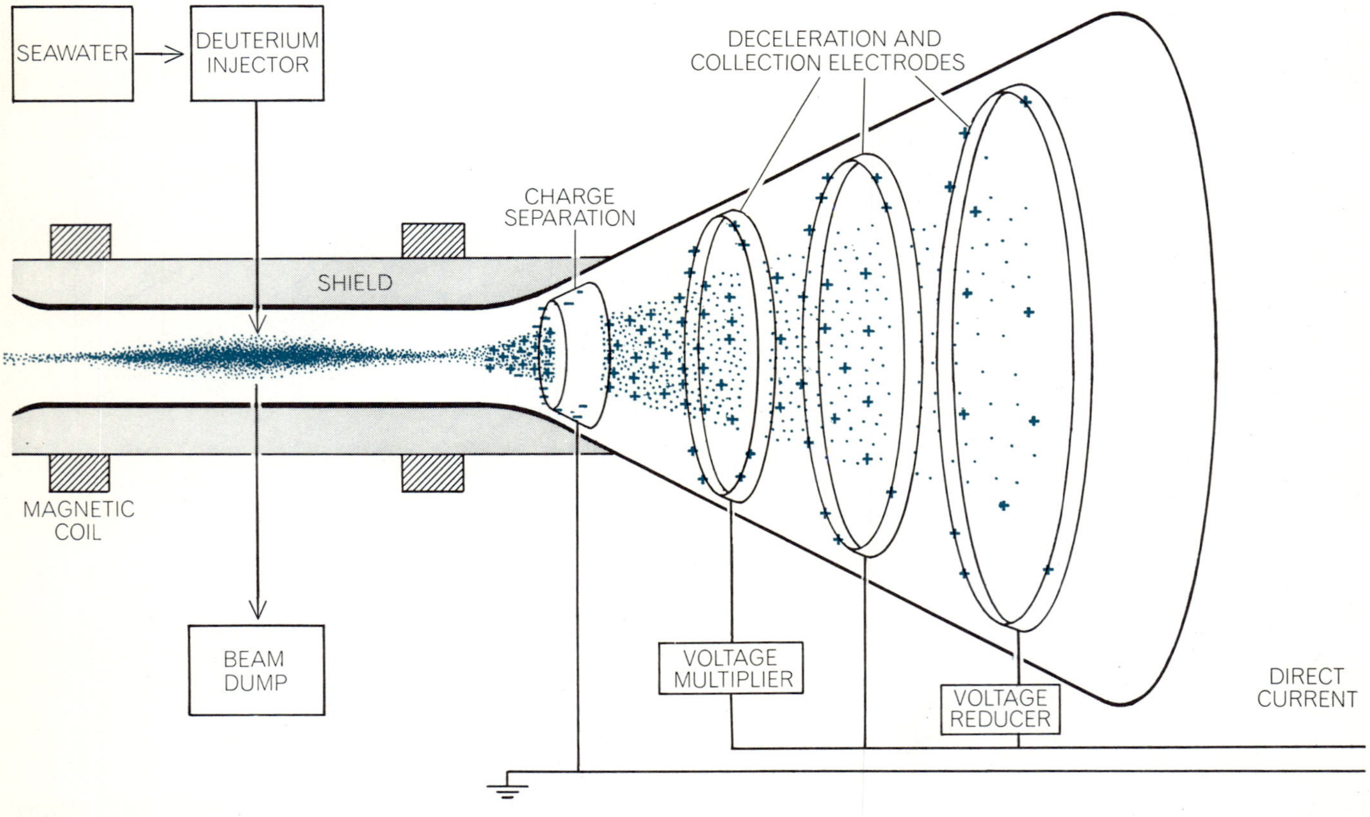

DIRECT ENERGY CONVERSION would be more suitable for fusion fuel cycles that release most of their energy in the form of charged particles. In this novel direct energy-conversion scheme, first proposed by Richard F. Post of the Lawrence Radiation Laboratory of the University of California at Livermore, the energetic charged particles (primarily electrons, protons and alpha particles) produced in the core of a linear fusion reactor would be released through diverging magnetic fields at the ends of the magnetic bottle, lowering the density of the plasma by a factor of as much as a million. A large electrically grounded collector plate would then be used to remove only the electrons. The positive reaction products (at energies in the vicinity of 400 kilovolts) would finally be collected on a series of high-voltage electrodes, resulting in a direct transfer of the kinetic energy of the particles to an external circuit.

eral idea here is to use these ultrahigh-density plasmas, possibly directly from the exhaust of a fusion reactor, to vaporize, dissociate and ionize any solid or liquid material [*see top illustration at right*]. The potential uses of such a fusion-torch capability are intriguing. For one thing, an operational fusion torch in its ultimate form could be used to reduce all kinds of wastes to their constituent atoms for separation, thereby closing the materials loop and making technologically possible a stationary-state economy. On a shorter term the fusion torch offers the possibility of processing mineral ores or producing portable liquid fuels by means of a high-temperature plasma system.

The fusion-torch concept could also be useful in transforming the kinetic energy of a plasma into ultraviolet radiation or X rays by the injection of trace amounts of heavy atoms into the plasma. The large quantity of radiative energy generated in this way could then be used for various purposes, including bulk heating, the desalting of seawater, the production of hydrogen or new chemical-processing techniques. Because such new industrial processes would make use of energy in the form of plasmas rather than in the form of, say, chemical solvents, they would be far less likely to pollute the environment. Although the various fusion-torch possibilities are largely untested and many aspects may turn out to be impractical, the concept is intended to stimulate new ideas for the industrial use of the ultrahigh-temperature plasmas that have already been developed in the fusion program as well as those plasmas that would be produced in large quantities by future fusion reactors.

Environmental Considerations

The environmental advantages of fusion power can be broken down into two categories: those advantages that are inherent in all fusion systems and those that are dependent on particular fuel cycles and reactor designs. Among the inherent advantages, one of the most important is the fact that the use of fusion fuel requires no burning of the world's oxygen or hydrocarbon resources and hence releases no carbon dioxide or other combustion products to the atmosphere. This advantage is shared with nuclear-fission plants.

Another advantage of fusion power is that no radioactive wastes are produced as the result of the fuel cycles contemplated. The principal reaction products would be neutrons, nonradioactive heli-

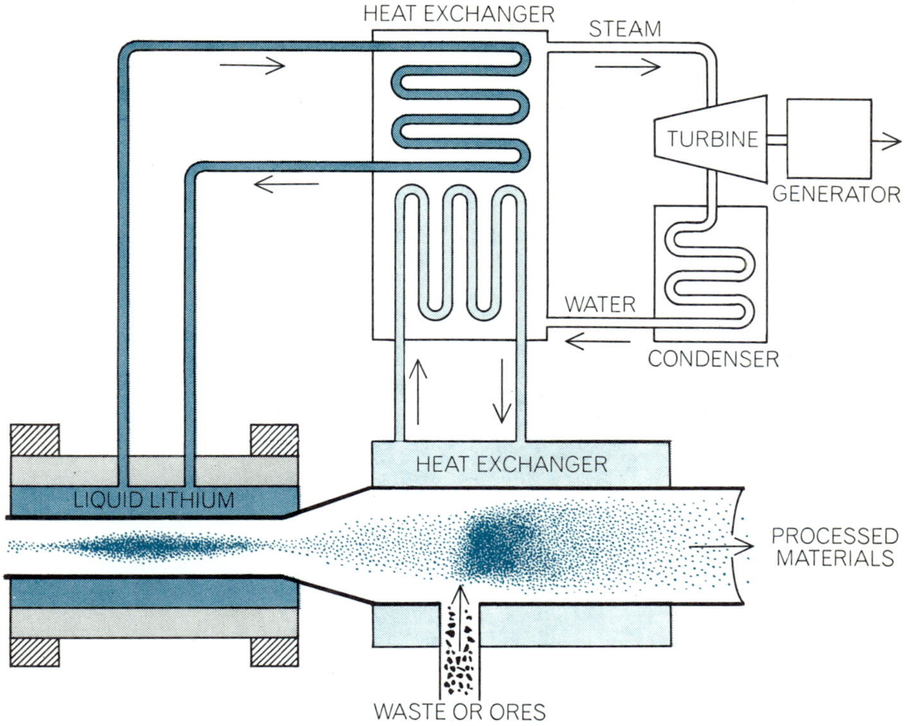

POTENTIAL NONPOWER USE of fusion energy is represented by the concept of the "fusion torch," which was put forward recently by the authors as a suggestion intended to stimulate new ideas for the industrial exploitation of the ultrahigh-temperature plasmas already made available by the fusion-research program as well as those that would be produced by fusion reactors. The general idea is to use some of the energy from these plasmas to vaporize, dissociate and ionize any solid or liquid material. In its ultimate form the fusion torch could be used to reduce any kind of waste to its constituent atoms for separation.

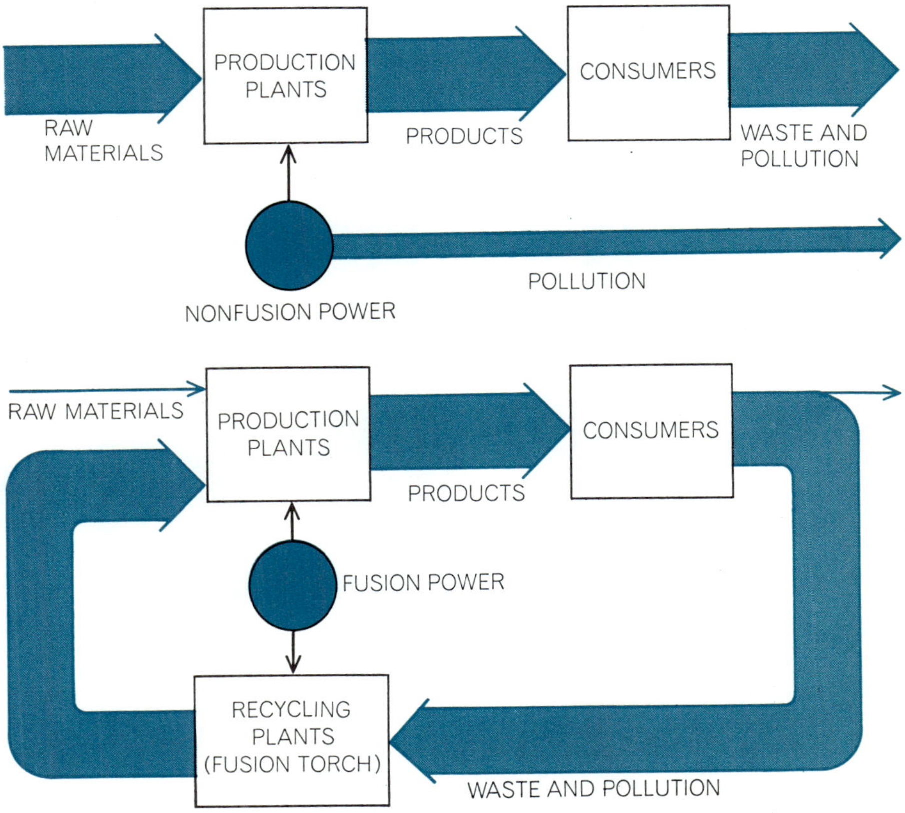

CLOSED MATERIALS ECONOMY could be achieved with the aid of the fusion-torch concept illustrated at the top of this page. In contrast to present systems, which are based on inherently wasteful linear materials economies (*top*), such a stationary-state system would be able to recycle the limited supply of material resources (*bottom*), thus alleviating most of the environmental pollution associated with present methods of energy utilization.

um and hydrogen nuclei, and radioactive tritium nuclei. It is true that tritium emits low-energy ionizing radiation in the form of beta particles (electrons), but since tritium is also a fusion fuel, it could be returned to the system to be burned. This situation is strongly contrasted with that in nuclear fission, which by its very nature must produce a multitude of highly radioactive waste elements.

Fusion reactors are also inherently incapable of a "runaway" accident. There is no "critical mass" required for fusion. In fact, the fusioning plasma is so tenuous (even in the "high density" machines) that there is never enough fuel present at any one time to support a nuclear excursion. This situation is also in contrast to nuclear-fission reactors, which must contain a critical mass of fissionable material and hence an extremely large amount of potential nuclear energy.

Among the system-dependent environmental advantages of fusion power must be counted the fact that the only radioactive fusion fuel considered so far is tritium. The amount of tritium present in a fusion reactor can range from near zero for a proton-lithium fuel cycle to a maximum for a deuterium-tritium cycle, where a "blanket" for the production of tritium must be included. Tritium, however, is one of the least toxic of the radioactive isotopes, whereas the fission fuel plutonium is one of the most toxic radioactive materials known.

The most serious radiological prob-

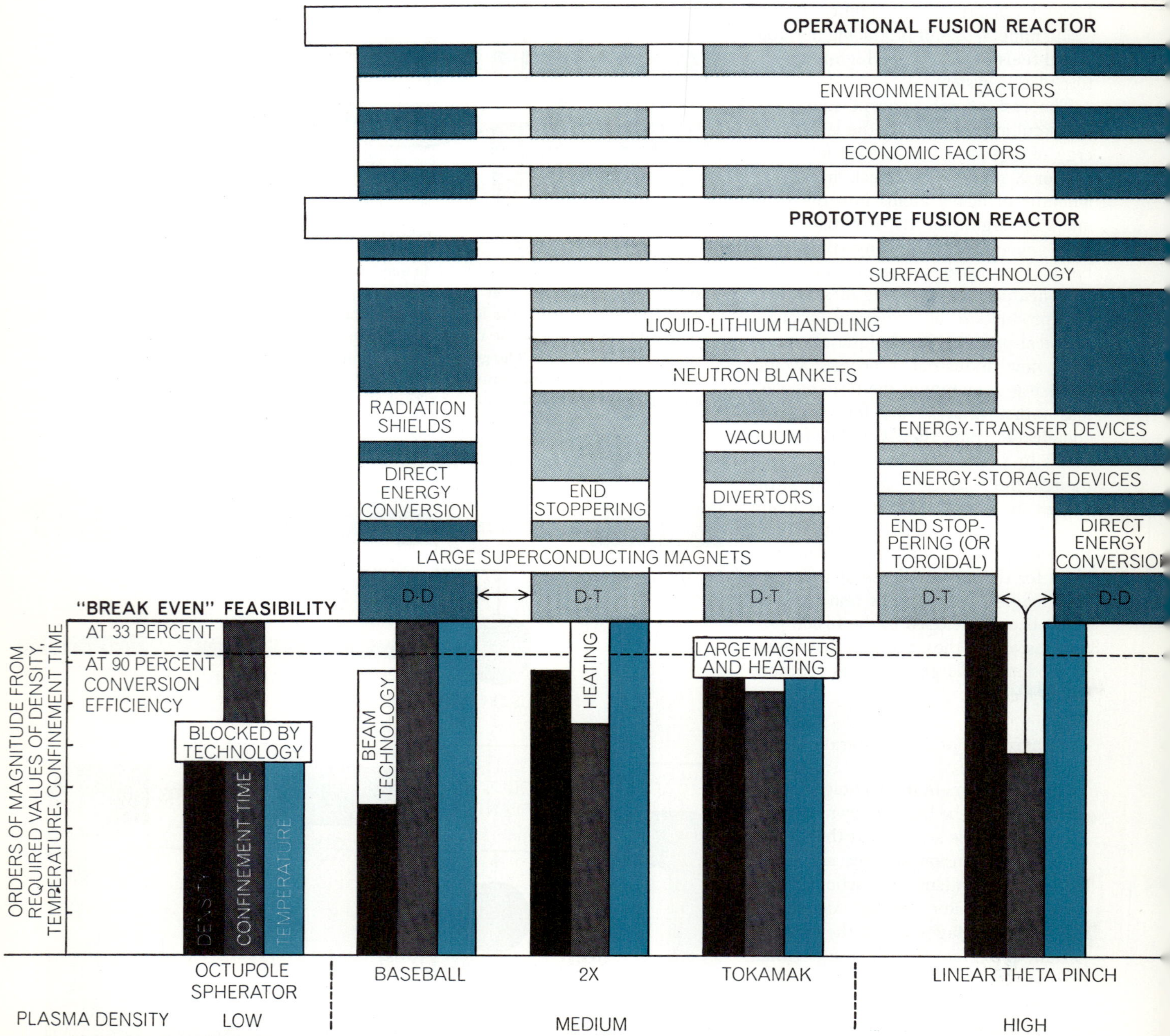

REMAINING PROBLEMS that must be solved before the goal of useful, economic fusion power can be achieved are depicted schematically in this illustration. The major experimental routes to the goal are ordered according to plasma density. Various experimental devices are represented by bars indicating the best combination of plasma density, confinement time and temperature achieved by each device; the logarithmic scale at lower left gauges how far each of these essential parameters is from the values needed to attain break-even feasibility. Technological problems that must be solved in each case are labeled. The achievement of a prototype reactor will be a function not only of plasma technology but also of the fuel cycle and the method of energy conversion chosen. Thus medium-density magnetic-mirror devices could be built to operate with either a deuterium-tritium (*D-T*) fuel mixture or a deuterium-deuterium (*D-D*) fuel mixture; the arrows signify these alternatives. If a D-D cycle is chosen, then direct energy conversion is possible, and once the converters are developed very few obstacles would remain to delay the construction of a prototype reactor. If, on the other hand, a D-T cycle is chosen, then conventional thermal energy conversion would be needed, and the listed technological lems for fusion would exist in a reactor burning and producing tritium. A representative rate of tritium consumption for a 2,000-megawatt deuterium-tritium thermal plant would be about 260 grams per day. Tritium "holdup" in the blanket and other elements of the tritium loop would dictate the tritium inventory. Holdup is estimated to be about 1,000 grams in a 2,000-megawatt plant. If necessary, the doubling time of breeding tritium could be less than two months in order to meet the needs of an expanding economy. The amount of tritium produced by the plant is controllable, however, and need not exceed the fuel requirements of the plant.

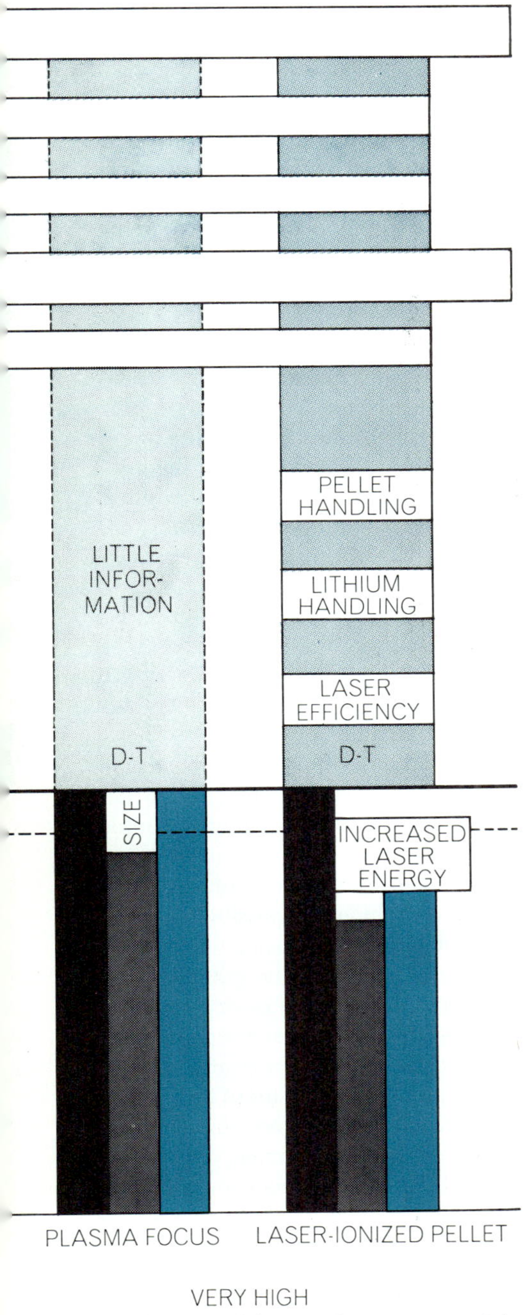

hurdles would have to be overcome. Other systems operating on the D-T cycle would have to climb past similar hurdles. The high-density linear theta-pinch device could take either the thermal-conversion path or the direct-conversion path (*arrows*). The final step, from a prototype to an operational reactor, would proceed through a region in which economic and environmental considerations can be expected to be paramount.

Careful design to prevent the leakage of tritium fuel from a deuterium-tritium reactor is mandatory. Engineering studies that take into account economic considerations indicate that the leakage rate can be reduced to .0001 percent per day. The conclusion is that even for an all-deuterium-tritium fusion economy the genetic dose rate from worldwide tritium distribution would be negligible.

In fact, for a given total power output the tritium inventory for an all-deuterium-tritium fusion economy (including both the inventory within the plant and that dispersed in the biosphere) would be between one and 100 times what it would be for an all-fission economy. It is true that tritium would be produced in a deuterium-tritium fusion reactor at a rate of from 1,000 to 100,000 times faster than in various types of fission reactor. Since tritium is burned as a fuel, however, it has an effective half-life of only about three days rather than the normal 12 years.

A technology-dependent but possibly serious limitation on deuterium-tritium fusion plants could be the release of tritium to the local environment. The level would be quite low but the long-term consequences from tritium emission to the environment in the vicinity of a deuterium-tritium reactor needs to be explored. In general the biological-hazard potential of the tritium fuel inventory in a deuterium-tritium reactor is lower by a factor of about a million than that of the volatile isotope iodine 131 contained in a fission reactor. Of course there is no expectation in either case that such a release would occur.

The radioactivity induced in the surrounding structures by a fusion reactor is dependent on both the fuel cycle and the engineering design of the plant. This radioactivity could range from zero for a fuel cycle that produces no neutrons up to very high values for a deuterium-tritium cycle if the engineering design is such that the type and amount of structural materials could become highly activated under neutron bombardment. Cooling for "after heat" will be required for systems that have intense induced radioactivity. Even if the cooling system should fail, however, there could be no nuclear excursion that would disperse the radioactivity outside the plant.

Other system-dependent environmental advantages of fusion power include safety in the event of sabotage or natural disaster, reduced potential for the diversion of weapons-grade materials and low waste heat. In fact, the potential exists for fusion systems to essentially eliminate the problem of thermal pollution by going to charged-particle fuel cycles that result in direct energy conversion. Finally, there is the advantage of the materials-recycling potential of the fusion-torch concept.

The Timetable to Fusion Power

The construction and operation of a power-producing controlled-fusion reactor will be the end product of a chain of events that is already to a certain extent discernible. For controlled fusion, however, there can never be an instant equivalent to the one that demonstrated the "feasibility" of a fission-power reactor (the Stagg Field experiment of Enrico Fermi in 1942). To reach the plasma conditions required for a net release of fusion power it is necessary to first develop many new technologies. In this context the term "scientific feasibility" cannot be precisely defined. To some investigators it means simply the achievement of the basic plasma conditions necessary to reach the break-even surface in the illustration on page 391. To others it represents reaching the same surface—but with a system that can be enlarged to a full-scale, economic power plant. To a few it represents the attainment of a full understanding of all the phenomena involved.

Although these differing interpretations of what is needed to give confidence in our ability to construct a fusion reactor may be somewhat confusing, each interpretation nevertheless contains a modicum of truth. To depict the complexity of this drive toward the goal of fusion power we have prepared the highly schematic illustration on the opposite page. The goal is to achieve useful, economic fusion power. The major routes to the goal are ordered in the illustration according to plasma density. Various individual experiments have climbed past various obstacles to reach positions close to the break-even level. In fact, in some instances two of the three essential parameters (density, temperature and confinement time) have already been achieved. The ignition temperature has been achieved in a number of cases. The rest of the climb to the break-even level in some cases involves a better understanding of the physics of the plasma-confinement system, but in others it may involve only engineering problems. Indeed, the location of the break-even level is a function of the technology used. Direct energy conversion, for example, would lower this level.

The next portion of the climb, the

construction of a prototype reactor, will be a function of the route taken to scientific feasibility. For instance, if a deuterium-tritium mixture is the fuel, this would require the development of components such as lithium blankets, large superconducting magnets, radiation-resistant vacuum liners, fueling techniques and heat-transfer technology. If fuels that release most of their energy in the form of charged particles are considered, however, then in the case of mirror reactors direct-conversion equipment may be part of a device used to demonstrate break-even feasibility. The step from that device to a prototype reactor could then be very short because the conversion equipment would be already developed. Other devices would face similar problems of differing magnitude in prototype construction. The final step from a prototype to an operational reactor would proceed through a much more nebulous region in which economic and environmental considerations would influence the comparative desirability of different power plants.

At present the main factor limiting the rate of progress toward fusion power is financial. The annual operating and equipment expenditures for the U.S. fusion program, when one uses the consumer price indexes to adjust these dollars for inflation, has remained fairly constant for the past eight years [*see illustration below*]. The total amount spent on the program since its inception is the cost equivalent of a single Apollo moon shot. The annual funding rate of about $30 million per year is the equivalent of 15 cents per person per year in the U.S.

The road to fusion power is a cumulative one in that successive advances can be built on earlier advances. At present the U.S. has a fairly broad program of investigations approaching the break-even surface for net energy release. It is essential that larger (and thus more expensive) devices be built if the goal of the break-even surface is to be reached. The surface should be broken through in a number of places so that the relative advantages of the possible routes beyond that surface to an eventual fusion-power reactor can be assessed.

Clearly the timetable to fusion power is difficult to predict. If the level of effort on fusion research remains constant or decreases slightly, the requirement for larger devices and advanced engineering will automatically cause a premature narrowing of the density range under investigation. This increases the risk of reaching the goal in a given time scale. To put it another way, it extends one's estimate of the probable time scale. If the level of fusion research expands sufficiently to maintain a fairly broad program across the entire density range, the probability of success increases and the probable time scale decreases. If fusion power is pursued as a "national objective," expanded programs could be carried out across the entire density range accompanied by parallel strong programs of research on the remaining engineering and materials problems to determine as quickly as possible the best routes to practical fusion-power systems. Therefore, depending on one's underlying assumptions on the level of effort and the difficulties ahead, the time it would take to produce a large prototype reactor could range from as much as 50 years to as little as 10 years.

There is at least one case in which the fusion break-even surface could be reached without making any new scientific advances and without developing any new technologies. This "brute force" approach, which might not be the optimum route to an eventual power reactor, would involve simply extending the length of the existing theta-pinch linear devices. It has been estimated that to reach the break-even surface by this method such a system would have to be about 2,000 feet long—less than a fifth of the length of the Stanford Linear Accelerator. This one fusion device, however, would cost an order of magnitude more than any experimental fusion device built to date. Even though a simple scaling of this type would introduce no new problems in plasma physics, one could not exclude the possibility of unexpected difficulties arising solely from the extended length of the system.

The length of such a device could be shortened by as much as 90 percent by installing magnetic mirrors at the ends, by increasing the diameter of the plasma or by making the system toroidal, but these steps would introduce new physical conditions. The system could also be shortened by the use of a direct energy-conversion approach, but this would introduce an unproved technology. At present a significant portion of the fusion-power program is concentrating on developing the new physics and technology that would reduce the cost of such break-even experiments. This continuing effort is sustained by the growing conviction that the eventual attainment of a practical fusion-power reactor is not blocked by the laws of nature.

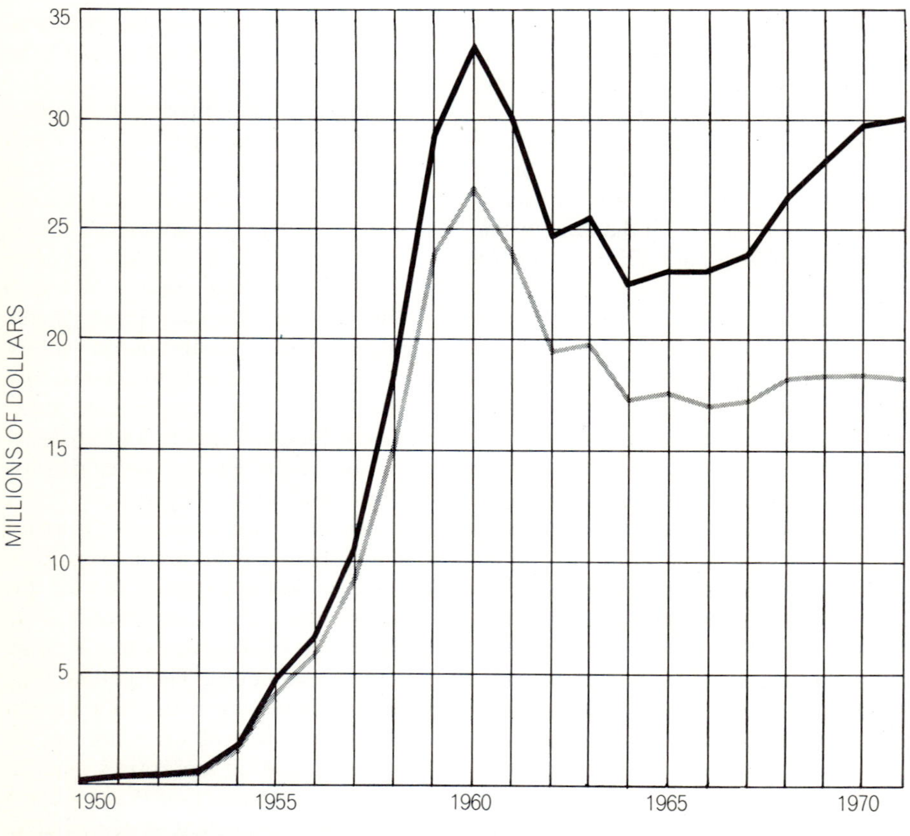

FINANCIAL SUPPORT is currently the main factor limiting the rate of progress toward the goal of fusion power. The solid curve shows the annual operating and equipment expenditures for the U.S. fusion program. The gray curve shows these expenditures adjusted for inflation. The adjustment shows that fusion research has been funded by the Atomic Energy Commission at an essentially constant rate for the past eight years. Smaller research programs have been funded by both private industry and other Government agencies.

Fusion by Laser

Experiments indicate that energy-releasing fusion reactions can be initiated and to some extent controlled without a confining magnetic field by focusing a powerful laser pulse on a frozen pellet of fuel

MOSHE J. LUBIN and ARTHUR P. FRAAS

June 1961

The rapid evolution of high-power pulsed lasers over the past decade has made available to workers in numerous fields a new tool whose potential usefulness has just begun to be explored. Prominent among the applications that have been proposed to date are a variety of schemes aimed at exploiting the fact that the focused light from such a laser is capable of heating a small amount of matter to extremely high temperatures: in some cases to more than 50 million degrees Kelvin! To the chemist, for example, such a capability means that chemical reactions can be initiated in less than a nanosecond (a billionth of a second) and can be studied under conditions previously considered unattainable.

To the plasma physicist the unprecedented heating capability of high-power pulsed lasers is particularly exciting. In principle it opens a promising new avenue of attack on the long-standing problem of how to produce the ultrahigh-temperature plasma needed to maintain thermonuclear, or fusion, reactions under controlled conditions. Recent experiments have shown that energy-releasing fusion reactions that may ultimately lead to the production of useful electrical power can be initiated and to some extent controlled within an "inertially confined" plasma obtained by focusing a powerful laser pulse on a dense frozen pellet consisting of a mixture of the heavy hydrogen isotopes deuterium (H^2) and tritium (H^3). In this article we shall review the current status of research on the application of high-power lasers to the generation of fusion power.

The case for fusion power and the progress that has been made over the past 20 years or so by nonlaser technologies toward achieving this goal have been discussed at length in several earlier articles in this magazine, the most recent of which appeared only a few months ago [see "The Prospects of Fusion Power," by William C. Gough and Bernard J. Eastlund, the article beginning on page 382]. Suffice it to say here that controlled fusion reactions involving light isotopes such as deuterium and tritium represent a potentially inexhaustible source of inexpensive, efficient, "clean" energy for supplying all mankind's future power requirements.

The fusion-power option, however, has not yet been shown to be technologically feasible. The difficulty is twofold. First, the task of heating the light-element fuel to a sufficiently high temperature at the required density so that it will begin to "burn" slowly has proved to be harder than was anticipated. The temperature required to initiate burning varies between 50 and 100 million degrees K., depending on the fuel. Second, once the fuel is ignited, the hot, dense, gaseous mixture of ions must be held together for a long enough time so that more energy is liberated through burning than is invested in the ignition process. Attempts at confinement by means of intense magnetic fields of various geometries have so far not yielded a practical solution. In spite of the difficulties encountered in heating a gaseous mixture to such temperatures and confining the ionized gas for large fractions of a second, however, the potential return on the investment of time and money in research on this problem is so great that all the major nations of the world have substantial controlled-fusion research programs.

Before describing how high-powered lasers can play a role in the solution of this problem it will be instructive to review briefly (1) the current state of the art in the development of high-power pulsed lasers, (2) the mechanism by which the energy from a laser beam interacts with a dense medium and (3) the requirements demanded of lasers in initiating controlled fusion reactions.

A laser is a device for generating or amplifying a beam of light whose waves are both monochromatic (all the same wavelength) and coherent (all in step). The light beam emitted by a laser can be made almost perfectly parallel, its divergence angle being theoretically limited only by diffraction effects. In principle such a beam can be focused to a spot with a diameter of only a few hundred-millionths of an inch. The laser produces its coherent light beam through the interaction of electromagnetic radiation with the laser medium. By elevating more atoms to an upper energy level than exist at a lower level the absorption of excitation radiation produces an "inverted" atomic population in the laser. The energy stored in the inverted population is then available to amplify a propagating light wave at a particular frequency. This frequency of emission is generally different from the frequency band over which the laser medium has absorbed excitation radiation. For example, a ruby laser absorbs "pumping" light in the green region of the optical spectrum but emits coherent light in the red region.

The small light pulse to be amplified is produced by a laser oscillator. For a laser to work as an oscillator some feedback mechanism must be provided. This is accomplished by the use of mirrors on both ends of the laser medium to provide a means by which waves at the emission frequency may travel back and forth through the laser. In this way oscillations are built up at the emission frequency by feeding on the inverted population until the stored energy in the laser medium is depleted, at which time emission ceases.

The first laser action in a solid material was observed in a ruby rod in 1960 by T. H. Maiman, who was then working at the Hughes Aircraft Company. Numerous other solid-state laser materials were discovered in rapid succession. The most important of these is neodymium-doped barium crown glass, in which laser action was first demonstrated in 1961 by Elias Snitzer of the American Optical Company. Whereas ruby is an expensive crystal to grow in any reasonable size, barium crown glass is comparatively inexpensive and can be manufactured in large sizes and quantities. Size becomes important in dealing with ultrahigh-power laser systems.

The end surface of the laser rod from which the coherent radiation is emitted can withstand only a limited amount of energy per square centimeter. Generally it is felt that impurities in the laser material contribute to significant absorption of the laser light, which ultimately leads to fracture of the laser medium. For example, the energy-handling capability of neodymium glass ranges between 10 and 100 joules per square centimeter, depending on the duration of the laser pulse.

At present solid-state ruby and neodymium-glass laser materials are used to obtain the highest peak-power output in pulsed operation. This is attributable in large part to the higher density of atoms available in solids to participate in the laser action. Liquids that sustain laser action hold promise for the future in high-power pulsed applications for this same reason; in addition they have the advantage of not being vulnerable to permanent structural damage. Unfortunately liquid lasers in the form of dye solutions or liquid glass are still in the initial stages of development.

Solid-state laser systems available at present are capable of delivering energies in excess of 1,000 joules in less than a nanosecond. This coherent energy flux is in the form of a highly collimated

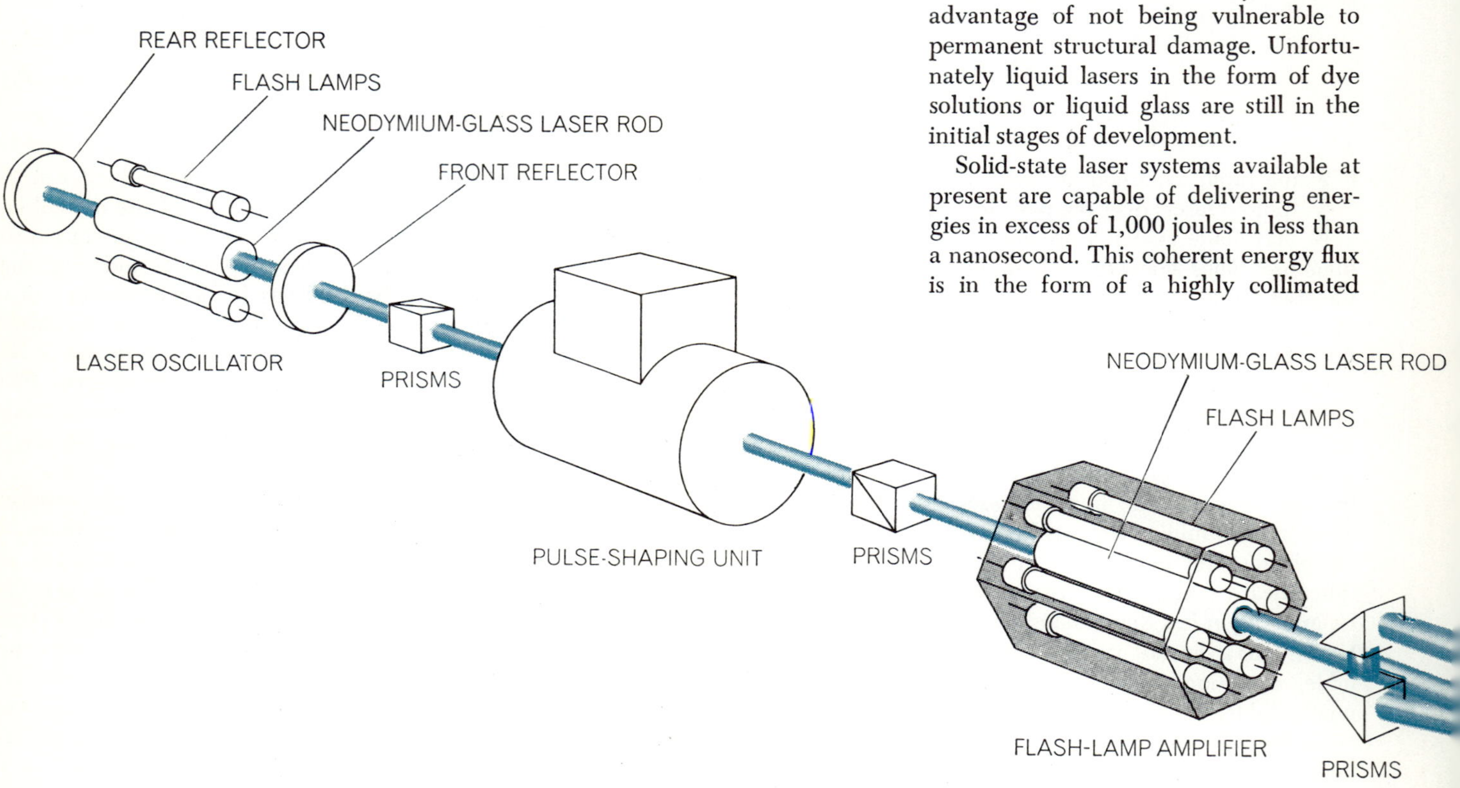

TYPICAL HIGH-POWER LASER SYSTEM shown on these two pages was designed for use in a plasma-heating experiment. The system consists of a string of neodymium-doped barium-crown-glass components, beginning with a laser oscillator (*extreme left*), in which a low-energy laser pulse is formed. The pulse is next "tailored," or shaped both in time and space to suit a particular application, before being amplified by additional laser rods and finally by a large disk amplifier. A suitable combination of prisms sends the pulse through the disk amplifier three times. The resulting beam, some 15 centimeters in diameter, is finally focused on a deuterium droplet inside a vacuum chamber (*extreme right*) to produce a hot plasma, or ionized gas, in which fusion reactions can take place. The fusion reactions are studied by means of the energetic neutrons they emit. The peak power currently available from such a laser system before focusing exceeds 10^{13} watts; when it is focused, it is possible to achieve power densities greater than 10^{17} watts per square centimeter.

DISK AMPLIFIER is capable of emitting an output pulse with an energy of more than 1,000 joules through an aperture 15 centimeters in diameter. The neodymium-glass laser disks are mounted at an angle to the incoming laser beam in order to minimize reflection at the same time that they are excited efficiently on their faces by the flash lamps located in the reflector tanks on each side of the disks. A hundred such amplifiers arranged in parallel could in principle achieve an energy output greater than 100,000 joules.

beam with a total divergence of less than a hundredth of an angular degree. Such a beam of light starting out six inches in diameter would be less than 18 inches in diameter after traveling a mile.

In the case of a ruby laser the wavelength of the emitted laser radiation is .6943 micron. This wavelength falls in the red region of the spectrum and is therefore visible. The neodymium glass used in high-power lasers emits radiation at 1.06 microns, which is in the infrared portion of the spectrum and is not directly visible to the human eye.

A typical high-power laser system [*see illustration below*] consists of an oscillator in which a laser pulse, appropriately shaped in space and time, is formed at low energy. The pulse is an envelope containing a burst of electromagnetic radiation oscillating at the

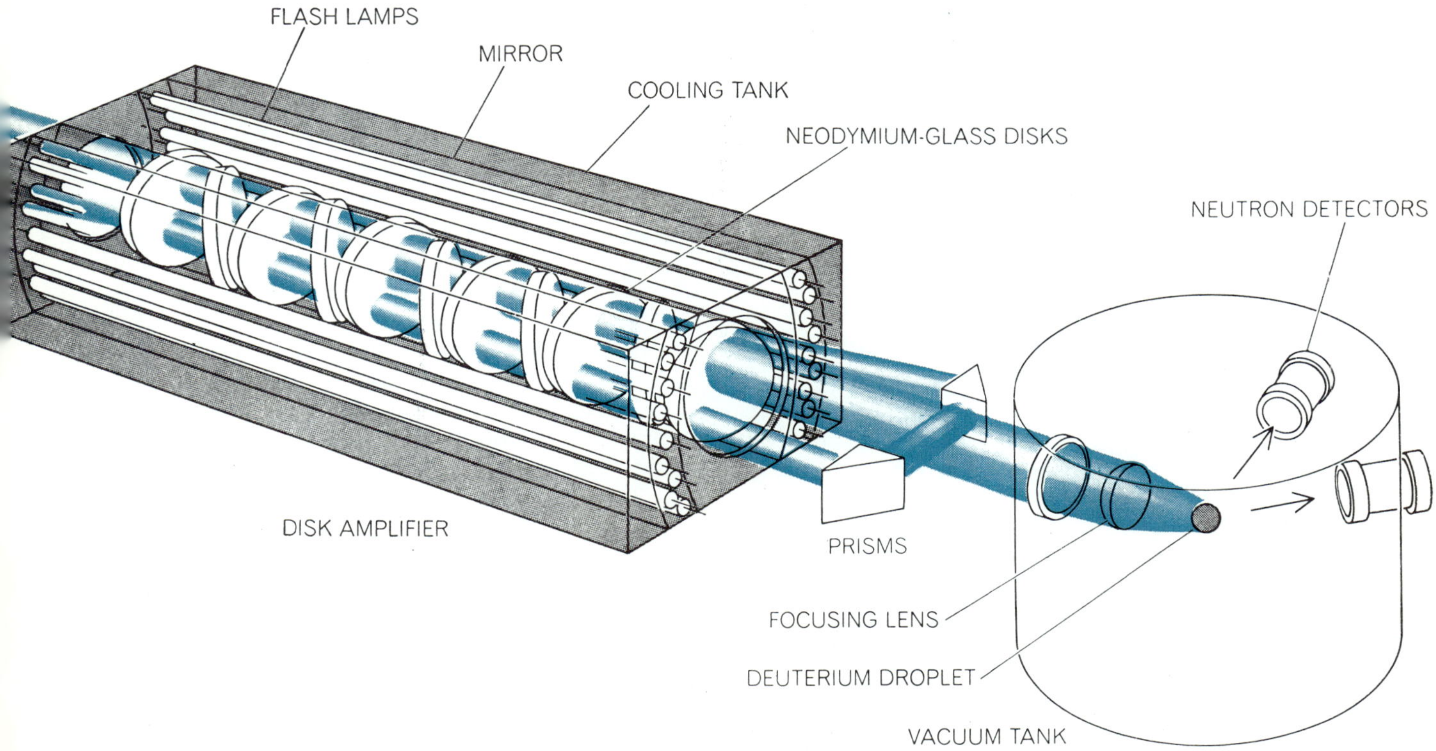

laser frequency. "Tailoring" a pulse to suit a particular application can be accomplished in a number of ways. Pulses lasting on the order of a nanosecond or longer can be reliably produced simply by chopping out a suitable portion of a fatter pulse with a fast electro-optical shutter. The shutter, activated by a high-voltage electrical pulse, is synchronized with the arrival of the longer pulse by monitoring the intensity of the laser radiation as a function of time. Such synchronization requires high-voltage switching on the time scale of a nanosecond.

Producing narrower pulses by this technique is unreliable. Instead a technique known as "mode-locking" is commonly employed [*see illustration below*]. As the energy in the laser cavity is built up and then decays, a string of such mode-locked pulses emerges from the partially transmitting mirror in the front of the cavity. An electro-optical shutter can be used here too, but only to "gate out," or select, a laser pulse with a duration far shorter than the time the shutter is open. One pulse or more can be gated out in this way. Here the duration of the laser pulse is determined solely by the components in the laser cavity. Pulses varying in duration from a billionth to a trillionth of a second have been produced in this fashion.

Once the appropriately shaped laser pulse emerges from the laser, it is directed into a string of laser amplifiers, each amplifier adding energy to the original pulse. The amplifiers usually have successively larger apertures, so that the lasing material can survive the increased energy without damage. The amplifying process itself can be called on to change the shape of the input pulse. If the intensity of the incoming pulse is large enough, most of the amplifier energy is deposited in the pulse's leading edge, thereby narrowing the width of the pulse.

The atoms in a neodymium-glass laser rod are excited by absorbing light from external flash lamps. Since the light enters the rod from the outside, more atoms near the outer edges of the rod are elevated to an excited energy state than are elevated in the interior. This undesirable situation becomes intolerable for rods more than two inches in diameter. In addition large rods are difficult to cool between pulses. One solution to the problem of exciting large-aperture amplifier stages is the disk amplifier [*see top illustration on preceding page*]. This type of amplifier consists of large neodymium-glass disks that are tilted with respect to the incoming laser beam in order to minimize reflection losses. At the same time the disks have a large projected area of minimal thickness facing the excitation flash lamps, which leads to uniform excitation. One such amplifier with an aperture of six inches is now capable of reaching a power output of 1,000 joules; 100 similar amplifiers could be arranged in parallel to achieve outputs of 100,000 joules.

Numerous available sources are capable of delivering such bursts of energy in a short time. None, however, equals the laser in the ease with which the output can be concentrated in a small volume. It is this ability to focus high-power radiation using optical elements such as lenses and mirrors that makes the laser uniquely attractive for the purpose of initiating fusion. The peak power in such a beam before focusing is more than 10^{13} watts, and when the beam is focused, it is possible to achieve power densities greater than 10^{17} watts per square centimeter. The focused energy results in a local electric field in the immediate vicinity of the focus on the order of 10^{10} volts per centimeter! It is difficult to grasp the magnitude of such enormous electric-field intensities; an example of their strength is that a free electron accelerated in a field of 10^{10} volts would reach a velocity comparable to the velocity of light in a fraction of an optical wavelength.

It is well known that nuclear-fusion fuels such as deuterium and tritium liberate more energy per nucleon (neutron or proton) than nuclear-fission fuels. Unfortunately these hydrogen isotopes only burn efficiently at high temperature. Below 10 million degrees K. the burning is too slow to be useful in an energy-producing process here on the

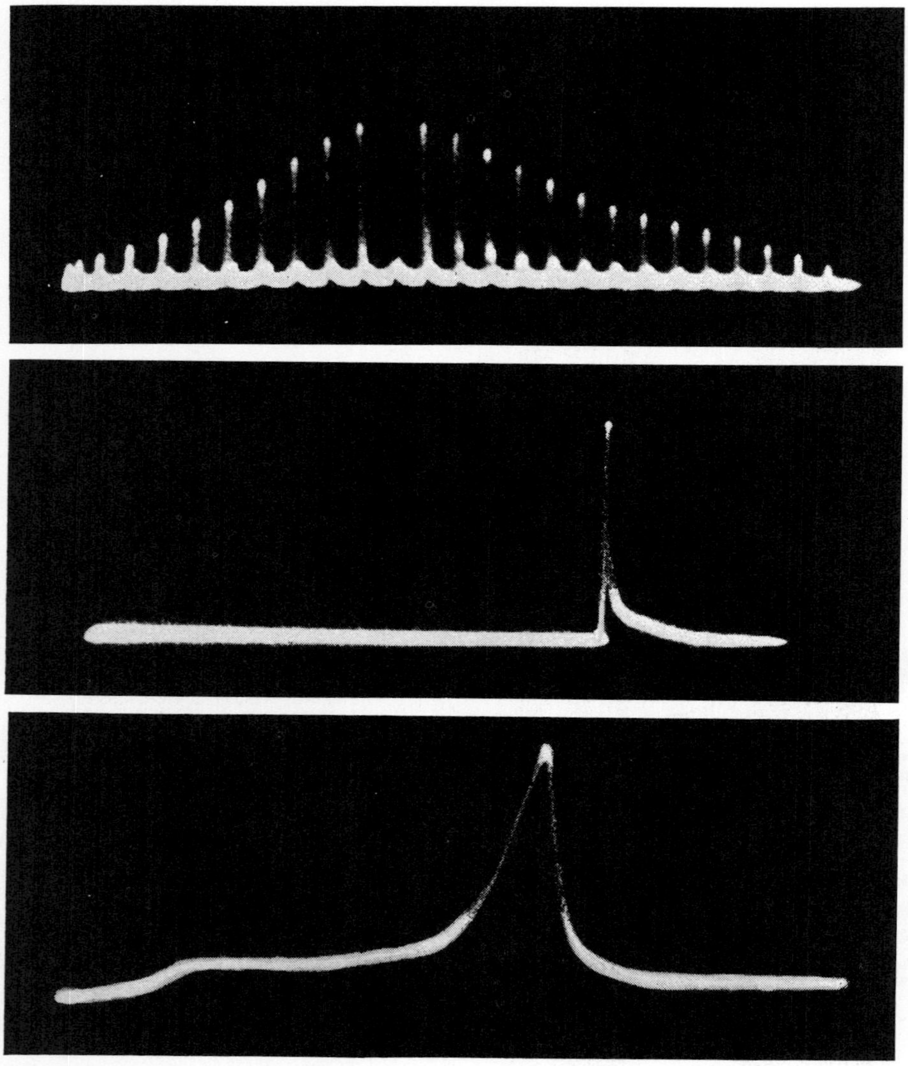

TAILORING OF A LASER PULSE is illustrated by this sequence of oscilloscope traces. A train of very brief "mode-locked" pulses is first produced in the oscillator section of the laser system (*top*). A single pulse is then extracted from the train (it is missing in the top trace) and is amplified (*middle*). The width of the pulse may vary between a billionth (10^{-9}) and a trillionth (10^{-12}) of a second. A low-power leading edge is often added to such a pulse (*bottom*) in order to vaporize the fuel droplet prior to heating by the main pulse.

earth. The sun can burn hydrogen efficiently at lower temperatures because of its large volume. In the limited size of a laboratory plasma one must consider burning isotopes at temperatures greater than 50 million degrees K.

The traditional approach to controlled fusion has been to begin by producing a plasma that is dilute and rather cool. The plasma is next trapped in a confining magnetic field. One then proceeds to heat the plasma to a higher temperature while holding it in place with a magnetic field that is made proportionately stronger. Our present experience and understanding only allow us to heat the plasma rather gently so as not to upset the delicate balance between the hot ionized gas and the magnetic field. Although our knowledge of the forces and conditions controlling this balance has increased greatly over the past 10 years, we are not yet sure of the proper magnetic-field configuration required to contain the hot plasma long enough for significant burning to occur.

When high-power pulsed lasers began to emerge as working systems, one of their first applications in the controlled-fusion program was the production of extremely clean, well-behaved plasmas to fill existing magnetic-confinement devices [*see top illustration at right*]. The question that was asked at the time was: "Can a plasma produced by the laser heating of a small droplet of thermonuclear fuel in a magnetic field serve as the plasma required for nearly steady-state, continuous fusion reactions?"

More recently, as the energy-producing capability of high-power pulsed laser systems has increased, a second question has arisen: "Is it possible to utilize the intense burst of focused coherent radiation from the laser to raise the temperature of a suitable deuterium-tritium target high enough to produce significant burning *without* the necessity of a confining magnetic field?"

To answer these questions one must first examine how high-frequency electromagnetic radiation interacts with a dense plasma made up of electrons and positive ions. The oscillating electric field in a light beam may be absorbed, reflected, scattered and/or refracted by a material surface. Our prime interest is in the absorption of this radiation and the conversion of the electromagnetic energy of the laser beam to the thermal energy of the fusion fuel. Once a few unbound electrons are produced on the surface of the solid hydrogen isotope, these free electrons rapidly pick up energy from the incident oscillating electric field. Their energy is then trans-

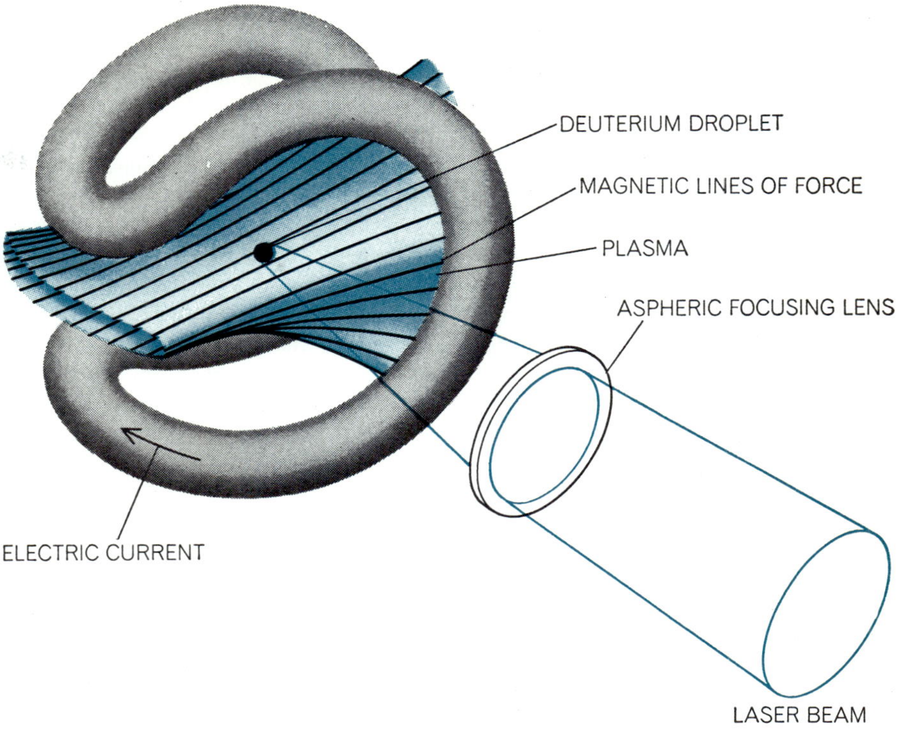

FIRST USE OF HIGH-POWER LASERS in the controlled-fusion program was to produce a plasma to fill existing magnetic-confinement devices such as the one shown in this schematic drawing. An electric current flowing in the "baseball seam" winding induces a magnetic field whose energy density is lowest at the center and increases outward in all directions, thus creating a magnetic "well" in which to confine the plasma, which is generated by laser-heating a fuel droplet at the center. In an experiment carried out at the University of Rochester in 1968 a device of this type was used to produce a confined plasma with a temperature of 10 million degrees Kelvin and a density of 10^{13} ions per cubic centimeter.

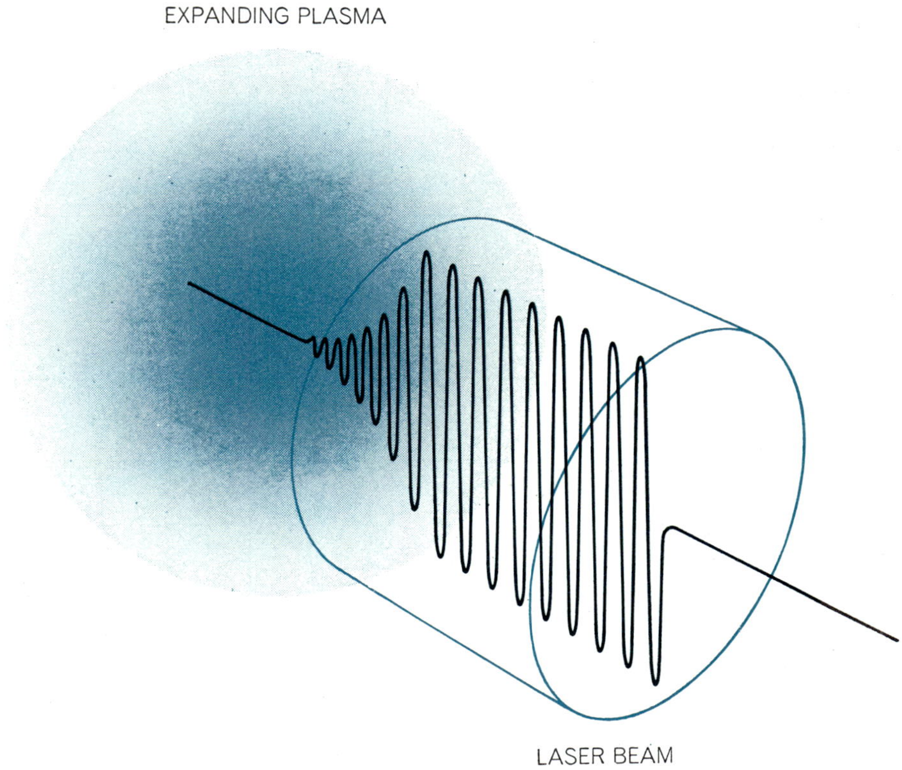

LASER PULSE IS ABSORBED very efficiently by a dense, expanding sphere of plasma, with most of the absorption taking place in a thin surface layer of plasma only about a hundredth of an inch thick. As the energy of the laser beam is absorbed by the plasma, the amplitude of the oscillating electric field (*black curve*) decreases rapidly within this layer.

ferred to the ions in the plasma medium by means of long-range attractive interactions. Thus the heavier ions also "feel" the effect of the laser beam through the mediation of the oscillating electrons. The transfer of this energy from the electrons to the ions can be much slower than the heating of the electrons by the laser beam. In fact, it is doubtful that in a free deuterium-tritium plasma effective transfer can occur on time scales of less than 10^{-11} second. This absorption process is called collisional absorption.

If the incident radiation is to be effectively absorbed, the plasma should be opaque to it. On the other hand, it is desirable that the laser radiation not be wasted by reflection. In more quantitative terms, it is desirable that the incident light wave lose all its energy to the electrons in their first few collisions with neighboring ions. This model enables us to estimate how thick a dense plasma must be to absorb all the incident laser light. When a plasma is surrounded by a vacuum, the density of electrons and ions increases rapidly from zero at the outer surface to a maximum in the bulk of the plasma. Most of the laser radiation is absorbed in this layer of increasing density [*see bottom illustration on preceding page*]. For complete absorption in a dense plasma at thermonuclear temperatures this layer need be only .005 inch thick.

The answer to the first question has been provided by the theoretical and experimental work of laboratories throughout the world. In the U.S. a group at the United Aircraft Research Laboratories under Alan F. Haught is

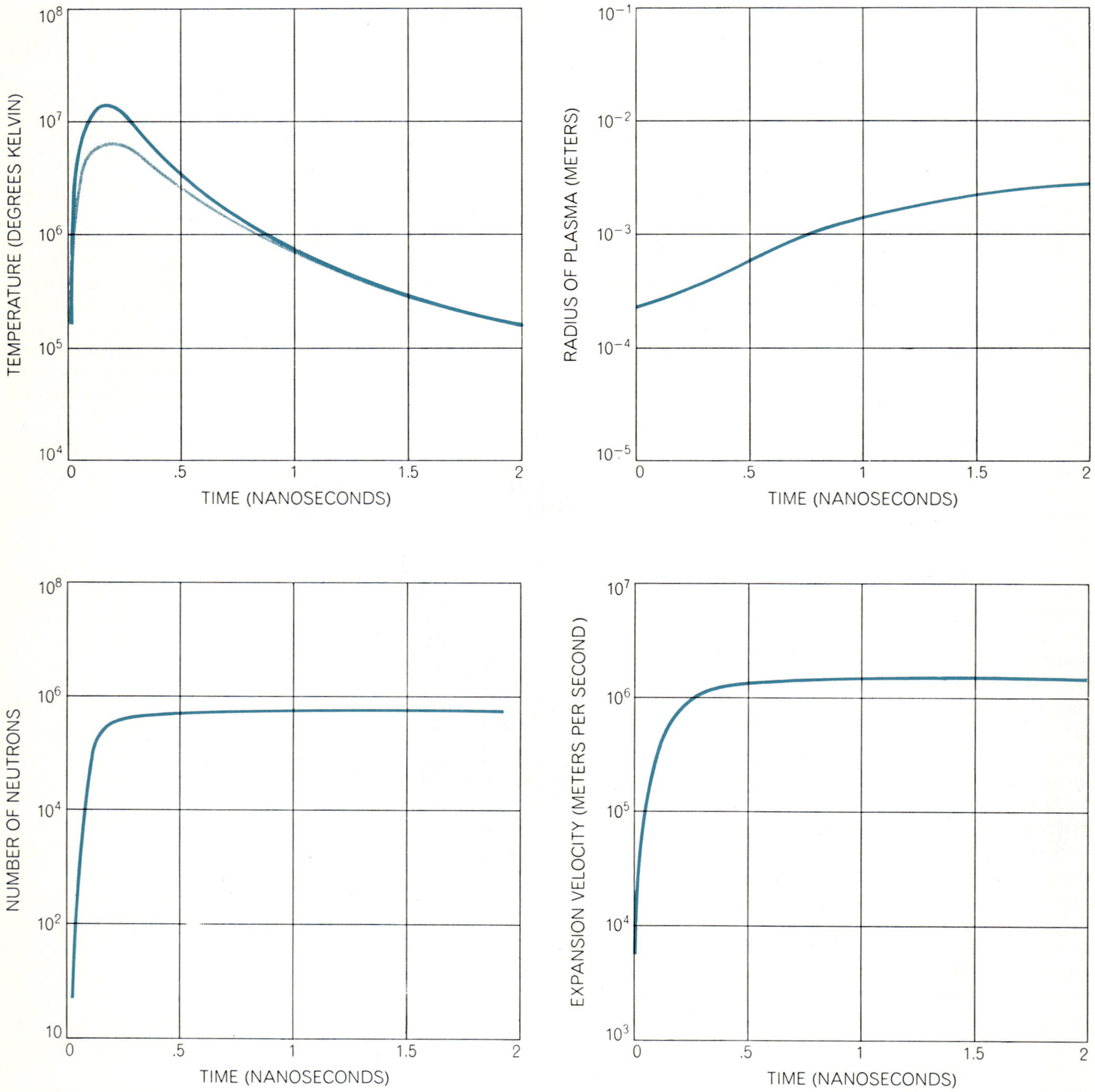

TYPICAL ABSORPTION HISTORY for a laser-heated deuterium fuel pellet is represented by these four graphs. The pellet, originally a tenth of a millimeter in diameter, was heated by a tailored laser pulse that lasted 10^{-10} second and had a peak amplitude of 10^{13} watts. Darker curve in first graph is electron temperature; lighter curve, ion temperature. The incoming pulse was absorbed solely by nonrelativistic processes and hence resulting neutron yield, a measure of success of burning, is a conservative estimate.

demonstrating that plasmas produced by the laser heating of small pellets can be confined in existing magnetic-field geometries over a wide range of temperatures. The resulting quasi-steady plasma, although not hot enough for significant controlled fusion reactions, can then be augmented and heated to higher temperatures by other methods. Thus clean, laser-produced plasmas can serve as the first step in the buildup to controlled fusion conditions. Since the laser plasma is only the catalyst that serves to turn on the steady-state fusion process, the low efficiency of the laser system is of no particular significance.

The second question—regarding the feasibility of laser-heating a small dense plasma to thermonuclear conditions without the necessity of a confining magnetic field—is receiving increased attention. The conditions required to achieve this result can best be understood by taking a step-by-step look at the heating process in a laser-produced plasma. In the typical experimental arrangement pulsed laser radiation is focused on a small fuel pellet of solid deuterium-tritium. The solid fuel pellet is converted to a dense plasma by the leading edge of the incident laser pulse, which is of sufficient duration to vaporize (but not significantly heat) the droplet. Once the droplet is in gaseous form the main heating pulse is applied.

The plasma does not remain stationary as it is heated. Detailed consideration of the absorption process shows that the dynamics of the expanding plasma heated by the incident radiation are vitally important to the time-dependence of the absorption. A typical absorption-time history for an initially solid droplet [*see illustration on opposite page*] shows that there is a time beyond which the plasma has expanded to a point of transparency to the incident laser light. The duration of usable laser energy for heating dense, freely expanding, small plasmas is bounded by two characteristic times. The first is the time it takes for the plasma to expand to the point where it is too dilute to continue to absorb a significant portion of the incident laser energy (a few nanoseconds). The second is the time associated with the electron-ion energy transfer. As we have mentioned, this time scale is on the order of 10^{-11} second. Hence a laser pulse with a duration of 10^{-10} second, bracketed by these two characteristic times, is well suited to this purpose. The laser energy coupled efficiently into the plasma appears initially as thermal energy, and this energy, coupled with the energy from fusion, is ultimately divided up among the fusion reaction products, radiation losses and expansion energy.

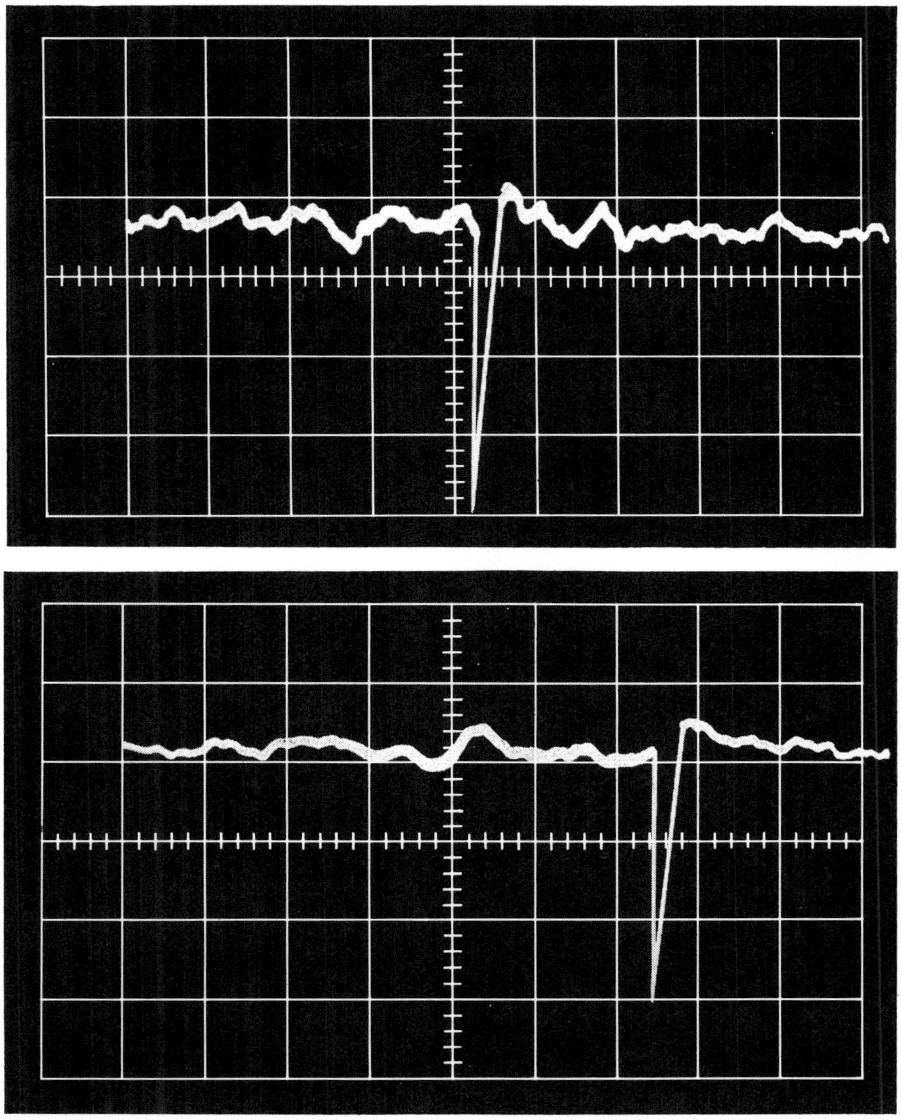

BURST OF NEUTRONS arriving successively at two detectors spaced 225 centimeters apart is signaled by the sharp deflections in these two oscilloscope traces. The difference in the arrival times is a measure of the energy of the neutrons and indicates that these particular neutrons were produced by deuterium-deuterium reactions in the experimental plasma. A similar experiment carried out with a pure hydrogen plasma yielded no neutron output.

One could in principle reduce the amount of energy that goes into expansion by using a strong containing magnetic field. To do so, however, would call for magnetic fields capable of exerting pressures of tens of millions of pounds per square inch. Such fields are not available at present.

Once the density and temperature of the ions are known as a function of time, the thermonuclear yield is easily determined. In particular, rigorous calculations on such typical configurations indicate that one can achieve a ratio of liberated energy to input energy that is greater than 1 at input energies of around 10^5 to 10^6 joules. The assumptions that form the basis of these calculations are currently being studied experimentally at a number of laboratories in the U.S. and abroad.

Neutrons resulting from fusion reactions are ideal "thermometers" to use in evaluating the success of a particular high-power heating experiment. For example, for every deuterium-tritium reaction a neutron with an energy of 14.1 million electron volts (MeV) is produced. The number of such reactions is strongly temperature-dependent. Neutrons produced by the interaction of laser light and a plasma were first reported by N. G. Basov at the Lebedev Institute in Moscow in 1963. The Russian work was followed by high-power laser-plasma neutron experiments at the Limeil Laboratory in France and at several places in the U.S., specifically the Livermore Laboratory of the University of California, the Los Alamos National Labora-

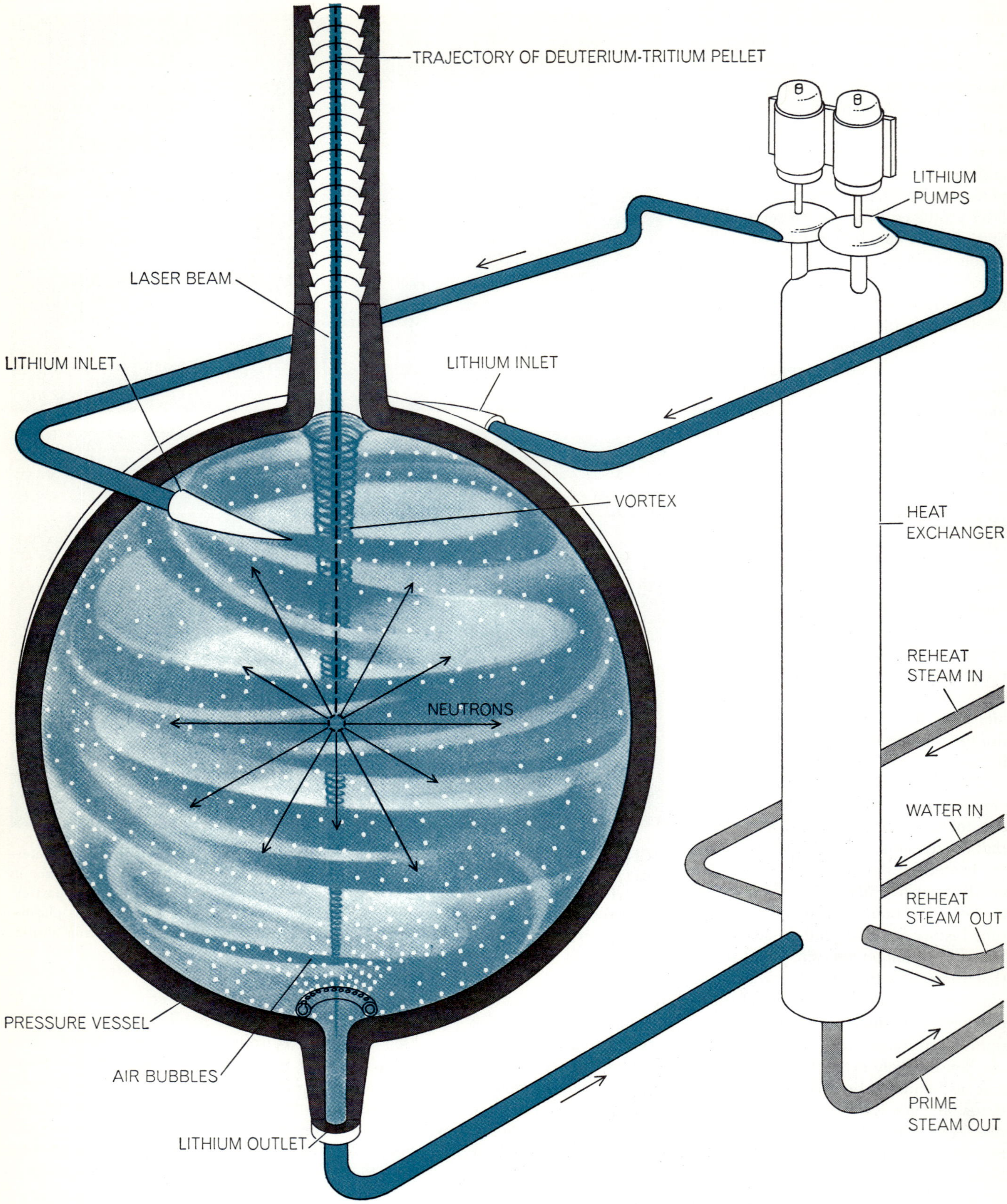

PROPOSED FUSION REACTOR was designed by workers at the Oak Ridge National Laboratory as a method for converting the fusion energy from laser-ignited deuterium-tritium pellets into useful electric power. The fusion energy would be absorbed in a pool of lithium, which would be contained in a cylindrical or spherical pressure vessel some 10 to 15 feet in diameter. A free-standing vortex would be maintained around a vertical axis by swirling the lithium at a sufficiently high velocity. A frozen pellet of deuterium-tritium would be injected into the center of the vortex cavity and would be ignited with a laser pulse when it reached the midplane. The energy deposited in the lithium as heat in the form of energetic neutrons (*black arrows*) would be removed by drawing off lithium from the bottom of the vessel, circulating it through heat exchangers and returning it through centrifugal pumps to tangential nozzles in the perimeter of the vessel. In this particular design the blast waves created by the explosion of the pellet would be attenuated to protect the pressure vessel by introducing shock-absorbing gas bubbles into the lithium pool through a perforated ring in the bottom of the vessel. The pellet-injection and laser systems would be protected by making the port for pellet injection quite long with a wall profile that would break the normal shock wave into many oblique shock waves, thus attenuating the primary blast wave.

tory, the Sandia Corporation and the University of Rochester. Laboratories around the world have been improving on those initial results. Total neutron yields in excess of 10^5 from the deuterium-deuterium reaction have been measured using targets of deuterium with incident laser-beam energies of between 50 and 250 joules. The interpretation of these results indicates a slightly better absorption than simple collisional theory predicts.

Of special interest is the detailed study of the absorption of the incident radiation. There are a number of important contributions to the absorption that may be more significant than the simple collisional process described above and that may hence affect the energy release. Nature, however, seems to favor a freely expanding dense plasma, since the majority of these special absorption processes increase the effectiveness of the incident laser beam.

At present lasers with a properly shaped pulse can deliver 10^3 joules, whereas at least 10^5 joules is needed for significant amounts of laser-produced fusion. This laser energy can be made available using present technology, but as yet no such working system exists. Although the experimental results are few, they appear to justify optimism.

Meaningful use can be made of the energy released from a dense centimeter-size fuel pellet heated by focused laser radiation in a number of different energy-conversion applications. For example, a central station generating electric power by means of controlled thermonuclear reactions from a periodic vaporizing of deuterium-tritium pellets would look quite different from a configuration designed for use in, say, space propulsion. As an illustration let us consider the feasibility of this general scheme for a controlled thermonuclear power plant.

A method for converting the fusion energy from laser-ignited deuterium-tritium pellets into electrical power was evolved at the Oak Ridge National Laboratory early in 1969 in conjunction with fusion-power feasibility studies that have been under way there since 1967. The Oak Ridge approach to fusion entails absorption of the energy from fusion in a pool of lithium, which in turn delivers the energy as heat to a thermodynamic cycle.

The lithium pool would be contained in a cylindrical or spherical pressure vessel 10 to 15 feet in diameter and would be swirled at a sufficiently high velocity to form a free vortex around its vertical axis [*see illustration on opposite page*]. By adjusting the swirl velocity distribution properly it should be possible to obtain a central cavity with a fairly uniform diameter of perhaps five centimeters through the region from the top of the vessel to well below the midplane. A frozen pellet of deuterium-tritium would be injected into the center of the vortex cavity and would be ignited with a laser pulse when it reached the midplane. The energy deposited in the lithium as heat would be removed by drawing off lithium from the bottom of the pressure vessel, circulating it through heat exchangers and returning it to the pressure vessel. The process would be repeated perhaps every 10 seconds. The large thermal inertia in the lithium circuit would act to maintain an essentially constant flow of heat to the thermodynamic cycle.

Drawing off the lithium from the bottom of the pressure vessel would help to stabilize the vortex. After circulating through the heat exchangers the lithium would be returned through pumps to tangential nozzles in the perimeter of the pressure vessel, thereby maintaining the desired vortex.

An obvious objection to this concept is that it would not serve to yield useful amounts of power because the amount of energy one might release in each explosion would have to be kept quite small or the pressure vessel would burst. A relatively simple analysis discloses that this is indeed the case unless some measures are taken to attenuate the blast wave before it strikes the wall of the pressure vessel. In fact, several steps can be taken to increase the rate at which the energy in the shock wave is degraded. One step would be to introduce a large number of gas bubbles in order to reduce the mean density of the liquid by about 5 percent. As the shock wave traversed a gas bubble some of its energy would go into spalling liquid from the inner surface of the bubble and projecting it through the void to strike the bubble wall at the other side, where much of the kinetic energy of the projected material would be converted to thermal energy. The extent to which this would attenuate the main shock wave is difficult to estimate, but simple tests indicate that a sufficiently high bubble density could be obtained to allow an increase in the energy released per explosion by as much as a factor of 10 over the corresponding value for a pool of bubble-free lithium.

The steps outlined here are designed to reduce the intensity of the blast wave before it impinges on the pressure vessel, but they would have little or no effect on the blast wave progressing upward through the cavity in the liquid lithium toward the laser and the pellet-injection system. Fortunately the low density of the lithium vapor will diminish the intensity of the blast wave. In addition the port for pellet injection and the laser beam can be made quite long, with a wall profile that would break the normal shock wave up into a host of oblique shock waves and thus dissipate the bulk of its energy.

Let us try to visualize in detail the sequence of events in the course of one explosion cycle, beginning with the injection of the deuterium-tritium pellet into the vortex. Perhaps 10 percent of the pellet would be vaporized as it moved along its trajectory as a consequence of the absorption of heat radiated to it by the hot lithium. The remainder of the pellet would be vaporized and ionized when it was struck by the laser beam. Some of the deuterium and tritium ions would fuse, and the fusion energy released would increase the temperature of the rest of the pellet material so that about 5 percent of the ions would fuse before plasma expansion terminated the reaction. About 75 percent of the energy from the fusion reaction would go into energetic neutrons, and this energy would be absorbed as those neutrons were slowed down in the inner region of the lithium. The absorbed energy would raise the temperature of the central lithium region a few hundred degrees in about a millionth of a second and would cause the lithium to expand; this expansion, however, should be largely absorbed by contraction of the bubbles so that no severe blast wave would be generated. About 25 percent of the energy released by the fusion reaction would appear as alpha particles; these would produce ion heating and, subsequently, X rays. The energy in the X rays would be absorbed in the first millimeter or two of the lithium layer, causing the lithium in that thin layer to vaporize. The vaporized lithium together with the expanding thermonuclear plasma would induce a weak blast wave in the lithium.

The velocity of sound in hot lithium is about 15,000 feet per second. The liquid would move outward from the explosion center at a lower velocity to form a spherical cavity. The displaced liquid would move into the upper portion of the vortex cavity. This would entail a good deal of sloshing, particularly in the region of the ports for the injection of the fuel pellet and the laser beam. The geometry of the injection passage de-

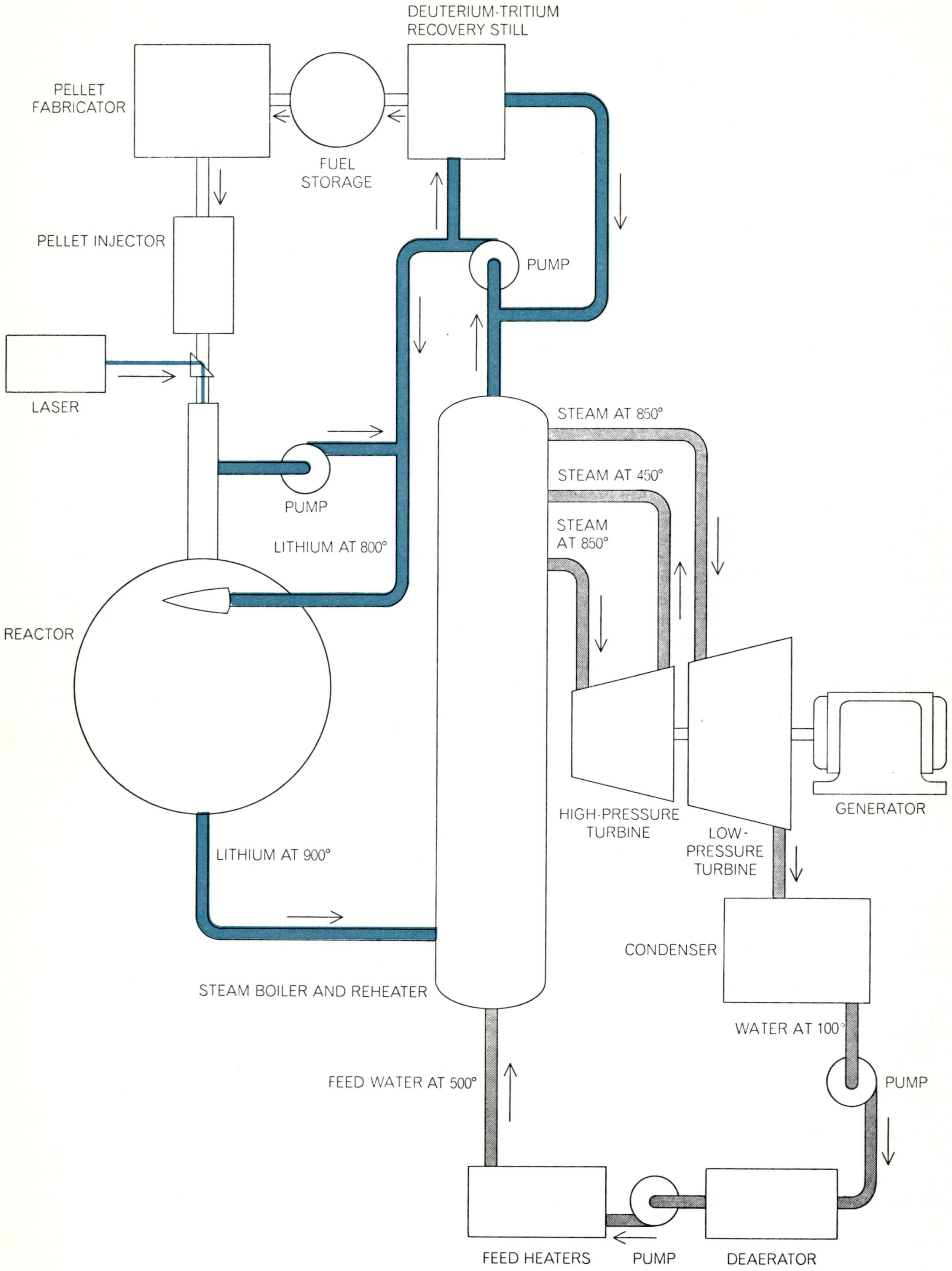

FULL-SCALE POWER PLANT incorporating many of the concepts discussed in this article might be based on a single fusion reactor in which deuterium-tritium pellets would be ignited by high-power laser pulses. The energy of the explosions would be absorbed in a tritium-breeding lithium blanket and used to generate 150 megawatts of electric power by means of a conventional steam cycle.

signed to keep the blast wave from moving up through the ports, however, would also be effective in inhibiting the liquid from sloshing up the port.

The rotational momentum of the lithium in the pressure vessel should help to reestablish the vortex. In addition the lithium through-flow in a typical case would be so large that about 50 percent of the lithium in the vessel would be replaced each cycle.

The pressure-vessel stress problems were examined by C. V. Chester and Lawrence Dresner at Oak Ridge. They quickly reached the conclusion that the proposed system presents so many analytical complexities, particularly if the effects of gas bubbles in the liquid are included, that it is doubtful an analytical model can be developed on purely theoretical grounds. Nonetheless, it does appear that all the phenomena involved are such that the scaling law commonly used for analysis of blast effects would apply. Hence test work has proceeded with small models.

Chester and Dresner designed a series of model tests using small steel vessels and ordinary explosive charges. The first tests were run with the model pressure vessel filled with bubble-free water. The amount of explosive was increased in small increments from about 1.5 grams to about 10 grams. The dilation of the vessel at the midplane was measured with a micrometer following each test, and the results were plotted as a function of the weight of charge detonated. A line drawn through the scatter band of points was passed through the zero dilation axis to define the maximum charge that could be detonated without stressing the vessel beyond the elastic limit. The tests indicated that this value was consistent with the value determined analytically, and that it corresponded to about two grams of explosive. Thus the simplified analytical model was deemed sound and suitable for scaling to full-size vessels.

A second series of tests was run with a thin layer of sponge rubber lining the inner wall of the pressure vessel. This cushioned the blast wave enough to increase to more than four grams the amount of explosive that could be used without stressing the vessel beyond the elastic limit.

A third series of tests was run with a perforated ring placed in the bottom of the model pressure vessel. Air was admitted to the ring to provide an annular curtain of bubbles in the region near the wall of the pressure vessel. A strain gage mounted on the outside of the model in the same horizontal plane as the explosive provided a good measure of the stress in the vessel initially with no air bubbles in the vessel and later with air bubbles filling about 5 percent of the vessel.

In extrapolating these results to a full-scale system—a pressure vessel 25 times larger, with a diameter of 12.5 feet and a wall 10 inches thick—the energy released from the explosion would be increased by a factor of 25^3, or 15,625. Allowing a safety factor of two, one could employ 15 kilograms of explosive in a full-scale system using bubble-free water at room temperature. This corresponds to an energy release of 15×10^5 calories per explosion. If the explosion were repeated at a frequency of one every 10 seconds, the power output would be 6.3 megawatts.

This value of 6.3 megawatts would be the energy in the blast wave for a system in which TNT would be exploded in water with no vortex or bubbles to cushion the explosion. With TNT all the energy would go into the blast wave, but in a fusion reactor about 80 percent of the energy would appear in the form of heat in the liquid as a consequence of the slowing down and absorption of fast neutrons. Most of this energy would simply go into heating the liquid and compressing the bubbles rather than a blast wave; hence the energy output of the reactor could be approximately five times the energy producing the blast wave, that is, about 30 megawatts. The model tests indicate that the cushioning effect of the bubbles ought to reduce the intensity of the blast wave by at least another factor of 2.5, and that the use of a spherical rather than a cylindrical vessel would give another factor of two, thus allowing an increase in the rated power output to perhaps 150 megawatts. Some further increase in power may be possible as a consequence of differences in compressibility between water and high-temperature lithium, but data are not in hand to estimate the extent of this effect.

The design of a full-scale power plant was derived from the concept outlined here within the limitations imposed by basic design considerations. For example, although deuterium is cheap and readily available, tritium is not. As a result, for a deuterium-tritium fusion reactor to be economically attractive it must breed tritium. This can be done because the energetic neutrons have a substantial probability of colliding with other neutrons in the course of slowing down in a natural lithium blanket. When a neutron is absorbed in the lithium, it yields tritium plus an alpha particle. Thus a breeding ratio of perhaps 1.3 would be obtained. If the lithium pool had a radius of at least a meter, there would be virtually no neutron losses from escape or absorption in structural material, and there would be no neutron damage to the pressure vessel. Hence lithium appears to be a particularly attractive choice for the fluid to absorb the energy of the explosion.

In the choice of material for the pressure vessel, extensive compatibility tests indicate that the two most promising candidates for use with lithium are Croloy (a chrome-molybdenum steel) and a niobium alloy containing 1 percent zirconium. The operating temperature with Croloy is limited by corrosion considerations to about 900 degrees F., whereas the niobium alloy could be employed with lithium up to at least 2,000 degrees F. Niobium is very expensive, however, and requires protection from oxidation; Croloy is preferable, at least for initial studies and experiments.

In choosing a thermodynamic cycle the first logical choice is a steam Rankine cycle. Croloy is widely used in existing fossil-fueled steam plants for steam temperatures up to 1,050 degrees F. Thus if an upper temperature limit of 900 degrees is adopted for the lithium system and a 50-degree temperature drop between the lithium and the steam circuit is accepted, the reactor could be coupled to a quite conventional steam system [*see illustration on opposite page*].

It might be argued that an intermediate fluid such as an inert salt should be used between the lithium and the steam circuit, because of the large energy release associated with the lithium-water reaction that would occur if there were a leak from one system into the other. The consequences of such a leak, however, appear no more serious than those associated with the heat exchangers between the sodium-potassium and the steam system employed in fast sodium-cooled fission reactor plants. The amount of radioactivity in the lithium would be small and the loss of tritium in such an accident would not be serious.

In order to keep the thermal stresses to a modest level in the vessels and piping of the lithium system it seems desirable to keep the average temperature rise in the lithium to about 100 degrees F. This could be accomplished by using a flow rate of 2,300 gallons per minute with two pumps operating in parallel.

A physically small but economically

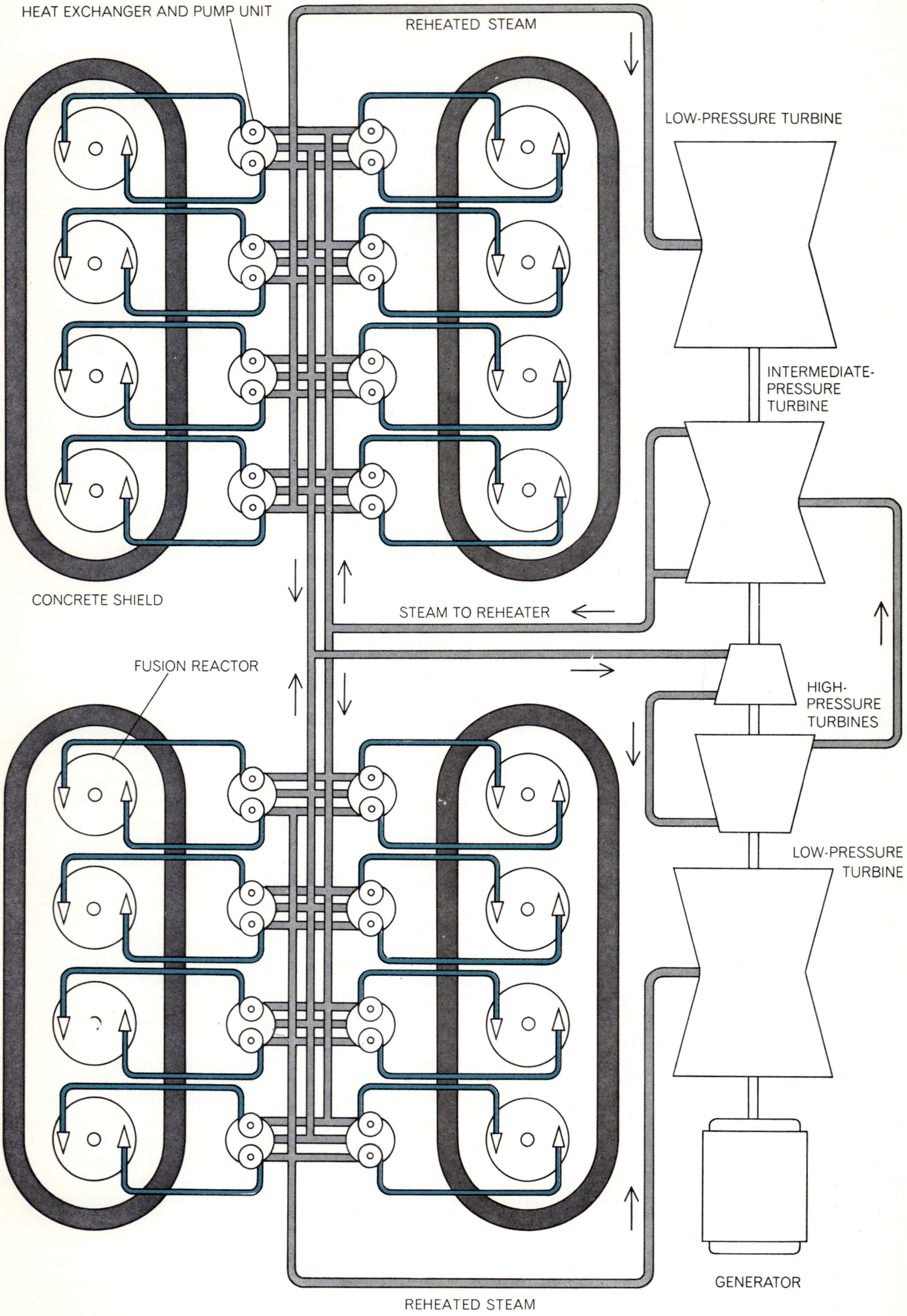
HEAT EXCHANGER AND PUMP UNIT
REHEATED STEAM
LOW-PRESSURE TURBINE
INTERMEDIATE-PRESSURE TURBINE
CONCRETE SHIELD
STEAM TO REHEATER
FUSION REACTOR
HIGH-PRESSURE TURBINES
LOW-PRESSURE TURBINE
GENERATOR
REHEATED STEAM

vital portion of the plant is the fuel-recovery and fuel-reprocessing system. It has been shown that both tritium and deuterium can be removed from lithium at low cost with a small, essentially conventional distillation system. After being compressed, the deuterium-tritium mixture can be liquefied with a cryogenic system. Fuel pellets can then be manufactured by allowing liquid droplets to fall through a vacuum chamber filled with cold helium gas, which would chill the droplet and freeze it. The electric power required for the cryogenic system appears to be less than a watt per kilowatt of thermal output from the reactor; hence it should not detract appreciably from the overall thermal efficiency of the power plant. It would, of course, be necessary to add deuterium and take off a deuterium-tritium mixture to maintain the proper composition of the fuel pellets.

For plants with an output greater than 150 megawatts it might be possible to make the cushion of bubbles more effective and thus increase the power output from a vessel of a given size by a factor of two or more. Power outputs of more than about 500 megawatts per vessel will require that the size and/or thickness of the vessel be increased. This will increase the difficulties of fabrication and consequently the unit cost in dollars per pound and dollars per kilowatt of output. The alternative is to use a number of relatively small vessels operated in parallel [*see illustration on opposite page*]. The latter approach is attractive because it would make possible modular construction with one standard size or more of shop-fabricated reactor vessels coupled with appropriately sized pumps, heat exchangers and connecting pipes. This approach is particularly attractive because large steam turbines are commonly supplied with steam through many steam pipes, since provisions for thermal expansion make it advantageous to keep the diameter—and hence the capacity—of individual steam pipes to a modest level.

It should be mentioned that the type of fusion reactor proposed here differs from both fission reactors and other types of fusion reactors in that there appears to be no theoretical advantage to the use of very large units. This constitutes an important advantage for the concept.

A laser-initiated fusion-power plant built of Croloy and operated to produce steam at 850 degrees F. would have an overall thermal efficiency of about 40 percent, which is approximately that of the better fossil-fueled plants in current operation. The efficiency could be increased dramatically if the system were built of the niobium alloy and operated at a temperature of about 1,800 degrees F. That temperature would be too high for use in a steam cycle because there would be enough dissociation of the hydrogen and oxygen in the steam to cause serious attack of any structural metal that would be economically attractive. It should be possible, however, to employ a binary-vapor cycle with a potassium-vapor Rankine cycle taking heat from the lithium at perhaps 1,800 degrees F. Such a system would have an overall thermal efficiency for the cycle of about 58 percent. This would cut the waste heat rejected per electrical kilowatt to about half that for conventional steam plants, and it opens the possibility of even higher efficiencies of heat utilization by integration with industrial and urban heating systems.

There is little point in developing the proposed power plant unless it looks attractive economically. If a suitable laser system can be built at a reasonable cost—a major question that cannot be resolved at this stage—it appears that the capital cost of the rest of the system should be no higher than the capital cost of more conventional plants. Certainly the cost of the steam system should be the same as that of similar steam systems in current use. The lithium circuit and steam boiler should cost about the same as the corresponding equipment projected for the circuit of the sodium-cooled fast-breeder fission reactor. Moreover, the pressure vessel would be relatively simple compared with those currently employed in water-cooled fission reactors. The weight of a spherical pressure vessel with an inside diameter of 12.5 feet and a wall thickness of 10 inches would be about 200,000 pounds. Assuming a 40 percent thermal efficiency, such a plant would yield an electrical output of about 60,000 kilowatts. Assuming a unit cost of $3 per pound, the vessel would cost $600,000, or about $10 per kilowatt. The cost of other items, such as the cryogenic systems for fuel recovery and pellet fabrication, appears to be a small fraction of the overall cost of the plant.

The operating cost for fuel should be low indeed. The cost of the deuterium and lithium would be about $200 per pound and $15 per pound respectively. This would yield a cost of only about three cents per million BTU (British thermal units) compared with current prices of about 40 cents per million BTU for fossil fuels. Inasmuch as capital charges are roughly the same as fuel costs in conventional fossil-fuel plants, this in turn indicates that the proposed laser-initiated fusion-power plant would be economically attractive even if the capital cost were twice as high.

One of the major problems associated with fission reactors stems from the large inventory of radioactive material inherently present and the potential hazard to the public that it represents. Because of this factor as much as 30 percent of the capital cost of a fission reactor plant may stem from elaborate provisions to prevent or contain any conceivable accident that might release radioactive material to the environment. The only radioactive material of consequence in the proposed fusion-power plant would be tritium, and estimates indicate that it would represent a total hazard potential that would be lower than that of a comparable fission reactor by a factor of about a million. This should reduce costs and greatly ease siting problems.

The design studies of full-scale laser-initiated fusion-power plants make the concept look attractive and therefore raise questions with respect to the development problems. Clearly the most vital are concerned with the laser and the pellet-ignition process. Can a sufficiently powerful laser be built and pulsed to ignite the pellet? If so, will the yield of fusion energy be many times more than the energy input to the laser? How effectively can the blast wave be attenuated by entraining a substantial fraction of gas bubbles in a swirling pool of lithium? These are the principal questions that must be answered experimentally before one can say whether or not the proposed concept is really feasible. There are, of course, many other difficult development problems, but none appears so difficult as to raise doubts about the feasibility of the concept.

THOUSAND-MEGAWATT POWER PLANT might be composed of 16 fusion-reactor modules, each with its associated heat exchanger and pump unit. The system would produce steam at a temperature of 850 degrees Fahrenheit and a pressure of about 1,200 pounds per square inch to drive a combination of high-pressure and intermediate-pressure turbines with one reheat to 850 degrees for a pair of low-pressure turbines. With the addition of a potassium-vapor "topping" cycle operating at a turbine-inlet temperature of 1,800 degrees the overall thermal efficiency of such a system could be brought as high as 58 percent.

39

Non-Military Uses of Nuclear Explosives

Research under the Plowshare program seeks constructive use for nuclear detonations. Underground explosions may be used for power production and mining; surface explosions may excavate harbors

GERALD W. JOHNSON
and HAROLD BROWN

December 1958

The nuclear reactor has become a symbol of the constructive uses of atomic energy; the nuclear bomb, a symbol of destruction. What peaceful end could ever be served by a nuclear explosion? In answering this question, let us reflect a moment on the precedent of an earlier expansion in the violence of explosives available to man's use. The fixation of atmospheric nitrogen, at the turn of the century, made possible the unlimited manufacture of chemical explosives for two world wars. But the fixation of nitrogen also relieved mankind of the prospect of nitrogen starvation. Synthetic fertilizers were regarded as the "good" side of this advance in science and technology; explosives, as the "bad." Yet it is not hard to think of peaceful and constructive uses for chemical explosives. In fact, the tonnage of these explosives consumed in mining and heavy construction now aggregates more than has ever been used for military purposes. Is it really impossible to conceive of such constructive uses for nuclear explosives?

Engineers have been setting ever larger charges of dynamite in recent years to accomplish more daring objectives more quickly and cheaply. The biggest so far on record is the 1,300-ton charge detonated last year in the Ripple Rock explosion, which removed a large, dangerous rock from an inland waterway near Vancouver, B.C. It is reported that the Chinese have used up to 10,000 tons in a single explosion for mining purposes. The biggest chemical explosions begin to approach the minimal nuclear explosion. With thermonuclear explosives we can think of undertaking projects 100 to 1,000 times larger than engineers have contemplated in the past. Indeed, the Soviet press has reported that nuclear explosions have been employed to "move mountains" in that country; no technical accounts, however, have been published to substantiate these claims.

In the U. S. the constructive uses of nuclear explosions are being actively explored, under the Plowshare program of the Atomic Energy Commission, by our group at the Livermore branch of the University of California Radiation Laboratory. In September, 1957, the detonation of a nuclear charge equivalent to 1,700 tons of TNT under a mesa in Nevada (Operation Rainier) demonstrated that a nuclear explosion could be successfully contained underground. Since then drilling and tunneling of the site has given us solid evidence to support our expectations of the constructive possibilities of such an explosion. The most recent series of nuclear weapons tests in Nevada, ending on the eve of the Geneva negotiations that look to the cessation of tests, included five underground shots in the energy-release range from 100 to 20,000 tons. The evaluation of these explosions promises to broaden the foundation for proceeding next to underground nuclear explosions designed for specific engineering purposes. In addition, the Plowshare program has been exploring the feasibility of large-scale excavation by surface and shallowly buried explosions. On the remote northwest coast of Alaska, if all goes well, nuclear explosives will excavate a new harbor by way of demonstration and experiment sometime in 1960. It is not too much to say that we are on the verge of a new period of "geographical engineering."

In defining the U. S. position on the discussion at Geneva, President Eisenhower proposed that the Plowshare experiments be exempted from any agreement to suspend the testing of nuclear weapons. These experiments, it has been announced, will be open to observation by invited representatives of other nations and their results will be fully disclosed through the scientific press.

The reconstructed history of the Rainier explosion provides a vivid picture of what happens when the enormous energy of a nuclear explosive is contained within the earth. The charge was placed in a small chamber at the end of a 1,600-foot tunnel which spiraled in on its objective in a manner such that the upheaval of the explosion would seal it off. In its first instants the explosion melted and vaporized some 700 tons of rock. The small chamber inflated to a hollow cavity 110 feet in diameter enclosed in a four-inch-thick shell of liquefied rock, which dripped from the ceiling in stalactites and condensed in glassy "raindrops" as it fell. The peak pressure of six million atmospheres developed in the cavity is indicated by the compression of this shell; samples of the fused rock expanded many times in volume when heated in the laboratory. As an assurance of the safety of future underground explosions, it was found that almost all of the radioactivity was concentrated in this hard, insoluble material. About one minute after the explosion the ceiling of the cavity collapsed under the burden of the tons of crushed and broken rock above it; successive caving produced a "chimney" which ran upward several hundred feet through the rock toward the top of the mesa. The shock of the detonation and the collapse of the shell together produced a large permeable region comprising at least 200,000 tons of material. Calculations based upon cores and tunnels drilled into the site show that about 50 per cent of the total energy of the explosion was transferred in heat to the surroundings. The large volume of water, trapped in the porous volcanic rock, quickly redistributed the heat to the masses of cold rubble surrounding the cavity, and the tremendous initial temperatures were reduced to the boiling point of water.

The first industrial possibility suggested by this experiment is that of elec-

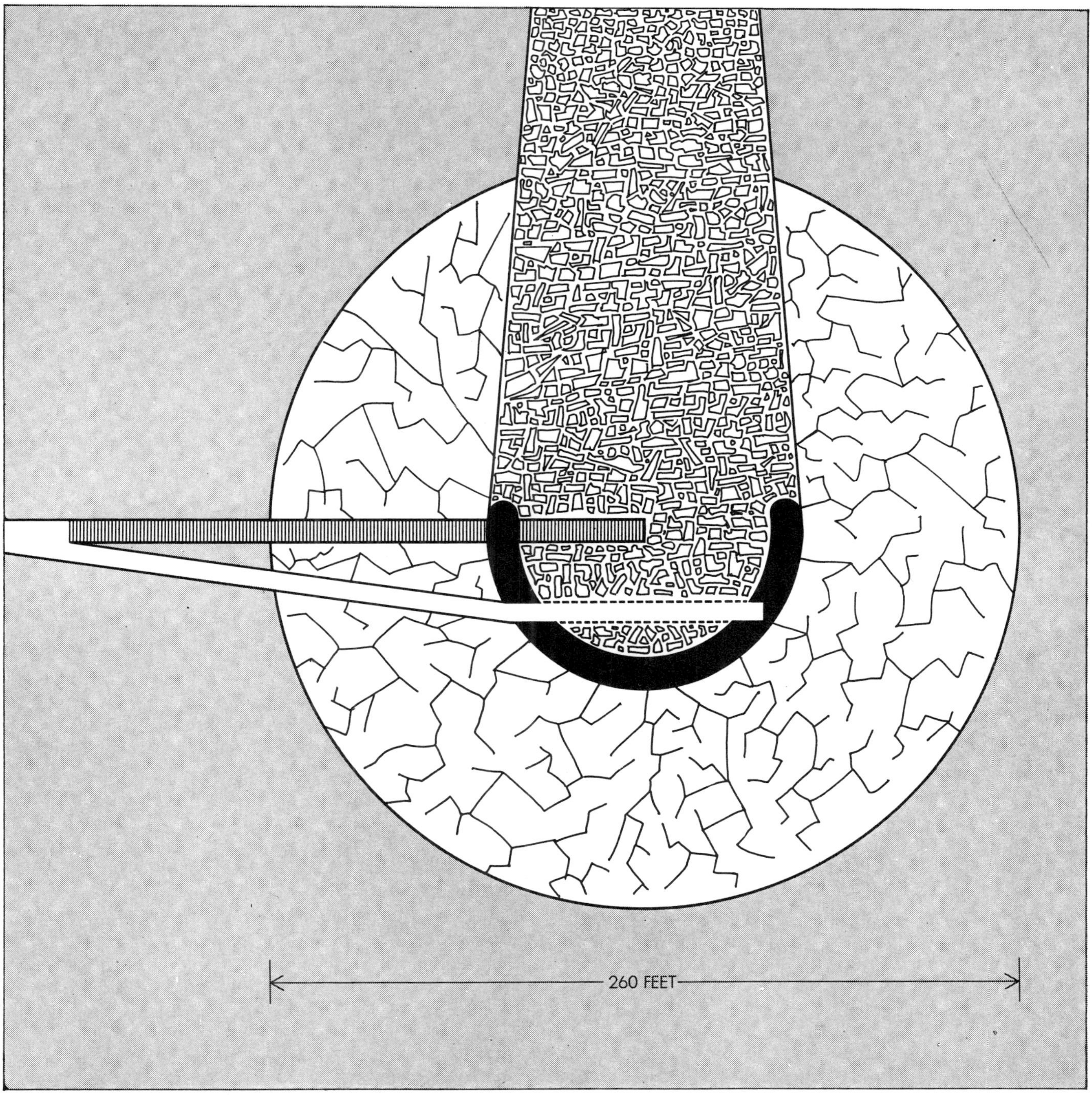

SITE OF RAINIER EXPLOSION was prepared by way of a tunnel designed to collapse during the explosion along the shaded stretch shown in this diagram. An exploratory tunnel driven below it has reached the zone of radioactive fused rock (*black semicircle*).

trical power production. On preliminary calculation, the economics of this route to nuclear power is so attractive that a number of large power companies are conducting studies along with our own. For maximum yield, the energy of the explosion must be trapped at the highest possible temperature. In the Rainier explosion at least half of the energy was released as heat at an initially high temperature, but the energy was quickly dissipated to the rubble of the collapsing cavity by the large quantity of water in in the rock. Workers in the field have proposed numerous ways to avoid this rapid heat dissipation. One calls for the construction of a cavern (or the location of a suitable natural cavern) that would survive the explosion. The cavern would have to be large enough to permit attenuation of the shock wave of the explosion before it strikes the walls. High-pressure steam or other gas, contained in the cavern, would be heated directly by passage of the shock. The shock wave of a 100-kiloton explosion in a chamber with a radius of 1,000 feet would exert an initial pressure of 600 pounds per square inch at the wall; this would be multiplied at least twice upon reflection to something more than 1,200 pounds per square inch. To contain this pressure an above-ground chamber would have to be built with walls of high-strength steel, 12 inches or more thick, and would weigh several million tons. Whether such a container could be built to withstand a multitude of explosions in series is dubious. For economic reasons alone it would be better to attempt its construction deep underground.

A simpler alternative is to return to the Rainier model and try to trap the heat in a natural formation underground. What is needed is an essentially waterless formation, such as a salt dome. In fact, it is now planned to set off the first Plowshare explosion in a thick salt-bed

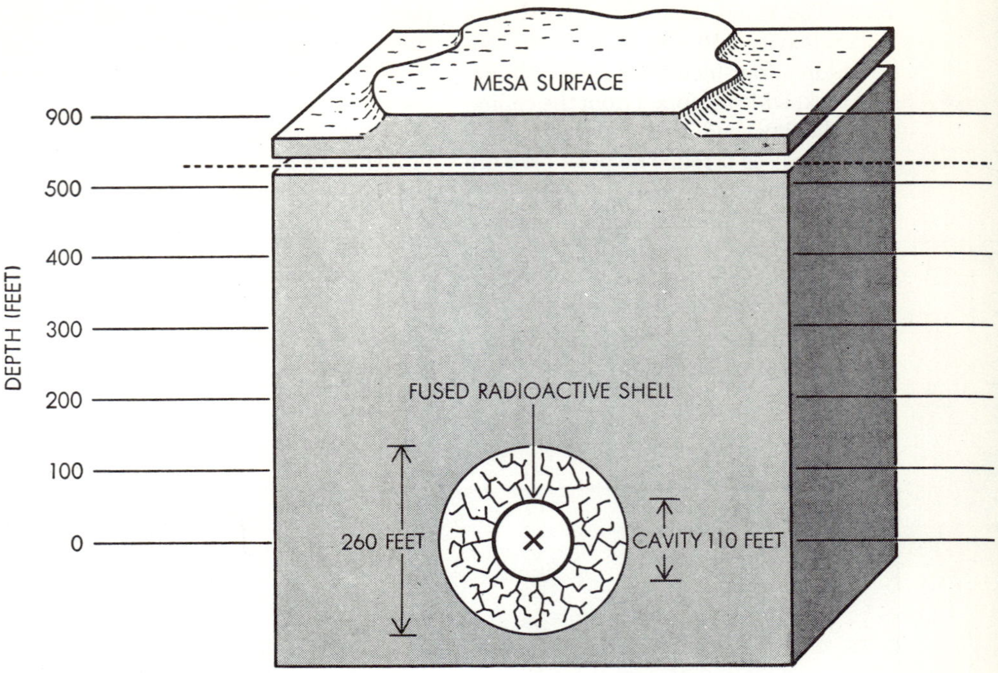

UNDERGROUND NUCLEAR EXPLOSION under a Nevada mesa (Operation Rainier) is shown in three stages. In its first instants (*left*) the explosion melted some 700 tons of

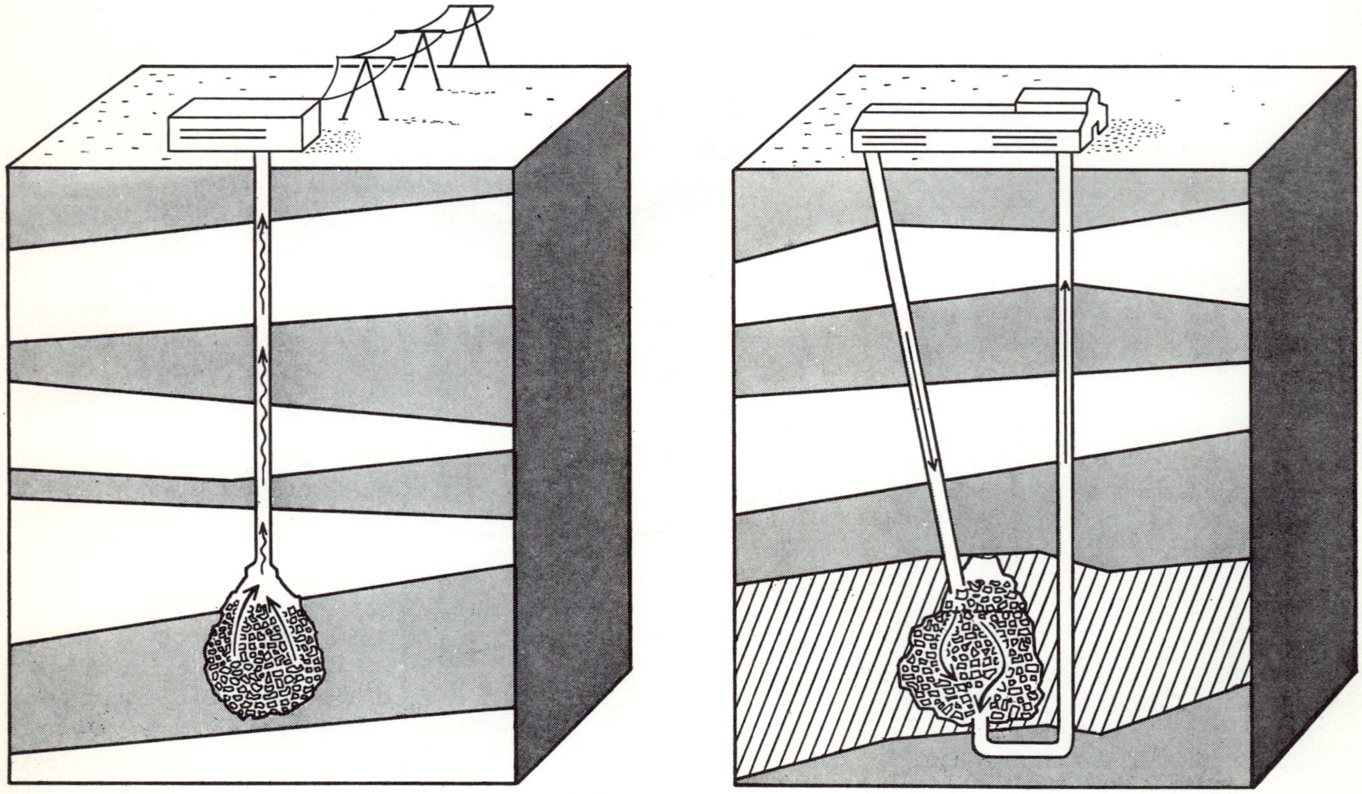

POSSIBLE INDUSTRIAL APPLICATIONS of nuclear explosions are illustrated. The heat of the explosion, trapped underground, may be converted to electricity by percolating a heat-transfer agent through the shattered rock (*left*). To extract minerals a leaching

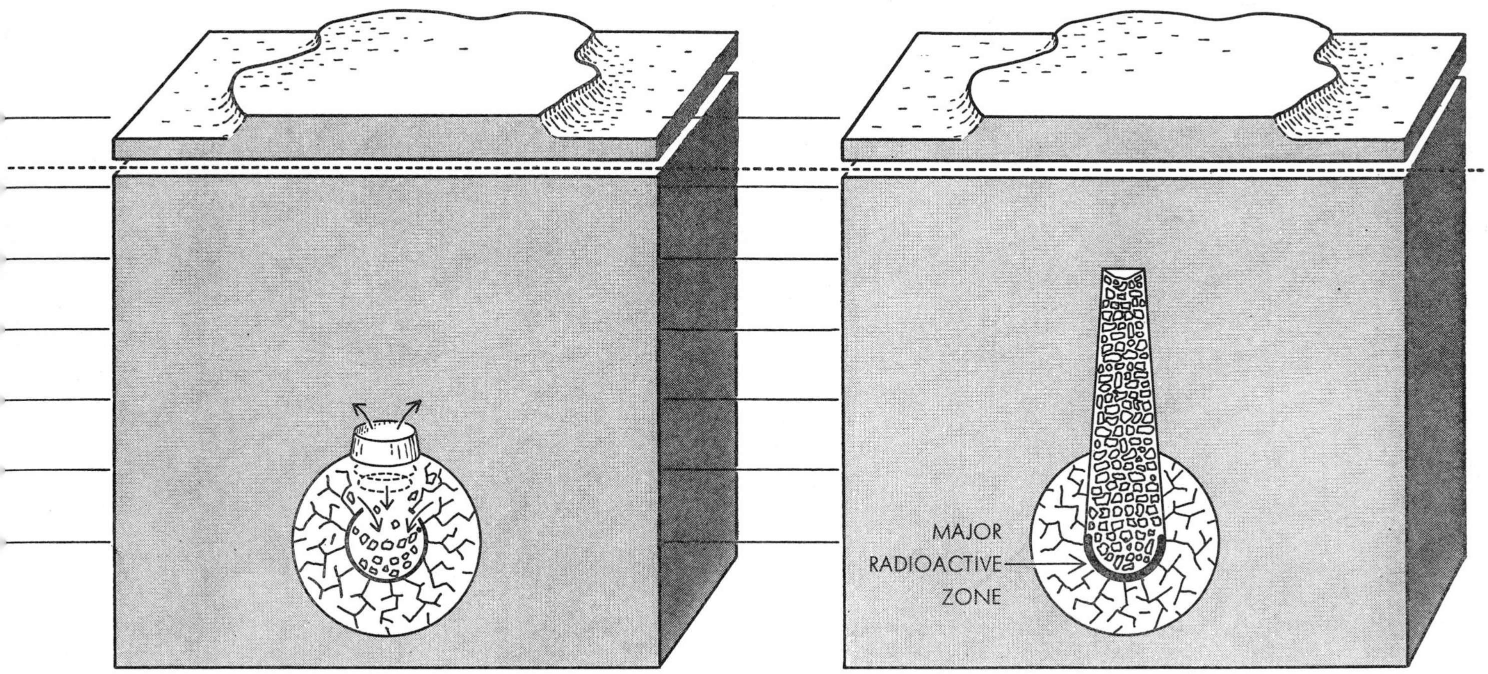

rock and compressed it in a four-inch shell enclosing a cavity 110 feet in diameter. After one minute (*center*), the roof of the cavity caved in under the burden of fractured rock. The cave-in then continued (*right*), running a "chimney" upward in the formation.

near Carlsbad, N.M. Each kiloton of energy released will raise 3,000 tons of salt to a temperature of 1,500 degrees Fahrenheit, thus melting it. A megaton device will therefore yield three million tons of melted salt, a mass of material 600 feet in diameter. The heat from such a thermal reservoir can be recovered by pumping a heat-transfer fluid, such as water or carbon dioxide gas, through the salt and thence to a turbine or other energy converter [*lower left illustration, page 412*]. In a limestone or dolomite formation, a nuclear explosion would evolve huge quantities of carbon dioxide gas from the rock itself. This gas can serve directly as a heat-transfer agent, and additional energy can be recovered from the calcium oxide residue of the rock by treating it with water.

Existing power plants which exploit

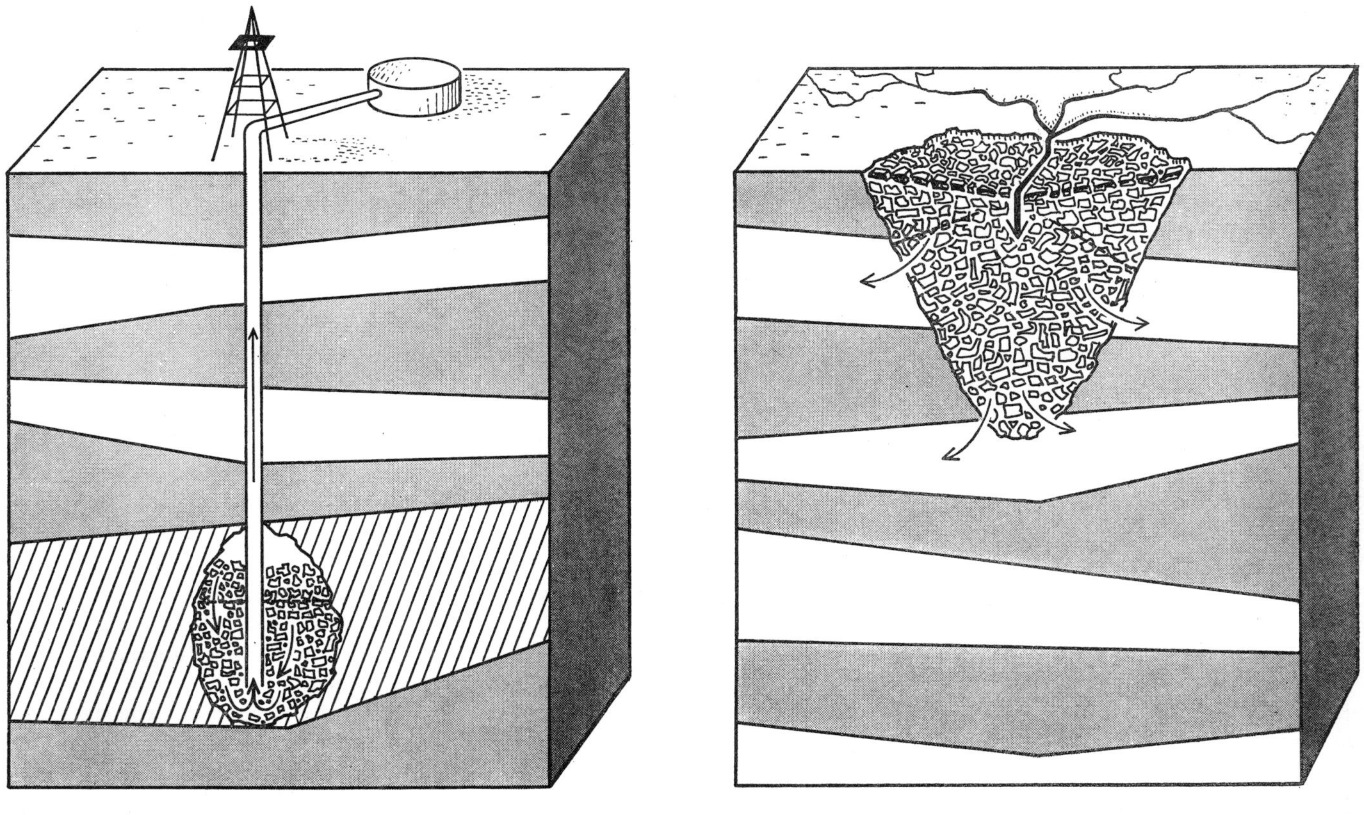

agent may be percolated through a shattered ore bed (*second from left*). An explosion in an oil-shale bed may shatter the shale for retorting (*third from left*). An explosion nearer the surface (*fourth*) may create a huge underground water-storage reservoir.

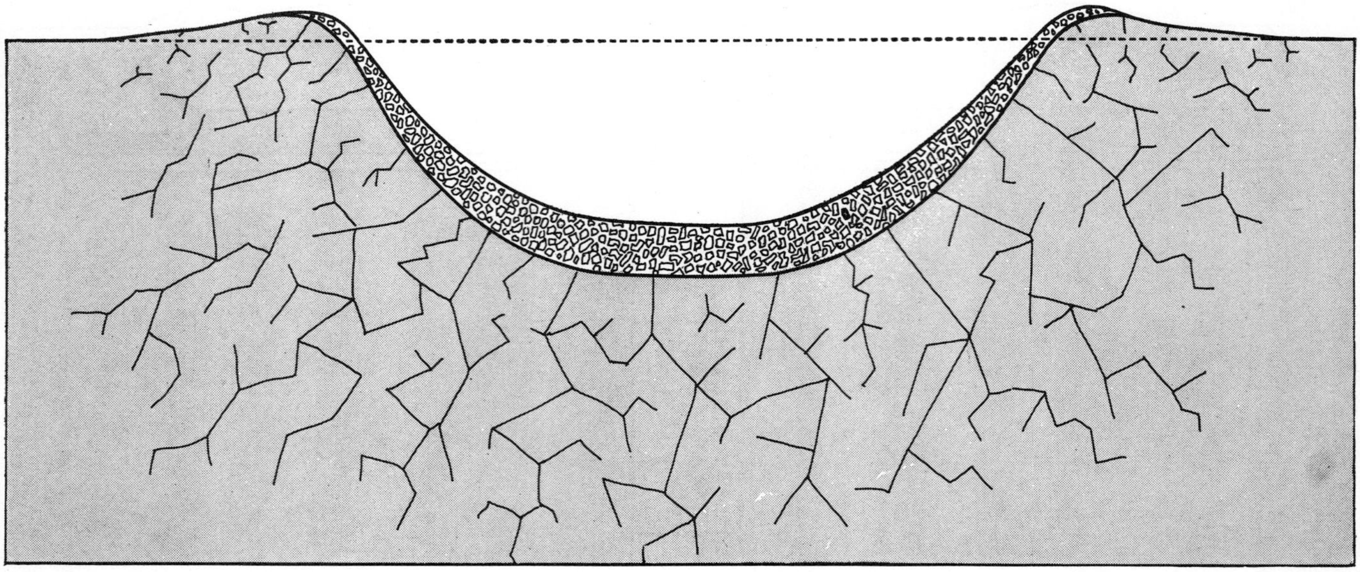

NUCLEAR EXPLOSION ON DRY LAND produced a crater of this proportion. The one-kiloton bomb was buried at a depth of about 50 feet. It blasted a crater some 300 feet in diameter and some 90 feet deep. The crater was partly filled in with its own debris.

natural underground heat provide ample precedent for this approach to electrical power production. The world's largest natural steam-power plant at Larderello, Italy, has been generating electricity from a volcanic heat-source since 1904; it produces 5 per cent of the country's power, and its 150,000-kilowatt capacity is now being doubled. In New Zealand a natural heat source is being opened up in the volcanic Wairakei region to produce power and direct boiler heat for pulp and paper production. The operating and engineering experience at these sites will contribute heavily to the technology of power generation by nuclear explosions. For one thing, they establish the impressive cost figure of .47 cent per kilowatt hour. This compares to .88 for gas or coal plants and .27 for hydroelectric stations in New Zealand. Since geothermal costs are all for plant and operations and include no fuel charges, it is clear that in calculating the economics of power from a thermonuclear explosion an extra figure must be added for the cost of explosives. If such explosions can be produced at a depth of 3,000 feet, which would probably be sufficient for containment, at a cost of $1 million, then the thermonuclear fuel cost would be .1 cent per kilowatt hour, resulting in a total cost of .57 cent per kilowatt hour.

Thermonuclear explosions might also be used to release geothermal energy and thereby achieve even more favorable results. From Larderello and Wairakei we know that steam plants can be operated efficiently at 400 degrees F. Based upon the Rainier explosion, a one-megaton detonation set off in a formation at this temperature and at a depth of 3,000 feet to ensure containment would produce about 12 million tons of broken rock. By percolating a heat-transfer fluid through this now-permeable mass of rock and converting the extracted heat at the efficiency standard of Larderello, a total of 8,000 million kilowatt hours of electrical energy could be derived from one explosion. Since the explosion itself contributes a little more than 1,000 million kilowatt hours to this total, the extraction of natural geothermal heat multiplies the explosion yield by a factor of eight. At the normal geothermal gradient of 100 degrees F. per mile it would require a hole 10 miles deep, about four times the feasible drilling depth, to reach 1,000 degrees. At many sites, however, 1,000 degrees can be reached at three miles. This is fully deep enough to contain a 30-megaton explosion. The heat reservoir created by a single such explosion would yield 2,400 million million kilowatt hours of energy, enough to operate a 500,000-kilowatt generating station for 15 years.

The Rainier experience can be applied even more directly to the technology of mining, which calls for a completely contained underground explosion and does not involve the special requirements of power production. Nuclear explosion provides a new way to extract the wealth of ore beds too deep or too poor for conventional mining. In a bed of low-grade copper the 200,000 tons of broken rock produced by a one-kiloton blast can be multiplied 10 times by preliminary tunneling to direct the energy of the explosion. The percolation of acidified water through the ore bed would then bring the copper to the surface in solution.

Nuclear explosions may be similarly employed to get at the huge reserves of petroleum in the Canadian tar sands and Colorado shales which presently lie beyond the reach of economical extraction. At only 15 per cent recovery, each 100-foot depth of the tar sands along the Athabaska River would yield 100 million barrels of oil per square mile. The oil is released when the tar sand is heated to only 200 degrees F. By firing directly in the sand or beneath it a fluid oil-field might be produced. We understand that the Canadian Government is planning to investigate this possibility. The oil shales present a more difficult problem, because the release of the oil requires a temperature of 750 degrees. The oil might be brought to the surface by controlled burning of the shale in the region shattered by the explosion. A megaton explosion at a depth of 3,000 feet could be expected to release directly about a million barrels of petroleum products and to produce, in addition, some 50 million tons of broken shale. Retorting of this mass of broken shale in place might release an additional 25 million barrels of petroleum products. It may also be that the yield of gas and petroleum from certain formations can be improved by judicious use of nuclear explosives.

An entirely new possibility is the creation of underground reservoirs and aquifers for storage of water, for flood control and for recharging water-bearing strata. The explosion would be set off in

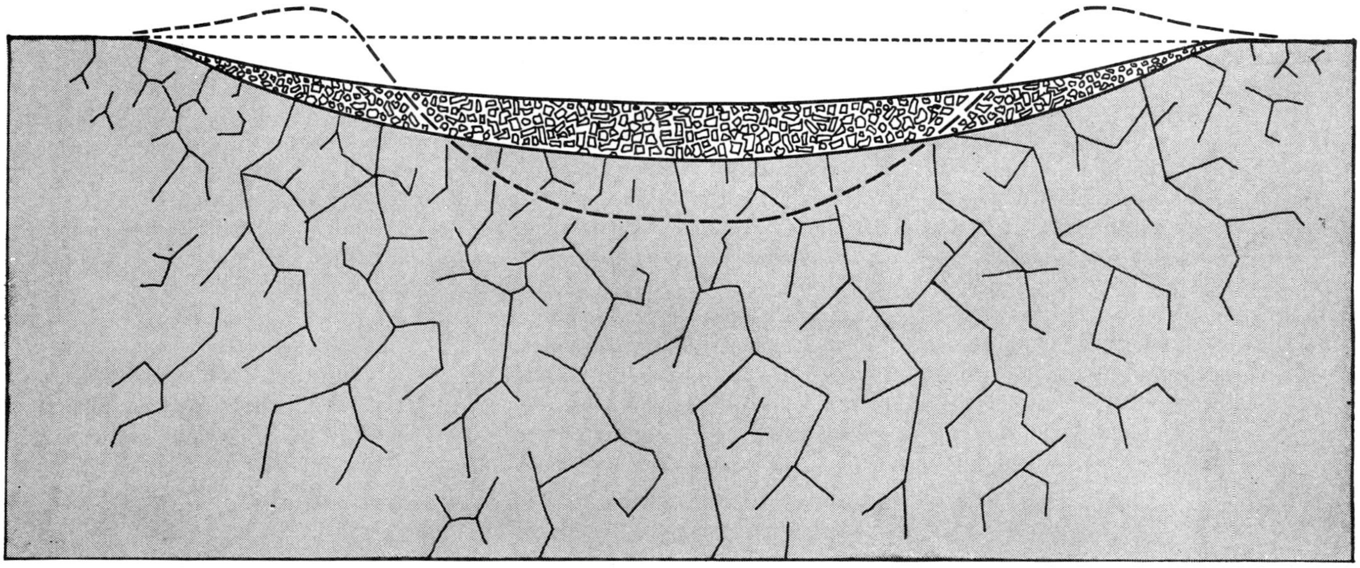

NUCLEAR EXPLOSION IN SHALLOW WATER would probably dig a wider and shallower crater. Among other things, the action of the water would later cause material around the crater to slump into it. Such a crater may be dug to make a harbor in Alaska in 1960.

a natural drainage-basin at such a depth that the progressive cave-in of the initial cavity would proceed completely to the surface. In a dry river bed in a desert area such a storage chamber would be filled during spring or storm runoff. With the water stored underground, evaporation losses would be reduced essentially to zero. Calculation shows that a 100-kiloton explosion would yield a storage capacity of 12,000 million gallons. Another use for nuclear explosions might be the conversion of fresh water from sea water in the heat reservoir of a deep underground explosion.

All these ideas, of course, depend upon the reduction of residual radioactivity to acceptable levels. In silicate rocks, as at the Rainier site, the radioactivity is almost entirely trapped in the rock melted in the first phase of the explosion. This material is highly refractory and insoluble and so should keep the residual activity from contaminating water, oil or leaching agents. At the same time the glassy radioactive rock may itself prove to be a valuable by-product. Enormous numbers of neutrons are produced in a thermonuclear explosion; by capturing these neutrons in suitable materials, buried with the explosive, specific isotopes could be produced in large quantities. The Rainier explosion is also pertinent here. Six months after the detonation a tunnel was driven to the edge of the radioactive sphere, and the radioactive glass was mined by hand. With rather primitive methods of shielding, using the tunnel material itself, all of the 700 tons of material might be mined.

Perhaps the most obvious constructive application of thermonuclear explosions is in earth-moving, that is, the production of craters to be used as harbors, canals or reservoirs. Surface explosions for these desirable ends, however, would have as undesirable side effects all the destructive consequences that make nuclear bombs such formidable weapons. As everyone knows by now, these comprise the incendiary effects of the fireball; the so-called "prompt" radiation at the instant of explosion, composed primarily of neutrons and gamma rays; the residual radiation due to fallout of fission products and radioactive isotopes produced by neutron capture in the surrounding soil, and the air-blast and ground-shock effects. None of these effects, of course, is essential to the objective of producing a crater. We are confident, however, that appropriate precautions in a given project can reduce each of them to acceptable levels. Surface and shallowly buried detonations in the kiloton range have been observed in lightly cemented, dry sand and gravel at the Nevada weapons-testing site. Several megaton shots have been fired on the surface of coral atolls at Eniwetok. These observations, extended by our much longer experience with chemical explosives, should help to minimize the undesirable effect of surface explosions.

To gauge the excavating power of nuclear explosives we have the data on a one-kiloton shot fired at a depth of approximately 50 feet in Nevada. This explosion removed 100,000 cubic yards of material, leaving a crater about 300 feet in diameter and 90 feet in depth. In general, the dimensions of the crater increase as the cube root of the power of the explosive. An explosion in a dry formation will produce a crater with a profile as shown in the illustration on page 32; in a wet formation the crater will have a shallower profile as shown in the illustration on page 33. At a burial depth of only 15 feet a one-kiloton explosive produced no incendiary effects beyond the rim of the crater. Significantly it left a crater with a diameter only 20 per cent less than that attained with a 50-foot burial depth. This result is helpful to the economics of nuclear excavation. Since the cost of burial is a large fraction of total cost, it is well that the effect of the fireball is suppressed by shallow burial.

Let us now apply these data to the construction of, say, a harbor for ocean-going vessels. Calculation shows that four 100-kiloton detonations fired at a depth of 50 feet would produce a channel 1,200 feet wide and 5,000 feet long. A one-megaton shot fired at a depth of 150 feet at the inland end of the chain would evacuate a turning basin 3,000 feet in diameter. Granting that costs of construction are difficult to estimate, this calculation provides an instructive comparison of nuclear and conventional earth-moving. Our harbor requires the excavation of 28 million cubic yards. At a low estimate of $2 per cubic yard, this gives a conventional earth-moving cost of $56 million. With thermonuclear explosives the cost might be as little as $5 million.

The burial depths that produce efficient cratering and minimize incendiary side-effects also remove "prompt" radiation hazards. These are reduced to acceptable levels by only a few feet of soil or water and by the fact that the blast and fall-out effects require observers to stand back at a distance at which the atmosphere fully attenuates the neutron and gamma-ray output. The radius at which air blast and ground shock will cause damage and public annoyance can be estimated in advance. Beyond 30 miles the earth-shaking effects of a megaton explosion would be of interest only to seismologists with their sensitive instruments. Air-blast effects are more difficult to predict; the shock waves may be focused in the atmosphere by wind and temperature gradients. The principal long-range nuisance of air blast is the breakage of windows. For a megaton explosion, the radius of window breaking is not much less than 30 miles even under the best meteorological conditions. Prohibitively large depths of burial would be required to produce a significant reduction of this nuisance.

Radioactive fall-out and the secondary radioactivity induced in the surrounding terrain by neutron radiation present the major safety problems. These hazards can be reduced by the use of thermonuclear explosives. Because they depend on fusion rather than fission, they produce less fall-out in ratio to yield. Their heavy neutron output can be reduced by surrounding the explosive with a neutron-absorbing blanket. Even with these measures there will be some local radioactivity. In each situation a careful study must be made of the effects on agriculture, fish and game, and on water supplies, to be sure that no continuing hazard is created. Based on experience to date, it seems clear that these effects can be restricted to acceptable magnitudes.

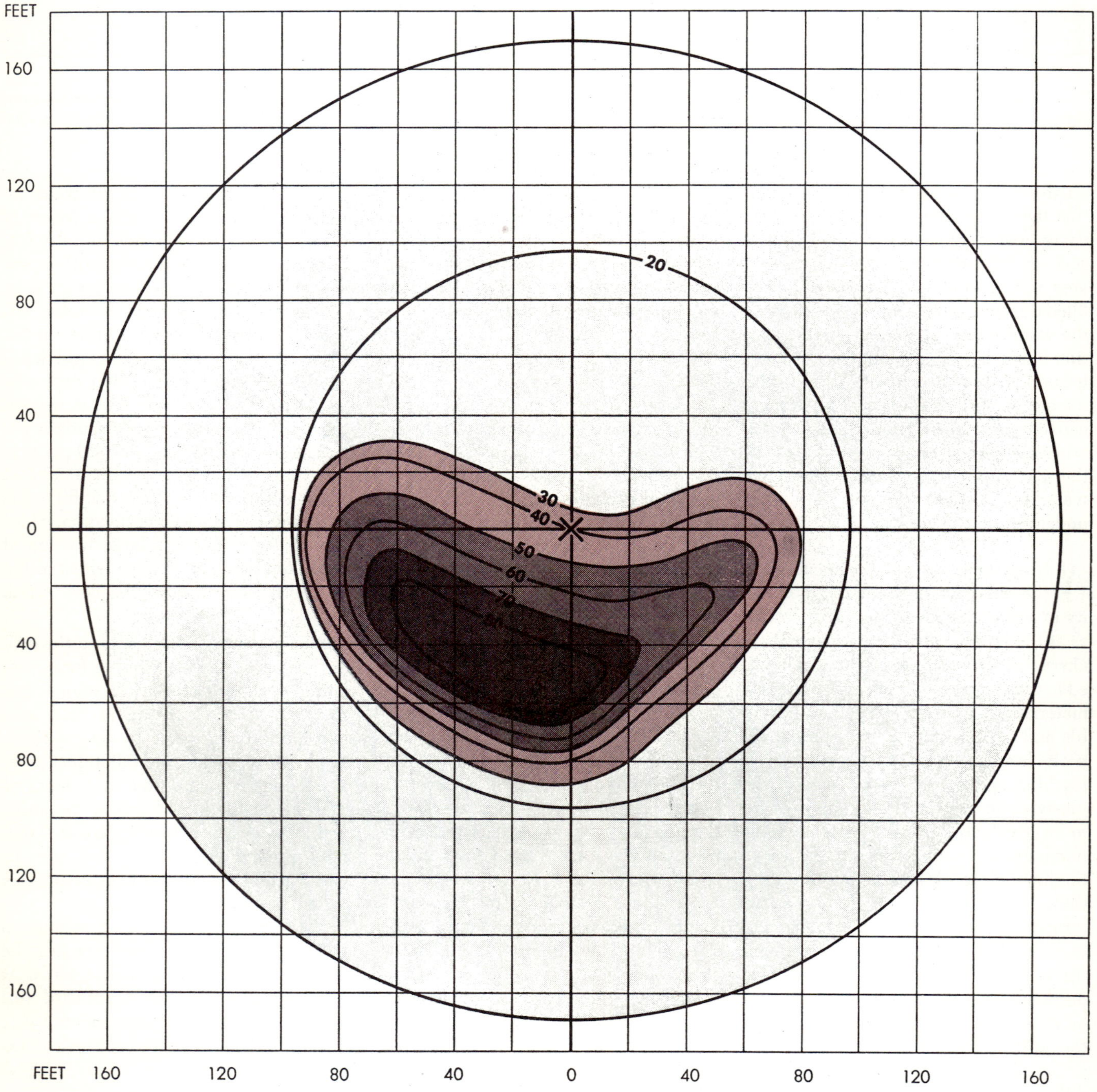

DISTRIBUTION OF TEMPERATURE at the site of the Rainier explosion after four months is shown in cross section. The temperature rose above the 17 degrees C. ambient temperature about 160 feet from ground zero and reached 80 degrees in explosion site.

Constructive Uses of Nuclear Explosives

PHILIP MORRISON

August 1968

A review of *The Constructive Uses of Nuclear Explosives,* by Edward Teller, Wilson K. Talley, Gary H. Higgins, and Gerald W. Johnson. New York: McGraw-Hill Book Company, 1968.

These four engineer-scientists of the Lawrence Radiation Laboratory at Livermore here present a useful account, on the level of a text for advanced engineering undergraduates, of nuclear explosions and their effects from the point of view of using the effects as engineering tools for surface construction of harbors and canals, for building underground storage vessels or for mineral extraction. Most of the material is obtained from the considerable body of theoretical and experimental work done under Project Plowshare, first conceived under the stress of the 1956 Suez crisis, they say, as a quick way to replace the blocked canal. Plowshare has often seemed to have a larger component of politics than of economics in it; the claimed potential of the peacetime developments, so far without a single success to their credit (up to the Gasbuggy shot in May), has been used here and abroad as an argument first against the partial ban of nuclear testing and then against the proposals for a treaty on non-proliferation. This book lies almost wholly at the engineering level, although there are those who might more conservatively estimate the radiation hazards.

Suppose you drill a shaft a yard wide and 2,500 feet deep into hard rock. Lower the 10-foot canister of the 100-kiloton explosive, weighing five tons, carefully into the hole. The Atomic Energy Commission estimates it will cost you about half a million dollars for the explosive. Plug the hole carefully with 50 feet of concrete and a pile of whatever you have handy. Fire! Deep in the earth a sphere of vaporized rock will form in a fraction of a second, its walls lined with molten rock. It will reach in that time a diameter of 300 feet. The molten rock will flow slowly down the walls and drip from the roof. After a brief period the unsupported roof will collapse, depositing its rubble to fill the bottom of an irregular chimney. Before these effects were observed it was thought that the molten rock—particularly if the shot were set off in salt—might simply seal the walls, form a molten pool at the base and sit there holding its heat. Then a new drill hole could bring in water to flash into steam, and thermonuclear energy would be at hand. It is not that easy. In 200 underground shots only one tight sphere remains. One even puffed radioactive gases in spite of the plugged drill hole.

There is a study of a new Panama canal to be dug by nuclear shots, one of which is to be 35 megatons! The savings over regular earth-moving techniques are said to be large, but neither development costs nor legal ones are considered. There is a curiously incomplete chapter on bomb physics, which handles Liouville's theorem, Thomas-Fermi equations of state and a good deal of unconventional hydrodynamics (it is not true that there is no photon-photon interaction at all, as stated) but barely lists the possible reactions of a thermonuclear explosion. Reading these chapters is a bit like seeing a badly cut film. But all in all there is no more up-to-date and complete text on nuclear explosions, their radioactivity and their general effects, particularly at the surface and underground. Air blast and fireball are of course better treated in the official AEC volume on effects.

The photographs of these underground shots are remarkable. Most awesome is the dome that bulges upward at the surface when the explosive is set off half a mile below.

Bibliographies

I. HISTORICAL BACKGROUND

Section 1. The Atom Bomb

Is the Atomic Bomb an Absolute Weapon?

FEAR, WAR, AND THE BOMB. P. M. S. Blackett. Whittlesey House, McGraw-Hill, 1949.

ONE WORLD OR NONE. Dexter Masters and Katharine Way. Whittlesey House, McGraw-Hill, 1946.

Arms Race V. Control

THE INTERNATIONAL CONTROL OF ATOMIC ENERGY. The Third Report of the United Nations Atomic Energy Commission to the Security Council, May 17, 1948. Department of State. U.S. Government Printing Office, 1948.

A REPORT ON THE INTERNATIONAL CONTROL OF ATOMIC ENERGY. Prepared for the Secretary of State's Committee on Atomic Energy by Chester I. Barnard, J. R. Oppenheimer, Charles A. Thomas, Harry A. Winne, and David E. Lilienthal. Doubleday and Company, 1946.

Section 2. The Hydrogen Bomb

The Hydrogen Bomb

ATOMIC ENERGY. George Gamow. Cambridge University Press, 1947.

The Hydrogen Bomb: II

ATOMIC ENERGY. George Gamow. Cambridge University Press, 1947.

ELEMENTARY NUCLEAR THEORY. H. A. Bethe, John Wiley and Sons, Inc., 1947.

The Hydrogen Bomb: III

THE HYDROGEN BOMB, Louis N. Ridenour in *Scientific American*; Vol. 182, No. 3, March, 1950 (this book, pages 51–55).

THE HYDROGEN BOMB: II. Hans A. Bethe in *Scientific American*; Vol. 182, No. 4, April, 1950 (this book, pages 56–61).

Section 3. Fallout

Ionizing Radiation and the Whole Animal

EVIDENCE FOR A HUMORAL FACTOR (OR FACTORS) CONCERNED IN RECOVERY FROM RADIATION INJURY: A REVIEW. Leon O. Jacobson in *Cancer Research*, Vol. 12, pages 315–325; 1952.

THE RELATIONSHIP OF X-RAY DOSE TO THE TIME OF DEVELOPMENT OF RADIATION SICKNESS FOLLOWING EXPOSURE TO A SINGLE DOSE OF X-RAYS. W. M. Court Brown and John D. Abbatt in *British Journal of Radiology*. Vol. 28, pages 153–158; 1955.

REPORT OF THE UNITED NATIONS SCIENTIFIC COMMITTEE ON THE EFFECTS OF ATOMIC RADIATION. General Assembly Official Records: Thirteenth Session. Supplement No. 17, 1958.

Ionizing Radiation and the Citizen

THE ABC OF NUCLEAR WEAPONS. H. W. B. Skinner in *The New Scientist*, Vol. 5, No. 119, pages 473–475; February 26, 1959.

THE BIOLOGICAL EFFECTS OF ATOMIC RADIATION. National Academy of Sciences, 1956.

GENETIC AND SOMATIC EFFECTS OF CARBON-14. Linus Pauling in *Science*, Vol. 128, pages 1,183–1,186; November 14, 1958.

GENETICS IN THE ATOMIC AGE. Charlotte Auerbach. Oliver and Boyd, 1956.

RECOMMENDATIONS OF THE INTERNATIONAL COMMISSION ON RADIOLOGICAL PROTECTION. *British Journal of Radiology*, Supplement No. 6; 1955.

WORLD-WIDE CAPABILITIES FOR PRODUCTION AND CONTROL OF NUCLEAR WEAPONS. Howard Simons in *Daedalus*, Vol. 88, No. 3, pages 385–409; Summer, 1959.

II. THE CURRENT STATE OF ARMS CONTROL

Section 4. First Steps in Arms Control

National Security and the Nuclear Test Ban

THE EFFECTS OF NUCLEAR WEAPONS. Edited by Samuel Glasstone. United States Atomic Energy Commission, April, 1962.

STEPS TOWARD DISARMAMENT. P. M. S. Blackett in *Scientific American*, Vol. 206, No. 4, pages 45–53; April, 1962.
WORLD PEACE THROUGH WORLD LAW. Louis B. Sohn and Grenville Clark. Harvard University Press, 1960.
A WORLD WITHOUT WAR. Walter Millis, Reinhold Niebuhr, Harrison Brown, James Real, and William O. Douglas. Washington Square Press, Inc. 1961.

The Detection of Underground Explosions

THE DETECTION AND RECOGNITION OF UNDERGROUND EXPLOSIONS. United Kingdom Atomic Energy Authority, 1965.
A DISCUSSION ON RECENT ADVANCES IN THE TECHNIQUE OF SEISMIC RECORDING AND ANALYSIS. *Proceedings of the Royal Society of London*, Series A, Vol. 290, No. 1422, pages 287–476; March 1, 1966.
PROLIFERATION. Andrew Martin and Wayland Young in *Disarmament and Arms Control*, Vol. 3, No. 2, pages 107–134; Autumn, 1965.

Section 5. SALT Phase I

Anti-Ballistic-Missile Systems

ADDRESS BY HONORABLE ROBERT S. MCNAMARA, SECRETARY OF DEFENSE, BEFORE UNITED PRESS INTERNATIONAL EDITORS AND PUBLISHERS, SAN FRANCISCO, SEPTEMBER 18, 1967. Office of Assistant Secretary of Defense (Public Affairs), 1967. Reprinted in *Science, Conflict, and Society*, Readings from *Scientific American* with introductions by Garrett Hardin, W. H. Freeman and Company, 1969.
THE EFFECTS OF NUCLEAR WEAPONS. Edited by Samuel Glasstone. United States Department of Defense and the United States Atomic Energy Commission, April, 1962.
STATEMENT OF SECRETARY OF DEFENSE ROBERT S. MCNAMARA BEFORE THE SENATE ARMED SERVICES COMMITTEE ON THE FISCAL YEAR 1969–73 DEFENSE PROGRAM AND 1969 DEFENSE BUDGET, U.S. Government Printing Office; January 22, 1968.

The Dynamics of the Arms Race

THE EFFECTS OF NUCLEAR WEAPONS. Edited by Samuel Glasstone. United States Department of Defense and the United States Atomic Energy Commission, April, 1962.
DEBATE: THE ANTIBALLISTIC MISSILE. Edited by Eugene Rabinowitch and Ruth Adams. Bulletin of the Atomic Scientists, 1968.
THE ESSENCE OF SECURITY. Robert S. McNamara. Harper and Row, Publishers, 1968.
ANTI-BALLISTIC-MISSILE SYSTEMS. Richard L. Garwin and Hans A. Bethe in *Scientific American*, Vol. 218, No. 3, pages 21–31; March, 1968 (this book, pages 164–174).
THE FUTURE OF THE STRATEGIC ARMS RACE: OPTIONS FOR THE 1970's. George W. Rathjens. Carnegie Endowment for International Peace, 1969.

Military Technology and National Security

THE ESSENCE OF SECURITY. Robert S. McNamara. Harper and Row, Publishers, 1968.
ABM: AN EVAULATION OF THE DECISION TO DEPLOY AN ANTI-BALLISTIC MISSILE SYSTEM. Edited by Abram Chayes and Jerome B. Wiesner, introduction by Edward M. Kennedy. Signet Books, 1969.
STRATEGIC AND FOREIGN POLICY IMPLICATIONS OF ABM SYSTEMS: HEARINGS BEFORE THE SUBCOMMITTEE ON INTERNATIONAL ORGANIZATION AND DISARMAMENT AFFAIRS OF THE COMMITTEE ON FOREIGN RELATIONS, UNITED STATES SENATE, NINETY-FIRST CONGRESS, FIRST SESSION. U.S. Government Printing Office, 1969.

The Limitation of Strategic Arms

DIPLOMATIC AND STRATEGIC IMPACT OF MULTIPLE WARHEAD MISSILES: HEARINGS BEFORE THE SUBCOMMITTEE ON NATIONAL SECURITY POLICY AND SCIENTIFIC DEVELOPMENTS OF THE COMMITTEE ON FOREIGN AFFAIRS HOUSE OF REPRESENTATIVES. NINETY-FIRST CONGRESS, FIRST SESSION. U.S. Government Printing Office, 1969.
STRATEGIC AND FOREIGN POLICY IMPLICATIONS OF ABM SYSTEMS: HEARINGS BEFORE THE SUBCOMMITTEE ON INTERNATIONAL ORGANIZATION AND DISARMAMENT AFFAIRS OF THE COMMITTEE ON FOREIGN RELATIONS, UNITED STATES SENATE, NINETY-FIRST CONGRESS, FIRST SESSION. Part 3. U.S. Government Printing Office, 1969.

The Limitation of Offensive Weapons

THE FUTURE OF THE STRATEGIC ARMS RACE: OPTIONS FOR THE 1970's. George W. Rathjens. Carnegie Endowment for International Peace, 1969.
SECURITY THROUGH LIMITATIONS. Harold Brown in *Foreign Affairs*, Vol. 47, No. 3, pages 422–432; April, 1969.
RACE TO OBLIVION. Herbert F. York. Simon and Schuster, Inc., 1970.
TOWARD A STRATEGIC ARMS LIMITATION AGREEMENT. Herbert Scoville, Jr. Carnegie Endowment for International Peace, 1970.

Reconnaissance and Arms Control

OBSERVATION SATELLITES: PROBLEMS AND PROSPECTS. Amrom H. Katz in *Astronautics*; April, June, July, August, September, October, 1960.
SECRET SENTRIES IN SPACE. Philip J. Klass. Random House, Inc., 1971.
RECONNAISSANCE, SURVEILLANCE AND ARMS CONTROL. Ted Greenwood. Adelphi Paper Number 88, The International Institute for Strategic Studies, 1972.

Missile Submarines and National Security

POLARIS AND POSEIDON, FBM FACTS. Strategic Systems Project Office. Navy Department, 1970.
SIPRI YEARBOOK OF WORLD ARMAMENTS AND DISARMAMENT 1969/70. Stockholm International Peace Research Institute. Humanities Press, 1971.
BEYOND SALT ONE. Herbert Scoville, Jr., in *Foreign Affairs*, Vol. 50, No. 3, pages 488–500; April, 1972.
REPORT ON ULMS. Members of Congress for Peace through Law. Washington, D.C., April, 1972.
TESTIMONY OF THE FEDERATION OF AMERICAN SCIENTISTS BEFORE DEFENSE SUBCOMMITTEE, APPROPRIATIONS COMMITTEE, APPROPRIATIONS COMMITTEE, U.S. House of Representatives on the FY 1973 Defense Program and Budget. Presented by Herbert Scoville. April, 1972.

Antisubmarine Warfare and National Security

FUNDAMENTALS OF SONAR. J. W. Horton. U.S. Naval Institute, 1959.
PRINCIPLES OF UNDERWATER SOUND FOR ENGINEERS. R. J. Urick. McGraw-Hill Book Company, 1967.
SIPRI YEARBOOK OF WORLD ARMAMENTS AND DISARMAMENT 1969/70. Stockholm International Peace Research Institute. Humanities Press, 1971.
ASW–THE CRUCIAL NAVAL CHALLENGE. Captain Robert H. Smith, USN ret., in *U.S. Naval Institute Proceedings*, Vol. 98, No. 5, pages 126–141; May, 1972.
MISSILE SUBMARINES AND NATIONAL SECURITY. Herbert Scoville, Jr., in *Scientific American*, Vol. 226, No. 6, pages 15–27; June, 1972 (this book, pages 235–247).

Section 6. Other Arms Control and Disarmament Issues

Extending the Nuclear-Test Ban

DEVELOPMENTS IN TECHNICAL CAPABILITIES FOR DETECTION AND IDENTIFYING NUCLEAR WEAPONS TESTS: HEARINGS BEFORE THE JOINT COMMITTEE ON ATOMIC ENERGY. Congress of the United States. U.S. Government Printing Office, 1963.

NUCLEAR TEST BAN TREATY: HEARINGS BEFORE THE COMMITTEE ON FOREIGN RELATIONS. United States Senate. U.S. Government Printing Office, 1963.

NATIONAL SECURITY AND THE NUCLEAR-TEST BAN. Jerome B. Wiesner and Herbert F. York in *Scientific American*, Vol. 211, No. 4, pages 27–35; October, 1964 (this book, pages 129–136).

PROSPECTS FOR A COMPREHENSIVE TEST BAN TREATY: HEARINGS BEFORE THE SUB-COMMITTEE ON ARMS CONTROL, INTERNATIONAL ORGANIZATIONS. United States Senate. U.S. Government Printing Office, 1971.

The Great Test-Ban Debate

AMERICAN SCIENTISTS AND NUCLEAR WEAPONS POLICY. Robert G. Gilpin. Princeton University Press, 1962.

DEVELOPMENTS IN TECHNICAL CAPABILITIES FOR DETECTION AND IDENTIFYING NUCLEAR WEAPONS TESTS: HEARINGS BEFORE THE JOINT COMMITTEE ON ATOMIC ENERGY. Congress of The United States. U.S. Government Printing Office, 1963.

NUCLEAR AMBUSH: THE TEST BAN TRAP. Earl H. Voss. Henry Regency Company, 1963.

NUCLEAR TEST BAN TREATY: HEARINGS BEFORE THE COMMITTEE OF FOREIGN RELATIONS. United States Senate. U.S. Government Printing Office, 1963.

DIPLOMATS, SCIENTISTS, AND POLITICIANS: THE UNITED STATES AND THE NUCLEAR TEST BAN NEGOTIATIONS. Harold Karan Jacobson and Eric Stein. The University of Michigan Press, 1966.

NUCLEAR DIPLOMACY: THE FIRST TWENTY-FIVE YEARS. George H. Quester. Dunellen Publishing Co., 1970.

Chemical and Biological Weapons

CHEMICAL AND BACTERIOLOGICAL (BIOLOGICAL) WEAPONS AND THE EFFECTS OF THEIR POSSIBLE USE: REPORT OF THE SECRETARY-GENERAL OF THE UNITED NATIONS. United Nations, 1969.

CHEMICAL-BIOLOGICAL WARFARE: U.S. POLICIES AND INTERNATIONAL EFFECTS. HEARINGS BEFORE THE SUBCOMMITTEE ON NATIONAL SECURITY POLICY AND SCIENTIFIC DEVELOPMENTS OF THE COMMITTEE ON FOREIGN AFFAIRS, HOUSE OF REPRESENTATIVES, NINETY-FIRST CONGRESS, FIRST SESSION. U.S. Government Printing Office, 1970.

HEALTH ASPECTS OF CHEMICAL AND BIOLOGICAL WEAPONS: REPORT OF A WORLD HEALTH ORGANIZATION GROUP OF CONSULTANTS. The American Public Health Association, Inc., 1970.

The Mekong River Plan

DEVELOPMENT OF THE WATER RESOURCES IN THE LOWER MEKONG BASIN. *Flood Control Series No. 12*. Economic Commission for Asia and the Far East.

ECONOMIC AND SOCIAL ASPECTS OF LOWER MEKONG DEVELOPMENT. A report by Gilbert F. White, Egbert de Vries, Harold B. Dunkerley and John V. Krutilla to the Committee for Co-ordination of Investigations of the Lower Mekong Basin. July, 1962.

THE LOWER MEKONG: CHALLENGE TO CO-OPERATION IN SOUTH EAST ASIA. C. Hart Schaaf and Russell H. Fifield. D. Van Nostrand Co., Inc., 1963.

THAILAND: ASPECTS OF LANDSCAPE AND LIFE. Robert L. Pendelton. American Geographical Society, 1962.

The Cratering of Indochina

ECOLOGICAL EFFECTS OF THE VIETNAM WAR. E. W. Pfeiffer in *Science Journal*, Vol. 5, No. 2, pages 33–38; February, 1969.

ECOLOGICAL EFFECTS OF THE WAR IN VIETNAM. Gordon H. Orians and E. W. Pfeiffer in *Science*, Vol. 168, No. 3931, pages 544–554; May 1, 1970.

IMPACT OF THE VIETNAM WAR. Committee Print of the U.S. Senate Committee on Foreign Relations. U.S. Library of Congress, June 30, 1971.

FORESTRY AND THE WAR IN SOUTH VIETNAM. Arthur H. Westing in *Journal of Forestry*, Vol. 69, No. 11, pages 777–783; November, 1971.

LAND WAR. E. W. Pfeiffer and Arthur H. Westing in *Environment*, Vol. 13, No. 9, pages 2–15; November, 1971.

HARVEST OF DEATH: CHEMICAL WARFARE IN VIETNAM AND CAMBODIA. J. B. Neilands, Gordon H. Orians, E. W. Pfeiffer, Alje Vennema and Arthur H. Westing. The Free Press, 1972.

III. PEACEFUL APPLICATIONS OF NUCLEAR TECHNOLOGY

Section 7. Plowshares and Pruning Hooks

Breeder Reactors

AN APPRAISAL OF THE ENRICO FERMI REACTOR. A. Amorosi in *Proceedings of the Second United Nations International Conference on the Peaceful Uses of Atomic Energy*, Vol. 9; 1959.

CONSTRUCTION DESIGN OF EBR-II: AN INTEGRATED UNMODERATED NUCLEAR POWER PLANT. Prepared by L. J. Koch in *Proceedings of the Second United Nations International Conference on the Peaceful Uses of Atomic Energy*, Vol. 9; 1959.

EXPERIMENTAL FAST REACTORS. A. I. Leipunsky and O. D. Kazachkovsky *et al.* in *Proceedings of the Second United Nations International Conference on the Peaceful Uses of Atomic Energy*, Vol. 9; 1959.

THE POSSIBILITIES OF SECURING LONG RANGE SUPPLIES OF URANIUM THORIUM AND OTHER SUBSTANCES FROM IGNEOUS ROCKS. H. Brown and L. T. Silver in *Proceedings of the International Conference on the Peaceful Uses of Atomic Energy*, Vol. 8, pages 129–132; 1956.

Fast Breeder Reactors

THE TECHNOLOGY OF NUCLEAR REACTOR SAFETY, VOL. I: REACTOR PHYSICS AND CONTROL. Edited by T. G. Thompson and J. G. Beckerley. The M.I.T. Press, 1964.

FAST REACTOR TECHNOLOGY: PLANT DESIGN. Edited by John G. Yevick. The M.I.T. Press, 1966.

AEC AUTHORIZING LEGISLATION, FISCAL YEAR 1971, HEARINGS BEFORE THE JOINT COMMITTEE ON ATOMIC ENERGY, PART 3. U.S. Government Printing Office, 1970.

Fusion Power

CONTROLLED FUSION RESEARCH: AN APPLICATION OF THE PHYSICS OF HIGH TEMPERATURE PLASMAS. Richard F. Post in *Reviews of Modern Physics*, Vol. 28, No. 3, pages 338–362; July, 1956.

The Prospects of Fusion Power

PROGRESS IN CONTROLLED THERMONUCLEAR RESEARCH. R. W. Gould, H. P. Furth, R. F. Post and F. L. Ribe in *Presentation Made before the President's Science Advisory Committee, December 15, 1970, and AEC's General Advisory Committee, December 16, 1970.*

WORLD SURVEY OF MAJOR FACILITIES IN CONTROLLED FUSION, *Nuclear Fusion*, Special Supplement 1970, STI/Pub/23. International Atomic Energy Agency, 1970.

WHY FUSION? William C. Gough in *Proceedings of the Fusion Reactor Design Symposium, Held at Texas Tech University, Lubbock, Texas, on June 2–5, 1970.*

Fusion by Laser

A POTASSIUM-STEAM BINARY VAPOR CYCLE FOR A MOLTEN-SALT REACTOR POWER PLANT. A. P. Fraas in *Transactions of the American Society of Mechanical Engineers: Series A, Journal of Engineering for Power*, Vol. 88, pages 355–366; October, 1966.

ATTENUATION OF SHOCK WAVES IN LONG PIPES BY ORIFICE PLATES, ROUGH WALLS, AND CYLINDRICAL OBSTACLES. L. Dresner and C. V. Chester. Oak Ridge National Laboratory ORNL-4288, July, 1968.

METHODS OF TRITIUM RECOVERY FROM MOLTEN LITHIUM. Riaz Farookhi and J. E. Rogers. Oak Ridge National Laboratory ORNL-MIT-66, December 18, 1968.

Non-Military Uses of Nuclear Explosives

NON-MILITARY USES OF NUCLEAR EXPLOSIONS. H. Brown and G. W. Johnson in University of California Radiation Laboratory Report No. 5,026, June 12, 1958.

Index